ORGANIZATIONAL BEHAVIOR

NINTH EDITION

Fred Luthans

George Holmes Distinguished Professor of Management
University of Nebraska

**McGraw-Hill
Irwin**

Boston   Burr Ridge, IL   Dubuque, IA   Madison, WI   New York   San Francisco   St. Louis
Bangkok   Bogotá   Caracas   Kuala Lumpur   Lisbon   London   Madrid   Mexico City
Milan   Montreal   New Delhi   Santiago   Seoul   Singapore   Sydney   Taipei   Toronto

McGraw-Hill Higher Education

A Division of The **McGraw-Hill** *Companies*

ORGANIZATIONAL BEHAVIOR

Published by McGraw-Hill, an imprint of The McGraw-Hill Companies, Inc., 1221 Avenue of the
Americas, New York, NY, 10020. Copyright © 2002, 1998, 1995, 1992, 1989, 1985, 1981,
1977, 1973 by The McGraw-Hill Companies, Inc. All rights reserved. No part of this publication
may be reproduced or distributed in any form or by any means, or stored in a data base
or retrieval system, without the prior written consent of The McGraw-Hill Companies, Inc.,
including, but not limited to, in any network or other electronic storage or transmission,
or broadcast for distance learning.
Some ancillaries, including electronic and print components, may not be available to customers
outside the United States.

This book is printed on acid-free paper.

1 2 3 4 5 6 7 8 9 0 DOW/DOW 0 9 8 7 6 5 4 3 2 1

ISBN 0-07-231288-2

Publisher: *John E. Biernat*
Senior editor: *John Weimeister*
Editorial assistant: *Tammy Higham*
Marketing manager: *Lisa Nicks*
Project manager: *Jean Hamilton*
Production supervisor: *Rose Hepburn*
Media technology producer: *Jenny R. Williams*
Designer: *Matthew Baldwin*
Cover design: *Joanne Schopler*
Cover Image: *© Masterfile*
Supplement coordinator: *Matthew Perry*
Printer: *R. R. Donnelley & Sons Company*
Typeface: *10.5/12 Times Roman*
Compositor: **TECH**BOOKS

Library of Congress Cataloging-in-Publication Data

Luthans, Fred.
   Organizational behavior / Fred Luthans.–9th ed.
      p. cm.
   Includes bibliographical references and index.
   ISBN 0-07-231288-2 (alk. paper)
   1. Organizational behavior. I. Title.

HD58.7 .L88 2001
658.4–dc21   2001024694

www.mhhe.com

About the Author

FRED LUTHANS is the George Holmes Distinguished Professor of Management at the University of Nebraska at Lincoln. He received his B.A., M.B.A., and Ph.D. from the University of Iowa and did some postdoctoral work at Columbia University. While serving in the armed forces, he taught at the U.S. Military Academy at West Point. He has been at the University of Nebraska since 1967, his entire academic career, and won the distinguished teaching award in 1986 and the excellence in graduate education award in 2000. A prolific writer, he has published a number of major books and about 150 articles in applied and academic journals. His book, *Organizational Behavior Modification,* coauthored with Robert Kreitner, won the American Society of Personnel Administration award for the outstanding contribution to human resource management, and a more recent book titled *Real Managers* is the result of a four-year research study that observed managers in their natural settings. *International Management,* coauthored with Richard Hodgetts and also published by Irwin/McGraw-Hill, is now in its fifth edition. His articles are widely reprinted and have brought him the American Society of Hospital Administration award. The co-editor-in-chief of the *Journal of World Business,* Professor Luthans is also the editor for *Organizational Dynamics* and is on the editorial board of several other journals. He has been very active in the Academy of Management over the years and was elected a Fellow in 1981. He is a former president of the Midwest Region. He was vice president, program chair of the National Academy meeting in Boston in 1984, and in 1986 was elected president. In 1997, Professor Luthans received the Academy of Management Distinguished Educator Award. In 2000 he became an inaugural member of the Academy's Hall of Fame for being one of the "Top Five" all-time published authors in the prestigious Academy journals. Also active in the Decision Sciences Institute (DSI), he was elected a Fellow in 1987. Professor Luthans has a very extensive research program at the University of Nebraska. Most recently, his studies with Alex Stajkovic on behavioral management (published in the October 1997 and June 2001 issues of the *Academy of Management Journal*) and self-efficacy (published in Vol. 124, 1998 of *Psychological Bulletin*) utilized meta-analysis techniques for theory building and application for performance improvement. He has been a visiting scholar at a number of universities in the United States and has lectured at universities and conducted workshops for managers in many countries around the world. Most recently, he has been actively involved in the former East Germany and Russia and in a U.S. A.I.D. program conducted in Albania and Macedonia. In addition, he has been on the Executive Committee of the annual Pan Pacific Conference since its beginning in 1984 and in 1995 was elected a Fellow. This international research and experience is reflected in his approach to the field of organizational behavior. He served on the Board of Directors of the Foundation of Administrative Research and currently on Senior Technologies, Inc. In addition, he is an active consultant and trainer to both private- (such as Wal-Mart and Ameritas Life Insurance, Inc.) and public-sector (such as the National Rural Electric Cooperative Association) organizations. Since 1998 he has been a Senior Research Scientist with the Gallup Organization. He is an avid golfer and University of Nebraska sports fan. He and his wife Kay, of 38 years, have four grown children and so far four granddaughters.

For
Kay, Kristin, Brett, Kyle, and Paige

PREFACE

Each time I do a new edition, I say to myself, "Fred, things have never changed so much and so fast. Since the last edition, this has to be the most dramatic changes we have ever experienced." Then to console myself about the work that lies ahead, I rationalize that in the next edition I won't have to make so darn many changes. Well, here we go again. Wow, I just cannot believe the amount of change we have experienced since the last edition. With all the hubbub surrounding the new millennium, it has all been said about the new environment, so I won't rehash it here again. However, let me simply say this: I have never put in so much time and effort, made so many changes, as I have in this ninth edition.

I will provide the details of these changes for you, but before I do, let me quickly state, in spite of all the many changes we have experienced in the last few years, the more things still remain the same. After all these years, I am more convinced than ever of the importance of organizational behavior theory, research, and application for high performance and competitive advantage. I am truly thankful that I was able to get in, pretty much on the ground floor, and have made my now over 35-year career in this, to me, still the most exciting and progressive academic discipline there is—organizational behavior.

Now, let me tell you why I am so excited about this particular edition. Before I get to the normal changes that all revisions tend to do, let me tell you, frankly with considerable personal pride, the *five* brand-new features of this ninth edition. To date, no other organizational behavior text has the following:

1. I am convinced at this stage of development of the field of OB, we need a complete theoretical framework to structure our introductory textbooks. Instead of a potpourri of chapters and topics, and maybe using an inductive (or should it be deductive?) sequencing, there is now the opportunity to have a sound conceptual framework to present our now-respectable body of knowledge. I have chosen the well-developed, very comprehensive social cognitive theory to structure this text. I present the background and theory building of this framework in the introductory chapter and also provide a new model (Figure 1.6) that fits in all the chapters. Importantly, the logic of this conceptual framework required two brand-new chapters and the rearrangement and combination of several others. For example, in the organizational context part there is a new Chapter 5, "Reward Systems," and in the cognitive processes part a new Chapter 9, "Positive Psychology Approach to OB: Optimism, Emotional Intelligence, and Self-Efficacy."

2. Besides having the first comprehensive theoretical framework for an introductory OB text, a second "first" for this edition is one or more OB Principles at the end of each chapter. Importantly, these principles are derived from meta-analytic research findings. These quantitative reviews usually include more than a hundred studies, thousands of subjects, and are stated in reader-friendly probability-of-success summary statements.

3. The third "first" goes way beyond most other texts that attempt to include real-world practices. Each chapter now starts off with "Best Practice Leader's Advice" on the chapter topic. Specifically, direct observations and advice from interviews with well-known practice leaders such as Jack Welch, Scott McNealy, Andy Grove, Admiral Louise Wilmont, Michael Porter, Lou Gerstner, Richard Branson, Percy

Barnevik, Michael Eisner, Peter Senge, Warren Bennis, and John Chambers, to name but a few, gain the readers' up-front interest and attention before going into the more theoretical, research-based chapter material.

4. The fourth "first" of this edition is to reinforce the best-practice theme by also having a "Consulting Best Practices" summary open up each major part of the text. Specifically, in addition to my long academic appointment at the University of Nebraska, in recent years I have also become a Senior Research Scientist with the Gallup Organization. Mostly known for the famous Gallup Poll, this world-class firm also has a very fast growing management consulting practice. About half of the "*Fortune* 50" are among Gallup's recent clients. With my input, Senior Analyst Dr. Dennis Hatfield drew from Gallup's tremendous survey research-base consisting of thousands of organizations and millions of people over the years. He provides Gallup's perspectives and current best practices relevant to each major part of the text.

5. The *fifth* "first" in this *ninth* edition, talk about *reinventing* yourself, reflects my continuing basic research program over the years. Chapter 9 is the first time that the topics of optimism, emotional intelligence, and self-efficacy have been given chapter status, and that the concepts of hope and happiness/subjective well-being (SWB), to my knowledge, have ever been covered in an introductory OB text. Because of my involvement in the emerging Positive Psychology movement through Gallup and my research collaboration with Alex Stajkovic of the University of Wisconsin–Madison on self-efficacy, I feel the time has come to introduce these powerful constructs into the mainstream organizational behavior literature.

Besides these truly significant five new features, the strength of the book over the years has been its up-to-date research base and its comprehensive coverage of key topics. This latest edition should enhance this reputation because it has been thoroughly revised and updated to include new research findings and the very latest topics. Besides the chapter-ending OB principles based on meta-analyses, this revision has made a conscious effort to include the results of other meta-analyses on topics where such studies have been conducted to date.

The reason for including meta-analysis results is that the field of organizational behavior has matured to the point where there are not just isolated studies but a stream of research on a number of topics that now need to be systematically (quantitatively) summarized for students and practitioners. For example, Alex Stajkovic and I have completed a meta-analysis of the studies with which I have been most closely associated with over the past 30 years, focusing on the positive effect that organizational behavior modification (O.B. Mod.) has on task performance. (This analysis is published in the October 1997 issue of the *Academy of Management Journal* and a follow-up research study conducted in the largest credit card processing company in the world is published in the June, 2001 issue of *AMJ.*) In addition, we conducted a meta-analysis (114 studies, 21,616 subjects) and found a very strong positive relationship between self-efficacy and task-related performance. (This is published in Vol. 124, No. 1, 1998 issue of *Psychological Bulletin.*) Both of these provide end-of-chapter OB Principles and with other such meta-analyses results are reported in discussions of research findings throughout the text.

Just as the actual practical side of management can no longer afford to evolve slowly, neither can the academic side of the field. With the world turned upside down for most organizations today, drastically new ideas, approaches, and techniques are needed both in the practice of management and in the way we study and apply the field of organizational behavior. This revision mirrors these needed changes.

Social Cognitive Conceptual Framework. The book contains 18 chapters in four major parts. Social cognitive theory explains organizational behavior in terms of both environmental, contextual events and internal cognitive factors, as well as the dynamics and outcomes of the organizational behavior itself. Thus, Part 1 provides the environmental and organizational context for the study and application of organizational behavior. The introductory chapter provides the new perspective, historical background, methodology, theoretical framework, and specific social cognitive model for the field of organizational behavior in general and specifically for this text. This is followed by two environmental context chapters:

> **Chapter 2,** "Information Technology and Globalization" (with new major sections on E-business, knowledge management, human/intellectual capital, and globalization) and
>
> **Chapter 3,** "Diversity and Ethics" (with updated material on diversity and a major new section on the impact of ethics on "bottom-line" outcomes).

After this broad environmental context is laid out, there are two chapters for the organizational context of the social cognitive framework:

> **Chapter 4,** "Design and Culture" (with new special emphasis given to the learning organization and horizontal, network, and virtual designs; best-practice cultures; and a new major section on the culture clashes from mergers and acquisitions) and
>
> **Chapter 5,** "Reward Systems" (a brand-new chapter with special emphasis given to money as a reward, the effectiveness of pay, the forms of "new pay," recognition systems, and benefits).

The second part of the text recognizes the micro-oriented cognitive processes of the social cognitive framework:

> **Chapter 6,** "Perception and Attribution" (with new emphasis on attribution theory and application);
>
> **Chapter 7,** "Personality and Attitudes" (with new major sections on the role of heredity and the brain, "Big Five" personality traits, the Myers-Briggs personality indicator, and organizational citizenship behavior);
>
> **Chapter 8,** "Motivational Needs and Processes" (with new major sections on extrinsic versus intrinsic motives, procedural justice, and motivation across cultures); and
>
> **Chapter 9,** the brand new chapter, not only for this text, but any other, on "Optimism, Emotional Intelligence, and Self-Efficacy." In addition to the focus on these three concepts, there are also major sections on emotion, multiple intelligences, general mental abilities, positive psychology, hope, and happiness/ subjective well-being (SWB).

Besides the major changes just mentioned, there are also a number of new organizational behavior topics such as emotional labor, PANA (positive and negative affectivity), agency theory, and explanatory attribution style.

Parts Three and Four are concerned with the dynamics and outcomes of organizational behavior in the social cognitive framework. Part Three contains the following:

> **Chapter 10,** "Communication" (with new material on information richness and complexity, communication styles, 360-degree feedback, knowledge sharing, and communication across cultures);
>
> **Chapter 11,** "Decision Making" (with new major sections on decision-making styles and creativity/innovation);
>
> **Chapter 12,** "Stress and Conflict" (with new material on stress and conflict from advanced technology and globalization, burnout, and work-family initiatives);

Chapter 13, "Power and Politics" (with new material on empowerment, trust, resource dependency, and the dynamics of power and politics in the new environment); and

Chapter 14, "Groups and Teams" (with new material on the punctuated equilibrium model of groups, group/team effectiveness, role conflict and ambiguity, social loafing, cross-functional teams, virtual teams, and cultural/global issues with the use of teams).

The final Part Four gives a new applied emphasis to the text. It focuses on *how* to manage and lead for high performance. These applied organizational behavior chapters, some of which were placed in other parts in the previous edition, include the following:

Chapter 15, "Managing Performance Through Job Design and Goal Setting" (with new material on the impact of information technology and telecommuting and major new sections on employee engagement/disengagement, high-performance work practices (HPWPs), applications of goal setting, and the new psychological contract and human capital perspective of work);

Chapter 16, "Behavioral Performance Management" (with new material on the role of social cognition, critical analysis of reinforcement theory, pay for performance, social recognition, and the contingencies with type of organization and interventions for O.B. Mod. effectiveness);

Chapter 17, "Effective Leadership Processes" (with new major sections on leadership across cultures and the GLOBE project); and

Chapter 18, "Great Leaders: Styles, Activities, and Skills" (with new major sections on leading in the new environment, leadership skills, career development programs, and new material on the role of humor/fun in leadership, the dark side of leadership in transitionary countries, leadership competencies, and unusual sources of leadership wisdom).

Pedagogical Features. Besides the many new features already described, there are also several strong pedagogical features carried over from the previous edition. To reflect and reinforce the applications orientation of the text, highlighted, mostly new, boxed real-world application examples appear in each chapter. In addition to these application boxes, the text also features experiential exercises at the end of each part. The exercises get participants involved in solving simulated problems or experiencing firsthand organizational behavior issues. New to this edition are end-of-chapter Internet exercises to get students involved in on-line relevant resources and vehicles for discussion and critique.

Besides the usual end-of-chapter short organizational behavior discussion cases, there is also at least one "Real Case" at the end of each chapter. These cases are drawn from recent real-world events (all are updated or are excerpted from current *Business Week* articles) and are intended to enhance the relevancy and application of the theories and research results presented in the chapter. These end-of-chapter real cases serve as both examples and discussion vehicles. It is suggested that students read them even if they are not discussed directly in class. The intent is that they can serve as supplemental readings as well as discussion cases.

This edition also contains learning objectives at the start of each chapter. These objectives should help students better focus and prepare for what follows in the chapter. Finally, the chapters have the usual end-of-chapter summaries and review and discussion questions.

Intended Audience. Despite the five new features and extensive revision throughout, the purpose and the intended audience of the book remain the same. As in the earlier editions, this edition is aimed at those who wish to take a totally up-to-date, research-based approach to organizational behavior and management. It does not assume the reader's prior knowledge of either management or the behavioral sciences. Thus, the book can be used effectively in the first or only course in either four-year or two-year colleges. It is aimed primarily at the required organizational behavior course, the behavioral follow-up elective course to the more traditional introductory management course, or it can be used in the organizational behavior course in the M.B.A. program. I would like to acknowledge and thank colleagues in countries around the world who have used previous editions of the book and point out that the enhanced international perspective and coverage should continue to make this new edition relevant and attractive. Finally, the book should be helpful to practicing managers who want to understand and more effectively manage their most important assets—their human resources.

Acknowledgments. Every author owes a great deal to others, and I am no exception. First and foremost, I would like to acknowledge the help on this as well as many other writing projects that I have received from Professor Richard M. Hodgetts of Florida International University. He has been an especially valued colleague and friend over the years. Second, I want to give special thanks to three of my former doctoral students—Don Baack of Pittsburg State University for his background work on some of the chapters, Steve Farner of Bellevue University for his help on the Internet Exercises, and Suzanne Peterson of Miami University for her help on the meta-analytic principles. Next, I would like to acknowledge the interaction I have had with my colleagues, Gwendolyn Combs, Colleen Jones, Douglas May, and Steve Sommer, in the organizational behavior area at the University of Nebraska. In particular, I would like to acknowledge the total support and standards of excellence provided by my department chairman, Sang M. Lee. Linda Rohn, Amy Leatherwood, and especially Cathy Watson from the Management Department staff have been very helpful. Dean Cynthia Milligan also has been very supportive. I can never forget the help, encouragement, and scholarly values I received from Professors Henry H. Albers and Max S. Wortman when starting out in my academic career. Over the years, I have been very lucky to have been associated with excellent doctoral students. I would like to thank them all for teaching me as much as I have taught them. In particular, I would like to mention besides Don Baack, Steve Farner and Suzanne Peterson, Doug Baker of Washington State University, Don Beard of University of Washington, Gwen Combs, University of Nebraska, Elaine Davis of Saint Cloud State University, Tim Davis of Cleveland State University, Mary Sully de Luque of Wharton, University of Pennsylvania, Nancy Dodd of Montana State University, Brooke Envick of St. Mary's University–Texas, Brenda Flannery of Minnesota State University–Mankato, Marilyn Fox of Minnesota State University–Mankato, Barron Harvey of Howard University, Elina Ibrayeva of Southwest State University, Avis L. Johnson of the University of Akron, Jim Jones of the University of Nebraska–Omaha, Barbara Kemmerer of Eastern Illinois University, Ed Knod of Western Illinois University, Robert Kreitner of Arizona State University, Diane Lockwood of Seattle University, Terry Maris, Ohio Northern University, Mark Martinko of Florida State University, Paul Marsnik of St. John's University, Harriette S. McCaul, Alisa Mosley of Jackson State University, James L. Nimnicht of Central Washington University, Robert Ottemann, University of Nebraska–Omaha, Rich Patrick of Nebraska Wesleyan University, Pam Perrewe of Florida State University, Doug Peterson of Indiana State University, Kendra Reed of University of Wisconsin–Madison, Laura Riolli-Saltzman of California State University–Sacramento, Lena Rodriguez of San Diego State University, Stuart A. Rosenkrantz, Bill Ruud of Boise State University, Bill Snavely of

Miami University, Charles Snyder of Auburn University, Chanhoo Song of Fairleigh Dickinson University, Alex Stajkovic of the University of Wisconsin–Madison, Carol Steinhaus, of Northern Michigan University, Linda Thomas of Bellevue University, Kenneth Thompson of DePaul University, Robert Waldersee of Queensland University of Technology, Australia, Dianne H. B. Welsh of John Carroll University, Don White of University of Arkansas, Steve Williams of Texas Southern University, and Melody Wollan of Clemson University. I am also very grateful to those professors who used the previous editions of the book and gave me valuable feedback for making this revision. Finally, as always, I am deeply appreciative and dedicate *Organizational Behavior,* ninth edition, to my wife and now-grown children and their families, who have provided me with a loving, supportive relationship and climate needed to complete this and other projects over the years.

CONTENTS IN BRIEF

CONTENTS

PART ONE

Environmental and Organizational Context

Consulting Best Practices

Beside the chapter opening "Best Practice Leader's Advice," another component of the best practice theme of this text are these part opening "Consulting Best Practices." The fast-growing, world-famous Gallup Organization provides its overall perspective and representative practices for each text part. Gallup is the recognized world leader in the measurement and analysis of human attitudes, opinions, and behavior. Best known for the Gallup Poll, in 1968 Dr. Donald Clifton founded Selection Research Inc. (SRI), which acquired the polling firm over 15 years ago to form today's Gallup Organization. Although the poll is still an important part, most of Gallup's work is providing consulting services to the world's (about 25 international offices) largest firms. About half the For-tune *50 firms have been or are Gallup clients and include such well-known firms as Best Buy, Blockbuster, Citigroup, Delta Air Lines, Fidelity, Marriott, Searle, Sears, Swissotel, and Toyota, to name but a few. The details and depth of Gallup's consulting practices can be found in the best-selling books* First, Break All the Rules *(Simon & Schuster, 1999) authored by Gallup Practice Leaders Marcus Buckingham and Curt Coffman and* Now, Discover Your Strengths *(The Free Press, 2001) by Buckingham and Donald Clifton. All the part opening Gallup perspectives for this text are written by Dr. Dennis Hatfield, a Gallup Senior Analyst, with some input by this author (Luthans, who in addition to his University of Nebraska position is a Gallup Senior Research Scientist). The following gives an introductory overview of the Gallup approach, and the other openers are more directly concerned with the theme of the respective part.*

An Introduction to the Gallup Approach

Gallup's approach to organizational consulting is built at the intersection of two disciplines, which are related, but seldom combined. Starting from one methodological "end" of the research spectrum, essentially sociological approaches are utilized to address research and practice questions related to brand, customer satisfaction and loyalty, and market characteristics. These methods, similar to our work in polling, allow us broad but highly accurate descriptions of the dynamics affecting brand and market. Although they do not allow the specificity of a particular "who," they do yield a vivid, relevant description of what is going on within the market, and what to do about it.

From the other "end" of the spectrum, Gallup has also been studying the talent of individuals for decades. In this methodology, we study top performers (objectively measured) in various roles. By discriminating the range of talent that correlates to excellent performance, we are able to help organizations place and develop individuals in optimal career trajectories, "growing them" according to their unique talents. Because talent is a pervasive human phenomenon, gender, age, culture, and other inclusiveness issues can be handled in a nondiscriminatory way. And because talent is precursor to acquisition of skills and competencies, focusing on talents significantly enhances an individual's career and the client organization's succession planning.

Gallup's Great Place to Work

Despite the importance of both the sociological and individual perspectives, Gallup believes it is the intersection of these two that is most important for organizations. We call it the "great place to work." As described in Buckingham and Coffman's *First, Break All the Rules,* Gallup consultants use the Q12® to provide a measure of the extent to which individuals are rightly placed and rightly managed, creating the great place to work. These Q12® questions are: (1) Do I know what is expected of me at work? (2) Do I have the materials and equipment I need to do my work right? (3) At work, do I have the opportunity to do what I do best every day? (4) In the last seven days have I received recognition or praise for good work? (5) Does my supervisor, or someone at work, seem to care about me as a person? (6) Is there someone at work who encourages my development? (7) At work, do my opinions seem to count? (8) Does the mission/purpose of my company make me feel like my work is important? (9) Are my coworkers committed to doing quality work? (10) Do I have a best friend at work? (11) In the last six months, have I talked with someone about my progress? (12) At work, have I had opportunities to learn and grow? (See Buckingham and Coffman, 1999, p. 28.)

Within thousands of business units, Gallup has found a strong significant relationship between these Q12® employee survey measures and key business performance outcomes: profit, productivity, retention, and customer satisfaction and loyalty. The right fit of talent and the right management of that talent has also been found to correlate with brand, productivity, profitability, and even specific areas such as safety.

The Gallup Path ®

Gallup sees its primary contribution to the engagement of organizational behavior lying along the Gallup Path ®. Having "linked" the steps of this path to the previously mentioned business performance outcomes, we describe it in terms of nine related "steps" or practices. We see the steps of the Path as: (1) identify strengths of individuals, (2) put them in a role of "right fit," (3) provide great managers, (4) provide *a great place to work*, and then have, (5) engaged associates, (6) loyal customers, (7) sustainable growth, (8) real profit increase, and (9) stock value increase. Although other dynamics of organizational behavior can and should be given attention and nurtured, Gallup focuses on these because of their clearly demonstrated connection to business performance outcomes, the localized, actionable measure the Q12® methodology provides, and the "linkage" of instruments and education used to support leaders in their organizational needs.

Examples of Gallup Best Practices in Action

Among Gallup's hundreds of clients are world-class global manufacturing companies based in both Asia and Europe. One of the Asian clients had built its North American success on product quality, assuming that customer loyalty would follow. In the absence of these results, and under pressure to find a way to increase the speed of effective management decision making, Gallup worked with them to help build a "great place to work." As discussed in *First, Break All the Rules,* we helped them identify their most effective managers. These best managers were trained to build a great place to work and given associated measures to enable self-awareness of increasingly effective performance. These mangers were developed to also think of themselves and others in terms of their strengths. Teams and practices of delegation and positioning were pursed in a way that took the talents of all individuals into account. The performance of "best fit" managers, in terms of strengths and talents, was significantly higher from the outset. In response to the Gallup training, the continued measurement shows significantly increased productivity, retention, and customer satisfaction.

In another example, a global European-based organization came to Gallup because of public confusion between two of its brands and some negative or ambivalent association with its lead brand in particular. In addition to helping them think about some of the usual strategic marketing and brand interventions, we also went into the organization itself. There we focused on the talent of the people in the organization. Leaders were amazed and delighted when we were able to show them that who is in the company, in terms of talent, has a brand effect, even when there is no direct contact between those associates and the customer. It would possibly have been more common to look only at their practices or competencies and then impose them on the lower groups. This more typical approach, however, overlooks the important question of how people impact outcome. It also misses the obvious issues that low performers are less likely to effectively implement the practices of the "stars," anyway. Of course it can help to know best practice. But best practice and desired competencies must be kept in conjunction with "best people," in terms of talent. This client is dealing with its brand and market challenges, in part by getting the right talent in place to support the brand. In summary, a key to the Gallup approach is that "best people" are where "best practices" come from.

CHAPTER 1

Introduction to Organizational Behavior

Learning Objectives

Provide an overview of the major challenges and the paradigm shift facing management now in the twenty-first century.

Outline an organizational behavior perspective for today's management.

Summarize the Hawthorne studies as the starting point of modern organizational behavior.

Explain the methodology that is used to accumulate knowledge and facilitate understanding of organizational behavior.

Relate the various theoretical frameworks that serve as a foundation for a model of organizational behavior.

Present the social cognitive model of organizational behavior that serves as the conceptual framework for the text.

Starting with Best Practice Leaders' Advice

The "Odd Couple" General Electric CEO Jack Welch and Sun Microsystems CEO Scott McNealy on the Interface Between the "New" and the "Old" Economy

Although recently retired, during Jack Welch's over 20 years of running General Electric, he became the most respected company leader of the "old" economy. GE, which has reinvented itself for the new economy under Welch's leadership, has hundreds of thousands of employees, with a diversity of businesses ranging from broadcasting to jet engines to credit cards to consumer electronics to lightbulbs. Sun Microsystems, with its double digit thousands of employees and CEO, Scott McNealy, represent the "new" economy. They manufacture computers that undergrid the Internet and are one of the elite companies that has helped create an information and communications infrastructure that supports a whole new way of doing business. These two friends and very successful CEOs will tell you that there's a lot to learn from each other's experience, as the new paradigm of business meets the old.

Q1:   *Four years ago, Jack was standing at the podium with Intel's Andy Grove at a Fortune 500 CEO Forum in San Francisco, and he basically told everyone, "I don't have a computer in my office, and I don't need a computer." Obviously Scott comes from a different place. Eight years ago he was presciently saying that e-mail is a killer application for business and spouting the slogan "The network is the computer." You guys are coming from two completely different places, and two dramatically different generations.*

Welch: So I'm basically the Neanderthal?

McNealy: . . . among other things . . .

Welch: And this dynamite stud has had the thing going for years. Is that what this [interview] is all about?

Q2:   *No, it's more that your two worlds are converging, and your growing friendship is highly symbolic. Scott's on the GE board now, and he's obviously a new kind of character for that body. And in the meantime you have transformed into "e-Jack," spurring GE to become a leader among traditional old-economy companies in embracing the Internet. When did you first use e-mail?*

Welch: I'd say 24 months ago. My wife had a major impact on my game. She was all over this computer stuff. Having a second wife 17 years younger than you can get you in the game faster. I wouldn't advise that technique for everyone, but it worked for me.

McNealy: Must've been 1982, when we set up shop at Sun.

Q5:   *How many e-mails a day do you get?*

McNealy: I get 200 or 300. I've got five direct reports right now, but I also have e-mail conversations going regularly with probably two-thirds of Sun's VPs, of which there are about 120.

Welch: I get 40 to 50. I have about 20 to 25 direct reports, but I use e-mail to reach down into the organization, too. I just got an e-mail this afternoon from the fellow who is running our Spanish plastics factory. He's been having some start-up difficulties in the past few months, and he was giving me the weekly progress report.

Q6:   *Jack, GE has a "geek mentoring" program in which 1,000 Internet-savvy employees work closely with senior managers one-on-one to show them the ropes of using the Internet. What role did that play in helping you get comfortable with the Internet?*

Welch: Don't call them geeks. They are 1,000 young people who were relatively new to the company but who were very good on the Web. It was an idea I copied from one of our guys in Europe who kept telling me about "his mentor." This was the president of an insurance company, and I wondered, what did he need with a mentor? Then he explained that he spent two or three hours with his mentor every week to learn the computer.

What we did with this was tip the organization upside down so the senior people are all working with somebody junior. So we get all the benefits and transparency of an upside-down organization. These guys all had mentors, they came in and did the stuff, and they learned a lot about new people, too.

Q7:   *So what exactly do you do on the Web now?*

Welch: Besides e-mail, I look at financial services Websites. I go to Yahoo. I go to chat rooms and see what they're saying about GE. I'm tempted to jump in, but I don't. I go on almost every night to see what the gossip is. I go to the CNBC site, too.

McNealy: You know, the Internet is really three things: First, it is messaging—namely, e-mail. Second, it's a medium for transactions. Now everybody is all geeked up about business-to-business, auctioning, and other online transactions and trading. Third, it is becoming an entertainment medium. These are all quite distinct activities. You go to Amazon, E*Trade, or eBay to transact; you go to Disney's Go.com to be entertained. Me, I'm almost entirely messaging-oriented, so e-mail is what the Net is to me.

Q8:   *Where do you think we are as an economy as far as e-business goes?*

Welch: First inning.

Q9:   *And GE is out front? Catching up? Way behind?*

Welch: Against our competitive playing field, we're ahead of the game. Against an absolute standard, we're behind the game.

Q10: *You're a GE director now, Scott. What's your appraisal of how GE is faring on the Net?*

McNealy: I usually entitle my speeches "You're All Hopelessly Behind Dot-Comming Your Businesses." And after I get everybody depressed, I tell the old "60-foot-tall-Internet-bear-in-the-woods" story, which goes like this: There's this big Internet grizzly charging down the path at you. So you stop and put on your tennis shoes so you can run faster. That's sort of what Jack's doing at GE. A competitor might warn that there's no way GE can outrun that bear, and that may be true. But Jack's reply to him should be, "I don't have to outrun the bear, I just have to outrun you." And I would say that GE very clearly is outrunning the other traditional hikers in its businesses. The fastest elephant is a very good thing to be.

But at the same time, you have to worry about death by a thousand cuts, which is also what the Internet is all about. There's not going to be one big thunderbolt that kills you. If you don't dot.com your business, if you don't put your employees online, if you don't put your customers online, if you don't put your service data online, each one of those things will come back to get you. Most of these thousand cuts are self-inflicted.

As a GE board member, one of my jobs is to yell, "Fire!" Because the whole economy is on fire, in every way you can imagine. But it's not a big bonfire, it's lots of tiny Bic lighters everywhere.

Q11: *So, Scott, what are you learning from Jack?*

McNealy: Jack has seen a movie I haven't seen. All of a sudden we're at 37,000 employees, we're growing at 20 percent-plus growth rates. . .the kinds of things that Jack has done, I'm beginning to have to deal with. It's a vast organization. You can't just call everyone into the lunchroom and stand on a chair and tell them, "Here's plan B." That's what I used to do.

It's a very, very different process. Jack has developed a learning organization that can spin on a dime, because he's got these black-belt, Green Beret-type folks infiltrated throughout the organization. So when the word comes down that this is the new initiative, away they go.

The other thing fantastic that Jack has done that I'm trying to do at Sun has to do with this: The bigger the boat gets, the more crisp, clear, and sparing you need to be about picking strategies and ideas to pursue. For GE, globalization was one, building a boundaryless organization was another, product service was another, Six Sigma quality, and now the Web. There have been just five companywide initiatives in Jack's whole career. My folks will tell you that I've got five initiatives per meeting.

So one thing I'm learning to do is to step back from spewing an idea a minute to focus on driving higher-level issues. For us, that's things like chip development, or availability as opposed to quality. I'm going to pick very few fights going forward, and I'm going to win them. That's the best thing I've learned from Jack.

All the speculation and speeches about launching into the new millennium have come and gone. Now trying to effectively manage 21st century organizations has become the harsh reality. Ask anyone today—management professors, practitioners, or students—what the major challenges are in this new environment, the answer will be very consistent: advanced information technology and globalization. As an afterthought, managing diversity and trying to solve ethical problems and dilemmas may also be mentioned. These are unquestionably major issues facing the management of today's organizations and are given major attention in this text. However, the field of organizational behavior in general, and the basic premise and assumptions of this text in particular, is that managing the people—the human resources of an organization—have been, are, and will continue to be, *the* major challenge and critical competitive advantage.

Information technology, globalization, diversity, and ethics serve as very important environmental or contextual dimensions for organizational behavior. However, as Sam Walton, the founder of Wal-Mart and richest person in the world when he died, declared to this author over lunch several years ago when asked what was the answer to successful organizations—"People are the key!" The technology can be purchased and copied, it levels the playing field. The people, on the other hand, cannot be copied. Although human bodies may be cloned in the future, their ideas, personalities, motivation, and organization cultural values cannot be copied. Becoming recognized as "human capital"[1] or "intellectual capital,"[2] the human resources of an organization and how they are managed represent the competitive advantage of today's and tomorrow's organizations.[3] As the ultimate "techie" Bill Gates astutely observed: "The inventory, the value of my company, walks out the door every evening."

Interestingly, whereas the technology dramatically changes, sometimes monthly or even weekly, the human side of enterprise has not and will not change that fast. As recently noted by well-known international management scholar Geert Hofstede, "Because management is always about people, its essence is dealing with human nature. Since human nature seems to have been extremely stable over recorded history, the essence of management has been and will be equally stable over time."[4] The nature of work and the workplace itself,[5] the traditional employment contract,[6] and the composition of the workforce[7] are all dramatically changing and given attention in this text. Yet, the overriding purpose of the first edition, now 30 years ago, of trying to better understand and effectively manage human behavior in organizations remains the essence of this ninth edition.

This introductory chapter gives the perspective, background, methodology, and approach to the field. After a brief discussion of the current environmental challenges and the paradigm shift facing management, the historical background is touched on. Particular attention is given to the famous Hawthorne studies, which are generally recognized to be the beginning of the systematic study and understanding of organizational behavior. Next, an overview of the methodology used in the scientific study of organizational behavior is given. The chapter concludes by defining exactly what is involved in organizational behavior and by providing a conceptual model for the rest of the text.

THE CHALLENGES FACING MANAGEMENT

The academic field of organizational behavior has been around for at least the past thirty years. However, as the accompanying OB in Action: "Some Things Never Really Change" clearly indicates, problems facing managers of human organizations have been around since the beginning of civilization. This case, with but a few word changes, is taken from the Old (not New) Testament of the Bible (Exodus 18:13–27), recognized by the Jewish, Christian, and Islam religions. The case took place over 3,000 years ago, the charismatic leader was Moses (when he led his people from Egypt to Palestine), the well-known consultant was Jethro, Moses' father-in-law, and the higher authority was God. Embedded in the case are many topics covered in this text—for example, charismatic leadership, management of conflict, empowerment, management of change, and nonfinancial incentives.

OB IN ACTION:

Some Things Never Really Change

A powerful, charismatic leader is having problems. A well-known consultant is called in to help. The consultant notices that the leader tries to handle all problems and conflicts of his people himself. People queue up before his office; because he is overwhelmed, he cannot handle all the business. So the consultant has a private talk with the leader and tells him to structure his organization by delegating authority, empowering subordinates to handle the workload. These subordinates should be selected not only on their leadership abilities, but also on their character: They should be truthful, not driven by material gain. The new structure should resolve all daily issues at the lowest possible level; only the big and difficult issues should be brought before the leader. He should focus on strategy—on dealing with the higher authority, on establishing new approaches and teaching these to the people, on showing them the way to go and the work to be done. The case states that the leader listens to the consultant and carries out the reorganization which is a success, and the consultant returns home.

Although the problems with human organizations and the solution over the ages have not really changed that much, the emphasis and surrounding environmental context certainly have changed. For example, in the 1980s and 1990s managers were preoccupied with restructuring their organizations to improve productivity and meet the competitive challenges in the international marketplace and quality expectations of customers. Although the resulting "lean and mean" organizations offered some short-run benefits in terms of lowered costs and improved productivity, if they continued to do business as usual they would not be able to meet current or future challenges. As a recent *Harvard Business Review* article argues, "These are scary times for managers."[8] The singular reason given for these frightening times—the increasing danger of disruptive change. Consider the following changes in the nature of work:

- The technological and human components of work are inextricably blended.
- Jobs are less tightly defined and programmed.
- Contingent workers comprise a significant proportion of the workforce.
- Customers influence the work that is performed within the organization and the standards applied to evaluating that work.
- Teams rather than individuals produce the basic units of work.
- Organizational charts fail to capture the networks of influence and relationships that characterize the workplace.[9]

All of these points represent disruptive change and require new thinking and new ways of managing. Take the disappearance of tightly defined and programmed jobs. The tendency is to think that this may be happening in the dot-com firms such as Amazon, but not in the mainline companies such as 60-year-old Koch Industries based in Wichita, Kansas, which is into chemicals, agriculture, financial services, and oil and gas. Yet the head of the Human Resources Department at Koch recently noted that they no longer use the old approach of a complex system of job classifications, pay grades, promotional charts, and job descriptions. Why doesn't either Amazon or Koch

Industries have defined jobs? Because the nature of work is changing so rapidly that rigid job structures impede the work to be done now, and that may drastically change the following year, month, or even week.[10]

The "nonjob" environment and the other points previously listed are already the reality for most organizations. The following changes may not yet be as common, but few would argue that this is a representative look at the workplace in the not-too-distant future:

- Knowledge workers will not have a traditional contractual relationship with employers. Instead, they will rent their professional skills and knowledge on a "freelance" basis to different companies at different times.
- The corporate headquarters will evolve into "heart centers," where emotional intelligence fuels creativity, innovation, and an enterprising spirit.
- Downsizing, upsizing, rightsizing, growth, and stabilization all will be welcome forms of "sizing" companies. People will have coping mechanisms that prepare them for any shift.
- In the 24/7 global environment, productivity will be driven by speed and efficiency rather than the number of staff hours dedicated to a project.
- Internet-speed workplaces will radically transform the world of work, making work across multiple time zones and irregular schedules more and more common.
- People won't work for organizations where they don't get a share of the profits and where work/life balance is not a given.
- Companies will no longer decide which benefits an employee needs. Instead, employees will log on to their company's website to customize their benefits programs.
- People will feel an increasing ownership of their destinies, lives, and careers. "Living skills" will be just as important as "professional skills."
- The boundaries between work and school will blur. Learning will be centered more around professions and trades, and there will be more mentor/apprentice relationships, with Internet-based coaching provided by people one has never met.
- A digital divide will emerge, separating employees who are tech-savvy and those who aren't. Smart companies will invest more in human capital and become virtual universities to narrow the gap.
- The *Fortune* list of companies will become less of an economic force. There will be new forms of stock trading, where businesses will be valued according to their contributions to the local and global communities.[11]

This new environment is disruptive, discontinuous change. It represents a new paradigm, a new way of thinking about the workplace.

UNDERGOING A PARADIGM SHIFT

The term *paradigm* comes from the Greek *paradeigma,* which translates as "model, pattern, or example." First introduced years ago by the philosophy of science historian Thomas Kuhn,[12] the term *paradigm* is now used to mean a broad model, a framework, a way of thinking, or a scheme for understanding reality.[13] In the words of popular futurist Joel Barker, a paradigm simply establishes the rules (written or unwritten), defines the boundaries, and tells one how to behave within the boundaries to be successful.[14] The impact of internationalization, information technology, diversity, and ethics given detailed attention in the next two chapters and a workforce recently described as a "blend of traditionally trained baby boomers, in-your-face Gen Xers, people with inadequate literacy skills from disadvantaged areas, and techies raised on computers,"[15] has led to a paradigm shift. In other words, for today's and tomorrow's organizations and management, there are new rules with different boundaries requiring new and different behavior inside the boundaries for organizations and management to be successful.

Those who study paradigm shifts, such as the shift that took place in the basic sciences from deterministic, mechanistic Cartesian-Newtonian to Einstein's relativity and quantum physics, note that "real controversy takes place, often involving substantial restructuring of the entire scientific community under conditions of great uncertainty."[16] Commonly called the "paradigm effect," a situation arises in which those in the existing paradigm may not even see the changes that are occurring, let alone reason and draw logical inferences and perceptions about the changes. This effect helps explain why there is considerable resistance to change and why it is very difficult to move from the old economy and management paradigm to the new. There is discontinuous change in the shift to the new paradigm. As one observer of the needed 21st-century organization noted:

> The depth of change required demands that those charged with charting a passage through hurricane-like seas do more than run up a new set of sails. What is involved equates to a quantum shift in, not just learning, but how we learn; not just doing things differently, but questioning whether we should be doing many of the things we currently believe in, at all; not just in drawing together more information but in questioning how we know what it is (we think) we know.[17]

This text on organizational behavior has the goal of helping today's and tomorrow's managers make the transition to the new paradigm. Some of the new paradigm characteristics include Chapter 2's coverage of information technology and globalization, Chapter 3's description of and suggestions for managing diversity and ethics, Chapter 4 on the organizational context of design and culture, and Chapter 5 on reward systems. The new paradigm sets the stage for the study, understanding, and application of the time-tested micro cognitive processes (Chapters 6–9), dynamics (Chapters 10–14), and the final part on managing and leading for high performance (Chapters 15–18). However, before getting directly into the rest of the text, we must know why management needs a new perspective to help meet the environmental challenges and the shift to the new paradigm. We must gain an appreciation of the historical background, methodology, and theoretical frameworks that serve as the basis of this text's perspective and model for organizational behavior.

A NEW PERSPECTIVE FOR MANAGEMENT

How is management going to meet the environmental challenges and paradigm shift outlined above?[18] Management is generally considered to have three major dimensions— technical, conceptual, and human. The technical dimension consists of the manager's functional expertise in accounting or engineering or marketing and increasingly in information technology. There seems little question that today's managers are competent in their functional specialization. When it comes to IT (information technology), although there has been and will be peaks and valleys in the dot-com firms and big high-tech firms, there is still a shortage of specialists and CIOs (chief information officers)[19] or CKOs (chief knowledge officers)[20] now and in the foreseeable future in the United States and abroad.[21] However, managers in general are beginning to close the learning gap on appreciating and understanding the role, if not the actual use, of electronic

OB IN ACTION:

The Four Horsemen of the New Economy

Not so long ago, it was a lot simpler to get a sense of how tech companies were doing. In the mainframe era, IBM was the dominant manufacturer and the industry's guiding light. In the 1990s, Microsoft and Intel, which made the software and chips for virtually all personal computers, were the best gauge of high tech's health. While all three remain forces to be reckoned with, they no longer provide definitive guidance about the tech economy.

Meet the new bosses: the Four Horsemen of the New Economy. More than any other collection of companies, Oracle, Sun Microsystems, EMC, and Cisco Systems represent the building blocks of Net business. Chances are, every company moving online will buy a piece of hardware or software from one of these four giants. Cisco makes the routers that do the heavy lifting—shuttling a corporation's data to and from the Net. Sun sells the Web servers that produce millions of Web pages. EMC is the storage king that holds the sea of ones and zeroes that make up digital information. And Oracle makes the database and e-commerce software that enables companies to digitize catalogs, process transactions, and move businesses online.

Over the past year, the stocks of the Four Horsemen have been up and down. With these kinds of stock valuations, even modest missteps are penalized. But let's be clear about what happened: While Oracle missed one number by a slight margin, its overall performance remains strong. By taking its own operations online and streamlining its business processes, it boosted profitability substantially. This past quarter, Oracle drove its operating margins up to 29.1% from 17.4% in the prior year's quarter. What's more, revenues for fiscal 2001 are projected to rise 20% to about $12 billion.

In the next six weeks, the three remaining Horsemen have experienced similar gyrations. How they perform should give a good indication of whether the current market turmoil is just a blip or a serious long-term problem. If Sun, EMC, and Cisco meet or exceed Wall Street's revenue growth expectations, the tech economy should remain strong. That should stabilize the queasy stock market. But if the four Horsemen miss their numbers, look out below.

Certainly, the high-tech industry is more complex and quicksilver than ever. But, regardless of short-term market antics, the Four Horsemen currently are providing the best barometer of the New Economy.

technology. This is particularly true of the so-called "Four Horsemen" of the new economy (see the accompanying OB in Action). The urgency of this technology component of management was brought out in a humorous hypothetical memo that recently appeared in a *Business Week* special issue on "Electronic Business: A Survival Guide":

> We have to get off our butts and get wired. Not just E-mail. Not just Web browsers or a Web site. I mean the big kahuna: electronic commerce. Our future depends on nothing less than transforming our company into a full-fledged E-business. Now. Or else we're roadkill.[22]

So, although managers are certainly more aware and becoming competent in their functional/technical component, few today would question that, at least in the past, most practicing managers either ignored the conceptual and human dimensions of their jobs or made some overly simplistic assumptions.

Following the assumptions that pioneering management scholar Douglas McGregor labeled many years ago as Theory X, most managers thought, and many still think, that their employees were basically lazy, that they were interested only in money, and that if you could make them happy, they would be high performers. When such Theory X assumptions were accepted, the human problems facing management were relatively clear-cut and easy to solve. All management had to do was devise monetary incentive plans, ensure security, and provide good working conditions; morale would then be high, and maximum productivity would result. It was as simple as one, two, three. Human relations experts, industrial psychologists, and industrial engineers supported this approach, and human resource managers implemented it.

Unfortunately, this approach no longer works with the current environmental demands under the new paradigm. Although no real harm has been done, and some good actually resulted in the early stages of organizational development, it is now evident that such a simplistic approach falls far short of providing a meaningful solution to the complex challenges.

The major fault with the traditional approach is that it overlooks and oversimplifies far too many aspects of the problem. Human behavior at work is much more complicated and diverse than is suggested by the economic-security–working-conditions approach. The new perspective assumes that employees are extremely complex and that there is a need for theoretical understanding backed by rigorous empirical research before applications can be made for managing people effectively. The transition has now been completed. The traditional human relations approach no longer has a dominant role in the behavioral approach to management. Few people would question that the organizational behavior approach, with its accompanying body of knowledge and applications, dominates the behavioral approach to management now and will do so in the foreseeable future. Unfortunately, still only a small minority of practicing managers and their organization cultures really buy into, fully implement, and then stick with a full-fledged organizational behavior, high-performance work practices approach to management.

Stanford professor Jeff Pfeffer has recently summarized the current status of the organizational behavior approach to real-world management as a "One-Eighth" situation.[23] and "The Knowing-Doing Gap."[24] By "One-Eighth" he means that roughly half of today's managers really believe and buy into the importance of the human side of enterprise and that the people are truly the competitive advantage of their organizations. Taken a step further, however, only about half of those who believe really do something about it. Thus, he says that only about one-fourth are fully implementing the high performance work practices (HPWPs) that flow from organizational behavior theory and research—such as, pay for performance, self-managed teams, 360 degree (multisource) feedback systems, and behavioral management. Most organizations have tried one or a few of the HPWPs emphasized in the chapters of Part 4 of this text, but only about a fourth fully implement the whole approach. So now we are down to one-fourth, where does the "One-Eighth" come from? Well, Pfeffer estimates that only about one-half of the one-fourth who implement the approach stick with it over time. Thus, only about one-eighth ($\frac{1}{2} \times \frac{1}{2} \times \frac{1}{2} = \frac{1}{8}$) of today's organizations believe it, do it, stick with it (the "3 Its"). The so-called "One-Eighth Organizations" have as their organizational cultural values the importance of human capital and the techniques in place to carry it out over time. Importantly, as Pfeffer well documents in his book the *Human Equation,* these one-eighth organizations are world class, the best in the world—such as, General Electric, Southwest Airlines, Gallup, and AES (a global developer and operator of power plants).

Today there is ample accumulated research findings and documented practices of the best firms to prove the value of the human factor. Pfeffer and Sutton felt compelled to try to explain why most managers today know this importance and how to implement the approach to improve organizational performance, but still are not doing it (i.e., *The Knowing-Doing Gap*). They identify five sources that seem to prevent the majority of managers from effective implementation and sustainability: (1) hollow talk, (2) debilitating fear, (3) destructive internal competition, (4) poorly designed and complex measurement systems, and (5) mindless reliance on precedent. They are convinced that if these obstacles (i.e., resistance to change) can be overcome, then "Competitive advantage comes from being able to do something others don't do. When most companies are stuck talking about what should be done, those that get down to business and actually *do* will emerge as star performers."[25] The purpose of this text is to present and translate what we know about organizational behavior and how to apply this knowledge. Hopefully, this will facilitate closing the gap with action. The starting point in any such journey should be with history and research methods.

HISTORICAL BACKGROUND: THE HAWTHORNE STUDIES

Most of today's organizational behavior texts have dropped any reference to history. Yet, the position taken here is that history always has important lessons to teach, and as was recently brought out again, "It is an interesting phenomenon that that which is touted as fundamentally 'new management practice' is essentially the readapting of existing 'old management truths'."[26] There is no question that the early management pioneers, such as Henri Fayol, Henry Ford, Alfred P. Sloan, and even the scientific managers at the end of the 19th century such as Frederick W. Taylor, recognized the behavioral side of management. However, they did not emphasize the human dimension; they let it play only a minor role in comparison with the roles of hierarchical structure, specialization, and the management functions of planning and controlling. An example would be the well known Nobel prize-winning French engineer turned executive Henri Fayol.

About the time of World War I Fayol headed up what was at that time the largest coal-mining firm in Europe. Writing the generally considered first book about management, he emphasized that the purpose of the organization was to get the work done in specialized, machinelike functions. He did not emphasize that the organization is made up of people; it is not a machine. Yet, perhaps the most widely recognized management expert in modern times, Peter Drucker, has stated, "The organization is, above all, social. It is people."[27] There were varied and complex reasons for the emergence of the importance of the organization as a social entity, but it is the famous Hawthorne studies that provide historical roots for the notion of a social organization made up of people and marks the generally recognized starting point for the field of organizational behavior.

The Illumination Studies: A Serendipitous Discovery

In 1924, the studies started at the huge Hawthorne Works of the Western Electric Company outside of Chicago. The initial illumination studies attempted to examine the relationship between light intensity on the shop floor of manual work sites and employee productivity. A test group and a control group were used. The test group in an early phase showed no increase or decrease in output in proportion to the increase or decrease of illumination. The control group with unchanged illumination increased output by the same amount overall as the test group. Subsequent phases brought the level of light down to moonlight intensity; the workers could barely see what they were doing, but productivity increased. The results were baffling to the researchers. Obviously, some variables in the experiment were not being held constant or under control. Something besides the level of illumination was causing the change in productivity. This something, of course, was the complex human variable.

It is fortunate that the illumination experiments did not end up in the wastebasket. Those responsible for the Hawthorne studies had enough foresight and spirit of scientific inquiry to accept the challenge of looking beneath the surface of the apparent failure of the experiments. In a way, the results of the illumination experiments were a serendipitous discovery, which, in research, is an accidental discovery. The classic example of serendipity is the breakthrough for penicillin that occurred when Sir Alexander Fleming accidentally discovered green mold on the side of a test tube. That the green mold was not washed down the drain and that the results of the illumination experiments were not thrown into the trash can be credited to the researchers' not being blinded by the unusual or seemingly worthless results of their experimentation. The serendipitous results of the illumination experiments provided the impetus for the further study of human behavior in the workplace.

Subsequent Phases of the Hawthorne Studies

The illumination studies were followed by a study in the relay room, where operators assembled relay switches. This phase of the study tried to test specific variables, such as length of workday, rest breaks, and method of payment. The results were basically the same as those of the illumination studies: each test period yielded higher productivity than the previous one. Even when the workers were subjected to the original conditions of the experiment, productivity increased. The conclusion was that the independent variables (rest pauses and so forth) were not by themselves causing the change in the dependent variable (output). As in the illumination experiments, something was still not being controlled that was causing the change in the dependent variable (output).

Still another phase was the bank wiring room study. As in the preceding relay room experiments, the bank wirers were placed in a separate test room. The researchers were reluctant to segregate the bank wiring group because they recognized that this would alter the realistic factory environment they were attempting to simulate. However, for practical reasons, the research team decided to use a separate room. Unlike the relay room experiments, the bank wiring room study involved no experimental changes once the study had started. Instead, an observer and an interviewer gathered objective data for study. Of particular interest was the fact that the department's regular supervisors were used in the bank wiring room. Just as in the department out on the factory floor, these supervisors' main function was to maintain order and control.

The results of the bank wiring room study were essentially opposite to those of the relay room experiments. In the bank wiring room there were not the continual increases in productivity that occurred in the relay room. Rather, output was actually restricted by the bank wirers. By scientific management analysis—for example, time and motion study—the industrial engineers had arrived at a standard of 7312 terminal connections per day. This represented $2\frac{1}{2}$ equipments (banks). The workers had a different brand of rationality. They decided that 2 equipments was a "proper" day's work. Thus, $2\frac{1}{2}$ equipments represented the management norm for production, but 2 equipments was the informal group norm and the actual output. The researchers determined that the informal group norm of 2 equipments represented restriction of output rather than a lack of ability to produce at the company standard of $2\frac{1}{2}$ equipments.

Of particular interest from a group dynamics standpoint were the social pressures used to gain compliance with the group norms. The incentive system dictated that the more a worker produced, the more money the worker would earn. Also, the best producers would be laid off last, and thus they could be more secure by producing more. Yet, in the face of this management rationale, almost all the workers restricted output. Social ostracism, ridicule, and name-calling were the major sanctions used by the group to enforce this restriction. In some instances, actual physical pressure in the form of a game called "binging" was applied. In the game, a worker would be hit as hard as possible, with the privilege of returning one "bing," or hit. Forcing rate-busters to play the game became an effective sanction. These group pressures had a tremendous impact on all the workers. Social ostracism was more effective in gaining compliance with the informal group norm than money and security were in attaining the scientifically derived management norm.

Implications of the Hawthorne Studies

Despite some obvious philosophical,[28] theoretical,[29] and methodological limitations by today's standards of research (which will be covered next), the Hawthorne studies did provide some interesting insights that contributed to a better understanding of human behavior in organizations.[30] For instance, one interesting aspect of the Hawthorne studies is the contrasting results obtained in the relay room and the bank wiring room. In the relay room, production continually increased throughout the test period, and the relay assemblers were very positive. The opposite was true in the bank wiring room; blatant restriction of output was practiced by disgruntled workers. Why the difference in these two phases of the studies?

One clue to the answer to this question may be traced to the results of a questionnaire administered to the subjects in the relay room. The original intent of the questions was to determine the health and habits of the workers. Their answers were generally inconclusive except that *all* the operators indicated they felt "better" in the relay test room. A follow-up questionnaire then asked about specific items in the test room situation. In discussions of the Hawthorne studies, the follow-up questionnaire results, in their entirety, usually are not mentioned. Most discussions cite the subjects' unanimous preference for working in the test room instead of the regular department. Often overlooked, however, are the workers' explanations for their choice. In order of preference, the workers gave the following reasons:

1. Small group
2. Type of supervision
3. Earnings
4. Novelty of the situation
5. Interest in the experiment
6. Attention received in the test room[31]

It is important to note that novelty, interest, and attention were relegated to the fourth, fifth, and sixth positions. These last three areas usually are associated with the famous Hawthorne effect. Many social scientists imply that the increases in the relay room productivity can be attributed solely to the fact that the participants in the study were given special attention and that they were enjoying a novel, interesting experience. This is labeled the *Hawthorne effect* and is, of course, a real problem with all human experimental subjects. But to say that all the results of the relay room experiments were due to such an effect on the subjects seems to ignore the important impact of the small group, the type of supervision, and earnings. All these variables (that is, experimental design, group dynamics, styles of leadership and supervision, and rewards), and much more separate the old human relations movement and the modern approach to the field of organizational behavior. So do the refinement and fine-tuning of the research methodology used to accumulate meaningful knowledge about organizational behavior.

RESEARCH METHODOLOGY

The understanding and effective application of organizational behavior depends on a rigorous research methodology. The search for the truth of why people behave the way they do is a very delicate and complex process. In fact, the problems are so great that many scholars, chiefly from the physical and engineering sciences, argue that there can be no precise science of behavior. They maintain that humans cannot be treated like chemical or physical elements; they cannot be effectively controlled or manipulated. For example, the critics state that, under easily controllable conditions, 2 parts hydrogen to 1 part oxygen will always result in water and that no analogous situation exists in human behavior. Human variables such as motives, learning, perception, values, and even "a Hawthorne Effect" on the part of both subject and investigator confound the controls that are attempted. For these reasons, behavioral scientists in general and organizational behavior researchers in particular are often on the defensive and must be very careful to comply with accepted methods of science.[32]

The Overall Scientific Perspective

Behavioral scientists in general and organizational behavior researchers in particular strive to attain the following hallmarks of any science:

1. The overall purposes are understanding/explanation, prediction, and control.
2. The definitions are precise and operational.
3. The measures are reliable and valid.
4. The methods are systematic.
5. The results are cumulative.

Figure 1.1 summarizes the relationship between the practical behavioral problems and unanswered questions facing today's managers, research methodology, and the existing body of knowledge. When a question arises or a problem evolves, the first place to turn for an answer is the existing body of knowledge. It is possible that the question can be answered immediately or the problem solved without going any further. Unfortunately, the answer is not always found in the body of knowledge and must be discovered through appropriate research methodology.

Although behavioral science in general compared to the physical and biological sciences is relatively young, and the field of organizational behavior is even younger—it's origins really only go back to the early 1970s—there is now enough accumulated knowledge that organizational behavior principles can be provided for the effective management of human behavior in organizations. As explained in the preface, this ninth edition is the first time research-based principles have been offered in an organizational behavior text. Interestingly, it is the research technique of meta-analysis providing the quantitative synthesis and testing of all available studies that permits the confident

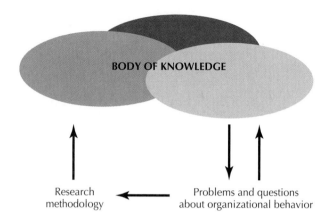

FIGURE 1.1

Simple relationships among problems, methodology, and knowledge.

stating of the principles presented in this text. As Williams points out, meta-analysis "shows what works and the conditions under which management techniques may work better or worse in the 'real world.' Meta-analysis is based on the simple idea that if one study shows that a management technique doesn't work and another study shows that it does, an average of those results is probably the best estimate of how well that management practice works (or doesn't work)."[33]

Although your author of this text believes there is now enough research studies in some areas of organizational behavior to be quantitatively synthesized through meta-analysis into guiding principles, it is also recognized that many questions and problems in organizational behavior cannot be answered or solved directly by existing knowledge. Thus, a working knowledge of research methodology becomes especially important to future managers, both as knowledgeable and critical consumers of the rapidly expanding literature reporting the results of organizational behavior research and as sophisticated practitioners who are capable of applying appropriate research methods to solve difficult problems in the workplace.

Starting with Theory

It has often been said (usually by theoreticians) that there is nothing as practical as a good theory. Yet students of organizational behavior are usually "turned off" by all the theories that pervade the field. The reason for all the theories, of course, is the still relative newness of the field and the complexity and multidimensionality of the variables involved.[34] The purpose of any theory, including those found in organizational behavior, is to explain and predict the phenomenon in question; theories allow the researcher to deduce logical propositions or hypotheses that can be tested by acceptable designs. Theories are ever changing on the basis of the research results. Thus, theory and research go hand in hand.

After pleading for more and stronger theory in organizational behavior, Sutton and Staw have pointed out that references, data, lists of variables or constructs, diagrams, and hypotheses are *not* theory. Instead, they point out that

> theory is the answer to queries of *why*. Theory is about the connections among phenomena, a story about why acts, events, structure, and thoughts occur. Theory emphasizes the nature of causal relationships, identifying what comes first as well as the timing of such events.

Strong theory, in our view, delves into the underlying processes so as to understand the systematic reasons for a particular occurrence or non-occurrence.[35]

Such theorizing is not easy. "Theorizing takes scientists on mental journeys between the world of observed events, such as falling apples, and the imagined world of hypothetical concepts, such as gravity. Bridging gaps between concrete experience and abstract concepts presents a challenge."[36] However, as Karl Weick, perhaps the most widely recognized theorist in organizational behavior, notes: a good theory explains, predicts, and delights.[37]

The Use of Research Designs

Research design is at the very heart of scientific methodology; it can be used to answer practical questions or to test theoretical propositions/hypotheses. The three designs most often used in organizational behavior research today are the experiment, the case, and the survey. All three have played important roles in the development of meaningful knowledge. The experimental design is borrowed largely from psychology, where it is used extensively; the case and survey designs have traditionally played a bigger role in sociology. All three designs can be used effectively for researching organizational behavior.

A primary aim of any research design is to establish a cause-and-effect relationship. The experimental design offers the best possibility of accomplishing this goal. All other factors being equal, most organizational behavior researchers prefer this method of testing hypotheses. Simply defined, an experiment involves the manipulation of independent variables to measure their effect on, or the change in, dependent variables, while everything else is held constant or controlled. Usually, an experimental group and a control group are formed. The experimental group receives the input of the independent variables (the intervention), and the control group does not. Any measured change in the dependent variable in the experimental group can be attributed to the independent variable, assuming that no change has occurred in any other variable and that no change has occurred in the control group. The controls employed are the key to the successful use of the experimental design. If all intervening variables are held constant or equal, the researcher can conclude with a high degree of confidence that the independent variable caused the change in the dependent variable.

The Validity of Studies

The value of any research study is dependent on its validity, that is, whether the study really demonstrates what it is supposed to demonstrate. In particular, a study must have both *internal validity* and *external validity* in order to make a meaningful contribution to the body of knowledge. A study has internal validity if there are no plausible alternative explanations of the reported results other than those reported. The threats to internal validity include but are not limited to:

1. *History.* Uncontrolled intervening events that occur between the time the preexperiment measurement is taken and the time the postexperiment measurement is taken.
2. *Maturation.* Changes in the subject or subjects with the mere passing of time, irrespective of the experimental treatment.
3. *Testing.* The effect of previous testing on a subject's present performance.
4. *Instrumentation.* Changes in measures of subject performance due to changes in the instruments or observers over time.

5. *Regression.*   Changes in performance due to subjects' going from extreme scores to more typical scores.
6. *Selection.*   Changes due to the differences in the subjects rather than the treatment.
7. *Ambiguity about direction of causation.*   Does A cause B, or does B cause A? This is a problem with correlational studies.
8. *Local history.*   Changes due to the unique situation when the experimental group received the treatment.[38]

Laboratory studies usually control these threats to internal validity better than field studies do. But, as Daniel Ilgen has pointed out, this control afforded by the laboratory is purchased at the price of generalizability and relevance. "As a result, many behavioral scientists decry the use of any laboratory research and dismiss results obtained from such as irrelevant or, worse yet, misleading for the understanding of naturally occurring human behavior."[39]

But, in general, the threats can be minimized, even in field settings, by *pretests* (these allow the investigator to make sure that the experimental and control groups were performing at the same level before the experimental manipulations are made, and they give measurement over time); *control groups* (these permit comparison with experimental groups—they have everything the same except the experimental manipulation); and *random assignment* (this pretty well ensures that the experimental and control groups will be the same, and it allows the correct use of inferential statistics to analyze the results). Thus, the threats to internal validity can be overcome with careful design of the study. This is not always true of external validity, which is concerned with the generalizability of the results obtained. In order for a study to have external validity, the results must be applicable to a wide range of people and situations.[40] Field studies tend to have better external validity than laboratory studies because at least the study takes place in a real setting.

In general, organizational behavior research can be improved by conducting studies longitudinally (over time) and attempting to design studies more from existing theory.[41] The best strategy is to use a number of different designs to answer the same question. The weaknesses of the various designs can offset one another and the problem of common method variance (the results are due to the design, rather than the variables under study) can be overcome.

Normally, the research would start with a laboratory study to isolate and manipulate the variable or variables in question. This would be followed by an attempt to verify the findings in a field setting. This progression from the laboratory to the field may lead to the soundest conclusions. However, free observation in the real setting should probably precede laboratory investigations of organizational behavior problems or questions. Specifically, in recent years qualitative methods are being suggested as a starting point or supplement, if not an alternative, to quantitatively-based and statistically analyzed methods of researching organizational behavior. Van Maanen explains that this qualitative approach "seeks to describe, decode, translate, and otherwise come to terms with the meaning, not the frequency, of certain more or less naturally occurring phenomena in the social world."[42] Multiple designs and multiple measures have the best chance for valid, meaningful research in organizational behavior.

DEFINING ORGANIZATIONAL BEHAVIOR

With a rich historical background such as the Hawthorne studies and an accepted scientific methodology as briefly outlined above, the field of organizational behavior is now an accepted academic discipline. As with any other relatively new academic endeavor,

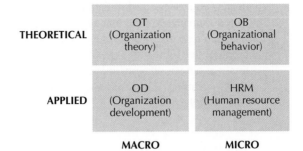

FIGURE 1.2
The relationship of
organizational behavior to
other closely related
disciplines.

however, there have been some rough spots and sidetracks along the way. Besides the healthy academic controversies over theoretical approach or research findings, perhaps the biggest problem that organizational behavior has had to face is an identity crisis. Exactly what is meant by organizational behavior? Is it an attempt to replace all management with behavioral science concepts and techniques? How, if at all, does it differ from good old applied or industrial psychology? Fortunately, these questions have now largely been answered to the satisfaction of most management academicians, behavioral scientists, and management practitioners.

Figure 1.2 shows in very general terms the relationships between and emphases of organizational behavior (OB) and the related disciplines of organization theory (OT), organization development (OD), and human resource management (HRM). As shown, OB tends to be more theoretically oriented and at the micro level of analysis. Specifically, OB draws from many theoretical frameworks of the behavioral sciences that are focused on understanding and explaining individual and group behavior in organizations. As with other sciences, OB accumulates knowledge and tests theories by accepted scientific methods of research. In summary, *organizational behavior* can be defined as the understanding, prediction, and management of human behavior in organizations.

The Relationship to Other Fields

Although Figure 1.2 is not intended to portray mutually exclusive domains for the related fields, because the lines are becoming increasingly blurred and there is not universal agreement of what belongs to what among academics or practitioners, most people in the field would generally agree with what is shown. Organization theory tends to be more macro-oriented than OB and is concerned primarily with organization structure and design. Yet, as in this text (Chapter 4 specifically and macro-oriented chapters such as 10–14), OT topics are included in the study and application of OB. Organization development, on the other hand, tends to be both more macro and more applied than OB. But also like OT, as in this text, OD topics are included in the study and application of OB. Finally, as shown, HRM tends to have a more applied focus than OB. The human resource management function is a part of practicing organizations as much as the marketing, finance, or operations functions are.

Human resource managers are hired and found with this title in practicing organizations; organizational behaviorists are not. Yet, somewhat confusingly, those managers who apply and draw from the field of organizational behavior (whether they be marketing managers, finance managers, hospital administrators, operations managers, store managers, academic administrators, office managers, *or* human resource managers) are called "human resource managers." They are called human resource managers and have a human resource management role (in addition to their other technical, functional role) because they all manage people. Thus, all managers, regardless of their technical function, are human resource managers in this view because they deal with human behavior in organizations. All managers need to have an understanding and perspective of organizational behavior.

The Behavioral Approach to Management

Organizational behavior represents the human side of management, not the whole of management. Other recognized approaches to management include the process, quantitative, systems, knowledge, and contingency approaches. In other words, organizational behavior does not intend to portray the whole of management. The charge that old wine (organizational psychology) has merely been poured into a new bottle (organizational behavior) has proved to be groundless. Although it is certainly true that all the behavioral sciences (anthropology, sociology, and especially psychology) make a significant contribution to both the theoretical and the research foundations of organizational behavior, it is equally true that organizational psychology should not be equated with organizational behavior. For example, organization structure and management processes (decision making and communication) play an integral, direct role in organizational behavior, as in this text (Part 3), but have at most an indirect role in organizational psychology. The same is true of many important dynamics and applications of organizational behavior. Although there will probably never be total agreement on the exact meaning or domain of organizational behavior—which is not necessarily bad, because it makes the field more dynamic and exciting—there is little doubt that organizational behavior has come into its own as a field of study, research, and application.

This text on organizational behavior attempts to provide the specific, necessary background and skills to make the managers of today and tomorrow as effective with the conceptual and human dimensions of management as they have been in the past with its technical, functional dimensions.

THEORETICAL FRAMEWORKS

Although organizational behavior is extremely complex and includes many inputs and dimensions, the cognitive, behavioristic, and social cognitive theoretical frameworks can be used to develop an overall model. After the theoretical frameworks are examined, the last section of the chapter presents an organizational behavior model that conceptually links and structures the rest of the text.

Cognitive Framework

The cognitive approach to human behavior has many sources of input. The micro-oriented chapters in the next part provide some of this background. For now, however, it can be said simply that the cognitive approach gives people much more "credit" than the other approaches. The cognitive approach emphasizes the positive and freewill aspects of human behavior and uses concepts such as expectancy, demand, and incentive.

Cognition, which is the basic unit of the cognitive framework, is the act of knowing an item of information. Under this framework, cognitions precede behavior and constitute input into the person's thinking, perception, problem solving, and information processing. Concepts such as cognitive maps can be used as pictures or visual aids in comprehending a person's "understanding of particular, and selective, elements of the thoughts (rather than thinking) of an individual, group or organization."[43]

The classic work of Edward Tolman can be used to represent the cognitive theoretical approach. Although Tolman believed behavior to be the appropriate unit of analysis, he felt that behavior is purposive, that it is directed toward a goal. In his laboratory experiments, he found that animals learned to expect that certain events would follow one another. For example, animals learned to behave as if they expected food when a certain cue appeared. Thus, Tolman believed that learning consists of the *expectancy* that a particular event will lead to a particular consequence. This cognitive concept of expectancy implies that the organism is thinking about, or is conscious or aware of, the goal. Thus, Tolman and others espousing the cognitive approach felt that behavior is best explained by these cognitions.

Contemporary psychologists carefully point out that a cognitive concept such as expectancy does not reflect a guess about what is going on in the mind; it is a term that describes behavior. In other words, the cognitive and behavioristic theories are not as opposite as they appear on the surface and sometimes are made out to be—for example, Tolman considered himself a behaviorist. Yet, despite some conceptual similarities, there has been a controversy throughout the years in the behavioral sciences on the relative contributions of the cognitive versus the behavioristic framework. As often happens in other academic fields, debate has gone back and forth through the years.[44]

Because of the recent advances from both theory development and research findings, there has been what some have termed a "cognitive explosion" in the field of psychology.[45] For example, a recent analysis of articles published in the major psychology journals found by far the greatest emphasis is on the cognitive school over the behavioral school starting in the 1970s.[46] Applied to the field of organizational behavior, a cognitive approach has traditionally dominated through units of analysis such as perception (Chapter 6), personality and attitudes (Chapter 7), motivation (Chapter 8), behavioral decision making (Chapter 11), and goal setting (Chapter 15). Very recently, there has been renewed interest in the role that cognitions can play in organizational behavior in terms of advancement in both theory and research on social cognition. This social cognitive process can be a unifying theoretical framework for both cognition and behaviorism. However, before getting into the specifics of social cognitive theory, which serves as the conceptual framework for this text, it is necessary to have an understanding of the behavioristic approach as well.

Behavioristic Framework

Chapter 16 discusses in detail the behavioristic theory in psychology and its application to organizational behavior. Its roots can be traced to the work of Ivan Pavlov and John B. Watson. These pioneering behaviorists stressed the importance of dealing with observable behaviors instead of the elusive mind that had preoccupied earlier psychologists. They used classical conditioning experiments to formulate the stimulus-response (S-R) explanation of human behavior. Both Pavlov and Watson felt that behavior could be best understood in terms of S-R. A stimulus elicits a response. They concentrated mainly on the impact of the stimulus and felt that learning occurred when the S-R connection was made.

Modern behaviorism marks its beginnings with the work of B. F. Skinner. Deceased for a number of years, Skinner is widely recognized for his contributions to psychology. He felt that the early behaviorists helped explain respondent behaviors (those behaviors elicited by stimuli) but not the more complex operant behaviors. In other words, the S-R approach helped explain physical reflexes; for example, when stuck by a pin (S), the person will flinch (R), or when tapped below the kneecap (S), the person will extend the lower leg (R). On the other hand, Skinner found through his operant conditioning experiments that the consequences of a response could better explain most behaviors than eliciting stimuli could. He emphasized the importance of the response-stimulus (R-S) relationship. The organism has to operate on the environment (thus the term *operant conditioning*) in order to receive the desirable consequence. The preceding stimulus does not cause the behavior in operant conditioning; it serves as a cue to emit the behavior. For Skinner and the behaviorists, behavior is a function of its contingent environmental consequences.

Both classical and operant conditioning and the important role of reinforcing consequences are given detailed attention in Chapter 16. For now, however, it is important to understand that the behavioristic approach is environmentally based. It posits that cognitive processes such as thinking, expectancies, and perception may exist but are not needed to predict and control or manage behavior. However, as in the case of the cognitive approach, which also includes behavioristic concepts, some modern behaviorists feel that cognitive variables can be behaviorized.[47] However, the social cognitive theory that has emerged in recent years incorporating both cognitive and behavioristic concepts and principles may be the most unifying and comprehensive framework for organizational behavior.

Social Cognitive Framework

The cognitive approach has been accused of being mentalistic, and the behavioristic approach has been accused of being deterministic. Cognitive theorists argue that the S-R model, and to a lesser degree the R-S model, is much too mechanistic an explanation of human behavior. A strict S-R interpretation of behavior seems justifiably open to the criticism of being too mechanistic, but because of the scientific approach that has been meticulously employed by behaviorists, the operant model in particular has made a tremendous contribution to the study and meaning of human behavior.[48] The same can be said of the cognitive approach. Much research has been done to verify its importance as an explanation of human behavior. Instead of polarization and unconstructive criticism between the two approaches, it now seems time to recognize that each can make an important contribution to the understanding, prediction, and control of human behavior. The social cognitive approach tries to integrate the contributions of both approaches.

Over 20 years ago we (Davis and Luthans) proposed a social learning approach to organizational behavior[49] and over 15 years ago we (Luthans and Kreitner) suggested a social learning approach to organizational behavior modification (O.B. Mod.).[50] Based on the work of Albert Bandura[51] and our own theory building and application to organizational behavior, social learning theory provided the conceptual framework for the last

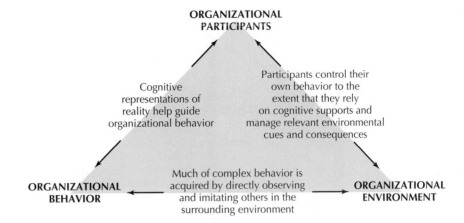

FIGURE 1.3
A social learning approach to organizational behavior.

six editions of this text. Social learning takes the position that behavior can best be explained in terms of a continuous reciprocal interaction among cognitive, behavioral, and environmental determinants. The person and the environmental situation do not function as independent units but, in conjunction with the behavior itself, reciprocally interact to determine behavior. Bandura explains that "it is largely through their actions that people produce the environmental conditions that affect their behavior in a reciprocal fashion. The experiences generated by behavior also partly determine what a person becomes and can do, which, in turn, affects subsequent behavior."[52] The triangular model shown in Figure 1.3 takes this work of Bandura and translates it into relevant units of analysis and variables in organizational behavior.

Bandura has taken his social learning and developed it into the more comprehensive social cognitive theory (SCT)[53] and we (Stajkovic and Luthans) have translated this SCT into the theoretical foundation for organizational behavior.[54] SCT is much more comprehensive than the cognitive or behavioristic approaches by themselves and its predecessor, social learning theory. Specifically, SCT recognizes the importance of behaviorism's contingent environmental consequences, but also includes cognitive processes of self-regulation. "The *social* part acknowledges the social origins of much of human thought and action (what individuals learn by being part of a society), whereas the *cognitive* portion recognizes the influential contribution of thought processes to human motivation, attitudes, and action."[55]

Similar to the social learning model in Figure 1.3, SCT explains organizational behavior in terms of the bidirectional, reciprocal causation among the organizational participants (e.g., unique personality characteristics such as conscientiousness), the organizational environment (e.g., the perceived consequences such as contingent recognition from the supervisor or pay for increased productivity), and the organizational behavior itself (e.g., previous successful or unsuccessful sales approaches with customers). In other words, like social learning, organizational participants are at the same time both products and producers of their personality, respective environments, and behaviors. Bandura goes beyond social learning with SCT by explaining the nature of the bidirectional reciprocal influences through the five basic human capabilities summarized in Figure 1.4.

FIGURE 1.4 The basic human capabilities according to Bandura's social cognitive theory (SCT).

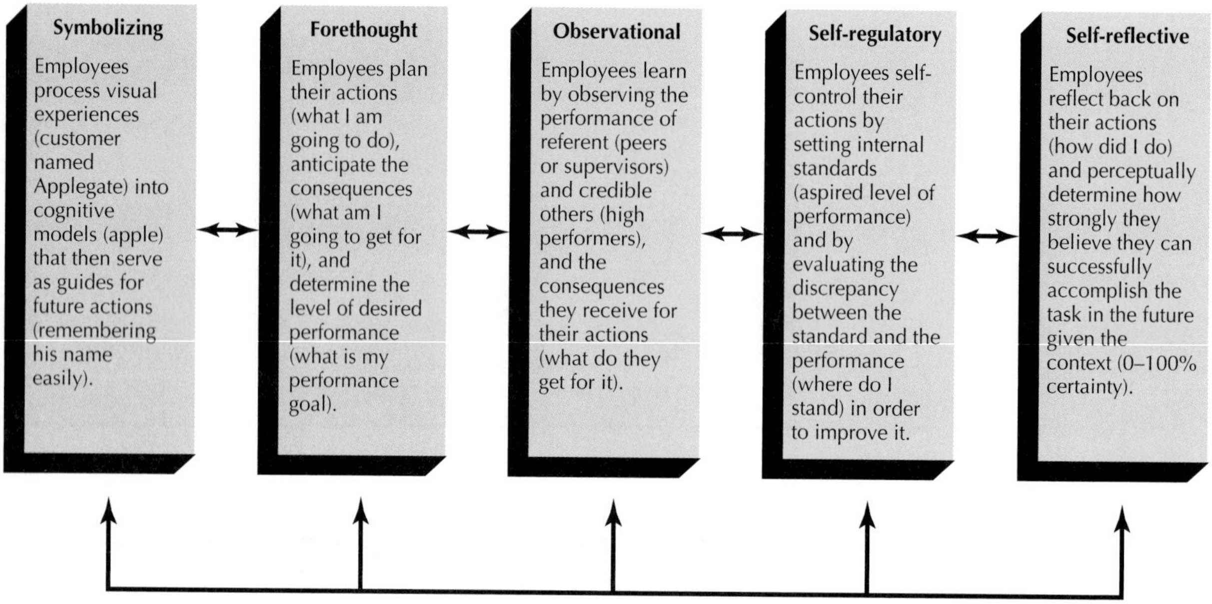

Symbolizing	Forethought	Observational	Self-regulatory	Self-reflective
Employees process visual experiences (customer named Applegate) into cognitive models (apple) that then serve as guides for future actions (remembering his name easily).	Employees plan their actions (what I am going to do), anticipate the consequences (what am I going to get for it), and determine the level of desired performance (what is my performance goal).	Employees learn by observing the performance of referent (peers or supervisors) and credible others (high performers), and the consequences they receive for their actions (what do they get for it).	Employees self-control their actions by setting internal standards (aspired level of performance) and by evaluating the discrepancy between the standard and the performance (where do I stand) in order to improve it.	Employees reflect back on their actions (how did I do) and perceptually determine how strongly they believe they can successfully accomplish the task in the future given the context (0–100% certainty).

Source: Alexander D. Stajkovic and Fred Luthans, "Social Cognitive Theory and Self-Efficacy: Going Beyond Traditional Motivational and Behavioral Approaches," *Organizational Dynamics,* Spring 1998, p. 65.

THE CONCEPTUAL FRAMEWORK FOR THE TEXT

The conceptual framework for this text is shown in Figure 1.5. As indicated, social cognitive theory is the foundation and consists of the reciprocal interaction among the environmental and organizational context (Part I, Chapters 2–5); cognitive processes (Part II, Chapters 6–9); and, importantly, the organizational behavior itself, which produces and is a product of the environmental/organizational context and the cognitive processes. At a more macro level are graphic depiction of the dynamics (not necessarily the outcomes) of organizational behavior (Part III, Chapters 10–14). Finally, at an applied level is the graphic representation of the role that managing and leading for high performance (Part IV, Chapters 15–18) plays in the conceptual framework for organizational behavior.

Obviously, this conceptual framework gives only a bare-bones sketch of organizational behavior rather than a full-blown explanation. Nevertheless, it can serve as a point of departure for how this text is organized. It helps explain why particular chapters are covered and how they relate to one another. As the chapters unfold, some of the fine points will become clearer and some of the seemingly simplistic, unsupported statements will begin to make more sense. Figure 1.5 serves merely as the welcoming mat to the study of the exciting, but still developing, field of organizational behavior.

FIGURE 1.5 A Conceptual Framework for the Study of Organizational Behavior

Environmental Context
  2. Info Tech & Globalization
  3. Diversity & Ethics
Organizational Context
  4. Design & Culture
  5. Reward System

Social Cognitive Theory

ORGANIZATIONAL BEHAVIOR

Dynamics

10. Communication
11. Decision Making
12. Stress & Conflict
13. Power & Politics
14. Groups & Teams

Managing & Leading for High Performance

15. Job Design & Goals
16. Behavioral Management
17. Leadership Processes
18. Great Leaders

Cognitive Processes
  6. Perception & Attribution
  7. Personality & Attitudes
  8. Motivational Needs & Processes
  9. Optimism, Emotional Intelligence
     and Self-Efficacy

Summary

This chapter first gives a brief overview of the significant challenges currently facing management. Besides the new workplace, environmental changes such as advanced information technology, globalization, and recognition and management of diversity and ethics represent a paradigm shift. This shift is characterized by new rules, new boundaries, and, importantly, new behaviors that are essential for organizations and managers to be successful or even survive. This new paradigm facing management requires a new perspective and an appreciation of the human, behavioral side of management. Thus, the field of organizational behavior becomes important now and in the future.

Organizational behavior is a relatively recent field of study and application. The beginnings are usually attributed to the famous Hawthorne studies, which had several phases (illumination, relay, bank wiring studies) and often-overlooked implications for modern management. Whereas the Hawthorne studies are often criticized for methodological flaws, today's organizational behavior field is characterized by rigorous scientific methodology. Both theory development and research designs are given considerable attention. Specifically, the threats to internal validity are attempted to be eliminated or minimized through carefully designed experiments. Field studies are used over laboratory studies whenever possible in order to have more external (generalizable) validity.

Because organizational behavior is a relatively new field, it must be precisely defined: the understanding, prediction, and management of human behavior in organizations. It is also important to see how OB (micro, theoretical) relates to other closely related disciplines such as organization theory or OT (macro, theoretical), organizational development or OD (macro, applied), and human resource management or HRM (micro, applied). Finally, it is important to provide a theoretical foundation to develop a specific model that can be used as a conceptual framework for this text. The cognitive, the behavioristic, and the emerging and more integrative social cognitive theories are used for such a foundation. The cognitive model gives the human being more "credit" and assumes that behavior is purposive and goal oriented. Cognitive processes such as expectancy and perception help explain behavior. The behavioristic approach deals with observable behavior and the environmental contingencies of the behavior. Classical behaviorism explained behavior in terms of S-R, whereas more modern behaviorism gives increased emphasis to contingent consequences, or R-S. The social cognitive approach emphasizes that the person, the environment, and the behavior itself are in constant interaction with one another and reciprocally determine one another. This social cognitive approach incorporates both cognitive and behavioristic elements and is used as the theoretical foundation for the organizational behavior model used as the conceptual framework to structure this text.

ENDING WITH META-ANALYTIC RESEARCH FINDINGS

OB PRINCIPLE: Because a number of important concepts and techniques have a stream of research findings that have had meta-analysis conducted on them, organizational behavior (OB) principles can now be stated.

Meta-Analysis Results: The end of each chapter will report the result of usually one but in some cases two or three meta-analyses. The above-stated principles, relevant to each chapter, are based on these meta-analytic findings. This results section will report the number of studies and participants and the meta-analytic average effect statistic *d*. Importantly, to make these meta-analytic results as user-friendly as possible, the *d* effect size is transformed using Grissom's (see source below) table to a percentage "probability of superior outcome of one treatment over another." Besides this percentage probability statement to support the "OB Principle," this section will also briefly discuss any moderating contingencies that were found and give the full citation of the meta-analysis in a source line like that below from Grissom's conversion of *d* to probability of success.

Conclusion: Each chapter "Ending with Meta-Analytic Research Findings" is patterned after this presentation: statement of OB Principle, Meta-Analysis Results, and Conclusion. The purpose of this conclusion is to tie the principle back to the chapter topic and make some final comments. The contribution of meta-analysis at this stage of development of the organizational behavior field is that it is able to draw overall, sound conclusions (i.e., state principles) from a large number of studies (often over 100) and usually thousands of subjects. Instead of just choosing one study here or there to support (or not support) a statement, meta-analysis provides a quantitative summary of individual studies across an entire body of research knowledge on a given concept (e.g., conscientiousness or self-efficacy) or technique (e.g., job characteristics model or organizational behavior modification). Many of the meta-analyses conducted to date on relevant topics in this text are included, but as research continues to accumulate, more meta-analytically derived OB principles will be forthcoming in the future.

Sources: Robert J. Grissom, "Probability of the Superior Outcome of One Treatment Over Another," *Journal of Applied Psychology*, Vol. 79, No. 2, 1994, pp. 314–316. For those wanting more information on meta-analysis, see: L. V. Hedges and I. Olkin, *Statistical Methods for Meta Analysis*, Academic Press, San Diego, 1985 and J. E. Hunter and F. L. Schmidt, *Methods of Meta-Analysis*, Sage, Beverly Hills, Calif., 1995. For a critical analysis and limitations of meta-analysis, see: P. Bobko and E. F. Stone-Romero, "Meta-Analysis May Be Another Useful Tool, But It Is Not a Panacea," in G. R. Ferris (Ed.), *Research in Personnel and Human Resources Management*, Vol. 16, JAI Press, Stamford, Conn., 1998, 359–397.

Questions for Discussion and Review

1. What are some of the major challenges facing today's and tomorrow's organizations and management? Briefly describe these developments.
2. What is a paradigm? How will the paradigm shift affect management? What are the implications of this paradigm shift for organizational behavior?
3. Why do you feel the Hawthorne studies made such an important historical contribution to the study of organizational behavior?

4. Why are theory development and rigorous scientific methodology important to the field of organizational behavior? What role does validity play in the design of research studies?

5. How does organizational behavior relate to, or differ from, organizational development? Organization theory? Human resource management?

6. In your own words, identify and summarize the various theoretical frameworks for understanding organizational behavior. How does the social cognitive approach differ from the cognitive approach? How does the social cognitive approach differ from the behavioristic approach?

7. Explain the model for organizational behavior that is used in this text.

Internet Exercise: Nonjobs in the New Economy

This chapter sets the tone for the new paradigm, new economy. One dramatic change in this environment has been the dramatic increase in the number of nonjob or "telecommuters," those that work from home. Inexpensive computers, the changing nature of jobs, and workers' demands for a more flexible schedule have all contributed to this trend. Go to http://www.tjobs.com/ and look at the jobs that they offer specifically designed around telecommuting. In fact, Putnam Investments has a page dedicated to jobs available at home. Visit their site at http://www.putnaminv.com/. Then, click on "career opportunities." You will also find many current articles on telecommuting at http://www.bluesuitmom.com. Browse through these sites, and consider the following questions.

1. Would you consider a job that kept you at home for a significant part of the workweek? What would be the advantages of this? Disadvantages?

2. As a manager, consider the challenges of managing those that work at home. What are your challenges? Consider, for example, how to monitor performance, motivate workers, and help them manage workplace problems.

3. Do you think the trend towards telecommuting will increase or decrease in the coming years? What impact will this have on some of the major topics in this text? Be as specific as you can by even looking at the table of contents and Figure 1.5.

REAL CASE:
The Case for
Optimism

The American economy will continue to have its ups and downs. Corporate spending on computers will wane. The golden touch of venture capitalists and other New Economy money mandarins will fade. But an Internet Depression? An economic catastrophe big enough to rival the Great Depression of the 1930s or Japan's Great Stagnation of the 1990s? That would require the economic equivalent of a Perfect Storm. And I wouldn't bet on it.

Michael J. Mandel's dark predictions of economic woe and policy ineptitude in *The Coming Internet Depression* rest on a series of worst-case assumptions. Unlike most economists, Mandel rightly recognizes that fast growth in a high-tech economy helps keep inflation low. Intense, perhaps unprecedented levels of competition prevent companies from raising prices. And management burns the midnight oil figuring out ways to run their businesses more efficiently by investing huge sums in high-tech gear and reorganizing the workplace. Productivity growth is currently so strong that unit labor costs are actually declining, even though the economy is at full employment.

Now, here's Mandel's ingenious twist that is key to his doleful outlook. Prices will soar when high-tech investment falls off sharply, venture-capital financing dries up, and the economy slows. No longer threatened by entrepreneurial rivals, companies will hike prices to shore up their earnings. The Fed, frightened that inflation is taking off, will tighten monetary policy. The economy will slump further, high-tech investment will plummet, the stock market will tumble, prices will rise further, the Fed will tighten again, and so on, in a vicious cycle that ends in depression.

But hold on. Just because faster economic growth is a force for price stability doesn't mean slower economic growth is inflationary. On the contrary, we can expect falling demand to force companies to hold down prices. What's more, global forces work in the same direction. Already, competition from goods manufactured cheaply in China by both local companies and foreign multinationals is putting downward price pressure on Japanese and American rivals. Japan is in the grips of a deflationary spiral. U.S. discount retailers are expanding into Europe and undercutting the Continent's established merchants. The Internet, with its promise of enormous efficiencies, is constantly expanding its reach. Management at General Electric, Charles Schwab, Wal-Mart, and other brand-name companies are spending billions restructuring their global operations around the World Wide Web. And they'll continue to shell out for greater efficiencies, even as the economy slows. "Technology spending would be the last thing we would cut," says Hardwick Simmons, president and CEO of Prudential Securities Inc.

What's more, the New Economy is remarkably resilient. Take labor. Companies are pursuing a variety of strategies to turn fixed labor costs into a variable expense. A quarter of all employees now keep schedules with varying work hours and work times, up from one-sixth a decade ago. Already, as of 1998, three-quarters of all companies used performance bonuses, about one-half offered profit sharing, and over one-third provided stock options, according to a Federal Reserve survey.

Mandel's depression scenario requires that investors turn skittish and abandon the market en masse. But investors are smarter than that. For years, a vocal group of economists and Wall Street seers warned that the U.S. stock market was a dangerous "bubble," especially considering the stratospheric valuations of dot-com companies. When the dot-com bubble burst, they warned, the crash would take both the New and the Old Economies down.

The technological revolution is still in its infancy, and several huge advances are just starting to take shape. Interactive television. Net-based medical care, or "e-health." Global wireless Internet services. These are giant industrial shifts, which take time to mature, and require progress in core technologies. Fortunately, researchers can collaborate on the Net to speed the pace of development. And that very process breeds fresh innovations—many of which promise further efficiency gains. Software companies, for example, are reinventing themselves as so-called application service providers, leasing their programs over the Net, and thus reducing delays, technical glitches, and costs for the customer. In Japan, which is ground zero for the wireless Internet, a whole new business category known as mobile e-commerce has been built around cell phones that surf the Net.

Economic disasters are fascinating. Some of the most fabled stories in economics are financial bubbles that ended in economic hardship, from America's railroad-building boom in the late 1860s and early 1870s to the Roaring Twenties and the Great Depression. But this bull market hasn't been a bubble. It has been a reflection of the New Economy. Right now, investors are reasonably knocking down stock prices, struggling to divine whether the economy will glide gracefully into a more moderate growth pattern, or, thanks to higher oil prices, endure a harder landing. Curl up with *The Perfect Storm* if you want a good read, but don't bet your portfolio that its economic equivalent will happen.

1. Based on your reading of this case and the current economic environment, which side would you agree with, the possibility of an Internet depression or the very slim (i.e., perfect storm) possibility? Support your argument.

2. What are the implications for organizational behavior of the statement "Companies are pursuing a variety of strategies to turn fixed labor costs into a variable expense"?
3. How and where does the economic environment fit into the social cognitive theory (SCT) that is used as the foundation and conceptual framework for this text?

ORGANIZATIONAL BEHAVIOR CASE: How Is This Stuff Going to Help Me?

Jane Arnold wants to be a manager. She enjoyed her accounting, finance, and marketing courses. Each of these provided her with some clear-cut answers. Now the professor in her organizational behavior course is telling her that there are really very few clear-cut answers when it comes to managing people. The professor has discussed some of the emerging challenges and the historical background and ways that behavioral science concepts play a big role in the course. Jane is very perplexed. She came to school to get answers on how to be an effective manager, but this course surely doesn't seem to be heading in that direction.

1. How would you relieve Jane's anxiety? How is a course in organizational behavior going to make her a better manager?
2. Why did the professor start off with a brief overview of emerging challenges?
3. How does a course in organizational behavior differ from courses in fields such as accounting, finance, or marketing?

ORGANIZATIONAL BEHAVIOR CASE: Too Nice to People

John has just graduated from the College of Business Administration at State University and has joined his family's small business, which employs 25 semiskilled workers. During the first week on the job, his dad called him in and said: "John, I've had a chance to observe you working with the men and women for the past two days and, although I hate to, I feel I must say something. You are just too nice to people. I know they taught you that human behavior stuff at the university, but it just doesn't work here. I remember when we discussed the Hawthorne studies when I was in school and everybody at the university got all excited about them, but believe me, there is more to managing people than just being nice to them."

1. How would you react to your father's comments if you were John?
2. Do you think John's father understood and interpreted the Hawthorne studies correctly?
3. What phases of management do you think John's father has gone through in this family business? Do you think he understands the significance of recent trends in the environment and how the new paradigm will affect his business?
4. How would you explain to your father the new perspective that is needed and how the study of organizational behavior will help the business be successful in the new paradigm?

ORGANIZATIONAL BEHAVIOR CASE: Conceptual Model: Dream or Reality?

Hank James has been section head for the accounting group at Yake Company for 14 years. His boss, Mary Stein, feels that Hank is about ready to be moved up to the corporate finance staff, but it is company policy to send people like Hank to the University Executive Development Program before such a promotion is made. Hank has enrolled in the program; one of the first parts deals with organizational behavior. Hank felt that after 14 years of managing people, this would be a snap. However, during the lecture on organizational behavior, the professor made some comments that really bothered Hank. The professor said:

> Most managers know their functional specialty but do a lousy job of managing their people. One of the problems is that just because managers have a lot of experience with people, they think they are experts. The fact is that behavioral scientists are just beginning to understand human behavior. In addition, to effectively manage people, we also have to somehow be able to better predict and control organizational behavior. Some models are now developed that we hope will help the manager better understand, predict, and manage organizational behavior.

Hank is upset by the fact that his professor apparently discounts the value of experience in managing people, and he cannot see how a conceptual framework that some professor dreamed up can help him manage people better.

1. Do you think Hank is justified in his concerns after hearing the professor? What role can experience play in managing people?
2. What is the purpose of conceptual frameworks such as those presented in this chapter? How would you weigh the relative value of studying theories and research findings versus "school-of-hard-knocks" experience for the effective management of people?
3. Using the conceptual framework presented in the chapter, how would you explain to Hank that this could help him better manage people in his organization?

CHAPTER 2

Environmental Context: Information Technology and Globalization

Learning Objectives

Examine the role that information technology plays in today's organizations.

Present the developments in knowledge management and human capital/intelligence.

Discuss the impact of globalization as an environmental context for organizational behavior.

Describe the meaning, role, and dimensions of culture as a context for international organizational behavior.

Starting with Best-Practice Leader's Advice

Intel's Andy Grove on the Impact of Information Technology and Globalization

Andrew S. Grove, the cofounder, past CEO, and current chairman of Intel, the world's largest microprocessor manufacturer, is perhaps the most qualified of anyone to comment on the impact of information technology and globalization. Dr. Grove has an impressive list of publications and academic teaching assignments to go along with his experience of leading one of the best known new-economy firms. He first makes some observations on the e-commerce environment and then globalization.

Q1:   *You have said that "E-commerce is the killer app of the connected PC universe." How do you view the impact of electronic commerce on advanced and emerging economies?*

Grove: I think a great deal depends on what policy makers in various countries do with their IT [information technology] investments, and even more importantly with their telecommunications infrastructure investments. Let's just look at the consumer connecting to this universe of Internet-connected PCs. For e-commerce to be a viable commercial means of doing business, it has to reach the end consumer. And the end consumer has real problems in almost all Asian countries, for example. One problem is the accessibility of telephone connections, which is being solved by the tens of millions of connections being deployed per year. But another problem that is not being solved is the cost of these connections.

    Today, the average computer costs approximately $1,000 and is used for four years. This corresponds to about $250 per year for the computer purchase, which is approximately the same annual cost as the $20 a month ISP subscription in the United States. So the computer cost and the Internet access charge are split 50-50. But in a hypothetical Asian country with a 10-cents-per-minute access charge, one-fifth of the total cost is associated with the computer, and 80 percent is associated with the access fee. So the biggest obstacle in popularizing e-commerce and making it truly a mass medium—the biggest economic factor separating people with and without computers—is telecommunications cost, and not computing cost. And it's a problem that urgently requires addressing.

    The point is that, in a world of a billion connected computers, providing electronic connections between these computers and embracing Internet commerce will become a competitive advantage to a society or country. In the past year, a lot of investments have been made to extend infrastructure and capability, in spite of the difficult economic climates in some regions of the world. But the penetration of electronic commerce is going to be limited by the cost effectiveness of the telecommunications infrastructure in different countries, different cultures, and different geographies.

Q2:   *Some people have said that globalization equals Americanization or colonization of other countries. What are your views on this?*

Grove: It's very easy to fight one cliché with another cliché, particularly older clichés. Electronic technology is a tool. It is a means by which buyer and seller get together, educator and student get together, and everyone in between. For a country to be colonized or defeated by a technology, two things have to happen: one party has to be aggressive about it and the other party has to be passive about it. So whether electronic technology provides a national competitive advantage to the United States or provides a worldwide improvement to the flow of commerce depends on the present and future actions of the various parties.

Q3:   *How can multinationals like Intel contribute to a healthy global economy?*

Grove: The global economy was created by multinationals. It continues to be created by multinationals. For many years, the majority of Intel's sales have been taking place outside the United States. The content of the personal computer is dominated 60 to 70 percent by products from different countries. If you tracked the flow of products that make up a personal computer, as with many industrial goods, they crisscross the globe several times before they land in front of the customer. All of this was created by multinational companies and by various business arrangements of multinational companies and regional manufacturers. For instance, we deal with producers in Korea, Taiwan, and Iran. So we have been the agent of this transnational form of business that we can call globalization, both as a seller and as a producer.

Q4:   *So you see multinationals as having a positive impact on the global economy?*

Grove: They have a positive impact as compared to any other alternative, to paraphrase Winston Churchill. The PC industry would have a hell of a time achieving its cost efficiency if it developed as a national industry with different standards. Likewise, the aircraft industry couldn't possibly have developed to its current standard if countries maintained their own production of airliners based on different national standards. The development costs and manufacturing costs of these complex industrial goods are so great that you have to amortize them by regarding the entire world as your market, and it is under that construct that regional competitive advantages come into play. For instance, Taiwan has developed particular expertise in PC subsystem manufacturing, Japan and Korea have developed regional expertise in memory manufacturing, and the United States has developed regional expertise in microprocessor manufacturing and the like. It's all under the umbrella of a very internationally constructed computing industry.

Today's environmental context for organizational behavior is markedly different from that of the past. As pointed out in the opening chapter, information technology, globalization, and diversity and ethics have forced management of all types of organizations to totally rethink their approach to both operations and human resources. Because of the paradigm shift, organizations are now more responsive to both their external and internal environments. This chapter examines information technology and globalization as the environmental context for organizational behavior.

THE ROLE OF INFORMATION TECHNOLOGY

The impact that the information technology explosion has had on organizations is truly amazing—with no end in sight. Obviously, technological breakthroughs in the last two centuries have had a dramatic impact. For example, followers of pioneering economist

Joseph Schumpeter's 50-year model note that the first wave in modern history (1780s–1840s) brought steam power that drove the Industrial Revolution; next came the railroads (1840s–1890s); followed by electric power (1890s–1930s); and then cheap oil and the automobile (1930s–1980s). Now the fifth wave is being powered by information technology. Yet this latest technological breakthrough is argued to have a faster (it took radio 38 years to reach 50 million users, TV 13 years, but the Web just 5 years)[1] and much different, more pervasive impact for three major reasons:

1. Information technology not only can be applied across all sectors of a given economy and the world (which is true of the other technologies as well), but it can affect every function within an organization. For example, information technology can improve not only the performance of a product such as an automobile (today's autos have more computer-processing power than the first lunar landing craft had in 1969), but also the design, engineering, manufacturing, and service of the auto. The same is true even in auto sales where it is estimated that over half of auto purchasers are influenced by the Internet, and the customer can order directly from the auto manufacturer.

2. The cost of computer-processing power has fallen by an average of about 30 percent a year in real terms; one estimate is that it now costs only one-hundredth of 1 percent of what it did in the early 1970s. Put into relative terms, if autos had developed and decreased in cost at the same pace as microprocessors over the past two decades, a typical car would now cost less than $5 and get 250,000 miles to the gallon.

3. Unlike other technological breakthroughs such as steam power or electricity, information technology can be both an input and a final product. It is capable of revolutionizing the production and distribution of entire industries, services, and organizational functions, but it also offers a vast range of new products and services of its own. In addition to all of these things, the Internet has itself become a new marketplace (e.g., eBay) and directly affects what managers do every day, ranging from locating a new supplier at the best price to coordinating a project on the other side of the world to collecting and managing customer data.[2]

The products range from cellular phones that allow managers to stay in touch with their field personnel no matter where they are, to lap (or even palm) personal computers that can handle inventory control and help employees communicate with each other via e-mail, to compact discs (CD-ROMs) that are able to store and retrieve billions of pieces of information, to the Internet, Intranet (discussed later), and Extranet (electronic interchange outside the organization's internal information system). In recent years, personal digital (or data) assistants (PDAs), which are wireless, handheld, and tied into the Internet, have made virtually all information available anytime, anywhere.

E-mail via PCs and PDAs has become commonplace in today's workplace; it is used to communicate with everyone, inside and outside the organization, around the world. The same is true of word processing and spreadsheets; this is simply the way business is conducted. In addition, at first electronic data interchange (EDI) and now B2B allows customers, suppliers, and manufacturers to communicate directly on a computer-to-computer systems basis. In today's organizations, written sales and order forms have been eliminated, information is being entered directly into computers, and these machines are being programmed to interpret information and make decisions. For example, at Wal-Mart all orders are placed electronically, and computers help the firm manage inventory. When reorders are necessary, the machines automatically place these orders by sending electronic messages to supplier computers. Besides these common tools of the Information Age, perhaps the biggest environmental impact on the field of organizational behavior is e-commerce or business, knowledge management, and human capital/intelligence.

E-Business

Herb Kelleher, the well-known founder and head of highly successful Southwest Airlines, was recently asked what will be the biggest business story of the 21st century. He replied:

> Even though I'm still into No. 2 pencils and legal notepads, I recognize the impact the Internet and e-commerce is having on business. Businesses globally have just brushed the tip of the iceberg when it comes to tapping the potential the Internet has to change the face of American business. About a third of the world's people now have Internet access; within five years, that number is expected to be more than 90 percent. That's a large base of customers residing only a few keyboard strokes away.[3]

Interestingly, Kelleher is referring to e-commerce with consumers, but that huge potential business actually pales by comparison to business-to-business electronic transactions. One recent *Business Week* estimate noted that e-business between businesses (or B2B) is five times greater than consumer e-commerce (B2C) and by 2003 will balloon to $1.3 trillion. That's 10 times consumer e-commerce, constituting 9 percent of all U.S. business trade—and more than the gross domestic product of either Britain or Italy. Around 2006 or so, B2B is projected to be 40 percent of all U.S. business.[4] Andy Grove, the well-known head of Intel who introduced this chapter as the "Best Practice Leader," even went so far to predict that in the future all companies will be Internet companies or they won't be businesses at all[5] (See accompanying Technology Application to see further what Grove is talking about.)

At the beginning of the century, hard-charging companies such as Cisco Systems (which became the most valuable company in the world in the spring of 2000, but of course has since experienced the roller coaster ride of the financial markets)[6] does about three-fourths of its entire business on the Internet, and Dell Computer does about half.[7] As founder and CEO Michael Dell is known for saying: Embrace information technology fully and make e-business a central focus, not a small side project, or watch everyone pass you by.

The well known dot-com firms such as Amazon, AOL, Netscape, and Yahoo are most closely associated with e-business and have redefined how business is done. For example, Yahoo cofounders Jerry Yang and David Filo gave their company a new, special identity from the "get-go." They not only offered their visitors a good search engine, but also the way they designed the pages and described the Web sites gave a sense of fun and discovery (i.e., the early "Netheads" culture). Here is a description of a typical Yahoo visit:

> A woman in Peoria, Illinois, pulls up Yahoo, checks the news and stock quotes bookmarked under her My Yahoo home page, and reviews e-mail in her account at yahoo.com. She's 30 today. Look: an e-card from Yahoo's Birthday Club—and $50 off at her favorite online store. Now that she's so much older and wiser, she decides to look for a bigger apartment in the Yahoo classifieds. And since she deserves a treat today, she bids on vintage pearl earrings in Yahoo's auction area.[8]

TECHNOLOGY APPLICATION

Get Wired or Get Whacked

Less than a decade ago, information technology was used primarily for data storage and retrieval. For example, insurance companies would put all of their policyholder contracts in computer memory and would then access this stored data to handle claims or to answer questions from customers regarding coverage. Retail firms would use their computers to keep track of sales and to alert the purchasing department when inventory levels reached reorder points. Airlines would use the machines to keep track of available seating space. All of these activities helped companies do a better job of managing operations. However, in large part information technology was a passive process. It was used simply to keep track of what was going on.

Today all of this has changed dramatically as information technology is being employed in a much more active way. For example, instead of just gathering and storing data, say to merely keep track of the expenses of salespeople and others who are required to travel on company business, firms are now having their people directly submit expenses electronically. For example, at Cisco Systems, after returning from a trip, employees log on to the system and report their out-of-pocket expenses. All other charges have been made to their corporate American Express card and are already in the computer system. Based on this information, the system then generates a report and within four days the employee receives reimbursement. By making the employee responsible for handling this activity, the company has doubled the number of expense claims it can process in a day and cut the cost of processing an expense report from $25 down to $3.

Businesses are also using the Internet to communicate with suppliers, partners, and customers, thus reducing both time and cost. One result is that the supply chains of the 1990s are now becoming supply webs today, and companies are tying their inventory operations directly into that of their suppliers. For example, at Wal-Mart, suppliers like Procter & Gamble (P&G) have direct computer access to the firm's inventory system. In this way, P&G is able to seamlessly identify when Wal-Mart inventory is likely to need replenishment, send a computer-generated order to its own manufacturing facilities to produce more of the product, and ship it to the correct Wal-Mart merchandise center.

Another current trend is the online ordering of inventory. Ford, General Motors, and Daimler-Chrysler now buy a large amount of their parts and materials from online suppliers. This approach is so efficient that it can cut as much as 16 percent off the costs of doing business the old way.

Customers are also getting into the act. For example, individuals and businesses that want to order computers from Dell Computer can configure their own PC online and track the assembly and shipping status of their order. This high-tech approach works so well that customer surveys report that Dell is ranked as the best company in this market.

Moreover, by freeing up employee time from mundane tasks such as order taking, a growing number of businesses are able to put their people to work on more important things such as analyzing sales trends and providing better customer service. Their goal is to take advantage of consumer online transactions, which are forecasted to rise to approximately $110–130 billion by the year 2003, a sharp increase over the $8 billion that was spent in 1998. The key to success is to create the needed technology system and train the employees to use it efficiently. As one expert recently put it, companies today are going to "get wired or get whacked."

Although the new economy dot-com firms dominate the popular media, e-business is also revolutionizing business models, processes and relationships along the whole length of the supply chain and the old economy firms per se (e.g., shipping, textiles, retailing, insurance, chemicals, and transportation). For example, online electronic stock trading completely transformed the consumer financial service business. The same impact is being felt in service companies. Over the years, FedEx has been state-of-the-art in its use of information technology.[9] The now more than 20-year-old information network Cosmos helped FedEx customer service reps keep track of packages, and in 1994 fedex.com was launched for customers to go online on two screens: one with a box where you could enter a tracking number and a second to show exactly where a specific package was. Today, fedex.com has over 8,000 pages tracking hundreds of thousands of packages on-site for customers in well over 200 countries. A program called interNetship helps business customers handle all their shipping needs without ever picking up the phone. It even lets them print out shipping labels from any recent Web browser. Web page views ("hits") at FedEx far outnumber calls to its 800 phone number.

The highly visible and successful firms such as Cisco, Microsoft, Dell, Yahoo, and FedEx are commonly used examples, but most businesses can never be totally electronic. Yet, there is little question that huge efficiencies and possible greater earnings are available to those organizations that make at least some of their processes electronic. For example, the marginal cost to a bank of a transaction over the Internet is a mere cent, compared with 27 cents by a cash machine, 52 cents by telephone and $1.14 by a bank teller.[10] Amazon.com still relies heavily on physical products and traditional distribution systems, but by making its selling and customer relationship entirely electronic, it has revolutionized the retail industry.

E-business is usually portrayed as a recent phenomena and is almost equated with today's Internet. Yet, it should be remembered that e-business was really born over 150 years ago when a telegraph operator tapped out a message to the next town when the train would be arriving. Next came telephones, shortwave radios, copiers, computers, and fax machines. All these electronic breakthroughs had a significant impact (e.g., the telegraph wiped out the Pony Express almost overnight, and shortwave radios greatly changed international business). In addition to not being new, it should also be recognized that Internet technology can be used not only for e-business, but also can be used strictly in-house as Intranets.

Intranets

Organizations today are using the wonders of the Internet, but without some of the problems. As one critical analysis pointed out, "Users are driven to distraction by the delays, the muddle and the brainless rubbish. Breakdowns of bits of the Net are hardly new, but when they happen these days a lot of people notice—as when America Online crashed leaving 6 million subscribers to twiddle their thumbs."[11]

To avoid the increasingly bothersome public access problems while taking advantage of what the Internet and Web technology can offer, almost all organizations are using an Intranet. These private Nets, or Intranets, use the infrastructure and standards of the Internet and World Wide Web, but are cordoned off from the public Internet through software programs known as "fire walls." With an Intranet, the organization's employees can venture out onto the Internet and all of its wealth of knowledge, and unauthorized users can't come into their Intranet.

Here are some of the major advantages of using Intranets:

1. An obvious advantage is the ability to slash the need for paper. Because Web browsers run on any type of computer and now PDAs, the same electronic information can be viewed by any employee. Thus, most documents—for example, internal phone books, procedure manuals, training materials, requisition forms—can be converted to electronic form on the Web and constantly updated at almost no cost.

2. Perhaps even more important, an organization's Intranet pulls all the computers, software, and databases into a single system that enables all employees to easily find and use information wherever it resides.[12]

To date, most organizations' Intranets are used for basic information sharing (e.g., employee benefits information or phone directories), but increasingly they are being used for competitive advantage. For example, Ford's Intranet contains its half-million product-design resources, production management tools, and strategic information assets. The giant auto firm's CIO (chief information officer) notes that the internal Web is the backbone of Ford's business today. The CEO holds a weekly "Let's Chat" open session on the Intranet for all employees who choose to participate. A more-focused example of this upward communication via the Intranet was the recent launch of the Mercury Sable. To send the message to all employees that Ford manages its business on the Intranet, top management is pushing for Web-only publication of divisional business plans, engineering best practices, and product development specs. In operations, every car and truck model has its own internal Web site to track design, production, quality control, and delivery processes. In the human resources part of the Ford Intranet, employees can access at any time updated benefit figures, new job postings, buy a new Ford or Mercury to their specifications, calculate merit pay, and submit anonymous critiques of their supervisors.[13]

In other words, the Intranet not only allows organizations to go "paperless" and thus cut costs, but also provides employees with user-friendly access to all the information and knowledge of the organization in order to make better decisions and improve customer service. Now, with this explosion of information available to everyone in the organization, the key competitive advantage and the real implication for organizational behavior is to manage the knowledge as effectively as possible.

Knowledge Management

Like many other concepts and practices in management and organizational behavior, the exact meaning and definition of knowledge management, or KM, is not always clear. A recent academic analysis of KM defines it as "the development of tools, processes, systems, structures and cultures explicitly to improve the creation, sharing, and use of knowledge critical for decision making."[14] Although this definition is comprehensive, the exact meaning of the term most often depends on the user. However, two generally recognized trends have emerged to represent KM in the literature and actual practice: (1) tangible knowledge assets captured and retained in organization structures and systems, e.g., R&D (research and development) outcomes, patents, copyrights, royalties, licenses, and information on employees, customers, suppliers, products and competitors; and (2) intangible knowledge or intelligence possessed by employees and other stakeholders (customers, suppliers, owners, consultants), e.g., their experience, skill, and ideas. These two dimensions are generally not used together in discussions in the literature by academics or when being described by practicing managers in the real world. The following summarizes the two approaches to KM.

Connectivity
- Computer networks, including LAN, WAN, or Internet access
- E-mail

Storage
- Data warehouses, data marts, and assorted databases
- Document management programs
- Electronic directories of "experts," such as corporate Yellow Pages and expert systems that compile information from experts in an intelligent database
- Large storage capacities, usually a corporate Intranet

Locators
- Browsers, which search through corporate Intranets
- Agents, software that seeks out information
- "Knowledge maps," indices that classify information and help users determine the location of the information
- Metadata or electronic card catalogues, which summarize and categorize data
- "Push" technology, which lets users request that all information on a particular topic be forwarded to them

Learning Vehicles
- Distance learning applications that help employees acquire knowledge

Recent Developments
- "Knowledge portals" available on employees' individual desktop PCs or PDAs for easy access to all useful data in the organization
- Software that transforms text and numbers into charts and graphs to make it easier to glean relevant information
- More sophisticated filters, browsers, and locators to make it possible for users to make queries and receive answers in regular language

FIGURE 2.1

The information technology behind the acquire and store approach to knowledge management.

(*Source:* Adapted from Jenny C. McCune, "Thirst for Knowledge," *Management Review,* April 1999, p. 12.)

KM as Acquiring and Storing Information.   Treating knowledge as a tangible asset, this approach to KM mainly employs technology, specifically information technology, to acquire and store information to be drawn upon by management decision makers and others to make products or deliver service to customers. Of the organizations that respond to surveys that they have a specific KM program in place (estimated to be over one-third and growing), the great majority mention programs such as (1) establishing repository databases and retrieval systems, (2) gathering information from customers, (3) creating and maintaining employee talent and skill profiles, and (4) creating and maintaining virtual or physical platforms for sharing and disseminating information.[15] A summary of the technology backup to this approach to KM is shown in Figure 2.1.

There is no question that this tangible asset, technology-based approach to KM has some problems. For example, the author of *Information Ecology: Mastering the Information and Knowledge Environment* decries that the technology often turns out to be an end in itself; "Our fascination with technology has made us forget the key purpose of information: to inform people."[16] The surveys of KM also point out obstacles such as knowing what information to gather, measurement issues, and making the information accessible and usable.[17] However, there are also many success stories from using this approach to KM. Here is a sampling of some of them:

- IBM consultants have reportedly cut proposal writing time from an average of 200 hours to 30 hours because they can share information.
- Eureka, an "expert" database compiled by Xerox for its copier repairers, has reduced average repair time by 50 percent.
- Technical support reps at Dell Computer Corp.'s Bray, UK, call center can solve more problems with a single call thanks to a knowledge base that advises the reps on what questions to ask and how to fix problems.

- W. L. Gore and Associates, Newark, Delaware, uses Lotus Notes and an Intranet that allows people in the field to quickly relay customers' needs to the product development team, which in turn can quickly devise customized products. This process could take weeks in the past. But now it takes only days, or even hours, to respond to custom orders.
- Internet portal Yahoo records every click made by every visitor, accumulating over 400 billion bytes of data per day—the equivalent of 800,000 books.
- Direct marketing giant Fingerhut has millions of names of repeat customers and stores up to 1,000 attributes on each one. Its data warehouse can hold 4.5 trillion bytes.[18]

The key theme in both the problems and successes of this technology-based KM is the sharing/accessibility of information/knowledge and the leveraging of this information/knowledge for desirable organizational outcomes.

KM as Sharing and Leveraging Information.　The problem is not that the technology-based KM is wrong; it is necessary for acquiring and retaining information. The problem is that it usually does not go far enough; it is not sufficient. Too often, as the accompanying Application example notes, the people behind the IT systems are forgotten. The other major approach to KM identified previously, the intangible intelligence (experience, skill, and ideas) of employees and other stakeholders, plays the major role in the more comprehensive sharing and leveraging approach to KM.

APPLICATION EXAMPLE

It's the People, Stupid

An Internet software executive recently noted he couldn't believe all the fuss about the auction site eBay Inc. "They're not *doing* anything," he said. "They just get people to show up together." Gee, is that all? eBay may have had a lot of luck on its side, but it understood one thing early on: It's the people, stupid. More than any other e-commerce site, eBay has created a community of people who can do business with each other on their own terms. In fact, it has amassed more than 16 million members solely from word of mouth.

People like eBay not just because it's fun but because they get a visceral sense that there's somebody behind the "Place Bid" button. And they're right. Almost every time someone buys something on eBay, they are shocked at the intensely personal service: Merchants offer to keep an eye out for other items the buyer might want, and if something's wrong with an order they fall all over themselves to fix it.

Indeed, remembering that buyers are people is even more critical for B2B sites. In a recent report, Boston Consulting Group Inc. said only 11 percent of the $4.8 trillion in B2B transactions it forecasts by 2004 will involve online price negotiations. The rest will be completed by phone or in person. Says BCG Vice-President Andy Blackburn: "In the end, you still have to have a conversation."

Does this mean the Web's vaunted efficiencies are a crock? Probably not. The Web can eliminate the need for people to punch a cash register or mop the linoleum. And ultimately, it will automate a lot more business processes. But golf games, power breakfasts, and phone calls will remain crucial business tools for a long time to come.

A former CEO of Hewlett-Packard (HP) noted that, "Successful companies of the 21st century will be those who do the best jobs of capturing, storing and leveraging what their employees know."[19] The resulting initiative for KM at HP was: "To create an environment where everyone is enthusiastic about sharing knowledge and leveraging the knowledge of others."[20]

The CIOs (chief information officers) have generally been charged to manage knowledge by trying to mesh and operationalize the hard data acquired and stored in information technology systems with the elusive intelligence of experienced, skilled, and creative employees stored in their heads. This has proved to be very difficult. A recent study of 200 executives from 158 large global firms found that the best way they have found to share and leverage knowledge into practical results is not from information technology but from informal employee networks, focus groups, and other workplace practices.[21] In other words, KM must recognize human/intellectual capital and how it can be effectively shared and leveraged.

Human/Intellectual Capital

The concept of human capital was introduced in the first chapter and basically recognizes that human resources have knowledge and intelligence through their experience, skills, and ideas. The value of this human capital depends on its contribution to competitive advantage or the core competence of a firm and its uniqueness (i.e., it can't be readily replaced or acquired on the open labor market).[22] Importantly, such human capital is not a cost factor of production, or even an asset. Rather, human resources can be thought of as investors in the business (contributing human capital) and expecting a return on this investment (e.g., salary, benefits, stock options, and pension payments).[23] At the firm level, the difference between the accounting book value (i.e., the tangible hard assets) and the market value (i.e., the value of the firm's stock in the financial markets) could be thought of as human/intellectual capital.[24] In recent years, companies having their market value 4 to even 10 times the book value (e.g., Microsoft during its peak years) is not unusual.[25] In other words, 40–90 percent of the firm's market value can be thought of as human capital and knowledge.

Unlike traditional financial capital or capital equipment and physical material resources, people take their intellectual capital home with them every night or when they leave or retire from the organization. As one KM expert points out, "The Company to some degree 'rents' intellectual capital, and takes ownership of it only when people convert their ideas into products, services or work processes."[26] However, when the employee leaves, the organization may feel it has a proprietary claim because of the loss of the intelligence.

Taking this proprietary view, Wal-Mart recently sued Amazon.com accusing the online retailer of stealing its executives and consultants in an effort to learn Wal-Mart's trade secrets (intelligence). The two giants settled out of court in this case, but the precedent was set for going beyond patents, copyrights, and specific nondisclosure, confidentiality contracts in intellectual property law to now legally recognize the value and ownership of human intelligence in the workplace. As one legal expert in this area noted, "Cases of corporate pillaging will become more and more common as market demand for specialized intellectual talent is placed at a premium, indicating a fundamental reassessment of the role and value of the employee within the workplace."[27] The confidentiality and transferability from one organization to another of human intelligence has traditionally been treated as a business ethics issue or at worst criminal corporate espionage. Now, however, proactive advice in the form of a "war room" mentality (as used by the Allied Powers in World War II) of militarylike strategic offensive and defensive organizational intelligence is being offered.[28] In any case, these developments in the recognition and reaction to human capital/intelligence have brought about a new contract, a "new deal" between employee and employer now and in the future.[29]

The pendulum swinging from the "hard" (e.g., computers, database management, data warehouses, Internet, and Intranet) to the "soft" (e.g., e-business, knowledge management, and human capital/intelligence) in the Information Age environmental context has an important impact on the study and application of organizational behavior. As the social cognitive model for organizational behavior presented at the end of Chapter 1 points out, this environmental context will affect and be affected by the organizational participants' cognitive processes (presented in the chapters of Part II) and be affected by the organizational behavior itself and its dynamics (chapters in Part III) and high-performance management (chapters in Part IV).

GLOBALIZATION

Besides information technology, the other major (at least equal to) environmental context impacting on organizational behavior is globalization. The advances made in information technology discussed so far and in air travel have truly made the world a smaller place. This has led to a borderless world—one big global marketplace. At the current rates of growth, it is estimated that trade *between* nations will exceed total commerce *within* nations by 2015 and "in industries such as semiconductors, automobiles, commercial aircraft, telecommunications, computers, and consumer electronics, it is impossible to survive and not scan the world for competitors, customers, human resources, suppliers, and technology."[30]

Today, well-known U.S.-based multinational corporations (MNCs) such as Mobil, Citicorp, Gillette, Dow Chemical, Hewlett-Packard, and Sara Lee have more than half their assets overseas, and most of these plus others such as Coca-Cola, Colgate-Palmolive, Exxon, Kodak, Proctor & Gamble, Texas Instruments, and even McDonald's obtain two-thirds or more of their sales from overseas.[31] The United Nations identifies 53,000 companies across the world as multinationals; collectively, they have 450,000 affiliates worldwide and, of course, e-business knows no boundaries. The top 100 global companies employ more than 6 million foreign nationals.[32] The shipping labels of one U.S. electronics company may best capture just how global the marketplace has become: "Made in one or more of the following countries: Korea, Hong Kong, Malaysia, Singapore, Taiwan, Mauritius, Thailand, Indonesia, the Philippines. The exact country of origin is unknown."[33]

The implications of this globalization on organizational behavior are profound and direct.[34] As the head of Brunswick Corporation recently declared, "Financial resources are not the problem. We have the money, products, and position to be a dominant global player. What we lack are the human resources. We just don't have enough people with needed global leadership capabilities."[35] GE's Jack Welch, arguably the best-known and respected corporate leader in modern times, stated before leaving GE: "The Jack Welch of the future cannot be like me. I spent my entire career in the United States. The next head of General Electric will be somebody who spent time in Bombay, in Hong Kong, in Buenos Aires. We have to send our best and brightest overseas and make sure they have the training that will allow them to be the global leaders who will make GE flourish in the future."[36] The same is true of countries outside the United States. As the accompanying International Application Example, Cracks in Mexico's

INTERNATIONAL APPLICATION EXAMPLE

Cracks in Mexico's Glass Ceiling

María Asunción Aramburuzabala, a vice-president of brewer Grupo Modelo, does her homework. When a chance to buy into Mexican media giant Grupo Televisa presented itself in April, she arrived at the company's offices armed with reams of numbers. For three hours, Aramburuzabala combed through the financials of each division with Televisa CFO Alfonso de Angoitia. "I was very surprised," he says. "She had already done a very detailed study." Nine weeks after that first meeting, Aramburuzabala got what she wanted: a 20.62% stake in Televisa holding company Grupo Televicentro along with three seats on its board.

With that deal, Aramburuzabala became a full member of the all-male club that is Mexican big business. Her family is one of the four that control Modelo, one of Mexico's largest publicly traded companies. Yet among the family-run giants that still dominate large swaths of Mexican industry, custom dictates that the corporate mantle pass from father to son. In cases where there are no male heirs, a son-in-law is next in line for the throne. When Aramburuzabala, 37, took over managing her family's interests, "people thought I was a little rich girl wanting to play at business and that I would soon get tired and stop," she recalls. But her purchase of the Televisa stake proves otherwise.

It has been a long time coming, but the feminist revolution is reaching the boardrooms of Mexico's family-run companies. Aramburuzabala is helping speed things along.

As Aramburuzabala breaks new ground for businesswomen in Mexico, there are other signs of change. Women are starting their own companies in record numbers while multinationals have promoted some of their female executives to top positions. For instance, Compaq Computer Corp.'s Mexican subsidiary has long had a woman chief executive, Barbara Mair. Since taking over in 1993, the 38-year-old Mair has pumped up sales from $65 million to $500 million last year. Despite her own success, Mair believes that Mexican women continue to limit themselves in their career choices. "They don't feel it's possible," she says.

Glass Ceiling, indicates, countries are beginning to realize that they need the talents of everyone in order to compete in the global economy.

Although there is a trend toward similar clothes, entertainment, and material possessions, and even general recognition that English is the international business language, there are still important differences in the ways in which people think and behave around the world. Even though it is meant to be humorous and recognizing the dangers of cultural stereotypes and overgeneralizations, which will be discussed next, the following does point to the differences, the cultural diversity, that managers exhibit around the world:

> The Swedes are "peacemakers," whereas Chinese business leaders hold that *Shang chang ru zhan chang* ("The marketplace is a battlefield"). In Japan, what is unspoken is all-important, while in France argument is a form of entertainment. German businessmen toil in structured environments (*Alles in Ordnung*—"all in order"), yet they might end the day by sunbathing nude in the city park.[37]

In other words, cultures around the world impact the organizational behavior of managers and employees quite differently than in the United States. There are even differences in the way in which knowledge about organizational behavior is accumulated. For example, it has been pointed out that European behavioral scientists tend to be more cognitive and/or psychoanalytically based, whereas their U.S. counterparts are more behavioristic and/or humanistically oriented.[38] In understanding and applying organizational behavior concepts in other countries around the world, one must be aware of the similarities and differences.

For example, a research study conducted by Welsh, Luthans, and Sommer found that U.S.-based extrinsic rewards and behavioral management approaches significantly improved the productivity of workers in a Russian factory, but a participative technique did not.[39] A follow-up critique concluded:

> What this study shows is that there are both potential benefits and problems associated with transporting U.S.-based human resource management theories and techniques to other cultures. On the one hand, the findings confirmed that the use of valued extrinsic rewards and improved behavioral management techniques may have a considerable impact on productivity among Russian workers in ways that are similar to American workers. On the other hand, participation had a counterproductive effect on Russian workers' performance.[40]

Another example would be that in some countries managers prefer to use—and may be more effective with—an autocratic leadership style rather than the typical U.S. manager's leadership style. Germany is a visible example. Typical U.S. managers who are transferred to Germany may find their leadership style to be too participative. German subordinates may expect them to make more decisions and to consult with them less. Research on obedience to authority (discussed in Chapter 7) found that a higher percentage of Germans were obedient than were their U.S. counterparts.[41] Similarly, a U.S. manager in Japan who decides to set up a performance-based incentive system that gives a weekly bonus to the best worker in each work group may be making a mistake. Japanese workers do not like to be singled out for individual attention and go against the group's norms and values. Perhaps this impact of similarities and differences across cultures was best stated by the cofounder of Honda Motor, T. Fujisawa, when he stated: "Japanese and American management is 95 percent the same, and differs in all important aspects."[42]

The starting point of how the globalization environment affects and is affected by organizational behavior is culture.

THE IMPACT OF CULTURE ON INTERNATIONAL ORGANIZATIONAL BEHAVIOR

Culture can be defined as the acquired knowledge that people use to interpret experience and generate social behavior. It is important to recognize that culture is learned and helps people in their efforts to interact and communicate with others in the society. When placed in a culture where values and beliefs are different, some people have a great deal of difficulty adjusting.[43] This is particularly true when U.S. businesspeople are assigned to a foreign country. There is considerable evidence that U.S. expatriates (those on a foreign assignment) have a much greater chance of failure than their European and Japanese counterparts.[44] These expatriates quickly learn that the values of U.S. culture are often quite different from those of their host country, and, even though increasing attention is being given to expatriate management,[45] U.S. multinational corporations (MNCs) are incurring millions of dollars of costs due to expatriate failures.[46]

Not as well publicized is the fact that those who enter the United States also suffer cultural shock and failures. Consider the problems experienced by expats being sent to the United States:

> It's ironic that this would be the case in a country with one of the world's most-traveled populations. Still, being sent to the United States on foreign assignment is not just a stressful business—it's a lonely one. From New Delhi to Cape Town to Minas Gerais, the observation is the same: Americans are friendly but hard to make friends with. We gregarious Americans don't truly bring international assignees into our lives, because we don't bring them into our homes after work.[47]

In other words, cultural differences are a two-way street. Cultural differences must be understood, and managers must be sensitive to them in order to be successful in the global economy. For example, there is recent research that shows that expatriate experience and levels of host-country language fluency, as expected, does significantly improve the expat adjustment process.[48]

How Do Cultures Vary?

There are several basic dimensions that differentiate national cultures. Before getting into these, it must be remembered that there are also differences within national cultures, and making generalizations or drawing stereotypes cannot only be wrong, but also lead to problems. As one international organizational behavior expert recently observed, "The longer I live in a country, the more uncomfortable I become making generalizations about the culture because 10 examples immediately come to mind where the generalization does not hold true."[49] However, noting broad differences, say between countries, can be done and can be helpful in international management. As another international organizational behavior expert countering the preceding quote noted, "When you're only looking within a country you only see the variation. But when you compare, let's say, a group of German managers with a group of French, you see the difference—and that is when your stereotypes get reinforced. Stereotypes are only meaningful by comparison."[50] The following sections examine and compare some of the most important differences between national cultures.

How People See Themselves.   In some countries of the world, people are viewed as basically honest and trustworthy. In others, people are regarded with suspicion and distrust. For example, a reason some people around the world regard the United States with suspicion and distrust may result from the way these people view themselves. They assume others are like them, that is, prepared to cut corners if they can get away with it. On the other hand, many other people of these countries are just the opposite. They do not lock their doors; they are very trusting and assume that no one will break in. It is forbidden to take the property of another person, and the people adhere strictly to that cultural value. In the United States, people also have a mixed view of other people. Most people from the United States still view others as basically honest but also believe that it is important to be alert for any sign of trouble.

When people travel outside their home country, they carry their values and language with them, just like their baggage. This results not only in confusion, but sometimes marketing disasters such as the following:

- McDonald's took more than a year to realize that Hindus in India do not eat beef. Only when it started making hamburgers out of lamb did sales flourish.
- A U.S. company sent an elaborate business proposal to Saudi Arabia bound in pigskin to dramatize its presentation. Because pigs are considered unclean by Muslims, the proposal was never even opened.

- In Africa, the labels on bottles show pictures of what's inside so that illiterate customers know what they're getting. When a baby food company showed a picture of an infant on the label, the product did not sell very well.
- An English firm tried to market a candy in the United States called "Zit." A Finnish product to unfreeze the car locks of American motorists was called "Super Piss." A Swedish manufacturer of vacuum cleaners proudly proclaimed, "Electrolux sucks."[51]

People's Relationship to Their World.   In some societies people attempt to dominate their environment. In other societies they try to live in harmony with it or are subjugated by it. People from the United States and Canada, for example, attempt to dominate their environment. In agriculture they use fertilizers and insecticides to increase crop yields. Most recently, many U.S. agribusiness firms have run into trouble because of genetic engineering of plants and animals. For example, Pioneer Hi-Bred International, a Des Moines, Iowa, agribusiness company, has encountered protestors in both Europe and the United States who oppose its genetic alteration of seeds that grow into the world's grains, fruits, and vegetables.[52]

Other societies, especially those in Asia, work in harmony with the environment by planting crops in the right places and at the right time. In still other societies, most notably developing countries, no action is taken regarding the subjugation of nature, so, for example, when the floods come, there are no dams or irrigation systems for dealing with the impending disaster. Also, when the Berlin Wall crumbled and Eastern Europe opened up, it was found that there was an ecological disaster there. For example, it was found that almost all the rivers were heavily polluted, in some areas 90 percent of the children suffered from respiratory and other pollution-related diseases, and sewage treatment was in a terrible state almost everywhere.[53] The former communist countries are still trying to dig their way out of this, in some cases irreversible, mess.

Besides the physical environment, there are also different cultural concerns for the preservation of values and the resistence to the intrusion of globalization itself. In the U.S., there have been small, but surprising, protests when the World Trade Organization (WTO) met at the beginning of the new century in Seattle, Washington, and then again when protesters showed up at the International Monetary Fund (IMF) and World Bank policy discussions in Washington, D.C. There has also been a grassroots negative reaction in France to the perceived invasion of U.S.-driven globalization of food, entertainment, and values into the French culture. The protests range from farmers trashing McDonald's franchises to 100 percent taxes on Coca-Cola in some French towns. In Europe, food and culinary eating traditions are closely linked with cultural identity. As one expert of French society noted, "There is a growing fear of being taken over by new types of technology and general ambivalence toward globalization, of which McDonald's has become a symbol."[54] The protests came to a head when a French Farmers Union leader was arrested for vandalizing a McDonald's under construction in Southern France, and an exploding bomb outside the drive-through killed a McDonald's employee near Dinan, France. Although the French government deplores any violence against the hugely successful U.S. multinational (there are over 800 profitable outlets in France alone), the minister of agriculture publically referred to the United States as home of the worst food in the world.[55]

Individualism versus Collectivism.   Some countries of the world have cultural values that encourage individualism. The United States, Great Britain, and Canada are examples. In other countries collectivism, or group orientation, is important. Japan, China, and the Israeli kibbutzim emphasize group harmony, unity, commitment, and loyalty.

The differences reflect themselves in many ways, such as in hiring practices. In countries where individualism is important, job applicants are evaluated on the basis of personal, educational, and professional achievements. In group-oriented societies applicants are evaluated on the basis of trustworthiness, loyalty, and compatibility with coworkers. Also in highly collectivistic cultures, employees tend to show considerable commitment to their organization, whereas in highly individualistic cultures, managers tend to be more mobile, going from job to job.[56] Unlike the individualistic United States, research in highly collectivistic Japan and China found employees do not seek or want to receive feedback about their individual performance.[57]

The Time Dimension.   In some societies people are oriented toward the past. In others they tend to be more focused on the present. Still others are futuristic in their orientation. People from the United States and Canada are most interested in the present and the near future. Businesspeople in these countries are particularly interested in where their companies are today and where they will be in 5 to 10 years. People who are hired and do not work out are often let go in short order. They seldom last more than one or two years. Most Europeans place more importance on the past than do North Americans. They believe in preserving history and continuing traditions. They are concerned with the past, present, and future. Many Asian countries are futuristic in their approach. The Japanese, for example, have very long term, future-oriented time horizons. When large Japanese firms hire employees, they often retain them for a long time, even for life. The firms will spend a great deal of money to train them, and there is a strong, mutual commitment on both sides.

Besides past, present, or future orientation, another way time varies by cultures is sequential versus synchronous. In cultures where sequential approaches are prevalent, people tend to do only one activity at a time, keep strict appointments, and show a strong preference for following plans as they are laid out and not deviating from them. In synchronous cultures, people tend to do more than one activity at a time, appointments are approximate and may be changed at any time, and schedules are not as important as relationships.[58] U.S. managers tend to be guided by sequential time orientation, which may be beneficial for careful planning and being on time, but may be a detriment to the speed necessary in today's competitive environment that may require synchronous activities and timing.

Public and Private Space.   Some cultures promote the use of public space; others favor private space. For example, in Japan bosses often sit together with their employees in the same large room. The heads of some of the biggest Japanese firms may leave their chauffeur-driven limousines at home and ride the crowded public subways to work in the morning so that they can be with their workers. In the Middle East there are often many people present during important meetings. These cultures have a public orientation. In contrast, North Americans have traditionally preferred private space. The more restricted or confined a manager was, the more important the individual was assumed to be. In recent years, this privacy orientation is changing in U.S. organizations as information technology (e.g., e-mail, intranets, and video conferencing) allows access to everyone and "open-door" and management-by-walking-around policies have become a reality. Also, with virtual teams becoming the rule rather than the exception in doing business electronically and under globalization, privacy is no longer an option. For example, a virtual team at Hewlett-Packard had members who were stationed throughout the world, in widely divergent time zones, who had to participate in meetings from their airplanes, hotels, work, and home.[59]

When comparing societies in terms of the dimensions discussed, it becomes obvious that there are major differences between the ways in which business is done from one corner of the world to another. The challenge for the field of organizational behavior "is not whether but to what extent and in what ways culture influences individual and group phenomena in organizations."[60] The point of departure of identifying cultural differences are the widely recognized dimensions provided by Geert Hofstede.

Hofstede's Cultural Dimensions

To date, the most common way to study and draw conclusions about organizational behavior across cultures and explain the differences that exist is to use Hofstede's framework. This well-known Dutch researcher conducted what is considered to be the largest organizationally based study ever done. Through a questionnaire measure he found differences in the behavior and attitudes of 116,000 respondents from 70 countries who worked for subsidiaries of IBM.[61] From this data, he identified four major cultural dimensions: individualism/collectivism, power distance, uncertainty avoidance, and masculinity/femininity.

There has been some reanalysis and criticism through the years of Hofstede's dimensions. For example, a study found that some of the dimensions are highly interrelated,[62] and, because all his data were collected from one company, the study has been criticized for not being representative of the various countries. However, Hofstede has countered such criticism by arguing that

> . . . samples for cross-national comparison need not be representative, as long as they are functionally equivalent. IBM employees are a narrow sample, but very well matched. . . . The only thing that can account for systematic and consistent differences between national groups *within* such a homogenous multinational population is nationality itself—the national environment in which people were brought up *before* they joined this employer. Comparing IBM subsidiaries therefore shows national cultural differences with unusual clarity.[63]

More recently, a critical analysis was made of some of the ways in which Hofstede made calculations of the indexes used in the cultural dimensions.[64] For example, it was found that he used extrapolated rather than available real values in calculating some of the scores for the United States. Had the actual values been used, the United States may be placed in the Germanic cultural cluster on some of the dimensions rather than the Anglo cluster. These and some ways that mathematical procedures were used to calculate the indexes raise questions about the seemingly uncritical acceptance of the Hofstede dimensions for cross-cultural analysis. It must also be remembered that "the position of a culture along a dimension is based on the averages for all the respondents in that particular country. Characterizing a national work culture does not mean that every person in the nation has all the characteristics ascribed to that culture—there are bound to be many individual variations."[65] In other words, care must be taken not to stereotype an entire country on the basis of this study. There are numerous subcultures and individual differences. Finally, it must be remembered that Hofstede's data are now more than 20 years old. Cultural values do have lasting power, but because of the turbulent environment in recent years, there seems little doubt that country clustering by cultural dimensions is undergoing change.[66] Yet, because Hofstede's dimensions are so well known and still widely used, they are discussed in the following sections in their relation to organizational behavior. Then Hofstede's framework is followed by a more recent conceptualization of cultural dimensions.

Individualism/Collectivism and Power Distance.   Individualism is the tendency to take care of oneself and one's immediate family. Collectivism is characterized by a tight social framework in which people distinguish between their own group and other groups. Power distance is the extent to which less-powerful members of organizations accept the unequal distribution of power, that is, the degree to which employees accept that their boss has more power than they do.

When Hofstede examined employees from 50 countries in terms of individualism and power distance, he found cultural clusters. Figure 2.2 shows that the United States has high individualism and small power distance (employees do not grant their bosses much power). This is in contrast, for example, to Mexico, which has high collectivism (tight group) and large power distance (a lot of power granted to the boss). Countries that are in the same circled-in area tend to be similar in terms of individualism/collectivism and power distance. Figure 2.2 illustrates that U.S. multinational firms doing business in Mexico would encounter much greater cultural differences than they would in France, but still less if they operated in Great Britain.

In general, Hofstede found that wealthy countries have higher individualism scores and poorer countries have higher collectivism scores. An exception would be Japan and, in the time since Hofstede gathered his data, the other now developed Asian countries, which have relatively high collectivism but have become quite well off. The collectivism cultural dimension would be more compatible with the new emphasis on teams in the workplace and might help explain why they work so well in Japan but

FIGURE 2.2

The position of selected countries on power distance and individualism.

(*Source:* Adapted from Geert Hofstede, "The Culture Relativity of Organizational Practices and Theories," *Journal of International Business Studies,* Fall 1983, p. 82. Used with permission.)

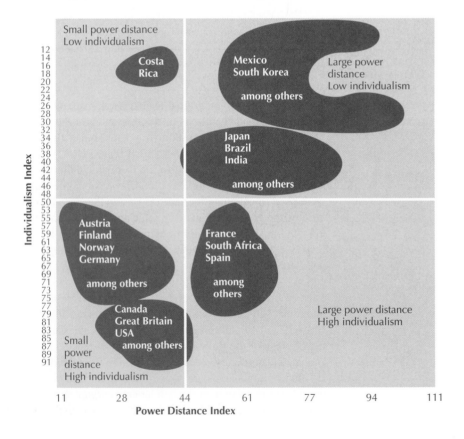

may not in the United States. However, small power distance cultures such as that of the United States may be more compatible with the newly emerging networked, flat structures, and empowerment dimensions of today's organizations.

Uncertainty Avoidance.   Another dimension of cultural difference identified by Hofstede is uncertainty avoidance. Uncertainty avoidance is the extent to which people feel threatened by ambiguous situations and the degree to which they try to avoid these situations by doing such things as:

- Providing greater career stability
- Establishing more formal rules
- Rejecting deviant ideas and behavior
- Accepting the possibility of absolute truths and the attainment of expertise[67]

In Japan, for example, where lifetime employment traditionally exists, at least in the large companies, there is high uncertainty avoidance. In the United States, by contrast, where there traditionally has been relatively high job mobility, there is low uncertainty avoidance. Also in Japan, the government has traditionally tried to reduce the uncertainty for business. However, as is the case with lifetime employment, this uncertainty avoidance climate for businesses in Japan may be changing as Japanese MNCs try to recover from their prolonged economic downturn and attempt to instill the cultural value of more risk taking, leading to more creativity and innovation to become more competitive.[68]

Figure 2.3 shows the position of selected countries on power distance and uncertainty avoidance. Countries like Great Britain, which has weak uncertainty avoidance

FIGURE 2.3

The position of selected countries on power distance and uncertainty avoidance.

(*Source:* Adapted from Geert Hofstede, "The Cultural Relativity of Organizational Practices and Theories," *Journal of International Business Studies,* Fall 1983, p. 84. Used with permission.)

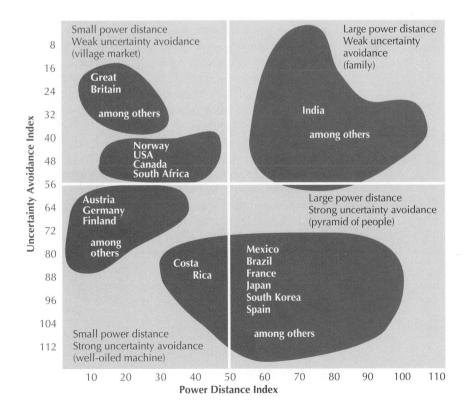

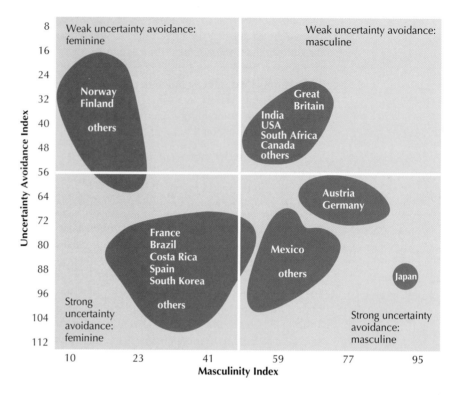

FIGURE 2.4

The position of selected countries on uncertainty avoidance and masculinity/femininity.

(*Source:* Adapted from Geert Hofstede, "The Cultural Relativity of Organizational Practices and Theories," *Journal of International Business Studies,* Fall 1983, p. 86. Used with permission.)

and small power distance, tend to have less hierarchy and more interaction between people. Additionally, risk taking is both expected and encouraged. Employees in large power distance and weak uncertainty avoidance cultures such as India tend to think of their organizations as traditional families. Employees in countries such as Mexico and Brazil tend to think of their organizations as pyramids of people rather than as families. Employees in countries such as Austria and Finland tend to work in organizations that are highly predictable without needing a strong hierarchy. Roles and procedures are clearly defined in these cultures.

Masculinity/Femininity. Hofstede also measured the impact of masculinity/femininity. Masculinity is the extent to which the dominant values of a society emphasize assertiveness and the acquisition of money and other material things. Femininity is the term used by Hofstede to refer to the extent to which the dominant values in a society emphasize relationships among people, concern for others, and interest in quality of work life. As shown in Figure 2.4, in masculine societies with strong uncertainty avoidance, such as Japan, the managers tend to be very assertive and materialistic. In feminine societies, such as Scandinavian countries like Norway, the workforce in factories is concerned with quality of work life.

Trompenaars's Cultural Dimensions

As noted, the Hofstede cultural dimensions have long been the standard classification scheme for cross-cultural analysis. However, the time has now come to look to a more up-to-date classification scheme for international organizational behavior. One of the most comprehensive (respondents were 15,000 managers from 28 countries) and recent comes from another Dutch researcher, Fons Trompenaars.[69] Similar to Hofstede, Trompenaars has identified five cultural dimensions from extensive data on how people deal with each other.[70]

Universalism versus Particularism.   Trompenaars labeled the cultural dimension of *universalism* as the belief that ideas and practices can be applied everywhere without modification. The other end of the continuum is *particularism,* which is the belief that circumstances dictate how ideas and practices should be applied. For example, highly universalist cultures would emphasize and be guided by strict, formal rules (e.g., in business dealings, contracts would be adhered to very closely and personnel in the organization would always strive to follow the rules and procedures). Highly particularistic cultures, on the other hand, would focus more on personal relationships and trust rather than on formal rules and legal contracts. Figure 2.5 shows that Trompenaars

FIGURE 2.5
Trompenaars's cultural dimensions by country (abbreviations below).
(*Source:* Adapted from information found in Fons Trompenaars, *Riding the Waves of Culture,* Irwin, New York, 1994).

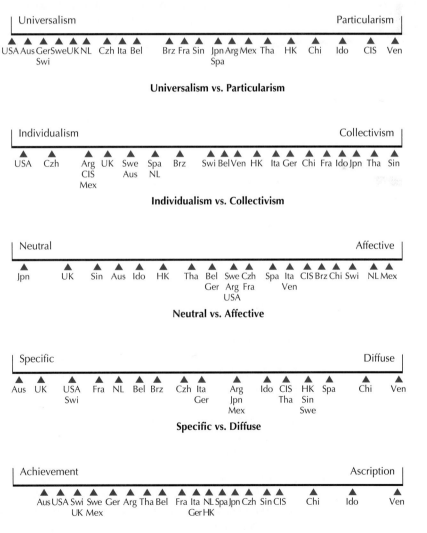

found highly universalist cultures to be the United States and European countries and highly particularist countries to be Venezuela, the republics of the former Soviet Union (CIS), and the Asian countries of Indonesia and China.

The cross-cultural implication is that the attitudes and style of management would be quite different in these two types of culture. Universalists would tend to have a "let's get down to business" attitude and not deviate from the rules and regulations, whereas particularists would tend to engage in a lot of small talk to get to know one another and let the situation dictate their actions. Particularists would be flexible and not let the rules get in the way of what is the right thing to do between friends. A recent study found that because the former Soviet Union (CIS) countries have high particularism, there may be a cultural fit with the effective use of high-performance work practices such as multisource (360 degree) feedback, pay-for-performance, self-managed work teams, and employee involvement/participation/empowerment.[71]

Individualism versus Collectivism.   Although Trompenaars derived these two dimensions differently than Hofstede, they still have the same basic meaning, but refinements are being made in terms of theory and measurement.[72] *Individualism* refers to people regarding themselves as individuals, while *collectivism* refers to people regarding themselves as part of a group. As shown in Figure 2.5, the United States, the former Czechoslovakia, Argentina, the republics of the former Soviet Union (CIS), and Mexico have high individualism. Importantly, these findings of Trompenaars are somewhat different from those of Hofstede. Although the definitions are very similar, the fact that there are differences (e.g., Mexico and Argentina are collectivist in Hofstede's findings but individualistic in Trompenaars's research) points out that cultural values may be shifting in some countries. For example, with Mexico now part of NAFTA and the global economy, this country may have moved from dominant collectivist cultural values to more individualist values. The same may be true of the former communist countries of Czechoslovakia and the republics of the former Soviet Union (CIS).

Contrary to assumptions and conventional wisdom about the former communist bloc in its transition to a market economy, these countries now have an increasing number of people with entrepreneurial, individualist values.[73] There is even growing evidence that the last remaining communist power—China—is also rapidly moving in this direction. For example, a study found that Chinese employees from the People's Republic ranked economic goals more highly than those from the United States and favored differentiated reward distributions more than their U.S. counterparts.[74]

The implications that these dimensions have for cross-cultural analysis would be in areas such as reward systems, decision making, and work design. For example, individualistic cultures would respond better to individually based pay-for-performance, individual executive decision making, and traditional work designs. In collectivistic cultures, however, it would be more appropriate to use a gainsharing reward plan, group problem solving, consensus decision making, and an autonomous teamwork design.

To date, most research in international organizational behavior has been concerned with these individualistic/collectivistic cultural differences. For example, here is a sample of research on organizational behavior concepts and variables covered in later chapters that considers individualism/collectivism:

1. *Attribution.*   One study comparing U.S. and Korean managers found that collectivistic-oriented Korean managers attributed greater personal responsibility for group failure than success and accepted greater personal responsibility for group failures than did individualistic U.S. managers.[75] In another study, American

students attributed academic success more often to ability than did Asian students.[76] Also, from their research findings, Kashima and Triandis argue that the self-serving bias (see Chapter 6) is less likely to be found in collectivistic cultures than in individualistic cultures.[77]

2. *Self-efficacy.*   Research by Earley found that collectivistic subjects who took part in individually oriented training programs had lower efficacy beliefs (see Chapter 9) and displayed lower effort and performance than did their collectivistic counterparts who took part in group-oriented training programs. Also, individualistic subjects had enhanced self-efficacy and displayed greater effort and performance when their training was oriented toward personal actions and potential.[78] Bandura emphasizes that "because there is variability within cultures, understanding how cultural background affects efficacy beliefs and functioning requires analysis of individual orientations as well as the prevailing cultural orientation. Regardless of cultural background, employees achieve the greatest sense of personal efficacy and productivity gains when training is congruent with their personal orientation."[79]

3. *Stress.*   One study comparing collectivistic Japanese and relatively individualistic Australian subjects found that the Japanese reported higher levels of stress when faced with making a decision by themselves.[80] In another study comparing salespersons from the United States and India, the U.S. subjects experienced more stress under formalization than did those from India.[81] In other words, bureaucratic structures were not stressors for the collectivistic Indian salespeople, but tended to be stressful for individualistic U.S. salespeople. Finally, a very large study found that role stressors varied more by country than by personal and organizational characteristics.[82]

4. *Goal setting and performance.*   There is research in collectivist cultures in general showing a tendency toward commitment to goals that serve the best interest of the group and in specific collectivistic cultures such as Israel where participative (as opposed to assigned) goal setting yield better performance outcomes and higher commitment.[83] Also, there is evidence that relational and interpersonal criteria such as good human nature, harmony in interpersonal relations, trustworthiness, respectful attitude, loyalty and deference toward superiors, effort and willingness to work, awareness of duties and obligations, gratitude, organizational citizenship, conformity, and contribution to team maintenance are more salient dimensions of performance in collectivist versus more task-related criteria in individualistic cultures.[84]

Neutral versus Affective.   Like individualism/collectivism, this Trompenaars cultural dimension is essentially self-explanatory. In a *neutral culture,* emotions are held in check and not outwardly expressed. As shown in Figure 2.5, the Japanese and British try not to outwardly show their feelings. However, in *affective cultures* the opposite is true; emotions are openly and naturally expressed. As shown in Figure 2.5, people in affective cultures, such as Mexicans, the Dutch, and the Swiss, tend to smile a great deal, talk loudly when they are excited, and greet each other enthusiastically.

Outsiders should not assume that those from neutral cultures are uninterested or unmotivated because of their nonexpressive demeanor, and vice versa. In other words, in communication and other interpersonal interactions, the nonverbal and verbal cues may have to be read quite differently in both highly neutral and highly affective cultures.

Specific versus Diffuse.   This cultural dimension is more subtle and difficult to interpret than the others. By a *specific culture,* Trompenaars means one in which individuals have a large public space they readily let others enter and share and a small private space they guard closely and share only with close friends and associates. A *diffuse culture* is one in which both public and private space are similar in size, and individuals guard their public space carefully, because entry into public space affords entry into private space as well.

As shown in Figure 2.5, Austria, the United Kingdom, the United States, and Switzerland are all specific cultures. In these specific cultures, outsiders are readily invited into a person's open, public space. Individuals in specific cultures often are open and extroverted; and there is a strong separation of work and private life. In diffuse cultures, such as in Venezuela, China, and Spain, people are not quickly invited into a person's open, public space, because once they are in, there is easy entry into the private space as well. Individuals in diffuse cultures often appear to be indirect and introverted, and work and private life are often closely linked.

In diffuse cultures, outsiders should respect a person's title, age, and background connections, and should not get impatient when people from the diffuse culture are being indirect or evasive. Conversely, when dealing with individuals from specific cultures, outsiders should try to get to the point and be efficient, learn to structure things, minimize the use of titles, and play down achievements or skills that are irrelevant to the situation.

Achievement versus Ascription.   The final major cultural dimension identified by Trompenaars is achievement/ascription. An *achievement culture* is one in which people are accorded status based on how well they perform their functions. An *ascription culture* is one in which status is attributed based on who or what a person is. Achievement cultures give high status to high achievers, such as the company's number-one salesperson or the manager of the unit with the highest profit. Ascription cultures accord status based on age, gender, or social connections. For example, in an ascription culture, a person who has been with the company the longest may be listened to more carefully because of the respect that others have for the individual's age and longevity with the firm. Also, individuals who have friends in top management may be afforded status because of whom they know. As shown in Figure 2.5, Austria, the United States, Switzerland, and the United Kingdom are achievement cultures, whereas Venezuela, Indonesia, and China are ascription cultures. The Chinese, for example, give considerable status to age and those with connections, or *guanxi.*[85]

The Hofstede and Trompenaars culture dimensions are useful in a general way (always realizing there are subcultures and individual differences) to recognize the similarities and differences around the world. The rest of the chapters in the book, especially Chapter 8 on motivation, Chapter 10 on communication, and Chapter 17 on leadership, will use these dimensions in the analysis of organization behavior across cultures.

Summary

This chapter examines the environmental context in terms of information technology and globalization. There have been some amazing breakthroughs in information technology in recent years. The personal computer, now even handheld through personal digital assistants (PDAs), have made e-mail, and the use of the Internet, Intranet, and Extranet everyday business tools. Of particular importance to the environmental context for the study of organizational behavior is e-business, emerging knowledge management, and the new emphasis on human/intellectual capital. E-business is dominated by business-to-business (B2B) transactions now and even more so in the future. Knowledge management (KM) is concerned with both tangible knowledge assets and intangible knowledge or intelligence possessed by employees and stakeholders. Not only is acquiring and storing data important, but the real key to effective KM is sharing and leveraging information and knowledge. The same can be said of human/intellectual capital. No longer just dependent on financial capital or capital equipment, today's organizations need human capital (employee experience, skills, and ideas/creativity) to be used and leveraged for competitive advantage.

Besides information technology, the international context in which organizational behavior operates is also becoming an increasingly important environmental context. Few would question that there is now globalization and that cultural differences must be recognized in the study and understanding of organizational behavior.

The discussion starts off by defining culture, which is the acquired knowledge that people use to interpret experience and generate social behavior. Although it must be remembered that it is difficult to make generalizations because of individual differences and the many subcultures operating in societies and countries, there are several dimensions of culture that do pretty well describe societal orientations. These dimensions are identified in the chapter as follows: how people see themselves; people's relationship to their world; individualism versus collectivism; the time dimension; and public and private space. These dimensions lead to organizational behavior differences across cultures. There are many reasons for these differences. The chapter draws heavily from the research of Hofstede, who found that people tend to differ on the basis of individualism/collectivism, power distance, uncertainty avoidance, and masculinity/femininity. However, because of the criticism of this widely recognized categorical scheme and the fact that Hofstede's data are now more than 20 years old, the more recent extensive work on cultural dimensions of countries by Fons Trompenaars is also presented. His dimensions include universalism/particularism, individualism/collectivism, neutral/affective, specific/diffuse, and achievement/ascription. These cultural dimensions are used to analyze the topics (especially motivation, communication, and leadership) across cultures in the rest of the book.

ENDING WITH META-ANALYTIC RESEARCH FINDINGS

OB PRINCIPLE: Conducting cross-cultural training can increase expatriate on-the-job performance and adjustment to an international assignment.

Meta-Analysis Results: [21 studies; 1,611 participants; $d = .79$ for performance, and $d = .91$ for adjustment]
*On average, expatriates who receive cross-cultural training have a **71 percent higher probability** of performing better and **74 percent higher chance** of better adjustment to the new culture than those who do not receive cross-cultural training.*

Conclusion: Under today's globalization, organizations must often depend on expatriates (those assigned to live and work away from their home country). However, expatriate failure in terms of poor performance and lack of adjustment causing early termination of the assignment is common. Experience and research has clearly indicated a major reason for these problems is the inability of expatriates and/or their families to understand and adjust to their new culture. Because most expats lack a true understanding of the customs, cultures, day-to-day conduct of business, and the work habits of the local people, they often make critical mistakes. Cultural blunders greatly hinder performance and also lead to frustration, stress, and eventual voluntary or nonvoluntary turnover. As the above meta-analysis of research indicates, cross-cultural training can help overcome such expatriate failure.

The cross-cultural training should occur both predeparture and periodically in-country during the assignment for both the expat and family members. The content should include language training, sensitivity training, history, current events and economic briefings, and cultural values and practices. The periodic in-country training should involve adjustment assessment, updates on everything, and Q and A. As this chapter indicates, globalization is a reality. As a result, not only traditional expatriates, but also all businesspeople will soon become members of the global community. These global managers will require the same type of expatriate cross-cultural training to make them effective performers.

Source: Adapted from S. P. Deshpande and C. Viswesvaran, "Is Cross-Cultural Training of Expatriate Managers Effective: A Meta-Analysis," *International Journal of Intercultural Relations,* Vol. 16, No. 3, 1992, pp. 295–310.

Questions for Discussion and Review

1. In what way is information technology an important environmental context for organizational behavior? Give examples.
2. Why do you think business-to-business (B2B) e-business has become so dominant?
3. What does it mean that Ford manages by its Intranet? Give some examples.
4. What are the two approaches to knowledge management (KM)?
5. How, if at all, is human capital different from the traditional use of the term *capital* in business firms?
6. What is meant by and what are some examples of globalization?
7. In your own words, what is meant by the term *culture?*
8. What are some basic dimensions that describe the cultural orientation of a society? Briefly describe each.
9. In what way do Hofstede's dimensions of individualism/collectivism, power distance, uncertainty avoidance, and masculinity/femininity help explain cultural differences? Define and give examples of these dimensions.

10. In what way do Trompenaars's dimensions of universalism/particularism, individualism/collectivism, neutral/affective, specific/diffuse, and achievement/ascription help explain cultural differences? Define and give examples of these dimensions.

Internet Exercise: Achieving Competitive Advantage Through IT

As pointed out in this chapter of the text, information technology (IT) has not only changed the way business does business, but also organizational behavior and human resource management. Using www.amazon.com, www.ebay.com, and one other firm of your choice, answer the following questions.

1. Obviously advanced information technology allowed these firms to gain competitive advantage. What challenges do they now face to sustain this advantage?
2. What issues covered in this text do these companies currently face? Are they entirely different types of companies with different issues than traditional companies? Or, are they just dot-com firms with the same "people" issues as traditional organizations?

REAL CASE:
Spread the
Knowledge

Memphis-based Buckman was one of the first companies to adopt a so-called knowledge-management system, which, after a decade in the corporate doghouse, is finally gaining respect. For years, many CEOS and management experts saw it as little more than a touchy-feely New Age management fad, able to do little for a company's bottom line. Now, thanks to the imperative to turn their companies into e-businesses, many CEOS are taking a second look. The attraction: By using the Net, companies can quickly and easily share, store, and retrieve the collective expertise of their people—which was previously hoarded by executives or locked away in employees' heads and file cabinets. "It's finally sinking in that it's not just about selling widgets anymore, but also the rich, experience-won information about the widgets, that will give a company its only real long-term prayer against rivals in the Information Economy," says Rashi Glaser, a professor at the University of California at Berkeley's Haas School of Business.

Companies large and small are jumping on the bandwagon. Industry leaders such as Chevron, Xerox, Johnson & Johnson, Royal Dutch/Shell, Ford, and Whirlpool also have major knowledge-sharing initiatives underway. In a recent Conference Board survey of 200 execs at 158 large multinationals, 80% said they had knowledge-management projects in the works, and many already have anointed chief knowledge officers or enlisted KM consultants. All told, says market researcher International Data Corp., consultants pulled in $1.8 billion in KM services last year. By 2003, the number should top $8 billion.

At Buckman, the payoff already is here. Revenues, which hit $400 million last year, have been growing about 5% annually in recent years, a slightly faster rate than its rivals can claim. Robert Buckman points to a 52% increase last year in the share of sales from products less than five years on the market, which he considers a measure of innovation. And he cites as proof statistics on employee productivity: Since 1992, sales per salesperson have gone up by 51 percent and sales per employee have increased by 34 percent. Operating profit per employee jumped 93 percent in the same period. All this has helped it to compete successfully with much larger and better-funded companies. "I don't think we'd be a player today if we hadn't done those things," says Robert H. Buckman, former Buckman CEO and currently the chairman of the executive committee of Bulab Holdings Inc., Buckman's parent company.

Despite its success, Buckman's experience offers important lessons in how tough it is to build a successful knowledge-sharing network. It takes time and often painful changes in corporate culture. On top of that, Buckman has found, the payoff may not always show up on the bottom line. Says Robert Buckman: "This is messy stuff. Think it's a technology problem? It's not. It's a cultural problem."

Others agree that convincing people to do things differently is the biggest hurdle. According to the Gartner Group, a full 50 percent to 70 percent of the work it takes to make a knowledge-management initiative a success will revolve around coaxing cultural changes. "Getting people to really share what they know is required now if you're going to start letting the Net modernize the organization," says Lawrence Prusak, IBM'S top knowledge guru.

1. In your own words, describe the Buckman Company's knowledge-management system. How, if at all, is this different from what this company should have been doing all along, before the advent of "Knowledge Management" in the "Information Age"?
2. Explain what is meant by the statement by Robert Buckman that "This is messy stuff. Think it's a technical problem? It's not. It's a cultural problem."
3. What impact do you think the study and application of organizational behavior can have in the information technology arena?

ORGANIZATIONAL BEHAVIOR CASE: How Far-Reaching Are Globalization and Technology?

Bob is the owner and operator of a medium-sized grocery store that has been in his family for more than 30 years. Currently his business is flourishing, primarily because it has an established customer base in a busy part of town. Also, Bob is a good manager. He considers himself to be highly knowledgeable about his business, having continuously adapted to the changing times. For example, he recently expanded his business by putting in a full-service deli. His philosophy is that by continuously providing customers with new products and services, he will always have a satisfied customer base to rely on.

At a management seminar he attended last year, the hot topic was globalization and the impact of technology on business. He has also been bombarded by the many television ads and mailers regarding the opportunities available on the Internet. For the most part, Bob doesn't think that globalization is an issue with his business, as he doesn't even intend to expand outside the city. Furthermore, he feels that the Internet has no applications in his branch of the retail industry and would simply be a waste of time.

1. Is Bob correct in his assessment of how globalization will impact his business?
2. Can you think of any Internet applications that Bob could profit from?
3. How could Bob's business be negatively impacted by both technology and globalization if he does not keep on top of these developments?

ORGANIZATIONAL BEHAVIOR CASE: I Want Out

When the Budder Mining Equipment company decided to set up a branch office in Peru, top management felt that there were two basic avenues the company could travel. One was to export its machinery and have an agent in that country be responsible for the selling. The other was to set up an on-site operation and be directly responsible for the sales effort. After giving the matter a great deal of thought, management decided to assign one of their own people to this overseas market. The person who was chosen, Frank Knight, had expressed an interest in the assignment, but had no experience in South America. He was selected because of his selling skills and was given a week to clear out his desk and be on location.

When Frank arrived, he was met at the airport by Pablo Gutierrez, the local who was hired to run the office and break Frank in. Pablo had rented an apartment and car for Frank and taken care of all the chores associated with getting him settled. Frank was very impressed. Thanks to Pablo, he could devote all his efforts to the business challenges that lay ahead.

After about six months, the vice president for marketing received a call from Frank. In a tired voice Frank indicated that even though sales were okay, he couldn't take it anymore. He wanted to come home. If nothing could be worked out within the next three months, Frank made it clear that he would resign. When his boss pressed him regarding the problems he was having, here is what Frank reported:

> Doing business over here is a nightmare. Everyone comes to work late and leaves early. They also take a two-hour rest period during the afternoon. All the offices close down during this afternoon break. So even if I wanted to conduct some business during this period, there would be no customers around anyway. Also, no one works very hard, and they seem to assume no responsibility whatsoever. There seems to be no support for the work ethic among the people. Even Pablo, who looked like he was going to turn out great, has proved to be as lazy as the rest of them. Sales are 5 percent over forecasted but a good 30 percent lower than they could be if everyone here would just work a little harder. If I stay here any longer, I'm afraid I'll start becoming like these people. I want out, while I still can.

1. In Frank's view, how important is the work ethic? How is this view causing him problems?
2. Why do the people not work as hard as Frank does? What is the problem?
3. What mistake is Frank making that is undoubtedly causing him problems in managing the branch office?

ORGANIZATIONAL BEHAVIOR CASE: Getting the Facts

When California-based Dalton & Dalton (D&D) was contacted by a large conglomerate in Taiwan, the president of D&D was quite surprised. For two years D&D had been looking for an overseas conglomerate that would be interested in building and selling its high-tech medical equipment under a licensing agreement. The company had been unsuccessful because the firms with whom it had spoken were not interested in investing any of their own money. They wanted D&D to provide the financial investment while they handled the actual manufacturing and selling.

The Taiwanese conglomerate has proposed to D&D that the two companies enter into a joint venture licensing agreement. The business deal will work in the following way:

- The Taiwanese will set up manufacturing facilities and create a marketing group to sell D&D's high-tech medical equipment.
- D&D will train 25 manufacturing and 25 salespeople from the conglomerate so that they understand how to make and sell this equipment. This training will take place in the United States.
- D&D will have the right to send people to the manufacturing facility to ensure that the equipment is being built according to specifications and will also have the right to travel with the salespeople to ensure that the equipment is being sold properly. (Specifically, D&D would be able to monitor the technical side of the sales presentation to ensure that the equipment is being properly represented and that the capabilities of the machinery are not being exaggerated.)

The arrangement sounds fine to the president of D&D. However, before she agrees to anything, she wants to get more information on how to do business with the Taiwanese. "If we're going to enter into a business venture with a foreign company, I think we owe it to ourselves to know something about their culture and customs. I'd like to know how to interact effectively with these people and to get an idea of the types of problems we might have in communicating with them. The better we understand them, the better the chances that there will be no misunderstandings between us."

1. If you were advising the president, what types of information would you suggest be gathered?
2. What types of culturally related problems are there that could result in misunderstanding between the two parties?
3. Overall, is the president right in suggesting that they learn more about the people of Taiwan and their culture before doing business with them?

CHAPTER 3

Environmental Context:
Diversity and Ethics

Learning Objectives

Identify what is meant by diversity and how it has become an important dynamic in the field of management and organizational behavior.

Examine diversity in today's organizations and the individual and organizational approaches to effectively managing diversity.

Discuss the meaning of ethics and the major factors of ethical behavior.

Describe major areas of ethical concern, including sexual harassment, discrimination in pay and promotion, and the privacy issue.

Relate some of the steps that can be taken to effectively address the major ethical concerns.

Starting with Best Practice
Leader's Advice

Admiral Louise Wilmot (Ret.) on Her Experiences in the Predominantly Male U.S. Navy

Rear Admiral Louise Wilmot was the highest-ranked and decorated woman in the U.S. Navy when she retired. She served in the navy for 30 years including holding positions such as Vice Chief of Naval Education and Training. Additionally, Wilmot was the first woman to ever command a naval base, the U.S. naval base in Philadelphia. Now retired from the navy, she serves as the Deputy Executive Director of Catholic Relief Services in Baltimore. Wilmot candidly discusses some of her experiences with sex discrimination and women in the military that have implications for all organizations.

Q1: *You have certainly had a very interesting and challenging career. You spent approximately 30 years in the United States Navy, an organization often described as one of the last male bastions in the world. The press tells us that this organization is rife with issues related to integration of women into the workforce—discrimination and harassment. Yet, you were a great success by anyone's standards. How did you achieve such a great level of success?*

Wilmot: With a good dose of naivete and tremendous enthusiasm! I didn't join the navy with the concept that I was joining an all-male organization. Certainly, my initial experiences in the navy didn't support that fact. I began my career in Women Officer's Candidate School, which primarily consisted of women training women.

At my first duty station, the Naval Air Station in Pensacola, Florida, there was a woman lieutenant commander, who was appointed to be the senior representative for women. She was wonderful and charismatic and took us under her wing. There also were some very senior enlisted women from whom I learned a lot. In those very early two years of my career in the navy, it never seemed to me that I was isolated.

Q2: *It's very interesting how our early experiences in organizations can impact our entire careers. In describing your early years, you talked about people who impacted your life. We read about the importance of mentors. When you entered the navy, there were no women admirals. You obviously couldn't look at a female role model and say, "That is where I shall stand one day." Was there an individual (or several), a woman or a man, whom you would describe as a mentor?*

Wilmot: Oh, yes. I had many mentors, male and female, in my career. I couldn't name just one because there were one or two at every place I served.

Q3: *It sounds like some women in the navy encountered resistance if not outright discrimination. Did you ever encounter discrimination in your years in the navy?*

Wilmot: Oh, yes. Many, many years ago when I was stationed at a NATO command I came smack into discrimination against women.

Q4: *Did you have any female bosses there?*

Wilmot: No, they were all men. I remember a situation in which there was an exercise requiring everybody to go to a remote site. The site had sleeping quarters. My boss said, "Well, you have to go take your turn at the remote site but you can't sleep out there. You will have to get on the bus and travel." I did. I was traveling from the city out to the remote site, which was an hour plus ride, performing the duty I was supposed to do, then getting back on the bus and coming back. I was subsisting on three or four hours of sleep.

Q5: *Do you think there are any jobs in the navy from which women should be excluded?*

Wilmot: No.

Q6: *Do you think the navy has achieved the goal of total equality now?*

Wilmot: No, I don't think any organization can say it has. Even though the navy has made tremendous efforts in recruiting, it hasn't reached its potential for minorities and women.

Q7: *What do you think are some of the key steps the organization should take to make that happen?*

Wilmot: First, the organization has to have the will to do it. The assets have to be put in recruiting. The organization has to be good at taking a very hard look at itself periodically, which I think the navy does. The leadership has to look at indicators to figure out if they are spinning their wheels or they've achieved some success.

Q8: *You mention the will to change as the first step in organizational change. Do you think the navy has the will to change?*

Wilmot: Yes, I do. There are a lot of competing, important things that need to be done, but someone must adopt the sacred trust to make things happen. They have to be listened to and they have to be heard. They can't be silenced or intimidated.

Q9: *Do you think that happens a lot? You tried to make things happen. Were there attempts to silence you?*

Wilmot: Yes, it happens a lot, sometimes due to peer pressure. I remember very distinctly one day when I was a student at the Navy War College. I was walking across a parking lot and a Marine officer fell in step with me. He said, "I have a question for you. Why do you have to be the point woman on the issue of women being in the military? Why do you take on every guest speaker? Why don't you let it ride?" I said, "Okay. I'll make a deal with you. If you'll take on our next speaker about the issue of women, I won't." Of course, he said, "No. It's not my issue." The point was, who was going to do it?

Q10:   *What do you think were some of the most important things that you did or that you were a catalyst for to wage war on racism, sexual harassment, and discrimination?*

Wilmot: When I was conducting an investigation of an officer who was anonymously accused of misconduct, an African-American lieutenant commander spoke on his behalf. After he gave me the factual information, he concluded by saying, "All my life in the navy I have had to fight racism, but I knew who my enemies were because they would stand up and say something to try and 'kill' me. What we are now dealing with are anonymous SOBs who are trying to take down this good man." I thought about this quite often. I felt that it was very important, especially when I was in the position of admiral, to take every opportunity to, first, give hope to those who were suffering from sexism and racism and, second, to let those anonymous racist and sexist SOBs out there know that I considered them cancers on the soul.

Q11:   *How do you think racist and sexist behavior impacts the navy from a strategic perspective?*

Wilmot: It's so destructive—anything that destroys your soul, destroys your being, and weakens your ability to be a cohesive unit. You can't permit this cancer, which is invisible, to attack your crew and to demoralize them—to make them think that this organization isn't what they thought it was.

Q12:   *If there was one piece of advice you were going to give a junior woman who was entering the navy today, what would that advice be?*

Wilmot: I like the advice that the World War I soldier gave at the Women's Memorial Dedication ceremony. She said, "Go for it." Similarly, I say, enjoy what you are doing. Think about what you want to do. Be aware that you have a legacy to leave and think about what that legacy is going to be. Realize that your time in the navy ends; someone relieves you, takes your place, and the navy moves on. I want a legacy where people say, "She came. She saw. She conquered. She left something good for us."

In the last few years, social issues have had a dramatic effect on the study and application of management and organizational behavior. In the past, diversity was treated primarily as a legal issue; that is, for about 40 years it has been directly against the law to discriminate against women, minorities, older employees, and those challenged by a disability. Now organizations are beginning to realize that diversity is not just something to deal with, but instead a reality to build on to make a stronger, more competitive enterprise. The same is true regarding ethics. By paying closer attention to ethical behavior and the way in which it is rewarded and managed, organizations can become more effective. In other words, the contemporary environmental context of diversity and ethics is no longer simply a "tack on" or afterthought in the study of organizational behavior; they play a central role in that discipline of study and application and therefore in framing the rest of this text.

This chapter first examines the nature of diversity, including the major reasons for its emergence and some of the age, gender, ethnicity, and educational characteristics. Next, the focus turns to managing diversity. The multicultural organization and individual (learning and empathy) and organizational (testing, training, mentoring, and work/family programs) approaches are given specific attention. The last part is devoted to ethics. After a discussion of the overall nature of ethics and ethical behavior, attention turns to the important ethical problems relevant to the field of organizational behavior, sexual harassment, discrimination in pay and promotion, and rights to privacy.

THE NATURE OF DIVERSITY

Diversity in the realm of organizational behavior has traditionally emphasized the differences among people in a group or organization. Now that the demographic projections of a few years ago have become a reality (the workforce is older and has an increasing percentage of women and racial/ethnic minorities), there is an emerging perspective on diversity as an all-inclusive mixture of differences and similarities.[1] This mixture idea of diversity is conceptualized in terms of a macro–micro continuum by R. Roosevelt Thomas as follows:

> A micro perspective looks at the individual component and a macro perspective looks at the mixture. To get at the true nature of diversity (comprising differences *and* similarities) requires an ability to assume both perspectives simultaneously; the micro facilitates identification of differences, and the macro enhances the ability to see similarities.[2]

This micro–macro conceptualization also holds for the conceptual framework for the entire field of organizational behavior. Figure 3.1 gives the major reasons for the diversity that exists in today's organizations.

Reasons for the Emergence of Diversity

As shown in Figure 3.1, a major reason for the emergence of diversity as an important challenge is changing demographics. Older workers, women, minorities, and those with more education are now entering the workforce in record numbers. The statistics on these demographic developments are covered in the next section. However, for now it

FIGURE 3.1
Major reasons for increasing diversity.

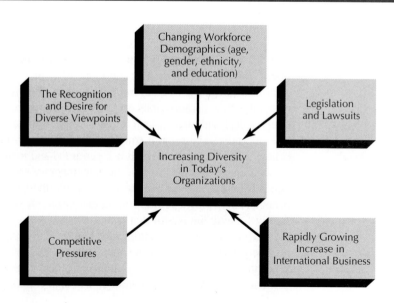

can be noted that the composition of today's and tomorrow's workforce is and will be much different from that of the past. For example, *USA Today* calculates a Diversity Index (based on population racial and ethnic probabilities) that shows now almost 1 out of 2 people randomly selected in the U.S. are racially or ethnically different, up from 1 out of 3 in 1980.[3] At the more micro level, assuming talent and ability are equally distributed throughout the population and that everyone has an equal opportunity, this means that there should be diversity in every level of an organization. As is discussed later in this chapter, such an assumption is not yet valid because diversity has not to date noticeably reached the upper levels of most organizations.

Another pragmatic reason for diversity in today's organizations stems from legislation and lawsuits. The political and legal systems have compelled organizations to hire more broadly and to provide equal opportunity for all employees. Although legislation going as far back as the Civil Rights Act of 1964 prohibited discrimination in employment, only recently have the full effects of that landmark law and other more recent legislation, such as the following, had an impact.

1. *Age Discrimination Act of 1978.* This law at first increased the mandatory retirement age from 65 to 70 and then was later amended to eliminate an upper age limit altogether.
2. *Pregnancy Discrimination Act of 1978.* This law gives full equal opportunity protection to pregnant employees.
3. *Americans with Disabilities Act of 1990.* This law prohibits discrimination against those essentially qualified individuals challenged by a disability and requires organizations to reasonably accommodate them.
4. *Civil Rights Act of 1991.* This law refined the 1964 act and reinstated burden of proof falls on employers to eliminate discrimination and ensure equal opportunity in employment to employees. It also allows punitive and compensatory damages through jury trials.
5. *Family and Medical Leave Act of 1993.* This law allows employees to take up to 12 weeks of unpaid leave for family or medical reasons each year.

These laws, along with lawsuits and the threat of lawsuits, have put teeth into diversity. Individuals and groups that have found themselves excluded from organizations or managerial positions can bring and have brought lawsuits in an effort to overcome discriminatory barriers and ensure themselves equal opportunity in employment. For example, successful lawsuits with resulting multimillion dollar penalties have in recent years been brought against Texaco, the City of Seattle, Mitsubishi, Boeing, Denny's, and Safeway.[4]

Still another reason for the emergence of the importance of diversity to organizations is the realization that diversity can help them meet the competitive pressures they currently face. Firms that aggressively try to hire and promote women and minorities are going to end up with a more talented and capable workforce than those that do not take such a proactive, affirmative action approach. For example, a recent large study by the American Management Association found that the more accurately the senior team of a company represents the demographics of its market, the more likely it is that the company will design products, market services, and create ad campaigns that score a hit.[5] Moreover, companies that gain a reputation for "celebrating diversity" are more likely to attract the best employees regardless of age, gender, or ethnicity. The most talented and qualified people will feel that opportunities are better with these firms than with others. In other words, diversity can provide an organization with competitive advantage.[6] For example, a recent study examined the relationships among racial diversity, business strategy, and firm performance in the banking industry.[7] It was found that racial diversity interacted with business strategy in determining company performance as measured in three different ways: productivity, return on equity, and market performance. This study concluded that the results demonstrated that diversity not only adds value but, in the proper context, also contributes to a firm's competitive advantage.

Stimulated by competitive pressures, organizations now recognize and strive to obtain diverse viewpoints in their decision-making processes and teams. Recent academic research points out the complex linkage between work group diversity and work group functioning,[8] but there is also growing practical evidence that diversity leads to innovation and often breakthrough competitive advantages. For example, women working for Reebok pointed out that there was no good shoe available for aerobics. The firm took this advice and began marketing aerobic shoes, which became very profitable and served as a breakthrough for Reebok in the very competitive athletic shoe industry. Another example occurred at the giant chemical firm DuPont, which used input from African-American employees to develop and successfully market agricultural products for small farmers in the South.

A final major reason for the emerging challenge of diversity is that more and more organizations are entering the international arena. A natural by-product of going international is increased diversity, in this case cultural diversity. If domestic organizations have and promote diversity, then, as they expand globally, they will be accustomed to working with people who have different cultures, customs, social norms, and mores. For example, a multicultural team at DuPont is given credit for gaining the firm about $45 million in new business worldwide. Among other things, this diverse team recommended an array of new colors for countertops that was very appealing to overseas customers.

The international arena is not a threatening place for diverse firms, a fact that is particularly important because of the major role that international operations and sales will play in the growth, and even survival, of companies in the global economy. As was pointed out in Chapter 2, the percentage of overall revenues from international operations and sales is increasing dramatically. Trade developments, such as NAFTA (North American Free Trade Agreement), the EU (European Union), and an increasingly unified Asia–Pacific Rim, are a sign of the times. The advantage of multinational companies that have and value cultural diversity becomes abundantly clear in this global, interconnected economy.

Specific Characteristics of Diversity

There are a number of demographic characteristics contributing to diversity. The most widely recognized involve age, gender, ethnicity, and education. A detailed description of these characteristics provides insights into the nature of diversity in the workplace.

Age.   The U.S. workforce is getting progressively older, and this trend will continue well into the 21st century. The percentage of employees under the age of 35 is declining, while the percent in the 35 to 54 age group is increasing. In fact, at the turn of the century about half the U.S. workforce is between 35 and 54 years old. This development is a result of a number of factors, including the baby boom generation following World War II, which accounts for the increasing number of workers in their fifties, and the declining birthrate among the post–baby boom generation, which helps explain the decline in the percentage of younger workers. A second contributing factor to an aging workforce is the nation's improved health and medical care, which is helping people live longer, more productive lives. Still another factor is the removal of mandatory retirement rules, allowing people who are capable of doing their jobs to continue working well into their sixties and beyond.

The changing age composition of the workforce is forcing organizations to make a number of adjustments. One is learning how to deal effectively with older workers. In the past this was not a problem because older workers were forced to retire. Now, with no mandatory retirement age, older employees have recourse when they are let go. As a result, the number of age discrimination complaints has increased dramatically. The Equal Employment Opportunity Commission has thousands of complaints each year, about 20 percent of all charges.[9] In order to reduce costs and increase productivity, many firms continue downsizing. The high-priced veterans are often let go and replaced by information technology or low-priced, newly educated or trained employees. The key here is that organizations cannot discriminate on the basis of age. Organizations must begin to listen to their older employees, determine how their needs are different from those of younger workers, and learn to draw from the expertise and experience that older employees can offer. McDonald's, for example, has taken advantage of the positive attributes of older employees. As the CEO notes, "We consider our seniors to be sensational role models for our younger people. They are tremendously patient and bring all their experience to the job."[10]

On the other side of the coin, organizations must also learn how to deal with younger employees, who have values markedly different from those of their older counterparts. The days of total loyalty and commitment to the company in exchange for guaranteed employment are a thing of the past. Young employees do not have such loyalty values, and organizations in recent years have made it clear that there is no such thing as lifetime employment. The era of downsizing has affected both older and younger employees.

Gender. Besides age composition, there are also changes occurring in gender composition. Women have been entering the workforce in record numbers over the last four decades. By 1975 they accounted for approximately 40 percent of the total and at the turn of the century women make up about half the workforce. This diversity development can and should dramatically change the policies and day-to-day practices of organizations.

Even though laws spelling out equal pay and opportunity for women have been on the books since the Equal Pay Act of 1963, companies are still finding that they must carefully examine their compensation and promotion policies and practices. For example, one of the major issues remaining is the *glass ceiling effect,* a term used in reference to women's being prevented from receiving promotions into top-management positions. This ceiling is often subtle and is uncovered only by looking at promotion statistics and seeing that women are greatly underrepresented in the executive suite. For example, if a firm has 10,000 employees of whom 5000 are women, and there are 150 senior-level managers of whom only one is a woman, there is good reason to believe that a glass ceiling exists. No matter how far up the organization a woman advances, there still seems to be this ceiling, not always visible, like glass, that halts her progress.

The same goes for pay. The latest statistics show that women are still being paid far less than men. Some analyses try to explain away this disparity by noting that many women do not have the same time on the job as men, so their salaries are lower. Another commonly cited reason is that many women want to spend time at home with their children, so they are willing to accept slower career progression and lower salaries. These types of reasons fall short of explaining the large disparities that still exist between men and women in the workplace. According to the National Committee on Pay Equity, by the end of the 1960s women were paid 69 cents for every dollar a man made. By the turn of the century this had only increased to 74 cents. At this rate, equality would not be reached until the 22nd century, except not even then for black and Hispanic women, who are now making only 63 cents and 54 cents, respectively, for every dollar white men earn.[11] Moreover, these pay gaps between men and women are not confined to lower-level jobs. *Working Women* recently reported pay differentials for men and women in a host of different occupations. These pay differentials are shown in Table 3.1. As the accompanying Diversity in Action indicates, this problem for women is true across the world. To meet the challenge of true equal pay and opportunity in employment, firms must continue to examine and change their policies and practices to eliminate gender bias and discrimination.[12]

TABLE 3.1 Salary Differentials for New-Economy Managerial Positions

Managerial Position	Male Salary	Female Salary	Differential
Advertising account executive	$48,800	$42,700	$6,100
Advertising media director	90,000	80,000	10,000
Business manager (magazine publisher)	44,349	39,829	4,520
Editorial director with 10+ years experience (magazine publisher)	90,287	77,393	12,894
Editorial director with 4–10 years of experience (magazine publisher)	70,231	59,921	10,310
Financial manager	60,008	36,556	23,452
Health care clinic manager	44,893	35,096	9,797
Information technology consultant	68,000	62,000	6,000
Information technology manager	74,000	67,000	7,000
Magazine production director	68,225	57,864	10,361
Office supervisor	36,712	28,023	8,689
Sales supervisor	35,932	23,608	12,324

Source: Adapted from 21st Annual Salary Survey, *Working Woman,* July/August 2000, pp. 55–70.

DIVERSITY IN ACTION

Equality Problems Here, There, and Everywhere

Many managers like to say that people are their company's most important asset, and research shows that this is an accurate statement. World-class organizations attract, train, and retain the most effective personnel. This, in turn, helps them outdistance their competitors—and stay ahead. Moreover, even if the competition wanted to close the gap, in many cases this is not possible because their organizational culture discourages the hiring and promotion of the most qualified personnel. As a result, these firms perform below their full potential.

The problems facing women and minorities in the U.S. are widely known. Unfortunately, the same can be said about other countries around the world. For example, in Chile women are seldom promoted into the upper ranks of management, and sexual harassment is extremely common. In fact, women there have few protections against unfair treatment in the workplace, and government legislation that would outlaw harassment has been stuck in committee for years. In Japan women fare no better. As one critic put it, "Japanese men have careers, while women are miscellaneous." Despite the passage of an antidiscrimination law in 1985 and its reinforcement in 1999 with amendments that include sanctions against sexual harassment, many Japanese firms still have a separate-track personnel management system for men and women. Men are hired with the assumption that they will build their careers with their companies, whereas women are separated into one of two categories: miscellaneous workers and career-track employees. The miscellaneous workers are typically receptionists or clerks. The career-track employees aim for management positions. However, research data shows that the latter do not fare very well. The latest government statistics report that only 1.2 percent of corporate development chiefs in Japan are women, a slight decline since 1995. Additionally, women hold less than 8 percent of all lower-level management positions. Nor do they do well in terms of compensation. Among salaried employees, Japanese women earn only 64 percent as much as their male counterparts, and this declines to 51 percent when part-time jobs are taken into account.

In recent years some firms have been sued by their employees for job discrimination. In Japan a woman who works for Sharp charged the firm with sex discrimination and ended up winning $55,000, the largest amount ever awarded by a Japanese court in such a case. In the United States hundreds of women working in a Mitsubishi auto plant in Illinois brought legal action against the Japanese firm. In the final settlement, the company paid $34 million to these employees and agreed to outside monitoring of complaints of harassment and discrimination. In another case, as a result of a 1998 lawsuit, Astra U.S.A., the international pharmaceutical firm, agreed to pay $10 million, issue an apology, and admit that it had fostered a hostile work environment for women.

Back in the United States, the Equal Employment Opportunity Commission recently issued a rebuke to Morgan Stanley Dean Witter & Company, saying that the firm discriminated against a female executive and possibly other women. This case is the latest in a number of high-profile accusations of gender-based discrimination made by women on America's famed Wall Street. Large groups of women have brought class-action cases during the last several years against Merrill Lynch & Company and the Salomon Smith Barney unit of Citigroup Inc. These were settled on terms requiring large payments by the firms as well as organizational reforms.

Nor are women the only ones who are taking action to ensure their equality in the work place. A group of black employees at the American icon Coca-Cola recently called for a boycott of Coke products worldwide. The call was in response to a racial discrimination suit that has been lodged against the firm. In particular, the employees want to see more minorities promoted into management positions and note that in the company's 100+year history there had been only one black senior vice president.

If people are really the firm's most important asset, why are some companies across the world facing these types of lawsuits? Are they saying one thing but doing another? The developments outlined show that if all companies do not back up this statement with concrete action, employees are likely to take matters into their own hands in an effort to ensure workplace equality for everyone.

Ethnicity.   The term *ethnicity* refers to the ethnic composition of a group or organization. Census statistics indicate that between 2000 and 2050 not only will the U.S. population increase from 281 to 392 million, but as the pie charts in Figure 3.2 show, the racial mix will change dramatically. Latinos are projected to far pass African Americans as the nation's largest minority. These changes in the racial mix of the overall population are reflected in the workforce.

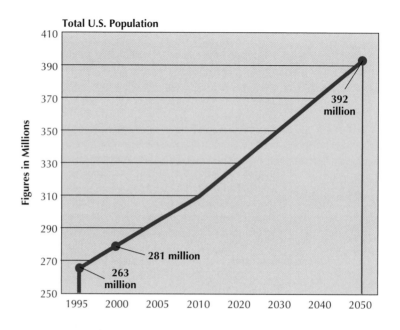

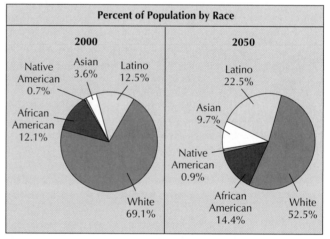

FIGURE 3.2
Overall population
growth and racial
composition.
(*Source:* U.S. Census
Bureau.)

In 1988, whites made up approximately 80 percent of the workforce, but by 2000, this declined to less than three-fourths, and by 2050, it will be about half. African Americans, who constituted approximately 12 percent of the workforce in 1988, have increased to around 14 percent at the turn of the century, and the Latino percentage has risen from 7 percent in 1988 to 10 percent in 2000. [These workforce percentages are slightly different from the total population percentages shown in Figure 3.2 because of ages eligible for the workforce.] Asians, who made up 1 percent of the workforce in 1988, have doubled their percentage by the turn of the century. During this 12-year period minorities account for about one-third of the new entrants into the workforce. These changing racial patterns point to greater workforce diversity. The challenge for management will be to deal with these ethnicity changes, as with the changes regarding gender, in terms of policies and practices concerning pay and promotions. Like women, minorities on the average are paid less and are less well represented in the upper-management ranks. A recent large study of women of color found that even those identified as being on a corporate "fast track" for promotion and pay report their workplace culture is uncomfortable and unsupportive.[13]

Education.   The educational level of the U.S. workforce has been rising. Paradoxically, however, whereas new entrants and existing employees have on average more education, the other end of the spectrum, those with little or no education or basic knowledge, is also increasing. For instance, some analysts have noted that whereas the top third of the nation's young people are the best educated in the world, the bottom third are at Third World standards. A survey by the Educational Testing Service of 3600 young people (ages 21 to 25) found that less than a third were able to determine the tip and the correct change for a two-item restaurant bill, and less than a quarter could interpret a complicated business schedule.[14] Young people are not the only ones who lack basic educational skills. It is estimated that there are over 25 million adult Americans who are functionally illiterate.

Education will be one of the major challenges that will face U.S. firms in the years ahead. On the one hand, there is the challenge to meet the expectations of the highly educated with shrinking opportunities for promotion because of the downsizing and flattening of organizations, and on the other hand, there is the challenge of bringing employees up to speed in knowledge-based organizations. As technology increases and the skills required to remain competitive in the quality-conscious, global economy continue to rise, companies will have to train and educate their employees. Those with high school educations will find that these skills will carry them only so far, and additional training and education are needed. Even engineers and other high-tech personnel will need to continually upgrade their knowledge. Businesses will also find that job redesign (covered in Chapter 15) and reengineering will be necessary in order to streamline the work, and the employees must be able to adjust to these expanding knowledge requirements. This challenge is why firms such as Motorola now require their employees to have at least 40 hours of education and training annually, and the budget to do so is around $100 million.

Other Characteristics of Diversity.   In addition to age, gender, ethnicity, and education, there are a number of other characteristics that describe diversity in the workforce. For example, for most employees English is the primary language used in communicating, but increasingly, for workers in south Texas, southern California, south Florida, and New York City, Spanish is the primary language. In dealing with these Hispanic employees, firms must exhibit care and accommodation to ensure effective communication. Also, those challenged with a disability are receiving increased attention. The Americans with Disabilities Act and changing workforce norms are helping companies focus on equal employment opportunities for these people. Other groups that are contributing to the growing diversity of the workplace include single parents, dual-career couples, and gays and lesbians. Finally, and often overlooked in discussions of diversity, there is the impact of multiculturalism in the global economy. Adler points out that under globalization, members of corporate boards, executives, managers, and workers now represent every nationality.[15] Managing this international diversity was given attention in Chapter 2.

MANAGING DIVERSITY

There are a number of approaches and specific steps that can be taken to effectively manage diversity. To begin with, a truly multicultural organization must be developed. After this foundation step is accomplished, then both individual- and organizational-level strategies and techniques can be employed.

Developing the Multicultural Organization

The foundation and point of departure for effectively managing diversity is the development of a truly multicultural organization.[16] A multicultural organization has been described as one that:

1. Reflects the contributions and interests of diverse cultural and social groups in its mission, operations, and product or service
2. Acts on a commitment to eradicate social oppression in all forms within the organization
3. Includes the members of diverse cultural and social groups as full participants, especially in decisions that shape the organization
4. Follows through on broader external social responsibilities, including support of other institutional efforts to eliminate all forms of social oppression[17]

Several stages have been identified in leading up to such a multicultural organization:[18]

1. *Exclusionary organization.* This type of organization is the furthest from a multicultural organization. It is devoted to maintaining the dominance of one group over all others on factors such as age, education, gender, or race. This organization is characterized by exclusionary hiring practices and other forms of discrimination. Even though such organizations are directly violating laws, they unfortunately still exist.
2. *Club organization.* This organization is characterized by the maintenance of privileges by those who traditionally have held power. These organizations may technically get around the laws by hiring and promoting women and minorities, but only those who are deemed to have the "right" credentials and perspectives.
3. *Compliance organization.* This type of organization is committed to removing some of the discriminatory practices that are inherent in the exclusionary and club organizations. For example, women and minorities are hired and promoted to give the impression of openness and fair play. However, the strategy is more of meeting the letter of the laws, not the spirit. For example, only tokenism is carried out; the basic exclusionary or club culture of the organization remains entrenched. For instance, a research study found *de facto* segregation in a bank.[19] White and African-American employees were assigned to supervisors of the same race in numbers that could not be attributed to mere statistical chance. Although the bank may not have done this deliberately, the fact remains that there was simply compliance going on, not the development of a true multicultural organization.
4. *Affirmative action organization.* This type of organization is committed to proactively eliminating discriminatory policies and practices and the inherent biases created by the exclusionary and club cultures. The affirmative action organization goes beyond the letter of the laws and proactively supports the growth and development of women, minorities, older employees, those challenged with a disability, and other

groups and individuals that have previously been denied equal access and opportunity. Affirmative action legislation has become a much-debated political issue. Recently, a number of court cases have ruled against affirmative action preferences in hiring.[20] Also, research has brought out that "employees who benefit from affirmative action efforts are often considered to be less competent and less qualified than their non–affirmative action peers."[21] This perception must be countered with unequivocally clear definitions and positive performance information or there will be a more subtle, but no less damaging, form of discrimination facing affirmative action hires. In other words, even though affirmative action may be a step in the right direction, it still may be falling short of creating truly multicultural organizations.

5. *Redefining organization.* This newly emerging organization is characterized by an examination of all activities for the purpose of evaluating their impact on all employees' opportunity to both participate in and contribute to their own and the firm's growth and success. Redefining the organization goes beyond being just proactively antiracist and antisexist. This approach questions the core cultural values of the organization as manifested in the mission, structure, technology, psychosocial dynamics, and products and services. The redefining organization not only deals with but recognizes the value of a diverse workforce; it engages in visionary planning and problem solving to tap the strength of the diversity. This approach involves both developing and implementing policies and practices that distribute power among all diverse groups in the organization.

6. *Multicultural organization.* The true multicultural organization is characterized by core cultural values and an ongoing commitment to eliminate social oppression throughout the organization. All members of diverse cultural and social groups are involved in the decisions that shape the mission, structure, technology, psychosocial dynamics, and products and services of the organization.

The true multicultural organization as defined is the stated ideal of an increasing number of organizations, although most are still in transition to this sixth stage. If carefully studied and objectively analyzed, most of today's organizations would still be best described by one of the other preceding forms discussed.

Moving toward and building a truly multicultural organization is perhaps the most important, but there are also some individual- and organization-level steps and techniques that can be used to effectively manage diversity. Unfortunately, to date, most of these diversity programs have fallen short of their objectives. For example, a recent study by the New York-based research organization Catalyst asked African-American women if diversity programs were effective in addressing subtle racism. A large majority (64 percent) said that they were not, and only 12 percent said that they had benefited from these programs to a great or very great extent.[22] The following sections provide some individual and organizational approaches that may help make managing diversity more effective.

Individual Approaches to Managing Diversity

Individual approaches to managing diversity typically take two interdependent paths: learning and empathy. The first is based on acquiring real or simulated experience; the second is based on the ability to understand feelings and emotions.

Learning.   Many managers are often unprepared to deal with diversity; because of their inexperience they are unsure of how to respond. To better prepare themselves, managers must work hard to learn and experience as much as they can about developing appropriate behavior. At the heart of this learning process is communication. Managers must openly communicate one-on-one with young and old employees, women, minorities, and those challenged with a disability in order to determine how best to understand and interact with them. In this way managers can learn more about a diverse group's personal values and how the individuals like to be treated.

Managers can also begin to develop a personal style that works well with each member of a diverse group. For example, to their amazement, many managers have learned that people who are challenged with a disability do not want special treatment. They want to be treated like everyone else, asking only for equal opportunities in employment. Many managers are unaware of their biased treatment of these employees. For example, after a review of the research literature in this area, the following conclusion was drawn:

> It should be noted that several of these studies have found that the physically challenged workers were more intelligent, motivated, better qualified, and had higher educational levels than their nonphysically challenged counterparts. While these findings may help account for the superior performance of those physically challenged, they may also reflect hidden biases whereby a physically challenged person must be overqualified for a specific job. In addition, they may reflect hesitancy to promote physically challenged individuals: the physically challenged may stay in entry-level jobs whereas similarly qualified nonphysically challenged individuals would be rapidly promoted.[23]

In this learning process, managers can also encourage diverse employees to give them candid feedback regarding how they are being treated. In this way, when the manager does something that an employee does not feel is proper, the manager quickly learns this and can adjust his or her behavior. This form of feedback is particularly important in helping organizations gain insights to effectively manage diversity.

Empathy.   Closely linked to the individual learning strategy is empathy, the ability to put oneself in another's place and see things from that person's point of view. Empathy is particularly important in managing diversity because members of diverse groups often feel that only they can truly understand the challenges or problems they are facing. For example, many women are discriminated against or harassed at work because of their gender, and, despite surface efforts to discourage these problems, discrimination and a "chilly climate" for women have become institutionalized through male-dominated management. Discrimination and harassment have in essence become the way things are done. These problems have sometimes resulted in sex bias or sexual harassment suits against organizations, and in recent years, the courts have favorably ruled on these charges.

Empathy is an important way to deal with more subtle problems because it helps the manager understand the diverse employee's point of view. For example, many women in business offices say that they are willing to get coffee for their male counterparts or bosses if they are on their way to the coffee room, but, importantly, they feel that they should be given similar treatment and have coffee brought to them on the same basis. Similarly, many managers try very hard to promote minorities into management positions and to give them work-related experiences that can help their careers. At the same time, however, these managers need to empathize with the fact that some minority members may be ambivalent or have mixed emotions about being promoted. They may like advancement in terms of pay and prestige, but at the same time they may be concerned about receiving special treatment, failing, or not living up to everyone's expectations. By learning how to empathize with these feelings and by offering encouragement, guidance, and after-the-fact backup support, the manager can play an important individual role in more effectively managing diversity.

Organizational Approaches to Managing Diversity

Organizational approaches to managing diversity include a variety of techniques. Some of the most common involve testing, training, mentoring, and programs designed to help personnel effectively balance their work and family lives. The following sections examine each of these techniques.

Testing.   A problem that organizations have encountered with the use of tests for selection and evaluation is that they are commonly culturally biased.[24] As a result, women and minorities may be able to do the job for which they are being tested even though their test scores indicate that they should be rejected as candidates. Most tests traditionally used in selection and evaluation are not suited or valid for a diverse workforce. As a result, in recent years a great deal of attention has been focused on developing tests that are indeed valid for selecting and evaluating diverse employees.

One way to make tests more valid for diverse employees is to use job-specific tests rather than general aptitude or knowledge tests. For example, a company hiring word processing personnel may give applicants a timed test designed to measure their speed and accuracy. The applicant's age, gender, or ethnic background are not screening criteria. This approach differs sharply from using traditional tests that commonly measure general knowledge or intelligence (as defined by the test). People from different cultures (foreign or domestic) often did poorly on the traditional tests because they were culturally biased toward individuals who had been raised in a white, middle-class neighborhood. Older applicants may also do poorly on such culturally biased tests. Job-specific tests help prevent diversity bias by focusing on the work to be done.

Besides being culturally unbiased, tests used in effectively managing diversity should be able to identify whether the applicant has the necessary skills for doing the job. The word processing example above is a good illustration because it measures the specific skills, not the subjective personal characteristics, required for the work. In some cases carefully conducted interviews or role playing can be used because this is the only effective way of identifying whether the person has the necessary skills. For example, a person applying for a customer service job would need to understand the relevant language of customers and be able to communicate well. The customer service job would also require someone who listens carefully, maintains his or her composure, and is able to solve problems quickly and efficiently. Carefully constructed and conducted interviews could be useful in helping identify whether the applicant speaks well, can communicate ideas, and has the necessary personal style for dealing effectively with customers. Role-playing exercises could be useful in helping identify the applicant's ability to focus on problems and solve them to the satisfaction of the customer. Also, the applicant could be given a case or exercise in a group setting to assess interpersonal skills. The point is that multiple measures and multiple trained raters would yield the most valid assessment of needed complex skills.

If pencil-and-paper tests are used, then to help ensure that they are not biased, scientific norming could be used. This is a process that ensures the tests are equivalent across cultures. As a result, all test questions have the same meaning regardless of the person's cultural background.

Training.   Recent surveys indicate that the majority of U.S. companies currently have diversity training. A comprehensive research study found those firms that adopted diversity training tended to have the following profile: (1) large size, (2) positive top-management beliefs about diversity, (3) high strategic priority of diversity relative to other competing objectives, (4) presence of a diversity manager, and (5) existence of a large number of other diversity supportive policies.[25] There are two ways in which this training can play a key role in managing diversity. One way is by offering training to diverse groups. Members from a diverse group can be trained for an entry-level skill or how to more effectively do their existing or future job. The other approach is to provide training to managers and other employees who work with diverse employees. In recent years a number of approaches have been used in providing such diversity training.

Most diversity training programs get the participants directly involved. An example is provided by Florida International University's Center for Management Development (CMD). This center provides diversity training for employers in south Florida, a geographic area where Latinos and African Americans constitute a significant percentage of the population. One of CMD's programs involves putting trainees into groups based on ethnic origin. Then each group is asked to describe the others and to listen to the way its own group is described. The purpose of this exercise is to gain insights into the way one ethnic group is perceived by another ethnic group. Each group is also asked to describe the difficulties it has in working with other ethnic groups and to identify the reasons for these problems. At the end of the training, both managers and employees relate that they have a better understanding of their personal biases and the ways in which they can improve their interaction with members of the other groups.

Another widely used approach is diversity board games, which require the participants to answer questions related to areas such as gender, race, cultural differences, age issues, sexual orientation, and disabilities. On the basis of the response, the game players are able to advance on the board or are forced to back up.[26] For example, in helping participants gain an understanding of the legal issues involved in employment practices, one game asks the players this question:

> Two white workers and one African-American worker were charged with theft of company property. The white employees were discharged, but the African-American employee was retained because of concerns about racial-discrimination lawsuits. The employer's action was:
> a. Illegal. The law prohibits racial discrimination.
> b. Legal. The law protects only minorities.
> c. Legal. This case involved theft.

The answer is "a" and participants who answer correctly are allowed to advance on the board or are given some form of reward such as a token that counts toward a higher score. The objective of these types of games is to acquaint the players in a nonthreatening manner with legal rules and restrictions regarding how to manage members of diverse groups.

Other training games help participants focus on cultural issues such as how to interact with personnel from other cultures. Here is an example:

> In Hispanic families, which one of the following values is probably most important?
> a. Achievement
> b. Money
> c. Being on time
> d. Respect for elders

The correct answer is "d." As participants play the game, they gain an understanding of the values and beliefs of other cultures and learn how better to interact with a diverse workforce.

In many cases these diversity-related games are used as supplements to other forms of training. For example, they are often employed as icebreakers to get diversity training sessions started or to maintain participant interest during a long program. Recent research has found that the major key to the success of diversity training is top management support for diversity; also important are mandatory attendance for all managers, long-term evaluation of training results, managerial rewards for increasing diversity, and a broadly inclusionary definition of diversity in the organization.[27] However, it must be remembered that awareness training is valuable to shift perceptions, but may not lead to behavioral change.[28] Allstate and other firms learned that the training must be linked to business outcomes in order to produce actual behavioral change.[29]

A major problem of training in general, and diversity training in particular, is the transfer problem. Those going through the diversity training may see the value and gain some relevant knowledge, but then do not transfer this training back to the job. A major reason for this transfer problem is a lack of confidence or self-efficacy (i.e., the trainees do not believe that they can successfully carry out the diversity training objectives back on the job in their specific environment). A recent field experiment by Combs and Luthans was designed to increase trainees' diversity self-efficacy. The results were that the training intervention significantly increased the trainees' (N = 276 in 3 organizations) measured diversity self-efficacy. More importantly, there was a strong positive relationship between the trained participants diversity self-efficacy and the number and difficulty of their stated intentions for initiating diversity goals in their specific environments of insurance and manufacturing firms and a government agency.[30] Chapter 9 will get into the self-efficacy psychological state in detail, but it is these types of organizational behavior concepts that are needed to improve important application areas such as diversity training.

Mentoring. A *mentor* is a trusted counselor, coach, or advisor who provides advice and assistance. In recent years, many organizations have begun assigning mentors to women and minorities.[31] The purpose of the mentor program is to help support members of a diverse group in their jobs, socialize them in the cultural values of the organization, and pragmatically help their chances for development and advancement. There are a number of specific benefits that mentors can provide to those they assist, including the following:

1. Identify the skills, interests, and aspirations the person has
2. Provide instruction in specific skills and knowledge critical to successful job performance
3. Help in understanding the unwritten rules of the organization and how to avoid saying or doing the wrong things
4. Answer questions and provide important insights
5. Offer emotional support
6. Serve as a role model
7. Create an environment in which mistakes can be made without losing self-confidence[32]

A number of organizations now require their managers to serve as mentors. Examples include Bell Laboratories, NCR, Hughes Aircraft, Johnson & Johnson, and Merrill Lynch. The formal process for establishing the mentoring program typically involves several steps. First, top-management support is secured for the program. Then mentors and their protégés are carefully chosen. The mentor, who provides the advice and guidance, is paired with an individual who is very likely to profit from the experience. Recent research on the networking strategies of minorities has implications for this step. It seems that highly successful, fast-track minorities are well connected to both minority and white informal circles, whereas their unsuccessful counterparts have very few, if any, network ties with other minorities.[33] In other words, this study would indicate that the effective mentor would be one who would be able to get the protégé involved in both the majority and the minority inner circles. Sometimes the advice has been to avoid association with other minorities, but this research would indicate the contrary.

The third step in an effective mentoring program would be to give both mentors and protégés an orientation. The mentors are taught how to conduct themselves, and the protégés are given guidance on the types of questions and issues that they should raise with their mentor so that they can gain the greatest value from the experience. Fourth, throughout the mentoring period, which typically lasts one year or less, mentor and protégé individually and together meet with the support staff of the program to see how well things are going. Fifth, and finally, at the end of the mentoring cycle, overall impressions and recommendations are solicited from both mentors and protégés regarding how the process can be improved in the future. This information is then used in helping the next round of mentors do a more effective job.

Work/Family Programs.　In the typical family today, both the mother and father have jobs. Initially the needs of the dual-career family were met through alternative work schedules, which allow the parents flexibility in balancing their home and work demands. The most common alternative work schedule arrangements are flextime, the compressed workweek, job sharing, and telecommuting, but there are also some newer programs that help balance work and family.

Flextime allows employees greater autonomy by permitting them to choose their daily starting and ending times within a given time period called a bandwidth, as shown in Figure 3.3. For example, consider the case of two parents who are both employed at a company that has a bandwidth of 7 A.M. to 7 P.M. Everyone working for the firm must put in his or her eight hours during this time period. For example, the father may go to work at 7 A.M. and work until 3 P.M., at which time he leaves and picks up the children from school. The mother, meanwhile, drops the children at school at 8:45 A.M. and works from 9:30 A.M. to 5:30 P.M. Thus both parents are able to adjust their work and

FIGURE 3.3
A flextime framework.

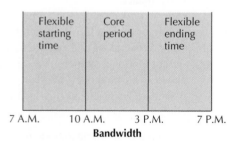

home schedules to fit within the bandwidth. The other characteristic of flextime is the core period, which is the time during which everyone must be at work. This period is typically the one with the heaviest workload, when the organization needs everyone there to meet work demands. If the core period in this case is 10 A.M. to 3 P.M. (see Figure 3.3), the two working parents will have no trouble wrapping their home-related responsibilities around this work requirement. Many companies are using this concept and similar ones to help their employees meet both organizational and personal demands.[34]

Another alternative work arrangement is the compressed workweek. This arrangement, which has been widely used in Europe, compresses the workweek into fewer days. For example, while the typical workweek is 40 hours spread over five days, a compressed workweek could be four 10-hour days. For those working a 35-hour week, the time could be compressed into three days of approximately 12 hours each. These arrangements give employees more time with their families, although their full impact on productivity, profitability, and employee satisfaction must still be determined.

Job sharing is the splitting of a full-time position between two people, each of whom works part-time. This arrangement is more common in professional positions in banking, insurance, and teaching. A husband and wife, or any two people, could share the job 50-50 or in any other combination. For example, parents who want to return to work on a part-time basis only have found job sharing to be an attractive employment alternative.

Still another alternative work schedule that is gaining in popularity is telecommuting. This entails receiving and sending work between home and the office and is currently being used to supplement the typical work arrangement. For instance, employees may come into the office on Monday and Tuesday, work out of their homes on Wednesday and Thursday via telecommuting, and come in again on Friday. By varying the on-site assignments of the personnel, companies are able to reduce the number of people who are in the building at any one time, thus cutting down on the amount of floor space and parking spots they need to rent. Some employees today have no office on a permanent basis.

Besides alternative work schedules, very innovative family-friendly programs are starting to emerge. When large numbers of women began entering the workforce a number of years ago, organizations were ill prepared for the resulting conflict that both women and men had between their work and family responsibilities. Today there are programs to help solve the reality of dual-career families and working parents. Table 3.2 provides a broad sampling of these work/family programs.[35] Of course, not all organizations are using these programs, but an increasing number are, and a few well-known firms such as the following have even more unique programs.[36]

1. PepsiCo has a "concierge service" (similar to hotels) that helps employees with errands or tasks that need to be done during the workday (e.g., getting an oil change, lining up a baby-sitter, or contracting for house repairs).
2. Eastman Kodak has a "humor room" where employees can read light, funny materials or engage in activities to take their minds off a stressful day.
3. Ben and Jerry's has a "Joy Gang" charged with creating happiness in the workplace. This group plans birthday and anniversary celebrations and creates other joyful events.

Recent research by Thomas and Ganster found work/family programs decrease family conflict, job dissatisfaction, and stress-related problems,[37] but it is difficult to

TABLE 3.2 Innovative Work/Family Programs

Child- or elder-care benefits	These may include child-care facilities at the work site and transportation of aging parents to a senior citizens center.
Adoption benefits	These include leave policies and reimbursement for legal fees, medical expenses, agency or placement fees, temporary foster care, and/or travel expenses.
Leave/time-off policies	These may include free time off for no reason or prior notice and paybacks for unused days off.
Convenience benefits	This refers to on-site services such as dry cleaning, ATM machines, postal services, and video rentals.
Life-cycle accounts	These are savings accounts designed to pay for specific life events, such as a college education. Often employers will match employee contributions.
Health promotion benefits	These include such things as fitness centers, health screenings, flu shots, and stress-management clinics.
Education assistance benefits	Examples include tutoring programs, tuition reimbursement, and scholarships.
Housing assistance	This refers to such items as relocation assistance, seminars, and preferred mortgage arrangements.
Group purchase programs	These include legal and financial planning assistance, discounts with local merchants, group auto and homeowners insurance, and fleet arrangements for auto purchases.
Casual day program	This would be dress-down days to have everyone relaxed in an on-the-job family atmosphere.

Source: Adapted from Carol Sladek, "A Guide to Offering Work/Life Benefits," *Compensation and Benefits Review,* January–February 1995, pp. 43–44.

empirically demonstrate the direct positive impact that these programs have on performance outcomes. However, a recent comprehensive research study did find a strong link between work/family programs and the use of high-commitment work systems containing employee involvement/participation and total quality initiatives.[38]

ETHICS AND ETHICAL BEHAVIOR IN ORGANIZATIONS

Ethics involves moral issues and choices and deals with right and wrong behavior. Only recently has ethics been fully integrated into the study of organizational behavior. It is now realized that not only individuals and groups but also a number of relevant factors from the cultural, organizational, and external environment determine ethical behavior. Cultural influences on ethical behavior come from family, friends, neighbors, education, religion, and the media. Organizational influences come from ethical codes, role models, policies and practices, and reward and punishment systems. The external forces having an impact on ethical behavior include political, legal, economic, and international developments. These factors often work interdependently in shaping the ethical behavior of individuals and groups in organizations. For example, minimum wage jobs may lock people into an economic existence that prevents them from bettering their lives. Is it ethical to pay people only a minimum wage? Or consider the facts that many obese workers report that they are discriminated against in the workplace[39] and that a research study found that applicants judged to be relatively less attractive were at a distinct disadvantage in decisions involving suitability for hiring and probable organizational progression.[40] Is it ethical to treat these workers differently, given that very limited legal protection is afforded to them and thus they have no recourse?

These questions help illustrate the problems and controversies in determining what ethical behavior is, and why good people sometimes do unethical things.[41] Moreover, while many people would argue that they are highly ethical in their own personal dealings, empirical research has found that such people are often viewed as unlikable by their peers in the organization.[42] Simply put, there is peer pressure on many people to be less ethical. Additionally, what one person or group finds unethical may be viewed differently by another individual or group. For example, a study investigated attitudes toward unauthorized copying of microcomputer software among both business executives and business faculty members. It was found that the faculty members did not view this to be as big an ethical problem as did the executives.[43]

These examples all help illustrate the elusiveness and contingent nature of determining guidelines for ethical behavior. Besides the obvious ethical concerns relating to the protection of the environment (the so-called "green" or "ecocentric" issues), the use of bribes, price fixing, and other illegal activities—and responding by drawing up and disseminating an ethical code—only recently has it been recognized that ethics is important in the study of organizational behavior. For example, with the arrival of the global economy, ethics has become a major concern for international management. (See the accompanying International Application Example.) Taking an organizational behavior perspective, Stajkovic and Luthans have proposed a social cognitive model of ethics across cultures.[44] This model uses national cultures as the social foundation for institutional (ethics legislation), organizational (codes of ethics), and personal (values and self-regulatory mechanisms) factors that interact to influence the perception of ethical standards and actual ethical behavior across cultures.

The Impact of Ethics on "Bottom-Line" Outcomes

Besides the morality issues surrounding ethics in the workplace,[45] there is increasing evidence that ethics programs and being ethical pays off for organizations. Although in the past the linkage between corporate social performance and bottom-line results has been vague or dependent on faith and anecdotal evidence, the cost of illegal, unethical practices is now clearly documented, and new research studies find a statistically significant relationship. For example, one study compared 67 *Fortune* 500 firms that were convicted of acts such as antitrust violations, product liabilities, and acts of discrimination with 188 firms in the same time period that were not. The results indicated that the convicted firms had significantly lower returns on assets and returns on sales.[46] Other recent studies have found a strong link between a company's ethical commitment and its market value added (MVA)[47] and the investment in social programs and the firm's financial outcomes.[48] The social programs involved community and employee relations, product characteristics, diversity, and the environment. One study focusing on the environment found a strong positive relationship between having preventative, proactive programs (e.g., pollution control and/or reduction of hazardous waste) and bottom-line profitability gains.[49]

This accumulating evidence on the value of ethical practices is leading to the development of theory, research, and measurement of corporate social performance (CSP).[50] In practice there are newly created ethics officer positions, and control systems are being suggested to monitor ethical behaviors.[51] However, in the framework of this chapter on diversity, ethics also has an impact on the way employees are treated and how they perform their jobs. In other words, ethics can affect the well-being of employees and their performance. In particular, the current social problems dealing with organizational participants concerning sexual harassment, discrimination in pay and promotion, and the right to privacy are especially relevant to the study of organizational behavior.

Is the Ethical Climate Getting Better or Worse?

Managing globally in the 21st century is turning out to be challenging, as everyone thought, but maybe for other reasons. One big international management issue has become the ethical behavior of managers—or lack of it. For example, in Vietnam there are ongoing trials of powerful bankers and business executives who are accused of bribing government officials and police officers in order to gain favorable treatment. At one recent trial of Vietnamese businesspeople, local reporters were taken aside and handed envelopes of cash worth more than a month's pay. They were asked to limit their articles to narrow accounts of court testimony. Unfortunately, in Vietnam business circles, such actions hardly raise eyebrows. They are considered a part of day-to-day life. In fact, as the Vietnamese economy has opened up over the last decade, opportunities for big payoffs have multiplied, part of the unbridled capitalism that has surged through the country. As a result, global managers doing business in Vietnam often consider bribery as a necessary evil.

The same is true in many other nations around the world. In too many developing countries, those who are willing to pay a bribe can still buy a government position. A common misperception is that unethical behavior is common in less developed counties, but it is not tolerated or found in more economically advanced countries. However, this does not seem to be the case. In a recent survey conducted by Transparency International, a Berlin-based organization that annually ranks countries based on how corrupt their officials are perceived to be, the United States, Germany, and Japan, the world's three largest economic powers, did not fare very well. The survey asked respondents to rank leading exporting nations on the basis of how likely it was that their companies would pay bribes in order to win contracts abroad. On a scale of 1 (very likely to pay bribes) to 10 (highly unlikely to do so), the United States was ranked in the middle of the pack, tied with Germany. Japan was rated even poorer. The lowest ratings went to China, South Korea, and Taiwan, whereas Sweden, Australia, Canada, and Austria were ranked as countries where bribes were least likely to be paid. The United States did better when countries were ranked on the basis of international corruption. Of the 99 nations that were ranked, Denmark was first, the United States was in 18th place (Germany was 14th and Japan was 25th), China was tied for 58th, Vietnam was tied for 75th, and Cameroon was rated as the most corrupt.

Businesspeople from all countries have criticized these types of rankings, contending in the case of bribes, for example, that respondents believe firms are making bribery payments because they are able to enter and do well in foreign markets where bribes are common. On the other hand, one of the cofounders of Transparency International has noted that the deep-seated suspicions of American business practices, in particular among some foreign executives, may not be groundless. He says, "They believe U.S. companies have honed sophisticated methods to circumvent the [law], such as setting up ventures unconnected to the contract they seek in which public officials or family members are silent equity partners." In any event, no matter how much someone believes (or does not believe) that global managers have high ethical standards, one is left to ponder the question: What is the ethical climate in international business and is it getting better or worse?

Sexual Harassment

Sexual harassment in the workplace can be defined as unwelcome sexual advances, requests for sexual favors, or other verbal or physical conduct of a sexual nature. This harassment has been prohibited as far back as the 1964 Civil Rights Act (as amended). Specifically, the guidelines to date provide that the above-mentioned activities constitute illegal sexual harassment when (1) submission to such conduct is made either explicitly or implicitly a term or condition of an individual's employment, (2) submission to or rejection of such conduct by an individual is used as the basis for employment decisions affecting such individual, or (3) such conduct has the purpose or effect of unreasonably interfering with an individual's work performance or creating a work environment that is intimidating, hostile, or offensive.[52]

In recent years, the publicity surrounding highly visable cases in the military, and the allegations against several public officials has increased everyone's awareness of sexual harassment. In the workplace, data reveal that almost three-fourths of working women report that they have been harassed at some point in their career.[53] A few of these instances have resulted in lawsuits. An example would be *Faragher v. City of Boca Raton,* in which the plaintiff resigned from her position as a lifeguard with the city of Boca Raton and brought action against the city and her immediate supervisor asserting the hostile-work-environment form of sexual harassment. In its decision, the Supreme Court gave specific directions as to the legal standards that must be met by an employer in attempting to avoid liability. The Court said that an employer may assert an affirmative action defense to limit liability. This defense is comprised of two elements: (1) that the employer exercise reasonable care to prevent and correct the problem behavior, and (2) that the employee unreasonably failed to take advantage of any preventative or corrective opportunities provided by the employer to avoid harm otherwise. However, legal counsel's interpretation also says the decision "clearly implies that employers are strictly liable for sexual harassment by supervisors or managers, even if the company was unaware of this harassment when it occurred."[54] In another significant case, *Oncale v. Sundowner Offshore Services,* the Supreme Court made clear the fact that if the plaintiff and defendant happened to be of the same sex, it was not a bar to Title VII sexual harassment claims.[55] Thus, these decisions reaffirm and strengthen the rights of employees to a work environment free of sexual harassment.

Although there seems to be increased awareness concerning the problem of sexual harassment and strict legislation being passed to prevent harassment, it does not appear that the sensitivity of today's organizations has kept pace. In fact, sexual harassment claims are rapidly increasing in corporate America every year. The Equal Opportunity Commission reports that this is the fastest-growing employee complaint. Recent statistics indicate that 90 percent of *Fortune* 500 firms have dealt with sexual harassment complaints and on average spend $200,000 on each complaint that is investigated and found valid.[56]

The negative impact of sexual harassment can be devastating to an organization in several ways. For starters, sexual harassment can bring costly lawsuits and public relations nightmares. For example, Mitsubishi recently agreed to pay $34 million to several hundred women who had alleged unheeded claims of sexual harassment over a period of years at the company's auto assembly plant in Normal, Illinois. Chevron agreed to pay $2.2 million to four women who alleged that they were victims of corporate retaliation for filing sexual harassment complaints.[57] Also, losses attributed to decreased productivity, increased absenteeism, lower morale, and higher turnover can be large. In addition to the 90 percent receiving compliants, approximately one-third of the *Fortune 500* companies have actually been sued for sexual harassment. These cases are said to come with a $6.7 million price tag for all of the related losses to the companies involved.[58]

Although recent surveys indicate that almost all firms now have sexual harassment policies in place and the vast majority of employees report they are well informed about their company's policies,[59] some firms can still be described as being "at risk." They have repeated problems concerning sexual harassment and seem to have a "deaf ear" syndrome. Characteristics of an organization with a "deaf ear" toward sexual harassment include having (1) inadequate policies and procedures that are poorly written and vague, (2) cumbersome reporting procedures, and (3) negative managerial reactions and rationalizations such as denying the harassment claims, blaming the victim, minimizing the seriousness of the offense, ignoring the habitual harasser, and retaliation against the victim.[60]

There are a number of steps that organizations are taking to ensure that their personnel do not engage in sexual harassment and, if they do, are dealt with properly. In particular, these initiatives include carefully complying with current legal requirements, as shown in Table 3.3. Prescriptions offered to increase responsiveness in order to eliminate especially the "deaf ear" syndrome include the following:[61]

1. *Examine the characteristics of "deaf ear" organizations.*   Managers should become familiar with potential problem indicators and remain vigilant in maintaining a work environment free of sexual harassment.
2. *Foster management support and education.*   Managers must realize that they set the standards of conduct through their behavior. Therefore, it is necessary to train and educate managers on what constitutes sexual harassment and what steps are necessary to resolve complaints. It is also critical to educate managers on the importance of overcoming the tendency to avoid, blame, deny, and retaliate against the victim.
3. *Stay vigilant.*   All managers should work to eliminate factors that contribute to a hostile work environment. As such, managers should monitor the work environment for any displays of a sexual nature and pay attention to potentially harassing verbal exchanges.
4. *Take immediate action.*   All reports of harassment should be taken seriously and acted on immediately. An employer who quickly investigates a claim of sexual harassment, verifies the claim, and promptly punishes the accused harasser can avoid

TABLE 3.3   Questions Asked by the EEOC When Considering a Charge of Harassment or Discrimination in the Workplace

- Does the employer have a policy that prohibits discrimination and harassment?
- Is the policy widely disseminated so that employees know what conduct is prohibited in the workplace?
- Does it contain a procedure whereby employees can file complaints to individuals other than their supervisors without fear of retaliation?
- Does it call for a prompt, thorough, and objective investigation of complaints?
- Does it ensure confidentiality, to the maximum extent possible, with respect to how the complaint will be handled?
- Does it call for prompt remedial action against the offender if the employer's investigation reveals wrongdoing?

liability for sexual harassment under the test for employer liability recently established by the U.S. Supreme Court.[62]

5. *Create a state-of-the-art policy.*   Organizations should develop a set of policies and procedures to fit the unique circumstances. Included within this policy should be a clear, nonlegalese definition of sexual harassment and use of realistic examples of various behaviors that have been identified by the courts as sexual harassment.

6. *Establish clear reporting procedures.*   Key features of "user-friendly" policies include clear procedures for filing complaints, mechanisms to ensure rapid investigation by impartial managers, and provisions for protecting the privacy of both accusers and accused.

To the extent the organizations follow these types of guidelines and focus on changing their cultures so as to address the ethical and legal challenge of sexual harassment, the problem can be largely prevented. However, because it is an ongoing challenge, organizations are finding that they must be continually alert to any sexual harassment so that they can begin taking immediate action to correct the situation.

Pay and Promotion Discrimination

As discussed earlier under characteristics of diversity, there remains a major problem concerning equality of pay and promotion opportunities for both women and minorities. Discrimination in the workplace on any basis is not only illegal; societal values clearly indicate that it is also morally wrong and unethical. Yet recent statistics indicate that although it has been about 40 years since the passage of the Equal Pay Act, there has been only a small improvement in the gap in wages and promotions between men and women. After analyzing the latest statistics on managers' earnings it was concluded, "By any measure of comparison—title, functional status, age, company ranking among them—women top earners are not only outnumbered, they earn less than their male counterparts."[63] Although women of color do worse than their male counterparts, both men and women of color have relatively lower earnings than white males. However, Hispanic women are well below white women, but Asian women are ahead of white and other women of color (but still only at about two-thirds of white males) and Asian men are ahead of Hispanic men and African-American men but are still behind white males.[64]

One of the most commonly cited reasons for the lack of promotion is the glass ceiling effect discussed earlier under the diversity discussion. The U.S. Department of Labor has even recognized glass ceilings as "artificial barriers based on attitudinal or organizational bias that prevent qualified [women] from advancing upward in their organization into [senior] management level positions."[65] Despite efforts to explain and deal with the problem, it continues to exist. The explanation that women have not yet had enough experience to reach the top of organizations no longer can be used. Although significant numbers of women have entered managerial positions for a sufficient number of years, women still are noticeably absent from the top levels of today's organizations. For example, in 1987, there were two women CEOs of *Fortune* 500 companies. At the turn of the century, there were still two CEOs and only 74 women out of 1,146 executive or senior vice presidents. In 1987, there were 11 women serving as inside directors for *Fortune* 500 firms. Ten years later, only eight women were serving in that capacity. That means that women hold just over half of 1 percent of the 1,250 inside-board-member positions in the *Fortune* 500. The number of female inside directors—an intermediate and usual requisite position in the succession to CEO—is astonishingly small.[66]

The facts of the glass ceiling speak for themselves. Recently, some of the academic explanations of why women are not reaching the top are being questioned. For example, some experts have argued that women have lower self- and organization-referent attitudes, and this is what holds them back. Noting that such conclusions have been based on laboratory studies of school-age children, a researcher on women in management counters this argument as follows:

> In fact, there is absolutely no reliable, empirical evidence based on truly comparable samples of men and women who are actually employed in work organizations that women's self- and organization-referent attitudes are systematically lower than men's. Indeed, my associates and I have demonstrated consistently that when the effects of organizational level or position are controlled, women's self- and organization-referent attitudes are usually more positive than men's. We believe strongly that the experiences women should have in the workplace . . . can counteract all or nearly all of the societal factors that have caused girls and women to manifest less positive attitudes in nonwork research settings.[67]

Other reasons for explaining the glass ceiling are also now being rejected as erroneous.[68] For example, the popular media have helped promote the belief that female managers choose family over career and this is why they are underrepresented in the upper ranks of management. However, there is accumulating evidence that the primary reason women leave their organizations is the lack of career advancement opportunities.[69] A research study comparing managerial women with children with those without children found:

> no differences in met expectations, turnover intentions, commitment, satisfaction, job characteristics, or perception of progress. However, women with children scored lower on job involvement and reported fewer work hours. While parenting demands may affect these variables, they may not necessarily affect work-related attitudes, professional attainment, attachment to the job, or commitment to the organization.[70]

In terms of parenting and dual-career families, there is also research evidence that fathers whose wives have jobs make significantly less money than fathers whose wives stay at home to take care of the children.[71] The suggestion is that "there may be a perception among employers that dads with non-employed spouses are more productive than male managers with employed spouses."[72] In other words, the fact that a woman works may even lead to salary discrimination against her husband. Thus dual-career families may be taking a double negative hit in their pay.

Another reason for the glass ceiling is the charge that women do not manifest the same leadership skills as men. Yet studies, such as one conducted by AT&T, have found no differences between male and female managers on their overall levels of leadership skills per se. In fact, what was found in this study was that women are better performers than men in many of the foundation skills required for effective leadership and management performance. Specifically, women were found to be superior to their male counterparts in interpersonal skills, perception of social cues, work involvement, behavior flexibility, personal impact, and freedom from prejudice against racial, ethnic, and other social groups.[73]

Not only has recent research brought into question some of the traditional explanations for the glass ceiling; it is also becoming clear that the widely recommended ways for dealing with the glass ceiling simply do not work. For example, although the affirmative action approach, which is perhaps the most commonly employed strategy for dealing with discrimination against women and minorities in the workplace, has had some success in enhancing the employment status of women and minorities,[74] these programs to date have fallen short of breaking the glass ceiling. A number of reasons can be cited for this result, including a lukewarm management commitment to the effort and the widely held belief that women promoted on the basis of affirmative action efforts would never have gotten there on their own ability. Another action strategy, gender training, often results in short-term results, at best, and sometimes only seems to magnify the differences between men and women. The same could be said for the seeding strategy of directly placing women into senior-level positions. This bypasses the glass ceiling, but the problem is that the seeding strategy typically involves putting women into upper-level staff rather than line jobs, where their authority and ability to use their talents are much more limited. They are viewed almost as interns, rather than full-fledged managers. This type of staff position may become a dead-end job.

The glass ceiling issue is not going to be solved overnight, but there are strategies and programs that firms must attempt to implement. One approach is to learn from those who have broken through the glass ceiling. For example, an extensive survey of executive women who hold titles of vice president or above in *Fortune* 1000 companies indicated that consistently exceeding performance expectations, developing a management style that men were comfortable with, seeking difficult or high visibility assignments, and having an influential mentor were critical success factors.[75] In addition, there must be a realization that the reasons for sex segregation patterns in organizations are neither simple not attributable just to women.[76] Organizations must design and implement programs that systematically attack discrimination and segregation at multiple levels of the structure.[77] A good example is provided by Sears Roebuck, which is now making a vigorous push to recruit and promote women. At the present time they constitute 22 percent of the senior officers, which is a decline from 26 percent in 1994. Some of the steps the company has recently taken to correct this trend include an overhauling of its management development process, the creation of a new mentoring program, and the promotion of 13 women into high-level management positions.[78]

Sound research is needed to draw valid conclusions concerning the best approach to eliminating pay and promotion discrimination rather than relying on hunches, opinions, and general intuition. Pragmatically, women also need to know the most effective steps to take in managing their careers. Some practical recommendations include:

1. Get a good education, be assertive, and do not be your own worst enemy.
2. Do not permit yourself to be intimidated, remain confident of your ability, and never be hostile or defensive.
3. Be willing to "do your time" in lower positions, but do not be afraid to change companies if you get dead-ended.
4. Once you have set a goal, do not let others intimidate you.
5. Obtain the support of family and friends.
6. Be willing to accept the responsibility that goes with a career decision.[79]

Finally, it is important to realize that women still report a number of significant barriers to upward progress including a lack of culture fit and not being included in informal networks. Moreover, researchers such as Lyness and Thompson report that career success, as measured by organizational level and compensation, are positively related to breadth of experience and developmental assignments, and women are still less likely to be given major assignments and increased authority.[80] The latest survey results reported six months into the new century do indicate some progress over at least the previous generations, but there is still a long way to go (see Diversity in Action Box).

DIVERSITY IN ACTION

Some Progress, But Still a Long Way to Go

Over the past decade there have been ever-growing attempts to obtain equal opportunity for everyone in the workplace. At the United Nations (UN), for example, there is an Office of Human Resources Management that is charged with ensuring that all UN employees throughout the world are treated equitably. This is quite a challenge, given that the agency has employees in almost 200 countries, and some of these nations have cultures that are openly hostile to such ideas as equal pay for equal work and the appointment of women into senior management positions.

In a recent *Wall Street Journal*/NBC News special survey on women in the workplace, more than 80 percent of Americans (and an even higher percentage of men) said that women in organizations had made considerable progress over the past generation. Moreover, these views were held across the board with no pockets of resistance from any particular responding group. At the same time, in this same survey most women reported that they have experienced discrimination (58 percent) and harassment (73 percent) on the job. They also said that progress for women was too slow. In particular, they noted that there is a significant pay gap between men and women, especially at the lower levels of the hierarchy, and that professional women continue to have difficulty gaining entry to the executive suite. In fact, reported the *Journal,* there are only two women chief executive officers among the *Fortune* 500 firms today.

Another finding from the survey, in contrast to the stereotyped view held by by some people, is that most women work out of economic necessity. About two-thirds of those polled said that they are the primary wage earner in their family or they have to work in order to make ends meet. Only 14 percent of women said they do not have to work, but do so for their own personal satisfaction. However, economic necessity was cited overwhelmingly by low-income women and African Americans.

At the same time, there are positive signs in some areas. For example, in the professional schools in universities such as medicine, law, and business, the percentage of women in the graduating classes has been increasing. In 1960 less than 6 percent of medical school graduates were women. By 1980 this had risen to over 23 percent, and today almost 43 percent of new doctors are women. The percentage of law school graduates has increased even faster. In 1960 women made up less than 3 percent of the graduating class. By 1980 they constituted just over 30 percent, and today approximately 45 percent of all law school graduates are women. The same pattern exists in business schools where in 1960 less than 3 percent of the graduating class consisted of women, but by 1980 this had risen to over 24 percent, and today it stands at 39 percent.

Despite some positive signs, there is quite a bit more that needs to be done. For example, only 41 percent of women (in contrast to 60 percent of men) report that women are treated professionally in the workplace and although 39 percent of men say that women are getting senior executive promotions, only 23 percent of women agree. Quite clearly, there has been some progress, but there is still a long way to go for organizations to tap the full potential of all their workforce.

Employee Privacy Issues

In addition to sexual harassment and discrimination in pay and promotion, which is in the domain of diversity, a more direct ethical issue involves privacy in the workplace. In recent years, a number of developments have occurred that directly influence employees' right to privacy. One such development is computer technology that now makes it easier than ever for employers to learn information about their employees. Another is mandatory drug testing, a policy that has been instituted by many organizations. A third is efforts of organizations to control the lifestyles of their employees.

Besides computer data banks that keep all types of personal information, another way that computer technology is having an impact on employee privacy is by allowing others to tap into one's communications. For example, millions of employees use electronic mail (e-mail) and have a password identification code that supposedly ensures them privacy. Unfortunately, these codes can and do get out, and the messages in the person's e-mail file can be read. In one case, two U.S. Nissan trainers had their e-mail messages reviewed by their supervisor, who found nasty comments made about himself. He rebuked the two trainers, who, in turn, sued the company for violation of their privacy. They charged that they had a reasonable expectation of privacy when using e-mail. There have been a number of court cases on this privacy issue, and it is still not yet resolved.[81] However, the latest survey data indicates an increase in employer storage and review of e-mail messages.[82]

Besides the ethical implications of e-mail, there are also privacy/ethical issues involved with firms' rights to and need for confidentiality of their own information. Particular attention is given to the conditions under which firms may share confidential business planning and operations data without operating in a collusive manner that might infringe on free trade, and the responsibility of information sharers to assure that transmitted information is accurate.[83] Still another ethical question for employers is to determine how much they want to monitor their employees' Internet usage. Nobody knows exactly how much time is wasted at the typical company, but the majority of HR managers in a recent survey said they had seen or heard of employees spending time surfing the Net as a diversionary activity. However, "cyberloafing" is not the only problem. There is the possibility of downloading virus-infected software and potential liability under sexual harassment and discrimination laws. These problems can end up costing an employer millions in IT or legal fees.[84]

The Electronic Communication Privacy Act (ECPA) makes employers potentially liable for invading employees' e-mail or stored communications. Although employers own these computer technologies, to prevent invasion of privacy they should have a policy in place that limits or prohibits employees' nonbusiness use of the Internet or e-mail, notifies employees of the company's right to monitor and review messages and online activities, requires MIS (management information systems) personnel to conduct periodic inspections and audits of both transmissions and stored e-mail to ensure that employees are complying with company policies, and requires that trusted MIS managers have access to all employees' e-mail passwords at all times.[85] In addition, the Internet and e-mail must not become mechanisms for sexual harassment via transmitting, downloading, or displaying unwelcome pornographic, profane, or sexually suggestive materials.

Another important privacy issue involves drug testing. There is little question that drug abuse can have a tremendous negative impact on performance. For example, recent data indicates that substance abusers have two to four times as many accidents as employees who do not use drugs and alcohol, can be linked to 40 percent of industrial fatalities, are absent from work two-and-a-half times more frequently, use three times the amount of sick leave, have workers' compensation claims five times higher than nonusers, and are generally less productive.[86] However, there is still the ethical question of whether substance abuse testing violates an employee's right to privacy.

Legally, drug testing, whether used with job applicants or randomly/periodically with existing employees, is a gray area. To date, there is no legislation that specifically addresses drug testing. Legal experts note that "in virtually all cases dealing with drug testing, the courts have applied a balancing test in which they balance the employer's need for the information against the intrusion into the employee's reasonable expectation for privacy."[87] Regardless of the legality, the ethical question is whether such testing violates an employee's right to privacy. An increasing number of firms do not feel that it does. They are requiring such testing for new employees, and many also make it a condition of employment that all workers be periodically tested. The American Management Association recently reported that about three-fourths of those firms' responding conduct drug tests, which has remained about the same over the past few years.[88] In addition, the federal government requires that all contractors that do more than $20,000 worth of government business conduct random tests on a cross section of the workers. Other organizations, such as Motorola, test all employees every three years, no matter how long they have been with the firm. As with the privacy issues surrounding e-mail, both the legal and ethical concerns could be reduced if employers are up front with employees about the reasons for drug testing (e.g., threats to health and safety) and fully communicate this before the testing takes place.

A relatively new threat to privacy comes in the form of companies' dictating the personal lifestyles of their employees. For example, can a company dismiss two employees who begin dating each other because it has a policy that forbids workers' fraternizing with each other? Can the firm refuse to hire smokers and/or make current employees quit smoking? Can the company insist that employees not race motorcycles or bungee jump? These are all examples of personal lifestyle choices that have gotten employees into trouble with their employers in recent years. In some cases the employers can enforce such policies because the workers are not legally protected.[89] For example, a growing number of firms now refuse to hire smokers and point to the additional costs in medical claims and sick days that result from smoking. Examples include Atlanta-based Lockheed Aeronautical Systems Co., which does not hire smokers in order to become smoke-free and improve the health of its employees, and Turner Broadcasting System has had a long-standing practice of hiring nonsmokers in order to have a healthy workforce that is consistent with their corporate culture. Similarly, some hospitals now offer their employees financial incentives if they have good lifestyle habits (no smoking, drinking in moderation, keeping weight within prescribed limits). The justification for these programs is based on lower health care and insurance costs and greater productivity. On the other hand, there are many people who oppose these lifestyle-related regulations on ethical grounds, feeling that the organization is attempting to dictate and control people's lives. Such privacy issues are likely to be an increasing ethical concern in the years ahead.

Summary

Two of the major dynamic realities facing modern organizations are diversity and ethics. Diversity exists when there is an all-inclusive mixture of differences and similarities in terms of age, gender, ethnicity, and/or education. There are a number of reasons for the rise of diversity in organizations, including the increasing number of women, minorities, and older employees in the workforce and legislative rulings that now require organizations to ensure equal opportunity to women, minorities, older employees, and those challenged by a disability. There are individual and organizational approaches to managing diversity. Approaches at the individual level include learning and empathy; at the organizational level, testing, training, mentoring, and the use of alternative work schedules and work/family programs can be implemented.

Ethics is involved with moral issues and choices and deals with right and wrong behavior. A number of cultural (family, friends, neighbors, education, religion, and the media), organizational (ethical codes, role models, policies and practices, and reward and punishment systems), and external forces (political, legal, economic, and international developments) help determine ethical behavior. These influences, acting interdependently, serve to help identify and shape ethical behavior in today's organizations. There is increasing evidence of the positive impact that ethical behavior and social programs have on "bottom-line" performance. Some of the major ethical issues especially relevant to the study of organizational behavior include sexual harassment, discrimination in pay and promotion, and the rights of privacy. Each of these ethical issues represents a challenge to today's organizations and must be given recognition and attention and be carefully managed.

ENDING WITH META-ANALYTIC RESEARCH FINDINGS

OB PRINCIPLE: Women and men currently differ in their perceptions of ethical business practices.

Meta-Analysis Results: [66 samples; 20,000 participants; $d = .22$] *On average, there is a **56 percent probability** that women will perceive higher ethical standards than men in evaluating business practices.* Results of a moderator analysis revealed that gender differences are smaller for samples of nonstudents than students. Moreover, gender differences in ethical perceptions also decline with age and work experience. Those who are older or who have considerable work experience display smaller gender differences in ethical perceptions.

Conclusion: As women have become established in the workforce, not only is there diversity, but also ethical perceptions are changing. In particular, the ethical climate has emerged as an important managerial and societal concern. How this ethical climate is perceived by organizational participants, both male and female, can become important to decision making and business practices. A growing body of research suggests that gender plays a role in perceptions of ethical climate. As the chapter points out, diverse input from society at large is affecting the cultural values of today's organizations. Thus, through early socialization, stereotypes associated with social role norms or actual organizational experiences, men and women may develop or bring diverse interests, traits, and values into the workplace. This learning and development may lead to differences in ethical perceptions regarding issues such as pay equity, bribery, and sexual harassment. However, over time as more men and women work together and assimilate into both the changing norms and cultures of both the overall society and organizations concerning working women, then the current differences in ethical perceptions will undoubtedly decrease.

Source: Adapted from George R. Franke, Deborah F. Crown and Deborah F. Spake, "Gender Differences in Ethical Perceptions of Business Practices," *Journal of Applied Psychology,* Vol. 82, No., 1, 1997, pp. 920–934.

OB PRINCIPLE: Employee integrity tests can predict unethical and deviant workplace behaviors and performance.

Meta-Analysis Results: [305 studies; 349,623 participants; $d = .84$ for overt tests; $d = .43$ for personality tests; and $d = .75$ when tests are related to performance] *On average, there is a **72 percent probability** that job applicants who score well on overt integrity tests will participate in less unethical and/or deviant behaviors than those who score poorly. Moreover, on average, there is a **62 percent probability** that job applicants who score well on personality-based integrity tests will participate in less unethical and/or deviant behaviors than those who score poorly.* Finally, not only does the use of integrity tests help predict unethical and/or deviant behavior, but they can also help organizations predict better performers. *On average, there is a **70 percent probability** that employees who score well on integrity tests will outperform those who score poorly.* Further analysis indicates the measurement method is a moderator. That is, measures of deviant behavior can be divided into external and self-report (admission) criteria. External criteria involves actual records of rule-breaking incidents, disciplinary actions, dismissals for theft, etc. Self-report criteria include all admissions of theft, past illegal actives,

98

and counterproductive behaviors. Interestingly, the validity of self-report measures was higher than those for external criteria—perhaps because not all thieves are caught or illegal activities detected.

Conclusion: Because unethical and deviant behavior can impact not only the well-being of employees, but can also have a detrimental affect on individual and organizational performance, the study of ethics has been receiving increased attention in organizational behavior. One way for organizations to screen out potentially unethical individuals is to give job applicants some form of overt or personality-based integrity/honesty test. These tests are commonly used to predict employee participation in illegal activity (e.g., theft), unethical behavior, excessive absences, drug abuse, or workplace violence. Over the past decade, the evidence for integrity test predictive validities has been strong. Overt integrity tests are designed to directly assess attitudes regarding dishonest behaviors. Examples are asking test takers questions such as the following: "Should a person be fired if caught stealing $5?" Personality-based integrity tests are designed to predict deviant behaviors at work by using personality measures such as reliability, conscientiousness, adjustment, trustworthiness, and sociability. The meta-analysis of research studies of both overt and personality integrity tests can help organizations to reduce unethical and/or deviant employee behavior as well as help them to predict better performers.

Source: Adapted from Deniz S. Ones, Chockalingman Viswesvaran, and Frank L Schmidt, "Comprehensive Meta-Analysis of Integrity Test Validities: Findings and Implications for Personnel Selection and Theories of Job Performance," *Journal of Applied Psychology Monograph,* Vol., 78, No., 4, 1993, pp. 679–703.

Questions for Discussion and Review

1. What is meant by diversity, and what are the major reasons that have made it such an important dimension of today's organizations?
2. What are some of the major characteristics of diversity?
3. How can diversity be effectively managed? Offer suggestions at both the individual and organizational levels.
4. What is meant by ethics, and what types of factors influence ethical behavior?
5. Many organizations are determined to eliminate sexual harassment. What are some steps that can be taken?
6. There are a number of misconceptions that people have about the glass ceiling. What are some of these? Also, what can organizations do to help break the glass ceiling?
7. Because privacy issues are likely to become increasingly important in the years ahead, what can organizations do to effectively deal with this ethical challenge?

Internet Exercise: Ethical Issues in the Workplace

Ethical issues are very much at the forefront of organizational behavior and of organizational decision making. One controversial issue concerns the monitoring of employees. Technology has now made it easy and inexpensive for employers to closely monitor the behaviors of employees. Visit the website http://www.aclu.org then click on "workplace rights" for news releases, pending legislation, and other relevant information for the American Civil Liberties Union perspective on this issue. Then, using your search engine, see if you can come up with other perspectives on employee monitoring.

1. Do you believe employers should be allowed to electronically monitor workers? Would you like to be monitored in this fashion?
2. Summarize the different perspectives that you found on the Internet. Be specific as to where you found this information.
3. Discuss other ethical issues that surfaced when looking at the ACLU website or others that you found.

REAL CASE:
A World of
Sweatshops

Walk through Tong Yang Indonesia (TYI) shoe factory, an 8,500-worker complex of hot, dingy buildings outside Jakarta, and company President Jung Moo Young will show you all the improvements he has made in the past two years. He did so at the behest of his biggest customer, Reebok International Ltd., to allay protests by Western activists who accuse the U.S. shoemaker of using sweatshops.

Last year, Jung bought new machinery to apply a water-based solvent to glue on shoe soles instead of toulene, which may be hazardous to workers who breathe it in all day. He installed a new ventilation system and chairs with back supports. In all, TYI, which has $100 million in annual sales, spent $2 million of its own money to satisfy Reebok. But to Jung's surprise, "The workers are more productive."

TYI's efforts show how much progress Western companies can make in cleaning up sweatshops. In the early 1990s, many companies adopted codes of conduct requiring contractors to fix harsh or abusive conditions. Based on recent visits to Asia, companies such as Reebok, Nike, Liz Claiborne, and Mattel have finally begun enforcing their codes.

The problem is that such companies are the exceptions. Although many multinationals operate facilities in Asia and Latin America that are as well-run as any in the West, too many still buy from factories with appalling practices—especially in such labor-intensive sectors as garments, shoes, and toys.

Even improvements in working conditions may not boost workers' pay. TYI gets around $13 for every pair of shoes it makes for Reebok, paying only $1 for labor. Still, TYI says that after paying for materials and overhead, its margins are just 10%. Says a TYI manager. "If we aren't cheap enough, [customers] will go to Vietnam or elsewhere."

1. What ethical responsibility do you think firms from the United States and other developed countries have in making sure their suppliers from developing countries are not badly exploiting workers?
2. How do you react to the statement at the end of the case by the Indonesian manager that "If we aren't cheap enough, customers will go to Vietnam or elsewhere"?
3. Besides the ethical, human rights issues, are there any implications in this case for the study and application of organizational behavior?

REAL CASE:
Not Treating Everyone
the Same

As recently as the 1980s, managers in some of the most productive organizations in the country used to pride themselves on treating all their employees equally. This typically meant holding the line on rules and regulations so that everyone conformed to the same set of guidelines. Moreover, when people were evaluated, they were typically assessed on the basis of their performance in the workplace. In recent years there has been a dramatic change in management's thinking. Instead of treating everyone the same, some organizations are now trying to meet the specific needs of employees. What is done for one individual employee may not be done for another. Additionally, instead of evaluating all employees on how well they work in the workplace, attention is being focused on how much "value added" people contribute, regardless of how many hours they are physically at the workplace. This new philosophy is also spilling over into the way alternative work arrangements are being handled.

An example is Aetna Life & Casualty, where workers are given the option of reducing their workweek or compressing the time into fewer days. Under this arrangement, a parent who wants to spend more time at home with the children can opt to cut working hours from 40 down to 30 per week or put in four 10 hour days and have a long weekend with the kids. In either case, these personal decisions do not negatively affect the employee's opportunities for promotion. Why is the company so willing to accommodate the personal desires of the workers? One of the main reasons is that Aetna was losing hundreds of talented people every year and felt that the cost to the company was too great. Something had to be done to keep these people on the payroll. As a result, today approximately 2000 of Aetna's 44,000 employees work part-time, share a job, work at home, or are on a compressed workweek arrangement. The company estimates that it saves approximately $1 million annually by not having to train new workers. Moreover, the company reported that in one recent year 88 percent of those employees who took family leave returned to work. An added benefit of this program is the fact that Aetna's reputation as a good place to work has been strengthened. The Families and Work Institute recently named Aetna one of the top four "family-friendly" companies.

Duke Power & Light is another good example of how companies are changing their approach to managing employees. Realizing that child care is a growing need among many employees, because in most households both parents now work, the company joined forces with other employers to build a child-care center. The firm has also changed its work schedule assignments. In the past, many employees reported that they hated working swing shifts: days one week, evenings the next, and then nights. So the firm created 22 work schedules and now lets employees bid on them annually, based on seniority. Some of these shifts are the traditional five-day week of eight-hour days. Others, however, are compressed workweek alternatives, including four 10-hour days and three 12-hour days. At the same time, the company has been turning more authority over to the personnel and has driven up its employee-to-manager ratio from 12 to 1 to 20 to 1. As a result, the company now has an attrition rate that is over three times lower than the industry average, and most of this attrition is a result of people's transferring to other jobs in the utility. As one manager put it, "We needed to recognize that people have lives." On the basis of results, it is obvious that the new arrangement is a win-win situation for both the workers and the firm.

1. How is the new management philosophy described in this case different from that of the old, traditional philosophy? Identify and describe the differences.
2. In what way are alternative work schedules proving helpful to managing diversity?
3. Do you think these new programs are likely to continue or will they taper off? Why?

ORGANIZATIONAL BEHAVIOR CASE: Changing with the Times

Jerry is director of marketing for a large toy company. Presently, his team of executives consists entirely of white males. The company says it is committed to diversity and equal opportunity. In a private conversation with Robert, the company president, about the makeup of top-level management in the marketing department, Jerry admitted that he tends to promote people who are like him.

Jerry stated, "It just seems like when a promotion opportunity exists in our department, the perfect person for the job happens to be a white male. Am I supposed to actively seek women and minorities, even if I don't feel that they are the best person for the job? After all, we aren't violating the law, are we?"

Robert responded, "So far the performance in your department has been good, and as far as I know, we are not violating any discrimination laws. Your management team seems to work well together, and we don't want to do anything to upset that, especially considering the big marketing plans we have for this coming fiscal year."

The big marketing plans Robert is referring to have to do with capturing a sizable share of the overseas market. The company thinks that a large niche exists in various countries around the world—and who better to fill that niche than an organization that has proved it can make top-quality toys at a competitive price? Now the marketing team has the task of determining which countries to target, which existing toys will sell, and which new toys need to be developed.

1. Do Jerry and Robert understand what "management of diversity" means? How would you advise them?
2. Considering the marketing plans, how could they benefit from a more diverse management team? Be specific.

CHAPTER 4

Organizational Context: Design and Culture

Learning Objectives

Explain the modern organization theories of open systems, information processing, contingency, ecology, and learning.

Present the emerging horizontal, network, and virtual designs of organizations.

Define organizational culture and its characteristics.

Relate how an organizational culture is created.

Describe how an organizational culture is maintained.

Explain some ways of changing organizational culture.

Starting with Best Practice
Leader's Advice

Harvard's Michael Porter's New Thinking on the Relation between Strategy and Structure

Harvard Business School professor and strategic management guru Michael Porter is a leading authority on competitive strategy and international competitiveness and is a widely recognized lecturer and consultant in these areas to business and government audiences across the globe. The youngest ever tenured professor in the Harvard Business School, he has authored over 50 articles and 15 books, including Competitive Strategy: Techniques for Analyzing Industries and Competitors *(1980) and* The Competitive Advantage of Nations *(1990), both leading works in their field. In this interview, Porter discusses some of his new ideas on the relation between strategy and organization structure.*

Q1:   *As you talk to organizational leaders and strategists throughout the world and begin pulling together what's happening, has your thinking been changing in any way? How have you been reformulating your ideas of what effective strategists do?*

Porter: I have become increasingly intrigued with the intersection of organization and strategy. We have tended to think that organization should follow and support strategy, and that is true. The more I've thought about it, however, the more I've come to realize that the challenge of developing a strategy is greatly affected by organizational issues. In short, I used to think that the biggest challenge in developing strategy was understanding the external environment, properly gauging how industry structure was changing, understanding the way competitors were moving, and so on. I still believe that these challenges are difficult and complex and require strategy tools and techniques. But the challenges go way beyond the external environment per se.

Q2:   *So you're now beginning to expand your emphasis to include organizational considerations?*

Porter: Yes, I've come to see that in many ways an equally formidable challenge in developing a sound strategy comes from within. There are a host of internal factors that constrain or divert managers from formulating effective strategies and making the choices on which every strategy depends.

Q3:   *Is this a total change in your thinking?*

Porter: No, but it is a significant extension. I was trained to think in terms of the classic Alfred Chandler—a company had a strategy and that strategy should then determine the kind of organizational structure, incentives, norms, and so forth that enterprises would adopt. There was always the acknowledgment of a feedback from structure to strategy, but this was a dotted line. I've come to see that, in many companies, what actually happens occurs in reverse order.

Q4:   *Could you give an example?*

Porter: The ways managers think about competition, the ways they measure their results, the structure in place, the incentives that are used to motivate people—all of these actually drive the choice of strategy or, more commonly, the choice of a *nonstrategy.* This became increasingly evident as I began to draw the distinction between strategic positioning and operational improvement. In my earlier work, it was clear that implementation was important and could be better or worse, but I saw strategy as the dominant driver of differences between companies. Now I've come to see that the distinction between strategy and implementation is the wrong distinction. There really is no meaningful distinction between strategy and implementation, because a strategy involves very fine-grained choices about how to configure particular activities and the overall value chains. The relevant distinction is not between strategy and implementation but between operational (or best practice) improvement and positioning.

Q5:   *Are you saying that best practices can be a part of strategy, but that strategy cannot be tied exclusively to best practices?*

Porter: Let me put it this way. Best practice improvement and strategy are not mutually exclusive. Both must be present. Best practice improvement is a hard game to win—it's very hard to sustain an advantage here because rivals are also motivated to do it. The real advantage normally comes in differences in strategic position supported by tailored activities, trade-offs, and fit. As this distinction has become more clear to me, I have come to see that the vast majority of what managers do is best practice improvement—trying to find universally good or the universally best way of competing, crowding out strategy in many companies.

Q6:   *Let me close by asking you: What are three things that managers will have to do better if they want to compete effectively in the 21st century?*

Porter: One is that they are going to have to get better at making strategic choices. After an era of operational improvement, we have to get back to strategy. Second, there is a need to restore the role of the general manager. In the last few decades we have seen the role of the general manager blur. Too many general managers see their jobs as doing deals and delegating. The role of the general manager in strategy is the primary role. Third, we will need to move beyond the era of cost and price and understand differentiation both as competitors and as customers. Imitation is undercutting real customer choice and prices. This is a by-product of operational effectiveness competition. Companies, in turn, have gone too far in paring down and beating up on their suppliers. There is a need to move to the next level of understanding that creating superior customer value, and justifying different price levels for different products, is an integral part of competing.

This chapter moves from the external environment to the organizational context for organizational behavior. Specifically, this chapter is concerned with organization design and culture. Organization structure represents the skeletal framework for organizational behavior. As the discussion of the conceptual framework in Chapter 1 points out, the organization design and culture are dominant environmental factors that interact with the personal cognitions and the behavior. The first half of the chapter presents the organization from the viewpoint of modern theory and design. As Chapter 2 points out, information technology and globalization have had a dramatic impact on organization structures. New theories, designs, and networks have emerged to meet the contemporary situation. For example, well-known companies, such as General Electric, have eliminated vertical structures and adopted horizontal designs, and the world of mergers and acquisitions has forever changed organization design and interorganizational relationships. For example, the German-U.S. firm DaimlerChrysler has acquired controlling interest in Japan's Mitsubishi Motors,[1] and AOL with its 22 million customers merged with old-line media giant Time Warner.[2] Importantly, the web that such mergers and acquisitions weave reaches to almost every industry and continent.

The modern approach to organization theory and design consists of very flexible networks and recognizes the interaction of information technology and people. For example, one organization theorist has noted: "Organization structure is more than boxes on a chart; it is a pattern of interactions and coordination that links the technology, tasks, and human components of the organization to ensure that the organization accomplishes its purposes."[3] There is also a renewed recognition for the role that structure (or lack of structure) plays in innovation, change, and learning in today's and future organizations.

The second half of the chapter is concerned with the cultural context that the organization provides for organizational behavior. After first defining what is meant by organizational culture, the discussion turns to the different types, how they are changing, and how they can be changed to meet the challenges of the new external environment and organization designs.

ORGANIZATION THEORY

Some organization theorists argue that the classical hierarchical, bureaucratic model of organizations was mistranslated and really was not meant to be an ideal type of structure. Instead, the hierarchical bureaucracy was an example of the structural form taken by the political strategy of rational-legal domination.[4] In other words, some of the original theories of classical hierarchical structure may contain underpinnings for modern organization theory.

Historical Roots

The real break with classical thinking on organizational structure is generally recognized to be the work of Chester Barnard. In his significant book, *The Functions of the Executive,* he defined a *formal organization* as a system of consciously coordinated activities of two or more persons.[5] It is interesting to note that in this often-cited definition, the words *system* and *persons* are given major emphasis. People, not boxes on an organization chart, make up a formal organization. Barnard was critical of the existing classical organization theory because it was too descriptive and superficial.[6] He was especially dissatisfied with the classical bureaucratic view that authority should come from the top down. Barnard, using a more analytical approach, took an opposite viewpoint. He maintained that authority really should come from the bottom up, rather than the top-down bureaucratic approach.

Besides authority, Barnard stressed the cooperative aspects of organizations. This concern reflects the importance that he attached to the human element in organization structure and analysis. It was Barnard's contention that the existence of a cooperative system is contingent on the human participants' ability to communicate and their willingness to serve and strive toward a common purpose.[7] Under such a premise, the human being plays the most important role in the creation and perpetuation of formal organizations.

From this auspicious beginning, modern organization theory has evolved in several directions. The first major development in organization theory was to view the organization as a system made up of interacting parts. The open-systems concept especially, which stresses the input of the external environment, has had a tremendous impact on modern organization theory. This development was followed by an analysis of organizations in terms of their ability to process information in order to reduce the uncertainty in managerial decision making. The next development in organization theory is the contingency approach. The premise of the contingency approach is that there is no single best way to organize. The organizational design must be fitted to the existing environmental conditions.

One of the modern theoretical approaches is a natural selection—or ecological—view of organizations. This organizational ecology theory challenges the contingency approach. Whereas the contingency approach suggests that organizations change through internal transformation and adaptation, the ecological approach says that it is more a process of the "survival of the fittest"; there is a process of organizational selection and replacement.[8]

Finally, are information processing and organizational learning. These most recent approaches to organization theory are based largely on systems theory and emphasize the importance of generative over adaptive learning in fast-changing external environments such as covered in Chapter 2 on information technology and globalization. All these organization theories serve as a historical foundation for the remaining discussion of the organizational context for organizational behavior.

The Organization as an Open System

Both the closed- and open-systems approaches are utilized in organization theory and practice. However, in today's dramatically changing environment an open-systems approach is becoming much more relevant and meaningful. The key for viewing organizations as open systems is the recognition of the external environment as a source of significant input. In systems terminology, the boundaries of the organization are permeable to the external environment (social, legal, technical, economic, and political).

The simplest open system consists of an input, a transformation process, and an output, which is depicted thus:

$$\text{input} \rightarrow \text{transformation process} \rightarrow \text{output}$$

A system cannot survive without continuous input, the transformation process, and output.

There are many types of inputs, transformation processes, and outputs. For example, one kind of input actually enters the open system in the "closed" sense. In other words, this type of input has a direct effect on the internal system rather than an outside effect—in systems jargon, it loads the system. Another type of input affects the system in an "open" sense. Generally, this input would consist of the entire environmental influence on the system. Still another kind of input takes the form of replacement or recycling. When a component of the system is ejected or leaves, the replacement becomes an input. This recycling process perpetuates the system. Specific examples of inputs into a business organization include monetary, material, informational, and human resources.

At the heart of the open system are the processes, operations, or channels that transform the inputs into the outputs. Here is where the internal organization design plays an important role. The transformation process consists of a logical network of subsystems, which lead to the output. The subsystems are translated into a complex systems network that transforms the inputs into the desired outputs.

The third and final major component of any simple open system is the output. This is represented by the product, result, outcome, knowledge, or accomplishment of the system. Specific examples of the outputs of a business organization system that correspond to the inputs of monetary, material, informational, and human resources are profit or loss, product or service sales, new products or services, and role behaviors.

The simple open-systems concept has universal applicability. Any biological, human, social, economic, or technical phenomenon can be conceptualized in open-systems terms. As has been shown, an economic institution receives inputs of people, raw materials, money, laws, information, and values. The system then transforms these inputs via organizational subsystems and processes into outputs, such as products, services, taxes, dividends, knowledge, and even pollution. From an organization design standpoint, the critical factor is the design of the transformation process. Oddly, this transformation design involves a closed-systems analysis. In other words, the closed system is a subsystem of the open system. The closed-systems aspects of the transformation process are concerned with the interrelated and interdependent organizational subsystems of structure, processes, and technology. These subsystems must be organized in such a way that they will lead to maximum goal attainment, knowledge, or output.

Although the approach has decreased in popularity in recent years, it has been pointed out that, to date, very little research on organizations has been guided by open-systems thinking.[9] It is not that the open-systems approach has proved to be wrong or lacking in some way but rather that "in order to most fruitfully utilize the systems paradigm of organizations, scholars in the field must re-examine their beliefs about the paradigm and, perhaps, re-educate themselves about how they should think about and study organizations as systems."[10] As has been pointed out, a new type of systems thinking has resurfaced in terms of organizational learning. As Peter Senge noted:

> What is changing today is the scope of systems thinking skills required. As power and authority are distributed more widely, it becomes increasingly important that people throughout the organization be able to understand how their actions influence others. To do so, local actors need better information systems so they can be aware of systemwide conditions.[11]

Before examining the learning organization, with which Senge is most closely associated, the information processing, contingency, and ecological approaches are examined.

Information Processing View of Organizations

The view of organizations as information processing systems facing uncertainty serves as a transition between systems theory, which has just been discussed, and contingency theory, which is discussed next. The information processing view makes three major assumptions about organizations.[12] First, organizations are open systems that face external, environmental uncertainty (for example, information technology or the new economy) and internal, work-related task uncertainty. Jay Galbraith defines task uncertainty as "the difference between the amount of information required to perform the task and the amount of information already possessed by the organization."[13] The organization must have mechanisms and be structured such that it can diagnose and cope with this environmental and task uncertainty. In particular, the organization through its knowledge management (KM), discussed in Chapter 2, must be able to acquire, store, interpret, and use the appropriate information to reduce the uncertainty. Thus, the second assumption is as follows: "Given the various sources of uncertainty, a basic function of the organization's structure is to create the most appropriate configuration of work units (as well as the linkages between these units) to facilitate the effective collection, processing, and distribution of information."[14] In other words, organizations in this view become information processing systems.

The final major assumption of this information processing approach deals with the importance of the subunits or various departments of an organization. Because the subunits have different degrees of differentiation (that is, they have different time perspectives, goals, technology, and so on), the important question is not what the overall organization design should be but, rather, "(a) What are the optimal structures for the different subunits within the organization (e.g., R&D, sales, manufacturing)?; (b) What structural mechanisms will facilitate effective coordination among differentiated yet interdependent subunits?"[15] and (c) How can the networked information technology becoming increasingly common in today's organizations actually replace or provide a substitute for the very concept of organization design as traditionally portrayed in theory and practice?

Taking the answers to these questions as a point of departure, Tushman and Nadler draw on relevant research to formulate the following propositions about an information processing theory of organizations:

1. The tasks of organization subunits vary in their degree of uncertainty.
2. As work-related uncertainty increases, so does the need for an increased amount of information, and thus the need for increased information processing capacity.
3. Different organizational structures have different capacities for effective information processing.
4. An organization will be more effective when there is a match between the information processing requirements facing the organization and the information processing capacity of the organization's structure.
5. If organizations (or subunits) face different conditions over time, more effective units will adapt their structures to meet the changed information processing requirements.[16]

These propositions summarize the information processing view of organizations. "The key concept is information, and the key idea is that organizations must effectively receive, process, and act on information to achieve performance."[17] Although the focal point of this approach is the interface between environmental uncertainty—both external and internal—and information processing, it is very closely related to systems, contingency, organizational learning, and knowledge management (KM), and some organization theorists would argue that it could even be subsumed under one of these.

Contingency and Ecological Organization Theories

All the modern organization theories focus on the environment, including the open-systems and information processing views. However, the modern contingency, ecological, and learning organization theories treat the environment differently. Contingency theories are proactive and are analogous to the development of contingency management as a whole; they relate the environment to specific organization structures. More specifically, the contingency models relate to how the organization designs adjust to fit with both the internal environment, such as work technology and processes, and the external environment, such as information technology (including the Internet) and globalization.

Some organization theorists feel that contingency theory should be replaced by an ecological view.[18] This approach is best represented by what is called "population ecology."[19] Very simply, this population-ecology approach can be summarized as follows:

1. It focuses on groups or populations of organizations rather than individual ones. For example, for the population of grocery organizations after World War II, there was an even split between "mom-and-pop" stores and supermarkets. The environment selected out the small "mom-and-pop" operations because they were not efficient, and only the supermarkets survived.
2. Organizational effectiveness is simply defined as survival.
3. The environment is assumed to be totally determining. At least in the short or intermediate term, management is seen to have little impact on an organization's survival.
4. The carrying capacity of the environment is limited. Therefore, there is a competitive arena in which some organizations will succeed and others will fail.[20]

Obviously, this ecology theory represents a much different view of organizations than the classical or even modern approaches. A more rational, proactive approach to management that is able to adapt the organization structure to fit the changing demands of the environment is more accepted and practical than environmental determination. Yet, in recent years, many organizations have not been able to keep up with the dramatic changes they are facing. For example, although the thousands of mergers and acquisitions and their resulting cultural clashes[21] (covered next in this chapter) and dysfunctional organizational outcomes dominate most of the business news reports, Drucker recently noted,

> Almost unnoticed by the public, and almost totally ignored by the business press and financial analysts, is that the real boom has been in alliances of all kinds, such as partnerships, a big business buying a minority stake in a small one, cooperative agreements in research or in marketing, joint ventures, and, often, handshake agreements with few formal and legally binding contracts behind them.[22]

These alliances and the significant impact of interconnected information technology and globalization, covered in Chapter 2, constitute a new paradigm for organization understanding and design. All these factors have impeded scientific progress in organization theory because, as Pfeffer pointed out: "The study of organizations is arguably paradigmatically not well developed, in part because of values that emphasize representativeness, inclusiveness, and theoretical and methodological diversity."[23] The learning organization represents the latest thinking in organization theory and is compatible with and directly relevant to the new paradigm environment facing today's organizations.

What Is Meant by a Learning Organization?

The organization portrayed as a learning system is not new.[24] In fact, at the turn of the century Frederick W. Taylor's learnings on scientific management were said to be transferable to workers to make the organization more efficient. However, the beginning of today's use of the term *learning organization* is usually attributed to the seminal work of Chris Argyris and his colleagues, who made the distinction between first-order, or "single-loop," and second-order, or dentero or "double-loop," learning.[25] The differences between these two types of learning applied to organizations can be summarized as follows:

1. Single-loop learning involves improving the organization's capacity to achieve known objectives. It is associated with routine and behavioral learning. Under single-loop, the organization is learning without significant change in its basic assumptions.

2. Double-loop learning reevaluates the nature of the organization's objectives and the values and beliefs surrounding them. This type of learning involves changing the organization's culture. Importantly, double-loop consists of the organization's learning how to learn.[26]

As indicated above, Peter Senge and his colleagues then proceeded to portray the learning organization from a systems theory perspective and made the important distinction between adaptive and generative learning.[27] The simpler adaptive learning is only the first stage of the learning organization, adapting to environmental changes. In recent years, many banks, insurance firms, and old-line manufacturing companies made many adaptive changes, but they experienced much difficulty under their basic assumptions, cultural values, and organization structure. They did not go beyond mere adaptive learning. The more important generative learning was needed. Generative learning involves creativity and innovation, going beyond just adapting to change to being ahead of and anticipating change.[28] The generative process leads to a total reframing of an organization's experiences and learning from that process.

With the theoretical foundation largely provided by Argyris (double-loop learning) and Senge (generative learning), we conducted a comprehensive review to identify the major characteristics of learning organizations.[29] Figure 4.1 shows the three major

FIGURE 4.1

Characteristics of learning organizations.

Source: Adapted from Fred Luthans, Michael J. Rubach, and Paul Marsnik, "Going Beyond Total Quality: The Characteristics, Techniques, and Measures of Learning Organizations," *The International Journal of Organizational Analysis,* January 1995, pp. 27–32.

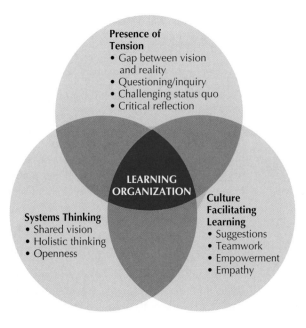

dimensions or characteristics of learning organizations that emerged out of the considerable literature. The presence of tension—Senge calls it "creative tension"—serves as a catalyst or motivational need to learn. As shown in Figure 4.1, this tension stems from the gap between the organization's vision (which is hopefully always being adjusted upward) and reality and suggests the learning organization's continually questioning and challenging the status quo. The systems characteristic of learning organizations recognizes the shared vision of employees throughout the whole organization and the openness to new ideas and the external environment. The third major characteristic shown in Figure 4.1 is an organizational culture conducive to learning. The culture of the organization places a high value on the process of learning and goes beyond mere lip service by setting mechanisms in place for suggestions, teams, empowerment, and, most subtly but importantly, empathy. This empathy is reflected by the genuine concern for and interest in employee suggestions and innovations that can be operationalized through reward systems.

Organizational Behavior in the Learning Organization

Taken to a more individual employee, organizational behavior level, the adaptive learning organization would be associated with employees' reacting to environmental changes with routine, standard responses that often result in only short-run solutions. In contrast, generative learning, with its emphasis on continuous experimentation and feedback, would directly affect the way personnel go about defining and solving problems. Employees in generative learning organizations are taught how to examine the effect of their decisions and to change their behaviors as needed. A good example is provided by the highly successful Taco Bell chain, which dramatically changed the way that managers and employees carry out their jobs.

> The selection process now focuses on hiring store managers who hold positive attitudes toward responsibility, teamwork, customer service, and sharing. . . . The role of the supervisor also changed from providing direction and control for the store managers to coaching and support. Store managers now receive training and support in communication, performance management, team building, coaching, and empowerment, and they can draw upon this training to improve their human resource skills.[30]

Learning organizations are also characterized by human-oriented cultural values such as these: (1) everyone can be a source of useful ideas, so personnel should be given access to any information that can be of value to them; (2) the people closest to the problem usually have the best ideas regarding how to solve it, so empowerment should be promoted throughout the structure; (3) learning flows up and down, so managers as well as employees can benefit from it; (4) new ideas are important and should be encouraged and rewarded; and (5) mistakes should be viewed as learning opportunities.[31] The last point of learning from failures is an especially important cultural value for people in the learning organization.

Learning Organizations in Action

There are a number of ways that the learning organization can be operationalized into the actual practice of management.[32] For example, managers must be receptive to new ideas and overcome the desire to closely control operations. Many organizations tend to do things the way they have done them in the past. Learning organizations break this mold and teach their people to look at things differently. For example, several years ago British Petroleum (BP) was bogged down in their bureaucratic structure and control procedures, accumulated a huge debt, and had some of the highest costs in the industry. Then a new CEO David Simon took over, sold off the firm's unrelated business, and implemented a corporate strategy mostly based on speed and rapid learning. BP was redesigned as follows:

> Functional and divisional walls that inhibited cooperation, resource sharing, and internal debate were leveled to promote forward thinking, the learning of new managerial competencies, and the adoption of risk taking behaviors. Most importantly, a rejuvenated senior management team began cultivating a new culture that emphasized knowledge sharing, open communications, team-building, and breakthrough thinking throughout the firm.[33]

By the turn of the century, BP had a learning-driven culture in place, the old bureaucratic boundaries were down, everyone in the firm shared knowledge with everyone else, and BP became the lowest-cost producer in the oil industry.

Another way to operationalize the learning process in organizations is to develop systemic thinking among managers. This involves the ability to see connections among issues, events, and data as a whole rather than a series of unconnected parts. Learning organizations teach their people to identify the source of conflict they may have with other personnel, units, and departments and to negotiate and make astute trade-offs both skillfully and quickly. Managers must also learn, especially, how to encourage their people to redirect their energies toward the substance of disagreements rather than toward personality clashes or political infighting. For example, in most successful firms today, interfunctional teams work on projects, thus removing the artificial barriers between functional areas and between line and staff.

Another practice of learning organizations is to develop creativity among personnel. Creativity is the ability to formulate unique approaches to problem solving and decision making. In generative learning organizations, creativity is most widely acknowledged as a requisite skill and ability. Two critical dimensions of creativity, which promote and help unleash creativity, are personal flexibility and a willingness to take risks. As a result, many learning organizations now teach their people how to review their current work habits and change behaviors that limit their thinking. Whereas typical organizations focus on new ways to use old thinking, learning organizations focus on getting employees to break their operating habits and think "outside the box." Creativity also includes the willingness to accept failure. Learning organizations see failure as feedback that contributes to future creativity, and managers encourage this behavior by providing a supportive environment. A cultural value or slogan such as "ready, fire, aim" depicts such an environment.

Still another practice is the development of a sense of confidence, as characterized by an awareness of personal and organizational values and a proactive approach to problem solving. In learning organizations such as General Electric, the firm clearly spells out its sense of mission and values. Then personnel are given the opportunity to identify and examine their own values. This helps employees better understand and work into the linkage between the two. In addition, personnel are taught to evaluate the effects of their behavior on others, so as to maximize their own effectiveness. In the process, they also learn how to solve problems before critical situations develop. This step-by-step approach helps employees analyze and evaluate situations with a view toward both addressing problems early and preventing their recurrence.

TABLE 4.1   Traditional versus Learning Organizations

Function	Traditional Organizations	Learning Organizations
Determination of overall direction	Vision is provided by top management.	There is a shared vision that can emerge from many places, but top management is responsible for ensuring that this vision exists and is nurtured.
Formulation and implementation of ideas	Top management decides what is to be done, and the rest of the organization acts on these ideas.	Formulation and implementation of ideas take place at all levels of the organization.
Nature of organizational thinking	Each person is responsible for his or her own job responsibilities, and the focus is on developing individual competence.	Personnel understand their own jobs as well as the way in which their own work interrelates with and influences that of other personnel.
Conflict resolution	Conflicts are resolved through the use of power and hierarchical influence.	Conflicts are resolved through the use of collaborative learning and the integration of diverse viewpoints of personnel throughout the organization.
Leadership and motivation	The role of the leader is to establish the organization's vision, provide rewards and punishments as appropriate, and maintain overall control of employee activities.	The role of the leader is to build a shared vision, empower the personnel, inspire commitment, and encourage effective decision making throughout the enterprise through the use of empowerment and charismatic leadership.

Source: Adapted from Peter M. Senge, "Transforming the Practice of Management," *Human Resource Development Quarterly,* Spring 1993, p. 9.

Senge summarizes the differences between learning organizations and traditional organizations in Table 4.1. These differences help illustrate why learning organizations are gaining in importance and why an increasing number of enterprises are now working to develop a generative learning environment. They realize the benefits that can result. The systems, information processing, contingency, and ecological theories are important to emerging organizations, but organizational learning goes a necessary step further to the understanding of today's organizations in the new paradigm environment.

MODERN ORGANIZATION DESIGNS

Along with organization theorists, many practicing managers are becoming disenchanted with traditional ways of designing their organizations. Up until a few years ago, most managers attempted only timid modifications of classical bureaucratic structures and balked at daring experimentation and innovation. However, many of today's managers have finally overcome this resistance to making drastic organizational changes. They realize that the simple solutions offered by the classical theories are no longer adequate in the new paradigm environment. In particular, the needs for flexibility, adaptability to change, creativity, innovation, knowledge, as well as the ability to overcome environmental uncertainty, are among the biggest challenges facing a growing number of modern organizations. The response has been horizontal, network, and virtual organization designs.

Horizontal Organizations

Horizontal designs replace the traditional vertical, hierarchical organization. The advanced information technology and globalization environment, discussed in Chapter 2, suggests the use of horizontal structure to facilitate cooperation, teamwork, and a customer rather than a functional orientation. Frank Ostroff, a McKinsey & Company consultant, along with colleague Douglas Smith, is given credit for developing some of the following guiding principles that define horizontal organization design.[34]

1. *Organization revolves around the process, not the task.* Instead of creating a structure around the traditional functions, the organization is built around its three to five core processes. Each process has an "owner" and specific performance goals.
2. *The hierarchy is flattened.* To reduce levels of supervision, fragmented tasks are combined, work that fails to add value is eliminated, and activities within each process are cut to the minimum.
3. *Teams are used to manage everything.* Self-managed teams are the building blocks of the organization. The teams have a common purpose and are held accountable for measuring performance goals.
4. *Customers drive performance.* Customer satisfaction, not profits or stock appreciation, is the primary driver and measure of performance.
5. *Team performance is rewarded.* The reward systems are geared toward team results, not just individual performance. Employees are rewarded for multiple skill development rather than just specialized expertise.
6. *Supplier and customer contact is maximized.* Employees are brought into direct, regular contact with suppliers and customers. Where relevant, supplier and customer representatives may be brought in as full working members of in-house teams.
7. *All employees need to be fully informed and trained.* Employees should be provided all data, not just sanitized information on a "need to know" basis. However, they also need to be trained how to analyze and use the data to make effective decisions.

Today, this horizontal structure has become a reality in an increasing number of organizations. For example, AT&T units are doing budgets based not on functions but on processes, such as the maintenance of a worldwide telecommunications network. Importantly, AT&T is also rewarding its people based on customer evaluations of the teams performing these processes, and GE, Motorola, and Xerox, among other firms, have moved to the principles of the horizontal design of organization.[35] For example, General Electric has scrapped the vertical structure that was in place in its lighting business and replaced the design with a horizontal structure that is characterized by over 100 different processes and programs. The Government Electronics group at Motorola has redesigned its supply-chain management organization so that it is now a process structure geared toward serving external customers. At Xerox new products are developed through the use of multidisciplinary teams; the vertical approach that had been used over the years is gone. These new ways of organizing are more relevant to today's environmental needs for flexibility, speed, and cooperation. A recent book on *The Horizontal Organization* suggests principles such as the following:

1. Make teams, not individuals, the cornerstone of organizational design and performance.
2. Decrease hierarchy by eliminating non-value-added work and by giving team members the authority to make decisions directly related to their activities within the process flow.
3. Emphasize multiple competencies and train people to handle issues and work in cross-functional areas.

4. Measure for end-of-process performance objectives, as well as customer satisfaction, employee satisfaction, and financial contribution.
5. Build a corporate culture of openness, cooperation and collaboration, a culture that focuses on continuous performance improvement and values employee empowerment, responsibility, and well-being.[36]

Network Designs

The network designs go beyond even horizontal structures and totally abandon the classical, hierarchical, functional structure of organization. The bureaucratic model worked fine in the previous era when there was less competition, more stable market conditions, and before the now boundaryless conditions of advanced information technology and globalization. To meet these challenges of revolutionary change, organizations are moving toward network structures.

Network organizations have been discussed in the academic literature for a number of years. For example, organization theorists Miles and Snow identified what they call the *dynamic network*.[37] This involves a unique combination of strategy, structure, and management processes. They more recently have described the network organization as follows: "Delayered, highly flexible, and controlled by market mechanisms rather than administrative procedures, firms with this new structure arrayed themselves on an industry value chain according to their core competencies, obtaining complementary resources through strategic alliances and outsourcing."[38] There is also research showing the impact that structure and information technology can have on network behavior and outcomes.[39]

With the advent of teams and outsourcing (concentrating on core competencies and forming outside partnerships to perform the peripheral activities and functions of the organization),[40] network designs are actually being used by practicing organizations. Tapscott and Caston note that such networked organizations are "based on cooperative, multidisciplinary teams and businesses networked together across the enterprise. Rather than a rigid structure, it is a modular organizational architecture in which business teams operate as a network of what we call client and server functions."[41] Table 4.2

TABLE 4.2   Traditional Hierarchical versus the Network Organization

Dimension/Characteristic	Traditional Organization	Network Organization
Structure	Hierarchical	Networked
Scope	Internal/closed	External/open
Resource focus	Capital	Human, information
State	Static, stable	Dynamic, changing
Personnel focus	Managers	Professionals
Key drivers	Reward and punishment	Commitment
Direction	Management commands	Self-management
Basis of action	Control	Empowerment to act
Individual motivation	Satisfy superiors	Achieve team goals
Learning	Specific skills	Broader competencies
Basis for compensation	Position in hierarchy	Accomplishment, competence level
Relationships	Competitive (my turf)	Cooperative (our challenge)
Employee attitude	Detachment (it's a job)	Identification (it's my company)
Dominant requirements	Sound management	Leadership

Source: Don Tapscott and Art Caston, *Paradigm Shift,* McGraw-Hill, New York, 1993, p. 11. Used with permission of McGraw-Hill.

FIGURE 4.2

The contrast between the hierarchical and network organization.

Source: Raymond E. Miles and Charles C. Snow, "The New Network Firm: A Spherical Structure Built on a Human Investment Philosophy," *Organizational Dynamics,* Spring 1995, p. 6. Used with permission of the publisher © 1995, American Management Association, New York. All rights reserved.

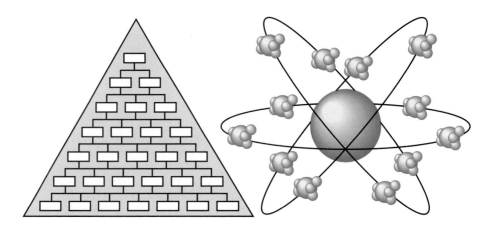

Rather than the old inflexible hierarchical pyramid, network organizations demand a flexible, spherical structure that can rotate competent, self-managing teams and other resources around a common knowledge base. Such teams, capable of quick action on the firm's behalf both externally and internally, provide a distinct competitive advantage.

compares the various dimensions and characteristics of the traditional, hierarchical organization with the network organization. Although the network design cannot readily be drawn, as can the classical hierarchical structures of the past, Figure 4.2 is an attempt to at least show the concept.

Miles and colleagues identified three types of radical redesign of today's organizations:[42]

1. *Greenfield redesign.* As the term implies, this means starting from just a piece of green field or from a clean slate, breaking completely from the classical structure and establishing a totally different design. Examples include such highly successful firms as Rubbermaid and Southwest Airlines. Rubbermaid's top management concluded that the key to success in their consumer plastic goods industry was constant product innovation and speed to market. They had to create a brand-new structure characterized by flexibility and empowerment to facilitate innovation, quality, and rapid responsiveness across a broad range of consumer markets. The same was turn for Southwest Airlines. Under the unique leadership of Herb Kelleher, the firm made a complete break from the floundering airline industry. Kelleher has been described as having enormous intellectual capabilities, a love for people, a playful spirit, and a commanding personality; he once arm-wrestled an opponent in an advertising slogan dispute rather than going to court.[43] Southwest created an organization that "flies in the face of bureaucracy: it stays lean, thinks small, keeps it simple—and more."[44]

2. *Rediscovery redesign.* This is a more usual type of redesign, whereby established companies such as General Electric return to a previously successful design by eliminating unproductive structural additions and modifications. For example, several of the most successful U.S. electronics firms such as Texas Instruments have reverted to some highly formalized, bureaucratic procedures in their product development process.[45]

3. *Network design.* Firms such as Ford and Harley-Davidson are not just redesigning in the "Greenfield" sense or rediscovering and extending their past. Instead, they

are undergoing efforts to disaggregate and partner. In the network approach, the firm concentrates on where it can add the greatest value in the supply chain, and it outsources to upstream and/or downstream partners who can do a better job. This network of the firm and its upstream and downstream partners can be optimally effective and flexible. Another network approach is to require internal units of the firm to interact at market prices—buy and sell to each other at prices equal to those that can be obtained by outsourcing partners. This "insourcing" approach to the internal network organization can be found in global firms such as the well-known and respected Swiss conglomerate Asea Brown Boveri (ABB). At Chase Bank there are "shared services" units that compete with outside vendors to furnish services to the bank's own operating units, and Delta Airlines has established a "business partners" unit to oversee its relations with some 250 vendors and 2,600 contracts for ground crew and customer services at 186 airports around the world.[46] Such global expansion challenges these multinational corporations to make sure they account for cultural differences (see International Application Example).

The network organization described is very close to what has become known as the virtual organization.

INTERNATIONAL APPLICATION EXAMPLE

One Size Doesn't Fit All—Even Hamburgers

There are some things in the world that seem to be the same regardless of geographic location. Whether a pilot is flying into Kennedy International in New York or Heathrow in the UK, one would assume the procedures for taking off and landing to be identical. The truth is, however, cultural differences may violate such assumptions. For example, most countries of the world have indeed agreed that English should be the universal language when pilots from anywhere are talking to air traffic controllers. On the other hand, French unions have encouraged their pilots to continue talking in French when landing at Charles de Gaulle airport. These culturally generated differences are not restricted to the airline industry.

Many multinational companies are finding that it is extremely difficult to take a product that sells well in the home country and achieve equal success in a foreign market. The customs, culture, and behaviors of people in these markets are often quite different from those in the home country. For example, when Office Depot and Office Max entered the Japanese market, they were convinced that their wide variety of products, convenient store layout, and low prices would help them attain a significant market share. They were wrong. One of their major Japanese competitors realized something that the big American multinationals did not—small business firms account for a significant percentage of the office supply market, and these firms were anxious to get the same big discounts on their purchases as did large firms. So the Japanese company created a catalogue business that was geared specifically to small firms. In these companies clerks did much of the purchasing of business equipment, and they were happy to be able to look through a catalog and place orders from their desk rather than traveling to the store. The Japanese company also realized that stationery accounted for a significant percentage of the office purchases of small firms, and in many cases there were young women, what the Japanese commonly refer to as "office ladies," who were responsible for this function. So the Japanese company created a "loyalty program" that was aimed directly at these women. If their firm placed an order for $1,000 of merchandise, the office lady was sent a teddy-bear clock. A purchase of $2,000 brought a box of chocolates. The women liked the attention that the company gave them and, in turn, bought almost exclusively from this Japanese firm.

Although chagrined by their efforts to compete effectively with their smaller Japanese rival, Office Depot and Office Max believed that they would be able to capture a large percentage of the remaining market—the walk-in customer. Again, they were foiled by their Japanese competitors. Unlike American customers, Japanese buyers do not mind shopping at small stores where the merchandise is crammed together. As a result, Office Depot and Office Max built large stores with wide aisles and ended up paying twice as much as their smaller competitors for rent and personnel salaries and were eventually forced to admit defeat. Their experience is not unique.

When Bob's Big Boy, the Michigan-based restaurant minichain, opened a series of units in Thailand, management was surprised to learn that local customers really did not care for the firm's hamburgers. Local customers would rather buy a sweet satay, noodle bowl, or grilled squid from a street vendor at one-fifth the cost. In fact, the owner of the Thai franchise system did not start making money until he began closely studying the potential customers who were walking past his restaurants. He then realized that these potential customers fell into two broad categories: European tourists and young Thai people. This resulted in his changing the menu of his restaurants. For German customers he began offering specialties such as spatzle, beef, and chocolate cake. For local Thais there were country-style specialties such as fried rice and pork omelets. The owner also added sugar and chile powder to Big Boy's burgers to better match Thai taste buds. Commenting on his eventual success, the adaptable owner recently noted, "We thought we were bringing American food to the masses. But now we're bringing Thai and European food to the tourists. It's strange, but you know what? It's working." And the reason is that the owner realizes market offerings have to be tailored to local demand. One size does not fit all.

The Virtual Organization

The term *virtual organization* has emerged not so much because it describes something distinct from network organizations but because the term itself represents the new Information Age and the partnering and outsourcing arrangements found in an increasing number of global companies.[47] Interestingly, the word *virtual* as used here comes not from the popular *virtual reality* but from *virtual memory,* which has been used to describe a way of making a computer's memory capacity appear to be greater than it really is. Virtual organizing requires a strong information technology platform.[48] The virtual organization is a temporary network of companies that come together quickly to exploit fast-changing opportunities.

Different from traditional mergers and acquisitions, the partners in the virtual organization share costs, skills, and access to international markets. Each partner contributes to the virtual organization what it is best at—its core capabilities.[49] Briefly summarized, here are the key attributes of the virtual organization:

1. *Technology.* Informational networks will help far-flung companies and entrepreneurs link up and work together from start to finish. The partnerships will be based on electronic contracts to keep the lawyers away and speed the linkups.
2. *Opportunism.* Partnerships will be less permanent, less formal, and more opportunistic. Companies will band together to meet all specific market opportunities and, more often than not, fall apart once the need evaporates.

3. *No borders.*   This new organizational model redefines the traditional boundaries of the company. More cooperation among competitors, suppliers, and customers makes it harder to determine where one company ends and another begins.
4. *Trust.*   These relationships make companies far more reliant on each other and require far more trust than ever before. They share a sense of "codestiny," meaning that the fate of each partner is dependent on the other.
5. *Excellence.*   Because each partner brings its "core competence" to the effort, it may be possible to create a "best-of-everything" organization. Every function and process could be world class—something that no single company could achieve.[50]

Importantly, virtual organizations can help competitiveness in the global economy. The alliances and partnerships with other organizations can extend worldwide, the spatial and temporal interdependence easily transcend boundaries, and the flexibility allows easy reassignment and reallocation to take quick advantage of shifting opportunities in global markets.[51]

Examples of virtual organizations include those already mentioned as well-known network organizations—Ford, Harley-Davidson, and ABB—and also, on a smaller scale, firms such as Clark Equipment, a manufacturer of forklifts and other industrial equipment; Semco, a Brazilian firm producing pumps, valves, and other industrial products; and the Australian firm Technical and Computer Graphics (TCG).[52] Other well-known examples include Nike and Reebok, who do very little of their own production but shift it to Asian firms. In the information technology industry, Sun Microsystems views itself as an intellectual holding company that designs computers and does all other functions (product ordering, manufacturing, distribution, marketing, and customer service) through contractual arrangements with partners located throughout the world, and Intel uses virtual teams with members from Ireland, Israel, England, France, and Asia working on a wide variety of projects.[53] As with the network organization, it is not really possible to show a virtual organization, but Figure 4.3 depicts graphically

FIGURE 4.3
An example of a virtual organization: Technical and Computer Graphics (TCG), an Australian-based multinational firm.
Source: Raymond E. Miles and Charles C. Snow, "The New Network Firm: A Spherical Structure Built on a Human Investment Philosophy," *Organizational Dynamics*, Spring 1995, p. 8. Used with permission of the publisher © 1995, American Management Association, New York. All rights reserved.

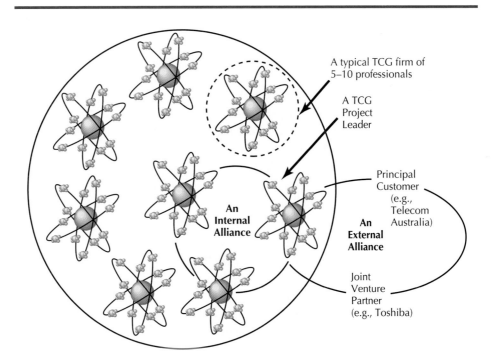

how TCG would look as a virtual organization. Because networks and virtual organizations both represent such radically different ways to structure firms, there are many challenges ahead, especially on the human side of these new structural forms.[54]

THE ORGANIZATIONAL CULTURE CONTEXT

Chapter 2's discussion of the globalization context included the dimensions of national cultures. Going from this macro to more of a micro cultural impact on organizational behavior is organizational culture. The remainder of the chapter defines organizational culture and examines the types and ways to change and manage organizational culture.

Definition and Characteristics

When people join an organization, they bring with them the values and beliefs they have been taught. Quite often, however, these values and beliefs are insufficient for helping the individual succeed in the organization. The person needs to learn how the particular enterprise does things. A good example is the U.S. Marine Corps. During boot camp, drill instructors teach recruits the "Marine way." The training attempts to psychologically strip down the new recruits and then restructure their way of thinking and their values. They are taught to think and act like Marines. Anyone who has been in the Marines or knows someone who has will verify that the Corps generally accomplishes its objective. In a less-dramatic way, today's organizations do the same thing. For example, as discussed in Chapter 2 under knowledge management (KM), the key challenge for the new economy, Information Age organizations is to instill and sustain a corporatewide culture that encourages knowledge sharing. As the partner in charge of Ernst & Young's knowledge-based business solution practice notes,"If you're going to have a rich knowledge-sharing culture, that can't just be a veneer on top of the business operation. You have to have people who can make sense out of it and apply it."[55]

Edgar Schein, who is probably most closely associated with the study of organizational culture, defines it as

> . . . a pattern of basic assumptions—invented, discovered, or developed by a given group as it learns to cope with its problems of external adaptation and internal integration—that has worked well enough to be considered valuable and, therefore, to be taught to new members as the correct way to perceive, think, and feel in relation to those problems.[56]

More recently, Joanne Martin emphasizes the differing perspectives of cultures in organizations. She notes:

> As individuals come into contact with organizations, they come into contact with dress norms, stories people tell about what goes on, the organization's formal rules and procedures, its formal codes of behavior, rituals, tasks, pay systems, jargon, and jokes only understood by insiders, and so on. These elements are some of the manifestations of organizational culture.[57]

However, she adds that there is another perspective of culture as well:

> When cultural members interpret the meanings of these manifestations, their perceptions, memories, beliefs, experiences, and values will vary, so interpretations will differ—even of the same phenomenon. The patterns or configurations of these interpretations, and the ways they are enacted, constitute culture.[58]

In other words, organizational culture is quite complex. Although there are a number of problems and disagreements associated with the conceptualization of organizational culture, most definitions, including the preceding, recognize the importance of shared norms and values that guide organizational participants' behavior. In fact, there is research evidence that not only are these cultural values taught to newcomers, but newcomers seek out and want to learn about their organization's culture.[59]

Organizational culture has a number of important characteristics. Some of the most readily agreed upon are the following:

1. *Observed behavioral regularities.*   When organizational participants interact with one another, they use common language, terminology, and rituals related to deference and demeanor.
2. *Norms.*   Standards of behavior exist, including guidelines on how much work to do, which in many organizations come down to "Do not do too much; do not do too little."
3. *Dominant values.*   There are major values that the organization advocates and expects the participants to share. Typical examples are high product quality, low absenteeism, and high efficiency.
4. *Philosophy.*   There are policies that set forth the organization's beliefs about how employees and/or customers are to be treated.
5. *Rules.*   There are strict guidelines related to getting along in the organization. Newcomers must learn those "ropes" in order to be accepted as full-fledged members of the group.
6. *Organizational climate.*   This is an overall "feeling" that is conveyed by the physical layout, the way participants interact, and the way members of the organization conduct themselves with customers or other outsiders.

Each of these characteristics has controversies surrounding it and varying degrees of research support. For example, there is controversy in the academic literature over the similarities and differences between organizational culture and organizational climate. However, there is empirical support for some of the characteristics, such as the important role that physical layout plays in organizational culture. Here is a real-world illustration:

> Nike Inc. serves as an excellent example of a company that successfully revealed its corporate culture through corporate design. Set on 74 sprawling acres amid the pine groves of Beaverton, Oregon, the Nike World campus exudes the energy, youth and vitality that have become synonymous with Nike's products. The campus is almost a monument to Nike's corporate values: the production of quality goods and, of course, fitness. Included in the seven-building campus is an athletic club with a track, weight rooms, aerobic studios, tennis, racquetball and squash courts, and a basketball court.[60]

The six characteristics of culture are not intended to be all-inclusive. Table 4.3 shows a list of the most-admired firms in the world. A recent study examined why companies were rated as most and least admired. Statistical analysis was conducted that compared the findings from a subjective opinion survey of reputation with what one might expect perceptions to be if they are based solely on financial performance. The financial measures that correlated most closely with the opinion of a firm's "reputation" were, in order, 10-year annual return to shareholders, profits as a percent of assets, total profits, and stock market value.[61] As the head of Coca-Cola, one of the most admired companies for several years in a row, declared: "I get paid to make the owners of Coca-Cola Co. increasingly wealthy with each passing day. Everything else is just fluff."[62] In other words, the importance of bottom-line financial performance remains an

TABLE 4.3   The World's Most-Admired Companies

Rank	Company	Industry
1	General Electric	Electronics, electrical equipment
2	Microsoft	Computers
3	Coca-Cola	Beverages
4	Intel	Computers
5	Berkshire Hathaway	Insurance: P&C
6	IBM	Computers
7	Wal-Mart	Retailers: general and specialist
8	Cisco Systems	Electronics, electrical equipment
9	Dell Computer	Computers
10	Merck	Pharmaceuticals
11	Lucent Technologies	Electronics, electrical equipment
12	AT&T	Telecommunications
13	Pfizer	Pharmaceuticals
14	Sony	Electronics, electrical equipment
15	Ford Motor	Motor vehicles
16	Toyota Motor	Motor vehicles
17	Johnson & Johnson	Pharmaceuticals
18	Procter & Gamble	Soaps, cosmetics
19	American Express	Securities, diversified financials
20	Home Depot	Retailers: general and specialist
21	Walt Disney	Entertainment
22	Southwest Airlines	Airlines
23	Hewlett-Packard	Computers
24	DaimlerChrysler	Motor vehicles
25	Citigroup	Securities, diversified financials

Source: Jeremy Kahn, "The World's Most Admired Companies," *Fortune,* October 11, 1999, p. 268.

important characteristic of corporate culture. However, as *Fortune* noted with a recent most-admired list, leadership on a global scale is really the key to being selected year after year. For example, in longtime winner GE's corporate culture, this leadership is synonymous with performance. As legendary chairman Jack Welch declared, "You've got to prove yourself every day."[63]

Uniformity of Culture

A common misconception is that an organization has a uniform culture. However, at least as anthropology uses the concept, it is probably more accurate to treat organizations "as if" they had a uniform culture. "All organizations 'have' culture in the sense that they are embedded in specific societal cultures and are part of them."[64] According to this view, an organizational culture is a common perception held by the organization's members. Everyone in the organization would have to share this perception. However, all may not do so to the same degree. As a result, there can be a dominant culture as well as subcultures throughout a typical organization.

A *dominant culture* is a set of core values shared by a majority of the organization's members. For example, most employees at Southwest Airlines seem to subscribe to such values as hard work, company loyalty, and the need for customer service. Southwest employees take to heart cultural values such as: irreverence is okay; it's okay to be yourself; have fun at work; take the competition seriously, but not yourself; and do whatever it takes for the customer.[65] Table 4.4 summarizes the FUNdamentals that are the core of the Southwest cultural values that are taught to the 25,000 associates who go through its

TABLE 4.4   The Southwest Airlines Core Cultural Values

Hire for attitudes, Train for skill.	The company deliberately looks for applicants with a positive attitude who will promote fun in the workplace and have the desire to "color outside the lines."
Do it Better, Faster, Cheaper.	Cost control is a personal responsibility for employees at Southwest and is incorporated into all training programs.
Deliver positively outrageous customer service (POS) to both internal and external customers!	The Southwest philosophy? Put your employees first and they will take care of the customers.
Walk a mile in someone else's shoes.	For example, a pilot works with ramp agents for a full day; a reservationist works in the University for People; a customer service agent helps the skycaps. And President Herb Kelleher frequently passes out peanuts and serves drinks on flights. He even helps the baggage handlers load and unload on holidays.
Take accountability and ownership.	A great value is placed on taking initiative, thinking for yourself, even if that means going against something in the policy manual. For instance, employees have been known to take stranded passengers back to their own homes in emergencies.
Celebrate and let your hair down.	Chili cook-offs, lavish Halloween productions, and Christmas parties in July are all tools for motivating people. When people have fun on the job, their productivity and performance improve.
Celebrate your mistakes as well as your triumphs.	Turning failures into personal growth is part of celebrating mistakes, a philosophy that encourages trying new ideas without the fear of repercussions.
Keep the corporate culture alive and well.	Members of the culture committee visit regularly at stations all across the country, infusing the corporate culture, reiterating the company's history and motivating employees to maintain the spirit that made the airline great.

Source: Adapted from Anne Bruce, "Southwest: Back to the FUNdamentals," *HR Focus,* March 1997, p. 11.

corporate University for People every year. At Hewlett-Packard, most of the employees share a concern for product innovativeness, product quality, and responsiveness to customer needs. At Wal-Mart stores, the associates—a term Wal-Mart uses for its employees that is very symptomatic of its culture—share a concern for customer service, hard work, and company loyalty. Those who work for Disney are: in the show, not on the job; wearing costumes, not uniforms; on stage or backstage, not at positions or workstations; cast members, not employees. When Disney cast members are presented with the riddle: "Ford makes cars, Sony makes TVs, Microsoft makes software, what does Disney make?"—all respond, "Disney makes people happy!"[66] These values create a dominant culture in these organizations that helps guide the day-to-day behavior of employees.

Important, but often overlooked, are the subcultures in an organization.[67] A *subculture* is a set of values shared by a minority, usually a small minority, of the organization's members. Subcultures typically are a result of problems or experiences that are shared by members of a department or unit. For example, even though GE has one of the most dominant overall corporate cultures of being boundaryless between the highly diversified divisions (e.g., ranging from power generation to media, plastics, financial services, aircraft engines, locomotives, medical equipment, and lighting and appliances), each also has a distinctive subculture. GE Capital, now contributing more than 40 percent of GE's total earnings, has a distinctive culture compared to the high-tech manufacturing cultures of aircraft engines and gas turbines.[68]

Subcultures can weaken and undermine an organization if they are in conflict with the dominant culture and/or the overall objectives. Successful firms, however, find that this is not always the case. Most subcultures are formed to help the members of a particular group deal with the specific day-to-day problems with which they are confronted. The members may also support many, if not all, of the core values of the dominant culture. In the case of GE, the success of the company is their "social architecture," which pulls the subcultures all together. As Jack Welch states, "GE is greater than the sum of its parts because of the intellectual capacity that is generated in the businesses and the sharing that goes on of that learning and the rapid action on that learning."[69]

CREATING AND MAINTAINING A CULTURE

Some organizational cultures may be the direct, or at least indirect, result of actions taken by the founders. However, this is not always the case. Sometimes founders create weak cultures, and if the organization is to survive, a new top manager must be installed who will sow the seeds for the necessary strong culture. Thomas Watson, Sr. of IBM is a good example. When he took over the CTR Corporation, it was a small firm manufacturing computing, tabulating, and recording equipment. Through his dominant personality and the changes he made at the firm, Watson created a culture that propelled IBM to be one of the biggest and best companies in the world. However, IBM's problems several years ago also were largely attributed to its outdated culture.[70] After Watson and his son, the leaders of IBM made some minor changes and modifications that had little impact and eventually left the company in bad shape. However, in recent years IBM, under the leadership of Lewis Gerstner, launched into a bold new strategy that changed IBM from top to bottom. Mr. Gerstner became convinced that "all the cost-cutting in the world will be unable to save IBM unless it upends the way it does business."[71] This cultural change at IBM has led to an outstanding turnaround. By the turn of the new millennium IBM was a top 10 most-admired company in the world and rated at the very top in international know-how.[72]

IBM is an example of an organization wherein a culture must be changed because the environment changes and the previous core cultural values are not in step with those needed for survival. IBM competitor Apple Computer is another good example. When Steve Jobs and his partner started Apple, they wanted to create a culture in which people could be creative, work on projects that interested them, and turn out a product that would be innovative. However, as they began broadening their horizons and trying to appeal to both the educational and the business market, the firm began to run into trouble. Its culture was not designed to compete in an increasingly cutthroat market. Steve Jobs was a thinker and creator, not an organizer and a manager. Apple began to lose money. A change in leadership and culture was needed. Jobs left Apple and directed his talents to starting a new venture, Next, Inc. Interestingly, Apple is still struggling, and several years ago the company brought Jobs back in an attempt to get things turned around. The following sections take a close look at how organizational cultures get started, maintained, and changed.

How Organizational Cultures Start

Although organizational cultures can develop in a number of different ways, the process usually involves some version of the following steps:

1. A single person (founder) has an idea for a new enterprise.
2. The founder brings in one or more other key people and creates a core group that shares a common vision with the founder. That is, all in this core group believe that

the idea is a good one, is workable, is worth running some risks for, and is worth the investment of time, money, and energy that will be required.

3. The founding core group begins to act in concert to create an organization by raising funds, obtaining patents, incorporating, locating space, building, and so on.

4. At this point, others are brought into the organization, and a common history begins to be built.[73]

Most of today's successful corporate giants in all industries basically followed these steps. Three well-known representative examples are Motorola, McDonald's, and Wal-Mart.

- *Motorola.*   Paul V. Galvin started the company in 1928. The founding product, a battery eliminator, was already on its way to total obsolescence in the first year of the firm. The founder had to have a new product within a year or two to survive. This constant renewal has become a core cultural value for Motorola. At age seven, Robert Galvin accompanied his father on business trips, and in 1940 Robert began working full-time for Motorola. In 1956 Bob Galvin became president and in 1964, chairman and CEO. He is given credit for being the architect for Motorola's quality efforts that resulted in a Malcolm Baldrige National Quality Award in 1988. Galvin described the cultural values of quality and customer service as follows: "The paramount idiom in our company (and it's not different than in a lot of other companies) is total customer satisfaction. And total in our case means total. It doesn't mean a lot, it doesn't mean best in class. It means everything."[74] Such cultural values have made Motorola a quality leader. The Galvins, father and son, have contributed much to this success. Characteristically, however, Bob Galvin noted: "Motorola is a thousand times bigger than when I came in as a kid. . . . We all made it happen. I helped a little."[75]

- *McDonald's.*   Ray Kroc worked for many years as a salesperson for a food supplier (Lily Tulip Cup). He learned how retail food operations were conducted. He also had an entrepreneurial streak and began a sideline business with a partner. They sold multimixers, machines that were capable of mixing up to six frozen shakes at a time. One day Kroc received a large order for multimixers from the McDonald brothers. The order intrigued Kroc, and he decided to look in on the operation the next time he was in their area. When he did, Kroc became convinced that the McDonald's fast-food concept would sweep the nation. He bought the rights to franchise McDonald's units and eventually bought out the brothers. At the same time, he built the franchise on four basic concepts: quality, cleanliness, service, and price. In order to ensure that each unit offers the customer the best product at the best price, franchisees are required to attend McDonald University, where they are taught how to manage their business. Here they learn the McDonald cultural values and the proper way to run the franchise. This training ensures that franchisees all over the world are operating their units in the same way. Kroc died a number of years ago, but the culture he left behind is still very much alive in McDonald's franchises across the globe. In fact, new employees receive videotaped messages from the late Mr. Kroc. Some of the more interesting of his pronouncements that reflect and carry on his values are his thoughts on cleanliness: "If you've got time to lean, you've got time to clean." About the competition he says: "If they are drowning to death, I would put a hose in their mouth." And on expanding he declares: "When you're green, you grow; when you're ripe, you rot."[76] So even though he has not been involved in the business for many years, his legacy lives on. Even his office at corporate headquarters is preserved as a museum, his reading glasses untouched in their leather case on the desk.

- *Wal-Mart.* Sam Walton, founder of Wal-Mart Stores, Inc., opened his first Wal-Mart store in 1962. Focusing on the sale of discounted name-brand merchandise in small-town markets, he began to set up more and more stores in the Sun Belt. At the same time, he began developing effective inventory control systems and marketing techniques. Today, Wal-Mart has not only become the largest retailer but also one of the biggest firms in the world. Although Sam died several years ago, his legacy and cultural values continue. For example, Walton himself stressed, and the current management staff continues to emphasize, the importance of encouraging associates to develop new ideas that will increase their store's efficiency. If a policy does not seem to be working, the company quickly changes it. Executives continually encourage associates to challenge the current system and look for ways to improve it. Those who do these things are rewarded; those who do not perform up to expectations are encouraged to do better. Today, Walton's founding values continue to permeate the organization. To make sure the cultural values get out to all associates, the company has a communication network worthy of the Pentagon. It includes everything from a six-channel satellite system to a private air force of numerous planes. Everyone is taught this culture and is expected to operate according to the core cultural values of hard work, efficiency, and customer service.

Although the preceding stories of cultural development are well known, in recent years the dot-com and high tech company lore is receiving most attention. Some, like Jeff Bezos's founding and cultural development of Amazon.com, are in some ways similar and in some ways different to the stories of Paul Galvin at Motorola or Sam Walton at Wal-Mart. They are similar in that both started from scratch with very innovative, "out of the box" ideas to build an empire and change the way business is done. They are different in terms of speed and style. Other corporate culture stories today are not necessarily about the founders, but about those who took their company to the next level. For example, John Chambers, the CEO of Cisco, is largely credited for taking this well known high tech firm from a market capitalization of $9 billion when he took over in 1995 to being the highest-valued corporation in the world five years later and then reposition the firm when the economy began to slump. The almost $500 billion increase in stockholder value was largely attributed to his old-school cultural values such as trust, hard work, and customer focus, but as the subsequent economic downturn and the rapid decline in the stock values of Cisco brought out, being at the right place at the right time in terms of the technology environment also had had a lot to do with Cisco's initial success. After the bubble had burst for Cisco and the other high tech and especially dot-com firms, those who had the strong, but flexible, cultures were the ones that survived the roller-coaster ride of the uncertain economy in recent years. Chambers indicated such desirable organizational cultural values when he declared, "I have no love of technology for technology's sake. Only solutions for customers."[77]

Maintaining Cultures through Steps of Socialization

Once an organizational culture is started and begins to develop, there are a number of practices that can help solidify the acceptance of core values and ensure that the culture maintains itself. These practices can be described in terms of several socialization steps. Figure 4.4 illustrates the sequence of these steps.

Selection of Entry-Level Personnel. The first step is the careful selection of entry-level candidates.[78] Using standardized procedures and seeking specific traits that tie to

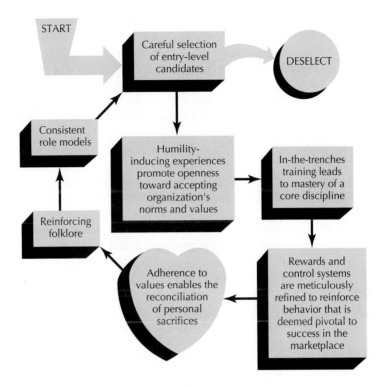

FIGURE 4.4

Steps of organizational culture socialization.

Source: Richard Pascale, "The Paradox of Corporate Culture: Reconciling Ourselves to Socialization." Copyright © by the Regents of the University of California. Reprinted from the *California Management Review,* Vol. 27, No. 2, Winter 1985, p. 38. By permission of the Regents.

effective performance, trained recruiters interview candidates and attempt to screen out those whose personal styles and values do not make a "fit" with the organization's culture. There is recent research indicating that newcomers' and their supervisors' perceptions of organization culture fit are related to organizational commitment and intention to leave the organization.[79] There is also accumulating evidence that those who have a realistic preview (called realistic job preview, or RJP) of the culture will turn out better.[80]

Placement on the Job.   The second step occurs on the job itself, after the person with a fit is hired. New personnel are subjected to a carefully orchestrated series of different experiences whose purpose is to cause them to question the organization's norms and values and to decide whether or not they can accept them. For example, many organizations with strong cultures make it a point to give newly hired personnel more work than they can handle. Sometimes these assignments are beneath the individual's abilities. At Procter & Gamble, for example, new personnel may be required to color in a sales territory map. The experience is designed to convey the message, "Although you're smart in some ways, you're in kindergarten as far as what you know about this organization." The objective is also to teach the new entrant into the culture the importance of humility. These experiences are designed to make newly hired personnel vulnerable and to cause them to move emotionally closer to their colleagues, thus intensifying group cohesiveness. Campus fraternities and the military have practiced this approach for years.

Job Mastery.   Once the initial "cultural shock" is over, the next step is mastery of one's job. This is typically done via extensive and carefully reinforced field experience. For example, Japanese firms typically put new employees through a training program for several years. As personnel move along their career path, their performance is evaluated, and additional responsibilities are assigned on the basis of progress. Quite often companies establish a step-by-step approach to this career plan, which helps reduce efforts by the personnel to use political power or to take shortcuts in order to get ahead at a faster pace. Highly successful "Coca-Cola slowly steeps its new employees in the company culture—in this case, an understanding of the trademark's image. The people system then ensures that only Coke managers who have been thoroughly socialized into worrying about the company as a whole get to make decisions affecting the company.[81]

Measuring and Rewarding Performance.   The next step of the socialization process consists of meticulous attention to measuring operational results and to rewarding individual performance. These systems are comprehensive and consistent, and they focus on those aspects of the business that are most crucial to competitive success and to corporate values. For example, at Procter & Gamble there are three factors that are considered most important: building volume, building profit, and making changes that increase effectiveness or add satisfaction to the job. Operational measures are used to track these three factors, and performance appraisals are tied to milestones. Promotions and merit pay are determined by success in each of these critical areas. Motorola personnel are taught to adhere to the core cultural values through careful monitoring of team performance and through continual training programs. Typically, in companies with a strong culture, those who violate cultural norms, such as overzealousness against the competition or harsh handling of a subordinate, are sent to the "penalty box." This typically involves a lateral move to a less-desirous location. For example, a branch manager in Chicago might be given a nebulous staff position at headquarters in Newark. This individual is now off-track, which can slow his or her career progress.

Adherence to Important Values.   The next step involves careful adherence to the firm's most important values. Identification with these values helps employees reconcile personal sacrifices brought about by their membership in the organization. They learn to accept these values and to trust the organization not to do anything that would hurt them. As Pascale observes: "Placing one's self 'at the mercy' of an organization imposes real costs. There are long hours of work, missed weekends, bosses one has to endure, criticism that seems unfair, job assignments and rotations that are inconvenient or undesirable."[82] However, the organization attempts to overcome these costs by connecting the sacrifices to higher human values such as serving society with better products and/or services. Today's firms in the global economy must give special attention to cultural differences around the globe, but maintain the core values. For example, when Wal-Mart Stores entered the German market a few years ago, it took along the "cheer"—Give me a W! Give me an A!, etc. Who's Number One? The customer!—which went over as well with the German associates as it did with their counterparts in the United States. However, the cultural value of greeting any customer within a 10-foot radius did not. German employees and shoppers were not comfortable with this Wal-Mart custom, and it was dropped from the German stores.[83]

Reinforcing the Stories and Folklore.   The next step involves reinforcing organizational folklore. This entails keeping alive stories that validate the organization's culture and way of doing things. The folklore helps explain why the organization does things a particular way. One of the most common forms of folklore is stories with morals the enterprise wants to reinforce. For example, Leonard Riggio, the CEO of Barnes &

Noble, often tells stories about his childhood experiences in Brooklyn and in particular his father's stint as a boxer. These often-told stories have been a great help to communicate a populist culture that needed to shed its elitist past. Also, Bill Hewlett of Hewlett-Packard is known for the often-told story of him using a bolt cutter to remove a lock that he encountered on the supply room. He left a note behind instructing that the door never be locked again to forever communicate the important cultural value of trust at H-P.[84]

Recognition and Promotion.   The final step is the recognition and promotion of individuals who have done their jobs well and who can serve as role models to new people in the organization. By pointing out these people as winners, the organization encourages others to follow their example. Role models in strong-culture firms are regarded as the most powerful ongoing training program of all. Morgan Stanley, the financial services firm, chooses role models on the basis of energy, aggressiveness, and team play. Procter & Gamble looks for people who exhibit extraordinary consistency in such areas as toughmindedness, motivational skills, energy, and the ability to get things done through others.[85] There is considerable research evidence that recognition can serve as a powerful reinforcer,[86] and thus those exhibiting cultural values that are given either formal recognition or even one-on-one social attention/recognition from relevant others can build and sustain the organizational culture.[87]

Changing Organizational Culture

Sometimes an organization determines that its culture has to be changed. For example, the current environmental context has undergone drastic change and either the organization must adapt to these new conditions or it may not survive. In fact, as Chapters 1 and 2 pointed out, it is no longer sufficient just to react to change. Today, as was pointed out in the earlier discussion in this chapter about organizational learning, organizations must have a culture that learns and anticipates change. New product development and information technology is changing so rapidly that any examples would be soon out of date. However, if the appropriate organization culture is in place, then such rapid change can be welcomed and accommodated with as little disruption and as few problems as possible. Perhaps one of the best examples of an organization culture built around change in innovative product development is 3M. Its culture supported its long-standing competency with sticky tape but also allowed innovative ventures into magnetic tape, film, coated abrasives, and the famous Post-it notes and now related products.[88]

Even though some firms such as 3M had a culture in place to anticipate change, moving to a new culture or changing old cultures can be quite difficult: a case can even be made that it really can't be done successfully. Predictable obstacles include entrenched skills, staffs, relationships, roles, and structures that work together to reinforce traditional cultural patterns. In addition, powerful stakeholders such as unions, management, or even customers may support the existing culture. The problems are compounded by the cultural clash that is the rule rather than exception in mergers and acquisitions (M&As).

The Case of Mergers and Acquisitions.   Although M&As were thought to have peaked in the 1980s, they have again become very common because the wide divergence in stock-market values between firms and globalization have left a climate for both friendly buyouts and hostile takeovers.[89] Besides the financial implications of M&As, the often-slighted or even ignored organizational culture implications can be dramatic. As one veteran of a number of recent M&As concluded about the cultural side of mergers: (1) you can't do too much, and (2) too little will be done. In the heat of the deal, he says, "people issues, as real as they are, become obscured."[90] The clash between the two cultures in a merger or acquisition can be focused into three major areas:

1. *Structure.* These factors from the two cultures include the size, age, and history of the two firms; the industry in which the partners come from and now reside; the geographic locations; and whether products and/or services are involved.
2. *Politics.* Where does the power and managerial decision making really reside? Corporate cultures range from autocratic extremes to total employee empowerment, and how this plays out among the partners will be important to cultural compatibility.
3. *Emotions.* The personal feelings, the "cultural contract" that individuals have bought into to guide their day-to-day thoughts, habits, attitudes, commitment, and patterns of daily behavior. These emotions will be a major input into the clash or compatibility of the two cultures.[91]

The potential (high probability) cultural clash from M&As will be greatly compounded when the partners are from different countries. With globalization now a reality (see Chapter 2), cross-border alliances are commonplace. Announcements of megamergers such as DaimlerChrysler, British Petroleum-Amoco, and Deutsche Bank-Bankers Trust reach the headlines, but the cultural clash aftermath seldom, if at all, is discussed. The highly visible DaimlerChrysler merger problems with advertising[92] and U.S.-government-sponsored research aimed at fuel efficiency and cleaner cars[93] is given attention, but the cultural issues are not given as much attention. Yet, the day-to-day cultural clashes at all levels are the reality. For example, the Mercedes-Benz plant in Vance, Alabama, represents the merger in microcosm. The German "wunderkind" plant manager deliberately selected German, U.S., and Canadian managers (some with Japanese auto firm experience) for his team. They have clashed not just over the operations system, but also on more subtle but explosive cultural issues such as image and decorum.[94] These are being worked out, but guidelines and help are still needed for meeting the challenge of managing the cultural change on both sides. More recently, as the Application Example: Cultural Clash of DaimlerChrysler vs. Mitsubishi indicates, DaimlerChrysler may not yet have learned their lesson.

The Case of Emerging Relationship Enterprises.   Today's networked global environment is going beyond formal M&As with what are being called "relationship enterprises."[95] Somewhat like virtual organization designs discussed earlier in the chapter, these relationship enterprises consist of a global network of independent companies that act as a single company with a common mission. Examples include the following:

- The aerospace industry at the turn of the century is controlled by two networks— Boeing (based in the U.S.) and Airbus (France). Importantly, each of these relationship enterprises consists of more than 100 partners around the world.
- In the telecommunications industry, the Global One joint venture, led by Sprint, Deutsche Telekom, and France Telecom, serves 65 countries and functions as one relationship enterprise to serve the global telecom needs of many corporations.

Cultural Clash of DaimlerChrysler vs. Mitsubishi

Jürgen E. Schrempp, the *über*-boss of car giant DaimlerChrysler, is a guy who likes to be in charge. He's the one, after all, who turned an equal partnership with Chrysler into an outright acquisition. So many investors figured it was just a matter of time before Schrempp tightened his hold on Mitsubishi Motors Corp., the cash-strapped Japanese carmaker that recently sold a third of its shares to DaimlerChrysler.

Sure enough, when Mitsubishi was assailed for covering up decades of customer complaints, Schrempp pounced. Under the new terms of the partnership, DaimlerChrysler is in the driver's seat—where it likes to be. Mitsubishi Motors President Katsuhiko Kawasoe is stepping down, and the new chief operating officer will be a Daimler veteran, Rolf Eckrodt, 58, chief of the Adtranz rail subsidiary. "This is developing quite positively for us," says one DaimlerChrysler executive. It's widely assumed that Eckrodt will be calling the shots: Germans 1, Japanese 0.

Well, maybe not. Look closely at Daimler's new commitment to Mitsubishi, and it's easy to see plenty of problems that could yet plague the relationship. It may turn out that this is one conquest Daimler could do without.

For starters, the revised alliance turns the rationale for the deal on its head. When DaimlerChrysler first announced the alliance in March, it said it expected to reap the benefits of Mitsubishi's know-how in manufacturing small cars at low cost. The idea was to use Mitsubishi as a convenient manufacturing partner for a new line of small cars, which would be sold under Daimler's Smart brand around the world. Daimler's purpose was not to overhaul Mitsubishi the way Renault's Carlos Ghosn has dramatically reshaped Nissan.

But now, Eckrodt will be leading what looks like a rescue mission. Eckrodt, whose latest achievement has been closing down Adtranz facilities to prepare the unprofitable unit for a sale to Bombardier Inc., will take along dozens of experts in finance, quality control, and manufacturing. And the Germans will have to get their hands dirty deciding Mitsubishi's car strategy, including the future of its small cars.

To some investors, this looks like a problem, given Daimler's limited success with its own line of small cars. "By their own admission, DaimlerChrysler has been unable to make money out of the A-Class and the Smart," says auto analyst Christopher Will at Lehman Brothers. "And now they're supposed to know how to run a small-car business?"

- In the airline industry, United, Lufthansa, SAS, Varig, Thai Airways, and others have formed into a relationship enterprise called Star Alliance. They provide the international traveler with seamless service anywhere on the planet and share systems, marketing, in-country operations, schedules, and frequent flier miles—everything except crews.[96]

In the near future such relationship enterprises will become common in more traditional industries such as chemicals, textiles, and food, as well as new frontier industries such as biotech and memory. The reason that this loose network of alliances is the trend over more formal M&As is because of legal terms (by law some countries do not allow majority purchase of their firms by foreigners), but mainly because of political nationalism and organizational cultural values. Pride and pragmatic needs are driving this new form of global alliance, but the perspective and management of the organizational cultures in this new relationship is a challenge. Issues such as trust, communication, and negotiation skills become very relevant and important to success. The organizations and managers in the global relations "must learn to communicate across the cultural divide; each must understand that the other perceives and interacts in a fundamentally different way."[97] Importantly, three-fourths of companies believe their alliances failed because of an incompatibility of country and corporate cultures.[98]

Guidelines for Change.   Despite the significant barriers and resistance to change, organizational cultures can be managed and changed over time. This attempt to change culture can take many different forms. Simple guidelines such as the following can be helpful:[99]

1. Assess the current culture.
2. Set realistic goals that impact on the bottom line.
3. Recruit outside personnel with industry experience, so that they are able to interact well with the organizational personnel.
4. Make changes from the top down, so that a consistent message is delivered from all management team members.
5. Include employees in the culture change process, especially when making changes in rules and processes.
6. Take out all trappings that remind the personnel of the previous culture.
7. Expect to have some problems and find people who would rather move than change with the culture and, if possible, take these losses early.
8. Move quickly and decisively to build momentum and to defuse resistance to the new culture.
9. Stay the course by being persistent.

Also, organizations attempting to change their culture must be careful not to abandon their roots and blindly abandon their core, but distinctive, competencies. For example, it is generally recognized that the reason "New Coke" failed was because it broke away from the tried-but-true Coca-Cola traditional culture. Pragmatically changing an organizational culture affects almost every aspect of the business. IBM, discussed earlier under creating and maintaining a corporate culture, remains the best example of a firm that has successfully undergone such a cultural change.

In the 1980s, the IBM "Big Blue" culture was recognized as the best in the world. Then, with the advent of PCs, the era of mainframes which IBM dominated was over. However, IBM was slow to recognize the need for cultural change to adapt to the PC market environment. Starting in 1991 and over the next four years, the computer giant lost $25 billion, the most money lost in the history of American business. IBM tried incremental changes to try to remake itself, but it wasn't until Lou Gerstner realized that total cultural change was necessary that IBM got back on track once again to be the premier firm that it is today.

Under Gerstner's leadership, IBM's culture became more customer oriented, faster at decision making, and quicker to apply the new technologies invented in its traditionally strong research and development labs.[100] As has been pointed out, the lesson from IBM for cultural change is that it takes patience, vigilance, and changing the parts of the culture that managers can control in the relatively short run: behavior and symbolic artifacts such as physical design and layout, dress codes, and who benefits (or doesn't) from company benefits and perks (e.g., stock options, parking spaces, and other such rewards and privileges).[101] In other words, the study of organizational behavior in general, and behavioral change management in particular, and reward systems (covered in the next chapter) play a big role in changing an organization's culture.

Summary

Organization theory is presented from the perspective of systems, information processing, contingency, ecological, and learning approaches. Systems theory emphasizes the impact of the external environment. The information processing approach emphasizes the importance of information flows in an organization to cope with internal differentiation and external environmental uncertainty. Contingency theory gives specific attention to adapting to the environment by relating it to organization structure and design. The ecological theory assumes environmental determinism; there is a natural selection and replacement of organizations. The most recent theoretical foundation for the learning organization draws on systems theory and emphasizes the importance of not only adaptive learning but also generative learning, leading to creativity, innovation, and staying ahead of change.

Modern organization designs are a marked departure from the classical models. The horizontal, network, and virtual organization designs have emerged to better meet the needs for flexibility and change in the new environment.

The second half of this chapter on the organization context is concerned with organizational culture. It is a pattern of basic assumptions that are taught to new personnel as the correct way to perceive, think, and act on a day-to-day basis. Some of the important characteristics of organizational culture are observed behavioral regularities, norms, dominant values, philosophy, rules, and organizational climate. Although everyone in an organization will share the organization's culture, not all may do so to the same degree. There can be a dominant culture, but also a number of subcultures. A dominant culture is a set of core values that are shared by a majority of the organization's members. A subculture is a set of values shared by a small percentage of the organization's members.

A culture typically is created by a founder or top-level manager who forms a core group that shares a common vision. This group acts in concert to create the cultural values, norms, and climate necessary to carry on this vision. In maintaining this culture, enterprises typically carry out several steps such as the following: careful selection of entry-level candidates; on-the-job experiences to familiarize the personnel with the organization's culture; mastery of one's job; meticulous attention to measuring operational results and to rewarding individual performance; careful adherence to the organization's most important values; a reinforcing of organizational stories and folklore; and, finally, recognition and promotion of individuals who have done their jobs well and who can serve as role models to new personnel in the organization.

In some cases organizations find that they must change their culture in order to remain competitive and even survive in their environment. The cultural change process at IBM demonstrates how this may be successfully accomplished.

ENDING WITH META-ANALYTIC RESEARCH FINDINGS

OB PRINCIPLE: Organizational configurations affect organizational performance.

Meta-Analysis Results: [33 studies; 40 organizations; $d = .55$] *On average, there is a **65 percent probability** that an identified organizational configuration will better predict performance of included organizations than if no configuration is identified and utilized.* Moderator analyses revealed that organizations' configurations contributed more to the explanation of performance to the extent that studies used broad definitions of configuration, single-industry samples, and longitudinal designs.

Conclusion: Organizational configurations are groups of firms sharing a common profile of organizational structural characteristics. The Miles and Snow typology describes four such configurations—defender, prospector, analyzer, and reactor. Each of these examine the relationship between strategy and structure. At the heart of configuration research is the relationship that firms have with their environments. Specifically, organizations that exist in environments where goals are attainable, resources are acquirable, internal processes are growing and thriving, and stakeholders are satisfied will be more effective than those that do not have such a configuration.

Source: Adapted from David J. Ketchen Jr., James G. Combs, Craig J. Russell, Chris Shook, Michelle A. Dean, Janet Runge, Franz T. Lohrke, Stefanie E. Naumann, Dawn Ebe Haptonstahl, Robert Baker, Brenden A. Beckstein, Charles Handler, Heather Honig and Stephen Lamoureux, "Organizational Configuration and Performance: A Meta-Analysis," *Academy of Management Journal,* Vol. 40, No. 1, 1997, pp. 223–240.

Questions for Discussion and Review

1. What was Chester Barnard's contribution to organization theory?
2. How does the open-systems theory differ from the information processing, contingency, ecological, and learning approaches? How does the open-systems concept apply to organizations? How does the contingency concept apply to organizations? How does the ecological concept apply to organizations? How does the learning concept apply to organizations?
3. How does a learning organization differ from a traditional organization?
4. Briefly define the horizontal, network, and virtual organization designs. How do these differ from the classical design? How do they better meet the challenges of the new environment?
5. What is meant by the term *organizational culture?* Define it and give some examples of its characteristics. What role may financial performance play in a firm's culture?
6. How does a dominant culture differ from a subculture? In your answer be sure to define both terms.
7. How do organizational cultures develop? What four steps commonly occur?
8. How do organizations go about maintaining their cultures? What steps are involved? Describe them.

Internet Exercise: The Structure and Culture of Organizations

As this chapter has discussed, there are dramatic differences in both the structure and culture of organizations. In part, the culture of an organization is determined by the structure. Some organizations tend to be hierarchical and rigid, whereas others are horizontal and flexible. Visit some corporate websites that describe various structural design components and corporate values. You can choose a specific firm such as General Electric or Dell Computers or search under "organization design" and/or "organization culture" to see where it leads you. Try to determine what the company's structure and culture may be.

1. Compare structure and culture of two or more firms. Which would you prefer to work for?
2. What other issues do the structure and culture have for other topics of organizational behavior (motivation, reward systems, etc.)?

REAL CASE:
Mike the Knife

Michael Treschow needs a second act. In his three years as CEO of Stockholm-based Electrolux Group, the world's biggest household appliance maker has undergone a radical restructuring. Faced with a bloated balance sheet and poorly managed acquisitions, Treschow has divested noncore assets worth $21 billion a year in sales, eliminated 14,500 jobs—10 percent of the Swedish company's workforce—and closed 27 plants and 50 warehouses. "Mike the Knife" is 57-year-old Treschow's nickname now, and in many ways it bespeaks a job well done. But what do you do with a knife when the cutting's all finished?

If Treschow isn't asking that question, a lot of investors are. They worry that Treschow may simply have run out of moves. Treschow's restructuring more or less complete, wringing out more cost savings isn't an option.

For many investors and industry watchers, Treschow has a clear path forward, and they wish he would take it. While Treschow is committed to new products and more cost-cutting, they believe acquisition is the smarter course. Analysts and investment bankers have been speculating for months that Treschow could spend up to $4 billion to acquire Maytag Corp., a rival appliance maker based in Newton, Iowa. Maytag, beset with sales and profitability problems, has seen its stock drop by more than half in recent months.

Treschow is not giving away his intentions toward Maytag. At least for now, Treschow says, his big push is toward Internet-savvy appliances that will take Electrolux from simple white boxes to high-margin, high-tech products. Electrolux and Ericcson now have a joint venture to supply networked apartments, with Net-connected appliances. In the works is Smartfridge, which allows consumers to surf the Net, replenish groceries, and watch TV via a screen in the door, and a robotic vacuum cleaner.

Nifty stuff. But in the long term, analysts say, a deal is the better option.

1. Do you agree with the downsizing of this company? Were any other options available?
2. What option do you think the company should now take? Do you agree with the financial analysts?
3. From an organizational behavior perspective, what do you think the company should do? What are some design and cultural issues?

REAL CASE:
A Fresh Face to
Shake Up the Culture

Warren E. Buffett is one of the most patient investors. But even he has had enough of the alarming decline of Gillette Co. Recently, Buffett and other board members asked CEO Michael C. Hawley to resign and installed 32-year company veteran Edward F. DeGraan as acting CEO. Now the question is where the board will find a permanent chief. Buffett is signaling a strong desire for an outsider.

This would be a radical step for Gillette, which has one of Corporate America's most insular cultures. But that very culture—though it provided the basis of Gillette's success for years—now bears as much blame for the company's troubles as any one individual. After two years of stagnant sales, repeatedly missed earnings forecasts, and a stock that has been cut in half, investors have lost confidence that the executives long steeped in Gillette's way of doing business will be able to bring needed change. "What Gillette needs now is some shaking up," argues Harvard Business School professor Rosabeth Moss Kanter.

Those who've risen to the top have invariably succeeded because they are masters at the growth formula that served Gillette so well for decades. Honed in the shaving market, which the company has dominated for nearly a century, the formula relies on the enormous engineering expertise to develop superior products for which Gillette charges a premium.

Problem is, although this formula still works in the blade business, "it clearly isn't working on some of their other categories," says Don Stuart, partner at marketing consultants Cannondale Associates. Exhibit A is Duracell, where Gillette rolled out a premium-priced battery, but still lost market share and saw margins fall.

The even deeper problem is that it's virtually the only way Gillette executives know how to do business. This cultural mind-set has made it difficult for insiders to find new solutions. "They need a large infusion of fresh blood," says Stuart.

The key challenge for the next CEO is to invent "a next-generation business design that will build a foundation for another 10 years of growth," says Adrian Slywotzky, a business strategy expert at Mercer Management Consulting. And that will likely require "an outsider who can bring in fresh insights, especially in marketing," argues Gary Stibel, founder and principal of the New England Consulting Group.

To be sure, parachuting in a high-profile outsider doesn't always work. Just look at C. Michael Armstrong's troubles at AT&T and George M. C. Fisher's rocky reign at Eastman Kodak Co. Still, Stibel predicts there will be outstanding candidates eager to become a hero at Gillette.

1. Do you agree with Professor Kanter that "What Gillette needs now is some shaking up"?
2. How can "a next-generation business design" be helpful? What might this design be?
3. From an organizational behavior perspective, how easy will it be to change the culture of Gillette? What may be needed besides a "fresh face"?

ORGANIZATIONAL
BEHAVIOR CASE:
The Outdated
Structure

Jake Harvey has a position on the corporate planning staff of a large company in a high-technology industry. Although he has spent most of his time on long-range, strategic planning for the company, he has been appointed to a task force to reorganize the company. The president and board of directors are concerned that they are losing their competitive position in the industry because of an outdated organization structure. Being a planning expert, Jake convinced the task force that they should proceed by first determining exactly what type of structure they have now, then determining what type of environment the company faces now and in the future, and then designing the organization structure accordingly. In the first phase they discovered that the organization is currently structured along classic bureaucratic lines. In the second phase they found that they are competing in a highly dynamic, rapidly growing, and uncertain environment that requires a great deal of flexibility and response to change.

1. What type or types of organization design do you feel this task force should recommend in the third and final phase of the approach to their assignment?
2. Explain how the systems, information processing, contingency, ecological, and learning theories of organization can each contribute to the analysis of this case.
3. Do you think Jake was correct in his suggestion of how the task force should proceed? What types of problems might develop as by-products of the recommendation you made in question 1?

ORGANIZATIONAL BEHAVIOR CASE: Keeping Things the Same

Metropolitan Hospital was built two years ago and currently has a workforce of 235 people. The hospital is small, but because it is new, it is extremely efficient. The board has voted to increase its capacity from 60 to 190 beds. By this time next year, the hospital will be over three times as large as it is now in terms of both beds and personnel.

The administrator, Clara Hawkins, feels that the major problem with this proposed increase is that the hospital will lose its efficiency. "I want to hire people who are just like our current team of personnel—hardworking, dedicated, talented, and able to interact well with patients. If we triple the number of employees, I don't see how it will be possible to maintain our quality patient care. We are going to lose our family atmosphere. We will be inundated with mediocrity, and we'll end up being like every other institution in the local area—large and uncaring!"

The chairman of the board is also concerned about the effect of hiring such a large number of employees. However, he believes that Clara is overreacting. "It can't be that hard to find people who are like our current staff. There must be a lot of people out there who are just as good. What you need to do is develop a plan of action that will allow you to carefully screen those who will fit into your current organizational culture and those who will not. It's not going to be as difficult as you believe. Trust me. Everything will work out just fine."

As a result of the chairman's comments, Clara has decided that the most effective way of dealing with the situation is to develop a plan of action. She intends to meet with her administrative group and determine the best way of screening incoming candidates and then helping those who are hired to become socialized in terms of the hospital's culture. Clara has called a meeting for the day after tomorrow. At that time she intends to discuss her ideas, get suggestions from her people, and then formulate a plan of action. "We've come too far to lose it all now," she told her administrative staff assistant. "If we keep our wits about us, I think we can continue to keep Metropolitan as the showcase hospital in this region."

1. What can Clara and her staff do to select the type of entry-level candidates they want? Explain.
2. How can Clara ensure that those who are hired come to accept the core cultural values of the hospital? What steps would you recommend?
3. Could Clara use this same approach if another 200 people were hired a few years from now?

ORGANIZATIONAL BEHAVIOR CASE: Out with the Old, In with the New

The Anderson Corporation was started in 1962 as a small consumer products company. During the first 20 years the company's R&D staff developed a series of new products that proved to be very popular in the marketplace. Things went so well that the company had to add a second production shift just to keep up with the demand. During this time period the firm expanded its plant on three separate occasions. During an interview with a national magazine, the firm's founder, Paul Anderson, said, "We don't sell our products. We allocate them." This comment was in reference to the fact that the firm had only 24 salespeople and was able to garner annual revenues in excess of $62 million.

Three years ago Anderson suffered its first financial setback. The company had a net operating loss of $1.2 million. Two years ago the loss was $2.8 million, and last year it was $4.7 million. The accountant estimates that this year the firm will lose approximately $10 million.

Alarmed by this information, Citizen's Bank, the company's largest creditor, insisted that the firm make some changes and start turning things around. In response to this request, Paul Anderson agreed to step aside. The board of directors replaced him with Mary Hartmann, head of the marketing division of one of the country's largest consumer products firms.

After making an analysis of the situation, Mary has come to the conclusion that there are a number of changes that must be made if the firm is to be turned around. The three most important are as follows:

1. More attention must be given to the marketing side of the business. The most vital factor for success in the sale of the consumer goods produced by Anderson is an effective sales force.
2. There must be an improvement in product quality. Currently, 2 percent of Anderson's output is defective, as against 0.5 percent for the average firm in the industry. In the past the demand for Anderson's output was so great that quality control was not an important factor. Now it is proving to be a very costly area.
3. There must be a reduction in the number of people in the operation. Anderson can get by with two-thirds of its current production personnel and only half of its administrative staff.

Mary has not shared these ideas with the board of directors, but she intends to do so. For the moment she is considering the steps that will have to be taken in making these changes and the effect that all of this might have on the employees and the overall operation.

1. What is wrong with the old organizational culture? What needs to be done to change it?
2. Why might it be difficult for Mary to change the existing culture?
3. What specific steps does Mary need to take in changing the culture? Identify and describe at least two.

CHAPTER 5

Organizational Context: Reward Systems

Learning Objectives

Discuss the theoretical background on money as a reward.

Present the latest research on the effectiveness of pay.

Describe some of the traditional methods of administering pay.

Relate some of the latest forms of "new" pay and their value in helping attract and retain talented employees.

Explain how recognition is used as an organizational reward.

Discuss the role of benefits as organizational rewards.

Starting with Best Practice
Leader's Advice

CEO William Stavropoulos on Dow Chemical's Reward System

Stavropoulos heads up Dow Chemical, the 100-year-old company with over $20 billion in sales, 2,400 product families and services (chemicals, plastics, energy, agricultural products, and environmental services), 115 manufacturing sites in 37 countries, and 43,000 employees. He started with Dow as a research chemist and worked his way up the corporate ladder through marketing and operations to become CEO in 1995. Below he describes the monetary reward system used by this well-known company.

Q1:   *In implementing your strategy at Dow, how do people learn about things such as the value of the company and how they are going to be evaluated?*

Stavropoulos: Well, we explain our values to everyone and show them how they're going to be used in the implementation process. It's a part of the leadership training we provide to all our employees. Additionally, everyone learns what the competencies are for their jobs and how they are going to be evaluated. Moreover, if people feel that they want to move to other jobs, there are jobs continually posted throughout the company. If you get the job, great. If not, you can find out which competencies you lack and how you can get them. And when you put the implementation process in the hands of the people, there is no limit to how far they can go.

Q2:   *What type of incentive pay can a Dow employee earn in a given year?*

Stavropoulos: It varies throughout the structure. In my case, I have more money at risk than someone in middle management. My variable pay would be in the neighborhood of 99 percent, whereas a secretary's variable pay might be 6 to 10 percent. There are gradations.

Q3:   *So a typical Dow employee in a good year could earn 25 percent variable pay?*

Stavropoulos: Oh, yes.

Q4:   *You used the term "at risk." Does that mean if someone doesn't make their goals, they lose this opportunity?*

Stavropoulos: Well, not just their failure to make the goals, but the company's failure as well. For example, last year we had a good year, but I only made 30 percent of my variable pay because we didn't make all of our company's goals.

Q5:   *If a person makes his or her goals as a lab manager, for example, but the company doesn't make its overall goals, how much might the individual make under these conditions?*

Stavropoulos: Maybe 15 percent.

Q6:   *But the person doesn't have much control over the company at large. Does that make some people uneasy because they feel they are doing fine but the company is not?*

Stavropoulos: Sure, but the answer is that we are all part of this thing. So if the company doesn't succeed, everyone ends up taking less. In the final analysis, the success of the firm determines whether people are going to have a job or not. But we also think it's fair that if you do something well, you are going to get paid. For example, we have special recognition awards or SRAs for short. We can give people cash on the spot. Just this morning, there was a woman here in the building who got an award equal to 50 percent of her monthly pay.

Q7:   *Where does the money come from for these SRAs? Does each manager have a small amount of money such as $1,000 from which these funds can be drawn?*

Stavropoulos: Actually, we have a big pot and we draw from it. And it does break down by business. In fact, we probably don't use the whole thing—but quite a few people get some in the form of cash or stock.

Although reward systems are not necessarily found in the first part of organizational behavior textbooks, it is placed here for two very important reasons. First, in the social cognitive theory presented in Chapter 1 as the conceptual framework for this text, the environment variable in the triadic reciprocal interaction model (along with the personal/cognitive and organizational behavior itself) consists of both the external and organizational contexts. The last chapter covered the structural design and culture of the organization, and especially in a social cognitive approach, the reward system covers the remaining major contextual variable for organizational behavior. Specifically, in social cognitive theory, reward consequences or contingencies play an important role in organizational behavior. For example, Bandura has noted that human behavior cannot be fully understood without considering the regulatory influence of rewards.[1] Although behavioral management is not covered until the last part of the book (Chapter 16), it can be said now that the organization may have the latest technology, well-designed structures, and a visionary strategic plan, but unless the people at all levels are rewarded, all these other things may become hollow and not be carried out for performance improvement. One way to put this importance of organizational rewards as simply as possible is to remember: you get what you reward![2]

The second major reason for putting organizational reward systems up front is to emphasize the emerging importance of human capital introduced in Chapters 1 and 2. Because intellectual/human capital is now recognized as being central to knowledge management and competitive advantage in the new paradigm environment, attention must be given to rewarding this capital to sustain/retain it and leverage it.[3] The importance of reward systems in the new paradigm is often overlooked, and that is why it is included here to conclude the introductory environmental context for the study and application of organizational behavior.

Certainly the tendency with most people, and often in actual organizational practice, is to equate organizational reward systems only with money. Obviously, money is the dominant reward and will be given first and foremost attention in this chapter. The theory, research, and analysis of all the ways money can be administered by today's organizations is given detailed attention. However, this is followed by the potentially powerful, and importantly much less costly, recognition rewards system.[4] Finally, the costly, but often not effective, use of benefits is presented.

PAY: THE DOMINANT ORGANIZATIONAL REWARD

Organizations provide rewards to their personnel in order to try to motivate their performance and encourage their loyalty and retention. Organizational rewards take a number of different forms including money (salary, bonuses, incentive pay), recognition, and benefits. This first part examines money as the most dominant reward system in today's organizations.

The Theoretical Background on Money as a Reward

Money has long been viewed as a reward and, for some people, it is more important than anything else their organization can give them. Newman and Hodgetts investigated motivation in the hospitality industry, for example, and found that workers here ranked good wages at the top of their list of important work factors.[5] This was in sharp contrast to industrial workers, who ranked interesting work as first (and good wages as fifth) in importance. So the role of money as a reward will often vary by both individual and industry, but one thing is clear: money is an important reward.[6] Commenting on this, Steve Kerr, Chief Learning Officer at General Electric, recently noted that, "Nobody refuses it, nobody returns it, and people who have more than they could ever use do dreadful things to get more."[7]

Money provides a rich basis for studying behavior at work because it offers explanations for why people act as they do.[8] For example, Mitchell and Mickel have noted that money is a prime factor in the foundation of commerce, that is, people organize and start businesses to make money.[9] Money is also associated with four of the important symbolic attributes for which humans strive: achievement and recognition, status and respect, freedom and control, and power.[10] In fact, in most of the management literature dealing with money, researchers have focused on money as pay and the ways in which pay affects motivation, job attitudes, and retention. In particular, money helps people attain both physical (clothing, automobiles, houses) and psychological (status, self-esteem, a feeling of achievement) objectives. As a result, money has been of interest to organizational behavior theorists and researchers who have studied the linkages between pay and performance by seeking answers to questions such as: How much of a motivator is money? How long lasting is its effects? What are some of the most useful strategies to employ in using money as a motivator?[11]

Money has also played an integral role in helping develop theories of organizational behavior. For example, if employees are interested in money, how much effort will they expend in order to earn it, and how much is "enough"? Moreover, if people work very hard but do not receive the rewards they expect, how much of a dampening effect will this have on their future efforts? Answers to these types of questions have helped develop some of the most useful theories of motivation, which will be covered in Chapter 8.

Another important perspective on money as a reward is provided by agency theory, a relatively new approach to understanding behavior by individuals and groups both inside and outside the organization. Specifically, *agency theory* is concerned with the diverse interests and goals that are held by an organization's stakeholders (stockholders, managers, employees) and the methods by which the enterprise's reward system is used to align these interests and goals. The theory draws its name from the fact that the people who are in control of large organizations are seldom the owners; rather, in almost every case, they are agents who are responsible for representing the interests of the owners.

Agency theory seeks to explain how managers differ from owners in using pay and other forms of compensation to effectively run the organization. For example, the owners of a corporation might be very interested in increasing their own personal wealth, and so they would minimize costs and work to increase the stock value of the enterprise. In contrast, their agents, the managers, might be more interested in expending organizational resources on activities that do not directly contribute to owner wealth. Agency theory also examines the role of risk and how owners and managers may vary in their approach to risk taking. For example, owners may be risk aversive and prefer conservative courses of action that minimize their chances of loss. Managers may be greater risk takers who are willing to accept losses in return for the increased opportunity for greater profits and market share; when their decisions are incorrect, the impact may be less than it would be on the owners and thus not greatly diminish their willingness to take risks.[12] Finally, agency theory examines the differences in time horizons between owners and managers. Owners may have longer time horizons because their goal is to maximize their value over time. Managers may have much shorter time horizons because their job tenure may require good short-term results, in addition to the fact that their bonuses or merit pay may be tied closely to how well they (or the organization) performed in the last four quarters.

Agency theory provides useful insights into pay as a reward.[13] This becomes increasingly clear when research on the effectiveness of pay is examined.

Research on the Effectiveness of Pay

Despite the tendency in recent years to downgrade the importance of pay as an organizational reward, there is ample evidence that money can be positively reinforcing for most people[14] and, if the pay system is designed properly to fit the strategies,[15] can have a positive impact on individual, team, and organizational performance.[16] For example, many organizations use pay to motivate not just their upper-level executives but everyone throughout the organization. Moreover, these rewards may not always have to be immediately forthcoming. Many individuals will work extremely hard for rewards that may not be available for another 5 or 10 years. As Kerr has noted:

> . . . such attractive rewards as large salaries, profit sharing, deferred compensation, stock grants and options, executive life and liability insurance, estate planning and financial counseling, invitations to meetings in attractive locations, and permission to fly first class or use the company plane, are typically made available only to those who reach the higher organizational levels. Do such reward practices achieve the desired results? In general, yes. Residents and interns work impossible hours to become M.D.s, junior lawyers and accountants do likewise to become partners, assistant professors publish so they won't perish, and Ph.D. students perform many chores that are too depressing to recount here to obtain their doctorates.[17]

Additionally, not only is money a motivator, but the more some people get, the more they seem to want. The idea here is that once money satisfies basic needs, people can use it to get ahead, a goal that is always just out of their reach, so they strive for more. Conversely, there is evidence that shows that if an organization reduces its pay, morale may suffer. So pay may need to continue to escalate. One researcher, for example, interviewed more than 330 businesspeople and found that employee morale can be hurt by pay cuts because the employees view this is an "insult" that impacts on their self-worth and value to the organization.[18] Simply put, morale is fragile, and when employees feel they are not being treated well, this can impact on their performance and hurt the bottom line.

There is also research showing that money means different things to different people.[19] Moreover, sometimes these "individual differences" end up affecting group efforts. For example, one study examined pay and performance information among baseball players.[20] Using statistical methods to control for such things as total team payroll, team talent, and market size,[21] the data were analyzed from 1,644 players on 29 teams over a nine-year period. It was found that, all other things being equal, the greater the pay spread on a team, the more poorly the players performed. These findings led to the conclusion that pay distributions have significant negative effects on player performance.

A similar study looked at the pay ranges of baseball teams in two leagues in Japan. This study found that the team with the smallest salary spread between the highest and lowest players was in first place in its league, whereas the team with the greatest pay spread was in the middle of the rankings.[22] On the other hand, interestingly, this study did not find a direct correlation between pay ranges and team performance. For example, the teams with the second smallest pay ranges were in fourth and fifth place, respectively, in their leagues.

Perhaps a better gauge of the effect of pay on performance of baseball teams may be total payroll. This reflects the overall salaries of the players; and if pay is indeed a motivator, would not a well-paid group outperform their less-well-paid counterparts? When applied to American baseball, for example, the New York Yankees have had the highest payroll in recent years, and their performance in these years has been spectacular as seen by their winning the World Series four times between 1996–2000. Compensation expert Edward Lawler echoes these sentiments, noting that there is a strong relationship between the total payroll of teams and how many games they win. "In a world of free agency, it takes a high payroll to attract and retain top talent. Thus, teams with the highest payrolls usually end up in the World Series."[23] Additionally, Lawler has argued that the rewarding of team performance is more important than the size of the pay differences among the individual players.

The question of pay ranges and their impact on productivity is one that merits more consideration as organizations seek to determine the effectiveness of pay on performance. It is also becoming important because a growing number of corporate shareholders are proposing resolutions that tie chief executive officer pay to a multiple of the lowest worker's pay, thus controlling the range between the lowest and highest paid person in the organization.[24]

Although money was probably overemphasized in classical management theory and motivation techniques, the pendulum now seems to have swung too far in the opposite direction. Money remains a very important[25] but admittedly complex potential motivator. The Application Example: Back to the Drawing Board provides some specific examples.

In terms of Maslow's well-known hierarchy of needs covered in Chapter 8, money is often equated only with the most basic requirements of employees. It is viewed in the material sense of buying food, clothing, and shelter. Yet, money has a symbolic as well as an economic, material meaning. It can provide power and status and can be a means to measure achievement. In the latter sense, as Chapter 16 will discuss in detail, money can be used as an effective positive reinforcement intervention strategy to improve performance.

APPLICATION EXAMPLE

Back to the Drawing Board

In recent years, top-level managers in many American corporations have experienced sharply increasing compensation. Much publicity was given to the huge pay earned by e-commerce executives that were tied into stock plans during the end of the last century and the beginning of the new at firms such as Amazon.com and Yahoo. A study of 365 of the largest corporations found that the compensation packages of the top two executives in each averaged over $10 million during that peak economic period. Firms such as Digital Equipment began to question their existing reward systems and made drastic changes.

For years Digital offered no cash bonuses to employees. Rewards were confined to annual salary increases and participation in the company's stock-option plan. The stock options were used to keep talented top-level managers. During the boom years of the 1970s and 1980s when the price of Digital stock kept going up, these options were very powerful rewards and were more than sufficient to retain good people. However, in the 1990s massive financial losses resulted not just in downsizing but in a severe dip in the company's stock price. Many of the Digital top-management group had options that had been issued at $40 to $90, but the price of the stock dropped to below $20, and thus the value of the options as a reward disappeared.

In an effort to resuscitate its ailing reward system, the company allowed managers on the plan to trade in their old stock options for ones that were redeemable at a gain. At the same time, Digital introduced cash bonuses as part of every employee's compensation package. Now, all Digital employees have some portion of their pay that is variable, and depending on the specific goals that the employee is pursuing, this extra variable-pay amount and more can be earned. At the same time, the company developed and implemented five principles that have helped it make the transition to the new reward system. They include the following:

1. *Manage expectations.* Over time the expectations of the personnel will change, and rewards will have to change with them.
2. *Explanations should be kept simple.* Compensation systems can be very complex and sophisticated. In explaining them, it is important to keep the plan short and simple so that everyone knows the benefits and drawbacks and can reach personal conclusions regarding what he or she needs to do in order to be rewarded.
3. *The program should be simple.* Employees have to be able to live and agree with the compensation system in practice, so it should have only one or two major objectives that are easy to implement and track.
4. *The program should be designed to meet the objectives.* It is not possible to have a successful cookie-cutter reward system; the system has to be designed to meet the needs of worldwide personnel, and this means it should be flexible enough to accommodate everyone.
5. *When in doubt, do it.* There are many reasons for not making changes in reward systems, and the greatest regret results from doing nothing or doing it only halfway rather than pushing past these doubts and implementing the approach that appears to be best—even if there is some doubt as to whether it will work as well as intended.

Beyond Maslow, more sophisticated analyses of the role of money are presented in cognitive terms. For example, a number of years ago some organizational psychologists concluded, based on their laboratory studies, that the use of extrinsic rewards such as money decreased the intrinsic motivation of subjects to perform a task.[26] Extrinsic and intrinsic motivation will be given specific attention in Chapter 8, but for now it is sufficient to know that the intrinsic motivation was usually measured in the laboratory by time spent on a task following the removal of the reward. However, through the years, there have been many criticisms of these studies, and a recent meta-analysis of 96 experimental studies concluded that "overall, reward does not decrease intrinsic motivation."[27] Although these studies used other rewards besides money, and the controversy still continues between the behavioral and cognitive schools of thought as outlined in Chapter 1, it is becoming clear that the real key in assessing the use of monetary rewards is not necessarily whether they satisfy inner needs but rather how they are administered.

In order for money to be effective in the organizational reward system, the system must be as objective and fair as possible[28] and be administered contingently on the employee's exhibiting critical performance behaviors.[29] This has been made particularly clear by Kerr, who notes that an effective pay system for rewarding people has to address three considerations. First, the organization must ask itself what outcomes it is seeking. Examples include higher profits, increased sales, and greater market share. Second, the enterprise must be able to measure these results. Third, the organization must tie its rewards to these outcomes. The problem for many of today's organizations is that they do still not know what they want to achieve or are unable to measure the results.[30]

Traditional Methods of Administering Pay

Traditionally, organizations have used two methods of administering pay: base pay and merit pay. These methods are then sometimes supplemented by pay-for-performance plans and "new pay" programs that extend, and in some cases radically revise, the traditional approaches.

Base wages and salary is the amount of money that an individual is paid on an hourly, weekly, monthly, or annual basis. For example, a person working on a part-time basis may earn $8.00 an hour. This is the hourly wage for that position. Most managers are paid on an annual salary basis, and the sum is broken down into weekly, biweekly, or monthly amounts. For example, a college graduate may be offered $36,000, which comes to just over $692 a week before taxes and other deductions.

Base pay is often determined by market conditions. For example, graduating engineers may be able to command $55,000 annually whereas engineering managers with 10 years of experience are paid $110,000. If base pay is not in line with the market rate, organizations may find that they are unable to hire and retain many of their personnel. At the same time, one of the major problems with base pay forms of compensation is that they tend to be most competitive at the entry level and are often less competitive thereafter. So an engineering manager who is making $105,000 may be $5,000 off the market when compared to what other engineering managers within the same region and similar job requirements are making, but the individual may also find that firms paying higher salaries prefer to develop their own management talent internally and do not hire from outside. In any event, most organizations have some form of merit pay system that is used to give annual salary increases, thus raising the base pay and preventing personnel from getting too far out of step with the market.

Merit pay is typically tied to some predetermined criteria. For example, a company may give all of its employees a cost-of-living allowance and then allocate additional funds for those who are judged "meritorious." The amount of merit pay can take one of two forms: a flat sum, such as $3,000, or a percentage of the base salary, such as 6 percent. In some cases companies use a combination of the two, such as giving everyone who qualifies for merit pay an additional 6 percent up to a maximum amount of $5,000. This approach ensures that those who are making lower salaries get larger percentage increases, whereas those earning higher salaries get a flat merit raise. For example, under the combination merit pay just described, a middle manager with a base salary of $50,000 will get an additional $3,000 (6 percent of $50,000), whereas a senior top-level manager with a base salary of $150,000 will get $5,000.

Merit pay has a number of major shortcomings. One is that the criteria for determining merit are often nebulous because the organization does not clearly spell out the conditions for earning this pay. An example is a firm that decides to give merit to its best employees. Unless the criteria for "best" are objectively spelled out, most of those who do not get merit money will feel left out because they believe they are among the best. A second, and related, problem is that it can often be difficult to quantify merit pay criteria. In particular, the work output of some people, production-line and salespeople being good examples, is easily measured, but the work output of others, such as accountants and other staff specialists, office personnel, and managers/supervisors, may be quite difficult to objectively measure. A second major problem is that merit pay can end up being "catch-up" pay. For example, everyone may be given a 2 percent across-the-board raise and then those whose pay is extremely low are given merit to get them closer to market value. This approach is common in enterprises that suffer salary compression brought on by the need to pay higher salaries to hire new personnel at the lower levels. Over time, the salary range between new hires and those who have been with the organization for, say, five years may be totally eliminated. So unless the longer-tenured employees are given more money, there is the likelihood that they will look for jobs at companies that are willing to pay them more based on their job experience.

In a way, merit pay is supposed to be a form of "pay for performance." Individuals who do superior work are given increases greater than the rest of their colleagues. However, because of the problems of linking merit pay with performance, many organizations have created specific pay-for-performance plans.

Pay for Performance

There are two basic types of "pay-for-performance" plans: individual incentive plans and group incentive plans. Individual incentive plans have been around for many years. They were particularly popular during the height of the scientific management movement over a hundred years ago in the form of piece rate incentive plans. For example, in those early days a person loading iron ingots in a steel mill could earn as much as 7 cents per long ton (2,200 pounds) under an incentive plan. As a result, a highly skilled loader could make 50 percent more money per day than an individual who was being paid a basic day rate.[31] So individuals who were willing to work hard and had the necessary stamina could opt for incentive pay that was determined by the amount of iron ore they were able to load each day.

Individual Incentive Pay Plans.   Like the piece rate incentive plan of the pioneering scientific managers, today's individual incentive plans also pay people based on output. Many salespeople work under an individual incentive pay plan earning, for example, 10 percent commission on all sales. At Lincoln Electric in Cleveland, Ohio, there is an individual incentive plan in effect that, in recent years, has helped some factory workers earn more than $100,000 annually.[32]

Pay for some jobs is based entirely on individual incentives. However, because of the risk factor, in the uncertain economy of recent years many companies have instituted a combination payment plan in which the individual receives a guaranteed amount of money, regardless of how the person performs. So a salesperson might be paid 10 percent of all sales with a minimum guarantee of $2,000 per month. Another popular approach is to give the person a combination salary/incentive such as $26,000 plus 5 percent of all sales. A third approach is to give the person a "drawing account" against which the individual can take money and then repay it out of commissions. An example would be a salesperson who is paid a flat 10 percent of all sales and can draw against a $25,000 account. If the first couple of months of the year are slow ones, the individual will draw on the account, and then as sales pick up the person will repay the draw from the 10 percent commissions received.

The Use of Bonuses.   Another common form of individual incentive pay is bonuses. The signing bonus is one of the biggest incentives for athletes and upper-level managers.[33] For example, Conseco Inc., the giant insurance company, recently paid Gary Wendt, a former executive at General Electric, a $45 million bonus for agreeing to join the company for at least five years as its chairman and chief executive officer. Additionally, Conseco will pay Wendt a bonus of between $8 million and $50 million at the end of his second year at the helm, depending on the firm's performance, and a minimum bonus of $2.8 million at the end of the fifth year.[34] Although this bonus package is extremely large, successful managers and individuals who can generate large accounts for a firm can also expect sizeable bonuses. For example, the PaineWebber Group recently recruited a top-producing brokerage team from its rival, Merrill Lynch, by offering the group a signing bonus of $5.25 million and an additional $2 million if they bring more customers to PaineWebber.[35]

The Use of Stock Options.   Another form of individual incentive pay is the stock-option plan. This plan is typically used with senior-level managers and gives them the opportunity to buy company stock in the future at a predetermined fixed price. The basic idea behind the plan is that if the executives are successful in their efforts to increase organizational performance, the value of the company's stock will also rise.[36] The rise of dot-com firms in the new economy discussed in Chapter 2 depended greatly on stock options to lure in and keep top talented managers and entrepreneurs. Table 5.1

TABLE 5.1   Examples of Unexercised Stock Options at Select Firms

Executive/Company	Value* (in thousands of dollars)	Executive/Company	Value* (in thousands of dollars)
Timothy Koogle Yahoo	$2,251,451	John Chambers Cisco Systems	482,453
Stephen Case America Online	1,263,767	Louis Gerstner IBM	481,350
Barry Diller USA Networks	1,033,984	Joseph Nacchio Qwest Communications International	467,546
Glen Meakem Freemarkets	751,140	William Esrey Spring Fon Group	452,837
Millard Drexler Gap	685,003	Jack Welch General Electric	436,357
Henry Silverman Cendant	684,683	Gerald Levin Time Warner	377,728

*Based on the stock price at the end of the company's fiscal year.
Source: Reported in *Business Week,* April 17, 2000, p. 106.

reports the value of some of the stock options that were not yet exercised by the spring of 2000, but of course a year later, if still not exercised, because the stock market decreased dramatically, these stock option values in many cases would have been halved or less.

Potential Limitations.   Although bonuses and stock options remain popular forms of individual pay, there are potential problems yet to be overcome. One obstacle is that these reward systems are practical only when performance can be easily and objectively measured. In the case of sales, commissions can work well. In more subjective areas such as clerical work and general supervision, they are of limited, if any, value. A second problem is that individual incentive rewards may encourage only a narrow range of behaviors. For example, a salesperson seeking to increase his or her commission may spend less time listening to the needs of the customer and more time trying to convince the individual to buy the product or service, regardless of how well it meets the buyer's needs. Bonuses are also proving unpopular in some situations such as educational compensation. Delegates to the National Education Association convention, for example, recently rejected the idea of linking job performance to bonuses. One reason is because the association believes that a bonus system will discourage people from teaching lower ability students or those who have trouble on standardized tests, as bonuses would be tied to how well students perform on these tests.[37]

Group Incentive Pay Plans.   As Chapter 14 will discuss in detail, in recent years there has been a growing trend toward the use of teams.[38] Organizations are increasingly aware that teams and teamwork can lead to higher productivity and better quality than do individuals working on their own. As a result, group-incentive pay plans have become increasingly popular. One of the most common forms of group pay is *gainsharing plans.*[39] These plans are designed to share with the group or team the cost savings from productivity improvements. The logic behind these plans is that if everyone works to reduce cost and increase productivity, the organization will become more efficient and have more money to reward its personnel.

The first step in putting a gainsharing plan into effect is to determine the costs associated with producing the current output. For example, if a computer manufacturer finds that it costs $30 million to produce 240,000 printers, the cost per printer is $125, and these data will be used as the base for determining productivity improvements. Costs and output are then monitored, while both the workers and the managers are encouraged to generate cost-saving ideas. Then, at some predetermined point, such as six months, costs and output are measured and productivity savings are determined. For example, if the firm now finds that it costs $14 million to produce 125,000 printers, the cost per unit is $112. There has been a savings of $13 per printer or $1,625,000. These gainsharing savings are then divided between management and the employees, say, on a 75:25 basis.

A number of organizations use gainsharing in one form or another. At Owens Corning, for example, the company has instituted a gainsharing plan designed to reduce costs and increase productivity in the production of fiberglass. Savings in the manufacturing cost per pound are then shared with the employees.[40] In another example, Weyerhaeuser, the giant forest and paper products company, employs what it calls "goalsharing" in its container board packaging and recycling plants. The company's objective is to enlist the workforce in a major performance improvement initiative designed to achieve world-class performance by reducing waste and controllable costs and increasing plant safety and product quality.[41]

Another common group incentive plan is *profit sharing*. Although these plans can take a number of different forms, typically some portion of the company's profits is paid into a profit-sharing pool, and this is then distributed to all employees. Sometimes this is given to them immediately or at year-end. Some plans defer the profit share, put it into an escrow account, and invest it for the employee until retirement.

A third type of group incentive plan is the *employee stock ownership plan* or *ESOP*. Under an ESOP the employees gradually gain a major stake in the ownership of the firm. The process typically involves the company taking out a loan to buy a portion of its own stock in the open market. Over time, profits are then used to pay off this loan. Meanwhile the employees, based on seniority and/or performance, are given shares of the stock. As a result, they eventually become owners of the company.

Potential Limitations. As noted earlier, group incentives plans are becoming increasingly popular. However, they have a number of shortcomings. One is that they often distribute rewards equally, even though everyone in the group may not be contributing to the same degree. So all of a team or defined group may get a gainsharing bonus of $2,700, regardless of how much each did to help bring about the productivity increases and/or reduced costs. A second shortcoming is that these rewards may be realized decades later as in the case of an employee's profit sharing that is placed in a retirement account. So their motivational effect on day-to-day performance may, at best, be minimal. A third shortcoming is that if group rewards are distributed regularly, such as quarterly or annually, employees may regard the payments as part of their base salary and come to expect them every year. If the group or firm fails to earn them, motivation and productivity may suffer because the employees feel they are not being paid a fair compensation.

Realizing that base pay, merit pay, and both individual and group forms of incentive pay all have limitations, organizations are now beginning to rethink their approach to pay as an organizational reward and formulate new approaches that address some of the challenges they are facing in today's environment.[42] The result has been the emergence of what are called new pay techniques.

New Pay Techniques

As noted earlier in this section, the standard base-pay technique provides for minimum compensation for a particular job. It does not reward above-average performance nor penalize below-average performance. Pay-for-performance plans correct this problem. In fact, in many cases, such as those in which pay is tied directly (i.e., contingently) to measured performance, pay-for-performance plans not only reward high performance but also punish low performance. Sometimes, of course, these plans are unfair in the sense that some jobs may be easy to do or carry very high incentives, thus allowing employees to easily earn high rates of pay, whereas in other cases the reverse is true. Similarly, in a group incentive arrangement in which all members are highly productive, the personnel will maximize their earnings, but in groups where some individuals are poor performers, everyone in the group ends up being punished.

Despite the downside to some of these pay-for-performance plans and the fact that they have been around for many years, they have become quite popular and can be considered new pay techniques. Examples include especially the group or team incentives such as gainsharing, profit sharing, employee stock-ownership plans, and stock-option plans. Recent surveys have found that a large majority of *Fortune* 1000 firms are using them.[43] Additionally, as organizations undergo continual changes brought about by technology, globalization, legislation, and the competitive pressures discussed in Chapters 1 and 2, many enterprises are rethinking and redesigning their pay plans to reflect 21st-century demands. What is emerging is a series of so-called "new pay" approaches.[44] The following is a brief summary of some of these.[45]

1. *Commissions beyond sales to customers.*   As with all of these new pay plans, the commissions paid to sales personnel are aligned with the organization's strategy and core competencies. As a result, besides sales volume, the commission is determined by customer satisfaction and sales team outcomes such as meeting revenue or profit goals.

2. *Rewarding leadership effectiveness.*   This pay approach is based on factors beyond just the financial success of the organization. It also includes an employee-satisfaction measure to recognize a manager's people-management skills.

3. *Rewarding new goals.*   In addition to being based on the traditional profit, sales, and productivity goals, rewards under this approach are aimed at all relevant employees (top to bottom) contributing to goals such as customer satisfaction, cycle time, or quality measures.

4. *Pay for knowledge workers in teams.*   With the increasing use of teams, pay is being linked to the performance of knowledge workers or professional employees who are organized into reengineering, product development, interfunctional, or self-managed teams. In some cases, part of this pay is initially given to individuals who have taken additional training, the assumption being that their performance will increase in the future as a result of these newly acquired knowledge or skills.[46]

5. *Skill pay.*   This approach recognizes the need for flexibility and change by paying employees based on their demonstrated skills rather than the job they perform. Although it is currently used with procedural production or service skills, the challenge is to apply this concept to the more varied, abstract skills needed in new paradigm organizations (e.g., design of information systems, cross-cultural communication skills).

6. *Competency pay.*   This approach goes beyond skill pay by rewarding the more abstract knowledge or competencies of employees, such as those related to technology, the international business context, customer service, or social skills.

7. *Broadbanding.*   This approach has more to do with the design of the pay plan than do the others. Formally defined as a compensation strategy, broadbanding "is the practice of collapsing the traditional large number of salary levels into a small number of salary grades with broad pay ranges."[47] So, for example, rather than having three levels of supervisors whose salary ranges are $25,000 to $40,000, $35,000 to $55,000, and $50,000 to $80,000, the company will have one supervisory salary grade that extends from $25,000 to $80,000. This allows a manager to give a salary increase to a supervisor without having to first get approval from higher management because the supervisor's salary puts the individual in the next highest salary level. Broadbanding sends a strong message that the organization is serious about change and flexibility, not only in the structural and operational processes but also in its reward system. Simply put, with broadbanding the organization puts its money where its mouth is.[48]

These new pay techniques are certainly needed to meet 21st-century challenges. If organizations expect customer satisfaction, leadership, satisfied employees, quality, teamwork, knowledge sharing, skill development, new competencies (e.g., technical, cross-cultural, and social), and employee growth without promotions, then they must reward these as suggested by the new pay techniques.

RECOGNITION AS AN ORGANIZATIONAL REWARD

Pay is an unquestionably important form of reward. However, it is not the only way in which organizations can reward their people. In addition to money, forms of recognition to identify and reward outstanding performance can be a vital, but too often overlooked, part of the organizational reward system. When people are asked what motivates them, money is always prominently featured on their list. However, both formal organizational recognition and social recognition used systematically by supervisors and managers is very important to their people and the success of organizations.

Recognition Versus Money

There are a number of reasons why recognition may be as, or even more, important than money as a reward for today's employees. One of the most obvious is that enterprises typically have pay systems that are designed to review performance and give incentive payments only once or twice a year. So if someone does an outstanding good job in July, the manager may be unable to give the person a financial reward until after the annual performance review in December. Nonfinancial rewards, on the other hand, such as genuine social recognition, can be given at any time.

Recognition rewards can take many different forms, can be given in small or large amounts, and in many instances are controllable by the manager. For example, in addition to social recognition and formal awards, a manager can give an employee increased responsibility. The employee may find this form of recognition motivational, and the result is greater productivity. As a follow-up, the manager can then give this employee even greater responsibility. Unlike many financial forms of reward, there is no limit to the number of people who can receive this type of reward or how often it is given. One expert on rewards puts it this way:

> You can, if you choose, make all your employees . . . eligible for nonfinancial rewards. You can also make these rewards visible if you like, and performance-contingent, and you needn't wait for high level sign-offs and anniversary dates, because nonfinancial rewards don't derive from the budget or the boss, and are seldom mentioned in employment contracts and collective bargaining agreements. Furthermore . . . if you inadvertently give someone more freedom or challenge than he can handle, you can take it back. Therefore, organizations can be bold and innovative in their use of nonmonetary rewards because they don't have to live with their mistakes.[49]

Research shows that there are many types of recognition that can lead to enhanced performance and loyalty.[50] One of these that is receiving increased attention is recognition of the fact that many employees have work and family responsibilities and when the organization helps them deal with these obligations, loyalty increases. This finding is particularly important in light of the fact that a recent survey has found that 25 percent of the most sought employees (highly educated, high-income professionals) report that they would change jobs for a 10 percent increase in salary and 50 percent would move for a 20 percent raise.[51]

This data is not an isolated example. Another recent survey of the attitudes and experiences of a large number of employees in business, government, and nonprofit organizations around the United States revealed the following: (1) only 30 percent feel an obligation to stay with their current employer; (2) individuals who are highly committed to their organization tend to do the best work; (3) workers who are discontent with their jobs are least likely to be productive; (4) employees in large organizations (100 or more people) tend to be less satisfied than their peers in small enterprises; (5) lower-level employees are less satisfied than those in higher-level positions; and (6) the things that the respondents would like their companies to focus on more include being fair to employees, caring about them, and exhibiting trust in them.[52]

Although research on the complexities of the relationship of satisfaction and commitment with outcomes will be given attention in Chapter 7, it is interesting to note here that groups such as the National Association for Employee Recognition have concluded that practicing human resource professionals and managers still seem to underestimate how useful recognition can be in motivating employees to achieve goals.[53] Moreover, recognition as a reward does not have to be sophisticated or time consuming. In fact, many firms that are now working to improve their recognition systems all use fairly basic and easy-to-implement programs. Steps such as the following need to be set up to effectively manage a reward and recognition program:[54]

1. When introducing new recognition procedures and programs, take advantage of all communication tools including Intranet and other knowledge-sharing networks—let everyone know what is going on.
2. Educate the managers so that they use recognition as part of the total compensation package.
3. Make recognition part of the performance management process, so that everyone begins to use it.
4. Have site-specific recognition ceremonies that are featured in the company's communication outlets such as the weekly newsletter and the bimonthly magazine.
5. Publicize the best practices of employees, so that everyone knows some of the things they can do in order to earn recognition.
6. Let everyone know the steps that the best managers are taking to use recognition effectively.
7. Continually review the recognition process in order to introduce new procedures and programs and scrap those that are not working well.
8. Solicit recognition ideas from both employees and managers, as they are the ones who are most likely to know what works well—and what does not.

Examples of Effective Formal Recognition Systems

Chapter 16 on behavioral performance management focuses on social recognition as an effective contingent reinforcer that supervisors/managers can use as a style in interpersonal relations to improve employee performance. In this chapter on organizational context, formal recognition programs implemented by organizations are the primary focus, along with money and benefits (covered next). Formal recognition is a vital part of the reward system that makes up the environmental component of the social cognitive framework for understanding and effectively managing organizational behavior (see Chapter 1).

Today there are a wide number of formal recognition systems that are being effectively used by organizations nationwide. Many of these are the result of continual modification, as organizations have altered and refined their reward systems to meet the changing needs of their workforce. However, all effective programs seem to have two things in common. First, they are designed to reward effective employee performance behavior and enhance employees' satisfaction and commitment. In other words, effective recognition systems lead to improved employee performance and retention. Second, they are designed to meet the specific and changing needs of the employees. Simply put, a recognition system that worked in the past or in one enterprise may have little value in another. This is why many firms have gone through a trial-and-error approach before they have settled into a unique system that works best today for their employees. Thus, recognition programs often vary widely from company to company—and many of them are highly creative. For example, one expert on implementing recognition systems offers the following creative, but practical, suggestions:[55]

1. Select a pad of Post-it Notes in a color that nobody uses and make it your "praising pad." Acknowledge your employees for work well done by writing your kudos on your praising pad.
2. Hire a caterer to bring in lunch once a week. Besides showing your respect and appreciation, this encourages mingling and the sharing of information, knowledge, ideas, and innovative solutions.
3. To get a team motivated during an important project, have them design a simple logo for the assignment. This will give the team not only a sense of camaraderie and cohesion, but also group identification and focus.

These tidbits represent useful suggestions, but many companies have gone much further by designing formal recognition systems that align their overall objectives (increased productivity, reduced cost, better-quality products and customer service, and even higher profitability) and employee performance behaviors. For example, at Dierbergs Family Market, a 16-store supermarket chain in Missouri, the firm has created what it calls the "Extra Step" program. This formal recognition program is designed to reward employees who are proactive in meeting customer needs. The objective of the program is twofold: make the company a place where employees love to work and keep customers coming back. In achieving this, the company rewards workers who go out of their way to do things for customers. For example, in one case, a customer left some of her purchases at one of the stores during a snowstorm. The store manager did not want any of the employees going out in the inclement weather, so he called a cab and paid the driver to deliver the packages she had left behind. In another case, an employee on his way to work recognized a good customer trying to change a flat tire. He went over, introduced himself as working for Dierbergs, and changed the tire for the customer.

These "extra steps" are rewarded by Dierbergs in a number of ways, including gift certificates, movie passes, and even lunch with the chief executive officer.[56] They also help the company achieve its objectives of increased revenues through word-of-mouth advertising (the best form, at no cost) and repeat business, customer satisfaction, and employee productivity and retention. Customer feedback has been overwhelmingly complimentary, and the firm's turnover rate has declined from almost 50 percent five years ago to 25 percent, in an industry where labor turnover is extremely high. For its efforts, Dierbergs was awarded the Arthur Andersen Award for Best Business Practices for Motivating and Retaining Employees.

Dierbergs is not alone. A growing number of firms are finding that well-structured and implemented employee recognition reward systems yield very positive cost-benefit results. In particular, formal recognition systems have become important in the hotel and restaurant industry, where annual turnover rates of 100 percent are typical. Firms that have implemented recognition systems have experienced dramatic improvement in retention of their best employees. For example, at the Hotel Sofitel Minneapolis the director of human resources has reported that thanks to the organization's recognition system, annual turnover has declined from 84 percent to 37 percent.[57] One of the most successful plans in its system is called the Sofitel Service Champions. This program is inexpensive to monitor and all employees participate. It works this way: When employees do something noteworthy, they are given a little slip of paper by a customer or a manager. This resembles a French franc (that goes with the Hotel's French theme), and when an employee gets three of these francs, he or she receives a $35 gift certificate that can be redeemed at one of the hotel's restaurants. Seven francs can be exchanged for dinner at one of the restaurants or a $35 gift certificate redeemable at any area store or restaurant. Ten francs entitles the person to a day off with pay or a $50 gift certificate that can be used in any store or restaurant in the area.

Another successful component in the Sofitel recognition system is the Team Member of the Month program. These members are chosen from one of the department teams within the hotel (e.g., housekeeping, receiving, room service, accounting, front office, etc). Each department director fills out a nomination form with the name of the team member who is believed to have done something outstanding that month. If chosen, the employee receives a $50 check, a special luncheon honoring the recipient in the employee cafeteria, a picture taken with the general manager and the direct report manager, which is placed in a display case, and a specially designated parking spot. If a person is nominated but does not win, the individual still remains eligible for the next three months. All monthly winners and nominees are tracked throughout the year and are eligible for the Team Member of the Year Award. This winner is given either $500 or a trip to one of the other Sofitel Hotels in North America.

A key success factor in such public recognition plans is that it is viewed as being fair, and those not recognized agree that recipients are deserving. At Sofitel the recognition programs are continually changed based on input from the employees. One of the recent additions to the recognition system at Sofitel is a recognition program called Department Appreciation Days. Each month, one department is chosen to be recognized by another. The recognition is typically something small and inexpensive, such as a jar of cookies, and has proven to be very popular with the personnel and departments that has led to constructive, friendly competition to win this award.

Other organizations use similar approaches to recognizing and praising their people. (See the accompanying OB in Action: Some Easy Ways to Recognize Employees.) For example, at the Fremont Hotel & Casino in Las Vegas, 75 percent of the human resource budget is set aside for recognition programs. One of these is called "Personality with a Hustle" and is designed to encourage employees to do everything they can to proactively help customers stay and play at the Fremont. Personnel who do so can end up being nominated as employee of the month. Winners are given $100, dinner for two at any of the company's restaurants, two tickets to a show, a special parking spot, and an Employee of the Month jacket. They are also eligible to win the Employee of the Year Award, which entitles them to an extra week's vacation, an all-expense-paid trip to Hawaii with $250 spending money, and a dinner for two with the company's chief executive officer.

In addition to these representative types of recognition systems, there are many other innovative, fun recognition awards in today's firms. At First Chicago, for example, there are Felix and Oscar awards (based on the characters in *The Odd Couple*) given to employees with the neatest and messiest work areas. At Chevron USA in San Francisco, an employee who is recognized for an outstanding accomplishment is immediately brought to a large treasure chest and is allowed to choose an item from the box: a coffee mug, pen-and-pencil set, gift certificate, or movie tickets. At Goodmeasure, a management consulting firm in Cambridge, Massachusetts, a person who does something outstanding is given an "Atta Person" award. At Mary Kay Cosmetics, pink Cadillacs, mink coats, and diamond rings are given to their leading sellers. At Hewlett-Packard, marketers send pistachio nuts to salespeople who excel or who close an

---

OB IN ACTION

Some Easy Ways to Recognize Employees

Employees never seem to tire of recognition. In psychological terms, they do not seem to become satiated, or filled up with recognition as they do with say with food or even money. For some, in fact, the more recognition they get, the more they want. Fortunately, it is not difficult to recognize people, and there are many ways in which it can be done. Some of the easiest and representative ways are the following:

1. Practice giving concentrated, focused recognition by calling deserving employees into your office and thanking them for doing an outstanding job. During this interaction focus is only on the detailed recognition and nothing else, so that the effect is not diluted by the discussion of other matters.
2. Buy a trophy and give it to the most deserving employee in the unit or department. Inscribe the individual's name on the trophy, but leave room for additional names. To help insure fairness and acceptance, at the end of a month, have this recipient choose the next member of the unit to be recognized and explain why this individual was chosen.
3. Recognize an employee who is located in another locale and does not get a chance to visit the home office very often. Deal with this "out of sight, out of mind" problem by faxing, e-mailing, or leaving a voice mail for the person that says "thank you for a job well done."
4. Write a note that recognizes an individual's contributions during the last pay period and attach this note to the person's paycheck.
5. When you get a raise or a promotion, acknowledge the role that was played by your support staff by taking all of them out to lunch. In sports, a smart quarterback who receives all the attention for a win will always recognize especially his line in front of him and may even take these "unsung heroes" out for dinner or buy them something.
6. Take a picture of someone who is being congratulated by his or her manager. Give a copy of the photo to the employee and put another copy in a prominent location for everyone to see.
7. Have a senior manager come by and attend one of your team meetings during which you recognize people for their accomplishments.
8. Invite your work team or department to your house on a Saturday evening to celebrate their completion of a project or attainment of a particularly important work milestone.
9. Recognize the outstanding skill or expertise of an individual by assigning the person an employee to mentor, thus demonstrating both your trust and your respect.
10. The next time you hear a positive remark made about someone, repeat it to that person as soon as possible.
11. Stay alert to the types of praise and recognition that employees seem to like the best and use these as often as possible.
12. Catch people doing things right—and let them know!

---

important sale. Salespeople at Octocom Systems in Chelmsford, Massachusetts, receive a place setting of china each month for meeting their quota. In a different, and for the long-run perhaps questionable, approach, at Microage Computer in Tempe, Arizona, employees who come to work late are fined, and this money is passed out to people who arrive on time. The Commander of the Tactical Air Command of the U.S. Air Force rewards individuals whose suggestions are implemented with bronze, silver, and gold buttons to wear on their uniforms.

In some cases, recognition awards are delivered on the spot for a job well done.[58] For example, at Tricon, a spinoff of PepsiCo that has become the world's largest restaurant company in units and second behind McDonald's in sales, the chief executive officer gave a Pizza Hut general manager a foam cheesehead for achieving a crew turnover rate of 56 percent in an industry where 200 percent is the norm. Commenting on the event, the CEO noted, "I wondered why anyone would be moved by getting a cheesehead, but I've seen people cry. People love recognition."[59] Yet, as pointed out at the beginning of this section, this powerful reward is still being underutilized, as seen by the results of a recent survey in which 96 percent of the respondents said that they had an unfulfilled need to be recognized for their work contributions.[60] A more visible, and much more costly form of organizational reward system involves the benefits that are provided to employees.

BENEFITS AS ORGANIZATIONAL REWARDS

Every permanent employee receives benefits, even though they often seem to be unaware[61] and not know the usually high monetary value of these benefits.[62] In fact, benefits constitute a large percentage of most company's expenses. In recent years these costs have been escalating (e.g., health insurance is usually cited as the biggest single cost increase firms have had in the last decade). Benefit costs range between 30 to 35 percent of wages and salaries. So a company that is paying an employee $70,000 annually is spending an additional $22,000 in benefits including life and health insurance, a pension plan, mandated government benefits such as Social Security, vacation time, and so forth.

Although some managers and small business owners question the high cost of benefits, many believe that it is money well spent because it is a vital part of the organization's reward system and helps attract, maintain, and retain outstanding employees. This reasoning is known as *efficiency wage theory* and holds that firms can save money and become more productive if they pay higher wages and better benefits because they are able to hire and leverage the best talent. This theory is particularly useful in explaining the importance of offering benefits that appeal to and are needed by today's employees to make them satisfied, stress free, and productive. For example, in recent years, with so many women in the workforce, a growing number of companies have been helping their people deal with family related challenges by providing on-site day care, dual parental maternity leave, and flexible work hours so individuals who have young children or elderly relatives who need their assistance can deal with these issues.

In general, the benefits portion of the organizational reward system can be categorized in a number of different ways. The following examines both the traditional and newly emerging benefits of today's organizational reward system.

Traditionally Offered Benefits

Commonly offered benefits are of two types: those that must be offered because they are required by law and those that most organizations typically have given to their personnel. When using benefits as part of the organizational reward system, these are standard offerings and, for the most part, do not differ from one organization to another.

Federal Government–Mandated Benefits. One traditional government mandated benefit is Social Security. The initial purpose of Social Security, officially known as the

Old Age Survivors and Disability Insurance Program, was to provide limited income to retired people to supplement such things as their personal savings, private pensions, and part-time work earnings. At the present time, employees are required to pay a Social Security tax of 7.65 percent on the first $72,600 they earn, and employers pay a like amount. Additionally, both employees and their employer pay 1.45 percent for Medicare taxes on all amounts above $72,600. In turn, this federal government–mandated program pays both a retirement benefit and Medicare benefits, although payments will vary depending on a number of factors. For example, a person retiring at the age of 62 will receive partial benefits, whereas someone retiring at the age of 65 is eligible for full benefits, The monthly payment at the turn of the century was around $1,400 per month for full benefits, and this may increase in the future given that much of the federal surplus in recent years has been earmarked to strengthen the Social Security system and ensure its long-term viability.

Another mandated benefit is workers' compensation. This is insurance that covers individuals who suffer a job-related illness or accident. Employers pay the cost of this insurance, and today over 110 million workers are protected under this program.[63]

Other mandated programs that are offered to employees do not specify a particular benefit, but they do require the employer to take specific types of actions. For example, the Family and Medical Leave Act of 1993 requires all organizations with 50 or more employees to grant any worker who has been employed there for at least one year an *unpaid* leave of up to 12 weeks for childbirth, the adoption of a child, to care for a family member with a serious health problem, or because of a personal health problem. During this period, all of the employee's existing health benefits must remain intact, and the individual must be allowed to return to the same or an equivalent job after the leave.

Another mandated program is the Employee Retirement Income Security Act of 1974, which requires that if an employer sets up a pension fund for employees and deducts contributions to that fund, the company must follow certain guidelines. These guidelines restrict the firm's freedom to take money out of the fund and provides formulas for employee vesting (when the employee has a right to the employer's contributions to the fund) and portability (the employee's ability to transfer funds to a different retirement account). A third mandated program is the result of the Pregnancy Discrimination Act of 1978, which protects a woman from being fired because she is pregnant. A fourth program is a result of the Economic Recovery Act of 1981, which allows employees to make tax-deductible contributions to a pension, savings, or an individual retirement account (IRA). All of these programs provide government–mandated benefits to employees.

Life, Disability, and Health Insurance.   Another major category of traditional benefits consists of insurance coverage. Most companies offer health insurance to their employees and pay a major portion of the premiums for this coverage. Life insurance is often based on the individual's annual salary so that the premium provides protection, for example, for two times the person's yearly salary. Additionally, employers often make disability insurance available for a minimum premium fee.

In recent years, health coverage costs have escalated, but have become an expected benefit. Even though firms are trying to manage for cost containment through copayment and preferred providers, to compete for top employees and retain the best, many employers are expanding coverage to encompass a variety of health care including prescription drugs, vision care products, mental health services, and dental care. A growing number also provide their employees the opportunity to join a health maintenance organization (HMO) that offers medical and health services on a prepaid basis. In some cases, companies pay the entire premium. However, in most instances the employer pays only a portion of the monthly premium, and the deductibles and a minor percentage of the cost of care is covered by the employees themselves.

Pension Benefits.   In addition to the pension benefits that are provided by Social Security, most organizations today have also established private pension plans. Contributions are generally made by both the employer and employee, and there are a variety of plans available. Two of the most popular are individual retirement accounts (IRAs) and 401(k) plans that allow employees to save money on a tax-deferred basis by entering into salary-deferral agreements with the employer. These built-up funds are then available to the employee in retirement and typically provide far more money than the monthly Social Security checks from the federal government.

Time-Off Benefit.   Another common benefit, often taken for granted by many, is paid time off. This benefit takes a number of different forms. One is vacation time. In many organizations employees are entitled to at least one week of vacation with pay after being with the firm for one year, and by the end of five years, most are given at least two weeks and, in some cases, as many as four. Moreover, some firms will pay, say, 1.5 times the person's weekly salary for every week of vacation that the individual foregoes, and some employers allow people to accumulate vacation time and, at some point, pay them for any unused time.

Another form of time off is paid religious holidays. Still another is paid sick leave. In many organizations individuals are given a predetermined number of sick days per year, such as six, whereas in others there is no limit. Finally, many firms give paid personal leave such as a day to attend the funeral of a friend or relative or simply for any personal reasons.

Newer Types of Benefits

In recent years, a number of "new" types of benefits have emerged and are gaining in popularity. One example of these is wellness programs, and another, mentioned earlier in this section, is assistance with family related responsibilities. These, in addition to others, are emerging as an important part of today's organizational reward system.

Wellness Programs.   Wellness programs, which will also be discussed in Chapter 12 on coping with stress, are a special type of benefit program that focuses on keeping employees from becoming sick.[64] There is considerable evidence that employees who exercise regularly are less likely to take sick days and thus reduce health insurance premiums and lost productive time. As a result, more and more firms are now encouraging their people to work out regularly by installing a gymnasium or workout center on the premises or offering to finance at least part of the cost of joining a local health club. Another wellness practice is to encourage employees to exercise by giving them a financial payment such as $1 for every mile they jog during the year. So a person who jogs three miles a day at the company gym will earn $15 a week. Some also encourage their people to keep their weight under control, and individuals who are too heavy are paid to lose the extra weight. For example, a firm may pay $10 for every pound an employee loses. Of course, once the individual has reached the weight recommended by the doctor, this weight must stay off. If the person gains it back, the individual may have to pay the firm $10 for every pound above the doctor's recommended limit. Many firms find that these are small sums to pay when contrasted with the cost of having someone, for example, out of work six days a year due to poor health. In fact, in order to encourage everyone to stay healthy, some organizations pay people for unused sick days. So those who are in good health have an incentive to maintain this status.

Life Cycle Benefits.   Another popular group of new benefits comes under the heading of what collectively are being called "life cycle" benefits. These are based on a person's stage of life and include such things as child care and elder care.

Child care benefits are extremely popular and many of the "best places to work" have on-site day care. Employees can drop off their child at the day care center, come by and have lunch with the child, and then pick up the youngster after work and drive home together. In a few instances, firms have even installed T.V. cameras so employees can view and keep track of their child throughout the day in the center. One of the primary benefits of this program is the elimination of day care costs, which can run well over $100 a week, as well as spending quality time with the child before, during, and after work, or, in the case of the T.V. monitored systems, during the work day.

Elder care takes a number of different forms. One of the most common is referral services, which can be used by an employee who has a disabled parent or one who needs constant care. Another form is long-term health care insurance, which provides for nursing homes or at-home care.

Another popular benefit is employee assistance programs (EAPs for short), which were originally designed to assist employees who had problems with alcohol. In recent times, EAPs deal with drug abuse and now have generally expanded into marital problems and financial planning. The purpose of these programs is to provide help to employees in dealing with personal problems that can negatively impact on their lives and their job performance. Unfortunately, the use of EAPs should be kept confidential so that employees are not hesitant to use the services for fear of career repercussions.

Other Benefits.   In recent years a number of other benefits have begun to appear, many of them offered by new economy and innovative companies. One is concierge services that help employees choose gifts for presents, get tickets to concerts, schedule home or auto repairs, and so forth.[65] Another is the use of tuition assistance to help employees obtain a college education.[66] A third is the use of noninsured benefit programs that help low-wage and part-time workers purchase medicines and medical assistance at a discount.[67] Still another example is prepaid legal plans that offer a variety of services such as legal advice, wills and estate planning, and investment counseling.[68]

Flexible, Cafeteria-Style Benefits.   Every organization has its own way of providing/administering the benefit package, but in recent years a growing number have begun offering flexible, cafeteria-style benefit plans. These are plans that allow employees self-control and choice over the benefits received. Employees are allowed to put together their own package by choosing those benefits that best meet their personal needs. Under this arrangement, the organization will establish a budgeted amount that it is willing to spend per employee, and the individual is then allowed to decide how to spend this money. For example, some employees may want more life insurance because they have a young family, whereas others may prefer to spend more on health insurance coverage because they have a spouse with a debilitating illness.

There is increasing evidence that these cafeteria-style programs can lead to increased satisfaction and reduced turnover.[69] However, organizations have also found that these plans can be somewhat expensive to administer because there are many different types of benefit packages, and someone has to keep track of what each person has chosen. Additionally, employees are usually allowed to make changes in their package on an annual basis, further complicating the problem of administering the benefits and the accompanying tax implications.[70] Finally, even though employees seem to like cafeteria-style benefit plans, there is no assurance that they always make rational decisions.[71] For example, young employees with families may opt to deal only with more immediate concerns such as better hospital coverage for their spouse and children and completely ignore the benefits of contributing to a retirement program for their future.

In summary, benefits are an important component of the organizational reward system. Unfortunately, because they are so common and everyone gets them, their value as a reward often goes unnoticed. Benefits unfortunately are taken for granted and are considered to be an entitlement and thus become a hollow reward for employee performance and retention.

Summary

This chapter examines reward systems as an important part of the organizational context for organizational behavior. For most organizations, pay dominates the organizational reward system. There is considerable evidence that pay is vital not only for hiring and retaining talented employees, but also if properly administered can have a positive impact on desirable outcomes such as productivity, quality, and customer service. In particular, pay provides employees with the opportunity to meet both lower-level maintenance and upper-level growth and achievement needs. The challenge for managers is to administer rewards properly. In particular, this means setting up pay systems that allow employees to know the outcomes that are to be rewarded, being able to measure these outcomes as fairly and objectively as possible, and tying monetary incentives directly to the results.

Pay administration takes several forms. Traditional methods include base salary and merit pay. Both of these, however, are often insufficient for retaining talented people. Organizations have to offer incentives for desirable outcomes. As a result, pay-for-performance systems are in place in many firms. These include both individual and group incentive plans. Common examples of individual incentives include commissions based directly on sales or work output, bonuses, and stock options. Group incentives include gainsharing, profit sharing, and employee stock ownership plans.

In recent years many organizations have realized that they must develop new pay approaches. One example is the use of commissions that go beyond sales such as customer service. Others include skill pay that is based on employees demonstrating completion of training and competency in particular job-related skills, competency pay that is based on rewarding people for abstract knowledge or competencies related to things such as technology or leadership, and broadbanding in which salary levels are collapsed into a small number of salary grades with broad pay ranges.

Another important but often overlooked component of organizational reward systems is recognition. In contrast to money, recognition is easier to control by the manager and can be easily altered to meet the individual employee needs. Social recognition is provided by managers/supervisors contingent on performing desirable behaviors and is given more detailed attention in Chapter 16 on behavioral performance management. As part of the organizational reward system discussed in this chapter, formal recognition systems can innovatively provide awards for desirable outcomes, and many actual examples were provided.

Benefits are the third major component of organizational reward systems. Some of these benefits are mandated by the federal government (e.g., Social Security and workers' compensation). However, numerous other benefits are received by today's permanent employees (not by temps, and this is a major problem for them). Examples include paid vacations, days off for religious holidays, personal leave, life and health insurance, and pensions. In addition there are benefits that have emerged in recent years that are proving quite popular. Examples include wellness programs, child care benefits, employee assistance programs (EAPs), tuition assistance, and prepaid legal expenses. In recent years the value of benefits as part of the reward system has increased, but so has the cost. The challenge for today's management is to make sure there is a favorable cost-benefit ratio and go beyond what is required by law to contribute to desired outcomes such as retention and performance.

ENDING WITH META-ANALYTIC RESEARCH FINDINGS

OB PRINCIPLE: The systematic administration of pay-for-performance reward systems can increase employee performance.

Meta-Analysis Results: [19 studies; 2,818 participants; (1) $d = 1.36$ for pay incentive in manufacturing firms; (2) $d = 1.82$ for pay incentive combined with performance feedback and social recognition in manufacturing settings; (3) $d = .42$ for pay incentive in service organizations; (4) $d = .89$ for pay incentive combined with performance feedback in service organizations (there were no studies with this combination in manufacturing); and (5) $d = .27$ for pay incentive combined with performance feedback and social recognition in service organizations] *On average, there is a:*

(1) **83 percent probability** *that a systematically administered pay-for-performance reward system to employees in manufacturing settings will increase their performance more than those who do not receive this approach;*

(2) **90 percent probability** *that a systematically administered pay combined with social recognition and feedback-for-performance reward system to employees in manufacturing settings will increase their performance more than those who do not receive this approach;*

(3) **62 percent probability** *that a systematically administered pay-for-performance reward system to employees in service organizations will increase their performance more than those who do not receive this approach;*

(4) **74 percent probability** *that a systematically administered pay combined with feedback-for-performance reward system to employees in service organizations will increase their performance more than those who do not receive this approach; and*

(5) **58 percent probability** *that a systematically administered pay combined with social recognition and feedback-for-performance reward system to employees in service organizations will increase their performance more than those who do not receive this approach.*

As the preceding probability statements reflect, moderator analyses revealed that the impact of the systematically administered pay (and it's combinations with social recognition and feedback) varied depending on the type of organization. As indicated, the pay-for-performance reward system had a bigger impact in manufacturing than in service organizations.

Conclusion: As discussed in this chapter, although there are a variety of techniques in organizational reward systems, pay is the one that comes to the forefront in any discussion or analysis. There is an automatic assumption that pay has a positive effect on employee performance. Despite this assumption and the popularity of money as a reward, managers are still searching for answers of effective ways to increase the incentive effects of money. Pay for performance or incentive pay is one answer because it supposedly links pay directly to performance results. It motivates employees because it gives something extra—compensation above and beyond basic wages or salaries. However, just as there have been problems with pay in general, as the chapter points out, there have also been mixed results with pay for performance. One way to improve pay for performance is to systematically administer the plan so that employees can clearly see the contingent (i.e., the if-then) relationship between their behaviors, the resulting performance, and what they are paid. One way to systematically administer such a pay-for-performance plan is through the behavioral management steps that will be given attention in Chapter 16. Such a systematic application of pay for performance, as was shown in the meta-analysis reported here, can have a positive impact on employee performance.

Source: Alexander D. Stajkovic and Fred Luthans, "A Meta-Analysis of the Effects of Organizational Behavior Modification on Task Performance," *Academy of Management Journal,* Vol. 40, No. 5, 1997, pp. 1122–1149.

Questions for Discussion and Review

1. In what way does agency theory provide understanding for pay as an important component of the organizational reward system?
2. Is pay an effective organizational reward? Does the fact that the chief executive officer makes 20 times as much as the lowest-paid member of the company have any effect on the value of pay as a determinant of organizational performance?
3. "The team with the highest payroll usually ends up in the World Series." How does this statement relate to the importance of pay as a reward?
4. Why have many organizations begun to supplement their traditional pay systems with "pay-for-performance" plans? Of these plans, what about individual vs. group incentives?
5. How can the so-called "new pay" techniques help solve some of the major challenges facing today's organizations? Give some specific examples.
6. Why have more and more firms begun developing recognition programs as part of their organizational reward system? Why not just give people more money?
7. What role do benefits play in the organizational reward system? How can these costly benefits contribute more to desirable organizational outcomes?

Internet Exercise: Rewards in the Workplace

Visit the website http://www.adcentive.com then click on "promotional ideas and info," then click on "idea store." Here you will find various ideas on how to use and implement various reward and incentive systems. Go to the idea store section to find various tips and programs currently being used by organizations.

1. From information you gained on the website, how do you think these suggestions could influence work behavior? Which ones do you think will work better than others? Why?
2. Using a search engine to go to specific companies, what other types of reward systems can you find? Give the specifics and critique their value to improving performance in the workplace.

REAL CASE:
Rewarding Teamwork
in the Plains

In the past, most reward systems have been geared to the individual employee. However, with the emergence of teams in most of today's organizations, systems are being revamped to reward teamwork. A good example is Behlen Manufacturing Company in Columbus, Nebraska. The 1,100 mostly production employees are organized into 32 teams. Some of these teams have only a handful of members, whereas others have as many as 60. Although each individual receives a base-pay component, which comes to about $8 an hour, the rest of the compensation is variable and is determined in a number of different ways, including how one's team is performing.

The centerpiece of the manufacturing company's variable-reward plan is gainsharing, an increasingly popular form of compensation whereby all members share a usually fixed percentage of the documented savings or performance gain accomplished by the team. Behlen employees can earn monthly gainsharing of up to $1 an hour when their teams meet productivity goals. The CEO explained this team reward system as follows: "If you're in a group that makes stock tanks, for example, from the start of the process to the end of the process, over all shifts, all month long, if the team achieves certain levels of productivity, each of its members is rewarded anywhere from 0 cents to $1 an hour for every hour worked in that area." Documentation of the gains is based on actual pounds of products, so that everyone on the team knows exactly how well their team is doing.

Another part of the company's variable-reward system involves profit sharing. Employees receive 20 percent of the profits. In recent years this has resulted in everyone's getting a profit-sharing bonus equivalent to three weeks' salary. Still another part of the reward package is the employee stock ownership plan. Each employee receives company stock equal in value to 2 percent of his or her base salary each year. Senior managers in the company participate in the same reward system as the workers, receiving the same proportional benefits. However, in the case of managers, performance is calculated on the gross margin of their business unit before selling and administrative costs are deducted.

How well has this company in the middle of the Great Plains performed with this organizational reward system? In each of the eight years this pay plan has been in place, performance has exceeded top management's expectations. In addition to the $5 million the firm saved because of safety, quality, and efficiency ideas that were submitted through the teams, the company has exceeded its profit goals each year. In fact, in the most recent year profits were $1 million greater than expectations. The CEO explained it this way, "As people focused in on their gainsharing opportunities—and they've understood their profit-sharing opportunities—we're seeing positive productivity improvements in every corner of the plant."

1. Explain the organizational reward system this firm uses.
2. Although this reward system has obviously been very effective, what more can be done? What specific recommendations would you make?
3. What if the agricultural economy goes bad and the sales of this agribusiness company greatly decreases? What will be the impact on the reward system this company uses, and what would you now recommend?

REAL CASE:
Different Strokes for
Different Folks

Organizations are finding that the best reward system entails a combination of money, recognition, and benefits. Money is important, of course, but if a person earns $50 in incentive pay every month, after a while this monetary reward may begin to lose some of its power. So financial rewards have to be altered and different ones offered. The same is true for recognition awards; although people never suffer from too much recognition, organizations have to be sure awards are fair, and highly creative organizations often ensure that change is built into the recognition system. The important thing that many firms have found is that what is truly rewarding for one person may not have the same impact for another. In short, there are individual differences when it comes to reward systems, and there have to be different strokes for different folks. Here are some representative innovative monetary and recognition rewards that have been offered by a variety of different enterprises.

- At Busch Gardens in Tampa, the company gives a Pat on the Back Award to employees who do an outstanding job and also has a copy of the notice of the award put in the employee's file.
- At Metro Motors in Montclair, California, the name of the Employee of the Month is put up on an electronic billboard over the dealership.
- At Colin Service Systems, a janitorial service in White Plains, New York, coworkers vote for the employees that they feel should be given awards as the Most Helpful Employee and the Nicest Employee, and executives make the presentations.
- At the Amway Corporation, on days when some workloads are light, the department's employees help out in other departments, and after accumulating eight hours of such work, employees get a personal thank you note from the manager of programs and services.
- At South Carolina Federal financial services in Columbia, the president and other top managers serve employees lunch or dinner as a reward for a job well done.
- At the Gunneson Group International, a total-quality consulting firm in Landing, New Jersey, when an employee refers business that results in a sale, the individual receives a cash award of 1 to 5 percent of the gross sale, depending on the value of the new business to the company.
- At QuadGraphics printing company in Pewaukee, Wisconsin, employees are paid $30 to attend a seminar devoted to quitting smoking, and the company gives $200 to anyone who quits for a year.
- At the Taylor Corporation, a printing company in North Mankato, Minnesota, in lieu of year-end bonuses, employees are allowed to make selections from a merchandise catalog.

1. Why are more and more companies complementing their monetary incentives with recognition awards in their organizational reward system?
2. How would you rate each of the examples? What are some strengths and weaknesses of each?
3. If you work for a human resource management consulting firm and are given the assignment to head up a project team to develop reward systems that would be appealing to new dot-com firms, what would you recommend?

ORGANIZATIONAL BEHAVIOR CASE: Huge Benefits, Little Understanding or Use

The Velma Company designs and manufactures high-tech communications equipment. The firm is a world-class supplier, and its three largest customers are *Fortune* 50 firms. Velma also has major clients in Japan and the European Union. Over the last five years the company's sales have tripled, and the biggest challenge it faces is hiring and retaining state-of-the-art people. In particular, there are two groups that are critical to the company's success. One is the design people who are responsible for developing new products that are more efficient and price competitive than those currently on the market. The other is the manufacturing people who build the equipment.

In an effort to attract and keep outstanding design people, Velma has a very attractive benefit package. All of their health insurance premiums and medical expenses are covered (no copay or deductibles). The company contributes 10 percent of their annual income toward a retirement program, and these funds are vested within 24 months. So a new design person who is earning $75,000 annually will have $7,500 put into a retirement fund by the company, and the individual can make additional personal contributions.

Each year all designers are given 100 shares of stock (the current sales price is $22) and an option to buy another 100 shares (the current strike price is $25 and this option is good for 10 years or as long as the person works for the firm, whichever comes first).

The manufacturing people are on a pay-for-performance plan. Each individual is paid $7 for each unit he or she produces, and the average worker can turn out three units an hour. There is weekend work for anyone who wants it, but the rate per unit does not change. In addition, the company gives all of the manufacturing people free health insurance and covers all medical expenses.

Another benefit is that everyone in the company is eligible for five personal days a year, and the company will pay for any unused days. Velma also has a large day care facility that is free for all employees, and there is a state-of-the-art wellness center located on the premises.

Last year the company's turnover was 9 percent, and the firm would like to reduce it by 50 percent this year. One proposed strategy is to strengthen the benefits package even more and make it so attractive that no one will want to, or could afford to, leave. Some top managers privately are concerned that the firm is already doing too much for these employees and are troubled by the fact that exit interviews with designers who left in the last year indicated that many of them were unaware of the benefits they were receiving. For example, most of the designers who have gone elsewhere reported that they were attracted to the stock offered them, yet they did not exercise the options to buy additional shares of Velma stock because they were not sure what the financial benefits were to them. The manufacturing people who left reported that $7 per unit was acceptable, although a higher rate would have resulted in their remaining with the firm. The manufacturing people also liked the stock that the company gave them, but were somewhat confused about the options they held.

Both groups—designers and manufacturing personnel—seemed pleased with the contribution that the company made to their retirement program, but most of them did not put any additional personal contributions into their retirement fund. When asked why, the majority of them were unaware that this could be done on a before-tax basis, thus temporarily shielding the contributions from taxes and making it easier to build a nest egg for the future. Finally, all of those who left said that they liked the child care benefit, although most of them did not have young children so they did not use it, and they thought the wellness center was also a good idea but they were so busy working that they admitted to never using the facilities.

1. Which benefits did the employees who were leaving seem to best understand and like?
2. Which benefits did they find confusing or of little value?
3. Based on your answers and other relevant considerations, what recommendations would you make to Velma's management regarding how they can do a better job of using the benefits package in their organizational reward system?

EXPERIENTIAL EXERCISES FOR PART 1

EXERCISE: Synthesis of Student and Instructor Needs*

Goals:
1. To "break the ice" in using experiential exercises
2. To initiate open communication between students and the instructor regarding mutual learning goals and needs
3. To stimulate the students to clarify their learning goals and instructional needs and to commit themselves to these
4. To serve as the first exercise in the "experiential" approach to management education

Implementation:
1. The class is divided into groups of four to six students each.
2. Each group openly discusses what members would like from the course and drafts a set of learning objectives and instructional aims. The group also makes up a list of learning/course objectives that they feel the instructor wants to pursue. (About 20 minutes.)
3. After each group has "caucused," a group spokesperson is appointed to meet with the instructor in an open dialogue in front of the class about course objectives.
4. The instructor meets with each group representative at the front of the classroom to initiate an open dialogue about the semester of learning. (About 30 minutes.) Several activities are carried out:
   a. Open discussion of the learning objectives of both the students and the instructor
   b. Recognition of the constraints faced by each party in accommodating these goals
   c. Identification of areas of goal agreement and disagreement, and feasible compromises
   d. Drafting a set of guidelines for cooperation between the parties, designed to better bring about mutual goal attainment

EXERCISE: Work-Related Organizational Behavior: Implications for the Course*

Goals:
1. To identify course topic areas from the participant's own work experience
2. To introduce experiential learning

Implementation:
Task 1: Each class member does the following:

1. Describes an experience in a past work situation that illustrates something about organizational behavior. (Some students have had only part-time work experience or summer jobs, but even the humblest job is relevant here.)

Source: "Synthesis of Student and Instructor Needs" was suggested by Professor Philip Van Auken and is used with his permission; "Work-Related Organizational Behavior: Implications for the Course" is from "Getting Acquainted Triads," in J. William Pfeiffer and John E. Jones (Eds.), *A Handbook of Structured Experiences,* Vol. 1, University Associates, San Diego, Calif., 1969, and "Defining Organizational Behavior," in James B. Lau, *Behavior in Organizations,* Irwin, Burr Ridge, Ill., 1975.

2. Explains what it illustrates about organizational behavior. (Time: five minutes for individuals to think about and jot down notes covering these two points.)

Task 2: The class forms into triads and each triad does the following:

1. Member A tells his or her experience to member B. Member B listens carefully, paraphrases the story back to A, and tells what it illustrates about organizational behavior. Member B must do this to A's satisfaction that B has understood fully what A was trying to communicate. Member C is the observer and remains silent during the process.
2. Member B tells his or her story to C, and A is the observer.
3. Member C tells his or her story to A, and B is the observer. (Each member has about five minutes to tell his or her story and have it paraphrased back by the listener. The instructor will call out the time at the end of each five-minute interval for equal apportionment of "airtime" among participants. (Total time: 15 minutes.)

Task 3: Each triad selects one of its members to relate his or her incident to the class. The instructor briefly analyzes for the class how the related story fits in with some topic to be studied in the course, such as perception, motivation, communication, conflict, or leadership. The topic areas are listed in the table of contents of this book.

EXERCISE: Organizations*

Goals:
1. To identify some of the important organizations in your life
2. To determine relevant, specific characteristics of organizations
3. To describe some of the important functions of management in organizations

Implementation: Read the "Overview" and "Procedure" sections. Complete the "Profile of Organizations" form, which follows these sections.

Overview: Undoubtedly, you have had recent experiences with numerous organizations. Ten to 15 minutes of reflective thinking should result in a fairly large list of organizations. Don't be misled by thinking that only large organizations, such as your college or General Motors, are relevant for consideration. How about the clinic, with the doctors, nurses, and secretary/bookkeeper? Or the corner garage or service station? The local bar, McDonald's, and the neighborhood theater are all organizations. You should have no difficulty listing several organizations with which you have had recent contact.

*Source: Reprinted with permission from Fremont E. Kast and James E. Rosenzweig, "Our Organizational Society," in *Experiential Exercises and Cases in Management,* McGraw-Hill, New York, 1976, pp. 13–15.

The second part of the exercise, however, is tougher. Describe several of the key characteristics of the organizations that you have listed. One of the major issues in studying and describing organizations is deciding *what* characteristics or factors are important. Some of the more common characteristics considered in the analysis of organizations are:

1. Size (small to very large)
2. Degree of formality (informal to highly structured)
3. Degree of complexity (simple to complex)
4. Nature of goals (what the organization is trying to accomplish)
5. Major activities (what tasks are performed)
6. Types of people involved (age, skills, educational background, etc.)
7. Location of activities (number of units and their geographic location)

You should be able to develop a list of characteristics that you think are relevant for each of your organizations.

Now to the third, final, and most difficult task. Think about what is involved in the management of these organizations. For example, what kinds of functions do their managers perform? How does one learn the skills necessary to be an effective manager? Would you want to be a manager in any of these organizations?

In effect, in this exercise you are being asked to think specifically about organizations you have been associated with recently, develop your own conceptual model for looking at their characteristics, and think more specifically about the managerial functions in each of these organizations. You probably already know a great deal more about organizations and their management than you think. This exercise should be useful in getting your thoughts together.

Procedure:

Step 1.   Prior to class, list up to 10 organizations (for example, work, living group, club) in which you have been involved or with which you have had recent contact.

Step 2.   Enter five organizations from your list on the form on page 174.

1. List the organization.
2. Briefly outline the characteristics that you consider most significant.
3. Describe the managerial functions in each of these organizations.

Step 3.   During the class period, meet in groups of five or six to discuss your list of organizations, the characteristics you consider important, and your descriptions of their management. Look for significant similarities and differences across organizations.

Step 4.   Basing your selections on this group discussion, develop a list entitled "What we would like to know about organizations and their management." Be prepared to write this list on the chalkboard or on big sheets of paper and to share your list with other groups in the class.

Profile of Organizations

	Organization	Key Characteristics	Managerial Functions
1.	_____	_____	_____
		_____	_____
		_____	_____
		_____	_____
2.	_____	_____	_____
		_____	_____
		_____	_____
		_____	_____
3.	_____	_____	_____
		_____	_____
		_____	_____
		_____	_____
4.	_____	_____	_____
		_____	_____
		_____	_____
		_____	_____
5.	_____	_____	_____
		_____	_____
		_____	_____
		_____	_____

EXERCISE: Using *Gung Ho* to Understand Cultural Differences*

Background: There is no avoiding the increasing globalization of management. Few, if any, current students of business can expect to pursue a successful career without some encounter of an international nature. Gaining early and realistic exposure to the challenges of cross-cultural dynamics will greatly aid any student of business.

The Pacific Rim will continue to play a dominant role in North American transnational organizations and global markets. The opening doors to China offer an unprecedented market opportunity. Korea, Singapore, and Taiwan continue to be unsung partners in mutually beneficial trading relationships. And, of course, Japan will always be a dominant player in the international arena.

An important aspect of cross-cultural awareness is understanding actual differences in interpersonal style and cultural expectations, and separating this from incorrect assumptions. Many embellished stereotypes have flourished as we extend our focus and attention abroad. Unfortunately, many of these myths have become quite pervasive, in spite of their lack of foundation. Thus, North American managers frequently and confidently err in their cross-cultural interactions. This may be particularly common in our interactions with the Japanese. For example, lifetime employment has long been touted as exemplifying the superior practices of Japanese management. In reality, only one-third of Japanese *male* employees enjoy this benefit, and in 1993, many Japanese firms actually laid off workers for the first time. Also, Japan is promoted as a collectivist culture

Source: Steven M. Sommer, University of California–Riverside. Used with permission.

founded on consensus, teamwork, and employee involvement. Yet Japan is at the same time one of the most competitive societies, especially when reviewing how students are selected for educational and occupational placement.

Films can provide an entertaining yet potent medium for studying such complex issues. Such experiential learning is most effective when realistic and identifiable with one's own likely experiences. Case studies can be too sterile. Role plays tend to be contrived and void of depth. Both lack a sense of background to help one "buy into" the situation. Films on the other hand can promote a rich and familiar presentation that promotes personal involvement. This exercise seeks to capitalize on this phenomenon to explore cross-cultural demands.

Procedure:	Step I. (110 minutes) Watch the film *Gung Ho.* (This film can be obtained at any video store.)

Step II. (30 minutes)   Use one of the following four formats to address the discussion topics.

Option A: Address each issue in an open class forum. This option is particularly appropriate for moderate class sizes (40 students) or for sections that do not normally engage in group work.

Option B: Divide the class into groups of four to seven to discuss the assigned topics. This is a better approach for larger classes (60 or more students). This approach might also be used to assign the exercise as an extracurricular activity if scheduled class time is too brief.

Option C: Assign one group to adopt the American perspective and another group to take the Japanese perspective. Using a confrontation meeting approach (Walton, 1987), have each side describe its perception and expected difficulties in collaborating with each other. Then, have the two sides break into small mixed groups to discuss methods to bridge the gap (or avoid its extreme escalation as portrayed in the film). Ideas should extend beyond those cited in the movie. Present these separate discussions to the class as a whole.

Option D: Assign students to groups of four to seven to watch the film and write a six-page analysis addressing one or more of the discussion topics.

Discussion topics:

1. In the opening scenes, Hunt observes Kaz being berated in a Japanese "management development center." According to at least one expert, this is a close representation of Japanese disciplinary practices. Would such an approach be possible in an American firm? How does this scene illustrate the different perspectives and approaches to motivation? To reinforcement? To feedback?

2. The concepts of multiculturalism and diversity are emerging issues in modern managerial environments. The importance of recognizing and responding to racial, ethnic, and other demographic factors has been widely debated in the popular press. What does *Gung Ho* offer to the discussion (both within and across the two groups)? How does each culture respond to different races, genders, cultures?

3. Individualism and collectivism represent two endpoints on a continuum used to analyze different cultural orientations. Individualism refers to a sense of personal focus, autonomy, and compensation. Collectivism describes a group focus, self-subjugation, obligation, and sharing of rewards. How do you see American and Japanese workers differing on this dimension? You might compare the reactions of the Japanese manager whose wife was about to give birth with those of the American worker who had planned to take his child to a doctor's appointment.

4. How does the softball game illuminate cultural differences (and even similarities)? You might consider this question in reference to topic 3; to approaches to work habits; to having "fun"; to behavioral norms of pride, honor, sportsmanship.

5. On several occasions we see George Wendt's openly antagonistic responses to the exercise of authority by Japanese managers. Discuss the concept of authority as seen in both cultures. Discuss expectations of compliance. How might George's actions be interpreted differently by each culture? Indeed, would they be seen as different by an American manager as compared with a Japanese manager?

6. Throughout the film, one gains an impression of how Americans and the Japanese might differ in their approach to resolving conflict. Separately describe how each culture tends to approach conflict, and how the cultures might be different from each other.

7. Experienced conflict between work and family demands has also gained attention as an important managerial issue. How do both cultures approach the role of work in one's life? The role of family? How does each approach balance competing demands between the two? Have these expectations changed over time (from 20 years ago, 40 years ago, 60 years ago)? How might they change now in the 21st century?

8. In reality, Japanese managers would be "shamed" if one of their subordinates was seriously injured on the job (the scene where the American worker's hand is caught in the assembly line belt). Taking this into account, what other issues in the film might be used to illustrate differences or similarities between American and Japanese management and work practices?

Supplemental Readings

Michael Gordon, L. Allen Slade and Neal Schmitt, "The 'Science of the Sophomore' Revisited: From Conjecture to Empiricism," *Academy of Management Review,* March 1986, p. 191.

Richard Hodgetts and Fred Luthans, "The Myth of Japanese Management," *Personnel,* April 1989, p. 42.

Leigh Stelzer and Joanna M. Banthin, "A *Gung Ho* Look at the Cultural Clash between Americans and Japanese," *Journal of Management Inquiry,* September 1992, p. 220.

Richard Walton, *Managing Conflict: Interpersonal Dialogue and Third Party Roles,* Addison-Wesley, Reading, Mass., 1987.

PART TWO

Cognitive Processes of Organizational Behavior

Consulting Best Practices

Gallup's Approach to the Importance of the Individual Great Manager Level of Analysis

This second major part of the text is concerned with the micro, individual level of analysis of organizational behavior. Gallup's research has found that human talents and motivation are garnered or squandered at the "local" level where managers create a great place to work, or not.

In studying this "great place to work," Gallup's research of great managers revealed that they did things differently from the "average." Based on this discovery, Gallup reduced this "great manager" discovery to "four keys." Gallup also created a "measuring stick" to provide objective numbers to guide managers. This Gallup instrument is correlated to positive business outcomes such as profitability, productivity, safety, retention, and customer loyalty, as studied in tens of thousands of business units and millions of employees.

The first of these four keys of what great managers do is to *select for talent.* Talent is the "soil" in which skills, knowledge, and competencies will grow, thrive, or, perhaps, languish. Great managers place and grow people according to their strengths. Although conventional wisdom puts greater emphasis in experience or "resumé" and what persons have learned to do, great managers look at the potential. Of course, Gallup provides measures for talent, so this understanding can be put alongside other standard evaluation processes.

The second key is to *define the right outcomes.* Great managers define people's work in terms of the desired results, how much the person measurably contributes, and how well it affected the customer. Great managers understand that real empowerment is not "permission to do what I told you, the way I said," but the freedom to find your best expression of what we saw as possible. Great managers help and encourage employees say how good they think they can be, and then support and help them get there.

The third key is to *focus on strengths.* In a recent consultation with a *Fortune* 50 company, Gallup was invited to come in at the last event of an 18-month mentoring process conducted for promising new executives. It was hoped a focus on strengths would save a process gone sour. For 18 months these "rising stars" had been given several lengthy unrelated psychological assessments that highlighted their inadequacies. After each examination, they were required to meet with their mentor and discuss how they could change their weaknesses. This, in spite of the fact that this organization's leaders did not want this new generation of executives to be like the older generation, to whom they were to submit in this mentoring process. The new executive participants were becoming very discouraged and the mentoring process was a failure. Little wonder. Great managers focus on people's strengths and help them get even better.

The fourth key is to *find the right fit.* Most corporate cultures were originally built on the premise that all careers should (or could) lead to the "top." But Gallup research shows that there is a significant difference between the talents of great managers, great teachers, and great engineers. Great managers create a culture where their people are placed in a job, and the role within that job, for the right fit of their strengths and are valued for their contributions.

These "four keys" of great managers function best where the managers themselves have the right talent and where there is valid measurement to support the practice. Managers need objective measures for human talent and to insure the "four keys" are being implemented in an effective manner. Gallup provides such instruments that are statistically related to positive business performance outcomes. This gives conceptual, behavioral, and financial coherence to the practice of great managers and the positive outcomes they create.

CHAPTER 6

Perception and Attribution

Learning Objectives

Define the overall nature of perception, explaining how it differs from sensation.

Discuss perceptual selectivity and organization.

Identify the dimensions of social perception, including stereotyping and halo.

Explain the attribution process.

Examine the processes and strategies of impression management.

Starting with Best Practice
Leader's Advice

IBM's CEO Lou Gerstner Foretells the Bursting of the Dot-Com Bubble

Lou Gerstner is widely known and greatly respected for his leadership in the dramatic turnaround of IBM in the mid-1990s and its regained world-class status today. In the 1970s and 80s, IBM was at the pinnacle of world business; its "Big Blue" culture was the envy of everyone. Then when the computer market paradigm shifted from mainframes to PCs, the entrenched culture prevented the needed changes. Some halfhearted changes were attempted, but IBM lost more than any firm in the history of business. Finally, Gerstner was brought in with no technical background and, after only one year of taking over, Big Blue was back on track and soon became a leader in the new economy. However, as indicated in his comments that follow, Gerstner warned that too many firms were misperceiving the dot-com bonanza. After these insightful comments, the dot-coms have indeed hit reality with the uncertain economy starting at the end of 2000.

Instead of the usual response to interviewer questions as found in the other chapters, Gerstner gave the following response termed "Blinded by Dot-Com Alchemy" as a guest editorial commentary in a recent issue of Business Week.

I was recently with the highly regarded chief executive of a major U.S. multinational who admitted to me that he has told his executive committee: "Do something with the Internet—anything." The CEO of another well-known Asian company—call it Acme Inc.—just confided to one of my colleagues that he was thinking of creating an Internet spin-off, Acme.com. When asked what he would put into it and what would remain in the parent company, he had no idea. Another CEO—this one at a large Japanese company—said recently that he had agreed to sign up with an online exchange because he thought his company would look dumb if it did nothing. But he confessed that he wasn't really sure what he had joined.

Something strange is happening here. Major businesses all over the world are starting to act in some very unbusinesslike ways. And many CEOs have an air of desperation about them. These execs are watching financial markets that have suspended—temporarily, at least—traditional methods of investment evaluation. As a result, each of these business leaders is under enormous investor pressure to do things like spin off a piece of the business, take the supply chain public, and drive up market value through some kind of quick strike—demonstrating to investors that Company X is participating in the New Economy.

I sympathize with their plight, but I think they're on dangerous ground. I would urge my fellow CEOs to take a deep breath and think hard about the long-term impact of their plans. Don't get me wrong. I'm convinced that e-business really is changing the entire basis of the global economy. At IBM, we've staked our future on it. But the point is, the real impact of the Internet is very different from what has been happening in stock markets around the world. These are two very distinct phenomena that are being treated by some as if they were one. They are not.

The first phenomenon—which has been building up over several years now—is this extraordinary, perhaps unprecedented, selectivity in investment. Some technology companies are increasing in value at incredible rates, while everything else is in a bear market. According to one mutual-fund manager, in 1999, the stocks of companies with no earnings were up an average of 52 percent, while stocks with real earnings were down. As a result, many CEOs of traditional companies are wondering what to do to give their stock price a boost.

The second phenomenon is, of course, e-business. It really does present CEOs with an extraordinary opportunity to transform their companies' competitiveness, to change the industries in which they operate, to fuel innovation, to open up alternative distribution channels. And to create entirely new cost structures. It is a fundamental change, one that occurs at the molecular level of business, making possible a transformation of the basic building blocks of economics, markets, and work.

What's fascinating about the past several months [late 1999, early 2000] is that some companies seem to be, against all reason, intermixing these two phenomena. They are confusing doing something—anything—about the Internet with the real work of transforming their businesses. In fact, the evidence suggests that even today's overheated stock market is smarter than that. By and large, it's not giving increased valuations to traditional companies that spin off their supply chains or launch e-commerce sites—even while the stocks of their technology partners (many of them barely past their initial public offerings) go through the roof. Of course, not all companies have been seduced by the lure of the magic market-cap wand. Many are hard at work creating alternative distribution channels, reinventing—not just spinning off—their supply chains, and more. This is a period of extraordinary change, with extraordinary opportunities. But, we can't seize them through dot-com alchemy.

This chapter focuses on the important cognitive processes of perception and attribution. As indicated in Chapter 1, cognitions are basically bits of information, and the cognitive processes involve the ways in which people process that information. In other words, the cognitive processes suggest that, like computers, humans are information processors. However, today's complex computers are still relatively simple information processing units when compared with *human information processing.*

People's individual differences and uniqueness are largely the result of the cognitive processes. Although there are a number of cognitive processes (imagination, perception, and even thinking), it is generally recognized that the perceptual process is a very important one that takes place between the situation and the behavior and is most relevant to the study of organizational behavior.[1] For example, the observation that a department head and an associate may react quite differently to the same top-management directive can be better understood and explained by the perceptual process. Also, recent research indicates that things such as organizational structure affect the perception of procedural fairness,[2] the language and labeling of the decision process affects perceptions of trustworthiness of the decision maker,[3] and the influence tactics used affect the perception of performance evaluation fairness.[4] In other words, many of the concepts and topics in organizational behavior affect the perceptual process and vice versa.

In this text, perception and attribution are presented as important cognitive processes in understanding organizational behavior. The environment (both antecedent and consequent) and other psychological processes, such as learning, motivation, and the whole of personality, are also important. However, although much of the material on perception is basic knowledge in the behavioral sciences, it has not received as much attention in the organizational behavior field. All the topics covered in this chapter are concerned with understanding organizational behavior, and they have many direct applications to organization and management practice. In particular, the concluding section of this chapter shows how the perceptual process can be applied to people's attempt to control or manage how others perceive them. Commonly called impression management, this application of the perceptual process can be an important strategy not only in getting selected for a position in an organization but also in becoming successful in life or in an organization.

The first major section presents a theoretical discussion of the general nature and significance of the perceptual process. The relationship between sensation and perception is clarified, and some of the important perceptual subprocesses are discussed. The second section covers the various aspects of perceptual selectivity and organization. The next section focuses on social perception—the phenomena of stereotypes and the halo effect. Attribution, which is given considerable attention in organizational behavior, uses social perception as a point of departure to explain or attribute how organizational participants explain their own and others' behavior. Finally, attention is given to impression management, which has direct implications for how people present themselves and affect the perceptions of others.

THE NATURE AND IMPORTANCE OF PERCEPTION

The key to understanding perception is to recognize that it is a unique *interpretation* of the situation, not an exact recording of it. In short, perception is a very complex cognitive process that yields a unique picture of the world, a picture that may be quite different from reality. Applied to organizational behavior, an employee's perception can be thought of as a "filter." Because perception is largely learned, and no one has the same learnings and experience, then every employee has a unique filter, and the same situations/stimuli may produce very different reactions and behaviors. Some analyses of employee behavior place a lot of weight on this filter:

> Your filter tells you which stimuli to notice and which to ignore; which to love and which to hate. It creates your innate motivations—are you competitive, altruistic, or ego driven? . . . It creates in you all of your distinct patterns of thought, feeling, and behavior. . . . Your filter, more than your race, sex, age, or nationality, is you.[5]

Recognition of the difference between this filtered, perceptual world and the real world is vital to the understanding of organizational behavior. A specific example would be the universal assumption made by managers that associates always want promotions, when, in fact, many really feel psychologically *forced* to accept a promotion. Managers seldom attempt to find out, and sometimes associates themselves do not know, whether the promotion should be offered. In other words, the perceptual world of the manager is quite different from the perceptual world of the associate, and both may be very different from reality. One of the biggest problems that new organizational leaders must overcome are the sometimes faulty or negative perceptions of them (see OB in Action for some real-world examples). If this is the case, what can be done about it? The best answer seems to be that a better understanding of the concepts involved should be developed. Direct applications and techniques should logically follow complete understanding. The place to start is to clearly understand the difference between sensation and perception and have a working knowledge of the major cognitive subprocesses of perception.

OB IN ACTION

New CEOs Need to Overcome Perception Problems

Can an organization continue to operate successfully after the leader who brought it to new heights decides to leave? For example, will General Electric still be the envy of the world business community with Jack Welch gone, or will the firm begin to flounder because the next head will not have Welch's insight and dynamism? Will Southwest Airlines be ranked as the best firm in its industry after Herb Kelleher retires, or will the management team that follows find it an impossible task to fill his shoes?

Incoming executives like to believe that they will be up to the task. Quite often they point to the fact that they have worked under the previous manager and they understand how to keep the magic alive. They are "insiders" who know the ropes. They have what it takes. Unfortunately, history shows that there is often a big perceptual gap between how these successors to a proven leader perceive themselves and the way the company's personnel, customers, and board of directors see them. In particular, many new chief executive officers (CEOs) have ineffective characteristics and habits that soon prove to be their undoing.

One of the major ones has been called "lifer syndrome." These executives have been with the organization for so long that when they take over, they are unable or unwilling to make the needed critical changes. The lifer has often been part of the culture for a decade or more and, for example, when one of their former peers/friends is unable to meet profit targets, the new CEO refuses to replace them. "I've known Lawrence for 10 years," he tells the board, "and I know I can work with him to straighten things out. He's always delivered for us in the past. It's just a matter of time before he does again." Several years ago "lifer" Robert Stempel after taking over as head of General Motors reportedly had this perception problem and the board soon had to replace him.

Another common perceptual problem often faced by new CEOs is "decision gridlock." This occurs when the CEO believes that by carefully analyzing situations, errors can be avoided and losses prevented. As a result, there are endless meetings and discussions regarding how to proceed, and in the final analysis very little gets done. The enterprise ends up suffering from "paralysis through analysis," and the CEO is unwilling to make decisions that change the organizational culture, streamline decision processes, and speed up manufacturing and marketing activities. In the early 1990s, John Akers at IBM thought things were going well, but decision gridlock resulted in IBM being battered by the competition. He was then replaced by Lou Gerstner, quoted in the chapter opening on Best Practice Leader's Advice who immediately began attacking decision gridlock. Refusing to spend time endlessly discussing and analyzing topics such as corporate vision, Gerstner quickly took action to simplify the structure, increase the speed of operations throughout the structure, encourage rapid decisions in critical areas, cut unneeded expenses, and both retain and build market share in the most lucrative niches. As a result of Gerstner's leadership, IBM's stock had risen by 1000 percent.

A third common perceptual problem is "poor people performance" and is typified by CEOs who think that their leadership style is bringing out the best in people when it is actually causing alarm and fear. When "Chainsaw" Al Dunlap took over Sunbeam Corporation, he did what he had done before: dramatically cut the workforce. What he failed to realize is that the personnel felt that these draconian measures were unnecessary and that the problem with Sunbeam was Dunlap's inability to effectively tap his most important resource, the people. As a result, he was unable to generate the cost savings he promised, and the stockholders eventually threw him out. The same happened to Ron Allen at Delta Airlines, who so infuriated the union that the board agreed that Allen had to go.

These actions are in sharp contrast to those of GE's Jack Welch, who used to be known as "neutron Jack" because like a neutron bomb, when he got done taking drastic action, the building and equipment were still there but the people were all gone. However, Welch also learned how to turn around an organization by identifying and developing effective personnel and keeping the focus on the human element. As he noted recently, "We spend all our time on people. The day we screw up the people thing, this company is over." This perception is well accepted at GE and has resulted in extraordinary longevity by its top executives. As a result, many industry analysts believe that GE will do well after Welch because the people who follow are not likely to have the perceptual problems that are so typical of new CEOs who fail.

Sensation versus Perception

There is usually a great deal of misunderstanding about the relationship between sensation and perception. Behavioral scientists generally agree that people's "reality" (the world around them) depends on their senses. However, the raw sensory input is not enough. They must also process these sensory data and make sense out of them in order to understand the world around them. Thus, the starting point in the study of perception should clarify the relationship between perception and sensation.

The physical senses are considered to be vision, hearing, touch, smell, and taste. There are many other so-called sixth senses. However, none of these sixth senses, such as intuition, are fully accepted by psychologists. The five senses are constantly bombarded by numerous stimuli that are both outside and inside the body. Examples of outside stimuli include light waves, sound waves, mechanical energy of pressure, and chemical energy from objects that one can smell and taste. Inside stimuli include energy generated by muscles, food passing through the digestive system, and glands secreting behavior-influencing hormones. These examples indicate that sensation deals chiefly with very elementary behavior that is determined largely by physiological functioning. Importantly, however, researchers now know that ears, eyes, fingers, and the nose are only way stations, transmitting signals that are then processed by the central nervous system. As one molecular biologist declares, "The nose doesn't smell—the brain does."[6] In this way, the human being uses the senses to experience color, brightness, shape, loudness, pitch, heat, odor, and taste.

Perception is more complex and much broader than sensation. The perceptual process or filter can be defined as a complicated interaction of selection, organization, and interpretation. Although perception depends largely on the senses for raw data, the cognitive process filters, modifies, or completely changes these data. A simple illustration may be seen by looking at one side of a stationary object, such as a statue or a tree. By slowly turning the eyes to the other side of the object, the person probably *senses* that the object is moving. Yet the person *perceives* the object as stationary. The perceptual process overcomes the sensual process, and the person "sees" the object as stationary. In other words, the perceptual process adds to, and subtracts from, the "real" sensory world. The following are some organizational examples that point out the difference between sensation and perception:

1. The division manager purchases a program that she thinks is best, not the program that the software engineer says is best.
2. An associate's answer to a question is based on what he or she heard the boss say, not on what the boss actually said.
3. The same team member may be viewed by one colleague as a very hard worker and by another as a slacker.
4. The same product may be viewed by the design team to be of high quality and by a customer to be of low quality.

Subprocesses of Perception

The existence of several subprocesses gives evidence of the complexity and the interactive nature of perception. Figure 6.1 shows how these subprocesses relate to one another. The first important subprocess is the *stimulus* or *situation* that is present. Perception begins when a person is confronted with a stimulus or a situation. This confrontation may be with the immediate sensual stimulation or with the total physical and sociocultural environment. An example is the employee who is confronted with his or her supervisor or with the total formal organizational environment. Either one or both may initiate the employee's perceptual process. In other words, this represents the stimulus situation interacting with the person.

In addition to the situation–person interaction, there are the internal cognitive processes of *registration, interpretation,* and *feedback.* During the registration phenomenon, the physiological (sensory and neural) mechanisms are affected; the physiological ability to hear and see will affect perception. Interpretation is the most significant cognitive aspect of perception. The other psychological processes will affect the interpretation of a situation. For example, in an organization, employees' interpretations of a situation are largely dependent on their learning and motivation and their personality. An example would be the kinesthetic feedback (sensory impressions from muscles) that helps manufacturing workers perceive the speed of materials moving by them in the production process. An example of psychological feedback that may influence an employee's perception is the supervisor's raised eyebrow or a change in voice inflection. Research has shown that both facial expressions and the specific situation will influence perceptions of certain emotions, such as fear, anger, or pain.[7] The behavioral termination of perception is the reaction or behavior, either overt or covert, which is necessary if perception is to be considered a behavioral event and thus an important part of organizational behavior. As a result of perception, an employee may move rapidly or slowly (overt behavior) or make a self-evaluation (covert behavior).

As shown in Figure 6.1, all these perceptual subprocesses are compatible with the social cognitive conceptual framework presented in Chapter 1. The stimulus or environmental situation is the first part; registration, interpretation, and feedback occur within the cognitive processes of the person; then there is the resulting behavior itself; and the environmental consequences of this behavior make up the final part. The subprocesses of registration, interpretation, and feedback are internal cognitive processes that are unobservable, but the situation, behavior, and environmental consequences indicate that perception is indeed related to behavior. Recent summaries of research using the meta-analysis technique have found empirical support for the relationship between cognitive

FIGURE 6.1 The subprocesses of perception.

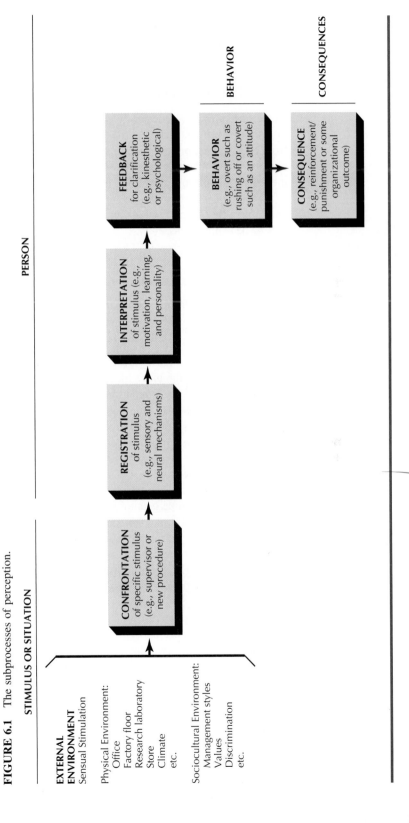

variables such as perception and behaviors.[8] Besides the subprocesses shown in the model, perceptual dimensions such as selectivity and organization, which are discussed next, help further clarify the cognitive aspects of perception.

PERCEPTUAL SELECTIVITY AND ORGANIZATION

Numerous stimuli are constantly confronting everyone. The noise of the air conditioner or computer printer, the sound of other people talking and moving, and outside noises from cars, planes, or street repair work are a few of the stimuli affecting the senses—plus the impact of the total environmental situation. Sometimes the stimuli are below the person's conscious threshold, a process called subliminal perception.

With all this stimulation impinging on people, how and why do they select out only a very few stimuli at a given time? Part of the answer can be found in the principles of perceptual selectivity.

Attention Factors in Selectivity

Various external and internal attention factors affect perceptual selectivity. The external factors consist of outside environmental influences such as intensity, size, contrast, repetition, motion, and novelty and familiarity.

1. *Intensity.* The intensity principle of attention states that the more intense the external stimulus, the more likely it is to be perceived. A loud noise, strong odor, or bright light will be noticed more than a soft sound, weak odor, or dim light. Advertisers use intensity to gain the consumer's attention. Examples include bright packaging and television commercials that are slightly louder than the regular program. Supervisors may raise their voices to gain attention. This last example also shows that other, more complex psychological variables may overcome the simple external variable. By speaking loudly, the supervisor may actually be turning the subordinates off instead of gaining their attention. These types of complications enter into all aspects of the perceptual process. As with the other psychological concepts, a given perceptual principle cannot stand alone in explaining complex human behavior. The intensity principle is only one small factor in the perceptual process, which is only a part of the cognitive processes, which are only a part of what goes into human behavior. Yet, for convenience of presentation and for the development of basic understanding, these small parts can be effectively isolated for study and analysis.

2. *Size.* Closely related to intensity is the principle of size. It says that the larger the object, the more likely it will be perceived. The largest machine "sticks out" when personnel view a factory floor. The maintenance engineering staff may pay more attention to a big machine than to a smaller one, even though the smaller one costs as much and is as important to the operation. A 6-foot 5-inch, 250-pound supervisor may receive more attention from his subordinates than a 5-foot 10-inch, 160-pound supervisor. In advertising, a full-page spread is more attention getting than a few lines in the classified section.

3. *Contrast.* The contrast principle states that external stimuli that stand out against the background or that are not what people are expecting will receive their attention. Figure 6.2 demonstrates this perceptual principle. The black circle on the right appears much larger than the one on the left because of the contrast with the

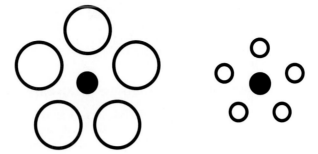

FIGURE 6.2
The contrast principle of
perception: Which black
circle is larger?

background circles. Both black circles are exactly the same size. In a similar manner, plant safety signs that have black lettering on a yellow background or white lettering on a red background are attention getting; and when the 6-foot 5-inch, 250-pound supervisor mentioned previously is placed next to a 5-foot 2-inch, 120-pound supervisor, the smaller one will probably receive as much notice as the bigger one. A worker with many years of experience hardly notices the deafening noise on the factory floor of a typical manufacturing operation. However, if one or more of the machines should come suddenly to a halt, the person would immediately notice the difference in noise level.

4. *Repetition.*   The repetition principle states that a repeated external stimulus is more attention getting than a single one. Thus, a worker will generally "hear" better when directions for a dull task are given more than once. This principle partially explains why supervisors have to give directions over and over again for even the simplest of tasks. Workers' attention for a boring task may be waning, and the only way they hear directions for the task is by the supervisors' repeating themselves several times. Advertisers trying to create a unique image for a product that is undifferentiated from its competitors—such as aspirin, soap, and deodorant—rely heavily on repetitious advertising.

5. *Motion.*   The motion principle says that people will pay more attention to moving objects in their field of vision than they will to stationary objects. Workers will notice materials being machined by a robot, but they may fail to give proper attention to the maintenance needs of the stationary machine next to them. In addition, the production line workers may devote their attention to the line of slowly moving materials they are working on and fail to notice the relatively nice working conditions (pastel-colored walls, music, and air-conditioning). Advertisers capitalize on this principle by creating signs that incorporate moving parts. Las Vegas at night is an example of advertisement in motion.

6. *Novelty and Familiarity.*   The novelty and familiarity principle states that either a novel or a familiar external situation can serve as an attention getter. New objects or events in a familiar setting or familiar objects or events in a new setting will draw the attention of the perceiver. Job rotation is an example of this principle. Research indicates that job rotation not only increased attention but also improved employees' acquisition of new skills at a large pharmaceutical company.[9] Changing workers' jobs from time to time will tend to increase the attention they give to the task. Switching from columns of numbers to color graphics may not motivate the managerial staff, but it will increase their attention until they become accustomed to the new method of presenting weekly performance data. The same is true in a

INTERNATIONAL APPLICATION EXAMPLE

Sometimes It Doesn't Translate

Although marketing people in the United States have produced some outstanding advertisements, it is not always possible to take these same ads and use them in other countries. Why not? Because the perceptions are not the same. Here are some classic examples:

1. "Schweppes Tonic Water" was initially translated to the Italian as "il water." However, the copywriters quickly corrected their mistake and changed the translation to "Schweppes Tonica." In Italian, "il water" means water in the bathroom commode.
2. When Pepsi-Cola ran an ad slogan of "Come Alive with Pepsi," it did very well in the United States. However, the company had to change its slogan in some foreign countries because it did not translate correctly. In German the translation of "come alive" is "come out of the grave." In Asia the phrase is translated "bring your ancestors back from the grave."
3. When General Mills attempted to capture the British markets with its breakfast cereal, it ran a picture of a freckled, red-haired, crew-cut, grinning kid saying, "See. kids, it's great!" The company failed to realize that the typical British family, not so child centered as the U.S. family, would not be able to identify with the kid on the carton. Results: Sales were dismally low.
4. General Motors initially had trouble selling its Chevrolet Nova in Puerto Rico. It failed to realize that although the name "Nova" in English means "star," in Spanish the word sounds like "no va," which means "it doesn't go."
5. Rolls-Royce attempted to market one of its models in Germany under the name "Silver Mist." It soon discovered that the word "mist" in German means "excrement."

foreign context. Recent meta-analysis indicates that culture may have a significant impact on perceptual interpretations. For example, collectivist countries tended to show higher levels of conformity than individualist countries.[10] The accompanying International Application Example: Sometimes It Doesn't Translate also shows some of the blunders U.S. advertising language has made in foreign countries.

The external attention getters in perceptual selectivity are fairly straightforward. More subtle is the concept of *set* in perceptual selectivity. It can be thought of as an internal form of attention getting and is based largely on the individual's complex psychological makeup. People will select out stimuli or situations from the environment that appeal to, and are compatible with, their learning, motivation, and personality. These internal attention factors are given specific attention in subsequent chapters. For now, however, let it be said that perceptual set has many direct implications for organizational behavior. In organizational life, some employees have learned to perceive the world around them in the same way. For example, one study found that the functional background (e.g., accounting, finance, marketing, human resources, and research and development) of a sample of managers significantly affected the changes they perceived in their organizations' effectiveness.[11] More recently, research has found contrary results of a predominantly negative relationship between areas of functional experience and perceptions.[12] In another study, the single sentence "I cannot recommend this young man too highly" was reproduced and distributed to several managers in the same

FIGURE 6.3
The role that learning
plays in perception.

organization. Although this statement is ambiguous and unclear, without exception all the managers interpreted this to be a positive recommendation.[13] They had all learned to perceive this statement the same way—positive and favorable.

In most cases, however, learning, motivation, and personality lead to extreme individual differences because of the way the individual is set to perceive. For example, Figure 6.3 brings out the role that set plays in perception. The three men in Figure 6.3 are drawn exactly equal in height. Yet they are perceived to be of different heights because the viewer has learned that the cues found in the picture normally imply depth and distance. A lot of what a person "sees" in the world is a result of past experience and learning. Even though the past experience may not be relevant to the present situation, it is nevertheless used by the perceiver.

Numerous instances of this situation occur in a modern organization. Participants may make the wrong perception, or perceive the same stimulus or situation in entirely different ways. A specific organizational example might be a poor output record in the operations department of a manufacturing plant. The engineer perceives the solution to this problem as one of improved systems design. The human resources manager perceives the solution as one of more training and better wage incentives. The department head perceives the solution to be more effective organizing, planning, and controlling. On the other hand, the workers may perceive the low output with pleasure because it is a way of "getting back" at their supervisor, whom they dislike. For the purpose of this discussion, it is not important who is right or wrong in this example; rather, the point is that all the relevant personnel perceive the *same* situation in completely *different* ways. The same can be said of words, abbreviations, and acronyms (see OB in Action).

Perceptual Organization

Whereas perceptual selectivity is concerned with the external and internal variables that gain an individual's attention, perceptual organization focuses on what takes place in the

OB IN ACTION

Are You a Generation Xer?

Words, abbreviations, and acronyms often mean different things to different people. One reason is because the term is occupational specific. For example, the term *OB* when used in a hospital means *obstetrics,* whereas in a College of Business it means *organizational behavior.* Similarly, in a medical unit *OD* means *overdose* as in the case of someone who has taken too much of a drug, whereas in a Department of Management the term means *organization development,* which is a long-range effort to improve an enterprise's problem-solving and renewal processes by effectively managing change and culture. Another reason why terms have different meanings is that their usage changes. So an acronym that had one meaning in 1980 might have quite another today. In the matrix following there are three columns. Before continuing, cover the two columns on the right so you cannot see them. Next, read the acronym in the left column and interpret its meaning. Then see whether your interpretation identifies you as a baby boomer (born between 1945–1964) or a Generation Xer (born between 1965–1981).

Abbreviation or acronym	Response by Baby Boomers	Response by Generation Xers
C.I.A.	Central Intelligence Agency—a governmental organization that is responsible for spying for the United States	Culinary Institute of America—a premier cooking school
T.L.C.	Tender loving care—something that is given by nurses to sick people	The Learning Channel—a popular television offering for children
4.0	A perfect grade point average for a college student	A version of a software program that may finally be bug free
10K	A 10-kilometer race	A year-end financial report
NATO	North American Treaty Organization—a group of countries (including the United States and the UK) that have banded together for mutual defense	The National Association of Theater Owners—a group of powerful movie exhibitors
I.R.A.	The Irish Republican Army—a radical political group	An Individual Retirement Account that allows people to make pretax contributions and thus build a nest egg for the future
LP	A vinyl, long-playing album	A limited partnership that offers tax benefits to participants
M.P.G.	Miles per gallon—it tells drivers how efficiently their car is performing	Multiplayer games that can keep children occupied for hours on their computer
W.W.F.	The World Wildlife Fund, a group of animal lovers	The World Wrestling Federation, the premier organization for sponsoring arena wrestling

perceptual process once the information from the situation is received. An individual seldom perceives patches of color or light or sound. Instead, the person will perceive organized patterns of stimuli and identifiable whole objects. For example, when a college student is shown a basketball, the student does not normally perceive it as the color brown or as grain-leather in texture or as the odor of leather. Rather, the student perceives a basketball that has, in addition to the characteristics named, a potential for giving the perceiver fun and excitement as either a participant or a spectator. In other words, the person's perceptual process organizes the incoming information into a meaningful whole. Similar to selectivity, there are several principles of perceptual organization.

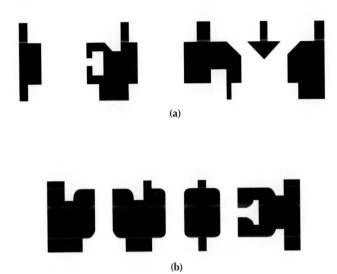

(a)

(b)

FIGURE 6.4
Illustrations of figure-ground.

Figure-Ground.   Figure-ground is usually considered to be the most basic form of perceptual organization. The figure-ground principle means simply that perceived objects stand out as separable from their general background. It can be effectively demonstrated as one is reading this paragraph. In terms of light-wave stimuli, the reader is receiving patches of irregularly shaped blacks and whites. Yet the reader does not perceive it this way. The reader perceives black shapes—letters, words, and sentences—printed against a white background. To say it another way, the reader perceptually organizes incoming stimuli into recognizable figures (words) that are seen against a ground (white page).

Another interesting figure-ground illustration is shown in Figure 6.4. At first glance, one probably perceives a jumble of black, irregular shapes against a white background. Only when the white letters are perceptually organized against a black background will the words FLY and TIE literally jump out with clarity. This illustration shows that perceptual selectivity will influence perceptual organization. The viewer is set to perceive black on white because of the black words (figures) throughout the book. However, in Figure 6.4 the reverse is true. White is the figure and black is the ground.

Perceptual Grouping.   The grouping principle of perceptual organization states that there is a tendency to group several stimuli together into a recognizable pattern. This principle is very basic and seems to be largely inborn. There are certain underlying uniformities in grouping. When simple constellations of stimuli are presented to people, they will tend to group them together by closure, continuity, proximity, or similarity.

1.   *Closure.*   The closure principle of grouping is closely related to the gestalt school of psychology. A basic gestalt principle is that a person will sometimes perceive a whole when one does not actually exist. The person's perceptual process will close the gaps that are unfilled from sensory input. In the formal organization, participants may either see a whole where none exists or not be able to put the pieces together into a whole that does exist. An example of the first case is the head of a project team who perceived complete agreement among the

members on a given project when, in fact, there was opposition from several members. The team leader in this situation closed the existing gaps and perceived complete agreement when, in fact, it did not exist. An example of the other side of the coin is the adage of not being able to see the forest (whole) because of the trees (parts). High degrees of specialization have often resulted in functionally oriented managers' losing sight of the whole organization's objectives. Specialists may get so caught up in their own little area of interest and responsibility that they may lose sight of the overall goal. They cannot close their part together with the other parts to perceive the whole. It is because of this problem that most organizations today have promoted interfunctional structures by emphasizing horizontal rather than traditional vertical, hierarchical structural arrangements. Chapter 4 on organization theory and design went into detail on some of these organizational designs.

2. *Continuity.* Continuity is closely related to closure. Some psychologists do not even bother to make a distinction between the two grouping principles. However, there is a slight difference. Closure supplies *missing* stimuli, whereas the continuity principle says that a person will tend to perceive *continuous* lines or patterns. This type of continuity may lead to inflexible, or noncreative, thinking on the part of organizational participants. Only the obvious, continuous patterns or relationships will be perceived. For example, a new design for some productive process or product may be limited to obvious flows or continuous lines. New, innovative ideas or designs may not be perceived. Continuity can greatly influence the systems design of a seamless organizational structure.

3. *Proximity.* The principle of proximity, or nearness, states that a group of stimuli that are close together will be perceived as a whole pattern of parts belonging together. For example, several employees in an organization may be identified as a single group because of physical proximity. Several workers who work on a particular process may be perceived as a single whole. If the output is low and the supervisor reports a number of grievances from the group, management may perceive all the workers on this process as one troublemaking group when, in fact, some of the workers are loyal, dedicated employees. Yet the fact remains that often department or work groups are perceived as a single entity because of physical proximity. As teams have become common in today's organizations, this principle of proximity will help identify them as a single entity. This perception may help solidify the team and promote teamwork. Chapter 14 on group dynamics and teams examines such processes in detail.

4. *Similarity.* The principle of similarity states that the greater the similarity of the stimuli, the greater the tendency to perceive them as a common group. Similarity is conceptually related to proximity but in most cases is stronger than proximity. In an organization, all employees who wear white collars may be perceived as a common group, when, in reality, each employee is a unique individual. Similarity also applies to minorities and women. There is a tendency to perceive minority and women employees as a single group, the famous "they." This of course can lead to stereotyping problems, which are discussed in a later section.

Perceptual Constancy.   Constancy is one of the more sophisticated forms of perceptual organization. It gives a person a sense of stability in a changing world. This principle permits the individual to have some constancy in a tremendously variable and highly complex world. Learning plays a much bigger role in the constancy phenomenon than in figure-ground or grouping phenomena.

FIGURE 6.5
Doodles illustrate the role
that context plays in
perception.

The size, shape, color, brightness, and location of an object are fairly constant regardless of the information received by the senses. It should be pointed out that perceptual constancy results from *patterns* of cues. These patterns are for the most part learned, but each situation is different, and there are interactions between the inborn and learned tendencies within the entire perceptual process.

If constancy were not at work, the world would be very chaotic and disorganized for the individual. An organizational example would be the worker who must select a piece of material or a tool of the correct size from a wide variety of materials and tools at varying distances from a workstation. Without perceptual constancy, the sizes, shapes, and colors of objects would change as the worker moved about and would make the job almost impossible.

Perceptual Context.   The highest, most sophisticated form of perceptual organization is context. It gives meaning and value to simple stimuli, objects, events, situations, and other persons in the environment. The principle of context can be simply demonstrated by doodles such as the one shown in Figure 6.5. The visual stimuli by themselves are meaningless. Only when the doodle is placed in a verbal context does it take on meaning and value to the perceiver. (The doodle in Figure 6.5 is the start of a "rat race.")

The organizational culture and structure provide the primary context in which workers and managers do their perceiving. Thus, a verbal order, an e-mail message, a new policy, a suggestion, a raised eyebrow, or a pat on the back takes on special meaning and value when placed in the context of the work organization. The preceding chapters presented the environmental and organizational context in which organizational participants perceive.

SOCIAL PERCEPTION

Although the selectivity and organization principles are closely related to social perception, this section gives recognition to social perception per se. The social aspects of perception are given detailed coverage because they play such an important role in organizational behavior. Social perception is directly concerned with how one individual perceives other individuals: how we get to know others.

Characteristics of Perceiver and Perceived

A summary of classic research findings on some specific characteristics of the perceiver and the perceived reveals a profile of the perceiver as follows:

1. Knowing oneself makes it easier to see others accurately.
2. One's own characteristics affect the characteristics one is likely to see in others.
3. People who accept themselves are more likely to be able to see favorable aspects of other people.
4. Accuracy in perceiving others is not a single skill.[14]

These four characteristics greatly influence how a person perceives others in the environmental situation.

There are also certain characteristics of the person being perceived that influence social perception. Research has shown that:

1. The status of the person perceived will greatly influence others' perception of the person.
2. The person being perceived is usually placed into categories to simplify the viewer's perceptual activities. Two common categories are status and role.
3. The visible traits of the person perceived will greatly influence others' perception of the person.[15]

These characteristics of the perceiver and the perceived suggest the extreme complexity of social perception. Organizational participants must realize that their perceptions of another person are greatly influenced by their own characteristics and the characteristics of the other person. For example, if a manager has high self-esteem and the other person is pleasant and comes from the home office, then the manager will likely perceive this other person in a positive, favorable manner. On the other hand, if the manager has low self-esteem and the other person is an arrogant salesperson, the manager will likely perceive this other person in a negative, unfavorable manner. Such attributions that people make of others play a vital role in their social perceptions and resulting behavior.

Participants in formal organizations are constantly perceiving one another. Managers are perceiving workers, workers are perceiving managers, line personnel are perceiving staff personnel, staff personnel are perceiving the line personnel, frontline employees are perceiving customers, customers are perceiving frontline employees, and on and on. There are numerous complex factors that enter into such social perception, but most important are the problems associated with stereotyping, the halo effect, and the cognitive process of causal attribution covered next.

Stereotyping

The term *stereotype* refers to the tendency to perceive another person (hence social perception) as belonging to a *single* class or category. The word itself is derived from the typographer's word for a printing plate made from previously composed type. In 1922, Walter Lippman applied the word to perception. Since then, "stereotyping" has become a frequently used term to describe perceptual errors. In particular, it is employed in analyzing prejudice. Not commonly acknowledged is the fact that stereotyping may attribute favorable or unfavorable traits to the person being perceived. Most often a person is put into a stereotype because the perceiver knows only the overall category to which the person belongs. However, because each individual is unique, the real traits of the person will generally be quite different from those the stereotype would suggest.

Stereotyping greatly influences social perception in today's organizations. Common stereotyped groups include managers, supervisors, knowledge workers, union members, young people, old people, minorities, women, white- and blue-collar workers, and all the various functional and staff specialists, for example, accountants, salespeople, computer programmers, and engineers. There may be a general consensus about the traits possessed by the members of these categories. Yet in reality there is often a discrepancy between the agreed-upon traits of each category and the actual traits of the members. In other words, not all engineers carry laptop computers and are coldly rational, nor are all human resource managers do-gooders who are trying to keep workers happy. On the contrary, there are individual differences and a great deal of variability among members of these and all other groups. In spite of this, other organization members commonly make blanket perceptions and behave accordingly. For example, one recent analysis noted that a major problem General Motors has is the institutionalized set of managerial beliefs about its customers, workers, foreign competitors, and the government. These perceptions cause the GM leadership to blame their problems on the famous stereotyped "them" instead of recognizing the need for fundamental corporate culture change.[16] There is also research indicating that long exposure to negative stereotypes may result in the members having an inferiority anxiety or lowered expectations.[17] There are numerous other research studies[18] and common, everyday examples that point out stereotyping and its problems that occur in organizational life.

The Halo Effect

The *halo effect* in social perception is very similar to stereotyping. Whereas in stereotyping the person is perceived according to a single category, under the halo effect the person is perceived on the basis of one trait. Halo is often discussed in performance appraisal when a rater makes an error in judging a person's total personality and/or performance on the basis of a single positive trait such as intelligence, appearance, dependability, or cooperativeness. Whatever the single trait is, it may override all other traits in forming the perception of the person. For example, a person's physical appearance or dress may override all other characteristics in making a selection decision or in appraising the person's performance. The opposite is sometimes called the "horns effect" where an individual is downgraded because of a single negative characteristic or incident.[19]

The halo effect problem has been given considerable attention in research on performance appraisal. For example, a comprehensive review of the performance appraisal literature found that halo effect was the dependent variable in over a third of the studies and was found to be a major problem affecting appraisal accuracy.[20] The current thinking on the halo effect can be summarized from the extensive research literature as follows:

1. It is a common rater error.
2. It has both true and illusory components.
3. It has led to inflated correlations among rating dimensions and is due to the influence of a general evaluation and specific judgments.
4. It has negative consequences and should be avoided or removed.[21]

Like all the other aspects of the psychological process of perception discussed in this chapter, the halo effect has important implications for the study and eventual understanding of organizational behavior. Unfortunately, even though the halo effect is one of the longest recognized and most pervasive problems associated with applications such as performance appraisal in the field of organizational behavior, a critical analysis of the considerable research concludes that we still do not know much about the impact of the halo effect[22] and attempts at solving the problem have not yet been very successful.[23] In other words, overcoming perceptual problems such as stereotyping and the halo effect remains an important challenge for effective human resources management.

ATTRIBUTION

Attribution refers simply to how people explain the cause of another's or their own behavior. It is the cognitive process by which people draw conclusions about the factors that influence, or make sense of, one another's behavior.[24] Applied to social perception, there are two general types of attributions that people make: *dispositional attributions,* which ascribe a person's behavior to internal factors such as personality traits, motivation, or ability, and *situational attributions,* which attribute a person's behavior to external factors such as equipment or social influence from others.[25] In recent years, attribution theories have been playing an increasingly important role in organizational behavior and human resource management,[26] but they are also recognized to influence perceptions. An examination of the various theories, types, and errors of attribution can contribute not only social perception, but also motivation (Chapter 8) and organization behavior in general.

Attribution Theory

Attribution theory is concerned with the relationship between personal, social perception and interpersonal behavior. There are a number of attribution theories, but they share the following assumptions:

1.   We seek to make sense of our world.
2.   We often attribute people's actions either to internal or external causes.
3.   We do so in fairly logical ways.[27]

Well-known social psychologist Harold Kelley stressed that attribution theory is concerned mainly with the cognitive processes by which an individual interprets behavior as being caused by (or attributed to) certain parts of the relevant environment. It is concerned with the "why" questions of organizational behavior. Because most causes, attributes, and "whys" are not directly observable, the theory says that people must depend on cognitions, particularly perception. The attribution theorist assumes that humans are rational and are motivated to identify and understand the causal structure of their relevant environment. It is this search for attributes that characterizes attribution theory.

Although attribution theory has its roots in all the pioneering cognitive theorists' work (for example, that of Lewin and Festinger), in de Charmes's ideas on cognitive evaluation, and in Bem's notion of "self-perception," the theory's initiator is generally recognized to be Fritz Heider. Heider believed that both internal forces (personal attributes such as ability, effort, and fatigue) and external forces (environmental attributes such as rules and the weather) combine additively to determine behavior. He stressed that it is the *perceived,* not the actual, determinants that are important to behavior. People will behave differently if they perceive internal attributes than they will if they perceive external attributes. It is this concept of differential ascriptions that has very important implications for organizational behavior.

Locus of Control Attributions

Using *locus of control,* work behavior may be explained by whether employees perceive their outcomes as controlled internally or externally. Employees who perceive internal control feel that they personally can influence their outcomes through their own ability, skills, or effort. Employees who perceive external control feel that their outcomes are beyond their own control; they feel that external forces such as luck or task difficulty control their outcomes. This perceived locus of control may have a differential impact on their performance and satisfaction. For example, studies by Rotter and his colleagues suggest that skill versus chance environments differentially affect behavior.[28]

In addition, a number of studies have been conducted in recent years to test the attribution theory–locus of control model in work settings. One study found that internally controlled employees are generally more satisfied with their jobs, are more likely to be in managerial positions, and are more satisfied with a participatory management style than employees who perceive external control.[29] Other studies have found that internally controlled managers are better performers,[30] are more considerate of subordinates,[31] tend not to burn out,[32] follow a more strategic style of executive action,[33] and have improved attitudes over a long period of time following promotions.[34] In addition, the attribution process has been shown to play a role in coalition formation in the political process of organizations. In particular, coalition members made stronger internal attributions, such as ability and desire, and nonmembers made stronger external attributions, such as luck.[35]

The implication of these studies is that internally controlled managers are somehow better than externally controlled managers. However, such generalizations are not yet warranted because there is some contradictory evidence. For example, one study concluded that the ideal manager may have an external orientation because the results indicated that externally controlled managers were perceived as initiating more structure and consideration than internally controlled managers.[36] In addition to the implications for managerial behavior and performance, attribution theory has been shown to have relevance in explaining goal-setting behavior,[37] leadership behavior,[38] and poor employee performance.[39] However, like other constructs in organizational behavior, attribution is now undergoing considerable refinement in the research literature. For example, recent studies have found that (1) attributions about poor performance are mediated by how responsible the employee is judged to be and how much sympathy the evaluator feels,[40] and (2) leaders providing feedback to poor performers is significantly affected by the performance attributions that are made.[41] A review article concludes that locus of control is related to the performance and satisfaction of organization members and may moderate the relationship between motivation and incentives.[42]

In addition, attributions are related to *organizational symbolism,* which in effect says that in order to understand organizations, one must recognize their symbolic nature.[43] Much of organization is based on attributions rather than physical or observed realities under this view.[44] For example, research has found that symbols are a salient source of information used by people in forming their impressions of psychological climate.[45]

Other Attributions

Attribution theory contributes a great deal to the better understanding of organizational behavior. However, other dimensions besides the internal and external locus of control also need to be accounted for and studied. Bernard Weiner, for example, suggested that a stability (fixed or variable) dimension must also be recognized.[46] Experienced employees will probably have a stable internal attribution about their abilities but an unstable internal attribution concerning effort. By the same token, these employees may have a stable external attribution about task difficulty but an unstable external attribution about luck.

Besides the stability dimension, Kelley suggests that dimensions such as consensus (do others act this way in a situation?), consistency (does this person act this way in this situation at other times?), and distinctiveness (does this person act differently in

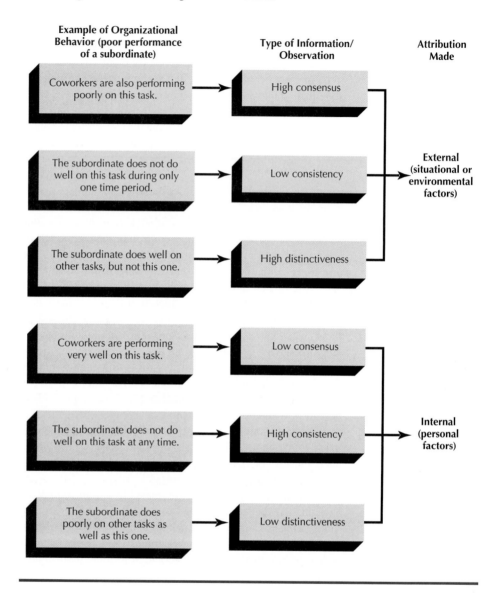

Example of Organizational Behavior (poor performance of a subordinate)

Coworkers are also performing poorly on this task.

The subordinate does not do well on this task during only one time period.

The subordinate does well on other tasks, but not this one.

Coworkers are performing very well on this task.

The subordinate does not do well on this task at any time.

The subordinate does poorly on other tasks as well as this one.

Type of Information/ Observation

High consensus

Low consistency

High distinctiveness

Low consensus

High consistency

Low distinctiveness

Attribution Made

External (situational or environmental factors)

Internal (personal factors)

FIGURE 6.6
Kelley's model of attribution.

other situations?) will affect the type of attributions that are made.[47] Figure 6.6 shows how this type of information affects the attributes that are made in evaluating employee behavior. To keep these dimensions straight, it can be remembered that consensus relates to other *people,* distinctiveness relates to other *tasks,* and consistency relates to *time.*[48] As shown in Figure 6.6, if there is high consensus, low consistency, and high distinctiveness, then attribution to external or situational/environmental causes will probably be made. The external attribution may be that the task is too difficult or that outside pressures from home or coworkers are hindering performance. However, if there is low consensus, high consistency, and low distinctiveness, then attributions to internal or personal causes for the behavior will probably be made. The supervisor making an internal attribution may conclude that the subordinate just doesn't have the ability, or is not giving the necessary effort, or does not have the motivation to perform well. There is some research evidence from field settings to directly support predictions from the Kelley model.[49]

In addition to Kelley, other well-known theorists, such as Weiner, use attribution theory to help explain achievement motivation and to predict subsequent changes in performance and how people feel about themselves.[50] Some research findings from Weiner's work include the following:

1. Bad-luck attributions (external) take the sting out of a negative outcome, but good-luck attributions (external) reduce the joy associated with success.
2. When individuals attribute their success to internal rather than external factors, they have higher expectations for future success, report a greater desire for achievement, and set higher performance goals.[51]

Attribution Errors

Social psychologists recognize two potent biases when people make attributions. The first is called the *fundamental attribution error.* Research has found that people tend to ignore powerful situational forces when explaining others' behavior.[52] People tend to attribute *others'* behavior to personal factors (for example, intelligence, ability, motivation, attitudes, or personality), even when it is very clear that the situation or circumstances caused the person to behave the way he or she did.

Another attribution bias that has emerged from the research is that people tend to present themselves favorably. This *self-serving bias* has been found in study after study; people readily accept credit when told they have succeeded (attributing the success to their ability and effort), yet often attribute failure to such external, situational factors as bad luck or the problem's inherent "impossibility."[53] For example, in explaining their victories, athletes commonly credit themselves, but they are more likely to attribute losses to something else—bad breaks, poor officiating, or the other team's superior effort.[54]

When something goes wrong in the workplace, there is a tendency for the boss to blame the problem on the inability or poor attitude of the subordinates, but the situation is blamed as far as he or she personally is concerned. The reverse is true of the subordinates. They blame the situation for their difficulties but make a personal attribution in terms of their boss. By the same token, if something goes well, the boss makes personal attributions for him- or herself and situational attributions for subordinates, and the subordinates make personal attributions for themselves but situational attributions for the boss. In other words, it is typical to have conflicting attributional biases among managers and subordinates in organizations.[55] As a way of creating more productive relationships, theorists and researchers suggest that efforts must be made to reduce divergent perceptions and perspectives among the parties through increased interpersonal interaction, open communication channels and workshops, and team-building sessions devoted to reducing attributional errors.[56] Although Martinko, in his book on *Attribution Theory,* demonstrates the validity and potential of attributional perspectives within an organizational context, theoretical, information processing, and situational factors all affect the attribution models of organizational behavior.[57] Despite this complexity, attribution theory does seem to have considerable potential for application and relevance, instead of being a purely academic exercise in theory building.

IMPRESSION MANAGEMENT

Whereas social perception is concerned with how one individual perceives other individuals and attribution is how people explain their own and others' behavior, *impression management* (sometimes called "self-presentation") is the process by which people attempt to manage or control the perceptions others form of them. There is often a tendency for people to try to present themselves so as to impress others in a socially desirable way. Thus, impression management has considerable implications for areas such as the validity of performance appraisals (is the evaluator being manipulated into giving a positive rating?) and is a pragmatic, political tool for one to build image and be successful.

The Process of Impression Management

As with other cognitive processes, impression management has many possible conceptual dimensions[58] and has been researched in relation to aggression, attitude change, attributions, social facilitation, and leadership.[59] Two separate components of impression management have been identified—impression motivation and impression construction.[60] Especially in an employment situation, subordinates may be motivated to control how their boss perceives them. The degree of this motivation to impression-manage will depend on such factors as the relevance the impressions have to the individual's goals, the value of these goals, and the discrepancy between the image one would like others to hold and the image one believes others already hold.[61]

Impression construction, the other major process, is concerned with the specific type of impression people want to make and how they go about doing it. Although some theorists limit the type of impression only to personal characteristics, others include such other things as attitudes, physical states, interests, or values. Using this broader approach, five factors have been identified as being especially relevant to the kinds of impressions people try to construct: the self-concept, desired and undesired identity images, role constraints, target's values, and current social image.[62] Although there is considerable research on how these five factors influence the type of impression that people try to make, there is still little known of how they select the way to manage others' perceptions of them. For example, do they directly tell their boss things such as "I'm really competitive and want to get ahead" or do they make indirect statements such as "I really like racquetball; it is really competitive." There is also research evidence indicating that managers who are high self-monitors (regulate and control themselves based on situational and interpersonal cues) are more sensitive and responsive to adjusting their self-presentations or impressions.[63] These high self-monitors were found to be more likely to be promoted, but they are also more likely to change employers or to make a job-related move to a different state or country.

Employee Impression Management Strategies

There are two basic strategies of impression management that employees can use. If employees are trying to minimize responsibility for some negative event or to stay out of trouble, they may employ a demotion-preventative strategy. On the other hand, if they are seeking to maximize responsibility for a positive outcome or to look better than they really are, then they can use a promotion-enhancing strategy.[64] The demotion-preventative strategy is characterized by the following:

1. *Accounts.* These are employees' attempts to excuse or justify their actions. Example excuses are not feeling well or not getting something done on time because of another higher-priority assignment.
2. *Apologies.* When there is no logical way out, the employee may apologize to the boss for some negative event. Such an apology not only gives the impression that the individual is sorry but also indicates that it will not happen again. The employee is big enough to face up to a problem and solve it.
3. *Disassociation.* When employees are indirectly associated with something that went wrong (for example, they are members of a committee or work team that made a bad decision), they may secretly tell their boss that they fought for the right thing but were overruled. Employees using this approach try to remove themselves both from the group and from responsibility for the problem.[65]

The promotion-enhancing strategies involve the following:

1. *Entitlements.* Under this approach, employees feel that they have not been given credit for a positive outcome. They make sure that it is known through formal channels. Or they may informally note to key people that they are pleased their suggestions or efforts worked out so well.
2. *Enhancements.* Here, employees may have received credit, but they point out that they really did more and had a bigger impact than originally thought. For example, their effort or idea not only served a customer well or met a difficult deadline, but can be used in the future to greatly increase profits.
3. *Obstacle disclosures.* In this strategy, employees identify either personal (health or family) or organizational (lack of resources or cooperation) obstacles they had to overcome to accomplish an outcome. They are trying to create the perception that because they obtained the positive outcome despite the big obstacles, they really deserve a lot of credit.
4. *Association.* Here, the employee makes sure to be seen with the right people at the right times. This creates the perception that the employee is well connected and is associated with successful projects.[66]

The preceding strategies help construct impressions or perceptions. The motivation on the part of employees may or may not be a deliberate attempt to enhance themselves in terms of political power, promotions, and monetary rewards. A recent analysis indicated that impression management might motivate employee citizenship behaviors (i.e., going beyond the normally required and rewarded behaviors for the good of the department or organization).[67] In other words, the motivation in this case may be to look good (impression management) instead of doing well for its own sake (citizenship behavior). Recent research indicates the specific impression management strategy that is used will depend on the situation (e.g., employment interview, performance appraisal or training session.)[68] Thus, managers should be aware of deliberate manipulation of perceptions when making evaluations of their people. By the same token, such impression management could be positively used to get ahead in an organization or keep good relations with customers.

Here are some guidelines that have been offered for organizational members that will help them recognize various impression management tactics and the motives behind them:

1. One should be on the lookout for high-probability impression management strategies. For example, recruiters should be careful to separate pure self-promotion and

legitimate claims of competence, and those in positions of power or status should be aware of subordinates' efforts to ingratiate themselves ("buttering up the boss" and "apple-polishing").

2. There should be an attempt to minimize personal, situational, and organizational features that foster undesirable impression management. For example, organizations in which task performance is ambiguous and/or resources are scarce tend to generate relatively high levels of ingratiation.

3. One should look for ulterior motives and avoid being overly influenced by impression management. For example, a manager who is able to distinguish between pure self-promotion and true competence is less likely to be biased by an invalid claim when appraising a staff member's performance.[69]

In total, there is no question that deliberately employing an impression management strategy can have a positive impact on performance evaluations and getting ahead in an organization.[70] Even something as simple as dressing for success can have an impact on both an individual's and even an organization's outcomes. In one research study of woman's choices of work attire, it was found that:

1. Women chose their attire to match their organizational level function, tasks, and special events of a particular day. Their knowledge of appropriate dress was based on group/societal norms, not written organizational rules or policies.

2. Women chose attire to help them perform their organizational roles. The women used dress to assume the role of employee and changed into other clothes for nonwork roles such as parent or volunteer.

3. Women expended considerable time and energy in shopping for appropriate clothing and planning what to wear to work. They feared reprimands from their supervisors if they wore clothes that were considered unprofessional.[71]

There is no question that dress codes in the workplace are changing. A recent national survey found almost half responded positively to the question "With the popularity of dress down day in the workplace, will the suit and tie ultimately disappear?"[72] To avoid "lawyer alerts" when suit clad attorneys call on high-tech, Internet firms (where dress is typically very casual), many law firms have recently gone to all-casual policies (usually simple slacks and shirts). One managing partner in a prestigious law firm in Cleveland said he got a standing ovation at the meeting in which he announced the casual-dress policy.[73] Yet, even though there will be cycles of dress codes, whatever it is, will still be used in impression management and social[74] and organizational identity. For example, Figure 6.7 uses the conspicuousness (the extent to which the dress of an organizational member stands out from the dress of nonmembers) and homogeneity (similarity) of dress to compare organizations.

In conclusion, probably the best advice is that offered by William Gardner at the end of his analysis of impression management. He states: "When selecting an image, never try to be something you're not. People will see through the facade. In sum, make every effort to put your best foot forward—but never at the cost of your identity or integrity!"[75] Put in other words, "We project the face that we believe is ours, hope is ours, and wish was ours—the persona that best suits our personality, weaknesses, stage in life, and immediate needs. T.S. Eliot had S. Alfred Prufrock say, 'There will be time/To prepare a face to meet the faces that you meet.'"[76]

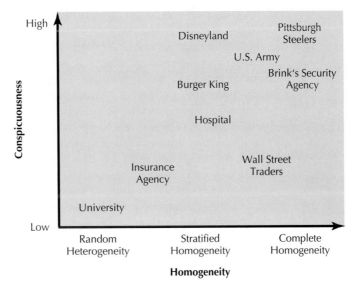

FIGURE 6.7

Comparing organizations on the basis of dress.

(*Source:* Anat Rafaeli and Michael G. Pratt, "Tailored Meanings: On the Meaning and Impact of Organizational Dress," *Academy of Management Review,* January 1993, p. 39. Used with permission.)

This figure is offered for illustrative purposes. Systematic observations are necessary to compare the exact locations of these various examples.

Summary

Perception is an important cognitive process. Through this complex process, persons make interpretations of the stimulus or situation they are faced with. Both selectivity and organization go into perceptual interpretations. Externally, selectivity is affected by intensity, size, contrast, repetition, motion, and novelty and familiarity. Internally, perceptual selectivity is influenced by the individual's motivation, learning, and personality. After the stimulus situation is filtered by the selective process, the incoming information is organized into a meaningful whole. Figure-ground is the most basic form of perceptual organization. Another basic form is the grouping of constellations of incoming stimuli by closure, continuity, proximity, and similarity. The constancy and context aspects of perceptual organization are more complex. The social context in particular plays an important role in understanding human behavior in organizations. Of particular importance to social perception are the two major problems of stereotyping (the tendency to perceive another person as belonging to a single class or category) and the halo effect (the tendency to perceive a person on the basis of one trait).

Attribution is a type of social perception concerned with how people explain the cause of another's or their own behavior. Attribution theory has a rich history from the cognitive pioneers in psychology. Applied to organizational behavior, locus of control (internal and external) attributions are very relevant, and research has found that internals tend to be more effective on a number of dimensions. Other types of attributions such as stability and consensus, consistency and distinctiveness have also received more recent attention in organizational behavior. So have the errors such as the fundamental attribution error (people tend to attribute others' behavior to personal factors) and self-serving bias (individuals take personal credit for successes, but attribute failure to the situation).

The last part of the chapter deals with controlling and constructing perceptions through impression management. Only recently recognized by the field of organizational behavior, impression management, or self-presentation, is the process by which people attempt to manage or control the perceptions others form of them. If employees are trying to minimize responsibility for some negative event or to stay out of trouble, they may employ a demotion-preventative strategy characterized by accounts, apologies, and/or disassociation. If they are seeking to maximize responsibility for a positive outcome or trying to look better than they really are, then they can use a promotion-enhancing strategy characterized by entitlements, enhancements, obstacle disclosures, and/or associations. Organization members should be aware of how impression management is being used on them and of impression management strategies that they can use. Although there is nothing wrong with looking as good as one can, one must always be true to oneself.

ENDING WITH META-ANALYTIC RESEARCH FINDINGS

OB PRINCIPLE: Appraisers attribute good performance to considerable ability and/or effort and poor performance to low ability and effort.

Meta-Analysis Results: [20 sets of results; 1,879 participants; $d = 1.09$] *On average, there is a **78 percent probability** that appraisers will attribute good performance to considerable ability and/or effort and poor performance to low ability and/or effort.* These results were found to be moderated by type of experimental setting. Results were stronger in lab settings than field settings.

Conclusion: Attribution theory is important for understanding perceptions in the workplace. Despite the stability of research findings and everyday behavior regarding attributional principles, many have questioned whether the theory holds up in actual workplace behaviors. Determining the generalizability of attribution principles is important because how and what individuals attribute causes of their own and others' behavior has implications for performance appraisal, motivation, leadership, and human performance. As you have learned in this chapter, attribution theory posits that, depending on the situation, individuals will attribute causes of their own and others' behavior to causes such as effort, ability, luck, or task difficulty. Attributions made may not always result in biases such as the self-serving bias and the fundamental attribution error, but being aware and understanding that these biases may be occurring will make attributions of one's own and others' behavior more effective.

Source: Christy L. De Vader, Allan G. Bateson and Robert G. Lord, "Attribution Theory: A Meta-Analysis of Attributional Hypotheses," in Edwin A. Locke (Ed.), *Generalizing from Laboratory to Field Settings,* Heath, Lexington, Mass., 1986.

Questions for Discussion and Review

1. Do you agree with the opening observation that people are human information processors? Why?
2. How does sensation differ from perception?
3. Give some examples of the external factors that affect perceptual selectivity.
4. Explain how perceptual constancy works.
5. What does stereotyping mean? Why is it considered to be a perceptual problem?
6. What is meant by the halo effect? Summarize the current thinking on this halo effect.
7. What is attribution theory? How can locus of control be applied to workers and managers?
8. What two major attribution errors or biases have surfaced? Give an example of each.
9. What is meant by impression management? What is meant by impression motivation and impression construction?
10. What are some of the major strategies employees can use in impression management?

Internet Exercise: Perceptual Illusions

Visit the website http://www.illusionworks.com It has detailed descriptions of the psychological reasons behind some of the perceptual illusions described in this chapter, as well as many practical, hands-on exercises. Be sure to go to the advanced section to see the detailed reasons behind why we perceive things in different ways.

1. What principles of perception discussed in the chapter are found or implied in the discussion on the website?
2. Consider times when a better understanding of the perception process could have prevented a large problem, either in a job you have had or in your personal life. How would this understanding have helped you avoid or solve the problem?

REAL CASE:
Dressing Down for
Success

It's so hard to dress for success these days. For Jack Steeg, vice-president for sales at the Internet-partner division of Dell Computer in Austin, Tex., choosing what to wear to work used to be a no-brainer. He'd put on a white shirt, tie, and suit and be done with it. But with the introduction of casual-dress rules, picking an office wardrobe has become a major task. That's why Steeg, 51, recently hired image consultant Sherry Maysonave to give him some pointers on choosing casual outfits that befit his station.

It's the ultimate sartorial irony: Less restrictive dress codes were supposed to make life more comfortable for everyone. Instead, with the old rules gone, many people are in a state of dress-down confusion. As a result, companies are refining their dress policies or hiring consultants such as Maysonave to help.

Of course, there are some general guidelines that will keep you from getting too far off the mark. Fashion experts say men usually can't go wrong with a sports coat in muted colors and flannel or gabardine trousers. Shirts, whether button-down or knit pullover, must have a collar. Women can wear pantsuits or tailored pants with a sweater set.

Beyond that, the rules get fuzzy. For one thing, they vary by region and industry. Not surprisingly, the East Coast and Midwest are more conservative than the West Coast. About 50 percent of financial, insurance, and real estate companies allow casual dress once a week, but just 34 percent permit it all the time, according to the Society for Human Resource Management. The SHRM says 44 percent of all businesses have adopted all-casual, all-the-time policies, up from 36 percent in 1998.

Companies have also learned that if they don't lay down specific policies, the words "dress casual" can be subject to wide interpretation.

Three years ago, when Development Counselors expanded its casual-Friday dress code to five days a week, its 25 employees were delighted. But then they started wearing just about anything they wanted—torn jeans, gym clothes, tube tops. Things got so out of hand that management formed a committee to devise an official dress policy. It then attached the new guidelines to the employee handbook.

Two years ago, the Austin office of Kennedy-Wilson International, a Los Angeles commercial real estate firm, adopted a casual-Friday policy and sent out a brief statement about appropriate dress, nixing such items as sundresses and jogging suits. More recently, when the office introduced a new arrangement—business casual Monday through Thursday and plain casual on Friday—they revised the requirements considerably. Example: Monday through Thursday, men have to wear shirts with collars and muted patterns; Friday, Hawaiian shirts are O.K.

When companies turn to image consultants, they are usually seeking guidance for more than just deciding whether, say, open-toed shoes are acceptable. They also must make sure policies aren't potentially discriminatory. Ideally, that means that if you indicate specific restrictions for women, you ought to do the same for men, and vice versa. "These things are sometimes held up in the legal department for weeks," says Isbecque. Some consultants conduct seminars for managers in how to enforce the rules. Isbecque, for example, leads role-playing exercises, holding up photographs of specific infractions and asking participants to demonstrate how they would confront a guilty employee. The bottom line is that although suits and ties may never regain their once ubiquitous presence in the workplace, companies are stopping well short of anything goes.

1. What is your reaction to the current status of dress codes in today's organizations? Give both sides, but on balance, what do you think the code should be?
2. From a perception standpoint, why do you think there is such variation in how employees interpret dress policies? What, if anything, should be done about these differing perceptions?
3. With the current status of dress codes in organizations, what implications are there for your use of impression management to get ahead in your career?

ORGANIZATIONAL BEHAVIOR CASE: Space Utilization

Sherman Adder, assistant plant manager for Frame Manufacturing Company, is chairperson of the ad hoc committee for space utilization. The committee is made up of the various department heads in the company. The plant manager of Frame has given Sherman the responsibility for seeing whether the various office, operations, and warehouse facilities of the company are being optimally utilized. The company is beset by rising costs and the need for more space. However, before okaying an expensive addition to the plant, the plant manager wants to be sure that the currently available space is being utilized properly.

Sherman opened up the first committee meeting by reiterating the charge of the committee. Then Sherman asked the members if they had any initial observations to make. The first to speak was the office manager. He stated: "Well, I know we are using every possible inch of room that we have available to us. But when I walk out into the plant, I see a lot of open spaces. We have people piled on top of one another, but out in the plant there seems to be plenty of room." The production manager quickly replied: "We do not have a lot of space. You office people have the luxury facilities. My supervisors don't even have room for a desk and a file cabinet. I have repeatedly told the plant manager we need more space. After all, our operation determines whether this plant succeeds or fails, not you people in the front office playing with your computer." Sherman interrupted at this point and said: "Obviously, we have different interpretations of the space utilization around here. Before further discussion I think it would be best if we have some objective facts to work with. I am going to ask the systems engineer to provide us with some statistics on plant and office layouts before our next meeting. Today's meeting is adjourned."

1. What perceptual principles are evident in this case?
2. What concept was brought out when the production manager accused the office personnel of playing with computers? Can you give other organizational examples of this concept?
3. Do you think that Sherman's approach to getting "objective facts" from statistics on plant and office layout will affect the perceptions of the office and production managers? How does such information affect perception in general?

ORGANIZATIONAL BEHAVIOR CASE: Same Accident, Different Perceptions

According to the police report, on July 9 at 1:27 P.M., bus number 3763 was involved in a minor noninjury accident. Upon arriving at the scene of the accident, police were unable to locate the driver of the bus. Because the bus was barely drivable, the passengers were transferred to a backup bus, and the damaged bus was returned to the city bus garage for repair.

The newly hired general manager, Aaron Moore, has been going over the police report and two additional reports. One of the additional reports was submitted by Jennifer Tye, the transportation director for the City Transit Authority (CTA), and the other came directly from the driver in the accident, Michael Meyer. According to Tye, although Mike has been an above-average driver for almost eight years, his performance has taken a drastic nosedive during the past 15 months. Always one to join the other drivers for an afterwork drink or two, Mike recently has been suspected of drinking on the job. Furthermore, according to Tye's report, Mike was seen having a beer in a tavern located less than two blocks from the CTA terminal at around 3 P.M. on the day of the accident. Tye's report concludes by citing two sections of the CTA Transportation Agreement. Section 18a specifically forbids the drinking of alcoholic beverages by any CTA employee while on duty. Section 26f prohibits drivers from leaving their buses unattended for any reason. Violation of either of the two sections results in automatic dismissal of the employee involved. Tye recommends immediate dismissal.

According to the driver, Michael Meyer, however, the facts are quite different. Mike claims that in attempting to miss a bicycle rider he swerved and struck a tree, causing minor damage to the bus. Mike had been talking with the dispatcher when he was forced to drop his phone receiver in order to miss the bicycle. Because the receiver broke open on impact, Mike was forced to walk four blocks to the nearest phone to report the accident. As soon as he reported the accident to the company, Mike also called the union to tell them about it. Mike reports that when he returned to the scene of the accident, his bus was gone. Uncertain of what to do and a little frightened, he decided to return to the CTA terminal. Because it was over a five-mile walk and because his shift had already ended at 3 P.M., Mike stopped in for a quick beer just before getting back to the terminal.

1. Why are the two reports submitted by Jennifer and Mike so different? Did Jennifer and Mike have different perceptions of the same incident?
2. What additional information would you need if you were in Aaron Moore's position? How can he clarify his own perception of the incident?
3. Given the information presented above, how would you recommend resolving this problem?
4. Can transportation director Jennifer Tye use impression management? What strategy would she use if her recommendation is accepted? If her recommendation is overruled?

Chapter 7

Personality and Attitudes

Learning Objectives

Define the overall meaning of personality.

Identify the "Big Five" personality traits and the Myers-Briggs types.

Describe the meaning of attitudes and their emotional, informational, and behavioral components.

Explain the antecedents of work-related attitudes, the functions they perform, and how they are changed.

Examine the major sources and outcomes of job satisfaction, organizational commitment, and prosocial, organizational citizenship behaviors.

Starting with Best Practice Leaders' Advice

Insights into the Personalities and Attitudes of Virgin's Richard Branson and ABB's Percy Barnevik

Two of the best known entrepreneurs and business visionaries in the world are the "New Europe's" Richard Branson and Percy Barnevik. The flamboyant Branson is known as much for his highly publicized around-the-world hot air ballon adventures, sense of humor, and wide-open/empowered management style as he is for founding the Virgin empire consisting of Virgin Atlantic Airways, Virgin Cola, Virgin Mega stores around the globe, hotels, video and book publishing, and radio and television production. Barnevick, on the other hand, has a different personality but an equally impressive track record. In 1987, he pulled off one of the world's biggest cross-border mergers by combining the Swedish engineering group ASEA with the Swiss competitor Brown, Boveri (thus ABB), added 70 more European and American firms, and covered global markets in electric power generation and transmission equipment, high-speed trains, automation and robotics, and environmental control systems. INSEAD's Manfred Kets de Vries asks personal questions that reveal the personalities and attitudes of these two charismatic leaders.

Q1 to Branson: *What do you see as your weaknesses? Do you have any characteristics that get in the way of your work?*

Branson: I suspect not being able to say no. Hopefully, I am getting better at it now. But there are so many wonderful ideas. I do love new projects; I love new ideas. . . . My weaknesses really go back to the fact that I have spread myself too thin. In a purely business sense, I suspect that if I just wanted to maximize profits, I should have stayed more focused on one area and really concentrated on that one area. That's the conventional way, and I'm sure that's what most business schools teach. Perhaps it's right. But it wouldn't have been half as much fun. . . . I must admit that I feel very much alive when I set out to achieve something. On reflection, it's really more the fight than the actual achieving. I love people and I just love new creative challenges. Some people ask, why keep battling on when you can take it easy? My reason, basically, is that I'm very fortunate to be in the position I am. I've learned a great deal and I've had great fun doing so. I'm in a unique position of being able to do almost anything I like and achieve almost anything I wish. I don't want to waste the position that I find myself in. I know that at age 80 or 90 I would kick myself if I just frittered away this second half of my life. I really do believe that fighting competition is exciting. And it's good for business. I think that Virgin can get in there and it can compete with the biggest and improve them—and hopefully survive alongside them, have fun, and pay the bills at the same time. Basically, I admire anyone who takes on either the establishment or something like a mountain and succeeds or fails. . . . I sometimes wake up at night and lie there and think, "Is it all a dream?" Because it has been pretty good to date. It just seems almost too much for one man in one lifetime. So, if I am to reflect, I have been very fortunate to have so many wonderful experiences. Every day is fascinating. Every day, I am learning something new.

Q2 to Branson: *When you leave Virgin, what kind of enduring mark do you want to leave behind? How do you want to be remembered?*

Branson: I think that it would be nice if Virgin can be remembered as a company that challenged the established way of doing things, and that built up a number of companies that were world leaders in their own fields. That doesn't necessarily mean being the biggest companies, but the best in that particular field. I also would like that the staff of Virgin would have very happy memories of the time that they spent working here.

Q1 to Barnevik: *What gets you excited at work?*

Barnevik: A lot of things. I know I am competitive. Beating the competition for a big project gets me excited; so does breaking into a new industry where we weren't previously. But what really gives me the greatest satisfaction is seeing young people whom I have promoted succeed. Then you have created something that will outlast an individual transaction. At the same time, I have had some of my biggest disappointments when people fail. . . . I want my people to constantly test their imagination, their ability to move further. To create this change mentality, this creative spirit, you have to show them that the environment, the competitors, the customers are changing. In order to survive we have to change. You know the expression, "When you are through changing you are through!"

Q2 to Barnevik: *Given your reputation of always being overprepared, do people in the company question some of your ideas? Do they dare to disagree?*

Barnevik: It's a difficult question to answer because all executives say, "Oh sure others disagree." Even the worst dictators tend to say something like that. Now, I appreciate that my characteristics are sometimes a little bit dominant. At times I can overwhelm people. I'm aware of the risk, sitting in my position, of not getting enough feedback and not having a sufficiently open attitude. Of course, it's comfortable, whatever position you are in, to have people agree with you. The temptation is always there. . . . In this organization for people who know me well, there is absolutely no problem about saying, "You're wrong. I disagree." But of course in an organization this size, there are many people who don't know me that well. In the Latin countries especially, and maybe in Germany, there is a tendency to be a little cautious so as not to offend the top guy. It's difficult to make people really speak their mind and tell you things openly, particularly unpleasant things. . . . I can only say that I am aware of the problem, that I work at it. With new people whom I don't know well, I go out of my way to try to build their confidence so that they don't worry about that aspect of the conversation. How successful I am in doing that is another matter.

Q3 to Barnevik: *What drives you?*

Barnevik: What gives me a sense of reward is to create something, to make some kind of lasting impact. Things like penetrating new countries, developing and commercializing new technologies, creating new opportunities. I don't work for the money and the prestige and all that. I guess it's like a person designing a house. People want to build something, create something that is worthwhile. That's what it all boils down to.

This chapter discusses the cognitive, personal variables of personality and attitudes. These two constructs are very popular ways to describe and analyze organizational behavior. Yet, like the other cognitive processes, personality and attitudes are quite complex. The aim of this chapter is to facilitate a better understanding of such complexities of today's employees. Such an analysis of personality and attitudes is vital to the study of organizational behavior.

The first section of the chapter defines and clarifies the concept of personality. The next section is devoted to personality development and the socialization process. This foundation of understanding of the complex personality and how it is developed is followed by the two major applications to organizational behavior, specifically, the "Big Five" personality traits that have been found to best relate to performance in organizations and the Myers-Briggs Type Indicator (MBTI) based on Carl Jung's personality theory, which has become a popular personal development and career assessment tool. The remaining sections of the chapter then focus on attitudes, starting with their nature and dimensions. This discussion is followed by a detailed analysis of the two most widely recognized attitudes to organizational behavior, job satisfaction and organizational commitment, and then the more recent relevant construct of prosocial/organizational citizenship behaviors.

THE MEANING OF PERSONALITY

Through the years there has not been universal agreement on the exact meaning of personality. Much of the controversy can be attributed to the fact that people in general and those in the behavioral sciences define "personality" from different perspectives. Most people tend to equate personality with social success (being good or popular, or having "a lot of personality") and to describe personality by a single dominant characteristic (strong, weak, or polite). When it is realized that thousands of words can be used to describe personality this way, the definitional problem becomes staggering. Psychologists, on the other hand, take a different perspective. For example, the descriptive-adjective approach commonly used by most people plays only a small part. However, scholars cannot agree on a definition of personality because they operate from different theoretical bases.

Some of the historically important ones include trait theory (observable patterns of behavior that last over time), Freud's psychoanalytic or psychodynamic theory (the unconscious determinants of behavior), and Carl Rogers and Abraham Maslow's humanistic theory (self-actualization and the drive to realize one's potential). Most recently, and the position taken in this chapter, is a more integrative theoretical approach drawing from all the historical theories, but more importantly, the self-concept including nature (heredity and physiological/biological dimensions) and nurture (environmental, developmental dimensions), dispositional traits, the social cognitive interactions between the person and the environment, and the socialization process.

In this text *personality* will mean how people affect others and how they understand and view themselves, as well as their pattern of inner and outer measurable traits and the person–situation interaction. How people affect others depends primarily on their external appearance (height, weight, facial features, color, and other physical aspects) and traits. In terms of external appearance, a very tall worker will have an impact on other people different from that of a very short worker. There is also evidence from meta-analysis that there are gender differences in certain personality characteristics.[1] Obviously, all the ramifications of perception covered in the last chapter enter into these physical aspects of personality.

The Role of Heredity and the Brain

Of more importance from the physiological/biological to the study of personality than the external appearance is the role of heredity and the brain. Although heredity's role in personality was traditionally downplayed, studies of twins in the last decade or so have led to some new interest. Identical twins share the same genetic endowment, but if they are raised apart (say through separate adoptions), then the similarities and differences can provide insight into the relative contribution of heredity vs. environment or nature vs. nurture. Although twin studies in general are open to criticism of political influence and lack of scientific controls,[2] most behavioral scientists now agree that genes play a role not only in physical characteristics and the brain, but also in personality. For example, a recent report by the American Psychological Association concludes, "Studies over the past 20 years on twins and adopted children have firmly established that there is a genetic component to just about every human trait and behavior, including personality, general intelligence and behavior disorders."[3] Now the debate is the relative contribution of each. However, maybe the debate should end, because it is not nature *or* nurture, but nature *and* nurture that contributes to one's personality.[4]

The brain, some call the last frontier because we still know relatively little about it, may hold more answers for personality than does heredity. Both evolutionary psychologists (those that suggest humans not only evolve and retain physically over the ages, but also psychologically) and neuropsychologists (those that explain psychological characteristics primarily through the brain) have traditionally not played a mainstream role in the study and understanding of personality. Recently, however, they are gaining attention because of rapid advances in their respective fields of study. Evolutionary psychologists are suggesting that humans may be "hardwired" from distant previous generations. As was recently noted in a *Harvard Business Review* article:

> Although human beings today inhabit a thoroughly modern world of space exploration and virtual realities, they do so with the ingrained mentality of Stone Age hunter-gatherers . . . an instinct to fight furiously when threatened, for instance, and a drive to trade information and share secrets. Human beings are, in other words, hardwired. You can take the person out of the Stone Age, but you can't take the Stone Age out of the person.[5]

The brain, because of recent breakthroughs in brain-scanning technology, is revealing specific regions that are linked to specialized roles. Although brain dominance theory has been around a long time and has probably been too oversimplified (e.g., the right-side creative brain and the left-side analytical or management brain), there is now general agreement that,

> The frontal lobes are the part of the brain that anticipates events and weighs the consequences of behavior, while deeper brain regions, including the seahorse-shaped hippocampus and the nearby amygdala, are associated with such things as memory, mood and motivation.[6]

There is little question that major inroads are being made in both the role that genetics and the brain play in human behavior in general, and personality in particular. However, at present the field of psychology as a whole and organizational behavior itself is still dominated by the developmental, "soft" or nurture side, which is also making advances in understanding and application. For example, five personality traits (the so-called "Big Five") have recently emerged from research as being especially related to job performance.[7] These specific traits will be given detailed attention after the more theoretical foundation components of personality of self-esteem, person-situation interaction and socialization are discussed.

Self-Esteem

People's attempts to understand themselves are called the *self-concept* in personality theory. The self is a unique product of many interacting parts and may be thought of as the personality viewed from within. This self is particularly relevant to the widely recognized self-esteem and the emerging self-variables of multiple intelligences, emotion, optimism, and especially efficacy, which are all relevant to the field of organizational behavior. These emerging self-variables are given specific attention in Chapter 9.

The more established, recognized *self-esteem* has to do with people's self-perceived competence and self-image. There is considerable research on self-esteem and even its societal implications. Two recent meta-analyses examined self-esteem by gender and race. The findings were that males score slightly higher than females on standard measures of global self-esteem[8] and, contrary to previous studies, more than a half million respondents indicated higher self-esteem scores for black than for white children, adolescents, and young adults.[9]

Applied to the analysis of personality, the research results have been mixed, and there is growing controversy about the assumed value of self-esteem. For example, one recent study found that people with high self-esteem handle failure better than those with low self-esteem.[10] However, an earlier study found that those with high self-esteem tended to become egotistical when faced with pressure situations[11] and may result in aggressive and even violent behavior when threatened.[12] After reviewing the research literature, Kreitner and Kinicki conclude, "High self esteem *can* be a good thing, but only if like many other human characteristics—such as creativity, intelligence, and persistence—it is nurtured and channeled in constructive and ethical ways. Otherwise, it can become antisocial and destructive."[13]

Self-esteem has obvious implications for organizational behavior. Although considered a global concept, there are attempts to specifically apply it to the organization domain. Called organization-based self-esteem (OBSE), it is defined as the "self-perceived value that individuals have of themselves as organization members acting within an organization context."[14] Those who score high on OBSE view themselves positively, and there may be some relation to performance and satisfaction on the job.[15] Also, both early[16] and the more recent studies indicate that self-esteem plays at least an important moderating role in areas such as emotional and behavioral responses and stress of organizational members.[17] As has been noted, "Both research and everyday experience confirm that employees with high self-esteem feel unique, competent, secure, empowered, and connected to the people around them."[18] By the same token, as the author of a recent book, *Self-Esteem at Work,* notes: "If your self-esteem is low and you aren't confident in your thinking ability, you are likely to fear decision making, lack negotiation and interpersonal skills and be reluctant or unable to change."[19]

As will be noted in Chapter 9, self-esteem is more of a global trait, whereas other self-variables, such as self-efficacy, are more situation and context specific. There seems little doubt that self-esteem plays an important role in one's personality, but, as pointed out earlier, the exact nature and impact is still to be determined. For now, the person–situation interaction and socialization are presented to serve as an important part of the social cognitive foundation for the rest of this chapter and for the more specific self-concepts of Chapter 9.

Person–Situation Interaction

The dimensions of personality traits and the self-concept add to the understanding of the human personality. The person–situation interaction dimension of personality provides further understanding. Each situation, of course, is different. The differences may seem to be very small on the surface, but when filtered by the person's cognitive mediating processes such as perception, they can lead to quite large subjective differences and diverse behavioral outcomes. In particular, this dimension suggests that people are not static, acting the same in all situations, but instead are ever changing and flexible. For example, employees can change depending on the particular situation they are in interaction with. For instance, it should be understood that even everyday work experience can change people. Especially today, with organizations transforming and entering into the new environment, those that can find, develop, and retain people who can fit into this dynamically changing situation will be most successful.[20] The next section dealing with the socialization process is especially relevant to today's important person–organization interaction.

The Socialization Process

Study of, and research on, the development of personality has traditionally been an important area for understanding human behavior. Modern developmental psychology does not get into the argument of heredity versus environment or of maturation (changes that result from heredity and physical development) versus learning. The human being consists of both physiological *and* psychological interacting parts. Therefore, heredity, environment, maturation, and learning *all* contribute to the human personality.

At least historically, the study of personality attempted to identify specific physiological and psychological stages that occur in the development of the human personality. This "stage" approach was theoretical in nature. There are many well-known stage theories of personality development. However, as with most aspects of personality, there is little agreement about the exact stages. In fact, a growing number of today's psychologists contend that there are *no* identifiable stages. Their argument is that personality development consists of a continuous process and the sequence is based largely on the learning opportunities available and the socialization process.

There is increasing recognition given to the role of other relevant persons, groups, and, especially, organizations that greatly influence an individual's personality. This continuous impact from the social environment is commonly called the *socialization process*. It is especially relevant to organizational behavior because the process is not confined to early childhood; rather, it takes place throughout one's life. In particular, evidence is accumulating that socialization may be one of the best explanations for why employees behave the way they do in today's organizations.[21] As Edgar Schein notes: "It is high time that some of our managerial knowledge and skill be focused on those forces in the organization environment which derive from the fact that organizations are social systems which do socialize their new members. If we do not learn to analyze and control the forces of organizational socialization, we are abdicating one of our primary managerial responsibilities."[22] A study found that the socialization tactics that organizations employ can have a positive, long-run impact on the adjustment of newcomers (i.e., lower role conflict and ambiguity, less stress, and higher job satisfaction and commitment).[23]

Socialization starts with the initial contact between a mother and her new infant. After infancy, other members of the immediate family (father, brothers, and sisters), close relatives and family friends, and then the social group (peers, school friends, and members of the work group) play influential roles. Of particular interest is Schein's idea that the organization itself also contributes to socialization.[24] He points out that the process includes only the learning of those values, norms, and behavior patterns that, from the organization's and the work group's points of view, are necessary for any new organization member to learn.

The following are widely accepted characteristics of the organizational socialization of employees:

1. Change of attitudes, values, and behaviors
2. Continuity of socialization over time
3. Adjustment to new jobs, work groups, and organizational practices
4. Mutual influence between new recruits and their managers
5. Criticality of the early socialization period[25]

Accordingly, organization members must learn such things as not to drive a Honda if they are working for Ford, not to criticize the company in public, and not to wear the wrong kind of clothes or be seen in the wrong kind of place.[26] They must understand "who holds power and who does not, which informal networks of communication are reliable and which are unreliable, and what political maneuvers they are likely to encounter in their department or unit. In short, if they wish to survive and prosper in their new work home, they must soon come to 'know the ropes.'"[27] The same is true for those in overseas assignments. They must be socialized into the correct conduct in dealing with the local culture. The accompanying International Application Example: Gift Giving in Western Europe provides some guidelines for correct behavior in that part of the world.

Specific techniques of socializing new employees would include the use of mentors or role models, orientation and training programs, reward systems, and career planning. Specific steps that can lead to successful organizational socialization would include the following:

1. Provide a challenging first job
2. Provide relevant training
3. Provide timely and consistent feedback
4. Select a good first supervisor to be in charge of socialization
5. Design a relaxed orientation program
6. Place new recruits in work groups with high morale[28]

Such deliberate socialization strategies have tremendous potential impact on socialization. A recent study found that those new employees attending a socialization training program were indeed more socialized than those who did not.[29]

In summary, the personality is a very diverse and complex cognitive process. It incorporates almost everything covered in this text, and more. As defined, personality is the whole person and is concerned with external appearance and traits, self, and

---

INTERNATIONAL APPLICATION EXAMPLE

Gift Giving in Western Europe

Culture is important in understanding the socialization not only of Americans but of those living in other countries as well. Western Europe is a good example. The United States does considerable business there, so it is very helpful for Americans working there to know how to act in this corner of the globe. For example, when you are doing business with Europeans, when is it acceptable to give a gift and how should it be done? The following are some useful guidelines for gift giving in Western Europe:

1. Do not give a business gift at the first meeting. This is considered bad manners.
2. If you are going to send flowers to your dinner hostess, send them ahead rather than handing them to her on your arrival. This gives her time to arrange and place them as she wants. It also prevents any embarrassment among the other guests who may show up at the same time you do and be empty-handed.
3. When sending flowers, be sure of your choice. In France, chrysanthemums are associated with mourning. In France and Germany, red roses are a gift only between lovers.
4. Good chocolates and liqueurs are excellent house gifts. If the occasion demands something more elaborate, small porcelain and silver gifts such as candlesticks are good choices.
5. Never give perfume or men's cologne as a gift. This is considered too personal for a business gift to or from either sex.
6. Do not enclose your business card with the gift. This is considered crass. Instead, write a note on a blank card.

---

situational interactions. Probably the best statement on personality was made many years ago by Kluckhohn and Murray, who said that, to some extent, a person's personality is like all other people's, like some other people's, and like no other people's.[30]

The "Big Five" Personality Traits

Although personality traits, long-term predispositions for behavior, have been generally downplayed and even totally discounted, in recent years there is gaining support for a five-factor trait-based theory of personality. Many years ago about 18,000 words were found to describe personality. Even after combining words with similar meanings, there still remained 171 personality traits.[31] Obviously, such a huge number of personality traits is practically unusable, so further reduction analysis found five core personality traits. Called the Five-Factor Model (FFM),[32] or in the field of organizational behavior and human resource management, the "Big Five," these traits have held up in many analyses over the years[33] and even across cultures.[34]

Table 7.1 identifies the "Big Five" and their major characteristics. Importantly, not only is there now considerable agreement on what are the core personality trait predispositions, but there is also accumulated research that these five best predict performance in the workplace.[35] Although the five traits are largely independent factors of a personality, like primary colors, they can be mixed in countless proportions and with other characteristics to yield a unique personality whole. However, also like colors, one may dominate in describing an individual's personality.

TABLE 7.1 The "Big Five" Personality Traits

Core Traits	Descriptive Characteristics of High Scorers
Conscientiousness	Dependable, hardworking, organized, self-disciplined, persistent, responsible
Emotional stability	Calm, secure, happy, unworried
Agreeableness	Cooperative, warm, caring, good-natured, courteous, trusting
Extraversion	Sociable, outgoing, talkative, assertive, gregarious
Openness to experience	Curious, intellectual, creative, cultured, artistically sensitive, flexible, imaginative

The real value of the "Big Five" to organizational behavior is that it does bring back the importance of predispositional traits,[36] and these traits have been clearly shown to relate to job performance. Importantly, it should also be noted that these five traits are stable. After about 30 years of age, the individual's personality profile will change little over time.[37] This does not intend to imply that the "Big Five" provide an ideal personality profile for employees over their whole career, because different traits are needed for different jobs. The key is still to find the right fit.[38] The following sections examine the research to date on the relationships of the various Big Five traits to dimensions of performance in organizations.

The Positive Impact of Conscientiousness.   There is general agreement that conscientiousness has the strongest, positive correlation (about .3) with job performance. A meta-analysis concluded that "individuals who are dependable, persistent, goal directed, and organized tend to be higher performers on virtually any job; viewed negatively, those who are careless, irresponsible, low achievement striving and impulsive tend to be lower performers on virtually any job."[39]

Put in relation to other organizational behavior areas as a personality trait per se, conscientious employees set higher goals for themselves, have higher performance expectations, and respond well to job enrichment (take on more responsibility, covered in Chapter 15) and empowerment strategies of human resource management. As would be expected, research indicates that those who are conscientious are less likely to be absent from work,[40] and a recent study found in international human resource management that conscientiousness of expatriates related positively to the rating of their foreign assignment performance.[41] Yet, there are also recent studies with nonsupporting and mixed results pointing to the complexity of this personality trait. For example, in a recent study conscientiousness was found not to be influential in determining managerial performance and in another study of Middle Eastern expatriate managers, conscientiousness was related to home-country ratings of the expats performance, but not the host-country ratings of the same expats.[42] In addition, studies had indicated that the individual's ability moderates the relationship between conscientiousness and performance (positive for high ability but zero or even negative for low ability), but the most recent study found no such moderator.[43] Another very recent study found the relationship of conscientiousness to job performance was strong when job satisfaction was low, but was relatively weak when satisfaction was high.[44]

Applied to peer evaluations, as hypothesized, a recent study found the raters' conscientiousness was negatively related with the level of the rating. In other words, conscientious raters did not give inflated evaluations, but those with low conscientiousness did.[45] Such multiplicative relationships with variables such as culture, ability, and job satisfaction indicate, like other psychological variables, that conscientiousness is complex and is certainly not the only answer for job performance. However, this is one area of personality where there is enough research evidence to conclude that conscientiousness should be given attention in personnel selection for most jobs, training, and appraisal of employees.

The Impact of the Other Traits.   Although conscientiousness has been found to have the strongest, consistent relationship with performance and thus has received the most attention, the remaining four traits also have some interesting findings. For example, a large study including participants from several European countries, many occupational groups, and multiple methods of measuring performance found both conscientiousness and emotional stability related to all the measures and occupations.[46] Yet, the absenteeism study that found conscientiousness had a desirable inverse relationship, the higher the extraversion trait the more absent the employee tended to be.[47]

The other traits have a more selective, but still logical impact. For example, those with high extraversion tend to be associated with management and sales success; those with high emotional stability tend to be more effective in stressful situations; those with high agreeableness tend to handle customer relations and conflict more effectively; and those open to experience tend to have job training proficiency and make better decisions in a training problem solving simulation.[48] Interestingly, with groups rather than individuals becoming more important in today's workplace, the "Big Five" may also be predictive of team performance. A recent study found that the higher the average scores of team members on the traits of conscientiousness, agreeableness, extraversion, and emotional stability, the better their teams performed.[49] In other words, depending on the situation, all the Big Five traits should be given attention in the study and application of organizational behavior.

Myers-Briggs Type Indicator (MBTI)

Whereas the "Big Five" has recently emerged from considerable basic research and has generally been demonstrated to significantly relate to job performance, the MBTI is based on a very old theory, has mixed at best research support,[50] but is widely used and very popular in real-world career counseling, team building, conflict management, and analyzing management styles.[51] The theory goes back to pioneering Swiss psychiatrist Carl Jung in the 1920s. He felt people could be typed into extraverts and introverts and that they had two basic mental processes—perception and judgment. He then further divided perception into sensing and intuiting and judgment into thinking and feeling. This yields four personality dimensions or traits: (1) introversion/extraversion, (2) perceiving/judging, (3) sensing/intuition, and (4) thinking/feeling. He felt that although people had all four of these dimensions in common, they differ in the combination of their preferences of each. Importantly, he made the point that one's preferences were not necessarily better than another's, only different.

About 20 years after Jung developed his theoretical types, in the 1940s the mother–daughter team of Katharine Briggs and Isabel Briggs-Myers developed about a 100-item personality test asking participants how they usually feel or act in particular situations in order to measure the preferences on the four pairs of traits yielding 16 distinct types. Called the Myers-Briggs Type Indicator or simply MBTI, the questions relate to how people prefer to focus their energies (extraversion vs. introversion); pay

TABLE 7.2   The Jung Theory Dimensions and the Meyers-Briggs Type Indicators

	Where do you get your energy?	
Extraversion (E) _____		*Introversion (I)*
Outgoing		Quiet
Interacting		Concentrating
Speaks, then thinks		Thinks, then speaks
Gregarious		Reflective
	How do you orient yourself to the outside world?	
Judging (J) _____		*Perceiving (P)*
Structured		Flexible
Time oriented		Open ended
Decisive		Exploring
Organized		Spontaneous
	What do you pay attention to and collect information on?	
Sensing (S) _____		*Intuiting (N)*
Practical		General
Details		Possibilities
Concrete		Theoretical
Specific		Abstract
	How do you evaluate and make decisions?	
Thinking (T) _____		*Feeling (F)*
Analytical		Subjective
Head		Heart
Rules		Circumstance
Justice		Mercy

attention and collect information (sensing vs. intuition); process and evaluate information and make decisions (thinking vs. feeling); and orient themselves to the outside world (judging vs. perceiving). Table 7.2 summarizes the characteristics of the four major dimensions, which in combination yield the 16 types. For example, the ESTJ is extraverted, sensing, thinking, and judging. Because this type likes to interact with others (E); sees the world realistically (S); makes decisions objectively and decisively (T); and likes structure, schedules, and order (J), this would be a manager type. The MBTI *Atlas* indicates that most managers studied were indeed ESTJs.

As Jung emphasized when formulating his theory, there are no good or bad types. This is a major reason the MBTI is such a psychologically nonthreatening, commonly used (millions take it every year) personality inventory. Although the MBTI has shown to have reliability and validity as a measure of identifying Jung's personality types[52] and predicting occupational choice (e.g., those high on intuition tend to prefer careers in advertising, the arts, and teaching), there still is not enough research support to base selection decisions or predict job performance.[53] Yet, the use of MBTI by numerous firms such as AT&T, Exxon, and Honeywell for their management development programs and Hewlett-Packard for team building seems justified. It can be an effective point of departure for discussion of similarities and differences and useful for personal development. However, like any psychological measure, the MBTI can also be misused. As one comprehensive analysis concluded, "Some inappropriate uses include labeling one another, providing a convenient excuse that they simply can't work with someone else, and avoiding responsibility for their own personal development with respect to working with others and becoming more flexible. One's type is not an excuse for inappropriate behavior."[54]

THE NATURE AND DIMENSIONS OF ATTITUDES

Both personality and attitudes are complex cognitive processes. The difference is that personality usually is thought of as the whole person, whereas attitudes may make up the personality.

The term *attitude* frequently is used in describing people and explaining their behavior. For example: "He has a poor attitude." "I like her attitude." "Our workers turn out poor-quality products because they have poor attitudes." More precisely, an *attitude* can be defined as a persistent tendency to feel and behave in a particular way toward some object. For example, George does not like working the night shift. He has a negative attitude toward his work assignment.

Attitudes can be characterized three ways. First, they tend to persist unless something is done to change them. For example, if George is transferred to the day shift, his attitude may become positive. Second, attitudes can fall anywhere along a continuum from very favorable to very unfavorable. At the present time, George's attitude may be moderately unfavorable. If he is transferred to the day shift, his attitude may change to highly favorable. Third, attitudes are directed toward some object about which a person has feelings (sometimes called "affect") and beliefs. In George's case this is the work shift. The following sections discuss the various dimensions of attitudes, including the basic components, antecedents, and functions, and, how attitudes can be changed. The remainder of the chapter will then examine the specific work-related attitudes of positive and negative affect (PA/NA), job satisfaction, organizational commitment, and organizational citizenship behaviors.

Components of Attitudes

Attitudes can be broken down into three basic components: emotional, informational, and behavioral. The emotional component involves the person's feelings or affect—positive, neutral, or negative—about an object. Emotion will be given specific attention as a type of intelligence (EI or EQ) in Chapter 9. In addition, the expression of emotions—either positive, like a customer service representative; negative, like a bill collector or police officer; or neutral, like an academic administrator or public servant—is also important to work behavior. The term *emotional labor* has emerged in recent years to represent the work people are asked to perform beyond their physical and mental contributions.[55] People in many service jobs are asked or even required to express emotions in interpersonal transactions other than those they are naturally feeling. Examples would include almost all jobs dealing with customers, patients, or clients. Service with a smile in all retailing, supermarkets, stores, restaurants, or airlines, and other emotions, such as concern in health care or sadness in the funeral business, are required of today's employees. Like traditional physical and mental labor, this emotional labor can take its toll in terms of exhaustion and stress.[56]

The informational component consists of the beliefs and information the individual has about the object. It makes no difference whether or not this information is empirically real or correct. A supervisor may believe that two weeks of training is necessary before a worker can effectively conduct a particular process. In reality, the average worker may be able to perform successfully after only four days of training. Yet the information the supervisor is using (that two weeks is necessary) is the key to his attitude about training.

The behavioral component consists of a person's tendencies to behave in a particular way toward an object. For example, the supervisor in the preceding paragraph may assign two weeks of training to all her new people.

It is important to remember that of the three components of attitudes, only the behavioral component can be directly observed. One cannot see another person's feelings (the emotional component) or beliefs (the informational component). These two components can only be inferred. For example, when the supervisor assigns a new employee to two weeks of training on the process, it is only inferred that (1) the supervisor has strong feelings about the length of training required and (2) the individual believes that this length of training is necessary. Yet understanding the antecedents of work-related attitudes is important in the study of organizational behavior.

Antecedents of Work-Related Attitudes: PA/NA

Traditionally, the situational determinants of attitudes received the most attention. In particular, Salancik and Pfeffer noted that the social context provided information to the employees to form their feelings, or affect (their job-related attitudes).[57] More recently, personality traits or affective (feelings) dispositions have been receiving increasing attention as antecedents of work-related attitudes. In particular, the dispositions of positive affectivity (PA) and negative affectivity (NA) have been found to be important antecedents to attitudes about one's job. As explained by George,[58] NA reflects a personality disposition to experience negative emotional states; those with high NA tend to feel nervous, tense, anxious, worried, upset, and distressed. Accordingly, those with high NA are more likely to experience negative affective states—they are more likely to have a negative attitude toward themselves, others, and the world around them. There is accumulating research supporting this biasing effect of NA.[59] For example, a recent study found that employees high in negative affectivity more often perceived themselves as victims and thus open themselves up to be more likely targets of coworkers' aggressive actions.[60]

Those with high PA have the opposite disposition and tend to have an overall sense of well-being, to see themselves as pleasurably and effectively engaged, and to experience positive attitudes. Whether PA is the bipolar opposite and independent of NA is still the subject of debate and interpretation of research results.[61] People do not necessarily move between opposite mood states, but can be both happy and unhappy. However, most of the time there are swings in mood or NA to PA or PA to NA. PAs do tend to perform better,[62] are less absent from work,[63] and are more satisfied,[64] whereas NAs may experience more stress.[65] There is even evidence that teams with a positive affective tone (i.e., the average PA of members is high) are more effective than teams with a negative affective tone.[66] In other words, one's mood or affective state may become a self-fulfilling prophecy as far as organization outcomes are concerned.

Functions of Attitudes

An understanding of the functions of attitudes is important to the study of organizational behavior. Based on extensive review of surveys of employers, an analysis concluded that "the most important consideration in hiring and the biggest deficit among new workforce entrants are the attitudes concerning work that they bring with them to their jobs."[67] Attitudes can help predict work behavior.[68] For example, if an attitude survey shows that workers are upset by a change in the work rules and the next week absenteeism begins to increase sharply, management may conclude that a negative attitude toward work rules led to an increase in worker absenteeism. An understanding of attitudes is also important because attitudes help people adapt to their work environment. Many years ago, Katz noted that attitudes serve four important functions in this process.[69]

The Adjustment Function.   Attitudes often help people adjust to their work environment. When employees are well treated, they are likely to develop a positive attitude toward management and the organization. When employees are berated and given minimal salary increases, they are likely to develop a negative attitude toward management and the organization. These attitudes help employees adjust to their environment and are a basis for future behaviors. For example, if employees who are well treated are asked about management or the organization, they are likely to say good things. Just the reverse would probably be true for those berated and given minimal salary increases. When Japanese firms did away with lifetime employment in recent years, Japanese workers had a very difficult time adjusting (see International Application Example).

INTERNATIONAL APPLICATION EXAMPLE

The Mental Effects of the Demise of Japanese Lifetime Employment Policies

In recent years not only has the economy been in a funk, but many Japanese employees seem to have growing fatigue and increased stress. According to the Japanese government, one-third of the working-age population now suffers from chronic fatigue and stress. In one hospital, doctors diagnosed 32 percent of the patients who were admitted in the internal medicine and psychological ward as suffering from this malady. This diagnosis was a result of the patients having at least six months of severe, continuous fatigue and depression in the absence of any known organic illness. According to the doctors, the explosion of chronic tiredness and fatigue is a postwar phenomenon and is a result of more than simple overwork. They attribute it to societal stress brought on by the nation's economic recession over the past decade, the amount of debt that many families accumulated during the nation's economic boom of the 1980s, and the need to work harder and harder in recent years in order to meet commitments and maintain living standards.

Adding to the problem is the fact that a growing number of Japanese employees are now facing the loss of their job. For decades Japanese firms took pride in their employment security policies, and their employees believed that they had been hired for a lifetime. However, by the beginning of the 1990s not only were Japanese firms beginning to lay off personnel, but a growing number of workers started reporting that they felt less loyalty to their employer and were more willing to seek jobs elsewhere. In 1987, the Japanese Labor Ministry reported that 53 percent of Japanese workers felt it was better to stay in one job as long as possible, even if they found their situation to be frustrating, and only 42 percent believed that it was all right to change jobs in order to more fully tap their talent and ability. However, in the latest poll by the Ministry, a mere 31 percent of employees believe that people should stay with their jobs whereas 63 percent feel that moving to another company or organization is all right.

One reason for the growing willingness to move may well be that employees realize that their employers no longer feel obligated to provide lifetime jobs. For example, when a production manager at the Shosiba Manufacturing Company, a midsized engine parts maker, was asked by his boss to quit his job, he was stunned by the request. It had long been the policy of the company to keep people employed until they were 60 years of age and then give them a large lump sum payment to finance their retirement. However, Shosiba did neither, and the production manager ended up joining the almost 3 million Japanese looking for work. Commenting on this fate, he said, "I'm angry. But I don't know where to direct my anger."

In another case, a 63-year-old alum of Kyoto University was told by his boss at Nippon Steel that he was being transferred from his engineering post to become a recruiter in the HR department. This was a major demotion, and the manager eventually left the company. Looking back on the way he was treated, he remarked, "The aim of Nippon Steel was to put people like us into such places so we would become unable to tolerate it and would quit."

A similar fate has been encountered by many other Japanese employees today, especially those 45 or more years of age. The impact has been particularly hard on well-educated, highly paid technical specialists and managers who joined their firms two or more decades ago and now have been let go. They are now regarded by other employers as too old to hire. Perhaps even worse than the loss of work and income is the loss of face. Many of these unemployed professionals feel a sense of shame and humiliation. Moreover, those who are able to find jobs often work at lower-level positions or manual labor where not only are their salaries less than half of what they used to earn, but their status has plummeted. Their previous experience is of no value in getting a new job, so they take what they can get such as driving a delivery truck or providing cleaning services in office buildings. Others, trying to get back into the labor force, turn to retraining programs but quite often they find that there are still not very many jobs, especially for older people. As a result, there appears to be a growing problem of chronic fatigue and stress resulting from a loss of face that are leading to serious societal mental health problems for Japan now and in the future.

The Ego-Defensive Function.   Besides helping employees adjust, attitudes also help them defend their self-images. For example, an older manager whose decisions are continually challenged by a younger subordinate manager may feel that the latter is brash, cocky, immature, and inexperienced. In truth, the younger subordinate may be right in challenging the decisions. The older manager may not be a very effective leader and may constantly make poor decisions. On the other hand, the older manager is not going to admit this but will try to protect the ego by putting the blame on the other party. As a result, the older manager will have a negative attitude toward the younger one. The same is undoubtedly true for the younger manager, who will feel that the boss is not doing a good job. This attitude helps the younger person protect the ego. If the subordinate were to change this perception and believe that the boss was doing a good job, this individual would also have to stop criticizing the boss. Quite obviously, this is something that the younger person does not want to do. So the attitude serves to justify the action and to defend the ego.

The Value-Expressive Function.   Attitudes provide people with a basis for expressing their values. For example, a manager who believes strongly in the work ethic will tend to voice attitudes toward specific individuals or work practices as a means of reflecting this value. A supervisor who wants a subordinate to work harder might put it this way: "You've got to work harder. That's been the tradition of the company since it was founded. It helped get us where we are today, and everyone is expected to subscribe to this ethic." A company president who believes strongly in the need to support the United Way campaign might tell the top-management team: "Everyone in this firm from top to bottom ought to support United Way. It's a wonderful organization and it does a great deal of good for our community. I don't know where we'd be without it." In both these cases, attitudes serve as a basis for expressing one's central values.

The Knowledge Function.   Attitudes help supply standards and frames of reference that allow people to organize and explain the world around them. For example, a union organizer may have a negative attitude toward management. This attitude may not be based on fact, but it does help the individual relate to management. As a result, everything that managers say is regarded by the union organizer as nothing more than a pack of lies, a deliberate distortion of the truth, or an attempt to manipulate the workers. Regardless of how accurate a person's view of reality is, attitudes toward people, events, and objects help the individual make sense out of what is going on.

Changing Attitudes

Employee attitudes can be changed, and sometimes it is in the best interests of management to try to do so. For example, if employees believe that their employer does not take care of them, management would like to change this attitude. Sometimes attitude change is difficult to accomplish because of certain barriers. After these barriers are identified, some ways of overcoming them and effectively changing attitudes are examined.

Barriers to Changing Attitudes.   There are two basic barriers that can prevent people from changing their attitude. One is called prior commitments, which occurs when people feel a commitment to a particular course of action and are unwilling to change. There is even theory and research support for *escalation of commitment,* the tendency for decision makers to persist with failing courses of action.[70]

The following scenario presents an example of escalation of commitment: The president of the company graduated from an Ivy League school and was personally instrumental in hiring the new head of the marketing department, who had graduated from the same school. Unfortunately, things are not working out well. The marketing manager is not very good. However, because the president played such a major role in hiring this manager, the chief executive is unwilling to admit the mistake. Using the ego-defensive function of attitudes, the president distorts all negative information received about the marketing manager and continues to believe that everything is going well and the right selection decision was made.

A second barrier is a result of insufficient information. Sometimes people do not see any reason to change their attitude. The boss may not like an associate's negative attitude, but the latter may be quite pleased with his or her own behavior. Unless the boss can show the individual why a negative attitude is detrimental to career progress or salary raises or some other desirable personal objective, this person may continue to have a negative attitude. This is particularly true when the attitude is a result of poor treatment by management. The associate will use the negative attitude to serve an adjustment function: "I can't respect a manager who treats me the way this one does."

Providing New Information.   Fortunately, there are ways in which the barriers can be overcome and attitudes can be changed. One of these is by providing new information. Sometimes this information will change a person's beliefs and, in the process, his or her attitudes. In one classic study it was found that union workers had an antimanagement attitude. However, when some of the workers were promoted into the management ranks, their attitudes changed.[71] They became aware of what the company was doing to help the workers, and, over time, this new information resulted in a change in their beliefs about management and in their attitude toward both the company and the union. They became more procompany and less prounion.

Use of Fear.   A second way of changing attitudes is through the use of fear. Some researchers have found that fear can cause some people to change their attitudes. However, the degree of fear seems to be important to the final outcome. For example, if low levels of fear arousal are used, people often ignore them. The warnings are not strong enough to warrant attention. If moderate levels of fear arousal are used, people often become aware of the situation and will change their attitudes. However, if high degrees of fear arousal are used, people often reject the message because it is too threatening and thus not believable. They essentially dig in their heels and refuse to be persuaded. A good example is provided in the case of antismoking commercials. The Department of Health and Human Services found that when it ran ads using patients who were dying of cancer, the message was so threatening to smokers that they shut it out; they refused to listen. As a result, the commercials did not have the desired impact. Health officials found that commercials using only moderate fear arousal were the most effective ones.

Resolving Discrepancies.   Another way in which attitudes can be changed is by resolving discrepancies between attitudes and behavior. For example, research shows that when job applicants have more than one offer of employment and are forced to choose, they often feel that their final choice may have been a mistake. However, this mild conflict, or dissonance, does not usually last very long. The theory of cognitive dissonance says that people will try to actively reduce the dissonance by attitude and behavior change.[72] Thus, when people take new jobs and begin working, they also start to have negative feelings toward the firms that were not chosen and positive ones toward the company that was chosen. The result may be that the new employees conclude they did indeed make the right choice.

Influence of Friends or Peers.   Still another way in which attitude changes can come about is through persuasion by friends or peers. For example, if Joe Smith has been padding his expense account and finds out that his friends in sales have not, he is likely to change his own attitude. This assumes that Joe likes his coworkers and they have some persuasive control over him. On the other hand, if Joe believes that the other salespeople are all lazy and would pad their accounts if they only knew how, he is unlikely to change his attitude toward doing so.

    Additionally, it is important to remember that when a particular matter is of personal interest to people, they are likely to reject extreme discrepancies between their current behavior and that of others. For example, if the other salespeople tell Joe that they never pad their expenses while he is padding his by several thousand dollars annually, Joe is unlikely to let them influence him. There are too many benefits to be achieved if he just keeps on doing what he has been doing. This is why unethical behavior is so difficult to combat.

The Co-opting Approach.   A final way in which attitude changes often take place is by co-opting, which means taking people who are dissatisfied with a situation and getting them involved in improving things. For example, Nancy feels that more needs to be done in improving employee benefits. As a result, the company appoints Nancy as a member of the employee benefits committee. By giving her the opportunity to participate in employee benefits decision making, the company increases the chances that Nancy's attitude will change. Once she begins realizing how these benefits are determined and how long and hard the committee works to ensure that the personnel are given the best benefits possible, she is likely to change her attitude.

JOB SATISFACTION

Specific employee attitudes relating to job satisfaction and organizational commitment are of major interest to the field of organizational behavior and the practice of human resource management. Whereas the discussion of attitudes so far has direct implications, the discussion of job satisfaction focuses on employees' attitudes toward their job and the discussion of organizational commitment focuses on their attitudes toward the overall organization. The more traditionally recognized job satisfaction is first discussed. Next is the discussion of the widely recognized attitude of organizational commitment. Finally, the more recent prosocial or organizational citizenship behaviors are presented to end this chapter.

What Is Meant by Job Satisfaction?

Locke gives a comprehensive definition of job satisfaction as involving cognitive, affective and evaluative reactions or attitudes and states it is "a pleasurable or positive emotional state resulting from the appraisal of one's job or job experience."[73] Job satisfaction is a result of employees' perception of how well their job provides those things that are viewed as important. It is generally recognized in the organizational behavior field that job satisfaction is the most important and frequently studied attitude.

Although recent theoretical analyses have criticized job satisfaction as being too narrow conceptually,[74] there are three generally accepted dimensions to job satisfaction. First, job satisfaction is an emotional response to a job situation. As such, it cannot be seen; it can only be inferred. Second, job satisfaction is often determined by how well outcomes meet or exceed expectations. For example, if organizational participants feel that they are working much harder than others in the department but are receiving fewer rewards, they will probably have a negative attitude toward the work, the boss, and/or coworkers. They will be dissatisfied. On the other hand, if they feel they are being treated very well and are being paid equitably, they are likely to have a positive attitude toward the job. They will be job-satisfied. Third, job satisfaction represents several related attitudes. Through the years five job dimensions have been identified to represent the most important characteristics of a job about which employees have affective responses. These are:

1. *The work itself.*   The extent to which the job provides the individual with interesting tasks, opportunities for learning, and the chance to accept responsibility
2. *Pay.*   The amount of financial remuneration that is received and the degree to which this is viewed as equitable vis-à-vis that of others in the organization

3. *Promotion opportunities.* The chances for advancement in the organization
4. *Supervision.* The abilities of the supervisor to provide technical assistance and behavioral support
5. *Coworkers.* The degree to which fellow workers are technically proficient and socially supportive[75]

Influences on Job Satisfaction

There are a number of factors that influence job satisfaction. For example, one study even found that if college students' majors coincided with their jobs, this relationship predicted subsequent job satisfaction.[76] However, the main influences can be summarized along the preceding five dimensions.

The Work Itself. The content of the work itself is a major source of satisfaction. For example, research related to the job characteristics approach to job design, covered in Chapter 15, shows that feedback from the job itself and autonomy are two of the major job-related motivational factors. Recent research has found that such job characteristics and job complexity mediate the relationship between personality and job satisfaction,[77] and if the creative requirements of employees' jobs are met, then they tend to be satisfied.[78] At a more pragmatic level, some of the most important ingredients of a satisfying job uncovered by surveys over the years include interesting and challenging work, and a recent survey found that career development (not necessarily promotion) was most important to both younger and older employees.[79]

Pay. Chapter 5 gave detailed attention to both pay and benefits. Wages and salaries are recognized to be a significant but cognitively complex[80] and multidimensional factor in job satisfaction.[81] Money not only helps people attain their basic needs but is also instrumental in providing upper-level need satisfaction. Employees often see pay as a reflection of how management views their contribution to the organization. Fringe benefits are also important, but they are not as influential. One reason undoubtedly is that most employees do not even know how much they are receiving in benefits. Moreover, most tend to undervalue these benefits because they do not realize their significant monetary value.[82] However, research indicates that if employees are allowed some flexibility in choosing the type of benefits they prefer within a total package, called a flexible or cafeteria benefits plan, there is a significant increase in both benefits satisfaction and overall job satisfaction.[83]

Promotions. Promotional opportunities seem to have a varying effect on job satisfaction. This is because promotions take a number of different forms and have a variety of accompanying rewards. For example, individuals who are promoted on the basis of seniority often experience job satisfaction but not as much as those who are promoted on the basis of performance. Additionally, a promotion with a 10 percent salary raise is typically not as satisfying as one with a 20 percent salary raise. These differences help explain why executive promotions may be more satisfying than promotions that occur at the lower levels of organizations. Also, in recent years with the flattening of organizations and accompanying empowerment strategies, promotion in the traditional sense of climbing the hierarchical corporate ladder of success is no longer available as it once was. Employees operating in the new paradigm, as outlined in Part I of this text, know that not only are traditional promotions not available, they are not even as desired. A positive work environment and opportunities to grow intellectually and broaden their skill base has for many become more important than promotion opportunities.[84]

Supervision.   Supervision is another moderately important source of job satisfaction. Chapter 18 discusses the impact of leadership skills. For now, however, it can be said that there seem to be two dimensions of supervisory style that affect job satisfaction. One is employee-centeredness, which is measured by the degree to which a supervisor takes a personal interest and cares about the employee. It commonly is manifested in ways such as checking to see how well the employee is doing, providing advice and assistance to the individual, and communicating with the associate on a personal as well as an official level. American employees generally complain that their supervisors don't do a very good job on these dimensions. There is considerable empirical evidence that one of the major reasons employees give for quitting a company is that their supervisor does not care about them.[85]

The other dimension is participation or influence, as illustrated by managers who allow their people to participate in decisions that affect their own jobs. In most cases, this approach leads to higher job satisfaction. For example, a meta-analysis concluded that participation does have a positive effect on job satisfaction. A participative climate created by the supervisor has a more substantial effect on workers' satisfaction than does participation in a specific decision.[86]

Work Group.   The nature of the work group or team will have an effect on job satisfaction. Friendly, cooperative coworkers or team members are a modest source of job satisfaction to individual employees. The work group, especially a "tight" team, serves as a source of support, comfort, advice, and assistance to the individual members. A "good" work group or effective team makes the job more enjoyable. However, this factor is not essential to job satisfaction. On the other hand, if the reverse conditions exist—the people are difficult to get along with—this factor may have a negative effect on job satisfaction.

Working Conditions.   Working conditions have a modest effect on job satisfaction. If the working conditions are good (clean, attractive surroundings, for instance), the personnel will find it easier to carry out their jobs. If the working conditions are poor (hot, noisy surroundings, for example), personnel will find it more difficult to get things done. In other words, the effect of working conditions on job satisfaction is similar to that of the work group. If things are good, there may or may not be a job satisfaction problem; if things are poor, there very likely will be.

Most people do not give working conditions a great deal of thought unless they are extremely bad. Additionally, when there are complaints about working conditions, these sometimes are really nothing more than manifestations of other problems. For example, a manager may complain that his office has not been properly cleaned by the night crew, but his anger is actually a result of a meeting he had with the boss earlier in the day in which he was given a poor performance evaluation. However, in recent years, because of the increased diversity of the workforce, working conditions have taken on new importance. Chapter 3 discussed many of the ways in which today's organizations are trying to make conditions more supportive and more nondiscriminatory/nonthreatening. There is also evidence of a positive relationship between job satisfaction and life satisfaction,[87] and that the direction of causality is that people who are satisfied with their lives tend to find more satisfaction in their work.[88]

Outcomes of Job Satisfaction

To society as a whole as well as from an individual employee's standpoint, job satisfaction in and of itself is a desirable outcome. However, from a pragmatic managerial and organizational effectiveness perspective, it is important to know how, if at all, satisfaction relates to outcome variables. For instance, if job satisfaction is high, will the employees perform better and the organization be more effective? If job satisfaction is low, will there be performance problems and ineffectiveness? This question has been asked by both researchers and practitioners through the years. There are no simple answers, and the results range from weak to strong. In examining the outcomes of job satisfaction, it is important to break down the analysis into a series of specific outcomes. The following sections examine the most important of these.

Satisfaction and Performance.   Do satisfied employees perform better than their less-satisfied counterparts? This "satisfaction–performance controversy" has raged over the years. Although most people assume a positive relationship, the research to date indicates that there is no strong linkage between satisfaction and performance. For example, the most-cited meta-analysis of the research literature a number of years ago found only a .17 best-estimate correlation between job satisfaction and performance.[89]

Conceptual, methodological, and empirical analyses have questioned and argued against these weak results.[90] Yet, to date an unpublished follow-up meta-analysis correcting for the potential problems and limitations of the first one does find a stronger relationship, but still not higher than the "Big Five" personality trait of conscientiousness discussed earlier in this chapter nor as high as the meta-analytic findings of other psychological constructs such as the relationship between self-efficacy (covered in Chapter 9) and performance (.38).[91]

Perhaps the best conclusion about satisfaction and performance is that there is definitely a relationship, probably higher than the well-known .17, but also not as high as conventional wisdom assumed concerning happy workers are productive workers. Moreover, the relationship may even be more complex than others in organizational behavior. For example, there seem to be many possible moderating variables, the most important of which are rewards. If people receive rewards they feel are equitable, they will be satisfied, and this is likely to result in greater performance effort.[92] Also, research evidence indicates that satisfaction may not necessarily lead to individual performance improvement but does lead to departmental[93] and organizational-level improvement.[94] Finally, there is still considerable debate whether satisfaction leads to performance or performance leads to satisfaction. The next chapter examines in detail these and other possible dimensions of this complex relationship.

Satisfaction and Turnover.   Does high employee job satisfaction result in low turnover? Unlike that between satisfaction and performance, research has uncovered a moderately negative relationship between satisfaction and turnover.[95] High job satisfaction will not, in and of itself, keep turnover low, but it does seem to help. On the other hand, if there is considerable job dissatisfaction, there is likely to be high turnover. Obviously, other variables enter into an employee's decision to quit besides job satisfaction. For example, age, tenure in the organization, and commitment to the organization (covered in the next major section), may play a role. Some people cannot see themselves working anywhere else, so they remain regardless of how dissatisfied they feel. Another factor is the general economy. When things in the economy are going well and there is little unemployment, typically there will be an increase in turnover because people will begin looking for better opportunities with other organizations. Even if they are satisfied, many people are willing to leave if the opportunities elsewhere promise to be better. On the other hand, if jobs are tough to get and downsizing, mergers, and acquisitions are occurring, as in recent years, dissatisfied employees will voluntarily stay where they are. On an overall basis, however, it is accurate to say that job satisfaction is important in employee turnover. Although absolutely no turnover is not necessarily beneficial to the organization, a low turnover rate is usually desirable because of the considerable training costs and the drawbacks of inexperience.

Satisfaction and Absenteeism.   Research has only demonstrated a weak negative relationship between satisfaction and absenteeism.[96] As with turnover, many other variables enter into the decision to stay home besides satisfaction with the job. For example, there are moderating variables such as the degree to which people feel that their jobs are important. For example, research among state government employees has found that those who believed that their work was important had lower absenteeism than did those who did not feel this way. Additionally, it is important to remember that although high job satisfaction will not necessarily result in low absenteeism, low job satisfaction is more likely to bring about absenteeism.[97]

Other Effects and Ways to Enhance Satisfaction.   In addition to those noted previously, there are a number of other effects brought about by high job satisfaction. Research reports that highly satisfied employees tend to have better physical health, learn new job-related tasks more quickly, have fewer on-the-job accidents, and file fewer grievances. Also on the positive side, it has been found that there is a strong negative relationship between job satisfaction and perceived stress.[98] In other words, by building satisfaction, stress may be reduced.

Overall, there is no question that employee satisfaction in jobs is in and of itself desirable. It cannot only reduce stress, but as the preceding discussion points out, may also help improve performance, turnover, and absenteeism. Based on the current body of knowledge, the following guidelines may help enhance job satisfaction.[99]

1. *Make jobs more fun.*   World-class companies such as Southwest Airlines have a fun culture for their employees. Management makes it clear that irreverence is okay; its okay to be yourself; and take the competition seriously, but not yourself.[100] Having a fun culture may not make jobs themselves more satisfying, but it does break up boredom and lessen the chances of dissatisfaction.

2. *Have fair pay, benefits, and promotion opportunities.*   These are obvious ways that organizations typically try to keep their employees satisfied. As Chapter 5 pointed out, an important way to make benefits more effective would be to provide a flexible, so-called cafeteria approach. This allows employees to chose their own distribution of benefits within the budgeted amount available. This way there would be no discrepancies between what they want, because it's their choice.

3. *Match people with jobs that fit their interests and skills.*   Getting the right fit is one of the most important, but overlooked, ways to have satisfied employees. This, of course, assumes that the organization knows what those interests and skills are. Effective human resource management firms such as Disney, Ford, IBM, and Kodak put considerable effort into finding out interests and skills of potential new hires, as well as existing employees, in order to make the match or fit with the right job.

4. *Design jobs to make them exciting and satisfying.*   Instead of finding people to fit the job as in point 3, this approach suggests designing jobs to fit the people. Most

people do not find boring, repetitive work very satisfying. Unfortunately, too many jobs today are boring and should be changed or eliminated as much as possible. Chapter 15 is concerned with designing jobs to help motivate and satisfy today's employees. Examples include providing more responsibility and building in more variety, significance, identity, autonomy, and feedback.

In summary, most organizational behavior scholars as well as practicing managers would argue that job satisfaction is important to an organization. Some critics have argued, however, that this is pure conjecture because there is so much we do not know about the positive effects of satisfaction. On the other hand, when job satisfaction is low, there seem to be negative effects on the organization that have been documented. So if only from the standpoint of viewing job satisfaction as a minimum requirement or point of departure, it is of value to the organization's overall health and effectiveness and is deserving of study and application in the field of organizational behavior.

ORGANIZATIONAL COMMITMENT

Although job satisfaction has received the most attention of all work-related attitudes, organizational commitment has become increasingly recognized in the organizational behavior literature. Whereas satisfaction is mainly concerned with the employee's attitude toward the job and commitment is at the level of the organization, a strong relationship between job satisfaction and organizational commitment has been found over the years.[101] Yet, there are always many employees who are satisfied with their jobs, but dislike, say, the highly bureaucratic organization they work for, or the software engineer may be dissatisfied with her current job, but be very committed to the overall visionary high-tech firm.

On balance, research studies and the field of organizational behavior in general treat satisfaction and commitment as different attitudes. In light of the new environment that includes downsizing, telecommuting, mergers and acquisitions, and globalization, organizational commitment has resurfaced as a very important topic of study and concern. Although some expert observers feel that *organizational* commitment is a dead issue because of the new environment and should be replaced by career commitment,[102] others such as the following see organizational commitment as the major challenge in the 21st century:

> Today's workplace is enveloped by the fear of downsizing, loss of job security, over-whelming change in technology and the stress of having to do more with less . . . managers [need to] establish the type of caring, spirited workplace that will ignite employee commitment.[103]

After first defining commitment and its dimensions, what research has found to date about its outcomes is then summarized.

The Meaning of Organizational Commitment

As with other topics in organizational behavior, a wide variety of definitions and measures of organizational commitment exist.[104] As an attitude, organizational commitment is most often defined as (1) a strong desire to remain a member of a particular organization; (2) a willingness to exert high levels of effort on behalf of the organization; and (3) a definite belief in, and acceptance of, the values and goals of the organization.[105] In other words, this is an attitude reflecting employees' loyalty to their organization

Listed below are a series of statements that represent possible feelings that individuals might have about the company or organization for which they work. With respect to your own feelings about the particular organization for which you are now working, please indicate the degree of your agreement or disagreement with each statement by checking one of the seven alternatives below each statement.*

FIGURE 7.1
Organizational
Commitment
Questionnaire (OCQ).
Source: R. T. Mowday,
R. M. Steers, and L. W.
Porter, "The Measure of
Organizational
Commitment," *Journal of
Vocational Behavior,* Vol. 14,
1979, p. 288. Used with
permission.

1. I am willing to put in a great deal of effort beyond what is normally expected in order to help this organization be successful.
2. I talk up this organization to my friends as a great organization to work for.
3. I feel very little loyalty to this organization. (R)
4. I would accept almost any type of job assignment in order to keep working for this organization.
5. I find that my values and the organization's values are very similar.
6. I am proud to tell others that I am a part of this organization.
7. I could just as well be working for a different organization as long as the type of work was similar. (R)
8. This organization really inspires the very best in me in the way of job performance.
9. It would take very little change in my present circumstances to cause me to leave this organization. (R)
10. I am extremely glad that I chose this organization to work for over others I was considering at the time I joined.
11. There's not too much to be gained by sticking with this organization indefinitely. (R)
12. Often, I find it difficult to agree with this organization's policies on important matters relating to its employees. (R)
13. I really care about the fate of this organization.
14. For me this is the best of all possible organizations for which to work.
15. Deciding to work for this organization was a definite mistake on my part. (R)

*Responses to each item are measured on a 7-point scale with scale point anchors labeled (1) strongly disagree; (2) moderately disagree; (3) slightly disagree; (4) neither disagree nor agree; (5) slightly agree; (6) moderately agree; (7) strongly agree. An "R" denotes a negatively phrased and reverse-scored item.

and is an ongoing process through which organizational participants express their concern for the organization and its continued success and well-being. Using this definition, it is commonly measured by the Organizational Commitment Questionnaire shown in Figure 7.1.

The organizational commitment attitude is determined by a number of personal (age, tenure in the organization, and dispositions such as positive or negative affectivity, or internal or external control attributions) and organizational (the job design, values, and the leadership style of one's supervisor) variables.[106] Even nonorganizational factors, such as the availability of alternatives after making the initial choice to join an organization, will affect subsequent commitment.[107]

Also, because of the new environment where many organizations are not demonstrating evidence of commitment to their employees, recent research has found that an employee's career commitment is a moderator between the perceptions of company policies and practices and organizational commitment.[108] For example, even though employees perceive supervisory support, they would also need to have a commitment to their careers, say in engineering or marketing, in order to have high organizational commitment.

Because of this multidimensional nature of organizational commitment, there is growing support for the three-component model proposed by Meyer and Allen.[109] The three dimensions are as follows:

1. *Affective commitment* involves the employee's emotional attachment to, identification with, and involvement in the organization.
2. *Continuance commitment* involves commitment based on the costs that the employee associates with leaving the organization. This may be because of the loss of senority for promotion or benefits.
3. *Normative commitment* involves employees' feelings of obligation to stay with the organization because they should; it is the right thing to do.

There is considerable research support for this three-component conceptualization of organizational commitment.[110] It also generally holds up across cultures.[111]

The Outcomes of Organizational Commitment

As is the case with job satisfaction, there are mixed outcomes of organizational commitment. Both early[112] and more recent research summaries[113] do show support of a positive relationship between organizational commitment and desirable outcomes such as high performance, low turnover, and low absenteeism. There is also evidence that employee commitment relates to other desirable outcomes, such as the perception of a warm, supportive organizational climate[114] and being a good team member willing to help.[115] Yet, as with satisfaction, there are some studies that do not show strong relationships between commitment and outcome variables[116] and others where there are moderating effects between organizational commitment and performance. For example, one study found a stronger relationship between organizational commitment and performance for those with low financial needs than for those with high ones.[117] Another study found that commitment to supervisors was more strongly related to performance than was commitment to organizations.[118] These and a number of other studies indicate the complexity of an attitude such as commitment. On balance, however, most researchers would agree that the organizational commitment attitude as defined here is a somewhat better predictor of desirable outcome variables than is job satisfaction[119] and thus deserves management's attention.

Guidelines to Enhance Organizational Commitment

As the opening discussion of commitment indicated, management faces a paradoxical situation: "On the one hand today's focus on teamwork, empowerment, and flatter organizations puts a premium on just the sort of self-motivation that one expects to get from committed employees; on the other hand, environmental forces are acting to diminish the foundations of employee commitment."[120] Dessler suggests the following specific guidelines to implement a management system that should help solve the current dilemma and enhance employees' organizational commitment:

1. *Commit to people-first values.* Put it in writing, hire the right-kind managers, and walk the talk.

2. *Clarify and communicate your mission.*   Clarify the mission and ideology; make it charismatic; use value-based hiring practices; stress values-based orientation and training; build the tradition.
3. *Guarantee organizational justice.*   Have a comprehensive grievance procedure; provide for extensive two-way communications.
4. *Create a sense of community.*   Build value-based homogeneity; share and share alike; emphasize barnraising, cross-utilization, and teamwork; get together.
5. *Support employee development.*   Commit to actualizing; provide first-year job challenge; enrich and empower; promote from within; provide developmental activities; provide employee security without guarantees.[121]

Organizational Citizenship Behaviors (OCBs)

An appropriate concluding section for this chapter covering both personality and attitudes are the prosocial/organizational citizenship behaviors, simply known as OCBs. This now very popular construct in organizational behavior was first introduced about 20 years ago with both a dispositional/personality and job attitudes theoretical foundation. Organ defines OCB as "individual behavior that is discretionary, not directly or explicitly recognized by the formal reward system, and that in the aggregate promotes the effective functioning of the organization."[122]

The personality foundation for these OCBs reflect the employee's predispositional traits to be cooperative, helpful, caring, and conscientious. The attitudinal foundation indicates that employees engage in OCBs in order to reciprocate the actions of their organizations. Both job satisfaction[123] and organizational commitment[124] clearly relate to OCBs. More important to OCBs, however, is that employees must perceive that they are being treated fairly, that the procedures and outcomes are fair. A number of studies have found a strong relationship between justice and OCBs.[125] It seems that procedural justice affects employees by influencing their perceived organizational support, which in turn prompts them to reciprocate with OCBs, going beyond the formal job requirements.[126]

Besides being extra-role or going beyond "the call of duty," other major dimensions are that OCBs are discretionary or voluntary in nature, and they are not necessarily recognized by the the formal reward system of the organization.[127] OCBs can take many forms, but the major ones could be summarized as: (1) altruism (e.g., helping out when a coworker is not feeling well), (2) conscientiousness (e.g., staying late to finish a project), (3) civic virtue (e.g., volunteering for a community program to represent the firm), (4) sportsmanship (e.g., sharing failure of a team project that would have been successful by following the member's advice), and (5) courtesy (e.g., being understanding and empathetic even when provoked).[128]

Obviously, such OCBs are valuable to organizations and, although they frequently go undetected by the reward system, there is evidence that individuals who exhibit OCBs do perform better and receive higher performance evaluations.[129] Also, OCBs do relate to group and organization performance and effectiveness.[130] However, as with job satisfaction and organizational commitment, there is still some criticism of the conceptualization and research on OCBs,[131] and more research is certainly warranted. Yet, as a summary statement, today's managers would be very wise in trying to enhance not only job satisfaction and organizational commitment, but also prosocial, organizational citizenship behaviors of their employees.

Summary

Personality and attitudes represent important micro, cognitively oriented variables in the study of organizational behavior. Personality represents the "whole person" concept. It includes perception, learning, motivation, and more. According to this definition, people's external appearance and traits, their inner awareness of self, and the person–situation interaction make up their personalities. Although the nature versus nurture debate continues, the findings of twin studies of the importance that heredity may play in personality and recent breakthroughs in neuropsychology that points to the importance of the brain in personality have led most psychologists to recognize nature *and* nurture. However, the nurture side still dominates. Self-esteem, the person–situation interaction, and the socialization process of personality development are all very relevant to the understanding and application of organizational behavior.

Besides the recent advances in the genetic and brain input into personality, the study of long-term predispositions has resurfaced in the form of the "Big-Five" personality traits. Conscientiousness, emotional stability, agreeableness, extraversion, and openness to experience have been found to significantly relate to job performance, especially conscientiousness. In addition, the Myers-Briggs Type Indicator (MBTI) remains a popular tool for personal and career development. Whereas the "Big-Five" is based on research, the MBTI is based on the historically important Carl Jung theory of personality types and mental processes. Both the "Big Five" and MBTI if carefully interpreted and used can make a contribution to the understanding and application of organizational behavior.

The second half of the chapter is more directly concerned with attitudes. Whereas personality deals with the whole person, an attitude is a persistent tendency to feel and behave in a particular way toward some object. Like personality, attitudes are a complex cognitive process that have three basic characteristics: they persist unless changed in some way; they range along a continuum; and they are directed toward an object about which a person has feelings, or affect, and beliefs. Attitudes also have three components: emotional, informational, and behavioral. Both situational and personality traits or dispositions, such as positive affectivity (PA) and negative affectivity (NA), are important antecedents to attitudes about one's job.

Attitudes often help employees adapt to their work environment. There are four functions that attitudes have in this process: (1) they help people adjust to their environment, (2) they help people defend their self-image, (3) they provide people with a basis for expressing their values, and (4) they help supply standards and frames of reference that allow people to organize and explain the world around them.

It is sometimes difficult to change attitudes. One reason is prior commitments. A second is insufficient information on the part of the person having an attitude to be changed. Research shows that some of the ways of bringing about attitude changes are providing new information, use of fear, resolving discrepancies between behavior and attitude, persuasion by friends or peers, and co-opting.

Job satisfaction is a pleasurable or positive emotional state resulting from the appraisal of one's job or job experience. A number of factors influence job satisfaction. Some of the major ones are the work itself, pay, promotions, supervision, the work group, and working conditions. There are a number of outcomes of job satisfaction. For example, although the relationship with productivity is not clear, low job satisfaction tends to lead to both turnover and absenteeism, whereas high job satisfaction often results in fewer on-the-job accidents and work grievances, less time needed to learn new job-related tasks, and less stress. There are also specific guidelines to enhance employee satisfaction such as making jobs fun, insuring fairness, getting the right fit, and design jobs to make them more exciting and satisfying.

Closely related to job satisfaction is the organizational commitment attitude. It involves the employees' loyalty to the organization and is determined by a number of personal, organizational, and nonorganizational variables. Now commitment is generally conceived as having three components: affective (emotional attachment), continuance (costs of leaving), and normative (obligation to stay). Like job satisfaction, the organizational commitment attitude is very complex and has mixed results, but in general, it is thought to have a somewhat stronger relationship with organizational outcomes such as performance, absenteeism, and turnover. Like satisfaction, organizational commitment can be enhanced.

The concluding section draws from both personality and attitudes. The extra-role, prosocial/organizational citizenship behaviors (OCBs) involve predispositional traits to be cooperative and conscientious and reflect through attitudes fair treatment from the organization. OCBs can take a number of forms such as altruism, conscientiousness, civic virtue, sportsmanship, and courtesy. Although there is still some criticism of the conceptualization and research of OCBs, there is growing evidence that OCBs positively relate to individual, group, and organizational performance.

ENDING WITH META-ANALYTIC RESEARCH FINDINGS

OB PRINCIPLE: Conscientious employees are effective performers.

Meta-Analysis Results: [117 studies; 19,721 participants; $d = .26$] *On average, there is a **57 percent probability** that conscientious employees will turn out to be better performers than those who do not have the conscientious personality trait.* Out of all the "Big Five" personality dimensions tested, only conscientiousness showed consistent relations with all job performance criteria across occupational groups.

Conclusion: Personality measures are widely used in employee analysis and selection because they contribute to the learning and understanding of today's employees. Though many personality traits have been investigated over the years, the Big Five personality dimensions (conscientiousness, extroversion, agreeableness, openness to experience, and emotional stability) have emerged as the most important because of their relationship with performance. However, consistent with what was discussed in this chapter, conscientiousness is the single strongest Big Five predictor of work performance. Conscientious people can be characterized as dependable, hardworking, responsible, persevering, and achievement oriented—all desirable qualities of effective, high-performing employees.

Source: Adapted from Murray R. Barrick and Michael K. Mount, "The Big Five Personality Dimensions and Job Performance: A Meta-Analysis," *Personnel Psychology,* Vol. 44, 1991, pp. 1–26.

OB PRINCIPLE: Employees who are satisfied with their jobs participate more in prosocial, organizational citizenship behaviors (OCBs).

Meta-Analysis Results: [28 studies; 6,746 participants; $d = .47$] *On average, there is a **63 percent probability** that employees who are satisfied in their jobs will participate in more prosocial, organizational citizenship behaviors (OCBs) than those who are not satisfied.* Self—versus other—ratings of organizational citizenship behaviors was a notable moderator of the relationship. Self-reports of citizenship behaviors tend to be inflated. Overall, the evidence provides support that measures of OCBs will be better related to job satisfaction than would in-role performance, with the exception that this applies mainly to nonmanagerial, nonprofessional employees.

Conclusion: Individuals who contribute to organizational effectiveness by doing things that are above and beyond their primary task or role are assets to their organizations. Examples of organization citizenship behaviors or OCBs are volunteering for extra job activities, helping coworkers, and making positive comments about the company. As this chapter has discussed, OCBs are of value to the organization because, although they are not viewed as a traditional measure of performance, they can still impact on an organization's performance by supporting ongoing task activities and influencing performance evaluations. Employees who exhibit citizenship behaviors such as helping others or making innovative suggestions receive higher performance ratings. Moreover, other attitudinal variables discussed in this chapter such as job satisfaction and organizational commitment predict and may lead to OCBs.

Source: Adapted from Dennis W. Organ and Katherine Ryan, "A Meta-Analytic Review of Attitudinal and Dispositional Predictors of Organizational Citizenship Behavior," *Personnel Psychology,* Vol. 48, 1995, pp. 775–802.

Questions for Discussion and Review

1. Critically analyze the statement that "the various psychological processes can be thought of as pieces of a jigsaw puzzle, and personality as the completed puzzle picture."
2. What is the comprehensive definition of "personality"? Give brief examples of each of the major elements.
3. What side would you prefer to argue in the nature versus nurture debate? What would be the major points each side would make? How would you resolve the controversy?
4. What are the "Big Five" personality traits? Which one seems to have the biggest impact on performance? How would knowledge of the "Big Five" help you in your job as a manager?
5. What are the four major dimensions of the Myers-Briggs Type Indicator (MBTI) that yield the 16 types? How can the MBTI be used effectively?
6. In your own words, what is an attitude? What are three characteristics and three components of attitudes?
7. Attitudes serve four important functions for individuals. What are these four functions?
8. What types of barriers prevent people from changing their attitudes? How can attitudes be changed?
9. What is meant by the term "job satisfaction"? What are some of the major factors that influence job satisfaction?
10. What are some of the important outcomes of job satisfaction?
11. What is organizational commitment? What three components have emerged to help better explain the complexities of commitment? Why may an understanding of organizational commitment be especially important in the years ahead?
12. What are organization citizenship behaviors (OCBs)? How do they come about and what are some examples?

Internet Exercise: Assessing Your Personality

This chapter was concerned with how personality traits may affect performance in the workplace. To understand this better, many organizations are using outside resources to assess employee personalities in an effort to get them into jobs that fit their characteristics. One such organization can be found at http://www.personality-tests-personality-profiles.com/home.htm. This site discusses the services that they provide, and provides some sample personality questions. Another interesting website is http://www.queendom.com/alltests.html. They have many different types of assessment tools that you can take online. Many of them are related to the workplace. Browse through these sites and take some of the tests. Then consider the following questions:

1. Did you learn anything that you didn't already know about yourself? If so, what? How do you think your personality will affect your work performance?
2. Is there anything you would like to change about yourself in order to improve yourself? If so, what? If not, what type of job would seem to be most suited to your personality?

3. Using your search engine, see if you can locate other websites that assess personality. How, if at all, do these personality assessments match up with what you have covered in this chapter on personality and attitudes?

REAL CASE:
It's All a Matter of
Personality

Largely because of downsizing, the survivors are working harder and longer hours every year—and although some get burned out and stressed, others seem to thrive on it. At Apple Computer, for example, development teams are well known for wearing T-shirts that proclaim, "90 Hours a Week and Loving It!" And high-tech firms are now coaxing double and triple time out of their employees, a practice that is spreading to other sectors of the economy. One of the best examples is provided by the increasing number of telecommuters who work at home. By giving employees PCs, cellular phones, pagers, and other devices, the company can stay in contact. However, many of these telecommuters are now finding that they are on call 24 hours a day. One of the new rules of survival in an increasing number of workplaces appears to be: If you don't have the personality to work round-the-clock, don't bother applying for a job here.

Of course, for some people work is extremely enjoyable, and they do not mind the new demands. Take the case of entrepreneur Wayne Huizenga, a self-made billionaire. Huizenga started out with a partner in the garbage collection business, confident that his firm could outperform the small mom-and-pop garbage companies and get their business. He was supremely confident of his own ability; it was not long before his plan started to come true. Wall Street did not think much of his ideas, however, and when he issued his first stock offering in 1971 it was to raise a mere $5 million. By the time Huizenga left in 1984, the market value of the firm's stock was $3 billion.

Huizenga's next move was to Blockbuster Entertainment. He was convinced that the movie rental business was a wave of the future. Again he was right. For a mere $18.5 million, he and his partners were able to buy the company—and soon thereafter sales took off, rising from $43 million annually to over $2 billion. By the time he sold out to Viacom in 1994, he had put another billion dollars in his pocket.

Now Huizenga is looking into new business ventures, including a garbage collection company, a security alarm firm, and a used-car operation. The latter is of particular interest to investors because it involves a novel approach to car buying. Huizenga is convinced that because the price of new cars is going up so quickly and more and more people are buying used cars, the big profit will be in the secondhand market. Whether he is right or wrong, Huizenga remains confident of his new investment decisions, and those who have bet with him in the past believe he has another set of winning strategies on the drawing board.

The same can be said for Steve Wynn of Mirage Resorts. Wynn's company was recently listed as one of *Fortune*'s 10 most admired firms in America. Why? Part of it is a reflection of Wynn's own personality. He is eternally optimistic and wants his people to be the same. Wynn's strategy is to keep everybody happy. If anyone is not, Wynn's employees are to fix it. As he tells his people, "If you see a hotel guest with the tiniest frown on her face, don't ask a supervisor, take care of it. Erase the charge, send the dinner back, don't charge for the room." In addition, Wynn sponsors elaborate parties to honor staffers who have kept the most customers happy. At one recent party for a Vietnamese woman who was being honored as employee of the year, Wynn brought in George and Barbara Bush to congratulate the lady. It cost a lot of money for the party, but, as Wynn puts it, "It's an investment."

1. Why do employees at firms such as Apple Computer work so hard and put in such long hours?
2. How would you describe Wayne Huizenga in terms of the self-concept, specifically self-esteem?
3. Why is job satisfaction and organizational commitment so high at Mirage Resorts? How does Steve Wynn manage to keep his employees so happy?

ORGANIZATIONAL BEHAVIOR CASE: Ken Leaves the Company

Good people—valuable employees—quit their jobs every day. Usually, they leave for better positions elsewhere. Take Ken, an experienced underwriter in a northeastern insurance company, who scribbled the following remarks on his exit interview questionnaire:

> This job isn't right for me. I like to have more input on decisions that affect me—more of a chance to show what I can do. I don't get enough feedback to tell if I'm doing a good job or not, and the company keeps people in the dark about where it's headed. Basically, I feel like an interchangeable part most of the time.

In answer to the question about whether the company could have done anything to keep him, Ken replied simply, "Probably not."

Why do so many promising employees leave their jobs? And why do so many others stay on but perform at minimal levels for lack of better alternatives? One of the main reasons—Ken's reason—can be all but invisible, because it's so common in so many organizations: a systemwide failure to keep good people.

Corporations should be concerned about employees like Ken. By investing in human capital, they may actually help reduce turnover, protect training investments, increase productivity, improve quality, and reap the benefits of innovative thinking and teamwork.

Human resource professionals and managers can contribute to corporate success by encouraging employees' empowerment, security, identity, "connectedness," and competence. How? By recognizing the essential components of keeping their best people and by understanding what enhances and diminishes those components.

Ken doubts that his company will ever change, but other organizations are taking positive steps to focus on and enhance employee retention. As a result, they're reducing turnover, improving quality, increasing productivity, and protecting their training investments.

1. Do you think that Ken's self-esteem had anything to do with his leaving the firm?
2. What do you think were Ken's satisfaction with and commitment to the job and firm he is leaving? How does this relate to the research on the determinants and outcomes of satisfaction and commitment?
3. What lesson can this company learn from the case of Ken? What can and should it now do?

ORGANIZATIONAL BEHAVIOR CASE: Doing His Share

When Ralph Morgan joined the Beacher Corporation, he started out as a process designer in operations. Ralph remained in this position for five years. During this time there were two major strikes. The first lasted 5 weeks; the second went on for 18 weeks. As a member of the union, Ralph was out of work during both of these periods, and in each case the strike fund ran out of money before a labor agreement was reached.

Last year Ralph was asked if he would like to apply for a supervisory job. The position paid $2500 more than he was making, and the chance for promotion up the line made it an attractive offer. Ralph accepted.

During the orientation period, Ralph found himself getting angry at the management representative. This guy seemed to believe that the union was too powerful and management personnel had to hold the line against any further loss of authority. Ralph did not say anything, but he felt the speaker was very ill informed and biased. Two developments have occurred over the last six months, however, that have led Ralph to change his attitude toward union–management relations at the company.

One was a run-in he had with a union officer who accused Ralph of deliberately harassing one of the workers. Ralph could not believe his ears. "Harassing a worker? Get serious. All I did was tell him to get back to work," he explained to the steward. Nevertheless, a grievance was filed and withdrawn only after Ralph apologized to the individual whom he allegedly harassed. The other incident was a result of disciplinary action. One of the workers in his unit came in late for the third day in a row and, as required by the labor contract, Ralph sent him home without pay. The union protested, claiming that the worker had really been late only twice. When Ralph went to the personnel office to get the worker's clock-in sheets, the one for the first day of tardiness was missing. The clerks in that office, who were union members, claimed that they did not know where it was.

In both of these cases, Ralph felt the union went out of its way to embarrass him. Earlier this week the manager from the orientation session called Ralph. "I've been thinking about bringing supervisors into the orientation meetings to discuss the union's attitude toward management. Having been on the other side, would you be interested in giving them your opinion of what they should be prepared for and how they should respond?" Ralph said he would be delighted. "I think it's important to get these guys ready to take on the union and I'd like to do my share," he explained.

1. What was Ralph's attitude toward the union when he first became a supervisor? What barriers were there that initially prevented him from changing his attitude regarding the union?
2. Why did Ralph's attitude change? What factors accounted for this?
3. Are workers who are recruited for supervisory positions likely to go through the same attitude changes as Ralph?

CHAPTER 8

Motivational Needs and Processes

Learning Objectives

Define motivation.

Identify the primary, general, and secondary needs.

Discuss the major content theories of work motivation.

Explain the major process theories of work motivation.

Present the contemporary equity and procedural justice theories.

Analyze work motivation across cultures.

Starting with Best Practice
Leader's Advice

Disney's CEO Michael Eisner on the Challenge of Motivating Employees

Everyone knows about Disney's theme parks and animated vintage films, but the "mouse that roared" largely under Eisner's visionary leadership, now owns other movie studios, cruise ships, 725 stores, a number of new theme parks, and media acquisitions (ABC, ESPN, Lifetime, E! Entertainment Television, and the Internet portal Go.com). Eisner made a name for himself in TV programming and as a motion picture producer before taking over the helm of Disney in 1984. He provides insights into the importance of motivating employees and how to do it.

Q1: *What aspect of running a large company is the most daunting?*

Eisner: Without a doubt, it's dealing on a day-to-day basis with the human equation—that is, making sure our cast members are committed and motivated, and that their emotions are engaged in the right ways. We make movies about conflict, ambition, envy, jealousy. In our movies, we look at what happens when healthy ambition turns into blind ambition, when normal needs for power turn into dictatorial power, when the appropriate search for opportunity turns into opportunism. That's in the movies. In the workplace, we don't want to go see the dark side of emotions if we can help it. We want ambition and power and opportunity to be under control. We want our top managers to be comfortable with themselves and to be an example for the entire workforce.

Q2: *When managers set an example of how to behave, does that allow more autonomy throughout the organization?*

Eisner: In some cases, yes. I'm a big believer in initiative and responsibility at every level. A ride operator at a Disney park should be able to adjust policies to address a guest's problems no less than a vice president of a division should be able to make decisions about how to move the organization forward.

But there have to be limits to autonomy. Our goal for senior management is to delegate authority—*authority* not autonomy—downward in the organization. Sometimes in large companies, too much gets delegated, especially now that empowerment is the rage. I just believe that those with the most experience should be given the most opportunity to handle really tough situations—situations that put a company or a division at risk.

I have had tremendous authority at every job I've ever had. I took it—because in the real world, most responsibility you take, you're not given. But I managed up as well as sideways and down. If I had a feeling that something was going to be more expensive, or was going over budget, or was going to put a project at risk, I told my boss and my boss's boss. I figured they had to have some talent. That's how they got to the top. There are not too many dumb bosses out there.

Q3:   *What about "being there"? Can you describe what that role involves?*

Eisner: Sometimes you just have to be there with your people. You have to be in the same room with them, look them in the eyes, hear their voices. I'll tell you one thing. Most of the bad decisions I've made, I've made while teleconferencing. In creative companies, you have to be able to read body language—see the look in people's eyes when an idea is launched, see whether they fall asleep.

   If you have an organization that is small enough, being there simply means having contact and exposure and being available. When the organization gets bigger, it is unbelievably frustrating to a leader that you can't be there for everyone. That's why you need a team of leaders running the organization, which is what we have. Our parks have a leader. Our movie and television business has a leader. Our Internet operations have a leader. ABC and ESPN have leaders. We have country managers. And what makes organizations great is the quality of that leadership spread across the top—not just at the very top.

   What I do is focus on the 40 people I have an impact on every day. I'm very available to them. And then I try to get out there as much as possible. Our management team is always moving around all over the company, which is all over the country and all over the world. We walk the parks, the hotels, and the stores. The most fun is going into the hotel kitchens late at night.

   I'm also using e-mail more to communicate with our whole cast—all 110,000 of them. Today I'm going to send something out about why we closed Walt Disney World for Hurricane Floyd. We've never closed the park before, and everyone wants to know why. They want to know what we did to protect our cast members and our guests down there. So I'll tell them. It's a great way to stay connected.

Q4:   *What does it mean to lead by being a nudge?*

Eisner: By nudging, I mean that I just don't forget things. I don't keep many notes, but once something is in my head, I can't get rid of it until I think it has been stuck into somebody else's head. I am constantly reminding people of ideas. I follow up and follow up because good ideas have a way of getting lost. They fall through the cracks, or they get mired in bureaucracy, and everyone is busy in their own orbit. So I nudge. Sometimes all that good ideas or good people need is an advocate who won't shut up.

Q5:   *The last role of a leader, you say, is being an idea generator. Should good ideas come from the top?*

Eisner: It's better if good ideas come from the top than bad ideas. But ideas can come from anywhere. The leader in a creative business should be creative. He or she should be spouting ideas all the time, just like everyone else. Many of us come up with ideas driving to work, walking around the house, watching our kids at sporting events, everywhere. It becomes addictive. Many of my ideas are simply bad, and, believe me, I am told so quickly. That kind of honesty in our team and culture must exist—a culture where your associates tell you that your last idea was all wet. I have no problem telling an associate that I hate his idea. So we must have an environment where criticism goes up as well as down. We all edit each other. Sometimes the ideas do make some sense, and we move forward with them.

Motivation is a basic psychological process. Few would deny that it is the most important focus in the micro approach to organizational behavior. In fact, a data-based comprehensive analysis concluded that "America's competitiveness problems appear to be largely motivational in nature."[1] Many people equate the causes of behavior with motivation; however, the causes of behavior are much broader and more complex than can be explained by motivation alone.

Along with perception, personality, attitudes, and learning, motivation is presented here as a very important process in understanding behavior. Nevertheless, it must be remembered that motivation should not be thought of as the only explanation of behavior. It interacts with and acts in conjunction with other mediating processes and the environment. It must also be remembered that, like the other cognitive processes, motivation cannot be seen. All that can be seen is behavior. Motivation is a hypothetical construct that is used to help explain behavior; it should not be equated with behavior. In fact, while recognizing the "central role of motivation," many of today's organizational behavior theorists "think it is important for the field to reemphasize behavior."[2]

This chapter presents motivation as a basic psychological process. The more applied aspects of motivation are covered in the last part of the book, on job design and goal setting. The first section of this chapter clarifies the meaning of motivation by defining the relationship among its various parts. The need–drive–incentive cycle is defined and analyzed. The next section is devoted to an overview of the various types of needs, or motives: primary, general, and secondary. The motives within the general and secondary categories are given major attention, and a summary of supporting research findings on these motives is included. The next two sections of the chapter present the content and process theories of work motivation giving particular attention to contemporary theories. Finally, the cross-cultural aspects of motivation are given attention. Specifically addressed are variances between motives across cultures and applications of motivation theories in international settings.

THE MEANING OF MOTIVATION

Today, virtually all people—practitioners and scholars—have their own definitions of motivation. Usually one or more of the following words are included: *desires, wants, wishes, aims, goals, needs, drives, motives,* and *incentives.* Technically, the term *motivation* can be traced to the Latin word *movere,* which means "to move." This meaning is evident in the following comprehensive definition: *motivation* is a process that starts with a physiological or psychological deficiency or need that activates a behavior or a drive that is aimed at a goal or incentive. Thus, the key to understanding the process of motivation lies in the meaning of, and relationships among, needs, drives, and incentives.

Figure 8.1 graphically depicts the motivation process. Needs set up drives aimed at incentives; this is what the basic process of motivation is all about. In a systems sense, motivation consists of these three interacting and interdependent elements:

1. *Needs.* Needs are created whenever there is a physiological or psychological imbalance. For example, a need exists when cells in the body are deprived of food

FIGURE 8.1
The basic motivation process.

NEEDS ⟶ **DRIVES** ⟶ **INCENTIVES**

and water or when the personality is deprived of other people who serve as friends or companions. Although psychological needs may be based on a deficiency, sometimes they are not. For example, an individual with a strong need to get ahead may have a history of consistent success.

2. *Drives.* With a few exceptions,[3] drives, or motives (the two terms are often used interchangeably), are set up to alleviate needs. A physiological drive can be simply defined as a deficiency with direction. Physiological and psychological drives are action oriented and provide an energizing thrust toward reaching an incentive. They are at the very heart of the motivational process. The examples of the needs for food and water are translated into the hunger and thirst drives, and the need for friends becomes a drive for affiliation.

3. *Incentives.* At the end of the motivation cycle is the incentive, defined as anything that will alleviate a need and reduce a drive. Thus, attaining an incentive will tend to restore physiological or psychological balance and will reduce or cut off the drive. Eating food, drinking water, and obtaining friends will tend to restore the balance and reduce the corresponding drives. Food, water, and friends are the incentives in these examples.

These dimensions of the basic motivation process serve as a point of departure for the content and process theories of work motivation. After discussion of primary, general, and secondary motives, those work-motivation theories that are more directly related to the study and application of organizational behavior and human resource management are examined.

PRIMARY MOTIVES

Psychologists do not totally agree on how to classify the various human motives, but they would acknowledge that some motives are unlearned and physiologically based. Such motives are variously called *physiological, biological, unlearned,* or *primary.* The last term is used here because it is more comprehensive than the others. However, the use of the term *primary* does not imply that these motives always take precedence over general and secondary motives. Although the precedence of primary motives is implied in some motivation theories, there are many situations in which general and secondary motives predominate over primary motives. Common examples are celibacy among priests and fasting for a religious, social, or political cause. In both cases, learned secondary motives are stronger than unlearned primary motives.

Two criteria must be met in order for a motive to be included in the *primary* classification: It must be *unlearned,* and it must be *physiologically based.* Thus defined, the most commonly recognized primary motives include hunger, thirst, sleep, avoidance of pain, sex, and maternal concern. Because people have the same basic physiological makeup, they will all have essentially the same primary needs. This is not true of the learned secondary needs.

GENERAL MOTIVES

A separate classification for general motives is not always given. Yet such a category seems necessary because there are a number of motives that lie in the gray area between the primary and secondary classifications. To be included in the general category, a motive must be unlearned but not physiologically based. Whereas the primary needs seek to reduce the tension or stimulation, these general needs induce the person to increase the amount of stimulation. Thus, these needs are sometimes called "stimulus motives."[4] Although not all psychologists would agree, the motives of curiosity, manipulation, activity, and affection seem best to meet the criteria for this classification. An understanding of these general motives is important to the study of human behavior—especially in organizations. General motives are more relevant to organizational behavior than are primary motives.

The Curiosity, Manipulation, and Activity Motives

Early psychologists noted that the animals used in their experiments seemed to have an unlearned drive to explore, to manipulate objects, or just to be active. This was especially true of monkeys that were placed in an unfamiliar or novel situation. These observations and speculations about the existence of curiosity, manipulation, and activity motives in monkeys were later substantiated through experimentation. In this case, psychologists feel completely confident in generalizing the results of animal experiments to humans. It is generally recognized that human curiosity, manipulation, and activity drives are quite intense; anyone who has reared or been around small children will quickly support this generalization.

Although these drives often get the small child into trouble, curiosity, manipulation, and activity, when carried forward to adulthood, can be very beneficial. If these motives are stifled or inhibited, the total society might become very stagnant. The same is true on an organizational level. If employees are not allowed to express their curiosity, manipulation, and activity motives, they may not be motivated. For example, sticking an employee behind a machine or a desk for eight hours a day may stifle these general motives.

The Affection Motive

Love or affection is a very complex form of general drive. Part of the complexity stems from the fact that in many ways love resembles the primary drives and in other ways it is similar to the secondary drives. In particular, the affection motive is closely associated with the primary sex motive on the one hand and with the secondary affiliation motive on the other. For this reason, affection is sometimes placed in all three categories of motives, and some psychologists do not even recognize it as a separate motive.

Affection merits specific attention because of its growing importance to the modern world. There seems to be a great deal of truth to the adages, "Love makes the world go round" and "Love conquers all." In a world where we suffer from interpersonal, intra-individual, and national conflict, and where quality of life, family values, and human rights are becoming increasingly important to modern society, the affection motive takes on added importance in the study of human behavior.

SECONDARY MOTIVES

Whereas the general drives seem relatively more important than the primary ones to the study of human behavior in organizations, the secondary drives are unquestionably the most important. As a human society develops economically and becomes more complex, the primary drives, and to a lesser degree the general drives, give way to the learned secondary drives in motivating behavior. With some glaring exceptions that have yet to be eradicated, the motives of hunger and thirst are not dominant among people living in the economically developed world. This situation is obviously subject to change; for example, the "population bomb," nuclear war, or the greenhouse effect may alter certain human needs. But for now, the learned secondary motives dominate.

Secondary motives are closely tied to the learning concepts that are discussed in Chapter 16. In particular, the learning principle of reinforcement is conceptually and practically related to motivation. The relationship is obvious when reinforcement is divided into primary and secondary categories and is portrayed as incentives. Some discussions, however, regard reinforcement as simply a consequence serving to increase the *motivation* to perform the behavior again,[5] and they are treated separately in this text. Once again, however, it should be emphasized that although the various behavioral concepts can be separated for study and analysis, in reality, concepts like reinforcement and motivation do not operate as separate entities in producing human behavior. The interactive effects are always present.

A motive must be learned in order to be included in the *secondary* classification. Numerous important human motives meet this criterion. Some of the more important ones are power, achievement, and affiliation, or, as they are commonly referred to today, *n Pow, n Ach,* and *n Aff.* In addition, especially in reference to organizational behavior, security and status are important secondary motives. Table 8.1 gives examples of each of these important secondary needs.

The Power Motive

The power motive is discussed first because it has been formally recognized and studied for a relatively long time. The leading advocate of the power motive was the pioneering psychologist Alfred Adler. Adler officially broke his close ties with Sigmund Freud and

TABLE 8.1   Examples of Key Secondary Needs

Need for Achievement
- Doing better than competitors
- Attaining or surpassing a difficult goal
- Solving a complex problem
- Carrying out a challenging assignment successfully
- Developing a better way to do something

Need for Power
- Influencing people to change their attitudes or behavior
- Controlling people and activities
- Being in a position of authority over others
- Gaining control over information and resources
- Defeating an opponent or enemy

Need for Affiliation
- Being liked by many people
- Being accepted as part of a group or team
- Working with people who are friendly and cooperative
- Maintaining harmonious relationships and avoiding conflicts
- Participating in pleasant social activities

Need for Security
- Having a secure job
- Being protected against loss of income or economic disaster
- Having protection against illness and disability
- Being protected against physical harm or hazardous conditions
- Avoiding tasks or decisions with a risk of failure and blame

Need for Status
- Having the right car and wearing the right clothes
- Working for the right company in the right job
- Having a degree from the right university
- Living in the right neighborhood and belonging to the country club
- Having executive privileges

Source: Adapted from Gary Yukl, *Skills for Managers and Leaders,* Prentice Hall, Upper Saddle River, N.J., 1990, p 41. The examples of need for status were not covered by Yukl.

proposed an opposing theoretical position. Whereas Freud stressed the impact of the past and of sexual, unconscious motivation, Adler substituted the future and a person's overwhelming drive for superiority or power.

To explain the *power need*—the need to manipulate others or the drive for being in charge of others—Adler developed the concepts of *inferiority complex* and *compensation*. He felt that every small child experiences a sense of inferiority. When this feeling of inferiority is combined with what he sensed as an innate (inborn) need for superiority, the two rule all behavior. The person's lifestyle is characterized by striving to compensate for feelings of inferiority, which are combined with the innate drive for power.

Although modern psychologists do not generally accept the tenet that the power drive is inborn and thus dominant, in recent years it has prompted renewed interest. The quest for power is readily observable in modern American society. The politician is probably the best example, and political scandals make a fascinating study of the striving for and the use of power in government and politics. However, in addition to politicians, anyone holding a responsible position in business, government, unions, education, or the military may also exhibit a considerable need for power. The power motive has significant implications for organizational leadership, as well as the informal, political aspects of organizations. Recent practitioner-oriented literature stresses the value of empowering employees and the use of power rewards (let employees make choices, set their own goals, and increase their responsibility) to motivate employees.[6] Further, as Chapter 13 brings out, there is a distinction to be made between social power and personal power. Social power, which is often a characteristic of effective leaders, is devoted to developing trust and respect from followers and is in conjunction with the leader's vision. Personal power is more oriented toward the ability to dominate others and for the personal gain of the leader.[7] Chapter 13 will examine in detail the theories and research of power. It has emerged as one of the most important dynamics in the study of organizational behavior.

The Achievement Motive

Whereas the power motive has been recognized and discussed for a long time, only very recently has there been any research activity. The opposite is true of the achievement motive. Although it has not been recognized for as long as the other motives, more is known about achievement than about any other motive because of the tremendous amount of research that has been devoted to it.[8] *Achievement* may be defined as the degree to which a person wishes to accomplish challenging goals, succeed in competitive situations, and exhibit the desire for unambiguous feedback regarding performance. An individual with a high need for achievement has higher levels of each element of the definition.

The Thematic Apperception Test (TAT) has proven to be a very effective tool in researching achievement. The TAT can effectively identify and measure the achievement motive.[9] The test works in the following manner: One picture in the TAT shows a young man plowing a field; the sun is about to sink in the west. The person taking the test is supposed to tell a story about what he or she sees in the picture. The story will project the person's major motives. For example, the test taker may say that the man in the picture is sorry the sun is going down because he still has more land to plow and he wants to get the crops planted before it rains. Such a response indicates high achievement. A low achiever might say that the man is happy the sun is finally going down so that he can go into the house, relax, and have a cool drink. The research approach to achievement has become so effective that it is often cited by psychologists as a prototype of how knowledge and understanding can be gained in the behavioral sciences.

David C. McClelland, a recently deceased Harvard psychologist, is most closely associated with study of the achievement motive, and, as Chapter 13 indicates, he also did considerable research on power as well. McClelland thoroughly investigated and wrote about all aspects of *n Ach* (achievement). A clear profile of the characteristics of the high achiever has emerged out of this extensive research. The derived specific characteristics of high achievers are summarized in the following sections.

Moderate Risk Taking.   Taking moderate risks is probably the single most descriptive characteristic of the person possessing high *n Ach*. On the surface it would seem that a high achiever would take high risks. However, once again research provides insights that are different from a seemingly commonsense explanation. The ring-toss game can be used to demonstrate risk-taking behavior. It has been shown that when ring tossers are told that they may stand anywhere they want to when they toss the rings at the peg, low and high achievers behave quite differently. Low achievers tend either to stand very close and just drop the rings over the peg or to stand very far away and wildly throw the rings at the peg. In contrast, high achievers almost always carefully calculate the exact distance from the peg that will challenge their own abilities. People with high *n Ach* will not stand too close because it would be no test of their ability simply to drop the rings over the peg. By the same token, they will not stand ridiculously far away because luck, not skill, would then determine whether the rings landed on the peg. In other words, low achievers take either a high or low risk, and high achievers take a moderate risk. This seems to hold true both for the simple children's game and for important adult decisions and activities in today's organizations.[10]

Need for Immediate Feedback.   Closely connected to high achievers' taking moderate risks is their desire for immediate feedback. People with high *n Ach* prefer activities that provide immediate and precise feedback information on how they are progressing toward their goals. Some hobbies and vocations offer such feedback, and others do not. High achievers generally prefer hobbies such as woodworking or mechanics, which provide prompt, exact feedback. They tend to shy away from the coin-collecting types of hobbies, which take years to develop. Likewise, high achievers tend to gravitate toward, or at least to be more satisfied in, jobs or careers, such as sales or certain managerial positions, in which they are frequently evaluated by specific performance criteria. On the other end of the scale, high *n Ach* persons are generally not to be found, or tend to be frustrated, in research and development or teaching vocations, where feedback on performance is very imprecise, vague, and long range.

Satisfaction with Accomplishments.   High achievers find accomplishing a task intrinsically satisfying in and of itself; they do not expect or necessarily want the accompanying material rewards. A good illustration of this characteristic involves money, but not for the usual reasons of wanting money for its own sake or for the material benefits that it can buy. Rather, high *n Ach* people look at money as a form of feedback or measurement of how they are doing. Given the choice between a simple task with a good payoff for accomplishment and a more difficult task with a lesser payoff, other things being equal, high achievers may choose the latter.

Preoccupation with the Task.   Once high achievers select goals, they tend to be totally preoccupied with their tasks until they are successfully completed. They cannot stand to leave a job half finished and are not satisfied with themselves until they have given their maximum effort. This type of dedicated commitment is often reflected in their outward personalities, which frequently have negative effects on those who come into contact with them. High achievers often strike others as being unfriendly and as "loners." They may be very quiet and may seldom brag about their accomplishments. They tend to be very realistic about their abilities and do not allow other people to get in the way of their goal accomplishments. Obviously, with this type of approach, high achievers do not always get along well with other people. Typically, high achievers make excellent salespersons but seldom good sales managers. There is some research evidence that cooperative efforts may be more effective than the competitive, individualistic efforts characteristic of high achievers.[11] Also, high achievers are likely to enjoy jobs with pay incentives that are clearly linked to performance and situations in which managers set challenging goals that, when reached, result in tangible rewards.

The accompanying Application Example: High Achievers in Action provides common strategies entrepreneurs use to start new businesses. Almost all such entrepreneurs have a relatively high need for achievement.

APPLICATION EXAMPLE

High Achievers in Action

One of the best examples of high achievers is entrepreneurs who start and manage their own businesses. Although many of these owner-managers do not stay in business more than five years, a large percentage are very successful and manage to keep their enterprises afloat for an indefinite period. How do successful entrepreneurs operate? By sidestepping the potential pitfalls and problems before they even open the doors of their new venture. Prior to starting, they take steps to ensure that the enterprise is able to survive the first two years—the most critical period for most small business ventures. Some of the strategic steps they take include the following:

1. *Draw up a five-year plan.* This assures entrepreneurs that they will have goals to aim for during the first 60 months of operation. The plan often has both annual and quarterly forecasts.
2. *Raise more money than is needed.* One of the biggest problems is running out of capital. To ensure that this does not happen, successful entrepreneurs allow for a margin of error by starting out with more money than they estimate will be needed. Then, if sales are not generated as quickly as forecasted, the new company has enough capital to tide it over.
3. *Test the market.* Successful entrepreneurs look over their market and ensure that there is sufficient demand for their goods or services. If the demand is weak, they look for different geographic locales. If the demand is strong, they look for specific target markets they can further exploit.
4. *Don't take "no" for an answer.* If the bank turns down an application for a loan, successful entrepreneurs find out why. If there is something wrong with their financial plan, they fix it. If their projected costs of operations are too high, they figure out ways of reducing them. They then return to the bank and get the loan—or find another financial institution that is willing to give them the loan.

Another interesting aspect of the achievement literature examines the effects of national achievement motives on economic growth. In one study, stories from children's primary school readers were compared across the dimensions of *n Ach* portrayed in the stories and indices of economic growth. In that study, and in others, a greater emphasis on achievement of young people was related to stronger economic growth in the years that followed.[12] Given the reported (but largely unsupported) concern associated with lower levels of achievement in today's so-called X-generation, this finding is particularly noteworthy.

The Affiliation Motive

Affiliation plays a very complex but vital role in human behavior.[13] *Affiliation* may be defined as the degree to which people seek approval from others, conform to their wishes, and avoid conflicts or confrontations with others. Those with high needs for affiliation express the greatest desire to be socially accepted by others. Sometimes this affiliation motive is equated with social motives and/or group dynamics. As presented here, the affiliation motive is neither as broad as is implied by the definition of social motives nor as comprehensive or complex as is implied by the definition of group dynamics.

The study of affiliation is further complicated by the view that some behavioral scientists hold that it is an unlearned motive. Going as far back as the Hawthorne studies, the importance of the affiliation motive in the behavior of organizational participants has been very clear. Employees, especially rank-and-file employees, have a very intense need to belong to, and be accepted by, the group. This affiliation motive is an important part of group dynamics, which is the subject of Chapter 14.

The Security Motive

Security is a very intense motive in a fast-paced, highly technological society such as is found in modern America. The typical American can be insecure in a number of areas of everyday living—for example, being liable for payments on a car or house, keeping a lover's or a spouse's affections, staying in school, getting into graduate school, or obtaining and/or keeping a good job. Job insecurity, in particular, has a great effect on organizational behavior. For example, the Chapter 7 discussion of organizational commitment indicates that, because of the downsizing mania of the last several years[14] and this era of temporary and contract workers, most employees at all levels are feeling very insecure about their jobs. On the surface, security appears to be much simpler than other secondary motives, for it is based largely on fear and is avoidance oriented. Very briefly, it can be said that people have a learned security motive to protect themselves from the contingencies of life and actively try to avoid situations that would prevent them from satisfying their primary, general, and secondary motives.

In reality, security is much more complex than it appears on the surface. There is the simple, conscious security motive described above, but there also seems to be another type of security motive that is much more complicated and difficult to identify. This latter form of security is largely unconscious but may greatly influence the behavior of many people. The simple, conscious security motive is typically taken care of by insurance programs, personal savings plans, and other fringe benefits at the place of employment. An innovative company such as the Washington, D.C.-based insurance company Consumers United Group never lays off its employees and has a minimum annual salary designed to give a family a secure, decent living. On the other hand, the more complex, unconscious security motive is not so easily fulfilled, but may have a greater and more intense impact on human behavior. Although much attention has been given to the simple security motive, much more understanding is needed concerning the role of the unconscious, complex security motive.

The Status Motive

Along with security, the status or prestige motive is especially relevant to a dynamic society. The modern affluent person is often pictured as a status seeker. Such a person is accused of being more concerned with the material symbols of status—the right clothes, the right car, the right address, and a swimming pool or the latest computer software and telecommunications equipment—than with the more basic, human-oriented values in life. Although the symbols of status are considered a unique by-product of modern society, the fact is that status has been in existence since there have been two or more persons on the earth.

Status can be simply defined as the *relative* ranking that a person holds in a group, organization, or society. Under this definition, any time two or more persons are together, a status hierarchy will evolve, even if both have equal status. The symbols of status attempt to represent only the relative ranking of the person in the status hierarchy. The definition also corrects the common misconception that "status" means "high status." Everyone has status, but it may be high or low, depending on how the relative positions are ranked.

How are status positions determined? Why is one person ranked higher or lower than another? In the final analysis, status determination depends on the prevailing cultural values and societal roles. Status-determining factors generally have quite different meanings, depending on the values of the particular culture. An example of the impact of cultural values on status is the personal qualities of people. In some cultures, the older people are, the higher their status. However, in other cultures, once a person reaches a certain age, the status goes downhill. It must be remembered that such cultural values are highly volatile and change with the times and circumstances. There are also many subcultures in a given society that may have values different from the prevailing values of society at large and correspondingly different statuses.

Intrinsic Versus Extrinsic Motives

Motives can be thought of as being not only generated by the needs discussed so far, but also by two separate but interrelated sets of sources. One method to characterize these two sources is to label them as being either "intrinsic" or "extrinsic" motives. Extrinsic motives are tangible and visible to others. They are distributed by other people (or agents). In the workplace, extrinsic motivators include pay, benefits, and promotions. Extrinsic motives also include the drive to avoid punishment, such as termination or being transferred. In each situation, an external individual distributes these items. Further, extrinsic rewards are usually contingency based. That is, the extrinsic motivator is contingent on improved performance, or performance that is superior to others in the same workplace. Extrinsic motivators are necessary to attract people into the organization and to keep them on the job. They are also often used to inspire workers to achieve at higher levels or to reach new goals, as additional payoffs are contingent on improved performance. They do not, however, explain every effort made by an individual employee.

Intrinsic motives are internally generated. In other words, they are motivators that the person associates with the task or job itself. Intrinsic rewards include feelings of responsibility, achievement, accomplishment, that something was learned from an experience, feelings of being challenged or competitive, or that something was an engaging task or goal. Performing meaningful work has long been associated with intrinsic motivation.[15]

It is important to remember that these two types of motivators are not completely distinct from one another. Many motivators have both intrinsic and extrinsic components. For example, a person who wins a sales contest receives the prize, which is the extrinsic motivator. At the same time, however, "winning" in a competitive situation may be the more powerful, yet internalized, motive.

To further complicate any explanation of intrinsic and extrinsic motivation, *cognitive evaluation theory* suggests a more intricate relationship. This theory proposes that a task may be intrinsically motivating, but that when an extrinsic motivator becomes associated with that task, the actual level of motivation may decrease.[16] Consider the world of motion pictures, where an actor often strives for many years to simply be included in a film. The intrinsic motive of acting is enough to inspire the starving artist. Once, however, the same actor becomes a star, the extrinsic motivators of money and perks would, according to cognitive evaluation theory, cause the individual to put less effort into each performance. In other words, according to this theory, extrinsic motivators may actually undermine intrinsic motivation. This may seem like a confusing outcome, but there is some research that supports this theoretical position.[17] However, as the meta analytically-based principle at the end of the chapter notes, there is considerable research evidence that extrinsic rewards may not detract from intrinsic motivation and at least for interesting, challenging tasks, extrinsic rewards may even increase the level of intrinsic motivation (see the end of the chapter OB Principle).

The seemingly contradictory findings make more sense when the concept of negative extrinsic motives is included. That is, threats, deadlines, directives, pressures, and imposed goals are likely to be key factors that diminish intrinsic motivation. For example, consider the difference between writing a book for fun versus writing a book that must be completed by a certain deadline in order to receive payment.[18] There are also a series of criticisms of the cognitive evaluation theory, including that it was built on studies using students as subjects rather than workers in the workplace setting and that actual decrements in intrinsic motivation were relatively small when extrinsic rewards were introduced.[19] Chapter 9 will extend this discussion into social cognitive variables such as self-efficacy, and Chapter 16 will use an extended reinforcement theory-based approach to behavioral performance management.

WORK-MOTIVATION APPROACHES

So far, motivation has been presented as a basic psychological process consisting of primary, general, and secondary motives; drives such as the *n Pow, n Aff,* and *n Ach* motives; and intrinsic and extrinsic motivators. In order to understand organizational behavior, these basic motives must be recognized and studied. However, these serve as only background and foundation for the more directly relevant work-motivation approaches.

Figure 8.2 graphically summarizes the various theoretical streams for work motivation. In particular, the figure shows three major approaches. The content theories go as far back as the turn of the century, when pioneering scientific managers such as Frederick W. Taylor, Frank Gilbreth, and Henry L. Gantt proposed sophisticated wage

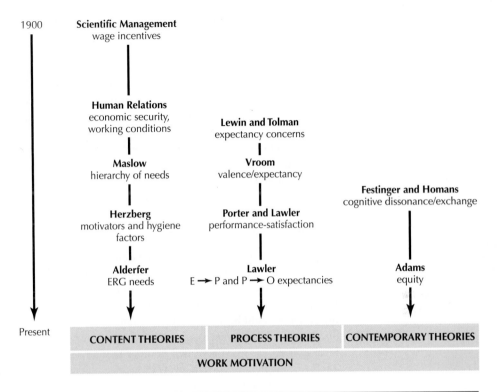

FIGURE 8.2

The theoretical development of work motivation.

incentive models to motivate workers. Next came the human relations movement, and then the content theories of Maslow, Herzberg, and Alderfer. Following the content movement were the process theories. Based mainly on the cognitive concept of expectancy, the process theories are most closely associated with the work of Victor Vroom and Lyman Porter and Ed Lawler. More recently, equity and its derivative procedural/organizational justice theories have received the most attention in work motivation.

Figure 8.2 purposely shows that at present there is a lack of integration or synthesis of the various theories. In addition to the need for integration, a comprehensive assessment of the status of work-motivation theory also noted the need for contingency models and group/social processes.[20] At present the content and process theories have become established explanations for work motivation, and there is continued research interest in equity and procedural justice theories, but no agreed-upon overall theory exists. The rest of the chapter gives an overview of the various theories of work motivation.

THE CONTENT THEORIES OF WORK MOTIVATION

The content theories of work motivation attempt to determine what it is that motivates people at work. The content theorists are concerned with identifying the needs/drives that people have and how these needs/drives are prioritized. They are concerned with the types of incentives or goals that people strive to attain in order to be satisfied and perform well. The content theories are referred to as "static" because they incorporate only one or a few points in time and are either past- or present-time oriented. Therefore, they do not necessarily predict work motivation or behavior, but they are still important to understanding what motivates people at work.

At first, money was felt to be the only incentive (scientific management), and then a little later it was felt that incentives include working conditions, security, and perhaps a democratic style of supervision (human relations). Subsequently, the content of motivation was deemed to be the so-called "higher-level" needs or motives, such as esteem and self-actualization (Maslow); responsibility, recognition, achievement, and advancement (Herzberg); and growth and personal development (Alderfer). A thorough study of the major content theories contributes to understanding and leads to some of the application techniques of motivation covered in the last part of the book.

Maslow's Hierarchy of Needs

Although the first part of the chapter discusses the most important primary, general, and secondary needs of humans, it does not relate them to a theoretical framework. Abraham Maslow, in a classic paper, outlined the elements of an overall theory of motivation.[21] Drawing chiefly on his clinical experience, he thought that a person's motivational needs could be arranged in a hierarchical manner. In essence, he believed that once a given level of need is satisfied, it no longer serves to motivate. The next higher level of need has to be activated in order to motivate the individual.

Maslow identified five levels in his need hierarchy (see Figure 8.3). They are, in brief, the following:

1. *Physiological needs.*   The most basic level in the hierarchy, the physiological needs, generally corresponds to the unlearned primary needs discussed earlier. The needs of hunger, thirst, sleep, and sex are some examples. According to the theory, once these basic needs are satisfied, they no longer motivate. For example, a starving person will strive to obtain a carrot that is within reach. However, after eating his or her fill of carrots, the person will not strive to obtain another one and will be motivated only by the next higher level of needs.

2. *Safety needs.*   This second level of needs is roughly equivalent to the security need. Maslow stressed emotional as well as physical safety. The whole organism

FIGURE 8.3

Maslow's hierarchy of needs.

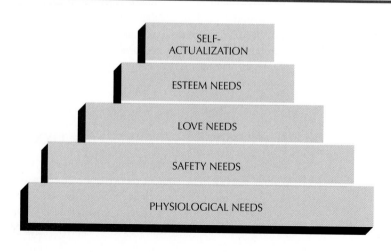

may become a safety-seeking mechanism. Yet, as is true of the physiological needs, once these safety needs are satisfied, they no longer motivate.

3. *Love needs.* This third, or intermediate, level of needs loosely corresponds to the affection and affiliation needs. Like Freud, Maslow seems guilty of poor choice of wording to identify his levels. His use of the word *love* has many misleading connotations, such as sex, which is actually a physiological need. Perhaps a more appropriate word describing this level would be *belongingness* or *social.*

4. *Esteem needs.* The esteem level represents the higher needs of humans. The needs for power, achievement, and status can be considered part of this level. Maslow carefully pointed out that the esteem level contains both self-esteem and esteem from others.

5. *Needs for self-actualization.* This level represents the culmination of all the lower, intermediate, and higher needs of humans. People who have become self-actualized are self-fulfilled and have realized all their potential. Self-actualization is closely related to the self-concepts discussed in Chapter 9. In effect, self-actualization is the person's motivation to transform perception of self into reality.

Maslow did not intend that his needs hierarchy be directly applied to work motivation. In fact, he did not delve into the motivating aspects of humans in organizations until about 20 years after he originally proposed his theory. Despite this lack of intent on Maslow's part, others, such as Douglas McGregor, in his widely read book *The Human Side of Enterprise,* popularized the Maslow theory in management literature. The needs hierarchy has had a tremendous impact on the modern management approach to motivation.

In a very rough manner, Maslow's needs hierarchy theory can be converted into the content model of work motivation shown in Figure 8.4. If Maslow's estimates are applied to an organization example, the lower-level needs of personnel would be

FIGURE 8.4
A hierarchy of work motivation.

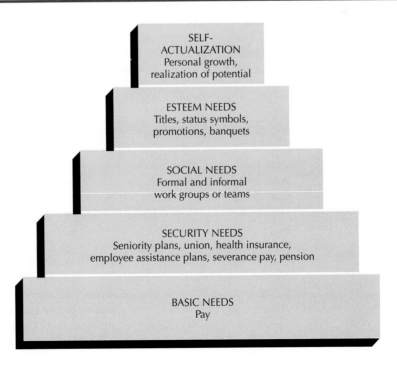

SELF-ACTUALIZATION
Personal growth, realization of potential

ESTEEM NEEDS
Titles, status symbols, promotions, banquets

SOCIAL NEEDS
Formal and informal work groups or teams

SECURITY NEEDS
Seniority plans, union, health insurance, employee assistance plans, severance pay, pension

BASIC NEEDS
Pay

generally satisfied (85 percent of the basic needs and 70 percent of the security needs), but only 50 percent of the social needs, 40 percent of the esteem needs, and a mere 10 percent of the self-actualization needs would be met.

On the surface, the content model shown in Figure 8.4 and the estimated percentages given by Maslow seem logical and still largely applicable to the motivation of employees in today's organizations. Maslow's needs hierarchy has often been uncritically accepted by writers of management textbooks and by practitioners. Unfortunately, the limited research that has been conducted lends little empirical support to the theory. About a decade after publishing his original paper, Maslow did attempt to clarify his position by saying that gratifying the self-actualizing need of growth-motivated individuals can actually increase rather than decrease this need. He also hedged on some of his other original ideas, for example, that higher needs may emerge after lower needs that have been unfulfilled or suppressed for a long period are satisfied. He stressed that human behavior is multidetermined and multimotivated.

Research findings indicate that Maslow's is not the final answer in work motivation. Yet the theory does make a significant contribution in terms of making management aware of the diverse needs of employees at work. As one comprehensive analysis concluded, "Indeed, the general ideas behind Maslow's theory seem to be supported, such as the distinction between deficiency needs and growth needs."[22] However, the number and names of the levels are not so important, nor, as the studies show, is the hierarchical concept. What is important is the fact that employees in the workplace have diverse motives, some of which are "high level." In other words, such needs as esteem and self-actualization are important to the content of work motivation. The exact nature of these needs and how they relate to motivation are not clear. At the same time, what does become clear from recent research is that layoffs and terminations (i.e., downsizing) can reduce employees to have concerns about basic-level needs such as security. Organizations that endeavor to reduce fears and other strong emotional responses during these moments through severance pay programs and outplacement services may be able to lessen the impact of individual terminations and layoffs, especially for those who remain with the company.[23]

To try to overcome some of the problems of the Maslow hierarchy, Alderfer has more recently proposed the ERG theory, which contains three well-known groups of needs. The ERG theory is covered after the discussion of Herzberg's two-factor theory.

Herzberg's Two-Factor Theory of Motivation

Herzberg extended the work of Maslow and developed a specific content theory of work motivation. He conducted a widely reported motivational study on about 200 accountants and engineers employed by firms in and around Pittsburgh, Pennsylvania. He used the critical incident method of obtaining data for analysis. The professional subjects in the study were essentially asked two questions: (1) When did you feel particularly good about your job—what turned you on; and (2) When did you feel exceptionally bad about your job—what turned you off?

Responses obtained from this critical incident method were interesting and fairly consistent. Reported good feelings were generally associated with job experiences and job content. An example was the accounting supervisor who felt good about being given the job of installing new computer equipment. He took pride in his work and was gratified to know that the new equipment made a big difference in the overall functioning of his department. Reported bad feelings, on the other hand, were generally

TABLE 8.2 Herzberg's Two-Factor Theory

Hygiene Factors	Motivators
Company policy and administration	Achievement
Supervision, technical	Recognition
Salary	Work itself
Interpersonal relations, supervisor	Responsibility
Working conditions	Advancement

associated with the surrounding or peripheral aspects of the job—the job context. An example of these feelings was related by an engineer whose first job was routine record keeping and managing the office when the boss was gone. It turned out that his boss was always too busy to train him and became annoyed when he tried to ask questions. The engineer said that he was frustrated in this job context and that he felt like a flunky in a dead-end job.

Tabulating these reported good and bad feelings, Herzberg concluded that job satisfiers are related to job content and that job dissatisfiers are allied to job context. Herzberg labeled the satisfiers *motivators,* and he called the dissatisfiers *hygiene factors.* The term *hygiene* refers (as it does in the health field) to factors that are preventive; in Herzberg's theory the hygiene factors are those that prevent dissatisfaction. Taken together, the motivators and the hygiene factors have become known as Herzberg's *two-factor theory of motivation.*

Relation to Maslow's Need Hierarchy.   Herzberg's theory is closely related to Maslow's need hierarchy. The hygiene factors are preventive and environmental in nature (see Table 8.2), and they are roughly equivalent to Maslow's lower-level needs (see Figure 8.5). These hygiene factors prevent dissatisfaction, but they do not lead to satisfaction. In effect, they bring motivation up to a theoretical zero level and are a necessary "floor" to prevent dissatisfaction, and they serve as a takeoff point for motivation.

FIGURE 8.5
The relationship between Alderfer's ERG needs, Maslow's five-level hierarchy, and Herzberg's two-factor theory.

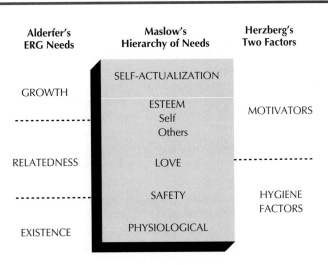

By themselves, the hygiene factors do not motivate. Only the motivators motivate employees on the job. They are roughly equivalent to Maslow's higher-level needs. According to Herzberg's theory, an individual must have a job with a challenging content in order to be truly motivated.

Contribution to Work Motivation.   Herzberg's two-factor theory casts a new light on the content of work motivation. Up to this point, management had generally concentrated on the hygiene factors. When faced with a morale problem, the typical solution was higher pay, more fringe benefits, and better working conditions. However, as has been pointed out, this simplistic solution did not really work. Management are often perplexed because they are paying high wages and salaries, have an excellent fringe-benefit package, and provide great working conditions, but their employees are still not motivated. Herzberg's theory offers an explanation for this problem. By concentrating only on the hygiene factors, management are not motivating their personnel.

There are probably very few workers or associates who do not feel that they deserved the raise they received. On the other hand, there are many dissatisfied associates and managers who feel they did not get a large enough raise. This simple observation points out that the hygiene factors seem to be important in preventing dissatisfaction but do not lead to satisfaction. Herzberg would be the first to say that the hygiene factors are absolutely necessary to maintain the human resources of an organization. However, as in the Maslow sense, once "the belly is full" of hygiene factors, which is the case in most modern organizations, dangling any more in front of employees will not motivate them. According to Herzberg's theory, only a challenging job that has the opportunities for achievement, recognition, responsibility, advancement, and growth will motivate personnel.

Critical Analysis of Herzberg's Theory.   Although Herzberg's two-factor theory remains a very popular textbook explanation of work motivation and makes sense to practitioners, it also is true that from an academic perspective the theory oversimplifies the complexities of work motivation. When researchers deviate from the critical incident methodology used by Herzberg, they do not get the two factors. Further, there is always a question regarding the samples utilized by Herzberg: Would he have obtained the results from low-complexity jobs such as truck drivers and third-shift factory workers or waitstaff personnel? Presumably both the hygiene factors and satisfiers could be substantially different when comparing these groups. Other factors that affect research results include the age of the sample and other factors that are not held constant or under control. In international settings, older workers in an Israli kibbutz preferred jobs that had better physical conditions and convenience. Also, Caribbean hotel workers reported being more interested in wages, working conditions, and appreciation for their work as key motivators.[24] These findings suggest that sample and setting may affect preferences for motivators and hygiene factors.

Finally, there seem to be job factors such as pay that lead to both satisfaction and dissatisfaction. For example, pay can be dissatisfying if not high enough, but also be satisfying as a form of achievement and recognition. These findings indicate that a strict interpretation of the two-factor theory is not warranted.

In spite of the obvious limitations, few would question that Herzberg has contributed substantially to the study of work motivation. He extended Maslow's needs hierarchy concept and made it more applicable to work motivation. Herzberg also drew attention to the importance of job content factors in work motivation, which previously had been badly neglected and often totally overlooked. However, even the context can be made to better fit the jobholder. For example, many Internet businesses never have employees directly interact with customers so their dress, appearance, and work space can be highly informal and designed according to personal choice.[25]

The job design technique of job enrichment is also one of Herzberg's contributions. Job enrichment is covered in detail in Chapter 15. Overall, Herzberg added much to the better understanding of job content factors and satisfaction, but, like his predecessors, he fell short of a comprehensive theory of work motivation. His model describes only some of the content of work motivation; it does not adequately describe the complex motivation process of organizational participants.

Alderfer's ERG Theory

An extension of the Herzberg and, especially, the Maslow content theories of work motivation comes from the work of Clayton Alderfer. He formulated a needs category model that was more in line with the existing empirical evidence. Like Maslow and Herzberg, he does feel that there is value in categorizing needs and that there is a basic distinction between lower-order needs and higher-order needs.

Alderfer identified three groups of core needs: existence, relatedness, and growth (hence ERG theory). The *existence needs* are concerned with survival (physiological well-being). The *relatedness needs* stress the importance of interpersonal, social relationships. The *growth needs* are concerned with the individual's intrinsic desire for personal development. Figure 8.5 shows how these groups of needs are related to the Maslow and Herzberg categories. Obviously, they are very close, but the ERG needs do not have strict lines of demarcation.

Alderfer is suggesting more of a continuum of needs than hierarchical levels or two factors of prepotency needs. Unlike Maslow and Herzberg, he does not contend that a lower-level need must be fulfilled before a higher-level need becomes motivating or that deprivation is the only way to activate a need. For example, according to ERG theory the person's background or cultural environment may dictate that the relatedness needs will take precedence over unfulfilled existence needs and that the more the growth needs are satisfied, the more they will increase in intensity. Further, Maslow's hierarchy suggested a process called satisfaction-progression, in which a person moves up the hierarchy after a lower-order need is being routinely met. Alderfer's approach adds what may be termed frustration-regression. When higher-order growth needs are stifled or cannot be met due to personal circumstances, the lack of ability, or some other factor, the individual is inclined to regress back to lower-order needs, and feel those needs more strongly. This would occur, for instance, when a person cannot move up the corporate ladder and is stuck in a mundane job. According to Alderfer's ERG model, that individual would be expected to then emphasize social relationships both on and off the job and become more enamored with pay and benefits.

There has not been a great deal of research on ERG theory. Although there is some evidence to counter the theory's predictive value, most contemporary analyses of work motivation tend to support Alderfer's theory over Maslow's and Herzberg's. Overall, ERG theory seems to include some of the strong points of earlier content theories but is less restrictive and limiting. The fact remains that the content theories in general lack explanatory power regarding the complexities of work motivation. They do, however, suggest the importance of meeting certain employee content needs on the job.

This would include providing enough financial remuneration so that workers can meet both basic needs and have some sense of security. Beyond simple survival, provisions for health insurance and retirement plans reassure employees regarding other aspects of life. Effective coordination of today's increasing use of teams and groups enhances socialization on the job, as do programs such as "casual" days. Finally, all of the content theories direct managers to share responsibility and empower employees in addition to recognizing their achievements. Thus, even though there may be several theoretical flaws in these content models, they still can offer valuable motivational insights into effective management of today's human resources.

THE PROCESS THEORIES OF WORK MOTIVATION

The content models attempt to identify what motivates people at work (for example, self-actualization, responsibility, and growth); they try to specify correlates of motivated behavior. The process theories, on the other hand, are more concerned with the cognitive antecedents that go into motivation or effort and, more important, with the way they relate to one another. As Figure 8.2 shows, the expectancy notion from cognitive theory makes a significant contribution to the understanding of the complex processes involved in work motivation. After the process theories are examined, equity and procedural/organizational justice theories are presented and analyzed as modern cognitive models of work motivation.

Vroom's Expectancy Theory of Motivation

The expectancy theory of work motivation has its roots in the cognitive concepts of pioneering psychologists Kurt Lewin and Edward Tolman, as shown in Figure 8.2, and in the choice behavior and utility concepts from classical economic theory. However, the first to formulate an expectancy theory directly aimed at work motivation was Victor Vroom. Contrary to most critics, Vroom proposed his expectancy theory as an alternative to content models, which he felt were inadequate explanations of the complex process of work motivation. At least in organizational behavior academic circles, his theory has become a popular explanation for work motivation and continues to generate considerable research.[26]

Figure 8.6 briefly summarizes the Vroom model. As shown, the model is built around the concepts of valence, instrumentality, and expectancy and is commonly called the *VIE theory.*

Meaning of the Variables.   By *valence,* Vroom means the strength of an individual's preference for a particular outcome. Other terms that might be used include *value, incentive, attitude,* and *expected utility.* In order for the valence to be positive, the person must prefer attaining the outcome to not attaining it. A valence of zero occurs when the individual is indifferent toward the outcome; the valence is negative when the individual prefers not attaining the outcome to attaining it. Another major input into the valence is the *instrumentality* of the first-level outcome in obtaining a desired second-level outcome. For example, a person would be motivated toward superior performance because of the desire to be promoted. The superior performance (first-level outcome) is seen as being instrumental in obtaining a promotion (second-level outcome).

Another major variable in the Vroom motivational process is *expectancy.* Although psychological theorists all agree that expectancies are mental, or cognitive,

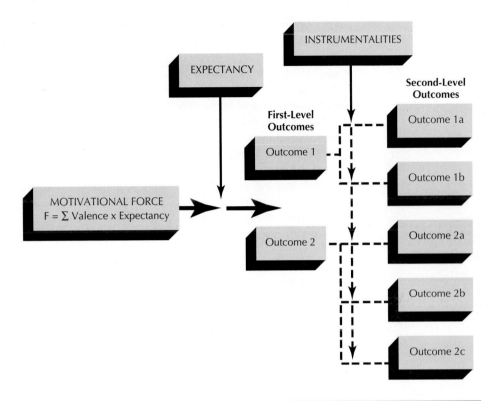

FIGURE 8.6
The Vroom expectancy,
or VIE, theory of work
motivation.

states, there is little agreement about the nature of these states.[27] Although at first glance the expectancy concept may seem to be the same as the instrumentality input into valence, it is actually quite different. Expectancy relates efforts to first-level outcomes (see Figure 8.6), whereas instrumentality relates first-level outcomes and second-level outcomes. In other words, expectancy in Vroom's theory is the probability (ranging from 0 to 1) that a particular action or effort will lead to a particular *first-level* outcome. *Instrumentality* refers to the degree to which a first-level outcome will lead to a desired *second-level* outcome. In summary, the strength of the motivation to perform a certain act will depend on the algebraic sum of the products of the valences for the outcomes (which include instrumentality) times the expectancies.

Implications of the Vroom Model for Organizational Behavior. Vroom's theory departs from the content theories in that it depicts a process of cognitive variables that reflects individual differences in work motivation. It does not attempt to describe what the content is or what the individual differences are. Everyone has a unique combination of valences, instrumentalities, and expectancies. Thus, the Vroom theory indicates only the conceptual determinants of motivation and how they are related. It does not provide specific suggestions on what motivates organizational members, as the Maslow, Herzberg, and Alderfer models do.

Although the Vroom model does not directly contribute much to the techniques of motivating personnel in an organization, it is of value in understanding organizational behavior. It can clarify the relationship between individual and organizational goals. For example, suppose workers are given a certain standard for production. By measuring the workers' output, management can determine how important their various personal goals (second-level outcomes such as money, security, and recognition) are; the instrumentality of the organizational goal (the first-level outcomes, such as the production standard) for the attainment of the personal goals; and the workers' expectancies that their effort and ability will accomplish the organizational goal. If output is below standard, it may be that the workers do not place a high value on the second-level outcomes; or they may not see that the first-level outcome is instrumental in obtaining the second-level outcomes; or they may think that their efforts will not accomplish the first-level outcome. Vroom feels that any one, or a combination, of these possibilities will result in a low level of motivation to perform. The model is designed to help management understand and analyze workers' motivation and identify some of the relevant variables; it does not provide specific solutions to motivational problems. Besides having an application problem, the model also assumes, as earlier economic theory did, that people are rational and logically calculating. Such an assumption tends to be very idealistic.

Importance of the Vroom Model.   Probably the major reason Vroom's model has emerged as an important modern theory of work motivation and has generated so much research is that it does not take a simplistic approach. The content theories oversimplify human motivation. Yet the content theories remain extremely popular with practicing managers because the concepts are easy to understand and to apply to their own situations. On the other hand, the VIE theory recognizes the complexities of work motivation, but it is relatively difficult to understand and apply. Thus, from a theoretical standpoint, the VIE model seems to help managers appreciate the complexities of motivation, but it does not give them much practical help in solving their motivational problems except simple prescriptions such as making sure employees know exactly what is expected of them.[28]

In some ways Vroom's expectancy model is like marginal analysis in economics. Businesspeople do not actually calculate the point where marginal cost equals marginal revenue, but it is still a useful concept for an economic theory of the firm. Likewise, the expectancy model attempts only to mirror the complex motivational process; it does not attempt to describe how motivational decisions are actually made or to solve actual motivational problems facing a manager.

The Porter-Lawler Model

Comments in Chapter 7 on job satisfaction refer to the controversy over the relationship between satisfaction and performance that has existed since the beginnings of the human relations movement. The content theories implicitly assume that satisfaction leads to improved performance and that dissatisfaction detracts from performance. The Herzberg model is really a theory of job satisfaction, but still it does not adequately deal with the relationship between satisfaction and performance. The Vroom model also largely avoids the relationship between satisfaction and performance. Although satisfactions make an input into Vroom's concept of valence and although the outcomes have performance implications, it was not until Porter and Lawler refined and extended Vroom's model (for example, the relationships are expressed diagrammatically rather than mathematically, there are more variables, and the cognitive process of perception plays a central role) that the relationship between satisfaction and performance was dealt with directly by a motivation model.

FIGURE 8.7 The Porter-Lawler motivation model.

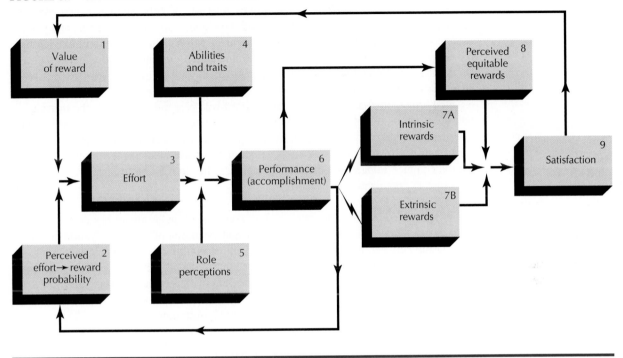

Porter and Lawler start with the premise that motivation (effort or force) does not equal satisfaction or performance. Motivation, satisfaction, and performance are all separate variables and relate in ways different from what was traditionally assumed. Figure 8.7 depicts the multivariable model used to explain the complex relationship that exists among motivation, performance, and satisfaction. As shown in the model, boxes 1, 2, and 3 are basically the same as the Vroom equation. It is important, however, that Porter and Lawler point out that effort (force or motivation) does not lead directly to performance. It is moderated by abilities and traits and by role perceptions. More important in the Porter-Lawler model is what happens after the performance. The rewards that follow and how these are perceived will determine satisfaction. In other words, the Porter-Lawler model suggests—and this is a significant turn of events from traditional thinking—that performance leads to satisfaction.

The model has had a fair degree of research support over the years. For example, a field study found that effort level and direction of effort are important in explaining individual performance in an organization.[29] Also, a comprehensive review of research verifies the importance of rewards in the relationship between performance and satisfaction. Specifically, it was concluded that performance and satisfaction will be more strongly related when rewards are made contingent on performance than when they are not.[30]

Implications for Practice.   Although the Porter-Lawler model is more applications oriented than the Vroom model, it is still quite complex and has proved to be a difficult way to bridge the gap to actual human resource management practice. To Porter and Lawler's credit, they have been very conscientious of putting their theory and research into practice. They recommend that practicing managers go beyond traditional attitude measurement and attempt to measure variables such as the values of possible rewards, the perceptions of effort–reward probabilities, and role perceptions. These variables, of course, can help managers better understand what goes into employee effort and performance. Giving attention to the consequences of performance, Porter and Lawler also recommend that organizations critically reevaluate their current reward policies. They stress that management should make a concentrated effort to measure how closely levels of satisfaction are related to levels of performance, and recently a practitioner-oriented article emphasized that the accuracy of role perceptions may be the missing link in improving employee performance.[31] The inference here is that employees need to better focus their efforts on high-impact behaviors and activities that result in higher performance. However, both studies[32] and comprehensive analyses[33] continue to point out the complex impact that the cognitive process has in relation to rewards and other outcomes in organizations.

Contributions to Work Motivation.   The Porter and Lawler model has definitely made a significant contribution to the better understanding of work motivation and the relationship between performance and satisfaction, but, to date, it has not had much impact on the actual practice of human resource management. Yet the expectancy models provide certain guidelines that can be followed by human resource management. For example, on the front end (the relationship between motivation and performance), it has been suggested that the following barriers must be overcome:

1. Doubts about ability, skill, or knowledge
2. The physical or practical possibility of the job
3. The interdependence of the job with other people or activities
4. Ambiguity surrounding the job requirements[34]

To help overcome these barriers, it is helpful to understand the role of other psychological variables such as self-efficacy (covered in the next chapter) plays in effort–performance relationships. A series of successes combined with positive feedback build the employee's sense of self-efficacy, which can, in turn, lead to a heightened sense that "I can do this." Greater effort may often be the result.[35] In addition to psychological constructs such as self-efficacy, there are also pragmatic considerations such as that the opportunity must be present to actually perform. Kurt Warner, MVP quarterback of the 2000 Super Bowl champion St. Louis Rams, probably had sufficient valance (pay plus the bonus check paid to Super Bowl winners), instrumentality or effort-performance calculations (ability combined with self-efficacy), and expectancy or performance-reward calculations (the belief that goal achievement would result in additional pay and recognition), yet still could not succeed until he was allowed to play due to the injury of the first-string quarterback.

In addition, on the back end (the relationship between performance and satisfaction), guidelines such as the following have been suggested:

1. Determine what rewards each employee values
2. Define desired performance
3. Make desired performance attainable
4. Link valued rewards to performance[36]

The last point is getting recognition in the management compensation plans of many big companies. At the same time, managers should be advised that an employee in a way calculates expectancies regarding future employment possibilities when seeking to leave a company, and more importantly, often sees a connection between performance and reward that invites less effort in a group or team situation. The reduced value is based on the belief that the person's own efforts are not sufficient to raise group performance levels, and that group incentives are less valuable than individualized rewards.

Managers may also take advantage of this process motivational approach by considering the use of nonmonetary rewards for performance. Many times workers may be inspired by being given first choice in selecting weeks for vacation, being allowed to choose when they will go to lunch (ahead of lower performers), and awarded certificates or "employee of the month" parking spaces. Recognition as a valence can be a powerful reward within the expectancy theory framework and was discussed in Chapter 5 and is given further detailed attention in Chapter 16.

CONTEMPORARY THEORIES OF WORK MOTIVATION

Although it is recognized that work-motivation theories are generally categorized into content and process approaches, equity and procedural justice theories have emerged in recent years and command most of the research attention. An understanding of these theoretical developments is now necessary to the study of work motivation in organizational behavior.

Equity Theory of Work Motivation

Equity theory has been around just as long as the expectancy theories of work motivation. However, equity has received relatively more recent attention in the organizational behavior field. As Figure 8.2 indicates, its roots can be traced back to cognitive dissonance theory and exchange theory. As a theory of work motivation, credit for equity theory is usually given to social psychologist J. Stacy Adams. Simply put, the theory argues that a major input into job performance and satisfaction is the degree of equity (or inequity) that people perceive in their work situation. In other words, it is another cognitively based motivation theory, and Adams depicts how this motivation occurs.

Inequity occurs when a person perceives that the ratio of his or her outcomes to inputs and the ratio of a relevant other's outcomes to inputs are unequal. Schematically, this is represented as follows:

$$\frac{\text{person's outcomes}}{\text{person's inputs}} < \frac{\text{other's outcomes}}{\text{other's inputs}}$$

$$\frac{\text{person's outcomes}}{\text{person's inputs}} > \frac{\text{other's outcomes}}{\text{other's inputs}}$$

Equity occurs when

$$\frac{\text{person's outcomes}}{\text{person's inputs}} = \frac{\text{other's outcomes}}{\text{other's inputs}}$$

Both the inputs and the outputs of the person and the other are based on the person's perceptions. Age, sex, education, social status, organizational position, qualifications, and how hard the person works are examples of perceived input variables. Outcomes consist primarily of rewards such as pay, status, promotion, and intrinsic interest in the job. In essence, the ratio is based on the person's *perception* of what the person is giving (inputs) and receiving (outcomes) versus the ratio of what the relevant other is giving and receiving. This cognition may or may not be the same as someone else's observation of the ratios or the same as the actual reality.

Equity as an Explanation of Work Motivation.   If the person's perceived ratio is not equal to the other's, he or she will strive to restore the ratio to equity. This "striving" to restore equity is used as the explanation of work motivation. The strength of this motivation is in direct proportion to the perceived inequity that exists. Adams suggests that such motivation may be expressed in several forms. To restore equity, the person may alter the inputs or outcomes, cognitively distort the inputs or outcomes, leave the field, act on the other, or change the other.

It is important to note that inequity does not come about only when the person feels cheated. For example, Adams has studied the impact that perceived overpayment has on equity. His findings suggest that workers prefer equitable payment to overpayment. Workers on a piece-rate incentive system who feel overpaid will reduce their productivity in order to restore equity. More common, however, is the case of people who feel underpaid (outcome) or overworked (input) in relation to others in the workplace. In the latter case, there would be motivation to restore equity in a way that may be dysfunctional from an organizational standpoint. For example, the owner of an appliance store in Oakland, California, allowed his employees to set their own wages. Interestingly, none of the employees took an increase in pay, and one service technician actually settled on lower pay because he did not want to work as hard as the others.

Research Support for Equity in the Workplace.   To date, research that has specifically tested the validity of Adams's equity theory has been fairly supportive. A comprehensive review found considerable laboratory research support for the "equity norm" (people review the inputs and outcomes of themselves and others, and if inequity is perceived, they strive to restore equity) but only limited support from more relevant field studies.[37] One line of field research on equity theory used baseball players. In the first study, players who played out their option year, and thus felt they were inequitably paid, performed as the theory would predict.[38] Their performance decreased in three of four categories (not batting average) during the option year, and when they were signed to a new contract, the performance was restored. However, a second study using the same type of sample, only larger, found the opposite of what equity theory would predict.[39] Mainly, performance improved during the option year. The reason, of course, was that the players wanted to look especially good, even though they felt they were inequitably paid, in order to be in a stronger bargaining position for a new contract. In other words, individuals faced with undercompensation may choose to decrease performance, but only to the extent that doing so will not affect the potential to achieve future rewards.[40] In any event, there are no easy answers nor is there 100 percent predictive power when applying a cognitive process theory such as equity.

Despite some seeming inconsistencies, recent studies using more sophisticated statistical techniques to estimate pay equity among ballplayers[41] and focusing more sharply on subsequent performance and other outcomes are more in line with equity theory predictions. For example, one study found a significant relationship between losing final-offer salary arbitration and postarbitration performance decline. The ballplayers who were losers in arbitration were also significantly more likely to change teams or leave major league baseball.[42] In another study of baseball and basketball players, it was found that the underrewarded players behaved less cooperatively.[43] This type of equity theory development and research goes beyond expectancy theory as a cognitive explanation of work motivation and serves as a point of departure for more specialized areas of current interest such as procedural justice.

The Relationship between Equity Theory and Procedural Justice

Recent theory development specifies that equity theory can be extended into what is now commonly known as procedural justice. Equity theory explains conditions under which decision outcomes (pay levels, pay raises, promotions) are perceived as being fair or unfair. Persons engaged in this type of thinking examine the results as opposed to how those results were achieved. Equity theory is based on a perception of *distributive justice,* which is an individual's cognitive evaluation regarding whether or not the amounts and allocations of rewards in a social setting are fair. In simple terms, distributive justice is one's belief that everyone should "get what they deserve." Culturally, the Judeo-Christian ethic is based, in part, on the notion that divine rewards accrue to those who lead good lives and behave appropriately, even while here are on earth. This reflects the distributive justice and equity perspectives.

Procedural justice is concerned with the fairness of the procedure used to make a decision. For example, a pay raise may be based on a sales representative selling more units of, for example, automobiles or houses. Some coworkers may consider this procedure to be unfair, believing management should instead base pay raises on dollar volume. This conclusion may be reached because selling 10 houses or cars for a low amount of money each contributes very little to company profits and are, at the same time, easier to sell. Selling high-priced cars or houses may take much longer to finalize, but the profits garned for the company are also higher. In this case it is not the outcome in dispute, which is the amount of the pay received. Instead, it is the perceived justice (fairness) of the procedure used to reach the outcome.

Procedural justice can raise issues of equality as opposed to equity. *Equality* means that in a promotion situation, males and females and all races would have equal opportunities to be selected, and that the criteria used would not discriminate. *Equity* would mean that the actual choice was fair, and that the criteria were correctly applied and therefore the most-qualified individual was promoted. The accompanying Managing Diversity and Ethics in Action box gives examples of how this is playing out in society at large.

Both equity theory and procedural justice can be combined into *organizational justice,* which suggests that the process and the outcomes of organizational decisions regarding the distribution of resources should be properly carried out. Organizational justice can help explain why employees retaliate against both inequitable outcomes and inappropriate processes. Retaliation in the form of theft, sabotage, forged time cards, and even violence toward an employer can be explained using the principles of organizational justice.[44]

Other Emerging Work Motivation Theories: Control and Agency

In addition to the micro-oriented expectancy and equity motivation theories coming out of cognitive psychology, there are other, more broad-based theories beginning to emerge in organizational behavior. Representatives of these recent theories are control theory and agency theory.

Treating Customers and Employees Fairly

One of the biggest challenges facing businesses these days is to treat all of their customers and employees in a fair and equitable manner. In particular, some firms are finding that past practices have been discriminatory, and they have not yet been corrected. One example is low-income people who have often been charged higher life insurance rates over the years.

In the recent settlement of a lawsuit brought by private class-action lawyers and state regulators, one of the country's largest life insurance firms, American General, agreed to make restitution to some policyholders, most of them minorities, who were charged higher premiums for life insurance than was the average customer. The company also agreed to provide financial restitution to policyholders who were sold policies where the total premiums were far greater than the benefit. For example, one policyholder had paid premiums of 90 cents a week for 32 years (a total of almost $1,500) for a policy that would have given her a $1,000 death benefit.

Beginning in the 1960s these types of policies were outlawed. However, some firms continued to sell them. In fact, American General found that some of the insurance firms that it acquired on its way to becoming the fourth-largest life insurer in the country were still selling these policies. On investigation, the company estimated that it had approximately five million policies on the lives of more than two million people and that on another 400,000 policies customers had paid, or would have paid, premiums that exceeded the face value of the policy. Under the agreement struck with the plaintiffs, American General agreed to give restitution to all of these policyholders, a settlement that returned over $200 million to them.

In another recent lawsuit, this one brought by the U.S. Labor Department, Sears, Roebuck agreed to pay a fine of $325,000 for violating child labor laws at more than 60 percent of the stores that investigators visited. In particular, federal inspectors found 227 teenagers working in violation of child-labor laws. The most common violation was that 16-year-old and 17-year-old workers were operating power-driven equipment, which is in violation of federal laws that bar anyone under the age of 18 from doing such work. The inspectors found that more than 200 Sears employees under the age of 18 were running power-driven paper balers, freight elevators, and forklifts—all machines that the Labor Department has declared as hazardous.

In the agreement that it signed with the Labor Department, Sears said it would appoint a manager to oversee child-labor compliance and said it would audit all of its stores in order to ferret out child-labor violations. Sears officials also pledged to improve its communications and training of managers and teenage workers in order to ensure total compliance.

Although these are all steps in the right direction, there are many advocates of equity in the workplace who argue that the biggest injustice is the pay system. As was brought out in Chapter 3, women and minorities are paid less. The most recent government data show that women earn considerably less of what men do for the same full-time work. There is an improvement over 20 years ago, but narrowing the pay gap is barely noticeable.

Female minorities fare even worse. At the beginning of this millennium black women were earning less then two-thirds of that paid to white men for the same work, and Hispanic women were even worse off. Quite obviously, treating people fairly is going to continue to be a challenge for today's organizations.

One version of *control theory,* like the other theories discussed so far, is essentially a cognitive phenomenon relating to the degree that individuals perceive they are in control of their own lives, or are in control of their jobs. Recent studies have shown that those who believe they have such personal control tolerate unpleasant events and experience less stress on the job than those who do not perceive such control.[45] There is also some evidence that perceived control will affect job satisfaction and absenteeism.[46] Another version of control theory, which also has implications for organizational behavior, relates to the more traditional management function of control. Traditional guidelines for effective management have included controlling both the inputs and outputs of organizations, but research has also analyzed strategically controlling human resources as well.[47] Especially relevant to today's workplace environment is that a sense of control seems very helpful when increasing job demands are placed on the employee. Thus, persons who are given more work, but also the control to complete that work, may not feel as negatively about their new assignments. On the other hand, more peripheral aspects of work control, such as when they start or stop a task or arrange the work flow, seem less related to work motivation.[48]

Similar to control theory's being taken from the traditional management literature, agency theory as applied to organizational behavior comes from the financial economics literature. As given attention in Chapter 5, an agency relationship involves one or more individuals (the principal) engaging another person or persons (the agent) to perform some service on their behalf.[49] The key to *agency theory* is the assumption that the interests of principals and agents diverge or may be in conflict with one another. The implications for organizational behavior involve how the principals (owners, board members, or top management) can limit divergence from their interests or objectives by establishing appropriate rewards or incentives for the agents (subordinates, middle management, or operating employees) for appropriate outcomes. There is beginning research evidence supporting an agency theory interpretation of areas in organizational behavior such as pay for performance,[50] compensation contracts,[51] foreign subsidiary compensation strategies,[52] and variable pay compensation strategies.[53] Like the other cognitive-based theories, agency theory helps us better understand the complex motivations of managers in today's organizations.

Recently, agency theory has been expanded to the macro level. It has been used to explain financing decisions in franchising operations[54] and to study the various forms of control that limit the decision-making authority of professional service organizations.[55] In the latter study, community control, bureaucratic control, and client control combined with the degree of self-control exhibited by the professional service agent to reduce decision-making autonomy.

One primary criticism of agency theory that has emerged is based on some recent research findings. That is, agency theory strongly emphasizes the roles that various forms of extrinsic motives play in shaping behaviors. Conversely, intrinsic motives, which may be quite powerful, are not accounted for in agency models. When combined with notions of control or the lack of control in a setting, the bias generated by an extrinsic-motive model may confuse any study or theoretical development.[56]

MOTIVATION ACROSS CULTURES

Motivation is of central importance in the study and application of international organizational behavior. There are two issues to be addressed when reviewing motivation in international settings. The first issue is concerned with the motives themselves. There is considerable evidence that the relative importance of motives varies across cultures. These differences in motives have implications for not only when providing incentives to workers but also whether or not motivational approaches hold across cultures. Some international experts believe that certain theories and application techniques are culture bound, meaning they may work well in the United States but not in other countries. Before examining these issues, however, the nature of work itself across cultures deserves consideration.

The Meaning of Work across Cultures

Traditionally in the United States, work has generally been equated with economic rewards. Although people have diverse needs and individual differences, North Americans can still be generally characterized as working because they want to earn money with which to buy things. Thus, for many North Americans, time on the job is money. This is often reflected in the ways they try to get as much done in as little time as possible. North Americans also like to have things spelled out for them so that they know what is expected and when tasks should be completed. As will be noted in Chapter 15, they respond to goals that help improve their performance levels.

Not all countries would use such a starting assumption in motivating their human resources. Although work is important to most people around the world, and the motivational theories and processes may or may not be similar, there are some important differences. For example, even the motives of employees between East and West Germany since the unification of the country seem to be quite different.[57]

The roles of work and the motivational processes of human resources in given cultures may also change over time. For example, in recent years downsizing and increased competitive pressures encountered by U.S. firms have caused the number of work hours per individual to rise. In contrast, in the same decade workloads decreased among Japanese workers.[58] This may change again as Japan seeks to bounce back from economic problems encountered for now over 10 years. Consequently, the nature and meaning of work in a given culture should be considered before beginning any other assessment of the nature of motivation.

Motivational Differences across Cultures

What contributes to the motivational differences across cultures? The roles of religion, uncertainty avoidance, and power distance provide some insight into this question.

The Role of Religion.   One explanation regarding motivational differences between cultures may come from religions and their accompanying values. For instance, some religions place greater emphasis on allowing events to develop in their own way, or just letting things happen. Many Hindus in India would follow this line of thinking. North Americans, on the other hand, are more likely to practice religions that teach them to try to control matters. Some religions teach that people will be reincarnated and will return; most North Americans believe they pass this way only once, so they want to get as much done here and now as they can. Some religions teach the importance of caring for others as much as oneself (collectivism); most North Americans believe the best way to help others is to ensure one's own success (individualism). These differing religious values may have an indirect and, in some cases, a direct impact on the motivational patterns of various individuals.

One international expert noted that the old Protestant work ethic, which may no longer be so dominant in North America and Western European countries as it once was, is alive and well in places such as Seoul, Soweto, and Santiago de Chile. He notes that it is operating in these formerly strong Buddhist and Catholic areas of the world, much as it did in North America and Western Europe. This may have occurred because it was crucial to integrate various religious values and attitudes with approaches that are conducive to success in high-growth, market economies.[59]

The Role of Uncertainty Avoidance.   Another factor that may contribute to motivational differences is related to the cultural value associated with avoiding ambiguity and uncertainty. How willing are people to face uncertainty? How much do they prefer to know what is happening and to not take too many risks? If the cultural values of employees make them willing to live with uncertainty, they may be motivated quite differently from those who prefer to know what is going on. For example, those who thrive on uncertainty may not have strong job security needs. Or, those with a low tolerance for ambiguity and uncertainly may respond more positively to objective job performance measures. A recent analysis concluded, "People who have high uncertainty avoidance prefer to specialize, avoid conflict, want clear instructions, and do not want competition. Some ways to reduce uncertainty about other people are to observe them, try to get information about them, and interact with them."[60]

Hofstede's research covered in Chapter 2 points out that this uncertainty avoidance cultural dimension or value varies from country to country. People in Latin countries (both in Europe and South America) generally do not like uncertainty. Neither do those from Mediterranean nations. On the other hand, those from countries including Denmark, Sweden, Great Britain, Ireland, Canada, and the United States function more effectively under conditions of uncertainty or ambiguity. Asian countries such as Japan and Korea tend to fall between these two extremes.[61]

The Role of Power Distance.   The third factor that contributes to motivational differences across cultures is power distance. Can the people in a particular country accept the fact that others have more power than they, or do they find this difficult to live with? People in the United States, Britain, Canada, and the Scandinavian countries have trouble accepting the idea that others have more power than they do. On the other hand, people in India, Mexico, Japan, and South Korea do not. This may explain why empowerment as a managerial style would be more accepted and motivational in those countries where smaller power distance exists, such as the United States and in Scandinavia. Cross-culturally, multinational companies may encounter difficulties when they try to motivate home country employees in Korea using empowerment tactics. On the other hand, a Korean corporation operating in the United States may have more effective results by empowering employees who are from North America.

In general, employees in the United States tend to fit the following profile using Hoefstede's cultural dimensions:

> relatively high masculinity and Protestant work ethic, high individualism, narrow power distances, low needs to avoid uncertainty, and high needs for continual stream of explicit information to be communicated from the context.

Starting in the 1990s, an explosive amount of new research examined differences in motivation cross-culturally by assessing a number of variables. These include degrees of Protestant work ethic, managerial feelings regarding the components of Theory X (autocratic styles) and Theory Y (democratic styles), competitiveness, propensity for saving, valuation of money, achievement through conformity, locus of control, needs for achievement, affiliation, dominance, and autonomy. Most of the time, there were no consistent patterns where cultural similaries emerge. Instead, many of these factors and motives tended to strongly vary by country or region, gender, and economic conditions in a given culture.[62] Because the development of motivation theories and techniques in the study of organizational behavior are largely U.S. based, and because motives may vary between cultures, one logical extension would be to determine the generalizability and/or the cultural contingencies.

Do Motivation Theories and Approaches Hold across Cultures?

The content and process theories and techniques of motivating human resources described in this chapter were largely developed by scholars in the United States and tested on U.S. employees. Nevertheless, there are some research findings and theories that would bring into question whether or not these theories and techniques hold equally well across cultures. Specifically our (Luthans and colleagues) study revealed that U.S.-based extrinsic motivators had a positive impact on Russian employees' performance, but a participative approach did not.[63] Other studies note that motivational processes such as those based on feelings of equity may be found not only in the United States, but also in Asian countries.[64] Most cross-cultural researchers, however, emphasize that there are more differences than similarities in various motivational theories and techniques. For example, after reviewing the cross-cultural motivation literature, Adler concluded, "American motivation theories, although too often assumed to reflect universal values, have failed to provide consistently useful explanations for behavior outside the United States."[65]

Most of the cross-cultural research on motivation has mainly been limited to the content theories such as Maslow's hierarchy of needs, Herzberg's two factors, and McClelland's achievement theory. The results of this research indicate that there are definitely variations of these content theories across cultures. For example, because the Chinese stress collective rather than individual needs, it has been suggested that Maslow's hierarchy, from most basic to highest, should be (1) belongingness (social), (2) physiological, (3) safety, and (4) self-actualization to society.[66]

The same has been suggested for Herzberg's two factors and McClelland's need for achievement; they should be recast in light of cultural differences. For instance, there is little question that an individual's sense of responsibility and need for achievement may vary by the culture in which the person was reared. For example, in the United States, Canada, and Great Britain, the need for achievement seems to be based on two culturally based characteristics: (1) a willingness to accept moderate degrees of risk and (2) a strong concern for performance. In a culture where uncertainty avoidance is a strongly held value, the first criterion is less likely to apply. As a result, individuals from countries such as Chile and Portugal may contain employees who base needs for achievement on other criteria and express differing views regarding what is associated with a high (or low) need for achievement.[67] The same type of modification would be necessary for cultures where needs for performance are neither as strongly nor as consistently held.

At the same time, the frameworks used to prepare these theories may be more universal. That is, people in all cultures experience need hierarchies (Maslow), encounter factors that prevent dissatisfaction and lead to motivation (Herzberg), and are associated with a level of achievement motivation (McClelland). It is not that these theories disappear or are not relevant across cultures, but rather that they have differing forms of content that must be incorporated when applying them within various cultures. In other words, all cultures have needs hierarchies, but the ordering of the needs may differ by culture, such as in the Chinese example just given. Further, many needs are relatively pervasive. For example, the need for achievement and the desire for interesting work are two highly motivating factors in many cultures. Thus, although employees in various countries may have differing absolute levels of needs, the relative ranks of the needs may be more consistent.[68]

The same may be true for the more sophisticated, but more generalizable process theories of motivation. As Adler points out: "Expectancy theories are universal to the extent that they do not specify the types of rewards that motivate a given group of workers."[69] There is one viewpoint that suggests that expectancy theory has limited use because it only applies to situations in which people have a strong need for personal control over work, yet the problem has not been limited to predictive validity of the theory. This may be due to the interaction between personal feelings of control combined with team and organizational outcomes and directives.[70] A similar conclusion seems to apply to theories of equity, attribution (Chapter 6), and reinforcement (Chapter 16). The process itself holds across cultures, but the content and successful application will be culture specific. For instance, in some cultures people are more sensitive to inequity, and the relative importance of equity as opposed to equality may vary, but in general people appear to value equity in almost any setting.[71] One new variation of the equity theory idea is related to a culturally based sense of entitlement, such as the one that may have developed in the Soviet Union during the years of its communist, centrally planned economy. In that situation, a worker may be inclined to believe that outcomes will routinely be greater than inputs, as many workers during that era received the benefits of guaranteed employment and free health care. When that happens, perceptions of equity are definitely altered.[72]

In summary, the key to understanding motivation in an international context is to explore the basic meaning of work first. Next, it is helpful to recognize the cultural dimensions that contribute to possible differences in motives. And finally, international human resource management should account for potential new ways to apply the motivation theories and approaches presented in this chapter by adapting them to the specific culture.

Summary

Motivation is probably more closely associated with the micro perspective of organizational behavior than is any other topic. A comprehensive understanding of motivation includes the need–drive–incentive sequence, or cycle. The basic process involves needs, which set drives in motion to accomplish incentives (anything that alleviates a need and reduces a drive). The drives, or motives, may be classified into *primary, general,* and *secondary* categories. The primary motives are unlearned and physiologically based. Common primary motives are hunger, thirst, sleep, avoidance of pain, sex, and maternal concern. The general, or stimulus, motives are also unlearned but are not physiologically based. Curiosity, manipulation, activity, and affection are examples of general motives. Secondary motives are learned and are most relevant to the study of organizational behavior. The needs for power, achievement, affiliation, security, and status are major motivating forces in the behavior of organizational participants.

Besides the various needs, motivation can also be broken down into its source— extrinsic and intrinsic. Extrinsic motives are the visible consequences external to the individual (e.g., money), usually contingently administered by others, to motivate the individual. Intrinsic motives are internal to the individual, and are self-induced to learn, achieve, or in some way better oneself.

When the theories are specifically focused on work motivation, there are several popular approaches. The Maslow, Herzberg, and Alderfer models attempt to identify specific content factors in the employee (in the case of Maslow and Alderfer) or in the job environment (in the case of Herzberg) that are motivating. Although such a content approach has surface logic, is easy to understand and can be readily translated into practice, the research evidence points out some definite limitations. There is very little research support for these models' theoretical basis and predictability. The trade-off for simplicity sacrifices true understanding of the complexity of work motivation. On the positive side, however, the content models have given emphasis to important content factors that were largely ignored by the human relationists. In addition, the Alderfer model allows more flexibility, and the Herzberg model is useful as an explanation for job satisfaction and as a point of departure for practical application.

The process theories provide a much sounder theoretical explanation of work motivation. The expectancy model of Vroom and the extensions and refinements provided by Porter and Lawler help explain the important cognitive variables and how they relate to one another in the complex process of work motivation. The Porter-Lawler model also gives specific attention to the important relationship between performance and satisfaction. Porter and Lawler propose that performance leads to satisfaction, instead of the human relations assumption of the reverse. A growing research literature is somewhat supportive of these expectancy models, but conceptual and methodological problems remain. Unlike the content models, these expectancy models are relatively complex and difficult to translate into actual practice, and, consequently, they have made a contribution but are not the final answer for motivation in the field of organizational behavior and human resource performance.

More recently, in academic circles, equity theory has received increased attention. Equity theory, which is based on perceived input–outcome ratios of oneself compared to relevant other(s), can lead to increased understanding of the complex cognitive process of work motivation but has the same limitation as the expectancy models for prediction and control in the practice of human resource management. More recently, this equity theory has been applied to the analysis of procedural justice in the workplace. Finally, control and agency theories, coming from other disciplines, are briefly discussed as representative of other approaches receiving recent research attention in organizational behavior.

The last part of the chapter recognizes the globalization environment. Cross-cultural studies of motivation are taking place in two areas. First, variances and similarities among motives and the relative importance of motives tend to indicate that there are routine differences in various cultures. Second, continuing research is oriented toward the understanding of which motivational theories are culture bound and which are more applicable to cultures other than the United States.

ENDING WITH META-ANALYTIC RESEARCH FINDINGS

OB PRINCIPLE: The process variables of cognitive motivation theories can predict work-related performance.

Meta-Analysis Results: [77 studies; *d* = .47] *On average, there is a **63 percent probability** that using Vroom's VIE (valence, instrumentality, expectancy) model of motivation will better predict work performance than if the model is not used.* However, further analysis indicates that the process variables independently may be even more related to performance.

Conclusion: As this chapter indicates, Vroom's VIE theory is the pioneering cognitive theory of work motivation, which focuses on the process variables that lead to employee performance. The theory is based on the cognition that people believe there are probability relationships and expectancies between the effort they put forth, the performance they achieve, and the outcomes they receive. Although the meta-analysis suggests that the VIE model per se may not have a great impact, the individual process variables of valence, expectancy, and instrumentality do hold up as probable predictors of performance, lending support to the cognitive theories of work motivation.

> *Source:* Adapted from Wendelien Van Eerde and Henk Thierry, "Vroom's Expectancy Models of Work-Related Criteria: A Meta-Analysis," *Journal of Applied Psychology,* Vol. 81, No. 5, 1996, pp. 575–586.

OB PRINCIPLE: On interesting, challenging tasks, providing extrinsic rewards can increase the level of intrinsic motivation.

Meta-Analysis Results: [13 studies; 729 participants; *d* = .34] *On average, there is a **60 percent probability** that administering extrinsic rewards such as money to employees performing interesting, challenging tasks will increase their level of intrinsic motivation more than those who do not receive extrinsic rewards.* However, a moderator analysis revealed that in some cases extrinsic rewards can actually decrease employees' intrinsic motivation by shifting the employee's focus away from wanting to perform well on a task because it is intrinsically interesting or challenging, to the desire for an external reward. Moreover, it is suggested that the extrinsic-intrinsic relationship depends on how intrinsic motivation is measured.

Conclusion: Although it is important that employees be genuinely interested and motivated to perform well, it is equally important that organizations reward people for their performance. However, the effects of combining extrinsic and intrinsic motivational techniques can be complex. Increasing levels of intrinsic motivation involves either increasing employees' level of competence that they can perform tasks, enhancing their perceptions of control over their behavior, or providing challenges in the work environment. Although in many cases providing extrinsic rewards adds to intrinsic motivation, organizations must be careful that the extrinsic rewards do not interfere with key cognitive processes. For example, employees who receive money for a job well done may attribute their performance to their motive for money rather than to a genuine interest or need for achievement. The result may be a decrease in intrinsic motivation on future tasks. This is perhaps one reason why organizations are turning

> *Source:* Adapted from Uco J. Wiersma, "The Effects of Extrinsic Rewards in Intrinsic Motivation: A Meta-Analysis," *Journal of Occupational and Organizational Psychology,* Vol. 65, 1992, pp. 101–114.

to alternatives to money to spark motivation. As this chapter indicates, work motivation is a complex process and there are no easy answers, but there is a probability that extrinsic rewards can increase intrinsic motivation on at least interesting and challenging tasks.

Questions for Discussion and Review

1. Briefly define the three classifications of needs, or motives. What are some examples of each?
2. What are the characteristics of high achievers?
3. How is status defined? What are some determinants of status?
4. What implications does the security motive have for modern human resource management?
5. What is the difference between an intrinsic and an extrinsic motive? Can both operate at the same time? If so, how?
6. In your own words, briefly explain Maslow's theory of motivation. Relate it to work motivation and Alderfer's ERG model.
7. What is the major criticism of Herzberg's two-factor theory of motivation? Do you think it makes a contribution to the better understanding of motivation in the workplace? Defend your answer.
8. In Vroom's model, what are valence, expectancy, and force? How do these variables relate to one another and to work motivation? Give realistic examples.
9. In your own words, briefly explain the Porter-Lawler model of motivation. How do performance and satisfaction relate to each other?
10. Briefly give an example of an inequity that a manager of a small business might experience. How would the manager strive to attain equity in the situation you describe?
11. How does equity theory relate to procedural justice? Why is this so important to today's employees?
12. Briefly describe control theory and agency theory. What implications can these two theories have for work motivation?
13. Which motivation theories do you believe are culture bound? Which are not? Explain your answer.

Internet Exercises: What Types of Jobs Motivate You?

Now that you have a foundation for understanding human motivation from the chapter, it is very useful to understand what motivates you. Go to the website http://company. monster.com/ and spend some time analyzing the jobs that they offer in your area of interest, and then answer the following questions.

1. Select one of the jobs listed. What motivational theories explain why or why not you would be a good, motivated employee in this job?
2. Would this job provide you motivation in each of Maslow's levels? How? How, if at all, would this job relate to Herzberg's two factors?
3. Using this job as a reference point, as best as you can trace through each step (the boxes in Figure 8.7) in the Porter and Lawler expectancy model of motivation.

REAL CASE:
"I'm Outta Here!"

Gone are the days of two-week notices, cleaning out your office, and giving a polite exit interview. With unemployment at its lowest level in modern history, job-hopping is at its highest rate in a decade. That means many workers with skills are getting downright nervy—even nasty—in the way they quit. For companies, this is adding only more throbbing to the biggest headache they have: finding and keeping good people. The bad blood and often very public departures are morale bombs for companies, causing bouts of second-guessing by those who remain behind and even hurting profitability—as it often costs twice ex-staffers' salaries to replace them.

There was a time when private, discreet, and diplomatic resignation letters expressed gratitude for the support and paycheck. And now? Companywide e-mails, heavy with invective about what's wrong with the organization, are popping up everywhere. That's the way Mike Drummond, 36, left his job as a telecommunications reporter for the *San Diego Union-Tribune*. After close to two years at the paper, he gave two weeks' notice and then fired off an e-mail to 2,000 *Union-Tribune* employees—from management to press operators. He groused about the high turnover rate among business news editors, blaming it on management's "unwillingness to advocate salary increases, flexible work hours, telecommuting, and other family-friendly remedies to stem the brain drain." After all, what did he care? He had a new offer from *Business 2.0*—which is paying him twice his newspaper salary—to try the slower pace of magazine journalism.

Increasingly, departing employees no longer feel compelled to sidestep sticky issues graciously when they say good-bye. Mark W. Lowder, vice-president of American Dairy Queen Corp.'s international division, says when some employees leave, they use the exit interview to seek revenge on a supervisor. Even so, that can sometimes help out the old cubemates. At Dairy Queen, after hearing repeatedly from departing staffers that salaries were too low, senior management started giving out raises, putting DQ pay on a par with the industry average, Lowder says.

Sometimes companies even have to abort bold strategies and settle for lesser ones because of employee churn. Mark Zivin, president of the Chicago-based software consulting group Business Productivity Systems Inc., decided to curtail growth three years ago because of high turnover and the subsequent morale problems it created. "One guy, we spent $20,000 plus training him, and he just walked out after five weeks," Zivin says.

1. Why do you think this brazen, somewhat rude exit behavior is occurring? What is the downside of such behavior? For the exiting person? For the organization?
2. The response to cut back a growth strategy at Business Productivity System is one way to handle the problems described with high turnover. From a motivational perspective, what is another approach? Be specific as to what motivation theories would be applicable.
3. What do you think of Dairy Queen's strategy of using higher pay as a way to prevent turnover? How would this strategy relate to the content and process theories of motivation? What about extrinsic versus intrinsic motivation? Are the motivation theories realistic in this sizzling job market?

ORGANIZATIONAL
BEHAVIOR CASE:
Star Salesperson

While growing up, Jerry Slate was always rewarded by his parents for showing independence. When he started school, he was successful both inside and outside the classroom. He was always striving to be things like traffic patroller and lunchroom monitor in grade school. Yet his mother worried about him because he never got along well with other children his own age. When confronted with this, Jerry would reply: "Well, I don't need them. Besides, they can't do things as well as I can. I don't have time to help them; I'm too busy improving myself." Jerry went on to do very well in both high school and college. He was always at or near the top of his class academically and was a very good long-distance runner for the track teams in high school and college. In college he shied away from joining a fraternity and lived in an apartment by himself. On graduation he went to work for a large insurance company and soon became one of the top salespersons. Jerry is very proud of the fact that he was one of the top five salespersons in six of the eight years he has been with the company.

At the home office of the insurance company, the executive committee in charge of making major personnel appointments was discussing the upcoming vacancy of the sales manager's job for the midwestern region. The human resources manager gave the following report: "As you know, the midwestern region is lagging far behind our other regions as far as sales go. We need a highly motivated person to take that situation over and turn it around. After an extensive screening process, I am recommending that Jerry Slate be offered this position. As you know, Jerry has an outstanding record with the company and is highly motivated. I think he is the person for the job."

1. Do you agree with the human resources manager? Why or why not?
2. Considering Jerry's background, what motives discussed in the chapter would appear to be very intense in Jerry? What motives would appear to be very low? Give specific evidence from the case for each motive.
3. What type of motivation is desirable for people in sales positions? What type of motivation is desirable for people in managerial positions?

ORGANIZATIONAL
BEHAVIOR CASE:
What Do They Want?

Pat Riverer is vice president of manufacturing and operations of a medium-size pharmaceutical firm in the Midwest. Pat has a Ph.D. in chemistry but has not been directly involved in research and new-product development for 20 years. From the "school of hard knocks" when it comes to managing operations, Pat runs a "tight ship." The company does not have a turnover problem, but it is obvious to Pat and other key management personnel that the hourly people are putting in only their eight hours a day. They are not working anywhere near their full potential. Pat is very upset with the situation because, with rising costs, the only way that the company can continue to prosper is to increase the productivity of its hourly people.

Pat called the human resources manager, Carmen Lopez, and laid it on the line: "What is it with our people, anyway? Your wage surveys show that we pay near the top in this region, our conditions are tremendous, and our fringes choke a horse. Yet these people still are not motivated. What in the world do they want?" Carmen replied: "I have told you and the president time after time that money, conditions, and benefits are not enough. Employees also need other things to motivate them. Also, I have been conducting some random confidential interviews with some of our hourly people, and they tell me that they are very discouraged because, no matter how hard they work, they get the same pay and opportunities for advancement as their coworkers who are just scraping by." Pat then replied: "Okay, you are the motivation expert; what do we do about it? We *have* to increase their performance."

1. Explain the "motivation problem" in this organization in terms of the content models of Maslow, Alderfer, and Herzberg. What are the "other things" that the human resources manager is referring to in speaking of things besides money, conditions, and fringe benefits that are needed to motivate employees?
2. Explain the motivation of the employees in this company in terms of one or more of the process models. On the basis of the responses during the confidential interviews, what would you guess are some of the expectancies, valences, and inequities of the employees in this company? How about Pat?
3. How would you respond to Pat's last question and statement if you were the human resources manager in this company?

ORGANIZATIONAL
BEHAVIOR CASE:
Tom, Dick, and Harry

You are in charge of a small department and have three subordinates—Tom, Dick, and Harry. The key to the success of your department is to keep these employees as motivated as possible. Here is a brief summary profile on each of these subordinates.

Tom is the type of employee who is hard to figure out. His absenteeism record is much higher than average. He greatly enjoys his family (a wife and three small children) and thinks they should be central to his life. The best way to describe Tom is to say that he is kind of a throwback to the hippie generation and believes deeply in the values of that culture. As a result, the things that the company can offer him really inspire him very little. He feels that the job is simply a means of financing his family's basic needs and little else. Overall, Tom does an adequate job and is very conscientious, but all attempts to get him to do more have failed. He has charm and is friendly, but he is just not "gung-ho" for the company. He is pretty much allowed to "do his own thing" as long as he meets the minimal standards of performance.

Dick is in many respects opposite from Tom. Like Tom, he is a likable guy, but unlike Tom, Dick responds well to the company's rules and compensation schemes and has a high degree of personal loyalty to the company. The problem with Dick is that he will not do very much independently. He does well with what is assigned to him, but he is not very creative or even dependable when he is on his own. He also is a relatively shy person who is not very assertive when dealing with people outside the department. This hurts his performance to some degree because he cannot immediately sell himself or the department to other departments in the company or to top management.

Harry, on the other hand, is a very assertive person. He will work for money and would readily change jobs for more money. He really works hard for the company but expects the company also to work for him. In his present job, he feels no qualms about working a 60-hour week, if the money is there. Even though he has a family and is supporting his elderly father, he once quit a job cold when his employer didn't give him a raise on the premise that he was already making too much. He is quite a driver. A manager at his last place of employment indicated that, although Harry did do an excellent job for the company, his personality was so intense that they were glad to get rid of him. His former boss noted that Harry just seemed to be pushing all the time. If it wasn't for more money, it was for better fringe benefits; he never seemed satisfied.

1. Can you explain Tom's, Dick's, and Harry's motivations by one or more of the work-motivation models discussed in this chapter?
2. Using Alderfer's ERG theory, what group of core needs seems to dominate each of these three subordinates?
3. How, if at all, would equity theory apply to the analysis of the motivations of Tom, Dick, and Harry?

CHAPTER 9

Positive Psychology Approach to OB: Optimism, Emotional Intelligence, and Self-Efficacy

Learning Objectives

Frame the chapter in terms of the positive psychology movement.

Discuss the theory, research, and application of optimism.

Provide, within the discussion of optimism, the related positive psychology concepts of hope and happiness/subjective well-being (SWB).

Present the theory, research, and application of emotional intelligence (EI).

Explain the specific roles that emotion and intelligence play in emotional intelligence.

Present the theory, research, and application of self-efficacy.

Give particular attention to the processes and sources of efficacy.

Starting with Best Practice
Leader's Advice

Daniel Goleman on the Importance of Employee Emotional Intelligence

Daniel Goleman is CEO of Emotional Intelligence Services and author of the best-selling books Emotional Intelligence *and* Working with Emotional Intelligence. *Dr. Goleman covered the behavioral and brain sciences for* The New York Times *for 12 years. He is now a consultant, author, and speaker drawing from his background in psychobiology. He provides insights from his experience with the role employees' EQ or EI (emotional intelligence) can play in today's organizations.*

Q1: *What was your primary goal for your book on* Working with Emotional Intelligence?

Goleman: To explore systematically, as I had for the first book, what the empirical data suggested was the importance of these skills. I was quite surprised myself to find out just how much emotional intelligence-based competencies affect performance for jobs of all kinds. They are twice as important as cognitive ability and technical expertise combined. The higher you go in an organization, the more it matters. So, for leadership positions, these skills account for close to 90 percent of what distinguishes the most outstanding leaders from average ones.

That puts a premium on getting people who have these abilities or on cultivating these abilities in the people you already have and value—which gets me to training.

I realize that there was really something significant that needed to be done in setting new standards for training in this area. Most companies say that they put a huge amount of effort into cultivating this range of emotional competencies.

Q2: *What are the emotional intelligence competencies?*

Goleman: [The competencies include] self-confidence, empathy, the need to get results, constant improvement, influence, and teamwork. These are the abilities that every organization needs to develop in people, and yet when you look at the track record of development efforts in those areas, it's disappointingly poor all too often.

Q3: *Isn't it a positive aspect of emotional intelligence for all of us that these skills can be learned?*

Goleman: Unlike IQ, which is basically the same throughout life, or personality, which does not change, emotional intelligence-based competencies are learned abilities. Confidence, for example, is a learned ability that improves job performance.

Q4: *The guidelines seem to require an intensely personal, customized, one-on-one approach. Is that really feasible for companies these days? It seems like it would be terribly expensive.*

Goleman: The guidelines have to be understood as a statement of the ideal, of the optimal. If you're dealing with top executives, for example, then you can do executive coaching.

You can afford to tailor training programs. On the other hand, I don't think [those methods are] only for people at the high end. I think there are ways to help people choose from menus and tailor their own programs, which can be done with large groups of people. In other words, you can find economies in putting these guidelines into practice that don't demand that you have an expensive executive coach for each person.

Q5:   *With so many young people entering the workforce, particularly in the next 5 to 10 years, are there specific ways one would teach these competencies to someone just out of college?*

Goleman: Just because older people learn more quickly, you shouldn't give up on young people. I think quite the opposite. There are signs that there has been a decline in emotional intelligence in the young people who are now entry-level in the workplace, relative to earlier generations. At the same time, these capabilities are more important than ever to companies' success, which says to me that you need to put more effort into helping new hires.

I often hear, for example, in the engineering community, that young people who are coming into companies aren't so good at teamwork, sharing data, helping out, and so on. They aren't good at receiving feedback; they take it as a personal attack. These are very basic skills that new hires need to master in order to do their best.

Q6:   *Do you plan to get into the specifics of how to teach someone how to be, for example, self-confident? How do we teach an attribute, as opposed to a fact or a process?*

Goleman: There are many packages now for doing exactly those tasks. We're not prescribing exactly which methods you should use, whether it's modeling or the cognitive behavioral model in which you help a person challenge his or her thoughts and start acting in ways that those thoughts are [preventing]. One of the biggest problems, for instance, is that people aren't given support for on-the-job practice. In order to change behavior, you have to give it weeks and months, not just a weekend seminar, and optimally you have to help people try out the new behavior on the job where it really counts. That's the way it's going to stick. And that's done too seldom.

Q7:   *You emphasize the importance of the opportunity to practice these new emotional intelligence skills.*

Goleman: People are given too few chances to practice on the job, to really make the new habit a lasting habit. They'll get a few days in a workshop, then maybe they'll get a few weeks of follow-up, but deep change and mastery takes months and months of practice. If the end goal is on-the-job performance, you want the new competence eventually to come naturally to people. That's not going to happen overnight. I believe that the follow-up period should be up to six months.

Just as the overall field of organizational behavior has become more comprehensive (as reflected in the new social cognitive theoretical framework for this text, given detailed attention in Chapter 1), there are a few important variables that have received attention in psychology for the past 15 to 20 years, but have just recently emerged to help in both the better understanding and the effective application of organizational behavior.

This new chapter (both to this text and the field of organizational behavior in general) draws from the recent positive psychology movement the constructs of optimism, emotional intelligence, and self-efficacy. Although positive psychology is most closely associated with optimism and its derivatives of hope and happiness/subjective well-being (SWB), closely related and especially relevant to organizational behavior are the popular positive-constructs of emotional intelligence (EI) and self-efficacy. All texts to date only give very brief mention, if at all, to these positive psychological constructs within the context of personality or individual differences. However, there is now enough theory and direct, or at least indirect, research evidence on the linkage to effective performance in the workplace that they deserve special attention along with the established cognitive variables of perception, personality, attitudes, and motivation. This chapter is framed in the positive psychology movement and then gives the theoretical background, research, and application of first optimism, then emotional intelligence and, finally, the construct most closely associated with social cognitive theory, self-efficacy.

POSITIVE PSYCHOLOGY

Mainly under the leadership of well-known psychologist Martin Seligman, the positive psychology movement has emerged from a reaction to the almost exclusive preoccupation that psychology has had on the negative, pathological aspects of human functioning and behaving. Seligman and a few others became concerned a few years ago that not enough attention was being given to the strengths, the positive features of people that make life worth living. They started positive psychology to shift at least some of the emphasis away from just the worst things in life to the study and understanding of some of the best things in life. The aim of *positive psychology* is to use scientific methodology to discover and promote the factors that allow individuals, groups, organizations, and communities to thrive. It is concerned with optimal human functioning instead of pathological human functioning.

In identifying the domain, Seligman and Csikszentmihalyi summarize the three levels of positive psychology as follows:[1]

1. *Valued subjective experiences.* Well-being, contentment, and satisfaction (in the past); hope and optimism (for the future); and flow and happiness (in the present).
2. *Positive individual traits.* The capacity for love and vocation, courage, interpersonal skill, aesthetic sensibility, perseverance, forgiveness, originality, future mindedness, spirituality, high talent, and wisdom.
3. *Civic virtues and the institutions that move individuals towards better citizenship.* Responsibility, nurturance, altruism, civility, moderation, tolerance, and work ethic.

These very "positive" goals have obvious implications not only for therapy, education, family life, and society at large, but, importantly, also for organizational life and behavior. Similar to Peter Frost's recent call for compassion in management and organizations,[2] there seems to be considerable, not only humanistic reasons, but also understanding and effective application reasons for why a positive psychology approach with its accompanying constructs can contribute to organizational behavior. Although many different tracks or approaches from positive psychology could be taken, this chapter first examines the most closely associated construct of optimism and its derivatives of hope and subjective well-being (SWB). The balance of the chapter then gives detailed attention to the positively oriented constructs of emotional intelligence and self-efficacy.

OPTIMISM

Although optimism has surfaced as probably the major component of the positive psychology movement, it has long been recognized by both psychologists and people in general. The positive impact of optimism on physical and psychological health and the attendant characteristics of perseverance, achievement, and motivation leading to academic, athletic, political, and occupational success are well documented. By the same token, pessimism is known to lead to passivity, failure, social estrangement, and, in its extreme, depression and mortality.

Not as well known, except for the psychological researchers in the area, is that optimism also can have drawbacks, dysfunctions, and costs. For example, well people tend to be optimistic about their future health and therefore often neglect needed nutritional and physical maintenance, or in an organization optimistic managers may become distracted from making the necessary action plans to attain goals.[3] So, whereas optimism has received growing attention in psychology, except for the general knowledge carryover, the field of organizational behavior has to date largely neglected optimism as an important concept and application in improving employee performance.

In defining optimism, contemporary psychologists go far beyond the old adage of the "power of positive thinking" popularized by widely read and heard writers a number of years ago, such as Norman Vincent Peale and Dale Carnegie, in recent times Tony Robbins and Steven Covey, and political leaders such as Franklin Roosevelt and Ronald Reagan. Psychology treats optimism as a cognitive characteristic in terms of a generalized positive outcome expectancy (see Chapter 8) and/or a positive causal attribution (see Chapter 6). Optimism is also often used in relation to other positive constructs such as emotional intelligence. Emotional intelligence expert Daniel Goleman, for instance, devotes considerable attention to the role of optimism in his discussions of emotional intelligence and even at one point refers to optimism as an emotionally intelligent attitude.[4] However, as University of Michigan psychologist Christopher Peterson points out in the most recent comprehensive analysis, "Optimism is not simply cold cognition, and if we forget the emotional flavor that pervades optimism, we can make little sense of the fact that optimism is both motivated and motivating."[5]

The Dimensions of Optimism

Most psychologists treat optimism as human nature and/or an individual difference. Unfortunately, like other psychological and organizational behavior concepts, there are still many unresolved issues surrounding optimism.

Optimism as Human Nature. Both the early philosophers (Sophocles, Nietzsche) and psychologists/psychiatrists (Freud, Allport, Erikson, Menninger) were generally negative about optimism. They felt that optimism was largely an illusion and that a more accurate perception of the hard facts of reality was more conducive to healthy psychological functioning. However, starting in the 1960s and 1970s, cognitive psychologists began to demonstrate that many people tend to have a more positive bias of themselves than cold reality, and that psychologically healthy people in particular have this positive bias. This positivity has gone all the way to being portrayed by some anthropologists, evolutionary psychologists, and neuropsychologists as inherent in the makeup of people—part of their basic human nature.[6]

Optimism as an Individual Difference.   More in tune with mainstream modern psychology is to treat optimism (as with other psychological constructs) as an individual difference; people have varying degrees of optimism. Treating optimism as an individual difference focuses on cognitively determined expectations and causal attributions. Seligman in particular is associated with the attributional approach. He uses the term *explanatory style* to depict how an individual habitually attributes the causes of failure, misfortune, or bad events.[7] This explanatory style is an outgrowth of Seligman's earlier work on *learned helplessness* (also covered in Chapter 12 on stress and conflict). He had found that dogs and then humans, when continually experiencing uncontrollable, punishing, aversive events, eventually learn to be helpless. This helplessness generalized to the point that even when the animals or humans could subsequently control and escape the aversive conditions, they still acted in a helpless manner. Importantly, however, not all the subjects learned to be helpless. About a third resisted; they persevered and refused to give in and be helpless. Seligman extended this work on learned helplessness into generalized causal attributions or explanatory styles of optimism and pessimism.

Here are the causal attributions or explanatory style pessimists and optimists tend to habitually use in interpreting personal bad events:[8]

1. *Pessimists* make *internal* (their own fault), *stable* (will last a long time), and *global* (will undermine everything they do) attributions.
2. *Optimists* make *external* (not their fault), *unstable* (temporary setback), and *specific* (problem only in this situation) attributions.

Research continues on explanatory style, and it has been found that the internality attribution does not hold up as well as the stability or globality.[9] Overall, however, no matter how optimism is measured, it has been shown to be significantly linked with desirable characteristics such as happiness, perseverance, achievement, and health.[10] Seligman himself has made a commitment to shift his own theory building and research from what can go wrong with people (e.g., learned helplessness, pessimism, and depression) to what can go right for people (e.g., optimism, health, and success).[11]

Some Unresolved Optimism Issues.   Even though there is considerably more research and definitive conclusions on optimism than, say, emotional intelligence, there is still much room for conceptual refinement and further research. Peterson identifies and summarizes three of the more important optimism issues as follows:[12]

1. *Little vs. big optimism.*   The magnitude and level of optimism may function quite differently. Little optimism involves specific expectations about positive outcomes (e.g., I will finish my assignment by 5 o'clock so I can watch the ball game tonight), whereas big optimism refers to more generic, larger expectations of positive outcomes (e.g., our firm can become the leader in the industry). Although there may be some relationship between little and big, there is also the distinct possibility of someone being a little optimist, but a big pessimist, or vice versa. There seems little question that the strategies, mechanisms, and pathways linking optimism to outcomes may differ (e.g., time management versus visionary leadership).
2. *Optimism vs. pessimism.*   Although the assumption is often made that optimism and pessimism are mutually exclusive, they may not be. Some people expect both good outcomes (optimism) *and* bad outcomes (pessimism) to be plentiful. Interestingly, explanatory style derived from attributions about bad events are usually independent of explanatory style based on attributions about good events. In other

words, attributions about bad events are identified as optimistic or pessimistic, but attributions about good events are not. It would seem that attributions about good events would be as, if not more, important to understanding optimism.

3. *Learning and sustaining optimism.*   Although optimism is sometimes portrayed as a stable personality trait (e.g., Scheier and Carver's dispositional optimism),[13] Seligman has led the way in popularizing *learned optimism*. This says that anyone, including pessimists, can learn the skills to be an optimist.[14] The social learning process of modeling (i.e., observing positive events and outcomes in one's relevant, valued environment) can contribute to the learning of optimism. By the same token, as Chapter 12 on stress will indicate, reducing and coping with bad events and stress can also help sustain optimism.

Overall, the past, present, and future of optimism as an exciting psychological construct for the better understanding and application of human functioning in general and for organizational behavior in particular seems very "optimistic."

Optimism in the Workplace

As discussed, there is no question that optimism is both motivated and motivating; has the desirable characteristics of happiness, perseverance, achievement, and health; makes external, unstable, and specific attributions of personal bad events; and is linked with positive outcomes such as occupational success. Obviously by extrapolating this profile, optimism could be a very positive force in the workplace. For example, optimists may be motivated to work harder; be more satisfied and have high morale; have high levels of aspiration and set stretch goals; persevere in the face of obstacles and difficulties; make attributions of personal failures and setbacks as temporary, not a personal inadequacy, and view it as a one-time unique circumstance; and tend to feel good and invigorated both physically and mentally. The accompanying Application Example: "Half-Empty" or "Half-Full" gives some real-world scenarios of such optimistic people in the workplace. There are some jobs and career fields where optimism would be especially valuable (e.g., sales, advertising, public relations, product design, customer service, and in the health and social services fields).

The Downside of Optimism.   Despite the overwhelming anecdotal evidence of the positive power of optimism in the workplace, it must be remembered that the academic literature does warn that in certain cases optimism can lead to meaningless or dysfunctional outcomes. For example, Peterson notes that optimistically driven behavior may be aimed at pointless pursuits (e.g., finish in the top five of the company golf league) or unrealistic goals (e.g., striving to attain an unattainable sales goal that results in stress, exhaustion, and high blood pressure).[15] Moreover, "realistic optimism" would result in more effective leadership than "false optimism." There are also certain jobs in which at least mild pessimism would be beneficial (e.g., some technical jobs such as safety engineering or jobs in financial control and accounting).

Seligman's Met Life Studies.   For studies of optimism in the workplace, Seligman again leads the way with his pioneering work at Metropolitan Life Insurance. After conferring with the president of this huge company, he was able to test the obvious hypothesis that optimism and its attendant motivation and perseverance were the keys to sales success. A shortened version of his theory-based Attributional Style Questionnaire (ASQ) was administered to 200 experienced Met Life sales agents. This

APPLICATION EXAMPLE

"Half-Empty" or "Half-Full"

Although to date there are not many research studies of the role of optimism in the workplace, it is nevertheless happening day to day in the way in which organizational participants interpret and react to events. Some people view the "glass" (everyday and important events) as half-full (optimists) and some as half-empty (pessimists). Here are some actual examples.

1. Take the case of two executives who were passed over for promotion because of negative evaluations from their boss.
    A. The "half-empty" exec reacted to the snub in a rage. He had fantasies of killing his boss, complained to anyone who would listen of his unfair treatment, and went on a drinking binge. He felt like his life was over. He avoided his boss and looked down when passing him in the hall. In an interview, however, he admitted "Even though I was angry and felt cheated, deep down I feared that he was right, that I was sort of worthless, that I had failed, and there was nothing I could do to change that."
    B. The "half-full" exec who did not get the promotion was also stunned and upset. But instead of going into a rage, he reasoned to himself, "I can't say I was surprised, really. He and I have such different ideas, and we've argued a lot." Instead of sulking, he openly discussed the setback with his wife to determine what went wrong and what he could do to correct it. He realized that maybe he was not giving his all at work and resolved to talk to the boss. Here is how it went: "I had some discussions with him and things went very well. I guess he was troubled about what he had done, and I was troubled about not working up to potential. Since then, things have been better for both of us."
2. Another "half-full" case is Anne Busquet of American Express. She was relieved of her duties as head of the Optima Card division when it was discovered that some of her employees had hidden millions of dollars in bad debt. Although not involved, she was held accountable and devastated by the setback. However, instead of quitting, she was still confident in her abilities and took a lower position trying to save the company's failing merchandising service division. She made a self-examination of what went wrong in the Optima Card division and concluded that maybe she was too strict and critical of her people. She reasoned that this style may have led her people to fear her to the point where they hid the losses. She resolved to soften her style and become more open, patient, and a better listener. Using this approach to manage the troubled merchandising service division, it reached profitability within two years.
3. Perhaps the greatest "half-full" case is Arthur Blank, the founder of Home Depot. In 1978, after personality clashes with his boss at the hardware chain Handy Dan's, he was fired. Instead of getting angry, he got even. He believed in his abilities and vision for this type of retailing. He did not give up after the setback at Handy Dan's. When an investor approached him, he jumped at the chance to put his talents to work and founded Home Depot. The rest is history.

The half-full optimists interpret bad events in terms of Seligman's explanatory style and, as the preceding three examples indicate, can result in future positive outcomes. Whereas the half-empty pessimists tend to give up and go into a downward spiral after problems or failures, the half-fulls view setbacks as a lesson to be learned for future success.

open-ended version of the ASQ was designed to determine the habitual explanatory style by asking the respondents to interpret six good and six bad vignettes in terms of personalization, permanence, and pervasiveness. Importantly, this test has been found to be very difficult to fake optimism; the right answers vary from test to test, and it does contain "lie scales" to identify those not telling the truth. Results were that agents who scored in the most optimistic half of the ASQ had sold 37 percent more insurance on average in their first two years than agents who scored in the pessimistic half. Agents who scored in the top 10 percent sold 88 percent more than the most pessimistic 10 percent.[16]

Despite the impressive findings from the initial study, Seligman was still not sure of the direction of causality from the correlational results (i.e., if the optimism caused the high performance or if the high performers became optimistic). He next conducted a pilot study on 104 new hires that took both the standard insurance industry test and the ASQ. Interestingly, he found that new insurance agents are more optimistic than any other group tested (e.g., car salespeople, commodity traders, West Point plebes, managers of Arby's restaurants, baseball stars, or world-class swimmers). Optimistic scorers were much less likely to quit (a big problem in the insurance industry where about half turn over the first year) and did as well as the industry test in predicting performance.

He next launched a full-blown study involving 15,000 applicants to Met Life taking both the industry test and the ASQ. One thousand were hired and, importantly, 129 more (called the "Special Force") that had scored in the top half of those taking the ASQ, but had failed the industry test were also hired. In the first year the optimists (those who scored in the top half of the ASQ) outsold the pessimists by only 8 percent, but in the second year by 31 percent. The "Special Force" (those who had flunked the industry test and would not have been hired except for scoring as optimists on the ASQ) outsold the pessimists in the regular force by 21 percent the first year and 57 percent the second. They sold about the same as the optimists in the regular force. Met Life, on the basis of Seligman's studies, then adopted the ASQ as an important part of their selection process of new agents.[17]

Other Research and Application in the Workplace.   With the exception of the comprehensive Met Life study, to date there has been very little research to directly test the impact of optimism in the workplace. One of the few studies examined competent managers and found that they attribute their failures to a correctable mistake, and then they persevere (i.e., an optimistic explanatory style).[18] Other work on optimism has been applied to leadership. For example, there has been recognition given in leadership theory to the importance of optimism,[19] and a recent field study found the measured optimism of military cadets had a significant relationship with their military science professors' rating of leadership potential.[20] There also have been only a few publicized applications of deliberate attempts to use optimism in HRM such as in the selection process. One example is the highly successful Men's Wearhouse discount retailer, where an HRM executive recently stated:

> We don't look for people with specific levels of education and experience. We look for one criterion for hiring: optimism. We look for passion, excitement, energy. We want people who enjoy life.[21]

Besides selection, another example is American Express Financial Advisors that reportedly uses optimism training with their associates.[22] For the future, there is a need for more research and systematic application in the workplace.

Hope: More than Sunny Advice

In the positive psychology movement, optimism has received the most attention, but recently the closely related concept of hope is also being recognized. Most people think of hope in terms of "hope for the best," a bit of sunny, be optimistic advice offered by friends, relatives, and counselors in times of trouble. In positive psychology, however, hope has taken on a specific meaning, and research so far indicates it has a very positive impact on academic achievement, athletic accomplishment, emotional health, the ability to cope with illness, and other hardships.[23] Although not yet part of the organizational behavior literature, like optimism, emotional intelligence, and self-efficacy, the construct of hope seems very relevant to human performance in the workplace.

Although hope draws from each of the positive psychology constructs, there are some conceptually important differences. From the perspective of emotional intelligence, Goleman states that, "having hope means that one will not give in to overwhelming anxiety, a defeatist attitude, or depression in the face of difficult challenges or setbacks."[24] In relation to optimism, Seligman states, "Whether or not we have hope depends on two dimensions of our explanatory style: pervasiveness and performance. Finding temporary and specific causes for misfortune is the art of hope."[25] The psychological meaning of hope draws from these and other earlier views about people's expectations that goals could be achieved[26] and Bandura's self-efficacy beliefs covered in the last third of the chapter. However, the definition and research on hope by C. Rick Snyder has become the most widely recognized.

Snyder believes that *hope* not only reflects the individual's determination that goals can be achieved, but also the person's belief that successful plans can be formulated and pathways identified in order to attain the goals. In simple terms, Snyder defines "being hopeful" as believing you can set goals, figure out how to achieve them, and motivate yourself to accomplish them.[27] Thus, this definition carefully makes the distinction between hope and the other positive psychological constructs. For example, in contrast to the especially close construct of optimism (in which Seligman suggests people are trying to distance themselves from past negative outcomes), under Snyder's definition of hope the individual is concentrating on reaching desired positive goal-related outcomes *and* in addition the agency (motivation and know how) and the thoughts about the pathways to the desired goal. Snyder also cites a number of research studies where measured hope contributed unique and additional variance beyond optimism and self-efficacy measures.[28]

Over the past decade, Snyder and his colleagues have developed a brief self-report "Hope Scale" with items such as "I energetically pursue my goals" and "There are lots of ways around any problem"[29] and conducted a number of research studies. This research finds a positive link between hope scores and goal expectancies, perceived control, self-esteem, positive emotions, coping, and achievement.[30] Although this growing research effort has mostly concentrated on academic, athletic, and mental and physical health, the carryover implications for the workplace seem quite clear. For example, there is already evidence that those with hope in stressful professions such as human services perform better[31] and survive with the most satisfaction, are less emotionally exhausted, and are most likely to stay.[32] Research is still needed on the role of hope in other types of work and would seem particularly relevant in the fields of entrepreneurship and international human resource management. Hope may play an important role in selection, especially for certain types of jobs, and because it is learned and statelike (can change) rather than a stable trait, can be enhanced by training and development to improve on-the-job performance and retention of valuable employees.

Happiness or Subjective Well-Being (SWB)

Although hope has received recent attention, in the positive psychology movement the more recognized, in addition to optimism, has been happiness. Similar to the distinction that psychology makes with the common usage of the term *hope,* psychological theory and research prefers to use the more precise and operationally defined term *subjective well-being* or simply *SWB* instead of happiness. As Seligman and Csikszentmihalyi recently noted: "In practice, subjective well-being is a more scientific-sounding term for what people usually mean by happiness."[33] Sometimes the terms are used interchangeably, but *SWB* is usually considered broader and is defined as people's affective (moods and emotions) and cognitive evaluations of their lives.[34] Under this psychological meaning, it is not necessarily what in reality happens to people that determines their happiness or subjective well-being, but instead how they emotionally interpret and cognitively process what happens to them that is the key. Like hope, SWB has not been in the mainstream of the organizational behavior literature, but unlike hope, there have been some work-related studies in the SWB research literature.

The Background on SWB.   Ed Diener's work over the past three decades is most closely associated with SWB.[35] As an important part of the positive psychology movement, SWB's increasing popularity and recent importance reflects societal trends valuing the good life and what makes people happy. Almost everyone now rates happiness over money (e.g., in a recent survey of 7,204 college students in 42 countries, only 6 percent rated money more important than happiness).[36] Academically, Diener and his research group made a break from simple feelings of happiness and just the demographic characteristics that correlate with it. Over 30 years ago, the derived profile of the happy person was dominated by descriptive demographics such as young, well-educated, either sex, married, and well paid.[37] Today, the interest is more on the processes that underlie life satisfaction. Specifically, there has been a shift away from *who* is happy (i.e., the demographics) to *when* and *why* people are happy and on *what* the processes are that influence SWB.[38] To recognize this comprehensive nature of SWB, Diener and colleagues have identified the following separate components:[39]

1. *Life satisfaction.*   The global judgments of one's life.
2. *Satisfaction with important domains.*   Examples would include work satisfaction.
3. *Positive affect.*   The experience of many pleasant emotions and moods.
4. *Low levels of negative affect.*   The experience of few unpleasant emotions and moods.

Diener and others have developed a number of valid measures of SWB components and combinations over the years. Although questionnaires are mostly used,[40] there are a few studies that use naturalistic experience sampling and even physiological measures, informants, and memory and reaction time. The research in recent years has mainly been concerned with SWB's underlying processes of personality, goals, adaptation, and coping.

Temperament and Personality Dispositions.   Personality has been found to be one of the strongest and most consistent predictors of SWB.[41] There is some evidence of a temperamental predisposition for SWB (i.e., some people may have a genetic predisposition to be happy or unhappy over the long run).[42] However, like the other correlates of SWB, no simple conclusions about the role of predisposition in SWB can be drawn because there are so many other interacting variables and processes. Personality traits (dispositions) such as extroversion have been found to be related with positive SWB and neuroticism with negative SWB.[43] Besides the "Big Five" (see Chapter 7) personality trait of extraversion, a recent meta-analysis also found another of the Big Five, agree-ableness, to equally predict SWB.[44] Yet, once again, the influence of personality traits on SWB are probably moderated (interact) with the environment and specific situation in which the individual is immersed.

The Role of Goals.   Another line of research in SWB is concerned with the goal process. Especially having implications for the workplace are recent studies that found that making progress toward goals is related to SWB[45] and having resources supporting one's important goals is a better predictor of SWB than having resources that are less related to one's important goals.[46] It also has been found that people feel better on days when they make progress toward goals that they value highly than they do on days when they are successful towards achieving goals that they value less.[47] Also, aspiration goals that are set too high or too low have been found to be detrimental to SWB (i.e., anxiety on the too-high end and boredom on the too-low end).[48] In other words, simply having goals and having the resources to pursue those goals is not enough to guarantee happiness or SWB.[49]

Adapting and Coping.   The third stream of research on SWB processes is adaptation and coping. Studies find that people adapt to most conditions fairly quickly. Although people do tend to react strongly to good and bad events, depending on their personality dispositions, they tend to adapt over time and return to their original level of SWB.[50] Recent adaptation studies have implications for the workplace. For example, one study found that in less than three months, the effects of major life events such as being pro-moted or fired lost their impact on SWB[51] and in another study recent changes in pay predicted job satisfaction, but mean levels of pay did not.[52]

  Coping strategies are more proactive than adaptation, and some strategies have been found to be more effective than others. For example, one study found that HIV caregivers that used a strategy of giving ordinary events a positive meaning and using problem-focused coping was related to positive SWB.[53]

  In summarizing the current understanding of and research findings on the three major processes of SWB, Diener and colleagues emphasize that any one of them alone seems necessary but not sufficient. They say the processes of genetics/personality dispositions, goals, and adaptation/coping are complementary to one another and need to be integrated in future research. The bottom line is that as of yet there is no simple an-swer to what causes SWB, and it is pointless to search for a single cause of happiness.[54]

SWB across Cultures.   Unlike the other constructs of positive psychology, SWB has been extensively studied across cultures. Using large samples from a number of coun-tries, here is a summary of some of the more interesting findings:[55]

1. Wealthier nations have higher levels of reported SWB.
2. Some countries were unexpectedly high or low in SWB, even after income was controlled. For example, the Latin American countries of Brazil, Chile, and Argentina were higher in SWB than predicted by their wealth, and Eastern Euro-pean nations including Russia were lower in SWB than predicted by their income.
3. Japan was an outlier with high income but relatively low SWB.
4. The developing nations in the most current survey—China, India, and Nigeria—did not show the extremely low SWB responses that were found in earlier studies.
5. SWB scores have not increased over the years in the countries where repeated sur-veys have been conducted, even though incomes have greatly increased in most of these countries.

6. Variables (e.g., self-esteem, referent others, marriage, and social support) correlate differently with SWB depending on the type of culture of the country (e.g., individualistic vs. collectivistic).

The explanations for these findings are fairly straightforward according to what is commonly known about these countries and cultures. Diener has recently made a call for a national index on SWB to be kept over time so that corporate leaders and government policy makers would be more likely to consider SWB in their decisions.[56]

SWB in Work.   Although not included in organizational behavior or HRM textbooks, SWB discussions do specifically mention work and the workplace as one of its domains, and there are a few research studies. In particular, SWB has a direct correlation to job satisfaction (covered in Chapter 7). A meta-analysis of 34 studies found an average correlation of .44 between job satisfaction and life satisfaction.[57] To determine whether job satisfaction leads to SWB or vice versa (i.e., the correlation studies do not yield the direction of causality), Judge and colleagues used sophisticated statistical designs. It was found that SWB was a significant predictor of job satisfaction five years later, but not vice versa.[58] Thus, it appears that people who are satisfied with their lives tend to find more satisfaction in their work.[59]

Besides job satisfaction, the effects of unemployment have also been studied. Multiyear statistical studies indicate that unemployment typically causes lower SWB.[60] Even though there is a bit better start in SWB, like optimism and hope, the potential research contribution that SWB can make to work, and the understanding and application of organizational behavior seems to be just scratching the surface.

EMOTIONAL INTELLIGENCE

Although not as directly associated with positive psychology as optimism, hope and SWB, the increasingly popular emotional intelligence is a newly emerging positive approach to organizational behavior. This section first examines its two conceptual components: emotion and intelligence. After examining these two important psychological dimensions separately, the synergy created by combining them into emotional intelligence becomes a very powerful positively-oriented construct for the understanding and application approach to organizational behavior.

The Role of Emotion

Emotion has been a major variable in psychology, but not organizational behavior, over the years. Similar to other psychological constructs, the exact definition and meaning of *emotion* is not totally agreed upon. However, most psychologists would agree that the best one word to describe emotion would be how a person *feels* about something. These emotional feelings are directed at someone or something, are not as broad as the term *affect* (as used in the discussion of positive and negative affect in Chapter 7 on personality), and are more intense and specific than the term *mood*. The specific differences between emotion, affect, and mood are summarized as follows:

> Emotions are reactions to an object, not a trait. They're object specific. You show your emotions when you're "happy about something, angry at someone, afraid of something." Moods, on the other hand, aren't directed at an object. Emotions can turn into moods when

you lose focus on the contextual object. So when a work colleague criticizes you for the way you spoke to a client, you might become angry at him [emotion]. But later in the day, you might find yourself just generally dispirited. This affective state describes a mood.[61]

Emotional Processing.   How do emotional reactions come about, and what are the inputs into emotional processing? A very simple, layperson's explanation of the process is that emotional feelings are in contrast with rational thinking. Put into popular terms, emotions come from the "heart" whereas rational thinking comes from the "head." For example, a young manager given a choice between two assignments may undergo the following cognitive processing: "my 'head' tells me to get involved with Project A because it has the best chance of succeeding and helping my career, but my 'heart' says that Project B will be more fun, I like the people better, and I can take more pride in any results we achieve." Obviously, such emotions often win out over rational thinking in what people decide, do, or how they behave.

Traditionally in psychology, both personality traits (e.g., extraversion/neuroticism or conscientiousness) and mood states (either positive or negative) have separate influences or emotional processing. Recently, however, to represent the more realistic complexity involved, it is suggested that: (1) mood states interact with individual differences in emotion-relevant personality traits to influence emotional processing, and/or (2) personality traits predispose individuals to certain mood states, which then influence emotional processing.[62] In other words, for (1) above, someone in a positive mood may have to have (or will be enhanced by) a personality trait such as conscientiousness in order to experience emotional happiness. For (2) above, the individual may have to have the personality trait such as extraversion in order to get into a positive mood state. This positive mood in turn will lead the person to experience emotional happiness. These moderation and meditation models of emotional processing help resolve some of the inconsistencies that have been found in the research using the separate influences of moods and personality traits for emotions.[63]

Types of Emotions.   Like the meaning of emotion, there is also not total agreement on the primary types of emotions. Table 9.1 summarizes the primary emotions and their descriptors most often mentioned in the psychology literature. Importantly, each of

TABLE 9.1   Types of Emotions

Positive Primary Emotions	*Other Descriptors*
Love/affection	Acceptance, adoration, longing, devotion, infatuation
Happiness/joy	Cheerfulness, contentment, bliss, delight, amusement, enjoyment, enthrallment, thrill, euphoria, zest
Surprise	Amazement, wonder, astonishment, shock

Negative Primary Emotions	*Other Descriptors*
Fear	Anxiety, alarm, apprehension, concern, qualm, dread, fright, terror
Sadness	Grief, disappointment, sorrow, gloom, despair, suffering, dejection
Anger	Outrage, exasperation, wrath, indignation, hostility, irritability
Disgust	Contempt, disdain, abhorrence, revulsion, distaste
Shame	Guilt, remorse, regret, embarrassment, humiliation

Source: Adapted from H. M. Weiss and R. Cropanzano, "Affective Events Theory," in B. M. Staw and L. L. Cummings (Eds.), *Research in Organizational Behavior,* Vol. 18, JAI Press, Greenwich, CT, 1996, pp. 20–22 and Daniel Goleman, *Emotional Intelligence,* Bantam Books, New York, 1995, pp. 289–290.

these emotions are very common in the workplace. For example:

- Juan has grown to *love* his paramedic emergency team as they solve one life-threatening crisis after another.
- Mary feels *happy* when her boss comments in front of the sales team that she just landed the biggest contract of the quarter.
- Jami is *surprised* to hear that the firm's stock price dropped two and one-half points today.
- George *fears* the new technological process that he believes may replace him.
- Trent feels *sad* for Alison because she does more than her share of the work, but gets no recognition from the supervisor.
- Lane is *angry* because he was passed over for promotion for the second time.
- Mark is *disgusted* with the favoritism shown to his colleague Steve when the regional sales manager assigns territories.
- Kent has a sense of *shame* for claiming expense reimbursement for a trip he did not take.

As shown by the preceding representative examples, the whole range of emotions are found in the workplace. In addition, it is probably not an exaggeration to state that most personal and many managerial/organizational decisions are based on emotional processes rather than rational thought processes. For example, career decisions are often based on emotions of happiness and affection or even fear, rather than what is rationally best for one's career.[64] As will be brought out in Chapter 11, management decisions are often driven by negative emotions such as fear or anger rather than marginal costs, return on investment, or other criteria that the traditional rational economic/finance models would suggest.[65]

The Categories and Continuum.   Besides identifying the different types of emotions, as shown in Table 9.1 they can be put into positive and negative categories. Whether a person feels a positive or negative emotion in the workplace has a lot to do with goal congruence (positive) or goal incongruence (negative).[66] For example, if salespeople meet or exceed their quota, they feel happy, are relieved, and like their customers, but if they fall short they may feel sad, disgusted, guilty, anxious and may blame or be angry with their boss and/or customers.

Emotions can also be conceptualized along a continuum. One classic emotional continuum is the following:[67]

Happiness—Surprise—Fear—Sadness—Anger—Disgust

Table 9.1 is arranged in the same order except with the positive extreme of love/affection on the front-end and the negative extreme of shame on the back-end.

The key is that the closer the primary emotions are related to one another, the more difficult it is for others to distinguish between them when expressed. For example, almost everyone can readily distinguish the facial expressions of positive versus negative categories of emotion, but may not readily interpret the differences within categories (e.g., between happiness and surprise or anger and disgust). Yet, going back to *emotional labor*[68] (covered in Chapter 7 referring to service personnel required to express false, not natural expression, positive emotions such as smiling), most seasoned customers can easily pick up the difference. For example most "Frequent Flyers" can tell the difference between a genuine, natural smile and "Have a nice day!" and a forced, false smile and insincere happy comment from an angry or disgusted reservationist or flight attendant. The nonverbal facial cues and tone of voice (see Chapter 10) are usually a loud and clear indication of what real emotions are being expressed.

Emotional labor not only has dysfunctional consequences for the employees doing it (e.g., stress and burnout),[69] but also detracts from effective customer service. World-class customer service firms such as Southwest Airlines recognize this by hiring only those with very positive personalities. As Herb Kelleher, the founder and charismatic leader of Southwest, declares: "We want people who can do things well with laughter and grace."[10] By putting humor and happiness at the top of their hiring criteria, Southwest knows, and the academic literature would support,[11] that their people will tend to express positive, genuine emotions (not emotional labor) in all their encounters with customers and coworkers.

Current Status and Future Application.   Although emotions are given primary attention in psychology, in the organizational behavior literature, with the exception of the increasing popularity of emotional labor and the impact of emotions in relation to stress,[72] emotion generally is only an indirect, subtopic in discussions of personality and individual differences. As one organizationalist behavior theorist/researcher recently noted:

> It's an underappreciated line of research. Emotions as part of the workplace have been ignored. They have either been seen as a commodity hiring smiling faces or something that gets in the way of rational decision making.[73]

This neglected status is unfortunate because most academics and practicing managers would agree with the systematic assessment that emotions permeate all of organizational life.[74]

Recently, and the reason emotions are singled out for special attention in this chapter, is the popularity of emotional intelligence and its relevance to the study and application to organizational behavior. Emotionally intelligent people not only can read the expressed emotions of other people as discussed in the previous section, but also have the maturity to hold their *felt emotions* in check and not *display* undesirable, immature negative emotions such as anger or disgust. This distinction between felt and displayed emotions[75] as well as the rest of the previous discussion on the meaning, cognitive processing, and types/categories/continuum of emotions, when combined with the next section on intelligence, serve as the foundation and point of departure for the important emerging role that emotional intelligence can play in organizational behavior.

The Role of Intelligence

Similar to emotion, intelligence has played a major role in psychology but a very minor, almost nonexistent, role in organizational behavior. About a hundred years ago, Alfred Binet created a written test to measure the "intelligence quotient" or IQ of grade school children in Paris. Eventually the U.S. Army used the test with recruits in Word War I, and then it was widely used in schools and businesses. IQ was assumed to be fixed at birth and went largely unchallenged as a predictor of school, job, and life success. It wasn't until about 20 years ago that the fixed, narrow IQ version of intelligence was seriously questioned, and sound theoretical and research-based alternatives were proposed.

Recognition of Multiple Intelligences.   The impetus for the new, expanded and positive perspective of intelligence in psychology and education is mostly attributed to

TABLE 9.2   Gardner's Multiple Intelligences

Original Intelligences	Characteristics	Famous Examples
1. **Logical/mathematical**	Processes analytically, calculates, quantifies	Scientist Albert Einstein
2. **Verbal/linguistic**	Thoughts through words, uses words to nurture	Consultant Tom Peters
3. **Interpersonal**	Understands others, processes through interaction, empathizes, humor	Entertainer Oprah Winfrey
4. **Intrapersonal**	Thinks in quiet, likes to be alone, goal oriented, independent, perseveres	Business Tycoon Howard Hughes
5. **Visual/spatial**	Uses mental models, thinks three dimensionally, pictures how to get places or solve problems	Architect Frank Lloyd Wright
6. **Musical**	Sensitivity to pitch, melody, rhythm, found in both performers and listeners	Composer Wolfgang Mozart
7. **Bodily/kinesthetic**	Physical movement, involves whole body, processes by jumping or dancing	Basketball Player Michael Jordan
"New" Intelligences	Characteristics	Famous Examples
8. **Naturalist**	Need to be with/survive in nature, strength in categorization in nature or urban world	Singer John Denver
9. **Existential**	Not religion per se, knowing why you are here, personal mission	Civil Rights Leader Martin Luther King
10. **Emotional**	Emotionally mature, recognize own anger, reacts to emotions of self and others	Pacifist Leader Mohandas Gandhi

Source: Adapted from Lou Russell, *The Accelerated Learning Fieldbook,* Jossey–Bass/Pfeiffer, San Francisco, 1999, pp. 60–70. For the original work see: Howard Gardner, *Frames of Mind: The Theory of Multiple Intelligences,* Basic Books, New York, 1983 and Howard Gardner, "Are There Additional Intelligences? The Case for Naturalist, Spiritual and Existential Intelligences," Unpublished White Paper, 1996. It should be noted that emotional intelligence is not necessarily recognized as an MI by Gardner.

Howard Gardner. In 1983 he published his breakthrough book, *Frames of Mind: The Theory of Multiple Intelligences.*[76] Binet's IQ basically measured two relatively narrow dimensions: mathematical/ logical and verbal/linguistic. As shown in Table 9.2, Gardner recognized these two plus five others. In developing these seven multiple intelligences or MIs, he found that intelligence was not entirely genetic and fixed at birth, but instead it could be nurtured and grown.

To be considered an intelligence under Gardner's approach, the following three criteria had to be met: (1) measurable, (2) valued by the person's culture, and (3) a strength that the person defaulted to when challenged to be creative or solve a problem. Gardner was careful to point out that his identified intelligences are: (1) a new kind of construct and should not be confused with a domain or discipline; (2) a capacity with component processes and should not be equated with a learning style, cognitive style, or working style; and (3) based wholly on empirical evidence that could be revised or added to on the basis of new empirical findings.[77] Importantly, the MIs are equal in importance and most people are strong in three or four and, because they are not fixed, there is always room for improvement in the others.

This expanded view of intelligence had a dramatic impact on psychology, and many educators have used MI as a new paradigm for schools and classrooms.[78] However, there have to date only been a very few applications of MI in the business world, mainly in training workshops such as at 3M, Coseco Insurance, and Northeast Utilities Service.[79] MI is seldom even acknowledged in the organizational behavior literature. However, with the recent addition of emotional intelligence or EI to Gardner's original seven (see Table 9.2), the recognition and theoretical foundation provided by Gardner's work becomes relevant and necessary to the understanding and application of EI in organizational behavior.

TABLE **9.3**   Cognitive Abilities Related to Job Performance

Mental Ability	Characteristics of Ability	Examples of Job Task
Verbal comprehension	Comprehend what is read or heard, understand what words mean and the relationships to one another	Supervisors following organization policy on sexual harassment
Numerical	Make fast and accurate arithmetic computations	Auto salespeople calculating the sales tax and their commission
Spatial visualization	Perceive spatial patterns, imagine how an object would look if position in space were changed	A builder describing a change to a customer
Perceptual speed	Quickly identify visual similarities and differences, Carry out tasks needing visual perception	A quality control engineer noting a product defect
Memory	Rote memory, retain and recall past incidents/experiences	A knowledge manager drawing from past experiences in the firm to advise a newly formed project team
Inductive reasoning	Identify logical sequence from specific to general	A scientist in the research department drawing from several independent studies to design an innovative product

Source: Adapted from M. D. Dunnette, "Aptitudes, Abilities, and Skills," in M. D. Dunnette (Ed.), *Handbook of Industrial and Organizational Psychology,* Rand McNally, Skokie Ill., 1976, pp. 478–483.

Intelligence as Cognitive Ability.   Although the field of organizational behavior has almost totally ignored multiple intelligences, there has been recognition and attention given over the years to the narrower concept of abilities. Applied to the workplace, *ability* refers to the aptitudes and learned capabilities needed to successfully accomplish a task. Both physical (e.g., manual dexterity, hand-eye coordination and body strength, stamina, and flexibility) and mental, intellectual, or cognitive abilities are recognized for jobs. However, with some obvious exceptions of jobs requiring considerable physical activity (e.g., in construction, manufacturing, repair services, sports or health clubs), the vast majority of jobs in today's workplace are concerned more with cognitive abilities.

Although some unique tasks require specific mental abilities (e.g., accounting tasks require numerical mental ability), most jobs, including those of an accountant or interior designer, require general mental ability (GMA). Over the years, psychologists have proposed numerous mental abilities, but those most widely recognized as underlying effective performance in jobs are summarized in Table 9.3.

Importantly, there is considerable research evidence that GMA tests are a good personnel selection and job training program predictor of overall job performance. Specifically, Schmidt and Hunter recently summarized 85 years of research and based on meta-analytic findings concluded that the highest validity for predicting job performance were: (1) GMA plus a work sample test; (2) GMA plus an integrity test; and (3) GMA plus a structured interview.[80] An additional advantage of (2) and (3) is that they can be highly predicative for both entry-level selection and selection of experienced employees. One further refinement is that GMA predictive validity is higher for more-complex jobs and lower for less-complex jobs.

The Meaning of Emotional Intelligence

As a point of departure for the important role that emotions have played in psychology over the years and Gardner's recognition of multiple intelligences is the recent emergence of emotional intelligence. Although its roots are usually considered to go back

TABLE 9.4   Goleman's Dimensions of Emotional Intelligence in the Workplace

EI Dimensions	*Characteristics*	*Workplace Example*
Self-awareness	Self-understanding; knowledge of true feelings at the moment	John recognizes that he is angry so he will wait to cool down and gather more information before making an important personnel decision.
Self-management	Handle one's emotions to facilitate rather than hinder the task at hand; shake off negative emotions and get back on constructive track for problem solution	Amber holds back her impulse to become visibly upset and raise her voice at the customer's unfair complaint and tries to get more facts of what happened.
Self-motivation	Stay the course toward desired goal; overcome negative emotional impulses and delay gratification to attain the desired outcome	Pat persisted to successful project completion in spite of the many frustrations from the lack of resources and top management support.
Empathy	Understand and be sensitive to the feelings of others; being able to sense what others feel and want	Because the head of the team knew her members were mentally if not physically exhausted, she took everyone bowling during an afternoon break and bought refreshments.
Social skills	The ability to read social situations; smooth in interacting with others and forming networks; able to guide others' emotions and the way they act	Jeremy could tell from the nonverbal cues from his staff members that they were not buying into the new policy being presented, so after the meeting he visited with each of them to explain how they will all benefit.

Source: Adapted from Daniel Goleman, *Emotional Intelligence,* Bantam Books, New York, 1995, pp. 43–44 and Daniel Goleman, *Working with Emotional Intelligence,* Bantam Books, New York, 1998, p. 318.

many years to what was called social intelligence, about a decade ago psychologists Peter Salovey and John Mayer are usually given credit with having the first comprehensive theory and definition of emotional intelligence. Taking off from a foundation in the theory of emotion and multiple intelligence, Salovey and Mayor defined emotional intelligence as "the subset of social intelligence that involves the ability to monitor one's own and others' feelings and emotions, to discriminate among them and to use this information to guide one's thinking and actions."[81] However, it was the publication of the 1995 best selling book *Emotional Intelligence* by psychologist/journalist Daniel Goleman that greatly popularized the construct. He defines *emotional intelligence* or EI as

> The capacity for recognizing our own feelings and those of others, for motivating ourselves, and for managing emotions well in ourselves and in our relationships.[82]

Table 9.4 summarizes the major EI dimensions that Goleman has determined to have the most relevant and biggest impact on understanding behavior in the workplace.

Importantly, Goleman, like Howard Gardner's recognition of multiple intelligences before him, makes a clear distinction between IQ and EI. The EI (or sometimes called EQ as a takeoff from IQ) literature carefully points out that the two constructs are certainly not the same but also not necessarily opposite from one another. As one summary of the analysis of IQ and EQ notes,

> Some people are blessed with a lot of both, some with little of either. What researchers have been trying to understand is how they complement each other; how one's ability to handle stress for instance, affects the ability to concentrate and put intelligence to use.[83]

Similar to the influence that neural activity and the brain play in IQ, Goleman also believes the brain pathways help process EI. However, whereas IQ mostly is associated with the more recent, on the thousands of years old evolutionary chain, neo-cortex (the thinking brain) located near the top of the brain, EI draws from the very early, in the evolution of the brain, inner subcortex more associated with emotional impulses. Importantly, however, unlike IQ, which is usually considered largely inherited and fixed, Goleman also recognizes the role that personality and behavioral theories play in EI. Thus, Goleman provides a very comprehensive theoretical foundation for EI that is based on the brain, but suggests that learning plays an important role in EI development as well. He states in his original book that

> Our genetic heritage endows each of us with a series of emotional set points that determines our temperament. But the brain circuitry involved is extraordinarily malleable; temperament is not destiny. The emotional lessons we learn as children at home and at school shape the emotional circuits, making us more adept—or inept—at the basics of emotional intelligence.[84]

In the second book, *Working with Emotional Intelligence,* he goes much further on the role of learning and the development of EI in maturing adults:

> Our level of emotional intelligence is not fixed genetically, nor does it develop only in early childhood. Unlike IQ, which changes little after our teen years, emotional intelligence seems to be largely learned, and it continues to develop as we go through life and learn from our experiences—our competence in it can keep growing. . . . There is an old-fashioned word for this growth in emotional intelligence: maturity.[85]

These seeming contradictions between the roles of genetic endowment, the brain, personality traits (that are pretty well set, see Chapter 7), and learning/development has drawn some criticism of Goleman's approach to EI.[86] However, there is recent evidence that college students (full-time, part-time, and adult executive education students) have significantly improved (a range of 50–300 percent) their measured (behavioral scoring and paper-and-pencil assessments) EI from the time they enter a program/curriculum designed to enhance their EI until they leave.[87] Goleman also cites "studies that have tracked people's level of emotional intelligence through the years show that people get better and better in these capabilities as they grow more adept at handling their empathy and social adroitness."[88] Even though there is still some controversy surrounding the development and measurement[89] of EI, the time has come for the field of organizational behavior to recognize the positive impact that EI can seem to have in the workplace.

Emotional Intelligence in the Workplace

EI has considerable appeal with real-world managers. When publishing *Emotional Intelligence* in 1995, Goleman had primarily aimed his book at the educational community, and it received a good response. However, he also received an unexpected overwhelming response from the business world. He recalls, "responding to a tidal wave of letters and faxes, e-mails and phone calls, requests to speak and consult, I found myself on a global odyssey, talking to thousands of people, from CEOs to secretaries, about what it means to bring emotional intelligence to work."[90] The appeal mostly came from the realization on the part of jobholders at all levels that both success and effectiveness has more to do with what Goleman described as EI (i.e., self-awareness, -regulation, and -motivation, empathy, and social skills) than with intelligence as traditionally depicted (IQ), technical expertise, or even experience.

Goleman's Approach to EI in the Workplace.   Based on the positive reaction from the field and using a combination of journalism (delving into facts and interviewing experts in hundreds of organizations and consulting firms) and academic theories/ research, Goleman published his next book on *Working with Emotional Intelligence*. In the first part he makes the case that EI counts for more that IQ or technical expert-ise for excellence in any job and especially for outstanding leadership. He then iden-tifies self-mastery job capabilities such as initiative, trustworthiness, self-confidence, and achievement drive that contribute to outstanding performance. Next, he identifies key relationship skills ("people skills") such as empathy, political awareness, leverag-ing diversity, team capabilities, and leadership that result in effective organizations. The final two parts deal with how to develop EI capabilities and organizations that are emotionally intelligent. He argues that not only are EI organizations the most effective and able to compete in the turbulent times ahead, but also they are the most satisfying and desirable places to work. He does caution that EI is not a magic bullet and then concludes:

> At the individual level, elements of emotional intelligence can be identified, assessed, and upgraded. At the group level, it means fine-tuning the interpersonal dynamics that make groups smarter. At the organizational level, it means revising the value hierarchy to make emotional intelligence a priority—in the concrete terms of hiring, training and develop-ment, performance evaluation and promotions.[91]

Initial Supporting Theory and Research.   Beyond Goleman's book, to date not much theory development or research has been done on EI in the workplace. A recent aca-demic, theoretical analysis has indicated that EI may help facilitate individual employee adaptation and change.[92] In terms of empirical research, there is some longitudinal evi-dence indicating EI to be a better predictor of life success (economic well-being, satis-faction with life, friendship, family life), including occupational attainments, than IQ.[93] This type of evidence has been extrapolated to the catchy phrase: "IQ gets you hired, but EQ gets you promoted."[94] Recent surveys do indicate that the majority of human resource managers believe this statement to be true,[95] and there is evidence that this value of EI may even hold for highly technical jobs such as the scientists and engineers at AT&T's Bell labs. When the 10 to 15 percent scientists/engineers judged to be "stars" were compared to everyone else, it was found that neither academic talent nor IQ was a good predictor of on-the-job productivity. Rather, the difference was that the stars used EI dimensions such as social skills to build a network of relationships and friends that they could call on and would get right back to them to help solve a prob-lem or handle a crisis.[96] Also, the well-known Center for Creative Leadership found that "derailed executives" (rising stars who flamed out) failed because of emotional in-telligence types of problems (poor working relations, too authoritarian, too ambitious, conflict with upper management) rather than a lack of technical ability.[97]

Conflict with Selection Research.   The findings and conclusions on the superiority of EI over IQ are in seeming conflict with the considerable empirical evidence and meta-analyses of Schmidt and Hunter. Discussed earlier in this chapter under intelligences, these well-known researchers on human resource selection unequivocally state after decades of studies that, "Other things equal, higher intelligence leads to better job performance on all jobs. Intelligence is the major determinant of job performance, and therefore hiring people based on intelligence leads to marked improvements in job per-formance."[98] Schmidt and Hunter do not address EI in their analyses to date, but one possibility to explain the conflict may lie in their definition of intelligence.

Schmidt and Hunter refer to intelligence in terms of general mental (or cognitive) ability (GMA), which is somewhat broader than the traditional views of IQ used in the comparisons with EI. They treat GMA as a *trait* that is relatively fixed and stable over time, whereas EI is portrayed and found to be more of a *state* that changes and can be developed over time. Thus, because EI may develop over time, it may eventually outweigh the fixed trait of GMA determined on entry into a job. An example of support of this statement would be the recent survey of 7,000 senior executives in 13 countries by a British researcher that concluded older, mature leaders are better able "to discuss sore points with key stakeholders and produce resolutions without resentment."[99] In other words, these older leaders may have developed EI over the years to become more effective in handling the increasingly common emotional encounters and issues, but their GMA stayed the same. These and other hypotheses need to be tested. However, at present there is no question that there is a tremendous amount of empirical evidence supporting the Schmidt and Hunter position on the value of GMA, and there is only starting, mostly qualitative, anecdotal evidence on the value of EI, especially in relation to its superiority over intelligence in predicting job performance.

Application to Leadership.   Most recently, Goleman has steered away from using EI as a selection tool and has moved into the broader-based domain of leadership. He drew a large random sample ($N = 3,871$) from a consulting firm database of 20,000 executives to find six distinct leadership styles that relate to the different components of EI.[100] Pioneering social psychologist David McClelland had earlier found that leaders with EI-related competencies were more effective than counterparts without them. For example, in one study of division heads of a global food and beverage company, McClelland had found that those leaders with EI competencies, 87 percent placed in the top third for bonuses based on performance, and their divisions on average outperformed yearly revenue targets by 15 to 20 percent.[101] Thus, based on these types of findings, Goleman felt it was important to identify the specific EI competencies associated with each style of leaderships as shown in Table 9.5.

TABLE 9.5   Relating Leadership Styles to EI

Leadership Styles	Characteristics	Competencies	Leadership Examples
Coercive	Directive; demands immediate compliance	Self-control, initiative, drive to achieve	In a crisis, this leader would be effective at getting things going (a program or an employee).
Authoritative	Leads the way; mobilizes people toward his/her vision	Self-confidence, empathy, change agent	This leader is effective in situations requiring a new vision or direction.
Affiliative	Creates harmony and cooperation; most concerned about the people	Empathy, relationship building, communication	This leader is effective at healing rifts between team members and motivating personnel in a crisis.
Democratic	Builds consensus through participation; gets everyone's input	Collaboration, team leadership, communication	This leader is effective in building consensus and buy in on important decisions and projects.
Pacesetting	Sets high standards; acts as a model for action	Conscientiousness, drive to achieve, initiative	This leader is effective at getting quick results from a highly motivated/competent team.
Coaching	Supports, facilitates and develops people; guides others to improve themselves for the future	Self-awareness, develops others, empathy	This leader is effective at helping employees to improve their performance and develop their strengths for the future.

Source: Adapted from Daniel Goleman, "Leadership that Gets Results," *Harvard Business Review,* March–April, 2000, pp. 82–83.

Other EI Applications.   Based on Goleman's popular influence and the slowly growing theoretical and empirical base, today's organizations are starting to implement various EI approaches. For example, the U.S. Air Force is beginning to develop and use EI tests to select applicants after finding that their recruiters who had high EI scores were 2.6 times more successful than those with lower EI.[102] Big corporations such as American Express, Bank of America, Ford, GE, CIGNA, Blue Cross Blue Shield, and McNeil/Johnson & Johnson are known for developing in house EI strategies. For example, Ford built collective emotional intelligence into their Lincoln Continental team (about 1,000 people and a $1 billion budget) that resulted in one of the first programs to meet or exceed all objectives.[103] In the service sector, Blue Cross Blue Shield uses an EI counseling/training approach to help their employees deal with change, emotionally charged work situations, and professional goals.[104] There are also applications of EI being made internationally. For example, EI training is conducted at both Hongkong Telecom and for Hong Kong government employees to better cope with and effectively resolve emotional issues and complaints.[105] Overall, there seems little doubt of the importance and applicability of EI in the workplace, but like the other positive psychology approaches to organizational behavior, there is a definite need for more theory development, valid measures, and especially, empirical research for the future.

SELF-EFFICACY

This final, but most theoretically developed and researched, positively-oriented psychological construct emerging for the field of organizational behavior is self-efficacy. It may also be most relevant, at least for this particular text on organizational behavior, because as was presented in Chapter 1, social cognitive theory serves both as the conceptual framework for this text and the theory from which self-efficacy is derived. It may be most important in this chapter because as Goleman himself states, self-efficacy is the underlying construct for both EI and, especially, optimism and Snyder says the same about his hope construct.[106] Largely due to the work of well-known psychologist Albert Bandura over the past three decades, self-efficacy has a widely acclaimed theoretical foundation,[107] an extensive body of knowledge gathered through basic research,[108] and proven effectiveness in a number of application areas, including the workplace.[109] After providing the meaning, process, and impact, the sources and development of self-efficacy are given attention, and finally, its application to human performance in organizations ends the chapter.

The Theoretical Background and Meaning of Self-Efficacy

Chapter 1 summarized Bandura's social cognitive theory (SCT). SCT incorporates both social/environmental and cognitive elements and the behaviors themselves. SCT explains psychological functioning in terms of environmental events; internal personal factors in the form of cognitive, affective, and biological variables; and behavioral patterns. These three (environment, personal cognitions, and behavior) operate as interacting determinants that influence one another bidirectionally. Embedded within SCT, along with the human's capabilities of symbolizing, forethought, and observational learning, is a self theory including both self-regulation and self-reflection. It is the capability for self-reflection—people reflect back on their actions/experience with a specific event/task to then cognitively process how strongly they believe they can successfully accomplish this event/task in the future—that serves as the theoretical basis for self-efficacy.[110]

Bandura strongly emphasizes that this self-efficacy is the most pervading and important of the psychological mechanisms of self-influence. He declares, "Unless people believe that they can produce desired effects and forestall undesired ones by their actions, they have little incentive to act. Whatever other factors may operate as motivators, they are rooted in the core belief that one has the power to produce desired results."[111]

The formal definition of self-efficacy that is usually used is Bandura's early statement of personal judgment or belief of "how well one can execute courses of action required to deal with prospective situations."[112] A somewhat broader, more workable definition for organizational behavior is provided by Stajkovic and Luthans: "*Self-efficacy* refers to an individual's conviction (or confidence) about his or her abilities to mobilize the motivation, cognitive resources, and courses of action needed to successfully execute a specific task within a given context."[113] Notice that this definition deals with efficacy on a specific task and context. To further clarify the exact meaning of self-efficacy as it is translated here for use in the organizational behavior field, specific versus general efficacy needs to be clarified. Earlier the differentiation between the various positive psychology constructs was briefly discussed, but the difference between self-efficacy and closely related established organizational behavior constructs such as self-esteem, expectancy motivation, and attribution/locus of control also needs to be addressed.

Specific versus General Self-Efficacy.   Specific self-efficacy follows Bandura's conceptualization and is widely recognized by almost all efficacy scholars and the psychology field as a whole.[114] In recent years, however, general self-efficacy has been used as another dimension of self-efficacy by a few efficacy researchers.[115] They suggest that in addition to specific self-efficacy, there is a generalized self-efficacy that reflects people's belief in successfully accomplishing tasks across a wide variety of achievement situations. It should be recognized that this generalized efficacy is quite different from Bandura's portrayal of self-efficacy. In particular, the accepted task specific version of self-efficacy is *statelike;* it is highly variable depending on the specific task and is cognitively processed by the individual before any effort is expended.

Bandura argues that self-efficacy represents a task and situation specific cognition.[116] On the other hand, general self-efficacy is conceptually the opposite; it is *traitlike.* That is, general efficacy is stable over time and across situations; in this regard it is like a personality trait.[117] Bandura contends with his years of theory building and basic research that "an efficacy belief is not a decontextualized trait."[118] However, Bandura and others point out that even though self-efficacy is not traitlike, this does not mean that specific self-efficacy evaluations never generalize.[119] Instead, although not necessarily stable across situations, efficacy judgments on one task may generalize to others depending on the situation, the task, and the person.

In summary, as presented here, self-efficacy is statelike and is aimed at specific tasks. For example, a systems analyst may have high self-efficacy on solving a particular programming problem, but low self-efficacy on writing up a report for the CIO (chief information officer) on how the problem was solved.

How Self-Efficacy Differs from Established Organizational Behavior Concepts.
At first glance self-efficacy appears very similar and is often confused with widely

recognized organizational behavior concepts, in particular, self-esteem (Chapter 7), expectancy motivation (Chapter 8), and attribution/locus of control (Chapter 6). A brief summary of the major differences will help clarify the exact meaning of self-efficacy.[120]

1. *Self-efficacy vs. self-esteem.*   Following from the preceding discussion of specific vs. general self-efficacy, there is no question that general self-efficacy is very similar to self-esteem, but the widely accepted specific self-efficacy as used here is quite different. The first difference is that self-esteem is a global construct of one's evaluation and belief of overall worthiness, whereas self-efficacy is one's belief about a task- and context-specific capability. Second, self-esteem is stable and traitlike, whereas self-efficacy is changing over time as new information and task experiences are gained and is statelike. Finally, self-esteem is aimed at any aspect of one's current self, whereas self-efficacy is a current assessment of one's future success at a task.[121] An example of the differences would be the salesperson who has high self-efficacy of selling a luxury item to low-income customers, but low self-esteem because he knows his career has been based on selling unneeded items to his customers and this takes away from their ability to buy some of the basic necessities for their families.

2. *Self-efficacy vs. expectancy concepts.*   Chapter 8 briefly discussed under expectancy theories of motivation the effort-performance (sometimes called E1) and behavior-outcome (sometimes referred to as E2) expectancy relationships. Although E1 and self-efficacy would both say that effort leads to performance, self-efficacy involves much more. Self-efficacy beliefs also involve perceptions of ability, skill, knowledge, experience with the specific task, complexity of the task, and more. In addition, self-efficacy has psychomotor reactions such as emotions, stress, and physical fatigue. With the E2 (behavior-outcome expectancy) there is even more pronounced differences. The process is different—efficacy is a judgment of one's ability to successfully execute a certain behavior pattern (i.e., "I believe I can successfully execute this task"), whereas the outcome expectancy is a judgment of the probable consequence such behavior will produce (i.e., "I believe that what I do will (or will not) lead to desired outcomes"). In other words, the individual's self-efficacy evaluation will usually come before any behavior outcome expectancies are even considered.[122]

3. *Self-efficacy vs. attribution/locus of control.*   The third close, but different, construct that is often confused with self-efficacy comes from attribution theory, specifically locus of control (see Chapter 6). Those who make internal attributions about their behavior and its consequences (success or failure) believe they are in control of their own fate (e.g., "It is my effort or ability that makes the difference") and assume personal responsibility for the consequences of their behavior. Externals, on the other hand, make attributions to the circumstances ("The task was too hard") or to luck and do not take personal responsibility for the consequences of their behavior. Bandura has argued that locus of control attributions are causal beliefs about action-outcome contingencies, whereas self-efficacy is an individual's belief about his or her abilities and cognitive resources that can be marshaled together to successfully execute a specific task.[123]

Although the differences outlined above may seem quite technical, they must be pointed out to make sure that self-efficacy is indeed a valid, independent construct and help clarify its exact meaning.

The Process and Impact of Self-Efficacy

The self-efficacy process affects human functioning not only directly, but has an indirect impact on other determinants as well. Directly, the self-efficacy process starts before individuals select their choices and initiate their effort. First, people tend to weigh, evaluate, and integrate information about their perceived capabilities. Importantly, this initial stage of the process has little to do with individuals' abilities or resources per se, but rather how they perceive or believe they can use these abilities and resources to accomplish the given task in this context. This evaluation/perception then leads to the expectations of personal efficacy which, in turn, determines:

1. The decision to perform the specific task in this context
2. The amount of effort that will be expended to accomplish the task
3. The level of persistence that will be forthcoming despite problems, disconfirming evidence, and adversity

In other words, from the preceding it can be seen that self-efficacy can directly affect:

1. *Choice behaviors* (e.g., decisions will be made based on how efficacious the person feels toward the options in, say, work assignments or even a career field)
2. *Motivational effort* (e.g., people will try harder and give more effort on tasks where they have high self-efficacy than those where the efficacy judgment is low)
3. *Perseverance* (e.g., those with high self-efficacy will bounce back, be resilient when meeting problems or even failure, whereas those with low self-efficacy tend to give up when obstacles appear)

In addition, there is research evidence that self-efficacy can also directly affect:[124]

4. *Facilitative thought patterns* (e.g., efficacy judgments influence self-talks such as those with high self-efficacy might say to themselves, "I know I can figure out how to solve this problem," whereas those with low self-efficacy might say to themselves, "I knew I couldn't do this, I don't have this kind of ability")
5. *Vulnerability to stress* (e.g., those with low self-efficacy tend to experience stress and burnout because they expect failure, whereas those with high self-efficacy enter into potential stressful situations with confidence and assurance and thus are able to resist stressful reactions)

These examples of the direct impact of self-efficacy on human functioning are right in line with high-performing individuals. Perhaps the best *profile of a high performer* on a given task would be the highly efficacious individual who really gets into the task (welcomes it and looks at it as a challenge); gives whatever effort it takes to successfully accomplish the task; perseveres when meeting obstacles, frustrations, or setbacks; has positive self-thoughts and talks; and is resistant to stress and burnout.

As if this high-performance profile is not enough, Bandura emphasizes that self-efficacy also plays a vital role in other important human performance determinants such as goal aspirations, the incentives in outcome expectations, and the perceived opportunities of a given project.[125] What level of goal is selected, how much effort is expended to reach the selected goal, and how one reacts/perseveres when problems are encountered in progressing toward the goal, all seem to be greatly affected by self-efficacy.[126] So does the outcome incentives people anticipate. Those with high self-efficacy expect to succeed and gain favorable, positive outcome incentives, whereas those with low self-efficacy expect to fail and conjure up negative outcome disincentives (i.e., "I won't get anything out of this anyway"). Especially relevant to strategy formulation, entrepreneurial start-ups, and struggling transitionary economies in postcommunist countries,[127] Bandura comments on the perceptions of opportunities as follows:

> People of high efficacy focus on the opportunities worth pursuing, and view obstacles as surmountable. Through ingenuity and perseverance they figure out ways of exercising some control even in environments of limited opportunities and many constraints. Those beset with self-doubts dwell on impediments which they view as obstacles over which they can exert little control, and easily convince themselves of the futility of effort. They achieve limited success even in environments that provide many opportunities.[128]

Whether direct or indirect through other processes, high self-efficacy is strongly related and very predictive of high performance. The extensive research solidly supports this conclusion. Not only does Bandura's seminal book on self-efficacy cite hundreds and hundreds of studies, but there are also a number of meta-analyses finding a strong positive relationship between self-efficacy and performance in different spheres of functioning under laboratory and naturalistic conditions.[129]

Sources of Self-Efficacy

Because Bandura has provided such a comprehensive, rich theoretical understanding, backed by years of research, there is common agreement on the principle sources of self-efficacy. Shown in Figure 9.1, it must be remembered from social cognitive theory that these four sources of efficacy only provide the raw data. The individual must select out, cognitively process, and self-reflect in order to integrate and use this information to make self-efficacy perceptual judgments and form beliefs. For example, the major input into self-efficacy of performance attainments, Bandura notes, "may vary depending on their interpretive biases, the difficulty of the task, how hard they worked at it, how much help they received, the conditions under which they performed, their emotional

FIGURE 9.1
The Major Sources of Information for Self-Efficacy

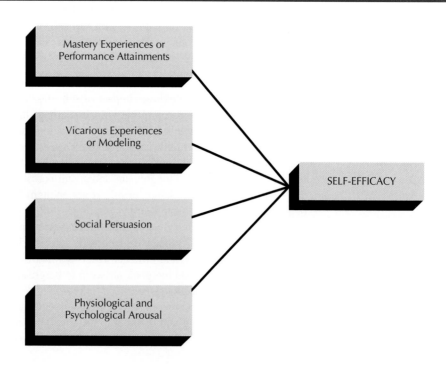

and physical state at the time, their rate of improvement over time, and selective biases in how they monitor and recall their attainments."[130]

In order of importance, the following briefly summarizes the major sources of information for self-efficacy:

1. *Mastery experiences or performance attainments.* This is potentially the most powerful for forming efficacy beliefs because it is direct information about success. However, once again, it should be emphasized that performance accomplishments do not directly equate with self-efficacy. Both situational (e.g., the complexity of the task) and cognitive processing (e.g., the perception of one's ability) concerning the performance will affect the self-efficacy judgment and belief. Bandura also points out that mastery experiences gained through perseverant effort and ability to learn form a strong and resilient sense of efficacy, but efficacy built from successes that came easily will not be characterized by much perseverance when difficulties arise and will change more quickly.[131]

2. *Vicarious experiences or modeling.* Just as individuals do not need to directly experience reinforced personal behaviors in order to learn (they can vicariously learn by observing and modeling relevant others who are reinforced), the same is true of acquiring efficacy. As stated by Bandura, "If people see others like themselves succeed by sustained effort, they come to believe that they, too, have the capacity to succeed. Conversely, observing the failure of others instills doubts about one's own ability to master similar activities."[132] It is important to emphasize that the more similar the model (e.g., demographics such as age, sex, physical characteristics, and education, as well as status and experience) and the more relevant the task being performed, the more effect there will be on the observer's efficacy processing. This vicarious source of information is particularly important for those with little direct experience (e.g., a new assignment) and as a practical strategy to enhance people's efficacy through training and development.

3. *Social persuasion.* Not as powerful a source of information as the previous two, and sometimes oversimplified as a "can-do" approach, people's belief in their efficacy can be strengthened by respected, competent others persuading them that they "have what it takes" on this particular task. On the other side of the coin, there is no question of the powerful impact that unkind words and negative feedback (e.g., "you can't do that") have in disabling and deflating one's confidence. Too often, a small negative comment or even nonverbal gesture can have a big impact on one's emotions and efficacy. Unfortunately, giving people positive feedback and pointing out their strengths for successfully accomplishing a task does not seem to be processed by most people with as much impact as the negative. However, by being genuine, providing objective information, and then taking follow-up actions to actually set up the individual for success and not failure, social persuasion can be selected and processed for building efficacy. Such social persuasion becomes more useful to fill in gaps when people begin to struggle or doubt themselves while pursuing a task than it is in trying to build one's efficacy for a new task.

4. *Physiological and psychological arousal.* People often rely on how they feel, physically and emotionally, in order to assess their capabilities. More than the other sources of information, if these are negative (e.g., the person is very tired and/or not physically well or is particularly anxious/depressed and/or feels under a lot of pressure) this will generally greatly detract from efficacy. On the other hand, if these physical and mental states are well off, they don't necessarily process as contributing much to the individual's efficacy. On balance, however, if the individual is

in excellent physical and mental condition, this can serve as a good point of departure to build efficacy other ways and may even in and of itself arouse a person's efficacy on a physically and/or psychologically demanding task.

Importantly for organizational behavior and human resource management, each of these sources of efficacy are highly malleable and changeable. As discussed earlier, specific self-efficacy is a state, not a trait. In other words, self-efficacy can definitely be enhanced through training and development targeted at these four sources. For example, as shown in Table 9.6, training expert Robert Mager has pinpointed specific training implications for each of the sources of self-efficacy. In fact, developing self-efficacy in trainees may be a solution to the long-standing problem of transferring training to the job. As Mager notes,

> People need a strong sense of efficacy before they will *try* to apply what they have learned and before they will try to learn new things. Belief in their ability to perform makes them less vulnerable to on-the-job conditions that aren't always supportive. It helps them to survive rejection. It helps them to persevere in the face of obstacles and setbacks.[133]

Self-efficacy not only has these important implications for training, but also for many other areas of today's workplace as well.

TABLE **9.6**   Implications of Self-Efficacy for Effective Training

Sources of Efficacy	*Key for Successful Training and Transfer to the Job*	*Training Recommendations*
1. **Mastery experience and performance attainment**	Trainees must learn they are the cause of their performance.	1. Plenty of practice so mastery (as defined by the training objectives) is reached. 2. Break learning into series of obtainable end points to help self-confirmation of skills. 3. Provide feedback on progress (not shortfalls) and contributions.
2. **Vicarious experience and modeling**	Model(s) used should have similar demographic attributes, and the training being done should be similar to what the trainees will be doing back on the job.	1. Carefully select models used in the training to have similar characteristics as the trainees. 2. Set up training so that trainees perceive performance is due to the capability of the model and not other factors. 3. Models should take a task-diagnostic perspective (i.e., focus on task and if mistake is made, interpret as way to learn rather than personal inadequacy).
3. **Social persuasion**	All comments have impact, so feedback must be phrased positively to build trainee confidence.	1. Set trainees up for success so feedback comments can be very positive. 2. Trainers must be careful and sensitive to keep positive things that are said and done in the presence of the trainee.
4. **Physical and psychological arousal**	Make sure trainees experiencing physical or psychological symptoms interpret them as the nature of the training task and not some personal inadequacy (i.e., lack of ability).	1. Trainees must understand that the need to exert considerable physical (or psychological) effort does not mean a lack of personal capability. 2. Getting trainees physically and psychologically fit may help arouse motivation to learn and be successful.

Source: Adapted from Robert F. Mager, "No Self-Efficacy, No Performance," *Training,* April 1992, pp. 34–36.

Implications for Self-Efficacy in the Workplace

Self-efficacy theory was first used over 25 years ago as a clinical framework "for analyzing changes achieved in fearful and avoidant behavior."[134] Psychotherapeutic treat-
ments such as desensitization, symbolic modeling, and firsthand mastery experiences
were clearly found to change behavior of clients through the common pathway of
perceived self-efficacy. However, the scope of self-efficacy quickly broadened beyond
this domain of clinical behavior change to be successfully applied in areas such as:
(1) the promotion of health and recovery from physical setbacks, (2) the control of eating, (3) resistance to addictive substances, (4) educational achievement, (5) athletic performance, and, importantly (6) for the study and application of organizational behavior
and performance in work settings.[135]

As previously noted, whereas the other positive psychology constructs have to date
relatively few research studies in the workplace, self-efficacy has a very well established
body of knowledge as to its applicability and positive impact on work-related performance.
Specifically, our (Stajkovic and Luthans) meta-analysis included 114 studies and 21,616
subjects.[136] The results indicated a highly significant .38 weighted average correlation between self-efficacy and work-related performance (see the OB principle based on this
meta-analysis at the end of this chapter for more details). When converted to the commonly used affect size estimate used in meta-analysis, the transformed value represents a
28 percent increase in performance due to self-efficacy.[137] By comparison, these results for
self-efficacy in the workplace represent a greater average gain in performance than the results from the meta-analyses of other popular organizational behavior interventions such as
goal setting (10.39%),[138] feedback (13.6%),[139] or organizational behavior modification
(17%),[140] and also seems to be a better predictor of work-related performance than the personality traits (e.g., the "Big Five") or relevant attitudes (e.g., job satisfaction or organizational commitment) commonly used in organizational behavior research.[141]

Although the workplace is given considerable attention in Bandura's 1997 book,
Self-Efficacy,[142] more recently he provided a focused review of the growing research literature of the direct and indirect impact that self-efficacy has on work-related personal
and organizational effectiveness.[143] This research review of the impact of self-efficacy
includes a wide range of organizational behavior topics such as career choice and development, new employee training, work design/job enrichment, supportive communication, teams (i.e., collective efficacy), innovation, entrepreneurship, leadership, and
stress. He then devotes considerable attention to the strategies and principles for developing and strengthening beliefs of personal efficacy in the workplace.

From this considerable body of theory and research on self-efficacy, the following
sections offer some practical implications and specific guidelines for the more effective
practice of managing human performance in today's and tomorrow's organizations.

Selection of Human Resources.   In hiring for a particular job, making an assignment to
a specific project, or promoting someone into an identifiable area of responsibility, assessing the person's present magnitude and strength of self-efficacy could be valuable input
into the selection decision. *Magnitude* measures the level of task difficulty that a person
believes he or she is capable of executing and *strength* indicates whether the magnitude
is strong and likely to produce perseverance when difficulties are encountered.[144]

Although most applicable to specific tasks within a job assignment or promotion,
self-efficacy scales could be set up for each of the major tasks or for the overall domain
of a given job. This scale would include, in ascending order, items that represent the
increasing levels of difficulty. The respondent would check for each item yes or

Number of Car Sales per month	Yes or No	Strength of Certainty (0–100%)
I believe I can sell 2		
I believe I can sell 4		
I believe I can sell 6		
I believe I can sell 8		
I believe I can sell 10		
I believe I can sell 12		
I believe I can sell 14		
I believe I can sell 16		
Totals		

FIGURE 9.2

An Example of a Self-Efficacy Scale Developed for an Auto Sales Position

no (magnitude) and then next to it 0–100% probability of attainment (i.e., strength). Figure 9.2 shows such a scale. The efficacy scores are derived by getting a total of the probability strengths for each item with a yes. This so-called Composite I method of scoring has been shown to be a valid measure of self-efficacy and more reliable than other measures.[145]

If regular questionnaire item scales are developed, they should be tailor-made for each specific selection purpose. Bandura advises that the content of such scales "must represent beliefs about personal abilities to produce specified levels of performance, and must not include other characteristics."[146] Of course, people should not be selected based only on their present self-efficacy assessment, but because it has been found to be such a good predictor of performance, self-efficacy could make a significant contribution to the selection process. This assessment could also be used as a training and development needs analysis.

Training and Development.   As discussed previously (see Table 9.6), because self-efficacy is a state (rather than a stable trait) and the sources have been identified (see Figure 9.1 and accompanying discussion), efficacy training and development can have considerable impact for employee performance management. Training can be set up around each (and in combination) of the sources of efficacy listed in Table 9.6.

Bandura recently categorized his approach to training and development into three areas.[147] First is what he calls *guided mastery,* which includes instructive modeling to acquire a skill or competency, guided skill perfection, and then transfering the training back to the job to insure self-directed success. Second, is for the more complex, but increasingly common for all levels in the modern workplace, ways to enhance efficacy for decision making and problem solving. He calls this *cognitive mastery modeling* to learn thinking skills and how to apply them by observing the decision rules and reasoning strategies successful models use as they arrive at solutions to problems and make effective decisions. For example, one study taught managers how to generate ideas to improve the quality of organizational functioning and customer service by providing them guidelines and practice in innovative problem solving.[148] Finally, he suggests the *development of self-regulatory competencies* (i.e., self-motivation or self-management). The development of this increasingly important self-management involves a variety of interlinked self-referent processes such as self-monitoring, self-efficacy appraisal, personal goal setting, and use of self-motivating incentives.[149] Whether using the more pragmatic training aimed at enhancing the four sources discussed earlier (Table 9.6

summarizes) or these more sophisticated approaches suggested by Bandura, there is proven effectiveness of this training and development of self-efficacy,[150] and the potential for the future seems unlimited.

Other Applications.   Besides selection and training/development, self-efficacy also has implications for stress management (Chapter 12), self-managed teams (Chapter 14), job design and goal setting (Chapter 15), and leadership (Chapters 17 and 18). One applications approach would be to enhance self-efficacy to better cope with stress[151] and facilitate productive teamwork[152] and collective efficacy[153] of self-managed teams. Another approach would be to use job designs that provide more responsibility, challenge, and empowered personal control over the work to enhance the jobholder's perception of self-efficacy.[154] In setting goals, goal difficulty and commitment will be affected by self-efficacy. By the same token, goal progress and attainment will in turn affect self-efficacy.[155]

Perhaps at least potentially the most significant, but still largely overlooked, implication for application lies in leadership efficacy. Although the importance of a leader's confidence has been recognized in the leadership literature over the years,[156] to date there has been very few attempts to measure and research the proposition drawn from self-efficacy theory and research presented here,[157] that leadership efficacy will have a strong positive impact on followers (e.g., the leader can serve as a model to enhance followers' self-efficacy) and performance outcomes. In conclusion, self-efficacy has implications for most of the remaining chapters in both Part 3, The Dynamics of Organizational Behavior, and Part 4, Managing and Leading for High Performance.

Summary

This chapter is concerned with three important positively-oriented psychological variables that have been around the field of psychology for awhile but are just emerging in organizational behavior—optimism, emotional intelligence, and self-efficacy. Most closely related to the recent positive psychology movement is optimism. Although optimism has been around for a long time and is associated with many positive things in life, its use as a psychological construct and its application to the workplace are relatively recent. Both motivated and motivating, optimism has some evidence not only of being part of human nature, but also more support for contributing to individual differences. The pioneering work of Seligman treats optimism in terms of cognitively determined expectancies and causal attributions (i.e., explanatory style). Specifically, pessimists make internal, stable, and global attributions of bad events, whereas optimists make external, unstable, and specific attributions. Although there can be some dysfunctional consequences such as stress from pursuing unattainable goals and there are some cases where a mild pessimist may be needed in organizations (e.g., safety engineer or accountant), in general, realistic optimism is very beneficial in life and in the workplace. Research is just starting, but evidence from Seligman's extensive work with sales agents at Metropolitan Life indicates the very positive impact that optimism can have on human performance in organizations.

Besides optimism, in the positive psychology movement, the closely related concepts of hope and happiness/subjective well-being (SWB). As used in psychology and its potential applicability to organizational behavior, hope is more than the sunny advice of "hope for the best." Although both Goleman and Seligman talk about hope in relation to EI and optimism respectively, the work of Snyder on hope as a stand alone construct is most recognized. He defines hope not only in terms of the person's determination that goals can be achieved, but also as the beliefs that successful plans can be formulated, pathways identified, and self-motivation exhibited in order to attain the goals. There has been such strong evidence of the relationship between hope and academic, athletic, and mental/physical health positive outcomes that the carryover to the workplace seems very promising for the future. The same is true of happiness or what positive psychologists prefer to call subjective well-being or SWB. Unlike hope, there have been some work-related studies in the SWB research literature. In particular, the work of Diener is most closely associated with SWB. As with the other positive constructs in this chapter, he is concerned with the underlying processes that influence life satisfaction, satisfaction with important domains (including work satisfaction), positive affect, and low levels of negative affect. Particular attention is given to the processes of personality, goals, adaptation, and coping. Unlike the other constructs, SWB has been extensively researched across cultures. As a domain of SWB, there have been studies related to work and the workplace. In particular, it has been found that SWB is a significant predictor of job satisfaction, and unemployment causes lower SWB.

Emotional intelligence or simply EI is first discussed in terms of its major components of emotion (feelings) and intelligence. Intelligence in particular has played a very minor role in organizational behavior. If recognized at all, the old, fixed dimensions of mathematical/logical and verbal/linguistic were assumed. The multiple intelligences, and emotional intelligence in particular, have only recently received attention. Broadly popularized by Goleman, EI is the capacity for understanding and managing one's own and others' emotions. There is increasing evidence that the characteristics of EI (e.g., self-awareness, self-motivation, empathy, and social skills) are not only superior to traditional IQ in predicting future life success, but in the workplace may also have considerable untapped potential for successful performance.

The last third of the chapter is devoted to the theory, research, and application of self-efficacy. The most comprehensive positively-oriented approach, social cognitive theory, posits that environmental, behavioral, and personal cognitive dimensions are in interaction and the self-reflective human capacity serves as the major theoretical underpinning of self-efficacy. Defined as the belief one has in his or her abilities to mobilize the motivation, cognitive resources, and courses of action necessary to successfully execute a specific task within a given context, self-efficacy is a state, not a trait. Through this theory building and extensive research of Bandura, four major sources of information to cognitively determine self-efficacy have been identified. These are, in order of importance, mastery experiences or performance attainments, vicarious experience or modeling, social persuasion, and physiological or psychological (emotional) arousal. Each of these can be used in training and development to enhance self-efficacy. Self-efficacy started off as a clinical technique to change client behavior, but soon was successfully applied to many other health, educational, and athletic pursuits. Unlike the other positively-oriented constructs, there is also a considerable research-derived body of knowledge on the strong positive relationship between self-efficacy and work-related performance. The Stajkovic and Luthans meta-analysis (114 studies, 21,616 subjects) found a highly significant .38 weighted average correlation that transforms to an impressive 28 percent gain in performance (higher than the results of meta-analyses of other popular organizational behavior interventions). With such substantial theory and research backup, there are important implications for effective practical applications of self-efficacy. Besides training and development to enhance self-efficacy and thus help the transfer of training to the job and increase performance, the measurement of self-efficacy could be used in the selection process. Self-efficacy can also be used to make job design, goal setting, teams, and stress management more effective. In total, as this chapter clearly indicates, the time has come for a positive psychology approach to join the mainstream of organizational behavior theory, research, and practice.

ENDING WITH META-ANALYTIC RESEARCH FINDINGS

OB PRINCIPLE: The higher employees' self-efficacy on a specific task, the better they
will perform.

Meta-Analysis Results: [114 studies; 21,616 participants; $d = .82$] *On average, there is a **72 percent probability** that employees with high self-efficacy on a specific task will have better performance than those with low self-efficacy.* The moderators found in the meta-analysis were task complexity and the setting for the study. Specifically, it was found that the more complex the task, the less, but still highly significant, impact self-efficacy will have on performance. Also, self-efficacy had a bigger impact in the studies conducted in laboratory settings than those in the field.

Conclusion: Although the positively-oriented constructs are becoming increasingly popular and important in the study and application of organizational behavior, to date, only self-efficacy has enough research to conduct a meta-analysis applicable to an OB principle. There seems little question that self-efficacy has become one of the very best predictors of human performance. In today's work environment characterized by uncertainty, change, and complex undertakings, organizations will be challenged to do their part in increasing employees' beliefs in their personal competence so that organizational performance goals can be realized. In addition to self-efficacy, the positive psychology constructs of optimism, hope, subjective well-being and emotional intelligence also show considerable promise for the understanding and effective application of organizational behavior.

Source: Adapted from Alexander D. Stajkovic and Fred Luthans, "The Relationship between Self-Efficacy and Work-Related Performance: A Meta-Analysis," *Psychological Bulletin,* Vol. 124, No.2, 1998, pp. 240–261.

Questions for Discussion and Review

1. How does optimism in positive psychology go beyond the old "power of positive thinking"? Give an example of where "little optimism" may be different from "big optimism." Besides sales, give an example of where optimism may be very beneficial to work performance.

2. In positive psychology, how does the concept of hope go beyond "sunny advice"? Why is the statement made in the discussion of hope that it may be particularly relevant to entrepreneurship and international human resource management?

3. What is subjective well-being (SWB)? What were some of the findings when SWB was studied across cultures? How do you explain the somewhat unusual findings?

4. What is an emotion? How do emotions differ from moods? Identify some primary emotions and give examples of how they may be expressed in the workplace.

5. What are Gardner's original seven intelligences? Which two are the most closely associated with traditional IQ? What are the three "new" intelligences? Which of the 10 do you feel are most relevant and important to an effective manager?

6. Very simply, what is emotional intelligence (EI)? What are the major dimensions of EI that are particularly relevant to the workplace? Why do you think EI may be more important than IQ for an effective manager?

7. What is self-efficacy? Why is it important to make the distinction that self-efficacy is a state rather than a trait? What implications does this have for the workplace?

8. Defend or argue against the statement that the characteristics of a highly efficacious employee may be "the best profile of a high performer." What is this profile and give an example of this in the workplace?

9. What are the four widely recognized sources of self-efficacy? How could each be used to enhance employee efficacy to increase performance?

10. Of the positive psychological constructs that are emerging for organizational behavior, which one do you think has the most potential for impacting employee performance? Why?

Internet Exercise: What is your IQ and EQ?

A good way to understand the value and the power of psychological variables is to first understand yourself. By first understanding yourself, you can better understand others. To compare and contrast your IQ with your EQ, there are a few such tests on the Web. Remembering that these are not scientifically valid and that you should only take them as interesting information and not too seriously, go to http://www.queendom.com for some cognitive exercises including an IQ test. To assess your emotional quotient, visit http://www.utne.com/azEq2.tmpl. This site has a short, multiple-choice assessment tool that is scored electronically. Following the test, be sure to read the detailed description of each answer.

1. Did the results surprise you? Considering that EQ can be learned, are there any areas you should try to improve on?

2. How do you think your close coworkers and/or friends would respond to these tests? Does that help you understand their behaviors better?

3. Do you agree with the text discussion that EQ (EI) may be more important than IQ and may be applicable to effective interpersonal relations and performance in the workplace? Why?

REAL CASE:
High Tech—High
Fear

Both the popular and academic press proclaim how wonderful advanced technology is for today's organizations. For example, B2B (business to business) processes can dramatically cut a firm's costs. Cisco reports that a quarter of its orders used to have to be reworked because of errors in its phone and fax ordering system. When the firm changed to online ordering, the error rate fell to 2 percent, representing a whopping savings of $500 million. In financial services, there is a seamless relationship between the various functions. There is also much publicity touting how online commerce can cut out layers of people for more efficient supply-chain management. Then there is e-tailing, which has completely streamlined and reduced the cost of the infrastructure of selling to customers. Even though the stock prices of e-businesses have proved to be highly volatile, the competitive advantages of e-business go on and on.

The other side, the dark side of this high tech revolution, however, is seldom mentioned. Although young employees who grew up with computers in their schools and homes may be adaptable and open to IT changes in the workplace, and certainly some middle-age and older employees at all levels welcome and are excited by the IT challenges, a significant number, if not most, of today's employees of all ages are not only resistant, but downright terrified. With the dramatic changes brought on by the new technological environment, today's employees have been thrust into a whole range of emotional reactions, from surprise to fear to anger to even shame. Competent, secure employees who were very optimistic and efficacious about their job duties in the old economy have become pessimistic and questioning of their abilities and cognitive resources necessary to be successful in this new high tech environment.

Here is a recent list of human problems associated with the advent of advanced technology in today's organizations:

1. Feelings of being overwhelmed, intimidated, and ashamed of not being able to keep up with job demands.
2. Some employees' belief that they are actually being enslaved, not empowered, by new technology.
3. Fears of appearing inept, unintelligent, or resistant to change.
4. A diminished ability to solve problems, fostering a sense of hopelessness and worry.
5. Loss of respect by the boss, peers, and subordinates.
6. Physiological disturbances brought on by longer hours, time pressures, and even hormone shifts brought on by being physically isolated.
7. Mood swings, depression, exhaustion, and attention deficits.

Obviously, these feelings, beliefs, fears, and physical/mental dysfunctions are taking their toll on the people affected, but there also may be an impact on quality, productivity, and retention.

1. What are the trade-offs in today's organizations between the positives and negatives of advanced technology? Does it really matter if some of the older employees are having a hard time adjusting; aren't they on their way out anyway and they can be replaced by the technology? On balance, what do you feel about the impact of technology?
2. In the "dark side" of IT presented in this case, there are many implications for optimism, hope, SWB, emotional intelligence and self-efficacy. Describe a specific example of each of these positive psychology constructs.
3. In general, how can the understanding of the positive constructs help overcome the list of problems presented in the case? How can the manager of a unit consisting of mostly older, computer-illiterate employees, who were very effective under the old system, use these concepts to make a more successful transition to a new, technologically sophisticated operating system?

ORGANIZATIONAL BEHAVIOR CASE: People Problems at HEI	After graduating with honors with a management major from State University, Ashley James accepted an entry-level position in the Human Resources Department of Hospital Equipment Inc. (HEI), a medium-sized manufacturer of hospital beds and metal furniture (bedstands, tables, cabinets, etc.). This hospital room product line has been a "cash cow" for HEI since the founding of the firm 35 years ago by James Robinson, Sr. In recent years, however, HEI's market share has become eroded by some of the big office furniture firms, both in the United States and abroad, who are starting to diversify into the health institution market.

Mr. Robinson has been easing into retirement the last couple of years. His only child, Rob, was made CEO three months ago. Rob came up through product engineering for two years and then headed up operations for the past four years. Rob had been a three-sport star athlete and student body president in high school. He then went on to State University where he graduated near the top of his class in mechanical engineering.

In his new leadership role at HEI, Rob's vision is to take the firm from being a low-tech bed and metal furniture manufacturer that is going downhill to become a high-tech medical equipment manufacturer. Rob is convinced that even though this would be a dramatic change for HEI, there is enough of a foundation and culture in place to at least start a new division focused initially on operating room equipment.

Rob's marketing manager had commissioned a study with a marketing research firm that concluded operating room equipment supply was not keeping up with demand and was way behind the rest of the health care supply industry in terms of innovative technology for patient comfort and care. The marketing manager, armed with this information, enthusiastically supported Rob's vision for the future of HEI. The finance and operations people are another story. The finance manager is very pessimistic. HEI is already under a cash flow strain because of decreasing revenues from their existing product line and, although they currently have very little long-term debt, with Robinson senior retiring, his contacts and long-term friends in the local lending community were gone. Only the big corporate banks with decision makers in other cities are left. The new head of operations, who has been very close to Robinson senior over the years and had basically run the show for Rob the past four years, is also very pessimistic. In a recent executive committee meeting where Rob had asked for input on his vision for HEI, this operations head angrily blurted out, "I know we have to do something! But medical equipment? I have absolutely no hope that our engineers or operating people have the capacity to move in this direction. As you know, almost all of our people have been with us at least 15 to 20 years. They are too set in their ways, and the only way we could start a new medical equipment division would be from scratch, and I certainly don't see the funding for that!"

After weighing his senior management team's advice, consulting with his dad, doing some research on his own, and tapping his network of friends in and outside the industry, Rob decided to go ahead with the planning of a new medical equipment division. He also decided that this new division would have to be run by present people and he would seek no outside funding. At this point, he called in the young Ashley James from the HR department and gave her the following assignment:

> Ashley, I know you haven't been around here very long, but I think you can handle the challenge that I am going to give you. As you probably know by now, HEI is having some difficulties, and I have decided we need to move in a new direction with a medical equipment division. As I see it, we have some real people problems to overcome before this will be a success. Having worked in operations the past several years, I am convinced we have enough raw talent in both engineering and at the operating level to make the transition and pull this off successfully. But I need your help. Did you come across anything in your program at State U. that had to do with getting people to be more positive, more optimistic, and confident? I really think this is the problem, starting with management and going right down the line. I want you to take a week to think about this, talk to everyone involved, do some research, and come back with a specific proposal of what HR can do to help me out on this. The very survival of HEI may depend on what you come up with.

1. Based on the limited information in this case, how would you assess the optimism, hope, EI, and self-efficacy of Rob? Of the operations manager? Give some specifics to back your assessment. What implications do these assessments have for the future of HEI?
2. What's your reaction to the finance manager's pessimism? What about the market manager's optimism? What implications does this have for Rob and the company?
3. Do you agree with Rob's decision? Would you like to work for him? Why or why not?
4. If you were Ashley, what specific proposal would you make to Rob? How would you implement such a proposal?

EXPERIENTIAL EXERCISES FOR PART 2

EXERCISE: Self-Perception and Development of the Self-Concept*

Goals:

1. To enable the students to consider their own self-concepts and to compare this with how they feel they are perceived by others.
2. To explore how the self-concept in personality is formed largely on the basis of feedback received from others (the reality that we "mirror ourselves in others").
3. To stimulate student thinking about how management of human resources may involve perception and personality.

Implementation:

1. The students take out a sheet of paper and fold it in half from top to bottom.
2. The students write "How I See Myself" and "How I Think Others See Me."
3. The students write down five one-word descriptions (adjectives) under each designation that, in their opinion, best describe how they perceive themselves and how others perceive them.
4. The students then share their two lists with their classmates (in dyads, triads, or the whole class) and discuss briefly. Each person may communicate what he or she is most proud of.
5. The instructor may participate in the exercise by sharing his or her list of adjectives.

*The exercise "Self-Perception and Development of the Self-Concept" was suggested by Philip Van Auken and is used with his permission.

EXERCISE: Motivation Questionnaire*

Goals:

1. To experience firsthand the concepts of one of the work-motivation theories—in this case, the popular Maslow hierarchy of needs.
2. To get personal feedback on your opinions of the use of motivational techniques in human resource management.

Implementation:

The following questions for the Motivation Questionnaire on the next page have seven possible responses:

1. Please mark one of the seven responses by circling the number that corresponds to the response that fits your opinion. For example, if you "strongly agree," circle the number "+3."
2. Complete every item. You have about 10 minutes to do so.

*The "Motivation Questionnaire" is reprinted from "Motivation: A Feedback Exercise," in John E. Jones and J. William Pfeiffer (eds.), *The Annual Handbook for Group Facilitators,* University Associates, San Diego, Calif., 1973, pp. 43–45, and is used with permission.

	Strongly Agree	Agree	Slightly Agree	Don't Know	Slightly Disagree	Disagree	Strongly Disagree
	+3	+2	+1	0	−1	−2	−3
1. Special wage increases should be given to employees who do their jobs very well.	+3	+2	+1	0	−1	−2	−3
2. Better job descriptions would be helpful so that employees will know exactly what is expected of them.	+3	+2	+1	0	−1	−2	−3
3. Employees need to be reminded that their jobs are dependent on the company's ability to compete effectively.	+3	+2	+1	0	−1	−2	−3
4. Supervisors should give a good deal of attention to the physical working conditions of their employees.	+3	+2	+1	0	−1	−2	−3
5. Supervisors ought to work hard to develop a friendly working atmosphere among their people.	+3	+2	+1	0	−1	−2	−3
6. Individual recognition for above-standard performance means a lot to employees.	+3	+2	+1	0	−1	−2	−3
7. Indifferent supervision can often bruise feelings.	+3	+2	+1	0	−1	−2	−3
8. Employees want to feel that their real skills and capacities are put to use on their jobs.	+3	+2	+1	0	−1	−2	−3
9. The company retirement benefits and stock programs are important factors in keeping employees on their jobs.	+3	+2	+1	0	−1	−2	−3
10. Almost every job can be made more stimulating and challenging.	+3	+2	+1	0	−1	−2	−3
11. Many employees want to give their best in everything they do.	+3	+2	+1	0	−1	−2	−3
12. Management could show more interest in the employees by sponsoring social events after hours.	+3	+2	+1	0	−1	−2	−3
13. Pride in one's work is actually an important reward.	+3	+2	+1	0	−1	−2	−3
14. Employees want to be able to think of themselves as "the best" at their own jobs.	+3	+2	+1	0	−1	−2	−3
15. The quality of the relationships in the informal work group is quite important.	+3	+2	+1	0	−1	−2	−3
16. Individual incentive bonuses would improve the performance of employees.	+3	+2	+1	0	−1	−2	−3
17. Visibility with upper management is important to employees.	+3	+2	+1	0	−1	−2	−3
18. Employees generally like to schedule their own work and to make job-related decisions with a minimum of supervision.	+3	+2	+1	0	−1	−2	−3
19. Job security is important to employees.	+3	+2	+1	0	−1	−2	−3
20. Having good equipment to work with is important to employees.	+3	+2	+1	0	−1	−2	−3

Scoring:

1. Transfer the numbers you circled in the questionnaire to the appropriate places in the following chart.

Statement No.	Score	Statement No.	Score
10	_____	2	_____
11	_____	3	_____
13	_____	9	_____
18	_____	19	_____
Total	_____	Total	_____
(Self-actualization needs)		(Safety needs)	
6	_____	1	_____
8	_____	4	_____
14	_____	16	_____
17	_____	20	_____
Total	_____	Total	_____
(Esteem needs)		(Basic needs)	
5	_____		
7	_____		
12	_____		
15	_____		
Total	_____		
(Belongingness needs)			

2. Record your total scores in the following chart by marking an *X* in each row below the number of your total score for that area of needs motivation.

	−12	−10	−8	−6	−4	−2	0	+2	+4	+6	+8	+10	+12
Self-actualization													
Esteem													
Belongingness													
Safety													
Basic													

Low
use

High
use

By examining the chart, you can see the relative strength you attach to each of the needs in Maslow's hierarchy. There are no right answers here, but most work-motivation theorists imply that most people are concerned mainly with the upper-level needs (that is, belongingness, esteem, and self-actualization).

PART THREE

Dynamics of Organizational Behavior

Consulting Best Practices

Gallup's Approach to the Dynamics of Organizational Behavior: The Use of Talent of Team

For Gallup, the first issue for the dynamics of organizational behavior is that the team be lead by an individual who has the right talent for the role. Among other talents, the team leader should have the talent we refer to as "team." In many situations, "teamwork" is a matter of belief, value, or policy. But if leaders are not "team leaders," the policies and beliefs about teamwork will be less than optimal. Certain individuals have this knack, or talent, to put people together so that the whole is greater than the sum of the parts. There is an essential leadership, talent issue at the center of a truly successful team practice.

The best teams are created when the unique talents of each individual are brought together for the desired outcome. Teams are not always more productive than individuals working separately. In Gallup's approach, the best teams are paradoxically related to the right way to handle individuals. To have a great team, each member of the team needs to have a self-awareness of their own best contribution to the team and an assurance that others know that their primary contributions are related to these talents. In this way, each member is attentive to his or her best contribution to and for the team. It is also true that team members do not labor under inappropriate expectations derived from the leader, teammates, or self. Put another way, people expect the best from me and the best for me, and in this way one is best positioned to respond in a successful manner.

In Gallup's research experience, teams built around issues of "fairness," each one gets their turn at every thing, will, by definition, create a more *average* performance. Teams built around "getting along" (personality) will tend to define success in terms of how "conflict free" their process is, aside from the fact it does not necessarily relate to increased productivity. These approaches, though common, may be more a reflection of the needs and limitations of the managers than they are adequate approaches to effective team building and improved performance.

Gallup has found that great team leaders pay attention to the difference in the talents that individuals bring to the table. Some people love to get things started. These same people frequently are bored with things long before they are finished. Their joy in life is "making things happen." Often these individuals are less interested in "permission" than "action." Often seen as "fire starters," they can be used well by moving them from team to team, timing their arrival at the point where the "analytical types" have things well in hand and are about to pass over into the paralysis of reanalyzing the analysis. Let the high-focus, detail people do cleanup operations. Such organizational behavior dynamics are talent based and create the greatest positive effect when people are encouraged to utilize their impact, rather than ignoring or actually seeking to thwart such inclinations. In a great "team," individuals are set up for success according to their strengths.

CHAPTER 10

Communication

Learning Objectives

Relate the perspective, historical background, and meaning of the communication process in organizations.

Describe modern communication technology.

Identify the dimensions of nonverbal communication.

Discuss the specific downward, upward, and horizontal (interactive) interpersonal communication processes.

Analyze communication across cultures.

Starting with Best Practice
Leader's Advice

Cisco Systems CEO John Chambers on Meeting Communication Challenges

Cisco, the well-known computer-networking equipment firm, has had its ups and downs in recent years, but continues to diversify into high-tech fields, such as fiber-optics communication equipment. However, because Cisco operates in such a dynamic industry where volatile markets are the norm, questions have been raised about its ability to continue to communicate and hold everything together at such a fast rate of change. Widely admired Cisco CEO John Chambers offers some of his valuable insights and experience on effective communication.

Q1:   *How do you manage differently today than when you took over in 1995?*

Chambers: Part of the answer may surprise you. A lot of the basics haven't changed. The approach that we started in '93 was one of segmenting the market, being number 1 and number 2 in each segment and each product area . . . and [devising] our strategy to make that happen . . . [We were] very much focused on how we used systems to gain competitive advantage and allow the scaling of the company to cookie-cut ideas. . . . We're not to the point where we actually can scale pretty rapidly. . . . It might surprise you, but there isn't a lot of difference . . . if you manage—let me use the term "lead" as opposed to "manage"—if you lead that way, whether you're 2,000 people, 20,000 or 100,000 people.

Q2:   *How does it work?*

Chambers: When a network is unstable, that's a critical A. When a network has the potential of becoming unstable and we've got to watch it, that's a B. So I get a report on all critical A accounts in the world. Now the fact that we focus on it so heavily helps us to resolve it quicker, but also helps us to prevent it. So I get a report each evening on anywhere from zero to 15 [accounts]. If there are only a few, then probably we haven't made enough new boxes out there. If it begins to get up to double digits, then we've got a customer-satisfaction issue coming our way. . . .

Then we pay every manager on customer satisfaction. It's amazing how that works. Once you say it's going to be part of their compensation, people say, "This must really be important," and secondly, "John's going to ask me about it all the time." And for either reason, they respond very well.

In our most recent survey, [customer-satisfaction scores] went up tremendously around the world. [There is a] one-to-one correlation between customer satisfaction and future revenues and profits.

The problem is that it lags 12 to 24 months, which is why most American companies don't pay as much attention to it as I believe they should.

Q3:   *With so many employees, how do you stay in touch with the front lines?*

Chambers: Well, probably if you add time together with the customers and with our own employees, that's probably 70 percent of my time. And sometimes they overlap. When you call on your customers, you're often with your local team. . . . I rank [each VP and senior VP] each quarter, top to bottom, about how many [customer] visits did they participate in and what their evaluation [was] from the customers.

Q4:   *Do you still meet with groups of frontline employees every month?*

Chambers: The birthday breakfasts are probably the most valuable sessions I do with employees. Once a month, anybody who has a birthday in that month can come and quiz [me] for about an hour and a half, and anything is fair game. We deliberately asked directors and VPs not to participate so that people who I don't get a chance normally to listen to can participate. And every single time I learn two or three things that either I need to do differently, or things that I thought were working one way weren't.

But again, it's building the culture. You want to lead by example. If you do that as a CEO, that will filter down through the leadership style of your team, where they'll do meetings with their employees and listen to their team.

Q5:   *How do you keep track of Cisco's diverse products and customers?*

Chambers: This is where the Web-based architecture is so key, because I can see an automatic roll-up [summary] of customer satisfaction very quickly any time I want. I can see an automatic roll-up of every order around the world and explode that down, not just by key geographies, and I look at every geography every day. So I look at my four key theaters, then I can explode it down to if I want to see by country or by city or by key customer, even down to an individual sales rep. . . . And then we, I, listen to constructive criticism probably more, not probably, definitely a lot more than you do compliments. Compliments are nice and I always need them, but I really listen to what we need to do better very, very carefully.

[The key is] how do you put a lot of the day-to-day activities down one layer, and then over time down two, and then over time down three? And now the decisions that [once] would have come to the CEO might be made by the first-line manager.

So for example . . . margins. Very often at the end of a quarter I might have realized that we had a problem in one of our product lines, that we didn't meet our margin expectations on it. Well, today the first-line manager can see who has responsibility for that product, either in engineering or in manufacturing [and] that the second week into the quarter our margins aren't in line with what we expected. They can explode that information down because of our use of Web-based architecture to understand exactly [what happened]: Are we discounting too heavily again? Is it because we're seeing more competition on a global basis, therefore we had to adjust, price-wise? . . . You can explode out your orders that are in the process so you can see: Will it correct itself or is it something that's going to get worse?

Well, those decisions used to come to the CFO and CEO two to three weeks after every quarter was closed. That now is done by the first-line manager any time they want to look into it. That's what empowerment is all about. That's what the Internet is about. It's about empowerment.

Communication is one of the most frequently discussed dynamics in the entire field of organizational behavior, but it is seldom clearly understood. In practice, effective communication is a basic prerequisite for the attainment of organizational strategies and human resource management, but it has remained one of the biggest problems facing modern management. Communication is an extremely broad topic and of course is not restricted to the organizational behavior field. Some estimates of the extent of its use go up to about three-fourths of an active human being's life, and even higher proportions of a typical manager's time. The comprehensive study reported in Chapter 18 that directly observed a wide cross section of what were called "Real Managers" in their day-to-day behaviors found that they devote about a third of their activity to routine communication—exchanging and processing routine information.[1] More important, however, is the finding that the communication activity made the biggest relative contribution to effective managers. Figure 10.1 summarizes these findings.

There seems little doubt that communication plays an important role in managerial[2] and organizational effectiveness. Yet, on the other side of the same coin, ineffective communication is commonly cited as being at the root of practically all the problems of the world. It is given as the explanation for lovers' quarrels, ethnic prejudice, war between nations, the generation gap, industrial disputes, and organizational conflict. These examples are only representative of the numerous problems attributed to ineffective communication. Obviously, this thinking can go too far: communication can become a convenient scapegoat or crutch. Not all organizational and interpersonal difficulties are the result of communication breakdown. Other matters discussed in this book—motivation, decision making, stress, organizational structure, to name but a few—can also contribute to problems. Yet it is also true that the communication process is a central problem in most human and organizational activities.

First, the background of the role of communication in management and organizational behavior is briefly discussed. This discussion is followed by a precise definition of communication and presentation of the two communication extremes—advanced communication media and technology and simple nonverbal communication. In communication technology, both management information systems (MIS) and telecommunications are

FIGURE 10.1

The contribution of communication activities to real managers' effectiveness.

Source: Fred Luthans, Richard M. Hodgetts and Stuart A. Rosenkrantz, *Real Managers,* Ballinger, Cambridge, Mass., 1988, p. 68. (Used with permission.)

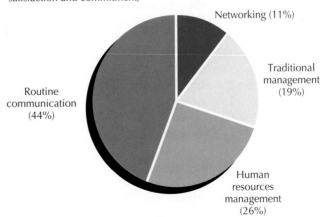

CONTRIBUTION TO REAL MANAGERS' EFFECTIVENESS
(*N* = 178, drawn from participant observation data related to combined effectiveness measure of unit performance and subordinate satisfaction and commitment)

Networking (11%)

Traditional management (19%)

Routine communication (44%)

Human resources management (26%)

given detailed attention. In the other extreme, nonverbal communication, body language and paralanguage are covered. Next, the heart of the chapter is concerned with interpersonal communication (downward, upward, and horizontal or interactive). An interpersonal process, as opposed to a linear information flow perspective of communication, is taken throughout. Finally, communication across cultures is recognized as important in today's global environment, and ways to make it more effective are offered.

BACKGROUND OF THE ROLE OF COMMUNICATION

Early discussions of management gave very little emphasis to communication. Although communication was implicit in the managerial function of command and the structural principle of hierarchy, the early theorists never fully developed or integrated it into management theory. At the same time, they did generally recognize the role of informal communication in relation to the problem of supplementing the formal, hierarchical channels. But the pioneering theorist Chester Barnard, in his classic *Functions of the Executive,* was the first to develop the idea of the central, important role communication plays in the organization.

Barnard's Contribution

Barnard was convinced that communication is the major shaping force in the organization. He ranked it with common purpose and willingness to serve as one of the three primary elements of the organization. To him, communication both makes the organization cooperative system dynamic and links the organization purpose to the human participants. Communication techniques, which he considered to be written and oral language, were deemed not only necessary to attain organizational purpose but also a potential problem area for the organization. In Barnard's words: "The absence of a suitable technique of communication would eliminate the possibility of adopting some purposes as a basis of organization. Communication technique shapes the form and the internal economy of organization."[3]

Barnard also interwove communication into his concept of authority. He emphasized that meaning and understanding must occur before authority can be communicated from manager to subordinate. He listed seven specific communication factors that are especially important in establishing and maintaining objective authority in an organization. He believed them, in brief, to be the following:

1.   The channels of communication should be definitely known.
2.   There should be a definite formal channel of communication to every member of an organization.
3.   The line of communication should be as direct and short as possible.
4.   The complete formal line of communication should normally be used.
5.   The persons serving as communication centers should be competent.
6.   The line of communication should not be interrupted while the organization is functioning.
7.   Every communication should be authenticated.[4]

Modern Perspective

Since the original contributions by Barnard, the dynamics of communication have been one of the central concerns, if not *the* central concern, of organizational behavior and

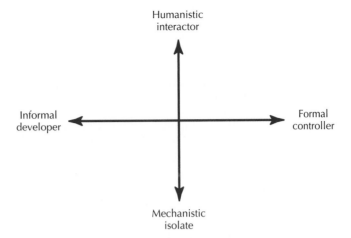

FIGURE 10.2
Managerial communication model: How managers communicate.

Source: Fred Luthans and Janet K. Larsen, "How Managers Really Communicate," *Human Relations,* Vol. 39, No. 2, 1986, p. 175.

management theorists. Except in the principles of those management textbooks that still rely heavily on a classical process framework, communication is given major attention. In addition, there has been a deluge of books and articles that deal specifically with interpersonal and organizational communication. Unfortunately, practically all this vast literature gives only a surface treatment of the subject and is seldom based on systematic research findings. For example, there have been complaints about an uncritical acceptance of the effectiveness of open communication, when a contingency perspective would be more in line with the evidence.[5]

One exception was the "Real Managers Study," reported in Chapter 18, and mentioned in the introductory comments of this chapter. One part of this study combined direct observation of managers in their natural setting with self-report measures to try to determine how they communicated.[6] The model shown in Figure 10.2 gives the results. The first dimension of the managerial communication model represents a continuum ranging from the humanistic interactor (who frequently interacts both up and down the organization system and exhibits human-oriented activities) to the mechanistic isolate (who communicates very little, except on a formal basis). The other dimension describes a continuum from the informal developer (who communicates spontaneously in all directions and exhibits activities related to developing his or her people) to the formal controller (who uses formally scheduled communication interaction and exhibits monitoring/controlling activities).[7] This empirically derived model describes two major dimensions of managerial communication. It provides a framework for *how* managers communicate on a day-to-day basis and can be used as a point of departure for formally defining communication and the interpersonal processes of communication in today's organizations.

The Definition of Communication

The term *communication* is freely used by everyone in modern society, including members of the general public, organizational behavior scholars, and management practitioners. In addition, as noted earlier, the term is employed to explain a multitude of sins both in the society as a whole and in work organizations. Despite this widespread usage, very few members of the general public—and not a great many more management people—can precisely define the term. Part of the problem is that communication experts have not agreed on a definition themselves.

FIGURE 10.3

The continuum of
communication in
organizational behavior.

Most definitions of "communication" used in organizational behavior literature stress the use of symbols to transfer the meaning of information. For example, one analysis stresses that communication is the understanding not of the visible but of the invisible and hidden. These hidden and symbolic elements embedded in the culture give meaning to the visible communication process.[8] Of equal, if not more, importance, however, is the fact that communication is a personal process that involves the exchange of behaviors. The personal aspects have been noted in no uncertain terms by most organizational behavior scholars. For example, Ivancevich and Matteson noted that "communication among people does not depend on technology but rather on forces in people and their surroundings. It is a process that occurs within people."[9] This personal perspective of communication has been made particularly clear by Nickerson, who has found that many people tend to assume that the other person has the same knowledge that they do, and they communicate on this basis.[10] The result is often communication breakdown.

In addition to being a personal process, communication has other implications. A communication expert emphasizes the *behavioral* implications of communication by pointing out that "the only means by which one person can influence another is by the behaviors he performs—that is, the communicative exchanges between people provide the sole method by which influence or effects can be achieved."[11] In other words, the behaviors that occur in an organization are vital to the communication process. This personal and behavioral exchange view of communication takes many forms.

The continuum in Figure 10.3 can be used to identify the major categories of communication that are especially relevant to the study of organizational behavior. On the one extreme is sophisticated communication media and technology, and on the other extreme is relatively simple nonverbal communication. The middle ground is occupied by interpersonal approaches, which represent the personal perspective taken in this chapter. An overview of the communication media and technology and nonverbal approaches is necessary to put the discussion of the interpersonal communication process into proper perspective.

COMMUNICATION MEDIA AND TECHNOLOGY

Chapter 2 covered the newly emerging advanced information technology found in today's organizations. The intent of this chapter is not to review or expand that discussion of IT, but instead is to simply recognize its tremendous importance and impact. After first discussing communication media, the application of IT to the communication processes is presented.

Choosing a Medium for Communication

In communicating effectively, it is important to choose the "right" medium—and there are a wide range of choices. The *Wall Street Journal* recently reported that the average U.S.

employee sends and receives over 200 messages daily.[12] The breakdown was as follows:

Telephone	51
E-mail	36
Voice mail	22
Postal mail	19
Interoffice mail	19
Fax	14
Post-it notes	12
Telephone message slips	9
Pager messages	8
Cell phone	4
Overnight couriers or messengers	4
Express mail	3

All are important, but the most effective medium for communication depends on the information richness and complexity.

The Matter of Information Richness.   The best choice of medium depends on the right degree of richness. *Information richness* can be defined as "the potential information-carrying capacity of data."[13] If the medium conveys a great deal of information, it is high in richness; if it conveys very little information, it is low in richness. So alternative media can have varying degrees of information richness.

Information richness can be measured by four factors. One is feedback, which can range from immediate to very slow. A second is the channel that is used to convey the information, and it can range from a combination of audio and visual to limited visual. A third is the type of communication, such as personal versus impersonal. The fourth is the language source that is used, including body language, natural, or numeric. Table 10.1 categorizes the information richness of five different types of media in terms of these four factors.

As shown in Table 10.1, the richest form of communication is face-to-face. It provides immediate feedback and serves as a check on how well the information has been comprehended. In addition, this form permits the parties to the communication to observe language cues such as body language and voice tone. Another form that is high in richness is the telephone, although it is not as rich as face-to-face communication. On the other hand, formal numeric media such as quantitative computer-generated reports or online video displays have low richness. These forms provide limited visual

TABLE 10.1   Information Richness for Different Media

Information Richness	Medium	Feedback	Channel	Type of Communication	Language Source
High	Face-to-face	Immediate	Visual, audio	Personal	Body, natural
High/ Moderate	Telephone	Fast	Audio	Personal	Natural
Moderate	Personal written	Slow	Limited visual	Personal	Natural
Moderate/ Low	Formal written	Very slow	Limited visual	Impersonal	Natural
Low	Formal numeric	Very slow	Limited visual	Impersonal	Natural

Source: Adapted from R. L. Daft and R. H. Lengel, "Information Richness: A New Approach to Managerial Behavior and Organization Design," in B. M. Staw and L. L. Cummings (Eds.), *Research in Organizational Behavior,* JAI Press, Greenwich, CT, 1984, p. 197.

information and impersonal data. However, with video streaming and real-time digitized (T.V.-like quality) people talking over the computer monitor, some of the richness of face-to-face communication can be captured online.

The Issue of Complexity.   In communicating information for the purpose of passing on data or discussing problem situations, managers must match their choice of media with the complexity of the issue. For instance, a highly complex situation would be the communication of a decision to downsize some of the company's divisions. Those who are going to be affected by the message will have questions, concerns, and fears that have to be addressed. So the company will have to communicate this situation in a deliberate, detailed way. On the other hand, low-complexity situations are routine and predictable and can be handled through the use of rules or standard operating procedures. An example is a communique to all salespeople reminding them that their expense reports are due by the 15th of the month. The challenge for the manager is to choose the appropriate medium.

Daft and Lengel have suggested that there are three zones of communication effectiveness.[14] The most effective zone is the one in which the complexity of the problem or situation is matched appropriately with the richness of the medium. For example, when faced with a simple situation, a manager should choose a medium that is low in richness. Conversely, if a problem is very complex, the manager should opt for a medium that is high in richness. If the individual does not match the situation and the medium correctly, the individual will be in one of the other two zones—the overload zone or the oversimplification zone.

The overload zone is one in which the medium provides more information than is necessary. An example is the use of face-to-face communication to convey a simple, routine matter such as reminding someone to attend a weekly meeting; an e-mail could easily accomplish this. The oversimplification zone is one in which the medium does not provide the necessary information. For example, posting a memo through the company Intranet relating that management has decided to downsize and terminate 10 percent of the workforce is going to cause a great deal of concern and anxiety. The personnel will want to know more about the decision, who will be affected, and how management intends to handle the matter. A more detailed, medium-rich approach is needed.

Research studies have revealed that media usage is significantly different across organizational levels.[15] Senior-level managers tend to spend much more time in face-to-face meetings than do lower-level managers. Given that these executives are far more likely to be dealing with ambiguous and complicated situations, these results are consistent with those noted here regarding the importance of matching the situation and the media richness.

Management Information Systems (MIS)

Closely related to media is communication technology applied through management information systems. Although management information systems do not have to be computerized, normally they are. With the common use of personal computers today and the Internet, almost all information processing is done by computers. MIS not only involves generating, processing, and transmitting information but in recent years has come to play a vital role in the strategy, and decision process and the management of knowledge in today's organizations. The system itself involves not only computer hardware and software but also information, knowledge, and people—both MIS personnel and users at all levels of the organization.

Although MIS is usually associated with integrated networks of information that support management decision making and e-business, MIS can also be used for strategic planning (for example, American Hospital Supply used MIS to change the perspective and direction of the company), improved customer service (for example, some airlines are providing gate agents with relevant information to personalize service at the gate, and Ritz Carlton Hotels and others in the hospitality industry are using it to personalize customer service), and communication per se. The next chapter, on decision making, devotes attention to how computerized systems, especially e-business, can support decision making, but for now it can be said that MIS can be used as part of the interpersonal and organizational communication systems. For example, managers can get on their firm's Intranet or the Internet to ask others for information about solving problems or can use the system to monitor the literature on particular technological developments. Some firms use a Yellow Pages type of component of their Intranet to identify those with experience on certain problems in order to share and leverage knowledge.

Telecommunications

Closely related to computerized MIS is the telecommunications explosion. In fact, the boundaries between computing and communicating are becoming very blurred. Today, computers communicate and telecommunication networks compute. In addition to computers, telecommunications use telephone and television technologies and both a wireless system and a wired system built around fiber-optic links.

The wireless communication technology is beginning to replace phones anchored by copper wires. However, there may be a price paid by working people for this wireless technology. One observer noted that wireless communication

> . . . could be a mixed blessing, freeing people from their desks yet chaining them to their jobs. Indeed, cellular companies are already building computerized systems that can automatically track a person's movements anywhere in North America, so the same telephone number will reach a person's desk phone or pocket phone wherever he or she roams. People will run, but they may not be able to hide.[16]

This communications technology explosion, sometimes called "a second communication revolution," is not confined to North America or to phones. Going beyond mere phones, the telecommunications revolution, or "personal communications services" (PCS), uses digital electronics of computers capable of sending data, images, and video to

> . . . an expanding family of nomadic computing devices—palm-size computers, electronic notepads and what some people call mutant devices that combine the features of a telephone, computer and pager.[17]

This blurring of audio, video, and computer technology is also found in CD-ROMs, which stands for Compact Disc Read-Only Memory (you can't record on them). From a communications standpoint, the key distinguishing feature of CD-ROMs is that they have enormous capacity. They can hold the equivalent of hundreds of disks. For example, one CD-ROM can contain all the phone numbers in the United States or a whole set of encyclopedias that can combine audio and video with the text. For instance, with a CD-ROM one can read about a composer such as Beethoven, see his picture, and hear his music all at the personal computer terminal. All the texts used in an M.B.A. (master of business administration) program can be put on one CD-ROM. However, with the Internet, much of CD-ROM technology has been leapfrogged and taken over by online communication.

In the wired world of fiber optics, information is transmitted as pulses of laser light through ultrapure glass fibers. Here is a description of what this fiber-optic system can do:

> The most advanced system today can transmit information at the rate of 3.4 billion bits per second, or the equivalent of 48,000 telephone conversations on a single pair of fibers. Of course, fiber optics will be important not so much for its role in accommodating voice traffic as for its role in accommodating the explosively growing traffic generated by facsimile, computer networking, and video.[18]

In other words, whether wireless or over fiber optics, the telephone, television, and computer will combine to form a very powerful, but potentially user-friendly, communication system.

Some of the telecommunication techniques widely used to communicate in today's organizations include telephone caller ID, electronic mail, voice messaging, and electronic bulletin boards. Electronic mail (e-mail) is so popular that every day millions of e-mail messages are sent,[19] and many executives report that they spend an hour or more daily reading and responding to them. Caller ID displaying the number of the person calling can be connected to a computer for many uses. American Express, for example, uses such a system at its customer relations center. When customers call, the computer uses the number to retrieve their name and bring up the AMEX file to the screen *before* the customer representative even picks up the phone.

Telecommuting

An outgrowth of the communications technology explosion with special relevance to organizational behavior is telecommuting. This development has resulted, among other things, in the creation of new words that have become part of the everyday language of business. Examples include: home page, browser, chat room, netiquette, URL, and search engine.[20] The term *telecommuting* is used and defined in many different ways and includes both flexible scheduling and the use of advanced information technology. Chapter 15 on job design will give specific attention to telecommuting, but for now here is a description of a typical telecommuter:

> Every morning the routine is the same. At 6:30 A.M. Jaye Gribble rolls out of bed, puts on a pot of coffee and jumps in the shower. While her hair is still wet, she eats breakfast and shuttles her son off to school, a block away. Then she heads to her office, a room on the ground floor of her house that has been outfitted with a PC, a modem and an extra phone line. The equipment and phone line were paid for by her employer, America West Vacation, Tempe, Ariz. At precisely 7:30, Gribble logs onto the company's computer network, dials into its phone system and starts to receive calls from clients around the country who want to book vacation packages. They have been forwarded to Gribble's phone line by an automatic call distributor in the central office, which divvies up incoming calls among both home-based and office-based agents. From her computer terminal, Gribble can make hotel and airline reservations for customers—even arrange rental cars. In short, she can do anything that in-office reservation agents can do without ever leaving her home.[21]

There are a number of both advantages and disadvantages to telecommuting for the organization, the employee, and the community.[22] Advantages for the organization include increasing retention rates; helping with ADA (Americans with Disabilities Act) compliance and EPA regulations; maximizing office space; reducing absenteeism, sick time, and overtime pay; and increasing employee productivity and job satisfaction.

The disadvantages for the organization include the facts that telecommuting decreases face-to-face communication and flexibility; demands greater coordination; is suitable only for certain jobs; and may be abused by employees.

Telecommuting can have either a very positive or very negative impact on employees. Pragmatically, it reduces/eliminates transportation costs and commuting time and is much more "family-friendly" and flexible in regard to child and elder care. From an organizational behavior standpoint, telecommuting allows the employee control over the work; the negatives are the sense of loneliness or "cabin fever," the absence of office support services, and the inability to participate in the interactive synergy and culture of the organization. The community experiences energy conservation and less commuting traffic, but there also may be a net loss of jobs and revenues.

In total, like other emerging approaches and techniques in today's workplace, telecommuting needs to be carefully planned, communicated, implemented, and controlled. A big part of successful implementation would involve a comprehensive telecommuting training system. This would involve an orientation program to fully communicate the purpose and answer all questions; a careful selection process to determine the suitability and commitment of the volunteers (a nonvoluntary program is usually disastrous); training programs for managers and supervisors so that they fully understand and commit to the program; and instruction in telecommuter skills, such as the procedures to be used and how to set up the home in terms of needed equipment and maintenance.[23] With the explosion of information technology and knowledge as well as the increase in virtual organizations, there seems little question that telecommuting will increase in the future.

NONVERBAL COMMUNICATION

The opposite end of the continuum from the tangible, often sophisticated communication media and technology is nonverbal communication. Although verbal communication has long been recognized as being important, nonverbal communication is being given increased attention in the study of communication. Sometimes called the "silent language," *nonverbal communication* can be defined as "nonword human responses (such as gestures, facial expressions) *and* the perceived characteristics of the environment through which the human verbal and nonverbal messages are transmitted."[24] Thus, whether a person says something or, equally important, does *not* say anything, communication still can take place.

Body Language and Paralanguage

There are many forms of nonverbal communication. Probably the most widely recognized is body language. Body movements convey meanings and messages. This form of communication includes facial expressions and what people do with their eyes, feet, hands, and posture. For example, good salespeople, advertisers, and even poker players capitalize on their knowledge of people's eyes. As explained by Preston:

> . . . when an individual is excited or aroused, the pupils of the eyes will dilate. When haggling over a price, the buyer will unconsciously signal an alert seller that a particular price is acceptable. . . . Some colors or shapes cause more excitement than others, and the reaction registers in the shopper's eyes. With this research information, marketing people redesign their products to better appeal to buyers in a competitive environment. Good poker players watch the eyes of their fellow players as new cards are dealt. The pupil dilation very often will show if the card being dealt improves the player's hand.[25]

Besides the obvious meanings attached to things such as a firm handshake or touching the other person when making an important point, at least one communication expert believes that what the person does with the lower limbs is the key to body language. He explains:

> That is where the tension and anxiety show. The person may claim to be relaxed, yet the legs are crossed tightly, and one foot thrusts so rigidly in the air that it appears to be on the verge of breaking off. *Insight:* People concentrate on hiding their tension from the waist up. Their real state is revealed in their legs and feet.[26]

Even a person's clothing can become important in body language. For example, in his best-selling book *Dress for Success,* John Molloy points out, "The most authoritative pattern is the pinstripe, followed in descending order by the solid, the chalk stripe and the plaid. If you need to be more authoritative, stick with dark pinstripes."[27] In addition to dress, physical appearance in general seems important. From her research with clients, one consultant concluded that physical attractiveness is "the single most important quality in determining your success at every stage in your life. People who are attractive are judged to be nicer people, more intelligent, more capable, more desirable mates and better employees."[28]

Besides the truly silent dimensions of nonverbal communication such as body language, time (for example, being late or early), or space (for example, how close one gets during a conversation or seating arrangements in a committee meeting), there are also *ways* in which people verbalize what are an important dimension of nonverbal communication. Sometimes called *paralanguage,* these include things such as voice quality, tone, volume, speech rate, pitch, nonfluencies (saying "ah," "um," or "uh"), laughing, and yawning. For example, tone of voice (genuine or fake) is important in customer service. Also, *who* says a word (for example, whether the boss or a coworker asks for "volunteers") and in what *environmental context* it is said (for example, in the boss's office or out on the golf course) make a difference.

Improving Nonverbal Effectiveness

The study of those with high emotional intelligence, or EI (discussed in Chapter 9), reveals that one of the key characteristics of these successful, effective people is their ability to read the nonverbal cues and react accordingly in a social situation.[29] Although EI is developed over time, as with other forms of communication, there are specific guidelines that can be used to increase the accuracy of interpreting others' nonverbal behavior. Here are some specific suggestions to improve nonverbal communication:

1. *Look at what is happening in the situation.* When nonverbal behavior is an emotional response, it reflects what is going on at the moment and can be used to better understand the person's nonverbal behavior.
2. *Consider the discrepancies between the nonverbal behavior and the verbal statements.* If there is a mismatch, then this should be a signal for closer examination of what is going on. Sometimes the nonverbal signals are more accurate than the verbal ones.
3. *Watch for subtleties in the nonverbal behavior.* For example, the difference between a real smile and a fake one can usually be detected.[30]

Cultural differences must also be recognized in nonverbal communication. For example, in the first of the author's numerous trips to Albania in 1992 to assist this Eastern European country in the transformation to a market economy,[31] the audience responded to talks on the importance of human resource management by shaking their heads from side to side. I interpreted this as: "Oh, wow, they don't agree with me. I have a problem here." However, at the end of my talk, the Albanians enthusiastically cheered and gave one of the warmest and most heartfelt receptions I have ever received. Later, when I expressed my puzzlement to some of them, saying that they didn't seem to be agreeing with me during the talk, I learned that in Albania shaking the head from side to side means "yes, I agree" and shaking it up and down means "no, I don't agree." This one nonverbal gesture, with a completely opposite meaning in this culture,

INTERNATIONAL APPLICATION EXAMPLE

Nonverbal and Verbal Communication

One of the best ways of coping with different cultures and customs is to be careful in the use of both verbal and nonverbal communication. This means saying and doing the right things and, perhaps even more important, not saying or doing the wrong things. Here are some guidelines that U.S. managers are finding useful in treading their way through the intercultural maze of foreign countries:

1. In Europe, act as if you are calling on a rich old aunt. Dress well, do not chew gum, do not smoke without first seeking permission, do not use first names unless invited to do so by the other party, be punctual to meetings, and, if you are unsure of the proper dress, err on the side of conservatism.
2. When in France, speak English to your hosts. They know how to speak English and typically are appalled at the performance of foreigners trying to communicate in their tongue. Stick to the language you know best. Also, be on time for all engagements. The French are sticklers for promptness.
3. Remember that Germans differ from the French in a number of ways. One of these is that they are even bigger sticklers for promptness. Also, remember that gentlemen walk and sit to the left of all women and men of senior business rank. Do not get on the wrong side.
4. In Britain, social events are not used for discussing business. This is left at the office. Also, remember that the British religiously keep engagement calendars, so if you are inviting some people to lunch or dinner, send your invitation well in advance or you are likely to find that date already filled in your prospective guest's calendar. If you are attending a formal dinner, it is common to toast Her Majesty's health after the main course. This is the signal that you may now smoke. Do not light up prior to this time. Also, remember that although promptness is valued, if you are invited to dinner at 8 P.M., you may show up five or ten minutes late, but it is not good manners to show up early.
5. In Italy, it is common to shake hands with everyone. However, do not expect them to remember your name. No one does on the first introduction. Also, get in the habit of calling people by their title. For example, university graduates often prefer to be addressed as such, and there are different titles depending on the individual's field of study.
6. In Spain, punctuality is taken seriously only when attending a bullfight. Most offices and shops close for siesta from 1:30 P.M. to 4:30 P.M., and restaurants do not usually reopen until after 9 P.M. or get into full swing before 11 P.M. An early dinner in Spain often ends around midnight; a late dinner goes into the wee hours of the morning. If you are invited to dinner and are unaccustomed to late hours, take an afternoon nap. You are going to need it if you hope to last through dessert.

had a huge impact on my reading the other person—especially when they then became inconsistent because they *sometimes* remembered that Americans had a different meaning for the direction of head shakes.

The following are a few guidelines affecting communication in various cultures: expect more physical closeness in Latin America; the use of "thumbs up" is fine almost anywhere except Australia; and take your hands out of your pockets when meeting a Japanese person. The accompanying International Application Example: Nonverbal and Verbal Communication gives some further guidelines for both nonverbal and verbal communication in foreign cultures. The last major section of the chapter will give detailed attention to communication in an international environment. Overall, nonverbal dimensions are extremely important to interpersonal communication and must be given as much recognition as the more technical transmissions from the advanced communication media and technology.

INTERPERSONAL COMMUNICATION

As shown in the continuum in Figure 10.3, interpersonal communication represents the middle ground between communication media and technology on the one extreme and nonverbal communication on the other. For the study of organizational behavior, interpersonal communication is most relevant.

In interpersonal communication, the major emphasis is on transferring information from one person to another. Communication is looked on as a basic method of effecting behavioral change, and it incorporates the psychological processes (perception, learning, and motivation) on the one hand and language on the other. However, it must be noted that the explosion of advanced information technology is also having an impact on this human interaction process. For example, in a recent University of Southern California commencement address by Disney's Michael Eisner, he noted:

> As any drama coach can tell you, when accompanied by varied intonation and facial expressions, identical words can come across completely differently. If a person says "you dope" with a smile over the dinner table, it can be endearing. But, in the hard, cold cathode-ray light of e-mail, the same two words stand there starkly and accusingly. I'm afraid that spell check does not check for anger, emotion, inflection or subtext.

A recent academic analysis noted: "Human communication has always been central to organizational action. Today, the introduction of various sophisticated electronic communication technologies and the demand for faster and better forms of interaction are visibly influencing the nature of [interpersonal] communication."[32] Thus, listening sensitivity and nonverbal communications are also closely associated with interpersonal communication. For example, Bill Marriott, Jr., of the highly successful hotel chain, spent nearly half his time listening and talking to frontline employees. It is important to note that he listened and then talked to his people.[33]

Importance of How to Talk to Others

In interpersonal communication, knowing *how* to talk to others can be very useful. One communication expert noted that when communicating with the boss, it is important to understand his or her preferred communication style. Here are some examples:[34]

1. *The Director:* This person has a short attention span, processes information very quickly, and is interested only in the bottom line. So it is best to present this type

of manager with a bulleted list of conclusions and forget all of the background information.

2. *The Free Spirit.*   This manager is a creative, big-picture type of person who likes to consider alternative approaches to doing things, but is not very good on follow-through. In communicating with this type of manager it is important to be patient and to be prepared for changes in direction. The manager often likes to assimilate what he or she is being told and to consider several alternatives before making a decision.

3. *The Humanist.*   This manager likes everyone to be happy and is very concerned with the feelings of others. So any suggestions or recommendations that are given to him or her will be passed around the entire department for full consensus before any action is taken. In dealing with this type of manager, patience and tact are very important.

4. *The Historian.*   This manager likes to know the whole picture and thrives on details. This individual wants to be given a thorough analysis and background information, especially if it is presented in linear fashion. This type of manager does not jump from subject to subject, but instead remains focused on the topic under consideration until it has been exhaustively reviewed and a decision is made.

In addition to these hints on how to talk with one's boss, the whole upward communication process is discussed later.

The Importance of Feedback

The often-posed philosophical question—Is there a noise in the forest if a tree crashes to the ground but no one is there to hear it?—demonstrates some of the important aspects of interpersonal communication. From a communications perspective, the answer is no. There are sound waves but no noise because no one perceives it. There must be both a sender and a receiver in order for interpersonal communication to take place. The sender is obviously important to communication, but so is the neglected receiver who gives feedback to the sender.

The importance of feedback cannot be overemphasized because effective interpersonal communication is highly dependent on it. Proper follow-up and feedback require establishing an informal and formal mechanism by which the sender can check on how the message was actually interpreted. Feedback makes communication a two-way process and is the problem with much of e-mail that turns out to be only one-way. As electronic communication becomes more interactive, such problems can be overcome. There is continuing research evidence that feedback not only improves communication but also, in turn, leads to more effective manager and organizational performance.[35] For example, when businesses have secret salaries so that no one knows what anyone else is earning, or family owned enterprises do not tell the employees how well the company is doing, many people believe that they are being paid less than they should.[36] On the other hand, when information is shared, even though this means giving up some control, the results are often well worth the effort.[37]

Table 10.2 summarizes some characteristics of effective and ineffective feedback for employee performance. The following list explains these characteristics in more detail:

1. *Intention.*   Effective feedback is directed toward improving job performance and making the employee a more valuable asset. It is not a personal attack and should not compromise the individual's feeling of self-worth or image. Rather, effective feedback is directed toward aspects of the job.

TABLE 10.2   Luthans and Martinko's Characteristics of Feedback for Effective and Ineffective Interpersonal Communication in Human Resource Management

Effective Feedback	Ineffective Feedback
1. Intended to help the employee	1. Intended to belittle the employee
2. Specific	2. General
3. Descriptive	3. Evaluative
4. Useful	4. Inappropriate
5. Timely	5. Untimely
6. Considers employee readiness for feedback	6. Makes the employee defensive
7. Clear	7. Not understandable
8. Valid	8. Inaccurate

2. *Specificity.*   Effective feedback is designed to provide recipients with specific information so that they know what must be done to correct the situation. Ineffective feedback is general and leaves questions in the recipients' minds. For example, telling an employee that he or she is doing a poor job is too general and will leave the recipient frustrated in seeking ways to correct the problem.

3. *Description.*   Effective feedback can also be characterized as descriptive rather than evaluative. It tells the employee what he or she has done in objective terms, rather than presenting a value judgment.

4. *Usefulness.*   Effective feedback is information that an employee can use to improve performance. It serves no purpose to berate employees for their lack of skill if they do not have the ability or training to perform properly. Thus, the guideline is that if it is not something the employee can correct, it is not worth mentioning.

5. *Timeliness.*   There are also considerations in timing feedback properly. As a rule, the more immediate the feedback, the better. This way the employee has a better chance of knowing what the supervisor is talking about and can take corrective action.

6. *Readiness.*   In order for feedback to be effective, employees must be ready to receive it. When feedback is imposed or forced on employees, it is much less effective.

7. *Clarity.*   Effective feedback must be clearly understood by the recipient. A good way of checking this is to ask the recipient to restate the major points of the discussion. Also, supervisors can observe facial expressions as indicators of understanding and acceptance.

8. *Validity.*   In order for feedback to be effective, it must be reliable and valid. Of course, when the information is incorrect, the employee will feel that the supervisor is unnecessarily biased or the employee may take corrective action that is inappropriate and only compounds the problem.

In recent years, multisource 360-degree feedback has become an increasingly popular process to communicate to a target manager about strengths and weaknesses. The multiple sources include peers (coworkers), managers, direct reports, and sometimes even customers (thus the term 360 degrees). This 360-degree feedback approach draws its conceptual roots from several different areas. One is the traditional organizational development technique of using surveys to assess employees' perceptions. These surveys measure items such as satisfaction with management, supervisors, pay, work procedures, or formal policies of the organization. The survey information is then fed back to those that generated it, with the goal of developing an action plan to improve the organization.

Another area in which 360-degree feedback has strong conceptual roots is in the performance appraisal literature. Today's environment has forced organizations to provide much more information than the traditional performance review, thus spawning such creative efforts as 360-degree feedback. It is now recognized that managers can improve their performance through increased multisource information.[38] Social cognitive theory (see Chapter 1), in particular the dimension of self-awareness, can also be used as an explanation.[39] Specifically, social cognitive theory posits that humans have the ability to assess their own capabilities and skills, and they often evaluate themselves quite differently than others do. Therefore, the 360-degree feedback provides managers with an external source of information designed to increase their self-awareness. This enhanced self-awareness may improve managerial effectiveness by providing individuals with another source of outside information regarding what others expect of him/her.

Other Important Variables in Interpersonal Communication

Besides feedback, other variables, such as trust, expectations, values, status, and compatibility, greatly influence the interpersonal aspects of communication. If the subordinate does not trust the boss, there will be ineffective communication.[40] The same is true of the other variables mentioned. People perceive only what they expect to perceive; the unexpected may not be perceived at all. The growing generation gap can play havoc with interpersonal communication;[41] so can status differentials and incompatibilities of any sort. Giving attention to, and doing something about, these interpersonal variables can spell the difference between effective and ineffective communication.

Because there are so many variables inherent in the interpersonal communication process, there is a need for a conceptual framework. One such framework for studying interpersonal communication is in terms of the downward, upward, and interactive processes.

DOWNWARD COMMUNICATION

Traditionally, one of the dominant themes of organizational communication has been the so-called downward process. However, when a personal perspective replaces a linear information flow perspective, the downward process is more accurately portrayed as interpersonal linkages, not just information flows, in the downward system. Today, of course, e-mail and other information technology have dramatically affected all organizational communication, including the downward personal process. It is commonplace for coworkers next door to one another, and sometimes even with desks next to each other, to send e-mails to communicate rather than to interact face-to-face. Obviously, this has some dysfunctional consequences from an interpersonal perspective and was previously discussed on what can be missed under nonverbal communication. Clicking the "Send" icon can also instantaneously distribute downward communication to as many people as are on the group address. Yet, even though this information technology drastically changes how the downward process is executed, the process itself remains the same. For example, if the recipient of an e-mail clicks "Delete" without opening the message, which is also becoming increasingly common, then communication as defined in this chapter did not occur. The following discussion recognizes the importance and impact of electronic communication, but is mainly concerned with the interpersonal process and only secondarily with the media and the methods.

The Purpose of the Downward Communication Process

Many years ago Katz and Kahn identified five general purposes of top-to-bottom communication in an organization:

1. To give specific task directives about job instructions
2. To give information about organizational procedures and practices
3. To provide information about the rationale of the job
4. To tell subordinates about their performance
5. To provide ideological information to facilitate the indoctrination of goals[42]

In the past, most organizations concentrated on and accomplished only the first two of these purposes; to a large extent, this is still the case today. In general, downward communication on job performance and the rationale-ideological aspects of jobs has been neglected, and may even be worse with e-mail.

A communication process that gives only specific directives about job instructions and procedures and fails to provide information about job performance or especially rationale-ideological information about the job has a negative organizational impact. This type of downward orientation promotes an authoritative atmosphere that tends to inhibit the effectiveness of the upward and horizontal processes of communication. Communicating the rationale for the job, the ideological relation of the job to the goals of the organization, and information about job performance to employees can, if properly handled, greatly benefit the organization. As Katz and Kahn point out: "If people know the reasons for their assignment, this will often insure their carrying out the job more effectively; and if they have an understanding of what their job is about in relation to their subsystem, they are more likely to identify with organizational goals."[43] This does not imply that management should tell production workers that their jobs are extremely important to the success of the company—that the company would fold unless they enter data correctly into the information system or weld a part properly. Obviously, this type of communication can backfire. The workers would justifiably reason: "Who are they trying to kid? My job isn't *that* important. It is just another hypocritical con job by management." What is meant is that providing *full* information about the job, its ramifications for the rest of the organization, and the quality of the employee's performance in it should be an important function of downward communication. Providing as much information as possible can be especially important in dealing with employees who are not native born, as seen in the International Application Example: Different Cultures, Different Meanings.

Media Used for Downward Communication

Besides the now universal application of communication technology, such as e-mail, discussed earlier, traditionally, downward communication systems relied on many types of print and oral media to disseminate information. Some examples of written media are organizational handbooks, manuals, magazines, newspapers, and letters sent to the home or distributed on the job; bulletin-board items, posters, and information displays; and standard reports, descriptions of procedures, and memos. Today, almost all of this type of downward communication is going online. As Chapter 2 indicated in the discussion of the Intranet, many of an organization's traditionally printed and distributed handbooks, newsletters, and information pieces are now being provided to employees through Web technology via personal computers. The same is true with bulletin boards and "chat rooms" on an Intranet or the Internet; they are replacing corkboards, posters, and information displays.

INTERNATIONAL APPLICATION EXAMPLE

Different Cultures, Different Meanings

As more and more organizations do business in the international arena, communication is going to become a growing problem. This is true not only for oral and written communication but for nonverbal communication as well. For example, many Americans are accustomed to conveying information by shrugging their shoulders, raising their eyebrows, clenching their fist with the thumb out and extended, or placing the thumb and index finger together to form an "O." Do international business people understand these nonverbal gestures? If so, do they give the gestures the same interpretation as do Americans?

One recent research study showed pictures of 20 gestures such as those described in the previous paragraph and asked people from various countries to identify them. The respondents were asked to write out their answers so that the responses could be compared both within and between international groups. If the gesture had no meaning, they were to indicate this also. In all, there were seven groups of respondents: Colombian, Venezuelan, Peruvian, Jamaican, Indian, Thai, and Japanese. The researchers found that of the 20 pictures, only one had the same meaning for all groups. Overall, the respondents identified 40 percent of the gestures the same way as in the United States and 40 percent differently. There were mixed responses on the remaining 20 percent. The results showed that the Thai and Japanese respondents agreed with the American meanings on fewer than half of the gestures, whereas the Venezuelan and Jamaican respondents agreed on about two-thirds of them.

This research points to the importance of communication in the international arena. There are people from many parts of the world who have very different meanings for the same nonverbal communications. For example, the "A-okay" sign that is conveyed by placing the thumb and forefinger in an "O" shape is an obscene gesture in Latin America and the Middle East, but a very common and positive gesture in the United States. Unless businesspeople are aware of the fact that nonverbal communications can differ radically from one part of the world to the next, there will continue to be communication breakdowns and, in some cases, considerable embarrassment.

Although telecommunications technology is increasingly becoming interactive, oral communication is still an important medium for downward communication. Examples of oral media used in the system are direct orders or instructions from managers, speeches,[44] meetings, closed-circuit television programs, public address systems, telephones, and personal computers. Arthur Morrissette, president and founder of Interstate Van Lines in Springfield, Virginia, has key managers address their employees every morning and extensively every couple of weeks; he even has a sing-along where employees belt out the lyrics to the company anthem.[45]

The numerous types of media give an indication of the avalanche of information that is descending on personnel from the downward system. This problem is being compounded by the availability, ease and speed of e-mail.

Ways to Improve Downward Communication

Quality and richness (discussed earlier) of information has often been sacrificed for quantity. Also, social psychology experiments over the years have clearly demonstrated people's willingness to ignore useful information and use useless information.[46] Some organizations have tried to solve their downward communication problems by the use of the communication technology discussed earlier. For example, the New York Transit Authority has an information system whereby if one of its buses breaks down, six months of service records are immediately available on a computer monitor at the service depot.[47] These information technologies help solve some of the information overload problem of the downward system. In addition, a research study found that although decision makers who perceive information overload may be more satisfied than those who perceive information underload, they may not perform as well.[48]

The biggest problem, however, is ignoring the importance of the receiver. This problem, of course, is symptomatic of taking a linear (in this case, downward) information flow perspective, as opposed to a personal perspective. After an extensive review of the literature, one communications researcher concluded that the downward flow of information can affect receivers in the following ways:

1. People's interpretations of communications follow the path of least resistance.
2. People are more open to messages that are consonant with their existing image, their beliefs, and their values.
3. Messages that are incongruent with values tend to engender more resistance than messages that are incongruent with rational logic.
4. To the extent that people positively value need fulfillment, messages that facilitate need fulfillment are more easily accepted than messages that do not.
5. As people see the environment changing, they are more open to incoming messages.
6. The total situation affects communication; a message interpreted as congruent in one situation may be interpreted as incongruent in another.[49]

If managers understand these impacts of communication on subordinates and do something about them, communication can become more effective. There is a series of studies indicating that if employees do get needed information (that is, if downward communication is effective), they perform better as individuals and in groups.[50] Unfortunately, there is recent research evidence indicating that managers are still not communicating very effectively with their people[51] and that organizations do not have policies governing the form of communication appropriate for specific circumstances.[52]

UPWARD COMMUNICATION

Just as downward communication becomes a dynamic interpersonal process, upward communication also becomes an interpersonal process. In the traditional view, the classical organizational structure formally provided for vertical information flows, downward and upward. However, in practice, except for feedback controls, the downward system completely dominated the upward system. Whereas the downward process is highly directive—giving orders, instructions, information, and procedures—the upward process is characteristically nondirective in nature. Although bureaucratic authority facilitates a directive atmosphere, a free, participative, empowered approach is necessary for effective upward communication.

Traditionally, bureaucratic authority has prevailed over the more participative, empowered styles, with the results that upward communication has often been outwardly stifled, badly misused, or conveniently ignored by management. Too often, employees simply fear to give upward communication, especially if it is bad news. An example would be the "computer company president who had to tell his chairperson—a substantial shareholder—and the assembled directors that results wouldn't be up to plan. The exec went about it the right way, providing a full explanation and detailed plans for getting back on track. The chairperson fired him on the spot anyway."[53] Moreover, even when they have good news or useful ideas, many people refuse to share them with their boss. Peter Lilienthal, president of InTouch Management Communication Systems, has reported that surveys conducted by his firm reveal that 90 percent of employees believe they have good ideas for improving the effectiveness of their firms, but only 50 percent of them ever share these ideas with the company.[54] A major challenge for the upward system is to encourage employees to come forth with their ideas.

Methods of Improving the Effectiveness of Upward Communication

The hierarchical structure is about the only formal method that the classical approach used to communicate upward, and, as has been pointed out, in practice this has not worked out well. Other techniques and channels for upward communication are necessary. The following are some possible ways to promote more effective upward communications:

1. *The grievance procedure.*   Provided for in most collective bargaining agreements in unionized organizations, but also in some nonunionized organizations as well, the grievance procedure allows employees to make an appeal upward beyond their immediate manager. It protects individuals from arbitrary action by their direct manager and encourages communication about complaints. A number of companies, such as FedEx, General Electric, and Borg-Warner, have instituted peer-review boards to resolve grievances. These boards consist of three peers (those on the same level or below) and two management representatives, and their decisions are binding on both parties.

2. *The open-door policy.*   Taken literally, this means that the manager's door is always open to employees. It is a continuous invitation for employees to come in and talk about anything that is troubling them. Unfortunately, in practice the open-door policy often turns out to be more fiction than fact. The manager may slap the employee on the back and say, "My door is always open to you," but in many cases both the employee and the manager know the door is really closed. It is a case where the adage "actions speak louder than words" applies.

3. *The use of e-mail.*   The use of e-mail today eliminates much of the intimidation of communicating upward. Most employees can and will directly e-mail to anyone in the organization, including upper-level management. Whereas most employees may have been reluctant before to make an appointment and meet face-to-face, or even pick up the phone, they now have no hesitation in tapping out an e-mail message to anyone.

4. *Counseling, attitude questionnaires, and exit interviews.*   The human resources department can greatly facilitate upward communication by conducting nondirective, confidential counseling sessions; periodically administering attitude questionnaires; and holding meaningful exit interviews for those who leave the organization. Much valuable information can be gained from these forms of communication.

5. *Participative techniques.*   Participative decision techniques can generate a great deal of communication. This may be accomplished by either informal involvement of employees or formal participation programs, such as the use of junior boards, union–management committees, suggestion boxes, and cross-functional teams. There is also empirical research evidence indicating that participants in communication networks are generally more satisfied with their jobs, are more committed to their organizations, and are better performers than those who are not involved in the communication process.[55]

6. *An empowerment strategy.* Closely related to participative techniques are the newly emerging empowerment strategies. Empowerment means different things, but it should involve not only giving employees the authority to make decisions, but also the resources, especially information, to get the job done and satisfy customers. This creates a climate of openness and trust that leads to improved upward communication by empowered employees. For example, at Harley-Davidson, workers are empowered to make multi-hundred-thousand-dollar machine purchases, and because of this trust, also communicate upward ideas and problem solutions to upper-level management.[56]

7. *The ombudsperson.* A largely untried in business firms, but potentially significant technique to enable management to obtain more upward communication, is the use of an ombudsperson. The concept has been used primarily in Scandinavia to provide an outlet for persons who have been treated unfairly or in a depersonalized manner by large, bureaucratic government. It has more recently gained popularity in American state governments, military posts, and universities. Although it is just being introduced in a few business organizations, if set up and handled properly, it may work where the open-door policy has failed. As business organizations become larger and more diverse, the ombudsperson may fill an important void that exists under these conditions.

Perhaps the best and simplest way to improve upward communication is for managers to develop good listening habits and systems for listening. For example, the top managers of a Canadian forest products company felt they were great communicators until an employee survey revealed differently. Here is what they did to solve the problem:

> The two owners undertook a series of thirty dinners in the course of the next year. Ten employees and their spouses, eventually including everyone at the mill, went to dinner with their bosses. After the meal, there was a sociable and often long and intense question-and-answer session. "We all wanted to be listened to," says the president. "By the end of the evening, I'd often see a remarkable change in attitude on the part of even the crustiest of the union guys."[57]

Some practical guidelines to facilitate active listening are (1) maintaining attention; (2) using restatement; (3) showing empathy; (4) using probes to draw the person out; (5) encouraging suggestions; and (6) synchronizing the interaction by knowing when to enter a conversation and when to allow the other person to speak.[58]

Types of Information for Upward Communication

Overall, employees can supply basically two types of information: (1) personal information about ideas, attitudes, and performance and (2) more technical feedback information about performance, a vital factor for the control of any organization. The personal information is generally derived from what employees tell their managers. Some examples of such information are:

1. What the persons have done
2. What those under them have done
3. What their peers have done
4. What they think needs to be done
5. What their problems are
6. What the problems of the unit are
7. What matters of organizational practice and policy need to be reviewed[59]

TABLE 10.3 New Communication Programs at AT&T Global Business
Communication Systems

Approach/Program	*Purpose*
Bureaucracy busters	Enable associates to submit suggestions for improving products, services, and processes
Shared ideas	Allow manufacturing associates to contribute suggestions for process/cost savings
Feedback surveys	Obtain associate feedback regarding work climate, leadership, customer satisfaction, and quality
Recognition programs	Provide recognition for both individual and team contributions
Solution technology planning	Promote innovation by collecting ideas that can result in product innovation
Chats with the president	Provide associates direct access to the head person in order to raise issues, offer suggestions, and ask questions
Answerline	Same as "chats with the president" except that the communication medium is the telephone or fax machine
Video/audio broadcasts	Encourage a dialogue with leadership on business directions, issues, and results

Source: Adapted from Sandra K. Nellis and Fred Lane, "A Second Look at AT&T's Global Business Communication Systems," *Organizational Dynamics,* Spring 1995, p. 75.

A growing number of innovative organizations are building upward feedback systems into their policies and practices. Here is what some representative firms are doing:

1. *AT&T.*   As part of the performance management program, questionnaires are developed and given organizationwide. These questionnaires are given to personnel in a unit and tap areas such as respect for the individual, dedication to helping customers, teamwork, innovation, and high standards of integrity. The manager receives the results as feedback about his or her unit. The manager then discusses the results in a one-on-one meeting with a facilitator and later in a meeting with his or her team. Other forms of feedback, developed within AT&T's Global Business Communication Systems, are provided in Table 10.3. These specific techniques indicate the efforts that this communications company is making to improve communication in-house.

2. *Massmutual Insurance.*   Over a four-year period, everyone from the CEO to first-level managers received 360-degree feedback (discussed earlier). A scientifically derived skills profile containing eight categories is filled out on each manager. At first, only the target manager saw the results, but now management are also able to review the feedback.

3. *AMOCO Corporation.*   Managers can voluntarily ask for feedback from their direct employees on a questionnaire concerning communication, teamwork, and leadership skills. Another questionnaire instrument called "the profiler," which can be filled out anonymously from one's computer terminal, provides feedback to managers participating in a training program called the Leadership Development Process. Recently, the firm has also implemented programs to share knowledge. One such program, called "Peer-Assist," has successful teams give briefings to new start-up teams; they shared tips and gained knowledge. Another is called "Connect," which is part of the Intranet that serves as a type of Yellow Pages directory to help locate those in the company who may have relevant knowledge and experience in a given problem or task.

4. *Deloitte & Touche.*   This professional services firm offers its office managers a standard questionnaire that they can either use as is or customize. Members of the

work group fill out the questionnaire, reflecting their attitudes and opinions. The results go only to the person being reviewed. Recently, however, some officers are providing the feedback results to the manager's advisor or mentor, who in turn helps set the manager's annual goal plan.

The other type of upward information, feedback for control purposes, such as accounting data, is necessary if the organization is to survive. As has been pointed out: "Decision centers utilize information feedback to appraise the results of the organization's performance and to make any adjustments to insure the accomplishment of the purposes of the organization."[60] The role that feedback communication plays is stressed earlier in this chapter. Its role in the decision process is covered in Chapter 11.

INTERACTIVE COMMUNICATION IN ORGANIZATIONS

The classical hierarchical organizational structure gave formal recognition only to vertical communication. Nevertheless, most of the classical theorists saw the need to supplement the vertical with some form of horizontal system. Horizontal communication is required to make a coordinated, cross-functional effort in achieving organizational goals. The horizontal requirement becomes more apparent as the organization becomes larger, more complex, and more subject to the flattening and networking of structures, covered in Chapter 4. Well-known companies such as General Electric, DuPont, Motorola, and Xerox have moved to such a horizontal model of organization. These and other modern network and team designs, formally incorporate horizontal flows into the structure. However, as is the case with vertical (downward and upward) flows in the organization structure, the real key to horizontal communication is found in people and behaviors. Because of the dynamic, interpersonal aspects of communication, the *interactive* form seems more appropriate than just the *horizontal* form. The horizontal flows of information (even in a horizontal structure) are only part of the communication process that takes place across an organization.

The Extent and Implications of Interactive Communication

Most management experts today stress the important but often overlooked role that interactive communication plays in today's organizations. In most cases the vertical communication process still overshadows the horizontal. For example, the study of "Real Managers" reported at the beginning of the chapter found that approximately 100 interactions per week reportedly occurred between managers and their employees (both to them and from them). "While there was far more communication downward (between managers and their employees) than upward (between managers and top managers above them in the organization), there were no specific differences determined by initiation of interaction."[61] The horizontal communication in this study was mainly represented by the networking activity (socializing/politicking and interacting with outsiders) that was shown to be related to successful managers (those promoted relatively fast) more than any other activity.[62] Other studies have also found a relationship, although complex, between communication activities and leadership.[63]

Just as in other aspects of organizational communication, there are many behavioral implications contained in the interactive process. Communication with peers, that is, with persons of relatively equal status on the same level of an organization, provides needed social support for an individual. People can more comfortably turn to a peer for social support than they can to those above or below them. The result can be good or bad for the organization. If the support is couched in terms of task coordination to achieve overall goals, interactive communication can be good for the organization. On the other hand, "if there are no problems of task coordination left to a group of peers, the content of their communication can take forms which are irrelevant to or destructive of organizational functioning."[64] In addition, interactive communication among peers may be at the sacrifice of vertical communication. Persons at each level, giving social support to one another, may freely communicate among themselves but fail to communicate upward or downward. In fact, in the study of "Real Managers," Figure 10.1 showed that networking had the least relative relationship with effective managers (those with satisfied and committed employees and high-performing units), but routine communication activities (exchanging and processing information) had the highest.[65]

The Purposes and Methods of Interactive Communication

Just as there are several purposes of vertical communication in an organization, there are also various reasons for the need for interactive communication. Basing his inquiry on several research studies, a communications scholar has summarized four of the most important purposes of interactive communication:

1. *Task coordination.* The department heads may meet monthly to discuss how each department is contributing to the system's goals.
2. *Problem solving.* The members of a department may assemble to discuss how they will handle a threatened budget cut; they may employ brainstorming techniques.
3. *Information sharing.* The members of one department may meet with the members of another department to give them some new data.
4. *Conflict resolution.* The members of one department may meet to discuss a conflict inherent in the department or between departments.[66]

The examples for each of the major purposes of interactive communication traditionally have been departmental or interdepartmental meetings, but in recent years they include teams and videoconferencing. Such meetings and teams that exist in most organizations have been the major methods of interactive communication. In addition, most organizations' procedures require written reports to be distributed across departments and to teams. The quantity, quality, and human implications discussed in relation to the vertical communication process are also inherent in interactive communication.

The Role of Communication Technology. Also like downward communication, communication technology via computers, telephones, and television has had a tremendous impact on interactive communication. Via their computer terminals, members of an organization at the same location or dispersed throughout the world can communicate with one another. For example, to stimulate sharing ideas and technological developments among its engineers, Hewlett-Packard has about 60 computer conferences running simultaneously.[67] Live interactive television hookups videoconferencing, and the use of "groupware" and chat rooms for interactive conferencing with PCs and PDAs (personal digital assistants, see Chapter 2) can now be used to hold meetings with participants at various geographical locations. This is less costly and time consuming than bringing everyone into one location and, because it can be face-to-face and interactive, it improves communication over traditional telephone conferencing. Intranets (see Chapter 2), which almost all firms of any size now have, are also moving from relatively static information sharing and publishing, e-mail, document management, and corporate directories to interactive collaboration.[68] There is more and more interactive, real-time communication on Intranets and Extranets (see Chapter 2) in the case of business to business (B2B).

The Role of the Informal Organization.   Because of the failure of the classical structures to meet the needs of interactive communication, not only have new organizational forms emerged, but the informal organization and groups have also been used to fill the void. Informal contacts with others on the same level are a primary means of interactive communication. The informal system of communication can be used to spread false rumors and destructive information, or it can effectively supplement the formal channels of communication. For example, communication experts recognize that the hallways of an organization encourage creative, open-ended interactions because of two reasons: (1) the hallway takes away some of the sense of hierarchy, making the participants seem more equal and (2) the hallway invites multiple perspectives—anyone who wanders by can join in, adding their ideas to the mix.[69] In general, the informal system can quickly disseminate pertinent information that assists the formal systems to attain goals. However, whether the informal system has negative or positive functions for the organization depends largely on the goals of the person doing the communicating. As in any communication system, the entire informal system has a highly personal orientation, and, as has been pointed out earlier, personal goals may or may not be compatible with organizational goals. The degree of compatibility that does exist will have a major impact on the effect that the grapevine or rumor mill has on organizational goal attainment.

Some organizational theorists are critical of the grapevine because its speed makes control of false rumors and information difficult to manage. By the same token, however, this speed factor may work to the advantage of the organization. Because the informal system is so personally based and directed, it tends to be much faster than the formal downward system of information flow. Important relevant information that requires quick responsive action by lower-level personnel may be more effectively handled by the informal system than by the formal system. Thus, the informal system is a major way that interactive communication is accomplished. The formal horizontal and upward systems are often either inadequate or completely ineffective. The informal system is generally relied on to coordinate the units horizontally on a given level. It may be enhanced, if necessary, by e-mail. However, most people are sensitive to the lack of security and privacy of e-mail and thus informal communication tends to remain word of mouth, even in this era of electronic communication.

COMMUNICATION ACROSS CULTURES

With globalization, the analysis and understanding of communication across cultures becomes critical. As Adler notes, "Communicating effectively challenges managers worldwide even when the work force is culturally homogeneous, but when employees speak a variety of languages and come from an array of cultural backgrounds, effective communication becomes considerably more difficult."[70] For example, the people at the home office of a multinational corporation, or MNC, and the nationals in the foreign branch or subsidiary may not have the same meanings for the same words. An example is that Japanese managers rarely come out with a direct "no" to another's request. A way they avoid saying "no" is to say "yes" and then follow the affirmative answer with a detailed explanation that in effect means "no."[71] Fortunately for North Americans and the British, English has become the language of international business, and of course the Internet knows no boundaries. Yet, there are still many communication problems and the following sections examine some of these breakdowns in and ways to improve communication across cultures.

Communication Breakdown across Cultures

There are a number of contributing factors leading to communication breakdown across cultures. Perhaps the best way to get at the root causes of this breakdown is through the concepts of perception, stereotyping, and ethnocentrism.

Perceptual Problems.   Chapter 6 is devoted specifically to perception, which is simply portrayed as a person's interpretation of reality and is said to be learned. People are taught to "see" things in a given way, and this will affect their interpretation (i.e., their perception) of reality. Some recent examples of such interpretations of reality would be Japanese stockbrokers who perceived that the chances of improving their careers are better with U.S. firms, so they have changed jobs. The same could be said for Hong Kong hoteliers who have begun buying U.S. properties. These Hong Kong hotel owners have the perception that if they can offer the same top-quality hotel service as back home, they can dominate the U.S. market. In other words, perceptions can affect international management, but misperceptions[72] due to cultural differences can also become a barrier to effective communication. For example, Adler suggests you read the following sentence and then very quickly count the number of Fs:

FINISHED FILES ARE THE RESULT OF YEARS OF SCIENTIFIC STUDY
COMBINED WITH THE EXPERIENCE OF YEARS.

She notes that most people who speak English as a second language see all six Fs but many who speak English as their first language pick up only three Fs; they miss the Fs in the word *of*. Those who speak English as their first language have been culturally conditioned to skip over the *of* because it is not needed to get the meaning of the sentence. Adler explains: "Once we see a phenomenon in a particular way, we usually continue to see it in that way. Once we stop seeing *of*'s, we do not see them again (even when we look for them); we do not see things that do exist."[73] Obviously, such misperceptions of reality are compounded when the individual attempts to communicate across cultures.

Stereotyping Problems.   Closely related to perception is another barrier to communication called stereotyping. Also covered in Chapter 6, stereotyping is the tendency to perceive another person as belonging to a single class or category. Stereotyping is a very simple, widely used way of constructing an assumed overall profile of other people. For example, ask people from the United States which people try to "keep a stiff upper lip during trying times" and the most common answer is the British. Ask people from the United States what country of the world is famous for its auto engineering and the most common answer is Germany.

Table 10.4 presents a matching quiz on the stereotyped images of people from around the world. Go ahead and take the test—the answers are found in footnote 75 at the end of the chapter. Of course, as Chapter 6 on perception pointed out, such stereotypes can be very misleading or unfair. To give one-word descriptions of an entire culture ignores individual differences and subcultures. However, rightly or wrongly, most people hold such views of other people. How did you score?

Ethnocentric Problems.   Ethnocentrism refers to the sense of superiority that members of a particular culture have. Those from many countries, for example, claim that people in the United States believe they are the best in everything regardless of what area is under discussion. Even the use of the term *American* as used by those in the United States reflects ethnocentrism, because all people in North, South, and Central American countries are Americans. However, although the United States may be the most visable example, all

TABLE **10.4**   A Matching Quiz of Brief Descriptive Stereotypes of People around the World[75]

Culture	Stereotyped Image
___ 1. United States	A. Demonstrative, talkative, emotional, romantic, bold, artistic
___ 2. English	B. Mañana attitude, macho, music lovers, touchers
___ 3. French	C. Inscrutable, intelligent, xenophobic, golfers, group-oriented, polite, soft-spoken
___ 4. Italians	D. Conservative, reserved, polite, proper, formal
___ 5. Latin Americans	E. Arrogant, loud, friendly, impatient, generous, hardworking, monolingual
___ 6. Asians	F. Arrogant, rude, chauvinistic, romantics, gourmets, cultural, artistic

cultures promote ethnocentrism through their value structures and nationalistic spirit. People are taught the "right" way to do things and, at least for them, it is regarded as the "best" way as well. When people interact with each other on an international basis, ethnocentrism can cause communication problems. Here are some examples of ethnocentrism in action that have been identified when U.S. businesspeople deal with Asians.[74]

1. Frustration with the language, the food, and local customs.
2. Quickly labeling the local ways of doing things as strange and inefficient, rather than trying to understand the rational basis behind them.
3. Failure to recognize that when Asians seem to say one thing and do another, they consider their behavior as face saving rather than misleading or dishonest.
4. U.S. businesspeople forming their own clubs at which they complain about the difficulties they face, rather than socializing with the local people to find out what the culture is really about.

Such ethnocentrism as in the preceding examples can lead to not only communication problems and how to solve them,[76] but also disputes between countries. For example, the United States and China have had disagreements over a number of issues in recent years. Because of their ethnocentric views, each side thinks it is right in areas such as human rights and selling armaments.

Improving Communication Effectiveness across Cultures

How can people doing business in other countries sensitize themselves to the culture of these nations and avoid making mistakes?[77] One of the most effective ways is by learning about the culture of that country before going there. Some firms have developed "cultural assimilator" training programs. These programmed learning approaches ask the participants to read about a particular situation and then choose one of four courses of action or type of language that they would use. After the participants have made the choice, they then immediately learn if it was right or wrong, along with an explanation. By being put through a couple of hundred situations that they are likely to encounter in the foreign country, they become somewhat sensitized to the culture of that country and are able to communicate more effectively. There is even evidence that speaking the language correctly is not enough. Pronunciation and accent are even important. More and more foreign-born managers' careers are being stalled because they have thick accents, even though their grammar and vocabulary skills are good.[78]

A second, and often complementary, approach is to provide the trainee with educational background material on the country, including social structure, religion, values, language, and history. In particular, these training programs are designed to help managers going to a foreign assignment create the right climate between themselves and those with whom they will be communicating. This type of training is becoming particularly important for women expatriates, whose numbers have been increasing in recent years. A recent suggestion is that MNCs include in their predeparture training for male expatriates some suggestions for enhancing the adjustment and success for women colleagues who will be joining them.[79] For example, a woman expatriate lawyer in Japan recounted how her male law partner, in initial meetings with Japanese clients, often mentions the name of the prestigious university from which she graduated and the important cases she had worked on. Given how important the university and previous experience are in establishing a person's status in the Japanese culture, this strategy was very effective in giving her immediate respect and subsequent success.[80]

Recent research indicates that both types of training methods have additive benefits in preparing managers for intercultural work assignments[81] and that cross-cultural training in general is quite effective.[82] A more recent training approach called "skill streaming" also seems to hold promise for learning culture-specific communication.[83] Originally developed to train individuals in prosocial behaviors (e.g., thank someone, apologize, ask a favor, or introduce oneself), this approach can be used to train expatriates in culture-specific prosocial communication. Techniques such as modeling, role playing, reinforcing feedback, and transfer of training can be applied in this skill-streaming approach to cultural training.[84] In the final analysis, however, the same principles and processes of communication discussed in this chapter hold across cultures, but the content and applications will differ by culture.

Summary

At every level of modern society, communication is a problem. One of the problems when applied to organizations has been the failure to recognize that communication involves more than just linear information flows; it is a dynamic, interpersonal process that involves behavior exchanges. Various communication media, management information systems, telecommunication, and nonverbal approaches are also important to communication in today's organizations. MIS involves not only generating, processing, and transmitting information but also strategy and decision making, and telecommunication involves an interaction among telephones (both wireless and fiber-optic), television, and, of course, computers. The explosion of advanced information technology is having a huge impact on communication in organizations; e-mail alone has revolutionized the way people communicate, let alone "groupware" and "chat rooms" on the Internet. Yet, communication is still a dynamic, interpersonal process. The three major dimensions of communication from this perspective are downward, upward, and interactive processes. Each has varied purposes and methods. The downward system is generally adequate in providing information, but better techniques are needed to improve the upward and horizontal systems. All three processes in organizations can greatly benefit from increased attention given to the dynamic, interpersonal aspects of communication. The same is true of communicating across cultures. There are a number of personal factors such as perception, stereotyping, and ethnocentrism that cause communication breakdown when global managers and expatriates attempt to communicate in other cultures. To help overcome these cultural obstecles, MNCs are using cultural assimilator training and newer approaches such as skill streaming.

ENDING WITH META-ANALYTIC RESEARCH FINDINGS

OB PRINCIPLE: Communicating feedback about performance to employees can improve their subsequent performance.

Meta-Analysis Results: [131 studies; 12,652 participants; $d = .41$] *On average, there is a **61 percent probability** that providing feedback (even negative) to employees about their performance will lead to better subsequent performance than those who do not receive performance feedback.* Cases in which providing feedback was not as effective can be explained by various cognitive processes. Specifically, when feedback is targeted at the task itself, it produces the strongest results. However, if feedback becomes more personal in nature, individuals may not respond as positively due to the self-evaluative mechanisms it activates.

Conclusion: Feedback is one form of interpersonal communication that can be used to effectively manage behavior and improve performance. In fact, feedback may be more valued by some employees than money. This is because people have a strong need to know how they are doing. If managers communicate performance standards to their employees and provide feedback about the progress being made, then there will be a positive impact on performance. If employees are doing well compared to the performance standard, they are likely to maintain current efforts or set new performance goals. In contrast, if they are currently not performing well, feedback can provide employees with the necessary information to reevaluate current strategies and try new ones. Similar to other forms of communication, feedback is most effective when it is positive, immediate, clear, and to the point.

Source: Adapted from Avraham N. Kluger and Angelo DeNisi, "The Effects of Feedback Interventions on Performance: A Historical Review, a Meta-Analysis, and a Preliminary Feedback Intervention Theory," *Psychological Bulletin,* Vol. 119, No. 2, 1996, pp. 254–284.

Questions for Discussion and Review

1. What role has information technology played and what role can it play in communication in organizations?
2. Compare and contrast the various telecommunication techniques for effective communication.
3. Why is feedback so important to communication? What are some guidelines for the effective use of feedback? How can 360-degree feedback help?
4. What are some of the major purposes and methods of downward communication?
5. What are some techniques for improving upward communication?
6. What are the major purposes and methods of interactive communication?
7. How do perception, stereotyping, and ethnocentrism affect communicating with employees across cultures?
8. How can multinational corporations sensitize their managers to the cultures of host countries before sending them on international assignments?

Internet Exercise: Communication in the Workplace

Visit the website http://www.employer-employee.com/comm101.htm where you will find current articles about various communication topics such as how to get a raise or how to get your idea across. Read a few of the articles, and see if you can develop some insights into the topics discussed in the chapter and specifically these questions.

1. How is advanced information technology affecting interpersonal communication in organizations?
2. Suppose you are employed in an entry-level management position in a large bank. What specific considerations (contingencies) would you identify of sending an e-mail versus talking in person to someone else in the bank.
3. From your reading, what advice would you give to the training department to help improve communication effectiveness of those being trained for an assignment overseas?

REAL CASE:
Online
Communication to
Share Knowledge

At the heart of Buckman Laboratory's knowledge-sharing system is an online discussion forum called K'Netix. It has 54 discussion groups that focus on Buckman's main products—chemicals for papermaking, leather-tanning, and water treatment. A salesperson might survey colleagues around the world for the inside skinny on a particular client, say, or get ideas on how to solve a customer problem. Typically, employees post 50 to 100 messages a day. That has helped the company amass an easily searchable database of inhouse expertise and past lessons learned that now contains more than 15,000 documents—all accessible by employees or customers via a Web browser. Before the online system was in place, "you would always be reinventing the wheel," says Cheryl Lamb, manager of Buckman's Knowledge Center.

Robert Buckman began experimenting with what he dubbed "knowledge sharing" in the mid-1980s, when he took charge of the company his father, Stanley, founded in 1945 and led until his death in 1978. Buckman's old way of distributing technical information—hiring PhDs and putting them on airplanes, Robert Buckman says—was getting too expensive as the company expanded globally. So Buckman began stationing people overseas. Today, 86 percent of its 1,300 employees work outside the home office.

With its staff scattered so far and wide, the company needed a way to keep people in touch. But getting the right information to the right people—fast—is easier said than done. For starters, in 1985, Robert Buckman told senior managers in Memphis to swap examples of innovative ideas through the company's e-mail system. But soon, the system became a network for chit-chat and gossip, and little else. "I realized the managers weren't going to share," he says. "They had information, but feared giving it up," because they felt they wouldn't get credit for their ideas.

So the CEO decided to adopt a more revolutionary strategy: empower the field staff to communicate with each other, rather than routing all information through managers in Memphis. He wanted his employees to share not just written reports but also the knowledge inside their heads gleaned from years of working in paper mills, tanneries, and treatment plants. "That's the real gold inside companies," he says. To pull that off, he set up a new computer system that linked the senior managers in Memphis plus Buckman's 1,300 employees around the world.

Once again, Buckman's efforts met resistance. Many managers resented having to yield their control over the flow of information—and refused to participate. "They didn't want to open their cabinets to people," says Dean Didato, vice president for leather chemicals. So the CEO decided to get tough. First, he ordered marketing manager Alison Tucker to start compiling weekly statistics detailing each employee's use of the knowledge-sharing network.

Finally, Robert Buckman set up a system to promote those who shared information—and to punish those who did not. The clincher: A few years ago, he took the system's 150 most frequent users to a Scottsdale, Arizona, resort for a week. Only then, he recalls, did the holdouts start getting the message.

1. Obviously, the "Information Age" has arrived. What impact do you think it has on organizational communication? What are some of the positives and the negatives?
2. Specifically cite examples from the case where the human dimension is dysfunctional for advanced communication technologies. How can these problems be overcome?
3. With such communication systems in place, what impact does interpersonal communication now play? Is this good or bad for organizational outcomes?

ORGANIZATIONAL BEHAVIOR CASE: Doing My Own Thing

Rita Lowe has worked for the same boss for 11 years. Over coffee one day, her friend Sara asked her, "What is it like to work for old Charlie?" Rita replied, "Oh, I guess it's okay. He pretty much leaves me alone. I more or less do my own thing." Then Sara said, "Well, you've been at that same job for 11 years. How are you doing in it? Does it look like you will ever be promoted? If you don't mind me saying so, I can't for the life of me see that what you do has anything to do with the operation." Rita replied, "Well, first of all, I really don't have any idea of how I am doing. Charlie never tells me, but I've always taken the attitude that no news is good news. As for what I do and how it contributes to the operation around here, Charlie mumbled something when I started the job about being important to the operation, but that was it. We really don't communicate very well."

1. Analyze Rita's last statement: "We really don't communicate very well." What is the status of manager–subordinate communication in this work relationship? Katz and Kahn identified five purposes of the manager–subordinate communication process. Which ones are being badly neglected in this case?
2. It was said in this chapter that communication is a dynamic, personal process. Does the situation described verify this contention? Be specific in your answer.
3. Are there any implications in this situation for upward communication and for interactive communication? How could feedback be used more effectively?

ORGANIZATIONAL BEHAVIOR CASE: Bad Brakes

Michelle Adams is the maintenance supervisor of a large taxicab company. She had been very concerned because the cabdrivers were not reporting potential mechanical problems. Several months ago she implemented a preventive maintenance program. This program depended on the drivers' filling out a detailed report in writing or into the office computer system when they suspected any problem. But this was not happening. On a number of occasions a cab left the garage with major problems that the previous driver was aware of but had not reported. Calling out the field repair teams to fix the breakdowns not only was costing the company much time and trouble but also was very unsafe in some cases and created a high degree of customer ill will. The drivers themselves suffered from a loss of fares and tips, and in some cases their lives were endangered by these mechanical failures. After many oral and written threats and admonishments, Michelle decided to try a new approach. She would respond directly to each report of a potential mechanical problem sent in by a driver with a return memo indicating what the maintenance crew had found wrong with the cab and what had been done to take care of the problem. In addition, the personal memo thanked the driver for reporting the problem and encouraged reporting any further problems with the cabs. In less than a month the number of field repair calls had decreased by half, and the number of turned-in potential problem reports had tripled.

1. In communication terms, how do you explain the success of Michelle's follow-up memos to the drivers?
2. Explain and give examples of the three communication processes in this company (that is, downward, upward, and interactive).

CHAPTER 11

Decision Making

Learning Objectives

Define the phases in the decision-making process.

Identify some models and styles of behavioral decision making.

Present the participative decision-making techniques.

Discuss the creative process and group decision-making techniques.

Starting with Best Practice
Leader's Advice

Ford's CEO Jacques Nasser on Decisions Needed to Drive Change

Originally from Lebanon, Jacques Nasser grew up in Melbourne, Australia, where he was a budding entrepreneur. During his teenage years he started a bicycle-making operation and discotheque. Then to his independent businessman father's surprise and consternation, Jacques joined Ford Australia as a financial analyst. However, the formative years served him well over the next 30 years as he worked his way through the ranks to become CEO of the huge automaker with 340,000 employees in 200 countries. Nasser describes the process and needed decisions to transform Ford into a 21st-century world-class firm.

Q1:   *Ford has been making cars for nearly a century. Why change the company's mind-set now?*

Nasser: If we don't, Ford as we know it won't be around in five years. That's the primary answer, and I would say it's pretty compelling. No company can survive in a world driven by rapidly changing consumer needs and tastes without having leaders at every level capable of fast decision making. If leaders think and move slowly or operate inefficiently—basically, if they don't keep up with consumers and competitors—then they won't be able to satisfy the capital markets' demand for both profitable growth and unassailable asset utilization. The capital markets are ruthless. They don't care about the stellar performance of one design team, or the financial results of a particular geographic region, or the amazing productivity of one molding plant. The capital markets value the health of a company as a whole. Is the company positioned to meet consumers' needs now and in the future? And can it meet those needs while bringing home great returns on the capital employed?

     Another point comes into play here, too. Increasingly, the markets value a global approach to business—an approach in which a company's units, divisions, teams, functions, and regions are all tightly integrated and synchronized across the borders. The markets reward the kinds of companies in which, for instance, a manager at an assembly plant in Cologne says, "It would definitely lower my costs to change such-and-such supplier, but it would damage our global strategy for raw material sourcing. I won't do it." When you have a whole company of people thinking like that, you know you're going to see the benefits in overall productivity. And even more important, you're going to see the benefits in innovation, because people will be asking themselves, "What can I do to make this whole company work better and smarter and faster? What creative ideas do I have that will really make us grow, not just in my area, but over there, in that division or that one?"

Q2: *Does that kind of questioning happen at Ford today?*

Nasser: More and more. But we still have way too much of the fiefdom perspective. I should note, by the way, that I myself used to have that view of our business. When I ran Ford Europe from 1992 to 1994, it was a fiefdom. Every three months or so, we'd get visitors from headquarters who would suggest new ways of thinking about and doing things. And we would wine and dine them and nod at everything they said. Finally, we'd get them on the plane home, and we wouldn't think about a word that they'd said until they came back again. We figured nobody knew more about how to run Ford Europe than we did. We were the experts. We can't do that anymore.

Q3: *The transformation effort at Ford, then, is undergirded by two concepts: employees should think like shareholders, and the company as a whole must be able to respond swiftly to—if not anticipate—consumers' needs. Those ideas aren't new. But is this the first time they've been introduced to Ford people?*

Nasser: We haven't had to introduce these concepts to our people until now. First let me make this clear: the last thing I want to imply is that the new executive team at Ford is a bunch of heroes on white horses, galloping in to save a company in distress. Ford has been in business for 95 years, and you can quibble with its degree of success, but the fact that a company is still around after 95 years is an accomplishment in itself. And when it comes to a global mind-set, Ford is actually ahead of most of its competitors.

Q4: *What about globalization of the economy?*

Nasser: Ford can't build the company if it holds on to a mind-set that doesn't respond swiftly to consumers' needs or pay attention to the capital markets. So that's why we're in the process of reinventing Ford as a global organization with a single strategic focus on consumers and shareholder value. That's not to say you wipe out national cultures or eliminate the idea that it makes sense to have people with expertise in one function or another, but it does mean you strive for some sort of Ford-wide corporate DNA that drives how we do things everywhere. That DNA has a couple of key components: a global mind-set, as I've said, and intuitive knowledge of Ford's customers, a relentless focus on growth, and the strong belief that leaders are teachers.

Q5: *Does having a single strategic focus necessarily mean that Ford intends to sell the same products across every market?*

Nasser: Just the opposite. As a matter of fact, it means that we can actually have products that are tailored to an individual market because we are able to leverage technologies and efficiencies around the world. Some aspects of Ford, however, will be common across markets. For instance, we will have the best practices in marketing and employee development. And all major decisions about brand positioning and technology will be made by a central group. Execution, however, will be local, with enough flexibility to ensure that local differences are accounted for. Let me give you an example. In order to have consistent Ford DNA around the world, we need to have consistent policies and practices on compensation. That said, different cultures come at compensation differently—in particular, they have different attitudes about the balance between fixed and variable compensation.

In this chapter, the important processes of decision making are given attention. A *process* is any action that is performed by management to achieve organizational objectives. Thus, like communication in the last chapter, decision making is an organizational process because it transcends the individual and has an effect on organizational goals. First, the overall decision-making process is explored. Then, the models and styles of behavioral decision making are described. Next, the traditional and modern participative techniques are presented. Finally, the creative process and group decision-making techniques are given attention.

THE DECISION-MAKING PROCESS

Decision making is almost universally defined as choosing between alternatives. It is closely related to all the traditional management functions. For example, when a manager plans, organizes, and controls, he or she is making decisions. The classical theorists, however, did not generally present decision making this way. Classical management theorists such as Fayol and Urwick were concerned with the decision-making process only to the extent that it affects delegation and authority, whereas Frederick W. Taylor alluded to the scientific method only as an ideal approach to making decisions. Like most other aspects of modern organization theory, the beginning of a meaningful analysis of the decision-making process can be traced to Chester Barnard. In *The Functions of the Executive,* Barnard gave a comprehensive analytical treatment of decision making and noted: "The processes of decision . . . are largely techniques for narrowing choice."[1]

Most discussions of the decision-making process break it down into a series of steps. For the most part, the logic can be traced to the ideas developed by Herbert A. Simon, the well-known Nobel Prize–winning organization and decision theorist, who conceptualized three major phases in the decision-making process:

1. *Intelligence activity.* Borrowing from the military meaning of "intelligence," Simon described this initial phase as consisting of searching the environment for conditions calling for decision making.
2. *Design activity.* During the second phase, inventing, developing, and analyzing possible courses of action take place.
3. *Choice activity.* The third and final phase is the actual choice—selecting a particular course of action from among those available.[2]

Closely related to these phases, but with a more empirical basis (that is, tracing actual decisions in organizations), are the stages of decision making of Mintzberg and his colleagues:

1. *The identification phase,* during which *recognition* of a problem or opportunity arises and a *diagnosis* is made. It was found that severe, immediate problems did not receive a very systematic, extensive diagnosis but that mild problems did.
2. *The development phase,* during which there may be a *search* for existing standard procedures or solutions already in place or the *design* of a new, tailor-made solution. It was found that the design process was a groping, trial-and-error process in which the decision makers had only a vague idea of the ideal solution.
3. *The selection phase,* during which the choice of a solution is made. There are three ways of making this selection: by the *judgment* of the decision maker, on the basis of experience or intuition rather than logical analysis; by *analysis* of the alternatives on a logical, systematic basis; and by *bargaining* when the selection involves a group of decision makers and all the political maneuvering that this entails. Once the decision is formally accepted, an *authorization* is made.[3]

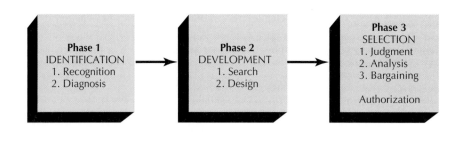

FIGURE 11.1

Mintzberg's empirically based phases of decision making in organizations.

Figure 11.1 summarizes these phases of decision making based on Mintzberg's research.

Whether expressed in Simon's or Mintzberg's phases, there seem to be identifiable, preliminary steps leading to the choice activity in decision making. Also, it should be noted that decision making is a dynamic process, and there are many feedback loops in each of the phases. "Feedback loops can be caused by problems of timing, politics, disagreement among managers, inability to identify an appropriate alternative or to implement the solution, turnover of managers, or the sudden appearance of a new alternative."[4] The essential point is that decision making is a dynamic process. This dynamic process has both strategic[5] and behavioral implications for organizations. Recent empirical research indicates that the decision process that involves making the right strategic choices does lead to successful decisions for the organization,[6] but there are still many problems of managers making the wrong decisions.[7] To go beyond the recent dominance of the role that information technology plays in the analysis and practice of effective decision making, this relevance to the study and application of organizational behavior is what has become known as behavioral decision making.

BEHAVIORAL DECISION MAKING

Why does a decision maker choose one alternative over another? Recently put another way, how do managers make the right decisions and learn from the wrong ones?[8] The answer to this question has been a concern of organizational behavior theorists as far back as March and Simon's classic book, *Organizations,* in 1958. Subsequently, however, the field became more interested in such topics as motivation and goal setting, and emphasis on decision making waned. The field of behavioral decision making was mainly developed outside the mainstream of organizational behavior theory and research by cognitive psychologists and decision theorists in economics and information science. Recently, however, there has been a resurgence of interest in behavioral decision making, and it has moved back into the mainstream of the field of organizational behavior.[9]

Whereas classical decision theory operated under the assumption of rationality and certainty, the new behavioral decision theory does not. Behavioral decision-making theorists argue that individuals have cognitive limitations and, because of the complexity of organizations and the world in general, they must act in situations where uncertainty prevails and in which information is often ambiguous and incomplete.[10] Sometimes this risk and uncertainty leads organizational decision makers to make questionable, if not unethical, decisions (see OB Application Example: Matching the Competition or Driving Them Out?). Because of this real-world uncertainty and ambiguity, a number of models of decision making have emerged over the years. The foundation and point of

OB Application Example:

Matching the Competition or Driving Them Out?

Decision making is no easy job, and sometimes it can end up creating ethical problems for a company. For example, in a growing number of Japanese firms such as Mazda, management has been eliminating jobs in order to reduce costs. At the same time, however, many workers feel that this is unethical because they joined the company under the premise that they would have lifetime employment. Meanwhile many U.S. firms have made the decision to radically change their culture, cut costs, and become more competitive. These decisions are upsetting many of the old guard in these firms who have been used to doing things "the old way." Yet the biggest ethical impact of decision making may well be in industries where competitive pricing has been more the rule than the exception. A good example is the airline industry.

In the highly competitive airline industry, when one company cuts fares, the others follow or lose business. And if the price cuts result in extremely low profits, or even losses, competitors will still follow suit because they hope to recover later on. Does this mean, then, that some airlines might cut their prices on routes in order to drive out the competition and then raise the rates back to high levels where they can recover their losses and even make substantial profits? This is not an easy question to answer, but in one recent action, the federal government has accused American Airlines of doing just this.

The government contends that American's management used its dominance of the Dallas–Forth Worth market to prevent weaker competitors from gaining a foothold. Then, when the competition had been run off, American Airlines raised prices and greatly increased its revenues. In substantiating these claims, the government accused American Airlines of using predatory tactics against three low-cost carriers that tried to compete with it on routes to cities from its Dallas–Fort Worth hub. For example, on an average nonstop one-way ticket between Dallas–Fort Worth and Colorado Springs it cost $158 before there was any competition. When American was confronted with low-cost rivals, the price dropped to $88. Then, when the competition had been driven from the field, the price of the ticket rose to $133. The same was true in the case of flights to and from Kansas City. Initially, the cost was $113 for a one-way ticket, but this dropped to $83 when American faced competition and later rose to $125 when the low-cost airlines were driven from the market.

In some of these cases, the cost of a ticket remained lower than it was initially. However, the government pointed out that with no competition, the increased passenger traffic substantially boosted revenues. For example, between Dallas–Fort Worth and Colorado Springs an average of 3,723 passengers flew the route monthly when American had no competition. When competitors entered the picture and prices dropped substantially, passenger traffic jumped to almost 20,000 per month. When American again dominated the field, demand dropped but there were still over 9,200 passengers per month. The same pattern of activity existed in the Kansas City and other markets. The government's argument was clear cut: Once American had driven the competition from the market, its gross revenue rose. For example, in the case of Colorado Springs, when there was no competition, American was grossing almost $600,000 a month. After the competition left the field, despite the decline in ticket prices American was grossing over twice as much. The same was true for the Kansas City and other routes. In Kansas City, American grossed just over $2.5 million before competition from the low-cost airlines and over $2.9 million after they left.

American Airlines claims that the government's case has no validity. They argue that the pricing decisions were not designed to drive competition out, but rather to help the company do business in a highly competitive environment. As one American spokesperson put it, "We simply matched the competition." The competition, quite obviously, disagrees.

departure for developing and analyzing the various models of behavioral decision making remains the degree and meaning of rationality.

Decision Rationality

The most often used definition of *rationality* in decision making is that it is a means to an end. If appropriate means are chosen to reach desired ends, the decision is said to be rational. However, there are many complications to this simple test of rationality. To begin with, it is very difficult to separate means from ends because an apparent end may be only a means for some future end. This idea is commonly referred to as the *means-ends chain* or *hierarchy*. Simon pointed out that "the means-end hierarchy is seldom an integrated, completely connected chain. Often the connection between organization activities and ultimate objectives is obscure, or these ultimate objectives are incompletely formulated, or there are internal conflicts and contradictions among the ultimate objectives, or among the means selected to attain them."[11]

Besides the complications associated with the means-ends chain, it may even be that the concept is obsolete. Decision making relevant to the national economy supports this position. Decision makers who seek to make seemingly rational adjustments in the economic system may in fact produce undesirable, or at least unanticipated, end results. Simon also warned that a simple means-ends analysis may have inaccurate conclusions.

One way to clarify means-ends rationality is to attach appropriate qualifying adverbs to the various types of rationality. Thus, *objective* rationality can be applied to decisions that maximize given values in a given situation. *Subjective* rationality might be used if the decision maximizes attainment relative to knowledge of the given subject. *Conscious* rationality might be applied to decisions in which adjustment of means to ends is a conscious process. A decision is *deliberately* rational to the degree that the adjustment of means to ends has been deliberately sought by the individual or the organization; a decision is *organizationally* rational to the extent that it is aimed at the organization's goals; and a decision is *personally* rational if it is directed toward the individual's goals.[12]

Models of Behavioral Decision Making

There are many descriptive models of behavioral decision making. In effect, these have become models for much of management decision-making behavior. The models attempt to describe theoretically and realistically how practicing managers make decisions. In particular, the models strive to determine to what degree management decision makers are rational. The models range from complete rationality, as in the case of the *economic rationality* model, to complete irrationality, as in the case of the *social* model. Figure 11.2 summarizes on a continuum the two major extremes and the in-between models of Simon's bounded rationality and the judgmental heuristics and biases model coming out of cognitive psychology. These models deal specifically with management decision-making behavior.

FIGURE 11.2
The continuum of decision-making behavior.

Economic rationality	Simon's bounded rationality model	Judgmental heuristics and biases model	Social model

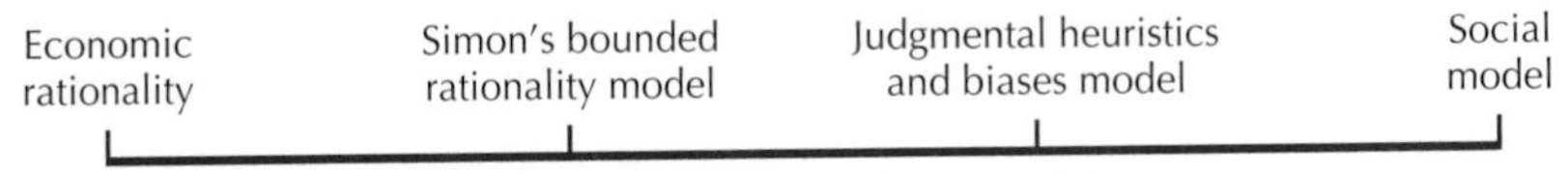

The Economic Rationality Model.   This model comes from the classical economics model, in which the decision maker is perfectly and completely rational in every way. Regarding decision-making activities, the following conditions are assumed:

1. The decision will be completely rational in the means-ends sense.
2. There is a complete and consistent system of preferences that allows a choice among the alternatives.
3. There is complete awareness of all the possible alternatives.
4. There are no limits to the complexity of computations that can be performed to determine the best alternatives.
5. Probability calculations are neither frightening nor mysterious.[13]

With this almost infallible ability, the decision maker always strives to maximize outcomes in the business firm, and decisions will be directed to the point of maximum profit where marginal cost equals marginal revenue (MC = MR).

Most economists and quantitative decision theorists do not claim that this depiction is a realistic descriptive model of modern decision-making behavior. But because this rational model and its accompanying quantitative methods have traditionally been embraced by the business schools, many of today's managers still equate "good" management decision making with this approach. Adherence to this approach, however, may be dangerous and may be a leading cause of many of today's problems.[14] As Peters and Waterman stated in their widely read *In Search of Excellence* book: "The numerative, rationalist approach to management dominates the business schools. It seeks detached, analytical justification for all decisions. It is right enough to be dangerously wrong, and it has arguably led us seriously astray."[15]

Obviously, Peters and Waterman are not saying "throw the rascal out," nor are other critics of the rational model. It has made and will continue to make a significant contribution to effective decision making. For example, the most successful consumer marketers, such as Procter & Gamble, Cheseibrough-Pond's, and Ore-Ida, are known for their rational approach and accompanying quantitative backup. The point that Peters and Waterman are making is that the rational model is not the be-all and end-all of effective decision making and that, if carried to the extreme, it may at least be misleading and at most be harmful to the decision-making process.

New Rational Techniques: ABC, EVA, and MVA.   Recently, traditional accounting and finance techniques based on the economic rationality model have been undergoing radical change. For example, well-known companies such as Daimler-Chrysler, Union Carbide, Hewlett-Packard, and General Electric have moved to a new type of accounting. To better manage costs, they now use activity-based costing, or what has become known as ABC. Traditionally, accounting identified costs according to the category of expense (for example, salaries, supplies, and fixed costs). ABC, on the other hand, determines costs according to what is paid for the different tasks employees perform. Under ABC, costs associated with activities such as processing sales orders, expediting supplier and/or customer orders, resolving supplier quality and/or delivery problems, and retooling of machines are calculated. Both the traditional and ABC methods reach the same bottom-line costs, but ABC provides decision makers a much more accurate breakdown of the cost data. For instance, B2B (business to business using the Internet) has been shown to greatly reduce identified acquisition and distribution costs of firms, and at Hewlett-Packard, when ABC showed that testing new designs and parts was extremely expensive, engineers changed their plans on the spot to favor components that required less testing, thus greatly lowering costs.

Another example of rethinking the traditional economic rationality used by management decision makers is the finance technique of economic value added, or EVA. A long-standing tenet of the economic model has been that a rational decision is one that results in earnings higher than the cost of capital. Traditionally, the cost of capital has simply been equated with the interest paid on borrowed capital. Under EVA, however, the true cost of all capital is determined. For example, the true cost of equity capital (the money provided by the shareholders) is the opportunity cost (what shareholders could earn in price appreciation and dividends if they invested in a similar company). Also, what a firm spends on research and development or employee training has been traditionally treated as expenses, but under EVA, it is treated as capital investments and is added into the cost of capital. The EVA is determined by subtracting this total cost of capital from the after-tax operating profit.

EVA has become popular because both companies and shareholders see it as a useful gauge for making decisions about issues ranging from acquisitions and divestitures to compensation.[16] Firms with a positive EVA are making rational decisions; those with a negative EVA are destroying capital and are in trouble. When CSX, Briggs and Stratton, and Coca-Cola moved to an EVA approach, the common stock value of these companies greatly increased.[17] Recently, because of the competition for capital, advocates say that EVA can be effectively used in the traditionally not-for-profit health care industry.[18]

A more recent and somewhat different measure is MVA (market value added). The difference between total market value (the amount that investors can take out of the company) and the invested capital (the total amount that investors have put into the company) is MVA. A positive MVA shows how much wealth has been created by the firm, and a negative balance shows how much capital has been wasted. Some top-ranked MVA firms include Coca-Cola, GE, Wal-Mart, Merck, and Microsoft.

MVA is usually directly related to EVA (a simple explanation is that MVA is the value the stock market places on the prospective stream of future EVAs). In the long run, firms with a strong EVA will also have a strong MVA. However, in the short run, EVA and MVA may be opposite. A firm may have a poor EVA, but stockholders may bet that the firm is making the right moves for the future and bid up the price of the stock, and thus the MVA is quite good. Examples are many of the dot-com firms that have negative EVA, but, because they are investing heavily in expensive advanced information technologies for the future, investors felt this would more than pay for itself in future earnings. The reverse could also be true. For example, many old economy firms have a strongly positive EVA, but this didn't impress investors, who made the decision to invest elsewhere because of the dim outlook of their future, and thus MVA was negative. In other words, even in these refinements of the economic rationality model, the human factor (i.e., the social decision-making model of rationality) still comes into the picture.

The Social Model.   At the opposite extreme from the economic rationality model is the social model drawn from psychology. Sigmund Freud viewed humans as bundles of feelings, emotions, and instincts, with their behavior was guided largely by their unconscious desires. Obviously, if this were the complete description, people would not be capable of making effective decisions.

Although most contemporary psychologists would take issue with the Freudian description of humans,[19] almost all would agree that psychological influences have a significant impact on decision-making behavior.[20] Furthermore, social pressures and influences may cause managers to make irrational decisions. The well-known conformity experiment conducted by Solomon Asch demonstrates human irrationality.[21] His study used several groups of seven to nine subjects each. They were told that their task was to compare the lengths of lines. All except one of the "subjects" in each group had pre-arranged with the experimenter to give clearly wrong answers on 12 of the 18 line-judgment trials. About 37 percent of the 123 naive subjects yielded to the group pressures and gave incorrect answers to the 12 test situations. In other words, more than one-third of the experimental subjects conformed to a decision they knew was wrong.

If more than one-third of Asch's subjects conformed under "right and wrong," "black and white" conditions of comparing the lengths of lines, a logical conclusion would be that the real, "gray" world is full of irrational conformists. It takes little imagination to equate Asch's lines with the alternatives of a management decision. There seems to be little doubt of the importance of social influences in decision-making behavior. In addition, there are many other psychological dynamics. For example, there seems to be a tendency on the part of many decision makers to stick with a bad decision alternative, even when it is unlikely that things can be turned around. Staw and Ross have identified four major reasons why this phenomenon, called *escalation of commitment,* might happen:[22]

1. *Project characteristics.* This is probably the primary reason for escalation decisions. Task or project characteristics such as delayed return on investment or obvious temporary problems may lead the decision maker to stick with or increase the commitment to a wrong course of action.
2. *Psychological determinants.* Once the decision goes bad, the manager may have information processing errors (use biased factors or take more risks than are justified). Also, because the decision maker is now ego-involved, negative information is ignored and defensive shields are set up.
3. *Social forces.* There may be considerable peer pressure put on decision makers and/or they may need to save face, so they continue or escalate their commitment to a wrong course of action.
4. *Organizational determinants.* Not only may the project or task characteristics lend themselves to the escalation of bad decisions—so may a breakdown in communication, dysfunctional politics, and resistance to change.

Certainly, the completely irrational person depicted by Freud is too extreme to be useful. However, escalation of commitment and other human dynamics covered throughout this text point out that there is little question of the important role that human complexity can and does play in management decision making.[23] Some management behavior is irrational but still very realistic. For example, the author and a colleague conducted two studies that showed that subjects in both laboratory and field settings who did not have much computer experience were more influenced in their decision activities by information presented by the computer than they were by information presented by noncomputer reporting procedures.[24] On the other hand, for those subjects with considerable computer experience, the reverse was true. In other words, decision makers are influenced in their choice activities even by the type of format in which information is presented to them. Managers without much computer experience may still be intimidated by the computer and place more value on information technology than is justified, while those with considerable computer experience may be highly skeptical and may underrate the importance of information technology.

Simon's Bounded Rationality Model. To present a more realistic alternative to the economic rationality model, Herbert Simon proposed an alternative model. He felt that management decision-making behavior could best be described as follows:

1. In choosing between alternatives, managers attempt to *satisfice,* or look for the one that is satisfactory or "good enough." Examples of satisficing criteria would be adequate profit or share of the market and fair price.
2. They recognize that the world they perceive is a drastically simplified model of the real world. They are content with this simplification because they believe the real world is mostly empty anyway.
3. Because they satisfice rather than maximize, they can make their choices without first determining all possible behavior alternatives and without ascertaining that these are in fact all the alternatives.
4. Because they treat the world as rather empty, they are able to make decisions with relatively simple rules of thumb or tricks of the trade or from force of habit. These techniques do not make impossible demands on their capacity for thought.[25]

In comparison with the economic rationality model, Simon's model is also rational and maximizing, but it is bounded. Decision makers end up satisficing because they do not have the ability to maximize. The case against maximizing behavior has been summed up by noting that objectives are dynamic rather than static; information is seldom perfect; there are obvious time and cost constraints; alternatives seldom lend themselves to quantified preference ordering; and the effect of environmental forces cannot be disregarded.[26] Simon's model recognizes these limitations. The traditional economic rationality model's assumptions are viewed as unrealistic. But in the final analysis, the difference between the economic rationality model and Simon's model is one of degree because, under some conditions, satisficing approaches maximizing, whereas in other conditions, satisficing and maximizing are very far apart.

Many economic, social, and organizational variables influence the degree to which satisficing becomes maximizing. An example of an economic variable is market structure. The more competitive the market, the more satisficing may approach maximizing. In an agricultural commodities market, satisficing will by necessity become maximizing. Economists generally recognize that in a purely competitive environment, profit maximization lends itself to the very survival of the firm. Thus, the decision maker must make maximizing decisions. In an oligopolistic market (for example, the automobile and steel industries), satisficing is different from maximizing. Oligopolistic firms can survive on the basis of adequate profit or share of the market. They do not have to operate at the point where marginal cost equals marginal revenue, and, in fact, they may be unavoidably prevented from maximizing.

Besides the economic market constraints, there are many socially based obstacles that prevent maximization in practice. Some of these social barriers are not consciously recognized by the management decision maker. Examples are resistance to change, desire for status, concern for image, organizational politics, and just plain stupidity. On the other hand, the decision maker may in some cases consciously avoid maximizing. Examples of the latter behavior include decisions that discourage competitive entry or antitrust investigation, restrain union demands, or maintain consumer goodwill. However, in the increasingly competitive global economy as described in Chapter 2, maximizing decisions are becoming more necessary.

Judgmental Heuristics and Biases Model.   Although Simon's bounded rationality model and the concept of satisficing are an important extension of the wholly economic rationality model, as Bazerman points out, it does not describe *how* judgment will be biased.[27] Thus, taking the bounded rationality model one step further, a cognitively based model that identifies specific systematic biases that influence judgment has emerged in the field of organizational behavior.

The judgmental heuristics and biases model is drawn mostly from Kahneman and Tversky, cognitive decision theorists, who suggested that decision makers rely on heuristics (simplifying strategies or rules of thumb).[28] Such judgmental heuristics reduce the information demands on the decision maker and realistically help in the following ways:

1. Summarize past experiences and provide an easy method to evaluate the present
2. Substitute simple rules of thumb or "standard operating procedures" for complex information collection and calculation
3. Save considerable mental activity and cognitive processing[29]

However, even though these cognitive heuristics simplify and help the decision maker, under certain conditions their use can lead to errors and systematically biased outcomes. Three major biases are identified that help explain how people's judgment deviates from a fully rational process. The following questions will help one better understand and will provide examples for the biases:

1. Are there more words in the English language that (*a*) begin with the letter *r* or (*b*) have *r* as the third letter?
2. On one day in a large metropolitan hospital, eight births were recorded by gender in the order of their arrival. Which of the following orders of births (B = boy, G = girl) was most likely to be reported?
   a. BBBBBBBB   b. BBBBGGGG   c. BGBBGGGB
3. A newly hired engineer for a computer firm in the Boston metropolitan area has four years of experience and good all-around qualifications. When asked to estimate the starting salary for this employee, my staff assistant (knowing very little about the profession or the industry) guessed an annual salary of $23,000. What is your estimate?
   $_____per year.[30]

Here are the three biases:

1. *The availability heuristic.*   This cognitive input into judgment refers to decision makers' tendencies to assess the frequency, probability, or likelihood of an event occurring by how readily they can remember it.[31] "An event that evokes emotions and is vivid, easily imagined, and specific will be more 'available' from memory than will an event that is unemotional in nature, bland, difficult to imagine, or vague."[32] An example would be a human resource manager's assessment of the probability of the effectiveness of a newly hired skilled worker from the local technical school, based on her recollection of the successes and failures of those graduates she has hired in recent years. This heuristic can be very valuable to decision makers because events that happen most frequently or are most vivid tend to lead to accurate judgments. By the same token, however, errors or bias results from this heuristic when the ease of recall is influenced by factors unrelated to the frequency of an event's occurrence.[33] For example, the most common response to question 1 above is (a), that there are more words that start with the letter *r*. However, the correct answer, by far, is (b); there are many more words with *r* as the third letter.[34] This is explained by the availability bias. More people can recall words that start with *r*, and it is difficult to think of those that have *r* as the third letter, so they falsely conclude that there must be more words that start with *r*. In other words, those words that start with *r* are more readily available in the typical person's memory, but this is a case where the remembered information is wrong and an error in judgment results.

2. *The representativeness heuristic.*   This second major heuristic uses decision rules of thumb based on the likelihood of an event's occurrence as judged by the similarity of that occurrence to stereotypes of similar occurrences. Managers would be using a representativeness heuristic when they predict the success of a new product on the basis of the similarity of that product to past successful and unsuccessful product types.[35] However, as with the availability heuristic, this representativeness thinking can be biased and lead to errors. For example, most people choose response (c) for question 2 because it appears to be most random. The reason is that both (a) and (b) are too ordered and are unlikely to occur. However, this is faulty logic. The correct response is that all three of the options are equally likely to occur. As explained by Northcraft and Neale, "the problem here is that we believe that a sequence of independent events (such as eight births) generated from a random process should resemble the essential characteristics of a random process, even when the sequence is too short for that process to express itself statistically. Decision makers expect a few examples of a random event to behave in the same way as large numbers of the event.[36]

3. *The anchoring and adjustment heuristic.*   In this heuristic, the decision maker makes a judgment by starting from an initial value or anchor and then adjusts to make the final decision. As Bazerman goes on to explain: "The initial value, or starting point, may be suggested from historical precedent, from the way in which a problem is presented, or from random information. For example, managers make salary decisions by adjusting from an employee's past year's salary."[37] However, as with the others, bias and resulting error in judgment can creep into this decision rule. For example, in question 3, most people do not think they are affected by the staff assistant's estimate. Yet Bazerman clearly found that they are. When he raised the staff assistant's estimate to $80,000, individuals gave much higher estimates, on average, than when the estimate was $23,000.[38] In other words, people use the staff assistant's estimate as an anchor (even though it is irrelevant information) and adjust from there.

Overall, even though the judgmental heuristics and biases model is based on relatively complex cognitive processing, it is quite descriptive of how managers actually make decisions. Despite the fact that this cognitive approach has only recently emerged in the mainstream of organizational behavior, there is a sound theoretical base and a growing stream of research.[39]

In the final analysis, all the decision models presented are appropriate under certain conditions and are used in combination with one another. This last one, however, has been largely ignored up to recent times. Obviously, it has to be taken into consideration for understanding decision making in today's organizations. Besides the heuristics and biases model, the various styles discussed next can also be helpful for not only understanding behavioral decision making, but making it more effective.

Decision-Making Styles

Besides the models of decision rationality, another approach to behavioral decision making focuses on the styles that managers use in choosing among alternatives. These styles reflect a number of psychological dimensions including how decision makers perceive what is happening around them and how they process information.[40] Specifically, behavioral decision-making styles can be categorized into two dimensions: value orientation and tolerance for ambiguity. The value orientation focuses on the decision maker's concern for task and technical matters as opposed to people and social concerns.

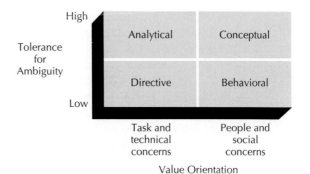

FIGURE 11.3
Decision-Making Styles

The tolerance for ambiguity orientation measures how much the decision maker needs structure and control (a desire for low ambiguity) as opposed to being able to thrive in uncertain situations (a desire for high ambiguity). These two orientations with their low and high dimensions are portrayed in the matrix shown in Figure 11.3, with four styles of decision making: directive, analytical, conceptual, and behavioral.

Directive Style.   Decision makers with a directive style have a low tolerance for ambiguity and are oriented toward task and the technical concerns. These decision makers tend to be efficient, logical, pragmatic, and systematic in their approach to problem solving. Directive decision makers also like to focus on facts and get things done quickly. They also are action oriented, tend to have a very short run focus, like to exercise power, want to be in control, and, in general, display an autocratic leadership style.

Analytical Style.   Analytical decision makers have a high tolerance for ambiguity and a strong task and technical orientation. These types like to analyze situations; in fact, they often tend to overanalyze things. They evaluate more information and alternatives than do directive decision makers. They also take a long time to make decisions, but they do respond well to new or uncertain situations. They also tend to have an autocratic leadership style.

Conceptual Style.   Decision makers with a conceptual style have a high tolerance for ambiguity and strong people and social concerns. They take a broad perspective in solving problems and like to consider many options and future possibilities. These decision makers discuss things with as many people as possible in order to gather a great deal of information and then rely on intuition in making their decisions. Conceptual decision makers are also willing to take risks and tend to be good at discovering creative solutions to problems. At the same time, however, they can foster an idealistic and indecisive approach to decision making.

Behavioral Style.   The behavioral style decision maker is characterized by a low tolerance for ambiguity and strong people and social concerns. These decision makers tend to work well with others and like situations in which opinions are openly exchanged. They tend to be receptive to suggestions, are supportive and warm, and prefer verbal to written information. They also tend to avoid conflict and be overly concerned with keeping everyone happy. As a result, these decision makers often have a difficult time saying no to people, and they do not like making tough decisions, especially when it will result in someone being upset with the outcome.

Style Implications.   Research reveals that decision makers tend to have more than one dominant style.[41] Typically managers rely on two or three decision styles, and these will vary by occupation, job level, and culture. These styles can be used to note the strong and weak points of decision makers. For example, analytical decision makers make fast decisions, but they also tend to be autocratic in their approach to doing things. Similarly, conceptual decision makers are innovative and willing to take risks, but they are often indecisive. These styles also help explain why different managers will arrive at different decisions after evaluating the same information. Overall, the analysis of decision-making styles is useful in providing insights regarding how and why managers make decisions, as well as offering practical guidelines regarding how to deal with various decision-making styles.

PARTICIPATIVE DECISION-MAKING TECHNIQUES

Most of the behaviorally oriented techniques, at least traditionally, have revolved around participation. Used as a decision-making technique, participation involves individuals or groups in the process. It can be formal or informal, and it entails intellectual and emotional as well as physical involvement. The actual amount of participation in making decisions ranges from one extreme of no participation, wherein the manager makes the decision and asks for no help or ideas from anyone, to the other extreme of full participation, where everyone connected with, or affected by, the decision is completely involved. In practice, the degree of participation will be determined by factors such as the experience of the person or group and the nature of the task. The more experience and the more open and unstructured the task, the more participation there will tend to be.[42]

In today's organizations there is an awakened interest in participation. Participative techniques have been talked about ever since the early human relations movement, and now, because of competitive pressures, the elimination of old hierarchical superior–subordinate relationships and the emergence of teams, horizontal structures, and boundary-spanning information technologies, organizations, teams, and individual managers are effectively using them.[43]

Participation techniques are being applied informally on an individual or a team basis or formally on a program basis. Individual participation techniques are those in which an employee somehow affects the decision making of a manager. Group participation utilizes consultative and democratic techniques. In consultative participation, managers ask for and receive involvement from their employees, but the managers maintain the right to make the decision. In the democratic form, there is total participation, and the group, not the individual head, makes the final decision by consensus or majority vote.

There are many positive and negative attributes of participative decision making. Balancing these attributes in evaluating the effectiveness of participative decision making is difficult because of moderating factors such as leadership style or personality of the parties involved; situational, environmental, and contextual factors;[44] and ideology.[45] Also, even though there is general research support,[46] the different forms of participative techniques can have markedly different outcomes. For example, informal participation was found to have a positive effect on employee productivity and satisfaction; representative participation had a positive impact on satisfaction, but not on productivity; and short-term participation was ineffective by both criteria.[47]

One problem is the tendency toward pseudoparticipation. Many managers ask for participation, but whenever subordinates take them up on it by making a suggestion or trying to make some input into a decision, they are put down or never receive any feedback. In some cases managers try to get their people involved in the task but not in the decision-making process. This can lead to a boomerang effect regarding employee satisfaction. If managers claim to want participation from their people but never let them become intellectually and emotionally involved and never uses their suggestions, the results may be negative. Also, participation can be very time consuming, and it has the same general disadvantages of committees such as pinpointing responsibility. From a behavioral standpoint, however, the advantages of participative decision making far outweigh the disadvantages. Most of the benefits are touched on throughout this text. Perhaps the biggest advantage is that the participative approach to decision making recognizes that each person can make a meaningful contribution to the attainment of organizational objectives.

CREATIVITY AND GROUP DECISION MAKING

By far, the most advances that have been made in decision making over the past several years have come from information technology. Management information systems (MIS) techniques, computerized decision support systems (DSS), data warehousing and mining, and expert systems are increasingly being used to help managers make better decisions. As Chapter 2 points out, such information-based approaches have had considerable impact and success. Yet, there are some recent research findings indicating that information technology such as DSS may not be the end-all solution to effective decision making. For example, one study found that more information was provided and exchanged by a group using DSS, but when compared with a group without DSS, no better decisions were made.[48] In another study, although the DSS improved the organization of the decision-making process, the DSS also led to less thorough and critical discussion.[49] However, today knowledge management is developing to more effectively process both tangible and intangible information (see Chapter 2), and everyday information technology tools (e-mail, word processing, spreadsheets, desktop publishing, PowerPoint/computerized presentation tools, and database programs) have become second nature. The key for effective decision makers is not to make them into information technologists, but make them into decision makers who can use information technology efficiently and effectively to make better decisions.[50]

Despite the increasing impact of advanced information technology on decision making, there is still a critical need for behaviorally oriented decision-making techniques. Unfortunately, only the participative behavioral techniques discussed so far have been available to managers, and there have been only a few scattered attempts to develop new techniques for helping make more creative and problem-solving types of decisions. Yet as knowledge management recognizes, it is these creative decisions that are still a major challenge facing modern management.

The Process of Creativity

A key challenge facing organizations in today's highly competitive environment is to be more creative and innovative. This is particularly true given the fact that many firms continue to downsize in an effort to become more efficient, but such a dramatic change on employees has been found to have a negative effect on the company's creativity.[51] Ironically, as the accompanying OB in Action box indicates, some firms have used creativity to eliminate the need to downsize at all.

Noted creativity researcher Teresa Amabile proposes that creativity is a function of three major components: expertise, creative-thinking skills, and motivation.[52] Expertise consists of knowledge: technical, procedural, and intellectual. Creative-thinking skills determine how flexibly and imaginatively people can deal with problems and

Application Example

Creative Decision Making to Eliminate Downsizing

Over the last decade, millions of workers have been laid off. In 1998 alone almost 700,000 Americans lost their jobs, and in recent years numbers have remained high. One of the major reasons for these layoffs has been downsizing. Unfortunately, growing research evidence questions whether layoffs due to downsizing really do produce long-run benefits for an organization. After all, the personnel can be let go only once, and even if the enterprise has some short-run cost savings from this one-time act, the long-run cost is being found to be greater than the short-term gain. In addition, the more indirect costs of loss of experience/knowledge and commitment of those remaining is much greater. Most organizations now agree with this argument and have begun looking for creative ways to eliminate the need for downsizing.

At Lincoln Electric, the Cleveland-based manufacturer of arc-welding products, for example, the company expanded internationally and suffered severe financial losses as a result. Rather than laying off anyone, however, the firm redeployed people from manufacturing operations into the sales department. Result: In their first year these new salespeople generated $10 million in revenue. Commenting on its creative approach to dealing with business setbacks, Lincoln's director of corporate relations said, "Our people are too valuable. The loss of one person costs us $100,000 to replace them. We don't do business that way." As a result, the company pulled out of its tailspin, returning a bonus to all employees and top management that has now averaged between 52 and 56 percent of salary for 65 straight years!

Rhino Products of Burlington, Vermont, is another example of a firm that has used creative decision making to deal with an economic downturn. When this specialty dessert maker realized that it could not keep its workforce intact, the management turned to Ben & Jerry's Ice Cream, a firm located nearby, and asked them if they would hire some of the Rhino personnel. For the next two years these workers learned new skills and gained a better understanding of customer needs and best practices, while still being able to keep their Rhino benefits and seniority. Then, as things improved for Rhino, they were brought back. Today Rhino is going strong and is introducing new products as well as increasing the size of its workforce.

Other firms are using similar types of creative approaches to prevent downsizing decisions from negatively affecting the personnel. Some of these include: (1) finding personnel who are interested in reduced hours, part-time work, job sharing, leaves of absence, or sabbaticals to work in the community; (2) networking with local employers regarding temporary or permanent redeployment; (3) using attrition effectively by examining whether a job needs to be filled or can be eliminated; (4) developing multistep, voluntary early retirement packages; and (5) cross training so trained people are ready to step into new job openings within the firm. Commenting on the use of these creative approaches, one expert in the field has recently noted that:

> Since all downsizing alternatives are grounded in a knowledge of each employee and his or her skills, a company must start with comprehensive employee assessment tools. A skills database that helps match people with business needs is the basis of effective redeployments. A tuned-in employer community—wider than just the downsizing firm—can retrain and reabsorb workers who have been downsized, thereby keeping downsizing to a minimum and addressing personnel shortages.

Drawing on these types of strategies, companies are finding that downsizing can be done efficiently and with minimum negative effects on the personnel. It is all a matter of learning how to use creative decision making.

make effective decisions. Motivation is the inner passion to solve the problem at hand, and this often results in decisions that are far more creative than expected.

Very simply, creativity results in people looking at things differently.[53] Research shows that, in contrast to the average person, creative people seem better able to do things such as abstracting, imaging, synthesizing, recognizing patterns, and empathizing.[54] They also seem to be good intuitive decision makers,[55] know how to take advantage of good ideas,[56] and are able to break old paradigms or ways of thinking and make decisions that sometimes seem to fly in the face of rationality. Such intuitive decision makers draw from their *tacit knowledge*. This type of knowledge is not readily explainable, is acquired through observation and experience, and seems to be in the unconscious.[57] Often, this tacit knowledge is important to effective decisions that rationality would discount. For example, banks have always focused on lending money to people who are good risks. However, what about lending to people who have little or bad credit and no collateral? This sounds like an irrational decision, but the ACCION bank has been doing just this by making microloans to small borrowers in the United States and Latin America for more than 30 years that more "rational" banks have turned down as bad credit risks. ACCION has done quite well helping small businesses to get started and to grow.[58]

How can today's decision makers increase their own creativity and generate more interesting and profitable solutions to difficult problems?[59] A number of useful ideas that have been offered by both successful professional managers and creativity researchers.[60] Michael Eisner, CEO and Chairman of the Walt Disney Company, has long contended creativity is not a "bolt out of the blue," but rather the result of careful thought and examination. In fact, early in his career one of his bosses wanted to have him fired because every time the boss suggested a new idea, Eisner would ask the manager if he could "think about it and get back to you." The boss was convinced that creativity was based on rapid responses, whereas Eisner believes that creativity is typically a result of careful, deliberate thought, an idea that is often echoed by many successful managers.[61] In fact, Eisner has often said, in contrast to stereotypical views of the creative process, that creativity is a disciplined process. In a recent interview, he explained his thinking this way:

> Discipline is good for the creative process, and time limits are good. An infinite amount of time to do a project does not always make it creatively better. The image of an artist being temperamental and acting like a 16-month-old child is usually false. It's a cliché that we've helped perpetrate in the movie business. Artists are always depicted as crazies. But in reality, insane artists are rare. In fact, some of the most creative people I've ever met—Steven Spielberg, George Lucas, I. M. Pei, Frank Stella, and Frank Gehry, just to name a few— are the most organized, mature individuals you'll ever meet. Not many creative people have the urge to cut off an ear.[62]

Creative ideas from both individuals and groups are scarce. One of the problems may be that students educated in business schools know how to crunch numbers, read a balance sheet, and now develop a Web page, but they have no knowledge of the creative process or how to develop creative solutions to problems. For example, General Foods held a competition in which student teams from prestigious business schools were given the charge to develop a new marketing plan that would stem the plunging sales of Sugar-Free Kool-Aid. Although they used quantitative analysis and the right terminology, they offered very few original ideas that the company could or would be able to use. The marketing manager concluded, "There were a couple of ideas that were of interest, but nothing we haven't looked at before."[63] A starting point for getting around this problem would be to understand the meaning and dimensions of creativity.

Psychological Definition and Analysis of Creativity

A simple, but generally recognized, psychological definition of *creativity* is that it involves combining responses or ideas of individuals or groups in novel ways.[64] Creative thinking reaches out beyond what is now known into what could be. It draws on observation, experience, knowledge, and the indefinable ability each person has to arrange common elements into new patterns. For instance, how would you respond to the problem of coming up with as many uses for a newspaper as possible? Compare your solution with the following proposal from a 10-year-old boy:

> You can read it, write on it, lay it down and paint a picture on it. . . . You could put it in your door for decoration, put it in the garbage can, put it on a chair if the chair is messy. If you have a puppy, you put newspaper in its box or put it in your backyard for the dog to play with. When you build something and you don't want anyone to see it, put newspaper around it. Put newspaper on the floor if you have no mattress, use it to pick up something hot, use it to stop bleeding, or to catch the drips from drying clothes. You can use a newspaper for curtains, put it in your shoe to cover what is hurting your foot, make a kite out of it, shade a light that is too bright. You can wrap fish in it, wipe windows, or wrap money in it. . . . You put washed shoes in newspaper, wipe eyeglasses with it, put it under a dripping sink, put a plant on it, make a paper bowl out of it, use it for a hat if it is raining, tie it on your feet for slippers. You can put it on the sand if you have no towel, use it for bases in baseball, make paper airplanes with it, use it as a dustpan when you sweep, ball it up for the cat to play with, wrap your hands in it if it is cold.[65]

Obviously, this boy describing the uses of a newspaper was very creative, but what caused his creativity?

Psychologists point out that it is much easier to provide examples of creativity than it is to identify causes. However, two widely recognized dimensions have been identified that can help explain the creative process:

1. *Divergent thinking.* This refers to a person's ability to generate novel, but still appropriate, responses to questions and problems. This is in contrast to convergent thinking, which leads to responses that are based mainly on knowledge and rational logic. In the preceding newspaper problem, convergent thinking would answer, "you read it," but divergent thinking would say, "make a kite out of it." The latter—divergent thinking—is considered more creative.
2. *Cognitive complexity.* This refers to a person's use of and preference for elaborate, intricate, and complex stimuli and thinking patterns. Creative people tend to have such cognitive complexity and display a wide range of interests, are independent, and are interested in philosophical or abstract problems. It is important to note, however, that creative people are not necessarily more intelligent (if intelligence is defined by standard tests of intelligence or grades in school, which tend to focus more on convergent thinking skills).[66]

Creativity Techniques for Management Decision Making

There are some techniques that managers can use to help them make more creative decisions. For example, a national survey of highly creative top managers found that they use techniques such as guided imagery, self-hypnosis, journal keeping, and lateral styles of thinking.[67] Not only does encouraging creativity help the organization; it may also help the employees. On the basis of interviews in several major Japanese companies, it was found that employee creativity is managed through deliberate structural means, not to effect direct economic outcomes to the organization, but to develop the employees' motivation, job satisfaction, and teamwork.[68] In other words, even though the Japanese are not known for their creative breakthroughs in product development or technology, they effectively structure their organizations to allow their people to creatively apply their ideas. A specific example of an organization structuring for creativity would be Toyota. This Japanese firm's designers think and work with sets of design alternatives rather than pursuing one alternative over and over. Toyota engineers gradually narrow the design sets until they come to a final solution. Analysis of the results of this seemingly slow and inefficient system conclude that the "set-based concurrent engineering" used by Toyota has made them quite effective auto developers.[69]

Other world-class auto manufacturers use similar creative approaches. A recent one is called *empathic design,* which relies heavily on visual information.[70] This creative technique is particularly useful when creating new products because it sidesteps the built-in problem associated with customer feedback. Most customers, when asked what new products they would like, typically respond in terms of the company's current products and suggest that they be made smaller or lighter or less expensive. Customers are notoriously poor in providing useful ideas for new products because their thinking is too closely linked to current products and their everyday uses.[71] Empathic design focuses on observing how people respond to products and services and drawing creative conclusions from the results. For example, when Nissan developed the Infinity J-30, it tested more than 90 samples of leather before selecting three that U.S. car buyers preferred. When Harley-Davidson builds a motorcyle it adjusts the motor so that it is pleasing to the customer's ears, that is, it sounds like a Harley (and it has sued competitors that have tried to imitate this sound).

By watching how people respond in the empathic approach, companies can generate more creative and consumer-pleasing offerings. This can be done in a number of ways. One is by taking pictures of people using the products. For example, when the Thermos Company had pictures taken of people using their charcoal grills, they saw that their units were much easier to use by men than by women, although women were often the ones doing the cooking. They then proceeded to redesign their grills so that they were equally appealing to women.

Envirosell, an international marketing research group, takes millions of photos every year of shoppers in retail stores to help answer the question: Who shops here and what do they like? Among other things, the research group has found that shoppers want wide aisles (they do not like to be bumped), good lighting (they like to see the merchandise clearly), and good signage (they want to know where things are located). Retail companies pay Envirosell large annual fees to provide them with marketing information regarding how to improve their sales. Where does Envirosell get these ideas? From analyzing the pictures of shoppers in their stores.[72] Instead of asking people questions about their shopping habits, the empathic design approach relies on observation to generate creative ideas and solutions. Table 11.1 provides some contrasts between the traditional method of asking customers questions and actually observing their behavior. Other creative approaches to decision making involve groups.

Group Decision Making

Creativity in decision making can apply to individuals or groups. Because individual decision making has largely given way to group decision making in today's organizations, an understanding of group dynamics and teams, as discussed in Chapter 14, becomes relevant to decision making. For example, that chapter's discussion of

TABLE 11.1   Inquiry versus Innovative Observation

Traditional Inquiry	*Innovative Observation*
People are often unreliable when it comes to explaining the types of goods and services they would be interested in purchasing.	Observers can rely on how people act in drawing conclusions regarding what types of products and services they would be willing to buy in the future.
People often give answers that they feel are acceptable to the questioner.	People give nonverbal clues through body language and spontaneous, unsolicited comments.
People are often unable to recall how they felt about a particular product or service that they received.	Observers can see how well people like a product or service based on the their reactions.
The questions that are asked can bias the responses.	There are no questions asked; all data are based on open-ended observation.
Peoples' routines are often interrupted by someone stopping them to ask questions.	People continue doing whatever they are doing, oblivious to the fact that they are being observed.
When comparing two similar products, respondents often have difficulty explaining why they like one better than the other.	By giving people an opportunity to use two similar products, observers can determine which is better liked or easier to use by simply watching how they behave.

Source: Adapted from Dorothy Leonard and Jeffrey F. Rayport, "Spark Innovation through Empathic Design," *Harvard Business Review,* November–December 1997, p. 111.

groupthink problems and phenomena such as the risky shift (that a group may make more risky decisions than individual members on their own) helps one better understand the complexity of group decision making.[73] In fact, a number of social decision schemes have emerged from social psychology research in recent years.[74]

These schemes or rules can predict the final outcome of group decision making on the basis of the individual members' initial positions. These have been summarized as follows:[75]

1. *The majority-wins scheme.*   In this commonly used scheme, the group arrives at the decision that was initially supported by the majority. This scheme appears to guide decision making most often when there is no objectively correct decision. An example would be a decision about what car model to build when the popularity of various models has not been tested in the "court" of public opinion.

2. *The truth-wins scheme.*   In this scheme, as more information is provided and opinions are discussed, the group comes to recognize that one approach is objectively correct. For example, a group deciding whether to use test scores in selecting employees would profit from information about whether these scores actually predict job performance.

3. *The two-thirds majority scheme.*   This scheme is frequently adopted by juries, who tend to convict defendants when two-thirds of the jury initially favors conviction.

4. *The first-shift rule.*   In this scheme, the group tends to adopt the decision that reflects the first shift in opinion expressed by any group member. If a car-manufacturing group is equally divided on whether or not to produce a convertible, it may opt to do so after one group member initially opposed to the idea changes her mind. If a jury is deadlocked, the members may eventually follow the lead of the first juror to change position.

Besides the listed schemes, there are also other phenomena, such as the status quo tendency (when individuals or groups are faced with decisions, they resist change and will tend to stick with existing goals or plans), that affect group decision making. Suggestions such as the following can be used to help reduce and combat the status quo tendency and thus make more effective group decisions:[76]

- When things are going well, decision makers should still be vigilant in examining alternatives.
- It can help to have separate groups monitor the environment, develop new technologies, and generate new ideas.
- To reduce the tendency to neglect gathering negative long-term information, managers should solicit worst-case scenarios as well as forecasts that include long-term costs.
- Build checkpoints and limits into any plan.
- When limits are reached, it may be necessary to have an outside, independent, or separate review of the current plan.
- Judge people on the way they make decisions and not only on outcomes, especially when the outcomes may not be under their control.
- Shifting emphasis to the quality of the decision process should reduce the need of the decision maker to appear consistent or successful when things are not going well.
- Organizations can establish goals, incentives, and support systems that encourage experimenting and taking risks.

In addition to simple guidelines such as these, group decision techniques such as Delphi and nominal grouping can also be used to help eliminate the dysfunction of groups and help them make more effective decisions.

The Delphi Technique

Although Delphi was first developed many years ago at the Rand Corporation's think tank, it has only recently become popularized as a group decision-making technique, for example, for long-range forecasting. Today, numerous organizations in business, education, government, health, and the military are using Delphi. No decision technique will ever be able to predict the future completely, but the Delphi technique seems to be as good a crystal ball as is currently available.

The technique, named after the oracle at Delphi in ancient Greece, has many variations, but generally it works as follows:

1. A group (usually of experts, but in some cases nonexperts may deliberately be used) is formed, but, importantly, the members are not in face-to-face interaction with one another. Thus, the expenses of bringing a group together are eliminated.
2. Each member is asked to make anonymous predictions or input into the problem decision the group is charged with.
3. Each member then receives composite feedback from what the others have inputted. In some variations the reasons are listed (anonymously), but mostly just a composite figure or list is used.
4. On the basis of the feedback, another round of anonymous inputs is made. These iterations take place for a predetermined number of times or until the composite feedback remains the same, which means everyone is sticking with his or her position.

A major key to the success of the technique lies in its anonymity. Keeping the responses of Delphi group members anonymous eliminates the problem of "saving face" and encourages the experts to be more flexible and thus to benefit from the estimates of others. In the traditional interacting group decision-making technique, the experts may be more concerned with defending their vested positions than they are with making a good decision.

Many organizations testify to the success they have had so far with the Delphi technique. Weyerhaeuser, a building supply company, has used it to predict what will happen in the construction business, and Smith, Kline, Beecham, a drug manufacturer, has used it to study the uncertainties of medicine. TRW, a highly diversified, technically oriented company, has 14 Delphi panels averaging 17 members each. The panels suggest products and services that have marketing potential and predict technological developments and significant political, economic, social, and cultural events. Besides business applications, the technique has been used successfully on various problems in government, education, health, and the military. In other words, Delphi can be applied to a wide variety of program planning and decision problems in any type of organization.

The major criticisms of the Delphi technique center on its time consumption, cost, and Ouija-board effect. The third criticism implies that, much like the parlor game of that name, Delphi can claim no scientific basis or support. To counter this criticism, Rand has attempted to validate Delphi through controlled experimentation. The corporation set up panels of nonexperts who use the Delphi technique to answer questions such as, "How many popular votes were cast for Lincoln when he first ran for president?" and "What was the average price a farmer received for a bushel of apples in 1940?" These particular questions were used because the average person does not know the exact answers but knows something about the subjects. The result of these studies showed that the original estimates by the panel of nonexperts were reasonably close to being correct, but with the Delphi technique of anonymous feedback, the estimates greatly improved.

The Nominal Group Technique

Closely related to Delphi is the nominal group approach to group decision making. The nominal group has been used by social psychologists in their research for many years. A nominal group is simply a "paper group." It is a group in name only because no verbal exchange is allowed between members. In group dynamics research, social psychologists would pit a fully interacting group against a nominal group (a group of individuals added together on paper but not interacting verbally). In terms of number of ideas, uniqueness of ideas, and quality of ideas, research has found nominal groups to be superior to real groups. The general conclusion is that interacting groups have certain dysfunctions that inhibit creativity. For example, one study found that the performance of participants in interactive groups was more similar, more conforming, than the performance of those in nominal groups.[77] Yet, except for idea generation, the interactive effect of real group members is known to have a significant positive effect on other variables. The latter type of effect is given attention in Chapter 14, on group dynamics and teams.

When the pure nominal group approach is expanded into a specific technique for decision making in organizations, it is labeled the *nominal group technique* (NGT) and consists of the following steps:

1. Silent generation of ideas in writing
2. Round-robin feedback from group members, who record each idea in a terse phrase on a flip chart or blackboard
3. Discussion of each recorded idea for clarification and evaluation
4. Individual voting on priority ideas, with the group decision being mathematically derived through rank ordering or rating[78]

The difference between this approach and Delphi is that the NGT members are usually acquainted with one another, have face-to-face contact, and communicate with one another directly in the third step. Although more research is needed, there is some evidence that NGT-led groups come up with many more ideas than traditional interacting groups and may do as well as, or slightly better than, groups using Delphi.[79] A study also found that NGT-led groups performed at a level of accuracy that was equivalent to that of the most-proficient members.[80] However, another study found that NGT-led groups did not perform as well as interacting groups whose participants were pervasively aware of the problem given the group and when there were no dominant persons who inhibited others from communicating ideas.[81] A recent study also found that individuals working alone and then formed into nominal groups were superior, but for computer-mediated idea generation, intact groups (such as a regular work group) generated more ideas (with higher quality) than those working in subgroups or than individuals in a nominal group.[82] Thus, as is true of most of the techniques discussed in this text, there are moderating effects. A review of the existing research literature on Delphi and NGT concluded:

> In general, the research on both Delphi and nominal group techniques suggests that they can help improve the quality of group decisions because they mitigate the problems of interacting groups—individual dominance and groupthink. A skillful chairperson, therefore, may adapt these techniques to particular decision-making situations.[83]

Summary

This chapter has been devoted to the process and techniques of decision making. Decision making is defined as choosing between two or more alternatives. However, viewed as a process, the actual choice activity is preceded by gathering information and developing alternatives. The models of behavioral decision making include the completely economic rationality model on one extreme, Herbert Simon's bounded rationality model and the judgmental heuristics and biases model in the middle range, and the irrationally based social model on the other extreme. Each of these models gives insights into decision-making rationality. For example, even the traditional accounting and finance techniques under the economic rationality model of decision making have recently given way in some companies to more effective activity-based costing (ABC), economic value added (EVA), and market value added (MVA) techniques. The same is true of the social models at the other extreme. Understanding human dynamics, such as irrational conformity or escalation of commitment, gives more credibility to the social model of decision making. However, Simon's bounded rationality, the judgmental heuristics and biases model from cognitive psychology, and the various management decision styles have emerged as having the biggest impact on behavioral decision-making theory and practice.

The techniques for decision making are currently being dominated by information technology. The behavioral techniques do not begin to approach the sophistication of these techniques. Yet it is the creative, problem-solving management decisions that are crucial for organizational success. Understanding the strengths and weaknesses of participative techniques and the creative individual and group decision-making process and techniques (Delphi and nominal grouping) can lead to more effective decision making for the future.

ENDING WITH META-ANALYTIC RESEARCH FINDINGS

OB PRINCIPLE: Using decision techniques such as devil's advocacy and dialectical inquiry can lead to better problem-solving decisions.

Meta-Analysis Results: [432 participants; $d = .22$] *On average, there is a **56 percent probability** that those who use the devil's advocacy and/or dialectical inquiry approach to solve problems will make higher-quality decisions than those who do not use these techniques.*

Conclusion: As this chapter points out, there are many different processes and techniques associated with decision making. Some are highly rational whereas others are irrationally based. Recently, behavioral decision-making techniques aimed at making creative, problem-solving decisions have gained increased attention. The devil's advocacy (DA) and dialectical inquiry (DI) approaches are two of the most commonly studied techniques for helping individuals to make more effective decisions. DA is a decision-making method in which an individual or group is assigned a role of critic who is supposed to criticize the proposed solution to problems. DI on the other hand, is a method whereby alternative solutions are generated that are purposely opposite to the proposed solution. Both approaches help to improve decision making because they force decision makers to identify and criticize assumptions of decisions. This increases the likelihood that the "best" decision will be made.

Source: Adapted from C. R. Schwenk, "Effects of Devil's Advocacy and Dialectical Inquiry on Decision Making: A Meta-Analysis," *Organizational Behavior and Human Decision Performance,* Vol. 47, 1990, pp. 161–176.

Questions for Discussion and Review

1. What are the three steps in Simon's decision-making process? Relate these steps to an actual decision.
2. Compare and contrast the economic rationality model and the social model. What are some recent refinements of these two extreme models?
3. Describe the major characteristics of Simon's bounded rationality model. Do you think this model is descriptive of the decision making of practicing executives?
4. Identify the three major judgmental biases. How do they differ from one another? Give an example of each in management decision making.
5. Identify and describe the four major management decision-making styles. What are some strengths and weaknesses of these styles?
6. What is the difference between divergent and convergent thinking, and what is their relationship to the process of creativity?
7. Explain a hypothetical situation in which Delphi and/or NGT could be used.

Internet Exercise: Decision Making in Organizations

Although decisions are made in organizations every day, it is oftentimes either the large decisions, such as laying off many workers, or bad decisions, such as evidenced recently in the Firestone Tire recall that receive all the attention. Using your search engine, come up with several organizations that have recently had a decision with negative or positive outcomes in the national news. Then, take these decisions, and consider the following:

1. What were the reasons behind the poor decisions? Which framework did the poor decisions fall under (rational, bounded rational, heuristic, or social)? Were the poor decisions the result of using an incorrect decision-making model? Analyze the same issues for the good decisions that you found.
2. Could the decisions be improved by using one of the group decision-making techniques discussed in your text? Don't forget to consider the downside to this, such as increased time to make the decision.
3. Did you find any specific organizations that had a pattern of wrong decisions? If so, discuss the possible reasons for this, based on the models discussed in your text.

REAL CASE:
Putting a Human
Face on Rational
Decisions

For more than two decades, behavioral economists such as Richard Thaler, Andrei Shleifer, Daniel Kahneman, and the late Amos Tversky have been pointing out all the ways in which people diverge from the hyperrational behavior that is assumed by conventional economics. They procrastinate on saving for retirement. They shop for hours to save pennies, then make snap decisions on big-ticket items. They run up huge credit-card debts even when they have ample savings to pay them off.

Behavioral economics says real people act like this because most of us lack the farsightedness or the willpower to do what the textbooks say we should. Makes sense, right? But even though it does a better job of describing reality, behavioral economics isn't part of the average economist's tool-box. One reason: Its psychological insights were never put into a formal language that economists could understand and work with. "The math was too complicated," says Colin F. Camerer, a business economist at the California Institute of Technology.

Now, behavioral economics is getting the mathematical rigor it needs to enter the mainstream of economics, where it can influence forecasting and policy decisions. That's thanks in large part to the formulations of Matthew Rabin, a 36-year-old economist at the University of California at Berkeley. Rabin, who wears tie-dyed T-shirts every day and does some of his best work at the counter of a San Francisco coffee shop, is considered a mathematical wizard by his colleagues. This year, Rabin won a $500,000 John D. & Catherine T. MacArthur Foundation "genius" fellowship in recognition of his work on formalizing behavioral economics.

A bedrock assumption of standard economics is that people attempt to maximize their well-being, using all available information and always acting with their long-term self-interest in mind. From this starting point, economists build models of all economic activity, from how people respond to price changes to what careers they pursue. In general, the assumption works pretty well. But not always. Rabin's goal is to improve the predictiveness of conventional economic models by plugging into them more realistic formulas for how people actually behave.

Take, for example, the exploding field of behavioral finance. Thaler, author of *The Winner's Curse: Paradoxes and Anomalies of Economic Life*, uses behavioral theories to explain what economists call the "equity premium puzzle": the odd fact that the long-term returns on equities are much higher than those on bonds—even more than their higher volatility would seemingly call for. Thaler says the answer to the puzzle is that people hate losses much more than they enjoy gains. So investors demand higher returns from stocks to compensate for their dread of losses. Likewise, sports fans who would not pay more than $200 for a Super Bowl ticket wouldn't sell one they own—i.e. "lose" it—for less than $400.

Rabin has made big contributions in the study of fairness. Imagine there's a drought. The more others conserve water, the more water a self-interested person could use without causing the reservoir to run dry. In fact, though, people are fair; they tend to conserve more when they see others conserving. That's what Rabin built into his formal model. Says Rabin: "People reciprocate public-spiritedness in others rather than counteract it." His model also takes into account that perceptions of unfairness breed retaliation, even when the cost of retaliating is very high.

Rabin's work on self-control problems such as procrastination is catching on most quickly. Cornell University economist Ted O'Donoghue and Rabin demonstrate that there's a good reason why many people put off the chore of financial planning—it takes a lot of work, and there's an insignificant cost of delaying the work until tomorrow. The difficulty comes from the fact that the same is true every day—and those small daily losses eventually add up to a tremendous sum. Rabin should know: He admits to having his own "severe procrastination problem." Rabin adds that people procrastinate longer on the most important things because the up-front effort is usually greatest.

O'Donoghue and Rabin recommend policies to fight procrastination, such as automatic enrollment in employee retirement plans, transaction deadlines, and on-the-job seminars on retirement planning. Economists once assumed such measures were unnecessary. But Thaler, who offers similar recommendations, says the steps "are designed to take into account people's humanness."

1. On the continuum of decision-making behavior (Figure 11.2), which model(s) is behavioral economics concerned with?
2. What is the "equity premium puzzle"? Can you give a personal example?
3. Why do you suppose that "work on self-control problems such as procrastination is catching on most quickly"? Can you provide an example and explanation of why people do this?
4. Why do you think it has taken so long for the "human face" to be widely recognized in decision-making analysis and practice?

REAL CASE:
The Banker Who
Can Say No

In 1997, Masamoto Yashiro, 71, was looking forward to a quiet retirement. Today the former Citibank Japan chief has a job that is anything but quiet: running money-center Shinsei Bank Ltd. Japanese politicians recently branded Yashiro a "national enemy." He has done the unthinkable: shown deadbeat corporate borrowers the door.

Hard-nosed banking is fine in the West, but this is Japan. And Shinsei, the reincarnation of Long-Term Credit Bank of Japan Ltd., was expected to play by the rules. But the bank, after being nationalized in 1998 with nearly $40 billion in debt, is now owned by a clutch of foreign investors, including Ripplewood Holdings, Mellon Bank, Paine Webber, and GE Capital. They are determined to set their own rules.

When the government recently sold the bank for $1.12 billion, it seemed a step forward in the campaign to modernize Japan's financial industry. It still might be. But six months later, Yashiro and his team face daunting challenges. The loan book Shinsei inherited from the government is shakier than promised. And Shinsei's effort to move out of the low-margin corporate loan business and into more profitable sectors like asset management and investment banking has been a struggle.

Yashiro has had to build a retail banking operation and investment bank mostly from scratch. But he has been distracted by vociferous political pressure to cut Shinsei borrowers some slack. "I can make myself a very liked person by saying: 'O.K., we'll forgive you, we love you,'" he says, but "then what happens to this bank?"

Hence Shinsei recently made a controversial decision to pull out of a $6 billion debt forgiveness scheme for retail giant Sogo Corp. The provisioning costs of swallowing its share of the Sogo loan would have wiped out Shinsei's projected $180 million profit for the fiscal year ending in March. But the withdrawal triggered Japan's second biggest corporate failure in history—and earned Shinsei the enmity of the political establishment.

It wasn't supposed to be this hard. After all, the government had assumed about half of Shinsei's debt, leaving it with supposedly sound assets of $120 billion. Shinsei had a strong capital adequacy ratio of 13 percent, well above the globally mandated 8 percent, as well as cash for growth. Yet trouble wasn't far off. One borrower, consumer-finance company Life Co., revealed a $1 billion negative net worth, double the estimate. Shinsei cut it off. Then when the bank opted to sell back its Sogo loan to the government, as it was entitled to do, it earned a drubbing from the ruling Liberal Democratic Party.

Not that Yashiro is going to fold. Companies without viable turnaround plans will be sent packing, he says with a grin, regardless of the backlash: "I have a very tough skin."

Credited with building up Citibank Japan's retail banking franchise, Yashiro was an obvious choice to run Shinsei. His goal is to achieve the same 120- to 160-basis-point return on assets that top Western banks earn, versus 30 in Japan. To get there, he has beefed up the consumer side by setting up telephone banking, offering mutual funds, and laying plans for online banking in 2001. On the investment banking side, Shinsei hopes to leverage its lending relationship with 450 corporate clients by offering to repackage and sell their assets and by helping them hedge against price shocks and currency moves.

Shinsei is a long way from taking on the major merger and acquisition advisers. And it has stiff local competition. Mizuho Holdings Inc., the three-way alliance among Industrial Bank of Japan, Fuji Bank, and Dai-Ichi Kangyo, is using its $1.2 trillion in assets to target similar niches.

Still, Shinsei seems to have the resources and talent to reemerge as a force in Japanese banking. Yashiro, who expects to take the bank public, even thinks he can deliver a profit for the government on its $2.3 billion worth of preferred shares. Of course, it would help if the politicians would stop carping from the sidelines.

1. What model of decision-making behavior (Figure 11.2) most closely describes the approach that Masamoto Yashiro is using in running this Japanese bank? Is this the appropriate way to run the bank? Why?
2. What decision style is Yashiro using? What are the strengths and weaknesses of this style? What style should he use if the bank becomes profitable? Why?
3. What creative techniques could Yashiro employ to reach his goals for the bank?
4. What implications do differing cultures have on the decision-making process, models, styles, and techniques? Give specific examples from this case from Japan compared to your own country of origin.

ORGANIZATIONAL BEHAVIOR CASE: Harry Smart— Or Is He?

Harry Smart, a very bright and ambitious young executive, was born and raised in Boston and graduated from a small New England college. He met his future wife, Barbra, who was also from Boston, in college. They were married the day after they both graduated cum laude. Harry then went on to Harvard, where he received an M.B.A., and Barbra earned a law degree from Harvard. Harry is now in his seventh year with Brand Corporation, which is located in Boston, and Barbra has a position in a Boston law firm.

As part of an expansion program, the board of directors of Brand has decided to build a new branch plant. The president personally selected Harry to be the manager of the new plant and informed him that a job well done would guarantee him a vice presidency in the corporation. Harry was appointed chairperson, with final decision-making privileges, of an ad hoc committee to determine the location of the new plant. At the initial meeting, Harry explained the ideal requirements for the new plant. The members of the committee were experts in transportation, marketing, distribution, labor economics, and public relations. He gave them one month to come up with three choice locations for the new plant.

A month passed and the committee reconvened. After weighing all the variables, the experts recommended the following cities in order of preference: Kansas City, Los Angeles, and New York. Harry could easily see that the committee members had put a great deal of time and effort into their report and recommendations. A spokesperson for the group emphasized that there was a definite consensus that Kansas City was the best location for the new plant. Harry thanked them for their fine job and told them he would like to study the report in more depth before he made his final decision.

After dinner that evening he asked his wife, "Honey, how would you like to move to Kansas City?" Her answer was quick and sharp. "Heavens, no!" she said, "I've lived in the East all my life, and I'm not about to move out into the hinterlands. I've heard the biggest attraction in Kansas City is the stockyards. That kind of life is not for me." Harry weakly protested, "But, honey, my committee strongly recommends Kansas City as the best location for my plant. Their second choice was Los Angeles and the third was New York. What am I going to do?" His wife thought a moment and then replied, "Well, I would consider relocating to or commuting from New York, but if you insist on Kansas City, you'll have to go by yourself!"

The next day Harry called his committee together and said, "You should all be commended for doing an excellent job on this report. However, after detailed study, I am convinced that New York will meet the needs of our plant better than Kansas City or Los Angeles. Therefore, the decision will be to locate the new plant in New York. Thank you all once again for a job well done."

1. Did Harry make a rational decision?
2. What model of behavioral decision making does this case support?
3. What decision techniques that were discussed in the chapter could be used by the committee to select the new plant site?

CHAPTER 12

Stress and Conflict

Learning Objectives

Define the meaning of stress.

Identify the extraorganizational, organizational, and group stressors.

Examine individual dispositions of stress.

Describe intraindividual and interactive conflict.

Discuss the effects of stress and conflict.

Present strategies for coping/managing stress and negotiation skills for conflict resolution.

Starting with Best Practice
Leader's Advice

Harvard's Robert H. Mnookin on Negotiation Strategies for Managers

Since the 1980s, the Program on Negotiation for Senior Executives based at Harvard Law School has been attended by more than 12,000 corporate executives and government officials. The program is taught by a cooperative arrangement of faculty from four prominent universities, which include Harvard, MIT, Tufts, and Simmons. Robert H. Mnookin, Williston Professor at Harvard Law School and chair of the steering committee of the program, discusses their experience with effective negotiation.

Q1:   *Typically, who attends the program on negotiation?*

Mnookin: People who hold important executive positions in their organizations. There's a broad range of titles and ages, and some 30 percent are women. They come because they realize that negotiation skills are fundamentally important: We all negotiate with customers, with suppliers, colleagues, subordinates, superiors. The people who attend our program are usually reasonably effective negotiators, but they want to both hone their skills and develop a conceptual framework to understand negotiations.

Q2:   *Are you saying there's literally a theory of negotiation?*

Mnookin: Certainly. There are three myths about negotiation, and our program gives the lie to all three. One of these myths is that there's not relevant theory in regard to negotiation. On the contrary, here at Harvard we're committed to developing theory that has practical, prescriptive applications to help people negotiate more effectively.

The core idea that we've been promoting for years is that most negotiations involve opportunities to expand the pie—in other words, they are not zero-sum games. It's also true that every negotiation involves distributive issues. No matter how big the pie gets, there'll be a question of who gets what size slice. But the important thing is the core idea that negotiations create value and have the potential for making both parties better off. Not necessarily equally, but not win-lose either. The win-lose mind-set can be disabling and lead to escalation and no deal at all.

Another myth is that people improve their negotiating skills through experience. I don't think they do. Certainly, they develop negotiation habits that sometimes serve them well, but when they don't they have no idea of why not. Instead, they blame the other side.

The third myth is that negotiation can't be taught. The response to our program demonstrates that's false. Having taught thousands of people, I think I can help even outstanding negotiators do it better. Indeed, the people who are very skilled often learn the most, because often it's a matter of tuning.

Q3:   *For those who face a negotiation before any chance of attending your course, what core advice would you give them?*

Mnookin: Prepare, prepare, prepare. As a lawyer, I'm astonished that lawyers who would spend weeks preparing for trial often go into a negotiation thinking it's something they can do on the fly. In preparing, there are a couple of key ideas. First, think very hard: If I don't reach a negotiated agreement with this person, what's my best alternative away from the table? We call that a BATNA, which stands for Best Alternative to a Negotiated Agreement. Sometimes you can improve your BATNA—for instance, if you're negotiating with your boss for a salary increase, and if you have two other offers for higher salaries, your alternatives are pretty darn good. That gives you more negotiating power at the table.

    Second, ask yourself: What are my interests here? What are the things that are important to me in going into this negotiation? Often, for instance, I have an important interest in preserving a good relationship, or I may have an interest in motivating an employee or in aligning an employee's incentives with the larger goals of the company. Thinking about what those interests are ahead of time is crucial.

    Then you must ask yourself about the other person's interests. You can't *know* what's most important to him, but you can ask: If I were in his shoes, knowing what I do know, what would be important to me? What would my interests be? One of the things you're going to learn at the negotiating table is to learn more about what the other person's interests are. In negotiations, I put a lot of effort into listening. I ask, "Tell me what's important to you." If somebody says, "I want X dollars," I say, "Tell me why the money's important. What other things are important to you?"

Q4:   *Are some people natural negotiators—salespeople, for instance?*

Mnookin: As in all human activities—whether oration or the high jump—some people are more gifted than others. Some people have very good interpersonal skills, are good at reading other people, are quick learners, and are skilled natural negotiators. People in sales have very good persuasive skills and are very good listeners, and listening skills are very valuable to a negotiator.

Q5:   *What's the biggest mistake inexperienced negotiators make?*

Mnookin: Not listening. They're good at talking, but not at listening, or demonstrating understanding; or they fail to learn about the other person's culture, if you're engaged in cross-cultural negotiations. Inexperienced negotiators tend to be very positional; they'll make demands without articulating the interests that underlie those demands. They also often go into negotiation with an adversarial mind-set that can be counterproductive. I go into negotiation with a problem-solving mind-set. I don't assume that the other person has the same interests as I do, nor do I assume there won't be distributive issues that have to be resolved. What I try to do is frame the negotiation as a shared problem and to see how the other person and I can work together to solve that problem. At the same time, I'm prepared to defend myself if I need to.

Traditionally, the field of organizational behavior has treated stress and conflict separately. Even though they are conceptually similar, and individuals, groups, and organizations in interaction are more associated with conflict, at the individual (intraindividual) level, they can be treated together. Therefore, this chapter combines stress and conflict. Conceptually, going from micro to macro, the discussion starts off with the meaning of stress and then examines the causes of stress. This is followed by both the intraindividual and interactive levels of conflict. Next, the effects of stress and conflict are examined, and the final part presents the ways of coping/managing stress and conflict with particular emphasis given to effective negotiation skills for resolving conflict.

THE EMERGENCE OF STRESS

A leading expert on stress, cardiologist Robert Eliot, gives the following prescription for dealing with stress: "Rule No. 1 is, don't sweat the small stuff. Rule No. 2 is, it's all small stuff. And if you can't fight and you can't flee, flow."[1] What is happening in today's organizations, however, is that the "small stuff" is getting to employees, and they are not going with the "flow." Stress has become a major buzzword and legitimate concern of the times.

New Environment Demands

There is considerable evidence that most managers report feeling work-related stress,[2] and the recent environment is making things worse. For example, globalization and strategic alliances have led to a dramatic increase in executive travel stress[3] and relocation.[4] The other major environmental impact of advanced information technology presented in the opening chapters has led to a new term of *technostress*.[5] Polls indicate that the exploding technology has created the following problems for today's employees at all levels:

- Loss of privacy
- Information inundation
- Erosion of face-to-face contact
- Continually having to learn new skills
- Being passed over for promotion because of their lack of knowledge

In addition to the feelings of technical inadequacy, one dot-com firm called DriveSavers has become an overnight success by solving computer crises (e.g., coaxing lost data from a hopelessly corrupted hard drive or rescuing files from a laptop submerged in 50 feet of water after a boat sank).[6] Besides globalization and advanced information technology, there is also evidence that increased diversification of the workforce may lead to unique stress problems[7] and that workers increasingly pressed into overtime work show significant higher levels of stress.[8]

This stress epidemic not only has a deteriorating impact on those affected and their families (which will be discussed later in the chapter), but is also very costly to organizations. The president of the American Institute of Stress at the New York Medical College recently noted that the cost of stress in the U.S. workplace

> . . . is estimated between $200 and $300 billion annually, as assessed by absenteeism, employee turnover, direct medical costs, workers' compensation and other legal costs, diminished productivity, accidents, etc., and is spread throughout the corporation, from the mailroom to the executive suite.[9]

In other words, stress in the workplace seems to be getting worse, and the costs are escalating. Before getting into the details, however, the exact meaning of stress is necessary.

What Stress Is, and Is Not

Stress is usually thought of in negative terms. It is thought to be caused by something bad (for example, a college student is placed on scholastic probation, a loved one is seriously ill, or the boss gives a formal reprimand for poor performance). This is a form of distress. But there is also a positive, pleasant side of stress caused by good things (for example, a college student makes the dean's list; an attractive, respected acquaintance asks for a date; an employee is offered a job promotion at another location). This is a form of *eu*stress. This latter term was coined by the pioneers of stress research from the Greek *eu,* which means "good." Applied to the workplace, a recent large study by researchers at Cornell University of 1,800 managers identified examples of "bad" stress as office politics, red tape, and a stalled career and "good" stress as challenges that come with increased job responsibility, time pressure, and high-quality assignments.[10] In other words, stress can be viewed in a number of different ways and has been described as the most imprecise word in the scientific dictionary. The word *stress* has also been compared with the word *sin:* "Both are short, emotionally charged words used to refer to something that otherwise would take many words to say."[11]

Although there are numerous definitions and much debate about the meaning of job stress,[12] Ivancevich and Matteson define *stress* simply as "the interaction of the individual with the environment," but then they go on to give a more detailed working definition, as follows: "an adaptive response, mediated by individual differences and/or psychological processes, that is a consequence of any external (environmental) action, situation, or event that places excessive psychological and/or physical demands on a person."[13] Note the three critical components of this definition: (1) it refers to a reaction to a situation or event, not the situation or event itself; (2) it emphasizes that stress can be impacted by individual differences; and (3) it highlights the phrase "excessive psychological and/or physical demands," because only special or unusual situations (as opposed to minor life adjustments) can really be said to produce stress.[14]

In another definition, Beehr and Newman define *job stress* as "a condition arising from the interaction of people and their jobs and characterized by changes within people that force them to deviate from their normal functioning."[15] Taking these two definitions and simplifying them for the purpose of this chapter, *stress* is defined as an adaptive response to an external situation that results in physical, psychological, and/or behavioral deviations for organizational participants.

It is also important to point out what stress is *not:*

1. *Stress is not simply anxiety.* Anxiety operates solely in the emotional and psychological sphere, whereas stress operates there and also in the physiological sphere. Thus, stress may be accompanied by anxiety, but the two should not be equated.

2. *Stress is not simply nervous tension.* Like anxiety, nervous tension may result from stress, but the two are not the same. Unconscious people have exhibited stress, and some people may keep it "bottled up" and not reveal it through nervous tension.

3. *Stress is not necessarily something damaging, bad, or to be avoided.* Eustress is not damaging or bad and is something people should seek out rather than avoid. The key, of course, is how the person handles the stress. Stress is inevitable; distress may be prevented or can be effectively controlled.[16]

What About Burnout?

As far as the increasingly popular term "burnout" is concerned, some stress researchers contend that burnout is a type of stress[17] and others treat it as having a number of components.[18] One stress and trauma support coordinator makes the distinction between stress and burnout as follows, "Stress is normal and often quite healthy. However, when the ability to cope with stress begins to let us down, then we may be on the road to burnout."[19] John Izzo, a former HR professional in the occupational development area, suggests that burnout may be the consequence of "losing a sense of the basic purpose and fulfillment of your work." He goes on to say that "Getting more balance or getting more personal time will help you with stress—but it will often not help you with burnout."[20] Research in this area shows that burnout is not necessarily the result of individual problems such as character or behavior flaws in which organizations can simply change people or get rid of them. In fact, Christina Maslach, a well-known stress researcher, says the opposite is probably true. She concludes that "as a result of extensive study, it is believed that burnout is not a problem of the people themselves but of the social environment in which people work."[21] She believes that burnout creates a sense of isolation and a feeling of lost control, causing the burned-out employee to relate differently to others and to their work.[22] Burnout is also most closely associated with the so-called helping professions such as nursing, education, and social work. So, even though technically burnout may be somewhat different from stress, the two terms will be treated the same here and used interchangeably.

Finally, conceptually similar to stress is conflict. Although there is some overlap in analyzing the causes and effects and managing stress and conflict, they are both covered in this chapter. The major difference, except for intraindividual conflict, is that conflict in the field of organizational behavior is more associated with disagreement or opposition at the interpersonal or intergroup level. After examining stressors, these levels of conflict are given attention.

THE CAUSES OF STRESS

The antecedents of stress, or the so-called stressors, affecting today's employees are summarized in Figure 12.1. As shown, these causes come from both outside and inside the organization, from the groups that employees are influenced by, and from employees themselves.

FIGURE 12.1
Categories of stressors
affecting occupational
stress.

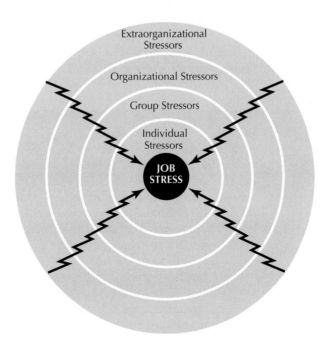

Extraorganizational Stressors

Although most analyses of job stress ignore the importance of outside forces and events, it is becoming increasingly clear that these have a tremendous impact. Taking an open-systems perspective of an organization (that is, the organization is greatly affected by the external environment), it is clear that job stress is not limited just to things that happen inside the organization, during working hours. Extraorganizational stressors include things such as societal/technological change, globalization, the family, relocation, economic and financial conditions, race and class, and residential or community conditions.

The phenomenal rate of change, which is given detailed attention in the introductory chapters, has had a great effect on people's lifestyles, and this of course is carried over into their jobs. Although medical science has increased the life spans of people and has eradicated or reduced the threat of many diseases, the pace of modern living has increased stress and decreased personal *wellness*. The concept of wellness has been defined as "a harmonious and productive balance of physical, mental, and social well-being brought about by the acceptance of one's personal responsibility for developing and adhering to a health promotion program."[23] Because people tend to get caught up in the rush-rush, mobile, urbanized, crowded, on-the-go lifestyle of today, their anxiety[24] and wellness in general has deteriorated; the potential for stress on the job has increased.

It is generally recognized that a person's family has a big impact on personality development. A family situation—either a brief crisis, such as a squabble or the illness of a family member, or long-term strained relations with the spouse or children—can act as a significant stressor for employees. Also, recent trends have made it increasingly difficult for employees to adequately balance the responsibilities of their jobs and their families. As employees are working longer hours and bringing more work home at night,[25] more and more pressure is being placed on work-family relationships[26] and more emphasis on the coordination of work and vacation schedules, and the search for elder and child care options has become prominent and very stressful.[27]

Relocating the family because of a transfer or a promotion can also lead to stress. For example, under globalization, expatriate managers (those with an assignment outside their home country) may undergo cultural shock and then when repatriated (relocated to the home country) may experience isolation; both are significant stressors.[28] For most people in recent years, their financial situation has also proved to be a stressor. Many people have been forced to take a second job ("moonlight"), or the spouse has had to enter the workforce in order to make ends meet. This situation reduces time for recreational and family activities. The overall effect on employees is more stress on their primary jobs.

Life's changes may be slow (getting older) or sudden (the death of a spouse). These sudden changes have been portrayed in novels and movies as having a dramatic effect on people, and medical researchers have verified that especially sudden life changes do in fact have a very stressful impact on people.[29] They found a definite relationship between the degree of life changes and the subsequent health of the person. The more change, the poorer the subsequent health. These life changes can also directly influence job performance. One psychologist, Faye Crosby, reports that divorce interferes with work more than any other trauma in a person's life. She says, "During the first three months after a spouse walks out, the other spouse—male or female—usually is incapable of focusing on work."[30]

Sociological variables such as race, sex, and class can also become stressors. As the workforce becomes increasingly diverse (see Chapter 3), potential stress-related issues include differences in beliefs and values, differences in opportunities for rewards or promotions, and perceptions by minority employees of either discrimination or lack of fit between themselves and the organization.[31] Researchers have noted over the years that minorities may have more stressors than whites.[32] Although a recent re-view of up-to-date evidence concludes that women experience more stress than men,[33] an earlier meta-analysis performed on 15 studies found no significant sex dif-ferences in experienced and perceived work stress.[34] There continues to be evidence that women perceive more job demands than men in both the male-dominated and female-dominated occupations.[35] Also, people in the middle and upper classes may have particular or common stressors. The same is true of the local community or region that one comes from. For example, one researcher identified the condition of housing, convenience of services and shopping, neighborliness, and degree of noise and air pollution as likely stressors.[36]

Organizational Stressors

Besides the potential stressors that occur outside the organization, there are also those associated with the organization itself. Although the organization is made up of groups of individuals, there are also more macrolevel dimensions, unique to the organization, that contain potential stressors. Figure 12.2 shows that these macrolevel stressors can be

FIGURE 12.2
Macrolevel organizational
stressors.

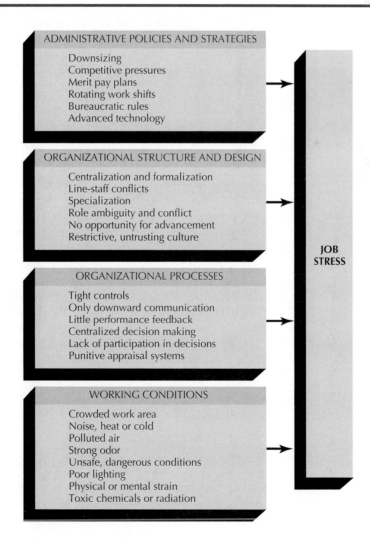

categorized into administrative policies and strategies, organizational structure and design, organizational processes, and working conditions. Some specific examples of these organizational stressors include responsibility without authority, inability to voice complaints, inadequate recognition, and lack of clear job descriptions or reporting relationships.[37] It should be noted that as organizations dramatically change to meet the environmental challenges outlined in the introductory chapters (globalization, information technology explosion, and diversity), there are more and more accompanying stressors for individual employees in their jobs. For example, a recent study by Deloitte and Touche found that 84 percent of U.S. companies were undergoing at least one major change intervention in their business strategy in order to compete in today's ultracompetitive environment. Programs such as reengineering, restructuring, and downsizing have become commonplace as the result of intense pressures to outperform the competition. Downsizing, in particular, has and continues to take its toll on employees. The actual loss of jobs, or even the mere threat of being laid off, can be extremely stressful for employees. Additionally, the "survivors" of downsizing "often experience tremendous pressure from the fear of future cuts, the loss of friends and colleagues, and an increase in workload."[38] In other words, downsizing often translates to longer hours and more stress for the survivors.[39]

Government data indicate that "an astonishing two-thirds of all American workers—over 75 million people—put in anything but traditional hours. Rather, they clock more than half their workday outside Ward Cleaver's time zone, the one that starts after breakfast and ends before supper, Monday through Friday."[40] Research indicates that such chronic occupational demands can lead to stress.[41]

Group Stressors

Chapter 14 will indicate the tremendous influence that the group has on behavior. The group can also be a potential source of stress. These group stressors can be categorized into two areas:

1. *Lack of group cohesiveness.* Starting with the historically famous Hawthorne studies, discussed in Chapter 1, it has become very clear that cohesiveness, or "togetherness," is very important to employees, especially at the lower levels of organizations. If an employee is denied the opportunity for this cohesiveness because of the task design, because the supervisor does things to prohibit or limit it, or because the other members of the group shut the person out, the resulting lack of cohesiveness can be very stress-producing.
2. *Lack of social support.* Employees are greatly affected by the support of one or more members of a cohesive group. By sharing their problems and joys with others, they are much better off. If this type of social support is lacking for an individual, the situation can be very stressful. There is even research indicating that the lack of social support is so stressful that it accounts for some health care costs.[42]

In addition to the group per se, group-level dynamics may become stressors. For example, one study found that organizational politics was a potential source of stress in the work environment.[43]

Individual Stressors: The Role of Dispositions

In a sense, the stressors discussed so far (extraorganizational, organizational, and group) all eventually get down to the individual level. There is also more research and agreement on possible situational dimensions and individual dispositions that may affect stress outcomes. For example, individual dispositions such as Type A personality patterns, personal control, learned helplessness, and psychological hardiness may all affect the level of stress someone experiences. In addition, the intraindividual level of conflict stemming from frustration, goals, and roles, covered next under conflict, definitely has implications as individual stressors.

Type A Characteristics.   The discussion of personality in Chapter 7 points out the complexity of, and individual differences in, personality dispositions and traits. Personality traits such as authoritarianism, rigidity, extroversion, supportiveness, spontaneity, emotionality, tolerance for ambiguity, anxiety, and the need for achievement have been uncovered by research as being particularly relevant to individual stress.[44] Most attention, however, has centered on the so-called Type A personality.

Although heart researchers have been working on the use of personality types and the resulting behavior patterns in order to predict heart attacks since the 1950s, in the late 1960s Friedman and Rosenman popularized the use of Type A and opposing Type B personalities in the study of stress. These types were portrayed as relatively stable characteristics, and initially Friedman and Rosenman's extensive studies found the Type A profile correlated highly with experienced stress and dangerous physical consequences.[45] In recent years, however, there is increasing evidence that Type As face no higher risk of heart disease than anyone else.

Table 12.1 gives the reader a chance to see whether he or she tends to be a Type A or a Type B personality. A majority of Americans are Type A, and an even higher percentage of managers are Type A; one study found that 60 percent of the managers sampled were clearly Type A and that only 12 percent were Type B.[46]

Friedman and Rosenman define the Type A personality as "an action-emotion complex that can be observed in any person who is aggressively involved in a chronic,

TABLE 12.1   Type A–Type B Self-Test

To determine your Type A or Type B profile, circle the number on the continuums (the verbal descriptions represent endpoints) that best represents your behavior for each dimension.

Am casual about appointments	1 2 3 4 5 6 7 8	Am never late
Am not competitive	1 2 3 4 5 6 7 8	Am very competitive
Never feel rushed, even under pressure	1 2 3 4 5 6 7 8	Always feel rushed
Take things one at a time	1 2 3 4 5 6 7 8	Try to do many things at once; think about what I am going to do next
Do things slowly	1 2 3 4 5 6 7 8	Do things fast (eating, walking, etc.)
Express feelings	1 2 3 4 5 6 7 8	"Sit" on feelings
Have many interests	1 2 3 4 5 6 7 8	Have few interests outside work

Total your score: _____ Multiply it by 3: _____. The interpretation of your score is as follows:

Number of points	Type of personality
Less than 90	B
90 to 99	B+
100 to 105	A−
106 to 119	A
120 or more	A+

Source: Adapted from R. W. Bortner, "A Short Rating Scale as a Potential Measure of Pattern A Behavior," *Journal of Chronic Diseases,* Vol. 22, 1966, pp. 87–91.

TABLE 12.2 Profiles of Type A and Type B Personalities

Type A Profile	Type B Profile
Is always moving	Is not concerned about time
Walks rapidly	Is patient
Eats rapidly	Doesn't brag
Talks rapidly	Plays for fun, not to win
Is impatient	Relaxes without guilt
Does two things at once	Has no pressing deadlines
Can't cope with leisure time	Is mild-mannered
Is obsessed with numbers	Is never in a hurry
Measures success by quantity	
Is aggressive	
Is competitive	
Constantly feels under time pressure	

incessant struggle to achieve more and more in less and less time, and if required to do so, against the opposing efforts of other things or other persons."[47] Table 12.2 briefly summarizes the Type A and Type B profiles. Obviously Type A employees (managers, salespersons, staff specialists, secretaries, or rank-and-file operating employees) experience considerable stress. They are the ones who:

1. Work long, hard hours under constant deadline pressures and conditions for overload.
2. Often take work home at night or on weekends and are unable to relax.
3. Constantly compete with themselves, setting high standards of productivity that they seem driven to maintain.
4. Tend to become frustrated by the work situation, to be irritated with the work efforts of others, and to be misunderstood by supervisors.[48]

By contrast, as shown in Table 12.2, Type B personalities are very laid back, they are patient and take a very relaxed, low-key approach to life and their job.

It is now accepted Type As per se do not predict heart problems, and in fact Type As may release and better cope with their stress than do Type Bs. The most recent studies indicate that it is not so much the impatience that is closely associated with Type As that leads to heart problems, but rather anger and hostility.[49] A leading medical researcher noted that the term "Type A" probably has outlived its usefulness. He stated: "Being a workaholic, being in a hurry, interrupting people, are not necessarily bad for your heart. What is bad is if you have high levels of hostility and anger, and you don't bother to hide it when dealing with other people."[50] This conclusion was supported by an organizational psychiatrist who, after extensive study of the causes of stress in Japanese, German, and American workers, concluded that "how workers handle their own aggression is the key factor in determining whether they will experience the kind of stress that can lead to heart attacks, high blood pressure and other health problems."[51] However, before completely dismissing the relationship of Type A to severe physical outcomes, it should be noted that anger, hostility, and aggression sometimes go along with a Type A personality.

Besides the debate surrounding the impact of Type A personality on health is the question of the performance and success of Type As versus Type Bs. It is pretty clear that Type As perform better[52] and are typically on a "fast track" to the top. They are more successful than Type Bs. However, at the *very* top they do not tend to be as successful as Type Bs, who are not overly ambitious, are more patient, and take a broader view of things.[53] The key may be to shift from Type A to Type B behavior, but, of course, most Type As are unable and *unwilling* to make the shift and/or to cope with their Type A characteristics.

Personal Control. Besides Type A personality patterns, another important disposition is an individual's perception of control. As mentioned in Chapter 7's discussion on job satisfaction, people's feelings about their ability to control the situation are important in determining their level of stress. In particular, if employees feel that they have little control over the work environment and over their own job, they will experience stress.[54] Studies have shown that if employees are given a sense of control over their work environment, such as being given a chance to be involved in the decision-making process that affects them, this will reduce their work stress.[55] A large study by Cornell University medical researchers found that those workers who experience a loss of control, especially in relatively low-level jobs, have triple the risk of developing high blood pressure. The researchers concluded that lack of control turns stress into physical problems. They also found that if a high-stress job included latitude to control the situation, there was no increase in blood pressure.[56] A study in a hospital setting also found that employee perceptions of the amount of control they experience at work relate to stress, which in turn affects physiological outcomes such as blood pressure as well as psychological outcomes such as job satisfaction.[57]

Learned Helplessness. The feeling of loss of control goes back to some of the classic research on learned helplessness conducted by Seligman.[58] Chapter 9 introduced this concept in relation to optimism. In conducting experiments on dogs who could not escape shock, Seligman found that they eventually accepted it and did not even try to escape. Later, when the dogs could learn to escape easily, they did not—they had learned to be helpless. Other studies found that people, too, can learn to be helpless,[59] which helps explain why some employees just seem to have given up and seem to accept stressors in their work environment, even when a change for the better is possible.

More recently, Seligman and his colleagues have concentrated on people's attributions for their lack of control. Specifically, they suggest that people are most apt to experience helplessness when they perceive the causes of the lack of control:

1. To be related to something about their own personal characteristics (as opposed to outside, environmental forces)
2. As stable and enduring (rather than just temporary)
3. To be global and universal (cutting across many situations, rather than in just one sphere of life)[60]

Further study and research on the sense of control in general and learned helplessness in particular will provide much insight into stress and how to cope with it.

Psychological Hardiness. Everyone has observed individual differences of people faced with stressors. Some people seem to go to pieces at the slightest provocation, whereas others seem unflappable in the face of extremely stressful situations. Those able to cope successfully with extreme stressors seem to have a "hardiness" disposition.

Kobasa and her colleagues studied executives under considerable stress who were both measurably hardy and nonhardy. She found that the hardy executives had a lower rate of stress-related illness and were characterized as having commitment (they became very involved in what they were doing); welcoming challenge (they believed that change rather than stability was normal); and feeling in control (they felt they could influence the events around them).[61] She suggests that the predisposition of psychological hardiness helps those with it to resist stress by providing buffers between themselves and stressors.

Such buffering drawn from hardiness may be an important quality as organizations now and in the future demand more and more from their employees at all levels. As has been noted:

> Why does the job seem so demanding? It isn't just long hours or clumsy direction from above, though there's plenty of that. All sorts of pressure, from the stress of participatory management techniques to the hyperkinesia of two-career marriages to the dismay of finding your workload increasing as you near 50, just when you thought you could adopt a more dignified pace, are working together to squeeze the oomph from heretofore steely-eyed achievers.[62]

Kobasa's research would say that those with hardiness will be able to survive and even thrive in such an environment, but those who do not possess hardiness may suffer the harmful outcomes of stress and conflict.

INTRAINDIVIDUAL CONFLICT

Although stress and conflict are treated differently, they are combined in this one chapter mainly because of the conceptual similarity between individual dispositional stressors and intraindividual conflict. After presenting the intraindividual forms of conflict in terms of frustration, goals, and roles, some more macro interactive conflict models are briefly reviewed as shown in Figure 12.3.

Conflict Due to Frustration

Frustration occurs when a motivated drive is blocked before a person reaches a desired goal. Figure 12.4 illustrates what happens. The barrier may be either overt (outward, or physical) or covert (inward, or mental-sociopsychological). The frustration model can

FIGURE 12.3
Level of conflict in
organizational behavior.

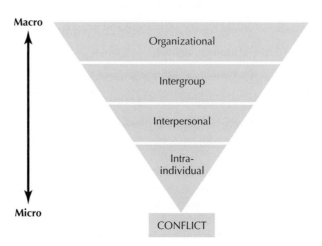

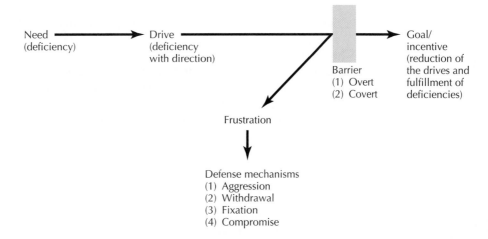

FIGURE 12.4
A model of frustration.

be useful in the analysis not only of behavior in general but also specific aspects of on-the-job behavior. Theft of company property and even violence on the job may be a form of an aggressive outcome to job frustration. For example, a summary article on violence in the workplace noted that in recent years more than a thousand Americans were murdered while on the job. Although the vast majority of these deaths were not the result of work-related incidents, homicide is still considered to be the second leading cause of death in the workplace (behind transportation accidents) and the leading cause of workplace death for women, and it has even been suggested that workplace homicide is the fastest-growing category of murder in the United States.[63]

In addition to aggression and violence, the withdrawal reaction to frustration may be a major explanation for the "motivational problem" of employees. They may be apathetic or have "retired on the job" because they are frustrated, not because they have no motivation. Many employees' motives have been blocked by dead-end jobs, high degrees of job specialization, or supervisors who put up barriers. Also, the fixation reaction to frustration may be used to explain irrational bureaucratic behavior. (The rules become the ends in themselves, and the frustrated employee pathetically adapts to the barriers.) Compromise can help explain midcareer changes (frustrated employees go around the barriers) or "living outside the job" (frustrated employees cannot achieve motivated goals on the job, so they seek fulfillment outside the job). These reactions to frustration often cost organizations a great deal because of the dysfunctions associated with aggression, withdrawal, and fixation. In the case of compromise, the employee's motivation is forced outside the organization. Although the discussion so far indicates the dysfunctional nature of frustration, such negativity should not be automatically assumed.

In some cases frustration may actually result in a positive impact on individual performance and organizational goals. An example is the worker or manager who has high needs for competence and achievement and/or who has high self-efficacy (see Chapter 9's discussion) in being able to do a job well. A person of this type who is frustrated on the job may react in a traditional defensive manner, but the frustration may result in improved performance. The person may try harder to overcome the barrier or may overcompensate, or the new direction or goal sought may be more compatible with the organization's goals. In addition, it should be remembered that defense mechanisms per se are not bad for the individual. They play an important role in the psychological adjustment process and are unhealthy only when they dominate the individual's personality. Also, those who have successfully overcome frustration in the past by learning that it is possible to surmount barriers or find substitute goals are more tolerant of frustration than those who have never experienced it, or than those who have experienced excesses in frustration. However, in general, a major goal of management should be to eliminate the barriers (imagined, real, or potential) that are or will be frustrating to employees. This goal may be accomplished through job redesign efforts (see Chapter 15) that are more compatible with employee motivation or leadership skills that get the frustrating barriers out of people's way.

Goal Conflict

Another common source of conflict for an individual is a goal that has both positive and negative features, or two or more competing goals. Whereas in frustration motives are blocked before the goal is reached, in goal conflict two or more motives block one another. For ease of analysis, three separate types of goal conflict are generally identified:

1. *Approach-approach* conflict, where the individual is motivated to approach two or more positive but mutually exclusive goals.
2. *Approach-avoidance* conflict, where the individual is motivated to approach a goal and at the same time is motivated to avoid it. The single goal contains both positive and negative characteristics for the individual.
3. *Avoidance-avoidance* conflict, where the individual is motivated to avoid two or more negative but mutually exclusive goals.

To varying degrees, each of these forms of goal conflict exists in the modern organization, but approach-avoidance is most relevant to the analysis of conflict.

Approach-avoidance conflict results from organizational goals having both positive and negative aspects for organizational participants. Basic research in psychology suggests that the positive aspects of a given organizational goal are stronger and more salient at a distance (in time and/or space) than the negative aspects. On the other hand, as a person gets nearer to the goal, the negative aspects become more pronounced, and at some point the individual may hesitate or fail to progress any further at the point where approach equals avoidance. For example, managers engaged in long-range planning typically are very confident of a goal (a strategic plan) they have developed for the future. Yet, as the time gets near to commit resources and implement the plan, the negative consequences seem to appear much greater than they did in the developing stage. Managers in such a situation may reach the point where approach equals avoidance. The result is a great deal of internal conflict and stress, which may cause indecision, physical reactions, or even depression.

Such approach-avoidance conflict and its aftermath are very common among decision makers and people in responsible positions in the fast-changing "new paradigm" organizations described in the chapters in the introductory part of the text. This era of global competition and advanced information technology has been depicted as one that involves trying to manage in the midst of chaos. As noted in a cover story of *Fortune,* "To the survivors, the revolution feels something like this: scary, guilty, painful, liberating, disorienting, exhilarating, empowering, frustrating, fulfilling, confusing, challenging."[64] In other words, as these terms indicate, many managers in recent years have been experiencing very mixed feelings, or approach-avoidance reactions. The accompanying Application Box: Dealing with Conflicting Goals gives some real-world examples.

APPLICATION EXAMPLE

Dealing with Conflicting Goals

How can managers deal with conflicting goals? One way is by recognizing that conflict exists in every organization and cannot be avoided. For example, many management experts argue that in order to bring about change, top executives have to be out front rallying the personnel and showing that they support the change. On the other hand, these same experts point out that change has to have a broad cadre of leaders at the middle and lower levels who are willing to carry the banner of change. So what is a leader to do: Get out front or encourage the personnel to assume this responsibility? The two approaches seem to be in conflict.

Or consider the independence versus interdependence conflict. Organizations demand that their managers act independently and assume personal initiative and responsibility for their units. However, when a manager initiates an action that steps on another unit's toes, the first manager often is called on the carpet and encouraged to "be more of a team player."

Another conflict is that of revenue growth versus cost containment. If managers spend all their time trying to grow the business, they face the criticism of not controlling their costs. If they put the primary focus on keeping expenses under control, they are asked why they are not increasing their revenue base.

What can managers do to deal with these conflicts? One way is to realize that conflict often forms into a central dilemma: empowerment versus alignment. Successful managers explore both approaches and balance their emphasis accordingly. For example, at General Motors there long has been a conflict between achieving low cost per unit through economies of scale (large-size enterprise) and responding to customer demands by reducing time to market. At IBM there has been an ongoing conflict between growing the business (raising revenues) and increasing profit (lowering costs). At Mercedes there has been a continual clash between factions in the firm who want to design and build quality cars (engineering emphasis) and those who argue that many people are unwilling to pay a premium for the car because they neither want nor appreciate such innovation (marketing emphasis). The successful manager often is the one who best can balance the conflicting demands while not losing sight of the organization's overall objectives. Through effective conflict management, the efforts of all concerned can be directed toward common goals that hopefully will be beneficial to both the people involved and the overall organization.

Role Conflict and Ambiguity

Closely related to the concept of norms (the "oughts" of behavior), *role* is defined as a position that has expectations evolving from established norms. People living in contemporary society assume a succession of roles throughout life. A typical sequence of social roles would be that of child, son or daughter, teenager, college student, boyfriend or girlfriend, spouse, parent, and grandparent. Each of these roles has recognized expectations that are acted out like a role in a play.

Besides progressing through a succession of roles such as those just mentioned, the adult in modern society fills numerous other roles at the same time. It is not uncommon for the adult middle-class male to be simultaneously playing the roles of husband, father, provider, son (to elderly parents), worker or manager, student (in a night program), coach of a Little League baseball team, church member, member of a social club, bridge partner, poker club member, officer of a community group, and weekend golfer. Women, of course, also have numerous, often conflicting, roles.[65] Although all the roles that men and women bring into the organization are relevant to their behavior, in the study of organizational behavior the organizational role is the most important. Roles such as digital equipment operator, clerk, team leader, salesperson, engineer, systems analyst, department head, vice president, and chairperson of the board often carry conflicting demands and expectations. There is recent research evidence that such conflict can have a negative impact on performance and be affected by cultural differences.[66]

There are three major types of role conflict. One type is the conflict between *the person and the role*. There may be conflict between the person's personality and the expectations of the role. For example, a production worker and member of the union is appointed to head up a new production team. This new team leader may not really believe in keeping close control over the workers, and it goes against this individual's personality to be hard-nosed, but that is what the head of production expects. A second type is *intrarole* conflict created by contradictory expectations about how a given role should be played. Should the new team leader be autocratic or democratic in dealing with the team members? Finally, *interrole* conflict results from the differing requirements of two or more roles that must be played at the same time. Work roles and non-work roles are often in such conflict. For example, a successful executive working for a computer company said that she often worked from 7:30 A.M. to 11:30 P.M. Her long hours led to the breakup of a relationship. When she got word that her mother was seriously ill, she remembered: "I had about five minutes to be upset before the phone started ringing again. You get so far into it, you don't even realize your life has gotten away from you completely."[67]

The production team leader and the fast-climbing executive obviously represent the extreme cases of organizational role conflict. Yet to varying degrees, depending on the individual and the situation, people in every other position in the modern organization also experience one or all three types of conflict. Staff engineers are not sure of their real authority. The clerk in the front office does not know whether to respond to a union organizing drive. The examples are endless. The question is not whether role conflict and ambiguity exist—they do, and they seem inevitable.[68] Rather, the key becomes a matter of determining how role conflict can be resolved or managed.[69]

INTERACTIVE CONFLICT

Besides the intraindividual aspects of conflict that are closely related to stress, the interactive aspects of conflict are also an important dynamic of organizational behavior. This section is specifically concerned with analyzing the interactive conflict that can result at the interpersonal and intergroup levels in today's organizations.

Interpersonal Conflict

Those who have interpersonal conflict most often attribute the cause to a personality problem or defect in the other party. For example, research from attribution theory, presented in Chapter 6, on the so-called fundamental attribution error suggests that people attribute others' behavior to personal factors such as intelligence, ability, motivation, attitudes, or personality. Whetten and Cameron, however, go beyond this surface explanation and propose that there are four major sources of interpersonal conflict.[70] These can be summarized as follows:

1. *Personal differences.* Everyone has a unique background because of his or her upbringing, cultural and family traditions, and socialization processes. Because no one has the same family background, education, and values, the differences can be a major source of conflict. Disagreements stemming from the differences "often become highly emotional and take on moral overtones. A disagreement about who is factually correct easily turns into a bitter argument over who is morally right."[71]

2. *Information deficiency.* This source of conflict results from communication breakdown in the organization. It may be that the two people in conflict are using different information or that one or both have misinformation. Unlike personal differences, this source of conflict is not emotionally charged and once corrected, there is little resentment.

3. *Role incompatibility.* This type of interpersonal conflict draws from both intraindividual role conflict (discussed in the previous section) and intergroup conflict (discussed in the next section). Specifically, in today's horizontal organizations, managers have functions and tasks that are highly interdependent. However, the individual roles of these managers may be incompatible. For example, the production manager and the sales manager have interdependent functions: one supports the other. However, the role of the production manager is to cut costs, and one way to do this is to keep inventories low. The sales manager, on the other hand, has the role of increasing revenues through increased sales. The sales manager may make delivery promises to customers that are incompatible with the low inventory levels maintained by production. The resulting conflict from role incompatibility may have to be resolved by higher-level management or systems development through advanced information technology.

4. *Environmental stress.* These types of conflict can be amplified by a stressful environment. In environments characterized by scarce or shrinking resources, downsizing, competitive pressures, or high degrees of uncertainty, conflict of all kinds will be more probable. "For example, when a major pet-food manufacturing facility announced that one-third of its managers would have to support a new third shift, the feared disruption of personal and family routines prompted many managers to think about sending out their résumés. In addition, the uncertainty of who was going to be required to work at night was so great that even routine management work was disrupted by posturing and infighting."[72]

Besides identifying some of the major sources of interpersonal conflict as in the preceding, it is useful to analyze the dynamics of individuals interacting with one another. One way to analyze their confronting others is through the response categories of (1) forcing (assertive, uncooperative); (2) accommodating (unassertive, cooperative); (3) avoiding (uncooperative, unassertive); (4) compromising (between assertiveness and cooperativeness); and (5) collaborating (cooperative, assertive).[73]

Intergroup Behavior and Conflict

In addition to interpersonal (which includes intragroup) conflict, social psychologists have been concerned about intergroup conflict for a number of years. Intergroup behavior is even specifically identified as follows: "Intergroup behavior occurs whenever individuals belonging to one group interact, collectively or individually, with another group or its members in terms of their reference group identification."[74]

Several antecedent conditions have been identified for explaining intergroup conflict. These can be summarized as follows:[75]

1. *Competition for resources.* Most organizations today have very limited resources. Groups within the organization vie for budget funds, space, supplies, personnel, and support services.

2. *Task interdependence.* If two groups in the organization depend on one another in a mutual way or even a one-way direction (as in a sequential technological process), there tends to be more conflict than if groups are independent of one another. The more diverse the objectives, priorities, and personnel of the interdependent groups (for example, research and production), the more conflict there tends to be.

3. *Jurisdictional ambiguity.* This may involve "turf" problems or overlapping responsibilities. For example, conflict might occur when one group attempts to assume more control or take credit for desirable activities, or give up its part and any responsibility for undesirable activities.

4. *Status struggles.* This conflict occurs when one group attempts to improve its status and another group views this as a threat to its place in the status hierarchy. One group may also feel it is being inequitably treated in comparison with another group of equal status in terms of rewards, job assignments, working conditions, privileges, or status symbols. Human resources departments justifiably often feel they are treated inequitably in relation to marketing, finance, and operations departments.

Groups in conflict behave differently from smoothly cooperating groups. Here is a real-world example:

> A division of Litton Industries needed to integrate West and East Coast operations in order to provide customers a full spectrum of services. The West Coast group had been running call centers for 30-some years, were hard working, but resistant to change. The East Coast operation was cobbled together through recent acquisitions and specialized in enterprise-wide process consulting. This East Coast group was freewheeling, risk-taking and could care less about Litton culture and tradition. The resulting conflict left virtually no communication or unified sense of direction between the two groups. Covert sabotage was routinely waged by both sides to dilute one another's effectiveness.[76]

There is recent research evidence that such groups in conflict change both internally and in their intergroup perceptions. For example, one study of 70 top management teams found internally that the degree of trust moderated the relationship between task conflict (the perception of disagreements about decisions made by the group) and relationship conflict (an emotional perception of interpersonal incompatibility).[77] Another study found that low intragroup cohesiveness and negative relationships across groups were significantly related to higher perceptions of intergroup conflict.[78] Overall, after searching the relevant literature, Daft identified the following characteristics of groups in conflict:

1. There is a clear distinction and comparison between "we" (the in-group) and "they" (the out-group).

2. A group that feels it is in conflict with another group becomes more cohesive and pulls together to present a solid front to defeat the other group.

3. The positive feelings and cohesion within the in-group do not transfer to the members of the out-group. The members of the out-group are viewed as the enemy rather than as neutrals.

4. Threatened group members feel superior—they overestimate their own strength and underestimate that of members of other groups.

5. The amount of communication between conflicting groups decreases. When there is communication, it is characterized by negative comments and hostility.
6. If a group is losing in a conflict, the members' cohesion decreases and they experience increased tension among themselves. They look for a scapegoat to blame their failure on.
7. The intergroup conflict and resulting hostility are not the result of neurotic tendencies on the part of individual members. These seem to be a product of group interaction, even when individuals in the group are normal and well adjusted.[79]

These findings from research help describe and provide an understanding of the behavior of conflicting groups in organizations, such as unions and management, operations and sales, office personnel and operating personnel, nurses and doctors, and faculty and administrators. Traditionally, such conflict was viewed as very simple and optimistic. It was based on the following assumptions:

1. Conflict is by definition avoidable.
2. Conflict is caused by troublemakers, boat rockers, and prima donnas.
3. Legalistic forms of authority such as "going through channels" or "sticking to the book" are emphasized.
4. Scapegoats are accepted as inevitable.[80]

Management traditionally relied on formal authority and classical organizational restructuring to solve their "conflict problem." Individual managers often became hypocritical in order to avoid conflicts from above or below. They tried to either ignore conflict or rationalize it away with the position that there is nothing that can be done about it.

Starting with the wide acceptance of the Argyris thesis that there is a basic incongruence between the needs and characteristics of adult, mature employees and the requirements of the modern formal organization, the behavioral approach to management began to reexamine its assumptions and concerns about conflict. This development has, at least indirectly, been caused by the overall societal concern with conflict on national, organizational, group, and individual bases. The outcome has been a new set of assumptions about organizational conflict, which are almost the exact opposite of the traditional assumptions. Some of the new assumptions about conflict are the following:

1. Conflict is inevitable.
2. Conflict is determined by structural factors such as the physical shape of a building, the design of a career structure, or the nature of a class system.
3. Conflict is integral to the nature of change.
4. A minimal level of conflict is optimal.[81]

Using such assumptions as a starting point, most experts today emphasize the importance of making a cost-benefit analysis of the conflict situation at any level and then setting up dispute systems[82] and, most recently, setting up systems through advanced information technology that eliminate conflict inherent in traditional (i.e., hierarchical and functional specializations) organization designs.

THE EFFECTS OF STRESS AND INTRAINDIVIDUAL CONFLICT

As has been pointed out, stress and conflict are not automatically bad for individual employees or their organizational performance. In fact, it is generally recognized that low levels of stress and conflict can even enhance job performance. For example, one study found that mild stress, such as getting a new supervisor or being involuntarily transferred, may have the positive result of an increased search for information in the job.[83] This may lead employees to new and better ways of doing their jobs. Also, mild stress may get employees' "juices" flowing and lead to increased activity, change, and overall better performance. People in certain jobs, such as in sales or creative fields (for example, newspaper journalists and television announcers who work under time pressures), would seem to benefit from a mild level of stress. People in other jobs, such as police officers or physicians, may not benefit from constant mild stress.

Research is also emerging that indicates that the level of difficulty, the nature of the task being performed, personal dispositions (such as Type A, personal control and learned helplessness, and psychological hardiness, discussed in previous sections), other psychological dispositions (such as negative affectivity[84]—see Chapter 7), and neuroticism[85] may affect the relationship between stress and performance. However, it is still safe to conclude that:

1. The performance of many tasks is in fact strongly affected by stress.
2. Performance usually drops off sharply when stress rises to high levels.[86]

It is the dysfunctional effects of high levels of stress and conflict that should be and are a major concern for contemporary society in general and for effective human resource management in particular. The problems due to high levels of stress and conflict can be exhibited physically, psychologically, or behaviorally by the individual.

Physical Problems Due to Stress and Conflict

Most of the attention and basic research over the years has been devoted to the impact that stress has on physical health. Specific physical health concerns that have been linked to stress include the following: (1) immune system problems, where there is a lessened ability to fight off illness and infection; (2) cardiovascular system problems, such as high blood pressure and heart disease; (3) musculoskeletal system problems, such as tension headaches and back pain; and (4) gastrointestinal system problems, such as diarrhea and constipation.[87] For example, heart attacks are a way of life (or death in this case) on stress-packed Wall Street. For the 5,000 people who work at the stock exchange, the heart attack death rate is 60 percent higher than the national rate for men between 18 and 65, and it was one of the first employers to install a defibrillator (used to restart the heart by electric shock).[88] There may even be a link between stress and cancer.[89]

Obviously, such serious physical ailments have a drastic effect on the individual; not always so obvious, but just as serious, are the effects that physical problems such as heart disease can have on the organization. Ivancevich and Matteson have provided the following worksheet for computing the costs of replacing employees lost to heart disease in a company employing 4,000 people.[90]

1.	Number of employees	4,000
2.	Men in age range 45 to 65 (0.25 × line 1)	1,000
3.	Estimated deaths due to heart disease per year (0.006 × line 2)	6
4.	Estimated premature retirement due to heart problems per year (0.003 × line 2)	3
5.	Company's annual personnel losses due to heart disorders (sum of lines 3 and 4)	9
6.	Annual replacement cost: the average cost of hiring and training replacements for experienced employees (line 5 × $25,000)	$225,000
7.	Number of employees who will eventually die of heart disease if present rate continues (0.5 × line 1)	2,000

These figures are just estimates, but they dramatically illustrate how heart disease alone can affect costs and sheer numbers of employees in a typical organization. Obviously, not all heart disease can be directly linked to stress; environmental conditions and the person's general state of health, heredity, and medical history also certainly contribute. However, there seems to be enough evidence that stress can and does contribute to this dreaded disease and to other physical problems as well.

Psychological Problems Due to Stress and Conflict

Although considerable attention has been given to the relationship between stress and physical health, especially within the medical community, not as much has been given to the impact of stress on mental health. Yet, at least indirectly if not directly, the psychological problems resulting from stress may be just as important, if not more important, to day-to-day job performance as the physical problems.

High levels of stress may be accompanied by anger, anxiety, depression, nervousness, irritability, tension, and boredom. One study found that stress had the strongest impact on aggressive actions, such as sabotage, interpersonal aggression, hostility, and complaints.[91] These types of psychological problems from stress, in turn, are especially relevant to poor job performance, lowered self-esteem,[92] resentment of supervision, inability to concentrate and make decisions, and job dissatisfaction.[93] These outcomes of stress can have a direct cost effect on the organization. For example, the National Centers for Disease Control reported that psychological stress is the source of numerous job-related insurance claims.[94] Recent court cases have also brought stress-related problems stemming from employment under the employer's workers' compensation insurance.[95] Experts are predicting that if the number of stress-related workers' compensation claims continues to grow at current rates, these claims will lead all other claims,[96] in an era when health care benefits for psychological problems have plummeted.[97]

Of even greater significance, the outcomes of stress can have a subtle, but very real, effect on the styles and effectiveness of managers in key positions. For example, managers who are under constant stress may become very moody, and their subordinates soon learn not to disturb them, even with important information, because they will just "bite your head off." Such managers may also realize, at times, that they are acting this way; they may feel that they are not living up to the expectations of their important position and suffer a loss of self-esteem. In this state they may also procrastinate and continue to put things off and not make needed decisions. And, finally, they may resent their boss for trying to get them back on track and begin to hate the job in general. Coworkers, subordinates, and bosses may become very disgusted with such a manager and explain the behavior away as being the result of a "rotten personality," when in fact the problems are the result of stress and conflict. If the manager had a heart attack, everyone would feel sorry and say that he or she was under too much stress, but a manager's moodiness, low self-esteem, inability to make a decision, and dissatisfaction with the boss and the job cause people to get angry and say that the manager is "no darned good" or "can't get along with anyone." Both a heart attack and a psychological problem may have the same cause (too much stress and conflict), and although people may react to them differently, the negative effect on performance is the same in the case of a psychological problem, or perhaps even worse.

Behavioral Problems Due to Stress and Conflict

As has been the case with other topics covered in this text, the *behavioral* unit of analysis may be most helpful—in this case, in analyzing the effects of job stress and conflict. Direct behaviors that may accompany high levels of stress include undereating or overeating, sleeplessness, increased smoking and drinking, and drug abuse. When it is realized that 6 percent of the population are alcoholics, that another estimated 10 percent are problem drinkers, and that 6 billion doses of amphetamines and barbiturates are consumed annually,[98] the potential problems for employee behavior caused by alcohol and drug abuse become dramatically clear. For example, one company had such a problem with on-the-job drinking that it bought a breath-alcohol meter to test its employees. The president of the union in this firm stated: "There were a couple of people who came to work drunk every day."[99] Although the meter has not been used yet, one worker was overheard to say, "I guess I'll have to stop going to the bar at lunchtime."[100] Besides being dangerous, as in this company, which used a lot of saws and punches, these problems may be manifested in tardiness, absenteeism, and turnover.

There is research evidence over the years indicating a relationship between stress and especially absenteeism and turnover.[101] For example, workers may experience stress and react by getting drunk and staying home from work the next day with a hangover. They then feel bad about this drinking. They may feel that they are letting everyone down "the morning after" and eventually quit or are fired from the job. In the meantime the absenteeism rate climbs, and subsequently the turnover rate increases, both of which are very costly to the organization in terms of filling in for absent workers and replacing those who have left. Staying away from a job that is causing stress or quitting the job is a "flight" reaction to the situation. Actually, this may be a healthier reaction than a "fight" reaction, in which the person may stay on the stress-producing job and become angry and/or aggressive.

Like the psychological problems resulting from stress and conflict, the behavioral problems are often not attributed to stress by coworkers or supervisors and generate little sympathy. But, also like the psychological and the physical symptoms of stress, the behavioral problems can be controlled, more effectively managed, and even prevented by the individual and the organization. These coping strategies are discussed next.

COPING STRATEGIES FOR STRESS AND CONFLICT

Much of the discussion so far in this chapter and, at least indirectly, a lot of the material in previous and subsequent chapters (for example, discussions of job design, goal setting, organizational behavior modification, group dynamics, communication skills, political strategies, leadership styles, organization processes and design, decision-making skills, control techniques, management of change, and organization development techniques) suggest ways to manage and cope more effectively with stress and conflict. There are even overall theories being developed on coping with stress,[102] and guidelines for converting stress into success.[103] The accompanying Application Example: Taking Time to Manage Time suggests some simple techniques, such as time management, that can be used to cope with stress, and there are many lists of steps to take in order to avoid stress and burnout found in the practitioner literature.[104]

Interactive behavior at both the interpersonal and intergroup levels resulting in conflict rather than stress per se has its own solutions for coping and managing. For example, a win-win strategy of conflict resolution or types of strategies such as avoidance, defusion, containment, or confrontation[105] are well known in conflict management. There continue to be many practitioner-oriented books[106] on resolving conflict in the workplace, but the more academic, research-based approach has concentrated on negotiation skills. After summarizing both the individual and organizational coping strategies for stress, the negotiation skills of conflict resolution conclude the chapter.

APPLICATION EXAMPLE

Taking Time to Manage Time

One of the major causes of stress for managers comes from time pressures. No matter how fast some managers work and how much time they put in, they are still unable to get all their work done. One of the most effective ways of dealing with this problem is the use of time management techniques. Today many organizations from Chase Manhattan to Exxon to Xerox are training their managers in how to get more done in less time. Some of the most helpful guidelines for effective time management are the following:

1. Make out a "to-do" list that identifies everything that must be done during the day. This helps keep track of work progress.
2. Delegate as much minor work as possible to subordinates.
3. Determine when you do the best work—morning or afternoon—and schedule the most difficult assignments for this time period.
4. Set time aside during the day, preferably at least one hour, when visitors or other interruptions are not permitted.
5. Have the secretary screen all incoming calls in order to turn away those that are minor or do not require your personal attention.
6. Eat lunch in the office one or two days a week in order to save time and give yourself the opportunity to catch up on paperwork.
7. Discourage drop-in visitors by turning your desk so that you do not have eye contact with the door or hallway.
8. Read standing up. The average person reads faster and more accurately when in a slightly uncomfortable position.
9. Make telephone calls between 4:30 and 5:00 P.M. People tend to keep these conversations brief so that they can go home.
10. Do not feel guilty about those things that have not been accomplished today. Put them on the top of the "to-do" list for tomorrow.

Individual Coping Strategies

Today, self-help remedies, do-it-yourself approaches, weight-loss clinics and diets, health foods, and physical exercise are being given much attention in the mass media. People are actually taking responsibility, or know they *should* be taking responsibility, for their own wellness. Individual coping strategies for dealing with stress make sense. In other words, most people don't have to be convinced of the value of taking charge and actually making a change in their lives.

Some specific techniques that individuals can use to eliminate or more effectively manage inevitable, prolonged stress are the following:

1. *Exercise.* Today, it is not whether you win or lose, but whether you get some good exercise that counts. People of all ages are walking, jogging, swimming, riding bicycles, or playing softball, tennis, or racquetball in order to get some exercise to combat stress. Although this seems to make a great deal of sense and many laypeople and physicians swear by it, there still is no conclusive evidence that exercise will directly reduce the chances of heart disease or stroke. But there seems little doubt that it can help people better cope with stress, even if only as a

result of the side effects, such as relaxation, enhanced self-esteem, simply getting one's mind off work for a while, and thus perform better in their daily tasks in the workplace.[107]

2. *Relaxation.* Whether a person simply takes it easy once in a while or uses specific relaxation techniques such as biofeedback or meditation, the intent is to eliminate the immediately stressful situation or manage a prolonged stressful situation more effectively. Taking it easy may mean curling up with a good book in front of a fireplace or watching something "light" (not a violent program or a sports program) on television. There is even some recent research evidence that those who do expressive writing about stressful events in their lives experience health benefits.[108] Meditation involves muscle and mental relaxation; the person slowly repeats a peaceful phrase or word or concentrates on a mental picture in a quiet location. There is some research evidence that such meditation can have a desirable physical[109] and mental[110] impact on people. Whether it can have a practical impact on job stress is yet to be determined. However, a number of firms are using it. For example, a stockbroker who regularly uses meditation stated: "It's widely known that this industry has a lot of stress. So where a lot of people drink alcohol, we meditate. It's not that we don't feel stress. It just doesn't hit us as much."[111]

3. *Behavioral self-control.* Chapter 16 gives specific attention to behavior management. By deliberately managing the antecedents and the consequences of their own behavior, people can achieve self-control. For example, sales managers who have a steady stream of customer complaints all day could change the antecedent by having an assistant screen all complaints and allow only exceptions to reach them. They could also manage the consequences by rewarding themselves with an extra break when they remain calm and collected after interacting with a particularly angry customer. Besides managing their own behavior to reduce stress, people can also become more aware of their limits and of "red flags" that signal trouble ahead. They can avoid people or situations that they know will put them under stress. In other words, this strategy involves individuals' controlling the situation instead of letting the situation control them.

4. *Cognitive therapy.* Besides behavioral self-control techniques, a number of clinical psychologists have entered the stress field with cognitive therapy techniques. Techniques such as Ellis's rational emotive model and cognitive behavior modification have been used as an individual strategy for reducing job stress.

5. *Networking.* One clear finding that has come out of social psychology research over the years is that people need and will benefit from social support.[112] Applied as a strategy to reduce job stress, this would entail forming close associations with trusted empathetic coworkers and colleagues who are good listeners and confidence builders. These friends are there when needed and provide support to get the person through stressful situations. Today, such alliances, especially if deliberately sought out and developed, are called *networks*. Although the relationship between social support and stress reduction appears complicated,[113] there is some research evidence that a networking strategy may be able to help people cope better with job stress[114] and be more effective[115] and successful managers.[116]

Organizational Coping Strategies

Organizational coping strategies are designed by management to eliminate or control organizational-level stressors in order to prevent or reduce job stress for individual employees. Earlier in the chapter, the organizational stressors were categorized in terms of overall policies and strategies, structure and design processes/functions, and working conditions (see Figure 12.2). It logically follows that each of these areas would be the focus of attention in developing organizational coping strategies. In other words, each of the specific stressors would be worked on in order to eliminate or reduce job stress. For example, in the policy area, attention would be given to making performance reviews and pay plans as equitable and as fair as possible. In the structural area, steps would be taken to back away from high degrees of formalization and specialization. The same would be done in the areas of physical conditions (for example, safety hazards would be removed, and lighting, noise, and temperature would be improved) and processes/functions (for example, communication and information sharing would be improved, and ambiguous or conflicting goals would be clarified or resolved).

Today, top firms such as Hewlett-Packard realize they are putting tremendous pressure on employees in competitive battles and are giving considerable effort to de-stress the organization.[117] H-P requires employees to have personal/leisure goals (e.g., weight loss, exercise, take time off for the family) as well as job goals. If employees fall short of their personal/leisure goals, supervisors are held responsible. When a milestone is reached e.g., leaving at 2:00 P.M. to take a daughter in-line skating, coworkers are encouraged to applaud with the same gusto as landing a big sales order. The Association for Fitness in Business estimates that 12,000 companies today offer stress-coping programs ranging from counseling services, lunchtime stress-management seminars, and wellness publications to elaborate company-run fitness centers where employees can sweat out the tension.[118] There is evidence that these stress management programs are increasing and they are being evaluated more rigorously.[119] Some are getting quite creative. For example, Pixar (the movie maker of *Toy Story* and *A Bug's Life*) created Pixar University (PU), an in-house operation with free classes for employees in data programming, tai chi, gesture drawing, improvisational acting, and juggling.[120]

In general, most firms today are trying to reduce stress and conflict through work-family initiatives. These involve both reorganization initiatives (e.g., restructuring of jobs and job duties, telecommuting, part-time work and job sharing, and flexible scheduling) and work and life benefit policies and programs (e.g., on-site child care and/or elder care, paid family and medical leave, release time for personal/family events, and limits on frequency and distance of business travel).[121]

Employee assistance programs (EAPs) have also become a very valuable organizational response to help employees cope with stress. EAPs are currently implemented in over half of U.S. organizations with 50 or more employees and have been found to consistently reduce absenteeism, health care costs, and disciplinary action.[122] EAPs typically provide employees with services such as confidential counseling and/or follow-up on issues of personal or work-related concerns. They also provide family workshops and consultations (related to marriage, single parenting, working parents), stress management workshops, relaxation seminars, and other kinds of support. Often, the mere presence of mind that EAPs provide—knowing that there is support available—can help ease some of the stress that employees face in today's environment.[123]

Besides work-family programs and EAPs, because of the stress resulting from downsizing in recent years, recent concern is also being given to both those who are let go and those who survive. For example, theoretical models[124] are being created and basic research[125] is being done on coping with job loss. One stream of research has examined the role that procedural justice (perceptions of fairness, discussed in Chapter 8) plays on those affected by downsizing. In three studies (of those already laid off, survivors of a firm that had downsized, and those scheduled to be laid off), it was found that fair procedural justice had a positive impact.[126] A summary of these studies noted:

> All three studies showed that the negative effects of layoffs can be blunted by the way company managers deal with the downsizing. Employees were more hostile when they thought procedures leading to the layoffs were not handled fairly, with sufficient notice and fair treatment of employees during downsizing. When procedures were seen as fair, employees still supported and trusted their firms even after the layoffs had occurred.[127]

Organizations experiencing downsizing need to be sure that those let go are as positive as possible so that there are not negative repercussions (e.g., in the community or even with customers). However, of even more concern are those suffering from what was described earlier as "survivor syndrome." As one survivor from a downsized firm describes this modern-day malady: "Just when we begin to think our jobs are safe, they change the rules on us. We don't know who's in charge, who we can trust or what we're supposed to be doing. The more unsettling it gets around here, the less productive we are."[128] The key issue is not only whether these survivors are stressed-out but also whether stress is affecting their performance.

Some guidelines to help downsized organizations combat the problems of survivor syndrome include the following:[129]

1. *Be proactive.* Before Compaq Computer in Houston laid off 2,000 employees, the corporate human resources department developed a comprehensive communication campaign and trained all managers not only in how to outplace people but also in how to help survivors.
2. *Acknowledge survivors' emotions.* The state of Oregon, which had cut back 1,000 employees, held workshops for survivors that allowed them to vent their frustrations and develop skills that would allow them to think of change as an opportunity for growth.
3. *Communicate after the downsizing.* After laying off 20 percent of its work force, Patagonia Inc., an outdoor apparel manufacturer in California, implemented a monthly (then twice-monthly) open forum during which employees can meet with the CEO during work hours to have their questions answered and hear about the firm's progress. In the jobholders' meetings at Pitney Bowes Inc., management gives an employee $50 for the toughest question asked.
4. *Clarify new roles.* Not only is there a need for communication of the big picture; it also is important to explain how each employee's job has changed, if at all, and relate how each individual contributes to the new big picture in the downsized organization.

NEGOTIATION SKILLS: GOING BEYOND CONFLICT MANAGEMENT

In recent years negotiation has moved from the industrial relations field to the forefront of necessary managerial skills. As Neale and Bazerman noted: "Everyone negotiates. In its various forms, negotiation is a common mechanism for resolving differences and allocating resources." They then define negotiation as "a decision-making process among interdependent parties who do not share identical preferences. It is through negotiation that the parties decide what each will give and take in their relationship."[130]

Although some organizational behavior scholars note that there are similarities between negotiation strategies and conflict management,[131] negotiation can go beyond just resolving conflict and become a managerial skill for personal and organizational success. For example, a manager can successfully negotiate a salary raise or a good price for supplies. After first noting some of the biases or errors that negotiators commonly make and the traditional negotiation techniques that have been used, the remainder of the chapter is devoted to the newly emerging skills needed for successful negotiation.

Traditional Negotiation Approaches

When negotiating, people in general and managers in particular tend to have certain biases and make certain errors, which prevents them from negotiating rationally and getting the most they can out of a situation. The research on these common mistakes can be summarized as follows:

1. Negotiators tend to be overly affected by the frame, or form of presentation, of information in a negotiation.
2. Negotiators tend to nonrationally escalate commitment to a previously selected course of action when it is no longer the most reasonable alternative.
3. Negotiators tend to assume that their gain must come at the expense of the other party and thereby miss opportunities for mutually beneficial trade-offs between the parties.
4. Negotiator judgments tend to be anchored on irrelevant information, such as an initial offer.
5. Negotiators tend to rely on readily available information.
6. Negotiators tend to fail to consider information that is available by focusing on the opponent's perspective.
7. Negotiators tend to be overconfident concerning the likelihood of attaining outcomes that favor the individual(s) involved.[132]

Besides these common bias problems, negotiators traditionally have taken either a distributive or a positional bargaining approach. Distributive bargaining assumes a "fixed pie" and focuses on how to get the biggest share, or "slice of the pie." With teams so popular in today's organizations, there is growing research on the effectiveness of teams in distributive bargaining. One study found that teams, more than individuals, developed mutually beneficial trade-offs among issues in the negotiation and discovered compatible interests. However, the common belief that teams have a relative advantage over individual opponents in negotiations was not supported by actual outcomes.[133] The conflict management strategies of compromising, forcing, accommodating, and avoiding, mentioned earlier, all tend to be associated with a distributive negotiation strategy. As noted by Whetten and Cameron:

> Compromise occurs when both parties make sacrifices in order to find a common ground. Compromisers are generally more interested in finding an expedient solution. . . . Forcing and accommodating demand that one party give up its position in order for the conflict to be resolved. When parties to a conflict avoid resolution, they do so because they assume that the costs of resolving the conflict are so high that they are better off not even attempting resolution.[134]

Closely related to distributed bargaining is the commonly used positional bargaining approach. This approach to negotiation involves successively taking, and then giving up, a sequence of positions. In its simplest form, this is what happens when one haggles in an open market. However, positional bargaining also happens in international diplomacy. Fisher and Ury note that such positional bargaining can serve a useful purpose: "It tells the other side what you want; it provides an anchor in an uncertain and pressured situation; and it can eventually produce the terms of an acceptable agreement."[135]

Both distributed and positional bargaining have simplistic strategies such as "tough person," or "hard"; "easy touch," or "soft"; or even "split the difference." Characteristics of the "hard" strategy include the following: the goal is victory, distrust others, dig in to your position, make threats, try to win a contest of will, and apply pressure. By contrast, the "soft" strategy includes these characteristics: the goal is agreement, trust others, change your position easily, make offers, try to avoid a contest of will, and yield to pressure.[136] The hard bargainer typically dominates and has intuitive appeal. However, both research[137] and everyday practice are beginning to reveal that more effective negotiation approaches than these traditional strategies are possible.

Contemporary Negotiation Skills

There are now recognized alternative approaches to traditionally recognized distributed and positional bargaining and the hard versus soft strategies in negotiation. Whetten and Cameron suggest an integrative approach that takes an "expanding the pie" perspective that uses problem-solving techniques to find win-win outcomes.[138] Based on a collaborating (rather than a compromising, forcing, accommodating, or avoiding) strategy, the integrative approach requires the effective negotiator to use skills such as (1) establishing superordinate goals; (2) separating the people from the problem; (3) focusing on interests, not on positions; (4) inventing options for mutual gain; and (5) using objective criteria.[139]

Recent practical guidelines for effective negotiations have grouped the techniques into degrees of risk to the user as follows:

1. Low-risk negotiation techniques
   a. Flattery—subtle flattery usually works best, but the standards may differ by age, sex, and cultural factors.
   b. Addressing the easy point first—this helps build trust and momentum for the tougher issues.
   c. Silence—this can be effective in gaining concessions, but one must be careful not to provoke anger or frustration in opponents.
   d. Inflated opening position—this may elicit a counteroffer that shows the opponent's position or may shift the point of compromise.
   e. "Oh, poor me"—this may lead to sympathy but could also bring out the killer instinct in opponents.
2. High-risk negotiation techniques
   a. Unexpected temper losses—erupting in anger can break an impasse and get one's point across, but it can also be viewed as immature or manipulative and lead opponents to harden their position.
   b. High-balling—this is used to gain trust by appearing to give in to the opponent's position, but when overturned by a higher authority, concessions are gained based on the trust.
   c. Boulwarism ("take it or leave it")—named after a former vice president of GE who would make only one offer in labor negotiations, this is a highly aggressive strategy that may also produce anger and frustration in opponents.
   d. Waiting until the last moment—after using stall tactics and knowing that a deadline is near, a reasonable but favorable offer is made, leaving the opponent with little choice but to accept.[140]

Besides these low- and high-risk strategies, there are also a number of other negotiation techniques, such as a two-person team using "good cop–bad cop" (one is tough, followed by one who is kind), and various psychological ploys, such as insisting that meetings be held on one's home turf, scheduling meetings at inconvenient times, or interrupting meetings with phone calls or side meetings.[141] There are even guidelines of if, when, and how to use alcohol in negotiations. As the president of Saber Enterprises notes, when the Japanese come over to negotiate, it is assumed that you go out to dinner and have several drinks and toast with sake.[142]

In addition to the preceding guidelines for effective negotiation skills, there is an alternative to positional bargaining and soft versus hard strategies that has been developed by the Harvard Negotiation Project. This alternative to traditional negotiation is called the *principled negotiation,* or *negotiation on the merits,* approach. There are four basic elements in this alternative approach to negotiation. Very simply, they are:

1. *People.*   Separate the people from the problem.
2. *Interests.*   Focus on interests, not positions.
3. *Options.*   Generate a variety of possibilities before deciding what to do.
4. *Criteria.*   Insist that the result be based on some objective standard.[143]

The principled skills go beyond hard versus soft and change the game to negotiation on the basis of merits. For example, in soft bargaining the participants are friends, in hard bargaining they are adversaries, but in the principled approach they are problem solvers; in soft bargaining the approach is to trust others, in hard bargaining there is distrust of others, but in the principled approach the negotiator proceeds independent of trust; and in the soft approach negotiators make offers, in the hard approach they make threats, but in the principled approach they explore common interests.[144] These principled negotiation skills can result in a wise agreement. As noted by Fisher and Ury:

> The method permits you to reach a gradual consensus on a joint decision *efficiently* without all the transactional costs of digging in to positions only to have to dig yourself out of them. And separating the people from the problem allows you to deal directly and empathetically with the other negotiator as a human being, thus making possible an *amicable* agreement.[145]

Along with social, emotional, behavioral, leadership, team, and communication skills, these negotiation skills are becoming increasingly recognized as important to management of not only conflict, but also effective management in general.

Summary

This chapter examines both stress and conflict. Although not always bad for the person (for example, the father of stress studies, Hans Selye, feels that complete freedom from stress is death) or the organization (low levels of stress may lead to performance improvement), stress is still one of the most important and serious problems facing the field of organizational behavior. Stress can be comprehensively defined as an adaptive response to an external situation that results in physical, psychological, and/or behavioral deviations for organizational participants. The causes of stress can be categorized into extraorganizational, organizational, and group stressors, as well as individual stressors and dispositions. In combination or singly, they represent a tremendous amount of potential stress impinging on today's jobholder—at every level and in every type of organization.

In addition to stress, the dynamics of interactive behavior at interpersonal and group levels, and the resulting conflict, play an increasingly important role in the analysis and study of organizational behavior. Conflict and stress are conceptually and practically similar, especially at the individual level. Conflict at the intraindividual level involves frustration, goal conflict, and role conflict and ambiguity. Frustration occurs when goal-directed behavior is blocked. Goal conflict can come about from approach-approach, approach-avoidance, or avoidance-avoidance situations. Role conflict and ambiguity result from a clash in the expectations of the various roles possessed by an individual and can take the forms of role conflict, intrarole conflict, or interrole conflict.

Interpersonal conflict is first examined in terms of its sources (personal differences, information deficiency, role incompatibility, and environmental stress). Then the analysis of interpersonal conflict is made through the response categories of forcing, accommodating, avoiding, compromising, and collaborating. Intergroup conflict has also become important. The antecedents to intergroup conflict are identified as competition for resources, task interdependence, jurisdictional ambiguity, and status struggles.

The effects of stress and intraindividual conflict can create physical problems (heart disease, ulcers, arthritis, and maybe even cancer), psychological problems (mood changes, lowered self-esteem, resentment of supervision, inability to make decisions, and job dissatisfaction), and/or behavioral problems (tardiness, absenteeism, turnover, and accidents). A number of individual and organizational strategies have been developed to cope with these stress-induced problems. Exercise, relaxation, behavioral self-control techniques, cognitive therapy techniques, and networking are some potentially useful coping strategies that individuals can apply to help combat existing stress. Taking a more proactive approach, management of organizations tries to eliminate stressors, reduce work-family conflict, and implement employee assistance programs (EAPs). A special concern for organizations today is to deal with the stress resulting from downsizing that affects both those laid off and the survivors. To manage this stress, downsizing organizations must fully communicate and display fair procedural justice for those let go. To counter survivor syndrome, downsized organizations can follow such guidelines as being proactive, acknowledging survivors' emotions, communicating after the cuts, and clarifying new roles. In any case, whether on an individual or an organizational level, steps need to be taken to prevent or reduce the increasing job stress facing today's employees.

The last part of the chapter is concerned with negotiation skills. Going beyond industrial relations and conflict management, negotiation skills are becoming increasingly recognized as important to effective management and personal success. Traditionally, negotiators have depended on distributed and positional bargaining. Relying on simplistic hard or soft strategies, this traditional approach is now being challenged by more effective alternative negotiation skills. Practical low-risk strategies include flattery, addressing the easy points first, silence, inflated opening position, and "oh, poor me." High-risk strategies include unexpected temper losses, high-balling, Boulwarism, and waiting until the last moment. In addition, alternatives to traditional distributed and positional bargaining are the integrative approach, which uses a problem-solving, collaborative strategy, and the principled, or negotiation on the merits, approach, which emphasizes people, interests, options, and criteria. These negotiation skills go beyond hard versus soft strategies and change the game, leading to a win-win, wise agreement.

ENDING WITH META-ANALYTIC RESEARCH FINDINGS

OB PRINCIPLE: Employees who work abnormally long hours per week will experience more health problems.

Meta-Analysis Results: [21 studies; 37,623 participants; $d = .26$] *On average, there is a **57 percent probability** that employees who work over 48 hours per week will experience more health problems than those who work fewer hours.* Further analysis also points out that longer working hours are often associated with poor lifestyle behaviors such as heavy smoking, inadequate diet, and lack of exercise, which further leads to health problems.

Conclusion: Due to increasing workloads, job insecurity, and pressures to perform, many individuals are working longer hours. As a result, there is much concern that stress and fatigue levels are on the rise, which leads to negative organizational outcomes such as absenteeism, decreased performance, and escalating medical expenses. Employees who become distressed mentally and physically due to working long hours experience work overload. Overload combined with prolonged exposure to other workplace stressors may result in health problems such as work-related injuries, accidents, and cardiovascular disease, along with mental disorders such as depression and anxiety. However, as this chapter on stress shows, individuals and organizations can buffer the ill effects of stress by enhancing coping strategies. Exercising regularly, eating a healthy diet, and taking time to relax are some ways individuals can reduce stress. Organizations, too, can help by establishing a supportive climate, having well-designed jobs, and reducing role conflict and role ambiguity.

Source: Adapted from Kate Sparks, Cary Cooper, Yitzhak Fried and Arie Shirom, "The Effects of Hours of Work on Health: A Meta-Analytic Review," *Journal of Occupational and Organizational Psychology,* Vol. 70, 1997, pp. 391–408.

OB PRINCIPLE: Type A personalities experience greater heart rate reactivity than Type Bs.

Meta-Analysis Results: [78 studies; 3,008 participants; $d = .22$] *On average, there is a **56 percent probability** that Type A personalities will experience greater heart rate reactivity (heart rate and blood pressure) than Type Bs.* Moderator analyses indicated that Type As showed especially greater cardiovascular reactivity in situations characterized as having positive or negative feedback and verbal harassment or criticism. Importantly, this study does not indicate that Type As necessarily have more heart attacks, just greater heart reactivity.

Conclusion: Cardiovascular disease is the leading cause of death among adults in Western industrialized countries. The role that stress and personality/behavior types such as A and B have with heart problems has received much attention. Because Type A behavior has the most obvious link with cardiovascular disease, identifying Type A characteristics and impact has been closely studied. As this chapter indicates, Type A personalities are hurried and competitive whereas Type Bs are more relaxed and related. Type A behavior would seem to be desired by organizations, and research has reveled that most managers are in fact Type As, except at the very top where Type Bs dominate, and in general perform better. However as this chapter on conflict and stress indicates, Type As may not necessarily need to change their personalities, which is likely an impossibility, but will need to learn to better cope with stressful situations that lead to emotional reactions such as anger in order to prevent physical problems such as heart disease. The key problem is anger, not just hyperactivity.

Source: Adapted from Scott A. Lyness, "Predictors of Differences between Type A and B Individuals in Heart Rate and Blood Pressure Reactivity," *Psychological Bulletin,* Vol. 114, No 2, 1988, pp. 266–295.

Questions for Discussion and Review

1. How is stress defined? Is it always bad for the individual? Explain.
2. What are the general categories of stressors that can affect job stress? Give some examples of each.
3. What are some of the dispositions that may influence an individual's reaction to stress? Give an example of each.
4. What is frustration? What are some of its manifestations? How can the frustration model be used to analyze organizational behavior?
5. Explain approach-avoidance conflict. Give a realistic organizational example of where it may occur.
6. What are some of the major sources of interpersonal conflict? Which do you think most relevant in today's organizations?
7. How do groups or teams in conflict behave? What are some antecedent conditions of intergroup conflict?
8. How do the traditional assumptions about conflict differ from the modern assumptions? What implications do these new assumptions have for the management of conflict?
9. Job stress can have physiological, psychological, and behavioral effects. Give an example of each and cite some research findings on the relationship between job stress and these outcomes.
10. Coping strategies for job stress exist for both the individual and the organizational levels. Summarize and evaluate these various strategies for preventing and/or more effectively managing stress.
11. A modern-day malady is survivor syndrome. What does this refer to, and how can organizations help combat it?
12. Compare and contrast the traditional versus the new negotiation skills. Why do you think the new skills lead to better agreements?

Internet Exercise: Managing Stress in Organizations

Visit the websites http://www.stress.org and http://www.stresstips.com. These sites provide information on the negative effects of stress in the workplace. They also have useful tips on how to manage stress in your personal life. While browsing through, consider the following:

1. What events in the workplace do you think cause the most stress? Does this match up with what is contained on the websites? Give some specific examples.
2. What things can an organization do to help manage stress? Which approach do you feel would be most effective? Are there any problems or a downside to any of these?

REAL CASE:
When Workers Just
Can't Cope

Until Congress passed the Americans with Disabilities Act (ADA) in 1990, most companies decided how to handle such problems on a case-by-case basis, often depending on such factors as just how challenged the employee was and how sympathetically the supervisor responded. And even the ADA didn't help employers much with deciding how far to go to accommodate people challenged with a disability. The law requires employers to make all "reasonable" accommodations for people with disabilities, including mental ones. But given how subjective and personal psychiatric issues can be, employers have struggled to develop clear policies about what to do in such cases.

In the past few years, the courts have begun to delineate how companies must act. The good news for employers is that the guidelines are surprisingly sympathetic to the dilemmas they face when someone shows signs of mental illness. If a worker becomes depressed or suicidal, the employer must try to find a way to help, by, for example, granting a short leave of absence or changing his or her work schedule. But companies don't have to lower work standards, tolerate misconduct, or give someone a make-work job—steps some employers have taken out of fear of a lawsuit, experts say. A key U.S. Supreme Court case last year further clarified the law by specifying that an employee suffering from mental illness isn't disabled if medication allows the person to function like anyone else. "Most courts are taking a narrow view of who is covered under the ADA," says Peggy Mastroianni, an associate legal counsel for the Equal Employment Opportunity Commission (EEOC).

Any signposts are welcome, because mental illness has posed one of the most difficult challenges to employers—and the courts—since the ADA took effect in mid-1992. Each year, clinical depression alone causes a loss of some 200 million working days in the United States, according to a report released by the International Labor Organization. Psychiatric claims filed with the EEOC doubled from 1993 to 1998, to 2,917 a year. This made them the single largest type of ADA claim, constituting 16.4 percent of all ADA discrimination cases, according to the commission.

Last year's Supreme Court decision went even further. The case involved two sisters who didn't qualify to be pilots at United Airlines Inc. because of poor vision. The court ruled that the sisters couldn't sue for discrimination under the ADA because their disability was correctable (with glasses or contacts). Since then, lower courts have applied the ruling to say that employers can consider the mitigating effects of interventions such as medication. In other words, if an antidepressant drug enables a depressed person to function normally, he or she isn't considered disabled and can't claim discrimination.

The new guidelines should help employers avoid being pushed into unreasonable actions. It's now clear that companies don't need to lower their standards to help a troubled employee, says K. Tia Burke, a Philadelphia management attorney who had one client company that did just that. Nor do employers have to invent light-duty jobs, as other clients have done, says Burke. "Many employers are so loath to get involved in these cases that they bend over backwards and provide more than what is reasonable," she says.

1. What responsibility do you think an employer has when an employee has mental illness? Do you agree with the current legal climate described in the case?
2. How can an employer manage to accommodate those with mental illness?
3. Can anything be learned from the study and management of stress and conflict that can be effectively applied to mental illness in the workplace?

REAL CASE:
Round-the-Clock
Stress

Many employees feel that on-the-job stress is difficult to control, but at least when they get home they can relax. However, as the nature of work changes, the home is no longer the sanctuary it once was. With advanced information technology and customer demands for 24-hour service, an increasing number of employees are on call at all times or working the "graveyard" shift that used to exist only for factory workers. For example, today there are numerous Wal-Mart stores, Walgreens drugstores, and supermarkets that never close. And consider the Heartland Golf Park in Deer Park, Long Island. A golfer who wants a late evening tee-off time can get one up to 3:00 A.M. The strategy has proven so popular that within 90 days of the time it was introduced, the wait time at midnight had grown to two and a half hours. Avid golfers do not mind, however, as the course is well lit and they can play as if it were high noon.

All around the country, businesses are realizing that there is a great deal of profit that can be added to the bottom line if they remain open outside of "normal" hours. One research firm estimates that this strategy can add 5 percent to overall profits, a hefty sum given that more and more businesses are finding their profit margins being narrowed by the competition.

In some cases, the decision to expand working hours has been a result of customer needs. Kinko's Inc., a privately held chain of photocopy shops, moved to a 24-hour schedule when people literally started banging on their doors after regular business hours and asking them to let them come in for desperately needed photocopies. As a news article recently put it, "The company's . . . stores are magnets for ambassadors of the night: everyone from dreamers pursuing secret schemes and second careers to executives putting the final touches on tomorrow's presentation." In Chicago, Kinko's set up an office in the lobby of the Stouffer Renaissance Hotel, a favorite spot of international executives. Customers from different time zones had been coming down at odd hours to ask the hotel to fax materials abroad and to help them with their desktop publishing. The hotel was not equipped to provide these services, so it asked Kinko's to help out. The guests are delighted with the new service, and the hotel is happy to be able to accommodate them thanks to their profitable arrangement with Kinko's.

Banks have also begun to offer 24-hour service. In addition to their ATM machines, which can be found just about everywhere, some banks now offer round-the-clock service: customers can call in and find out within 10 minutes whether they qualify for a new-car loan. A growing number of banks also offer after-hours customer services ranging from safe deposit boxes to $1,000 credit lines to overdraft protection. All the customer has to do is call in at any hour and provide the necessary information.

Some critics are concerned that this development will result in increasing costs to business and added stress to employees. After all, when people work late at night or put in a 15-hour day, they are likely not only to make far more mistakes than if they were on a 9-to-5 schedule but also to become fatigued and burned out. Nevertheless, at the present time approximately two-thirds of all U.S. workers, around 75 million people, do not work traditional 9-to-5 hours—and the number is definitely growing. Additionally, organizations that are engaged in international business, such as brokerage firms, are finding that their operations in Europe and Asia require them to keep odd hours. A U.S.-based broker must be up or on call in the wee hours of the morning because Europe's stock exchanges are doing business. By the time the broker wraps up trading on the Pacific Stock Exchange in the early evening (Eastern Standard Time), there are only a few hours before the Asian stock exchanges open. Simply put, in an increasing number of businesses, it is possible to work round-the-clock—and, of course, to pick up the stress that goes along with this lifestyle.

1. How would a Type A personality feel if his or her organization suddenly announced that everyone was to be on call 24-hours a day because the company was moving to round-the-clock customer service?
2. How would psychological hardiness help people deal with these emerging round-the-clock operations?
3. What are some ways employees and their organizations could cope with the stress caused by these new round-the-clock developments?

ORGANIZATIONAL BEHAVIOR CASE: Sorry, No Seats Are Left; Have a Nice Flight

Jim Miller has been a ticket agent for Friendly Airlines for the past three years. This job is really getting to be a hassle. In order to try to reduce the mounting losses that Friendly has suffered in recent months, management have decided to do two things: (1) overbook their flights so that every seat possible will be filled and (2) increase their service to their customers and live up to their name. Jim, of course, is at the point of application of this new policy. When checking in passengers, he is supposed to be very courteous and friendly, and he has been instructed to end every transaction with the statement, "Have a nice flight." The problem, of course, is that sometimes there are more passengers holding confirmed reservations checking in than there are seats on the plane. Rightfully, these people become extremely upset with Jim and sometimes scream at him and even threaten him. During these confrontations Jim becomes "unglued." He breaks into a sweat, and his face turns bright red. The company guidelines on what to do in these situations are very vague. When Jim called his supervisor for advice, he was simply told to try to book passengers on another flight, but be friendly.

1. Is Jim headed for trouble? What would be some physical, psychological, and behavioral outcomes of this type of job stress?
2. What could the company do to help reduce the stress in Jim's job?
3. What individual coping strategies could Jim try in this situation?

ORGANIZATIONAL BEHAVIOR CASE: A Gnawing Stomachache

Sandy Celeste was 30 years old when her divorce became final. She was forced to go to work to support her two children. Sandy got married right after graduating from college and had never really held a full-time job outside the home. Nevertheless, because of her enthusiasm, education, and maturity, she impressed the human resources manager at Devon's Department Store and was immediately hired. The position involves supervising three departments of men's and women's clothing. Sandy's training consisted of approximately two months at another store in the Devon chain. She spent this training period both selling merchandise and learning the supervisor's responsibilities. On the first day of her supervisory job, Sandy learned that, because of size constraints at the store, six clothing departments are all located in the same area. In addition to Sandy, there are two other supervisors in the other departments. These three supervisors share the service of 28 full- and part-time salespeople. Because the various departments are so jammed together, all the salespeople are expected to know each department's merchandise. Devon's merchandising philosophy is that it will not finish one department or storewide sale without starting another. Both the clerks and the supervisors, who work on a commission and salary basis, are kept busy marking and remarking the merchandise as one sale stops and another starts. To make matters worse, Devon's expects the employees to remark each item just prior to closing time the night after a big sale. The pressure is intense, and customers are often neglected and irritated. However, all the salespeople realize that when the customer suffers, so do their commissions. As a supervisor, Sandy is expected to enforce the company's policy rigidly. Soon after taking the position as supervisor, Sandy began to experience severe headaches and a gnawing stomachache. She would like to quit her job, but realistically she can't because the pay is good and she needs to support her children.

1. To what do you attribute Sandy's health problems? What are some possible extraorganizational, organizational, group, and individual stressors?
2. Is there anything that this company could do to alleviate stress for its supervisors? What individual coping strategies could Sandy try?

ORGANIZATIONAL
BEHAVIOR CASE:
Drinking Up the
Paycheck

James Emery is the father of four children. He was raised in a hardworking immigrant family. His needs for achievement and power were developed while he was growing up. Now he finds himself in a low-paying, dead-end assembly line job with a large manufacturing firm. It is all he can do to get through the day, so he has started daydreaming on the job. On payday he often goes to the tavern across the street and generally spends a lot of money. The next day he is not only hung over but also very depressed because he knows that his wife cannot make ends meet and his children often go without the essentials.

Now he cannot take it any longer. At first he thought of going to his boss for some help and advice, but he really does not understand himself well enough, and he certainly does not know or trust his boss enough to discuss his problems openly with him. Instead, he went to his union steward and told him about his financial problems and how much he hated his job. The steward told James exactly what he wanted to hear. "This darn company is the source of all your problems. The working conditions are not suited for a slave, let alone us. The pay also stinks. We are all going to have to stick together when our present contract runs out and get what we deserve—better working conditions and more money."

1. Explain James's behavior in terms of the frustration model.
2. Cite a specific example of role conflict in this case.
3. What type of conflict resolution strategy is the union steward suggesting? Do you think the real problems facing James are working conditions and pay? Why or why not?
4. What, if anything, can be done to help the James Emerys of the world? Keep your answer in terms of human resources management.

ORGANIZATIONAL
BEHAVIOR CASE:
Arresting the
Neighbor's Kid

Barney Kohl is a police officer assigned to the juvenile department of a large city. Part of the oath that Barney took was to uphold the law consistently for all people. The scope of his job includes investigation of youth drug traffic, alcoholism, and vandalism. Barney is also involved in the community outreach program, which works to build greater understanding and cooperation between the police department and the youth of the community.

Last night, Barney ran into one of the most difficult, if not the most dangerous, problems he has ever faced. While on patrol, he received a radio report to investigate some possible vandalism at a junior high school. On reaching the scene he found five youths, aged 12 to 15, engaged in malicious acts of vandalism. They were throwing rocks through the windows and had splashed paint against the walls. After calling backup units, he proceeded to chase and arrest the vandals. He was successfully holding the group at bay and was waiting for the backup unit to arrive when he noticed that one of the offenders was his neighbor's son. The city has a parents' responsibility law that makes parents financially liable for the damage caused by their children's actions. The damage looked as if it would be considerable, probably running into the thousands of dollars. Barney knows his neighbor can't afford the costs because he has a physical disability and is out of work. He also knows this incident will lead to great problems in the neighbor's family and, of course, would place a great strain on his own and his family's relationship with the neighbors.

1. What kind of conflict is this police officer experiencing? What should he do?
2. How do you explain the youths' behavior in terms of the frustration model?
3. If you were asked to conduct a training seminar for police officers on the management of conflict, what topics would you cover? What strategies would you suggest?

CHAPTER 13

Power and Politics

Learning Objectives

Define power and its relationship to authority and influence.

Identify the various classifications of power.

Discuss the contingency approach to power.

Describe the empowerment of employees.

Relate the political implications of power.

Present some political strategies for power acquisition in modern organizations.

Starting with Best Practice Leader's Advice

Ida Castro, Chairwoman of the Equal Employment Opportunity Commission, on the Power and Politics of Building an Effective EEOC

The first woman to head the EEOC, Ida Castro came up through the U.S. Department of Labor, serving as deputy assistant secretary, director of the Office of Workers' Compensation Programs, and most recently head of the Women's Bureau. A former professor at Rutgers, she also was senior legal counsel for the Health and Hospital Corp. of New York City, the nation's largest municipal health care system. This experience in the political system is evident as she describes attempts to make the EEOC a more powerful and effective government agency to insure equal opportunity in employment for everyone.

Q1: What are the toughest challenges facing you and the agency?

Castro: Probably my greatest challenge is turning the agency around internally. The agency has experienced more than 20 years of resource starvation. We have issues of staff allocation, training, and professional development. We also have issues in relation to technology, where the agency is far behind the private sector. Because we are so far behind in technology, I believe staff training is key. We have a staff that is committed to the agency, but many staff members have been with us for many years and require some updating of their skills.

Q2: The agency received a budget increase of $37 million for fiscal year 1999. Will this additional money fund all the projects that the agency needs?

Castro: The $37 million is more than welcome and puts us on the right track. The money will help us expand our services and strengthen our staff in very significant ways. But is it enough? And is it the total solution to our problem? The answer to those questions would be "no." Again, the history of starvation in this agency has caused great impact. We have been able, thanks to the leadership of my predecessor, to make significant inroads on the issue of backlog. But we still, on average, take 310 days to process a charge, and that is too long.

Q3: During a recent commission meeting, three different groups representing the interests of employers brought up their concerns about overlaps in the Americans with Disabilities Act (ADA) and the Family and Medical Leave Act (FMLA). Are there overlaps? What can the commission do to clear up employers' confusion in this area?

Castro: I don't think there are overlaps, but certainly there is interplay. And I think that we have been addressing that, somewhat. I think the agency has to be a little bit more aggressive in disseminating information about the interplay between the laws. I would be willing to explore making sure that future guidance and outreach documents tend to at least flag where such interplay exists and, to the extent possible, explain the interplay in laypersons' terms. We've already done that with some of our guidance materials and will certainly flag those common issues in the agency's upcoming reasonable accommodation guidance.

Q4: *A key element of the EEOC strategic plan is to improve communication and outreach to employers. The agency has already improved its Web page and increased its educational programs. What needs to be done to futher improve communication with employers?*

Castro: My goal in working with the employer community—first and foremost—is to establish a trust relationship. My goal is that everyone will perceive this agency as fair and efficient and as the premier enforcement agency for antidiscrimination laws in this country. During my confirmation hearing, I told the Senate committee that I was aware small and midsize businesses tended to perceive the EEOC as "the enemy" and as an agency that exercises undue power. Personally, I don't believe that to be true. I think this agency has been fair in its application of resources. There have been some cases that have been publicized in a manner that may have affected that image. We don't need to be battling in a public forum over issues that may not be real issues and are merely perceptions or misconceptions of what the agency is doing. There may be ample opportunity for us to disagree on real issues. I say if we're going to disagree, then let's do it over real issues and have some real and meaningful dialogues. And let's not base these discussions merely on perceptions. The way we can make positive changes is by making an honest effort to reach out and listen carefully to what employers have to say.

Q5: *Over the past couple of years, the EEOC has received some negative publicity from several cases. How might the agency avoid criticism like this in the future?*

Castro: I think the EEOC would benefit from an expanded dialogue with those who work with us, so that we can clarify a number of things. If we are in full dialogue with all employers and employees, if people understand their rights and their responsibilities under the law, then we can change these negative perceptions. We do have to enforce the law, mind you, so there will be people who may not be too happy with us. But if people sense and know that we are fair and we are efficient, then we will have less, as you called it, "negative publicity."

Q6: *The EEOC was praised for its handling of the Mitsubishi Motors sexual harassment case. What did the agency do right, and does this set a model on how the EEOC should handle cases like this in the future?*

Castro: I think when the case is a strong, solid case, and the EEOC comes forward assertively and firmly, then it does the world good. The Mitsubishi case not only benefited the agency—which is a narrow way of looking at it—it resolved the issue for the affected women and generated a high level of publicity and public discourse that makes other workplaces understand their responsibilities and compels them to eliminate this type of insidious behavior. Do I want more cases that will help me do all of that? It's an interesting question, because it would be like saying, well, I want discrimination. I don't want discrimination. But if we find similar instances, yes, I would want to proceed and handle the case fairly, efficiently, and firmly.

Over the years, groups, informal organization, interactive behavior, conflict, and stress have received considerable attention as important dynamics of organizational behavior; power and politics, however, have not. As Rosabeth Kanter observed a number of years ago, "Power is America's last dirty word. It is easier to talk about money—and much easier to talk about sex—than it is to talk about power."[1] Yet it is becoming clear, and anyone who has spent any time in a formal organization can readily verify, that organizations are highly political, and power is the name of the game. Power and politics must be brought "out of the closet" and recognized as an important dynamic in organizational behavior. For example, the dynamics of power—how to use it and how to abuse it—were discovered by Joseph O'Donnell, who was abruptly fired from his high-level executive position with JWT Group Inc. when he proposed stripping the CEO and chairman Don Johnston of his day-to-day operating duties. In other cases, however, such a grab for power has worked. Lewis Glucksman, for instance, pushed Peter Peterson from the head of Lehman Brothers several years ago, and every day, in organizations at all levels, power plays and political moves take place.

The first part of the chapter defines what is meant by power and describes how power is related to authority and influence. The next part concentrates on the various classifications of power. Particular attention is given to the French and Raven classification of the sources of power. After an examination of some of the research results on power types, attention is given to some contingency approaches (for example, the influenceability of the target and an overall contingency model of power). Next, the popular approach of empowering employees is presented. The last part is concerned with organizational politics. Particular attention is given to a political perspective of power in today's organizations and to specific political strategies used in the acquisition of power.

THE MEANING OF POWER

Although the concepts in the field of organizational behavior seldom have universally agreed-upon definitions, *power* may have even more diverse definitions than most. Almost every author who writes about power defines it differently. Going way back, for example, the famous pioneering sociologist Max Weber defined power as "the probability that one actor within a social relationship will be in a position to carry out his own will despite resistance."[2] More recently, a search of the literature on power found it referred to as the ability to get things done despite the will and resistance of others or the ability to "win" political fights and outmaneuver the opposition. The power theorists stress the positive sum of power, suggesting it is the raw ability to mobilize resources to accomplish some end without reference to any organized opposition.[3] Pfeffer, the organizational behavior theorist perhaps most closely associated with the study of power, simply defined power as a potential force and in more detail "as the potential ability to influence behavior, to change the course of events, to overcome resistance, and to get people to do things that they would not otherwise do."[4]

Usually definitions of power are intertwined with the concepts of authority and influence. For example, the preceding definition uses the word *influence* in describing power, the pioneering management theorist Chester Barnard defined power in terms of "informal authority," and many organizational sociologists define authority as "legitimate power."[5] These distinctions among concepts need to be cleared up in order to better understand power.

The Distinctions among Power, Authority, and Influence

In Chapter 8 the power motive is defined as the need to manipulate others and have superiority over them. Extrapolating from this definition of the need for power, "power" itself can be defined as the ability to get an individual or group to do something—to get the person or group to change in some way. The individual who possesses power has the ability to manipulate or change others. Such a definition of power distinguishes it from authority and influence.

One of the primary sources of definitional controversy revolves around the question: Is power the *observed influence* over others, or is it merely the *potential to influence?* An argument can be made that those individuals who have the most power are the least likely to need to demonstrate outward evidence that they hold it. Their mere presence is enough to change the behaviors of others without lifting a finger or saying a word. This makes the study of power much more difficult, but at the same time conceptually should not be ignored.[6] An employee who takes the back stairs to avoid confronting an intimidating coworker is being influenced without the coworker even knowing of the power held over the frightened coworker.

Authority legitimatizes and is a source of power. Authority is the right to manipulate or change others. Power need not be legitimate. In addition, the distinction must be made between top-down classical, bureaucratic authority and Barnard's concept of bottom-up authority based on acceptance. In particular, Barnard defined *authority* as "the character of a communication (order) in a formal organization by virtue of which it is accepted by a contributor to or 'member' of the organization as governing the action he contributes."[7]

Such an acceptance theory of authority is easily differentiated from power. Grimes notes: "What legitimizes authority is the promotion or pursuit of collective goals that are associated with group consensus. The polar opposite, power, is the pursuit of individual or particularistic goals associated with group compliance."[8]

Influence is usually conceived of as being broader in scope than power. It involves the ability to alter other people in general ways, such as by changing their satisfaction and performance. Influence is more closely associated with leadership than power is, but both obviously are involved in the leadership process. Thus, authority is different from power because of its legitimacy and acceptance, and influence is broader than power, but it is so conceptually close that the two terms can be used interchangeably.

The preceding discussion points out that an operational definition of power is lacking, and this vagueness is a major reason power has been largely ignored in the study of organizational behavior. Yet, especially when it is linked to the emerging concern for organizational politics, the study of power can greatly enhance the understanding of the ways in which organizations function.

The Classifications of Power

Most discussions of power often begin and sometimes even end with a review of the five categories of the sources of social power identified by psychologists John French and Bertram Raven.[9] Describing and analyzing these five classic types of power (reward, coercive, legitimate, referent, and expert) serves as a necessary foundation and point of departure for the entire chapter. Most of the examples and applications to organizational behavior derive from the following five types of power.

Reward Power.   This source of power is based on a person's ability to control resources and reward others. In addition, the target of this power must value these rewards. In an organizational context, managers have many potential rewards, such as pay increases, promotions, valuable information, favorable work assignments, more responsibility, new equipment, praise, feedback, and recognition available to them. In operant learning terms, this means that the manager has the power to administer positive reinforcers. In expectancy motivation terms, this means that the person has the power to provide positive valences and that the other person perceives this ability.

To understand this source of power more completely, one must remember that the recipient holds the key. If managers offer their people what they think are rewards (for example, a promotion with increased responsibility), but the people do not value them (for example, they are insecure or have family obligations that are more important to them than a promotion), then managers do not really have reward power. By the same token, managers may not think they are giving rewards to their people (they calmly listen to chronic complainers), but if they perceive this to be rewarding (the managers are giving them attention by intently listening to their complaining), the managers nevertheless have reward power. Also, managers may not really have the rewards to dispense (they may say that they have considerable influence with top management to get their people promoted, but actually they don't), but as long as their people think they have it, they do indeed have reward power.

Coercive Power.   This source of power depends on fear. The person with coercive power has the ability to inflict punishment or aversive consequences on another person or, at least, to make threats that the other person believes will result in punishment or undesirable outcomes. This form of power has contributed greatly to the negative connotation that power has for most people. In an organizational context, managers frequently have coercive power in that they can fire or demote people who work for them or dock their pay, although the legal climate and unions have stripped away some of this power. A manager can also directly or indirectly threaten an employee with these punishing consequences. In operant learning terms, this means that the person has the power to administer punishment or negatively reinforce (terminate punishing consequences, which is a form of negative control). In expectancy motivation terms, this means that power comes from the expectation on the part of the other person that they will be punished for not conforming to the powerful person's desires. For example, there is fear of punishment when the rules, directives or policies of the organization are not carefully followed. It is probably this fear that gets most people to arrive at work on time and to look busy when the boss walks through the area. In other words, much of organizational behavior may be explained in terms of coercive power rather than reward power.

Legitimate Power.   This power source, identified by French and Raven, stems from the internalized values of the other persons that give the legitimate right to the agent to influence them. The others feel they have the obligation to accept this power. It is almost identical to what is usually called authority and is closely aligned with both reward and coercive power because the person with legitimacy is also in a position to reward and punish. However, legitimate power is unlike reward and coercive power in that it does not depend on the relationships with others but rather on the position or role that the person holds. For example, people obtain legitimacy because of their titles (captain or executive vice president) or position (oldest in the family or officer of a corporation) rather than their personalities or how they affect others.

Legitimate power comes from three major sources. First, the prevailing cultural values of a society, organization, or group determine what is legitimate. For example, in some societies, the older people become, the more legitimate power they possess. The same may be true for a certain physical attribute, gender, or job. In an organizational context, managers generally have legitimate power because employees believe in the value of private property laws and in the hierarchy where higher positions have been designated to have power over lower positions. The same holds true for certain functional positions in an organization. An example of the latter would be engineers who have legitimacy in the operations area of a company, whereas accountants have legitimacy in financial matters. The prevailing values within a group also determine legitimacy. For example, in a street gang the toughest member may attain legitimacy, whereas in a work group the union steward may have legitimacy.

Second, people can obtain legitimate power from the accepted social structure. In some societies there is an accepted ruling class. But an organization or a family may also have an accepted social structure that gives legitimate power. For example, when blue-collar workers accept employment from a company, they are in effect accepting the hierarchical structure and granting legitimate power to their supervisors.

A third source of legitimate power can come from being designated as the agent or representative of a powerful person or group. Elected officials, a chairperson of a committee, and members of the board of directors of a corporation or a union or management committee would be examples of this form of legitimate power.

Each of these forms of legitimate power creates an obligation to accept and be influenced. But, in actual practice, there are often problems, confusion, or disagreement about the range or scope of this power. Consider the following:

> An executive can rightfully expect a supervisor to work hard and diligently; may he also influence the supervisor to spy on rivals, spend weekends away from home, join an encounter group? A coach can rightfully expect [her] players to execute specific plays; may [she] also direct their life styles outside the sport? A combat officer can rightfully expect his men to attack on order; may he also direct them to execute civilians whom he claims are spies? A doctor can rightfully order a nurse to attend a patient or observe an autopsy; may he [or she] order [him or] her to assist in an abortion against [his or] her own will?[10]

These gray areas point to the real concern that many people in contemporary society have regarding the erosion of traditional legitimacy. These uncertainties also point to the complex nature of power.

Referent Power.   This type of power comes from the desire on the part of the other persons to identify with the agent wielding power. They want to identify with the powerful person, regardless of the outcomes. The others grant the person power because he or she is attractive and has desirable resources or personal characteristics.

Advertisers take advantage of this type of power when they use celebrities, such as movie stars or sports figures, to provide testimonial advertising. The buying public identifies with (finds attractive) certain famous people and grants them power to tell them what product to buy. For example, a review of research has found that arguments, especially emotional ones, are more influential when they come from beautiful people.[11]

Timing is an interesting aspect of the testimonial advertising type of referent power. Only professional athletes who are in season (for example, baseball players in the summer and early fall, football players in the fall and early winter, and basketball players in the winter and early spring) are used in the advertisements, because then they are very visible, they are in the forefront of the public's awareness, and consequently they have referent power. Out of season the athlete is forgotten and has little referent power. Exceptions, of course, are the handful of superstars (for example, Shaquille

O'Neal, Michael Jordan, Wayne Gretzky, and Tiger Woods) who transcend seasons and have referent power all year long, and even after they have retired.

In an organizational setting, referent power is much different from the other types of power discussed so far. For example, managers with referent power must be attractive to their people so that they will want to identify with them, regardless of whether the managers later have the ability to reward or punish or whether they have legitimacy. In other words, the manager who depends on referent power must be personally attractive to subordinates.

Expert Power.   The last source of power identified by French and Raven is based on the extent to which others attribute knowledge and expertise to the power holder. Experts are perceived to have knowledge or understanding only in certain well-defined areas. All the sources of power depend on an individual's perceptions, but expert power may be even more dependent on this than the others. In particular, the target must perceive the agent to be credible, trustworthy, and relevant before expert power is granted.

Credibility comes from having the right credentials; that is, the person must really know what he or she is talking about and be able to show tangible evidence of this knowledge. There is basic research indicating the significant positive impact that credibility has on perceived power[12] and much evidence from everyday experience. For example, if a highly successful football coach gives an aspiring young player some advice on how to do a new block, he will be closely listened to—he will be granted expert power. The coach has expert power in this case because he is so knowledgeable about football. His evidence for this credibility is the fact that he is former star player and has coached championship teams. If this coach tried to give advice on how to play basketball or how to manage a corporation, he would have questionable credibility and thus would have little or no expert power. For avid sports fans or players, however, a coach might have general referent power (that is, he is very attractive to them), and they would be influenced by what he has to say on any subject—basketball or corporate management. For example, successful coaches such as basketball's Pat Riley and Rick Pitino have written best-selling books aimed at effective business management.

In organizations, staff specialists have expert power in their functional areas but not outside them. For example, engineers are granted expert power in production matters but not in personnel or public relations problems. The same holds true for other staff experts, such as computer experts or accountants. For example, the computer person in a small office may be the only one who really understands the newest software and how to use it, and this knowledge gives him or her considerable power.

As already implied, however, expert power is highly selective, and, besides credibility, the agent must also have trustworthiness and relevance. By trustworthiness, it is meant that the person seeking expert power must have a reputation for being honest and straightforward. In the case of political figures, scandals could undermine their expert power in the eyes of the voting public. In addition to credibility and trustworthiness, a person must have relevance and usefulness to have expert power. Going back to the earlier example, if the football coach gave advice on world affairs, it would be neither relevant nor useful, and therefore the coach would not have expert power in this domain.

It is evident that expertise is the most tenuous type of power, but managers and especially staff specialists, who seldom have the other sources of power available to them, often have to depend on their expertise as their only source of power. As organizations become increasingly technologically complex and specialized, the expert power of the organization members at all levels may become more and more important. This is formally recognized by some companies that deliberately include lower-level staff members with expert power in top-level decision making. For example, Andy Grove, the head of Intel, has stated: "In general, the faster the change in the know-how on which a business depends, the greater the divergence between knowledge and position power is likely to be. Since our business depends on what it knows to survive, we mix 'knowledge-power people' with 'position-power people' daily, so that together they make the decisions that will affect us for years to come."[13]

It must also be remembered that French and Raven did recognize that there may be other sources of power. For instance, some organizational sociologists recognize the source of power of task interdependence (where two or more organizational participants must depend on one another). An example would be an executive who has legitimate power over a supervisor, but because the executive must depend on the supervisor to get the job done correctly and on time, the supervisor also has power over the executive. There is research evidence that those in such an interdependent relationship with their boss receive better pay raises[14] and even that such interdependence can enhance the quality of the professor–student relationship.[15]

Closely related to interdependence is the use of information as a source of power. A person who controls the flow of information and/or interprets data before it is presented to others has such information power. Information power is distinguished from expert power because the individual merely needs to be in the "right place" to affect the flow and/or distribution of information, rather than having some form of expertise over the generation or interpretation of the information.[16]

Besides recognizing that there may be additional sources of power, French and Raven also point out that the sources are interrelated (for example, the use of coercive power by managers may reduce their referent power and there is research evidence that high coercive and reward power may lead to reduced expert power),[17] and the same person may exercise different types of power under different circumstances and at different times.

Recent research indicates that French and Raven's five bases of power may be summed to develop a measure of global power.[18] This more global measure was found to be internally consistent and significantly related to each of the five individual power bases. It also accounted for additional variance in studies of the relationship between power and other variables such as resistance, compliance, and control. Additional research has found the role that procedural justice may play in the bases of power. One study indicates that although the bases of power are related to affective work reactions, they are also mediated by perceptions of procedure justice.[19] This means employees are inclined to form evaluative perceptions regarding the fairness of actions exhibited by power holders and respond accordingly. Specifically, when the actions seem fair or justifiable, employees respond more favorably to the power influences being utilized by their supervisors. These findings and the previous discussion of the impact of the situation and time lead to the contingency models of power in organizations.

Contingency Approaches to Power

As in other areas of organizational behavior and management, contingency approaches to power have emerged. For example, Pfeffer simply says that power comes from being in the "right" place. He describes the right place or position in the organization as one where the manager has:

1. Control over resources such as budgets, physical facilities, and positions that can be used to cultivate allies and supporters

2. Control over or extensive access to information—about the organization's activities, about the preferences and judgments of others, about what is going on, and who is doing it
3. Formal authority[20]

There is some research support[21] for such insightful observations, and there are also research findings that lead to contingency conclusions such as the following:

1. The greater the professional orientation of group members, the greater relative strength referent power has in influencing them.
2. The less effort and interest high-ranking participants are willing to allocate to a task, the more likely lower-ranking participants are to obtain power relevant to this task.[22]

Besides these overall contingency observations, there is increasing recognition of the moderating impact of the control of strategic contingencies such as organizational interdependence and the extent to which a department controls critical operations of other departments[23] or the role of influence behaviors in the perception of power.[24] Also, the characteristics of influence targets (that is, their influenceability) have an important moderating impact on the types of power that can be successfully used. An examination of these characteristics of the target and an overall contingency model is presented next.

Influenceability of the Targets of Power.   Most discussions of power imply a unilateral process of influence from the agent to the target. It is becoming increasingly clear, however, that power involves a reciprocal relationship between the agent and the target, which is in accordance with the overall social cognitive perspective taken in this text. The power relationship can be better understood by examining some of the characteristics of the target. The following characteristics have been identified as being especially important to the influenceability of targets:[25]

1. *Dependency.*   The greater the targets' dependency on their relationship to agents (for example, when a target cannot escape a relationship, perceives no alternatives, or values the agent's rewards as unique), the more targets are influenced.
2. *Uncertainty.*   Experiments have shown that the more uncertain people are about the appropriateness or correctness of a behavior, the more likely they are to be influenced to change that behavior.
3. *Personality.*   There have been a number of research studies showing the relationship between personality characteristics and influenceability. Some of these findings are obvious (for example, people who cannot tolerate ambiguity or who are highly anxious are more susceptible to influence, and those with high needs for affiliation are more susceptible to group influence), but some are not (for example, both positive and negative relationships have been found between self-esteem and influenceability).
4. *Intelligence.*   There is no simple relationship between intelligence and influenceability. For example, highly intelligent people may be more willing to listen, but, because they also tend to be held in high esteem, they also may be more resistant to influence.
5. *Gender.*   Although traditionally it was generally thought that women were more likely to conform to influence attempts than men because of the way they were raised, there is now evidence that this is changing.[26] As women's and society's views of the role of women are changing, there is less of a distinction of influenceability by gender.

6. *Age.* Social psychologists have generally concluded that susceptibility to influence increases in young children up to about the age of eight or nine and then decreases with age until adolescence, when it levels off.

7. *Culture.* Obviously, the cultural values of a society have a tremendous impact on the influenceability of its people. For example, some cultures, such as Western cultures, emphasize individuality, dissent, and diversity, which would tend to decrease influenceability, whereas others, such as many in Asia, emphasize cohesiveness, agreement, and uniformity, which would tend to promote influenceability. As the accompanying International Application Example: Taking as Long as It Takes indicates, controlling the agenda and time in foreign cultures may be used to gain power and influenceability.

These individual differences in targets greatly complicate the effective use of power and point up the need for contingency models.

INTERNATIONAL APPLICATION EXAMPLE

Taking as Long as It Takes

In recent years many American firms doing business internationally have found, to their chagrin, that their overseas hosts have been using the agenda to gain power over visiting dignitaries. Here is a story related by a business lawyer who recently returned from Japan.

"I went to Japan to negotiate a licensing agreement with a large company there. We had been in contact with these people for three months and during that time had hammered out a rough agreement regarding the specific terms of the contract. The president of the firm thought that it would be a good idea if I, the corporate attorney, went to Tokyo and negotiated some of the final points of the agreement before we signed. I arrived in Japan on a Sunday with the intention of leaving late Friday evening. When I got off the plane, my hosts were waiting for me. I was whisked through customs and comfortably ensconced in a plush limousine within 30 minutes.

"The next day began with my host asking me for my return air ticket so his secretary could take care of confirming the flight. I was delighted to comply. We then spent the next four days doing all sorts of things—sightseeing, playing golf, fishing, dining at some of the finest restaurants in the city. You name it, we did it. By Thursday I was getting worried. We had not yet gotten around to talking about the licensing agreement. Then on Friday morning we had a big meeting. Most of the time was spent discussing the changes my hosts would like to see made in the agreement. Before I had a chance to talk, it was time for lunch. We finished eating around 4 P.M. This left me only four hours before I had to leave for the airport. During this time I worked to get them to understand the changes we wanted made in the agreement. Before I knew it, it was time to head for the airport. Halfway there my host pulled out a new contract. "Here are the changes we talked about," he said. "I have already signed for my company. All you have to do is sign for yours." Not wanting to come home empty-handed, I signed. It turned out that the contract was much more favorable to them than to us. In the process, I learned a lesson. Time is an important source of power. When you know the other person's agenda, you have an idea of what the individual's game plan must be and can work it to your advantage. Since this time, I have all my reservations and confirmations handled stateside. When my host asks me how long I will be staying, I have a stock answer, 'As long as it takes.' "

Required Sources of Power	Process of Power	Target's Influenceability	Required Conditions
Reward Coercive ——— Compliance Means-ends-control		Wants to gain a favorable reaction; wants to avoid a punishing one from the agent	The agent must have surveillance over the target
Referent ——— Identification Attractiveness		Finds a self-satisfying relationship with the agent; wants to establish and maintain a relationship with the agent	The agent must have salience; the agent must be in the forefront of the target's awareness
Expert Legitimate ——— Internalization Credibility		Goes along with the agent because of consistency with internal values	The agent must have relevance

FIGURE 13.1
An overall contingency model of power based on the French-Raven and Kelman theories.

An Overall Contingency Model for Power.   Many other contingency variables in the power relationship besides the target could be inferred from the discussion of the various types of power, for example, credibility and surveillance. All these variables can be tied together and related to one another in an overall contingency model.

The classic work on influence process, by social psychologist Herbert Kelman,[27] can be used to structure an overall contingency model of power. The model in Figure 13.1 incorporates the French and Raven sources of power with Kelman's sources of power, which in turn support three major processes of power.

According to the model, the target will *comply* in order to gain a favorable reaction or avoid a punishing one from the agent. This is the process that most supervisors in work organizations must rely on. But in order for compliance to work, supervisors must be able to reward and punish (that is, have control over the means to their people's ends) and keep an eye on them (that is, have surveillance over them).

People will *identify* not in order to obtain a favorable reaction from the agent, as in compliance, but because it is self-satisfying to do so. But in order for the identification process to work, the agent must have referent power—be very attractive to the target—and be salient (prominent). For example, a research study by Kelman found that students were initially greatly influenced by a speech given by a very handsome star athlete; that is, they identified with him. However, when the students were checked several months after the speech, they were not influenced. The handsome athlete was no longer salient; that is, he was no longer in the forefront of their awareness, and his previous words at the later time had no influence. As discussed earlier, except for the handful of superstars, athletes are soon forgotten and have no power over even their most avid fans. Once they have graduated or are out of season, they lose their salience and, thus, their power.

Finally, people will *internalize* because of compatibility with their own value structure. But, as Figure 13.1 shows, in order for people to internalize, the agent must have expert or legitimate power (credibility) and, in addition, be relevant. Obviously, this process of power is most effective. Kelman, for example, found that internalized power had a lasting impact on the subjects in his studies.

Researchers have had problems constructing ways to measure compliance, identification, and internalization.[28] However, this model of power does have considerable relevance as to how and under what conditions supervisors and managers influence their people. Many must depend on compliance because they are not attractive or do not possess referent power for identification to work. Or they lack credibility or do not have expert or legitimate power for internalization to occur. Kelman's research showed that internalization had the longest-lasting impact and, as shown in the model, does not need surveillance or salience. In other words, what is generally considered to be leadership (covered in the last two chapters) is more associated with getting people not just to comply but also to identify with the leader and, even better, to internalize what the leader is trying to accomplish in the influence attempt. This internalization would be especially desirable in today's highly autonomous, flat organizations with cultures of openness, empowerment, and trust.

The Two Faces of Power

Besides the sources and situational, or contingency, nature of power, there are also different types of power that can be identified. Well known, recently deceased, social psychologist David McClelland did, as Chapter 8 points out, considerable work on the impact of the motivational need for power (what he called *n Pow*). His studies indicated that there are two major types of power, one negative and one positive.

As the introductory comments point out, over the years power has often had a negative connotation. The commonly used term "power-hungry" reflects this negative feeling about power. According to McClelland, power

> . . . is associated with heavy drinking, gambling, having more aggressive impulses, and collecting "prestige supplies" like a convertible. . . . People with this personalized power concern are more apt to speed, have accidents, and get into physical fights. If . . . possessed by political officeholders, especially in the sphere of international relations, the consequences would be ominous.[29]

McClelland felt that this negative use of power is associated with *personal power*. He felt that it is primitive and does indeed have negative consequences.

The contrasting "other face" of power identified by McClelland is *social power*. It is characterized by a "concern for group goals, for finding those goals that will move people, for helping the group to formulate them, for taking some initiative in providing members of the group with the means of achieving such goals, and for giving group members the feeling of strength and competence they need to work hard for such goals."[30] Under this definition of social power, the manager may often be in a precarious position of walking a fine line between an exhibition of personal dominance and the more socializing use of power. McClelland accumulated some empirical evidence that social power managers are quite effective. In some ways this role power may play in organizational effectiveness is in opposition to the more humanistic positions, which emphasize the importance of democratic values and participative decision making. There is also more recent empirical evidence that would counter McClelland's view. One study found that those with a high need for power may suppress the flow of information, especially information that contradicts their preferred course of action, and thus have a negative impact on effective managerial decision making.[31]

The negative use of power can also show up in situations such as sexual harassment. Unwelcome conduct of a sexual nature takes place when someone uses coercive power to threaten another with negative consequences if they do not submit to sexual advances. This is known as *quid pro quo* harassment. A hostile work environment (sexual jokes, leering, posters) is another inappropriate use of one's power over another. In all such inappropriate circumstances, harassment is based on power being used to intimidate another, especially those in a subordinate formal position. However, regardless of some of the controversy surrounding power, it is clear that power is inevitable in today's organizations. How power is used and what type of power is used can vitally affect human performance and organizational goals.

THE SPECIAL CASE OF EMPOWERMENT

Closely related to social power is the popular technique of employee empowerment. Empowerment may be defined as "recognizing and releasing into the organization the power that people have in their wealth of useful knowledge and internal motivation."[32] Empowerment is the authority to make decisions within one's area of responsibility without first having to get approval from someone else. Although empowerment is similar to traditional delegated authority, there are two characteristics that make it unique. One is that employees are encouraged to use their own initiative, and, as they say at Cummins Engine, "Just do it."[33] The second is that empowered employees are given not only the authority, but also the resources, so they are able to make decisions and have the power to get them implemented. The Application Example: Just Doing It provides some specific examples of how Baldrige National Quality Award-winning companies apply such empowerment.

Empowerment programs can transform a stagnant organization into a vital one by creating a "shared purpose among employees, encouraging greater collaboration, and, most importantly, delivering enhanced value to customers."[34] To do so, the organization must overcome certain obstacles, such as becoming impatient, assuming employees have all the needed skills without first checking to make sure they are qualified, and creating confusion through contradictory rewards and the model's behaviors. This means there must be a linkage of the power with self-reliance, managerial authority, and expecting individual contributor commitment.[35] In order for this to occur, empowerment must become embedded in an organization's cultural values operationalized through participation, innovation, access to information, and accountability.

The Complexity of Empowerment

Empowerment assumes that employees are willing to accept responsibility and improve their daily work processes and relationships. A recent survey revealed that almost all U.S. workers do feel personally responsible and want to improve quality and performance. Many companies are now discovering that empowerment training can be extremely useful in showing employees how to participate more actively and make things happen. There is also empirical research evidence that where participation is part of an empowerment program, manufacturing performance improves,[36] and managers perceive that they are indeed empowered.[37]

A good example comes from the chemical division of Georgia-Pacific, where a quality and environmental assurance supervisor and a plant operator who had received empowerment training began participating through sharing ideas for more effectively preparing test samples of a certain chemical. Once they finalized their ideas, they used their empowerment status to produce a demonstration video. After seeing the video, management asked the two employees to share the tape with quality assurance supervisors in other plants. In turn, the supervisor and operator encouraged these other employees to provide feedback on the video and to share their own ideas. As a result, a more efficient system of preparing test samples was developed companywide.

APPLICATION EXAMPLE

Just Doing It

Empowerment involves both giving employees the authority to make decisions and providing them with the financial resources to implement these decisions. For example, at the Ritz-Carlton hotel chain, employees are authorized to spend up to $2000 to handle a customer-related problem. This amount is usually more than sufficient for such common solutions as mailing a shirt to a guest who checked out and accidentally left a shirt or blouse in the room or bringing a guest with a cold a pot of herbal tea and some aspirin. At Zytec, a Minnesota-based designer and supplier of electronic equipment, employees can spend up to $1000 on customer service–related matters. When this sum of money is depleted, the personnel are given another $1000, and this continues indefinitely. So the funds are really continuous and are available to handle all customer-related needs.

At AT&T Universal Card Services, employees are put into teams that plan strategies for improving customer service. These teams identify "top-10" problems and then formulate strategies for dealing with them. When a particular customer service problem is solved, it is removed from the top-10 list and another is put in its place. In attacking these problems, team members are empowered to make those decisions that will reduce costs and increase customer delight (one of the company's primary objectives).

At Solectron, a small manufacturer of complex circuit boards and subsystems for computers and other electronic products, line workers are empowered to stop the production line any time they feel it is necessary. Meanwhile, customer service employees have full authority to return or replace products without getting approval from their boss; and manufacturing employees are trained to use statistical process control techniques and make whatever decisions they feel are justified based on their findings. Additionally, engineers and sales representatives are trained to interact effectively with customers and to make whatever decisions are needed to satisfy customer requirements.

At Motorola, empowered teams are given authority to carry out a wide array of functions, including creating production schedules and job assignments, setting up equipment and conducting routine maintenance, developing and managing budgets, and training new employees. In handling customer-related problems, the employees are provided funds that they can spend as they deem appropriate. In some cases, Motorola personnel are authorized to go as high as $5000, and these monies are replaced on a daily basis.

At the same time, care must be given to the effects on other managers. For example, many middle managers find themselves in a dilemma of dealing with two cultures when empowerment strategies are enacted. The first tells them to "relinquish control" whereas another demands that they "maintain control." These contrasting values create role conflicts that must be resolved in order for the program to succeed.[38] Empowerment and participation have been found to work best when they open new avenues for action among all members of the organization and strengthen their resolve to go along with the new ideas.[39] Some critics argue that power and empowerment are only evoked when there is consonance between the "poetic" and the "rhetoric" of an organization, which means that a person's interpretative framework must account for every aspect of the program. Because there is a conflict between relinquishing and maintaining control, and the two demands must be resolved for the employee to feel empowered, care must be taken not to neutralize empowerment and render it impotent.[40]

Innovation Implications.   Empowerment encourages innovation because employees have the authority to try out new ideas and make decisions that result in new ways of doing things. For example, in one major consumer goods company, two engineers used their empowered status to design and test a new household product. After spending over $25,000 on the project, they realized that the product did not perform up to expectations. The design was faulty and performance was poor. The next day the president of the company sent for both of them. When they entered the executive office, they found they were guests of honor at a party. The president quickly explained that he appreciated all their efforts and even though they were not successful, he was sure they would be in the future. By encouraging their innovative efforts through empowerment, the president helped ensure that these two employees would continue to bring new ideas to the market. This climate for innovation is greatly facilitated by empowering employees.

Access to Information.   When employees are given access to information as a vital part of their empowerment, their willingness to cooperate is enhanced. At firms such as General Mills, self-managed work teams are given any information they need to do their jobs and improve productivity. This includes information as far ranging as profit and loss statements, manufacturing processes, and purchasing procedures. In addition, if employees desire additional training, even if the training is peripheral to their main jobs, it is provided. As a result of this accessibility to information, work teams are able to manage and control operations more effectively than under the old hierarchical bureaucratic and secretive, only on a need-to-know basis, information. With "open-book" cultural values and Intranet technology, empowered employees have all the organization's information (and knowledge) available to do their jobs as effectively as possible.

Accountability and Responsibility.   Although employees are empowered to make decisions they believe will benefit the organization, they must also be held accountable and responsible for results. This accountability is not intended to punish mistakes or to generate immediate, short-term results. Instead, the intent is to ensure that the associates are giving their best efforts, working toward agreed-upon goals, and behaving responsibly toward each other. When these behaviors are exhibited, management is able to continue empowering employees to proceed at their own pace and in their own ways. Empowering employees should raise the level of trust in the organization. Empowered employees feel that "we are in this thing together" and are almost compelled to act responsibly.[41] Trust is a must in today's open, empowered organizations, that are in very competitive markets.

Putting Empowerment into Action

There are a number of ways that managers can implement empowerment. Two common approaches are: (1) *kaizen* and "just do it" principles (JDIT), and (2) trust building. The goal is to tie empowerment with an action-driven results approach. This approach is found at Cummins Engine. The company provides a five-day training program in which *kaizen* (a Japanese term that means "continuous improvement") is combined with JDIT. The principles or operational guidelines utilized include: (1) discard conventional, fixed ideas about doing work; (2) think about how to do it rather than why it cannot be done; (3) start by questioning current practices; (4) begin to make improvements immediately, even if only 50 percent of them can be completed; and (5) correct mistakes immediately.[42]

The first day of the Cummins empowerment training program begins with a discussion about what *kaizen* and JDIT principles mean. Participants learn about the need for teamwork and the use of group problem solving. The second day is spent applying these ideas to a work area where improvement is needed. Cross-functional JDIT teams of three to five people are sent to the work floor to observe, document, and evaluate work practices. The third day is used to implement ideas that were identified and evaluated on the work floor. The next day is spent evaluating the improvements that have been initiated and making any final changes so that the new way of doing the work is more efficient than the previous method. The final day of the program is devoted to making presentations of the results to an audience of managers, explaining the changes that were made, and showing the results that were obtained.

Trust building is also vital. Violations of trust between employers and employees (sometimes called "organizational infidelity") means the terms of the psychological contract that has been built have been ignored or have been broken. Once this occurs, perceptions of rewards and contributions are reevaluated, usually resulting in reduced effort and lower commitment to the company.[43]

"Optimal trust" occurs when managers and employees reach an agreement where trust is counterbalanced with distrust, as there is always at least a degree of suspicion in organizational relationships. Reaching optimal levels of trust involves finding the point where distrust is low enough to not be disruptive and trust is strong enough to move forward with confidence.[44] Distrust is a major disruption to any change, including empowerment. Even at the highest levels of the organization, distrust can negatively affect operations. Unless trust is restored, the effects linger for a long time.[45]

Trust building matches the principles of empowerment. Professional and collaborative relationships can be built across functional and hierarchical lines when trust is present. This grants the ability to disseminate ideas and information quickly throughout the organization. A shared mind-set develops that encourages people to continually challenge old processes and take prudent risks in creating something new. This fosters the ability to form quality ad hoc teams that share knowledge and tackle problems.[46]

At the extreme, some organizations encourage silliness and fun to build trust. Matt Weinstein and Luke Barber are management consultants who help companies build better environments for empowerment using such unusual tactics as bringing champagne to work to celebrate an employee's greatest failure to get rid of the negative stigma. They have set up dance-in-the-hallway sessions, candy prizes, and dress-up days, where workers showed up in Elvis costumes, biker togs, and nun outfits to release stress. When work is fun, employees feel more relaxed and truly empowered.[47]

Although empowerment implementation programs widely vary, they are all based on careful evaluations of the benefits and drawbacks of the process and the degree to which the organization's members are prepared to accept the ideas. The accompanying Application Example: Empowerment and Trust indicates that today's employees seem ready, and even demand, a high degree of empowerment and trust. However, some organizations have found that high degrees of empowerment work extremely well whereas others have discovered that the organization operates most efficiently with less empowerment. To account for these differences, Bowen and Lawler have suggested that organizations first identify at which of four levels of empowerment they should operate: (1) very little involvement, as reflected by traditional production-line firms; (2) moderate involvement, as reflected by organizations that employ suggestion programs and

APPLICATION EXAMPLE

Empowerment and Trust

If an organization wants to tap the full potential of their human resources and maintain their loyalty, how should people be managed? There are many answers to this question. For example, some researchers have noted that an ideal leader does things such as: develops and empowers people, shares authority, and encourages constructive challenge. Others, such as the well-known leadership guru Warren Bennis, contend that leaders have to build trust, and this is a two-way street. Managers have to believe in their employees and employees have to feel that the boss will never let them down.

Some insight into the question of how people should be managed may be found in a recent large interview study involving several hundred firms. Employees responded that their productivity and tenure with their employer was determined by how well they are treated by their boss. Forty percent of those who said they had poor bosses also reported that they would be willing to leave their company and take a job elsewhere if the opportunity arose. In contrast, of those who said their bosses were excellent, only 11 percent said they would be willing to leave.

The lesson from these findings is clear. Being a tough manager may have worked well a decade ago when corporate America was being "lean and mean" by laying off workers. However, that era is now over. As one analyst put it, "The American workplace has evolved to a kinder, gentler state." Additionally, recent survey data shows that most workers rate having a caring boss as more important than either money or fringe benefits.

In particular, employees report that they have strong loyalty to companies that help them develop their skills, provide them mentors, and adjust work schedules to meet their personal needs. Consider the case of Mary Morse, a software engineer at Autodesk, a computer-aided design company in San Rafael, California. Her first manager guided her through a six-month internship, accommodating her college schedule, and providing time off during finals week. Her next boss asked her how much she wanted as a starting salary and paid her $5,000 above this amount. Then this boss's supervisor approached Mary and asked if she could be her mentor. When Mary agreed, the supervisor had her write out a list of short-term and long-term objectives and then began working with her to ensure that these goals were met. Mary's third boss spent time talking to her about her career ambitions, and when she indicated that she wanted to move from designing and writing computer code to becoming a software engineer, he recommended classes and gave her the time off to attend them. So when Mary was wooed by a competitive firm that, among other things, offered her options for 7,000 shares of stock at less than $1 a share, she turned them down. Looking back at her decision and the options that became worth over $1 million, Mary still feels she made the right decision to stay with her current employer. She is not alone.

Recent research shows that people with poor bosses are four times more likely to leave their companies than are those with caring bosses. And that is why so many firms are now getting on the band wagon. For example, Macy's West, a division of Federate Department Stores in San Francisco, recently began a pilot program of assigning mentors to new managers and telling all managers that up to 35 percent of their compensation would now be linked to how well they retained the people under them. And at the International Paper plant in Moss Point, Mississippi, there are morning training sessions on positive reinforcement that are designed to change the way many supervisors manage by making these individuals friendlier and more approachable. The reason for these developments was best summed up by one of Mary Morse's managers at Autodesk, who said, "Job satisfaction and being challenged means as much to me as the money part of it—just so long as I feel rewarded." Simply put, a kind, caring approach can go a long way in motivating people.

quality circles; (3) fairly substantial involvement, as reflected in organizations where jobs are designed so that employees can employ a variety of skills and have a great deal of autonomy in carrying out those jobs; and (4) high involvement, as reflected by organizations in which personnel share information and work together to solve problems and complete tasks.[48]

In general, empowerment can be viewed as the sharing of social power in an organization. Individual employees share goals and combine efforts to reach those goals. This fosters creativity and a stronger stake in the organization's outcomes and future.

POLITICAL IMPLICATIONS OF POWER

Power and politics are very closely related concepts. A popular view of organizational politics is how one can pragmatically get ahead in an organization. Alvin Toffler, the noted author of *Future Shock, The Third Wave,* and *Powershift,* observed that "companies are always engaged in internal political struggles, power struggles, infighting, and so on. That's normal life."[49] There is even the view that there may be an inverse relationship between power and politics. For example, a recent publication aimed at practicing human resources (HR) managers noted that in this era of competing for limited resources, HR managers who lack power must use more politics. "Those who lack political skills will gain a reputation for folding under pressure and having no convictions."[50] Such political skills largely deal with the acquisition of power. In this latter view, power and politics become especially closely intertwined. A recognition of the political realities of power acquisition in today's organizations and an examination of some specific political strategies for acquiring power are of particular interest for understanding the dynamics of organizational behavior.

A Political Perspective of Power in Organizations

The classical organization theorists portrayed organizations as highly rational structures in which authority meticulously followed the chain of command and in which managers had legitimatized power. The discussion in Chapter 14 of informal managerial roles and organization portrays another, more realistic view of organizations. It is in this more realistic view of organizations that the importance of the political aspects of power comes to the forefront. As Pfeffer notes: "Organizations, particularly large ones, are like governments in that they are fundamentally political entities. To understand them, one needs to understand organizational politics, just as to understand governments, one needs to understand governmental politics."[51]

The political perspective of organizations departs from the rational, idealistic model. For example, Walter Nord dispels some of the dreams of ideal, rationally structured, and humanistic organizations by pointing out some of the stark realities of political power. He suggests four postulates of power in organizations that help focus on the political realities:

1. Organizations are composed of coalitions that compete with one another for resources, energy, and influence.
2. Various coalitions will seek to protect their interests and positions of influence.
3. The unequal distribution of power itself has dehumanizing effects.
4. The exercise of power within organizations is one very crucial aspect of the exercise of power within the larger social system.[52]

In other words, the political power game is very real in today's organizations. Researchers on organizational politics conclude that

> . . . politics in organizations is simply a fact of life. Personal experience, hunches, and anecdotal evidence for years have supported a general belief that behavior in and of organizations is often political in nature. More recently, some conceptual and empirical research has added further support to these notions.[53]

Some of today's large corporations have even formalized their political nature by creating political action committees (PACs) to support certain government positions. For example, one CEO created a stir when he proposed a PAC and purportedly suggested that employees who don't contribute "should question their own dedication to the company and their expectations."[54] But like other aspects of organizational dynamics, politics is not a simple process; it can vary from organization to organization and even from one subunit of an organization to another. A comprehensive definition drawing from the literature is that "organizational politics consists of intentional acts of influence undertaken by individuals or groups to enhance or protect their self-interest when conflicting courses of action are possible."[55] The political behavior of organizational participants tends to be opportunistic for the purpose of maximizing self-interest.[56]

Research on organizational politics has identified several areas that are particularly relevant to the degree to which organizations are political rather than rational. These areas can be summarized as follows:[57]

1. *Resources.* There is a direct relationship between the amount of politics and how critical and scarce the resources are. Also, politics will be encouraged when there is an infusion of new, "unclaimed" resources.
2. *Decisions.* Ambiguous decisions, decisions on which there is lack of agreement, and uncertain, long-range strategic decisions lead to more politics than routine decisions.
3. *Goals.* The more ambiguous and complex the goals become, the more politics there will be.
4. *Technology and external environment.* In general, the more complex the internal technology of the organization, the more politics there will be. The same is true of organizations operating in turbulent external environments.
5. *Change.* A reorganization or a planned organization development (OD) effort or even an unplanned change brought about by external forces will encourage political maneuvering.

The preceding implies that some organizations and subunits within the organization will be more political than others. By the same token, however, it is clear that most of today's organizations meet these requirements for being highly political. That is, they have limited resources; make ambiguous, uncertain decisions; have unclear yet complex goals; have increasingly complex technology; and are undergoing drastic change. This existing situation facing organizations makes them more political, and the power game becomes increasingly important. Miles states: "In short, conditions that *threaten* the status of the powerful or *encourage* the efforts of those wishing to increase their power base will stimulate the intensity of organizational politics and increase the proportion of decision-making behaviors that can be classified as political as opposed to rational."[58] For example, with the political situation of today's high-tech, radically innovative firms, it has been suggested that medieval structures of palace favorites, liege lordship, and fiefdoms may be more relevant than the more familiar rational structures.[59] The next section presents some political strategies for power acquisition in today's organizations.

Specific Political Strategies for Power Acquisition

Once it is understood and accepted that contemporary organizations are in reality largely political systems, some very specific strategies can be identified to help organization members more effectively acquire power. For example, one recent research study found that a supervisor-focused political strategy resulted in higher levels of career success, whereas a job-focused political strategy resulted in lower levels of success.[60] Another recent taxonomy of political strategies included the following:[61]

1. *Information strategy*—targets political decision makers by providing information through lobbying or supplying position papers or technical reports
2. *Financial incentive strategy*—targets political decision makers by providing financial incentives such as honoraria for speaking or paid travel
3. *Constituency building strategy*—targets political decision makers indirectly through constituent support such as grassroots mobilization of employees, suppliers, customers, or public relations/press conferences

For over 20 years, various political strategies for gaining power in organizations have been suggested. Table 13.1 gives a representative summary of these strategies. Research is also being done on political tactics. For example, Yukl and Falbe derived eight political, or influence, tactics that are commonly found in today's organizations. These tactics are identified in Table 13.2. Yukl and his colleagues found that the consultation and rational persuasion tactics were used most frequently[62] and along with inspirational appeal were most effective.[63] Some modern organization theorists take more analytical approaches than most of the strategies suggested in Table 13.1 and Table 13.2, and they depend more on concepts such as uncertainty in their political strategies for power. For example, Pfeffer's strategies include managing uncertainty, controlling resources, and building alliances.[64] Others take a more pragmatic approach, such as the analysis that

TABLE 13.1   Political Strategies for Attaining Power in Organizations

Taking counsel
Maintaining maneuverability
Promoting limited communication
Exhibiting confidence
Controlling access to information and persons
Making activities central and nonsubstitutable
Creating a sponsor–protégé relationship
Stimulating competition among ambitious subordinates
Neutralizing potential opposition
Making strategic replacements
Committing the uncommitted
Forming a winning coalition
Developing expertise
Building personal stature
Employing trade-offs
Using research data to support one's own point of view
Restricting communication about real intentions
Withdrawing from petty disputes

TABLE 13.2   Political Tactics Derived from Research

Tactics	Description
Pressure tactics	Using demands, threats, or intimidation to convince you to comply with a request or to support a proposal.
Upward appeals	Persuading you that the request is approved by higher management, or appealing to higher management for assistance in gaining your compliance with the request.
Exchange tactics	Making explicit or implicit promises that you will receive rewards or tangible benefits if you comply with a request or support a proposal, or reminding you of a prior favor to be reciprocated.
Coalition tactics	Seeking the aid of others to persuade you to do something, or using the support of others as an argument for you to agree also.
Ingratiating tactics	Seeking to get you in a good mood or to think favorably of the influence agent before asking you to do something.
Rational persuasion	Using logical arguments and factual evidence to persuade you that a proposal or request is viable and likely to result in the attainment of task objectives.
Inspirational appeals	Making an emotional request or proposal that arouses enthusiasm by appealing to your values and ideals or by increasing your confidence that you can do it.
Consultation tactics	Seeking your participation in making a decision or planning how to implement a proposed policy, strategy, or change.

Source: Adapted from Gary Yukl and Cecilia M. Falbe, "Influence Tactics and Objectives in Upward, Downward, and Lateral Influence Attempts," *Journal of Applied Psychology,* Vol. 75, 1990, p. 133. Used with permission.

suggests that successful political behavior involves keeping people happy, cultivating contacts, and wheeling and dealing.[65] Law Professor Theresa Beiner recently coined the term "reindeer games" (from the song "Rudolf the Red-Nosed Reindeer") to describe, like in the song, social activities that provide some, but not all, employees with opportunities to interact with other organization members, which helps build an individual's power base. For example, a boss who invites three male subordinates to play a round of golf and does not include a female subordinate is engaged in a reindeer game that could be considered discriminatory in terms of gaining access to the inner circle of power and influence.[66]

One of the more comprehensive and relevant lists of strategies for modern managers comes from DuBrin.[67] A closer look at a sampling of his and other suggested strategies provides important insights into power and politics in modern organizations.

Maintain Alliances with Powerful People.   As has already been pointed out, the formation of coalitions (alliances) is critical to the acquisition of power in an organization. An obvious coalition would be with members of other important departments or with members of upper-level management. Not so obvious but equally important would be the formation of an alliance with the boss's secretary or staff assistant, that is, someone who is close to the powerful person. An ethnographic study of a city bus company found that a series of dyadic alliances went beyond the formal system and played an important role in getting the work done both within and between departments.[68] For example, alliances between supervisors and certain drivers got the buses out on the worst winter snow days and kept them running during summer vacation periods when drivers were sparse.

Embrace or Demolish.   Machiavellian principles can be applied as strategies in the power game in modern organizations. One management writer has applied these principles to modern corporate life. For example, for corporate takeovers, he draws on Machiavelli to give the following advice:

> The guiding principle is that senior managers in taken-over firms should either be warmly welcomed and encouraged or sacked; because if they are sacked they are powerless, whereas if they are simply downgraded they will remain united and resentful and determined to get their own back.[69]

Divide and Rule.
This widely known political and military strategy can also apply to the acquisition of power in a modern organization. The assumption, sometimes unwarranted, is that those who are divided will not form coalitions themselves. For example, in a business firm the head of finance may generate conflict between marketing and production in hopes of getting a bigger share of the limited budget from the president of the company.

Manipulate Classified Information.
The observational studies of managerial work have clearly demonstrated the importance of obtaining and disseminating information.[70] The politically astute organization member carefully controls this information in order to gain power. For example, the CIO (chief information officer) may reveal some new pricing information to the design engineer before an important meeting. Now the CIO has gained some power because the engineer owes the CIO a favor. In the new Information Age, the amount of information being generated is growing rapidly; how it is managed can provide power. Specifically, knowledge managers such as this CIO can become powerful in new economy firms.

Make a Quick Showing.
This strategy involves looking good on some project or task right away in order to get the right people's attention. Once this positive attention is gained, power is acquired to do other, usually more difficult and long-range, projects. For example, an important but often overlooked strategy of a manager trying to get acceptance of a knowledge management program (see Chapter 2) is to show some quick, objective improvements in the quality of a product, service, or process.

Collect and Use IOUs.
This strategy says that the power seeker should do other people favors but should make it clear that they owe something in return and will be expected to pay up when asked. The "Godfather" in the famous book and movie of that name and Tony Soprano of the popular HBO T.V. series very effectively used this strategy to gain power.

Avoid Decisive Engagement (Fabianism).
This is a strategy of going slow and easy—an evolutionary rather than a revolutionary approach to change. By not "ruffling feathers," the power seeker can slowly but surely become entrenched and gain the cooperation and trust of others.

Attacking and Blaming Others.
A political tactic some people try is to make others "look bad" in order to make themselves "look good." Blaming and attacking deflects responsibility onto others. It is unethical and unacceptable, but is also a common practice in many organizations.

Progress One Step at a Time (Camel's Head in the Tent).
This strategy involves taking one step at a time instead of trying to push a whole major project or reorganization attempt. One small change can be a foothold that the power seeker can use as a basis to get other, more major things accomplished.

Wait for a Crisis (Things Must Get Worse before They Get Better). This strategy uses the reverse of "no news is good news"; that is, bad news gets attention. For example, many deans in large universities can get the attention of central administration and the board of regents or trustees only when their college is in trouble, for instance, if their accreditation is threatened. Only under these crisis conditions can they get the necessary funding to move their college ahead.

Take Counsel with Caution. This suggested political strategy is concerned more with how to keep power than with how to acquire it. Contrary to the traditional prescriptions concerning participative management and empowerment of employees, this suggests that at least some managers should avoid "opening up the gates" to their people in terms of shared decision making. The idea here is that allowing subordinates to participate and to have this expectation may erode the power of the manager.

Be Aware of Resource Dependence. The most powerful subunits and individuals are those that contribute valuable resources. Controlling the resources other persons or departments need creates considerable bargaining power.

All of these political tactics are part of the games and turf wars that take place in today's organizations. On one level they are inevitable and cannot be prevented. On another, however, they are counterproductive and dysfunctional. They can impede participation and empowerment programs and cause people to waste time and resources. Consequently, many managers believe they must take steps to stop the game playing and turf wars through trust-building and goal-sharing programs.[71] These efforts are especially warranted in a situation in which an organization is undergoing a crisis. Effective crisis management must, at some level, include social-political and technological-structural interventions, mainly aimed at disruptive dysfunctional political agendas of individuals, groups, and/or departments in order to resolve the crisis.[72] Recently, some knowledgeable observers have even suggested that managers would benefit from reading Shakespeare in order to understand the intrigues and intricacies of political tactics used in today's organizations.[73]

A Final Word on Power and Politics

Obviously, the strategies discussed are only representative, not exhaustive, of the many possible politically based strategies for acquiring power in organizations. Perhaps even more than in the case of many of the other topics covered in the text, there is little research backup for these ideas on power and, especially, politics.[74] There is also a call for a framework and guidelines to evaluate the ethics of power and politics in today's organizations. This ethical concern goes beyond the notions of success or effectiveness. For example, of the 10 most unethical activities one study identified, three are directly political: (1) making arrangements with vendors for the purposes of personal gain; (2) allowing differences in pay based on friendships; and (3) hiring, training, and promoting personal favorites rather than those who are most qualified.[75]

To help overcome the negative impact that organizational politics can have on the ethics of an organization, the following guidelines can be used:

1. Keep lines of communication open.
2. Role-model ethical and nonpolitical behaviors.
3. Be wary of game players acting only in their own self-interests.
4. Protect individual privacy interests.
5. Always use the value judgment, "Is this fair?"[76]

As one analysis pointed out: "When it comes to the ethics of organizational politics, respect for justice and human rights should prevail for its own sake."[77]

Besides the possible ethical implications of power and politics carried to the extreme, there are, as previously mentioned, dysfunctional effects such as morale being weakened, victors and victims being created, and energy and time spent on planning attacks and counterattacks instead of concentrating on getting the job done.[78] There is also evidence that politics may play a large role in both base-pay and incentive-pay decisions,[79] and in one company the power struggles and political gamesmanship were the death knell of a gainsharing plan.[80] There is some empirical evidence that those managers who are observed to engage in more political activity are relatively more successful in terms of promotions but are relatively less effective in terms of subordinate satisfaction and commitment and the performance of their unit.[81] There is research evidence that this finding of the importance of political maneuvering in getting ahead in the organization, but detracting from effective performance of the unit, may hold across cultures (at least in Russia).[82]

The dynamics of power continue to evolve. In particular, information technology and the Internet/Intranet provide information access that was not previously available. Organizations with fewer boundaries and wider, even global, access to intellectual capital have political systems and processes that are altered considerably.[83] Also, the ups and downs of the economy in both the United States and the rest of the world (especially Asia) have dramatically changed traditional power bases and processes. In the current social environment, many employees are as interested in jobs with meaning as they are with scoring political points and gaining power. In other words, today's organizational participants' passion for the good life may be replacing their ruthless search for power.[84]

One thing about power and politics, however, remains certain: modern, complex organizations tend to create a climate that promotes power seeking and political maneuvering. And, in today's environment, these political activities extend beyond the traditional boundaries of an organization. For example, Microsoft learned, the hard way, that ingratiation political tactics may have been much more successful than simply trying to bully government regulators when antitrust law violations were being investigated. Other new economy firms such as Cisco are learning from Microsoft's mistakes; it makes sense to investigate and carefully implement the best political approach when seeking to deal with outside agencies and individuals who could alter or harm a firm's inside operations and growth.[85] Power and politics are a fact of modern organizational life, and it is hoped that future research will be forthcoming and will help managers better understand their dynamics, meaning, and successful application.

Summary

This chapter examines one of the most important and realistic dynamics of organizational behavior—power and politics. "Power" and "politics" have a number of different meanings. Power can be distinguished from authority and influence, but most definitions subsume all three concepts. Most of the attention given to power over the years has centered on the French and Raven classification of social power types: reward, coercive, legitimate, referent, and expert. More recently, some contingency models for power have been developed, which take into consideration the influenceability of the targets of power (that is, their dependency, uncertainty, personality, intelligence, gender, age, and culture). Overall contingency models are also beginning to emerge.

Closely related to the contingency models of the French and Raven power types is the view of power by McClelland. He suggests that there are two faces of power: negative personal power and positive social power. Finally, the special case of empowerment is given attention. This popular approach goes beyond merely delegating authority to make decisions to include participation, innovation, access to information, and accountability/responsibility.

Politics is very closely related to power. This chapter gives particular attention to a political perspective of power in modern organizations, in terms of resources, decisions, goals, technology, external environment, and change, and to strategies for the acquisition of power. Some specific political strategies are to maintain alliances with powerful people, embrace or demolish, divide and rule, manipulate classified information, make a quick showing, collect and use IOUs, avoid decisive engagement, attacking and blaming others, progress one step at a time, wait for a crisis, take counsel with caution, and be aware of resource dependence. Above all, it should be remembered that both power and politics represent the realities of modern organizational life. The study of these important dynamics can significantly improve the understanding of organizational behavior.

ENDING WITH META-ANALYTIC RESEARCH FINDINGS

OB PRINCIPLE: Individualistic cultural values result in less conformity in the power and politics of organizations.

Meta-Analysis Results: [133 studies; 4,627 participants; $d = .41$]. *On average, there is a **61 percent probability** that strong individualistic cultural values will result in lower levels of conformity in the power and politics of organizations than when individualistic cultural values are weak (i.e., collectivist cultural values dominate).* Moderator analyses revealed that within just the United States, conformity is stronger the larger the size of the majority and the greater the proportion of female respondents. Interestingly, levels of conformity have declined in the United States since the 1950s when the infamous "organization man" and the "man in the gray flannel suit" dominated the power and politics of large corporations.

Conclusion: As discussed in this chapter, there are many dynamic complexities involved in organizational power and politics. One such dimension is conformity. The power to gain acceptance and cooperation through conforming to group and/or organizational norms can make a functional contribution to organizational effectiveness. However, conformity can also be mind-numbing and dysfunctional in terms of stifling innovation or going along with unethical decisions. Powerful, politically astute managers must be able to read and make a fit with the prevailing cultural values in order to use or minimize conformity. Participants may feel a certain pressure to conform even at the expense of their better judgment or ethical standards. Although the pressure to conform appears to have declined in the United States over the decades, it still seems to be a product of cultural values. Certain societies do not tolerate dissidence and stress collective thought and action. Others foster values of independence and freedom of ideas. From a power and politics perspective, conformity can be either a strength or a weakness for the effectiveness of organizations. Conformity can contribute to the power of a manager, and a political strategy is to attain conformity to desired standards and ways of behaving.

Source: Adapted from Rod Bond and Peter B. Smith, "Culture and Conformity: A Meta-Analysis of Studies Using Asch's (1952b, 1956) Line Judgement Task," *Psychological Bulletin,* Vol. 119, No. 1, 1993, pp. 111–137.

Questions for Discussion and Review

1. How would you define *power* in your own words? How does power differ from authority? From influence?
2. Identify, briefly summarize, and give some realistic examples of each of the French and Raven power types.
3. Using the contingency model of power, who would you use to advertise products in the fall, winter, spring, and summer? Explain your choices.
4. Describe employee empowerment, giving specific attention to its operationalization and implications for effective outcomes. How, if at all, is empowerment related to traditional delegation? To social power?

5. In the chapter it is stated: "The political power game is very real in today's organizations." Explain this statement in terms of the discussion in the chapter and any firsthand experience you have had to verify it.

6. Identify three or four of the political strategies that are discussed in the chapter. Explain how these might actually help someone acquire power in today's organization. How would these work in dot-com firms?

Internet Exercise: The Uses and Abuses of Power

Using the classic French and Raven five sources of power discussed in this chapter as the framework, how can some jobs effectively use one or more of these five types to be more or less effective? For example, an airline captain may be much more effective by having high levels of legitimate and expert power. A different type or style of manager, such as a new product design team leader, may be more effective by having high levels of referent power, but be ineffective with use of legitimate power. You might look under some of the job listings for managers at such sites as www.monster.com or America's Job Bank at www.ajb.dni.us/ to get some examples of specific jobs to analyze in terms of power.

1. For each of the five types of power, list a specific job listing found on the Web that would benefit from its use.

2. Consider managers that you have worked for in the past. What type of power did they have? Was it effective?

3. If you could be strong in one power category, which type would it be? Does this depend on the organization you work for? Why or why not?

REAL CASE:
Fighting Back

One of the areas in which organizations are finding power to be an extremely important consideration in today's knowledge management is the protection of intellectual property, specifically patent protection. When a firm secures a patent, it gains knowledge power over the marketplace. However, if this patent cannot be defended against violators, it has little value. A good example of a patent protection battle is that of Fusion Systems, a small, high-tech American firm, and Mitsubishi, the giant Japanese conglomerate.

Several years ago, Fusion developed a core technology that allowed it to manufacture high-intensity ultraviolet lamps powered by 500 to 6000 watts of microwave energy. The company obtained patents in the United States, Europe, and Japan. One of its first big orders came from the Adolph Coors Company for lamp systems to dry the printed decoration on beer cans. Other customers included Hitachi, IBM, 3M, Motorola, Sumitomo, Toshiba, NEC, and Mitsubishi. The last purchased Fusion's lamp system and immediately sent it to the research and development lab to be reverse engineered. Once Mitsubishi had stripped down the product, it began filing patent applications that copied and surrounded Fusion's high-intensity microwave lamp technology. Fusion was unaware of what was going on until it began investigating and found that Mitsubishi had filed nearly 300 patent applications directly related to its own lamp technology. When Fusion tried to settle the matter through direct negotiations, the firm was unsuccessful. In addition, Mitsubishi hired the Stanford Research Institute to study the matter and the Institute concluded that the Japanese company's position was solid. However, the chairman of the applied physics department at Columbia University, who was hired by Fusion, disagreed and—after reviewing the patent materials from both companies—concluded that Mitsubishi had relied heavily on technology developed at Fusion and that Mitsubishi's lamp represented no significant additional breakthrough.

Mitsubishi then offered Fusion a deal: Mitsubishi would not sue Fusion for patent infringement if Fusion would pay Mitsubishi a royalty for the privilege of using "its" patents in Japan. Mitsubishi would then get a royalty-free, worldwide cross-license of all of Fusion's technology. Fusion responded by going to the Office of the U.S. Trade Representative and getting help. The company also found a sympathetic ear from the Senate Finance Committee and the House Republican Task Force on Technology Transfer, as well as from the secretary of commerce and the American ambassador to Japan. As the dispute was dragged through the courts, Mitsubishi began to give ground in the face of political pressure. At the same time, Fusion continued to develop innovations in its core field of expertise and remains the leader in both Japanese and worldwide markets. The company believes that as long as it maintains the exclusive rights to this technology, competitors will not be able to erode its market power.

1. What type of power does a patent provide to a company? Is this the same kind of power that people within a firm attempt to gain?
2. What types of political strategies has Mitsubishi used to try to gain power over Fusion? Using the material in Table 13.1, identify and describe three.
3. How has Fusion managed to retaliate successfully? Using the material in Table 13.2, identify and describe three tactics it has employed.

ORGANIZATIONAL BEHAVIOR CASE: Throwing Away a Golden Opportunity

Roger Allen was a man on the move. Everyone in the firm felt that someday he would be company president. To listen to his boss, Harry Walden, it was only a matter of time before Roger would be at the helm.

The current president of the firm was a marketing person. She had worked her way up from field salesperson to president by selling both the product and her competency to customers and the company alike. In a manner of speaking, the marketing department was the "well-oiled" road to the top. Roger was the number-one salesperson and, according to the grapevine, was due to get Harry Walden's job when the latter retired in two years. However, Roger was not sure that he wanted to be vice president of marketing. Another slot was opening up in international sales. Roger knew nothing about selling to Europe, but this was the firm's first venture outside the United States, and he thought he might like to give it a try. He talked to Harry about it, but the vice president tried to discourage him. In fact, Harry seemed to think that Roger was crazy to consider the job at all. "Rog," he said, "that's no place for you. Things are soft and cozy back here. You don't have to prove yourself to anyone. You're number one around here. Just sit tight and you'll be president. Don't go out and make some end runs. Just keep barreling up the middle for four yards on each carry, and you'll score the big touchdown." Roger was not convinced. He thought perhaps it would be wise to discuss the matter with the president herself. This he did. The president was very interested in Roger's ideas about international marketing. "If you really think you'd like to head up this office for us, I'll recommend you for the job."

After thinking the matter over carefully, Roger decided that he would much rather go to Europe and try to help establish a foothold over there than sit back and wait for the stateside opening. He told his decision to Harry. "Harry, I've talked to the president, and she tells me that this new opening in international sales is really going to get a big push from the company. It's where the action is. I realize that I could sit back and take it easy for the next couple of years, but I think I'd rather have the international job." Harry again told Roger that he was making a mistake. "You're throwing away a golden opportunity. However, if you want it, I'll support you."

A week later, when the company selected someone else from sales to head the international division, Roger was crushed. The president explained the situation to him in this way: "I thought you wanted the job and I pushed for you. However, the other members of the selection committee voted against me. I can tell you that you certainly didn't sell Harry very strongly on your idea. He led the committee to believe that you were really undecided about the entire matter. In fact, I felt rather foolish telling them how excited you were about the whole thing, only to have Harry say he'd talked to you since that time and you weren't that sure at all. When Harry got done, the committee figured you had changed your mind after talking to me, and they went on to discuss other likely candidates."

1. Who had power in this organization? What type of power did Harry Walden have?
2. Do you think Roger played company politics well? If so, why didn't he get the international sales job?
3. At this point, what would you do if you were Roger? What political strategies could be used?

CHAPTER 14

Groups and Teams

Learning Objectives

Describe the basic nature of groups: the dynamics of group formation and the various types of groups.

Discuss the implications that research on groups has for the practice of management.

Explain the important dynamics of informal groups and organizations.

Analyze the impact of groupthink.

Present the newly emerging team concept and practice.

Starting with Best Practice
Leader's Advice

Continental Airlines' CEO Gordon Bethune on the Value of Teams

Continental Airlines has the distinction of going from one of the worst to one of the most admired companies in the world. Continental has recently received many awards in its industry, including Airline of the Year and Best Managed U.S. Carrier. Continental has also been ranked first in customer service in recent years in the J. D. Power Airline Customer Satisfaction study. CEO and then Chairman of the Board Gordon Bethune was named one of the top 25 global managers by Business Week *and was ranked sixth among the top 50 CEOs in 1999 by* Worth *magazine. In this interview, Bethune discusses his experience with teams in the success of Continental.*

Q1: Continental's Working Together program involves a lot of teamwork. How do you view teams?

Bethune: Running an airline is the biggest team sport there is. It's not an approach, it's not reorganization, and it's not a daily team plan. We are like a wristwatch—lots of different parts, but the whole has value only when we all work together. It has no value when any part fails. So we are not a cross-functional team, we're a company of multifunctions that has value when we all work cooperatively—pilots, flight attendants, gate agents, airport agents, mechanics, reservation agents. And not to understand that about doing business means you're going to fail. Lots of people have failed because they don't get it. It's like basic human nature: if you take someone for granted or treat them like they have less value than someone else, they'll go to extraordinary lengths to show you you're wrong. People who try to manage our business and ascribe various values to different functions and treat some with disdain because they are easy to replace might some day find the watch doesn't work—it might be the smallest part that's broken, but the whole watch doesn't work.

Q2: How do you get teams working in a great way?

Bethune: We are analogous to a football team. Everyone has a different assignment but that is the game. In a larger sense we are all on a team, and we instill that down to the head of departments. We have a fairly collegial style of management. I have four or five people I work with closely—our president and chief operating officer, the chief financial officer, the head of legal and public relations, and the head of operations. We collectively agree on things or we just don't do them because each one of them sees things in their knothole from their functional perspective. If we all say yes, it's probably OK. I read once that four or five really smart guys working together could beat any one guy. And 14 or so are too many and you might go the wrong way. So we have four or five of us who, each in our definition of smart, brings smarts to the table. And we've got the best management team in the United States. It works, it shows in the records, it's not me being a proud parent. Just look at the data.

Q3:   *What do you see as some of the challenges of teams?*

Bethune: We all have to identify and agree on the definition of success. The biggest disconnect in any enterprise is when people have different definitions of success. Let's take organized labor and the corporate office. How does organized labor define success—number of dues collected, number of jobs? Is that the way you write the income statement? No, that's not a definition, so it's not unusual, then, to have different viewpoints and different directions you want to go in when you don't decide on how you keep score. So here's the big issue: you define how you keep score and define success and how you reward employees, and that's what you're going to get. Before I became CEO, Continental said: "We are going to be the lowest cost airline." So we had a mantra of low cost is everything, it's the Holy Grail. It's like having only one instrument like an air speed indicator on an airplane—air speed is important but it isn't the only thing. So, you're doing pretty well when you hit the mountain, right? When that happens, you say, wait a minute, cost isn't everything. Let's say we're in the pizza business. If I'm rewarded by making the product cost less, I'll take the cheese off the pizza and get paid. That's not what you wanted.

I was on a panel at Texas A&M University with Roger Clemens. Roger is one of the world's best pitchers. The students were asking: "How do you get people to change their behavior and do things you want them to do?" I said: "Why do you think Roger throws strikes?" Because that's how you keep score, that's how you win the game, that's how Roger gets paid. If you change the rules to four balls you're out, three strikes you walk, what do you think Roger's going to do? He isn't going to do the same thing as before because people want to win. You tell them what the metric is—how you keep score, how you get paid—and you get out of the way.

Q4:   *Are most of your teams of a permanent nature whereas others are temporary?*

Bethune: We are all permanent.

Q5:   *You have had great success turning around Continental. What strategies do you have to sustain that success, particularly with regard to your Working Together program?*

Bethune: The Working Together program says that you've got to have people work as a team, and every person on the team has to know what's going on. So we started telling all our employees what's going on every day—how our stock did, our on-time performance, baggage handling, and so on. Everybody knows every day. Every Friday evening, I put out a voice mail that's also e-mailed all around the company. It's from the CEO's perspective—what happened and where we're going. Every month in Houston we have an open house, and every month we send employees a newsletter to their home. Every six months the president and I go to seven major domestic cities and give a formal presentation. It is also available on videotape for employees to take home. At Continental, we spend 100 percent of our time working together as a team, trying to figure out how to beat our competitors.

Q6:   *What do you see as your greatest current challenge as CEO of Continental?*

Bethune: I suspect it's the sustainability of our winning team and how to keep the focus and discipline of 48,000 men and women who are probably the best at what they do and keeping them the best. That's a challenge for me.

This chapter approaches organizational behavior dynamics from the perspective of the group—both informal and formal—and the increasingly popular team concept and practice. The first section examines the way groups are formed, the various types of groups, some of the dynamics and functions of groups, and the findings of research on groups. The next section explores the dynamics of informal roles and organization. This discussion is followed by an analysis of the impact of groupthink. The balance of the chapter is devoted specifically to teams. The distinction is made between work groups and teams, and specific attention is devoted to self-managed and cross-functional teams. The way to make these teams more effective through training and evaluation is discussed.

THE NATURE OF GROUPS

The group is widely recognized as an important sociological unit of analysis in the study of organizational behavior. Studying groups is especially valuable when the dynamics are analyzed. Group dynamics are the interactions and forces among group members in social situations. When the concept is applied to the study of organizational behavior, the focus is on the dynamics of members of both formal or informal work groups and, now, teams in the organization.

The popularity of work groups and teams is soaring. Although they were first used in corporate giants such as Toyota, Motorola, General Mills, and General Electric, recent surveys indicate that the great majority of American manufacturers now utilize teams and that they are being widely used in the service sector as well. Yet, as with many other areas of organizational behavior, the study and application of groups is undergoing considerable controversy and change. For example, in a commentary about the status of groups in the field of organizational behavior, Alderfer noted:

> Groups and group dynamics are a little like the weather—something that nearly everyone talks about and only a few do anything about. Research, practice, and education about group dynamics are currently in a state of ferment. In the world of practice, we hear leaders speaking out to encourage teamwork, to support empowering people, and to establish organizational cultures that promote total quality management. Each of the initiatives depends on understanding groups well and acting effectively with them.[1]

In addition, today's social environment surrounding groups is changing. For example, there is the assumption that Generation Xers are difficult to manage in groups because they have low needs for group affiliation, high needs for individual achievement, and "doing their own thing." The solution may be found in the careful construction of rewards and performance measures in order to obtain cooperation and collaboration.[2]

The Meaning of a Group and Group Dynamics

Instead of quickly moving to teams per se, the discussion begins with groups and their dynamics, an understanding of which is basic to the field of organizational behavior. The term *group* can be defined in a number of different ways, depending on the perspective that is taken. A comprehensive definition would say that if a group exists in an organization, its members:

1. Are motivated to join
2. Perceive the group as a unified unit of interacting people

3.   Contribute in various amounts to the group processes (that is, some people contribute more time or energy to the group than do others)
4.   Reach agreements and have disagreements through various forms of interaction[3]

Just as there is no one definition of the term *group,* there is no universal agreement on what is meant by *group dynamics.* Although Kurt Lewin popularized the term in the 1930s, through the years different connotations have been attached to it. One normative view is that group dynamics describes *how* a group *should* be organized and conducted. Democratic leadership, member participation, and overall cooperation are stressed. Another view of group dynamics is that it consists of a set of *techniques.* Here, role playing, brainstorming, focus groups, leaderless groups, group therapy, sensitivity training, team building, transactional analysis, and the Johari window are traditionally equated with group dynamics, as are the emerging self-managed teams. A recent example of a new group technique is called "creative abrasion," which is the search for a clash of ideas rather than "personal abrasion," or the clash of people. The goal here is to develop greater creativity from the group.[4] A third view is the closest to Lewin's original conception. Group dynamics are viewed from the perspective of the internal nature of groups, how they form, their structure and processes, and how they function and affect individual members, other groups, and the organization. The following sections are devoted to this third view of group dynamics and set the stage for the discussion of work teams.

The Dynamics of Group Formation

Why do individuals form into groups? Before discussing some very practical reasons, it would be beneficial to examine briefly some of the classic social psychology theories of group formation, or why people affiliate with one another. The most basic theory explaining affiliation is *propinquity.* This interesting word means simply that individuals affiliate with one another because of spatial or geographical proximity. The theory would predict that students sitting next to one another in class, for example, are more likely to form into a group than are students sitting at opposite ends of the room. In an organization, employees who work in the same area of the plant or office or managers with offices close to one another would more probably form into groups than would those who are not physically located together. There is some research evidence to support the propinquity theory, and on the surface it has a great deal of merit for explaining group formation. The drawback is that it is not analytical and does not begin to explain some of the complexities of group formation. Some theoretical and practical reasons need to be explored.

Theories of Group Formation.   A more comprehensive theory of group formation than mere propinquity comes from the classic theory of George Homans based on activities, interactions, and sentiments.[5] These three elements are directly related to one another. The more activities persons share, the more numerous will be their interactions and the stronger will be their sentiments (how much the other persons are liked or disliked); the more interactions among persons, the more will be their shared activities and sentiments; and the more sentiments persons have for one another, the more will be their shared activities and interactions. This theory lends a great deal to the understanding of group formation and process. The major element is *interaction.* Persons in a group interact with one another not just in the physical propinquity sense, but also to accomplish many group goals through cooperation and problem solving.

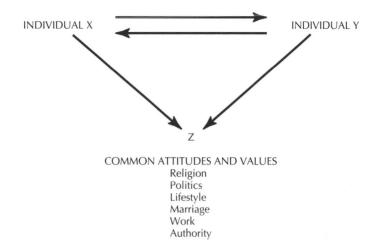

INDIVIDUAL X   INDIVIDUAL Y

Z

COMMON ATTITUDES AND VALUES
Religion
Politics
Lifestyle
Marriage
Work
Authority

FIGURE 14.1
A balance theory of
group formation.

There are many other theories that attempt to explain group formation. Most often they are only partial theories, but they are generally additive in nature. One of the more comprehensive is Theodore Newcomb's *balance theory* of group formation.[6] The theory states that persons are attracted to one another on the basis of similar attitudes toward commonly relevant objects and goals. Figure 14.1 shows this balance theory. Individual X will interact and form a relationship/group with individual Y because of common attitudes and values (Z). Once this relationship is formed, the participants strive to maintain a symmetrical balance between the attraction and the common attitudes. If an imbalance occurs, an attempt is made to restore the balance. If the balance cannot be restored, the relationship dissolves. Both propinquity and interaction play a role in balance theory.

Still another theoretical approach to group formation from social psychology is *exchange theory.*[7] Similar to its functioning as a work-motivation theory, discussed in Chapter 8, exchange theory of groups is based on reward–cost outcomes of interaction. A minimum positive level (rewards greater than costs) of an outcome must exist in order for attraction or affiliation to take place. Rewards from interactions gratify needs, whereas costs incur anxiety, frustration, embarrassment, or fatigue. Propinquity, interaction, and common attitudes all have roles in exchange theory.

Besides these more established social psychology explanations for group formation, there are also some generally recognized identifiable stages of group development.[8] These stages can be briefly summarized as follows:

1. *Forming.*   This initial stage is marked by uncertainty and even confusion. Group members are not sure about the purpose, structure, task, or leadership of the group.
2. *Storming.*   This stage of development, as indicated by the term, is characterized by conflict and confrontation. (In the usually emotionally charged atmosphere, there may be considerable disagreement and conflict among the members about roles and duties.)
3. *Norming.*   Finally, in this stage the members begin to settle into cooperation and collaboration. They have a "we" feeling with high cohesion, group identity, and camaraderie.
4. *Performing.*   This is the stage where the group is fully functioning and devoted to effectively accomplishing the tasks agreed on in the norming stage.

5. *Adjourning.*   This represents the end of the group, which in ongoing, permanent groups will never be reached. However, for project teams or task forces with a specific objective, once the objective is accomplished, the group will disband or have a new composition, and the stages will start over again.

Practicalities of Group Formation.   Besides the conceptual explanations for group formation and development, there are some very practical reasons for joining and/or forming a group. For instance, employees in an organization may form a group for economic, security, or social reasons. Economically, workers may form a group to work on a project that is paid for on a group-incentive plan such as gainsharing,[9] or they may form a union to demand higher wages. For security, joining a group provides the individual with a united front in combating indiscriminant, unilateral treatment. The adage that there is strength in numbers applies in this case. The most important practical reason individuals join or form groups is, however, that groups tend to satisfy the very intense social needs of most people. Workers, in particular, generally have a very strong desire for affiliation. This need is met by belonging to a group or becoming a member of a team. Research going as far back as the Hawthorne studies revealed that the affiliation motive has a major impact on human behavior in organizations. Chapter 8 also discusses this motive.

An alternative model that has most recently been proposed as an explanation for group formation processes is called the *punctuated equilibrium model*.[10] According to this approach, groups form in a first phase in which a target or mission is set and then are not altered very easily, due to a process called inertia, or systematic resistance to change. At some midpoint, the second phase begins. This phase commences when group members suddenly recognize that if they don't change tactics, the group's goal or mission will not be accomplished. This "midlife crisis" in the group's existence is exemplified by changes made in tactics followed by bursts of activity and energy designed to complete the task. The name of the model is derived from the equilibrium that exists in the first half of the group's life and the punctuated efforts and behavioral modifications in the second phase. Although there is just preliminary research on the punctuated equilibrium model, it has considerable intuitive appeal based on the common experiences most people have had in working on group projects.

Models of the dynamics of group formation and functioning should progress further when issues such as demographic diversity and globalization are incorporated. One recent analysis noted that "fault lines" within groups may form around individual member characteristics and lead to subgroup conflicts among members.[11] Diversity is the primary source of differences in member characteristics leading to such conflict. On the international front, another study notes that group efficacy, or the group's belief in its ability to perform effectively, as well as actual performance, may be impacted by intercultural variables such as collectivism and task uncertainty.[12] Further, there may be a relationship between personal efficacy (see Chapter 9) and collective efficacy. For example, one recent study by Bandura and his colleagues revealed that socioeconomic status enhanced perceived personal efficacy, which in turn contributed substantially to a sense of collective efficacy to effect social change through unified action.[13]

Types of Groups

There are numerous types of groups. The theories of group formation that were just discussed are based partly on the attraction between two persons—the simple dyad group.

Of course, in the real world groups are usually much more complex than the dyad. There are small and large groups, primary and secondary groups, coalitions, membership and reference groups, in- and out-groups, and formal and informal groups. Each type has different characteristics and different effects on its members.

Primary Groups.   Often the terms *small group* and *primary group* are used interchangeably. Technically, there is a difference. A small group has to meet only the criterion of small size. Usually no attempt is made to assign precise numbers, but the accepted criterion is that the group must be small enough for face-to-face interaction and communication to occur. In addition to being small, a primary group must have a feeling of comradeship, loyalty, and a common sense of values among its members. Thus, all primary groups are small groups, but not all small groups are primary groups.

Two examples of a primary group are the family and the peer group. Initially, the primary group was limited to a socializing group, but then a broader conception was given impetus by the results of the Hawthorne studies. Work groups definitely have primary group qualities. Research findings point out the tremendous impact that the primary group has on individual behavior, regardless of context or environmental conditions. An increasing number of companies, such as General Mills, FedEx, Chaparral Steel, and 3M, have begun to use the power of primary groups by organizing employees into *self-managed teams.* Importantly, these teams are natural work groups with all the dynamics described so far. The team members work together to perform a function or produce a product or service. Because they are self-managing, they also perform functions such as planning, organizing, and controlling the work. For example, at 3M self-managed teams are empowered to take corrective actions to resolve day-to-day problems; they also have direct access to information that allows them to plan, control, and improve their operations. The last part of the chapter discusses this team concept and practice in detail.

Coalitions.   Although recent research indicates that the social structure will affect the increasingly popular strategic alliance formation patterns between organizations,[14] at a more micro level, coalitions of individuals and groups within organizations have long been recognized as an important dimension of group dynamics. Although the concept of coalition is used in different ways by different theorists, a comprehensive review of the coalition literature suggests that the following characteristics of a coalition be included:[15]

1. Interacting group of individuals
2. Deliberately constructed by the members for a specific purpose
3. Independent of the formal organization's structure
4. Lacking a formal internal structure
5. Mutual perception of membership
6. Issue-oriented to advance the purposes of the members
7. External forms
8. Concerted member action, act as a group

Although the preceding have common characteristics with other types of groups, coalitions are separate, usually very powerful, and often effective entities in organizations. For example, a study found that employees in a large organization formed into coalitions to overcome petty conflicts and ineffective management in order to get the job done.[16]

Other Types of Groups.   Besides primary groups and coalitions, there are also other classifications of groups that are important to the study of organizational behavior. Two important distinctions are between membership and reference groups and between in-groups and out-groups. These differences can be summarized by noting that membership groups are those to which the individual actually belongs. An example would be membership in a craft union. Reference groups are those to which an individual would like to belong—those he or she identifies with. An example would be a prestigious social group. In-groups are those who have or share the dominant values, and out-groups are those on the outside looking in. All these types of groups have relevance to the study of organizational behavior, but the formal and informal types are most directly applicable.

There are many formally designated work groups, such as committees, in the modern organization. The functional departmental committees (finance, marketing, operations, and human resources) and now cross-functional teams are examples, as are standing committees such as the public affairs committee, grievance committee, or executive committee. Teams, however, have emerged as the most important type of group in today's organizations.

Informal groups form for political, friendship, or common interest reasons. For political purposes, the informal group may form to attempt to get its share of rewards and/or limited resources. Friendship groups may form on the job and carry on outside the workplace. Common interests in sports or ways to get back at management can also bind members into an informal group. The dynamics of these informal groups are examined in more detail in an upcoming section.

Implications from Research on Group Dynamics

Starting with the Hawthorne studies discussed in Chapter 1, there has been an abundance of significant research on groups that has implications for organizational behavior and performance. Besides the Hawthorne studies, there are numerous research studies on group dynamics that indirectly contribute to the better understanding of organizational behavior.[17] In general, it can be concluded from research over the years that groups have a positive impact on both individual employee effectiveness (help learn about the organization and one's self, gain new skills, obtain rewards not available to individuals, and fulfill important social needs) and organizational effectiveness (strength in numbers of ideas and skills, improved decision making and control, and facilitating change as well as organizational stability).[18]

In addition to the somewhat general conclusions, there are some specific studies in social psychology that seem to have particular relevance to organizational behavior. The seminal work of social psychologist Stanley Schachter seems especially important for the application of group dynamics research to human resource management.

The Schachter Study.   In a classic study, Schachter and his associates tested the effect of group cohesiveness and induction (or influence) on productivity under highly controlled conditions.[19] *Cohesiveness* was defined as the average resultant force acting on members in a group. Through the manipulations of cohesiveness and induction, the following experimental groups were created:

1.   High cohesive, positive induction (Hi Co, + Ind)
2.   Low cohesive, positive induction (Lo Co, + Ind)
3.   High cohesive, negative induction (Hi Co, − Ind)
4.   Low cohesive, negative induction (Lo Co, − Ind)

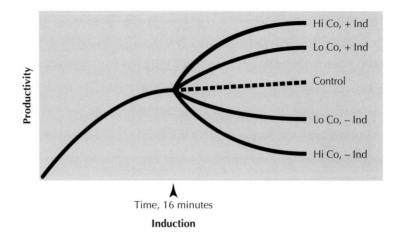

FIGURE 14.2
The "pitchfork" results
from the Schachter study.

The independent variables in the experiment were cohesiveness and induction, and the dependent variable was productivity. Figure 14.2 summarizes the results. Although Schachter's experiment did not obtain a statistically significant difference in productivity between the high and low cohesive groups that were positively induced, a follow-up study that used a more difficult task did.[20]

Implications of the Schachter Study.   The results of this classic study contain some very interesting implications for group/team performance in today's organizations. The "pitchfork" productivity curves in Figure 14.2 imply that highly cohesive groups have very powerful dynamics, both positive and negative, for group performance. On the other hand, the low-cohesive groups are not so powerful. A meta-analysis of a number of studies over the years found that group cohesiveness had a highly significant positive effect on performance.[21] However, of even more importance to group performance is the variable of induction. The findings of this study indicate that performance depends largely on how the high- or low-cohesive group is induced.

At least for illustrative purposes, leadership may be substituted for induction. If this is done, the key variable for the subjects' performance in the Schachter experiment becomes leadership. A highly cohesive group that is given positive leadership will have the highest possible productivity. On the other side of the coin, a highly cohesive group that is given poor leadership will have the lowest possible productivity. A highly cohesive group is analogous to a time bomb in the hands of management. The direction in which the highly cohesive group goes, breaking production records or severely restricting output, depends on how it is led. The low-cohesive group is much safer in the hands of management. Leadership will not have a serious negative or positive impact on this group. However, the implication is that if management wishes to maximize productivity, it must build a cohesive group and give it proper leadership and, importantly, over time this highly cohesive group may become self-managing.

This discussion does not imply that subjects doing a simple task in a laboratory setting can be made equivalent to managing human resources in modern, complex organizations. This, of course, cannot and should not be attempted. On the other hand, there are some interesting insights and points of departure for organizational behavior analysis that can come out of laboratory investigations such as Schachter's. For instance,

TABLE 14.1 Factors That Increase and Decrease Group Cohesiveness

Factors That Increase Group Cohesiveness	*Factors That Decrease Group Cohesiveness*
Agreement on group goals	Disagreement on goals
Frequency of interaction	Large group size
Personal attractiveness	Unpleasant experiences
Intergroup competition	Intragroup competition
Favorable evaluation	Domination by one or more members

Source: Andrew D. Szilagyi, Jr., and Marc J. Wallace, Jr., *Organizational Behavior and Performance,* 5th ed., Scott, Foresman/Little, Brown, Glenview, Ill., 1990, pp. 282–283.

the results of Schachter's study can be applied in retrospect to the pioneering work on scientific management of Frederick W. Taylor or to the Hawthorne studies. Taylor accounted only for the Hi Co, − Ind productivity curve when he advocated "breaking up the group." If his scientific management methods could be considered + Ind, the best productivity he could obtain would be that of Lo Co, + Ind. In other words, in light of the Schachter study, Taylor's methods could yield only second-best productivity.

In the Hawthorne studies, both the relay room operatives and the bank wirers were highly cohesive work groups. As is brought out in Chapter 1, a possible explanation of why one highly cohesive work group (the relay room workers) produced at a very high level and the other highly cohesive group (the bank wirers) produced at a very low rate is the type of induction (supervision) that was applied. Both leadership and group dynamics factors, such as cohesiveness, can have an important impact on group performance in organizations. Table 14.1 briefly summarizes some of the major factors that can increase and decrease group cohesiveness. In addition, there are some recent research findings regarding the effects of time on group cohesion. In one study, a longer time together gave group members the opportunity to engage in meaningful interactions. Importantly, for today's environment for groups, surface-level diversity issues (age, gender, race differences) were found to weaken over time, whereas deep-level diversity differences (attitudes and values) became stronger.[22]

Group/Team Effectiveness

Besides the basic research coming out of social psychology, a more specific focus on the impact that groups/teams have on employee behavior, especially the contribution to satisfaction and performance, has also received attention. The following is an overall summary of the way to use groups to enhance satisfaction and performance:[23]

1. Organizing work around intact groups
2. Having groups charged with selection, training, and rewarding of members
3. Using groups to enforce strong norms for behavior, with group involvement in off-the-job as well as on-the-job behavior
4. Distributing resources on a group rather than an individual basis
5. Allowing and perhaps even promoting intergroup rivalry so as to build within-group solidarity

A review of the research literature determined three factors that seem to play the major role in determining group effectiveness: (1) task interdependence (how closely group members work together); (2) outcome interdependence (whether, and how, group performance is rewarded); and (3) potency (members' belief that the group can be effective).[24]

To assess group or team effectiveness first requires careful specification of criteria. Effective groups are characterized as being dependable, making reliable connections between the parts, and targeting the direction and goals of the organization. This is accomplished when members "buy in," achieve coordination, have the desired impact, and exhibit the kind of vitality that sustains the organization over time as the environment shifts or changes.[25] Factors that affect the success level of any given group include the type of task being performed and the composition of the group itself. Teams with self-leadership have been found to have varying levels of success, depending on whether the group's task is primarily conceptual or primarily behavioral in nature.[26] The composition of the group has been found to be optimal when there is a mix of member types. Groups with only one type, such as task "shapers" (those who define group tasks) are less successful than those with shapers, coordinators, completer-finishers, and team players.[27]

Well-known leadership guru Warren Bennis argues that effective groups have shared dreams and manage conflict by abandoning individual egos in the pursuit of a dream. They also are protected from the "suits," or corporate leaders, have real or invented enemies, see themselves as underdogs who are winning, and pay a personal price to succeed.[28] Their leaders provide direction, meaning, trust, hope and display a bias toward action, risk taking, and urgency. Others suggest that "hot groups," those that accomplish breakthrough performance, are ones in which members see distinction and importance in their work, that the tasks captivate members, and that the tasks take priority over interpersonal relationships. Building hot groups requires less micromanaging, more informal (as opposed to formal) feedback, and role modeling of successful hot group behaviors by experienced members working with other new groups. Leadership in this approach is less intrusive and emphasizes group rather than individual rewards, and, as a result, groups can "turn on a dime" and get things done more quickly.[29]

Some aspects of effectiveness may be influenced by how groups form. When they are established, social comparisons and competition exists between members. These may have an impact on the organizational citizenship behaviors (see Chapter 7) exhibited by group members. Citizenship behaviors include altruism, conscientiousness (or being a "good soldier"), courtesy, sportsmanship, and civic virtue, which are also involved in looking out for the welfare of the group and the organization. Perceptions of fairness in group practices may impact such citizenship behaviors, which in turn help maintain the group's performance levels.[30]

Group effectiveness may also be influenced by the conditions of adaptation to nonroutine events. Previous group literature suggested three behaviors as keys to adapting to unusual circumstances or events: (1) information collection and transfer, (2) task prioritization, and (3) task distribution. In one recent study of airline crews using flight simulations, it was found that the timing of key adaptive group behaviors was more strongly associated with performance than the behaviors themselves.[31] In other words, information must be collected at the right time, prioritized properly, and tasks divided in a frame that allows for successful adaptation to unusual events.

THE DYNAMICS OF INFORMAL GROUPS

Besides the formally designated groups and teams, informal groups in the workplace play a significant role in the dynamics of organizational behavior. The major difference between formal and informal groups is that the formal group has officially prescribed goals and relationships, whereas the informal one does not. Despite this distinction, it is a mistake to think of formal and informal groups as two distinctly separate entities. The two types of groups coexist and are inseparable. Every formal organization has informal groups, and every informal organization eventually evolves some semblance of formal groups.

Norms and Roles in Informal Groups

With the exception of a single social act such as extending a hand on meeting, the smallest units of analysis in group dynamics are norms and roles. Many behavioral scientists make a point of distinguishing between the two units, but conceptually they are very similar. *Norms* are the "oughts" of behavior. They are prescriptions for acceptable behavior determined by the group. Norms will be strongly enforced by work groups if they:

1. Aid in group survival and provision of benefits
2. Simplify or make predictable the behavior expected of group members
3. Help the group avoid embarrassing interpersonal problems
4. Express the central values or goals of the group and clarify what is distinctive about the group's identity[32]

A role consists of a pattern of norms; the use of the term in organizations is directly related to its theatrical use. A role is a position that can be acted out by an individual. The content of a given role is prescribed by the prevailing norms. Probably *role* can best be defined as a position that has expectations evolving from established norms.

Informal Roles and the Informal Organization

Informal roles vary widely and are highly volatile. An example of informal roles found in today's teams would include the following:[33]

1. *Contributor.* This task-oriented team member is seen as very dependable. He or she enjoys providing the team with good technical information and data, is always prepared, and pushes the team to set high performance goals.
2. *Collaborator.* This team member focuses on the "big picture." He or she tries to remind others of the vision, mission, or goal of the team but is flexible and open to new ideas, is willing to work outside the defined role, and is willing to share the glory with other team members.
3. *Communicator.* This positive, people-oriented team member is process-driven and is an effective listener. He or she plays the role of facilitator of involvement, conflict resolution, consensus building, feedback, and building an informal relaxed atmosphere.
4. *Challenger.* Known for candor and openness, this member questions the team's goals, methods, and even ethics. He or she is willing to disagree with the leader or higher authority and encourages well-conceived risk taking.

Like the formal organization, the informal organization has both functions and dysfunctions. In contrast to formal organization analysis, the dysfunctional aspects of informal organization have received more attention than the functional ones. For example, conflicting objectives, restriction of output, conformity, blocking of ambition, inertia, and resistance to change are frequently mentioned dysfunctions of the informal organization. More recently, however, organizational analysis has begun to recognize the functional aspects as well. For example, the following list suggests some practical benefits that can be derived from the informal organization:[34]

1. Makes for a more effective total system
2. Lightens the workload on management
3. Fills in gaps in a manager's abilities
4. Provides a safety valve for employee emotions
5. Improves communication

Because of the inevitability and power of the informal organization, the functions should be exploited in the attainment of objectives rather than futilely combated by management. As one analysis of leadership points out: "Informal social networks exert an immense influence which sometimes overrides the formal hierarchy. . . . Leadership goes beyond a person's formal position into realms of informal, hidden, or unauthorized influence."[35]

THE DYSFUNCTIONS OF GROUPS AND TEAMS

So far, the discussion has been mostly about the positive impact and the functional aspects of groups and teams. However, there are a number of recognized dysfunctions that should also be recognized. Of particular interest in work groups and teams are norm violation and role ambiguity/conflict, groupthink, risky shift, and social loafing.

Norm Violation and Role Ambiguity/Conflict

Group norms that are violated can result in antisocial behaviors. At the extreme, these include sexual harassment and theft. Others include lying, spreading rumors, withholding effort, and absenteeism. A recent study found group members who are chronically exposed to antisocial behaviors are more likely to engage in them, and dissatisfaction with coworkers may also rise, especially when those coworkers exhibit more antisocial activities than the person in question.[36]

There may also be gaps between the prescribed role as dictated by norms and the individual's reaction to the role. *Role ambiguity* occurs when the individual employee is unclear about the dictates of a given situation, or, in more common terms, "doesn't know what he's supposed to be doing." Unclear job descriptions, incomplete orders given by a manager, and inexperience all contribute to role ambiguity. Such ambiguity can affect the person's ability to function effectively in a group or team. Also, *role conflict* occurs when the employee or team member is: (1) asked to perform conflicting tasks or (2) required to perform a task that conflicts with his or her own personal values. In group settings, the odds of role conflicts increase, especially when the group engages in unethical or antisocial behaviors and when the members of the group stress one set of norms while the leader and rules of the formal organization emphasize others.

The Groupthink, Conformity Problem

A dysfunction of highly cohesive groups and teams that has received a lot of attention has been called *groupthink* by well-known social psychologist Irving Janis. He defines it as "a deterioration of mental efficiency, reality testing, and moral judgment that results from in-group pressures."[37] Essentially, groupthink results from the pressures on individual members to conform and reach consensus. Groups and teams that are suffering from groupthink are so bent on reaching consensus that there is no realistic appraisal of alternative courses of action in a decision, and deviant, minority, or unpopular views are suppressed.

Janis has concluded that a number of historic fiascos by government policy-making groups (for example, Britain's do-nothing policy toward Hitler prior to World War II, the unpreparedness of U.S. forces at Pearl Harbor, the Bay of Pigs invasion of Cuba, and the escalation of the Vietnam war) can be attributed to groupthink. The Watergate affair during the Nixon administration, the Iran–Contra affair during the Reagan administration, and the Whitewater affair in the Clinton administration are also examples. The decision process by which NASA launched the space shuttle *Challenger* on its fateful mission can be analyzed in terms of the characteristics of groupthink. For example, conformity pressures were in evidence when NASA officials complained to the contractors about delays. Other symptoms of groupthink shown in Table 14.2— illusions of invulnerability and unanimity and mindguarding—were played out in the *Challenger* disaster by management's treatment and exclusion of input by the engineers.

Although historically notorious news events can be used to dramatically point out the pitfalls of groupthink, it may also occur in committees and work groups in business firms or hospitals or any other type of organization. Initially, there was at least some partial support of the groupthink model when applied to areas such as leader behavior and decision making.[38] However, recently there have been criticisms of the groupthink model coming from the organizational behavior literature. First of all, there has been very little research conducted to test the propositions of groupthink, most notably because it is so difficult to incorporate all of the items mentioned as the indicators of the phenomenon into one study. Further, some of the results provide only very limited evidence for the model, and the continued uncritical acceptance of groupthink may be an example of groupthink itself.[39] At this point, some organizational behavior theorists/researchers are calling for either elimination of the groupthink model, reformulation of how it works, or revitalization of the approach used.[40] One such approach would be to integrate the assumptions into the general group decision-making and problem-solving literature to see if they would provide support for conformity/groupthink. These analyses suggest that the popularity of the groupthink model may come from its intuitive appeal rather than research support. Studies should be used to replicate the research in order to confirm previous findings, and these studies should be cumulative over time. Without this type of research rigor, unconditional acceptance of any model or theory may exist, even when empirical findings are sketchy at best.

TABLE 14.2 Symptoms of Groupthink

1. There is the *illusion of invulnerability.* There is excessive optimism and risk taking.
2. There are *rationalizations* by the members of the group to discount warnings.
3. There is an unquestioned belief in the group's *inherent mortality.* The group ignores questionable ethical or moral issues or stances.
4. Those who oppose the group are *stereotyped* as evil, weak, or stupid.
5. There is *direct pressure* on any member who questions the stereotypes. Loyal members don't question the direction in which the group seems to be heading.
6. There is *self-censorship* of any deviation from the apparent group consensus.
7. There is the *illusion of unanimity.* Silence is interpreted as consent.
8. There are *self-appointed mindguards* who protect the group from adverse information.

Source: Adapted from Irving L. Janis, *Groupthink,* 2d ed., Houghton Mifflin, Boston, 1982, pp. 174–175.

Risky Shift Phenomenon

Even before excessive risk taking was brought out by groupthink, the so-called "risky shift phenomenon" of groups was recognized. Research going back many years has shown that, contrary to popular belief, a group may make more risky decisions than the individual members would on their own.[41] This conclusion, of course, must be tempered by the values attached to the outcomes, but most of the research over the years finds that group discussion enhances the initial tendency of individual members in a given direction.[42] Called group-induced attitude polarization, this means that, for example, if an employee has a prounion (or antiunion) attitude before group discussion, the group discussion results in an even more extreme attitude in the same direction.

Dysfunctions in Perspective

Such symptoms as risky shift, polarization, and the others found in groupthink should make groups take notice and be very careful of the dysfunctions of groups. To help overcome the potentially disastrous effects, free expression of minority and unpopular viewpoints should be encouraged and legitimatized. Companies such as General Electric, Bausch & Lomb, Apple Computer, Ford, Johnson & Johnson, and United Parcel Service are known for not only tolerating, but formally encouraging, conflict and debate during group/team work and committee meetings.

Although many studies show that successful companies advocate such open conflict and healthy debate among group members, other studies point to the value of consensus. This apparent contradiction may be resolved by recognizing the following:

> Consensus may be preferred for smaller, non-diversified, privately held firms competing in the same industry while larger firms dealing with complex issues of diversification may benefit from the dissent raised in open discussions. Larger firms in uncertain environments need dissent while smaller firms in more simple and stable markets can rely on consensus.[43]

Social Loafing

Another more recently recognized dysfunction associated with groups and teams is called social loafing. This problem occurs when members reduce their effort and performance levels when acting as part of a group. Primary causes include lack of performance feedback within the group, tasks that are not intrinsically motivating, situations in which the performances of others will cover for the reduced effort given by some members, and the "sucker effect" of not wanting to do more than the perception of effort being given by others. There is a cultural component inherent in such social loafing. Research has found that cultures dominated by individual, self-interest values are more likely to have groups that experience loafing. On the other hand, more collectivist cultures, which are dominated by a "we feeling" and group goals lead to a stronger focus on the collective good, and therefore endure less loafing by group members.[44]

Social loafing is more likely to appear in large teams, where individual contributions are more difficult to identify. To reduce the impact of members shirking their duties and ensure that they are fully contributing members of the team, it has been suggested to keep teams smaller in size, specialize tasks so that individual member contributions are identifiable, measure individual performance, and select only motivated employees when building teams.[45]

TEAMS IN THE MODERN WORKPLACE

The discussion so far on group dynamics serves as the background and foundation for teams, and the terms *groups* and *teams* have been used interchangably. However, teams have become so popular in today's organizations that they deserve special attention. The term *team,* of course, is not new to organizations, and teamwork has been stressed throughout the years. For example, the well-known quality guru Joseph Juran first took his "Team Approach to Problem Solving" to the Japanese in the 1950s and then in the 1980s to the United States. Today, teams are becoming increasingly popular. Estimates of the prevalence and type of teams among *Fortune* 1000 companies are as follows:

1. Almost all use project teams (diverse managerial/professional employees working on projects for a defined, but typically extended, period of time).
2. A large majority use parallel teams (employees working on problem-solving or quality teams in parallel to the regular organizational structure).
3. A majority use permanent work teams (self-contained work units responsible for manufacturing products or providing services).[46]

After first defining what is meant by a team and critically analyzing self-managed teams found in today's organizations, the ways to train self-managed teams and make them more effective are discussed.

The Nature of a Team

Although the term *team* is frequently used for any group, especially to get individuals to work together and to motivate them, some team experts make a distinction between teams and traditional work groups. For example, the authors of a book on the use of teams for creating high-performance organizations note that the difference between a work group and a team relates to performance results. They note:

> A working group's performance is a function of what its members do as individuals. A team's performance includes both individual results and what we call "collective work-products." A collective work-product is what two or more members must work on together . . . [it] reflects the joint, real contribution of team members.[47]

They go on to note these specific differences between work groups and teams:

1. The work group has a strong, clearly focused leader; the team has shared leadership roles.
2. The work group has individual accountability; the team has individual and mutual accountability.
3. The work group's purpose is the same as the organization's; the team has a specific purpose.
4. The work group has individual work-products; the team has collective work-products.
5. The work group runs efficient meetings; the team encourages open-ended, active problem-solving meetings.
6. The work group measures effectiveness indirectly (for example, financial performance of the overall business); the team measures performance directly by assessing collective work-products.
7. The work group discusses, decides, and delegates; the team discusses, decides, and does real work.[48]

The point is that teams do go beyond traditional formal work groups by having a collective, synergistic (the whole is greater than the sum of its parts) effect.

The use of teams to produce products started in well-known, quality-conscious corporate giants, such as Toyota in Japan and Motorola and General Electric in the United States, and has quickly spread. Companies as different as Xerox (office equipment), Monsanto (chemicals), Hewlett-Packard (computers), and Johnsonville Sausage use self-managed, sometimes called autonomous, teams. As with other popular management approaches, such as MBO (management by objectives) or TQM (total quality management), after the initial excitement, it has now become clear that although self-managed teams are important, they are not *the* answer. There is increasing attention being given to the dynamics of groups/teams (already discussed) and the emergence of cross-functional, virtual, and self-managed teams.

Cross-Functional Teams

As part of the movement toward horizontal designs (see Chapter 4) and the recognition of dysfunctional bureaucratic functional autonomy, the focus has shifted to the use of cross-function teams. These teams are made up of individuals from various departments or functional specialities. For example, the U.S. Navy discovered that it was able to improve productivity by establishing cross-functional teams to manage and improve the core processes that affect both external customers and mission performance.[49] At Massachusetts General, one of the nation's most prominent hospitals, doctors on the emergency-trauma team have created a "seamless" approach between the various functions for treating critical patients who are brought in with life-threatening gunshot and knife wounds.[50] The accompanying Application Example: Greater Productivity through Cross-Functional Teams provides details on these and other examples.

The key to ensuring successful performance of cross-functional teams is found in two sets of criteria: one inside the team and one in the organization at large. To improve coordination with cross-functional teams, organizations must carry out five steps. These include: (1) choosing the membership carefully, (2) clearly establishing the purpose of the team, (3) ensuring that everyone understands how the group will function, (4) conducting intensive team building up front so that everyone learns how to interact effectively, and (5) achieving noticeable results so that morale remains high and the members can see the impact of their efforts.[51]

Virtual Teams

With the advent of advanced information technology, the requirement that groups be made up of members in face-to-face interaction is no longer necessary. Members can now communicate at a distance through electronic means, such as e-mail, chat rooms, phone conferencing, faxes, satellite transmissions, and websites. Knowledge-based tasks performed by members in remote locations can become members of so-called virtual teams. Also, those performing in telecommuting jobs often include responsibilities to serve on virtual teams. Virtual teams are increasingly evident in global and partnered operations.

One key to effective use of virtual teams is called *synchronous technologies,* which allow members to interact at the same time, or in real time. Audio and videoconferencing are examples of synchronous technologies, whereas asynchronous technologies, such as e-mail, chat rooms, group calendars, bulletin boards, and Web pages may be used when delayed interaction is acceptable. The low cost of e-mail makes it an excellent candidate for collecting data, generating ideas, and sometimes for negotiating technical and interpersonal conflicts.[52] Virtual teams can be effective because they are

Greater Productivity through Cross-Functional Teams

Over the last five years, cross-functional teams have become increasingly popular—and for good reason. Research shows that by combining the abilities and skills of individuals, all of whom can contribute different inputs to the team, it is possible to reduce the time needed to get things done while simultaneously driving up productivity and profit.

Hewlett-Packard is a good example of the use of effective teams. Although the firm has long been admired as one of the best companies in America, its distribution organization was second rate. On average, it took 26 days for an H-P product to reach the customer, and employees had to shuttle information through a tangle of 70 computer systems. This is when the firm decided to reorganize the distribution process and reduce delivery time. Two H-P managers who assumed responsibility for the project assembled a team of 35 people from H-P and two other firms and then began examining the work flow. First, they looked at the way things were being done currently and began noting ways of eliminating work steps and shortening the process. Next, the team completed a two-week training and orientation program to familiarize team members with the current process. Then the team redesigned the entire work process and got everyone on the cross-functional team to buy in. Finally, they implemented the process and then made changes to correct errors remaining in the system. In the process, they were allowed to empower the workforce and managed to get delivery time down to eight days. This enabled the firm to cut its inventories by nearly 20 percent while increasing service levels to customers.

Another good example of cross-functional teams is provided by the emergency-trauma team at Massachusetts General Hospital. On an average day, about 200 patients show up at the emergency room, and about one-third of them end up in the trauma center. At the center there is a group of doctors, nurses, and technicians who come together and work as a "seamless" team. Each person begins a task—checking out a wound, running an IV, hooking up a machine. Then someone takes the lead and decides the strategy for treatment. Usually this is a doctor, but the direction can come from an intern or a nurse who is well versed in the applicable field. As an attending physician puts it, "Nobody bosses everybody around. If someone has a thought that's useful, we are open to suggestions." The job is intense, but it is also rewarding, and the personnel enjoy a high degree of professionalism and an environment in which they are able to use their abilities to deal with situations that require rapid and skilled decisions if lives are to be saved.

A third example is the U.S. Navy SEALs (the acronym refers to the commandos' all-terrain expertise: sea, air, land). These individuals are put through months of rigorous physical training in which each is taught how to use his skills to contribute to the team effort. Commenting on those who fail to measure up to the rigorous demands, one SEAL officer notes, "If you are the sort of person who sucks all the energy out of the group without giving anything back, then you are going to go away." The result of this effort is a high-performance team that is able to fulfill a host of different functions from teaching Namibian game wardens how to track down poachers to training Singaporean army regulars to combat potential terrorists.

In each case, the contribution of each team member greatly influences the success of the group effort. And by submerging their own identities in the group's activities, each individual is able to achieve both personal and group goals.

flexible and are driven by information and skills rather than time and location.[53] However, caution must be paid when assembling a virtual group. They should match the task at hand. Internet chat rooms, for example, may create more work and result in poorer decisions than face-to-face meetings and telephone conferences unless there is adequate training and some experience with the technology.[54]

Self-Managed Teams

As evident from the term, as part of the empowerment movement and more egalitarian cultural values in an increasing number of organizations, teams are being set up or are evolving into being self-managed. A self-managed work team can be defined as "a group of employees who are responsible for managing and performing technical tasks that result in a product or service being delivered to an internal or external customer."[55] For example, at Hewlett-Packard and Harley-Davidson, self-managed teams are empowered to hire, organize, and purchase equipment without management direct approval. The results from these teams have reportedly been very positive.[56]

Although there has been considerable such testimonial evidence of the value of self-managed teams,[57] supporting research and documented experience are now starting to emerge. To date, both the research and practice literature has been quite favorable to self-managed teams. For example, recent studies of the empowerment of self-managed teams found increased job satisfaction, customer service, and team organizational commitment,[58] and a comprehensive meta-analysis covering 70 studies concluded that self-managed teams had a positive impact on productivity and specific attitudes related to the team, but not on general attitudes, absenteeism, or turnover.[59] This finding on the impact on productivity is impressive, and more recent studies also find a more favorable impact on attitudes as well,[60] but there are still practical problems to overcome. For example, an in-depth interview survey of 4500 teams at 500 organizations uncovered a host of individual and organizational factors behind self-managed team ineffectiveness.[61] Individual problems included the following:

1. Team members aren't willing to give up past practices or set aside power and position.
2. Not all team members have the ability, knowledge, or skill to contribute to the group. Team functioning slows because some members shoulder more responsibility than others.
3. As team members, workers often face conflicts or challenges to their own personal beliefs. What works for the group often does not work for the individual.[62]

Organizational-level problems uncovered by this survey included compensation and reward systems that still focused solely on individual performance; thus there was little incentive for teams to perform well.[63] A survey of 300 large companies found that only 9 percent of them were pleased with their team-based compensation.[64] The next and final section explores how to make all types of teams more effective.

How to Make Teams More Effective

The effectiveness of teams may be measured based on the extent to which the team achieves its objectives and performs on behalf of the overall organization. Previous research has, at times, failed to note the ways in which teams are embedded in overall organizations.[65] Consequently, studies of team effectiveness may not have revealed a complete picture of the nature of team success.

For teams to be more effective, they must overcome some of the problems and dysfunctions that groups in general encounter.[66] Long-standing models of team effectiveness include creating the right environment where support, commitment, reward systems, communication systems, and physical space are all in sync to allow the team to work in a productive atmosphere.[67] Tasks should be designed to be interdependent, team size should be kept small (10 members or less), and members should be selected based on both being motivated and competent. Further, team cohesion should be built by either establishing homogenous groups or overcoming potential problems associated with diversity, by encouraging interaction and contact, and by making the group seem somewhat "exclusive," so that the members are happy to be included.[68] Also, team success naturally tends to build greater cohesion, as does the presence of external competition and challenges. In particular, there is now enough research evidence and practical experience to indicate the following ways to enhance team effectiveness: (1) team building, (2) collaboration, (3) leadership, and (4) understanding of cultural issues in global situations.

Team Building.   Team building begins with the understanding that work groups require time and training before they develop into productive and cohesive units. There is a definite learning curve in building an effective team.[69] At first, some employees may be unwilling to join or buy into the group. Only when they see success and team member satisfaction will this feeling change. Once established, some form of accountability must be present. Managers should expect to see some uncertainty in the team, which may last for up to two years, and during that time there may even be a dip in productivity. As the team matures, members learn the basics of team work, understand their roles more clearly, make more effective group decisions, and pursue group goals.[70]

Effective team building establishes a sense of partnership[71] and allows members to see the team as a unit and as an attractive work arrangement.[72] Team building succeeds when individuals share collective intelligence[73] and experience a sense of empowerment.[74] Team building involves rapid learning, which takes place when there is a free-flowing generation of ideas.[75] Quality team-building programs must fit with the corporate culture, have well-designed goals, allow members to translate skills to the workplace, often take place in a separate environment, and may even move employees outside of a comfort zone, but not so much that they cannot learn. Programs such as rope climbing and even cooking classes may help members of some teams bond and learn to work together.[76]

An example of an effective team training approach would be the 10-step model shown in Table 14.3. GE, in its Electrical Distribution and Control Division, has successfully used this training model. According to the trainers, the trained GE teams "are made up of dedicated people who enjoy working together, who maintain high standards, and who demonstrate high productivity and commitment to excellence."[77]

Besides going through the steps of training, teams also must be monitored and evaluated on a continuous basis. Five key areas that should be monitored and measured include: (1) the team's mission, (2) goal achievements, (3) feelings of empowerment, (4) communications, and (5) roles and norms that are positive.[78]

Team-building processes can take place in levels as high as corporate boards. To do so, members should be emotionally intelligent (see Chapter 9), rather than just have raw intelligence (i.e., IQ), and feel they are part of a real team with clear, stable boundaries requiring interdependent tasks.[79] Members must learn to do what they promise, even when it means a personal sacrifice may be involved.[80] Boards that function as effective teams can create a major competitive advantage for the firm.[81]

Collaboration.   Effective group leaders do not act alone. They assemble a group of highly talented people and figure out how to get the most creative efforts out of everyone

TABLE 14.3 Training Guidelines for Developing Effective Self-Managed Teams

Steps of Training	Summary
1. Establish credibility.	The trainers must first establish their knowledge and believability.
2. Allow ventilation.	The trainees must have their anxieties and unresolved issues cleared before starting.
3. Provide an orientation.	The trainers should give specific verbal directions and provide clear expectations and models of behavior.
4. Invest in the process.	Early on, have the team identify its problems and concerns.
5. Set group goals.	The trainees create, through consensus, their own mission statement and then set goals and specific activities and behaviors to accomplish these goals.
6. Facilitate the group process.	The trainees are taught about how groups function and are given techniques, such as nominal grouping and paired comparison.
7. Establish intragroup procedures.	This involves setting up a meeting format that might include reporting minutes, making announcements, discussing problems and issues, proposing solutions, taking action, and making new assignments.
8. Establish intergroup processes.	Although the team is self-managed, leaders must be selected in order to interact with others, such as supervisors, managers, and other teams.
9. Change the role of the trainers.	As the team becomes more experienced and empowered, the trainers take on a more passive role.
10. End the trainers' involvement.	At this point, the team is on its own and is self-managing.

Source: Adapted from Paul E. Brauchle and David W. Wright, "Training Work Teams," *Training and Development,* March 1993, pp. 65–68.

by effectively organizing their collaborative efforts.[82] The process of collaboration involves learning how to improve interpersonal interactions in group settings while committing to a common agenda. Various developmental milestones may indicate that these collaborative skills are being learned and effectively applied.[83]

Group Leadership.   Whether the assigned head of the team or the emergent leader in self-managed teams, there are two key ways in which leaders may affect performance of groups: (1) how they select members and (2) the tactics they use to affect those members.[84] Tactics that help create a more team-oriented climate include eliminating or reducing special offices for the group heads, major differences in perks and privileges, and a decline in the use of designated leader titles.[85] At the same time, leaders need to continue to be clear and decisive even as they work with different people, different teams, and different environments. Effective leaders know both how to teach[86] and how to share the glory by acknowledging group success.[87]

Cultural/Global Issues.   There is evidence suggesting that certain cultures contain values that lead to resistance to teams.[88] For example, in one study of managers from Mexico, the great majority of leaders indicated they believed there would be significant problems if their companies adopted self-directed work teams.[89] Clearly such cultural obstacles must be overcome to build effective teams. As revealed in a recent study of a German-Japanese joint venture, national culture remains a key factor in explaining patterns of relationships exhibited in teams.[90] To facilitate such group efforts, recent research indicates that creating a "hybrid" team culture can be linked to improved performance.[91] In this study, a U-shaped relationship existed between team heterogeneity and team effectiveness, where homogenous and highly heterogeneous teams outperformed moderately heterogeneous groups in the long run. Therefore, as noted in the preceding leadership discussion, selection of group members seems to play an important role in the effectiveness of the group.

To help overcome some of the problems associated with more individualistic cultures, it is advisable to allow groups to form voluntarily or for members to join voluntarily. Those who volunteer are more likely to be cooperative and experience greater satisfaction, motivation, and fewer disciplinary problems. Further, group goal-setting processes may also serve to increase motivation and satisfaction when they build group or collective efficacy.[92]

As the review of these four processes indicates, there is a great deal left to be learned about how to build more effective teams. At the same time, the use of teams to accomplish tasks continues to grow. This makes the study of teams and performance remain as an important area for more organizational behavior research.

Summary

Groups represent an important dynamic in the study and application of organizational behavior. Group formation, types, and processes; the dynamics of informal roles and organization; and the dysfunctions of work groups and teams are all of particular relevance to the study of organizational behavior. Group formation can be theoretically explained by propinquity; as a relationship among activities, interactions, and sentiments; as a symmetrical balance between attraction and common attitudes; and as a reward–cost exchange. Participants in an organization also form into groups for very practical economic, security, and social reasons. Many different types of groups are found in modern organizations. Conceptually, there are primary groups, coalitions, and others such as membership and reference groups. Groups have been researched over the years, and findings from classic social psychology studies, such as the one conducted by Schachter, have implications for organizational behavior.

The last half of the chapter discusses and analyzes the dynamics of informal groups and teams. Informal norms and roles and the informal organization are very relevant to and often represent the real organization. Informal structure coexists with every formal structure. Traditionally, only the dysfunctional aspects of informal organization have been emphasized. More recently, the functional aspects have also been recognized.

The dynamics of the dysfunctions of groups and teams were examined in terms of norm violation resulting in antisocial behaviors, role ambiguity/conflict, group think conformity, the risky shift phenomenon, and social loafing. The remainder of the chapter focused on teams per se. Initially, most publicity was given to quality circles, but now self-managed teams are in the spotlight. Self-managed teams are beginning to become an established form of doing work to meet the high-tech, quality challenges facing both manufacturing and service organizations. To date, self-managed teams have a quite successful track record. In addition to self-managed teams, cross-functional and virtual teams are examples of new team forms that have also achieved success. Building effective teams requires long-standing principles regarding the creation of the proper environment in which support, commitment, rewards, communication, physical space, group size, membership, and cohesion are emphasized. Then, team effectiveness may be enhanced using team-building programs, collaboration, and effective leadership and by accounting for cultural and global issues when teams are formed.

ENDING WITH META-ANALYTIC RESEARCH FINDINGS

OB PRINCIPLE: Highly cohesive groups and teams are good performers.

Meta-Analysis Results: [16 studies; 372 groups; $d = .92$] *On average, there is a **74 percent probability** that highly cohesive groups and teams will have better performance than when cohesiveness is low.* This relationship was found to be particularly straightforward, as no moderator variables were found.

Conclusion: Theoretically, cohesive groups or teams should be motivated to advance group objectives and to fully participate in group activities. Thus, of particular interest is the relationship between group and team cohesiveness and performance. Group cohesion enables a group or team to exercise effective control over its members in relationship to its behavioral norms and needed teamwork. Less-cohesive groups, on the other hand, have greater difficulty exercising control over their members and enforcing standards of behavior. Moreover, as this chapter points out, one liability of cohesive groups is the tendency to develop groupthink, a dysfunctional process. Because cohesive groups tend to identify strongly with the group, the group members may prefer concurrency in decisions at the expense of critically evaluating other's suggestions for the best interest of the group. Nevertheless, group cohesion typically enhances members' satisfaction and improves organizational performance due to the strong motivation to maintain good, close relationships with other members.

Source: Adapted from Charles R. Evans and Kenneth L. Dion, "Group Cohesion and Performance: A Meta-Analysis," *Small Group Research,* Vol. 22, No. 2, 1991, pp. 175–186.

Questions for Discussion and Review

1. Briefly discuss the major theoretical explanations for group formation. Which explanation do you think is most relevant to the study of organizational behavior? Defend your choice.
2. What implications does the Schachter study have for the study of organizational behavior?
3. What are some functions of the informal organization? What are some dysfunctions?
4. What are some of the major symptoms of groupthink? Can you give an example from your own experience where groupthink may have occurred?
5. What is social loafing? How can it be overcome?
6. How, if at all, do teams as used in today's organizations differ from traditional work groups?
7. What are two ways to make and maintain self-managed teams' effectiveness?
8. Describe a cross-functional team and a virtual team. Why are these types of teams growing in popularity?
9. How should team effectiveness be measured?

Internet Exercise: Work Environment in Team-Based Organizations

Many organizations are recognizing the value of teamwork. In fact, many companies have promoted their team environment on their Web page. Go to www.IBM.com and look at their description of the organization under employment opportunities. Notice the emphasis that they put on group and team dynamics. A much smaller but interestingly unique organization is Custom Research, Inc. Their Web page is www.cresearch.com. Note how they emphasize the use of teams. Using these two examples of teams in action as background and a point of departure, answer the following questions. (This would be an especially good exercise to use groups to discuss and arrive at answers.)

1. In these team environments, it takes longer to get tasks done. Is this an important consideration in determining whether or not a team approach is effective? Why or why not?
2. Besides time, what are some other important dynamics? Give two specific strengths and two weaknesses of teams in the workplace.
3. Does the type of organization and its work/projects make a difference on how and when to use teams? Use IBM vs. Custom Research as examples in your answer.

REAL CASE:
There Are Teams, and
There Are Teams

One of the most difficult challenges for multinational managers is that of understanding how to manage groups and teams across cultures. What works in the home country often has no value in other cultures. For example, in the late-1990s, while the Japanese economy continued to stagger, a number of U.S.-based multinational firms entered the Japanese market to take advantage of the weak competition. Large U.S. retailers set up super stores in Japan with a wide variety of offerings and low prices. However, Japanese customers found these stores to be too big and impersonal for many types of goods and preferred to shop at smaller, locally owned stores. As a professor of marketing at a Japanese business school put it, "Retailing is such a local business, it's not that easy to succeed."

The same challenges of appealing to Japanese customers also hold true for managing Japanese employees. What works in the United States often has little value in Japan. For example, in the United States it is common for firms to have work groups compete against each other and to reward the winning teams. In Japan's collectivist cultural values, openly competing with others is frowned on. Those who win feel embarrassed and those who lose feel a sense of shame and loss of face. A good example is provided by an American manager who was in charge of a major department in a Japan-based, multinational bank. The manager, in an effort to increase the profits of his department came up with a fairly simple idea. It involved combining two different futures contracts to create an arbitrage position (i.e., the simultaneous purchase and sale of the same securities and foreign exchange in different markets to then profit from unequal prices). A number of the bank's non-Japanese competitors were making money with this type of strategy, and the manager felt that his bank could do the same. Unfortunately, this is not what happened. When he presented this idea to the senior-level management group, the Japanese managers convinced the rest of their colleagues to veto it. Their reasoning was grounded in an understanding of Japanese culture. Because two different futures would have to be traded by two different departments, one group would make money on the trade and the other would lose. So even though the overall bank would profit from the two transactions, the Japanese managers realized that the group that lost money would be embarrassed in front of its peers and lose face.

This same situation applies when Japanese firms compete against each other for a local market. There is great social pressure for each of the competing firms to retain their relative position. Thus Sony would not attempt to dislodge Mitsubishi and become the largest competitor in a particular industry. Only when Japanese firms go international do they compete strongly for market share—and this is against local competitors in the foreign market and not each other.

Performance appraisal is another good example. If an American employee does not do a good job, the person may be replaced. However, this seldom happens in Japan. So when American and Japanese firms create a joint venture and assign teams to the undertaking, the Japanese do not use the same type of individual performance requirements. The Americans want results but the Japanese are often more interested in everyone in the team being cooperative and helpful. Harmony is more important than productivity, and seldom is any direct action taken against poorly performing individual employees. However, the peers/teammates may subtly get the low performer straigtened out in an informal setting such as over drinks or on a fishing trip.

Another difference between American and Japanese teams is that U.S. managers try very hard to let their people know what is to be done, when it is to be completed, and how progress or performance will be determined. For example, the boss might say, "I want your team to take a look at our major competitors and tell me three products that they are likely to bring to market over the next six months." The Japanese manager will be much more indirect and vague. The Japanese exec might say something like, "What product changes do you think we can expect from the competition in the future?" As a result of these directives, the American team will generate a fairly short, well-focused report that contains a great deal of specific information. The Japanese team will submit a very long, detailed report that covers all aspects of the competition and provides a wealth of information on a host of products that may be introduced into the marketplace over the next year.

1. Based on the information in the case and your reading of the chapter, what would you recommend to be included in the following assignments you are given as a member of a large multinational corporation training department?
   a. How would you make the teams of the Japanese subsidiary more effective?
   b. How would you make the cross-functional team that is working on new product development for both the U.S. and Japanese markets as effective as possible?
2. How do you personally react to the statement in the case that "the Japanese are more interested in everyone in the team being cooperative and helpful. Harmony is more important than productivity"?
3. How do you explain that the Japanese have been using teams way before the United States, but they have had economic problems for the past decade? How would you explain to the CEO of your company that you recommend the use of teams in light of the prolonged Japanese competitive problems?

ORGANIZATIONAL BEHAVIOR CASE: The Schoolboy Rookie

Kent Sikes is a junior at State University. He has taken a summer job in the biggest factory in his hometown. He was told to report to the warehouse supervisor the first day at work. The supervisor assigned him to a small group of workers who were responsible for loading and unloading the boxcars that supplied the materials and carried away the finished goods of the factory.

After two weeks on the job, Kent was amazed at how little work the workers in his crew accomplished. It seemed that they were forever standing around and talking or, in some cases, even going off to hide when there was work to be done. Kent often found himself alone unloading a boxcar while the other members of the crew were off messing around someplace else. When Kent complained to his coworkers, they made it very plain that if he did not like it, he could quit, but if he complained to the supervisor, he would be sorry. Although Kent has been deliberately excluded from any of the crew's activities, such as taking breaks together or having a Friday afternoon beer after work at the tavern across the street, yesterday he went up to one of the older members of the crew and said, "What gives with you guys, anyway? I am just trying to do my job. The money is good, and I just don't give a hang about this place. I will be leaving to go back to school in a few weeks, and I wish I could have gotten to know you all better, but frankly I am sure glad I'm not like you guys." The older worker replied, "Son, if you'd been here as long as I have, you would be just like us."

1. Using some of the theories, explain the possible reasons for the group formation of this work crew. What types of groups exist in this case?
2. Place this work group in the Schachter study. What role does the supervisor play in the performance of this group?
3. What are the major informal roles of the crew members and Kent? What status position does Kent have with the group? Why?
4. Why hasn't Kent been accepted by the group? Do you agree with the older worker's last statement in the case? Why or why not?

ORGANIZATIONAL BEHAVIOR CASE: The Blue-Ribbon Committee

Mayor Sam Small is nearing completion of his first term in office. He feels his record has been pretty good, except for the controversial issue of housing. He has been able to avoid doing anything about housing so far and feels very strongly that this issue must not come to a head before the next election. The voters are too evenly divided on the issue, and he would lose a substantial number of votes no matter what stand he took. Yet with pressure increasing from both sides, he has to do something. After much distress and vacillation, he has finally come upon what he thinks is an ideal solution to his dilemma. He has appointed a committee to study the problem and make some recommendations. To make sure that the committee's work will not be completed before the election comes up, it was important to pick the right people. Specifically, Sam has selected his "blue-ribbon" committee from a wide cross section of the community so that, in Sam's words, "all concerned parties will be represented." He has made the committee very large, and the members range from Ph.D.s in urban planning to real estate agents to local ward committeepersons to minority group leaders. He has taken particular care in selecting people who have widely divergent, outspoken, public views on the housing issue.

1. Do you think Sam's strategy of using this group to delay taking a stand on the housing issue until after the election will work? Why or why not?
2. What are some of the important dynamics of this group. Do you think the group will arrive at a good solution to the housing problems facing this city?
3. Do you think they will suffer from groupthink?
4. What types of informal roles is Sam exhibiting? Do you think he is an effective manager? Do you think he is an effective politician? Is there a difference?

EXPERIENTIAL EXERCISES FOR PART 3

EXERCISE: Groups and Conflict Resolution*

Goals:

1. To compare individual versus group problem solving and decision making
2. To analyze the dynamics of groups
3. To demonstrate conflict and ways of resolving it

Implementation:

1. Divide any number of people into small groups of four or five.
2. Take about 15 minutes for individual responses and 30 minutes for group consensus.
3. Each individual and group should have a worksheet. Pencils, a flip chart (newsprint or blackboard), marker pens, or chalk may also be helpful to the groups.

Process:

1. Each individual has 15 minutes to read the story and answer the 11 questions about the story. Each person may refer to the story as often as needed but may not confer with anyone else. Each person should circle "T" if the answer is clearly true, "F" is the answer is clearly false, and "?" if it isn't clear from the story whether the answer is true or false.
2. After 15 minutes each small group makes the same decisions using group consensus. Allow 30 minutes for group consensus. No one should change his or her answers on the individual questions. The ground rules for group decisions are as follows:
   a. Group decisions should be made by consensus. It is illegal to vote, trade, average, flip a coin, etc.
   b. No individual group member should give in only to reach agreement.
   c. No individual should argue for his or her own decision. Instead, each person should approach the task using logic and reason.
   d. Every group member should be aware that disagreements may be resolved by facts. Conflict can lead to understanding and creativity if it does not make group members feel threatened or defensive.

Scoring:

1. After 30 minutes of group work, the exercise leader should announce the correct answers. Scoring is based on the number of correct answers out of a possible total of 11. Individuals are to score their own individual answers, and someone should score the group decision answers.
   The exercise leader should then call for:
   a. The group-decision score in each group.
   b. The average individual score in each group.
   c. The highest individual score in each group.

Source: Alan Filley, *Interpersonal Conflict Resolution,* Scott, Foresman, Glenview, Ill., 1975, pp. 139–142, as adapted from William H. Haney, *Communication and Organizational Behavior,* Irwin, Burr Ridge, Ill., 1967, pp. 319–324.

2. Responses should be posted on the tally sheet. Note should be taken of those groups in which the group score was (1) higher than the average individual score or (2) higher than the best individual score. Groups should discuss the way in which individual members resolved disagreements and the effect of the ground rules on such behavior. They may consider the obstacles experienced in arriving at consensus agreements and the possible reasons for the difference between individual and group decisions.

The story:

A businessman had just turned off the lights in the store when a man appeared and demanded money. The owner opened a cash register. The contents of the cash register were scooped up, and the man sped away. A member of the police force was notified promptly.

Statements about the story:

1.	A man appeared after the owner had turned off his store lights.	T	F	?
2.	The robber was a man.	T	F	?
3.	A man did not demand money.	T	F	?
4.	The man who opened the cash register was the owner.	T	F	?
5.	The store owner scooped up the contents of the cash register and ran away.	T	F	?
6.	Someone opened a cash register.	T	F	?
7.	After the man who demanded the money scooped up the contents of the cash register, he ran away.	T	F	?
8.	Although the cash register contained money, the story does *not* state *how much*.	T	F	?
9.	The robber demanded money of the owner.	T	F	?
10.	The story concerns a series of events in which only three persons are referred to: the owner of the store, a man who demanded money, and a member of the police force.	T	F	?
11.	The following events in the story are true: someone demanded money, a cash register was opened, its contents were scooped up, and a man dashed out of the store.	T	F	?

Tally Sheet

Group Number	Group Score	Average Individual Score	Best Individual Score	Group Score Better Than Average Indiv.?	Group Score Better Than Best Indiv.?

EXERCISE: NASA Moon Survival Task*

Goals: The challenge in decision making is to obtain the best information within limits of time and other resources. This is often very difficult because information does not exist in pure form. It is always filtered through people who may or may not get along with each other and who might not even care about a good decision. This exercise is a means to help you look at the process of gathering information, working out group procedures, analyzing different contributions, and handling conflict and motivation. The exercise is intended to help you examine the strengths and weaknesses of individual decision making versus group decision making.

Instructions: You are a member of a space crew originally scheduled to rendezvous with another ship on the lighted surface of the moon. Because of mechanical difficulties, however, your ship was forced to land at a spot some 200 miles from the rendezvous point. During landing, much of the equipment aboard was damaged, and because survival depends on reaching the main ship, the most critical items available must be chosen for the 200-mile trip.

Implementation: 1. On the next page are listed the 15 items left intact and undamaged after the landing. Your task is to rank them in terms of their importance to your crew in reaching the rendezvous point.
2. In the first column (step 1) place the number 1 by the most important item, the number 2 by the second most important, and so on, through number 15, the least important. You have 15 minutes to complete this phase of the exercise.
3. After the individual rankings are completed, participants should be formed into groups having from four to seven members.
4. Each group should then rank the 15 items as a team. This group ranking should be a consensus after a discussion of the issues, not just the average of each individual ranking. Although it is unlikely that everyone will agree exactly on the group ranking, an effort should be made to reach at the least a decision that everyone can live with. It is important to treat differences of opinion as a means of gathering more information and clarifying issues and as an incentive to force the group to seek better alternatives.
5. The group ranking should be listed in the second column (step 2).
6. The third phase of the exercise consists of the instructor's providing the expert's rankings, which should be entered in the third column (step 3).

Scoring: 1. Each participant should compute the difference between the individual ranking (step 1) and the expert's ranking (step 3), and between the group ranking (step 2) and the expert's ranking (step 3).
2. Then add the two "difference" columns—the smaller the score, the closer the ranking is to the view of the experts.

Source: This exercise was developed by Jay Hall, Teleometrics International, and was adapted by J. B. Ritchie and Paul Thompson, *Organization and People,* 2d ed., West, St. Paul, Minn., 1980, pp. 238–239. Also see James B. Lau and A. B. Shani, *Behavior in Organizations,* 4th ed., Irwin, Burr Ridge, Ill., 1988, pp. 94–99.

NASA Tally Sheet

Items	Step 1 Your individual ranking	Step 2 The team's ranking	Step 3 Survival expert's ranking	Step 4 Difference between Steps 1 and 3	Step 5 Difference between Steps 2 and 3
Box of matches					
Food concentrate					
50 feet of nylon rope					
Parachute silk					
Portable heating unit					
Two .45-calibre pistols					
One case dehydrated Pet milk					
Two 100-lb. tanks of oxygen					
Stellar map (of the moon's constellation)					
Life raft					
Magnetic compass					
5 gallons of water					
Signal flares					
First aid kit containing injection needles					
Solar-powered FM receiver-transmitter					
TOTAL (The lower the score, the better)				**Your score**	**Team score**

EXERCISE: TGIF (Thank God It's Friday!)*

Goals:

This exercise provides an opportunity to experience and explore several facets of group dynamics. Although the activity itself is recreational in nature, it reflects many of the same challenges faced by managerial groups and contemporary empowered and self-managed teams. That is, the exercise calls on decision-making and interpersonal behavior skills necessary to effectively manage a collaborative work effort.

Implementation:

The activity itself involves the spelling out of a list of common or well-known phrases and items. Each quotation includes a number, and that number is the clue to solving the puzzle. For example, the sample puzzle is presented as "7 D. of the W."

The number 7 is part of the phrase and provides the clue that the saying is "7 days of the week." Another common item is "12 E. in a D." which stands for "12 eggs in a dozen."

Source: Professor Steven M. Sommer, University of California–Riverside, developed the exercise around the two anonymous activity sheets. Used with permission.

Activity Sheet A

Instructions: Each equation below contains the initials of words that will make it correct. Finish the missing words. For example:

7 - D. of the W.   Would be *7 days of the week.*

1.   26 - L. of the A.   _____

2.   7 - W. of the A. W.   _____

3.   1001 - A. N.   _____

4.   54 - C. in a D. (with the J.)   _____

5.   12 - S. of the Z.   _____

6.   9 - P. in the S. S.   _____

7.   13 - S. of the A. F.   _____

8.   88 - P. K.   _____

9.   18 - H. on a G. C.   _____

10.   32 - D. F. at which W. F.   _____

11.   90 - D. in a R. A.   _____

12.   200 - D. for P. G. in M.   _____

13.   8 - S. on a S. S.   _____

14.   3 - B. M. (S. H. T. R.)   _____

15.   4 - Q. in a G.   _____

16.   24 - H. in a D.   _____

17.   1 - W. on a U.   _____

18.   5 - D. in a Z. C.   _____

19.   57 - H. V.   _____

20.   11 - P. on a F. T.   _____

21.   1000 - W. that a P. is W.   _____

22.   29 - D. in F. in a L. Y.   _____

23.   64 - S. on a C. B.   _____

24.   40 - D. and N. of the G. F.   _____

Procedure:

1.   (Five minutes). Students should break up into groups of four or five.
2.   Do not read the discussion questions before doing the task.
3.   (Twenty to thirty minutes). The groups solve as many items on one of the following activity sheets (A or B) as possible.
4.   (Five minutes). The instructor reads off the answers to the list. Groups may propose alternative solutions.
5.   (Fifteen minutes). In a class forum, the groups discuss and compare their experiences by responding to the discussion questions.
6.   As a follow-up activity, use the alternate list. The follow-up may be used to show effective group development, effective teamwork (after discussing problems that may have surfaced with the first list), or the power of groups over individuals (have students complete the list on their own, then as a group).

Activity Sheet B

1. $\dfrac{\text{EZ}}{\text{i i i i i i i}}$	2. $\begin{array}{c}\text{T}\\\text{O}\\\text{U}\\\text{C}\\\text{H}\end{array}$	3. Moth cry cry cry	4. $\dfrac{\text{Black}}{\text{coat}}$
5. Time Time	6. $\text{L}^{\text{A}}\text{N}_{\text{D}}$	7. Hurry ↑	8. Me Quit
9. Le vel	10. $\dfrac{\text{Knee}}{\text{light}}$	11. $\dfrac{\text{Man}}{\text{Board}}$	12. He's/Himself
13. R|e|a|d|i|n|g	14. AGES	15. $\begin{array}{c}\text{R}\\\text{ROAD}\\\text{A}\\\text{D}\end{array}$	16. $\dfrac{\text{O}}{\begin{array}{c}\text{M.A.}\\\text{B.A.}\\\text{PH.D}\end{array}}$
17. $\dfrac{\text{WEAR}}{\text{LONG}}$	18. DICE DICE	19. ECNALG	20. CYCLE CYCLE CYCLE
21. CHAIR	22. $\begin{array}{c}\text{T}\\\text{O}\\\text{W}\\\text{N}\end{array}$	23. ii ii o o	24. $\dfrac{\text{Stand}}{\text{I}}$

Discussion questions:

1. How did the group try to solve the list? Did you plan out your approach? Did you explore answers as a group, divide parts among individuals? Or did each member try to solve the entire list individually and then pool answers? Did people take on different roles? Recorder? Encourager? Idea generator? Spy?

2. How important was it for the group to solve all 24 puzzles? Did the team initially set a goal to finish the list? How challenging was this exercise? What happened as you approached completion? Did commitment go up? As the last few unsolved items became frustrating, did the group start to lose its desire?

3. Describe the climate or personality of the group. Was everyone in agreement about how hard to work? How many to finish? Did members begin to react differently

to the frustrations of getting the list completed? Did some argue to finish? Did others tell the team to quit?

4. Did some members try to dominate the process? The suggested solutions? How well did you get along in doing the exercise? Was there conflict? Did members fight fair in debating different answers? Was each discovery of a correct answer a source of excitement and pride? Or was it a sense of relief, a step closer to getting it over with?

5. Did the group develop any rules to regulate behavior? Was there a process of group development in which members discussed the assignment before beginning to tackle it? What changes in behaviors or expectations occurred as time progressed and the group became more or less focused on the activity? Did a form of self-discipline emerge to keep the team focused, to prevent being embarrassed in relation to other groups?

6. To what extent did public evaluation of performance become important? Did you begin to monitor how well other groups were doing? Did your group try to spy on their answers? Did you negotiate any trades?

EXERCISE: Power and Politics*

Goals:

1. To gain some insights into your own power needs and political orientation
2. To examine some of the reasons people strive for power and what political strategies can be used to attain it

Implementation:

Answer each of the following question with "mostly agree" or "mostly disagree," even if it is difficult for you to decide which alternative best describes your opinion.

	Mostly Agree	Mostly Disagree
1. Only a fool would correct a boss's mistakes.	___	___
2. If you have certain confidential information, release it to your advantage.	___	___
3. I would be careful not to hire a subordinate with more formal education than myself.	___	___
4. If you do a favor, remember to cash in on it.	___	___
5. Given the opportunity, I would cultivate friendships with powerful people.	___	___
6. I like the idea of saying nice things about a rival in order to get that person transferred from my department.	___	___
7. Why not take credit for someone else's work? They would do the same to you.	___	___
8. Given the chance, I would offer to help my boss build some shelves for his or her den.	___	___
9. I laugh heartily at my boss's jokes, even when they are not funny.	___	___
10. I would be sure to attend a company picnic even if I had the chance to do something I enjoyed more that day.	___	___
11. If I knew an executive in my company was stealing money, I would use that against him or her in asking for favors.	___	___
12. I would first find out my boss's political preferences before discussing politics with him or her.	___	___
13. I think using memos to zap somebody for his or her mistakes is a good idea (especially when you want to show that person up).	___	___

Source: Reprinted with permission from Andrew J. DuBrin, *Human Relations,* Reston, Reston, Va., 1978, pp. 122–123.

14. If I wanted something done by a coworker, I would be willing to say, "If you don't get this done, our boss might be very unhappy." _____ _____
15. I would invite my boss to a party at my house, even if I didn't like him or her. _____ _____
16. When I'm in a position to, I would have lunch with the "right people" at least twice a week. _____ _____
17. Richard M. Nixon's alleged bugging of the Democratic headquarters would have been a clever idea if he hadn't been caught. _____ _____
18. Power for its own sake is one of life's most precious commodities. _____ _____
19. Having a high school named after you would be an incredible thrill. _____ _____
20. Reading about job politics is as much fun as reading an adventure story. _____ _____

Scoring:

Each statement you check "mostly agree" is worth 1 point toward your power and political orientation score. If you score 16 or over, it suggests that you have a strong inclination toward playing politics. A high score of this nature would also suggest that you have strong needs for power. Scores of 5 or less would suggest that you are not inclined toward political maneuvering and that you are not strongly power-driven.

A caution is in order. This questionnaire is designed primarily to encourage you to think carefully about the topic of power and politics. It lacks the scientific validity of a legitimate, controlled test.

PART FOUR

Managing and Leading for High Performance

Consulting Best Practices

Gallup's Approach to Managing for High Performance

Because this last part of the text is concerned with both managing and leading for high performance, and this is Gallup's major practice with clients, we will first look at the managing part and then at the leading part.

Managing for high performance starts with measurement. When the match of talent is right, people will do more of, and get better at, the things we measure. But what sort of things? In Gallup's practice, we seek to work in a context defined by outcomes. Because of this, it is imperative that every employee know their customers—both internal or external. From this relationship, right expectations can be created in ways that allow for measurement of quantity and quality of the person's performance. Once the "what" question is answered, objective, mutually agreed-upon measures can be developed. At Gallup, we believe "if you have a job that cannot be measured, you probably have a nonjob!"

Notice that the measurement is not about compliance to process. Except where issues such as safety are concerned, the idea is to allow room for initiative, creativity, individualization, and improvement of the systems and processes to the employee. We focus on the performance.

We have found that focusing on quantity alone can be counterproductive. Consequently, we always include quality assessment. It is the customer who determines quality. Of course, some issues are expected to manifest themselves in most any work environment—timelines, accuracy, responsiveness, and the like. Frequently, we find that other items such as "personal touch" may be included. When people get to see how much they are producing, and how well their efforts are being received, they have both a benchmark and a reason to see "how much better they can get."

At Gallup, we recommend reward systems that respond to the fact that people are differently motivated. Some choose to compete against themselves, for instance, whereas others choose to compete "in the wider arena." In addition to articulating systems in this way, we also pay attention to how people like to receive their recognition. Public recognition for winning against others can be largely counterproductive when given to a person who dislikes comparison to others and who is a "private person."

It is important to measure the right things, because you will get more of what you measure. Some issues, such as safety, can be tricky. Measuring "reduction of reported incidents" can get you exactly that: fewer reports! Likewise, in call centers certain companies have learned the hard way that rewarding short "duration of call" can be very harmful to customer service, creating only an appearance of high performance.

Intrinsic motivation is actually a presupposition of Gallup's approach to measurement and recognition. Because Gallup believes in matching a "right fit" for a person's talent for the desired outcomes, Gallup seeks to situate persons in roles that are "natural" to them. In this way, employees have the inner satisfaction of doing what they do well. They get good measures in their work, usually from the very start, and because their talent is a "fit," they have the requisite ability to keep growing and improving in their role. As this continues, rapid improvement becomes a "base" of motivation, which underwrites the measurement and recognition systems.

Obviously, Gallup does not support the notion that promotion should be used as a reward. Neither should people be rewarded for tenure. High performance is the key issue; measurement of outcomes, and individually appropriate recognition is the means.

Gallup's Approach to Leadership for Effective Performance

Gallup's approach to leadership is not so much focused on the achievement of a goal, but rather it is the continuation of a journey. This journey includes improvement of performance and growth of the organization. However, in Gallup's point of view, these are managed outcomes that accompany the leadership process. At the center, leadership is more about the business of creating hope, possibility, and future. There is no "arrival" here, though various milestones are obtained along the way. Leadership at its best not only transforms individuals and organizations towards their highest aspirations, but it also creates moments of vision and comprehension that allow people to transcend to new, as yet unattained, levels of experience and performance.

In Gallup's research, leadership has been shown to be the "main driver" of employee retention and loyalty. In a rapidly changing, high-turnover environment, leadership has emerged as a "higher level" construct that influences employees through future, vision, values, and creation of culture constructed around these, and with behaviors that demonstrate regard, respect, and value for employees.

Leaders as Talent

Gallup's approach to leadership is largely based on the study of human talent. Although it may appear a "trait approach" at first glance, talent is not rooted in personality or "style." A talent, for Gallup, is a measurable, stable constellation of thought, feeling, and behavior. Talent is, in Gallup's methodology, the "soil" in which various skills and competencies can be "planted." It is the talents of the individual that create the basis for which "skills" will thrive, which will "do ok," and which will "languish." Talent, in its dominant or "signature" dimension, is much more about what people will do, rather than what they might do or might be managed or coerced to do. Possessing a methodology that allows us to measure talent in a reliable way, Gallup focuses on those talents that demonstrably distinguish top performing or successful leaders from the "average."

Leaders vs. Managers

A necessary first step is to distinguish leadership from management. Gallup has found that managers and supervisors exert their greatest and most significant influence in what could be called the "first synapse," the relationship between themselves and the individuals they manage. Leaders, on the other hand, exert their influence "over a distance." Although the literature recognizes indirect leadership (the influence of a focal leader on individuals not directly reporting to him or her), Gallup views this "leadership at a distance" not as an "indirect function" of leaders, but as *the principle activity of leaders.*

Who are leaders? For Gallup, leaders are individuals who successfully bring a constituency (more than an immediate group) to a commonly shared "destination" that initially "inhabited the future." Though all human beings may have such a capacity in some measure, and use it on some localized scale, it is also true that for certain individuals these capacities are so manifest that they can and frequently do exercise them over considerable range or distance. Those who "can do" are leaders. To be sure, the situation, Zeitgeist, context, followers, and other variables do matter. That is why true leaders need the talent to navigate these challenges, and that is why Gallup measures not only the talents of the leader but also various related measures within the leader's constituency.

Gallup has developed methodologies related to the measurement of management and leadership. These methodologies allow leaders to have measured information of their own talent and critical, leverageable points within their constituency. In all this, Gallup feels, it is critical to keep managerial issues separated and clarified for managerial functioning and to deal with leadership in a similar way. Happily, these methods and measures have critical "intersections" between issues and functions and between managers and leaders, allowing for full organizational use of the information for effective outcomes.

The Leader-Situation Fit

Gallup would agree with the contingency theories that there must be a "fit" between the leader and the situation. It is also important for a leader to use his or her talent in a manner that is "fitting" for the situation. Self-awareness is a significant ingredient in leadership success, as are the talents that serve to modulate the effective use of other talents. Gallup's studies would suggest that the ability to "modulate" one's talent for a wide range of situations is what typifies a successful leader. When the talents of an individual are the right "fit" for the role and used in a manner "fitting" to a role and the situation, Gallup refers to it as leadership "strengths." Hence, the measurement of talent has a predictive value for job placement, development, and succession planning.

Gallup's Identified Demands of Leadership

The process of leadership, in Gallup's assessment, proceeds on the leader's response to seven demands. The first demand is that the leader *know one's self.* The process of continual development in the area of self-awareness is, in Gallup's research, of great importance. To know one's strengths and nonstrengths and act accordingly is to use oneself optimally and to limit the vulnerabilities caused by "blind spots" and "denial." Knowledge of strengths grounds the leader's self in authentic, ethical presence to others.

Leaders also need to *make sense of experience,* for themselves and others. A central reason is the reduction of fear in the organization. Anxiety can distract and dissipate human energy, drawing it away from productive engagement. Leaders reduce fear by having parsimonious explanations of "realities" that could otherwise be problematic. It is not necessary that the leader always have all the answers, but people need to know that their leaders are "aware and attentive" to the things that matter.

Leaders need to *mentor and be mentored.* Particularly in today's world of rapid change, leaders themselves continue their own growth when they make themselves available to the development of others. A best way to be focused on current and future issues is to be intimately acquainted with the fears and dreams of the rising stars of one's origination. Additionally, leaders also need others who can challenge their own trajectory. These mentoring relationships support the continued growth of leaders.

Successful leaders build their constituency strategically and continually. For leaders, every day is recruiting day. There are no leaders who do not have followers, and following is a choice. Leaders win loyalty through personal trust and to the vision and values they espouse. Leaders' behavioral congruency with words is required in this process. Leaders understand that "friends may come and go, but enemies tend to accumulate."

Leaders *harness the values* of the people in the organization. As the future is best expressed as an "embodiment" of organizational purpose or mission, leaders bring to the surface, to "resonance," this aspect of the human experience. Leaders lift up and clarify the shared human reason and passion for the endeavor. This gives meaning, purpose, and direction to the people. Leadership taps into heartfelt motivations and helps to enhance employee engagement.

Leaders work the effervescence of *vision*. For leaders, in Gallup's view, visioning is an ongoing process. Emerging from the values and purpose of the organization is an expression of a desirable, mutually shared image of a possible, shared future. As the organization proceeds, the vision reshapes as the continuity of values finds increasingly fresh and expansive expressions of possibility. Although specific goals support the pursuit of vision and should be achieved, vision always remains at the horizon of possibility. It is the work of leaders to make this be so.

Leaders challenge their people with *audacious goals*. Successful leaders use challenging, stretch goals to tell their people that they believe in them. This is a critically important message. Far-reaching goals that feel detached from the organization's mission and vision may be perceived as the leaders' "ego trip." But when leaders successfully create a continuity of values, vision, policy, action, and challenge, remarkable things can be achieved; future direction and hope can be created; and organizational effectiveness can be enhanced.

CHAPTER 15

Managing Performance through Job Design and Goal Setting

Learning Objectives

Discuss the background of job design as an approach to managing for high performance.

Define the job enrichment and job characteristics approaches to job design.

Present the quality of work life (QWL), sociotechnical, and high performance work practices (HPWPs) approaches to job design.

Explain goal-setting theory and guidelines from research.

Describe the application of goal setting to overall systems performance.

Starting with Best Practice
Leader's Advice

GE's Steve Kerr on Designing Jobs and Setting Goals for Performance Improvement

Steve Kerr is Vice President of Corporate Leadership Development and Chief Learning Officer for General Electric. Among his responsibilities is GE's renewal leadership education center. Dr. Kerr is also a highly respected academic. Before coming to GE, he was an organizational behavior professor and prolific researcher on the faculties of Ohio State, Southern California, and Michigan. He is able to draw from both his academic research and real-world experience in commenting on ways today's organizations can improve performance through job design and goal setting.

Q1:   *Can you tell us about the GE workout program? How did the program begin and what were its purposes?*

Kerr: Workout emerged when GE began downsizing its operations. A lot of people became concerned that all of the work would now fall on the shoulders of those who remained. So the company started looking for ways to streamline things by getting rid of low-value work. The term *workout* refers to the company's efforts to reduce the amount of work people have to do by getting rid of bureaucratic red tape and minutia. We did this through workout sessions.

Q2:   *Is GE still using workout, and is it as widely used as it was before?*

Kerr: It's still being used, but it's gone through a series of changes. In Stage 1, it was done in a formal realm of business; and we used to take it off site—i.e., at "unnatural places." In Stage 2, we would train the trainers to do it inside their own businesses. We called this stage "unnatural acts in natural places." We were still creating artificial events, but conducted by people in their own site. When a transition is done correctly, the initiative should eventually move to Stage 3: "natural acts in natural places." People doing it naturally as a way of life. We seldom do workouts in a formal, explicit, centrally driven way anymore. Most of the businesses do use it on a regular basis, not because they're getting pressure from corporate, but because they have found it really does motivate people. It mobilizes them and helps them come up with good ideas. So, they're doing it for the right reasons. And if someone up top were to ask me how many workouts got done at GE, I would say I'm delighted to tell you I have no idea. It's unorchestrated. It's now all natural acts.

Q3:   *Is GE now moving toward team-based organizations, or do you think you've been doing that for quite a while?*

Kerr: Collectively the corporation is, but again it varies a lot by business. We have some businesses that are still getting good use from the entrepreneurial kind of spirit. Other businesses rely heavily on the team concept companies' best practices. And then you decide. So I would say there's much more exposure to team practices in GE, but it's still up to the businesses whether they want to make use of it. I don't think there's any corporate requirement that they do so.

Q4:   *Are there any other key elements in your boundaryless organization perspective that we haven't talked about?*

Kerr: Well, one is the way American organizations are built on the assumption that people can and want to ascend hierarchically. The big rewards are always moving up, moving up. That's where the perks are; that's where the power is. Yet in a downsized world, you're not going to be able to validate people's careers with rapid promotions. So, what the smart companies are doing is disconnecting rewards and hierarchical advancement. We have to help people understand that they're going to have a satisfying career without vaulting up some hierarchy that's not going to be there.

Q5:   *GE has been touting stretch goals for years, yet you say they can be destructive. What gives?*

Kerr: Most organizations don't have a clue about how to manage stretch goals. It's popular today for companies to ask their people to double sales or increase speed to market threefold. But then they don't provide their people with the knowledge, tools, and means to meet such ambitious goals. We all agree that generally you get more output by committing more input, but now corporate America seems to be trying to get more output just by demanding more output. Ask them to explain the incongruity, and they say, "We're smarter now. We're not going to give you more people, or money, or physical space; we're not going to give you more of any resource, so your solution is going to have to be to work smarter, get out of the box, and be creative."

Q6:   *Why bother with stretch goals in the first place if they're going to harm workers?*

Kerr: Well, if done right, a stretch target, which basically is an extremely ambitious goal, gets your people to perform in ways they never imagined possible. It's a goal that, by definition, you don't know how to reach. You might, for instance, ask people to cut costs by half or reduce product-development time from years to months. Stretch goals are an artificial stimulant for finding ways to work more efficiently. They force you to think "out of the box." . . . There's plenty of evidence that if you don't find dramatically new ways of doing business, you're not going to be in business. And if you don't intrude artificially into what's going on, you probably won't come up with out-of-the-box ideas. So clearly some intervention is needed.

Q7:   *What's the right approach?*

Kerr: No. 1, don't set goals that stress people crazily. No. 2, if you do set goals that stretch them or stress them crazily, don't punish failure. No. 3, if you're going to ask them to do what they have never done, give them whatever tools and help you can.

There are meta-analytic research findings supporting the conventional wisdom that good old work experience is related to job performance.[1] (In other words, the more relevant experience jobholders have, the better job they tend to do.) However, there is also an established body of knowledge supporting the idea that certain job designs and goal setting can enhance performance. This chapter focuses on improving performance through these two important application techniques: job design and goal setting. These two techniques are singled out because more research has been generated in these two areas than anywhere else in the entire field of organizational behavior. It is becoming increasingly clear that appropriately designing jobs can have a positive impact on both employee satisfaction and quality of performance. The same is true of goal setting, which has been held up as a prototypical model for how theory and basic research can lead to improved performance. The purpose of this chapter is to provide some of the background, review the related research, and spell out some of the effective applications for these important areas of the field of organizational behavior.

JOB DESIGN

Job design may be defined as the methods that management uses to develop the content of a job, including all relevant tasks, as well as the processes by which jobs are constructed and revised. Job design is an increasingly important application technique in the study of organizational behavior, especially in light of various recent trends. Most importantly, the nature of work is changing because of the intrusion of advanced information technology as discussed in Chapter 2, especially the Internet, Intranet, and e-business. Consequently, two new developments have emerged. The first is a blurring of the distinction between on-work and off-work time. A person carrying a cell phone and/or PDA (personal digital assistant) and a home office containing a fax machine and Internet access is "at work" even when not in the office and is "on-call" practically every moment of the day. This includes drive time and time spent in airports or while flying across the world. The second development, which is tied to the first, is the rising number of telecommuting jobs or teleworking, in which the employee performs substantial amounts of work at home. Today in the United States, there are over 16 million telecommuters who work at home at least one day a month (40 million on a global basis), and about 8 million are full-time telecommuters. These numbers are expected to greatly increase in the years ahead.[2] Ford and Delta Airlines are among the first of many to give employees personal computers for home use. These recent trends create new challenges for job design models, which are already based on an extensive and growing theoretical and research base, and are being widely applied to the actual practice of management.

Initially, the field of organizational behavior paid attention only to job enrichment approaches to job design. Now, with *quality of work life* (QWL) becoming a major societal issue in this country and throughout the world, job design has taken a broader perspective. Figure 15.1 summarizes the various dimensions and approaches to job design, starting with the historically significant job engineering. Job enrichment still dominates the job design literature on organizational behavior, but from the perspective of job characteristics rather than from Herzberg's motivators. The social information processing approach recognizes some of the theoretical complexity in job design, and the QWL approach recognizes the overall importance of the climate or culture and the role of more specific sociotechnical and team techniques in job design.

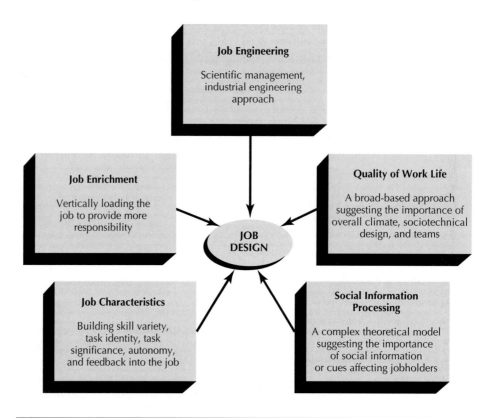

FIGURE 15.1
Various approaches to job design.

Background on Job Design

Ideas about job design appeared in the literature as early as the 1700s. In particular, British economist Adam Smith noted in his landmark economics book, *The Wealth of Nations,* that the assembly of straight pins could be dramatically increased if each worker was assigned a small, routine, repeated task. Thus, one individual held the job of "wire straightener," and a second was a "wire cutter." A third was assigned the job of sharpening the pin head, and so forth. This type of specialized job design dramatically increased productivity and set the stage for the scientific management movement that began well over a hundred years ago. Pioneering scientific managers such as Frederick W. Taylor and Frank Gilbreth systematically examined jobs with techniques such as time and motion analysis. Their goal was to maximize human efficiency in jobs. Taylor suggested that task design might be the most prominent single element in scientific management.

The scientific management approach evolved into what is now generally called *job engineering.* This industrial engineering approach is concerned with product, process, and tool design; plant layout; standard operating procedures; work measurement and standards; worker methods; and human–machine interactions. It has been the dominant form of job design analysis for over 100 years; it went hand in hand with automation in the previous generation, and it has been closely associated with cybernation (automatic feedback control mechanisms) and sophisticated computer applications involving artificial intelligence (AI), expert systems, and computer-assisted design (CAD). These computer systems have had a positive impact by reducing task and workflow uncertainty.[3] At first blue-collar production jobs, and then white-collar office and service jobs as well, became highly specialized (the employee did one or a very few tasks) and standardized (the employee did the task the same way every time).

The often-cited example of the employee on the assembly line putting a nut on a bolt as the product moves by on the conveyor belt became quite common in manufacturing plants across the country. The same types of specialized jobs became common in banks, offices, hospitals, schools, and every other kind of organizational setting. The consensus was that these highly specialized, standardized jobs were very efficient and led to a high degree of control over workers. Until recent times, few people questioned this traditional engineering approach to job design. Top management could readily determine and see immediate cost savings from job engineering. But side effects on quality, absenteeism, and turnover were generally ignored.

Starting in the 1950s, some practicing managers, such IBM founder Thomas Watson, sought to extend some of the principles of job engineering. Two of the more popular methods in the 1950s and 1960s were job rotation and job enlargement. These programs were designed to take advantage of specialization of labor from the job engineering approach, but also to reduce some of the negative effects these engineered jobs have on employee satisfaction and performance.

Job Rotation.   This simpliest form of job redesign involves moving employees from one relatively simple job to another after short time periods (one hour, half-days, every day). For example, at McDonalds, an employee may cook French fries one day, fry hamburgers the next, wait on the front counter during the next shift, and draw soft drinks the next. This form of job rotation has several advantages. First, the odds of injury are reduced, as each worker must refocus on a new task throughout the workday. Further, the incidence of repetitive strain injuries (e.g., carpal tunnel syndrome) may also be reduced. Second, as employees learn sets of tasks, they are more flexible and able to cover for someone who is absent or who quits. Third, supervisors who are promoted from the ranks know more about how the entire operation works. A manager promoted from the ranks at McDonalds after only six months on the job has probably been exposed to every production task performed at the unit. The primary disadvantage of job rotation is that each individual task eventually becomes as boring as the rest of the simple tasks. In other words, over the long term there is no substantial difference between cooking French fries and frying hamburgers. Consequently, job satisfaction and/or performance may decline. Rotation does, however, have some recent research showing a positive impact,[4] and it is a better alternative to job redesign than doing nothing.

Job Enlargement.   This process involves increasing the number of tasks each employee performs. A sales clerk who waits on customers, finalizes the sale, helps with credit applications, arranges merchandise, and reorders stock has an enlarged job, when compared to a checkout clerk or a shelf stocker at Wal-Mart. Workers in enlarged jobs are able to utilize more skills in performing their tasks. Many times, however, enlargement reduces the efficiency with which tasks are completed, thereby slowing work down. Imagine being waited on individually at Wal-Mart. The company's competitive advantage for low labor costs compared to a full-service department store would be quickly and dramatically reduced. However, enlargement does not necessarily result in improved employee satisfaction and commitment. For example, one of the major by-products of recent downsizing is enlarged jobs assigned to the members of the organization who remain. The survivors with anxiety of "I'm next" and greatly enlarged jobs are less, rather than more, satisfied and committed to the organization.

New Challenges.   Both job rotation and enlargement are known as horizontal loading programs. Each incorporates tasks from the same job level (horizontally) in terms of skill and responsibility. Although boredom at work may still be a significant problem,[5] in the last several years attention has shifted to new, demanding challenges facing employees in jobs. For example, because of the downsizing of organizations and increasingly advanced information technology, jobs have suddenly become much more demanding, and employees must think in different ways to adapt to unpredictable changes. For example, in manufacturing, assembly line methods are being replaced by flexible, "customized" production and computer-integrated manufacturing (CIM). This new manufacturing approach requires workers to deal with an ever-increasing line of products and sophisticated technology. Similar job changes have occurred in the white-collar service industry. For example, bank tellers must not only demonstrate facility with computers but also be marketers and customer service representatives—rather than just number-crunchers and clerks.

For both academicians and practitioners, job design takes on special importance in today's human resource management. It is essential to design jobs so that stress (covered in Chapter 12) can be reduced, motivation (covered in Chapter 8) can be enhanced, and satisfaction and commitment of employees (covered in Chapter 7) and their performance can be improved so that organizations can effectively compete in the global marketplace.

Job Enrichment

Job enrichment represents an extension of the earlier, more simplified job rotation and job enlargement techniques of job design. Because it is a direct outgrowth of Herzberg's two-factor theory of motivation (see Chapter 8), the assumption is that in order to motivate personnel, the job must be designed to provide opportunities for achievement, recognition, responsibility, advancement, and growth. The technique entails "enriching" the job so that these factors are included. In particular, *job enrichment* is concerned with designing jobs that include a greater variety of work content; require a higher level of knowledge and skill; give workers more autonomy and responsibility in terms of planning, directing, and controlling their own performance; and provide the opportunity for personal growth and a meaningful work experience. As opposed to job enlargement, which horizontally loads the job, job enrichment *vertically* loads the job; there are not necessarily more tasks to perform, but more responsibility and accountability. For example, instead of having workers do a mundane, specialized task, then passing off to another worker doing another minute part of the task, and eventually having an inspector at the end, under job enrichment, the worker would be given a complete module of work to do (job enlargement) and, importantly, would inspect his or her own work (responsibility) and put a personal identifier on it (accountability).

As with the other application techniques discussed in this text, job enrichment is not a panacea for all job design problems facing modern management. After noting that there are documented cases where this approach to job design did not work, Miner concluded that the biggest problem is that traditional job enrichment has little to say about when and why the failures can be expected to occur.[6] Some of the explanations that have been suggested include that job enrichment is difficult to truly implement, that many employees simply prefer an old familiar job to an enriched job, and that employees in general and unions in particular are resistant to the change. Some employees have expressed preferences for higher pay rather than enriched jobs, and others enjoy their current patterns of on-the-job socialization and friendships more than they do increased responsibility and autonomy. Essentially, job enrichment can inhibit a person's social life at work.

Despite some potential limitations, job enrichment is still a viable approach, and recent research provides continuing evidence that it has mostly beneficial results (more employee satisfaction and customer service, less employee overload, and fewer employee errors).[7] There is even a recent study that found employees were more creative when they worked in an enriching context of complex, challenging jobs and a supportive, noncontrolling supervisory climate.[8] However, management must still use job enrichment selectively and give proper recognition to the complex human and situational variables. The job characteristics models of job enrichment are a step in this direction.

The Job Characteristics Approach to Task Design

To meet some of the limitations of the relatively simple Herzberg approach to job enrichment (which he prefers to call *orthodox job enrichment,* or OJE), a group of researchers began to concentrate on the relationship between certain job characteristics, or the job scope, and employee motivation. J. Richard Hackman and Greg Oldham developed the most widely recognized model of job characteristics,[9] shown in Figure 15.2. This model recognized that certain job characteristics contribute to certain psychological states and that the strength of employees' need for growth has an important moderating effect. The core job characteristics can be summarized briefly as follows:

1. *Skill variety* refers to the extent to which the job requires the employee to draw from a number of different skills and abilities as well as on a range of knowledge.
2. *Task identity* refers to whether the job has an identifiable beginning and end. How complete a module of work does the employee perform?
3. *Task significance* involves the importance of the task. It involves both internal significance—how important is the task to the organization?—and external significance—how proud are employees to tell relatives, friends, and neighbors what they do and where they work?

FIGURE 15.2
The Hackman-Oldham job characteristics model of work motivation.

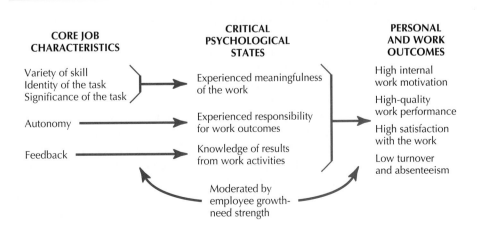

4. *Autonomy* refers to job independence. How much freedom and control do employees have to, for example, schedule their own work, make decisions, or determine the means to accomplish objectives?

5. *Feedback* refers to objective information about progress and performance and can come from the job itself or from supervisors or an information system.

The critical psychological states can be summarized as follows:

1. *Meaningfulness.*   This cognitive state involves the degree to which employees perceive their work as making a valued contribution, as being important and worthwhile.

2. *Responsibility.*   This state is concerned with the extent to which employees feel a sense of being personally responsible or accountable for the work being done.

3. *Knowledge of results.*   Coming directly from the feedback, this psychological state involves the degree to which employees understand how they are performing in the job.

In essence, this model says that certain job characteristics lead to critical psychological states. That is, skill variety, task identity, and task significance lead to experienced meaningfulness; autonomy leads to the feeling of responsibility; and feedback leads to knowledge of results. The more these three psychological states are present, the more employees will feel good about themselves when they perform well. Hackman states: "The model postulates that internal rewards are obtained by an individual when he *learns* (knowledge of results) that he *personally* (experienced responsibility) has performed well on a task that he *cares* about (experienced meaningfulness)."[10] Hackman then points out that these internal rewards are reinforcing to employees, causing them to perform well. If they don't perform well, they will try harder in order to get the internal rewards that good performance brings. He concludes: "The net result is a self-perpetuating cycle of positive work motivation powered by self-generated rewards. This cycle is predicted to continue until one or more of the three psychological states is no longer present, or until the individual no longer values the internal rewards that derive from good performance."[11] Not only did Hackman and Oldham provide original research supporting the existence of these relationships, but recent research has found strong support for the linkages between the core job dimensions and the critical psychological states, and between these states and the predicted outcomes.[12] (Also see the OB Principle at the end of this chapter).

An example of an enriched job, according to the Hackman-Oldham characteristics model, would be that of a surgeon. Surgeons must draw on a wide variety of skills and abilities; usually surgeons can readily identify the task because they handle patients from beginning to end (that is, they play a role in the diagnosis, perform the operation, and are responsible for postoperative care and follow-up); the job has life-and-death significance; there is a great deal of autonomy, as surgeons have the final word on all decisions concerning patients; and there is clear, direct feedback during the operation itself (real-time monitoring of the vital signs and the "scalpel"–"scalpel" type of feedback communication) and afterwards, because, of course, the patient's recovery and subsequent health determine the success of the operation. According to this explanation, these job characteristics determine the surgeon's considerable motivation—not the needs developed while growing up nor his or her valences, instrumentalities, and expectancies as postulated by the process theories discussed in Chapter 8.

At the other extreme would be most traditional blue-collar and white-collar jobs. All five job characteristics would be relatively minimal or nonexistent in the perceptions of many such jobholders and thus can help explain the motivation problem with these low-level jobs. In other words, the job design, not just the person holding the job, helps explain the motivation to perform under this approach.

Diagnosing and Measuring Task Scope

There are several ways that the Hackman-Oldham model can be used to diagnose the degree of task scope that a job possesses. For instance, a manager could simply assess a particular job by clinically analyzing it according to the five core dimensions, as was done in the example of the surgeon's job. Others have suggested a specific checklist, which would include such items as the use of inspectors or checkers, labor pools, or narrow spans of control to help pinpoint deficiencies in the core dimensions.[13] More systematically, Hackman and Oldham have developed a questionnaire, the Job Diagnostic Survey (JDS), to analyze jobs. The questions on this survey yield a quantitative score that can be used to calculate an overall measure or job enrichment, or what is increasingly called *job scope*—to differentiate it from Herzberg-type job enrichment. The formula for this motivating potential score (MPS) is the following:

$$\text{MPS} = \left(\frac{\text{skill variety} + \text{task identity} + \text{task significance}}{3} \right) \times \text{autonomy} \times \text{feedback}$$

Notice that the job characteristics of skill variety, task identity, and task significance are combined and divided by 3, whereas the characteristics of autonomy and feedback stand alone. Also, because skill variety, task identity, and task significance are additive, any one or even two of these characteristics could be completely missing or measured as zero, and the person could still experience meaningfulness, but if either autonomy or feedback were missing, the job would offer no motivating potential (MPS = 0) because of the multiplicative relationships.

The JDS is a widely used instrument that measures task characteristics or task scope. More than 200 empirically based studies have examined the impact that the motivating potential of a job has on job satisfaction and performance. Most of the support for the model comes from Hackman and his colleagues, who claim that people on enriched jobs (according to their characteristics as measured by the JDS) are definitely more motivated and satisfied and, although the evidence is not as strong, may have better attendance and performance effectiveness records.[14] In one study—one of the very few that has looked at the long-term impact—some fairly encouraging results were found. Using about a thousand tellers from 38 banks of a large holding company, the following results were obtained from the job redesign intervention:

1. Perceptions of changed job characteristics increased quickly and held at that level for an extended period. Thus, employees perceive meaningful changes that have been introduced into their jobs and tend to recognize those changes over time.
2. Satisfaction and commitment attitudes increased quickly, but then diminished back to their initial levels.
3. Performance did not increase initially but did increase significantly over the longer time period. The implication here is that managers and researchers need to be more patient in their evaluation of work redesign interventions.[15]

In addition to this large longitudinal study, meta-analyses of the job characteristics model have found general support for the model and for its effects on motivation and satisfaction and performance outcomes.[16] More recently, the relationship between the perception of job characteristics and job satisfaction were studied and revealed some additional insights. The employee's perception of the job may explain increases in both overall and intrinsic job satisfaction. Therefore, employees who have experienced increased job characteristics may have satisfaction in the short term because their perceptions regarding the job have been aroused.[17] However, other studies that try to theoretically refine and extend the job characteristics model have mixed results on both the prescribed moderators/critical psychological states[18] (see Figure 15.2) and outcomes.[19] The model also did not hold cross-culturally when it failed to increase the performance of a group of Russian factory workers.[20] Despite the mixed results, the job characteristics model on balance has considerable positive research evidence and, along with goal setting (covered in the last half of this chapter), remains one of the most effective application techniques for managing human resources for high performance.

Practical Guidelines for Redesigning Jobs

Specific guidelines such as those found in Figure 15.3 are offered to redesign jobs. Such easily implementable guidelines make the job design area popular and practical for more effective human resource performance management. An actual example would be the application that was made in a large department store.[21] In a training session format, the sales employees' jobs were redesigned in the following manner:

1. *Skill variety.*   The salespeople were asked to try to think of and use
   a. Different selling approaches
   b. New merchandise displays
   c. Better ways of recording sales and keeping records
2. *Task identity.*   The salespeople were asked to
   a. Keep a personal record of daily sales volume in dollars
   b. Keep a record of number of sales/customers
   c. Mark off an individual display area that they considered their own and keep it complete and orderly

FIGURE 15.3
Specific guidelines for redesigning jobs for the more effective practice of human resource management.

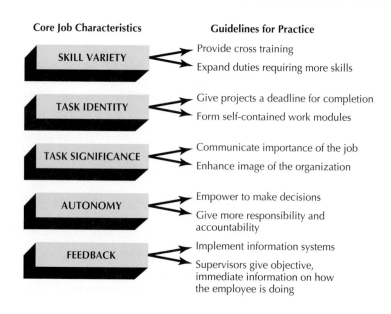

3. *Task significance.* The salespeople were reminded that
   a. Selling a product is the basic overall objective of the store
   b. The appearance of the display area is important to selling
   c. They are "the store" to customers; they were told that courtesy and pleasant-ness help build the store's reputation and set the stage for future sales
4. *Autonomy.* The salespeople were
   a. Encouraged to develop and use their own unique approach and sales pitch
   b. Allowed freedom to select their own break and lunch times
   c. Encouraged to make suggestions for changes in all phases of the policy and operations
5. *Feedback from the job itself.* Salespeople were
   a. Encouraged to keep personal records of their own sales volume
   b. Encouraged to keep a sales/customer ratio
   c. Reminded that establishing a good rapport with customers is also a success; they were told that if the potential customer leaves with a good feeling about the store and its employees, the salesperson has been successful
6. *Feedback from agents.* Salespeople were encouraged to
   a. Observe and help each other with techniques of selling
   b. Seek out information from their boss and relevant departments on all phases of their jobs
   c. Invite customer reactions and thoughts concerning merchandise, service, and so forth

Both the salespeople's functional (conversing with customers, showing merchandise, handling returns, and so forth) and dysfunctional (socializing with coworkers or visi-tors, idly standing around, being gone for no legitimate reason) performance behaviors moved in the desired directions, and a subanalysis also indicated they were more satis-fied. A control group of salespeople, with everything else the same except that they did not have their jobs redesigned, showed no change in their performance behaviors. Thus, this study provided evidence that the job characteristics approach can be practically ap-plied with desirable performance and satisfaction results.[22] Such well-known companies as 3M, AT&T, Xerox, and Motorola are also among those that have actually implemented job design changes in accordance with the job characteristics model.[23]

Engagement, Disengagement, and Social Information Processing

A theoretical approach to untangling the relationship between the design of a job and its subsequent impact on employee satisfaction and performance is concerned with the times when personal engagement and disengagement occur while on the job. William Kahn notes that most previous views of job design take what is essentially a static view (a still photo, no change or movement) of dynamic organizational involvements (a mo-tion picture, where things are changing and moving).[24] That is, most previous theory building and research suggests that employees are fairly constant in how involved they are in their jobs, how committed they are to their organizations, and/or how alienated they have become while at work.[25] Instead, it is more realistic to assume that reactions to work ebb and flow and are constantly changing. People have days when they are more tuned into tasks and times when they are much more distant or removed from what is going on.

Personal engagement occurs when organizational members place themselves in the role physically, cognitively, and emotionally during role (job) performance.[26] In a study involved with counselors at a youth camp compared to members of an architec-tural firm, Kahn was able to describe circumstances in which personal engagement was quite high—physically, cognitively and emotionally. One camp counselor reported high engagement when teaching a high-skill scuba class, placing himself physically (diving), cognitively (teaching while looking for ideal diving conditions), and emotionally (explaining the wonders of the ocean while worrying about the safety of the divers) into the task. An architectural contractor reported the same feelings physically by "flying around the office" working on the task, cognitively by seeking methods to improve the design of the project, and emotionally by providing a supportive, team-building envi-ronment for others. Simply stated, in both instances these employees were able to fully engage themselves into their jobs.

Three psychological conditions enhance the likelihood that employees will be-come engaged in their job. These conditions are perceived meaningfulness, safety, and availability. Psychological meaningfulness is a feeling that one is receiving a return on investment from one's self from physical, cognitive, and emotional energy. *Meaningful-ness* is the experience that a task is worthwhile, useful, and/or valuable. Psychological *safety* is present when a worker is able to show or employ one's self without fear of negative consequences to self-image, status, and/or a career. Safety and trust of others are built in situations that are predictable, consistent, clear, and nonthreatening. Psycho-logical *availability* means the individual has the sense that sufficient personal physical, emotional, and cognitive resources are available to engage in a particular moment. Items that reduce psychological availability included depletion of physical energy, per-sonal insecurity, and the intrusion of an outside life (personal problems taking away from energy that could be given to the job). Positive self-in-role experiences would heighten the employment experience from a personal emotional standpoint. Further stronger personal engagement logically results in greater effort and intensity on the job, which makes it a "win-win" situation for the employee and the organization.

Psychological disengagement may be best summarized by the phrase merely "go-ing through the motions" while at work. In other words, disengagement occurs in situa-tions where the individual psychologically uncouples from the job, withdrawing in order to defend one's self physically, cognitively, and emotionally during a role performance. Personal disengagement appears to be a type of defense mechanism, in which the employee's actions are robotic, burned out, apathetic, detached, and effortless.[27] People who are at a given moment personally disengaged are emotionally distant, hiding what they think and feel to the point of stifling any sense of energy or creativity that might be given to the job. Many of the dissatisfiers described by Herzberg in Chapter 8 (poor pay and working conditions, oppressive supervision) are candidates for creating disengagement.

Importantly, it should be noted that degrees of engagement and disengagement rise and fall over time while on the same job. Also, future research may investigate cir-cumstances under which engagement is a disadvantage to the organization. Two possi-bilities include employees who are too intense and make life miserable for others around them or the salesperson who becomes highly engaged while driving down the highway talking on a cell phone. This individual is much more likely to become in-volved in a traffic accident. Further, key role shapers such as a supervisor may influence the circumstances under which an employee remains engaged or becomes disengaged from a task or job. Negative interactions with a supervisor are strong candidates to form periods of disengagement.

Kahn's analysis of engagement relies heavily on the individual becoming socially involved with coworkers and clients. In other words, degrees of in-the-role involvement are socially constructed. This view draws from the earlier work on the social information processing (SIP) perspective of job design.[28] From a *social information processing* perspective, three major causes of employee perceptions, attitudes, and behaviors on the job are:

1. Cognitive perceptions of the real task environment
2. Past actions, reinforcements received, and learning experiences
3. The information provided in the immediate social context

Salancik and Pfeffer, who developed the SIP perspective many years ago, argue that the third point deserves the most weight. Note that it is the "immediate" social context that influences the individual, in the same sense that personal engagement and disengagement might be affected by the prevailing situation. Kahn's description of engagement includes dimensions of social systems, interpersonal relationships, group and intergroup dynamics, and interactions with supervisors. Therefore, both engagement theory and SIP suggest that social information and social cues have major influences on employees' perceptions of and reactions to their jobs.

The SIP model of job design has generated considerable research over the years.[29] As with other models, results have been mixed.[30] Some studies support the notion that social cues, such as negative and positive coworker comments, affect perceptions of jobs. It would not be surprising to find that these social cues also help define the terms of engagement and disengagement at any given time, especially when combined with objective job characteristics such as found in the Hackman and Oldham model.[31]

QUALITY OF WORK LIFE, SOCIOTECHNICAL DESIGN AND HPWPs

So far, the discussion of job design has revolved mainly around job enrichment, job characteristics, engagement, and social information processing. The concern for quality of work life (QWL) and the accompanying sociotechnical approach to job design and high-performance work practices (HPWPs) take a more macro perspective.

Quality of Work Life (QWL)

The quality of work life (QWL) perspective does not advocate one particular job design technique. Instead, QWL is more concerned with the overall work climate or culture. *QWL* may be described as a concern about the impact of work on people and organizational effectiveness combined with an emphasis on participation in problem solving and decision making.[32] There is considerable evidence that employees who are truly empowered and work within a participatory, problem-solving framework are more committed to both the organization and, if they are union members, to the union.[33]

The overriding purpose of a QWL program is to change and improve the work climate so that the interface of people, technology, and the organization makes for a more favorable work experience and desired outcomes. There is still debate as to how this is actually accomplished and what is meant by *quality* in QLW (quality could be better pay or it could be feeling more engaged, as per the previous section). Still, there are several applications that have been undertaken. In the area of human resource management, job sharing, flextime, and four-day–10-hour workweeks are examples of attempts to improve the quality of work experience. In organizational behavior, the sociotechnical approach and the more recent high-performance work practices (HPWPs) approach deserve specific attention.

Sociotechnical Design

The sociotechnical approach to job design was made popular a number of years ago by the experiences of the Swedish Saab and Volvo automobile plants. Volvo CEO Pehr Gyllenhammer led the sociotechnical changes in his firm after becoming convinced that the company was experiencing severe absenteeism and turnover related to a conflict between the values of workers, who wanted more meaningful jobs, and the technological work processes needed to build cars efficiently.

The changes made at Volvo reflected more natural work modules, which were served by autonomous work groups who assigned and inspected their own work. Each member of the group worked toward the same group goals, and all were paid the same except the leader. After some initial smaller programs, an entire plant utilized the new approach. Soon after, turnover and absenteeism were reduced, and workers reported an improved quality of work life. Top management believed the transformation was successful, even though no systematic analysis of results was performed. Company leaders reported "false starts, errors, outright failures, and periodically, brilliant breakthroughs" at Volvo.[34] Objectively, the fact remains that the new plant experienced the lowest assembly costs of all of Volvo's facilities.

Although the Volvo project is the most famous historically, some companies in the United States also pioneered sociotechnical approaches. One widely reported example took place at the General Foods plant in Topeka, Kansas. The plant made Gaines pet food and was redesigned to accommodate shared responsibility, autonomous work groups, and a group coach rather than supervisor. Status symbols such as parking privileges were also abolished.

Initial results at the General Foods plant were very favorable. Employees expressed positive work attitudes, and management noted that fewer workers were needed to run the operation. Rejects dipped to way below industry norms, resulting in large cost savings. Unfortunately, soon the success began to erode. Some managers at the plant were openly hostile to the plan, because it undermined their authority. Over time the program was eventually dropped.

More recent approaches to the sociotechnical approach involve the use of autonomous, self-managed teams. Early applications were made at Proctor & Gamble, Digital Equipment, and TRW. Later the influence of quality circles from Japan led other companies to try teams in their sociotechnical initiative. Most combined autonomy with empowerment strategies, including General Mills, FedEx, 3M, and Hewlett-Packard. Many experienced improved productivity as well as costs savings.[35] The Japanese model of quality circles never caught on in the United States, and the team emphasis covered in Chapter 14 has emerged and is considered more of what has become known as a HPWP rather than a sociotechnical approach or technique.

High-Performance Work Practices (HPWPs)

The High Performance Work Practices (HPWPs) (sometimes the term *system* is used instead of *practice*) are designed to improve an organization's financial and operational performance.[36] HPWPs' methods are probably the most inclusive of all job design methods described thus far. Although there are many definitions, a recent comprehensive review concluded that the best definition is "an organization system that continually aligns its strategy, goals, objectives, and internal operations with the demands of its external environment to maximize organizational performance."[37] The primary emphasis of an HPWP is to achieve a fit between people, technology, information, and work. There must be a further match in which the firm's internal environment meshes and fits with the demands of the external environment, including supporting customer needs and expectations.[38]

As the definitions suggest, HPWPs must become a way of thinking about people, work, and performance. In this vein, a total organizational culture must be devised, highlighting variables including a focus on the organization's strategy, a systematic organizational design, encouragement of innovation, measures of internal and external customer service, cooperation, teamwork, and a new organizational value system. In addition, this culture supporting HPWPs incorporates higher levels of open communication and trust, and leaders must be focused on both employees and the organization's needs. Recent analyses have found that HPWPs are indeed positively related with both financial and operational performance.[39]

There are several key aspects of HPWPs that are especially relevant to organizational behavior research, theory building, and practice. First, the approach expands understanding of the "fit" concept between people and technology to include other elements of the work experience, notably the organization's culture, which may be related to the quality of work life. Second, this approach highlights empowerment in addition to team-based and nonfinancial rewards. Further, employees are to be rewarded for their specific competencies and for learning. The HPWPs' perspective also emphasizes the disadvantages associated with people doing jobs that do not match their competencies. For instance, many organizations have recently experienced the problem of managers performing too many low-level activities, which is sometimes called "scut work." This misallocation of time reduces the emphasis on the strategic focus that should be engaging senior and middle managers.[40]

Most importantly, perhaps, is that HPWPs insist on effective human resource management selection and evaluation practices. This includes multiple selectors and effective training of selectors (e.g., as found in an assessment center) and innovative performance evaluations and ways to provide feedback (e.g., 360-degree feedback systems as discussed in Chapter 10). The goal of HPWPs is to go beyond simply trying to fit employees with existing technological structures within the organization. In addition, the fit should exist with organizational processes, information flows, and managerial operations.

One body of organizational behavior literature that may be integrated into the HPWPs' literature is that associated with realistic job previews (RJPs). One recent meta-analysis revealed that effective RJPs were related to higher performance as well as to lower attrition from the recruitment process, initial job expectations, voluntary turnover, and all turnover.[41] This bodes well for the operational and financial goals associated with HPWPs, as RJPs may lead to the required "fit" more often.

Further, the new workplace seems to be especially well suited to HPWPs. As Chapters 2 and 4 indicated, advanced information technologies including websites, e-mail, teleconferencing, digital networks, and e-business mean that traditional organizational structures and technologies are being reconfigured. In this new environment, organizations become boundaryless for not only information flows, but also for human interaction. Individual employees may go beyond traditional boundaries to conduct research, receive instructions, cooperate with friends and peers within and outside an industry or country, and develop innovations. The natures of many "jobs" have changed or become "nonjobs," from something relatively static to a constantly emerging new form in which learning or knowledge acquisition and sharing must be supplemented with new skills and also emotional intelligence and self-efficacy (see Chapter 9) to accept and effectively apply needed concepts, processes, and practices. Consequently, the emphasis on innovation and managerial efforts to select for best fit, reward competencies, develop employees, and set quality performance targets, as suggested by the HPWPs' literature, matches well with the new information technology-driven workplace.[42]

Finally, the HPWPs' approach may help explain certain international organizational behavior concerns. For example, one recent study conducted in the former Soviet Union suggests that the major remedies for the struggles encountered by many members of the Commonwealth of Independent States (CIS) in the transition to market-based economies may be, in part, culturally based.[43] Specifically, in Russia, where economic woes continue more than 10 years after the fall of communism, there are several cultural dimensions that need to be recognized in order to understand the typical Russian workplace environment. Specifically, the Russian culture is characterized as being high in "particularism," which is the belief that circumstances dictate how ideas and practices should be applied (see Chapter 2). In other words, relationships and trust are more important than rules. Trompenaars, who investigated the nature of the CIS culture, concluded that most managers and entrepreneurs (mostly younger people) in the postcommunist cultures are high on individualism, seeking to care for themselves and their immediate families and expecting others to do the same.[44] Russians also tend to be more emotional and work within a diffuse culture in which public and private space are deemed similar, so that individuals are inclined to guard public space carefully. And finally, the managerial class in Russia tends to be higher in the culture dimension called ascription, where status is derived from age, gender, and social connections rather than achievements.

Because of these cultural dimensions, several of the variables from HPWPs may have a good fit with the Russian situation and achieve positive results. Specific HPWPs that would seem to be applicable to the Russian workplace include multisource (360-degree) feedback, pay for performance, self-managing work teams, and employee empowerment.[45] When properly administered to reflect the cultural dimensions of CIS states, the culture of the organization may be aligned to fit with the culture of the region to enhance human resource performance.

The HPWPs' approach narrows down for effective practice what began as some very broad ideas regarding the quality of work life. By incorporating concepts associated with QWL and sociotechnical approaches, self-managed work teams, empowerment, and culture (both country and organizational) into an overall system, future theory building and research can be value adding. Studies can be devised to investigate conditions under which all of these elements have been effectively incorporated into a system that accounts for the smallest element (the job design) within the context of an organization and its environment. The other major motivational technique that is not only very popular, but through sophisticated basic and applied research has been shown to improve individual and organizational performance, is goal setting.

GOAL SETTING

Goal achievement is a factor that influences the success levels of individual employees, departments and business units, and the overall organization. A goal is a performance target that an individual or group seeks to accomplish at work. Goal setting is the process of motivating employees by establishing effective and meaningful performance targets. It is often given as an example of how the field of organizational behavior should progress from a sound theoretical foundation to sophisticated research to the actual application of more effective management practice.

There has been considerable theoretical development of goal setting, coming mainly from the cognitively based work of Edwin Locke and his colleagues. To test the theory, there has been considerable research in both laboratory and field settings on the various facets of goal setting. Finally, and important to an applied field such as organizational behavior, goal setting has become an effective tool for the practice of human resource management and an overall performance system approach.

Theoretical Background of Goal Setting

A 1968 paper by Locke is usually considered to be the seminal work on a theory of goal setting.[46] He suggests that goal-setting theory really goes back to scientific management at the turn of the century. Locke credits its first exponent, Frederick W. Taylor, with being the "father of employee motivation theory,"[47] and he says that Taylor's use "of tasks was a forerunner of modern-day goal setting."[48]

Although Locke argues that expectancy theories of work motivation (see Chapter 8) originally ignored goal setting and were nothing more than "cognitive hedonism,"[49] his theoretical formulation for goal setting is very similar. He basically accepts the purposefulness of behavior, which comes out of Tolman's pioneering cognitive theorizing, and the importance of values, or valence, and consequences. Thus, as in the expectancy theories of work motivation, *values and value judgments,* which are defined as the things the individual acts on to gain and/or to keep, are important cognitive determinants of behavior. Emotions or desires are the ways the person experiences these values. In addition to values, *intentions* or *goals* play an important role as cognitive determinants of behavior. It is here, of course, where Locke's theory of goal setting goes beyond expectancy theories of work motivation, because people strive to attain goals in order to satisfy their emotions and desires. Goals provide a directional nature to people's behavior and guide their thoughts and actions to one outcome rather than another. The individual then responds and performs according to these intentions or goals, even if the goals are not attained. Consequences, feedback, or reinforcement are the result of these responses.

Major Dimensions of Goal-Setting Theory.   Figure 15.4 summarizes the goal-setting theory. Meta-analysis and a recent review provides support for the theory.[50] A number

FIGURE 15.4
Locke's goal-setting theory of work motivation.

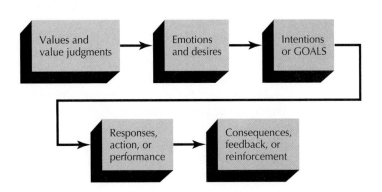

of years ago a survey of scholars in the field of organizational behavior was conducted to rate 15 major work-motivation theories on the criteria of scientific validity and practical usefulness. Goal-setting theory was ranked first in validity and second in practical usefulness.[51]

As previously noted, except for the concept of intentions or goals, Locke's theory is very similar to the other process theories (most notably the expectancy theories). In particular, recent refinements of goal theory involving difficulty[52] and overall goal-setting research[53] use the concepts of expectancy, valence, and instrumentality, as defined in Chapter 8. Also, attribution theory, as discussed in Chapter 6, has been applied to goal setting.[54] Although the expectancy theories are frequently used as a theoretical foundation for goal setting, Locke carefully points out that goal setting is not the only, or necessarily the most important, concept of work motivation. He notes that the concepts of need and value are the more fundamental concepts of work motivation and are, along with the person's knowledge and premises, what determine goals.[55]

Refinements of Goal-Setting Theory. Unlike many other theorists, Locke is continually refining and developing his theory. Recently he has given attention to the role that commitment plays in the theory. He recognized from the beginning that if there is no commitment to goals, goal setting will not work. However, to clarify some of the confusion surrounding its use, Locke and his colleagues defined commitment as "one's attachment to or determination to reach a goal, regardless of the goal's origin" and developed a cognitive model to explan the process.[56] Now it is recognized that commitment is a moderator of the goal–performance relationship,[57] and a meta-analysis found that goal commitment significantly affects goal achievement.[58]

Locke is an ardent supporter of the cognitive interpretation of behavior and is an outspoken critic of other theories, for he says that goal setting is really the underlying explanation for the other theories—whether that be Vroom's VIE theory, Maslow's or Herzberg's motivation theories, or, especially, operant-based behaviorism.[59]

Although Locke is critical of operant-based behaviorism as being too mechanistic, he is supportive of Bandura's expanded social cognitive theory[60] as being compatible with goal-setting theory. As pointed out in Chapter 1, this social cognitive theory is the framework and conceptual model for this text. Locke recognizes the comprehensive nature of social cognitive theory. In particular, he feels that social cognitive theory not only includes goal setting but adds the important dimensions of role modeling, with significant effects on goal choice and goal commitment as well as self-efficacy, which affects goal choice, goal commitment, and response to feedback.[61]

Research on the Impact of Goal Setting

Locke's theory has generated considerable research. In particular, a series of laboratory studies by Locke and his colleagues and a series of field studies by Locke's associate Gary Latham and other colleagues have been carried out to test the linkage between goal setting and performance.[62] Over the past decade, numerous studies have been conducted to refine and extend goal-setting theory and practice. The following sections briefly summarize this work.

The Importance of Specific Goals. Specific goals have been found to be more effective than vague or general goals, such as "do your best," as well as no goals at all. Specific goals result in higher levels of performance.[63] For instance, salespeople should have goals in dollar amounts or units of volume, production departments should have targeted and defined goals in terms of numbers, percentages and dates, and all other departments should incorporate measurable objectives or specific metrics and dates rather than things such as "try as hard as you can" or "try to do better than last year."

The Importance of Difficult and Challenging Goals.   Besides clearly stated goals, performance targets should also be challenging rather than easy or routine. At the same time, goals should be reachable and not so difficult that pursing them becomes frustrating. The accompanying OB in Action: Using Stretch Goals gives some practical guidelines.

Recent research indicates some moderators of the relationship between goal difficulty and subsequent performance. Two forms of feedback can enhance goal achievement: (1) process feedback and (2) outcome feedback. Process feedback is related to information as to how the individual or unit is proceeding in attempting to reach the goal, whereas outcome feedback is information related to and stated in terms of the actual

---

APPLICATION EXAMPLE

Using Stretch Goals

Goal setting is widely recognized as a technique to improve performance. However, there are a number of problems associated with the indiscriminate use of ambitious goals. Steven Kerr, a noted organizational behavior researcher and now Chief Learning Officer for General Electric who is interviewed to start this chapter, has noted that many organizations fail to effectively use what can be called "stretch goals." The goals are set very high, but the needed support to accomplish them is often missing. For example, top management may ask their people to increase output by 25 percent but fail to provide them with the knowledge, tools, and means to reach such ambitious goals. As a result, the only way that people can meet these new and demanding challenges is by working longer—often on their own time. In fact, notes Kerr, everywhere in America people are working evenings and weekends in order to meet the goals that the organization has set for them.

This is not necessary, however, if the enterprise carefully examines what needs to be done and how it has to occur. Kerr recommends three rules that can help organizations create stretch goals and reach them without exhausting and burning out their human resources. These include (1) do not set goals that overly stress people; (2) if goals require people to stretch, do not punish them if they fail; and (3) if they are being asked to do things that they have never done before, give them whatever tools and help are available.

How should goals be set? Kerr believes that easy goals are too simple and do not improve performance and that difficult goals may be *so* difficult that people cannot attain them—so they give up. Stretch goals force them to go beyond what they are accustomed to doing, and thus improve performance, but, importantly, they are also attainable. At the same time, the organization has to be willing to reward the personnel for attaining the stretch goals. How can this be done? One way is with money. Financial rewards are very direct and encourage individuals to continue their efforts. However, if management decide that they will give back to those involved one-third of the performance gain (i.e., gainsharing), they must stick to this and not back down when big gains are realized. If organizations follow these simple suggestions of using stretch goals and pay for performance, they can increase their productivity and employees can be challenged and rewarded for their efforts.

goal itself.[64] Other researchers have investigated the role that competition plays in moderating the goal difficulty–performance relationship, but results have been mixed. One study revealed that the lack of competition combined with difficult goals led to higher performance, whereas another found no effects related to competition.[65]

In still another research stream, perceived goal difficulty had negative effects on self-reports of job performance. In other words, an employee who thought a job was highly difficult reported performing at a lower level. However, goal difficulty, when combined with goal clarity, led to increased reports of effort, which in turn led to more positive self-reports of performance in the same study.[66]

Goal Acceptance, Participation, and Commitment.   Specific goals are most likely to affect performance when employees accept and are committed to them. This ownership and acceptance of goals are best accomplished through a participative process.[67] Self-commitment can be given to assigned goals as well as to personal or self-set goals, especially when goals are equivocal. Commitment tends to run higher when goals are specific as opposed to general or broad. Monetary incentives can also increase commitment to goals if the goals are perceived as being achievable.[68]

Self-efficacy and Goals.   As was given detailed attention in Chapter 9, self-efficacy is the perception or belief of the individual that he or she can successfully accomplish a specific task and is associated with goal commitment.[69] People exhibiting higher levels of self-efficacy tend to set more challenging personal goals and are more likely to achieve them, and commitment to self-set personal goals is normally also higher than commitment to goals set by others (imposed goals).[70] Self-efficacy is also related to imposed goals. Some individuals may reject imposed goals, but if they have self-efficacy still maintain high personal goals. Further, if the imposed goal is impossible, personal goals and self-efficacy may be reduced, along with performance.[71]

Objective and Timely Feedback.   Studies have also found objective and timely feedback is preferable to no feedback and, as noted earlier, can be related to the process used to achieve a goal or the content (degree of achievement) of the goal. It is probably fair to say that feedback is a necessary but not sufficient condition for successful application of goal setting.[72] In one recent research study it was found that daily feedback had positive influences on both productivity and employee satisfaction.[73]

Other Moderators in Goal Setting.   Although the practical guidelines from goal-setting theory and research are probably as direct as any in the entire field of organizational behavior, there are still some moderating variables that should be recognized in the relationship between goal setting and performance, and there are some contradictory findings.[74] For example, a study by Latham and Saari revealed that a supportive management style had an important moderating effect, and that, contrary to results in previous studies, specific goals did not lead to better performance than a generalized goal such as "do your best."[75] However, another study did yield a significant relationship between goal levels and performance.[76] Leader style may also affect goal commitment. Recent research revealed that an interaction between leader-member exchange and goal commitment accounted for a significant amount of variance in the performance level of a sales force.[77] Another analysis indicated that there are also some unexplored areas, such as the distinction between quantity and quality goals[78] and task complexity,[79] that may limit and make the application of goal setting more complex.

A Word of Caution Regarding Goal Setting.   In the words of Ambrose and Kulik, who have made a recent comprehensive review of goal-setting research, there are boundary conditions that surround the relationships between goal setting and perform- ance that should be carefully noted for effective application.[80] First, one study noted that goals can narrow an individual's focus to perform only behaviors directly associ- ated with goal attainment, at the cost of other desirable behaviors. This type of tunnel vision was revealed in a study in which students were given a specific goal of correct- ing the grammar on a recruiting brochure. They did so at the expense of improving the content of the brochure. Those with a more general goal (e.g., make it better) worked on both the content and the grammar.[81] Furthermore, difficult goals increases the level of risk managers and employees are willing to take, and this increase may be counter- productive.[82] Also, a study found that goals inhibited subjects from helping others who were requesting assistance, which has implications for teamwork.[83] Other studies have found that difficult goals may lead to stress, put a perceptual ceiling on performance, cause the employees to ignore nongoal areas, and encourage short-range thinking, dis- honesty, or cheating.[84] However, Locke and Latham do provide specific guidelines of how these potential pitfalls can be overcome by better communication, rewards, and setting examples.[85] On balance, there has been impressive support for the positive im- pact of setting specific, difficult goals that are accepted and of providing feedback on progress toward goals.

Other Performance Management Techniques Associated with Goal Setting

Much of the discussion so far has been directly concerned with goal-setting theory, re- search findings and application for performance improvement of an individual manager or work unit. However, there are also other performance management techniques related to goal setting. One is *benchmarking,* which is a form of goal setting, though it is meant to be more inclusive and is often portrayed as part of total quality management. *Benchmarking* is the process of comparing work and service methods against the best practices and outcomes for the purpose of identifying changes stated as specific goals that will result in higher-quality output. Importantly, benchmarking incorporates the use of goal setting to set targets that are pursued, identified, and then used as the basis for future action. The benchmarking process involves looking both inside and outside the organization for ways of improving performance.

Benchmarking has several elements that are similar to the high-performance work practices (HPWPs) described earlier in the chapter. Both are integrative approaches designed to incorporate performance management techniques into the managerial system. In HPWPs, the emphasis is more focused on human resource management for performance improvement. With benchmarking, the idea is to en- able the organization to learn from others and then to formulate specific change goals based on procedures and work assignments that have been observed in world- class organizations. Companies that have effectively used benchmarking include IBM and Magnavox. IBM benchmarked its efforts in comparison to Xerox, Motorola, 3M, Hewlett-Packard, and some Japanese firms that utilized just-in-time inventory controls.[86] Magnavox benchmarked a series of HR practices, which they turned into 14 training measures that are now commonly called metrics, again with strong evidence of success.[87]

A *stretch target* or goal, already mentioned, is another currently popular tech- nique associated with goal setting. *Stretch targets* may be defined as objectives or goals that force organizations to significantly alter their processes in ways that involve a whole new paradigm of operations.[88] In a manner similar to benchmarking, stretch targets seek to integrate and align the internal operation and culture with external best practices. Examples of stretch targets include enhancing motivation, performance, and creative decision making through specific numbers, percentages and dates.

One area of application associated with goal setting with international implications is that of *goal source.* Questions remain as to how to implement goal-setting programs across cultures. During a goal-setting program, subordinates often receive information from a supervisor or leader. If that leader (the goal source) is distrusted, the message may be rejected. If the leader or goal source is trusted, goal acceptance and commitment and performance may be higher. One recent study conducted in England confirmed that English workers, who were more likely to trust a shop steward than a supervisor due to several key historical and cultural reasons, did indeed accept goals and perform at higher rates when the steward helped deliver the goals.[89] This goal source impact applied in a cross-cultural environment would suggest that, depending on cultural dimensions such as power distance (discussed in Chapter 2), home country nationals involved in the goal setting process may have more of an impact on home country employees than would expatriates or those from another country home office.

The Application of Goal Setting to Organizational System Performance

In addition to the impact of goal setting on individual and work unit performance through the techniques discussed so far, goal setting is also the basis for the traditionally used management-by-objectives, or MBO, approach to planning, control, personnel appraisal, and overall system performance. However, MBO has been around for many years and thus preceded much of the theory and research on goal setting per se. Management by objectives is usually attributed to the well-known management writer and consultant Peter Drucker, who coined the term and suggested that a systematic approach to setting of objectives and appraising by results would lead to improved organizational performance and employee satisfaction. Today, the term *MBO* may no longer be used. Instead, MBO has evolved into an overall systems performance approach using goal setting and appraisal by results. For example, Locke and Latham noted that "MBO can be viewed as goal setting applied to the macro or organizational level."[90]

The application of goal setting and appraisal by results of overall organizational systems generally follows the series of systematic steps outlined in Figure 15.5. As shown, once the overall objectives have been set and the organization is developed to the point of accommodating the performance system, individual objectives are set. These individual objectives are determined by each manager–subordinate pair, starting at the top and going down as far as the system is to be implemented. The scenario for this process would be something like the following: The boss would contact each of his or her subordinates and say:

> As you know, we have completed our system performance improvement orientation and development program, and it is now time to set individual objectives. I would like you to develop by next Tuesday a proposed set of objectives for your area of responsibility. Remember that your set of objectives should be in line with the organization's overall objectives developed by the top management team, which you have a copy of, and should be able to contribute to the objectives that you interact with, namely, my objectives, the other units' objectives on your same level, and your subordinates' objectives. Your objectives should be stated in quantifiable, measurable terms and should have a target date. I will also

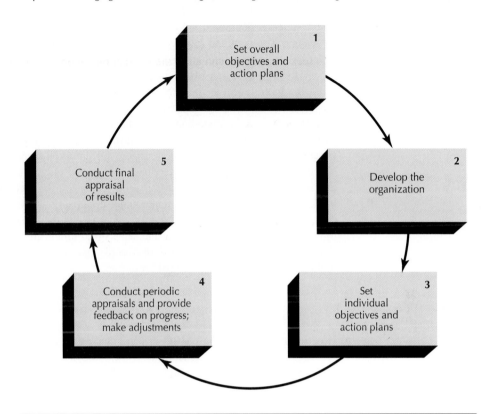

FIGURE 15.5
The application of goal setting (or MBO) to system performance.

have some suggestions that I think should be given top priority for your area of responsibility. We will sit down and have an open give-and-take session until we reach a *mutually* agreeable set of objectives for your area of responsibility.

In line with the goal-setting research, these objectives, as indicated above, should be specific, difficult, owned, and accepted. Like the overall objectives, this set of individual objectives should also be accompanied by action plans developed to spell out how the objectives are to be specifically accomplished.

Although the goal-setting dimension is most closely associated with this approach to system performance, as shown in Figure 15.5, feedback and appraisal by results also play an important role. Individuals will be given feedback and will be appraised on the basis of how they perform in accordance with the objectives that are set. This feedback and appraisal process takes place on both a periodic (at least every quarter in most systems) and an annual basis. The appraisal sessions attempt to be diagnostic rather than purely evaluative. This means simply that the subordinate's manager assesses the reasons why objectives were either attained or not attained, rather than giving punishments or rewards for failure or success in meeting objectives.

Periodic reviews are conducted in order to provide feedback and evaluate progress toward the attainment of objectives. They provide the opportunity to make the necessary changes in objectives. Every organization is operating in such a dynamic environment that objectives set at the beginning of the period (usually the fiscal year) may be rendered obsolete in a few months because of changing conditions. Priorities and conditions are constantly changing; these must be monitored in the periodic review sessions, and the needed changes must be made. Constant revision of the individual objectives and, to a lesser degree, of the overall objectives creates a living system that is adaptable to change. At the annual review session, an overall diagnosis and evaluation is made according to results attained, and the system starts over again.

The early research results on MBO-type performance systems were mixed.[91] However, more recent analyses conclude that overall goal-setting systems have a slightly positive effect on employee satisfaction, but a much larger, but still modest, effect on performance,[92] and a meta-analysis (details found in the principles that follow) on MBO found that 68 out of 70 studies showed productivity gains.[93] Successful MBO programs are the result of the same processes that are linked to goal-setting theory—specific goals and target dates, feedback, participative decision making, commitment, and acceptance. Of these, the participation dimension for successful MBO is especially vital. When Chevron needed to make major organizational changes in a very short period of time, the management team relied on what they termed "direct participation" to get things done quickly and, at the same time, solicit high employee involvement.[94] The bonding of individual goals with overall organizational objectives and processes is highlighted in this successful MBO program.

Impact on the Psychological Contract

Goal setting in general and MBO in particular create psychological contracts with employees. In any exchange situation at work, there are both formal and informal expectations regarding what is given and, especially in relation to the new perspective of *human capital* discussed in the introductory chapters, what should be received in return. Imposing new goals may violate existing views of what is present in the psychological contract, creating either resistance to the program or a renegotiation of the rewards to be received. Note that any linkage between goals and performance has a psychological contract implied in the relationship. Organizations that routinely demand higher performances yet fail to respond with rewards to their human capital can expect increasingly negative responses and reactions.[95]

A number of other instances of contract violations may inhibit the success rates of goal setting and MBO. These violations include restructuring, downsizing, increased reliance on temporary workers, and globalization. Goal setting in part constructs a social role at work that is intertwined with other elements of a psychological contract. Consequently, successful applications of goal-setting programs must account for how resulting processes will affect existing psychological contracts of employees.[96]

Summary

This chapter deals with two of the most important application areas that have emerged for high-performance organizations. The first part examines job design. Although the concern for designing jobs goes back to the scientific management movement at the turn of the twentieth century, the recent concern for human resource management as a competitive advantage has led to renewed interest in, and research on, job design. The older job engineering and job enlargement and rotation approaches have given way to first a job enrichment approach and then a job characteristics approach that relates to psychological or motivational states leading to improved employee satisfaction and performance. Characteristics such as skill variety, task identity, task significance, autonomy, and feedback have been found by research to be related to employee satisfaction and quality of work. But the way employees perceive these characteristics and the importance of moderating variables such as growth-need strength are being shown to have an important impact on the relationship between job scope and job satisfaction and employee performance. Also, theoretically based approaches such as engagement and social information processing (SIPA) have emerged to account for social effects. Increased attention is being given to the impact of a more macrooriented perspective, and incorporating QWL concerns is the sociotechnical approach to job design. Sociotechnical projects at Volvo in Sweden and at General Foods and other companies in this country have important historical significance. There has been a surge of interest in self-managed teams and other high-performance work practices (HPWPs) as companies try to use HRM-based approaches to meet their competitive problems. These HPWPs' applications have reportedly been very successful. Yet, as is true of the other techniques discussed in this text, more systematic research is needed for the future.

The last part of the chapter deals with the theory, research, and applications of goal setting. Basing his approach on a cognitive perspective, Locke has developed a goal-setting theory of motivation. This theory emphasizes the important relationship between goals and performance. Laboratory and field studies have generally verified this relationship. In particular, the most effective performance seems to result when specific, difficult goals are accepted and when feedback on progress and results is provided. An extension and systematic application of the goal-setting approach are benchmarking, stretch targets, and MBO, which has evolved into a total performance system approach with a positive, but modest, impact on satisfaction and performance. The goal setting and other performance-enhancing approaches may have an overlooked impact on the psychological contract. To be successful, the human capital must also benefit and receive a return (reward).

ENDING WITH META-ANALYTIC RESEARCH FINDINGS

OB PRINCIPLE: The use of job enrichment/redesign strategies can reduce employee turnover.

Meta-Analysis Results: [20 studies; 6,492 participants; $d = .35$] *On average, there is a **60 percent probability** that organizations that implement job enrichment/redesign techniques will experience less turnover than organizations that do not use such techniques.* Further analysis indicated no moderators of the relationship between job enrichment and turnover.

Conclusion: Excessive turnover is very costly to organizations in terms of lost productivity, increased training time, increased recruitment and selection time, lost work efficiency, and other indirect costs such as customer service and commitment. Unfortunately, companies trying to reduce turnover are often left with little practical guidance as to how to meet this challenge. Although raising salaries, implementing orientation programs, utilizing exit interviews, establishing training programs, and improving selection do help to reduce turnover, job enrichment/redesign may be an effective, but often overlooked, strategy for reducing turnover. As you have learned in this chapter, job enrichment/redesign strategies include vertical loading or increasing the depth of a job by adding personal responsibility for employees' own work. This may involve planning, organizing, controlling, and evaluating a job. A contingency approach is necessary because jobs vary in the degree to which they can be easily enriched or redesigned and not all people will respond favorably to increased responsibilities. However, enriching jobs may enhance employees' motivation, satisfaction, performance, and what this principle states—retention.

Source: Adapted from Glenn M. McEvoy and Wayne F. Cascio, "Strategies for Reducing Turnover: A Meta-Analysis," *Journal of Applied Psychology,* Vol. 70, No. 2, 1985, pp. 342–353.

OB PRINCIPLE: The more employees perceive their work to be designed according to the characteristics in the job characteristics model (JCM), the more motivated and satisfied they will be.

Meta-Analysis Results: [72 studies; over 18,000 participants; $d = 1.6$] *On average, there is an **87 percent probability** that employees who perceive the characteristics found in the job characteristics model (JCM) to be high, the higher their internal work motivation and overall job satisfaction will be compared to those who do not perceive these job characteristics.* Further analysis indicated that the critical psychological states of the JCM played a mediating role between job characteristics and outcomes.

Conclusion: The well-researched job characteristics model posits that the five core job dimensions (task identity, task significance, skill variety, feedback, and autonomy) designed into a job influence the critical psychological states of experienced meaningfulness, knowledge of results, and experienced responsibility, which in turn will affect work outcomes. The five job characteristics are measured by the perceptions of the jobholder and are combined into a single index called a motivating potential score (MPS). This MPS reflects the overall potential the job has to influence the employee's motivation and satisfaction. Overall, the job characteristics model represents a way to predict employee motivation and satisfaction and hopefully organizational outcomes such as quality of work and absenteeism/turnover.

Source: Adapted from Yitzhak Fried and Gerald R. Ferris, "The Validity of the Job Characteristics Model: A Review and Meta-Analysis," *Personnel Psychology,* Vol. 40, 1987, pp. 287–322.

OB PRINCIPLE: Difficult, specific task goals will lead to a higher level of performance than routine, general goals such as "do your best."

Meta-Analysis Results: [Over 50 studies; over 5,800 participants; d range = .44 to .58] *On average, there is a **62 to 66 percent probability** that difficult and specific goals (if accepted) will lead to higher levels of task performance than easy or general "do-your-best" goals.* The setting (laboratory versus field) was found to be a moderator of the relationship, with lab studies in general having stronger findings.

Conclusion: Like job design (i.e., the JCM), goal setting has considerable research backup, but unlike the JCM, is a very commonly used motivational technique for enhancing human performance in today's organizations. Goals help clarify the sense of purpose and mission that is essential to success in the workplace. As the listed principle indicates, goal difficulty and goal specificity have been found to be strongly related to task performance across a wide variety of tasks and settings. This is because specific and challenging goals serve to focus employees' attention on exactly what is to be accomplished and to bring out their best performance. Moreover, as this chapter points out, goals must be specific and measurable so that employees know exactly what the goal is and can track their progress toward goal achievement. Goal setting as an indicator of performance represents one of the strongest and most consistent OB principles today. In addition, there are not many areas of the field of organizational behavior in which goal setting cannot play a role. For example, goal setting is widely recognized in areas such as cognitive motivation theories, self-efficacy, feedback-seeking behavior, job design, and behavioral management. In many ways, goal setting can be used as a prototype of how theory, research, and application should be done in organizational behavior.

Source: Adapted from Anthony J. Mento, Robert P. Steel, and Ronald J. Karren, "A Meta-Analytic Study of the Effects of Goal Setting on Task Performance: 1966–1984," *Organizational Behavior and Human Decision Processes,* Vol. 39, 1987, pp. 52–83.

OB PRINCIPLE: The use of management by objectives (MBO) can improve organization performance.

Meta-Analysis Results: [70 studies; $d = 2.6$]. *On average, there is a **97 percent probability** that organizations that properly implement an MBO system will outperform those that don't use MBO.* Further analysis found that top-management commitment was a moderator. When top management is committed to MBO, the average increase in performance is greater than when such support is missing.

Conclusion: Management by objectives (MBO) has been around for many years but still represents an applied method of goal setting and is an effective tool for performance management. Specifically, MBO is a management system that combines goal setting, participative decision making, and objective feedback. It is a process whereby managers and subordinates jointly set goals, share information, and discuss strategies that lead to goal attainment. Although MBO has been criticized by some for being a "fad" that does not achieve desired results, MBO supporters suggest that mixed results are due to different or poor implementation of MBO rather than to the process itself. Overall, the research on MBO has been quite strong as indicated, and although it may be called something else in recent years, there is compelling evidence that this is an OB principle to which organizations should pay attention.

Source: Adapted from Robert Rodgers and John E. Hunter, "Impact of Management by Objectives on Organizational Productivity," *Journal of Applied Psychology Monograph,* Vol. 76, No. 2, 1991, pp. 322–336.

Questions for Discussion and Review

1. Compare and contrast the engineering versus the enrichment approach to job design.
2. What are the core job characteristics in the Hackman-Oldham model? How do you calculate the motivating potential of a job? How would a professor's job and a janitor's job measure up on these characteristics? Be specific in your answer.
3. Describe the circumstances under which employees may become engaged and/or disengaged from their jobs.
4. Considering that former employees at the General Foods plant indicate there may be some problems with sociotechnical design, what do you think the future holds for this type of approach? Do you think QWL standards will and should be legislated? Why?
5. In your own words, describe the theory behind goal setting. What has the research generally found in testing goal setting?
6. Summarize the five basic steps of the overall performance system of MBO. What have been the research findings on this approach?
7. How does goal setting relate to benchmarking, stretch targets and psychological contracts?

Internet Exercise: What Is the Motivation Potential of Jobs at Southwest Airlines?

Many companies have employment opportunities listed on their website. Go to http://www.southwest.com/careers/ and look at the job openings at Southwest Airlines. Using the Hackman and Oldham job design model with identity, significance, skill variety, autonomy, and feedback, analyze the jobs listed according to each characteristic.

1. From a job design standpoint, which job would seem to have the most motivation potential? The least?
2. Of the jobs that you consider poorly designed, discuss some ways that they might be improved.
3. Compare these jobs to other companies that post jobs on their websites. Using a search engine, go to company websites in manufacturing and the public sector that provide job openings and/or descriptions. Do you think some industries tend to have more motivating potential jobs than others?

REAL CASE:
I Can't Believe they
Redesigned the
Whole Thing

General Motors Corp.'s new Grand River plant, now being built in Lansing, Mich., is shaped like the letter "T." It might just as well be a "W"—for worker. Either way, the shape of the new factory—GM's first in the U.S. in 14 years—shows how crucial labor remains in the era of high-tech manufacturing.

Indeed, when workers begin assembling Cadillac Cateras there next year, GM's newest plant will not only be its most worker-friendly, it will be the company's first major step toward upgrading its creaky manufacturing practices.

The reason for the T-shape? In older rectangular factories, trucks arrived at the back door, and goods were unloaded and stored in a warehouse area. From there, supplies were wheeled to the line as they were needed. The new layout allows trucks to pull straight up to the factory where they will be used. This isn't just a convenience. It eliminates the need for forklifts, a chronic source of injuries.

Keeping the fully stocked supply trucks parked outside—like jets at so many airport gates—allows GM to shrink the plant size. The $558 million building will be about half as large as a traditional GM factory, and the paint and body shops will be in different buildings connected to the assembly line by conveyors. This makes the lines easier to modify and provides better access to work areas.

It's easy to see why GM is billing Grand River as its most employee-focused operation ever. For one thing, the company is spending big so that the assembly benches in front of each worker can be individually raised and lowered. It has splashed out $12 million on training alone. And long before the factory walls were complete, the carmaker invited 200 United Auto Workers members to help design workstations and layouts. The new plant is so popular that transfer requests outnumber the anticipated openings, says Art Baker, an officer with UAW Local 652.

GM's worker-friendly goals, however, are facing some fresh challenges as the company rolls toward a more radical makeover. In 1999, GM proposed a concept called "Yellowstone", a Dell-like plan that called for parts suppliers to build subassemblies near the main factory. These would then be snapped together by UAW workers to make customized vehicles in a fraction of the time required today. But the union choked on the proposal, seeing it as a way to replace high-paying union jobs with cheaper, nonunion ones at outside suppliers. When the UAW threatened to strike, GM compromised by coming up with the Lansing plant.

Perhaps GM didn't get everything it wanted. But it didn't back down on the most important elements in the Yellowstone plan, according to Daron Gifford, global automotive practice leader for Deloitte Consulting. The key isn't really who builds what, or where. It's about making inventory leaner. And Grand River accomplishes that, he says.

The Lansing plant will also help on the productivity front—and it comes at a propitious time. GM had some of the biggest gains in productivity last year, says Ronald E. Harbour of *The Harbour Report,* an auto manufacturing survey. From the perspective of layout and materials flow, "this is a big leap beyond any of their other plants," Harbour says.

But the auto giant is banking on more than boosting productivity and getting forklifts out of the way. "GM is erecting this plant to be a model for its competitive manufacturing strategies," President and CEO G. Richard Wagoner Jr. said at a plant unveiling earlier this year. If the model works, GM might finally get some respect for its assembly plants.

1. The case indicates that GM feels this Grand River plant is its "most employee-focused operation ever." Based on what you read in the chapter and this brief description of the plant, do you agree with this statement? What else would you recommend could/should have been done?
2. How would you balance the trade-off of manufacturing efficiency versus employee involvement? What would lead to maximum productivity? Employee retention?
3. Do you believe that GM was correct in compromising with the UAW on the "Yellowstone" concept? Why?

REAL CASE:
Making It a Nice
Place to Work

There are a number of ways in which organizations are trying to apply techniques to improve performance. For example, redesigning traditional, bureaucratic organizations and specialized jobs has emerged as a way to enhance employee satisfaction and performance. This can be done by restructuring the organization so that it is a more enjoyable, pleasant place in which to work. This is actually being accomplished in a number of different ways in the real world.

At Inhale Therapeutic Systems, a small start-up company in northern California that focuses on novel drug-delivery technology, everyone, including the president of the company, sits in large cubicles (they call them "bullpens") with four other people of various ranks and functions. There are no walls or barriers between any of them. This arrangement forces people to talk to each other, while limiting the amount of time they spend gossiping, and reduces the need to write memos and use e-mail—as, in most cases, the people to whom these messages would be directed are sitting in the same bullpen. Every nine months the company reshuffles everyone and assigns new bullpen partners. This arrangement has seemed to promote teamwork and reduce office politics.

At West Bend Mutual Insurance Company top management decided to make the workplace as comfortable as possible for people. Management put money where their mouth was by purchasing equipment that allows those in certain workstations to adjust the temperature, fresh air, and noise levels. Researchers from Rensselaer Polytechnic Institute have studied the impact of these changes and concluded that those who are allowed to control their own climate are at least 3 percent more productive than those who are not. The company management believe that these productivity increases are even higher, probably more in the range of 5 to 10 percent. In addition, the novel workstations have become an asset in recruiting and retaining workers.

Other companies are approaching the motivation challenge by asking: What else can we do to make the organization an enjoyable place to work? At Sun Microsystems, some members of top management are asking an even more radical question. Noting that many of their employees are never in the office because they are out in the field with clients or working from home, they ask: Why should we heat, cool, and clean offices when so few people ever use them? This has led management to consider reducing office space; if personnel who never come to the office need to get together for occasional meetings or face-to-face interactions, they can rent space at hotels or conference centers. Although this may not be the route Sun eventually takes, it does show that the old way of having everyone in their office from 9 to 5 may become a thing of the past.

An interesting issue that is beginning to emerge concerns "too much of a good thing." Is it possible that the new work arrangements such as those at Inhale Therapeutic Systems or West Bend Insurance will result in facilitating so much interaction that people become overstimulated or distracted? Moreover, the changes that are being made today may soon be outmoded by changes in tomorrow's technology, resulting in the need to reorganize the workplace again. On the positive side, however, some work design experts note:

> The good news . . . is that those involved in forging the new workplace realize there is no ideal, no cookie-cutter workplace template they can plop on top of organizations. And it's a rare alternative-office space that doesn't get adapted as trial runs reveal elements that don't work or could work better. "One thing we've realized is that not only must we assess what's possible but how far and how fast it can move." That would seem to signal an end to the age of the corporate "edifice complex" and a new era of workspaces that work.

1. How does redesign of jobs lead to improved performance and job satisfaction? In your answer include a discussion of Figure 15.2.
2. How do the examples in this case relate to the job characteristics model as discussed in this chapter?
3. Are we likely to see more workplace redesign in the future? Why or why not?

| ORGANIZATIONAL BEHAVIOR CASE: The Rubber Chicken Award | Kelly Sellers is really fed up with his department's performance. He knows that his people have a very boring job, and the way the technological process is set up leaves little latitude for what he has learned about vertically loading the job through job enrichment. Yet he is convinced that there must be some way to make it more interesting to do a dull job. "At least I want to find out for my people and improve their performance," he thinks.

The employees in Kelly's department are involved in the assembly of small hair dryer motors. There are 25 to 30 steps in the assembly process, depending on the motor that is being assembled. The process is very simple, and currently each worker completes only |

one or two steps of the operation. Each employee has his or her own assigned workstation and stays at that particular place for the entire day. Kelly has decided to try a couple of things to improve performance. First, he has decided to organize the department into work teams. The members of each team would be able to move the workstations around as they desired. He has decided to allow each team to divide the tasks up as they see fit. Next, Kelly has decided to post each team's performance on a daily basis and to reward the team with the highest performance by giving them a "rubber chicken" award that they can display at their workbenches. The production manager, after checking with engineering, has reluctantly agreed to Kelly's proposal on a trial basis.

1. Do you think Kelly's approach to job redesign will work? Rate the core job dimensions from the Hackman-Oldham model of Kelly's employees before and after he redesigned their jobs. What could he do to improve these dimensions even more?
2. How do you explain the fact that Kelly feels he is restricted by the technological process but still redesigned the work? Is this an example of sociotechnical job redesign?
3. What will happen if this experiment does not work out and the production manager forces Kelly to return to the former task design?

ORGANIZATIONAL BEHAVIOR CASE: Specific Goals for Human Service

Jackie Jordan is the regional manager of a state human services agency that provides job training and rehabilitation programs for the hearing impaired. Her duties include supervising counselors as well as developing special programs. One of the difficulties that Jackie has had was with a project supervisor, Kathleen O'Shean. Kathleen is the coordinator of a threeyear federal grant for a special project for the hearing impaired. Kathleen has direct responsibility for the funds and the goals of the project. The federal agency that made the grant made continuance of the three-year grant conditional on some "demonstrated progress" toward fulfilling the purpose of the grant. Jackie's problem with Kathleen was directly related to this proviso. She repeatedly requested that Kathleen develop some concrete goals for the grant project. Jackie wanted these goals written in a specific, observable, and measurable fashion. Kathleen continually gave Jackie very vague, nonmeasurable platitudes. Jackie, in turn, kept requesting greater clarification, but Kathleen's response was that the work that was being done was meaningful enough and took all her time. To take away from the work itself by writing these specific goals would only defeat the purpose of the grant. Jackie finally gave up and didn't push the issue further. One year later the grant was not renewed by the federal government because the program lacked "demonstrated progress."

1. Do you think Jackie was right in requesting more specific goals from Kathleen? Why or why not?
2. Do you think the federal government would have been satisfied with the goal-setting approach that Jackie was pushing as a way to demonstrate progress?
3. Would you have handled the situation differently if you were Jackie? How?

CHAPTER 16

Behavioral Performance Management

Learning Objectives

Define the theoretical processes of learning: behavioristic, cognitive, and social.

Discuss the principle of reinforcement, with special attention given to the law of effect, positive and negative reinforcers, and punishment.

Analyze organizational reward systems, emphasizing both monetary and nonfinancial rewards.

Present the steps and results of behavioral performance management, or organizational behavior modification (O.B. Mod.).

Starting with Best Practice
Leader's Advice

Ed Lawler, Director of the Center for Effective Organizations, on the Complexities of Using Pay in Performance Management

Since receiving his doctorate under the direction of Professor Lyman Porter at the University of California, Berkeley in 1964, Dr. Lawler has had a distinguished academic (Yale, Michigan, and since 1978, Southern California) and consulting career. He has published over 200 articles and 30 books, but is best known for his research and practical application on the use of pay as a reward. Although pay is only one of the reinforcers used in behavioral management, as Lawler points out, it can be an effective, but complex way to improve human performance in today's organizations.

Q1: *Is pay dissatisfaction inevitable?*

Lawler: Yes. Typically 50 percent or more of employees are unhappy either with their pay or with the way they're being paid. Still, one can do better and worse. At some companies, 70 percent to 80 percent of employees are unhappy. But if your sole goal is making your workforce happy, you may be struggling for a long time. . . . The problem is that, when it comes to determining how fair their pay is, people make comparisons that are inherently dissatisfying—we always find somebody who's doing better than we are, and we always feel that we should be doing as well as everybody. Even CEOs, who are very well paid, especially in the United States, will say to me, "I work as hard as Michael Jackson or Michael Jordan, and have more responsibility besides." And then they say their compensation is determined by the market. If I were to debate them, I would point out that unlike Jackson or Jordan, they don't pass the box office test—that is, directly produce revenue or profit. . . . For me, the problem is not the dollar difference between the top and the rest of the organization, but that the trajectory is different for the two—that is, the top is doing very well whereas the rest of the organization is either not improving or dropping in pay, because they're on different reward systems and a different payoff lever. What one hears in the ranks is, "If we pull off this turnaround, they'll get rich, but we'll be right here at the same pay level, so why should I get excited about this big market opportunity?" That's a common but awfully deadly attitude to have in a corporation, and I'm glad to see that more and more corporations— about 20 percent of the *Fortune* 1,000, I think—have stock-option plans that cover all employees.

Q2: *What else can a company do to recruit and retain good people?*

Lawler: Traditional companies should not try to compete with the dot-coms, because they'll lose that competition and mess up their internal systems besides; but I also say to traditional companies that they ought to spruce up their value proposition. At the least, they should try to create what I call a serial monogamy mentality, in which you hope somebody will stay 5 to 10 years, but you don't expect them to stay for a career. Think in terms not of loyalty to the company but, rather, of commitment to the job or the task.

Q3:   *Where does job satisfaction come into play?*

Lawler: Decades of research have shown that motivation occurs as a result of what people *think* will happen to them when they perform well. Their current level of satisfaction is a determinant of whether they stay with the organization, but not necessarily a major determinant of how they're going to perform in the future. . . . Yes, you want people at least moderately satisfied with their pay or else they'll leave, but the key question is: Do they trust that by performing better or helping the company perform better, they'll get better pay treatment in the future? It's that trust factor that's critical and so hard to build. Part of it is how you treat people generally, but specifically it comes down to the pay system: Has it got credibility, is there a good set of metrics, is there a good way of converting performance into pay changes or stock-option grants, and so on?

Q4:   *You talk about the need for people to feel at least moderately satisfied with their pay. Given the superheated state of many sectors of the job market, can you expect that without paying people their market value?*

Lawler: You've got to pay people close to their market value—80 percent or 85 percent of it—or they'll leave. In the hot market for talent, every company faces an interesting dilemma: whether to update existing employee pay to the external market or, rather, wait for a threat to leave and then match the competing job offer. Over three years, if an employee is in a hot specialty, you may be paying him 25 percent or 30 percent below market value despite merit increases every year. What's the organization to do? The right thing is to make a market adjustment. But the tendency is not to do that. . . . A lot of companies get tied up in their pay ranges, in the philosophy of paying for the job, not the person. "Geez," they say, "if I give this person a 15 percent or 20 percent raise, that would put him at the top of his range, so I couldn't give him any more merit increases, and we'd have to adjust the entire pay range." I argue that the idea of job-based pay ranges is obsolete anyway, and the key issue is focusing on individuals and skills and knowledge in determining market value, which then facilitates matching the market because the market for people changes more than the market for jobs. . . . Many high-tech companies have a philosophy of identifying a core group of employees—say, 10 percent or 20 percent—who are considered absolutely essential, and they'll do everything they can to keep them. Many in this core group are technology people, people who are capable of leading new product-development teams or who have cross-functional skills. Then there's another 75 percent to 80 percent who are valuable contributors—you'd like to have them around, but if they leave, they can be replaced. You still have to worry about the market value of these people, because replacement costs are high, but you don't have to lock them in with premium wages and lots of stock.

Q5:   *But won't the 80 percent resent the 20 percent?*

Lawler: The core/noncore approach should be not a stated policy, but rather something that can be deduced by the grapevine. People will realize that some people get special deals. But try to keep the boundary between the anointed and unanointed as porous as possible, so you can fall out of the core group if you don't stay current and can gain access to it if you perform well or develop desirable skills.

In a sense, this whole text on organizational behavior is concerned with the *what* and *how* of managing and leading people for high performance in today's organizations. Certainly many of the chapters (e.g., Chapter 5 on Reward Systems, Chapter 8 on Motivation, Chapter 9 on positive psychology concepts, and all of the chapters in Part 3) are directly, or at least indirectly, concerned with how to manage human resources more effectively. The same could be said of popular techniques that have strong consulting advocates such as the late Edwards Deming's "Total Quality Management," Steven Covey's "The Seven Habits of Highly Effective People," or Peter Senge's "Learning Organizations." Both the academic or consulting solutions to high performance are not necessarily wrong, although the academic approaches may not be directly applied enough, and the popular writers' techniques tend to be "quick fixes" and "fads" without research backup that come with a splash and then, unfortunately, go. In contrast, this last part of the text (with the last chapter on job design and goal setting, this chapter on behavioral management, and the next two chapters on leadership) focuses on theoretically based, research supported, and broadly sustainable application approaches to managing and leading for high performance. Similar to job design and goal setting, behavioral management meets these criteria. As one behavioral management advocate strongly points out:

> Behavior Performance Management is not a good idea to be tried for a while and then cast aside for some other good idea. It is a science that explains how people behave. It cannot go away anymore than gravity can go away. In a changing world, the science of behavior must remain the bedrock, the starting place for every decision we make, every new technology we apply, and every initiative we employ in our efforts to bring out the best in people.[1]

The purpose of this chapter is to provide an overview of learning theory and principles that serve as a foundation and point of departure for presenting the behavioral management approach. The first section summarizes the theories of learning: behavioristic, cognitive, and social cognitive. Next, the principles of reinforcement and punishment are given attention, followed by a discussion of both monetary and nonfinancial rewards. The last part of the chapter is devoted specifically to behavioral management. Both the steps of organizational behavior modification, or O.B. Mod., and the results of its basic research and application are given attention.

LEARNING THEORY BACKGROUND

Although learning theory has not been as popular in organizational behavior as motivation or personality theories, both scholars and practitioners would agree on its importance to both the understanding and effective development and management of human resources. In fact, practically all organizational behavior is either directly or indirectly affected by learning. For example, a worker's skill, a manager's attitude, a staff assistant's motivation, or an accountant's mode of dress are all learned. With the application of learning processes and principles, employees' behavior can be analyzed and managed to improve their performance.

The most basic purpose of any theory is to better explain the phenomenon in question. When theories become perfected, they have universal application and should enable prediction and control. Thus, a perfected theory of learning would have to be able to explain all aspects of learning (how, when, and why), have universal application (for example, to children, college students, managers, and workers), and predict and control learning situations. To date, no such theory of learning exists. Although there is general agreement on some principles of learning—such as reinforcement—that permit prediction and control, there is still a degree of controversy surrounding the theoretical understanding of learning in general and some of the principles in particular. This does not mean that no attempts have been made to develop a theory of learning. In fact, the opposite is true. The most widely recognized theoretical approaches incorporate the behavioristic and cognitive approaches and the emerging social cognitive theory that Chapter 1 indicated serves as the conceptual framework for this text. An understanding of these learning theories is important to the study of organizational behavior in general and behavioral performance management in particular.

Behavioristic Theories

The most traditional and researched theory comes out of the behaviorist school of thought in psychology (see Chapter 1). Most of the principles of learning and organizational reward systems, covered in Chapter 5, and the behavioral performance management approach discussed in this chapter are based on behavioristic theories, or behaviorism.

The classical behaviorists, such as the Russian pioneer Ivan Pavlov and the American John B. Watson, attributed learning to the association or connection between stimulus and response (S-R). The operant behaviorists, in particular the well-known American psychologist B. F. Skinner, give more attention to the role that consequences play in learning, or the response-stimulus (R-S) connection.[2] The emphasis on the connection (S-R or R-S) has led some to label these the *connectionist theories* of learning. The *S-R* deals with classical, or respondent, conditioning, and the *R-S* deals with instrumental, or operant, conditioning. An understanding of these conditioning processes is vital to the study of learning and serves as a point of departure for understanding and modifying organizational behavior.

Classical Conditioning.   Pavlov's classical conditioning experiment using dogs as subjects is arguably the single most famous study ever conducted in the behavioral sciences. A simple surgical procedure permitted Pavlov to measure accurately the amount of saliva secreted by a dog. When he presented meat powder (unconditioned stimulus) to the dog in the experiment, Pavlov noticed a great deal of salivation (unconditioned response). On the other hand, when he merely rang a bell (neutral stimulus), the dog did not salivate. The next step taken by Pavlov was to accompany the meat with the ringing of the bell. After doing this several times, Pavlov rang the bell without presenting the meat. This time, the dog salivated to the bell alone. The dog had become classically conditioned to salivate (conditioned response) to the sound of the bell (conditioned stimulus). Thus, *classical conditioning* can be defined as a process in which a formerly neutral stimulus, when paired with an unconditioned stimulus, becomes a conditioned stimulus that elicits a conditioned response; in other words, the S-R connection is learned. The Pavlov experiment was a major breakthrough and has had a lasting impact on the understanding of learning.

Despite the theoretical possibility of the widespread applicability of classical conditioning and its continued refinement and application to areas such as marketing today,[3] most modern theorists agree that it represents only a very small part of total human learning. Skinner in particular felt that classical conditioning explains only respondent (reflexive) behaviors. These are the involuntary responses that are elicited by a stimulus. Skinner felt that the more complex, but common, human behaviors cannot be explained by classical conditioning alone. When explaining why he was abandoning a stimulus-response psychology, Skinner noted, "The greater part of the behavior of an organism was under the control of stimuli which were effective only because they were correlated with reinforcing consequences."[4] Thus, Skinner, through his extensive research, posited that *behavior was a function of consequences,* not the classical conditioning eliciting stimuli. He felt that most human behavior affects, or operates on, the environment to receive a desirable consequence. This type of behavior is learned through operant conditioning.

Operant Conditioning.   *Operant conditioning* is concerned primarily with learning that occurs as a consequence of behavior, or R-S. It is not concerned with the eliciting causes of behavior, as classical, or respondent, conditioning is. The specific differences between classical and operant conditioning may be summarized as follows:

1. In classical conditioning, a change in the stimulus (unconditioned stimulus to conditioned stimulus) will elicit a particular response. In operant conditioning, one particular response out of many possible ones occurs in a given stimulus situation. The stimulus situation serves as a cue in operant conditioning. It does not elicit the response but serves as a cue for a person to emit the response. The critical aspect of operant conditioning is what happens as a consequence of the response. The strength and frequency of classically conditioned behaviors are determined mainly by the frequency of the eliciting stimulus (the environmental event that precedes the behavior). The strength and frequency of operantly conditioned behaviors are determined mainly by the consequences (the environmental event that follows the behavior).

2. During the classical conditioning process, the unconditioned stimulus, serving as a reward, is presented every time. In operant conditioning, the reward is presented only if the organism gives the correct response. The organism must operate on the environment (thus the term *operant conditioning*) in order to receive a reward. The response is instrumental in obtaining the reward. Table 16.1 gives some examples of classical (S-R) and operant (R-S) conditioning.

TABLE 16.1   Examples of Classical and Operant Conditioning

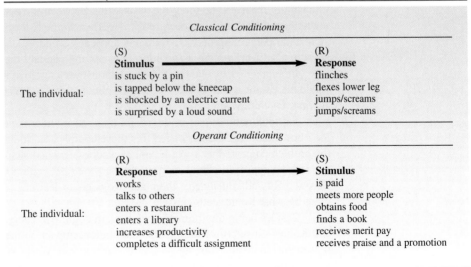

	Classical Conditioning	
	(S) **Stimulus** ⟶	(R) **Response**
The individual:	is stuck by a pin is tapped below the kneecap is shocked by an electric current is surprised by a loud sound	flinches flexes lower leg jumps/screams jumps/screams
	Operant Conditioning	
	(R) **Response** ⟶	(S) **Stimulus**
The individual:	works talks to others enters a restaurant enters a library increases productivity completes a difficult assignment	is paid meets more people obtains food finds a book receives merit pay receives praise and a promotion

Operant conditioning has a much greater impact on human learning than classical conditioning. Today, even though Skinner died in 1990, he remains somewhat controversial[5] and his views are commonly misrepresented,[6] the operant theory is still being refined and expanded,[7] historical analyses recognize some limitations but also definite contributions,[8] and applications are being made in areas such as marketing[9] and performance management.[10] Operant conditioning also explains, at least in a very simple sense, much of organizational behavior. For example, it might be said that employees work eight hours a day, five days a week, in order to feed, clothe, and shelter themselves and their families. Working (conditioned response) is instrumental only in obtaining the food, clothing, and shelter.

Some significant insights can be gained directly from operant analysis. The consequences of organizational behavior can change the environmental situation and greatly affect subsequent employee behaviors.[11] Managers can analyze the consequences of organizational behavior to help accomplish the goals of prediction and control. Some organizational behavior researchers are indeed using the operant framework to analyze the effectiveness of managers at work.[12] In addition, this theory serves as the framework for operationalizing much of behavioral performance management presented in this chapter.

Cognitive Theories

As in Chapter 1 for understanding organizational behavior in general, the cognitive theories must also be covered to understand learning and, especially as an input into social cognitive theory, to better understand behavioral performance management.[13] Edward Tolman is widely recognized as a pioneering cognitive theorist. He felt that *cognitive learning* consists of a relationship between cognitive environmental cues and expectation. He developed and tested this theory through controlled experimentation. In fact, even though behaviorists are mostly associated with animal subjects in their research, Tolman was one of the first to use the now-famous white rat in psychological experiments. He found that a rat could learn to run through an intricate maze, with purpose and direction, toward a goal (food). Tolman observed that at each choice point in the maze, expectations were established. In other words, the rat learned to expect that certain cognitive cues associated with the choice point might eventually lead to food. If the rat actually received the food, the association between the cue and the expectancy was strengthened, and learning occurred. In contrast to the S-R and R-S learning in the classical and operant approaches, Tolman's approach could be depicted as S-S (stimulus-stimulus), or learning the association between the cue and the expectancy.

In another early, classic study to demonstrate cognitive learning, Wolfgang Kohler used chimps presented with a problem of obtaining an out-of-reach suspended banana. At first the chimps attempted to jump for it, but soon gave up and seized a box that had been placed in another part of the room, dragged it under the object, mounted it, and took down the fruit. Kohler called this more complex learning "insight." The solution to the problem appeared as a whole, not as a series, gradual shaping of new responses as the operant approach would suggest. At the time (1927), famous social philosopher/critic Bertrand Russell concluded, "there are two ways of learning, one by experience, and the other by what Kohler calls 'insight.'"[14]

Besides being the forerunner of modern cognitive theory, Tolman's S-S connection and Kohler's insightful learning also had a great impact on the early human relations movement. Industrial training programs starting after World War II (and in many respects still today) drew heavily on their ideas. Programs were designed to strengthen the relationship between cognitive cues (supervisory, organizational, and job procedures) and worker expectations (incentive payments for good performance). The theory was that the worker would learn to be more productive by building an association between taking orders or following directions and expectancies of monetary reward for this effort. The same is true for the creativity, problem-solving groups that have been so popular over the years (see Chapter 11 on decision-making groups); they have drawn heavily from the notion of insightful learning.

Today, the cognitive sciences focus more on the structures and processes of human competence (for example, the role of memory and information processing) rather than on the acquisition and transition processes that have dominated learning theory explanations.[15] In organizational behavior, the cognitive approach has been applied mainly to motivation theories. Expectations, attributions and locus of control, and goal setting (which are in the forefront of modern work motivation) are all cognitive concepts and represent the purposefulness of organizational behavior. Many researchers are currently concerned about the relationship or connection between cognitions and organizational behavior.[16]

Social Learning and Social Cognitive Theory

As brought out in Chapter 1, social learning theory served as the conceptual framework for the past six editions of this text. However, similar to the theory building in social psychology, primarily from the extensive work of widely recognized psychologist Albert Bandura,[17] this edition of the text and this overview of learning recognizes the evolution to the more comprehensive social cognition. After first recognizing social learning, the discussion turns to social cognition and its derivatives of modeling and self-efficacy.

Social Learning.   This theoretical approach to learning was the first to combine and integrate both behaviorist and cognitive concepts and emphasized the interactive, reciprocal nature of cognitive, behavioral, and environmental determinants. It is important to recognize that social learning theory recognizes and draws from the principles of classical and operant conditioning. But equally important is the fact that social learning theory went beyond classical and operant theory by recognizing that there is more to learning than direct learning via antecedent stimuli and contingent consequences. Social learning theory posits that learning can also take place via vicarious, or modeling, and self-control processes (see Chapter 1). Thus, social learning theory agrees with classical and operant conditioning processes, but says they are too limiting and adds vicarious, modeling, and self-control processes.

Social Cognition.   This theory has emerged in recent years to go beyond social learning theory. Social cognitive theory extends learning and/or modifying behavior by giving more attention to the self-regulatory mechanisms. Specifically, as was presented in Chapter 1, social cognitive theory identifies five capabilities that people use to initiate, regulate, and sustain their own behavior: (1) symbolizing, (2) forethought, (3) vicarious/modeling learning, (4) self-regulation, and (5) self-reflection.[18] These human capabilities recognize cognitive processes, social learning, and self-efficacy. A closer look at social learning through the social cognitive derivatives of modeling and self-efficacy can lead to the better understanding of learning and provide the theoretical underpinning of behavioral performance management.

Modeling Processes.   The vicarious, or modeling, processes essentially involve observational learning. "Modeling in accordance with social learning theory can account for certain behavior acquisition phenomena that cannot be easily fitted into either operant or respondent conditioning."[19]

Many years ago, Miller and Dollard suggested that learning need not result from discrete stimulus-response or response-consequence connections. Instead, learning can take place through imitating others. Bandura states:

> Although behavior can be shaped into new patterns to some extent by rewarding and punishing consequences, learning would be exceedingly laborious and hazardous if it proceeded solely on this basis. . . . [It] is difficult to imagine a socialization process in which the language, mores, vocational activities, familial customs and educational, religious and political practices of a culture are taught to each new member by selective reinforcement of fortuitous behavior, without benefit of models who exemplify the cultural patterns in their own behavior. Most of the behaviors that people display are learned either deliberately or inadvertently, through the influence of example.[20]

Bandura has done considerable research demonstrating that people can learn from others.[21] This learning takes place in two steps. First, the person observes how others act and then acquires a mental picture of the act and its consequences (rewards and punishers). Second, the person acts out the acquired image, and if the consequences are positive, he or she will tend to do it again. If the consequences are negative, the person will tend not to do it again. These positive and negative consequences, of course, are where there is a tie-in with operant theory. But because there is cognitive, symbolic representation of the modeled activities instead of discrete response-consequence connections in the acquisition of new behavior, modeling goes beyond the operant explanation. In particular, Bandura concludes that *modeling* involves interrelated subprocesses, such as attention, retention, and motoric reproduction, as well as reinforcement.

Self-Efficacy.   Although given detailed attention in Chapter 9, self-efficacy has recently been recognized as a construct in behavioral performance management as well.[22] Bandura has defined *self-efficacy* as the "beliefs in one's capabilities to organize and execute the courses of action required to produce given attainments."[23] In particular, when faced with a specific task or job, an employee's efficacy will determine whether the necessary behavior will be initiated, how much effort will be expended and sustained, and how much persistence and resilience there will be when there are obstacles or even failure.[24] In other words, people who believe they can perform well on a task (high self-efficacy) do better than those who think they will fail (low self-efficacy). Importantly for the field of organizational behavior, a stream of research studies metaanalyzed has found a strong relationship between self-efficacy and work-related performance.[25] Also, those with high self-efficacy have the tendency to remain calm in a stressful situation.[26] In other words, there is considerable evidence that those employees with high self-efficacy tend to persevere and end up doing a good job without suffering stress or burnout. Unlike predisposed personality traits, efficacy is a state that can be trained and developed. As discussed in detail in Chapter 9, the input into efficacy is recognized to be mastery experiences, vicarious/modeling learning, social persuasion, and physiological/psychological arousal.[27] Both managers and their employees who experience success, are trained through modeling, and are encouraged and aroused on a given task or job, will have their efficacy enhanced and will perform well. There seems to be considerable practical implications for understanding and developing self-efficacy in managers and employees for performance improvement.[28]

PRINCIPLES OF LEARNING: REINFORCEMENT AND PUNISHMENT

Reinforcement and punishment play a central role in the learning process and provide principles for behavioral performance management. Most learning experts agree that reinforcement is more important than punishment and is the single most important concept and application principle. Yet there is still some controversy over its theoretical explanation. The first theoretical treatment given to reinforcement in learning and the framework that still dominates today is pioneering psychologist Edward Thorndike's classic law of effect.

Laws of Behavior

In Thorndike's own words, the *law of effect* is simply stated thus: "Of several responses made to the same situation, those which are accompanied or closely followed by satisfaction [reinforcement] . . . will be more likely to recur; those which are accompanied or closely followed by discomfort [punishment] . . . will be less likely to occur." From a strictly empirical standpoint, most behavioral scientists, even those with a strict cognitive orientation, generally accept the validity of this law. It has been demonstrated time after time in highly controlled learning experiments and is directly observable in everyday learning experiences. Sometimes called the laws of behavior, desirable, or reinforcing, consequences will increase the strength of the preceding behavior, and increase its probability of being repeated in the future. Undesirable, or punishing, consequences will decrease the strength of the preceding behavior and decrease its probability of being repeated in the future. Sometimes a third law is added: If the behavior is followed by no consequence (neither a positive nor a negative contingent consequence) the behavior will extinguish over time (thus this is called the extinction principle or law).[29]

Critique of Reinforcement Theory

Although there is wide acceptance of the laws of behavior, there may be some occasions when a person's cognitive rationalizations might neutralize them. For example, people with inaccurate self-efficacy beliefs may not be affected by the consequences of their actions. In the workplace, this is a real problem for managers. Those with inaccurate or false self-efficacy beliefs who experience performance failures time after time will not learn from their mistakes or respond to the manager's comments on how to correct the problem. They have high self-efficacy (they believe that their behaviors are appropriate to successfully accomplish the task), but they are wrong.[30] In addition to this type of cognitive processing that may neutralize the law of effect, there is some disagreement when it is carried a step further and used as an overall theory or an absolute requirement for learning.

Both Tolman's and Kohler's classic studies providing initial support for cognitive theories, presented earlier, discounted the need for incremental reinforcement as necessary for learning to occur. For example, Tolman conducted place learning, latent learning, and transposition experiments in an attempt to demonstrate that reinforcement was not a precondition for learning to occur. Specifically, in the place-learning he trained a rat to turn right in a T maze in order to obtain the reward of food. Then he started the rat from the opposite part of the maze. According to operant theory, the rat should have turned right because of past conditioning. However, the rat turned toward where the food had been placed. Tolman concluded that the behavior was purposive; the rat had formed a cognitive map to figure out how to get to the food. Over time, the behaviorists were able to counteract Tolman's studies with more controlled (e.g., sterile mazes, etc.) experiments, and Kohler's conclusions about insight were also explained away by a reinforcement history alternative explanation.[31]

More recently, Deci[32] and Deci and Ryan,[33] through their cognitive evaluation theory and laboratory research studies, have posited that external consequences (i.e., rewards) have a negative impact on intrinsically motivated (see Chapter 8) behavior dealing with task persistence and creativity. These findings generated considerable follow-up research with mixed findings. One review of about 100 studies found some rewards may have a detrimental effect, but an equal number found no effect or a positive effect.[34] The conclusion from this extensive review was that (1) the detrimental effects of rewards occur under highly restricted, easily avoidable conditions; (2) mechanisms of classical and operant conditioning are basic for understanding incremental and detrimental effects of reward on task motivation; and (3) positive effects of rewards on performance are easily attainable using procedures derived from behavioral theory.[35]

Finally, a meta-analysis of 96 studies found that the only detrimental effect of rewards was the time spent carrying out laboratory activity following a performance-independent (i.e., a noncontingent) reward.[36] There is also systematic analysis that discounts cognitive evaluation theory when compared to operant theory explanations.[37] Yet, despite this considerable empirical and theoretical counterevidence, an unconvinced few such as popular author Alfie Kohn continue to write (not do research) with titles such as *Punished by Rewards* and "Why Incentive Plans Cannot Work."[38] Based on his own assumptions and the now-countered Deci and Ryan theory and research, and in stark contrast to the large body of reinforcement theory and research, he makes unequivocal statements such as: "The bottom line is that any approach that offers a reward for better performance is destined to be ineffective."[39]

Unfortunately, Kohn's largely unsupported statements do not fall on deaf ears in the real world. This is because practicing managers have indeed experienced some implementation problems with pay-for-performance programs.[40] For example, after an extensive review of the relevant literature, Lawler concluded that process/design problems, not the underlying theory of reinforcement or the supporting basic research, limit the effectveness of pay for performance.[41] There is also a recent research study that found that highly dispersed reward systems (i.e., very large differences between highest and lowest payouts) may have a negative effect on both individual and organizational performace, especially when collaborative efforts (such as in teams) are important.[42] Yet, once again, it is not that the theory/research on reinforcement is wrong, but rather it is the implementation that can cause problems. As Bandura points out, "To say that [only] thought guides action is an abbreviated statement of convenience rather than a conferral of agency of thought,"[43] because "if people acted . . . on the basis of informative cues but remained unaffected by the results of their actions, they would be insensible to survive very long."[44] As a final summary statement, it can be said that the theory of reinforcement, like learning in general, is not perfect and still needs development. However, it can also be said that reinforcement does serve as a good theoretical foundation and guiding principle, and the implementation issues need to be overcome by effective behavioral performance management.

Reinforcement as Used in Behavioral Management

The terms *rewards* and *reinforcers* are often used interchangeably and loosely, but in behavioral performance management have very precise definitions and usage. An often-cited circular definition of reinforcement says that it is anything the person finds rewarding. This definition is of little value because the words *reinforcing* and *rewarding* are used interchangeably, but neither one is operationally defined. A more operational definition can be arrived at by reverting to the laws of behavior. Specifically, *reinforcement* in behavioral management is defined as anything that both increases the strength and tends to induce repetitions of the behavior that preceded the reinforcement. A *reward,* on the other hand, is simply something that the person who presents it deems to be desirable.

Reinforcement is functionally defined. Something is reinforcing only if it strengthens the behavior preceding it and induces repetitions. For example, a manager may ostensibly reward an employee who found an error in a report by publicly praising the employee. Yet on examination it is found that the employee is embarrassed and chided by coworkers, and error-finding behavior decreases in the future. In this example, the "reward" is not reinforcing. Besides clearing up differences between reinforcers and rewards, behavioral management also requires making the distinction between positive and negative reinforcers.

Positive and Negative Reinforcers

There is much confusion surrounding the terms *positive reinforcement, negative reinforcement,* and *punishment.* First of all, it must be understood that reinforcement, positive *or* negative, strengthens the behavior and increases the probability of repetition. But positive and negative reinforcers accomplish this impact on behavior in completely different ways. *Positive reinforcement* strengthens and increases behavior by the *presentation* of a desirable consequence. *Negative reinforcement* strengthens and increases behavior by the threat of the use of an undesirable consequence or the *termination or withdrawal* of an undesirable consequence. Figure 16.1 briefly summarizes the differences between positive and negative reinforcement and punishment. Giving recognition and attention to an employee for the successful completion of a task could be an example of positive reinforcement (if this does in fact strengthen and subsequently increase this task behavior). On the other hand, a worker is negatively reinforced for getting busy when the supervisor walks through the area. Getting busy terminates being "chewed out" by the supervisor.

Negative reinforcement is more complex than positive reinforcement, but it should not be equated with punishment. In fact, they have opposite effects on behavior. Negative reinforcement strengthens and increases behavior, whereas punishment weakens and decreases behavior. However, both are considered to be forms of

FIGURE 16.1
Summary of the operational definitions of positive and negative reinforcement and punishment.

Contingent / Consequence of	Reward (something desirable)	Noxious stimuli (something aversive and undesirable)
Application	POSITIVE REINFORCEMENT Behavior increases	PUNISHMENT Behavior decreases
Withdrawal	PUNISHMENT Behavior decreases	NEGATIVE REINFORCEMENT Behavior increases

negative control of behavior. Negative reinforcement is really a form of social black-mail, because the person will behave in a certain way in order not to be punished. A clearer understanding of punishment will help further clarify how it differs from negative reinforcement.

The Use of Punishment

Punishment is one of the most used but least understood and badly administered aspects of behavioral management. Whether in rearing children or dealing with subordinates in a complex organization, parents and supervisors or managers often revert to punishment instead of positive reinforcement in order to modify or control behavior. Punishment is commonly thought to be the reverse of reinforcement but equally effective in altering behavior. However, this simple analogy with reinforcement is not warranted. The reason is that punishment is a very complex phenomenon and must be carefully defined and used.

The Meaning of Punishment.   *Punishment* is anything that weakens behavior and tends to decrease its subsequent frequency. Punishment usually consists of the application of an undesirable or noxious consequence, but as shown in Figure 16.1, it can also be defined as the withdrawal of a desirable consequence. Thus, taking away certain organizational privileges from a manager who has a poor performance record could be thought of as punishment.

Regardless of the distinction between punishment as the application of an undesirable consequence and as the withdrawal of a desirable consequence, in order for punishment to be effective, there must be a weakening of, and a decrease in, the behavior that preceded it. Just because a supervisor criticizes a subordinate and thinks this is a punishment, it is not necessarily the case unless the behavior that preceded the criticism weakens and decreases in subsequent frequency. In many situations when supervisors think they are punishing employees, they are in fact reinforcing them because they are giving attention, and attention tends to be very reinforcing. This explains the common complaint that supervisors often make: "I call Joe in, give him heck for goofing up, and he goes right back out and goofs up again." What is happening is that the supervisor thinks Joe is being punished, when operationally, what is obviously happening is that the supervisor is reinforcing Joe's undesirable behavior by giving him attention and recognition. Punishment, like reinforcement, is defined and operationalized by its effects on behavior, not by what the person thinks is or should be punishment.

Administering Punishment.   Opinions on administering punishment range all the way from the one extreme of dire warnings never to use it to the other extreme that it is the only effective way to modify behavior. As yet, research has not been able to support either view completely. However, there is little doubt that the use of punishment tends to cause many undesirable side effects. Neither children nor adults like to be punished. The punished behavior tends to be only temporarily suppressed rather than permanently changed, and the punished person tends to get anxious or uptight and resentful of the punisher. Thus, the use of punishment as a strategy to control behavior is a lose-lose approach. Unless the punishment is severe, the behavior will reappear very quickly, but the more severe the punishment, the greater the side effects such as hate and revenge.

To minimize the problems with using punishment, persons administering it must always provide an acceptable alternative to the behavior that is being punished. If they do not, the undesirable behavior will tend to reappear and will cause fear and anxiety in the person being punished. The punishment must always be administered as close in time to the undesirable behavior as possible. Calling subordinates into the office to give them a reprimand for breaking a rule the week before is not effective. All the reprimand tends to do at this time is to punish them for getting caught. The punishment has little effect on the rule-breaking behavior. When punishment is administered, it should be remembered that there is also an effect on the relevant others who are observing the punishment.

Guidelines for Discipline.   A rule of thumb for effective behavioral management should be: always attempt to reinforce instead of punish in order to change behavior. Furthermore, the use of a reinforcement strategy is usually more effective in accelerating desirable behaviors than the use of punishment is for decelerating undesirable behaviors because no bad side effects accompany reinforcement. As one comprehensive analysis of punishment concluded: "In order to succeed, [punishment] must be used in an orderly, rational manner—not, as is too often the case, as a handy outlet for a manager's anger or frustration. If used with skill, and concern for human dignity, it can be useful."[45] In behavioral management, discipline is a learning experience, never purely a coercive experience to prove mastery or control over others. Perhaps the best practical advice is the old red-hot-stove rule of discipline—like the stove, punishment should give advance warning and be immediate, consistent, and impersonal. In addition, most modern approaches stress that punishment should be situationally applied (a crew of nineteen-year-old high school dropouts should be treated differently from a $100,000-per-year professional) and progressive. The progressive discipline may start off with a clarifying verbal discussion, then move to a written contract signed by the person being disciplined, next move to time off with or without pay, and then only as a last step end in termination.

THE ROLE OF ORGANIZATIONAL REWARD SYSTEMS

Because positive reinforcement consequences are so important to employee behavior, organizational reward systems become critical to behavioral performance management. The organization may have the latest advanced information technology, well-thought-out strategic plans, detailed job descriptions, and comprehensive training programs, but unless the people are reinforced for their performance-related behaviors, the "up-front" variables (technology, plans, and so on) for the rules that govern[46] or the establishing operation (i.e., there is enough motivation)[47] of their behavior, there will be little impact. In other words, going back to Skinner's original conception, the antecedent cues (technology, plans, and the like) have power to control or provide rules and establishing operation for behavior only if there are reinforcing consequences. As one behavioral management consultant points out:

> A company is always perfectly designed to produce what it is producing. If it has quality problems, cost problems, productivity problems, then the behaviors associated with those undesirable outcomes are being reinforced. This is not conjecture. This is the hard, cold reality of human behavior.[48]

The challenge for performance management is to understand this behavioral reality, eliminate the reinforcers for the undesirable behaviors, and more importantly and effectively, reinforce the desirable behavior. Thus, organizational reward systems become a key, often-overlooked, factor in bringing about improved performance and success.

Chapter 5 is specifically devoted to reward systems that are a vital part of the organizational environment (along with structure and culture) in the social cognitive model for this text. As was pointed out, money (pay) dominates organizational reward systems. The following sections analyze both monetary and nonfinancial reinforcers that can be used in behavioral performance management.

Analysis of Money as a Reinforcer

Unfortunately, about the only reinforcing function that traditional monetary reward systems (covered in Chapter 5) such as base-pay techniques provide is to reinforce employees for walking up to the pay window or for opening an envelope and seeing their paycheck or direct deposit stub every two weeks or every month. These traditional pay plans certainly have come up short of having the intended impact on improving employee performance at all levels.[49] Yet, despite the problems with traditional pay approaches, recent analyses of the research studies concludes that money contingently administered can have a positive effect on employee behavior.[50] However, there are even short-comings with merit pay mainly due to implementation issues such as poor measurement of performance, lack of acceptance of supervisory feedback, limited desirability of merit increases that are too small, a lack of linkage between merit pay and performance, and potential unintended consequences such as focusing only on merit-related activities and behaviors.[51] Some compensation practitioners argue that merit pay only makes employees unhappy because they view it as an unfair way to reward for past performance instead of being geared to improved future performance.[52] Also, a laboratory study of merit pay led to the following conclusions:

1. Unless a merit raise is at least 6 to 7 percent of base pay, it will not produce the desired effects on employee behavior.
2. Beyond a certain point, increases in merit-raise size are unlikely to improve performance.
3. When merit raises are too small, employee morale will suffer.
4. Cost-of-living adjustments, seniority adjustments, and other nonmerit components of a raise should be clearly separated from the merit component.
5. Smaller percentage raises given to employees at the higher ends of base-pay ranges are demotivating.[53]

In other words, both the traditional base- and merit-pay plans have some problems.

The "New Pay" plans covered in Chapter 5 (e.g., pay for performance at both the individual and group levels, paying for customer and/or employee satisfaction, pay for knowledge, skill pay, competency pay, and broadbanding) have overcome many of the problems.[54] For example, a large study sponsored by the American Compensation Association was able to place a dollar value on the positive impact of pay-for-performance plans. The value of the performance improvement translates into a 134 percent net return on what is paid out to employees (excluding the costs associated with training, communications, and consulting), or, for every $1 of payout, a gain of $2.34 was attained.[55]

In terms of basic research, a recent field experiment conducted by Stajkovic and Luthans in the biggest credit card processing firm in the world found the following:

1. A traditionally administered pay-for-performance plan (i.e., announced through normal channels in terms of the amount of pay that would be received for various levels of performance) did increase performance by 11 percent; but

2. The same plan that was implemented through the behavioral performance management approach discussed next (i.e., specifying the critical performance behaviors that would lead to monetary consequences) had a significantly higher 32 percent increase in performance.[56]

In other words, because the performance behaviors strengthened and increased, the theory and principles of reinforcement explain that money can indeed be a powerful reinforcer. Importantly, money may not be a reinforcer when administered through the traditional pay plans, but when made contingent on identified performance behaviors as in behavioral performance management, money can be a powerful reinforcer.

The same could be said for the very expensive benefit plans in the organizational reward system (see Chapter 5). Flexible benefit plans and those that depend on performance may have better intended results.[57] Instead of benefits taking on an entitlement mentality, an increasing number of firms (18 percent according to a recent American Compensation Association survey) are making the amount and choice of benefits dependent on employee performance. For example, under Owens-Corning's "Rewards and Resources Program," workers get to clearly see how their work is reinforced with extra pay in the form of more benefit choices.[58]

Nonfinancial Rewards

As Chapter 5 pointed out, money is the most obvious organizational reward, but the nonfinancial rewards are receiving increased attention. In fact, one comprehensive review of surveys that ask the value employees place on various rewards found that nonfinancial rewards were ranked much higher than financial ones.[59] For example, one study of 1500 employees in a wide variety of work settings found personalized, instant recognition from managers as being the most important reward of the 65 evaluated. However, more than half of these same employees reported that they seldom, if ever, received such personal recognition from their managers.[60] Also, a staffing company reported that the number-one reason employees give for leaving companies is the lack of praise and recognition.[61] Also in the same Stajkovic and Luthans research study cited previously, it was found that both social recognition (24 percent) and performance feedback (20 percent) had a significantly higher relative performance increase than did the traditionally administered pay for performance (11 percent).[62] In other words, there is little doubt that the nonfinancials can be very powerful, but are often overlooked, as a reinforcer in behavioral performance management.

Table 16.2 summarizes some of the major categories of nonfinancial rewards. Notice that even though these are considered nonfinancial, they may still cost the organization. This is true of the consumables, manipulatables, and visual and auditory rewards. The job design category is a special case and is usually not, but could be, considered as an organizational reward. Chapter 15 was devoted to these and they are not included here as part of behavioral performance management. On the other hand, the social recognition and attention and performance feedback categories are relatively easy to apply in behavioral performance management, cost nothing (except for

TABLE 16.2 Categories of Nonfinancial Rewards

Consumables	Manipulatables	Visual and Auditory	Job Design	Formal Recognition	Performance Feedback	Social Recognition and Attention
Coffee-break treats	Desk accessories	Office with a window	Jobs with more responsibility	Formal acknowledgment of achievement	Nonverbal performance information	Friendly greetings
Free lunches	Wall plaques	Piped-in music	Job rotation	Feature in house newsletter	Verbal performance information	Informal recognition
Food baskets	Company car	Internet and e-mail for personal use	Special assignments	Story in newspaper/TV	Written reports	Solicition of suggestions
Easter hams	Watches	Redecoration of work environment	Cross training	Celebrations/banquets	Performance evaluations/appraisals (including 360 degree)	Solicitation of advice
Christmas turkeys	Trophies	Company literature	Knowledge training	Letters of commendation	Performance charts and graphs	Compliment of work progress
Dinners for the family on the company	Commendations	Private office	Authority to schedule own work	Acknowledgment/praise in front of others	Meters/counters or performance information	Pat on the back
Company picnics	Rings/tie pins	Popular speakers or lecturers	Flexible hours		Self-information from performance or problem solutions	Smile
After-work wine and cheese parties	Appliances and furniture for the home	Book club discussions	Flexible breaks			Verbal or nonverbal recognition or praise
Time off	PC for the home/personal use		Job sharing			
Trips	Home shop tools		Participation in decisions			
Entertainment/Sports events	Garden tools		Participation in teams			
Education classes	Clothing		Self-managed teams			
	Club privileges					
	Use of company recreation facilities					
	Use of company convenience center					
	Use of company facilities for personal projects					

preparing some of the performance feedback), and may be even more powerful than the cost-based nonfinancial rewards. These two are major reinforcers and deserve special coverage.

Social Recognition and Attention.   Informally providing contingent recognition and attention (and praise, if genuine) tend to be very powerful reinforcers for most people. In addition, few people become satiated or filled up with these. However, similar to monetary reinforcers, social reinforcers should be administered on a contingent basis to have a positive effect on employee performance. For example, a pat on the back or verbal praise that is insincere or randomly given (as under the old human relations approach) may have no effect or even a punishing "boomerang" effect. But genuine social reinforcers, contingently administered for performance of the target behavior, can be a very effective positive reinforcer for most employees and improve their performance. The added benefit of such a strategy, in contrast to the use of monetary rewards, is that the cost of social reinforcers to the organization is absolutely nothing.

Importantly, this informal *social* recognition based on a valued person's (e.g., boss, peer, subordinate, friend, spouse, etc.) attention and appreciation may have not only a bigger impact as a reinforcer in behavioral management than money, but also than formal recognition programs. Unlike valued social recognition and attention, formal recognition programs, especially over time, can easily turn into being phoney, not valued by the recipient, or go against group and/or cultural norms. As Luthans and Stajkovic recently noted:

> A formal recognition award such as the "Golden Banana" at Hewlett-Packard or "Employee of the Month" given at many companies can initially be a reinforcer, but over time may cross the line and become an empty reward and be perceived even in a negative light. The first few Employee of the Month recipients may be very deserving instances that everyone would agree with, but over time selections become more and more controversial and subjective, usually resulting in selecting less-qualified or not-qualified employees. At this point company politics often come into play and those who truly deserved the recognition feel betrayed. In this case, the program would actually produce negative effects (e.g., "rewarding A while hoping for B"). Also, from a (collectivistic) cultural values and individual differences standpoint, although everyone may like to be recognized for their efforts and achievements, not everyone likes to be singled out in the public way that usually goes along with formal recognition.[63]

With the increasing use of teams, there is also recent evidence that they may be providing social reinforcement to their members that yields organizationally desirable outcomes. For example, in the American Compensation Association research study cited earlier, team suggestion plans, under the umbrella of an organizational performance reward plan or operating independently, were found to be particularly powerful contributors to organizational success. Importantly, the team suggestion plans, which typically used nonfinancial rewards, outperformed the individually based plans, which typically used financial rewards, by 4 to 1.[64] For example, the average value per idea adopted from team suggestion plans using nonfinancial rewards was an impressive $46,200 for a major airline, $14,500 for a manufacturer, $19,344 for a newspaper, and $19,266 for a bank.[65]

Performance Feedback.   There is little question that despite the tremendous amount of data being generated by today's advanced information systems, individuals still receive very little, if any, feedback about their performance (see Chapter 10 on communication). People generally have an intense desire to know how they are doing; they engage in feedback-seeking behavior.[66] Even though feedback has been found to be complex in research studies,[67] it is generally accepted that feedback enhances individual performance in behavioral management.[68] A comprehensive review (30 laboratory and 42 field experiments) concluded that performance feedback had a positive effect.[69] Also, as cited earlier, the very recent Stajkovic and Luthans study found, although not as high as contingently administered money and social recognition reinforcers, the performance feedback intervention still yielded a highly significant 20 percent performance improvement.[70] Importantly, this was significantly higher than the traditionally administered pay for performance (11 percent). As a general guide line for behavioral management, the performance feedback should be as *p*ositive, *i*mmediate, *g*raphic, and *s*pecific—thus, the acronym PIGS—as possible to be effective.[71]

Despite the recognized importance, there is still disagreement among scholars as to whether feedback per se is automatically reinforcing or too simplistic.[72] For example, after reviewing the existing research literature on feedback, one researcher concluded that its impact is contingent on factors such as the nature of the feedback information, the process of using feedback, individual differences among the recipients of the feedback, and the nature of the task.[73] One study, for instance, found that self-generated feedback with goal setting had a much more powerful effect on technical or engineering employees than externally generated feedback with goal setting.[74] Also, another study found subjects rated specific feedback more positively than they rated nonspecific feedback and preferred feedback that suggested an external cause of poor performance to feedback that suggested an internal cause.[75] And the source of the feedback seems important as well.[76] Not only are the amount and the frequency of feedback generated by a source important, but also the consistency and usefulness of the information generated, as a study found. Individuals viewed feedback from formal organizations least positively, from coworkers next, then from supervisors and tasks, with the best being self-generated feedback.[77] As Chapter 10 on communication pointed out, feedback from multiple sources may be most effective,[78] and the 360-degree feedback systems (the individual is anonymously appraised not only by the boss but also by subordinates, peers, and sometimes customers) can be automated on a software system to provide more timely, objective, and less-costly feedback. Also, studies have found that choice of reward interacting with feedback had a positive impact on task performance in a laboratory exercise,[79] but workers in highly routine jobs in fast-food restaurants who received positive feedback did not improve their performance.[80] Despite these qualifications and contingencies, a general guideline regarding performance feedback is that it can be a very effective reinforcer for behavioral performance management.

BEHAVIORAL PERFORMANCE MANAGEMENT, OR O.B. MOD.

Behavioral performance management is based on behavioristic, social learning, and social cognitive theories, and especially the principles of reinforcement. Figure 16.2 graphically depicts the historical development and theory building up to the present influence of Bandura's social cognitive theory. The full-blown organizational behavior modification, or O.B. Mod. model, is shown in Figure 16.3. The simplified steps are

FIGURE 16.2
Chronological Develop-
ment of Conceptual
Foundation for O.B.
Mod.

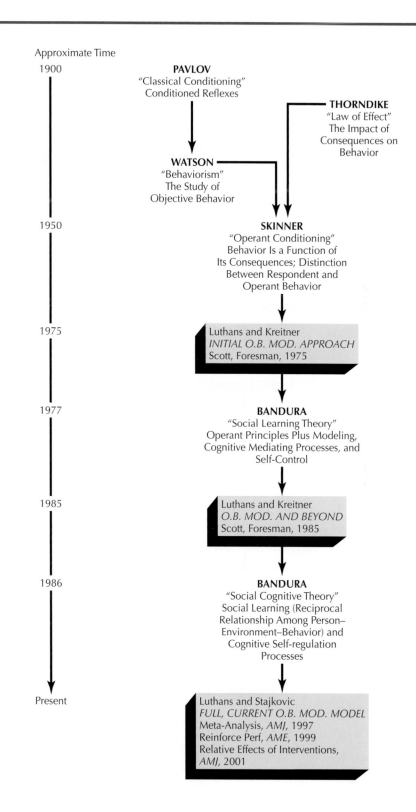

Approximate Time

1900 — **PAVLOV** "Classical Conditioning" Conditioned Reflexes

THORNDIKE "Law of Effect" The Impact of Consequences on Behavior

WATSON "Behaviorism" The Study of Objective Behavior

1950 — **SKINNER** "Operant Conditioning" Behavior Is a Function of Its Consequences; Distinction Between Respondent and Operant Behavior

1975 — Luthans and Kreitner *INITIAL O.B. MOD. APPROACH* Scott, Foresman, 1975

1977 — **BANDURA** "Social Learning Theory" Operant Principles Plus Modeling, Cognitive Mediating Processes, and Self-Control

1985 — Luthans and Kreitner *O.B. MOD. AND BEYOND* Scott, Foresman, 1985

1986 — **BANDURA** "Social Cognitive Theory" Social Learning (Reciprocal Relationship Among Person– Environment–Behavior) and Cognitive Self-regulation Processes

Present — Luthans and Stajkovic *FULL, CURRENT O.B. MOD. MODEL* Meta-Analysis, *AMJ*, 1997 Reinforce Perf, *AME*, 1999 Relative Effects of Interventions, *AMJ*, 2001

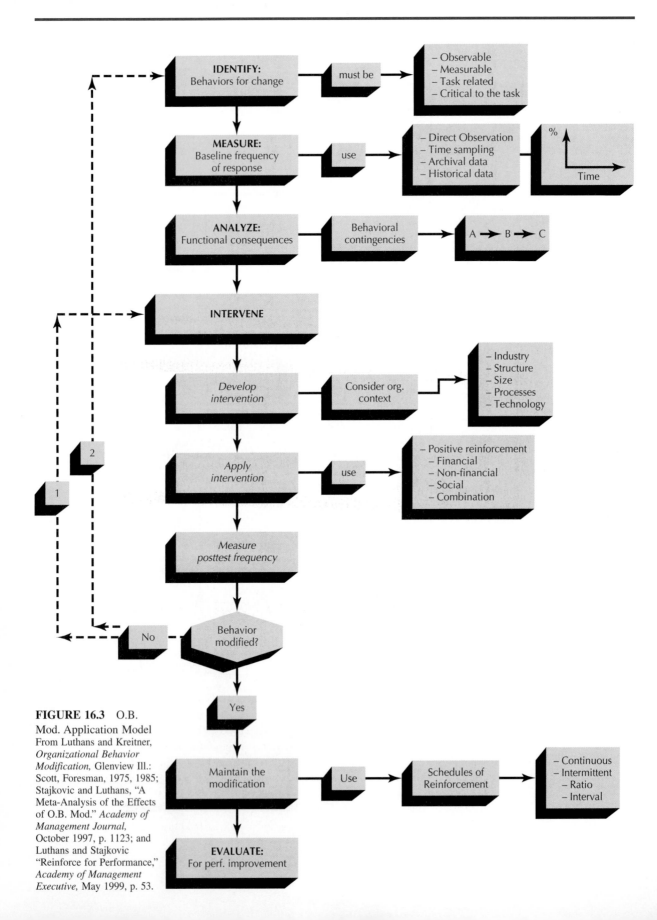

FIGURE 16.3 O.B. Mod. Application Model From Luthans and Kreitner, *Organizational Behavior Modification,* Glenview Ill.: Scott, Foresman, 1975, 1985; Stajkovic and Luthans, "A Meta-Analysis of the Effects of O.B. Mod." *Academy of Management Journal,* October 1997, p. 1123; and Luthans and Stajkovic "Reinforce for Performance," *Academy of Management Executive,* May 1999, p. 53.

FIGURE 16.4

Major steps of Luthans's O.B. Mod. Approach to Behavioral Performance Management

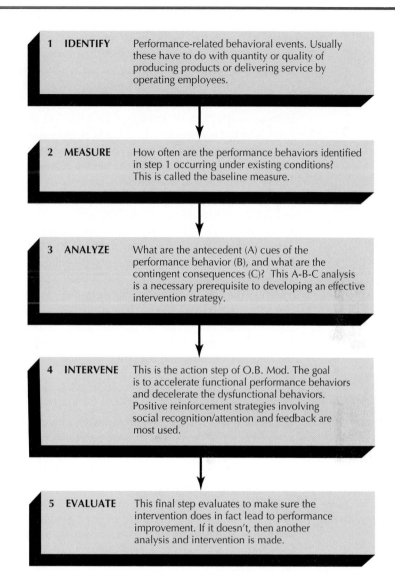

1 IDENTIFY	Performance-related behavioral events. Usually these have to do with quantity or quality of producing products or delivering service by operating employees.
2 MEASURE	How often are the performance behaviors identified in step 1 occurring under existing conditions? This is called the baseline measure.
3 ANALYZE	What are the antecedent (A) cues of the performance behavior (B), and what are the contingent consequences (C)? This A-B-C analysis is a necessary prerequisite to developing an effective intervention strategy.
4 INTERVENE	This is the action step of O.B. Mod. The goal is to accelerate functional performance behaviors and decelerate the dysfunctional behaviors. Positive reinforcement strategies involving social recognition/attention and feedback are most used.
5 EVALUATE	This final step evaluates to make sure the intervention does in fact lead to performance improvement. If it doesn't, then another analysis and intervention is made.

depicted in Figure 16.4. There are other systematic approaches to behavioral performance management based on academic work and consultants.[81] However, with the exception of studies published over the years in the *Journal of Organizational Behavior Management, The Behavior Analyst,* the *Journal of Applied Behavior Analysis,* and to a lesser degree the *Journal of Experimental Analysis of Behavior,* none of which use a consistent, identifiable model of behavioral management applied to the workplace, research studies on the O.B. Mod. model per se are the most published in the organizational behavior literature. In a recent meta-analysis, 19 studies with 115 effect sizes and a total sample size of 2,818 subjects met the O.B. Mod. inclusion criteria (see the principles at the end of the chapter for details and results).[82] The following discussion summarizes the steps of applying the O.B. Mod. approach to behavioral performance management.

Step 1: Identification of Performance Behaviors

In this first step the critical behaviors that make a significant impact on performance (making or selling a product or providing a service to clients or customers) are identified. In every organization, regardless of type or level, numerous behaviors are occurring all the time. Some of these behaviors have a significant impact on performance, and some do not. The goal of the first step of O.B. Mod. is to identify the critical behaviors—the 5 to 10 percent of the behaviors that may account for up to 70 or 80 percent of the performance in the area in question.

The process of identifying critical behaviors can be carried out in a couple of ways. One approach is to have the person closest to the job in question—the immediate supervisor or the actual jobholder—determine the critical behaviors. This goes hand in hand with using O.B. Mod. as a problem-solving approach for the individual manager or a team. Its advantages are that the person who knows the job best can most accurately identify the critical behaviors, and, because that person is participating, he or she may be more committed to carrying the O.B. Mod. process to its successful completion.

Another approach to identifying critical behaviors would be to conduct a systematic *behavioral audit*. The audit would use internal staff specialists and/or outside consultants. The audit would systematically analyze each job in question, in the manner that jobs are analyzed using job analysis techniques commonly employed in human resource management. The advantages of the personal approach (where the jobholder, immediate supervisor, and/or team makes a vital input into the audit) can be realized by the audit. In addition, the advantages of information from those closest to the action and consistency can be gained.

Regardless of the method used, there are certain guidelines that can be helpful in identifying critical behaviors. First, only direct performance behaviors are included. A team's lack of commitment and teamwork or someone's "goofing off" all the time is unacceptable. Only direct performance behaviors such as absenteeism or attendance, tardiness or promptness, or, most importantly, doing or not doing a particular task or procedure that leads to quantity and/or quality outcomes play the major role in O.B. Mod. Something like goofing off is not acceptable because it is not operationally measurable. It could be broken down into measurable behaviors such as not being at the workstation, being tardy when returning from breaks, spending time at the water cooler, disrupting coworkers, playing computer games or surfing for personal reasons, and even socializing with coworkers. However, for a behavior to be identified as a critical behavior appropriate for O.B. Mod., there must be a positive answer to the questions (1) Can it be directly measured? and (2) Does it have a significant impact on a performance outcome?

Most organizations do not have problems with their technology or the ability or training of their people, but they have many behaviorally related performance problems. Functional behaviors (those that contribute to performance goals) need to be strengthened and accelerated in frequency, and dysfunctional behaviors (those that detract from, or are detrimental to, performance goals) need to be weakened and decelerated in frequency. As in the initial step of any problem-solving process, these behaviors must be properly identified or the subsequent steps of O.B. Mod. become meaningless for attaining the overall goal of performance improvement.

Step 2: Measurement of the Behavior

After the performance behaviors have been identified in step 1, they are measured. A *baseline measure* is obtained by determining (either by observing and counting or by extracting from existing records) the number of times that the identified behavior is occurring under present conditions. Often this baseline frequency is in and of itself very revealing. Sometimes it is discovered that the behavior identified in step 1 is occurring much less or much more frequently than anticipated. The baseline measure may indicate that the problem is much smaller or much bigger than was thought to be the case. In some instances, the baseline measure may cause the "problem" to be dropped because its low (or high) frequency is now deemed not to need change. For example, attendance may have been identified in step 1 as a critical behavior that needed to be improved. The supervisor reports that the people "never seem to be here." The baseline measure, however, reveals that on average there is 96 percent attendance, which is deemed to be acceptable. In this example, the baseline measure rules out attendance as being a problem. The reverse, of course, could also have occurred. Attendance may have been a much bigger problem than anticipated.

The purpose of the baseline measure is to provide objective frequency data on the critical behavior. A baseline frequency count is an operational definition of the strength of the behavior under existing conditions. Such precise measurement is the hallmark of any scientific endeavor, and it separates O.B. Mod. from more subjective human resource management approaches, such as participation. Although the baseline is established before the intervention to see what happens to the behavior as a result of the intervention, it is important to realize that measures are taken after the intervention as well. Busy managers may feel that they do not have time to record behavioral frequencies objectively, but, at least initially, they should record them in order to use the O.B. Mod. approach effectively. Most measures, however, can be taken from existing, archival data (e.g., quality and productivity numbers) that are gathered for other purposes and can be easily obtained for this measurement step of O.B. Mod.

Step 3: Functional Analysis of the Behavior

Once the performance behavior has been identified and a baseline measure has been obtained, a functional analysis is performed. A *functional analysis* identifies both the antecedents (A) and consequences (C) of the target behavior (B), or, simply stated, an A-B-C analysis is performed. As discussed under behavioristic learning theory and operant conditioning, both the antecedent and the consequent environments are vital to the understanding, prediction, and control of human behavior in organizations. In Table 16.3 a simple operant-based A-B-C functional analysis is shown. Remember that in an operant approach, cognitive mediating processes do not play a role. Such an omission may detract from the comprehensive understanding of organizational behavior and the analysis of modeling and self-control processes, but for pragmatic application, an A-B-C functional analysis may be sufficient.[83] In the A-B-C functional analysis, A is the antecedent cue, B is the performance behavior identified in step 1, and C is the contingent consequence. Table 16.3 identifies some of the As, Bs, and Cs for attendance and absenteeism. A review of absenteeism found work unit size, worker responsibility, and organizational scheduling to be three potential antecedent influences that could be used to improve employee attendance, and feedback, rewards, and punishers to be effective attendance control procedures.[84]

This functional analysis step of O.B. Mod. brings out the problem-solving nature of the approach. Both the antecedent cues that emit the behavior, and sometimes control it, and the consequences that are currently maintaining the behavior must be identified and understood before an effective intervention strategy can be developed. In this step, the question may be asked as to whether the employee can do the identified performance behavior if his/her life depended on it. If the answer is "no," then there may be an

TABLE 16.3 An Example of Functional Analysis

Functional Analysis of Attendance Behaviors		
A ⟶	*B* ⟶	*C*
Antecedent Cues	*Behaviors*	*Consequences*
Awareness of any consequence	Going to bed on time	Reward programs
Advertising	Setting the alarm	Contingent time off
Meetings	Waking up	Gifts and prizes
Memorandums	Getting dressed	Preferred jobs
Orientation	Getting children off	Social
Bulletin board	to school	Attention
Observation of any consequence	Leaving home	Recognition
Social status and pressure	Getting a baby-sitter	Praise
Temporal cues	Driving to work	Feedback
Special events	Reporting to work	Data on attendance
Weather		

Functional Analysis of Absenteeism Behaviors		
A ⟶	*B* ⟶	*C*
Antecedent Cues	*Behaviors*	*Consequences*
Illness/accident	Getting up late	Discipline programs
Hangover	Sleeping in	Verbal reprimands
Lack of transportation	Staying home	Written reprimands
Traffic	Drinking	Pay docks
No day care facilities	Fishing/hunting	Layoffs
Family problems	Working at home	Dismissals
Company policies	Visiting	Social consequences from
Group or personal norms	Caring for sick child	coworkers
Seniority/age		Escape from and avoidance
Awareness/observation of		of working
any consequence		Nothing

Source: Fred Luthans and Mark Martinko, "An Organizational Behavior Modification Analysis of Absenteeism," *Human Resources Management,* Fall 1976, p. 15. Used with permission.

"A" problem (i.e., equipment, training, even expectations) that must be attended to. However, this is usually not the case. The employees can do the behavior if their lives depend on it, but they are not doing it. Then this becomes a "C" problem. They know how to do the desired performance behavior and there is all the necessary support to do it, but there are not reinforcing consequences. This lack of reinforcing consequences is the major problem and challenge facing behavioral management. The accompanying Application Example: Functional Analysis in Action gives the functional analysis of a production supervisor's problem of his workers' taking unscheduled breaks.

Step 4: Development of an Intervention Strategy

The first three steps in an O.B. Mod. approach are preliminary to this action step, the intervention. The goal of the intervention is to strengthen and accelerate functional performance behaviors and/or weaken and decelerate dysfunctional behaviors. There are several strategies that can be used, but the main ones are positive reinforcement and punishment–positive reinforcement.

A Positive Reinforcement Strategy. Positive, not negative, reinforcement is recommended as an effective intervention strategy for O.B. Mod. The reason is that positive

APPLICATION EXAMPLE

Functional Analysis in Action

In an actual case of an O.B. Mod. application, a production supervisor in a large manufacturing firm identified unscheduled breaks as a critical behavior affecting the performance of his department. It seemed that workers were frequently wandering off the job, and when they were not tending their machines, time—and irrecoverable production—was lost. When a baseline measure of this critical behavior was obtained, the supervisor was proved to be right. The data indicated that unscheduled breaks (defined as leaving the job for reasons other than to take a scheduled break or to obtain materials) were occurring in the department on a relatively frequent basis. The functional analysis was performed to determine the antecedent(s) and consequence(s) of the unscheduled-break behavior.

It was found that the clock served as the antecedent cue for the critical behavior. The workers in this department started work at 8 A.M., they had their first scheduled break at 10 A.M., and they had lunch at noon. They started again at 1 P.M., had a break at 3 P.M., and quit at 5 P.M. The functional analysis revealed that almost precisely at 9 A.M., 11 A.M., 2 P.M., and 4 P.M., a number of workers were leaving their jobs and going to the rest room. In other words, the clock served as a cue for them to take an unscheduled break midway between starting time and the first scheduled break, between the first scheduled break and lunch, between lunch and the scheduled afternoon break, and between the afternoon break and quitting time. The clock did not cause the behavior; it served only as a cue to emit the behavior. On the other hand, the behavior was under stimulus control of the clock because the clock dictated when the behavior would occur. The consequence, however, was what was maintaining the behavior. The critical behavior was a function of its consequences. The functional analysis revealed that the consequence of the unscheduled-break behavior was escaping from a dull, boring task (that is, the unscheduled-break behavior was being negatively reinforced) and/or meeting with coworkers and friends to socialize and have a cigarette (that is, the unscheduled-break behavior was being positively reinforced). Through such a functional analysis, the antecedents and consequences are identified so that an effective intervention strategy can be developed.

reinforcement represents a form of *positive control of behavior,* whereas negative reinforcement represents a form of *negative control of behavior.* Traditionally, and to a large extent still today, organizations depend on negative control. People come to work in order not to be fired, and they look busy when the supervisor walks by in order not to be punished. Under positive control, the person behaves in a certain way in order to receive the desired consequence. Under positive control, people come to work in order to be recognized for making a contribution to their department's goal of perfect attendance, or they keep busy whether the supervisor is around or not in order to receive incentive pay or because they get social recognition/attention and feedback for the good job. Positive control through a positive reinforcement intervention strategy is much more effective and longer lasting than negative control. It creates a much healthier and more productive organizational climate.

A positive reinforcer used as an O.B. Mod. intervention strategy could be anything, as long as it increases the performance behavior. Most often money is thought of as the logical, or sometimes the only, positive reinforcer available to managers using this approach. However, as the discussion of monetary reward systems in Chapter 5 and earlier in this chapter points out, money is potentially a very powerful reinforcer, but it often turns out to be ineffective because it is not contingently administered as a consequence of the behavior being managed. Besides money, positive reinforcers that are also very powerful, readily available to all behavioral managers, and cost nothing are the social reinforcers (attention and recognition) and performance feedback. These reinforcers (money, recognition, and feedback) can be and, as has been demonstrated through research,[85] have been used as an effective O.B. Mod. strategy to improve employee performance.

A Punishment–Positive Reinforcement Strategy.   There is little debate that a positive reinforcement strategy is the most effective intervention for O.B. Mod. Yet realistically it is recognized that in some cases the use of punishment to weaken and decelerate undesirable behaviors cannot be avoided. This would be true in the case of something like unsafe behaviors that need to be decreased immediately. However, as was pointed out earlier, so many negative side effects such as hate and revenge accompany the use of punishment that it should be avoided if at all possible. Punished behavior tends to be only temporarily suppressed; for example, if a supervisor reprimands a subordinate for some dysfunctional behavior, the behavior will decrease in the presence of the supervisor but will surface again when the supervisor is absent. In addition, a punished person becomes very anxious and uptight; reliance on punishment may have a disastrous impact on employee satisfaction and create unnecessary stress.

Perhaps the biggest problem with the use of punishment, however, is that it is very difficult for a supervisor to switch roles from punisher to positive reinforcer. Some supervisors and managers rely on a negative approach so much in dealing with their subordinates that it is almost impossible for them to administer positive reinforcement effectively. This is a bad situation for the management of human resources because the use of positive reinforcement is a much more effective way of changing employee behavior. If punishment is deemed necessary, the desirable alternative behavior (for example, safe behavior) should be positively reinforced at the first opportunity. Use of this combination strategy will cause the alternative desirable behavior to begin to replace the undesirable behavior in the person's behavioral repertoire. Punishment should never be used alone as an O.B. Mod. intervention. If punishment is absolutely necessary, it should only be used in combination with positive reinforcement.

Step 5: Evaluation to Ensure Performance Improvement

A glaring weakness of most human resource management programs is the absence of any systematic, built-in evaluation. A comprehensive analysis of the evaluation of human resources programs concluded that the traditional approach has been "to review a program with one or two vice presidents at the corporate office, various managers in the field, and perhaps a group of prospective trainees. It continues to be used until someone in a position of authority decides that the program has outlived its usefulness. All of this is done on the basis of opinion and judgment."[86] Such haphazard evaluations have resulted in the termination of some effective programs and the perpetuation of some ineffective ones. In either case, there are severe credibility problems, and today all programs dealing with people, whether they are government social service programs or human resource management programs, are under the pressure of evaluation and accountability. Human resource managers no longer have the luxury of just trying something new and different and hoping they can improve performance. Today there is pressure for everything that is tried to be proved to have value. As in the case of the validity of selection and appraisal techniques, systematic evaluations of all human resource management techniques should have been done all along.

O.B. Mod. attempts to meet the credibility and accountability problems head-on by including evaluation as an actual part of the process. In this last step of the approach, the need for Kirkpatrick's well-known four levels of evaluation (reaction, learning, behavioral change, and performance improvement) is stressed. The reaction level refers simply to whether the people using the approach and those having it used on them like it. If O.B. Mod. is well received and there is a positive reaction to it, there is a better chance of its being used effectively. In addition, reaction evaluations are helpful because (1) positive reactions help ensure organizational support, (2) they can provide information for planning future programs, (3) favorable reactions can enhance the other levels of evaluation (learning, behavioral change, and performance improvement), and (4) they can provide useful comparative data between units and across time.[87]

The second level of evaluation is learning, which is especially important when first implementing an O.B. Mod. approach. Do the people using the approach understand the theoretical background and underlying assumptions and the meaning of, and reasons for, the steps in the model? If they do not, the model will again tend to be used ineffectively. The third level is aimed at behavioral change. Are behaviors actually being changed? The charting of behaviors started in step 2 of the O.B. Mod. process gives objective data for this level of evaluation. The fourth and final level, performance improvement, is the most important. The major purpose of O.B. Mod. is not just to receive a favorable reaction, learn the concepts, and change behaviors. These dimensions are important mainly because they contribute to the overriding purpose, which is to improve performance. "Hard" measures (for example, data on quantity and quality, turnover, absenteeism, customer complaints, employee grievances, safety, length of patient stay, number of clients served, and rate of return on investment) and scientific methodology are used whenever possible to systematically evaluate the impact of O.B. Mod. on performance.

Application of Behavioral Management

There is a considerable body of research that has evaluated the effectiveness of behavioral performance management in general and the five-step O.B. Mod. approach in particular. It has been widely applied in manufacturing as well as in nonmanufacturing, service-oriented organizations. In addition to the direct application of O.B. Mod. as described, considerable basic research has been conducted on operant and social learning and social cognitive variables in experimental psychology. For many years and in very recent times, a number of studies have assessed the application of the behavioral management approach to improving employee performance in a number of different areas. The following summarizes these areas:[88]

1. *Employee productivity.* Most applications by far have focused on performance output. The considerable number of research studies clearly indicate that employee productivity or task completion is positively affected by behavioral management techniques. The performance improvement is for both quantity and quality of employee output and cuts across virtually all organizational settings and all intervention techniques.

2. *Absenteeism and tardiness.* This is probably the second-biggest area of application. Studies that have examined this area have typically used small monetary incentives

or lottery incentive systems for attendance or promptness and/or punishers for absenteeism or tardiness. One extensive search of this literature found very positive results.[89] The six most sound methodological studies reported an 18 to 50 percent reduction in the absence rate and a 90 percent reduction in the frequency of tardiness. One study found a positive, causal impact that an O.B. Mod. program had on the attendance of employees in a bank.[90]

3. *Safety and accident prevention.* Most organizations, especially manufacturing firms and others in which dangerous equipment is used, are very concerned about safety. However, because accidents occur at such a relatively low frequency, most studies have focused on reducing identifiable safety hazards or increasing safe behaviors (for example, wearing earplugs, which went from 35 to 95 percent compliance according to one study;[91] wearing hard hats; and keeping the safety guard in place on dangerous equipment). A review of the research indicates the considerable success that behavioral management techniques have had in these areas.[92] Some actual company examples are Boston Gas, where employees without accidents are eligible for lottery drawings; Virginia Power, where employees can win from $50 to $1000 for safe work habits; Southern New England Telecommunications, which gives gift coupons to employees without accidents; and Turner Corporation, a New York-based engineering and construction firm, where employees can earn company stock if they meet safety goals. All these companies report lower accident rates through the use of a behavioral management approach. Recently, Southern Fineblanking, a 225-employee metal stamping plant in South Carolina, reported after implementing a behavioral management program aimed at safety that there was a 33 percent reduction in accidents, and the average cost per injury decreased from $1,400 to $500.[93]

4. *Sales performance.* Sales managers and trainers have traditionally relied on internal motivation techniques to get their salespeople to improve their performance. For example, one behavioral performance management consultant tells about a company that gave its sales personnel a typical high-powered, multimedia training program, which supposedly taught them effective selling skills. However, when the enthusiastic trainees finished the program and actually tried the things presented to them in the program, they received little, if any, feedback or reinforcement. Within a few weeks the enthusiasm began to wane, and, most important, actual sales performance began to decline.[94] In other words, even though these salespeople had probably acquired effective selling skills during their training, the environment did not support (reinforce) the use of these skills. A behavioral performance management approach, in which important selling behaviors such as customer approach, suggestive statements, and closing statements are identified, measured, analyzed, intervened in, and evaluated, would be an alternative to the motivation-skill-teaching approach. A comprehensive review of the behavioral approach to sales in restaurants, retail stores, wholesale establishments, and telephone operations found considerable success.[95] When a combination of antecedent and consequence intervention strategies was used, dramatic improvements were shown in areas such as wine and dessert sales, average customer transactions, customer assistance, sales forecasting, sales-call frequency, sales of telephone services, and airline reservations. A study of fast-food restaurants also found that antecedent prompts ("Can I get you some fries with that?") significantly increased consumer purchases.[96] The successful application of O.B. Mod. to the selling, absent-from-the-workstation, and idle-time behaviors of clerks in a large retail store was also found.[97]

Although these results are not exhaustive and do not always reflect the exact O.B. Mod. model outlined in this chapter, they are representative of the growing application of the behavioral performance management approach. In addition, comprehensive reviews generally support the findings.[98]

Research Findings on O.B. Mod.

The specific O.B. Mod. model has been directly tested and has been found to have positive performance results in both manufacturing[99] and service organizations (retail, banking and hospital).[100] The O.B. Mod. approach has also "gone international" and has been shown to have a positive impact on the performance behaviors and output of Russian factory workers[101] and retail clerks.[102]

Most recently the Stajkovic and Luthans meta-analysis mentioned earlier and in the principles at the end of the chapter (19 studies over the past 20 years) examined the relationship between O.B. Mod. as defined here and task performance.[103] The overall results indicated that O.B. Mod. resulted, on average, in an impressive 17 percent increase in task performance across all the studies. As shown in Table 16.4, further analysis revealed that O.B. Mod. had a stronger average effect in manufacturing firms than in service organizations, but the O.B. Mod. approach was highly significant in both. The difference in application effectiveness of O.B. Mod. between manufacturing and service organizations was explained as

> (1) the definition and accurate assessment of performance outcomes; and (2) the nature of the employee behaviors and work processes involved in the delivery of performance outcomes. The first point refers to the difference between the definition and measurement of the more vague and complex service organization performance outcomes (e.g., customer satisfaction, return business) versus tangible performance outcomes (e.g., productivity and quality) in manufacturing organizations. The second point refers to the difference between specifying service delivery employee behaviors and processes that go into making a tangible product. Service performance behaviors and outcomes are more complex and less identifiable than those found in manufacturing organizations.[104]

So, although O.B. Mod. may be more difficult to apply in service than in manufacturing organizations, it still works in both, and the challenge is to make it even more effective in service applications.

TABLE **16.4** Percentage Performance Improvement in Manufacturing and Service Organizations According to Different Types of O.B. Mod. Reinforcers

Type of Organization	Overall Effect	Monetary (I)	Performance Feedback (II)	Social Atten/Recog. (III)	Simultaneous application of I & II	Simultaneous application of II & III	Simultaneous application of I, II, & III
Manufacturing	33%	39%	41%	(No studies)	(No studies)	41%	44%
Service	13%	14%	6%	15%	30%	30%	9%

Note 1. Overall effectiveness of O.B. Mod. in terms of performance improvement regardless of type of organization and reinforcer is 17 percent.

Note 2. All percentages presented in this table are based on the value of the unbiased average effect size statistic ($d.$) (from Hedges and Olkin's 1985 meta-analysis book) respectively for each category. All $d. < .05$ statistical significance.

Source: Adapted from Alexander D. Stajkovic and Fred Luthans, "A Meta-Analysis of the Effects of Organizational Behavior Modification on Task Performance, 1975–1995," *Academy of Management Journal,* Vol. 40, No. 5, 1997, pp. 1122–1149; and Fred Luthans and Alexander D. Stajkovic, "Reinforce for Performance: The Need to Go Beyond Pay and Even Rewards," *Academy of Management Executive,* Vol. 13, No. 2, 1999, p. 54.

The results in Table 16.4 also show the differential effects of the three reinforcement interventions and their combinations. In manufacturing, it is interesting, and important to cost-conscious human resource management, to note that the nonfinancial reinforcers (performance feedback and feedback used in combination with social attention/recognition) had about the same effect as the use of money or money in combination with feedback and social attention/recognition. In service organizations, the differential effects are more complicated, but again it is interesting to note that the monetary and the social attention/recognition had about the same impact, and when the social attention/recognition was combined with the feedback, it had twice as big an impact as money alone and the same as money combined with feedback. In other words, in both manufacturing and service applications of O.B. Mod., nonfinancial reinforcers may have as big an impact on performance improvement as the costly financial ones. The overall implications of these findings from the meta-analysis are that behavioral management systematically applied through steps such as the O.B. Mod. model can help meet the performance improvement challenges facing today's organizations.

Summary

Learning is a major psychological process, but it has not been as popular in the study of organizational behavior as constructs such as personality, attitudes, or motivation. Also, it has not been generally recognized that there are different types of learning and different theoretical explanations of learning (behavioristic, cognitive, and social). Despite the controversy surrounding learning theory, there are many accepted principles of learning that are derived largely from experimentation and the analysis of operant conditioning. Reinforcement is generally recognized as the single most important principle in the learning process and is most relevant to behavioral performance management. On the basis of the classic law of effect, or "Laws of Behavior," reinforcement can be operationally defined as anything that increases the strength of a behavior and that tends to induce repetitions of the behavior that preceded the reinforcement. Reinforcers may be positive (the application of a desirable consequence) or negative (termination or withdrawal of an undesirable consequence), but both have the impact of strengthening the behavior and increasing its frequency. Punishment, on the other hand, decreases the strength and frequency of the behavior. There is also the special case of extinction (no consequence) that also will decrease the behavior over time.

The major direct application of learning theories and the reinforcement principle in particular is behavioral performance management. Both financial and nonfinancial (social attention/recognition and performance feedback) are important, but somewhat complex, reinforcers that must be carefully applied in behavioral performance management. Behavioral management can be effectively applied through the O.B. Mod. steps: identify the performance-related behavior; measure it to determine the baseline frequency; functionally analyze both the antecedents and the consequences of the behavior (A-B-C); intervene through a positive reinforcement strategy to accelerate the critical performance behaviors; and evaluate to make sure the intervention is, in fact, increasing performance. The behavioral management approach in general and O.B. Mod. in particular have been demonstrated to have a significant positive impact on employee performance in both manufacturing and nonmanufacturing, service-oriented organizations.

ENDING WITH META-ANALYTIC RESEARCH FINDINGS

OB PRINCIPLE: The use of organizational behavior modification (O.B. Mod.) increases employee performance.

Meta-Analysis Results: [19 studies; 2,818 participants; $d = .51$] *On average, there is a **64 percent probability** that utilizing the five-step O.B. Mod. model to systematically manage performance-related employee behavior will lead to higher performance than not using the O.B. Mod. approach.* Further analysis indicated that the effect of O.B. Mod. interventions on performance is moderated by the type of organization and contingent reinforcer used. The effect of O.B. Mod. was found to be greater in manufacturing over service organizations. There were no significant differences among monetary, feedback, and social recognition interventions in manufacturing, but certain combinations had a bigger impact in service organizations.

Conclusion: As you have learned in this chapter, the overriding premise of reinforcement theory is that behavior is a function of its contingent consequences. This is an external, behavioral paradigm as opposed to the internal, cognitive paradigm that served as the foundation for the topics of perception, attribution, personality, attitudes, and motivation. Whereas job design and goal setting are application techniques for the cognitive paradigm, O.B. Mod. represents an effective method of applying the behavioral paradigm to manage employee behavior for performance improvement. In particular, by training supervisors and managers in the five-step O.B. Mod. model of identifying, measuring, analyzing, intervening, and evaluating, there is a proven way to improve performance. Importantly, besides monetary reward interventions, no-cost performance feedback and social attention/recognition are found to be effective ways to improve employee performance using the O.B. Mod. approach to behavioral performance management.

Source: Adapted from Alexander D. Stajkovic and Fred Luthans, "A Meta-Analysis of the Effects of Organizational Behavior Modification on Task Performance," *Academy of Management Journal,* Vol. 40, No. 5, 1997, pp. 1122–1149.

OB PRINCIPLE: The use of nonfinancial interventions of feedback and social recognition administered in an O.B. Mod. approach improves employee performance.

Meta-Analysis Results: [19 studies; 2,818 participants; (1) $d = 1.48$ for feedback in manufacturing; (2) $d = 1.49$ for feedback simultaneously applied with social recognition in manufacturing; (3) $d = .19$ for feedback in service organizations; (4) $d = .53$ for feedback simultaneously applied with social recognition in service organizations; and (5) $d = .44$ for social recognition in service organizations (there were no studies with social recognition only in manufacturing)] *On average, there is a: (1) **85 percent probability** that employees receiving performance feedback only in manufacturing firms; (2) **85 percent probability** that employees receiving simultaneous feedback and social recognition in manufacturing; (3) **55 percent probability** that employees receiving feedback in service organizations; (4) **65 percent probability***

Source: Adapted from Alexander D. Stajkovic and Fred Luthans, "A Meta-Analysis of the Effects of Organizational Behavior Modification on Task Performance," *Academy of Management Journal,* Vol. 40, No. 5, 1997, pp. 1122–1149.

that employees receiving simultaneous feedback and social recognition in service organizations; and (5) **62 percent probability** *that employees receiving social recognition only in service organizations will perform better than those employees whose behavior is not contingently reinforced by performance feedback and/or social recognition.*

Conclusion: Providing contingently administered nonfinancial rewards of performance feedback and social attention/recognition are perhaps the most overlooked methods of effectively increasing employee performance. Although financial incentives, when administered contingently, can be powerful reinforcers, so can no-cost feedback and social attention/recognition. In fact, many employees, depending on the situation, respond more positively to the nonfinancial rewards than they do to money. In addition to performance, studies have shown that a major reason why employees leave organizations is due to a lack of feedback on how they are doing and recognition from their supervisors. All employees want to be informed of how they are doing, noticed, and given attention for their contributions. Thus, effective supervisors and managers are taking advantage of feedback and social attention/recognition as alternatives to costly and often poorly administered incentive pay and pay-for-performance plans.

Questions for Discussion and Review

1. Do you agree with the statement that learning is involved in almost everything that everyone does? Explain.
2. What are the major dimensions of behavioristic, cognitive, social learning, and social congnitive theories?
3. What is the difference between classical and operant conditioning?
4. What is the difference between positive and negative reinforcement? What is the difference between negative reinforcement and punishment? Provide some examples.
5. What could be done to make money more effective as a reinforcer for behavioral management?
6. What are some examples of nonfinancial reinforcers? How can these be used to improve employee performance?
7. What are the five steps of O.B. Mod.? Briefly summarize the critical dimensions of each step that will help improve employee performance.
8. In what areas has behavioral management been successfully applied?
9. Summarize the results of the meta-analysis on O.B. Mod. What recomendations would you make to the HRM department based on these findings?

Internet Exercise: Applying Behavior Management Principles to Athletic Performance

The principles of reinforcement and behavior management can and should be found in all sports. Using a search engine, go to the websites of various sports and see how reinforcement does and should play a role in the performance of the athletes. For example, you might compare golfers (http://www.pgatour.com) with football (http://www./nfl.com) players.

1. What specific reinforcers drive the behavior and resulting performance of the athletes in the sport you chose?
2. How might the reinforcers be different for college vs. professional athletes?
3. How could a coach effectively use behavioral management? Give some specific examples by sport.

REAL CASE:
Rewarding Big Time
for Failure

After seeing the obscene severance packages given to CEOs who ostensibly were let go, failure has never looked more lucrative.

Indeed, if the meteoric growth in executive pay already seemed troubling, the growing phenomenon of corporate boards showering generous parting gifts on failed CEOs is insulting not just to us workers, but to shareholders as well. The latest evidence: On Aug. 25, Procter & Gamble Co. disclosed that it gave just-ousted CEO Durk I. Jager a $9.5 million bonus—even though Jager lasted no more than 17 months at the helm and with P&G's stock down 50%, costing P&G shareholders more than $70 billion in wealth. But P&G looks downright penurious compared to Conseco Inc., which earlier this year gave a $49.3 million going-away gift to Stephen C. Hilbert, whose ill-fated move into subprime lending has left the insurer's recovery in question.

But if there's any villain here, it isn't Jager or Hilbert. It's the boards of their former companies, who by approving such generous parachutes, are sending the perverse message that failure has its reward. "This is the fault of the boards," argues Nell Minow, a Washington (D.C.)-based shareholder activist. For activists such as Minow, this is pure and simple corporate log-rolling. Many boards are peopled by CEOs serving as outside directors looking out for their own.

For their part, corporate directors say that the huge payouts aren't always undeserved. In the case of M. Douglas Ivester—who received a $25.5 million severance from Coca-Cola Co. last December, according to Executive Compensation Advisory Services, despite his bungling of a European contamination scare and his unwillingness to slash Coke's overhead—directors chose to take the long view of his performance. "The fellow broke his back for Coke for 25 years and made significant contributions," argues New York investment banker Herbert A. Allen, a Coke board member. Directors such as Allen also fret that trying to penalize a failed CEO would only make it more difficult to recruit outside executives. "You'd get a bad reputation in the community from which you hire very quickly," he says.

Granted, as former Coke CEO Roberto C. Goizueta's right-hand man, Ivester did a yeoman's job. But for that, Ivester had been amply rewarded, to the tune of $100 million-plus, according to *Business Week* estimates, by the time of his ouster. And despite the magnanimous intent, these are not cost-free transactions: By one estimate, Mattel Inc. will have to sell 600,000 additional Barbie dolls each year for the next decade just to cover the $1.2 million annual pension being given to ex-CEO Jill E. Barad as part of a broader $50 million severance.

Directors should take the lead of Sunbeam Corp., which after firing Albert J. Dunlap in the face of a disastrous restructuring and allegations of accounting improprieties, resisted his demands that he be allowed to accelerate all of his outstanding options. (Dunlap has since sued.) "No one should expect to make a fortune for failing at their job," argues Charles M. Elson, a Sunbeam director and law professor at the University of Delaware. Of course, because few situations are as extreme as that at Sunbeam, most CEOs can probably bank on a good-bye kiss from former employers, regardless of their performance.

1. What is your reaction to these severance packages? Can you justify them?
2. How do these examples fit with reinforcement theory and behavioral management discussed in this chapter?
3. Using the O.B. Mod. Model as a point of reference, what would you propose to be a fair contract for a CEO of a major corporation? Is this realistic at this level of management?

ORGANIZATIONAL BEHAVIOR CASE: Contrasting Styles

Henry Adams has been a production supervisor for eight years. He came up through the ranks and is known as a tough but hardworking supervisor. Jane Wake has been a production supervisor for about the same length of time and also came up through the ranks. Jane is known as a nice, hardworking boss. Over the past several years these two supervisors' sections have been head and shoulders above the other six sections on hard measures of performance (number of units produced). This is true despite the almost opposite approaches the two have taken in handling their workers. Henry explained his approach as follows:

> The only way to handle workers is to come down hard on them whenever they make a mistake. In fact, I call them together every once in a while and give them heck whether they deserve it or not, just to keep them on their toes. If they are doing a good job, I tell them that's what they're getting paid for. By taking this approach, all I have to do is walk through my area, and people start working like mad.

Jane explained her approach as follows:

> I don't believe in that human relations stuff of being nice to workers. But I do believe that a worker deserves some recognition and attention from me if he or she does a good job. If people make a mistake, I don't jump on them. I feel that we are all entitled to make some errors. On the other hand, I always do point out what the mistake was and what they should have done, and as soon as they do it right, I let them know it. Obviously, I don't have time to give attention to everyone doing things right, but I deliberately try to get around to people doing a good job every once in a while.

Although Henry's section is still right at the top along with Jane's section in units produced, personnel records show that there has been three times more turnover in Henry's section than in Jane's section, and the quality control records show that Henry's section has met quality standards only twice in the last six years, while Jane has missed attaining quality standards only once in the last six years.

1. Both these supervisors have similar backgrounds. On the basis of learning theory, how can you explain their opposite approaches to handling people?
2. What are some of the examples of punishment, positive reinforcement, and negative reinforcement found in this case? If Jane is using a reinforcement approach, how do you explain this statement: "I don't believe in that human relations stuff of being nice to workers"?
3. How do you explain the performance, turnover, and quality results in these two sections of the production department?

ORGANIZATIONAL BEHAVIOR CASE: Volunteers Can't Be Punished

Jenette Jackson is head of a volunteer agency in a large city, in charge of a volunteer staff of over 25 people. Weekly, she holds a meeting with this group in order to keep them informed and teach them the specifics of any new laws or changes in state and federal policies and procedures that might affect their work, and she discusses priorities and assignments for the group. This meeting is also a time when members can share some of the problems with and concerns for what they are personally doing and what the agency as a whole is doing. The meeting is scheduled to begin at 9 A.M. sharp every Monday. Lately, the volunteers have been filtering in every five minutes or so until almost 10 A.M. Jenette has felt she has to delay the start of the meetings until all the people arrive. The last few weeks the meetings haven't started until 10 A.M. In fact, at 9 A.M., nobody has shown up. Jenette cannot understand what has happened. She feels it is important to start the meetings at 9 A.M. so that they can be over before the whole morning is gone. However, she feels that her hands are tied because, after all, the people are volunteers and she can't push them or make them get to the meetings on time.

1. What advice would you give Jenette? In terms of reinforcement theory, explain what is happening here and what Jenette needs to do to get the meetings started on time.
2. What learning theories (operant, cognitive, and/or social) could be applied to Jenette's efforts to teach her volunteers the impact of new laws and changes in state and federal policies and procedures?
3. How could someone like Jenette use modeling to train her staff to do a more effective job?

ORGANIZATIONAL BEHAVIOR CASE: Up the Piece Rate

Larry Ames has successfully completed a company training program in O.B. Mod. He likes the approach and has started using it on the workers in his department. Following the O.B. Mod. model, he has identified several performance behaviors, measured and analyzed them, and used a positive reinforcement intervention strategy. His evaluation has shown a significant improvement in the performance of his department. Over coffee one day he commented to one of the other supervisors, "This contingent reinforcement approach really works. Before, the goody-goody people up in human resources were always telling us to try to understand and be nice to our workers. Frankly, I couldn't buy that. In the first place, I don't think there is anybody who can really *understand* my people—I certainly can't. More important, though, is that under this approach I am only nice *contingently*—contingent on good performance. That makes a lot more sense, and my evaluation proves that it works." The other supervisor commented, "You are being reinforced for use of the reinforcement technique on your people." Larry said, "Sure I am. Just like the trainer said: `Behavior that is reinforced will strengthen and repeat itself.' I'm so reinforced that I am starting to use it on my wife and kids at home, and you know what? It works there, too."

The next week Larry was called into the department head's office and was told, "Larry, as you know, your department has shown a substantial increase in performance since you completed the O.B. Mod. program. I have sent our industrial engineer down there to analyze your standards. I have received her report, and it looks like we will have to adjust your rates upward by 10 percent. Otherwise, we are going to have to pay too much incentive pay. I'm sure you can use some of the things you learned in that O.B. Mod. program to break the news to your people. Good luck, and keep up the good work."

1. Do you think Larry's boss, the department head, attended the O.B. Mod. program? Analyze the department head's action in terms of O.B. Mod.
2. What do you think Larry's reaction will be now and in the future? How do you think Larry's people will react?
3. Given the 10 percent increase in standards, is there any way that Larry could still use the O.B. Mod. approach with his people? With his boss? How?

ORGANIZATIONAL
BEHAVIOR CASE:
A Tardiness Problem

You have been getting a lot of complaints recently from your boss about the consistent tardiness of your work group. The time-sheet records indicate that your people's average start-up time is about 10 minutes late. Although you have never been concerned about the tardiness problem, your boss is really getting upset. He points out that the tardiness reduces the amount of production time and delays for the start-up of the production process. You realize that the tardiness is a type of avoidance behavior—it delays the start of a very boring job. Your work group is very cohesive, and each of the members will follow what the group wants to do. One of the leaders of the group seems to spend a lot of time getting the group into trouble. You want the group to come in on time, but you don't really want a confrontation on the issue because, frankly, you don't think it is important enough to risk getting everyone upset with you. You decide to use an O.B. Mod. approach.

1. Trace through the five steps in the O.B. Mod. model to show how it could be applied to this tardiness problem. Make sure you are specific in identifying the critical performance behaviors and the antecedents and consequences of the functional analysis.
2. Do you think the approach you have suggested in your answer will really work? Why or why not?

CHAPTER 17

Effective Leadership Processes

Learning Objectives

Define leadership.

Present the background and classic studies of leadership.

Discuss the traditional theories of leadership, including the trait, group and exchange, contingency, and path-goal approaches.

Identify modern theoretical processes for leadership, such as charismatic, transformational, social cognitive, and substitutes for leadership.

Examine leadership across cultures giving special attention to the GLOBE project.

Starting with Best Practice
Leader's Advice

Learning Organization Guru Peter Senge on the Role of the Leadership Process

MIT's Peter Senge's best-selling book The Fifth Discipline: The Art and Practice of the Learning Organization *catapulted him into becoming one of the most sought after speakers and consultants in the world. His open-systems thinking is primarily centered around the value of organization learning. However, as the following comments indicate, he also has strong views on how the leadership process should occur at all levels in order for the organization to be successful in today's environment.*

Q1: *You say a major key to the learning organization is systems thinking. People like Herbert Simon, Buckminster Fuller, and Kenneth Boulding were talking about systems thinking in the 1960s, so the concept shouldn't be entirely new to everyone in the business world. Conceptually, at least, don't most people understand that things affect each other? Don't they already know that their organizations are complex systems?*

Senge: There is a big difference between an idea and a capability. Reading an article about nuclear physics doesn't make me a nuclear physicist. This is a problem we have in business all the time: People go off to a two- or three-day training program and think they can do something. The only thing you can do after two or three days of training is something trivial—by definition.

The issue is how to move from concept to capability. It's been the death of many good ideas. The problem is that you and I have spent our whole lives being nonsystems thinkers. That's not easy to change. But if you can shift your assumptions and really embrace systems thinking—the way you see yourself and the world around you—you begin to see that no one is ever in control. Organizations revolve around someone trying to be in control. Complex systems aren't controllable. They can't be figured out. Systems thinking is a radical shift, and it can't be brought about by rational analytical tools.

That's why we talk about five disciplines. You have to master the disciplines if you are going to be open to the idea of complexity and real systems insights. You'll spend a lifetime working at it. It's hard to accept that we don't have control of the systems we're part of. Control is not possible with human beings and living systems.

Q2: *Yet the defining business icon has been the heroic CEO who sits astride a giant corporation—a huge system—and steers it brilliantly along the course he chooses. Michael Eisner at Disney, Jack Welch at GE, Bill Gates at Microsoft, John Reed at CitiCorp, Mike Armstrong at AT&T . . . the list goes on and on. Are you suggesting these people aren't really very important to the success of the companies they run?*

Senge: I'm not saying they're not important. There is a big difference between saying that GE's success is not due entirely to Jack Welch and saying that Jack Welch doesn't matter. But the fact is, much of the renown these CEOs have gained is an artifact of the media. It's hard for the *Wall Street Journal* to write a story about General Electric; it would be a story about thousands of people doing thousands of things. But it's easy to write a story about Jack Welch. The business media is addicted to this cult of the hero leader. Leo Tolstoy had an incisive critique about 150 years ago in *War and Peace.* He said that we don't have any idea how to talk about the forces of history, so instead we talk about a few individuals and pretend this is an explanation.

It is more helpful to talk about leadership communities. There are three different types of leaders in such a community. Executive leaders are one, and they do matter. But they matter in ways that aren't treated very well in the public discussions. They are designers and mentors. They're ultimately responsible for the climate or the overall environment.

The most important leaders are line leaders—local managers who decide how people spend their time and whether or not innovations really get integrated into the business. CEOs make speeches and reorganize, but have very little impact on the day-to-day operation in any kind of business. That's why you see so many reorganizations. It's one of the few things a CEO can do.

The third kind of leader is hard for most people to understand. We've called them networkers—people who spread new ideas.

Q3: *Line managers—the second type of leaders you mention—are deluged with ideas about how to run or how to change an enterprise. How do they sort out all the possible things they might act on? How do they decide what to do?*

Senge: The real question is, Are people serious enough to start to develop their own capability? If they're looking for an answer, they should go find a consultant who will sell them an answer. And they'll get another answer next year, and another answer the year after that. Or, they can start to think that there are some deeper issues that are causing problems for them—problems caused because of how they think and how they interact with people. They can start thinking about things at that deeper level and then start to make some headway. But managers are under pressure for quick fixes: "Tell me three things I need to do!" And there will always be someone out there to sell it to them. Oscar Wilde put it very well: "For every complex question there is a simple answer, and it's wrong."

Q4: *So trying to line up the variables that may be influencing a situation, and sorting them out rationally or logically or statistically—that sort of thing doesn't help?*

Senge: What I mean is that you can't fight complexity with complexity. You have to fight it with learning, with know-how. Take something simple you know how to do, like walking. Write down three steps to explain walking. You can't do it. Michael Polanyi, the famous philosopher, had a wonderful line about this kind of personal knowledge: "We know far more than we can ever tell." That's the essence of personal knowledge, of human know-how—it can't be reduced to simple how-to answers and steps.

Learning occurs when people engage in complicated undertakings and find a way to reflect on how they're doing it—and perhaps engage a coach or mentor who has some tools and methods for learning. Those tools are different from answers. Answers are for lazy people who don't want to learn how to use a thinking method to learn how to deal with a practical problem. I have zero respect for trying to find an "answer."

There is a profound difference between having an answer and having an approach you can use to deal with a complicated and different practical problem.

This chapter on leadership processes and the next on great leaders styles, activities, and skills are an appropriate conclusion to the study of organizational behavior. Leadership is the focus and conduit of most of the other areas of organizational behavior. The first half of the chapter deals with the definition and classical background. The last half then presents the major theoretical processes of leadership. Particular attention is devoted to both traditional and modern theories of leadership.

WHAT IS LEADERSHIP?

Leadership has probably been written about, formally researched, and informally discussed more than any other single topic. Despite all this attention given to leadership, there is still considerable controversy. Some organizational behavior theorists do not even recognize leadership. For example, an academic article started with this assumption: "The social construct of leadership is viewed as a myth that functions to reinforce existing social beliefs and structures about the necessity of hierarchy and leaders in organizations."[1] In another more recent article, leadership guru Warren Bennis gives the title "The End of Leadership" to make his point that effective leadership cannot exist without the full inclusion, initiatives, and the cooperation of employees. In other words, one cannot be a great leader without great followers.[2] In spite of the seeming discontent at least with the traditional approaches to leadership theory and practice, throughout history the difference between success and failure, whether in a war, a business, a protest movement, or a basketball game, has been attributed to leadership. A recent Gallup survey indicates that most employees believe that it is the leader, not the company, that guides the culture and creates situations where workers can be happy and successful.[3] The intensity of today's concern about leadership is pointed out by recent observations such as the following:

> Desperate for answers, corporations and consultants are drawing up lists of so-called leadership competencies, from "thinking outside of the box" to "musical listening," which means hearing the emotional content behind someone's words. But also how to avoid the IBM trap of indoctrinating people with irrelevant skills?[4]

Regardless of all the attention given to leadership and its recognized importance, it does remain pretty much of a "black box," or unexplainable concept. It is known to exist and to have a tremendous influence on human performance, but its inner workings and specific dimensions cannot be precisely spelled out. Despite these inherent difficulties, many attempts have been made over the years to define leadership. Unfortunately, almost everyone who studies or writes about leadership defines it differently. About the only commonality is the role that influence plays in leadership.[5]

In recent years, many theorists and practitioners have emphasized the difference between managers and leaders. For example, as Bennis has noted: "To survive in the twenty-first century, we are going to need a new generation of leaders—leaders, not managers. The distinction is an important one. Leaders conquer the context—the volatile, turbulent, ambiguous surroundings that sometimes seem to conspire against us and will surely suffocate us if we let them—while managers surrender to it."[6] He then

TABLE 17.1 Some Characteristics of Managers versus Leaders in the Twenty-First Century

Manager Characteristics	Leader Characteristics
Administers	Innovates
A copy	An original
Maintains	Develops
Focuses on systems and structure	Focuses on people
Relies on control	Inspires trust
Short-range view	Long-range perspective
Asks how and when	Asks what and why
Eye on the bottom line	Eye on the horizon
Imitates	Originates
Accepts the status quo	Challenges the status quo
Classic good soldier	Own person
Does things right	Does the right thing

Source: Adapted from Warren G. Bennis, "Managing the Dream: Leadership in the 21st Century," *Journal of Organizational Change Management,* Vol. 2, No. 1, 1989, p. 7.

goes on to point out his thoughts on some specific differences between leaders and managers, as shown in Table 17.1. Obviously, these are not scientifically derived differences, but it is probably true that an individual can be a leader without being a manager and a manager without being a leader.

Although many specific definitions could be cited, most would depend on the theoretical orientation taken. Besides influence, leadership has been defined in terms of group processes, personality, compliance, particular behaviors, persuasion, power, goal achievement, interaction, role differentiation, initiation of structure, and combinations of two or more of these.[7] As George B. Weathersby, the past president of the American Management Association, notes, "the nature of work has dramatically changed due to a number of factors, one of which is increasing turnover in the rank-and-file and managerial levels. In an environment in which work may evolve to employment on a project-by-project basis, the need for visionary leaders who are able to communicate, encourage, and persuade (rather than command) is going to continue to intensify."[8]

Perhaps as good a definition as any comes from a *Fortune* article, which states: "When you boil it all down, contemporary leadership seems to be a matter of aligning people toward common goals and empowering them to take the actions needed to reach them."[9] An equally good definition of leadership is implied in hockey great Wayne Gretzky's famous quote: "I don't go where the puck is; I go to where the puck is going to be." But, as Bennis recently pointed out, "the issue is not just interpreting and envisioning the future, or knowing where the puck is going to be, but being able to create the kind of meaning for people, the values that make sense to them, where there's enough trust in the system so it's going to stick."[10] Whatever specific definition is used is not important. What is important is to interpret leadership in terms of the specific theoretical process and to realize that leadership, however defined, does make a difference.

THE HISTORICALLY IMPORTANT STUDIES ON LEADERSHIP

Unlike many other topics in the field of organizational behavior, there are a number of studies and a considerable body of knowledge on leadership. A review of the better-known classic studies can help set the stage for the traditional and modern theories of leadership.

The Iowa Leadership Studies

A series of pioneering leadership studies conducted in the late 1930s by Ronald Lippitt and Ralph K. White under the general direction of Kurt Lewin at the University of Iowa has had a lasting impact. Lewin is recognized as the father of group dynamics and as an important cognitive theorist. In the initial studies, hobby clubs for ten-year-old boys were formed. Each club was submitted to all three different styles of leadership—authoritarian, democratic, and laissez-faire. The authoritarian leader was very directive and allowed no participation. This leader tended to give individual attention when praising and criticizing, but tried to be friendly or impersonal rather than openly hostile. The democratic leader encouraged group discussion and decision making. This leader tried to be "objective" in giving praise or criticism and to be one of the group in spirit. The laissez-faire leader gave complete freedom to the group; this leader essentially provided no leadership.

Unfortunately, the effects that styles of leadership had on productivity were not directly examined. The experiments were designed primarily to examine patterns of aggressive behavior. However, an important by-product was the insight that was gained into the productive behavior of a group. For example, the researchers found that the boys subjected to the autocratic leaders reacted in one of two ways: either aggressively or apathetically. Both the aggressive and apathetic behaviors were deemed to be reactions to the frustration caused by the autocratic leader. The researchers also pointed out that the apathetic groups exhibited outbursts of aggression when the autocratic leader left the room or when a transition was made to a freer leadership atmosphere. The laissez-faire leadership climate actually produced the greatest number of aggressive acts from the group. The democratically led group fell between the one extremely aggressive group and the four apathetic groups under the autocratic leaders.

Sweeping generalizations on the basis of the Lippitt and White studies are dangerous. Preadolescent boys making masks and carving soap are a long way from adults working in a complex, modern organization. Furthermore, from the viewpoint of today's behavioral science research methodology, many of the variables were not controlled. Nevertheless, these leadership studies have important historical significance. They were the first attempts to determine, experimentally, what effects styles of leadership have on a group. Like the Hawthorne studies presented in Chapter 1, the Iowa studies are too often automatically discounted or at least marginalized because they were experimentally crude. The value of the studies was that they were the first to analyze leadership from the standpoint of scientific methodology, and, more important, they showed that different styles of leadership can produce different, complex reactions from the same or similar groups.

The Ohio State Leadership Studies

At the end of World War II, the Bureau of Business Research at Ohio State University initiated a series of studies on leadership. An interdisciplinary team of researchers from psychology, sociology, and economics developed and used the Leader Behavior Description Questionnaire (LBDQ) to analyze leadership in numerous types of groups and situations. Studies were made of Air Force commanders and members of bomber crews; officers, noncommissioned personnel, and civilian administrators in the Navy Department; manufacturing supervisors; executives of regional cooperatives; college administrators; teachers, principals, and school superintendents; and leaders of various student and civilian groups.

The Ohio State studies started with the premise that no satisfactory definition of leadership existed. They also recognized that previous work had too often assumed that *leadership* was synonymous with *good leadership*. The Ohio State group was determined to study leadership, regardless of definition or of whether it was effective or ineffective.

In the first step, the LBDQ was administered in a wide variety of situations. In order to examine how the leader was described, the answers to the questionnaire were then subjected to factor analysis. The outcome was amazingly consistent. The same two dimensions of leadership continually emerged from the questionnaire data. They were *consideration* and *initiating structure*. These two factors were found in a wide variety of studies encompassing many kinds of leadership positions and contexts. The researchers carefully emphasize that the studies show only *how* leaders carry out their leadership function. Initiating structure and consideration are very similar to the time-honored military commander's functions of mission and concern with the welfare of the troops. In simple terms, the Ohio State factors are task or goal orientation (initiating structure) and recognition of individual needs and relationships (consideration). The two dimensions are separate and distinct from each other.

The Ohio State studies certainly have value for the study of leadership. They were the first to point out and emphasize the importance of *both* task and human dimensions in assessing leadership. This two-dimensional approach lessened the gap between the strict task orientation of the scientific management movement and the human relations emphasis, which had been popular up to that time. Interestingly, when Colin Powell, usually considered one of the most effective and admired leaders of recent years, speaks of his own leadership process, he uses this two-dimensional approach. However, on the other side of the coin, the rush for empirical data on leadership led to a great dependence on questionnaires in the Ohio State studies to generate data about leadership behaviors, and this may not have been justified. For example, Schriesheim and Kerr concluded after a review of the existing literature that "the Ohio State scales cannot be considered sufficiently valid to warrant their continued uncritical usage in leadership research."[11] In addition to the validity question is the almost unchallenged belief that these indirect questionnaire methods are in fact measuring leadership *behaviors* instead of simply measuring the questionnaire respondent's behavior and/or perceptions of, and attitudes toward, leadership. A multiple-measures approach, especially observation techniques as outlined in the next chapter, seems needed and has been used in recent years.

The Early Michigan Leadership Studies

At about the same time that the Ohio State studies were being conducted, a group of researchers from the Survey Research Center at the University of Michigan began their studies of leadership. In the original study at the Prudential Insurance Company, 12 high–low productivity pairs were selected for examination. Each pair represented a high-producing section and a low-producing section, with other variables, such as type of work, conditions, and methods, being the same in each pair.

Nondirective interviews were conducted with the 24 section supervisors and 419 clerical workers. Results showed that supervisors of high-producing sections were significantly more likely to be general rather than close in their supervisory styles and be employee-centered (have a genuine concern for their people). The low-producing-section supervisors had essentially opposite characteristics and techniques. They were found to be close, production-centered supervisors. Another important, but sometimes overlooked, finding was that employee satisfaction was *not* directly related to productivity.

The general, employee-centered supervisor, described here, became the standard-bearer for the traditional human relations approach to leadership. The results of the Prudential studies were always cited when human relations advocates were challenged to prove their theories. The studies have been followed up with hundreds of similar studies in a wide variety of industrial, hospital, governmental, and other organizations. Thousands of employees, performing unskilled to highly professional and scientific tasks, have been analyzed. Rensis Likert, the one-time director of the Institute for Social Research of the University of Michigan, presented the results of the years of similar research in his books and became best known for his "System 4" (democratic) leadership style.

TRADITIONAL THEORIES OF LEADERSHIP

The Iowa, Ohio State, and Michigan studies are three of the historically most important leadership studies for the study of organizational behavior. Unfortunately, they are still heavily depended on, and leadership research has not surged ahead from this relatively auspicious beginning. Before analyzing the current status of leadership research, it is important to also examine the theoretical development that has occurred through the years.

There are several distinct theoretical bases for leadership. At first, leaders were felt to be born, not made. This so-called "great person" theory of leadership implied that some individuals are born with certain traits that allow them to emerge out of any situation or period of history to become leaders. This evolved into what is now known as the *trait theory* of leadership. The trait approach is concerned mainly with identifying the personality traits of the leader. Dissatisfied with this approach, and stimulated by research such as the Ohio State studies, researchers switched their emphasis from the individual leader to the group being led. In the group approach, leadership is viewed more in terms of the leader's behavior and how such behavior affects and is affected by the group of followers.

In addition to the leader and the group, the situation began to receive increased attention in leadership theory. The situational approach was initially called *Zeitgeist* (a German word meaning "spirit of the time"); the leader is viewed as a product of the times and the situation. The person with the particular qualities or traits that a situation requires will emerge as the leader. The Application Example: The "Right Stuff" gives some views on this approach. This view has much historical support as a theoretical basis for leadership and serves as the basis for situational—and now, contingency—theories of leadership. Fiedler's contingency theory, which suggests that leadership styles must fit or match the situation in order to be effective, is the best known. A more recent situational, or contingency, theory takes some of the expectancy concepts of motivation that are discussed in Chapter 8 and applies them to leadership and situations. Called the path-goal theory of leadership, it is an attempt to synthesize motivational and leadership processes. The following sections examine these widely recognized trait, group, contingency, and path-goal theories of leadership.

APPLICATION EXAMPLE

The "Right Stuff"

Considerable research over the years has been devoted to trying to determine what makes leaders effective. In practice, good leaders often are described as simply having the "right stuff." How does a leader get this "stuff"? Many training experts in industry and practicing managers believe that the "right stuff" may be a mystery yet can be learned through careful observation. For example, Yotaro Kobayashi, chairman of Japan's Fuji Xerox, says that he learned a great deal by observing other leaders up close. Consultants and popular authors such as Steven Covey, widely recognized for his best-selling book *Seven Habits of Highly Effective People,* believe that effective leadership can be learned if people know how they should behave and then practice this behavior. Stanley Bing, a practicing executive, has done a takeoff on Covey's well-known list—what he humorously calls "the seven habits of highly offensive people." But writing seriously, Bing notes that many successful leaders seem to have most, if not all, of the habits he has identified as follows:

1. *Empower your inner child.*   Children are open, genuine, and not afraid to say what is on their mind. Successful leaders employ many of these same behaviors.
2. *Be slightly weird.* Effective leaders have their own approach to doing things, such as eating a hot dog without any condiments such as mustard or ketchup, drinking coffee out of an expensive mug, or having a cloth napkin at their desk that they use whenever they eat anything. These personal habits are unique to the leader and may make the individual appear somewhat weird in comparison with his or her peer group. However, these slightly odd habits also give the person a degree of uniqueness that seems to pay off when managing people.
3. *Embrace compensation.*   Everyone likes money, but successful leaders can talk about it. Moreover, they do not get upset when a meeting agenda is altered at the last minute so more discussion can be given to the topic of compensation because they feel comfortable dealing with the issue.
4. *Focus carefully.*   Successful leaders can handle more than two or three things at the same time because they are able to filter out extraneous information and focus on critical issues. This allows them to handle more items than the average leader.
5. *Speak openly.*   Effective leaders say what they are thinking. This helps them deal with important issues rather than trying to figure out a way of tactfully dodging them.
6. *Don't get even—get mad.*   Good leaders let off steam and move along to the next issue. They do not waste their time trying to get even for petty grievances, and they use their anger to help focus and energize their people.
7. *Keep up on the latest developments.*   Successful leaders know the latest business jargon and trends. They read at least one new business book every six months—and usually more than one. So they are up on the latest trends and developments.

Trait Theories of Leadership

The scientific analysis of leadership started off by concentrating on leaders themselves. Eventually, however, the "great person" theory gave way to a more realistic trait approach to leadership. Under the influence of the behavioristic school of psychological thought, researchers accepted the fact that leadership traits are not completely inborn but can also be acquired through learning and experience. Attention turned to the search for universal traits possessed by leaders. The results of this voluminous research effort were generally very disappointing. Only intelligence seemed to hold up with any degree of consistency. When these findings are combined with those of studies on physical traits, the conclusion seems to be that leaders are bigger and brighter than those being led, but not too much so. For example, this line of research concluded that the leader was more intelligent than the average of the group being led, but, interestingly, is not the most intelligent of the group. Political analysts indicate that candidates should not come across as too intelligent to be electable, and the most intelligent member of a criminal gang is not the leader, but usually a lieutenant of the leader, the "brains" of the outfit.

When the trait approach is applied to organizational leadership, the result is even cloudier. One of the biggest problems is that all managers think they know what the qualities of a successful leader are. Obviously, almost any adjective can be used to describe a successful leader. However, it should be recognized that there are semantic limitations and that there is no evidence of a cause-and-effect relationship between observed traits and successful leadership. A possible exception may be the attention recently being given to multiple intelligences, especially emotional intelligence, or EQ, discussed in Chapter 9. Research on EQ seems to indicate that emotional characteristics such as empathy, graciousness, optimism, and being able to read the nonverbal cues in a social situation are associated with effective leaders.[12] Another recent study suggests that self-efficacy, discussed in Chapter 9, may also be related to leadership effectiveness. Specifically, this study found that self-rated leadership efficacy of military cadets was a valid predictor of their leadership evaluation by others.[13]

In general, however, research findings do not agree on which traits are generally found in leaders or even on which ones are more important than others. Similar to the trait theories of personality, except for the recent emergence of the "big five" discussed in Chapter 7, the trait approach to leadership has provided some descriptive insight but has little analytical or predictive value. The trait approach is still alive, but now the emphasis has shifted away from personality traits and toward job-related skills. Katz has identified the technical, conceptual, and human skills needed for effective management.[14] Yukl includes skills such as creativity, organization, persuasiveness, diplomacy and tactfulness, knowledge of the task, and the ability to speak well.[15] These skills have become very important in the application of leadership theory and are given specific attention in the next chapter.

Perhaps the newest iteration of the trait idea is the study of leader "competencies," as opposed to characteristics or skills. One stream of research has identified several key competencies that are related to leadership effectiveness both in the United States and other cultures:[16]

1. Drive, or the inner motivation to pursue goals
2. Leadership motivation, which is the use of socialized power to influence others to succeed
3. Integrity, which includes truthfulness and the will to translate words into deeds
4. Self-confidence that leads others to feel confidence, usually exhibited through various forms of impression management directed at employees
5. Intelligence, which is usually focused in the ability to process information, analyze alternatives, and discover opportunities
6. Knowledge of the business, so that ideas that are generated help the company to survive and thrive
7. Emotional intelligence, based on a self-monitoring personality, making quality leaders strong in situation sensitivity, and the ability to adapt to circumstances as needed

Importantly, these competencies seem to hold in the new environment facing organizational leaders, but require further theory building and research.

Group and Exchange Theories of Leadership

The group theories of leadership have their roots in social psychology. Classic exchange theory, in particular, serves as an important basis for this approach. Discussed in previous chapters, this means simply that the leader provides more benefits/rewards than burdens/costs for followers. There must be a positive exchange between the leaders and followers in order for group goals to be accomplished. Pioneering theorist Chester Barnard applied such an analysis to managers and subordinates in an organizational setting more than a half-century ago. More recently, this social exchange view of leadership has been summarized as follows:

> Exchange theories propose that group members make contributions at a cost to themselves and receive benefits at a cost to the group or other members. Interaction continues because members find the social exchange mutually rewarding.[17]

This quotation emphasizes that leadership is an exchange process between the leader and followers. Social psychological research can be used to support this notion of exchange. Table 17.2 compares and contrasts the theory and research on the three domains of leadership. Importantly, although traditionally ignored, there is considerable

TABLE 17.2 Summary of the Three Domains of Leadership

	Leader-Based	Follower-Based	Relationship-Based
What is leadership?	Appropriate behavior of the person in leader role	Ability and motivation to manage one's own performance	Trust, respect, and mutual obligation that generates influence between parties
What behaviors constitute leadership?	Establishing and communicating vision; inspiring, instilling pride	Empowering, coaching, facilitating, giving up control	Building strong relationships with followers; mutual learning and accommodation
Advantages	Leader as rallying point for organization; common understanding of mission and values; can initiate wholesale change	Makes the most of follower capabilities; frees up leaders for other responsibilities	Accommodates differing needs of subordinates; can elicit superior work from different types of people
Disadvantages	Highly dependent on leader; problems if leader changes or is pursuing inappropriate vision	Highly dependent on follower initiative and ability	Time-consuming; relies on long-term relationship between specific leaders and members
When appropriate?	Fundamental change; charismatic leader in place; limited diversity among followers	Highly capable and task-committed followers	Continuous improvement of teamwork; substantial diversity and stability among followers; network building
Where most effective?	Structured tasks; strong leader position power; member acceptance of leader	Unstructured tasks; weak position power; member nonacceptance of leader	Situation favorability for leader between two extremes

Source: Adapted from George B. Graen and Mary Uhl-Bien, "Development of Leader–Member Exchange (LMX) Theory of Leadership over 25 Years: Applying a Multi-Level Multi-Domain Perspective," *Leadership Quarterly,* Vol. 6, No. 2, 1995, p. 224.

evidence that followers affect leaders and there is considerable theory and research on the relationship, or exchange-based, approach to leadership.

Followers' Impact on Leaders. A few important research studies indicate that followers/subordinates may actually affect leaders as much as leaders affect followers/subordinates. For example, one study found that when subordinates were not performing very well, the leaders tended to emphasize the task or initiating structure, but when subordinates were doing a good job, leaders increased emphasis on their people or consideration.[18] In a laboratory study it was found that group productivity had a greater impact on leadership style than leadership style had on group productivity,[19] and in another study it was found that in newly formed groups, leaders may adjust their supportive behavior in response to the level of group cohesion and arousal already present.[20] In other words, such studies seem to indicate that subordinates affect leaders and their behaviors as much as leaders and their behaviors affect subordinates. Some practicing managers, such as the vice president of Saga Corporation, feel that subordinates lack followership skills, and there is growing evidence that these skills are becoming increasingly important.[21] In other words, it is probably not wise to ignore followership. Most managers feel that subordinates have an obligation to follow and support their leader. As the CEO of Commerce Union Corporation noted in a *Wall Street Journal* article: "Part of a subordinate's responsibility is to make the boss look good."

The Vertical Dyad Linkage Model. Relevant to the exchange view of leadership is the vertical dyad linkage (VDL) approach,[22] more recently called leader–member exchange (LMX).[23] The VDL or LMX theory says that leaders treat individual subordinates differently. In particular, leaders and subordinates develop dyadic (two-person) relationships that affect the behavior of both leaders and subordinates. For example, subordinates who are committed and who expend a lot of effort for the unit are rewarded with more of the leader's positional resources (for example, information, confidence, and concern) than those who do not display these behaviors.

Over time, the leader will develop an "in-group" of subordinates and an "out-group" of subordinates and treat them accordingly. Thus, for the same leader, research has shown that in-group subordinates report fewer difficulties in dealing with the leader and perceive the leader as being more responsive to their needs than out-group subordinates do.[24] Also, leaders spend more time "leading" members of the in-group (that is, they do not depend on formal authority to influence them), and they tend to "supervise" those in the out-group (that is, they depend on formal roles and authority to influence them).[25] Finally, there is evidence that subordinates in the in-group (those who report a high-quality relationship with their leader) assume greater job responsibility, contribute more to their units, and are rated as higher performers than those reporting a low-quality relationship.[26]

This exchange theory has been around for some time now, and although it is not without criticism,[27] in general, the research continues to be relatively supportive.[28] However, as traditionally presented, VDL or LMX seems to be more descriptive of the typical process of role making by leaders, rather than prescribing the pattern of downward exchange relations optimal for leadership effectiveness.[29] Research is also using more sophisticated methodologies[30] and suggests that task characteristics moderate the LMX–performance relationship.[31]

LMX ideas have been expanded significantly in other areas as well (e.g., by examining the characteristics of subordinates in the dyad and through the study of similarities between the leader and follower within in-group relationships). For instance, regarding subordinates, those exhibiting higher levels of self-efficacy were more likely to form in-group relationships with leaders, who perceived the followers to be more likable and to be more similar in personality to the leader.[32] In another study, perceived similarities between the leader and the follower predicted higher quality leader–member exchanges and the cognitive factors of implicit theories and self-schemas along with perceived similarities led to greater liking of the subordinate.[33] Also, research has found that the *perception* of similarity seems to be a more important factor than the actual demographic similarities.[34]

Graen and his colleagues have emphasized that LMX has evolved through various stages: (1) the discovery of differentiated dyads; (2) the investigation of characteristics of LMX relationships and their organizational implications/outcomes; (3) the description of dyadic partnership building; and (4) the aggregation of differentiated dyadic relations to group and network levels.[35] New insights into the manner in which leaders differentiate between employees in order to form in-groups and out-groups may in part be explained by social network analysis. Positive social networks and exchange processes assist leaders in selecting those who may become part of the inner life of an organization.[36] Also, the fourth stage recognizes the new cross-functional or network emphasis in organizations and even external relations with customers, suppliers, and other organizational stakeholders. Research that identifies leader–follower relationships that are best suited to specific environmental contingencies is still needed.[37]

Finally, from the social cognitive perspective taken by this text, it should be remembered that leader–member exchanges are a reciprocal process. Evidence of this process of interaction suggests that leaders may be inclined to change subordinate self-concepts in the short term to achieve performance goals and more enduring changes. At the same time, subordinates reciprocally shape leaders' self-schemas through their responses, both as individuals and through collective or group reactions.[38] These and other elements of the continual negotiation between the leader and followers, which is also recognized by the psychological contract concept discussed in Chapter 15, deserve additional consideration in the future.

Contingency Theory of Leadership

After the trait approach proved to fall short of being an adequate overall theory of leadership, attention turned to the situational aspects of leadership. Social psychologists began the search for situational variables that affect leadership roles, skills, behavior, and followers' performance and satisfaction. Numerous situational variables were identified, but no overall theory pulled it all together until Fred Fielder proposed a widely recognized situation-based, or contingency, theory for leadership effectiveness.

Fielder's Contingency Model of Leadership Effectiveness.   To test the hypotheses he had formulated from previous research findings, Fiedler developed what he called a *contingency model of leadership effectiveness.* This model contained the relationship between leadership style and the favorableness of the situation. Situational favorableness was described by Fiedler in terms of three empirically derived dimensions:

1. The *leader–member relationship,* which is the most critical variable in determining the situation's favorableness
2. The *degree of task structure,* which is the second most important input into the favorableness of the situation
3. The *leader's position power* obtained through formal authority, which is the third most critical dimension of the situation[39]

Situations are favorable to the leader if all three of these dimensions are high. In other words, if the leader is generally accepted and respected by followers (high first dimension), if the task is very structured and everything is "spelled out" (high second dimension), and if a great deal of authority and power are formally attributed to the leader's position (high third dimension), the situation is favorable. If the opposite exists (if the three dimensions are low), the situation will be very unfavorable for the leader. Fiedler was convinced through his research that the favorableness of the situation in combination with the leadership style determines effectiveness.

Through the analysis of research findings from all types of situations, Fiedler was able to discover that under very favorable *and* very unfavorable situations, the task-directed, or hard-nosed and authoritarian, type of leader was most effective. However, when the situation was only moderately favorable or unfavorable (the intermediate range of favorableness), the human-oriented or democratic type of leader was most effective. Figure 17.1 summarizes this relationship between leadership style and the favorableness of the situation.

Why is the task-directed leader successful in very favorable situations? Fielder offered the following explanation:

> In the very favorable conditions in which the leader has power, informal backing, and a relatively well-structured task, the group is ready to be directed, and the group expects to be told what to do. Consider the captain of an airliner in its final landing approach. We would hardly want him to turn to his crew for a discussion on how to land.[40]

As an example of why the task-oriented leader is successful in a highly unfavorable situation, Fiedler cited

> . . . the disliked chairman of a volunteer committee which is asked to plan the office picnic on a beautiful Sunday. If the leader asks too many questions about what the group ought to do or how he should proceed, he is likely to be told that "we ought to go home."[41]

The leader who makes a wrong decision in this highly unfavorable type of situation is probably better off than the leader who makes no decision at all. In essence, what Fiedler's model suggests is that in highly unfavorable situations, the effective leader

FIGURE 17.1
Fiedler's contingency model of leadership.

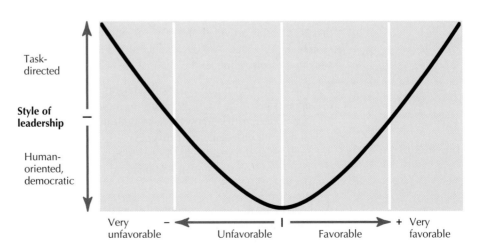

Favorableness of the situation

takes charge and makes the decisions that need to be made to accomplish the task without asking for input or trying to keep everyone happy.

Figure 17.1 shows that the human-oriented, democratic leader is effective in the intermediate range of favorableness. An example of such situations is the typical committee or unit. In these situations, the leader may not be wholly accepted by the other members of the group, the task may not be completely structured, and some authority and power may be granted to the leader. Under such a relatively unfavorable, but not extremely unfavorable, situation, the model predicts that a human-oriented, democratic type of leader will be most effective. The same would be true of a moderately favorable situation. Such moderately unfavorable or favorable situations are most common for supervisors and managers. The implication is that in general the human-oriented, democratic style of leadership would be most effective in managing human resources in the large majority of organizational situations.

Research Support for the Contingency Model.   As is true of any widely publicized theoretical development, Fiedler's model has stimulated a great deal of research. Not surprisingly, the results are mixed and a controversy has been generated. Fielder and his students have provided almost all the support for the model over the years. For example, to defend the validity of his theory, he cites 30 studies in a wide variety of teams and organizations (Navy teams, chemical research teams, shop departments, supermarkets, heavy machinery plant departments, engineering groups, hospital wards, public health teams, and others) and concludes that "the theory is highly predictive and that the relations obtained in the validation studies are almost identical to those obtained in the original studies."[42] With one exception, which Fiedler explains away, he maintains that the model correctly predicted the correlations that should exist between the leader's style and performance in relation to the identified favorableness of the situation. As predicted, his studies show that in very unfavorable and very favorable situations, the task-oriented leader performs best. In a moderately favorable and moderately unfavorable situations, the human-oriented leader is more effective. Although Fiedler recognizes that there is increasing criticism of his conclusions, he maintains that "methodologically sound validation studies have on the whole provided substantial support for the theory."[43] Meta-analytic investigations of the predictions of the model have yielded support,[44] mixed results,[45] and nonsupport.[46]

Fiedler's Contingency Theory in Perspective.   Overall, there seems little question that Fiedler has provided one of the major breakthroughs for leadership theory, research, and practice. Although some of the criticism is justified, there are several reasons that Fiedler's model has made a contribution:

1.   It was the first highly visible leadership theory to present the contingency approach.
2.   It emphasized the importance of both the situation and the leader's characteristics in determining leader effectiveness.
3.   It stimulated a great deal of research, including tests of its predictions and attempts to improve on the model, and inspired the formulation of alternative contingency theories.[47]

At the very least, Fiedler conducted considerable empirical research, and more recently he proposed another contingency theory.[48]

In Fiedler's recent cognitive resource theory (CRT), he identifies the situations under which a leader's cognitive resources, such as intelligence, experience, and technical expertise, relate to group and organizational performance. Based on Fiedler and his colleagues' research, CRT predicts the following:

1. More intelligent leaders develop better plans, decisions, and action strategies than less intelligent leaders.
2. Intelligence contributes more strongly to group performance if the leader is directive and the group members are motivated and supportive of the leader.
3. Interpersonal stress distracts the leader from the task and the leader's intelligence will contribute more highly if the leader has relatively stress-free relationships with superiors and subordinates.[49]

As is the case with his original contingency model, CRT has been criticized,[50] but it also will generate more research and, one hopes, make meaningful linkages to practice.

Path-Goal Leadership Theory

The other widely recognized theoretical development from a contingency approach is the path-goal theory derived from the expectancy framework of motivation theory. Although Georgopoulos and his colleagues at the University of Michigan's Institute for Social Research used path-goal concepts and terminology many years ago for analyzing the impact of leadership on performance, the modern development is usually attributed to Martin Evans and Robert House, who wrote separate papers on the subject.[51] In essence, the path-goal theory attempts to explain the impact that leader behavior has on subordinate motivation, satisfaction, and performance. The House version of the theory incorporates four major types, or styles, of leadership.[52] Briefly summarized, these are:

1. *Directive leadership.* This style is similar to that of the Lippitt and White authoritarian leader. Subordinates know exactly what is expected of them, and the leader gives specific directions. There is no participation by subordinates.
2. *Supportive leadership.* The leader is friendly and approachable and shows a genuine concern for subordinates.
3. *Participative leadership.* The leader asks for and uses suggestions from subordinates but still makes the decisions.
4. *Achievement-oriented leadership.* The leader sets challenging goals for subordinates and shows confidence that they will attain these goals and perform well.

This path-goal theory—and here is how it differs in one respect from Fiedler's contingency model—suggests that these various styles can be and actually are used by the same leader in different situations.[53] Two of the situational factors that have been identified are the personal characteristics of subordinates and the environmental pressures and demands facing subordinates. With respect to the first situational factor, the theory asserts:

> Leader behavior will be acceptable to subordinates to the extent that the subordinates see such behavior as either an immediate source of satisfaction or as instrumental to future satisfaction.[54]

And with respect to the second situational factor, the theory states:

> Leader behavior will be motivational (e.g., will increase subordinate effort) to the extent that (1) it makes satisfaction of subordinate needs contingent on effective performance, and (2) it complements the environment of subordinates by providing the coaching, guidance, support, and rewards which are necessary for effective performance and which may otherwise be lacking in subordinates or in their environment.[55]

Using one of the four styles contingent on the situational factors as outlined, the leader attempts to influence subordinates' perceptions and motivate them, which in turn leads to their role clarity, goal expectancies, satisfaction, and performance. This is specifically accomplished by the leader as follows:

1. Recognizing and/or arousing subordinates' needs for outcomes over which the leader has some control
2. Increasing personal payoffs to subordinates for work-goal attainment
3. Making the path to those payoffs easier to travel by coaching and direction
4. Helping subordinates clarify expectancies
5. Reducing frustrating barriers
6. Increasing the opportunities for personal satisfaction contingent on effective performance[56]

In other words, by doing the preceding, the leader attempts to make the path to subordinates' goals as smooth as possible. But to accomplish this path-goal facilitation, the leader must use the appropriate style contingent on the situational variables present. Figure 17.2 summarizes this path-goal approach.

As happened with the expectancy theory of motivation, there was a surge of research on the path-goal theory of leadership. So far, most of the research has concentrated only on parts of the theory rather than on the entire theory. For example, a sampling of the research findings indicates the following:

1. Studies of seven organizations have found that *leader directiveness* is (a) positively related to satisfactions and expectancies of subordinates engaged in ambiguous tasks and (b) negatively related to satisfactions and expectancies of subordinates engaged in clear tasks.
2. Studies involving 10 different samples of employees found that *supportive leadership* will have its most positive effect on satisfaction for subordinates who work on stressful, frustrating, or dissatisfying tasks.
3. In a major study in an industrial manufacturing organization, it was found that in nonrepetitive, ego-involving tasks, employees were more satisfied under *participative leaders* than under nonparticipative leaders.

FIGURE 17.2
A summary of path-goal relationships.

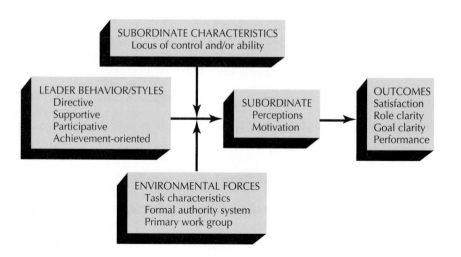

4. In three separate organizations it was found that for subordinates performing ambiguous, nonrepetitive tasks, the higher the *achievement orientation of the leader,* the more subordinates were confident that their efforts would pay off in effective performance.[57]

The more recent reviews of the research on the path-goal theory are not as supportive as the preceding. For example, Schriesheim and DeNisi note that only a couple of hypotheses have really been drawn from the theory, which means that it may be incapable of generating meaningful predictions.[58] Another note of pessimism offered by these reviewers is that only one of the two hypotheses has received consistent empirical support. Also, a comprehensive review of 48 studies demonstrated that the mixed results of the individual studies, when cumulated, were transformed into support for continued testing of path-goal theory.[59]

Overall, the path-goal theory, like the other established theories presented in this chapter, seems to need more research, but it certainly warrants continued attention in the coming years. One analysis concluded that leaders will be perceived most favorably by their subordinates, and succeed in exerting most influence over them, when they behave in ways that closely match (1) the needs and values of subordinates and (2) the requirements of a specific work situation.[60] In other words, the path-goal theory, like the expectancy theory in work motivation, may help better explain the complexities of the leadership process.

MODERN THEORETICAL PROCESSES OF LEADERSHIP

Despite a relative degree of acceptance of the contingency and path-goal theories of leadership and the great (at least relative to other areas in organizational behavior) amount of research that has been conducted, few would disagree today that leadership is still in trouble. Leadership is currently being attacked on all fronts—in terms of theories relating to it, research methods for studying it, and applications. For example, a recent comprehensive review of the traditional theories concluded that many of the tests conducted to identify moderating effects were judged to be inappropriate and that most of the results reported in this domain have not been replicated.[61] The time has come for alternative theories, research methods, and applications for leadership studies.

Besides the established trait, group, contingency, and path-goal theories of leadership, a number of other theories have emerged in recent years. These include the charismatic, transformational, social cognitive, and substitutes theories of leadership. An overview of each of these provides better understanding of the complex leadership process.

Charismatic Leadership Theories

Charismatic leadership is a throwback to the old conception of leaders as being those who "by the force of their personal abilities are capable of having profound and extraordinary effects on followers."[62] Although the charismatic concept, or charisma, goes as far back as the ancient Greeks and is cited in the Bible, its modern development is often attributed to the work of Robert House.[63] On the basis of the analysis of political and religious leaders, House suggests that charismatic leaders are characterized by self-confidence and confidence in subordinates, high expectations for subordinates, ideological vision, and the use of personal example. Followers of charismatic leaders identify with the leader and the mission of the leader, exhibit extreme loyalty to and confidence in the leader, emulate the leader's values and behavior, and derive self-esteem from their relationship with the leader.[64]

Recently, Bass has extended the profile of charismatic leaders by including business leaders such as Jack Welch or Bill Gates or women who have become top-level executives. In particular, he notes that charismatic leaders have superior debating and persuasive skills as well as technical expertise and that they foster attitudinal, behavioral, and emotional changes in their followers.[65] A *Fortune* article humorously describes a manager with charisma as follows:

> He attended some middling college. Doesn't have an MBA. But he has an aura. He persuades people—subordinates, peers, customers, even the S.O.B. you both work for—to do things they'd rather not. People charge over the hill for him. Run through fire. Walk barefoot on broken glass. He doesn't demand attention, he commands it.[66]

Because of the effects that charismatic leaders have on followers, the theory predicts that charismatic leaders will produce in followers performance beyond expectations as well as strong commitment to the leader and his or her mission. Recent research indicates that the impact of such charismatic leaders will be enhanced when the followers exhibit higher levels of self-awareness and self-monitoring, especially when observing the charismatic leaders' behaviors and activities.[67] House and his colleagues provide some support for charismatic theory,[68] but as with the other leadership theories, complexities are found[69] and more research is needed. For example, one recent study that assessed charismatic leader behaviors, individual level correlates, and unit-level correlates (outcomes) in the military yielded only limited support for the theory's propositions and led the researchers to conclude that greater sensitivity to multiple constituencies of leaders is needed in theories and studies focused on charismatic leadership.[70] Also, extensions of the theory are being proposed. For example, Conger and Kanungo treat charisma as an attributional phenomenon and propose that it varies with the situation.[71] Leader traits that foster charismatic attributions include self-confidence, impression-management skills, social sensitivity, and empathy. Situations that promote charismatic leadership include a crisis requiring dramatic change[72] or followers who are very dissatisfied with the status quo. For example, a recent study in a university setting revealed a situation in which a charismatic leader was able to successfully implement a technical change, but at the same time suffered through major political turmoil, which appeared to be side effects of the technical change. This suggests that studies of charismatic leadership must be considered in the context in which the leader operates, and the nature of the task or work being performed should be included in the analysis.[73]

Included in the extensions of charismatic leadership is also the recognition of a dark side.[74] Charismatic leaders tend to be portrayed as wonderful heroes, but as Table 17.3 shows, there can also be unethical characteristics associated with charismatic leaders. With regard to meeting the challenge of being ethical, it has been noted that charismatic leaders

> . . . deserve this label only if they create transformations in their organizations so that members are motivated to follow them and to seek organization objectives not simply because they are ordered to do so, and not merely because they calculate that such compliance is in their self-interest, but because they voluntarily identify with the organization, its standards of conduct and willingly seek to fulfill its purpose.[75]

This transformation idea is also picked up by Bass, who suggests that charismatic leadership is really just a component of the broader-based transformational leadership, covered next.[76]

TABLE 17.3 Ethical and Unethical Characteristics of Charismatic Leaders

Ethical Charismatic Leader	Unethical Charismatic Leader
• Uses power to serve others • Aligns vision with followers' needs and aspirations • Considers and learns from criticism • Stimulates followers to think independently and to question the leader's view • Open, two-way communication • Coaches, develops, and supports followers; shares recognition with others • Relies on internal moral standards to satisfy organizational and societal interests	• Uses power only for personal gain or impact • Promotes own personal vision • Censures critical or opposing views • Demands own decisions be accepted without question • One-way communication • Insensitive to followers' needs • Relies on convenient, external moral standards to satisfy self-interests

Source: Jane M. Howell and Bruce J. Avolio, "The Ethics of Charismatic Leadership: Submission or Liberation?" *Academy of Management Executive,* May 1992, p. 45. Used with permission.

Transformational Leadership Theory

Identifying charismatic characteristics of leaders can become very important as organizations transform traditional ways of being led to meet the challenge of dramatic change. In recent years, the heads of IBM, GM, American Express, Westinghouse, Eli Lilly, Allied Signal, Kodak, and Tenneco all lost their jobs because they failed to lead their firms through the successful transformations necessary for the new environment discussed in the first part of the text. On the other hand, the CEOs of Ameritech, Pepsico, and GE led their companies through successful transformations. For example, Bill Weiss transformed Ameritech while achieving five years of record earnings, and GE's Jack Welch transformed his firm into the requirements of the new economy. Transformational leadership theory serves as the foundation for these important developments as organizations progress in the 21st century.

Burns initially identified two types of political leadership: transactional and transformational.[77] The more traditional transactional leadership involves an exchange relationship between leaders and followers, but transformational leadership is based more on leaders' shifting the values, beliefs, and needs of their followers. Table 17.4 summarizes the characteristics and approaches of transactional versus transformational leaders. On the basis of his research findings, Bass concludes that in many instances (such as relying on passive management by exception), transactional leadership is a prescription for mediocrity and that transformational leadership leads to superior performance in organizations facing demands for renewal and change. He suggests that fostering transformational leadership through policies of recruitment, selection, promotion, training, and development will pay off in the health, well-being, and effective performance of today's organizations.[78]

Most of the research on transformational leadership to date has relied on Bass's questionnaire, which has received some criticism,[79] or qualitative research that simply describes leaders through interviews. An example of the latter were the interviews with top executives of major companies conducted by Tichy and Devanna. They found that effective transformational leaders share the following characteristics:

1. They identify themselves as change agents.
2. They are courageous.
3. They believe in people.
4. They are value driven.

TABLE 17.4 Characteristics and Approaches of Transactional versus Transformational Leaders

---

Transactional Leaders

1. *Contingent reward:* Contracts exchange of rewards for effort, promises rewards for good performance, recognizes accomplishments.
2. *Management by exception* (active): Watches and searches for deviations from rules and standards, takes corrective action.
3. *Management by exception* (passive): Intervenes only if standards are not met.
4. *Laissez-faire:* Abdicates responsibilities, avoids making decisions.

Transformational Leaders

1. *Charisma:* Provides vision and sense of mission, instills pride, gains respect and trust.
2. *Inspiration:* Communicates high expectations, uses symbols to focus efforts, expresses important purposes in simple ways.
3. *Intellectual stimulation:* Promotes intelligence, rationality, and careful problem solving.
4. *Individual consideration:* Gives personal attention, treats each employee individually, coaches, advises.

Source: Bernard M. Bass, "From Transactional to Transformational Leadership: Learning to Share the Vision," *Organizational Dynamics,* Winter 1990, p. 22. Used with permission.

5. They are lifelong learners.
6. They have the ability to deal with complexity, ambiguity, and uncertainty.
7. They are visionaries.[80]

Only recently has empirical research begun to support these characteristics. For example, field studies have shown that transformational leaders more frequently employ legitimating tactics and engender higher levels of identification and internalization[81] (see Chapter 13) and have better performance.[82] Recent studies are refining these general findings. For example, in a study comparing male and female sales managers, females were inclined to form unique relationships with each of their individual subordinates that were independent of their group memberships, suggesting transformational and contingent reward patterns that were somewhat different from their male counterparts.[83] In other studies, transformational leadership produced indirect effects on the organizational citizenship behaviors (OCBs) of subordinates (see Chapter 7), with the relationship being moderated by perceptions of procedural justice and trust, and extraversion and agreeableness of the "Big Five Personality Traits" (see Chapter 7) positively related to transformational leadership.[84] Conceptual analysis indicates that contextual factors may influence receptivity to transformational leadership tactics, and therefore they should be considered and accounted for when research is being conducted.[85] In addition, other theories are also starting to gain attention to help explain the complex process of leadership.

A Social Cognitive Approach

Just as social cognitive theory was used in Chapter 1 to provide the overall conceptual framework for this text on organizational behavior,[86] it can also provide a model for the continuous, reciprocal interaction between the leader (including his or her cognitions), the environment (including subordinates/followers and organizational-level variables), and the behavior itself.[87] These interactions are shown in Figure 17.3. This would seem to be a comprehensive and viable theoretical foundation for understanding leadership.[88] Any of the other theoretical approaches, standing alone, seem too limiting. For example, the one-sided, cognitively based trait theories suggest that leaders are causal

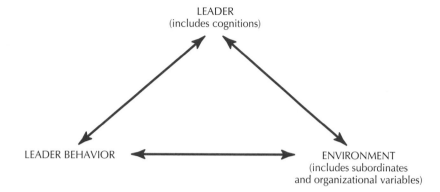

FIGURE 17.3
A social cognitive
approach to leadership.

determinants that influence subordinates independent of followers' behaviors or the situation. The contingency theories are a step in the right direction, but even they for the most part have a unidirectional conception of interaction, in which leaders and situations somehow combine to determine leadership behavior. Even those leadership theories that claim to take a bidirectional approach (either in the exchange sense between the leader and the group or in the contingency sense between the leader and the situation) actually retain a unidirectional view of leadership behavior. In these theories, the causal input into the leader's behavior is the result of the interdependent exchange, but the behavior itself is ignored as a leadership determinant.

As far as leadership application for the social cognitive approach is concerned, unlike the more limited A-B-C (antecedent-behavior-consequence) functional analysis used in the operant approach (see Chapter 16), in the social cognitive view, recognition is given to the role of cognitive processes such as symbolizing, forethought, and especially self-efficacy (see Chapter 9). The successful application of this social cognitive approach "depends upon the leader's ability to bring into awareness the overt or covert antecedent cues and contingent consequences that regulate the leader's and subordinate's performance behavior."[89] More specifically, in this leadership application, the followers are actively involved in the process, and together with the leader they concentrate on their own and one another's *behaviors,* the environmental contingencies (both antecedent and consequent), and their cognitions such as self-efficacy. Some examples of this approach are the following:

1. The leader identifies the environmental variables that control his or her own behavior.
2. The leader works with the subordinate to discover the personalized set of environmental contingencies that regulate the subordinate's behavior.
3. The leader and the subordinate jointly attempt to discover ways in which they can manage their individual behavior to produce more mutually reinforcing and organizationally productive outcomes.[90]
4. The leader enhances the efficacy of subordinates through setting up successful experiences, modeling, positive feedback and persuasion, and psychological and physiological arousal that can lead to performance improvement. This success with subordinates can in turn lead to leadership efficacy.[91]

In such an approach, the leader and the subordinate have a negotiable, reciprocal, interactive relationship and are consciously aware of how they can modify (influence) each other's behavior through cognitions and the contingent environment.

Although some work has been done on the theoretical development of a social cognitive approach to leadership, research and application are still developing. Only time will tell whether it will hold up as a viable, researchable approach to leadership. However, because of its growing importance as a theoretical foundation for the fields of psychology and organizational behavior as a whole and because it recognizes the interactive nature of all the variables of previous theories, a social cognitive approach to leadership would seem to have considerable potential for the future.

Substitutes for Leadership

Because of dissatisfaction with the progress of leadership theory and research in explaining and predicting the effects of leader behavior on performance outcomes, some of the basic assumptions about the importance of leadership per se have been challenged. In particular, Kerr and Jermier proposed that there may be certain "substitutes" for leadership that make leader behavior unnecessary and redundant, and "neutralizers" that prevent the leader from behaving in a certain way or that counteract the behavior.[92] These substitutes or neutralizers can be found in subordinate, task, and organization characteristics. Figure 17.4 gives specific examples of possible substitutes and neutralizers according to supportive/relationship leadership and instrumental/task leadership.

As shown, subordinate experience, ability, and training may substitute for instrumental/task leadership. For example, craftspersons or professionals such as accountants or software engineers may have so much experience, ability, and training that they do

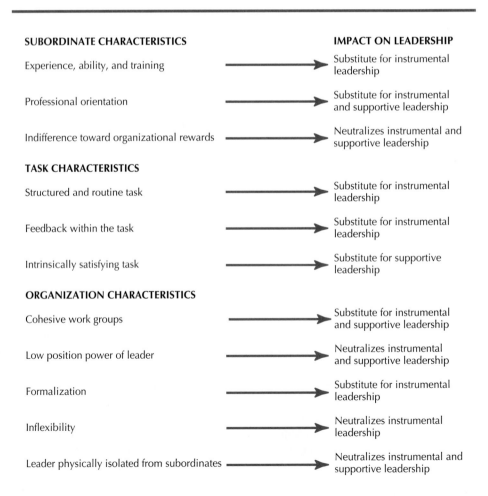

FIGURE 17.4
Kerr and Jermier's substitutes and neutralizers for leadership.

SUBORDINATE CHARACTERISTICS

Experience, ability, and training ⟶ Substitute for instrumental leadership

Professional orientation ⟶ Substitute for instrumental and supportive leadership

Indifference toward organizational rewards ⟶ Neutralizes instrumental and supportive leadership

TASK CHARACTERISTICS

Structured and routine task ⟶ Substitute for instrumental leadership

Feedback within the task ⟶ Substitute for instrumental leadership

Intrinsically satisfying task ⟶ Substitute for supportive leadership

ORGANIZATION CHARACTERISTICS

Cohesive work groups ⟶ Substitute for instrumental and supportive leadership

Low position power of leader ⟶ Neutralizes instrumental and supportive leadership

Formalization ⟶ Substitute for instrumental leadership

Inflexibility ⟶ Neutralizes instrumental leadership

Leader physically isolated from subordinates ⟶ Neutralizes instrumental and supportive leadership not need instrumental/task leadership to perform well and be satisfied. Those subordinates who don't particularly care about organizational rewards (for example, professors or musicians) will neutralize both supportive/relationship and instrumental/task leadership attempts. Tasks that are highly structured and automatically provide feedback substitute for instrumental/task leadership, and those that are intrinsically satisfying (for example, teaching) do not need supportive/relationship leadership. There are also a number of organizational characteristics that substitute for or neutralize leadership.

There has been further analysis of the leader substitutes concept,[93] and Kerr and Jermier have provided some empirical support from field studies of police officers.[94] They found that substitutes such as feedback from the task being performed had more impact on certain job-related activities than leader behaviors did. Other studies have also been interpreted (post hoc) to support organizational characteristics such as formalization as leader substitutes.[95] More recent direct tests have yielded mixed results.[96] One study using hospital personnel with a wide variety of skills and backgrounds and in a wide variety of professions found several potential substitutes to predict subordinate satisfaction and commitment, but only one of the single substitutes (organizational formalization) rendered leadership impossible and/or unnecessary.[97] A follow-up study found that worker professionalism was an important moderator variable. It also found that professionals differed from nonprofessionals in that intrinscially satisfying work tasks and importance placed on organizational rewards were strong substitutes for leaders' support.[98]

Overall, the substitutes notion puts leadership back into proper perspective and may help explain the relatively poor track record of leadership research. In particular, the leadership situation (subordinate, task, or organization) may replace or counteract the leader's behavior in affecting subordinate satisfaction and performance. It has recently been noted that "the idea of leadership substitutes and neutralizers helps to account for the largely mixed results of research on most leadership theories. Studies of leadership that ignore the effect of neutralizers and substitutes may fail to uncover hypothesized relationships because the particular leadership process is irrelevant, rather than because the theory is invalid."[99]

In other words, some things are beyond leaders' control; leaders do not have mystical powers over people. The situation does play a role. By the same token, leaders can have a considerable impact. The substitutes idea does not negate leadership; it just puts a more realistic boundary on what leadership is capable of achieving from subordinates. Some styles, behaviors, activities, and skills of leadership are more effective than others. The next chapter examines these effective approaches to the actual practice of leadership.

Leadership Across Cultures

Leadership takes on added significance in a global economy. As leadership guru Warren Bennis noted: "Given the nature and constancy of change and the transnational challenges facing American business leadership, the key to making the right choices will come from understanding and embodying the leadership qualities necessary to succeed in the volatile and mercurial global economy."[100] Research to date reveals both similarities and differences when leadership activities and styles are examined across cultures.

In their classic study, Haire, Ghiselli, and Porter studied managerial attitudes regarding different leadership styles in 14 countries. National groupings alone explained 28 percent of the variance in managerial attitudes.[101] Later research revealed that the degree of participation used by managers was different across eight countries.[102] In a more current study conducted by the author (Luthans) and colleagues, participative management techniques were actually ineffective in a Russian factory.[103] Further, the author's (Luthans) Real Managers Study, presented in detail in the next chapter,[104] was replicated in a Russian factory.[105] In a manner similar to U.S. managers studied (although the relative frequencies were a little different), the Russian managers were observed to perform, in order, traditional management, communication, human resources, and networking activities. Also, as was the case with the U.S. managers studied, the degree of networking activities conducted by Russian managers was related to their success levels within the organization. Still, the relationship between the activities of various Russian managers and their subsequent levels of effectiveness were similar, but less clear.[106] In other words, there are a number of factors that potentially contribute to differences in effective leader processes across cultures. Some that have been studied include personal values, the manager's background, and interpersonal skills.

Personal Values.   The personal values held by a manager shape his or her perception of a situation, influence the analysis of alternative solutions to a problem, and affect the ultimate decision made by the leader.[107] At the same time, the personal values of followers influence their leader, and these values are different across cultures. A recent study of similar U.S.-owned manufacturing plants located in five different cultures (Italian, Mexican, Spanish, United States, and British) revealed that the overall leadership approaches of the host-country nationals reflected the expectations of the local culture and workforce.[108]

Backgrounds of the Managers.   U.S. managers come from all economic backgrounds—lower, middle, and upper class. Although most are college educated, there is no guarantee that attending a given school will lead to success, as promotion is often based on performance. Whereas degrees from prestigious schools may offer a distinct advantage, U.S. managers come from a wide variety of colleges. The same may not be true in other countries. For example, in France managers are often chosen from the graduates of the *grandes ecoles*.[109] In Japan, graduates of prestigious schools have much better chances to become top managers in the larger corporations, and in Korea many top business leaders are educated in the United States.

Besides educational background, class and family status also can have an influence. U.S. managers come from all classes, but the same is not true in other countries. Family name and class are important in France. In India, it is common to accept the authority of elders, and this is revealed through little delegation of authority in many companies. In Scandinavian countries, however, differing family patterns are reflected in participatory decision-making styles and the routine delegation of authority by leaders.

Interpersonal Skills.   There is considerable evidence that managers differ across cultures in their interpersonal skills. Leaders vary in their views of rules and procedures, deference to authority, levels of dependence and independence, use of objectivity versus intuition, willingness to compromise, and other interpersonal tactics. A U.S. supervisor on an oil rig in Indonesia learned this lesson the hard way. In a moment of anger, he shouted at his timekeeper to take the next boat to shore. Immediately, a mob of outraged Indonesian coworkers grabbed fire axes and went after the supervisor. He escaped by barricadding himself in his quarters. The leadership lesson this American learned was: never berate an Indonesian in public.[110] Even transformational and transactional tactics used by leaders may vary in their levels of success in differing cultures.[111]

As these preliminary research studies reviewed indicate, there is reason to believe that cultural issues in leadership should be studied to reveal both differences between cultures and specific within-country practices that will help expatriate leaders succeed. The accompanying International Application Example shows how communication will differ across cultures. Today's global leaders need to recognize such

International Application Example

How Business Leaders Communicate across Cultures

One of the biggest challenges facing leaders doing business internationally is that the nationals of each country typically use their language and speech in a different way. In one culture people will lower their voice to indicate the seriousness of a situation, whereas in another culture they will speak very loudly to convey the same message. In one culture people will talk rapidly and be regarded as highly credible, whereas in another they will speak slowly and achieve the same result. The challenge in dealing with business leaders across cultures is to know how they use their language to communicate and what they are looking for from the other person. Here are some specific examples.

British The British tend to use a reserved tone in speaking and like to understate things. They also have a fondness for conceding points early to their opponents in order to take the steam out of the others' arguments. British business leaders are very good at being vague in order to maintain politeness and to avoid confrontation. When trying to influence them, use of humor and anecdotes and the offers of reasonable prices and good quality works best.

Spaniards and Italians Spaniards and Italians like to use a broad vocabulary and employ their hands, arms, and facial expressions when conveying their message. In particular, business leaders let others clearly understand how they feel about things. When trying to persuade others to a particular point of view, these business leaders appeal directly and strongly to good sense, a warm heart, and generosity. Additionally, these business leaders often insist that others make a decision right away.

Germans German business leaders rely on logic, but they also place strong importance on gathering a great deal of information to back up their positions. They like to present their points in a thorough and detailed way so that there is little opportunity for counterarguments, although effective negotiators find it very effective to work with German business leaders to find common ground and thus ward off a "win-lose" situation. German business leaders are influenced by technical information, good prices, high quality, and specific delivery dates.

Scandinavians Scandinavian business leaders like to list the pros and cons of a position before providing the other person with their decision on the matter. They are also very slow to give up on their position because they feel that they have more than ample support for it. They also like to forego the niceties and get down to the business at hand. Quite often their presentations are factual, succinct, and well thought through. In persuading Scandinavian business leaders, it is important to emphasize quality, design, technical information, and delivery dates.

Japanese Japanese business leaders are extremely polite and almost never say no. On the other hand, the fact that they smile a great deal does not mean that they agree with the other person. Those who deal with Japanese business leaders on a regular basis find that they are greatly influenced by presentations that help them understand how something works or why it is a good idea or how it will be profitable for them. Two of the main things that outsiders need to focus on when dealing with Japanese business leaders are good price and politeness.

Finally, it is important to remember that business leaders from each culture have their own attention span, and if someone goes beyond this time period, they may find themselves losing out. For example, the British have a moderate time span, about 40 minutes. Scandinavians have a somewhat longer span, about 50 minutes. The Japanese typically give others about an hour before they begin losing interest. The Germans are the longest of all in this regard, tending to have attention spans of about 75 minutes. So when interacting with business leaders across cultures, attention must be given to both content and length and communications must be adapted accordingly.

differences. The next step in the process is to systematize the study of leadership across cultures to build contingency models similar to what has been done with international human resource management.[112]

Project GLOBE and the Future of International Leadership Studies

Recently, a major international research project under the general direction of Robert House, called Global Leadership and Organizational Effectiveness or GLOBE, started publishing its findings.[113] The meta-goal of the GLOBE program is to develop, over time, an empirically based theory to describe, understand, and predict the impact of cultural variables on leadership, organizational processes, and the effectiveness of the leader and the processes. Over the past decade, 170 country-based coinvestigators (CCIs) gathered data from 18,000 managers from 62 countries. The CCIs were responsible for leading the study in the specific culture in which each had expertise.

The first goal of the GLOBE project was to develop societal and organizational measures of culture and leader attributes that were appropriate to use across all cultures. The opening investigation suggested nine dimensions of cultures that differentiate societies and organizations. These identified dimensions were:

1. *Power distance,* or the degree to which members of a collective expect power to be distributed equally
2. *Uncertainty avoidance,* which is the extent a society, organization, or groups relies on norms, rules, and procedures to alleviate the unpredictability of future events
3. *Humane orientation,* reflected in the degree to which a collective encourages and rewards individuals for being fair, altruistic, generous, caring, and kind to others
4. *Collectivism I,* described as the degree to which organizational and societal institutional practices encourage and reward the collective distribution of resources and collective actions
5. *Collectivism II,* which is the degree to which individuals express pride, loyalty, and cohesiveness in their organizations or families
6. *Assertiveness,* defined as the degree to which individuals are assertive, confrontational, and aggressive in their relationships with others
7. *Gender egalitarianism,* expressed as the degree a collective minimizes gender inequality
8. *Future orientation,* or the extent to which individuals engage in future-oriented behaviors such as delaying gratification, planning, and investing in the future
9. *Performance orientation,* suggested by the degree to which a collective encourages and rewards group members for performance improvement and excellence

The first six dimensions were originally defined by Hofstede[114] (see Chapter 2). One dimension Hofstede called "masculinity" has been relabeled as two constructs, assertiveness and gender egalitarianism, by the GLOBE researchers. Following the development and validation of the scale used to measure leader and cultural variables, pilot studies were conducted to empirically assess the psychometric properties of the dimensions that had been established.

The second phase of the program was a further assessment of the leader and cultural scales. Unobtrusive measures were created to identify the latent constructs, manifest indicators, and qualitative indicators that could be used to assess the nine cultural dimensions, nine organizational practices, organizational contingencies including technology, the environment, and the size of the organization, plus societal culturally endorsed implicit leadership theories. In addition, hypotheses were developed regarding the relationships between various societal dimensions, organizational dimensions, and the culturally endorsed implicit theories that had been identified.

Phase three of the project was designed to study organizational cultures along with measures of leader and work-unit effectiveness, as well as individual cognitive, emotional, and evaluative responses to leader behaviors. The goal is to study leader behaviors within organizations and cultures longitudinally.

Phase four is based on phase three, in which universally perceived behaviors that impede or facilitate outstanding leadership will be identified. Also, phase three is oriented toward identifying actual leader practices and universal organizational practices leading to positive or negative cognitive, affective, and performance consequences. Further, efforts will be made to identify those perceived behaviors and practices that are culture specific. Once these parameters are in place, it should be possible, in phase four, to experimentally test responses to various leader behaviors and practices, so that stronger causal inferences can be made. The researchers hope to find answers, in phase four, to the following questions:

1. Are there any universally effective leader behaviors?
2. What are the effects of violating strongly held culturally endorsed preferences for leader behaviors?
3. What types of consistent specific preferences for leader behaviors are present across cultures?

Some of the preliminary findings released by the GLOBE team suggest 21 specific leader attributes and behaviors that are universally viewed as contributing to leadership effectiveness. Eleven of these were closely associated with what was termed "global charismatic/value-based leadership." Subsequent research revealed strong support for the hypothesis that charismatic/value-based leadership is universally endorsed by subject participants. The same was true for team-oriented leadership and humane/participative leadership. Eight specific leader characteristics were universally viewed as impediments to leader effectiveness. Then, 35 other specific leader characteristics were identified as contributors to success in some cultures and impediments in others.

The general findings of the completed portions of the GLOBE project are that cultural dimensions do exist that can be identified and measured. Cultural differences can be studied through etic (across cultures) or emic (within cultures, or country-specific information) approaches. Cultural differences strongly influence the ways in which people think about their leaders as well as societal norms that exist concerning the status, influence, and the privileges granted to leaders. Although work remains to complete the project, the preliminary findings yielded by the pilot studies and beginning published articles[115] indicate a great deal of promise for furthering understanding of how leaders can effectively operate in various cultures.

Other smaller international research efforts are also emerging in recent years. For example, Bass has examined the nature of the transactional-transformational leadership paradigm across national boundaries.[116] Also, Church and Wacalawski investigated the relationship between leader style (transformational versus transactional) and subsequent organizational practices and outcomes, which supports the preliminary findings presented in the GLOBE report.[117] And finally, still another study suggests that there are indeed leadership concepts that are culturally endorsed, in which similar cultures share similar leadership concepts.[118] Clearly, the study of leadership across cultures is a growing and important body of knowledge for the leadership field.

Summary

This chapter presents and analyzes the processes of leadership. The classic research studies on leadership set the stage for the theoretical development of leadership. The trait theories concentrate on the leaders themselves but, with the possible exception of intelligence and emotional maturity (EQ) characterized by empathy/interpersonal sensitivity, and self-confidence or self-efficacy, really do not come up with any agreed-upon traits of leaders. In recent times the trait approach has resurfaced in terms of leader skills and competencies.

The group and exchange theories emphasize the importance of followers, and although the vertical dyad linkage (VDL or LMX) model still generates research, the group and exchange theories in general are recognized to be only partial theories. Today, the widely recognized theories of leadership tend to be more situationally based. In particular, Fiedler's contingency model made a significant contribution to leadership theory and potentially to the practice of human resource management. The path-goal approach also made an important contribution to leadership understanding. It incorporates expectancy motivation concepts.

All the established theories of leadership continue to provide understanding and a foundation for the practice of leadership in today's organizations. However, in recent years a number of alternative theories have emerged to supplement and, in some cases, facilitate better understanding of the various processes of effective leadership. In particular, the charismatic, transformational, social cognitive, and substitutes approaches have received increasing attention. Charismatic leaders (characterized as having qualities beyond the usual appointed leader) get extraordinary commitment and performance from followers. The charismatic leaders, however, as a group are considered only a subsection of the larger group of transformational leaders characterized by charisma, inspiration, and intellectual and individualized stimulation. These transformational leaders are felt to be especially suited to today's organizations as they experience dramatic change. The social cognitive theory of leadership incorporates the leader, the situation, and the behavior itself. This social cognitive approach emphasizes the importance of behavior and the continuous, interacting nature of all the variables in leadership. The substitutes approach recognizes that certain subordinate, task, and organizational characteristics may substitute for or neutralize the impact that leader behavior has on subordinate performance and satisfaction. All of these leadership theories need more research to provide a better understanding of the complexities involved and to make the applications to practice more effective.

Finally, studies of international leadership indicate the importance of recognizing differences both across cultures and within cultures leadership studies. The GLOBE project in particular is an example of a very comprehensive research program designed to discover the nature of leader effectiveness by identifying both universal and culture-specific variables that are associated with effective leadership processes.

ENDING WITH META-ANALYTIC RESEARCH FINDINGS

OB PRINCIPLE: The leader's level of intelligence will influence others' perception of the leader's effectiveness.

Meta-Analysis Results: [13 studies; over 1,533 participants; $d = 1.21$] *On average, there is an **80 percent probability** that highly intelligent leaders will be perceived as more effective leaders than those of less intelligence.* Further analysis, although not as strong, also supported that the traits of dominance and masculinity/femininity are also significantly related to perceptions of leadership effectiveness.

Conclusion: According to the "Great Person" theory of leadership, leaders are born and not made. Such historically important theories suggest that leaders are blessed with inherent traits or abilities that distinguish them from others. Physical attributes such as height, appearance, and age along with personality traits such as dominance and introversion/extroversion have all been considered as potential leadership attributes. Although these lines of inquiry have yielded some interesting findings, no generalizations, with the possible exception of intelligence as found in this meta-analysis, have emerged. However, the evidence has been somewhat stronger regarding leader skills and abilities and states such as emotional intelligence and self-efficacy studied in Chapter 9.

Source: Adapted from Robert G. Lord, Christy L. De Vader, and George M. Alliger, "A Meta-Analysis of the Relation between Personality Traits and Leadership Perceptions: An Application of Validity Generalization Procedures," *Journal of Applied Psychology,* Vol. 71, No. 3, 1986, pp. 402–410.

OB PRINCIPLE: Leader–member exchange (LMX) is positively related to job performance, satisfaction, and commitment.

Meta-Analysis Results: [(1) 12 studies; 1,909 participants, $d = .91$ for performance ratings (leader LMX); (2) 30 studies; 4,218 participants; $d = .58$ for performance ratings (member LMX); (3) 8 studies; 982 participants; $d = .19$ for objective performance; (4) 27 studies; 5,302 participants; $d = 1.59$ for satisfaction with supervision; (5) 33 studies; 6,887 participants; $d = 1.03$ for overall satisfaction; and (6) 17 studies; 3,006 participants; $d = .75$ for organizational commitment.] *On average, there is a: (1) **74 percent probability** that the leader's perception of LMX will be more related to members' rated performance than for those leaders who do not perceive LMX; (2) **66 percent probability** that the members' perception of LMX will be more related to their rated performance than for those who do not perceive LMX; (3) **55 percent probability** that perceived LMX will be more related to objective performance (e.g., quantity or quality of work) than if LMX is missing; (4) **87 percent probability** that perceived LMX will be more related to member satisfaction with supervision than if LMX is absent; (5) **77 percent probability** that perceived LMX will be more related to member overall satisfaction than if LMX is not perceived; and (6) **70 percent probability** that perceived LMX will be more related to member organizational commitment than if LMX is absent.* Further moderator analysis indicates that the strength of this relationship depends on the measurement used. When perceptions of LMX are measured from a leader's perspective, the relationship between LMX and performance ratings of members is stronger than when perceptions are measured from the member's point of view.

Conclusion:

LMX perceptions of the leader's relationship with members and those in the in-group and out-group are important because of the linkages between leadership processes and outcomes of performance, satisfaction and commitment. In particular, perceptions of a supervisor or leader regarding an employee's performance become criteria on which important decisions are made. A tendency for a supervisor to rate someone favorable as a result of being in the in-group can translate into favorable outcomes for in-group members and negative outcomes for out-group members. Furthermore, creating positive or negative expectations about an employee through the development of LMX perceptions may change the actual performance level of employees (i.e., become a self-fulfilling prophecy) and not just affect performance ratings. This LMX process highlights the importance of interpersonal relationships between leaders and their followers.

Source: Charlotte R. Gerstner and David V. Day, "Meta-Analytic Review of Leader-Member Exchange Theory: Correlates and Construct Issues," *Journal of Applied Psychology,* Vol. 82, No. 6, 1997, pp. 827–844.

Questions for Discussion and Review

1. Briefly summarize the findings of the three classic leadership studies.
2. How do the group theories differ from the trait theories of leadership?
3. Name and describe the main "competencies" that may be associated with a leader's effectiveness.
4. What are the three critical situational variables identified by Fiedler? If these are very favorable, what is the most effective style to use?
5. In simple terms, what is the path-goal theory of leadership? What is the leader's function in this conceptualization?
6. What are the major differences between traditional transactional leaders and emerging transformational leaders? Can you clarify these differences in how today's organizations are led?
7. What are the three variables in the social cognitive approach to leadership? How do they relate to one another? How can this approach be applied to the practice of human resource management?
8. What is meant by "substitutes for," and "neutralizers of," leadership? Give some subordinate, task, and organizational examples of these substitutes and neutralizers.
9. What is the GLOBE project? What cultural dimensions have been identified by the GLOBE researchers? What preliminary findings have been found by this GLOBE research effort?

Internet Exercise: Leading in Times of Crisis

Most organizations at one time or another face crisis situations in which leaders must make important choices to insure the very survival of the organization. Consider the recent examples of Firestone Tire' defective tire problems or Microsoft's antitrust court battles and how quality leadership either fixed, or at least helped, these organizations minimize their losses. Either following up on these two examples or a current "organizational crisis" that is in progress, search both the popular and/or business press (e.g., www.businessweek.com or www.fortune.com) and then the specific firm's website for stories about the crisis. By examining quotes and other relevant information about such things as speed of reaction and placing of blame and/or responsibility for the crisis, look for leadership traits or leadership issues. Then, consider the following questions.

1. What style is the leader using in order to solve the crisis? Does it seem effective? Why or why not? What would you have done differently if you were the leader in charge?

2. Frame the issue in the context of Fiedler's theory and specific contingency model of leadership (Figure 17.1). Does the leadership style in use fit the situation as defined by Fielder? If not, could this explain why the organization is not solving the problem?

REAL CASE: No Organization Chart and an 80-Blank-Pages Policy Manual	Ask Michael E. Marks about his company's procedures for making a big capital investment, and he is likely to refer you to the Flextronics International Corporate Policy Manual. It has 80 pages—all of them blank. Although Marks is Flextronics' chairman and CEO, he says he sometimes lets subordinates such as Humphrey W. Porter, the head of Flextronics' European operations, do multimillion-dollar acquisitions without showing him the paperwork. He disdains staff meetings at his San Jose (Calif.) headquarters, and he refuses to draw up an organization chart delineating his managers' responsibilities.

One might think Marks's style is too casual for a fast-growing conglomerate. This is a giant that owns dozens of factories scattered over four continents and has big contracts with some of the most demanding corporate customers on earth, from Cisco Systems Inc. to Siemens. What's more, Flextronics seems to be announcing a breakthrough deal a month. This year alone, the company has spent $5.5 billion to acquire electronics manufacturing plants, design firms, and component makers in the United States, Europe, and Asia. It also has landed huge manufacturing contracts with Motorola Inc. and Microsoft Corp.

As Marks sees it, the business of global contract manufacturing is all about speed. The time it takes to get a prototype into mass production and onto retail shelves across the globe can determine whether a leading-edge digital gadget succeeds or flops. And with the Internet and corporate makeovers rapidly reconfiguring entire industries, Marks thinks it's a bigger sin to miss important opportunities than to make a mistake or two. So he doesn't want to tie down his top managers with bureaucracy. One of Marks's favorite dictums: "It's not the big who eat the small. It's the fast who eat the slow."

So far, Marks has managed to craft the right balance. A Harvard MBA who had run several small electronics makers, Marks helped engineer a takeover of Singapore-domiciled Flextronics in 1993, when it was nearly bankrupt. After turning the company around, he began to rebuild. Flextronics became a favored supplier to companies like Cisco, 3Com, and Palm. Marks then parlayed Flextronics' zooming stock price into aggressive acquisitions. In seven years, sales have soared from $93 million towards $10.5 billion this year. Its stock, meanwhile, has soared from under $10 in 1998 to the mid-70s currently. This year, Flextronics is poised to become the world's second-largest contract manufacturer, after Milpitas (Calif.)-based Solectron Corp. Besides the industrial parks in Hungary, it also has huge manufacturing campuses in Mexico, China, and Brazil.

The basketball hoop hanging in Marks's modest, somewhat disheveled office seems to sum up his self-image. Marks is a passionate player—even though he stands all of 5 ft. 2 in. Likewise, in the business world, Marks seems determined to prove a point. One way or another, he's convinced he can retain the agile management style of a start-up, while making Flextronics a global enterprise that can play in the big leagues.

1. Based on your reading of the case, describe the leadership process used by Michael Marks. Do you think he is successful because of or in spite of his leadership approach?

2. What leadership theories covered in the chapter would best support Marks? Give specific examples.
3. How do you think Marks would do in another industry such as automobiles or retail?

The results are in. America doesn't know Jack. John F. Welch, that is, General Electric Co.'s lame-duck chairman and all-time, intergalactic champ memoir-peddler. Sure, Time Warner Inc.'s book publishing unit may think enough of him and his reputation as one of America's foremost management thinkers to pay him a $7.1 million advance payment—more than the advances paid to either Pope John Paul II or General Colin L. Powell for their memoirs. But a new *Business Week*/Harris Poll discovered Welch's broad public recognition probably wouldn't necessarily put sales of the Welch tome in the same league as the works of Stephen King or Mary Higgins Clark.

In fact, just 11 percent of the folks surveyed online said they were very familiar or even somewhat familiar with Welch. That's the same number drawn by Amazon.com Inc. CEO Jeffrey P. Bezos even after he was named *Time* magazine's Person of the Year last December. Welch's recognition factor was also way below Microsoft Corp.'s Bill Gates (97 percent) and Federal Reserve Chairman Alan Greenspan (76 percent). Even New York Yankees boss George Steinbrenner (68 percent) left Welch in the dust. Moreover, those who had some familiarity with Welch were hard pressed to say just what he does. Only 36 percent were able to identify him as the chief executive of America's most valuable company. More than half simply didn't know.

Welch is no stranger to *Business Week*, of course. For one thing, his book's coauthor is, Senior Writer John A. Byrne. And Welch has appeared on the cover four times since becoming GE's chief in 1981—a sure sign that we think what he has to say is worth readers' time. But what about asking someone who might have to sell Welch's book? At The Bookery in Indialantic, Fla., owner Renee Shaw hadn't a clue who Welch was, even though her July 17 *Publishers Weekly* carried news of the $7.1 million deal. Can Time Warner sell the estimated 1.6 million copies of Welch's wisdom needed to make a profit of the book? "It ain't gonna fly," she concluded. Maybe 100,000 copies will sell—"at best."

She may be right. Then again, betting against Welch has never proved very smart. And even the BW poll shows clearly that many who know him respect him. Among the subset of poll respondents who said they did have some familiarity with Welch, one-third agreed with one or both of these glowing statements: "He is one of America's best managers," and "His ideas have helped make U.S. corporations far more competitive." And why not? Welch runs his business by the numbers, so why not judge him the same: In a little over 15 years, a $10,000 investment in the Standard & Poor's 500-stock index would have grown to $91,000; the same investment in GE would have netted $347,000. Americans may not recognize Welch, but they certainly can recognize success.

1. Why are these corporate leaders popular (and not according to the poll)? How would you rank them? Why?
2. Since this survey was taken, GE acquired Honeywell, and Jack Welch had a positive *60 Minutes* program devoted to him. What has happened recently with the rest of them? Do you think the rankings are now different?
3. Each of these leaders are quite different. What theories in the book would support their rise to the top of the corporate world?

CHAPTER 18

Great Leaders: Styles, Activities, and Skills

Learning Objectives

Relate the style implications from the classic studies and modern theories of leadership.

Present the widely recognized traditional styles of leadership, including those from the managerial grid and the life-cycle approach.

Discuss the findings on leadership roles and activities.

Examine the relationship that activities have with successful and effective leaders.

Identify the skills needed for effective leadership of today's organizations.

Analyze the various approaches to leadership development.

Starting with Best Practice
Leader's Advice

Leadership Guru Warren Bennis on Great Leaders vs. the Situation

Warren Bennis has had a long and distinguished academic and professional career. He has written numerous articles and about 25 books on leadership. His publications include the book Leaders, *a best-seller, and* An Invented Life: Reflections on Leadership and Change, *a collection of essays that was nominated for the Pulitzer Prize. The* Wall Street Journal *names him as one of the top 10 speakers on management. In this interview Bennis talks about the great person versus situation debate in leadership.*

Q1: *How do you think the challenges that are being faced by leaders have changed over the last 25 years?*

Bennis: Well, two of the most obvious challenges are those of dealing with globalization and galloping technology. However, a third challenge—even more interesting in my opinion—is the whole area of employee involvement, employee participation, and empowerment. Of course, today these are not new ideas. But 25 years ago, the concept of worker participation was just beginning to take off.

Q2: *Has this idea developed the way you thought it would?*

Bennis: Yes and no. It certainly has progressed from being an esoteric idea to one that is widely taken for granted. This certainly did not surprise me. However, at the same time, there have been dramatic changes in the environment—and these have had a significant impact. In particular, I see the notion of empowerment on a collision course with many of the ideas associated with downsizing, restructuring, and reengineering.

Q3: *Warren, you've given us interesting insights to leadership challenges of the future and the past. In looking at all of this as a totality, are leaders good leaders regardless of the time period in which they emerge? Or would a successful world leader, say Winston Churchill, fail in Great Britain today because he lacks the skills needed at this point in time?*

Bennis: You've presented an interesting dilemma, and in answering your question let me contrast the views of Leo Tolstoy, the Russian novelist, with those of Thomas Carlyle, the great British historian. Tolstoy believed that men were always the effect—rather than a cause—of events. Events have their own historical force and, at best, a leader can guide the way. This viewpoint of situationalism is sharply different from that of Carlyle, who believed that history is a succession of biographies. Every institute is the "length and breadth of one great man." I personally lean toward Carlyle's view and believe that great leaders create the situation. And not necessarily where the situation is currently, but where it is headed. As my favorite management philosopher, Wayne Gretzky, put it, "It's not where the puck is; it's where the puck will be."

An effective leader is an individual who can see through the fog of reality to interpret events and be able to make sense of the blurring and ambiguous complexity. And to be able to do this has nothing to do with whether we're living in 2020 or today. Moreover, even if you have the best vision in the world, if you can't generate trust, it doesn't matter. And it's not just trust in an abstract sense. It's the ability to connect with people in their gut and in their heart and not just in their head.

There's a leader I know who runs one of the country's largest transportation firms. He read an article of mine where I quoted Gretzky, and he said to me, "You know, I really appreciate your quote, but I run a company where I think we know where the puck is going to be, but I can't get the union, the workforce, or anybody to actually go with me on that vision." He talked in very negative terms about his overall operation, but never acknowledged the fact that the people in the firm do not trust him. They see him as a "revolving SOB"—an SOB regardless of the angle from which they look at him. So he has the vision and the ability to see through the fog of reality, but he can't get the people to follow him. And this is the issue of not just interpreting and envisioning the future, or knowing where the puck is going to be, but being able to create the kind of meaning for people, the values that make sense to them, where there's enough trust in the system so it's going to stick. So I'm not saying that situations are not important. But I am saying that the effective leader has to be able to size up that situation, forge a new path to see where the puck is going, and then have a message and vision that has meaning to the workforce. And there has to be trust in the system. Without that, you can call for the spirits from the vasty deep forever—and they won't come.

Q4:   *So, in closing, you feel that over the last 25 years the challenges of the leader remain similar to what they have been in terms of not just vision but the development of trust?*

Bennis: Absolutely, and that's particularly true in this era of reengineering and downsizing, where trust continues to be a major concern for the employees. If leaders can't establish that trust, then participation and empowerment will be cynical relics of a distopian nightmare. The problem is squarely in the hands of management, and it's a challenge that will confront us well into the 21st century.

The preceding chapter presented the background and the traditional and modern theoretical processes of leadership. This chapter serves as the follow-up application. Specifically, this chapter deals with the various styles, activities, and skills of leaders/managers.

First, the style implications from the classic studies and theories of the preceding chapter are examined. Then, the main part of the chapter presents and analyzes the widely recognized styles of leadership. This discussion is followed by an examination of roles and activities, with special attention given to successful and effective leaders/managers. The last part of the chapter focuses on the leadership skills that are increasingly being recognized as necessary for today's dramatically changing organizations. Very simply, the differences among styles, activities, and skills express the *ways* leaders influence followers. Roles and activities are *what* leaders do, and skills are concerned with *how* leaders can be effective.

In this chapter the terms *leaders* and *managers* are used interchangeably, although the preceding chapter pointed out the distinction between managers and leaders, and there is even empirical evidence that there may be a difference.[1] Nevertheless, as Richard Teerlink, the highly successful leader of Harley-Davidson, noted: "In the business environment of the future, everyone will be in a leadership role."[2] Thus, this chapter on *leadership* styles, activities, and skills is also on *management* styles, activities, and skills. After first discussing the modern context for leadership, the chapter will give equal attention to styles, activities, skills, and development of great leaders.

Leadership in the New Environment

There is no question that leadership roles are changing in the new environment and organizational contexts outlined in the first part of the book. One recent analysis argues that five key leadership roles will shape managerial successes (and failures) in the next decade. They include: (1) a strategic vision to motivate and inspire, (2) empowering employees, (3) accumulating and sharing internal knowledge, (4) gathering and integrating external information, and (5) challenging the status quo and enabling creativity.[3] Others suggest that even the small-business leader faces a shifting role, moving from a local to a global focus, following the market, seeking innovation, being open, staying intent on the quality of the execution rather than the idea, remaining inquisitive and innovative, and being a networker rather than the lone ranger.[4] There are also pessimists that note a trend in which many young, capable new employees actively avoid the prospect of becoming a leader or manager, because the idea of managing itself is obsolete, exhausting, irrelevant, and an unfashionable career choice.[5] The same is true for what young people expect from their leaders. As the accompanying OB in Action indicates, the values and beliefs of the young "Generation Xer's" are much different than the "baby boomers" who are in leadership positions. In such a shifting environment, the understanding of leader styles, activities, and skills for effectiveness becomes an increasingly complex and challenging task.

Several new trends affect the study of leadership. As mentioned in Chapter 15, many jobs are now being performed away from the work site, at home, by telecommuters. These individuals do not have the same day-to-day personal contacts with leaders that more traditional employees experience. Motivational processes, incentives, and leadership tactics must be modified in telework. Further, the growing world of e-business has spawned an entirely new kind of leader: the e-boss, who focuses on speed, technology, high risk taking, and megaprofits in short periods of time. Jeff Bezos, CEO of Amazon.com, is a prime example of this new type of e-manager. He is a self-described "techie nerd" who takes high risks, but also generously rewards his people who have become very wealthy. At the same time, major swings in stock values, new competitors, governmental regulation, and other factors make the roles of e-leaders such as Bezos substantially different from those who are in more traditional settings.

More and more organizations are utilizing technology to e-manage their operations. For example, GM has created a new system, known as ROS (Retail Operating System), which provides reference materials for procedures and resources to meet customer expectations so the GM area contact representatives can keep in closer contact with various retailers. The modules include information regarding organizational development, market development, business administration, sales operations, service operations, and parts operations.[6] In a manner similar to Kerr's view regarding substitutes for

OB In Action

With GenXers, It's a Whole New Ball Game

Leading human resources in the 21st century is going to be a major challenge for every enterprise. In addition to the changes that are taking place in the environment in terms of technology and competitive strategies, organizations are finding that their incoming personnel are more demanding than ever before—and they can get away with it because if the company does not accede to their demands, they will go somewhere else. These young individuals, known as "Generation Xer's," were born between 1965–1981. They have grown up during the computer revolution, the advent of MTV sound bites, and a business world that has gone haywire with corporate downsizing and massive layoffs. As a result, they have learned to expect change—and they are willing to deal with it.

Today there are approximately 44 million Generation Xers in the United States and many of them are being led by baby boomers, who are individuals born between 1945–1964. The values and beliefs of the two groups differ sharply. Although overgeneralizations and stereotypes can be wrong, it is generally agreed that baby boomers tend to be more loyal to their organizations and want to know what their bosses want done. Their attitude is one of "Thank you for the job opportunity. I'll try to please you." Generation Xers tend to have a different mind-set. Their attitude and approach may best be represented by the statement, "Here's what I want to stay with the company and if I'm not happy and having fun, I'll take my skills elsewhere."

How can today's leaders deal effectively with Generation Xers? Experts who have studied the beliefs and attitudes of young GenX employees have found that there are a number of things that organizations can do in order to hire and retain them. These include:

1. Challenge them with assignments that let them use their entrepreneurial instincts and their strong pragmatism.
2. Create a team concept with a great deal of interaction with other employees so that they will enjoy their work.
3. Build their confidence by letting them use their problem-solving skills.
4. Explain to them what needs to be done and the outcomes in terms of pros and cons, so that they understand the trade-offs they are going to have to make.
5. Show them what they are doing is important to the organization and how their work relates to other areas.
6. Encourage them to participate in the planning process and to contribute their ideas and suggestions.
7. Explain the rationale behind instructions and directives so that they not only understand what needs to be done, but why it needs to be done.
8. Pair them up with older workers in a buddy system because they get along well with these people.
9. Help them understand the career paths that are available in the organization and offer them counseling and guidance so that they can make informed decisions regarding where they want to go and how they can get there.
10. Give them prompt feedback on their work: when they do a good job, praise them; when they make mistakes, show them how to avoid repeating them in the future.

Many of the management approaches that worked well in the 1990s have limited value in leading the young GenX workforce today. As many managers are now discovering, with GenXers it's a whole new ball game!

leadership (see Chapter 17), technology is being used to enhance the tactics used by traditional leaders. Consequently, organizational behavior theory building and research must adapt to the new types of leaders and organizations, which continue to experience these new patterns and trends in organizational life.[7]

LEADERSHIP STYLES

The classic leadership studies and the various leadership theories discussed in the preceding chapter all have direct implications for what style the manager or supervisor uses in human resource management. The word *style* is very vague. Yet it is widely used to describe successful leaders. For example, the leadership style of Steve Jobs, a founder of Apple Computer, was discribed as follows:

> Sometimes it's hard to tell whether Steve Jobs is a snake-oil salesman or a bona fide visionary, a promoter who got lucky or the epitome of the intrepid entrepreneur. What's indisputable is that he possesses consummate charm, infectious enthusiasm, and an overdose of charisma.[8]

This vivid description also points out the difficulty of attaching a single style to a leader. This complexity is also brought out in meta-analyses of gender and leadership that do not wholly support stereotypes of the styles and effectiveness of men and women leaders.[9] Styles also differ from one culture to another. The following sections describe how leadership styles have been studied and evaluated over the years.

Style Implications of the Classic Studies and the Modern Theories

Chapter 1 discusses the major historical contributions to the study of organizational behavior. Most of this discussion has indirect or direct implications for leadership style. For example, the Hawthorne studies were interpreted in terms of their implications for supervisory style. Also relevant is the classic work done by Douglas McGregor, in which Theory X represents the traditional authoritarian style of leadership and Theory Y represents an enlightened, humanistic style. The studies discussed at the beginning of the preceding chapter are also directly concerned with style. The Iowa studies analyzed the impact of autocratic, democratic, and laissez-faire styles, and the studies conducted by the Michigan group found the employee-centered supervisor to be more effective than the production-centered supervisor. The Ohio State studies identified consideration (a supportive type of style) and initiating structure (a directive type of style) as being the major functions of leadership. The trait and group theories have indirect implications for style, and the human-oriented, democratic and task-directed styles play an important role in Fiedler's contingency theory. The path-goal conceptualization depends heavily on directive, supportive, participative, and achievement-oriented styles of leadership.

The same is true of charismatic and transformational leaders. They have an inspirational style with vision, and they "do the right thing" for their people. Table 18.1 summarizes the charismatic leader style according to three major types of behavior, with illustrative actions. An example of such a style in recent times would be Paul O'Neil of ALCOA. He espoused a clear vision for his firm, anchored on quality, safety, and innovation. He made his vision compelling and central to the company, set high expectations for his management team and employees throughout the organization, and provided continuous support and energy for his vision through meetings, task forces,

TABLE 18.1   Nadler and Tushman's Charismatic Leadership Styles

Types of Charismatic Leadership Styles	Meaning	Examples
Envisioning	Creating a picture of the future—or a desired future state—with which people can identify and that can generate excitement	Articulating a compelling vision Setting high expectations
Energizing	Directing the generation of energy, the motivation to act, among members of the organization	Demonstrating personal excitement and confidence Seeking, finding, and using success
Enabling	Psychologically helping people act or perform in the face of challenging goals	Expressing personal support Empathizing

videotapes, and extensive personal contact.[10] Another example of new leadership in action is Hewlett-Packard's CEO Carly Fiorina. She is known for her bold, some would say radical, style the way she reorganized HP.[11]

A rough approximation of the various styles derived from the studies and theories discussed so far can be incorporated into the continuum shown in Table 18.2. For ease of presentation, the styles listed may be substituted for the expressions "boss-centered" and "employee-centered" used by Tannenbaum and Schmidt in their classic leadership continuum shown in Figure 18.1. The verbal descriptions and the relationship between authority and freedom found in Figure 18.1 give a rough representation of the characteristics of the various styles of leadership. Importantly, as shown in the contingency theories, both sides can be effective. An example would be the long-term success of GE's Jack Welch, who admitted he was more involved in the day-to-day operations of his corporation than would be the traditional boss-centered leader.[12] In any case, this depiction can serve as background for a more detailed examination of the specific application of styles to the effective practice of human resource management.

One thing is certain: leadership style can make a difference, both positively and negatively. For example, a survey found that senior executives view their companies' leadership styles as pragmatic rather than conceptual, and conservative rather than risk taking. These same executives felt that to meet their current and future challenges, the

TABLE 18.2   Summary Continuum of Leadership Styles Drawn from the Classic Studies and Theories of Leadership

Boss-Centered	*Employee-Centered*
Theory X ⟷	Theory Y
Autocratic ⟷	Democratic
Production-centered ⟷	Employee-centered
Close ⟷	General
Initiating structure ⟷	Consideration
Task-directed ⟷	Human relations
Directive ⟷	Supportive
Directive ⟷	Participative

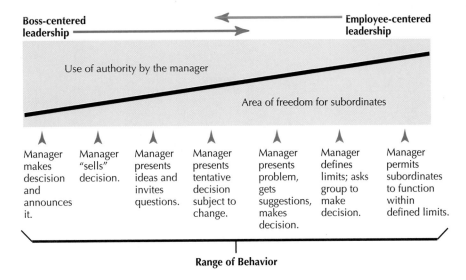

FIGURE 18.1
The Tannenbaum and Schmidt continuum of leadership behavior.

styles should be the other way around.[13] In contrast to the leaders in the classical bureaucracies, leaders of today's organizations, described in Chapter 4, "must be more entrepreneurial; more accountable; more customer- , process- , and results-focused; biased toward action; empowering; communicative; technologically sophisticated; on fire about innovation and continuous improvement; strong in the use of guidance, suggestion, and influence; and sparing in the use of pure authority."[14] To be otherwise may have dire consequences for the organization as well as for its individual members. One recent study of abusive leadership, characterized as a sustained display of hostile verbal and nonverbal behaviors, excluding physical contact, indicates a series of potential long-term undesirable outcomes, including employees with lower job and life satisfaction, lower normative and affective commitment, conflicts between work and family, and psychological distress.[15] Consequently, as Bennis has noted: "Never before has American business faced so many challenges, and never before have there been so many choices in how to face those challenges. We must look now at what it is going to take not just to regain global leadership, but simply to stay a player in the game."[16] The following sections examine the widely recognized leadership styles available to today's managers to meet these challenges.

Managerial Grid Styles

One very popular approach to identifying leadership styles of practicing managers is Blake and Mouton's classic managerial grid. Figure 18.2 shows that the two dimensions of the grid are "concern for people" along the vertical axis and "concern for task" along the horizontal axis. These two dimensions are equivalent to the consideration and initiating structure functions identified in the last chapter by the Ohio State studies and the employee-centered and task-centered styles used in the Michigan studies.

The five basic styles identified in the grid represent varying combinations of concern for people and task. The 1,1 manager has minimum concern for people and task; this style is sometimes called the "impoverished" style. The opposite is the 9,9 manager. This individual has maximum concern for both people and task. The implication

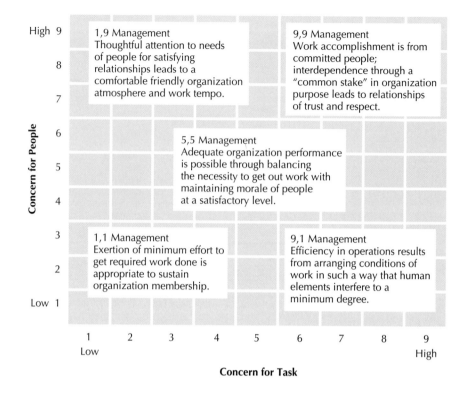

FIGURE 18.2
The Blake and Mouton managerial grid.

is that the 9,9 is the best style of leadership, and Blake and Mouton have stated in no uncertain terms: "There should be no question about which leadership style is the most effective. It's that of the manager whom we call, in the terminology of the Managerial Grid, a 9,9 team builder."[17] Blake and Mouton provided empirical evidence that their interactive notion of leadership style (that is, concern for people interacting with concern for task) has more predictive validity than additive situational approaches.[18] The 5,5 manager is the "middle-of-the-roader," and the other two styles represent the extreme concerns for people (1,9, "country club" manager) and task (9,1, "task" manager). A manager's position on the grid can be determined by a questionnaire developed by Blake and Mouton. The International Application Example: Balancing People and Profits offers an example of the managerial grid approach to international negotiations.

Hersey and Blanchard's Life-Cycle, or Situational, Approach

Another popular approach to management-style training and development is the *life-cycle* (later termed the *situational*) approach to leadership.[19] It is an extension of the managerial grid approach. Following the original Ohio State studies and the grid approach, Hersey and Blanchard's approach identifies two major styles:

1. *Task style.* The leader organizes and defines roles for members of the work group; the leader explains the tasks that members are to do and when, where, and how they are to do them.
2. *Relationship style.* The leader has close, personal relationships with the members of the group, and there is open communication and psychological and emotional support.

Balancing People and Profits

One of the most interesting examples of current leadership practices is provided by those individuals in the international arena who are negotiating business deals. Quite often, they fit into one of two groups: businesspeople from other countries who are seeking opportunities to invest and national leaders who are seeking to attract investment. For example, Lou Gerstner, the current head of IBM, is working closely with Toshiba of Japan to develop a series of technological projects related to memory chips and liquid crystal displays, and Jack Welch, of greatly admired General Electric, is expanding operations into China, India, Mexico, and other developing nations. Each would like to enter into a contract that enhances his position, and this is where effective leadership enters the picture.

These CEOs are not alone. In recent years Russia and the other republics of the former Soviet Union have worked very hard to attract foreign investment. CEOs from PepsiCo, Archer Daniels Midland, United Telecommunications, and Chevron, to name but a few, have all negotiated with the Russians and others about investment opportunities there. The problem for many of these business leaders is that the political power base continues to change, and thus there is considerable risk. On the one hand, they must talk to the head of the Russian government, but on the other hand, other senior-level government officials in Russia and especially the other republics have local authority and can block decisions made in Moscow. Moreover, leaders on both sides of these international negotiations must balance a concern for the local people with a concern for the work to be done and the profits that must be earned in order to attract the initial foreign investment.

Another very visible example of international negotiating is provided by Bill Richardson, a former professional baseball player and congressman. Mr. Richardson has been a negotiator for the U.S. government with none other than Saddam Hussein and Fidel Castro. Richardson has found that there are some useful rules that can be extremely helpful when negotiating with such notorious international strongmen. Six of his recommendations would seem to be of considerable value to business people everywhere:

1. *Be a good listener.* It is important to respect the other person's point of view and to know what makes this adversary tick.
2. *Come away with something.* In many cases it will not be possible to obtain the primary goal (e.g., freeing a U.S. citizen from the local jail), but it is often possible to secure the promise of a future meeting so that the negotiations can continue.
3. *Use leverage.* In many cases the other side has demands or a point of view that they want others to know about, and the negotiator can gain leverage by promising to pass along these messages to the parties for whom they are intended, thus making it more likely that the adversary will want to continue negotiating.
4. *Know your adversary.* By getting background on the other people, knowing how they are likely to act and what is likely to solicit a positive response from them, you can strengthen your negotiating position.
5. *Earn the other side's respect.* It is important to show that you are skilled and tough and do not back down at every threatening gesture made by the other side. In this way, they know you are firm and they are likely to respect you—and, in turn, your position.
6. *Get others involved.* Quite often strong international figures are isolated and do not know what is going on throughout their country. By involving others in the negotiations, it is possible, if things start to collapse, for leaders to turn to their advisors and say, "I thought we had a deal, but things seem to be unraveling. Help me out here, will you?"

Taking the lead from some of Fiedler's work on situational variables, Hersey and Blanchard incorporated the maturity of the followers into their model. The level of maturity is defined by three criteria:

1. Degree of achievement motivation
2. Willingness to take on responsibility
3. Amount of education and/or experience

Although they recognize that there may be other important situational variables, Hersey and Blanchard focus only on this maturity level of work group members in their model.

Figure 18.3 summarizes the situational approach. The key for leadership effectiveness in this model is to match up the situation with the appropriate style. The following summarizes the four basic styles:

1. *Telling style.* This is a high-task, low-relationship style and is effective when followers are at a very low level of maturity.

FIGURE 18.3
Hersey and Blanchard's situational leadership model.

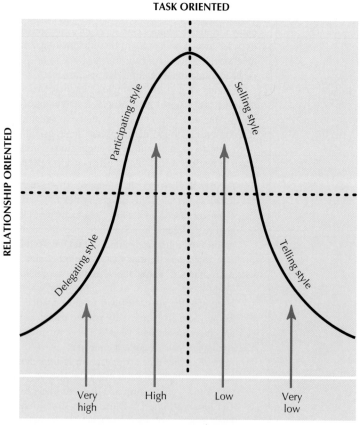

TASK ORIENTED

Participating style

Selling style

RELATIONSHIP ORIENTED

Delegating style

Telling style

Very high   High   Low   Very low

Maturity Level of Followers
(need for achievement, willingness to accept
responsibility, and education/experience)

2. *Selling style.* This is a high-task, high-relationship style and is effective when followers are on the low side of maturity.
3. *Participating style.* This is a low-task, high-relationship style and is effective when followers are on the high side of maturity.
4. *Delegating style.* This is a low-task, low-relationship style and is effective when followers are at a very high level of maturity.

Like the grid approach, Hersey and Blanchard's approach includes a questionnaire instrument that presents 12 situations that generally depict the various levels of maturity of the group; respondents answer how they would handle each situation. These responses follow the four styles. How closely respondents match the situation with the appropriate style will determine their effectiveness score.

Even though this situational leadership model has some practical implications for the management of change,[20] the theoretical rationale is generally criticized as being "weak, because Hersey and Blanchard have neglected to provide a coherent, explicit rationale for the hypothesized relationships."[21] They also, by their own admission, highly oversimplify the situation by giving only surface recognition to follower maturity. Also, as in the grid approach, there is a noted absence of any empirical tests of the model. One review of all facets of the approach was particularly critical of the instrument that Hersey and Blanchard used to measure leader effectiveness,[22] and an empirical test did not find support for the underlying assumptions or predictions.[23] Overall, however, as is true of the other style approaches, this situational approach seems to be of some value in training and development work in that it can point out the need for flexibility and take into consideration the different variables affecting leaders. Yet, this type of approach has limited utility for identifying or predicting leadership effectiveness.

Leadership Styles in Perspective

Blake and Mouton's managerial grid and Hersey and Blanchard's life cycle represent the established approaches to leadership style. These have been around for a number of years, but are still relevant in the prescriptive sense of what managers should do, even in today's emerging organizations. However, there is a general lack of research support. Recently, noted leadership researchers House and Podsakoff have summarized the behaviors and approaches of great leaders that they drew from the more modern theories (e.g., charismatic and transformational) and research findings as follows:[24]

1. *Vision.* Great leaders articulate an ideological vision that is congruent with the deeply held values of followers, a vision that describes a better future to which the followers have a moral right.
2. *Passion and self-sacrifice.* Great leaders display a passion for, and have a strong conviction of, the moral correctness of their vision. They engage in outstanding or extraordinary behavior and make extraordinary self-sacrifices in the interest of their vision and the mission.
3. *Confidence, determination, and persistence.* Great leaders display a high degree of faith in themselves and in the attainment of the vision they articulate. Theoretically, such leaders need to have a very high degree of self-confidence and moral conviction because their mission usually challenges the status quo

and, therefore, is likely to offend those who have a stake in preserving the established order.

4. *Image building.*   Great leaders are self-conscious about their own image. They recognize that they must be perceived by followers as competent, credible, and trustworthy.

5. *Role modeling.*   Leader image building sets the stage for effective role modeling because followers identify with the values of role models who are perceived positively.

6. *External representation.*   Great leaders act as the spokesperson for their organization and symbolically represent the organization to external constituencies.

7. *Expectations of and confidence in followers.*   Great leaders communicate high performance expectations to their followers and strong confidence in their followers' ability to meet such expectations.

8. *Selective motive arousal.*   Great leaders selectively arouse those motives of followers that are of special relevance to the successful accomplishment of the vision and mission.

9. *Frame alignment.*   To persuade followers to accept and implement change, great leaders engage in frame alignment. This refers to the linkage of individual and leader interpretive orientations such that some set of followers' interests, values, and beliefs, as well as the leader's activities, goals, and ideology, becomes congruent and complementary.

10. *Inspirational communication.*   Great leaders often, but not always, communicate their messages in an inspirational manner using vivid stories, slogans, symbols, and ceremonies.

These 10 leadership behaviors and approaches are not specific styles per se, but cumulatively they probably represent what is currently known about the most effective style of today's leaders/managers. In any case, there is accumulating evidence that a leader's style can make a difference. For example, studies have found that the leader's style is the key to the formulation and implementation of strategy[25] and even plays an important role in work group members' creativity[26] and team citizenship.[27] Even humor and fun may play a role in leader effectiveness.[28] There have been many anecdotal reports regarding the positive effects of humor at world-class companies such as Southwest Airlines, Ben & Jerry's Ice Cream, and Sun Microsystems. For example, recognized leader Scott McNealy of high-tech Sun Microsystems wears a Java "decoder" ring that has the motto "Kick butt and have fun." He also plays in an intramural squirt gun war with engineers. Admired leader Herb Kelleher of Southwest Airlines often shows up at meetings and on holidays in a variety of costumes, including the Easter Bunny, and arm wrestled an opponent in a trademark dispute in front of a big audience. Based on such an approach, one recent study of 115 Canadian financial managers and their 322 subordinates revealed a significant relationship between humor and individual performance as well as with work unit performance.[29] The note of caution in the study, however, was that humor and fun only meshed with a more active and involved leader style. In other words, there is little doubt that the *way* (style) leaders influence work group members can make a difference in their own and their people's performance.

In recent years, however, except for continued use as a training vehicle, the concern for styles of leadership has given way to the importance of the roles and activities of leadership and the skills of effective leaders. The rest of the chapter is concerned with this *what* (roles and activities) and *how* (skills) of leadership.

THE ROLES AND ACTIVITIES OF LEADERSHIP

In answer to the question of what do leaders really do, separate observational studies by Henry Mintzberg and the author (Luthans) were conducted. These studies provide direct empirical evidence of the roles (Mintzberg) and activities (Luthans) of leaders/managers.

Leader/Manager Roles

On the basis of his direct observational studies (as opposed to the questionnaire/interview studies so commonly used in leadership research), Mintzberg proposes the three types of managerial roles shown in Figure 18.4.[30] The *interpersonal roles* arise directly from formal authority and refer to the relationship between the manager and others. By virtue of the formal position, the manager has a *figurehead role* as a symbol of the organization. Most of the time spent as a figurehead is on ceremonial duties such as greeting a touring class of students or taking an important customer to lunch. The second interpersonal role is specifically called the *leader role.* In this role the manager uses his or her influence to motivate and encourage subordinates to accomplish organizational objectives. In the third type of interpersonal role the manager undertakes a *liaison role.* This role recognizes that managers often spend more time interacting with others outside their unit (with peers in other units or those completely outside the organization) than they do working with their own leaders and subordinates.

Besides the interpersonal roles flowing from formal authority, Figure 18.4 shows that managers also have important *informational roles.* Most observational studies find that managers spend a great deal of time giving and receiving information. As *monitor,* the

FIGURE 18.4
Mintzberg's managerial roles.

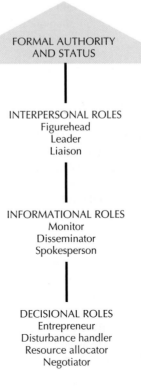

manager is continually scanning the environment and probing subordinates, bosses, and outside contacts for information; as *disseminator,* the manager distributes information to key internal people; and as *spokesperson,* the manager provides information to outsiders.

In the *decisional role,* the manager acts upon the information. In the *entrepreneurial role* in Mintzberg's scheme, the manager initiates the development of a project and assembles the necessary resources. As *disturbance handler,* on the other hand, instead of being proactive like the entrepreneur, the manager is reactive to the problems and pressures of the situation. As disturbance handler, the manager has a crisis management type of role; for example, the employees are about to strike, or a major subcontractor is threatening to pull out. As *resource allocator,* the manager decides who gets what in his or her department. Finally, as *negotiator,* the manager spends time at all levels in the give-and-take of negotiating with subordinates, bosses, and outsiders. For example, a production manager may have to negotiate a grievance settlement with the union business agent, or a supervisor in a social services department may have to negotiate certain benefit payments that one of the counselors wants to give a client.

These informal managerial roles suggested by Mintzberg get much closer to describing what managers/leaders really do than the formally described and prescribed functions. Mintzberg's work has definitely shed some light on what leaders do, but as he stated in a retrospective commentary about the 10 roles: "We remain grossly ignorant about the fundamental content of the manager's job and have barely addressed the major issues and dilemmas in its practice."[31] More recent studies have used leadership roles such as vision setter, motivator, analyzer, and task master.[32] These roles were then tested concerning their relationships to three dimensions of firm performance. The results were that leaders with high behavioral complexity—the ability to play multiple, competing roles—produce the best performance, particularly with respect to business performance (growth and innovation) and organizational effectiveness.[33] Another more recent study identified the roles of senior-level executives as mobilizer, ambassador, driver, auditor, and servant.[34] The results indicated that higher-level executives are rated more favorably than are their subordinates in all five roles and that there were no differences in the ratings of executives in public versus private organizations.[35]

The Activities of Successful and Effective Leaders

Closely related to the study and identification of leader/manager roles are their day-to-day activities. The author (Luthans) and his colleagues conducted a comprehensive study to answer three major questions: (1) What do managers do? (2) What do successful managers do? and (3) What do effective managers do?[36] Answers to these questions can provide insights and specific descriptions of the daily activities of successful (those promoted relatively rapidly in their organizations) and effective (those with satisfied and committed subordinates and high-performing units) managers or leaders.

What Do Managers Do?   The so-called "Real Managers Study" first used trained observers to freely observe and record for one varied hour per day over a two-week period the behaviors and activities of 44 managers from all levels and types of Midwest organizations. These included retail stores, hospitals, corporate headquarters, a railroad, government agencies, insurance companies, a newspaper office, financial institutions, and manufacturing plants. The voluminous data gathered from the free-observation logs were then reduced through the Delphi technique (described in Chapter 11) into 12 categories with observable behavioral descriptors, as shown in Table 18.3. These

TABLE 18.3 Managerial Activities and Behavioral Descriptors Derived from Free Observation of Real Managers

1. **Planning/Coordinating**
   a. setting goals and objectives
   b. defining tasks needed to accomplish goals
   c. scheduling employees, timetables
   d. assigning tasks and providing routine instructions
   e. coordinating activities of each work group member to keep work running smoothly
   f. organizing the work

2. **Staffing**
   a. developing job descriptions for position openings
   b. reviewing applications
   c. interviewing applicants
   d. hiring
   e. contacting applicants to inform them of being hired or not
   f. "filling in" where needed

3. **Training/Developing**
   a. orienting employees, arranging for training seminars, etc.
   b. clarifying roles, duties, job descriptions
   c. coaching, mentoring, walking work group members through task
   d. helping work group members with personal development plans

4. **Decision Making/Problem Solving**
   a. defining problems
   b. choosing between two or more alternatives or strategies
   c. handling day-to-day operational crises as they arise
   d. weighing the trade-offs; cost-benefit analyses
   e. actually deciding what to do
   f. developing new procedures to increase efficiency

5. **Processing Paperwork**
   a. processing mail
   b. reading reports, in-box
   c. writing reports, memos, letters, etc.
   d. routine financial reporting and bookkeeping
   e. general desk work

6. **Exchanging Routine Information**
   a. answering routine procedural questions
   b. receiving and disseminating requested information
   c. conveying results of meetings
   d. giving or receiving routine information over the phone
   e. staff meetings of an informational nature (status update, new company policies, etc.)

7. **Monitoring/Controlling Performance**
   a. inspecting work
   b. walking around and checking things out, touring
   c. monitoring performance data (e.g., computer printouts, product, financial reports)
   d. preventive maintenance

8. **Motivating/Reinforcing**
   a. allocating formal organizational rewards
   b. asking for input, participation
   c. conveying appreciation, compliments
   d. giving credit where due
   e. listening to suggestions
   f. giving positive performance feedback
   g. increasing job challenge
   h. delegating responsibility and authority
   i. letting work group members determine how to do their own work
   j. sticking up for the group to managers and others, backing a work group member

9. **Disciplining/Punishing**
   a. enforcing rules and policies
   b. nonverbal glaring, harassment
   c. demotion, firing, layoff
   d. any formal organizational reprimand or notice
   e. "chewing out" a work group member, criticizing
   f. giving negative performance feedback

10. **Interacting with Outsiders**
    a. public relations
    b. customers
    c. contacts with suppliers, vendors
    d. external meetings
    e. community service activities

11. **Managing Conflict**
    a. managing interpersonal conflict between work group members or others
    b. appealing to higher authority to resolve a dispute
    c. appealing to third-party negotiators
    d. trying to get cooperation or consensus between conflicting parties
    e. attempting to resolve conflicts between a work group member and self

12. **Socializing/Politicking**
    a. non-work-related chitchat (e.g., family or personal matters)
    b. informal "joking around," B.S. ing
    c. discussing rumors, hearsay, grapevine
    d. complaining, griping, putting others down
    e. politicking, gamesmanship

Source: Fred Luthans and Diane Lee Lockwood, "Toward an Observation System for Measuring Leader Behavior in Natural Settings," in J. G. Hunt, D. Hosking, C. Schriesheim, and R. Stewart (Eds.), *Leaders and Managers,* Pergamon, New York, 1984, p. 122.

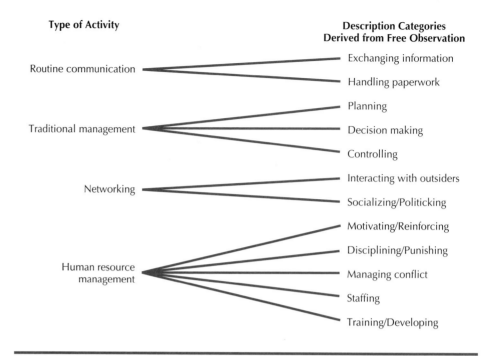

Type of Activity

Routine communication

Traditional management

Networking

Human resource management

Description Categories Derived from Free Observation

Exchanging information

Handling paperwork

Planning

Decision making

Controlling

Interacting with outsiders

Socializing/Politicking

Motivating/Reinforcing

Disciplining/Punishing

Managing conflict

Staffing

Training/Developing

FIGURE 18.5
Luthans's conceptual categories of real managers' activities.

empirically derived behavioral descriptors were then conceptually collapsed into the four managerial activities shown in Figure 18.5. Briefly summarized, these activities are as follows:

1. *Communication.* This activity consists of exchanging routine information and processing paperwork. Its observed behaviors include answering procedural questions, receiving and disseminating requested information, conveying the results of meetings, giving or receiving routine information over the phone, processing mail, reading reports, writing reports/memos/letters, routine financial reporting and bookkeeping, and general desk work.

2. *Traditional management.* This activity consists of planning, decision making, and controlling. Its observed behaviors include setting goals and objectives, defining tasks needed to accomplish goals, scheduling employees, assigning tasks, providing routine instructions, defining problems, handling day-to-day operational crises, deciding what to do, developing new procedures, inspecting work, walking around inspecting the work, monitoring performance data, and doing preventive maintenance.

3. *Human resource management.* This activity contains the most behavioral categories: motivating/reinforcing, disciplining/punishing, managing conflict, staffing, and training/developing. Because it was not generally permitted to be observed, the disciplining/punishing category was subsequently dropped from the analysis. The observed behaviors for this activity include allocating formal rewards, asking for input, conveying appreciation, giving credit where due, listening to suggestions, giving positive feedback, providing group support, resolving conflict between work group members, appealing to higher authorities or third parties to resolve a dispute, developing job descriptions, reviewing applications, interviewing applicants, filling in where needed, orienting employees, arranging for training, clarifying roles, coaching, mentoring, and walking work group members through a task.

4. *Networking.* This activity consists of socializing/politicking and interacting with outsiders. The observed behaviors associated with this activity include non-work-related chitchat; informal joking around; discussing rumors, hearsay, and the grapevine; complaining, griping, and putting others down; politicking and games-manship; dealing with customers, suppliers, and vendors; attending external meetings; and doing/attending community service events.

The preceding lists of activities empirically answer the question of what managers really do. The activities include some of the classic activities identified by pioneering theorists such as Henri Fayol[37] (the traditional activities), as well as more recent views by modern leadership theorists such as Henry Mintzberg[38] (the communication activities) and John Kotter[39] (the networking activities). As a whole, however, especially with the inclusion of human resource management activities, this view of real managers' activities is more comprehensive than previous studies of leader/manager activities.

After the nature of managerial activities was determined through the free observation of the 44 managers, the next phase of the study was to determine the relative frequency of these activities. Data on another sample of 248 real managers (not the 44 used in the initial portion of this study but from similar organizations) were gathered. Trained participant observers filled out a checklist based on the managerial activities shown in Table 18.3 at a random time, once every hour, over a two-week period (80 observation periods). As shown in Figure 18.6, the managers were found to spend about a third of their time and effort in routine communication activities, a third in traditional management activities, a fifth in human resource activities, and a fifth in networking activities. This relative-frequency analysis—based on observational data of a large sample—provides a fairly confident answer to the question of what real managers do. The environmental changes since this Real Managers Study was conducted have undoubtedly had an impact on managerial work.[40] However, although globalization has affected the scope and advanced information technology has affected the means and the speed of communication and other areas such as decision making, the identified activities themselves should remain relevant and valid.

What Do Successful Managers Do? Important though it is to get an empirical answer to the basic question of what leaders/managers do, of even greater interest is determining what successful and effective leaders/managers do. Success was defined in terms of the speed of promotion within an organization. A success index on the sample

FIGURE 18.6

Relative distribution of managers' activities.

Source: Fred Luthans, Richard M. Hodgetts and Stuart A. Rosenkrantz, *Real Managers,* Ballinger, Cambridge, Mass., 1988, p. 27. Used with permission.

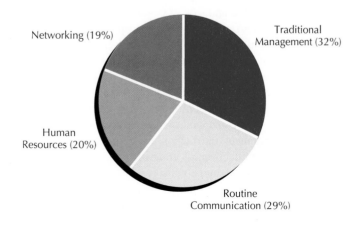

Networking (19%)

Traditional Management (32%)

Human Resources (20%)

Routine Communication (29%)

in the study was calculated by dividing the managers' levels in their respective organizations by their tenure (length of service) there. Thus, a manager at the fourth level of management who had been with the organization for five years would be rated more successful than a manager at the third level who had been at that level for 25 years. Obviously, there are some potential problems with such a measure of success, but for the large sample of managers, this was an objective and useful measure.

To answer the question of what successful managers do, several types of analyses were conducted. In all these analyses, the importance of networking in real managers' success was very apparent. Of the four major activities, only networking had a statistically significant relationship with success.[41] Overall, it was clear that networking made the biggest relative contribution to manager success and, importantly, human resource management activities made the least relative contribution.

What does this mean? It means that in this study of real managers, using speed of promotion as the measure of success, it was found that successful managers spend relatively more time and effort socializing, politicking, and interacting with outsiders than did their less-successful counterparts. Perhaps equally important, the successful managers did not give relatively as much time or attention to the traditional management activities of planning, decision making, and controlling or to the human resource management activities of motivating/reinforcing, staffing, training/developing, and managing conflict. In other words, for the managers in this study, networking seems to be the key to success (as defined by rapid promotion). It should be noted that many managers aspire to success rather than being effective. One reason is that personal pride and mobility is at stake. Bedeian and Armenakis note what they call the "cesspool syndrome," in which organizations in decline lose their best employees first, leaving behind the "dreck," which then floats to the top.[42] Consequently, although being successful as opposed to effective may seem less desirable to the organization, from an individual manager's perspective, it may be part of an effective career strategy.

What Do Effective Managers Do?   Although the operational measure of success used in the study was empirical and direct, the definition and measurement of effectiveness offers little agreement on criteria or measures. To overcome as many of the obstacles and disagreements as possible, for a sample of the managers, the study used a combined effectiveness index that represented the two major—and generally agreed upon—criteria of both leadership theory/research and practice: (1) getting the job done through high quantity and quality standards of performance, and (2) getting the job done through people, requiring their satisfaction and commitment.

In particular, a standardized organizational effectiveness questionnaire[43] that measures the unit's quality and quantity of performance, job satisfaction questionnaire,[44] and organizational commitment questionnaire[45] were used. This multiple-measures index was employed in the study to answer the most important question of what effective managers do. It was found that communication and human resource management activities made by far the largest relative contribution to the managers' effectiveness and that the traditional management activities, and especially the networking activities, made by far the least relative contribution.[46] In other words, if effectiveness is defined as the perceived quantity and quality of the performance of a manager's unit and his or her work group members' satisfaction and commitment, then the biggest relative contribution to leadership effectiveness comes from the human-oriented activities—communication and human resource management.

Another intriguing finding from this part of the study, alluded to earlier, was that the least relative contribution to the managers' measured effectiveness came from the networking activity. This, of course, is in stark contrast to the results of the successful manager analysis. Networking activity had by far the strongest relative relationship to success, but the weakest to effectiveness. On the other hand, human resource management activities had a strong relationship to effectiveness (second only to human-oriented communication activities) but had the weakest relative relationship to success. In other words, the successful managers in this study did not perform the same activities as the effective managers (in fact, they did almost the opposite). These contrasting profiles may have significant implications for understanding the performance problems facing today's organizations.

Implications Across Cultures and for Entrepreneurs.   The Real Managers Study is obviously bound by the definitions that were used, and, of course, one could question the generalizability of the findings and conclusions to all managers. As far as generalizability across cultures goes, a replication of this study that observed Russian managers in a large textile factory found very similar results.[47] This study provides evidence that the activities identified for the successful and effective U.S. managers may hold across cultures.

Besides holding across cultures, there is also a recent study of the activities of U.S. entrepreneurs (those who started and sustained their own business for at least seven years) using the same methodology found basically the same results as the Real Managers Study.[48] However, even though the activities and their frequency of occurence seem to hold both across cultures and for entrepreneurs as well as managers, more evidence is needed to draw any definitive conclusions about generalizability.

In the global arena, there are always confounding cultural variables. For example, there may be what has been called a "dark side" to leadership, which seems to be in evidence in postcommunist countries.[49] This negative side of leadership includes power bases derived from the communist era, which demands loyalty at any cost. This form of leadership creates an increasing escalation of commitment to various courses of action (e.g., the Russian armed conflicts with Afghanistan and Chechnya) and takes advantage of a halo effect derived from leaders and a sense of nationalism ("Mother Russia" combined with the popularity of the Stalin legacy). Under this "dark" approach, opposition is quickly removed. Follower characteristics can also contribute to this dark side; they view change with suspicion and worry that unsuccessful attempts at free enterprise are indicative of weak and ineffective leadership.

A very recent analysis argues that the Russian economy must be built through a transformation in the leadership.[50] Centralized decision making must be curtailed, a culture of empowerment should be created, autocratic leader practices must be reduced, trust must be developed, accountability training needs to be introduced, and follower responses of learned helplessness must be eliminated and replaced with an entrepreneurial spirit. Obviously such changes will take many years and are going to be highly difficult to accomplish. These needed changes in leadership have recently called for "minishock therapy" for the entire Russian culture and economy.[51] Both domestically and internationally, knowing *what* leaders do, which was the purpose of the Real Managers Study, must be supplemented with *why* they are doing it.[52]

Implications of the Real Managers Study.   Despite some limitations, there seem to be a number of implications from the Real Managers Study for the application of leadership in today's organizations. Probably the major implication stems from the significant difference between the activities of successful and effective managers. The most obvious implication from this finding is that more attention may need to be given to formal reward systems so that effective managers are promoted. Organizations need to tie formal rewards (especially promotions) to performance in order to move ahead and meet the challenges that lie ahead. This can be accomplished most pragmatically in the short run by performance-based appraisal and reward systems and in the long run by developing cultural values that support and reward effective performance, not just successful socializing and politicking. An important goal to meet the challenges of the years ahead might be as simple as making effective managers successful.

Besides the implications for performance-based appraisal and reward systems and organizational culture, much can be learned from the effective managers in the study. In particular, it is important to note the relative importance that they gave to the human-oriented activities of communication and human resource management. The effective managers' day-to-day activities revolved around their people—keeping them informed, answering questions, getting and giving information, processing information, giving feedback and recognition, resolving conflicts, and providing training and development. In other words, these effective managers provide some answers to how to meet the challenges that lie ahead. Human-oriented leadership skills may be of considerable value in meeting the challenges of global competition, of information technology and knowledge management. The next section focuses on these leadership skills.

LEADERSHIP SKILLS

As the preceding chapter indicates, there is now recognition in both leadership theory and practice of the importance of skills—*how* leaders behave and perform effectively. Both styles and roles/activities are closely related to skills and can be used as a point of departure for the discussion of skills. First, some of the commonly recognized leadership skills are identified; then, a number of techniques are suggested for enhancing the effectiveness of leadership.

What Skills Do Leaders Need?

As mentioned in Chapter 17, the research on leader traits has given way to attempts to identify leader skills. There are many lists of such skills in the practitioner-oriented literature. For example, one such list of suggested leadership skills critical to success in the global economy includes the following:[53]

1. *Cultural flexibility.* In international assignments this skill refers to cultural awareness and sensitivity. In domestic organizations the same skill could be said to be critical for success in light of increasing diversity. Leaders must have the skills not only to manage but also to recognize and celebrate the value of diversity in their organizations.
2. *Communication skills.* Effective leaders must be able to communicate—in written form, orally, and nonverbally.
3. *HRD skills.* Because human resources are so much a part of leadership effectiveness, leaders must have human resource development (HRD) skills of developing a learning climate, designing and conducting training programs, transmitting information and experience, assessing results, providing career counseling, creating organizational change, and adapting learning materials.
4. *Creativity.* Problem solving, innovation, and creativity provide the competitive advantage in today's global marketplace. Leaders must possess the skills to not only

be creative themselves but also provide a climate that encourages creativity and assists their people to be creative.

5. *Self-management of learning.* This skill refers to the need for continuous learning of new knowledge and skills. In this time of dramatic change and global competitiveness, leaders must undergo continuous change themselves. They must be self-learners.

This list is up to date and is as good as any other; however, as an academic analysis recently noted: "The prevailing conceptualizations of skills required for successful managerial performance hinders our understanding of the phenomenon."[54] To get around this problem, Whetten and Cameron provide a more empirical derivation of effective leadership skills. On the basis of an interview study of more than 400 highly effective managers, the 10 skills most often identified were the following:[55]

1. Verbal communication (including listening)
2. Managing time and stress
3. Managing individual decisions
4. Recognizing, defining, and solving problems
5. Motivating and influencing others
6. Delegating
7. Setting goals and articulating a vision
8. Self-awareness
9. Team building
10. Managing conflict

Follow-up studies and related research have found skills similar to the 10 listed. Through statistical techniques, the results of the various research studies were combined into the following four categories of effective leadership skills:

1. Participative and human relations (for example, supportive communication and team building)
2. Competitiveness and control (for example, assertiveness, power, and influence)
3. Innovativeness and entrepreneurship (for example, creative problem solving)
4. Maintaining order and rationality (for example, managing time and rational decision making)[56]

Commenting on these various leadership skills identified through research, Whetten and Cameron note three characteristics:

1. The skills are behavioral. They are not traits or, importantly, styles. They consist of an identifiable set of actions that leaders perform and that result in certain outcomes.
2. The skills, in several cases, seem contradictory or paradoxical. For example, they are neither all soft- nor all hard-driving, oriented neither toward teamwork and interpersonal relations exclusively nor toward individualism and entrepreneurship exclusively.
3. The skills are interrelated and overlapping. Effective leaders do not perform one skill or one set of skills independent of others. In other words, effective leaders are multiskilled.[57]

On the basis of this background, Whetten and Cameron then develop models for both personal and interpersonal leadership skills. Figure 18.7 and Figure 18.8 show these models. As shown, the personal skills of developing self-awareness, managing stress, and solving problems creatively overlap with one another, and so do the interpersonal skills of communicating supportively, gaining power and influence, motivating

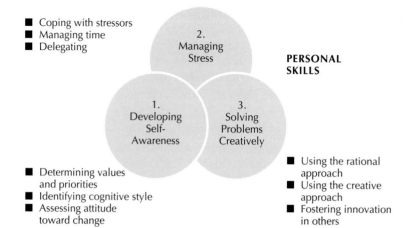

FIGURE 18.7

Whetten and Cameron model of personal skills.

Source: David A. Whetten and Kim S. Cameron, *Developing Management Skills,* 2d ed., HarperCollins, New York, 1991, p. 17. Used with permission.

others, and managing conflict. These models not only can be used to summarize what skills were found to be important in effective leaders but also can serve as guidelines for needed skill development in the future.

Besides the skills discussed so far that take a personal and interpersonal perspective, "career streams" should be recognized at the organization level. Among the keys from an organizational point of view are finding the right fit between the individual, the position, and the company's needs.[58] Also, firms developing leaders and seeking to retain them should be aware of what is called the "Pied Piper effect," where job hopping by an effective leader can lead to defections and attrition among the subordinates who were under the departed leader.[59] Leadership skills and career development programs may need to be extended to include recruitment, training, and even postcorporate career components (i.e., what to pursue after one's corporate career comes to an end).[60] Leadership skills and career development have become more critical than ever.

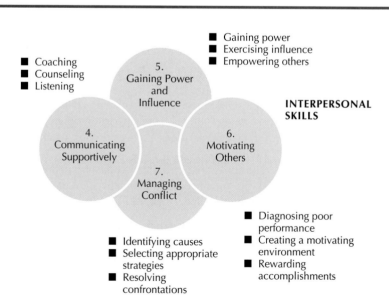

FIGURE 18.8

Whetten and Cameron model of interpersonal skills.

Source: David A. Whetten and Kim S. Cameron, *Developing Management Skills,* 2d ed., HarperCollins, New York, 1991, p. 16. Used with permission.

Leadership Skills and Career Development Programs

One consistent need that has emerged in recent years is a foreboding lack of leadership talent under development. As an example, one recent survey indicates that the number of 35- to 44-year old executives will fall by 15 percent in the next decade, creating a major reduction in the leadership talent pool.[61] One answer offered is to create options that extend the careers of current leaders while developing a means to attract and train those to replace them. However, as witnessed during the Clinton administration by the tragic plane crash in the Balkans that killed Secretary of Commerce Ron Brown and 16 corporate executives, there are always unexpected events that many companies are not prepared to handle. In the case of the fallen executives, most of the organizations that they represented were not able to fill the void and floundered for several years.[62]

Organizational behavior and human resource experts are being asked to identify methods to train and develop leaders for the new economy. Zand suggests that the three primary areas to be developed are knowledge, trust, and power, which he refers to as the "leadership triad."[63] Regardless of the label, numerous techniques are under consideration. One method suggested is to develop an acceleration pool, in which key leadership competencies, the understanding of job challenges, and organizational knowledge bases are enhanced.[64] The acceleration pool utilizes information gained in assessment centers to identify potential new leaders along with the strengths and weaknesses individual candidates possess. From there it is possible to speed up the process by which they are trained to move into leadership positions.

There does seem to be merit in identifying key individual differences that are predictive of success. For example, a recent study of male cadets in a military college indicated that physical fitness, prior influence experiences, and great self-esteem were predictive of effectiveness in later leadership roles.[65] Another study revealed that attitudes toward leadership and experience were related to leader emergence at a rate that was much stronger than the traditionally assumed prerequisite of masculine gender role characteristics.[66] These studies are representative of the continuing body of research that will assist in leader training and development in the coming years.

Others believe an entire new development system should be used. Believing that most traditional leadership programs fail because they start with competencies and focus on individuals, one group of trainers recommends a different approach. Instead of individuals, the goal is to deliver leadership development by beginning with business results and working back to abilities.[67] In other words, it is more valuable to clarify the business purpose and desired outcomes first, and then move leader trainees toward methods of achieving these outcomes. What this and other new approaches indicate is that many companies are trying to make leader development programs more effective. One current survey indicated that only 35 percent of the companies surveyed were satisfied with their investments in leadership development programs, leaving a great deal of room for improvement.[68]

The most recent mainstream approach to leadership development is centered on competencies. In this approach, there are three ways that competencies have been derived: (1) research based, (2) strategy based, and (3) values based. Research-based competencies are derived from behavioral data gathered from successful leaders. Strategy-based competency models derive information from key informants regarding strategic company issues and directions. The values-based model focuses on the company's cultural values, as interpreted by company leaders. Briscoe and Hall argue for the need to go beyond these three with what they call "metacompetancies."[69] Under this new approach, leaders would be trained utilizing a learning-based model. Continuous learning emphasizes flexibility and identity, so strong that the individual leader is able to "learn how to learn" and therefore adapt to continually changing circumstances as found in today's environment. Other competencies are not abandoned, but rather are augmented by this learning and knowledge-acquisition-based approach.

Another recently emerging method of leader development is coaching. When the relationship between a coach and a client is built on mutual trust, respect, and freedom of expression, the potential for heightened learning increases.[70] The goal of effective coaching is to move away from the concept that "managing equals controlling" and forward to the idea that "managing equals creating a context for coaching."[71] It is the partnership and the climate that are the keys to effective coaching development systems.

Tactics that support effective coaching include accessibility, attention, validation, empathy, support, compassion, and consistency. A supportive coach can reduce the loneliness of the CEO's role by creating bonds that help the leader renew energy levels and provide new challenges.[72] Also, effective coaches clarify boundaries and expectations for leaders, limiting leaders' efforts to definable targets and time frames for learning.[73] To obtain the greatest value from a coaching approach to leader development, some of the more important practices include a strategic focus for coaching efforts, integrating coaching into existing HR systems, building reliable "pools" of coaches, and systematically evaluating the results.[74]

This is an era in which CEO succession will become an even more vital concern for many organizations.[75] Indeed, many European firms that are family based have become targets for takeovers due to leadership succession problems.[76] In these environments, coaching systems can be effectively used to help identify and place the right new chief executive into the job (i.e., make the fit).

Other Techniques for Developing Leadership Effectiveness

Besides the skill development programs, other techniques involving training, job design, and behavioral management, discussed in previous chapters, can also be used. For example, leaders can undergo personal growth training that may involve a combination of psychological exercises and outdoor adventures. This approach is aimed at empowering participants to take greater responsibility for their own lives and ultimately their organizations.[77] As revealed in the following reflection of a personal growth training participant, these popular programs may be wrongly equating the thrills involved with effective leadership:

> I peer over the edge of the cliff, trying to be logical. The harness to which I am attached seems sturdy. I have just watched several other participants jump. Although they appeared anxious at first, they not only survived the leap—they seemed to enjoy it. I also trust the safety of the system because I trust that the training company does not want me to die. Okay, given that assessment, let's take the risk. It might even be fun. And somehow, I might become a better leader. So off the edge I go.[78]

Despite the potential for the "thrill" becoming an end in itself, there are arguments that personal training contributes to effective leadership. One recent professional book argues that bringing "peace, fulfillment, and awakening to all aspects of your life" are important components of transformational leadership,[79] and another suggests that too much attention may be paid to external aspects of leadership at the expense of internal matters. The argument is that for leaders, *who they are* is just as important as *what they do*.[80]

Although such personal growth training is controversial, there is no question that leaders need to use training techniques with their people. The Japanese, of course, have traditionally placed a high priority on training of all kinds. Recently, however, world-class United States corporations have also become committed to the importance of training. For example, all employees at the highly successful Quad/Graphics firm spend considerable time every week in training sessions—on their own time—to improve themselves and make their company more competitive. A major component of the Motorola "quality revolution" was that spending on employee training went to $100 million per year, with 40 percent directly devoted to the skills and procedures needed to produce a no-defect product or to provide timely, error-free, courteous service to internal and external customers. Old job-rotation training programs have also come to life following the adage that there is no training experience better than "walking a mile in the other person's shoes." The same goes for cross training and the newer "pay-for-knowledge" approaches (see Chapter 5) that an increasing number of U.S. firms are beginning to implement.

Besides training, job redesign is another important technique leaders can use effectively. Covered in Chapter 15, this approach attempts to manage the job rather than the extremely complex person who holds the job. From enriching the job by building in more responsibility, the more recent approach is to concentrate on the characteristics of identity, variety, significance, autonomy, and feedback identified by Hackman and his colleagues and covered in Chapter 15. There has been a stream of research to support the concept that when employees perceive these characteristics in their job, they do high-quality work. Leaders need to give special attention to the autonomy and feedback characteristics of their people's jobs. Autonomy involves empowering their subordinates to make decisions and solve their own problems, in other words, giving them more control over their own job. Feedback can be built into some jobs, but leaders also must provide specific, immediate performance feedback of their people.

The behavioral management approach, covered in Chapter 16, can also be effectively used by leaders to meet the challenges ahead. The organizational behavior modification (O.B. Mod.) techniques based on the principles of operant conditioning and social cognitive theory were shown in Chapter 16 to have excellent results on human performance in organizations. It is important to note that O.B. Mod. interventions have used mainly nonfinancial rewards—feedback systems and contingent recognition/attention in both manufacturing and service organizations.

Besides drawing from the established job design and behavioral management approaches, the search for effective leadership practices has recently gone to some unusual sources for leadership wisdom.[81] Examples include: *Leadership Lessons from Star Trek, The Next Generation,* and even stranger sources such as *Goldilocks on Management* and *Beep! Beep! Competing in the Age of the Road Runner.* Also, the leadership style exhibited in the HBO TV hit *The Sopranos* has been examined, as well as an application of the principles of "Tough Love," which are ordinarily reserved for troubled and rebellious teenagers. Besides marketing books, these titles should remind researchers and practitioners of the wide variety of approaches to leadership that have yet to be explored.

Leadership is clearly important in a wide variety of settings beyond business and industry. Recent studies indicate the importance of effective leadership in educational programs at the college and university level,[82] in urban renewal programs,[83] and during the transformational process from college students to those in military settings.[84] There are also many similarities between the capabilities of effective business leaders and political leaders, including the tendency to be a visionary with strong communications skills, even though there are also key differences.[85] The question remains, however, as to whether or not one set of skills (business) can be readily adapted to the political world.

The intent of this discussion is not to give an exhaustive list of leadership skills and techniques. All the styles, roles/activities, and skills discussed in this chapter and the theories in the preceding chapter, plus the techniques discussed in the job design and behavioral management chapters, are relevant and can be effective. Obviously, there are many other leadership skills and techniques that can be relevant to high performance organizations. In total, how leaders apply their skills and techniques can and will make a difference in the challenges that lie ahead.

Summary

This chapter is concerned with leadership styles (the way leaders/managers influence followers/employees), activities (what leaders/managers do in their day-to-day jobs), and skills (how leaders/managers can be effective). Leadership styles have been studied the longest and are derived from both the classic leadership studies and the modern theories. Examples of well-known approaches to leadership styles include Blake and Mouton's managerial grid and Hersey and Blanchard's situational, or life-cycle, model. Both of these approaches to style have been around for a long time but still have implications for the practice of leadership. The grid is valuable mainly because it allows managers to describe their styles. Hersey and Blanchard's approach shows how well managers can match the appropriate style with the maturity level of the group being led. However, these approaches to style lack the research backup to make significant contributions to effective practice.

The shift in attention from styles to roles and activities reflects a more empirical emphasis on what leaders really do. Through observational methodology, Mintzberg identified interpersonal (figurehead, leader, liaison), informational (monitor, disseminator, spokesperson), and decisional (entrepreneur, disturbance handler, resource allocator, negotiator) roles. Closely related is the observational study of leader/manager activities. The author's (Luthans) Real Managers Study investigated the question of what leaders/managers do in their day-to-day activities and what successful and effective leaders/managers do. It was found that the managers spend about a third of their time and effort in communication activities, a third in traditional management activities, a fifth in human resource management activities, and a fifth in networking activities. The analysis of successful managers (those rapidly promoted) found that networking made the biggest relative contribution to their rise and human resource management activities the least. In contrast, however, the analysis of effective managers (those with satisfied and committed subordinates and high-performing units) found that communication and human resource management activities made the largest relative contribution and networking the least. This difference between successful and effective managers has considerable implications for how one gets ahead in an organization (networking involves socializing/politicking and interacting with outsiders) and the reward systems of organizations (the effective managers may not be promoted as fast as the politically savvy ones).

The last part of the chapter is concerned with leadership skills—how leaders behave and perform effectively. Although there are many skills, such as cultural flexibility, communication, HRD, creativity, and self-management of learning, the more research-based skills identified by Whetten and Cameron seem most valuable. Their personal skills model, involving developing self-awareness, managing stress, and solving problems creatively, and the interpersonal skills model, involving communicating supportively, gaining power and influence, motivating others, and managing conflict, are especially comprehensive and useful. Recently, leadership skill development, especially centered on competencies and coaching, has been receiving increased attention. Finally, the more widely recognized organizational behavior techniques found in other chapters (for example, training, job design, and behavioral management) can also be effectively used by leaders.

ENDING WITH META-ANALYTIC RESEARCH FINDINGS

OB PRINCIPLE: Leaders with a charismatic style have high-performing followers and organizations.

Meta-Analysis Results: [32 studies; 4,611 participants; $d = 1.0$] *On average, there is a **76 percent probability** that leaders with a highly charismatic style will have better performing followers and organizations than leaders with a less-charismatic style.*

Conclusion: Charismatic leadership theory represents a recent attempt to define what types of characteristics and skills leaders possess that allow them to have profound effects on followers. Charismatic leadership results when leaders use their personal abilities and unique talents to increase levels of achievement and performance on the part of followers. Similar to trait theories of leadership, some say charisma is a natural born gift of chosen leaders. Others, however, suggest that charisma can be developed. Regardless, because of the great source of influence that a charismatic leadership style can have on followers, it is important that leaders do not use their charisma for their own self-interest. As this chapter points out, the "dark side" of leadership is a product of leaders who use their powerful influence in manipulative and potentially destructive ways. The key for this approach to leadership is to recognize the potential for good and bad, but that for the discontinuous change needed in today's economy, the vision provided and the devotion of followers assured, make the charismatic style of leadership more important than ever.

Source: J. B. Fuller, C. E. P. Patterson and D. Stringer, "A Quantitative Review of Research on Charismatic Leadership," *Psychological Reports,* Vol. 78, 1996, pp. 271–287.

Questions for Discussion and Review

1. What are some styles of charismatic leadership? What do they mean? Give an example.
2. Briefly identify the major styles from Blake and Mouton's grid and from Hersey and Blanchard's life-cycle model. Which style is best?
3. What are the major categories of roles identified by Mintzberg? What are some of the subroles when leaders/managers give and receive information?
4. Use the Real Managers Study to briefly answer the following: What do managers do? What do successful managers do? What do effective managers do?
5. What are some of the needed skills for leaders/managers to be effective? What are the three major characteristics of these skills?
6. How can a competency and coaching approach develop leaders and make them more effective?

Internet Exercise: Leaders as Coaches

The last few years have seen an increase in the popularity of viewing leaders as coaches. For practical information on coaching, visit http://www.coachu.com/. This is an organization that specializes in training coaches as managers. You also can look at the International Coaching Federation, at http://www.coachfederation.com/. Based on what you have found, answer the following questions.

1. Would you like to be led by a "coach" as these organizations define it? What would be some advantages and disadvantages of viewing leaders this way?
2. Based on your own leadership style, would you make a good coach? Why or why not?
3. Discuss a situation in which a coaching approach to leadership would be particularly effective. What would be a situation where a coaching approach would seem to be ineffective?

REAL CASE:
Jeanne P. Jackson:
A Retailing Leader

When Jeanne P. Jackson, the merchant who transformed Banana Republic into a chic, urbane shopping destination, joined Walmart.com this spring as CEO, some analysts considered it an odd mix of cultures. But while the world's biggest discounter is a far cry from upscale Banana, Jackson, 49, felt immediately at home when she attended a Saturday morning management meeting at Wal-Mart Stores Inc. headquarters in Bentonville, Ark., before taking the job. To her amazement, then-CEO David D. Glass was sifting through store-by-store sales reports. "David Glass is concerned about how many lawn mowers were being sold in Poughkeepsie last week. I was blown away," says Jackson, who considers herself a fanatic about retail detail after 22 years in the business.

Up until that day, Jackson had rejected repeated overtures to lead Walmart.com, established by Wal-Mart and venture capital firm Accel Partners. But Accel managing partner James W. Breyer says the companies persisted because Jackson "was absolutely our first choice."

No wonder. Jackson had established herself as a superstar since joining Gap Inc. in 1995. In one gutsy move, she persuaded Banana Republic's parent to open large, expensive flagship stores in key markets to sell the Banana Republic lifestyle. Banana Republic grew rapidly under her leadership, jumping from an estimated $750 million in sales to $1.5 billion in four years. That included reviving the chain's lapsed catalog. "She has taken [Banana Republic] from a niche brand to a mega-brand," says Gap Executive Vice-President Ronald R. Beegle. In 1998, Jackson took over Gap's Direct division, which included managing its Internet sites.

The daughter of a Colorado architect, Jackson stumbled into retailing. While working her way through Harvard Business School, she caught the attention of a department store CEO who was attending an executive program. He frequented the campus pub, managed by Jackson and three male partners. Jackson was there first thing in the morning as the short-order cook, and she was back at night as the bartender. Anyone so tireless should be in retailing, he told her. Jackson was persuaded to give up her plan to go into packaged goods, and joined Federated's vaunted management training program. She later did stints at Saks Fifth Avenue, Walt Disney, and Victoria's Secret.

A mother of two who now travels to Arkansas almost every other week, Jackson hasn't changed much from those early days. She'll need that energy and quick mind as she attempts to extend the largest bricks-and-mortar brand onto the Web. Says Russell Stravitz, who hired her at Federated's Bullock's unit in Los Angeles: "The world is watching, and the pressure is on."

1. Why do you think this retailing leader made this move to Wal-Mart?
2. How would you evaluate her background?
3. Evaluate her self-described "fanatic about retail detail." How would this and other details in the case fit into what you have learned in this chapter about what leaders really do?

REAL CASE:
He's the Best—
Or Is He?

Mention the word *leadership* in reference to CEOs and it often conjures up the names of people such as Carly Fiorina of HP or some other chief executive of one of America's most admired firms. However, there are many effective leaders who are not well known but are considered extremely effective. A good example is Steve Wynn, whose face is known to millions from his television advertising appearances but otherwise goes unrecognized.

Steven Wynn is head of Mirage Resorts Inc., an empire that consists mainly of up-scale resort hotels in Las Vegas and, over the next few years, other cities in Nevada, New Jersey, and Mississippi. To most people who are familiar with his face, he is an advertising pitchman who urges viewers to come out to one of his casinos. However, Wynn is a lot more than this. He has taken bold risks to build his casino empire and has always been an astute risk taker. During the 1980s he linked up with the infamous "junk bond king" Michael Milken and used junk bonds to finance his rise in the casino business. Then, when interest rates subsided, he replaced the troubled bonds with lower-interest securities.

At the same time Wynn has shown that he can be very effective in managing in-house operations. One of the key areas on which he focuses a great deal of attention is employee relations. He contends that "you can never go wrong indulging your employ-ees." Throughout the company, personnel are given "Gotcha Awards," which usually entail an extra day off or a gift certificate. These awards are given simply for doing their jobs in a highly competent manner. As Wynn's director of human resources at the Las Vegas Mirage puts it, "We reward the ordinary, not just the extraordinary." In addition, employees at the Mirage are given fresh, free meals in the hotel's gleaming new cafeteria, which is in sharp contrast to employees at other hotels, who are typically fed with leftovers from the guest buffet. Moreover, Employees and Supervisors of the Year are treated to Hawaiian vacations and a lavish banquet that costs upward of $400,000.

Wynn's winning approach also extends to day-to-day work activities. His hotels op-erate under a system that uses "planned insubordination." This unusual approach requires supervisors to explain to subordinates why a task should be accomplished. And if the workers find that the explanation is unsatisfactory, they are not required to do that job. Do the personnel like this idea? They must, given that turnover at Wynn's operations runs around 12 percent annually whereas it is twice this for the industry at large. In addition, jobs at the Mirage are so coveted that employees are willing to work there for pay that is at or below market rates. And although 40 percent of the workers belong to unions, not a single grievance has been filed against the company in more than four years.

On the other side of the coin, some people complain that Wynn's leadership style can be offensive. He has been accused of erupting into anger and launching verbal as-saults at subordinates over minor matters such as a burned-out lightbulb or a dirty ashtray. He explains these behaviors by noting, "I've always been emotional and passionate. I guess it's a fear that I'll become isolated and not know what's going on." Outsiders who have worked with him simply say that he wants to get things done immediately and that his passion becomes almost maniacal at times, resulting in his outbursts.

Regardless of the strengths and weaknesses of his leadership style, Wynn's empire continues to grow, and he is likely to remain a major force in the gambling and casino in-dustry for many years to come. One reason may have been explained best by an expert on the gaming business who remarked, "I see Steve Wynn as the prototypical charismatic leader, a kind of Henry Ford of the gambling industry. Yet he has these ticks, and he wants to make everything perfect. He may scream at you and humiliate you, but he's also the best person to work for if you want to learn to do things the right way."

1. In terms of the various leadership styles described in the chapter, how would you de-scribe Steve Wynn?
2. If you were making any suggestions to him regarding how he could improve his lead-ership style, what would you tell Wynn?
3. Which of the three major skills in Figure 18.7 would be of most value to Wynn?

ORGANIZATIONAL
BEHAVIOR CASE:
The Puppet

Rex Justice is a long-term employee of the Carfax Corporation, and for the last several years he has been a supervisor in the financial section of the firm. He is very loyal to Carfax and works hard to follow the company policies and procedures and the orders of the managers above him. In fact, upper-level management think very highly of him; they can always count on Rex to meet any sort of demand that the company places on him. He is valued and well liked by all the top managers. His employees in the financial section have the opposite opinion of Rex. They feel that he is too concerned with pleasing the upper-level brass and not nearly concerned enough with the needs and concerns of the employees in his department. For example, they feel that Rex never really pushes hard enough for a more substantial slice of the budget. Relative to other departments in the company, they feel they are underpaid and overworked. Also, whenever one of them goes to Rex with a new idea or suggestion for improvement, he always seems to have five reasons why it can't be done. There is considerable dissatisfaction in the department, and everyone thinks that Rex is just a puppet for management. Performance has begun to suffer because of his style and leadership. Upper-level management seem to be oblivious to the situation in the finance section.

1. How would you explain Rex's leadership style in terms of one or more of the approaches discussed in the chapter?
2. What advice would you give Rex to improve his approach to leadership?
3. Could a leadership training program be set up to help Rex? What would it consist of?

EXERCISE: Job Design Survey*

Goals:

1. To experience firsthand the job characteristics approach to job design, in this case through the Hackman-Oldham Job Diagnostic Survey (JDS).

2. To get personal feedback on the motivating potential of your present or past job and to identify and compare its critical characteristics.

Implementation:

1. Please describe your present job (or a job you have held in the past) as objectively as you can. Circle the number that best reflects the job.

   a. How much *variety* is there in your job? That is, to what extent does the job require you to do many things at work, using a variety of your skills and talents?

   1- - - - - - -2- - - - - -3- - - - - -4- - - - - -5- - - - - -6- - - - - -7

   | Very little; the job requires me to do the same routine things over and over again. | Moderate variety. | Very much; the job requires me to do many different things, using a number of different skills and talents. |

   b. To what extent does your job involve doing a "*whole*" and *identifiable piece of work*? That is, is the job a complete piece of work that has an obvious beginning and end, or is it only a small part of the overall piece of work, which is finished by other people or by machines?

   1- - - - - - -2- - - - - -3- - - - - -4- - - - - -5- - - - - -6- - - - - -7

   | My job is only a tiny part of the overall piece of work; the results of my activities cannot be seen in the final product or service. | My job is a moderate-sized "chunk" of the overall piece of work; my own contribution can be seen in the final outcome. | My job involves doing the whole piece of work, from start to finish; the results of my activities are easily seen in the final product or service. |

   c. In general, *how significant or important* is your job? That is, are the results of your work likely to significantly affect the lives or well-being of other people?

   1- - - - - - -2- - - - - -3- - - - - -4- - - - - -5- - - - - -6- - - - - -7

   | Not very significant; the outcomes of my work are not likely to have important effects on other people. | Moderately significant. | Highly significant; the outcomes of my work can affect other people in very important ways. |

   d. How much *autonomy* is there in your job? That is, to what extent does your job permit you to decide *on your own* how to go about doing the work?

   1- - - - - - -2- - - - - -3- - - - - -4- - - - - -5- - - - - -6- - - - - -7

   | Very little; the job gives me almost no personal "say" about how and when the work is done. | Moderate autonomy; many things are standardized and not under my control, but I can make some decisions. | Very much; the job gives me almost complete responsibility for deciding how and when the work is done. |

   e. To what extent does doing the *job itself* provide you with information about your work performance? That is, does the actual *work itself* provide clues about how well you are doing—aside from any feedback coworkers or supervisors may provide?

   1- - - - - - -2- - - - - -3- - - - - -4- - - - - -5- - - - - -6- - - - - -7

   | Very little; the job itself is set up so that I could work here forever without finding out how well I am doing. | Moderately; sometimes doing the job provides feedback to me; sometimes it does not. | Very much; the job is set up so that I get almost constant feedback as I work about how well I am doing. |

2. The five questions above measure your perceived skill variety, task identity, task significance, autonomy, and feedback in your job. The complete JDS uses several questions to measure these dimensions. But to get some idea of the motivating potential, use your scores (1 to 7) for each job dimension and calculate as follows:

$$\text{MPS} = \frac{\text{skill variety} + \text{task identity} + \text{task significance}}{3} \times \text{autonomy} \times \text{feedback}$$

Next, plot your job design profile and MPS score on the following graphs. These show the national averages for all jobs. Analyze how you compare and suggest ways to redesign your job.

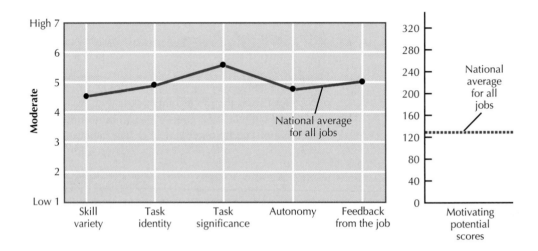

*The "Job Design Survey" is drawn from J. R. Hackman and G. R. Oldham, "Development of the Job Diagnostic Survey," *Journal of Applied Psychology,* Vol. 60, 1975, pp. 159–170.

EXERCISE: Role Playing and O.B. Mod.*

Goal: To experience the application of the O.B. Mod. approach to human resource management.

Implementation: This role-playing situation involves two people: Casey, the supervisor of claims processing in a large insurance firm, and Pat, an employee in the department. One person will be selected to play the role of Casey, and another will play Pat. The information on and background for each of the participants follow. When the participants have carefully read their roles, the supervisor. Casey, will be asked to conduct a performance-related discussion with Pat, Those who are not playing one of the roles should carefully observe the conversation between Casey and Pat and provide the information requested below. The observers should not necessarily read the roles of Casey and Pat.

1. List those words, phrases, or sentences that Casey used that seem particularly reinforcing.
2. List any words, phrases, or sentences used by Casey that may have been punishing.
3. List any suggestions that you have for improving Casey's future conversations with employees.
4. Using the steps of O.B. Mod (identify, measure, analyze, intervene, and evaluate), how would you (or your group) improve the human performance in this claims department? Be as specific as you can for each step. You may have to fabricate some of the examples.

Role-playing situation for Casey: After reading the following information, you are to conduct a performance-related discussion with Pat in order to reward increased productivity.

You are the supervisor of 20 people in the claims processing department of a large insurance company. Several weeks ago, you established standards for claims processing and measured each employee's work output. One employee, Pat Nelson, had particularly low output figures and averaged less than 80 percent of standard during the baseline data collection period. Your target for rewarding Pat was an 85 percent average for a one-week period. During the first two weeks, Pat failed to meet this goal. Now, in

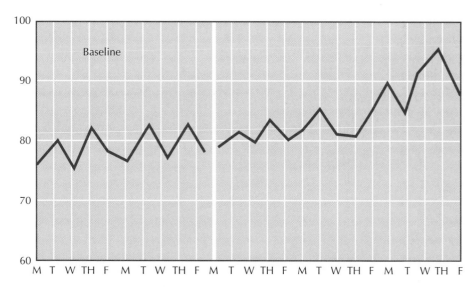

*"Role Playing and O.B. Mod." is adapted from Fred Luthans and Mark J. Martinko, *The Power of Positive Reinforcement,* McGraw-Hill, New York, 1978, pp. 35–38.

the third week after you have decided to use this approach, Pat has achieved the new goal. Pat's performance is illustrated in the graph.

Role-playing situation for Pat:

After reading the following information, you are to be interviewed by your supervisor concerning your performance.

You are Pat Nelson, an employee in the claims processing department of a large insurance company. Recently your supervisor, Casey Parks, instituted a new system of measuring performance in the department. Most of the other employees have already discussed their performance with Casey, but for some reason Casey has not yet talked with you. Now this morning, Casey wants to have a talk about your performance. You are somewhat anxious about what Casey will have to say. You know that you are not the best employee in the department, but you do make your best effort. You hope that Casey will recognize this and not be too hard on you.

EXERCISE: Leadership Questionnaire*

Goal: To evaluate oneself in terms of the leadership dimensions of task orientation and people orientation.

Implementation:
1. Without prior discussion, fill out the Leadership Questionnaire. Do *not* read the rest of this until you have completed the test.
2. In order to locate yourself on the Leadership Style Profile Sheet, you will score your own questionnaire on the dimensions of task orientation (T) and people orientation (P).

Scoring: The scoring is as follows:
1. Circle the item number for items 8, 12, 17, 18, 19, 30, 34, and 35.
2. Write the number 1 in front of a *circled item number* if you responded S (seldom) or N (never) to that item.
3. Also write a number 1 in front of *item numbers not circled* if you responded A (always) or F (frequently).
4. Circle the number 1s that you have written in front of the following items: 3, 5, 8, 10, 15, 18, 19, 22, 24, 26, 28, 30, 32, 34, and 35.
5. *Count the circled number 1s.* This is your score for the level of your concern for people. Record the score in the blank following the letter P at the end of the questionnaire.
6. *Count the uncircled number 1s.* This is your score for your concern for the task. Record this number in the blank following the letter T.
7. Next, look at the Leadership Style Profile Sheet at the end of the exercise, and follow the directions.

*Source: Reprinted with permission from J. William Pfeiffer and John E. Jones (eds.), *A Handbook of Structured Experiences for Human Relations Training.* Vol. 1. University Associates, San Diego, Calif., 1974. The questionnaire was adapted from Sergiovanni, Metzeus and Burden's revision of the Leadership Behavior Description Questionnaire, *American Educational Research Journal,* Vol. 6, 1969, pp. 62–79.

Leadership Questionnaire

Name_____Group_____

Directions: The following items describe aspects of leadership behavior. Respond to each item according to the way you would most likely act if you were the leader of a work group. Circle whether you would most likely behave in the described way always (A), frequently (F), occasionally (O), seldom (S), or never (N). Once the test is completed, go back to number 2 under Implementation.

A	F	O	S	N	1.	I would most likely act as the spokesperson of the group.
A	F	O	S	N	2.	I would encourage overtime work.
A	F	O	S	N	3.	I would allow members complete freedom in their work.
A	F	O	S	N	4.	I would encourage the use of uniform procedures.
A	F	O	S	N	5.	I would permit the members to use their own judgment in solving problems.
A	F	O	S	N	6.	I would stress being ahead of competing groups.
A	F	O	S	N	7.	I would speak as a representative of the group.
A	F	O	S	N	8.	I would needle members for greater effort.
A	F	O	S	N	9.	I would try out my ideas in the group.
A	F	O	S	N	10.	I would let the members do their work the way they think best.
A	F	O	S	N	11.	I would be working hard for a promotion.
A	F	O	S	N	12.	I would tolerate postponement and uncertainty.
A	F	O	S	N	13.	I would speak for the group if there were visitors present.
A	F	O	S	N	14.	I would keep the work moving at a rapid pace.
A	F	O	S	N	15.	I would turn the members loose on a job and let them go to it.
A	F	O	S	N	16.	I would settle conflicts when they occur in the group.
A	F	O	S	N	17.	I would get swamped by details.
A	F	O	S	N	18.	I would represent the group at outside meetings.
A	F	O	S	N	19.	I would be reluctant to allow the members any freedom of action.
A	F	O	S	N	20.	I would decide what should be done and how it should be done.
A	F	O	S	N	21.	I would push for increased production.

A	F	O	S	N	22.	I would let some members have authority which I could keep.
A	F	O	S	N	23.	Things would usually turn out as I had predicted.
A	F	O	S	N	24.	I would allow the group a high degree of initiative.
A	F	O	S	N	25.	I would assign group members to particular tasks.
A	F	O	S	N	26.	I would be willing to make changes.
A	F	O	S	N	27.	I would ask the members to work harder.
A	F	O	S	N	28.	I would trust the group members to exercise good judgment.
A	F	O	S	N	29.	I would schedule the work to be done.
A	F	O	S	N	30.	I would refuse to explain my actions.
A	F	O	S	N	31.	I would persuade others that my ideas are to their advantage.
A	F	O	S	N	32.	I would permit the group to set its own pace.
A	F	O	S	N	33.	I would urge the group to beat its previous record.
A	F	O	S	N	34.	I would act without consulting the group.
A	F	O	S	N	35.	I would ask that group members follow standard rules and regulations.
T_____				P_____		

Variations:

1. Participants can predict how they will appear on the profile prior to scoring the questionnaire.
2. Paired participants already acquainted can predict each other's scores. If they are not acquainted, they can discuss their reactions to the questionnaire items to find some bases for this prediction.
3. The leadership styles represented on the profile sheet can be illustrated through role playing. A relevant situation can be set up, and the "leaders" can be coached to demonstrate the styles being studied.
4. Subgroups can be formed of participants similarly situated on the shared leadership scale. These groups can be assigned identical tasks to perform. The work generated can be processed in terms of morale and productivity.

T-P Leadership Style Profile Sheet

Name _____Group _____

Directions: To determine your sytle of leadership, mark your score on the concern for task dimension (T) on the left-hand arrow below. Next, move to the right-hand arrow and mark your score on the concern for people dimension (P). Draw a straight line that intersects the P and T scores. The point at which that line crosses the shared leadership arrow indicates your score on that dimension.

Shared leadership results from balancing
concern for task and concern for people

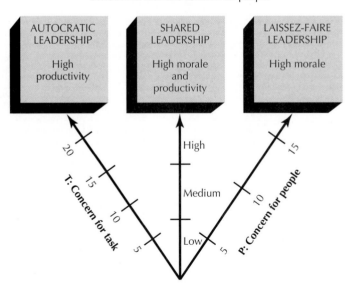

EXERCISE: Paper Plane Corporation

Goals:

1. To work on an actual organizational task
2. To experience the dynamics of performance.

Implementation:

Unlimited groups of six participants each are used in this exercise. These groups may be directed simultaneously in the same room. Approximately a full class period is needed to complete the exercise. Each person should have assembly instructions and a summary sheet, which are shown on the next page, and ample stacks of paper (8½ by 11 inches). The physical setting should be a room large enough so that the individual groups of six can work without interference from the other groups. A working space should be provided for each group.

1. The participants are doing an exercise in production methodology.
2. Each group must work independently of the other groups.
3. Each group will choose a manager and an inspector, and the remaining participants will be employees.
4. The objective is to make paper airplanes in the most profitable manner possible.
5. The facilitator will give the signal to start. This is a 10-minute, timed event utilizing competition among the groups.
6. After the first round, everyone should report his or her production and profits to the entire group. Each person also should note the effect, if any, of the manager in terms of the performance of the group.
7. This same procedure is followed for as many rounds as time allows.

Paper Plane Corporation: Data sheet

Your group is the complete work force for Paper Plane Corporation. Established in 1943, Paper Plane has led the market in paper plane production. Presently under new management, the company is contracting to make aircraft for the U.S. Air Force. You must establish an efficient production plant to produce these aircraft. You must make your contract with the Air Force under the following conditions:

1. The Air Force will pay $20,000 per airplane.
2. The aircraft must pass a strict inspection made by the facilitator.
3. A penalty of $25,000 per airplane will be subtracted for failure to meet the production requirements.
4. Labor and other overhead will be computed at $300,000.
5. Cost of materials will be $3000 per bid plane. If you bid for 10 but make only 8, you must pay the cost of materials for those that you failed to make or that did not pass inspection.

Summary sheet:

Round 1:
Bid: _____ Aircraft @ $20,000 per aircraft = _____
Results: _____ Aircraft @ $20,000 per aircraft = _____
Less: $300,000 overhead
_____ × $3000 cost of raw materials
_____ × $25,000 penalty
Profit: _____

Round 2:
Bid: _____ Aircraft @ $20,000 per aircraft = _____
Results: _____ Aircraft @ $20,000 per aircraft = _____
Less: $300,000 overhead
_____ × $3000 cost of raw materials
_____ × $25,000 penalty
Profit: _____

Round 3:
Bid: _____ Aircraft @ $20,000 per aircraft = _____
Results: _____ Aircraft @ $20,000 per aircraft = _____
Less $300,000 overhead
_____ × $3000 cost of raw materials
_____ × $25,000 penalty
Profit: _____

INSTRUCTIONS FOR AIRCRAFT ASSEMBLY

STEP 1: Take a sheet of paper and fold it in half; then open it back up.

STEP 2: Fold upper corners to the middle.

STEP 3: Fold the corners to the middle again.

STEP 4: Fold in half.

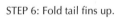

STEP 5: Fold both wings down.

STEP 6: Fold tail fins up.

COMPLETED AIRCRAFT

Chapter 1 Footnote References and Supplemental Readings

1. For example, see: Eilene Zimmerman, "What Are Employees Worth? Companies and Academics Are Working on Ways to Measure Human Capital," *Workforce,* February 2001, pp. 32–36; Thomas O. Davenport, *Human Capital: What It Is and Why People Invest It,* Jossey-Bass, San Francisco, 1999; and David P. Lepak and Scott A. Snell, "The Human Resource Architecture: Toward a Theory of Human Capital Allocation and Development," *Academy of Management Review,* Vol. 24, 1999, pp. 31–48.

2. For example, see: Stephen L. Cohen and Nena K. Backer, "Making and Mining Intellectual Capital," *Training & Development,* September 1999, pp. 46–50 and William Miller, "Building the Ultimate Resource," *Management Review,* January 1999, pp. 42–45.

3. For example, see: Jeffrey Pfeffer, *The Human Equation,* Harvard Business School Press, Boston, 1998; Jay B. Barney and Patrick M. Wright, "On Becoming a Strategic Partner: The Role of Human Resources in Gaining Competitive Advantage," *Human Resource Management,* Spring 1998, pp. 31–46; and Donald A. Marchand, William J. Kettinger and John Rollins, "Information Orientation: People, Technology and the Bottom Line," *Sloan Management Review,* Summer, 2000, pp. 69–80.

4. Geert Hofstede, "Problems Remain, but Theories Will Change: The Universal and the Specific in 21st-Century Global Management," *Organizational Dynamics,* Summer 1999, p. 34.

5. For example, see: Sharon Leonard, "Is America's Work Ethic Changing?" *HR Magazine,* April 2000, p. 224; Michael Hitt, "The New Frontier: Transformation of Management for the New Millennium," *Organizational Dynamics,* Winter 2000, pp. 7–17; and Marina Whitman, *New World, New Rules: The Changing Role of the American Corporation,* Harvard Business School Press, Boston, 1999.

6. Peter Cappelli, *The New Deal at Work: Managing the Market-Driven Workforce,* Harvard Business School Press, Boston, 1999; Peter Cappelli, "Managing Without Commitment," *Organizational Dynamics,* Vol. 28, No. 4, 2000, pp. 11–24; and Denise M. Rousseau and Michael B. Arthur, "The Boundaryless Human Resource Function: Building Agency and Community in the New Economic Era," *Organizational Dynamics,* Spring 1999, pp. 7–18.

7. John F. Viega, Karla Fox, John N. Yanouzas, and Kim Eddleston, "Toward Greater Understanding in the Workplace," *Academy of Management Executive,* May 1999, pp. 81–87; Dan Baugher, Andrew Varanelli, Jr. and Ellen Weisbord, "Gender and Cultural Diversity Occurring in Self-Formed Work Groups," *Journal of Managerial Issues,* Vol. 12, No. 4, Winter 2000, pp. 391–407; and Robert J. Grossman, "Race in the Workplace," *HR Magazine,* March 2000, pp. 41–45.

8. See Suzy Wetlaufer, "Business as Usual Isn't Usual at All," *Harvard Business Review,* March-April 2000, p. 10; and Clayton Christensen and Michael Overdorf, "Meeting the Challenge of Disruptive Change," *Harvard Business Review,* March-April 2000, pp. 66–76.

9. See Daniel R. Ilgen and Elaine D. Pulaskos (Eds.), *The Changing Nature of Performance: Implications for Staffing, Motivation, and Development,* Jossey-Bass, San Francisco, 1999.

10. Shari Caudron, "Jobs Disappear," *Workforce,* January 2000, pp. 30–32.

11. The future scenarios come from Leif Edvinsson, Calla Farren, and Jim O'Connell and are reported in Louisa Wah, "Workplace of the Future," *Management Review,* January 2000, p. 9. Also see: Peter Senge and Goran Carstedt, "Next Industrial Revolution," *MIT Sloan Management Review,* Winter 2001, pp. 24–38.

12. Thomas S. Kuhn, *The Structure of Scientific Revolutions,* 2d ed., University of Chicago Press, Chicago, 1970. Kuhn discussed paradigms as far back as 1962.

13. Don Tapscott and Art Caston, *Paradigm Shift: The Promise of Information Technology,* McGraw-Hill, New York, 1993, p. xii.

14. Joel A. Barker, *Future Edge,* Morrow, New York, 1992, p. 32.

15. Patricia A. McLagan, "Portfolio Thinking," *Training & Development,* February 2000, p. 44.

16. Norman Clark, "Similarities and Differences between Scientific and Technological Paradigms," *Futures,* February 1987, p. 28.

17. John D. Burdett, "Beyond Values—Exploring the Twenty-First Century Organization," *Journal of Management Development,* Vol. 17, No. 1, 1998, p. 28.

18. See Peter Drucker, *Management Challenges for the 21st Century,* Harper Business, New York, 1999.

19. E. J. Heresniak, "Why Don't CIOs Fit?" *Across the Board,* July/August 1999, p. 51.

20. Dede Bonner, "Enter the Chief Knowledge Officer," *Training & Development,* February 2000, pp. 36–40.

21. Andrew Kakabadse and Mada Korac-Kakabadse, "IS/IT Professionals: Work, Practice and Skills," *Journal of Management Development,* Vol. 19, No. 2, 2000, p. 100.

22. Robert Hof, "What Every CEO Needs to Know About Electronic Business," *Business Week,* March 22, 1999, p. EB9. Also see: David Feeny, "E-opportunity," *MIT Sloan Management Review,* Winter 2001, pp. 41–51.

23. Pfeffer, *The Human Equation. op. cit.*

24. Jeffrey Pfeffer and Robert Sutton, *The Knowing-Doing Gap,* Harvard Business School Press, Boston, 2000. Also see: Harlow B. Cohen, "The Performance Paradox," *Academy of Management Executive,* Vol. 12, No. 3, 1998, pp. 30–40.

25. Pfeffer and Sutton, *The Knowing-Doing Gap. op. cit.*

26. Rikki Abzug and Susan Phelps, "Everything Old Is New Again: Barnard's Legacy—Lessons for Participative Leaders," *Journal of Management Development,* Vol. 17, No. 3, 1998, p. 209.

27. Peter F. Drucker, "Toward the New Organization," *Leader to Leader,* Winter 1997, p. 8.

28. For example, see Lyle Yorks and David Whitsett, "Hawthorne, Topeka, and the Issue of Science versus Advocacy in Organizational Behavior," *Academy of Management Review,* January 1985, pp. 21–30.

29. Gary W. Yunker, "An Explanation of Positive and Negative Hawthorne Effects: Evidence from the Relay Assembly Test Room and Bank Wiring Observation Room Studies," *Academy of Management Best Papers Proceedings,* 1993, pp. 179–183.

30. H. McIlvaine Parsons, "Hawthorne: An Early OBM Experiment," *Journal of Organizational Behavior Management,* Vol. 12, No. 1, 1992, pp. 27–44.

31. C. E. Turner, "Test Room Studies in Employee Effectiveness," *American Journal of Public Health,* June 1933, p. 584.

32. See David Klahr and Herbert Simon, "Studies of Scientific Discovery: Complementary Approaches and Convergent Findings," *Psychological Bulletin,* Vol. 125, No. 5, 1999, pp. 524–543.

33. Chuck Williams, *Management,* South-Western College Publishing, Cincinnati, OH, 2000, pp. 5–6.

34. See Katherine J. Klein, Henry Tosi, and Albert A. Cannella, Jr., "Multi-level Theory Building: Benefits, Barriers, and New Developments," *Academy of Management Review,* Vol. 24, No. 2, 1999, pp. 243–248.

35. Robert I. Sutton and Barry M. Staw, "What Theory Is Not," *Administrative Science Quarterly,* Vol. 40, 1995, p. 378.

36. Robert Folger and Carmelo J. Turillo, "Theorizing as the Thickness of Thin Abstraction," *Academy of Management Review,* Vol. 24, No. 4, 1999, p. 742.

37. Karl E. Weick, "Definition of Theory," in Nigel Nicholson (Ed.), *Blackwell Dictionary of Organizational Behavior,* Blackwell, Oxford, England, 1995. Also see Karl E. Weick, "What Theory Is Not, Theorizing Is," *Administrative Science Quarterly,* Vol. 40, 1995, pp. 385–390; Karl E. Weick, "That's Moving Theories that Matter," *Journal of Management Inquiry,* Vol. 8, No. 2, 1999, pp. 134–142; and Karl E. Weick, "Theory Construction as Disciplined Reflexivity: Tradeoffs in the 90s," *Academy of Management Review,* Vol. 24, No. 4, 1999, pp. 797–808.

38. Thomas D. Cook and Donald T. Campbell, "The Design and Conduct of Quasi-Experiments and True Experiments in Field Settings," in M. D. Dunnette (Ed.), *Handbook of Industrial and Organizational Psychology,* Rand McNally, Chicago, 1976, pp. 224–246. Also see Terence R. Mitchell, "An Evaluation of the Validity of Correlational Research Conducted in Organizations," *Academy of Management Review,* April 1985, pp. 192–205 and Frank L. Schmidt, C. Viswesvaran and Deniz E. Ones, "Reliability Is Not Validity and Validity Is Not Reliability," *Personnel Psychology,* Vol. 53, 2000, pp. 901–912.

39. Daniel R. Ilgen, "Laboratory Research: A Question of When, Not If," in Edwin A. Locke (Ed.), *Generalizing from Laboratory to Field Settings,* Lexington Books, Lexington, Mass., 1986, p. 257.

40. For example, see Frank L. Schmidt, Kenneth Law, John E. Hunter, Hannah R. Rothstein, Kenneth Pearlman and Michael McDaniel, "Refinements in Validity Generalization Methods: Implications for the Situational Specificity Hypothesis," *Journal of Applied Psychology,* February 1993, pp. 3–12.

41. Michael West, John Arnold, Martin Corbett and Ben Fletcher, "Editorial: Advancing Understanding about Behavior at Work," *Journal of Occupational and Organizational Psychology,* March 1992, pp. 1–3.

42. J. Van Maanen, "Reclaiming Qualitative Methods for Organizational Research," *Administrative Science Quarterly,* Vol. 24, 1979, pp. 520–526.

43. Colin Eden, "On the Nature of Cognitive Maps," *Journal of Management Studies,* May 1992, p. 262. Also see C. Marlene Fiol and Anne Sigismund Huff, "Maps for Managers: Where Are We? Where Do We Go from Here?" *Journal of Management Studies,* May 1992, pp. 267–285.

44. An example arguing for cognition would be Robert Epstein, *Cognition, Creativity and Behavior,* Praeger, Westport, CT, 1996 and for modern behaviorism Christina Lee, *Alternatives to Cognition: A New Look at Explaining Human Social Behavior,* Erlbaum, Mahwah, NJ, 1998 and Valentin Dragoi and J. E. R. Staddon, "The Dynamics of Operant Conditioning," *Psychological Review,* Vol. 106, No. 1, 1999, pp. 20–61. Also see: John A. Bargh and Melissa J. Ferguson, "Beyond Behaviorism: On the Automaticity of Higher Mental Processes," *Psychological Bulletin,* Vol. 126, No. 6, 2000, pp. 925–945.

45. Ronald E. Riggio, *Introduction to Industrial/Organizational Psychology,* Scott, Foresman/Little, Brown, Glenview, Ill., 1990, p. 16 and Andrew R. McGill, Michael D. Johnson, and Karen A. Bantel, "Cognitive Complexity and Conformity: The Effects on Performance in a Turbulent Environment," *Academy of Management Best Papers Proceedings,* 1993, pp. 379–383.

46. Richard W. Robins, Samuel D. Gosling, and Kenneth H. Clark, "An Empirical Analysis of Trends in Psychology," *American Psychologist,* Vol. 54, No. 2, 1999, pp. 117–128.

47. For example, see: Arthur W. Staats, "Psychological Behaviorism and Behaviorizing Psychology," *The Behavior Analyst,* Vol. 17, No. 1, 1994, pp. 93–112.

48. Richard J. DeGrandpre, "A Science of Meaning: Can Behaviorism Bring Meaning to Psychological Science?" *American Psychologist,* Vol. 55, No. 7, 2000, pp. 721–739.

49. See Tim R. V. Davis and Fred Luthans, "A Social Learning Approach to Organizational Behavior," *Academy of Management Review,* April 1980, pp. 281–290.

50. Robert Kreitner and Fred Luthans, "A Social Learning Approach to Behavior Management: Radical Behaviorists Mellowing Out," *Organizational Dynamics,* Autumn 1984, pp. 61–75 and Fred Luthans and Robert Kreitner, *Organizational Behavior Modification and Beyond,* Scott, Foresman, Glenview, Ill., 1985.

51. Albert Bandura, "Social Learning Theory," in J. T. Spence, R. C. Carson and J. W. Thibaut (Eds.), *Behavioral Approaches to Therapy,* General Learning Press, Morristown, N.J., 1976; Albert Bandura, *Social Learning Theory,* Prentice Hall, Upper Saddle River, N.J., 1977; and Albert Bandura, "The Self System in Reciprocal Determinism," *American Psychologist,* April 1978, pp. 344–358.

52. Bandura, *Social Learning Theory, op. cit.* p. 9.

53. Albert Bandura, *Social Foundations of Thought and Action: A Social-Cognitive Theory,* Prentice Hall, Upper Saddle River, N.J., 1986 and Albert Bandura, "Social Cognitive Theory: An Agentic Perspective," *Asian Journal of Social Psychology,* Vol. 2, 1999, pp. 21–41.

54. See Alexander D. Stajkovic and Fred Luthans, "Social Cognitive Theory and Self-Efficacy: Going Beyond Traditional Motivational and Behavioral Approaches," *Organizational Dynamics,* Spring 1998, pp. 62–74.

55. Ibid., p. 63.

Chapter 2 Footnote References and Supplemental Readings

1. See Peter M. Senge and Goran Carstedt, "Innovating our way to the Next Industrial Revolution," *MIT Sloan Management Review,* Winter 2001, pp. 24–38 and Richard Oliver, "Happy 150th Birthday, Electronic Commerce!" *Management Review,* July-August 1999, pp. 12–13.

2. "The World Economy: The Hitchhiker's Guide to Cybernomics," *The Economist,* September 28, 1996, pp. 4,8. Also see: Jeremy Hope and Tony Hope, *Competing in the Third Wave: The Ten Key Management Issues of the Information Age,* Harvard Business School Press, Boston, 1997; Adam Cohen, "Wireless Summer," *Time,* May 29, 2000, pp. 58–66; and "E-Management, Inside the Machine," *The Economist,* November 11, 2000, pp. 5–21.

3. "The Best Is Yet to Come," *Management Review,* December 1999, p. 17

4. Robert D. Hof, "What Every CEO Needs to Know about Electronic Business," *Business Week,* March 22, 1999, p. EB9.

5. Oren Harari, "The Year in Management," *Management Review,* February 2000, p. 16.

6. Scott Thurm and E. S. Browning, "Cisco Passes Microsoft to Be No. 1," *Wall Street Journal,* March 28, 2000, p. C-1 and "Waking up to Equity Risk," *The Economist,* March 10, 2001, pp. 17–18.

7. Harari, "The Year in Management," p. 16.

8. Jane Hodges, "9 Ways to Win on the Web," *Fortune,* May 24, 1999, p. 121.

9. Ibid. p. 124. Also see David Feeny, "Making Business Sense of the E-Opportunity," *MIT Sloan Management Review,* Winter 2001, pp. 41–51.

10. "The New Economy: Untangling E-conomics," *The Economist,* September 23, 2000, p. 11.

11. "Why the Net Should Grow Up," *The Economist,* October 19, 1996, p. 17.

12. Amy Cortese, "Here Comes the Internet," *Business Week,* February 26, 1996, pp. 76–77.

13. Mary J. Cronin, "9 Ways Win on the Web," *Fortune,* May 24, 1999, p. 115.

14. David DeLong and Patrica Seemann, "Confronting Conceptual Confusion and Conflict in Knowledge Management," *Organizational Dynamics,* Vol. 29, No. 1, 2000, p. 33.

15. "Survey on Knowledge Management," *Management Review,* April 1999, p. 21.

16. Thomas O. Davenport, *Information Ecology: Mastering the Information and Knowledge Environment,* Oxford University Press, New York, 1997. Also see Daniel Tobin, *The Knowledge-Enabled Organization,* AMACOM, New York, 1998.

17. "Survey on Knowledge Management," p. 21.

18. Reported in Jenny C. McCune, "Thirst for Knowledge," *Management Review,* April 1999, p. 11 and Thomas O. Davenport, Jeanne G. Harris and Ajay K. Kohli, "How Do They Know Their Customers So Well?" *MIT Sloan Management Review,* Winter 2001, p. 63.

19. Marilyn Martiny, "Knowledge Management at HP Consulting," *Organizational Dynamics,* Autumn 1998, p. 71.

20. Ibid.

21. "Knowledge Sharing Isn't Always Best Handled By the Technology-Minded," *Wall Street Journal,* March 23, 2000, p. A1.

22. David P. Lepak and Scott A. Snell, "The Human Resource Architecture: Toward a Theory of Human Capital Allocation and Development," *Academy of Management Review,* Vol. 24, No. 1, 1999, pp. 35–36 and Eilene Zimmerman, "What Are Employees Worth?" *Workforce,* February 2001, pp. 32–36.

23. Thomas O. Davenport, *Human Capital: What It Is and Why People Invest It,* Jossey-Bass, San Fancisco, 1999.

24. F. Horibe, *Managing Knowledge Workers,* Wiley, New York, 1999.

25. See Brian Becker, Mark A. Huselid and David Ulrich, *The HR Scorecard,* Harvard Business School Press, Boston, 2001, pp. 8–10 and B. Lev, "Knowledge Management: Fad or Need," *Research Technology Management,* Vol. 43, No. 5, 2000, pp. 9–10.

26. William C. Miller, "Fostering Intellectual Capital," *HR Focus,* January 1998, p. 9.

27. Michael Hickins, "Gray Matter Stolen," *Management Review,* September 1999, p. 6.

28. Steven M. Shaker and Mark P. Gembicki, *The War Room Guide to Competitive Intelligence,* McGraw-Hill, New York, 1999.

29. See Peter Cappelli, *The New Deal at Work: Managing the Market-Driven Workplace,* Harvard Business School Press, Boston, 1999.

30. Hal B. Gregersen, Allen J. Morrison, and J. Stewart Black, "Developing Leaders for the Global Frontier," *Sloan Management Review,* Vol. 40, No. 1, 1998, pp. 21–22.

31. Reported in *Management Review,* October 1999, pp. 46–47.

32. Reported in *Workforce,* January 2000, p. 48.

33. Murray Weidenbaum, "All the World's a Stage," *Management Review,* October 1999, p. 45.

34. See Nancy J. Adler, *International Dimensions of Organizational Behavior,* 3d ed., South-Western, Cincinnati, OH, 1997.

35. Gregersen, Morrison, and Black, p. 22.

36. Ibid.

37. Robert Rosen, with Patricia Digh, Marshall Singer, and Carl Phillips, *Global Literacies,* Simon & Schuster, New York, 2000.

38. Charles J. Cox and Cary L. Cooper, "The Irrelevance of American Organizational Sciences to the UK and Europe," *Journal of General Management,* Winter 1985, pp. 29–30.

39. Dianne H. B. Welsh, Fred Luthans, and Steven M. Sommer, "Managing Russian Factory Workers: The Impact of U.S.-Based Behavioral and Participative Techniques," *Academy of Management Journal,* February 1993, pp. 58–79.

40. Lisa A. Mainiero, "Participation? Nyet: Rewards and Praise? Da!" *Academy of Management Executive,* August 1993, p. 87. Also see Snejina Michailova, "Contrasts in Culture: Russian and Western Perspectives on Organizational Change," *Academy of Management Executive,* Vol. 14, No. 4, 2000, pp. 99–112.

41. David G. Myers, *Social Psychology,* 3d ed., McGraw-Hill, New York, 1990, pp. 226–227.

42. Quoted in Nancy J. Adler, Robert Doktor, and S. Gordon Redding, "From the Atlantic to the Pacific Century: Cross-Cultural Management Reviewed," *Journal of Management,* Vol. 12, No. 2, 1986, p. 295.

43. For example, see Stephen J. Mezias, Ya-Ru Chen, and Patrice Murphy, "Toto, I Don't Think We're in Kansas Anymore," *Journal of Management Inquiry,* Vol. 8, No. 3, 1999, pp. 323–333.

44. Susan C. Schneider and Kazuhiro Asakawa, "American and Japanese Expatriate Adjustment: A Psychoanalytic Perspective," *Human Relations,* Vol. 48, No. 10, 1995, p. 1109. Also see Rita Bennett, Anne Aston and Tracy Colquhoun, "Cross-Cultural Training," *Human Resource Management,* Summer/Fall 2000, pp. 239–250.

45. Reyer A. Swaak, "Expatriate Management: The Search for Best Practices," *Compensation & Benefits Review,* March–April 1995, pp. 21–29. Also see Mark E. Mendenhall and Günter K. Stahl, "Expatriate Training and Development," *Human Resource Management,* Summer/Fall 2000, pp. 251–265.

46. Reyer A. Swaak, "Expatriate Failures: Too Many, Too Much Cost, Too Little Planning," *Compensation & Benefits Review,* November–December 1995, pp. 47–55.

47. Martha Finney, "Culture Shock in America?" *Across the Board,* May 2000, p. 29. Also see AAhad M. Osman-Gani, "Developing Expatriates for the Asia-Pacific Region: A Comparative Analysis of Multinational Enterprise Managers from Five Countries Across Three Continents," *Human Resource Development Quarterly,* Fall 2000, pp. 213–233.

48. Margaret A. Shaffer, David A. Harrison, and K. Matthew Gilley, "Dimensions, Determinants, and Differences in the Expatriate Adjustment Process," *Journal of International Business Studies,* Vol. 30, No. 3, 1999, pp. 557–581.

49. Joyce S. Osland, in Allan Bird, Joyce S. Osland, Mark Mendenhall, and Susan C. Schneider, "Adapting and Adjusting to Other Cultures," *Journal of Management Inquiry,* Vol. 8, No. 2, 1999, p. 153.

50. Susan C. Schneider, in Ibid.

51. These examples are found in Jim Holt, "Gone Global?" *Management Review,* March 2000, p. 13 and are drawn from Rosen, *Global Literacies.*

52. Marlene Piturro, "What Are You Doing About the New Global Realities?" *Management Review,* March 1999, p. 19.

53. Mark Maremont, "Eastern Europe's Big Cleanup," *Business Week,* March 19, 1990, pp. 114–115.

54. "French Fight for Soul Against Big Mac Attacks," *Lincoln Journal Star,* September 9, 1999, p. 4E.

55. John-Thor Dahlburg, "Culture Clash in France Turns Deadly," *Denver Post,* April 22, 2000, p. 16A.

56. Geert Hofstede, *Cultures and Organizations: Software of the Mind,* McGraw-Hill U.K., London, 1991.

57. J. R. Bailey, C. C. Chen and S. G. Dou, "Conceptions of Self and Performance-Related Feedback in the U.S., Japan and China," *Journal of International Business Studies,* Vol. 28, 1997, pp. 605–625.

58. Fons Trompenaars, *Riding the Waves of Culture,* Irwin, New York, 1994. Also see Richard M. Hodgetts and Fred Luthans, *International Management,* 4th ed., Irwin/McGraw, Boston, 2000, p. 130.

59. See Kim Kiser, "Working on World Time," *Training,* March 1999, p. 31.

60. Zeynep Aycan, "Cross-Cultural Industrial and Organizational Psychology," *Journal of Cross-Cultural Psychology,* Vol. 31, No. 1, 2000, p. 111.

61. Geert Hofstede, *Culture's Consequences: International Differences in Work Related Values,* Sage, Beverly Hills, Calif., 1980. For a review and extension of Hofstede's work, see Robert G. Westwood and James E. Everett, "Culture's Consequences: A Methodology for Comparative Management Studies in Southeast Asia?" *Asia Pacific Journal of Management,* May 1987, pp. 187–202, and his more recent book, *Cultures and Organizations.*

62. Ryh-song Yeh and John J. Lawrence, "Individualism and Confucian Dynamism: A Note on Hofstede's Cultural Root to Economic Growth," *Journal of International Business Studies,* 3d Quarter 1995, pp. 655–669.

63. Hofstede, *Cultures and Organizations,* pp. 251–252.

64. Fred Luthans, Alexander D. Stajkovic and Kendra Reed, "Country Clustering Revisited: A Critical Analysis of Hofstede's Cultural Dimensions," *Proceedings of Decision Sciences Institute,* 1996, Orlando, Fla., pp. 367–369.

65. Derek S. Pugh and David J. Hickson, *Writers on Organizations,* 4th ed., Sage, Newbury Park, Calif., 1989, p. 94.

66. For example, see Irene K. H. Chew and Joseph Putti, "Relationship of Work-Related Values of Singaporean and Japanese Managers in Singapore," *Human Relations,* Vol. 48, No. 10, 1995, pp. 1149–1170.

67. Adler, op. cit., p. 51.

68. Ikujiro Nonaka and Hiro Takeuchi, *The Knowledge-Creating Company: How Japanese Companies Foster Creativity and Innovation for Competitive Advantage,* Oxford University Press, New York, 1995.

69. Fons Trompenaars, *Riding the Waves of Culture,* Irwin, New York, 1994.

70. The discussion on Trompenaars's dimensions is drawn from *Ibid* and Lisa Hoecklin, *Managing Cultural Differences,* Addison-Wesley, Workingham, England, 1995. Also see Hodgetts and Luthans, op. cit., which summarizes these dimensions.

71. Fred Luthans, Kyle Luthans, Richard M. Hodgetts, and Brett Luthans, "Can HPWPs (High Performance Work Practices) Help in the Former Soviet Union? A Cross-Cultural Fit Analysis," *Business Horizons,* September–October, 2000, pp. 53–60.

72. Theodore M. Singelis, Harry C. Triandis, Dharm P. S. Bhawuk and Michele J. Gelfond, "Horizontal and Vertical Dimensions of Individualism and Collectivism: A Theoretical and Measurement Refinement," *Cross-Cultural Research,* August 1995, pp. 240–275.

73. For example, see Sheila M. Puffer and Stanislav V. Shekshnia, "The Fit between Russian Culture and Compensation," *International Executive,* March/April 1996, p. 235; Elena Avraamova, "Russian Elites Amid Social and Economic Reform," *International Studies of Management and Organization,* Vol. 25, No. 4, pp. 27–43; and Igor Filatotchev, Robert E. Hoskisson, Trevor Buck and Mike Wright, "Corporate Restructuring in Russian Privatizations," *California Management Review,* Winter 1996, pp. 87–105.

74. Chao C. Chen, "New Trends in Rewards Allocation Preferences: A Sino-U.S. Comparison," *Academy of Management Journal,* April 1995, pp. 408–428. Also see Cliff Chen, "Should Mainland Chinese Be Rewarded the Way Americans Are?" *Academy of Management Executive,* February 1996, pp. 84–85.

75. S. H. Nam and R. T. Mowday, "Culture and Managerial Attributions of Personal Responsibility for Group Success and Failure," presented at *Western Academy of Management,* San Jose, Calif., 1993.

76. W. Yan and E. Gaier, "Causal Attributions for College Success and Failure: An Asian-American Comparison," *Journal of Cross-Cultural Psychology,* Vol. 25, No. 1, 1994, pp. 146–158.

77. Y. Kashima and H. C. Triandis, "The Self-Serving Bias in Attributions as a Coping Strategy: A Cross-Cultural Study," *Journal of Cross-Cultural Psychology,* Vol. 17, 1985, pp. 83–97.

78. P. Christopher Earley, "Self or Group? Cultural Effects of Training on Self-Efficacy and Performance," *Administration Science Quarterly,* Vol. 39, 1994,

pp. 89–117. Also see P. Christopher Earley, "East Meets West Meets Mideast: Further Explorations of Collectivistic and Individualistic Work Groups," *Academy of Management Journal,* Vol. 36, 1993, pp. 319–348.

79. Albert Bandura, *Self-Efficacy: The Exercise of Control,* W. H. Freeman, New York, 1997, p. 471.

80. M. H. B. Radford, L. Mann, Y. Ohta and Y. Nakane, "Differences between Australian and Japanese Students in Decisional Self-Esteem, Decisional Stress, and Coping Styles," *Journal of Cross-Cultural Psychology,* Vol. 24, 1993, pp. 287–297.

81. S. Agarwol, "Influence of Formalization on Role Stress, Organizational Commitment, and Work Alienation of Salespersons: A Cross-National Comparative Study," *Journal of International Business Studies,* 4th Quarter 1993, pp. 715–739.

82. Mark F. Peterson and Peter B. Smith, "Role Conflict, Ambiguity, and Overload: A 21-Nation Study," *Academy of Management Journal,* February 1996, pp. 37–63.

83. This research literature is summarized in Aycan, "Cross-Cultural Industrial and Organizational Psychology," op. cit., pp. 119–120.

84. Ibid., p. 120.

85. Irene Y. M. Yenng and Rosalie L. Tung, "The Importance of Guanxi/Connections," *Organizational Dynamics,* Autumn 1996, pp. 54–65.

Chapter 3 Footnote References and Supplemental Readings

1. R. Roosevelt Thomas, Jr., *Redefining Diversity,* AMACOM, New York, 1996.

2. R. Roosevelt Thomas, Jr., "Redefining Diversity," *HR Focus,* April 1996, p. 6.

3. Haya ElNassar and Paul Overberg, "Index Charts Growth in Diversity," *USA Today,* March 15, 2001, p. 3A

4. Special Report on Diversity, *HR Focus,* 1998, p. 55.

5. "Diversity Boosts Performance," *HR Focus,* May 1999, p. 5.

6. See Joan Crockett, "Winning Competitive Advantage Through a Diverse Workforce," *HR Focus,* May 1999, pp. 9–10.

7. Orlando C. Richard, "Racial Diversity, Business Strategy, and Firm Performance: A Resource-Based View," *Academy of Management Journal,* Vol. 43, No. 2, 2000, pp. 164–177.

8. Lisa Hope Pelled, Kathleen M. Eisenhardt and Katherine R. Xin, "Exploring the Black Box: An Analysis of Work Group Diversity, Conflict, and Performance," *Administrative Science Quarterly,* Vol. 44, 1999, pp. 1–28 and Dan Baugher, Andrew Varanelli and Ellen Weisbord, "Gender and Culture Diversity Occurring in Self-Formed Work Groups," *Journal of Managerial Issues,* Vol. 12, No. 4, 2000, pp. 391–407.

9. Sheldon Steinhauser, "Minimizing Your Potential for Age Discrimination Lawsuits," *HR Focus,* August 1998, p. 3.

10. Kenneth Labich, "Making Diversity Pay," *Fortune,* September 9, 1996, p. 180.

11. Reported in Molly Ivins, "Pay Gap a Very Real Problem," *Lincoln Journal Star,* May 9, 1999, p. 8c.

12. Jeanne M. Brett and Linda K. Stroh, "Women in Management: How Far Have We Come and What Needs to be Done as We Approach 2000?" *Journal of Management Inquiry,* Vol. 8, No. 4, December 1999, pp. 392–398.

13. "Women of Color Doubt Diversity Commitment," *HR Focus,* May 1999, p. 5.

14. For more on this topic, see Lynn R. Offermann and Marilyn K. Gowing, "Organizations of the Future: Changes and Challenges," *American Psychologist,* February 1990, pp. 95–108.

15. Nancy J. Adler, *International Dimensions of Organizational Behavior,* 3d ed., South-Western, Cincinnati, Ohio, 1997, p. 123.

16. Patricia L. Nemetz and Sandra L. Christensen, "The Challenge of Cultural Diversity: Harnessing a Diversity of Views to Understand Multiculturalism," *Academy of Management Review,* April 1996, pp. 434–462.

17. Bailey W. Jackson, Frank LaFasto, Henry G. Schultz and Don Kelly, "Diversity," *Human Resource Management,* Spring/Summer 1992, p. 22.

18. Ibid., pp. 22–24.

19. Joel Lefkowitz, "Race as a Factor in Job Placement: Serendipitous Findings of 'Ethnic Drift,' " *Personnel Psychology,* Vol. 47, No. 3, 1994, pp. 497–513.

20. See Larry Reynolds, "Bye-Bye Affirmative Action?" *HR Focus,* July 1998, p. 8.

21. David Nye, "Affirmative Action and the Stigma of Incompetence," *Academy of Management Executive,* February 1998, p. 88. The research is based on Madeline E. Heilman, Caryn J. Block and Peter Stathatos, "The Affirmative Action Stigma of Incompetence: Effects of Performance Information Ambiguity," *Academy of Management Journal,* Vol. 40. No. 3, 1997, pp. 603–625. Also see Myrtle P. Bell, David A. Harrison and Mary E. McLaughlin, "Forming, Changing, and Acting on Attitudes Toward Affirmative Action Programs in Employment: A Theory-Driven

Approach," *Journal of Applied Psychology,* Vol. 85, No. 5, 2000, pp. 784–798.

22. Heather Golden and Steve Hinkle, "Reactions to Affirmative Action: Substance and Semantics," *Journal of Applied Social Psychology,* Vol. 31, No. 1, 2001, pp. 73–88 and Robert J. Grossman, "Is Diversity Working?" *HR Magazine,* March 2000, p. 49.

23. Sara M. Freedman and Robert T. Keller, "The Handicapped in the Workforce," *Academy of Management Review,* July 1981, p. 453.

24. Charlene Marmer Solomon, "Testing at Odds with Diversity Efforts?" *Personnel Journal,* April 1996, pp. 131–140.

25. Sara Rynes and Benson Rosen, "A Field Survey of Factors Affecting the Adoption and Perceived Success of Diversity Training," *Personnel Psychology,* Vol. 48, 1995, p. 247.

26. Dawn Gunsch, "Games Augment Diversity Training," *Personnel Journal,* June 1993, pp. 76–83.

27. Rynes and Rosen, op. cit., p. 247.

28. D.P. Frost, "Review Worst Diversity Practices to Learn from Others' Mistakes," *HR Focus,* April 1999, p. 12.

29. Louisa Wah, "Diversity: A Competitive Weapon at Allstate," *Management Review,* July–August 1999, pp. 24–30.

30. Gwendolyn M. Combs and Fred Luthans, "The Impact of Self-Efficacy on Diversity Training Efficacy," Paper Presented at the Academy of Management Annual Meeting, Organizational Behavior Division, Washington D.C., 2001.

31. Susan Caminiti, "Straight Talk," *Working Woman,* September 1999, p. 69.

32. Richard M. Hodgetts and K. Galen Kroeck, *Personnel and Human Resource Management,* Dryden, Fort Worth, Tex., 1992, p. 403 and Suzanne M. Crampton, "Women in Management," *Public Personnel Management,* Vol. 28, No. 1, Spring 1999, p. 92.

33. Herminia Ibarra, "Race, Opportunity, and Diversity of Social Circles in Managerial Networks," *Academy of Management Journal,* June 1995, pp. 673–703.

34. Sarah Fister Gale, "Formalized Flextime: The Perk that Brings Productivity," *Workforce,* February 2001, pp. 39–42.

35. See Carol Sladek, "A Guide to Offering Work/Life Benefits," *Compensation and Benefits Review,* January-February 1995, pp. 43–44.

36. Ibid.

37. For example, see Linda Thiede Thomas and Daniel C. Ganster, "Impact of Family-Supportive Work Variables on Work-Family Conflict and Strain: A Control Perspective," *Journal of Applied Psychology,* Vol. 80, 1995, pp. 6–15.

38. Paul Osterman, "Work/Family Programs and the Employment Relationship," *Administrative Science Quarterly,* Vol. 40, 1995, pp. 681–700. Also see Dawn S. Carlson and K. Michele Kacmar, "Work-Family Conflict in Organizations," *Journal of Management,* Vol. 26, No. 5, 2000, pp. 1031–1054.

39. Wade Lambert, "Obese Workers Win On-the-Job Protection Against Bias," *Wall Street Journal,* November 12, 1993, pp. B1, 7.

40. Cynthia M. Marlowe, Sandra L. Schneider and Carnot E. Nelson, "Gender and Attractiveness Biases in Hiring Decisions: Are More Experienced Managers Less Biased?" *Journal of Applied Psychology,* Vol. 81, No. 1, 1996, pp. 11–21.

41. David M. Bersoff, "Why Good People Sometimes Do Bad Things: Motivated Reasoning and Unethical Behavior," *Personality and Social Psychology Bulletin,* January 1999, pp. 28–39.

42. Linda Klebe Trevino and Bart Victor, "Peer Reporting of Unethical Behavior: A Social Context Perspective," *Academy of Management Journal,* March 1992, pp. 38–64.

43. G. Stephen Taylor and J. P. Shim, "A Comparative Examination of Attitudes toward Software Piracy among Business Professors and Executives," *Human Relations,* April 1993, pp. 419–433.

44. Alexander D. Stajkovic and Fred Luthans, "Business Ethics across Cultures: A Social Cognitive Model," *Journal of World Business,* Spring 1997, pp. 17–34.

45. See Edward F. Boyle, "Morality in the Workplace," *Perspectives on Work,* Vol. 1, No. 1, 1997, pp. 22–25.

46. Melissa A. Baucus and David A. Baucus, "Paying the Piper: An Empirical Examination of Longer-term Financial Consequences of Illegal Corporate Behavior," *Academy of Management Journal,* February 1997, pp. 129–151.

47. Reported in "Ethics Linked to Financial Performance," *Management Review,* July-August 1999, p. 7.

48. Sandra A. Waddock and Samuel B. Graves, "The Corporate Social Performance-Financial Performance Link," *Strategic Management Journal,* April 1997, pp. 303–319.

49. Bernadette M. Ruf, Krishnamurty Muralidhar and Karen Paul, "The Development of a Systematic, Aggregate Measure of Corporate Social Performance," *Journal of Management,* Vol. 24, No. 1, 1998, pp. 119–133.

50. See: Abagail McWilliams and Donald Siegel, "Corporate Social Responsibility: A Theory of the Firm Perspective," *Academy of Management Review,* Vol. 26, No. 1, 2001, pp. 117–127 and "Ethics vs. Ethical," *HR Focus,* April 1998, p. 7.

51. Gary R. Weaver, Linda Klebe Trevino and Philip L. Cochran, "Corporate Ethics Programs as Control Systems," *Academy of Management Journal,* February 1999, pp. 41–57; James C. Wimbush, "The Effect

of Cognitive Moral Development and Supervisory Influence on Subordinates' Ethical Behavior," *Journal of Business Ethics,* Vol. 18, 1999, pp. 383–395; and Sandra Waddock and Neil Smith, "Corporate Responsibility Audits," *Sloan Management Review,* Winter 2000, pp. 75–83.

52. "Guidelines on Discrimination on the Basis of Sex," *Equal Employment Opportunity,* Washington, D.C., November 10, 1980, p. 2 and Janice Anderson Huebner, "How to Avoid Sexual Harassment Traps," *HR Focus,* March 1995, p. 15.

53. Brigid Moynahan, "Creating Harassment-Free Work Zones," *Training and Development Journal,* May 1993, p. 67.

54. "Sexual Harassment Revisited," *Management Review,* October 1998, p. 6 and Peter W. Dorfman, Anthony T. Cobb and Roxanne Cox, "Investigations of Sexual Harassment Allegations: Legal Means Fair—or Does It?" *Human Resource Management,* Spring 2000, pp. 33–49.

55. William A. Carmell, "Another Look at Sexual Harassment: Implications of the 1998 Supreme Court Decisions," *Diversity Factor,* Spring 1999, pp. 34–38.

56. Brian B. Stanko and Mark Schneider, "Sexual Harassment in the Public Accounting Profession," *Journal of Business Ethics,* Vol. 18, 1999, p. 186.

57. Ellen Peirce, Carol A. Smolinski and Benson Rosen, "Why Sexual Harassment Complaints Fall on Deaf Ears," *Academy of Management Executive,* August 1998, p. 41.

58. Patricia M. Buhler, "The Manager's Role in Preventing Sexual Harassment," *Supervision,* April 1999, pp. 16–18.

59. "Sexual Harassment Charges (and Dismissals) Escalate," *HR Focus,* April 1999, p. 4. Also see Jasmine Tata, "She said, He said. The Influence of Remedial Accounts of Third-Party Judgments of Coworker Sexual Harassment," *Journal of Management,* Vol. 26, No. 6, 2000, pp. 1133–1156.

60. Peirce, Smolinski and Rosen, op. cit., pp. 43–48.

61. Ibid., pp. 51–52.

62. Susan E. Long, "Quick Reaction by Employer Prevents Sexual Harassment Liability," *HR Focus,* April 1999, p. 3.

63. *HR Focus,* February 1999, p. 16.

64. Katherine Giscombe and Adrienne D. Sims, "Breaking the Color Barrier," *HR Focus Special Report on Diversity,* 1998, p. S9.

65. "A Report on the Glass Ceiling Initiative," *Office of Information and Public Affairs,* U.S. Department of Labor, Washington, D.C., 1991, p. 1.

66. Dan R. Dalton and Catherine M. Daily, "Not There Yet," *Across the Board,* November/December 1998, pp. 16–20.

67. Robert A. Snyder, "The Glass Ceiling for Women: Things That Don't Cause It and Things That Won't Break It," *Human Resource Development Quarterly,* Spring 1993, p. 99. Also see Timothy J. Keaveny and Edward J. Inderrieden, "Gender Differences in Pay Satisfaction and Pay Expectations," *Journal of Managerial Issues,* Vol. 12, No. 3, Fall 2000, pp. 363–379.

68. See Debra E. Meyerson and Joyce K. Fletcher, "A Modest Manifesto for Shattering the Glass Ceiling," *Harvard Business Review,* January-February 2000, pp. 127–136.

69. C. Trost, "Women Managers Quit, Not for Family, but to Advance Their Corporate Climb," *Wall Street Journal,* May 2, 1990, pp. B1–2 and H. M. Rosin and K. Korabik, "Marital and Family Correlates of Women Managers' Attribution from Organizations," *Journal of Vocational Behavior,* Vol. 37, 1990, pp. 104–120.

70. Karen Korabik and Hazel M. Rosin, "The Impact of Children on Womens' Career Behavior and Organizational Commitment," *Human Resource Management,* Winter 1995, p. 513.

71. Linda K. Stroh and Jeanne M. Brett, "Dual-Earner Dads versus Traditional Dads: Can We Account for Differences in Salary Progression?" Academy of Management Meeting, 1994 and Marilyn W. Barrett, "Dual-Earner Dads May Be the Latest Victims of Salary Discrimination," *Academy of Management Executive,* May 1995, pp. 71–72.

72. Barrett, op. cit., p. 71.

73. Ann Howard and Douglas Bray, *Managerial Lives in Transition,* Guilford, New York, 1988.

74. Alison M. Konrad and Frank Linnehan, "Formalized HMR Structures," *Academy of Management Journal,* June 1995, pp. 787–820.

75. Belle Rose Ragins, Bickley Townsend, and Mary Mattis, "Gender Gap in the Executive Suite: CEOs and Female Executives Report on Breaking the Glass Ceiling," *Academy of Management Executive,* February 1998, p. 29.

76. Robin J. Ely, "The Power in Demography: Women's Social Constructions of Gender Identity at Work," *Academy of Management Journal,* June 1995, pp. 589–634.

77. Nancy D. Marlow, Edward K. Marlow, and J. Aline Arnold, "Career Development and Women Managers: Does 'One Size Fit All'?" *Human Resource Planning,* Vol. 18, No. 2, 1996, pp. 38–49.

78. Joann Cleaver, "Top 25 Companies for Executive Women," *Working Woman,* December/January 2000, p. 51.

79. Crampton, op. cit., pp. 100–101.

80. Karen S. Lyness and Donna E. Thompson, "Climbing the Corporate Ladder: Do Female and

Male Executives Follow the Same Route?" *Journal of Applied Psychology,* Vol. 85, No. 1, 2000, pp. 86–101.

81. See: Thomas J. Hodson, Fred Englander and Valerie Englander, "Ethical, Legal and Economic Aspects of Employer Monitoring of Employee Electronic Mail," *Journal of Business Ethics,* Vol. 19, 1999, pp. 90–108.

82. "Electronic Monitoring and Surveillance," *Management Review,* October 1998, p. 38.

83. Kimbal P. Marshall, "Has Technology Introduced New Ethical Problems?" *Journal of Business Ethics,* Vol. 19, 1999, p. 87.

84. Samuel Greengard, "Use Common Sense When Providing Employees Internet Access," *Workforce,* April 1999, pp. 95–98.

85. Barry D. Weiss, "Four Black Holes in Cyberspace," *Management Review,* January 1996, p. 31.

86. "Substance Abuse in the Workplace," *HR Focus,* 1999, p. 4.

87. Larry Michaels, "Will Drug Testing Pass or Fail in Court?" *Personnel Journal,* April 1996, p. 141.

88. "Illegal or Controlled Substances," *Management Review,* October 1998, pp. 33–34.

89. Lee Smith, "Can Smoking or Bungee Jumping Get You Canned?" *Fortune,* August 9, 1993, p. 92.

Chapter 4 Footnote References and Supplemental Readings

1. Scott Miller and Norihiko Shirouzu, "Daimler to Take Controlling Stake in Mitsubishi for $1.95 Billion," *Wall Street Journal,* March 27, 2000, p. A-21.

2. Nick Wingfield, "AOL's Lure? Two Worlds: Cash and Customers," *Wall Street Journal,* April 3, 2000, p. B12.

3. Robert Duncan, "What's the Right Organization Structure?" *Organizational Dynamics,* Winter 1979, p. 59.

4. Richard M. Weiss, "Weber on Bureaucracy: Management Consultant or Political Theorist?" *Academy of Management Review,* April 1983, pp. 242–248.

5. Chester I. Barnard, *The Functions of the Executive,* Harvard University Press, Cambridge, Mass., 1938, p. 73.

6. Ibid., p. vii.

7. Ibid., p. 82.

8. Glen R. Carroll, "Organizational Ecology in Theoretical Perspective," in Glen R. Carroll (Ed.), *Ecological Models of Organizations,* Ballinger, Cambridge, Mass., 1988, pp. 1–2.

9. Donde P. Ashmos and George P. Huber, "The Systems Paradigm in Organization Theory: Correcting the Record and Suggesting the Future," *Academy of Management Review,* October 1987, pp. 607–621.

10. Ibid., p. 618. Also see Ron Zemke, "Systems Thinking," *Training,* February 2001, pp. 40–46.

11. Peter M. Senge, "Transforming the Practice of Management," *Human Resource Development Quarterly,* Spring 1993, p. 12.

12. These assumptions are identified in Michael L. Tushman and David A. Nadler, "Information Processing as an Integrating Concept in Organization Design," *Academy of Management Review,* July 1978, pp. 614–615.

13. Jay Galbraith, *Designing Complex Organizations,* Addison-Wesley, Reading, Mass., 1973, p. 5.

14. Tushman and Nadler, op. cit., p. 614.

15. Ibid., p. 615.

16. Ibid. For a more future orientation, see: David A. Nadler and Michael L. Tushman, "The Organization of the Future," *Organizational Dynamics,* Summer 1999, pp. 45–60.

17. James L. Gibson, John M. Ivancevich and James H. Donnelly, Jr., *Organizations,* 6th ed., Business Publications, Plano, Tex., 1988, p. 513.

18. Carroll, op. cit.

19. For the original presentation of this model, see Michael T. Hannon and John J. Freeman, "The Population Ecology of Organizations," *American Journal of Sociology,* March 1977, pp. 929–964.

20. Stephen P. Robbins, *Organization Theory,* 3d ed., Prentice Hall, Upper Saddle River, N.J., 1990, p. 226.

21. See Stephanie Overman, "Learning Your M&ABC's," *HR Focus,* August 1999, pp. 7–8.

22. Peter F. Drucker, "The Unrecognized Boom," *Across the Board,* January 2000, p. 15.

23. Jeffrey Pfeffer, "Barriers to the Advance of Organizational Science: Paradigm Development as a Dependent Variable," *Academy of Management Review,* October 1993, pp. 599–620.

24. See Philip M. Mirvis, "Historical Foundations of Organizational Learning," *Journal of Organizational Change Management,* Vol. 9, No. 1, 1996, pp. 13–31.

25. See Chris Argyris and Donald Schon, *Organizational Learning,* Addison-Wesley, Reading, Mass., 1978 and Chris Argyris, *Overcoming Organizational Defenses,* Allyn & Bacon, Needham Heights, Mass., 1990.

26. For the historical background on the learning organization and the distinctions between single-loop and double-loop learning, see Dave Ulrich, Mary Ann

Von Glinow, and Todd Jick, "High-Impact Learning," *Organizational Dynamics,* Autumn 1993, p. 53.

27. See Peter M. Senge, *The Fifth Discipline: The Art and Practice of the Learning Organization,* Doubleday, New York, 1991 and Peter M. Senge, "The Leader's New Work: Building Learning Organizations," *Sloan Management Review,* Fall 1990, pp. 7–23.

28. Ronald Recardo, Kathleen Molloy and James Pellegrino, "How the Learning Organization Manages Change," *National Productivity Review,* Winter 1995/1996, pp. 7–14 and Cameron M. Ford and dt ogilvie, "The Role of Creative Action in Organizational Learning and Change," *Journal of Organizational Change Management,* Vol. 9, No. 1, 1996, pp. 54–62.

29. Fred Luthans, Michael J. Rubach, and Paul Marsnik, "Going Beyond Total Quality: The Characteristics, Techniques, and Measures of Learning Organizations," *The International Journal of Organizational Analysis,* January 1995, pp. 24–44.

30. Michael E. McGill, John W. Slocum, Jr. and David Lei, "Management Practices in Learning Organizations," *Organizational Dynamics,* Summer 1992, p. 9.

31. Tom Kramlinger, "Training's Role in a Learning Organization," *Training,* July 1992, p. 48.

32. Calhoun W. Wick and Lu Stanton Leon, "From Ideas to Action: Creating a Learning Organization," *Human Practice of the Learning Organization,* Doubleday, New York, 1991 and Peter M. Senge, "The Leader's New Work: Building Learning Organizations," *Sloan Management Review,* Fall 1990, pp. 7–23.

33. David Lei, John W. Slocum and Robert A. Pitts, "Designing Organizations for Competitive Advantage: The Power of Learning and Unlearning," *Organizational Dynamics,* Winter 1999, p. 25.

34. See John A. Byrne, "The Horizontal Corporation," *Business Week,* December 20, 1993, pp. 78–79.

35. Ibid., p. 78.

36. Frank Ostroff, *The Horizontal Organization,* Oxford University Press, New York, 1999.

37. Raymond E. Miles and Charles C. Snow, "Organizations: New Concepts for New Forms," *California Management Review,* Spring 1986, p. 62. Also see Raymond E. Miles and Charles C. Snow, "Causes of Failure in Network Organizations," *California Management Review,* Summer 1992, pp. 53–72.

38. Raymond E. Miles and Charles C. Snow, "The New Network Firm: A Spherical Structure Built on a Human Investment Philosophy," *Organizational Dynamics,* Spring 1995, pp. 5–18.

39. Keith G. Provan and Juliann G. Sebastian, "Networks within Networks: Service Link Overlaps, Organizational Cliques, and Network Effectiveness," *Academy of Management Journal,* Vol. 41, No. 4, 1998, pp. 453–463 and Gillian Symon, "Information and Communication Technologies and the Network Organization," *Journal of Occupational and Organizational Psychology,* Vol. 73, 2000, pp. 389–414.

40. See Timm Runnion, "Outsourcing Can Be a Productivity Solution for the '90s," *HR Focus,* November 1993, p. 23.

41. Tapscott and Caston, op. cit., p. 75. Also see Shawn Tully, "The Modular Corporation," *Fortune,* February 8, 1993, pp. 106–115.

42. Raymond E. Miles, Henry J. Coleman, Jr. and W. E. Douglas Creed, "Keys to Success in Corporate Redesign," *California Management Review,* Spring 1995, pp. 133–140.

43. Kevin Freiberg and Jackie Freiberg, *Nuts,* Bard Press, Austin, Tex., 1996, p. xix.

44. Ibid., p. 75.

45. Paul S. Adler, "Building Better Bureaucracies," *Academy of Management Executive,* Vol. 13, No. 4, 1999, pp. 40–41.

46. Michael Useem and Joseph Harder, "Leading Laterally in Company Outsourcing," *Sloan Management Review,* Winter 2000, p. 25.

47. See William H. Davidow and Michael S. Malone, *The Virtual Corporation,* Harper Business, New York, 1992 and M. Lynne Markus, Brook Manville and Carole E. Agres, "What Makes a Virtual Organization Work?" *Sloan Management Review,* Fall 2000, pp. 13–26.

48. N. Venkatraman and John C. Henderson, "Real Strategies for Virtual Organizing," *Sloan Management Review,* Fall 1998, pp. 33–48.

49. Carl Long and Mary Vickers-Koch, "Using Core Capabilities to Create Competitive Advantage," *Organizational Dynamics,* Summer 1995, pp. 7–22.

50. See "The Virtual Corporation," *Business Week,* February 8, 1993, pp. 98–102.

51. Marie-Claude Boudreau, Karen D. Loch, Daniel Robey, and Detmar Straud, "Going Global: Using Information Technology to Advance the Competitiveness of Virtual Transnational Organization," *Academy of Management Executive,* Vol. 12, No. 4, 1998, p. 122.

52. Miles, Coleman, and Creed, op. cit., pp. 138–142.

53. Boudreau, Loch, Robey and Straud, op. cit., pp. 122–123.

54. Jeannie Coyle and Nicky Schnarr, "The Soft-Side Challenges of the 'Virtual Corporation,'" *Human Resource Planning,* Vol. 18, No. 1, 1995 pp. 41–42.

55. Quoted in Louisa Wah, "Making Knowledge Stick," *Management Review,* May 1999, p. 24.

56. Edgar H. Schein, *Organizational Culture and Leadership,* Jossey-Bass, San Francisco, 1985, p. 9.

57. Joanne Martin, *Cultures in Organizations,* Oxford University Press, New York, 1992, p. 3.

58. Ibid.

59. Elizabeth Wolfe Morrison, "Longitudinal Study of the Effects of Information Seeking on Newcomer

Socialization," *Journal of Applied Psychology,* April 1993, pp. 173–183.

60. Genevieve Soter Capowski, "Designing a Corporate Identity,"*Management Review,* June 1993, p. 37.

61. Jennifer Reese, "America's Most Admired Corporations," *Fortune,* February 8, 1993, p. 44.

62. Ibid.

63. Jeremy Kahn, "The World's Most Admired Companies," *Fortune,* October 11, 1999, p. 272.

64. Nancy C. Morey and Fred Luthans, "Refining the Displacement of Culture and the Use of Scenes and Themes in Organizational Studies," *Academy of Management Review,* April 1985, p. 221.

65. Freiberg, op. cit., p. 151.

66. John Guaspari, "We Make People Happy," *Across the Board,* April 2000, p. 53.

67. Jennifer A. Chatman and Sigal G. Barsade, "Personality, Organizational Culture, and Cooperation: Evidence from a Business Simulation," *Administrative Science Quarterly,* Vol. 40, 1995, pp. 423–443.

68. "General Electric," *Merrill, Lynch & Co.,* May 25, 2000, pp. 10–11.

69. "GE Chief Has Electric Presence," *The Honolulu Advertiser,* April 17, 2000, p. B6.

70. Carol J. Loomis, "Dinosaurs?" *Fortune,* May 3, 1993, pp. 36–42.

71. "A Spanner in the Works," *The Economist,* October 23, 1993, p. 75.

72. Kahn, op. cit., pp. 268; 275.

73. Schein, op. cit., p. 210.

74. Kenneth R. Thompson, "A Conversation with Robert W. Galvin," *Organizational Dynamics,* Spring 1992, p. 58.

75. Ibid., p. 69.

76. Robert Johnson, "McDonald's Combines a Dead Man's Advice with Lively Strategy," *Wall Street Journal,* December 18, 1987, p. 1.

77. Andy Serwer, "There's Something about Cisco," *Fortune,* May 15, 2000, p. 118.

78. This process is described in Richard Pascale, "The Paradox of 'Corporate Culture': Reconciling Ourselves to Socialization," *California Management Review,* Winter 1985, pp. 29–38.

79. Annelies E. M. Van Vianen, "Person-Organization Fit: The Match Between Newcomers' and Recruiters' Preferences for Organizational Cultures," *Personnel Psychology,* Vol. 53, 2000, p. 13.

80. See Gregory B. Northcraft and Margaret A. Neale, *Organizational Behavior,* Dryden, Chicago, 1990, pp. 460–461, for a review of this literature and Robert Vandenberg and Vida Scarpello, "The Matching Model: An Examination of the Processes Underlying Realistic Job Previews," *Journal of Applied Psychology,* February 1990, pp. 60–67, for more research.

81. Peter Cappelli and Anne Crocker-Hefter, "Distinctive Human Resources Are Firms' Core Competencies," *Organizational Dynamics,* Winter 1996, p. 18.

82. Pascale, op. cit., p. 32.

83. Jenny C. McCune, "Exporting Corporate Culture," *Management Review,* December 1999, p. 53.

84. These and other examples are found in Robert F. Dennehy, "The Executive as Storyteller," *Management Review,* March 1999, pp. 41–42.

85. For more on this process, see Richard Pascale, "Fitting New Employees into the Company Culture," *Fortune,* May 18, 1984, pp. 28–43.

86. Fred Luthans and Alexander D. Stajkovic, "Provide Recognition for Performance Improvement," in Edwin A. Locke (ed.), *Handbook of Principles of Organizational Behavior,* Blackwell, London, 2000.

87. Kenneth Thompson and Fred Luthans, "Organizational Culture: A Behavioral Perspective," in Benjamin Schneider (Ed.), *Organizational Climate and Culture,* Jossey-Bass, San Francisco, 1990, pp. 319–344.

88. Frank J. Barrett, "Creating Appreciative Learning Cultures," *Organizational Dynamics,* Autumn 1995, p. 42.

89. "Raiders of the Lost Decade: '80s-Style Mergers Return," *Wall Street Journal,* March 29, 2000, p. C1.

90. Quoted in Sylvia DeVoge and Scott Spreier, "The Soft Realities of Mergers," *Across the Board,* November/December 1999, p. 27.

91. Mark N. Clemente and David S. Greenspan, "M&A's: Preventing Culture Clash," *HR Focus,* February 1999, p. 9.

92. Sally Beatly, "Car Makers Face Possible Pile-Up of Ad Agencies," *Wall Street Journal,* May 8, 1998, pp. B-1; B-9.

93. John J. Fialka, "Deal Beclouds Joint Research By Big Three," *Wall Street Journal,* May 8, 1998, pp. B-1; B-2.

94. Douglas A. Blackmon, "A Factory in Alabama Is the Merger in Microcosm," *Wall Street Journal,* May 8, 1998, pp. B-1; B-10.

95. Cyrus F. Freidheim, Jr., "The Battle of the Alliances," *Management Review,* September 1999, pp. 46–51.

96. *Ibid.,* p. 47.

97. Andrew Rosenbaum, "Testing Cultural Waters," *Management Review,* July–August 1999, p. 42.

98. Reported in Gail Dutton, "Building a Global Brain," *Management Review,* May 1999, p. 36.

99. Patrick Flanagan, "The ABC's of Changing Corporate Cultural," *Management Review,* July 1995, p. 61.

100. D. Q. Mills, "The Decline and Rise of IBM," *Sloan Management Review,* June 1996, pp. 78–82.

101. Chuck Williams, *Management,* Southwestern, Cincinnati: 2000, pp. 68, 70.

Chapter 5 Footnote References and Supplemental Readings

1. Albert Bandura, *Social Foundations of Thought and Action.* Prentice Hall, Upper Saddle River, N.J., 1986, p. 228.

2. Fred Luthans and Alexander D. Stajkovic, "Reinforce for Performance: The Need to Go Beyond Pay and Even Rewards," *Academy of Management Executive,* Vol. 13, No. 2, 1999, pp. 49–57.

3. Thomas B. Wilson, *Rewards that Drive High Performance: Success Stories from Leading Organizations.* American Management Association, New York, 1999 and Eilene Zimmerman, "What Are Employees Worth?" *Workforce,* February 2001, pp. 32–36.

4. See: Bob Nelson, *1001 Ways to Reward Employees,* Workman, New York, 1994 and Fred Luthans and Alexander Stajkovic, "Provide Recognition for Performance Improvement," in E. Locke (Ed.), *Handbook of Principles and Organizational Behavior,* Blackwell, Oxford, UK, 2000, pp. 166–180.

5. Diann R. Newman and Richard M. Hodgetts. *Human Resource Management: A Customer-Oriented Approach.* Prentice Hall, Upper Saddle River, N.J., 1998, p. 227.

6. See for example Betty Sosnin, "A Pat(ent) on the Back," *HR Magazine,* March 2000, pp. 107–112, and Jeff Barbian, "C'mon, Get Happy," *Training,* January 2001, pp. 92–96.

7. Stephen Kerr, "Organization Rewards, Practical, Cost-Neutral Alternatives That You May Know, But Don't Practice," *Organizational Dynamics,* Summer 1999, p. 68.

8. Patricia K. Zingheim and Jay R. Schuster, *Pay People Right! Breakthrough Reward Strategies to Create Great Companies,* Jossey-Bass Publishers, San Francisco, 2000.

9. Terence R. Mitchell and Amy E. Mickel, "The Meaning of Money: An Individual-Difference Perspective," *Academy of Management Review,* July 1999, p. 569.

10. Ibid.

11. Thomas J. Hackett and Donald G. McDermott, "Seven Steps to Successful Performance-Based Rewards," *HR Focus,* September 1999, pp. 11–12.

12. Matt Bloom and George T. Milkovich, "Relationships Among Risk, Incentive Pay, and Organizational Performance," *Academy of Management Journal,* June 1998, pp. 283–297.

13. Also see John R. Deckop, Robert Mangel and Carol C. Cirka, "Getting More Than You Pay For: Organizational Citizenship Behavior and Pay-for-Performance Plans," *Academy of Management Journal,* August 1999, pp. 420–428.

14. A. Furnham and M. Argyle, *The Psychology of Money,* Routledge, London, 1998.

15. Edward E. Lawler III, "The New Pay: A Strategic Approach," *Compensation and Benefits Review,* July–August 1995, pp. 14–21. Also see Jack Dolmar-Connell, "Developing a Reward Strategy that Delivers Shareholder and Employee Value," *Compensation and Benefits Review,* March–April 1999, pp. 46–53.

16. Nina Gupta and Jason D. Shaw, "Financial Incentives are Effective," *Compensation and Benefits Review,* March–April 1998, pp. 27–32; "Pay Preview," *The Economist,* August 29, 1998, pp. 59–60; and Harry G. Barkema and Luis R. Gomez-Mejia, "Managerial Compensation and Firm Performance," *Academy of Management Journal,* April 1998, pp. 135–145.

17. Kerr, op. cit., p. 74.

18. "Cutting Pay Could Hurt Morale," *HR Focus,* December 1999, p. 5.

19. Mitchell and Mickel, op. cit., pp. 568–578.

20. Matt Bloom, "The Performance Effects of Pay Dispersion on Individuals and Organizations," *Academy of Management Journal,* March 1999, pp. 25–40.

21. For more on this see Christy Eidson, "A Lesson from the Ballpark," *Across the Board,* November/December 1999, p. 35.

22. Susumo Yoshida, "How Does It Play in Japan?" *Across the Board,* November–December 1999, p. 37.

23. Lawler quoted in Eidson, op. cit., p. 38.

24. For more on this see Phyllis Gail Doloff, "Missionary Zeal," *Across the Board,* April 2000, p. 30.

25. Michele Himmelberg, "Incentives Play Larger Role in Wages," *Lincoln Journal Star,* May 9, 1999, Section D, p. 1–2.

26. E. L. Deci, "The Effect of Contingent and Non-Contingent Rewards and Controls on Intrinsic Motivation," *Organizational Behavior and Human Performance,* Vol. 8, 1970, pp. 218–219 and E. L. Deci, *Intrinsic Motivation,* Plenum, New York, 1975.

27. Judy Cameron and W. David Pierce, "Reinforcement, Reward, and Intrinsic Motivation: A Meta-Analysis," *Review of Educational Research,* Fall 1994, p. 363.

28. Bob Filipczak, "Why No One Likes Your Incentive Program," *Training,* August 1993, pp. 19–25.

29. Luthans and Stajkovic, "Reinforce for Performance: The Need to Go Beyond Pay and Even Rewards," op. cit. and Alexander Stajkovic and Fred Luthans, "The Differential Effects of Incentive Motivators on Work Performance," *Academy of Management Journal,* June 2001.

30. Kerr, op. cit., p. 61.

31. See, for example, Charles A. Wrege and Richard M. Hodgetts, "Frederick W. Taylor's 1899 Pig Iron Observations: Examining Fact, Fiction, and Lessons for the New Millennium," *Academy of Management Journal,* Vol. 43, No. 6, 2000, pp. 1283–1291.

32. Richard M. Hodgetts, "A Conversation with Donald Hastings of the Lincoln Electric Company," *Organizational Dynamics,* Winter 1997, pp. 68–74.

33. Also see Shirliey Fung, "How Should We Pay Them?" *Across the Board,* June 1999, pp. 37–41.

34. Calmetta Y. Coleman, "Conseco Package Has $45 Million for CEO Wendt," *Wall Street Journal,* July 11, 2000, p. A4.

35. Charles Gasparino and Pui-Wing Tam, "Hot Broker Market Fuels Questions About Pay," *Wall Street Journal,* March 28, 2000, pp. C1, C4.

36. Also see "Stock Options Can Be too Much of a Good Thing," *HR Focus,* March 1999, p. 5.

37. Dirk Johnson, "Teachers Reject Linking Job Performance to Bonuses," *New York Times,* July 6, 2000, p. A16.

38. Judith A. Honeywell-Johnson and Alyce M. Dickinson, "Small Group Incentives: A Review of the Literature," *Journal of Organizational Behavior Management,* Vol. 9, No. 2, 1999, pp. 89–120.

39. Denis Collins. *Gainsharing and Power: Lessons from Six Scanlon Plans,* Cornell University Press, Ithaca, N.Y., 1998 and Dong-One Kim, "Determinants of the Survival of Gainsharing Programs," *Industrial and Labor Relations Review,* Vol. 53, No. 1, October 1999, pp. 21–42.

40. Patricia K. Zingheim and Jay R. Schuster, "Value Is the Goal," *Workforce,* February 2000, p. 59.

41. Ibid., p. 57. Also see Michael J. Guadioso, "How a Successful Gainsharing Program Arose from an Old One's Ashes at Bell Atlantic (Now Verizon) Directory Graphics," *Journal of Organizational Excellence,* Winter 2000, pp. 11–18.

42. "Fresh Wrinkles in Performance Pay," *Leader to Leader,* Winter 1997, pp. 61–62 and Harry G. Barkema and Luis R. Gomez-Mejia, "Managerial Compensation and Firm Performance: A General Research Framework," *Academy of Management Journal,* April 1998, pp. 135–145.

43. Paul Gavejian, "Compensation: Today and Tomorrow," *HR Focus,* November 1998, pp. 55–56.

44. See, for example, Suzanne J. Peterson, "Supervisory 'New Pay' for Performance: Operationalization, Application and Empirical Evaluation." Paper presented at Midwest Academy of Management, 1999.

45. These techniques are drawn from Patricia K. Zingheim and Jay R. Schuster, "Introduction: How Are the New Pay Tools Being Deployed?" *Compensation and Benefits Review,* July–August 1995, pp. 10–11, and Fred Luthans and Alexander D. Stajkovic, "Reinforce for Performance: The Need to Go Beyond Pay and Even Rewards," *Academy of Management Executive,* May 1999, pp. 49–57.

46. For additional insights into the effectiveness of these plans see Brian Murray and Barry Gerhart, "An Empirical Analysis of a Skill-Based Pay Program and Plant Performance Outcomes," *Academy of Management Journal,* January 1998, pp. 68–78.

47. Susan Haslett, "Broadbanding: A Strategic Tool for Organizational Change," *Compensation and Benefits Review,* November–December 1995, p. 40.

48. Richard M. Hodgetts, "A Conversation with Steve Kerr," *Organizational Dynamics,* Spring 1996, p. 69.

49. Kerr, op. cit., p. 68.

50. Fred Luthans and Alexander D. Stajkovic, "Provide Recognition for Performance Improvement." in E. Locke (Ed.), *Handbook on Principles of Organizational Behavior,* Blackwell, Oxford UK, 2000, pp. 166–179.

51. "Employee Loyalty Hangs on Company Recognition that There Is Life Beyond Work," *HR Focus,* August 1999, p. 5.

52. http://www.recognition.org/walker.htm. July 2000.

53. Brenda Paik Sunoo, "Praise and Thanks—You Can't Give Enough," *Workforce,* April 1999, p. 56 and David Robinson, "Thoughtful Appreciation can Keep Workers Happy," *Suday World Herald,* March 11, 2001, p. 13-G.

54. "Companies Are Working to Improve Recognition Programs," *The Conference Board,* p. 7, and Paul A. Gilster, "Online Incentives Sizzle—and You Shine," *Workforce,* January 2001, pp. 44–47.

55. "Morale Maintenance," *Across the Board,* January 2000, p. 79.

56. Sunoo, op. cit., p. 58.

57. Jeanne Bursch and Adrianne Van Strander, "Well-Structured Employee Reward/Recognition Programs Yield Positive Results," *HR Focus,* November 1999, pp. 1, 14.

58. These examples can be found in Bob Nelson, *1001 Ways to Reward Employees.* Workman Publishing, New York, 1994.

59. K. Barron, "Praise and Poodles with that Order," *Forbes,* September 20, 1999, p. 153.

60. Kyle Luthans, "Recognition: A Powerful, but Often Overlooked Leadership Tool to Improve Employee Performance," *Journal of Leadership Studies,* Winter 2000, p. 36.

61. See for example Jennifer Laabs, "Demand Performance for Benefits," *Workforce,* January 2000, pp. 42–46.

62. "Strengthen Links Between Benefits and Strategy," *HR Focus,* June 1999, p. 12.

63. *New York Times Almanac,* New York Times Company, New York, 2000, p. 176.

64. "A Step Above the Basics," *HR Focus,* November 1999, p. 11.

65. "Pampering Employees with Concierge Services," *HR Focus,* December 1999, p. S3.

66. "Companies Use Tuition Assistance to Strengthen Retention Rates," *HR Focus,* December 1999, p. S4.

67. "Non-Insured Benefit Programs Add Value for Employees," *HR Focus,* December 1999, p. S5.

68. "Legal Benefit Plans Help Attract and Retain Employees," *HR Focus,* December 1999, p. S7.

69. Alison E. Barber, Randall B. Dunham and R. A. Formisano, "The Impact of Flexible Benefits on Employee Satisfaction: A Field Study," *Personnel Psychology,* Vol. 45, 1992, pp. 55–57.

70. See Carolyn Hirschman, "Kinder, Simpler Cafeteria Rules," *HR Magazine,* January 2001, pp. 74–79.

71. Also see Melissa W. Barringer and George T. Milkovich, "A Theoretical Exploration of the Adoption and Design of Flexible Benefit Plans: A Case of Human Resource Innovation," *Academy of Management Review,* January 1998, pp. 305–324.

Chapter 6 Footnote References and Supplemental Readings

1. For example, see Colin Eden and J. C. Spender. (Eds.), *Managerial and Organizational Cognition: Theory, Methods, and Research,* Sage, London, 1998.

2. Marshall Schminke, Maureen L. Ambrose and Russell S. Cropanzano, "The Effect of Organizational Structure, on Perceptions of Procedural Fairness," *Journal of Applied Psychology,* Vol. 85, No. 2, 2000, pp. 294–304.

3. Kimbery D. Elsbach and Greg Elofson, "How the Packaging of Decision Explanations Affects Perceptions of Trustworthiness," *Academy of Management Journal,* Vol. 43, No. 1, 2000, pp. 80–89.

4. James H. Dulebohn and Gerald R. Ferris, "The Role of Influence Tactics in Perceptions of Performance Evaluations' Fairness," *Academy of Management Journal,* Vol. 42, No. 3, 1999, pp. 288–303.

5. Marcus Buckingham and Curt Coffman, *First Break All The Rules,* Simon and Schuster, New York, 1999, pp. 76, 78.

6. The quote is found in Shannon Brownlee with Traci Watson, "The Senses," *U. S. News and World Report,* January 13, 1997, p. 52.

7. James M. Carroll and James A. Russell, "Do Facial Expressions Signal Specific Emotions? Judging Emotion from the Face in Context," *Journal of Personality and Social Psychology,* Vol. 70, No. 2, 1996, pp. 205–218.

8. Min-Sun Kim and John E. Hunter, "Attitude-Behavior Relations: A Meta-Analysis of Attitudinal Relevance and Topic," *Journal of Communication,* Winter 1993, pp. 101–142 and Min-Sun Kim and John E. Hunter, "Relationships among Attitudes, Behavioral Intentions, and Behavior," *Communication Research,* June 1993, pp. 331–364.

9. Michael A. Campion, Lisa Cheraskin and Michael J. Stevens, "Career Related Antecedents and Outcomes of Job Rotation," *Academy of Management Journal,* December 1994, pp. 1518–1542.

10. Rod Bond and Peter B. Smith, "Culture and Conformity: A Meta-Analysis of Studies Using Asch's Line Judgment Task," *Psychological Bulletin,* Vol. 119, No. 1, 1996, pp. 111–137.

11. Mary J. Walker, George P. Huber and William H. Glick, "Functional Background as a Determinant of Executives' Selective Perception," *Academy of Management Journal,* August 1996, pp. 943–974.

12. Janice M. Beyer, Prithviraj Chattopadhyay, Elizabeth George, William H. Glick, dt ogilvie and Dulce Pugliese, "The Selective Perception of Managers Revisited," *Academy of Management Journal,* Vol. 40, No. 3, 1997, pp. 716–737.

13. John Swanda, *Organizational Behavior,* Alfred, Sherman Oaks, Calif., 1979, p. 91.

14. Sheldon S. Zalkind and Timothy W. Costello, "Perception: Some Recent Research and Implications for Administration," *Administrative Science Quarterly,* September 1962, pp. 227–229.

15. Ibid., p. 230.

16. James O'Toole, "Hump? What Hump?" *Across the Board,* October 1999, p. 8.

17. See: Claude M. Steele, "A Threat in the Air: How Stereotypes Shape Intellectual Identity and Performance," *American Psychologist,* June 1997, p. 617.

18. For example, see Linda A. Jackson, Linda A. Sullivan and Carole N. Hodge, "Stereotype Effects on Attributions, Predictions, and Evaluations: No Two Social Judgments Are Quite Alike," *Journal of Personality and Social Psychology,* July 1993, pp. 69–84.

19. Angelo S. DeNisi and Ricky W. Griffin, *Human Resource Management,* Houghton Mifflin, Boston, 2001, p. 251.

20. J. John Bernardin and Peter Villanova, "Performance Appraisal," in Edwin A. Locke (Ed.), *Generalizing from Laboratory to Field Settings,* Lexington (Heath), Lexington, Mass., 1986, pp. 45, 53.

21. Kevin R. Murphy, Robert A. Jako and Rebecca L. Anhalt, "Nature and Consequences of Halo Error: A Critical Analysis," *Journal of Applied Psychology,* April 1993, p. 218.

22. Ibid., pp. 218–225.

23. Rick Jacobs and Steve W. J. Kozlowski, "A Closer Look at Halo Error in Performance Ratings," *Academy of Management Journal,* March 1985, pp. 201–212.

24. Donald L. McCabe and Jane E. Dutton, "Making Sense of the Environment: The Role of Perceived Effectiveness," *Human Relations,* May 1993, pp. 623–643.

25. Spencer A. Rathus, *Psychology,* 4th ed., Holt, Rinehart & Winston, Fort Worth, Tex., 1990, pp. 613–614.

26. For summaries of this literature, see James C. McElroy and Charles B. Shrader, "Attribution Theories of Leadership and Network Analysis," *Journal of Management,* Vol. 12, No. 3, 1986, pp. 351–362 and Christy L. DeVader, Allan G. Bateson, and Robert G. Lord, "Attribution Theory: A Meta-Analysis of Attributional Hypotheses," in Edwin A. Locke (Ed.), *Generalizing from Laboratory to Field Settings,* Lexington (Heath), Lexington, Mass., 1986, pp. 63–81. Also see new attributional analysis in areas such as workplace violence: Mark Martinko and Kelly Zellars, "Toward a Theory of Workplace Violence: A Social Learning and Attributional Perspective," *Academy of Management Proceedings,* 1996, pp. 419–423; work exhaustion: Jo Ellen Moore, "Why Is This Happening? A Causal Attribution Approach To Work Exhaustion Consequences," *Academy of Management Review,* Vol. 25, No. 2, 2000, pp. 235–349; empowerment and learned helplessness: Constance R. Campbell and Mark J. Martinko, "An Integrative Attributional Perspective of Empowerment and Learned Helplessness: A Multimethod Field Study," *Journal of Management,* Vol. 24, No. 2, 1998, pp. 173–200; and across cultures: Incheol Choi, Richard E. Nisbett and Ara Norenzayan, "Causal Attribution Across Cultures: Variation and Universality," *Psychological Bulletin,* Vol. 125, No. 1, 1999, pp. 47–63.

27. David G. Myers, *Social Psychology,* 2d ed., McGraw-Hill, New York, 1990, p. 71.

28. Julian B. Rotter, Shephard Liverant and Douglas P. Crowne, "The Growth and Extinction of Expectancies in Chance-Controlled and Skilled Tasks," *Journal of Psychology,* July 1961, pp. 161–177.

29. Terence R. Mitchell, Charles M. Smyser and Stan E. Weed, "Locus of Control: Supervision and Work Satisfaction," *Academy of Management Journal,* September 1975, pp. 623–631.

30. The higher performance of internally controlled managers was verified by the use of student subjects in a study by Carl R. Anderson and Craig Eric Schneier, "Locus of Control, Leader Behavior and Leader Performance among Management Students," *Academy of Management Journal,* December 1978, pp. 690–698. For a more recent study, see Gary Blau, "Testing the Relationships of Locus of Control to Different Performance Dimensions," *Journal of Occupational and Organizational Psychology,* June 1993, pp. 125–138.

31. Margaret W. Pryer and M. K. Distenfano, "Perceptions of Leadership, Job Satisfaction, and Internal–External Control across Three Nursing Levels," *Nursing Research,* November–December 1971, pp. 534–537.

32. Eli Glogow, "Research Note: Burnout and Locus of Control," *Public Personnel Management,* Spring 1986, p. 79.

33. Danny Miller, Manfred F. R. Kets DeVries, and Jean-Marie Toulouse, "Top Executive Locus of Control and Its Relationship to Strategy-Making, Structure, and Environment," *Academy of Management Journal,* June 1982, pp. 237–253.

34. Simon S. K. Lam and John Schaubroeck, "The Role of Locus of Control in Reactions to Being Promoted and to Being Passed Over," *Academy of Management Journal,* Vol. 43, No. 1, 2000, pp. 66–78.

35. John A. Pearce and Angelo S. DeNisi, "Attribution Theory and Strategic Decision Making: An Application to Coalition Formation," *Academy of Management Journal,* March 1983, pp. 119–128.

36. Douglas E. Durand and Walter R. Nord, "Perceived Leader Behavior as a Function of Personality Characteristics of Supervisors and Subordinates," *Academy of Management Journal,* September 1976, pp. 427–428.

37. Dennis L. Dossett and Carl I. Greenberg, "Goal Setting and Performance Evaluation: An Attributional Analysis," *Academy of Management Journal,* December 1981, pp. 767–779.

38. Bobby J. Calder, "An Attribution Theory of Leadership," in Barry Staw and Gerald Salancik (Eds.), *New Directions in Organizational Behavior,* St. Clare Press, Chicago, 1977, pp. 179–204; James C. McElroy, "A Typology of Attribution Leadership Research," *Academy of Management Review,* July 1982, pp. 413–417; Gregory Dobbins, "Effects of Gender on Leaders' Responses to Poor Performers: An Attributional Interpretation," *Academy of Management Journal,* September 1985, pp. 587–598; and James C. McElroy and Charles B. Shrader, "Attribution Theories of Leadership and Network Analysis," *Journal of Management,* Vol. 12, No. 3, 1986, pp. 351–362.

39. Terence R. Mitchell and Robert E. Wood, "Supervisors' Responses to Subordinate Poor Performance:

A Test of an Attribution Model," *Organizational Behavior and Human Performance,* February 1980, pp. 123–138, and Jeffrey A. Lepine and Linn Van Dyne, "Peer Responses to Low Performers: An Attributional Model of Helping in the Context of Groups," *Academy of Management Review,* Vol. 26, No. 1, 2001, pp. 67–84.

40. C. Ward Struthers, Bernard Weiner and Keith Allred, "Effects of Causal Attributions on Personnel Decisions: A Social Motivation Perspective," *Basic and Applied Social Psychology,* Vol. 20, No. 2, 1998, pp. 155–166.

41. Sherry E. Moss and Mark J. Martinko, "The Effects of Performance Attributions and Outcome Dependence on Leader Feedback Following Poor Subordinate Performance," *Journal of Organizational Behavior,* Vol. 19, 1998, pp. 259–274.

42. Paul E. Spector, "Behavior in Organizations as a Function of Employees' Locus of Control," *Psychological Bulletin,* May 1982, pp. 482–497. Also see Leslie Kren, "The Moderating Effects of Locus of Control on Performance Incentives and Participation," *Human Relations,* September 1992, p. 991.

43. Peter J. Frost, "Special Issue on Organizational Symbolism," *Journal of Management,* Vol. 11, No. 2, 1985, pp. 5–9.

44. Farzad Moussavi and Dorla A. Evans, "Emergence of Organizational Attributions: The Role of Shared Cognitive Schema," *Journal of Management,* Spring 1993, pp. 79–95.

45. Suzyn Ornstein, "Organizational Symbols: A Study of Their Meanings and Influences on Perceived Psychological Climate," *Organizational Behavior and Human Decision Processes,* October 1986, pp. 207–229.

46. Bernard Weiner, *Theories of Motivation,* Rand McNally, Chicago, 1972, Chap. 5.

47. Harold H. Kelley, "The Process of Causal Attribution," *American Psychologist,* February 1973, pp. 107–128.

48. Robert Kreitner and Angelo Kinicki, *Organizational Behavior,* 2d ed., Irwin, Homewood, Ill., 1992, p. 148.

49. Mitchell and Wood, op. cit.

50. Bernard Weiner, "An Attribution Theory of Achievement Motivation and Emotion," *Psychological Review,* October 1985, pp. 548–573.

51. See Kreitner and Kinicki, op. cit., p. 150, for a summary of this research.

52. Myers, op. cit., pp. 74–77.

53. Ibid., p. 82.

54. B. Mullen and C. A. Riordan, "Self-Serving Attributions for Performance in Naturalistic Settings," *Journal of Applied Social Psychology,* Vol. 18, 1988, pp. 3–22.

55. Gary Johns, "A Multi-Level Theory of Self-Serving Behavior in and By Organizations," *Research in Organizational Behavior,* Vol. 21, 1999, pp. 1–38.

56. James L. Bowditch and Anthony F. Buono, *A Primer On Organizational Behavior,* 3rd Ed., Wiley, New York, 1994, p. 90.

57. Mark J. Martinko, (Ed.), *Attribution Theory: An Organizational Perspective,* St. Lucie Press, Delray Beach, Fla., 1995.

58. For example, see Kimberly D. Elsbac and Robert Sutton, "Acquiring Organizational Legitimacy through Illegitimate Actions: A Marriage of Institutional and Impression Management Theories," *Academy of Management Journal,* October 1992, pp. 699–738 and Kenneth J. Dunegan, "Framing, Cognitive Modes, and Image Theory: Toward an Understanding of a Glass Half Full," *Journal of Applied Psychology,* June 1993, pp. 491–503.

59. For example, see R. F. Baumeister, "A Self-Presentational View of Social Phenomena," *Psychological Bulletin,* Vol. 91, 1982, pp. 3–26; R. F. Baumeister (Ed.), *Public Self and Private Self,* Springer-Verlag, New York, 1986; B. R. Schlenker, *Impression Management: The Self-Concept, Social Identity, and Interpersonal Relations,* Brooks/Cole, Monterey, Calif., 1980; and William L. Gardner and Bruce J. Avolio, "The Charismatic Relationship: A Dramaturgical Perspective," *Academy of Management Journal,* Vol. 23, No. 1, 1998, pp. 32–58.

60. Mark R. Leary and Robin M. Lowalski, "Impression Management: A Literature Review and Two-Component Model," *Psychological Bulletin,* Vol. 107, No. 1, 1990, pp. 34–47.

61. Ibid., pp. 38–39.

62. Ibid., pp. 40–42.

63. Martin Kilduff and David V. Day, "Do Chameleons Get Ahead? The Effects of Self-Monitoring on Managerial Careers," *Academy of Management Journal,* August 1994, pp. 1047–1060.

64. Robert A. Giacalone, "Image Control: The Strategies of Impression Management," *Personnel,* May 1989, pp. 52–55.

65. Ibid., p. 54.

66. Ibid., pp. 54–55.

67. Mark C. Bolino, "Citizenship and Impression Management: Good Soldiers or Good Actors?" *Academy of Management Review,* Vol. 24, No. 1, 1999, pp. 82–98.

68. K. Michele Kacmar and Dawn S. Carlson, "Effectiveness of Impression Management Tactics Across Human Resource Situations," *Journal of Applied Social Psychology,* Vol. 29, No. 6, 1999, pp. 1293–1315.

69. These guidelines are adapted from William L. Gardner, "Lessons in Organizational Dramaturgy: The Art of Impression Management," *Organizational Dynamics,* Summer 1992, pp. 43–44.

70. Sandy J. Wayne and Robert C. Liden, "Effects of Impression Management on Performance Ratings: A Longitudinal Study," *Academy of Management Journal*, February 1995, pp. 232–260 and Dwight D. Frink and Gerald R. Ferris, "Accountability, Impression Management, and Goal Setting in the Performance Evaluation," *Human Relations*, No. 10, 1998, p. 1259.

71. Anat Rafaeli, Jane Dutton, Celia V. Harquail and Stephanie Mackie-Lewis, "Navigating by Attire: The Use of Dress by Female Administrative Employees," *Academy of Management Journal*, Vol. 40, No. 1, pp. 9–45, and Sherry Sullivan, "Do Clothes Really Make The Woman? The Use of Attire to Enhance Work Performance," *Academy of Management Executive*, Vol. 11, No. 4, 1997, pp. 90–91.

72. "Execs Believe Suit and Tie Will Soon Be Obsolete," *HR Focus*, March 1999, p. 4.

73. "Casual Dress Spreads to Many Old-Line Law Firms," *Wall Street Journal*, March 21, 2000, p. A1.

74. Michael G. Pratt and Anat Rafaeli, "Organizational Dress as a Symbol of Multilayered Social Identities," *Academy of Management Journal*, Vol. 40, No. 4, 1997, pp. 862–898.

75. Gardner, op. cit., p. 45.

76. John Wareham, "The Mirrors of Ourselves," *Across the Board*, April 2000, p. 49.

Chapter 7 Footnote References and Supplemental Readings

1. Alan Feingold, "Gender Differences in Personality: A Meta Analysis," *Psychological Bulletin*, Vol. 116, No. 3, 1994, pp. 429–456.

2. See: "What We Learn from Twins: The Mirror of Your Soul," *The Economist*, January 3, 1998, pp. 74–76.

3. Beth Azar, "Nature, Nurture: Not Mutually Exclusive," *APA Monitor*, May 1997, p. 1. Also see "Who Wants to Be a Genius," *The Economist*, January 13, 2001, pp. 77–78.

4. Ibid. See also W. Andrew Collins, Eleanor E. Maccoby, Laurence Steinberg, E. Mavis Hetherington and Marc H. Bornstein, "Contempory Research on Parenting: The Case for Nature and Nurture," *American Psychologist*, February 2000, pp. 218–232.

5. Nigel Nicholson, "How Hardwired Is Human Behavior?" *Harvard Business Review*, July–August 1998, p. 135. Also see Barbara Decker Pierce and Roderick White, "The Evolution of Social Structure: Why Biology Matters," *Academy of Management Review*, Vol. 24, No. 4, 1999, pp. 843–853.

6. Mark Nichols, "Secrets of the Brain," *McClean's*, January 22, 1996, p. 44. Also see Marcus Buckingham and Donald O. Clifton, *Now, Discover Your Strengths*, The Free Press, New York, 2001, pp. 50–56.

7. Murray R. Barrick and Michael K. Mount, "The Big Five Personality Dimensions and Job Performance: A Meta-Analysis," *Personnel Psychology*, Vol. 44, 1991, p. 1 and Michael K. Mount and Murray R. Barrick, "Five Reasons Why the 'Big Five' Article Has Been Frequently Cited," *Personnel Psychology*, Vol. 51, 1998, pp. 849–857.

8. Kristen C. Kling, Janet Shibley Hyde, Carolin J. Showers and Brenda N. Buswell, "Gender Differences in Self-Esteem: A Meta-Analysis," *Psychological Bulletin*, Vol. 125, No. 4, 1999, pp. 470–500.

9. Bernadette Gray-Little and Adam R. Hafdahl, "Factors Influencing Racial Comparisons of Self-Esteem: A Quantitative Review," *Psychological Bulletin*, Vol. 126, No. 1, 2000, pp. 26–54.

10. See: P. G. Dodgson and J. V. Wood, "Self-Esteem and the Cognitive Accessibility of Strength and Weaknesses after Failure," *Journal of Personality and Social Psychology*, July 1998, pp. 178–197.

11. B. R. Schlenker, M. F. Weigeld and J. R. Hallam, "Self-Serving Attributions in Social Context: Effects of Self-Esteem and Social Pressure," *Journal of Personality and Social Psychology*, May 1990, pp. 855–863.

12. For example, see R. F. Baumeister, L. Smart and J. M. Boden, "Relation of Threatened Egotism to Violence and Aggression: The Dark Side of High Self-Esteem," *Psychological Review*, January 1996, pp. 5–33.

13. Robert Kreitner and Angelo Kinicki, *Organizational Behavior*, 5th ed., Irwin/McGraw-Hill, Burr Ridge, Ill., 2001, p. 139.

14. J. L. Pierce, D. G. Gardner, L. L. Cummings and R. B. Dunham, "Organization-Based Self-Esteem: Construct Definition, Measurement, and Validation," *Academy of Management Journal*, September 1989, p. 625.

15. For example, see T. A. Judge, E. A. Locke, C. C. Durham and A. N. Kluger, "Dispositional Effects on Job and Life Satisfaction: The Role of Core Evaluations," *Journal of Applied Psychology*, February 1998, pp. 17–34.

16. K. W. Mossholder, A. G. Bedeian and A. A. Armenakis, "Role Perceptions, Satisfaction, and Performance: Moderating Effects of Self-Esteem and Organizational Level," *Organizational Behavior and Human Performance*, Vol. 28, 1981, pp. 224–234 and K. W.

Mossholder, A. G. Bedeian and A. A. Armenakis, "Group Process–Work Outcome Relationships: A Note on the Moderating Impact of Self-Esteem," *Academy of Management Journal,* Vol. 25, 1982, pp. 575–585.

17. Jon L. Pierce, Donald G. Gardner, Randall B. Dunham, and Larry L. Cummings, "Moderation by Organization-Based Self-Esteem of Role Condition–Employee Response Relationships," *Academy of Management Journal,* April 1993, pp. 271–288; Daniel C. Ganster and John Schaubroeck, "Work Stress and Employee Health," *Journal of Management,* Vol. 17, 1991, pp. 235–271; and Daniel C. Ganster and John Schaubroeck, "Role Stress and Worker Health: An Extension of the Plasticity Hypothesis of Self-Esteem," *Journal of Social Behavior and Personality,* Vol. 6, 1991, pp. 349–360.

18. Roy J. Blitzer, Colleen Petersen and Linda Rogers, "How to Build Self-Esteem," *Training and Development,* February 1993, p. 59. However, for some of the measurement issues see Richard W. Robins, Holly M. Hendin and Kali H. Trzesniewski, "Measuring Global Self Esteem," *Personality and Social Psychology Bulletin,* Vol. 27, No. 2, 2001, pp. 151–161.

19. Nathaniel Branden, *Self-Esteem at Work,* Jossey-Bass, San Francisco, 1998, quoted in Perry Pescarella, "It All Begins with Self-Esteem," *Management Review,* February 1999, p. 60.

20. Amy L. Kristof, "Person–Organization Fit: An Integrative Review of Its Conceptualizations, Measurement, and Implications," *Personnel Psychology,* Vol. 49, 1996, pp. 1–49.

21. Cheryl L. Adkins, "Previous Work Experience and Organizational Socialization: A Longitudinal Examination," *Academy of Management Journal,* June 1995, pp. 839–862.

22. Edgar H. Schein, "Organizational Socialization and the Profession of Management," in David Kolb, Irwin Rubin and James McIntyre (Eds.), *Organizational Psychology: A Book of Readings,* Prentice Hall, Upper Saddle River, N.J., 1971, pp. 14–15.

23. Blake E. Ashforth and Alan M. Saks, "Socialization Tactics: Longitudinal Effects on Newcomer Adjustment," *Academy of Management Journal,* February 1996, pp. 146–178.

24. Schein, op. cit., p. 3.

25. Daniel C. Feldman and Hugh J. Arnold, *Managing Individual and Group Behavior in Organizations,* McGraw-Hill, New York, 1983, pp. 79–80.

26. Schein, op. cit., p. 3.

27. Robert A. Baron, *Behavior in Organizations,* 2d ed., Allyn & Bacon, Boston, 1986, p. 65.

28. Feldman and Arnold, op. cit., pp. 83–86.

29. Howard J. Klein and Natasha A. Weaver, "The Effectiveness of an Organization Level Orientation Training Program in the Socialization of New Hires," *Personnel Psychology,* Vol. 53, 2000, p. 47.

30. Clyde Kluckhohn and H. A. Murray, "Personality Formation: The Determinats," C. Kluckhohn and H. A. Murray (Eds.), *Personality,* Knopf, New York, 1948, p. 35.

31. G. W. Allport and H. S. Odbert, "Trait Names: A Psychological Study," *Psychological Monographs,* Vol. 4, 1936, pp. 211–214.

32. See J. M. Digman, "Personality Structure: Emergence of the Five-Factor Model," *Annual Review of Psychology,* Vol. 41, 1990, pp. 417–440.

33. See Barrick and Mount, op. cit.; Mount and Barrick, op. cit.; R. J. Schneider and L. M. Hough, "Personality and Industrial/Organizational Psychology," *International Review of Industrial and Organizational Psychology,* Vol. 10, 1995, pp. 75–129; M. Zuckerman, D. M. Kuhlman, J. Joireman, P. Teta and M. Kraft, "A Comparison of Three Structural Models for Personality: The Big Three, The Big Five, and The Alternative Five," *Journal of Personality and Social Psychology,* October 1993, pp. 757–768; and Gregory M. Hurtz and John J. Donovan, "Personality and Job Performance: The Big Five Revisited," *Journal of Applied Psychology,* Vol. 85, No. 6, 2000, pp. 869–879.

34. S. V. Paunonen et al., "The Structure of Personality in Six Cultures," *Journal of Cross-Cultural Psychology,* May 1996, pp. 339–353, and G. Saucier and F. Ostendorf, "Hierarchical Subcomponents of the Big Five Personality Factors: A Cross-Language Replication," *Journal of Personality and Social Psychology,* April 1999, pp. 613–627.

35. See Barrick and Mount, op. cit. and Mount and Barrick, op. cit. Also see J. F. Salgado, "The Five-Factor Model of Personality and Job Performance in the European Community," *Journal of Applied Psychology,* Vol. 82, 1997, pp. 30–45.

36. Robert J. House, Scott A. Shane, and David M. Herold, "Rumors of the Death of Dispositional Research Are Vastly Exaggerated," *Academy of Management Review,* January 1996, p. 203.

37. Robert R. McCrae and Paul T. Costa, Jr., "The Stability of Personality: Observations and Evaluations," *Current Directions in Psychological Science,* December 1994, p. 173.

38. Marcus Buckingham and Curt Coffman, *First, Break All The Rules,* Simon and Schuster, New York, 1999, pp. 177–214, and S. B. Gustafson and M. D. Mumford, "Personal Style and Person-Environment Fit: A Pattern Approach," *Journal of Vocational Behavior,* April 1995, pp. 163–188.

39. Mount and Barrick, op. cit., p. 851.

40. T. A. Judge, J. J. Martocchio and C. J. Thoresen, "Five-Factor Model of Personality and Employee

Absence," *Journal of Applied Psychology,* Vol. 82, 1998, pp. 745–755.

41. Paula M. Caligiuri, "The Big Five Personality Characteristics as Predictors of Expatriate's Desire to Terminate the Assignment and Supervisor-Rated Performance," *Personnel Psychology,* Vol. 53, 2000, p. 67.

42. Ivan T. Robertson, Helen Baron, Patrick Gibbons, Rab MacIver and Gill Nyfield, "Conscientiousness and Managerial Performance," *Journal of Occupational Psychology,* Vol. 73, 2000, pp. 171–180, and Maxine Dalton and Meena Wilson, "The Relationship of the Five-Factor Model of Personality to Job Performance for a Group of Middle Eastern Expatriate Managers," *Journal of Cross Cultural Psychology,* Vol. 31, No. 2, 2000, pp. 250–258.

43. Michael K. Mount, Murray R. Barrick and J. Perkins Strauss, "The Joint Relationship of Conscientiousness and Ability with Performance: Test of the Interaction Hypothesis," *Journal of Management,* Vol. 25, No. 5, 1999, pp. 707–721.

44. Michael K. Mount, Amy E. Colbert, James K. Harter and Murray R. Barrick, "Does Job Satisfaction Moderate the Relationship Between Conscientiousness and Job Performance." Paper presented to Academy of Management Annual Meeting, Toronto, Canada, August 2000.

45. H. John Bernardin, Donna K. Cooke and Peter Villanova, "Conscientiousness and Agreeableness as Predictors of Rating Leniency," *Journal of Applied Psychology,* Vol. 85, No. 2, 2000, pp. 232–234.

46. Salgado, op. cit.

47. Judge, Martocchio and Thoresen, op. cit.

48. See Salgado, op. cit., Barrick and Mount, op. cit. and Mount and Barrick, op. cit. For the decision-making simulation study showing the positive relationship with openness, see Jeffrey A. Lepine, Jason A. Colquitt and Amir Erez, " Adaptability to Changing Task Contexts: Effects of General Cognitive Ability, Conscientiousness, and Openness to Experience," *Personnel Psychology*, Vol. 53, 2000, pp. 563–593.

49. M. R. Barrick, G. L. Stewart, M. J. Neubert and M. K. Mount, "Relating Member Ability and Personality to Work-Team Processes and Team Effectiveness," *Journal of Applied Psychology,* Vol. 83, 1998, pp. 377–391.

50. For example, see: W. L. Gardner and M. J. Martinko, "Using the Myers-Briggs Type Indicator To Study Managers: A Literature Review and Research Agenda," *Journal of Management,* Vol. 22., 1996, pp. 45–83, and R. Zemke, "Second Thoughts About the MBTI," *Training,* April 1992, pp. 42–47.

51. See Debra L. Nelson and James Campbell Quick, *Organizational Behavior,* 3rd ed., South-Western,

Cincinnati, 2000, pp. 88–92 for an extensive treatment of the MBTI. The discussion and Table 7.2 is adapted from this source.

52. See: J. B. Murray, "Review of Research on the Myers-Briggs Type Indicator," *Perceptual and Motor Skills,* Vol. 70, 1990, pp. 1187–1202 and J. G. Carlson, "Recent Assessment of the Myers-Briggs Type Indicator," *Journal of Personality Assessment,* Vol. 49, 1985, pp. 356–365.

53. Gardner and Martinko, op. cit. and Zemke, op. cit.

54. Nelson and Quick, op. cit., p. 92.

55. J. A. Morris and D. C. Feldman, "The Dimensions, Antecedents, and Consequences of Emotional Labor," *Academy of Management Review,* Vol. 21, 1996, pp. 986–1010.

56. See Karen Pugliesi, "The Consequences of Emotional Labor: The Effects on Work Stress, Job Satisfaction, and Well Being," *Motivation and Emotion,* Vol. 23, No. 2, 1999, pp. 125–153; J. A. Morris and D. C. Feldman, "Managing Emotions in the Workplace," *Journal of Managerial Issues,* Fall, 1997, pp. 257–274; K. D. Grimsley, "Service With a Forced Smile," *Washington Post,* October 18, 1998, p. A1.

57. Gerald Salancik and Jeffrey Pfeffer, "A Social Information Processing Approach to Job Attitudes and Task Design," *Administrative Science Quarterly,* June 1978, pp. 224–253.

58. Jennifer M. George, "Personality, Affect, and Behavior in Groups," *Journal of Applied Psychology,* Vol. 75, No. 2, 1990, p. 108.

59. Larry J. Williams, Mark B. Gavin and Margaret L. Williams, "Measurement and Nonmeasurement Processes with Negative Affectivity and Employee Attitudes," *Journal of Applied Psychology,* Vol. 81, No. 1, 1996, pp. 88–101.

60. Karl Aquino, Steven L. Grover, Murray Bradfield and David G. Allen, "The Effects of Negative Affectivity, Hierarchical Status, and Self-Determination on Workplace Victimization," *Academy of Management Journal,* Vol. 42, No. 3, 1999, pp. 260–272.

61. James A. Russell and James M. Carroll, "On the Bipolarity of Positive and Negative Affect," *Psychological Bulletin,* Vol. 125, No. 1, 1999, pp. 3–30.

62. B. M. Staw and S. G. Barsade, "Affect and Managerial Performance: A Test of the Sadder-but-Wiser vs. Happier-and-Smarter Hypotheses," *Administrative Science Quarterly,* Vol. 38, 1993, pp. 304–331.

63. J. M. George, "Mood and Absence," *Journal of Applied Psychology,* Vol. 74, 1989, pp. 287–324.

64. Jason D. Shaw, Michelle K. Duffy, G. Douglas Jenkins, Jr. and Nina Gupta, "Positive and Negative Affect, Signal Sensitivity, and Pay Satisfaction,"

Journal of Management, Vol. 25, No. 2, 1999, pp. 189–206, and Howard M. Weiss, Jeffrey P. Nicholas and Catherine S. Daus, "An Examination of the Joint Effects of Affective Experiences and Job Beliefs on Job Satisfaction and Variations in Affective Experiences Over Time," *Organizational Behavior and Human Decision Processes,* Vol. 78, No. 1, April 1999, pp. 1–24.

65. M. J. Burke, A. P. Brief and J. M. George, "The Role of Negative Affectivity in Understanding Relations Between Self-Reports of Stressors and Strains," *Journal of Applied Psychology,* Vol. 78, 1993, pp. 402–412.

66. J. M. George, "Personality, Affect, and Behavior in Groups," *Journal of Applied Psychology,* Vol. 75, 1990, pp. 107–116.

67. Peter Cappelli, "Is the 'Skills Gap' Really about Attitudes?" *California Management Review,* Summer 1995, p. 110.

68. See Min-Sun Kim and John E. Hunter, "Relationships among Attitudes, Behavior Intentions, and Behavior," *Communication Research,* June 1993, pp. 331–364, and Min-Sun Kim and John E. Hunter, "Attitude–Behavior Relations: A Meta-Analysis of Attitudinal Relevance and Topic," *Journal of Communication,* Winter 1993, pp. 101–142.

69. D. Katz, "The Functional Approach to the Study of Attitudes," *Journal of Opinion Quarterly,* Summer 1960, pp. 163–204.

70. Joel Brockner, "The Escalation of Commitment to a Failing Course of Action: Toward Theoretical Progress," *Academy of Management Review,* January 1992, pp. 39–61.

71. S. Lieberman, "The Effect of Changes in Roles on the Attitudes of Role Occupants," *Human Relations,* November 1956, pp. 385–402.

72. Leon Festinger, *A Theory of Cognitive Dissonance,* Stanford University Press, Stanford, Calif., 1957.

73. E. A. Locke, "The Nature and Cause of Job Satisfaction," in M. D. Dunnette (Ed.), *Handbook of Industrial and Organizational Psychology,* Rand McNally, Chicago, 1976, p. 1300.

74. Andrè Bussing, Thomas Bissls, Vera Fuchs and Klaus M. Perrar, "A Dynamic Model of Work Satisfaction: Qualitative Approaches," *Human Relations,* Vol. 52, No. 8, 1999, p. 999.

75. P. C. Smith, L. M. Kendall and C. L. Hulin, *The Measurement of Satisfaction in Work and Retirement,* Rand McNally, Chicago, 1969.

76. Mary Ann M. Fricko and Terry A. Beehr, "A Longitudinal Investigation of Interest Congruence and Gender Concentration as Predictors of Job Satisfaction," *Personnel Psychology,* September 1992, pp. 99–118.

77. Timothy A. Judge, Joyce E. Bono and Edwin A. Locke, "Personality and Job Satisfaction: The Mediating Role of Job Characteristics," *Journal of Applied Psychology,* Vol. 85, No. 2, 2000, pp. 237–249.

78. Christina E. Shalley, Lucy L. Gilson and Terry C. Blum, "Matching Creativity Requirements and the Work Enviroment: Effects on Satisfaction and Intentions to Leave," *Academy of Management Journal,* Vol. 43, No. 2, 2000, pp. 215–223.

79. "IT Workers Expect Career Development and Job Satisfaction," *HR Focus,* August 1999, p. 4.

80. Shawn M. Carraher and M. Ronald Buckley, "Cognitive Complexity and the Perceived Dimensionality of Pay Satisfaction," *Journal of Applied Psychology,* Vol. 81, No. 1, 1996, pp. 102–109, and A. Furnham and M. Argyle, *The Psychology of Money,* Routledge, London, 1998.

81. See Timothy A. Judge, "Validity of the Dimensions of the Pay Satisfaction Questionnaire: Evidence of Differential Prediction," *Personnel Psychology,* Summer 1993, pp. 331–355, and Terence R. Mitchell and Amy E. Mickel, "The Meaning of Money: An Individual Difference Perspective," *Academy of Management Review,* July 1999, pp. 568–578.

82. Brenda Major and Ellen Konar, "An Investigation of Sex Differences in Pay Expectations and Their Possible Causes," *Academy of Management Journal,* December 1984, pp. 777–792.

83. Alison E. Barber, Randall B. Dunham and Roger A. Formisano, "The Impact of Flexible Benefits on Employee Satisfaction: A Field Study," *Personnel Psychology,* September 1992, pp. 55–76.

84. "Executives Heed Employee Priorities," *HR Focus,* August 1999, p. 4.

85. See Marcus Buckingham and Curt Coffman, *First, Break All the Rules,* Simon and Schuster, New York, 1999, p. 264.

86. Katharine I. Miller and Peter R. Monge, "Participation, Satisfaction, and Productivity: A Meta-Analytic Review," *Academy of Management Journal,* December 1986, p. 748.

87. M. Tait, M.Y. Padgett and T. T. Baldwin, "Job and Life Satisfaction: A Reevaluation of the Strength of the Relationship and Gender Effects as a Function of the Date of the Study," *Journal of Applied Psychology,* June 1989, pp. 502–507.

88. T. A. Judge and S. Watanabe, "Another Look at the Job Satisfaction–Life Satisfaction Relationship," *Journal of Applied Psychology*, Vol. 78, 1993, pp. 939–948.

89. M. T. Iffaldano and P. M. Muchinsky, "Job Satisfaction and Job Performance: A Meta-Analysis," *Psychological Bulletin,* Vol. 97, 1985, pp. 251–273.

90. For example, see T. A. Judge, K. A. Hanisch and R. D. Drankoski, "Human Resources Management and Employee Attitudes," in G. R. Ferris, S. D. Rosen and D. T. Barnum (Eds.), *Handbook of Human Resources Management,* Blackwell Publishers, Oxford, England, 1995; C. L. Hulin, "Adaptation, Persistence, and Commitment in Organizations," in M. D. Dunnette and L. M. Hough (Eds.), *Handbook of Industrial and Organizational Psychology,* 2nd Ed., Vol. 2, Consulting Psychologist Press, Palo Alto, CA; and M. M. Petty, G. W. McGee and J. W. Cavender; "A Meta-Analysis of the Relationships Between Individual Job Satisfaction and Individual Performance," *Academy of Management Review,* Vol. 9, 1984, pp. 712–721.

91. Alexander D. Stajkovic and Fred Luthans, "Self-Efficacy and Work-Related Performance: A Meta-Analysis," *Psychological Bulletin,* Vol. 124, No. 2, 1998, pp. 240–261.

92. P. M. Podsakoff and L. J. Williams, "The Relationship between Job Performance and Job Satisfaction," in E. A. Locke (Ed.), *Generalizing from Laboratory to Field Settings,* Lexington Books, Lexington, Mass., 1986.

93. Dennis J. Adsit, Manuel London, Steven Crom and Dana Jones, "Relationships between Employee Attitudes, Customer Satisfaction and Departmental Performance," *Journal of Management Development,* Vol. 15, No. 1, 1996, pp. 62–75.

94. Cheri Ostroff, "The Relationship between Satisfaction, Attitudes, and Performance: An Organizational Level Analysis," *Journal of Applied Psychology,* December 1992, pp. 963–974.

95. For an example of a study that verifies the relationship between satisfaction and turnover, see Thomas W. Lee and Richard T. Mowday, "Voluntarily Leaving an Organization: An Empirical Investigation of Steers and Mowday's Model of Turnover," *Academy of Management Journal,* December 1987, pp. 721–743. Also see Robert P. Tett and John P. Meyer, "Job Satisfaction, Organizational Commitment, Turnover Intention, and Turnover: Path Analyses Based on Meta-Analytic Findings," *Personnel Psychology,* Summer 1993, pp. 259–294, and P. W. Hom and R. W. Griffith, *Employee Turnover,* Southwestern, Cincinnati, 1995, pp. 35–50.

96. R. D. Hackett, "Work Attitudes and Employee Absenteeism: A Synthesis of the Literature," *Journal of Occupational Psychology,* 1989, pp. 235–248.

97. C. W. Clegg, "Psychology of Employee Lateness, Absenteeism, and Turnover: A Methodological Critique and an Empirical Study," *Journal of Applied Psychology,* February 1983, pp. 88–101.

98. M. A. Blegen, "Nurses' Job Satisfaction: A Meta-Analysis of Related Variables," *Nursing Research,* January–February 1993, pp. 36–41.

99. These guidelines are structured and drawn from Jerald Greenberg and Robert A. Baron, *Behavior in Organizations,* 7th ed., Prentice Hall, Upper Saddle River, N.J., 2000, pp. 179–180.

100. Kevin Freiberg and Jackie Freiberg, *Nuts,* Bord Press, Austin, Tex., 1996, p. 151.

101. Edwin A. Locke and Gary P. Latham, *A Theory of Goal Setting and Task Performance,* Prentice Hall, Upper Saddle River, N.J., 1990, pp. 249–250, and R. P. Tett and J. P. Meyer, "Job Satisfaction, Organizational Commitment, Turnover Intention, and Turnover: Path Analysis Based on Meta-Analytic Findings," *Personnel Psychology,* Summer 1993, pp. 259–293.

102. K. Carson, P. Carson, C. Roe, B. Birkenmeier and J. Philips, "Four Commitment Profiles and Their Relationships to Empowerment, Service Recovery and Work Attitudes," *Public Personnel Management,* Vol. 28, No. 1, 1999, pp. 1–13.

103. ADL Associates, *Commitment: If You Build It . . . Results Will Come,* ADL Associates, Lewisville, TX, 1998, p.6.

104. See Thomas E. Becker, Donna M. Randall and Carl D. Riegel, "The Multidimensional View of Commitment and the Theory of Reasoned Action: A Comparative Evaluation," *Journal of Management,* Vol. 21, No. 4, 1995, pp. 617–638.

105. R. T. Mowday, L. W. Porter and R. M. Steers, *Employee–Organization Linkages,* Academic Press, New York, 1982.

106. For example, see Fred Luthans, Donald Baack, and Lew Taylor, "Organizational Commitment: Analysis of Antecedents," *Human Relations,* Vol. 40, No. 4, 1987, pp. 219–236, and Joan E. Finegan, "The Impact of Person and Organizational Values on Organizational Commitment," *Journal of Occupational and Organizational Psychology,* Vol. 73, 2000, pp. 149–169.

107. Gregory B. Northcraft and Margaret A. Neale, *Organizational Behavior,* Dryden, Chicago, 1990, p. 472.

108. Eunmi Chang, "Career Commitment as a Complex Moderator of Organizational Commitment and Turnover Intention," *Human Relations,* Vol. 52, No. 10, 1999, p. 1257.

109. J. P. Meyer and N. J. Allen, "A Three-Component Conceptualization of Organizational Commitment," *Human Resource Management Review,* Vol. 1, 1991, pp. 61–89.

110. For some tests of the Meyer and Allen model, see Rich D. Hackett, Peter Bycio and Peter Hausdoft, "Further Assessments of a Three-Component Model of Organizational Commitment," *Academy of*

Management Best Papers Proceedings, 1992, pp. 212–216, Mark John Somers, "A Test of the Relationship between Affective and Continuance Commitment Using Non-Recursive Models," *Journal of Occupational and Organizational Psychology,* June 1993, pp. 185–192, and N. J. Allen and J. P. Meyer, "Affective, Continuance and Normative Commitment to the Organization: An Examination of Construct Validity," *Journal of Vocational Behavior,* Vol. 49, 1996, pp. 252–276.

111. See J. Ko, J. L. Price and C. W. Mueller, "Assessment of Meyer and Allen's Three Component Model of Organizational Commitment in South Korea," *Journal of Applied Psychology,* Vol. 82, 1997, pp. 961–973, and Abubakr M. Sulimand and Paul A. Iles, "The Multi-Dimensional Nature of Organisational Commitment in a Non-Western Context," *Journal of Management Development,* Vol. 19, No. 1, 2000, pp. 71–82.

112. R. T. Mowday, R. M. Steers and L. W. Porter, "The Measurement of Organizational Commitment," *Journal of Vocational Behavior,* Vol. 14, 1979, pp. 224–247.

113. J. E. Mathieu and D. M. Zajac, "A Review and Meta-Analysis of the Antecedents, Correlates, and Consequences of Organizational Commitment," *Psychological Bulletin,* Vol. 108, 1990, pp. 171–199; J. P. Meyer and J. J. Allen, *Commitment in the Workplace: Theory, Research and Application,* Sage, Thousand Oaks, Calif., 1997; B. Benkhoff, "Ignoring Commitment Is Costly: New Approaches Establish the Missing Link Between Commitment and Performance," *Human Relations,* Vol. 50, No. 6, 1997, pp. 701–726; M. J. Somers, "Organizational Commitment, Turnover and Absenteeism: An Examination of Direct and Interaction Effects," *Journal of Organizational Behavior,* Vol. 16, 1995, pp. 49–58 and L. Lum, J. Kervin, K. Clark, F. Ried and W. Sirola, "Explaining Nursing Turnover Intent: Job Satisfaction, Pay Satisfaction, or Organizational Commitment?" *Journal of Organizational Behavior,* Vol. 19, 1998, pp. 305–320.

114. Fred Luthans, La Vonne K. Wahl and Carol S. Steinhaus, "The Importance of Social Support for Employee Commitment," *Organizational Development Journal,* Winter 1992, pp. 1–10.

115. See J. W. Bishop and K. D. Scott, "How Commitment Affects Team Performances," *HR Magazine,* February 1997, pp. 107–111.

116. For example see Donna M. Randall, Donald B. Fedor and Clinton O. Longenecker, "The Behavioral Expression of Organizational Commitment," *Journal of Vocational Behavior,* Vol. 36, 1990, pp. 210–224.

117. Joan F. Brett, William L. Cron and John W. Slocum, Jr., "Economic Dependency on Work: A Moderator of the Relationship between Organizational Commitment and Performance," *Academy of Management Journal,* Vol. 38, No. 1, 1995, pp. 261–271.

118. Thomas E. Becker, Robert S. Billings, Daniel M. Eveleth and Nicole L. Gilbert, "Foci and Bases of Employee Commitment: Implications for Job Performance," *Academy of Management Journal,* April 1996, pp. 464–482.

119. Lynn McMarlane Shore, George C. Thornton and Lucy A. Newton, "Job Satisfaction and Organizational Commitment as Predictors of Behavioral Intentions and Employee Behavior," *Academy of Management Proceedings,* 1989, pp. 229–333 and Locke and Latham, op. cit., p. 250.

120. Gary Dessler, "How to Earn Your Employees' Commitment," *Academy of Management Executive,* Vol. 13, No. 2, 1999, p. 65.

121. Ibid., pp. 66.

122. D.W. Organ, *Organizational Citizenship Behavior: The Good Soldier Syndrome,* Lexington Books, Lexington, Mass., 1988, p. 4.

123. D.W. Organ and K. Ryan, "A Meta-Analytic Review of Attitudinal and Dispositional Predictors of Organizational Citizenship Behavior," *Personnel Psychology,* Winter 1995, pp. 775–802.

124. See C. O. Reilly and J. Chatman, "Organizational Commitment and Psychological Attachment: The Affective Compliance, Identification, and Internalization on Pro-Social Behavior," *Journal of Applied Psychology,* Vol. 71, 1986, p. 493 and Randall, Fedor and Longenecker, op. cit.

125. For reviews of this literature see, L. VanDyne, L. L. Cummings and J. McLean Parks, "Extra-Role Behaviors: In Pursuit of Construct and Definitional Clarity," in L. L. Cummings and B. M. Staw (Eds.), *Research in Organizational Behavior,* Vol. 17, JAI Press, Greenwich, Conn., 1995, and Maureen L. Ambrose and Carol T. Kulick, "Old Friends, New Faces: Motivation Research in the 1990's," *Journal of Management,* Vol. 25, No. 3, 1999, p. 245.

126. Robert H. Moorman, Gerald L. Blakely and Brian P. Niehoff, "Does Perceived Organizational Support Mediate the Relationship Between Procedural Justice and Organizational Citizenship Behavior?" *Academy of Management Journal,* Vol. 41, No. 3, 1998, pp. 351–357.

127. D.W. Organ, "Organizational Citizenship Behavior: It's Construct Clean-Up Time," *Human Performance,* Vol. 10, 1997, pp. 85–98.

128. See: E. W. Morrison, "Role Definition and Organizational Citizenship Behavior: The Importance of Employee's Perspective," *Academy of Management Journal,* Vol. 37, 1994, pp. 1543–1567 and summarized by Greenberg and Baron, op. cit., pp. 372–373.

129. T. D. Allen and M. C. Rush, "The Effects of Organizational Citizenship Behavior on Performance Judgments: A Field Study and a Laboratory Experiment," *Journal of Applied Psychology,* Vol. 83, 1998, pp. 247–260.

130. See P. M. Podsakoff and S. B. MacKenzie, "Organizational Citizenship Behaviors and Sales Unit Effectiveness," *Journal of Marketing Research,* Vol. 31, No. 3, 1994, pp. 351–363; and Sandra M. Walz and Brian P. Niehoff, "Organizational Citizenship Behaviors and Their Effect on Organizational Effectiveness in Limited-Menu Restaurants," *Academy of Management Best Paper Proceedings,* 1996, pp. 307–311; P. M. Podsakoff, M. Ahearne and S. B. MacKenzie,

"Organizational Citizenship Behavior and the Quantity and Quality of Work Group Performance," *Journal of Applied Psychology,* April 1997, pp. 262–270; and Linn Van Dyne and Jeffrey A. LePine, "Helping and Voice Extra-Role Behaviors: Evidence of Construct and Predictive Validity," *Academy of Management Journal,* Vol. 41, No. 1, 1998, pp. 108–119.

131. See: Mark C. Bolino, "Citizenship and Impression Management: Good Soldiers or Good Actors?" *Academy of Management Review,* Vol. 24, No. 1, 1999, pp. 82–98 and Linn Van Dyne and Soon Ang, "Organizational Citizenship Behavior of Contingent Workers in Singapore," *Academy of Management Journal,* Vol. 41, No. 6, 1998, pp. 692–703.

Chapter 8 Footnote References and Supplemental Readings

1. John B. Miner, Bahman Ebrahimi and Jeffrey M. Wachtel, "How Deficiencies in Motivation to Manage Contribute to the United States' Competitiveness Problem (and What Can be Done about It)," *Human Resource Management,* Fall 1995, p. 363.

2. Martin G. Evans, "Organizational Behavior: The Central Role of Motivation," *Journal of Management,* Vol. 12, No. 2, 1986, p. 203.

3. The most frequently cited exception is the need for oxygen. A deficiency of oxygen in the body does not automatically set up a corresponding drive. This is a fear of high-altitude pilots. Unless their gauges show an oxygen leak or the increased intake of carbon dioxide sets up a drive, they may die of oxygen deficiency without a drive's ever being set up to correct the situation. The same is true of the relatively frequent deaths of teenagers parked in "lovers' lanes." Carbon monoxide leaks into the parked automobile, and they die from oxygen deficiency without its ever setting up a drive (to open the car door).

4. Spencer A. Rathus, *Psychology,* 4th ed., Holt, Rinehart & Winston, Fort Worth, Tex., 1990, p. 312.

5. Ronald E. Riggio, *Introduction to Industrial/Organizational Psychology,* Scott Foresman/Little, Brown, Glenview, Ill., 1990, p. 175.

6. Dean R. Spitzer, "Power Rewards: Rewards That Really Motivate," *Management Review,* May 1996, pp. 45–50.

7. Robert J. House and N. R. Aditya, "The Social Scientific Study of Leadership: Quo Vidis?" *Journal of Management,* Vol. 23, No. 4, 1997, pp. 409–473.

8. For examples of recent research on the achievement motive, see N. T. Feather, "Authoritarianism and Attitudes toward High Achieverism," *Journal of Personality and Social Psychology*, July 1993,

pp. 152–164 and Daniel Turban and Thomas L. Keon, "Organizational Attractiveness: An Interactionist Perspective," *Journal of Applied Psychology,* April 1993, pp. 184–193.

9. William Spangle, "Validity of Questionnaire and TAT Measures of Need for Achievement: Two Meta-Analyses," *Psychological Bulletin,* Vol. 112, No. 1, 1992, pp. 140–154.

10. For example, see Wayne Grossman, "Does Incentive Compensation Lower Executives' Willingness to Take Risks?" *Academy of Management Executive,* November 1995, pp. 91–92 and Randolph P. Beatty and Edward J. Zajac, "Managerial Incentives, Monitoring and Risk Bearing: A Study of Executive Compensation, Ownership, and Board Structure in Initial Public Offerings," *Administrative Science Quarterly,* Vol. 39, 1994, pp. 313–335.

11. David W. Johnson, Geoffrey Maruyama, Roger Johnson, Deborah Nelson and Linda Skon, "Effectiveness of Cooperative, Competitive, and Individualistic Goal Structures on Achievement: A Meta-Analysis," *Psychological Bulletin,* Vol. 89, No. 1, 1981, pp. 47–62.

12. R. de Charms and G. H. Moeller, "Values Expressed in American Children's Readers: 1800–1950," *Journal of Abnormal and Social Psychology,* Vol. 64, 1962, pp. 136–142.

13. Shawn C. O'Connor and Lorne K. Rosenblood, "Affiliation Motivation in Everyday Experience: A Theoretical Comparison," *Journal of Personality and Social Psychology,* Vol. 70, No. 3, 1996, pp. 513–522.

14. For example, see Kim S. Cameron, "Investigating Organizational Downsizing: Fundamental Issues," *Human Resource Management Journal,* Summer 1994, pp. 183–188 and James R. Morris, Wayne F. Cascio, and Clifford E. Young, "Downsizing After All These

Years," *Organizational Dynamics,* Winter 1999, pp. 78–87.

15. Lyman W. Porter, Edward E. Lawler, III and J. R. Hackman, *Behavior in Organizations*, McGraw-Hill, New York, 1975.

16. R. de Charms, *Personal Causation: The Internal Affective Determinants of Behavior,* Academic Press, New York, 1968. An example of recent measures of intrinsic and extrinsic motivation can be found in Frederic Guay, Robert J. Vallerand and Celine Blanchard, "On the Assessment of Situational Intrinsic and Extrinsic Motivation: The Situational Motivation Scale (SIMS)," *Motivation and Emotion,* Vol. 24, No. 3, 2000, pp. 175–213.

17. P. C. Jordan, "Effects of an Extrinsic Reward on Intrinsic Motivation: A Field Experiment," *Academy of Management Journal,* 1986, pp. 405–412.

18. Richard M. Ryan and Edward L. Deci, "Self-Determination Theory and the Facilitation of Intrinsic Motivation, Social Development, and Well-Being," *American Psychologist,* Vol. 55, 2000, pp. 68–78.

19. For example, see Daniel J. Bernstein, "Of Carrots and Sticks: A Review of Deci and Ryan's Intrinsic Motivation and Self-Determination in Human Behavior," *Journal of The Experimental Analysis of Behavior,* Vol. 54, 1990, pp. 323–332.

20. Terence R. Mitchell, "Motivation: New Directions for Theory, Research, and Practice," *Academy of Management Review,* January 1982, p. 86.

21. A. H. Maslow, "A Theory of Human Motivation," *Psychological Review,* July 1943, pp. 370–396.

22. Robert A. Baron, *Behavior in Organizations,* 2d ed., Allyn & Bacon, Boston, 1986, p. 78.

23. A. J. Kinicki, G. E. Prussia, and F. M. McKee-Ryan, "A Panel Study of Coping with Involuntary Job Loss," *Academy of Management Journal,* Vol. 43, No. 1, 2000, pp. 90–100.

24. Maureen L. Ambrose and Carol T. Kulik, "Old Friends, New Faces: Motivation Research in the 1990s," *Journal of Management,* Vol. 25, No. 3, 1999, pp. 231–292. Also see Kennon M. Sheldon, Andrew J. Elliot, Youngmee Kim and Tim Kasser "What Is Satisfying About Satisfying Events? Testing 10 Candidate Psychological Needs," *Journal of Personality and Social Psychology,* Vol. 80, No. 2, 2001, pp. 325–339.

25. For example, see S. Caudron, "Be Cool!" *Workforce,* April 1998, pp. 50–61.

26. Some examples of research using Vroom's concepts include Mark E. Tubbs, Donna M. Boehne and James G. Dahl, "Expectancy, Valence, and Motivational Force Functions in Goal-Setting Research: An Empirical Test," *Journal of Applied Psychology,* June 1993, pp. 361–373; N. T. Feather, "Expectancy-Value Theory and Unemployment Effects," *Journal of Occupational and Organizational Psychology,* December 1992, pp. 315–330; and Anthony J. Mento, Howard J. Klein, and Edwin A. Locke, "Relationship of Goal Level to Valence and Instrumentality," *Journal of Applied Psychology,* August 1992, pp. 395–405.

27. Anthony Dickinson, "Expectancy Theory in Animal Conditioning," in Stephen B. Klein and Robert R. Mowrer (Eds.), *Contemporary Learning Theories,* Erlbaum, Hillsdale, N.J., 1989, p. 280.

28. For example, see Dean R. Spitzer, "The Seven Deadly Demotivators," *Management Review*, November 1995, pp. 56–60.

29. Gary Blau, "Operationalizing Direction and Level of Effort and Testing Their Relationships to Individual Job Performance," *Organizational Behavior and Human Decision Processes,* June 1993, pp. 152–170.

30. Philip M. Podsakoff and Larry Williams, "The Relationship between Job Performance and Job Satisfaction," in Edwin Locke (Ed.), *Generalizing from Laboratory to Field Settings,* Lexington Books, Lexington, Mass., 1986, p. 244. Also see Edwin A. Locke and Gary P. Latham, A *Theory of Goal Setting and Task Performance,* Prentice Hall, Upper Saddle River, N.J., 1990, pp. 265–267 and E. Brian Peach and Daniel A. Wren, "Pay for Performance from Antiquity to the 1950's," *Journal of Organizational Behavior Management,* Vol. 12, 1992, pp. 5–26.

31. Oren Harari, "The Missing Link in Performance," *Management Review,* March 1995, pp. 21–24.

32. Erik P. Thompson, Shelly Chaiken and J. Douglas Hazlewood, "Need for Cognition and Desire for Control as Moderators of Extrinsic Reward Effects: A Person $\times$ Situation Approach to the Study of Intrinsic Motivation," *Journal of Personality and Social Psychology,* June 1993, pp. 987–999.

33. James N. Baron and Karen S. Cook, "Process and Outcome: Perspectives on the Distribution of Rewards in Organizations," *Administrative Science Quarterly*. Vol. 37, 1992, pp. 191–197.

34. James M. McFillen and Philip M. Podsakoff, "A Coordinated Approach to Motivation Can Increase Productivity," *Personnel Administrator,* July 1983, p. 46.

35. K. A. Karl, A. M. O'Leary-Kelly, and J. J. Martoccio, "The Impact of Feedback and Self-Efficacy on Performance in Training," *Journal of Organizational Behavior,* Vol. 14, 1993, pp. 379–394, and T. Janz, "Manipulating Subjective Expectancy Through Feedback: A Laboratory Study of the Expectancy-Performance Relationship," *Journal of Applied Psychology,* Vol. 67, 1982, pp. 480–485.

36. Robert A. Baron, *Behavior in Organizations,* Allyn & Bacon, Boston, 1983, p. 137.

37. Michael R. Carrell and John E. Dittrich, "Equity Theory: The Recent Literature, Methodological

Considerations, and New Directions," *Academy of Management Review,* April 1978, pp. 202–210.

38. Robert G. Lord and Jeffrey A. Hohenfeld, "Longitudinal Field Assessment of Equity Effects on the Performance of Major League Baseball Players," *Journal of Applied Psychology,* February 1979, pp. 19–26.

39. Dennis Duchon and Arthur G. Jago, "Equity and Performance of Major League Baseball Players: An Extension of Lord and Hohenfeld," *Journal of Applied Psychology,* December 1981, pp. 728–732.

40. Maureen L. Ambrose and Carol T. Kulik, "Old Friends, New Faces: Motivation Research in the 1990s," *Journal of Management,* Vol. 25, No. 3, 1999, pp. 231–292.

41. Larry W. Howard and Janis L. Miller, "Fair Pay for Fair Play: Estimating Pay Equity in Professional Baseball with Data Envelopment Analysis," *Academy of Management Journal,* August 1993, pp. 882–894.

42. Robert D. Bretz, Jr. and Steven L. Thomas, "Perceived Equity, Motivation, and Final-Offer Arbitration in Major League Baseball," *Journal of Applied Psychology,* June 1993, pp. 280–287.

43. Joseph W. Harder, "Play for Pay: Effect of Inequity in a Pay-for-Performance Context," *Administrative Science Quarterly,* June 1992, pp. 321–335.

44. See Jerald Greenberg and Robert A. Baron, *Behavior in Organizations,* 7th ed. Prentice-Hall, Upper Saddle River, N.J., 2000, pp. 142–148; A. Furnham, B. D. Kirkcaldy, and R. Lynn, "National Attitudes to Competitiveness, Money, and Work Among Young People: First, Second, and Third World Differences," *Human Relations,* Vol. 47, 1994, pp. 119–132; J. Greenberg, *The Quest for Justice on the Job.* Sage, Thousand Oaks, Calif., 1997; and R. Cropanzano and J. Greenberg, "Progress in Organizational Justice: Tunneling Through the Maze," in C. L. Cooper and I. T. Robertson (Eds.), *International Review of Industrial and Organizational Psychology,* Vol. 12, Wiley, New York, 1997.

45. See "Control in the Workplace and Its Health-Related Aspects," in S. L. Sauter, J. J. Hurrell and C. L. Cooper (Eds.), *Job Control and Worker Health,* Wiley, Chichester, England, 1989, pp. 129–159; D. C. Ganster and M. R. Fusilier, "Control in the Workplace," in C. L. Cooper and I. T. Robertson (Eds.), *International Review of Industrial and Organizational Psychology,* Wiley, Chichester, England, 1989, pp. 235–280; and Marilyn L. Fox, Deborah J. Dwyer, and Daniel C. Ganster, "Effects of Stressful Job Demands and Control on Physiological and Attitudinal Outcomes in a Hospital Setting," *Academy of Management Journal,* April 1993, pp. 289–318.

46. D. J. Dwyer and D. C. Ganster, "The Effects of Job Demands and Control on Employee Attendance and

47. For example, see Scott A. Snell, "Control Theory in Strategic Human Resource Management: The Mediating Effect of Administrative Information," *Academy of Management Journal,* June 1992, pp. 292–327.

48. Leisa D. Sargent and Deborah J. Terry, "The Effects of Work Control and Job Demands on Employee Adjustment and Work Performance," *Journal of Occupational and Organizational Psychology,* Vol. 71, 1998, pp. 219–236.

49. For some of the original development of agency theory, see M. C. Jensen and W. H. Meckling, "Theory of the Firm, Managerial Behavior, Agency Costs, and Ownership Structure," *Journal of Financial Economics,* Vol. 3, 1976, pp. 305–360. For recent applications of agency theory to the management literature, see Charles W. L. Hill and Thomas M. Jones, "Stakeholder-Agency Theory," *Journal of Management Studies,* March 1992, pp. 131–154.

50. See H. L. Tosi and L. R. Gomez-Mejia, "The Decoupling of CEO Pay and Performance: An Agency Theory Perspective," *Administrative Science Quarterly,* Vol. 34, 1989, pp. 169–189 and Luis R. Gomez-Mejia and David B. Balkin, "Determinants of Faculty Pay: An Agency Theory Perspective," *Academy of Management Journal,* December 1992, pp. 921–955.

51. Judi McLean Parks and Edward J. Conlon, "Compensation Contracts: Do Agency Theory Assumptions Predict Negotiated Agreements?" *Academy of Management Journal,* June 1995, pp. 821–838.

52. Kendall Roth and Sharon O'Donnell, "Foreign Subsidiary Compensation Strategy: An Agency Theory Perspective," *Academy of Management Journal,* June 1996, pp. 678–703.

53. Linda K. Stroh, Jeanne M. Brett, Joseph P. Baumann and Anne H. Reilly, "Agency Theory and Variable Pay Compensation Strategies," *Academy of Management Journal,* June 1996, pp. 751–767.

54. J. C. Combs and D. J. Ketchen, Jr., "Can Capital Scarcity Help Agency Theory Explain Franchising? Revisiting the Capital Scarcity Hypothesis," *Academy of Management Journal,* Vol. 42, No. 2, 1999, 196–207.

55. Anurag Sharma, "Professional as Agent: Knowledge Assymetry in Agency Exchange," *Academy of Management Review,* Vol. 22, No. 3, 1997, pp. 758–798.

56. Chip Heath, "On the Social Psychology of Agency Relationships: Lay Theories of Motivation Overemphasis Extrinsic Incentives," *Organizational Behavior and Human Decision Processes,* Vol. 78, No. 1, April 1999, pp. 25–62.

57. Michael Frese, Wolfgang Kring, Andrea Soose and Jeannette Zempel. "Personal Initiative at Work:

Differences between East and West Germany," *Academy of Management Journal,* February 1996, pp. 37–63.

58. Christopher J. Chipello, "Japan's Quality of Life," *The Wall Street Journal,* January 28, 1992, p. A9.

59. Peter Berger, quoted in "What Is Culture's Role in Economic Policy?" *The Wall Street Journal,* December 22, 1986, p. 1.

60. Lillian H. Chaney and Jeanette S. Martin, *Intercultural Business Communication,* Prentice Hall, Upper Saddle River, N.J., 1995, p. 44.

61. Simcha Ronen, *Comparative and Multinational Management,* Wiley, New York, 1986, p. 170.

62. Maureen L. Ambrose and Carol T. Kulik, "Old Friends, New Faces: Motivation Research in the 1990s," *Journal of Management,* Vol. 25, No. 3, 1999, pp. 231–292.

63. Dianne H. B. Welsh, Fred Luthans and Steven M. Sommer, "Managing Russian Factory Workers: The Impact of U.S.-Based Behavioral and Participative Techniques," *Academy of Management Journal,* February 1993, pp. 58–79.

64. K. I. Kim, H. J. Park and N. Suzuki, "Reward Allocations in the United States, Japan, and Korea: A Comparison of Individualistic and Collectivistic Cultures," *Academy of Management Journal,* Vol. 33, No. 2, 1990, pp. 198–199 and Greenberg and Baron, op. cit., p. 145.

65. Nancy J. Adler, *International Dimensions of Organizational Behavior,* 3d ed., South-Western, Cincinnati, Ohio, 1997, p. 166.

66. Edwin C. Nevis, "Cultural Assumption and Productivity: The United States and China," *Sloan Management Review,* Spring 1983, pp. 17–29.

67. G. Hofstede, "Motivation, Leadership, and Organization: Do American Theories Apply Abroad?" *Organizational Dynamics,* Summer 1980, p. 55.

68. A. Sagie, D. Elizur and H. Yamauchi, "The Structure and Strength of Achievement Motivation: A Cross-Cultural Comparison," *Journal of Organizational Behavior,* Vol. 17, 1996, pp. 431–444.

69. Adler, op. cit., p. 165.

70. N. A. Boyacigiller and N. J. Adler, "The Paraochial Dinosaur: Organizational Science in a Global Context," *Academy of Management Review,* Vol. 16, No. 3, 1991 pp. 262–290.

71. Kim, Park and Suzuki, op. cit., pp. 198–199, and Greenberg and Baron, op. cit., p. 145.

72. S. L. Mueller and L.D. Clarke, "Political-Economic Context and Sensitivity to Equity: Differences Between the United States and the Transition Economics of Central and Eastern Europe," *Academy of Management Journal,* Vol. 42, No. 3, 1998, pp. 319–329.

Chapter 9 Footnote References and Supplemental Readings

1. Martin E. P. Seligman and Mihaly Csikszentmihalyi, "Positive Psychology," *American Psychologist,* January 2000, p. 5.

2. Peter Frost, "Why Compassion Counts!" *Journal of Management Inquiry,* Vol. 8, No.2, June 1999, pp. 127–133.

3. See G. Oettingen, "Positive Fantasy and Motivation," in P. M. Gollwitzer and J. A. Bargh (Eds.), *The Psychology of Action: Linking Cognition and Motivation to Behavior,* Guillford Press, New York, 1996, pp. 236–259.

4. Daniel Goleman, *Emotional Intelligence,* Bantam Books, New York, 1995, p. 89.

5. Christopher Peterson, "The Future of Optimism," *American Psychologist,* January 2000, p. 45.

6. For example, see: Lionel Tiger, *Optimism: The Biology of Hope,* Simon & Schuster, New York, 1979, and S. E. Taylor, *Positive Illusions,* Basic Books, New York, 1989.

7. Martin E. P. Seligman, *Learned Optimism,* Pocket Books, New York, 1998 (originally published in 1991).

8. Ibid.

9. Christopher Peterson, "Meaning and Measurement of Explanatory Style," *Psychological Inquiry,* Vol. 2, 1991, pp. 1–10.

10. Peterson, "The Future of Optimism," op. cit., p. 47.

11. See Martin E. P. Seligman, *Helplessness: On Depression, Development and Death,* Freeman, San Francisco, 1975, and Seligman and Csikszentmihalyi, "Positive Psychology," op. cit., and Seligman, *Learned Optimism,* op. cit.

12. Peterson, op. cit., pp. 49–52.

13. M. F. Scheier and C. S. Carver, "The Effects of Optimism on Psychological and Physical Well-Being," *Cognitive Theory and Research,* Vol. 16, 1992, pp. 201–228.

14. See Selgiman, *Learned Optimism,* op. cit.

15. Peterson, op. cit., pp. 50–51.

16. Seligman, *Learned Optimism,* op. cit., pp. 99.

17. Ibid., pp. 102–104.

18. See: Richard Boyatzis, *The Competent Manager: A Model for Effective Performance,* Wiley, New York, 1982, and Lyle M. Spencer Jr. and Signe M. Spencer, *Competence at Work: Models for Superior Performance,* Wiley, New York, 1993.

19. For example, see R. J. House and B. Shamir, "Towards the Integration of Transformational, Charismatic, and Visionary Theories," in M. M. Chemers and R. Ayman (Eds.), *Leadership Theory and Research: Perspectives and Directions,* Academic Press, San Diego, Calif., 1993, pp. 81–108.

20. Martin M. Chemers, Carl B. Watson and Stephen T. May, "Dispositional Affect and Leadership Effectiveness: A Comparison of Self Esteem, Optimism, and Efficacy," *Personality and Social Psychology Bulletin,* Vol. 26, No. 3, 2000, pp. 267–277.

21. E. Ransdell, "They Sell Suits with Soul," *Fast Company,* October 1998, pp. 66–68.

22. Daniel Goleman, *Working with Emotional Intelligence,* Bantam Books, New York, 1998, p. 128.

23. Reported in Alan Bavley, "Researcher: Hope Leads to Greater Success," *Lincoln Journal Star,* March 24, 2000, p. 1A, 8A.

24. Goleman, *Emotional Intelligence,* op. cit., p. 87.

25. Seligman, *Learned Optimism,* op. cit., p. 48.

26. For example, see E. Statland, *The Psychology of Hope,* Jossey-Bass, San Francisco, 1969, and J. R. Averill, G. Catlin and K. K. Chon, *Rules of Hope,* Springer-Verlag, New York, 1990.

27. C. R. Snyder, *The Psychology of Hope: You Can Get There from Here,* Free Press, New York, 1994. Also see Peterson, "The Future of Optimism," op. cit., p. 48 for a summary of Snyder's work.

28. See C. R. Snyder (Ed.), *Handbook of Hope: Theory, Measures, and Applications,* Academic Press, San Diego, 2000, pp. 13–17.

29. For the latest version of the "Hope Scale," see C. R. Snyder, S. C. Sympson, F. C. Ybasco, T. F. Borders, M. A. Babyak and R. L. Higgins, "Development and Validation of the State Hope Scale," *Journal of Personality and Social Psychology,* Vol. 70, 1996, pp. 321–335.

30. For examples of recent studies see: L. A. Curry, C. R. Snyder, D. L. Cook, B. C. Ruby and M. Rehm, "Role of Hope in Academic and Sport Achievement," *Journal of Personality and Social Psychology,* Vol. 73, 1997, pp. 1257–1267.

31. Spencer and Spencer, op. cit.

32. S. Kirk and G. Koeske, "The Fate of Optimism: A Longitudinal Study of Case Managers' Hopefulness and Subsequent Morale," *Research in Social Work Practice,* January 1995. Also see S. Taylor and J. D. Brown, "Illusion and Well-Being: A Social Psychological Perspective on Mental Health." *Psychological Bulletin,* Vol. 103, 1988, 193–210.

33. Seligman and Csikszentmihalyi, op. cit., p. 9.

34. Ed Diener, "Subjective Well-Being: The Science of Happiness and a Proposal for a National Index," *American Psychologist,* January 2000, p. 34.

35. See Ibid., and Ed Diener, Eunkook M. Suh, Richard E. Lucas and Heidi L. Smith, "Subjective Well-Being: Three Decades of Progress," *Psychological Bulletin,* Vol. 125, No. 2, 1999, pp. 276–302. The discussion in this section largely draws from these two articles.

36. See Diener, op. cit., p. 34, and E. Suh, E. Diener, S. Oishi and H. Triandis, "The Shifting Basis of Life Satisfaction Judgements Across Cultures: Emotions Versus Norms," *Journal of Personality and Social Psychology,* Vol. 74, 1998, pp. 482–493.

37. W. Wilson, "Correlates of Avowed Happiness," *Psychological Bulletin,* Vol. 67, 1967, pp. 294–306.

38. Diener, op. cit., p. 40.

39. Ibid., p. 34.

40. For a review of the measures, see Ibid., pp. 34–36. For the commonly used Satisfaction with Life Scale see W. Pavot and E. Diener, "Review of the Satisfaction with Life Scale," *Psychological Assessment,* Vol. 5, 1993, pp. 164–172.

41. Diener, et. al., op. cit., p. 279.

42. See: A. Tellegen, D. T. Lykken, T. J. Bouchard, K. J. Wilcox, N. L. Segal and S. Rich, "Personality Similarity in Twins Reared Apart and Together," *Journal of Personality and Social Psychology,* Vol. 54, 1988, pp. 1031–1039, and D. Lykken and A. Tellegen, "Happiness Is a Stochastic Phenomenon," *Psychological Science,* Vol. 7, 1996, pp. 186–189.

43. See Diener, et. al., op. cit., p. 280 for a review, and D. Watson and L. A. Clark, "Negative Affectivity: The Disposition to Experience Negative Affective States," *Psychological Bulletin,* Vol. 96, 1984, pp. 465–490, and D. Watson and L. A. Clark, "Extraversion and Its Positive Emotional Core," in R. Hogan, J. Johnson and S. Briggs (Eds.), *Handbook of Personality Psychology,* Academic Press, San Diego, 1997, pp. 767–793.

44. Kristina M. DeNeve and Harris Cooper, "The Happy Personality: A Meta-Analysis of 137 Personality Traits and Subjective Well-Being," *Psychological Bulletin,* Vol. 124, 1998, pp. 197–229.

45. N. Cantor and C. A. Sanderson, "Life Task Participation and Well Being: The Importance of Taking Part in Daily Life," in D. Kahneman, E. Diener and N. Schwarz (Eds.), *Well Being: The Foundations of Hedonic Psychology,* Russell Sage Foundation, New York, 1999.

46. E. Diener and F. Fujita, "Resources, Personal Strivings, and Subjective Well-Being: A Monothetic and Idiographic Approach," *Journal of Personality and Social Psychology,* Vol. 68, 1995, pp. 926–935.

47. S. Oishi, E. Diener, E. Suh and R. E. Lucas, "Values as a Moderator in Subjective Well-Being," *Journal of Personality,* Vol. 67, 1999, pp. 157–184.

48. R. A. Emmons, "Abstract Versus Concrete Goals: Personal Striving Level, Physical Illness, and Psychological Well-Being," *Journal of Personality and Social Psychology,* Vol. 62, 1992, pp. 292–300, and M. Csikszentmihalyi, *Flow: The Psychology of Optimal Experience,* Harper Perennial, New York, 1990.

49. Diener et. al., op. cit., p. 285.

50. See Diener, op. cit., p. 37.

51. E. Suh, E. Diener and F. Fujita, "Events and Subjective Well-Being: Only Recent Events Matter," *Journal of Personality and Social Psychology,* Vol. 70, 1996, pp. 1091–1102.

52. See Diener, op. cit., p. 37 and A. E. Clark, "Are Wages Habit Forming? Evidence from Micro Data," *Journal of Economic Behavior and Organization,* Vol. 39, pp. 179–200.

53. S. Folkman, "Positive Psychological States and Coping with Severe Stress," *Social Science and Medicine,* Vol. 45, 1997, pp. 1207–1221.

54. This summary of SWB is found in Diener et. al., op. cit., pp. 294–295.

55. See Diener, op. cit., pp. 39–40; Ed Diener, Marissa Diener and Carol Diener, "Factors Predicting the Subjective Well-Being of Nations," *Journal of Personality and Social Psychology,* Vol. 69, 1995, pp. 851–864; E. Diener and S. Oishi, "Income and Subjective Well-Being Across Nations," in E. Diener and E. Suh (Eds.), *Subjective Well-Being Across Nations,* MIT Press, Cambridge, MA, in press; and E. Diener and M. Diener, "Cross Cultural Correlates of Life Satisfaction and Self-Esteem," *Journal of Personality and Social Psychology,* Vol. 68, 1995, pp. 653–663.

56. Diener, op. cit., pp. 40–41.

57. M. Tait, M. Y. Padgett and T. T. Baldwin, "Job Satisfaction and Life Satisfaction: A Reexamination of the Strength of the Relationship and Gender Effects as a Function of the Date of the Study," *Journal of Applied Psychology,* Vol. 74, 1989, pp. 502–507.

58. T. A. Judge and C. L. Hulin, "Job Satisfaction as a Reflection of Disposition: A Multiple Source Causal Analysis," *Organizational Behavior and Human Decision Processes,* Vol. 56, 1993, pp. 388–421, and T. A. Judge and S. Watanabe, "Another Look at the Job Satisfaction–Life Satisfaction Relationship," *Journal of Applied Psychology,* Vol. 78, 1993, pp. 939–948.

59. M. J. Stones and A. Kozma, "Happy Are They Who Are Happy: A Test Between Two Causal Models of Happiness and Its Correlates," *Experimental Aging Research,* Vol. 12, 1986, pp. 23–29.

60. Clark, op. cit. and A. E. Clark and A. J. Oswald, "Unhappiness and Unemployment," *Economic Journal,* Vol. 104, 1994, pp. 648–659.

61. Stephen P. Robbins, *Organizational Behavior,* 9th ed., Prentice Hall, Upper Saddle River, N.J., 2001, p. 104. Also see N. H. Frijda, "Moods, Emotion Episodes and Emotion," in M. Lewis and J. M. Haviland (Eds.), *Handbook of Emotions,* Guliford Press, New York, 1993, pp. 381–403.

62. See Cheryl L. Rusting, "Personality, Mood, and Cognitive Processing of Emotional Information," *Psychological Bulletin,* Vol. 124, No. 2, 1998, pp. 165–196.

63. Ibid.

64. See: J. M. Kidd, "Emotion: An Absent Presence in Career Theory," *Journal of Vocational Behavior,* June 1998, pp. 275–288.

65. The classic analysis of the limits of rational models is found in Herbert A. Simon, *Administrative Behavior,* 2d ed., Macmillan, New York, 1957, and Herbert A. Simon, *The New Science of Management Decision,* Harper, New York, 1960.

66. See: R. S. Lazarus, *Emotion and Adaptation,* Oxford University Press, New York, 1991, and J. A. Russell and L. F. Barrett, "Core Affect, Prototypical Emotional Episodes, and Other Things Called Emotion: Dissecting the Elephant," *Journal of Personality and Social Psychology,* May 1999, pp. 805–819.

67. R. D. Woodworth, *Experimental Psychology,* Holt, New York, 1938.

68. See J. A. Morris and D. C. Feldman, "The Dimensions, Antecedents, and Consequences of Emotional Labor," *Academy of Management Review,* Vol. 21, 1996, pp. 986–1010.

69. Karen Pugliese, "The Consequences of Emotional Labor: Effects on Work Stress, Job Satisfaction, and Well-Being," *Motivation and Emotion,* Vol. 23, No. 2, 1999, pp. 125–153.

70. Quoted in Kevin Friberg and Jackie Friberg, *Nuts!,* Bard Press, Austin, TX, 1996, p. 65.

71. For example, see Rusting, op. cit. and Joanne Martin, Kathleen Knopoff and Christine Beckman, "An Alternative to Bureaucratic Impersonality and Emotional Labor: Bounded Emotionality at the Body Shop," *Administrative Science Quarterly,* Vol. 43, 1998, pp. 429–469.

72. For example, see Louisa Wah, "The Emotional Tightrope," *Management Review,* January 2000, pp. 38–42, and Cheryl Comeau-Kirschner and Louisa Wah, "Holistic Management," *Management Review,* December 1999, pp. 27–32.

73. Quoted in Carla D'nan Bass, "Expert: Forced Emotions Draining," *Lincoln Journal Star,* February 27, 2000, p. 1D.

74. See B. E. Ashforth and R. R. Humphrey, "Emotion in the Workplace: A Reappraisal," *Human Relations,* Vol. 48, 1995, pp. 97–125.

75. See A. R. Hochschild, "Emotion Work, Feeling Rules, and Social Structure," *American Journal of Sociology,* November 1979, pp. 551–575, and L. A. King, "Ambivalence Over Emotional Expression and Reading Emotions," *Journal of Personality and Social Psychology,* March 1998, pp. 753–762.

76. Howard Gardner, *Frames of Mind: The Theory of Multiple Intelligences,* Basic Books, New York, 1983. A 10th anniversary edition, with a new introduction was published in 1993.

77. Howard Gardner, "Reflections on Multiple Intelligences: Myths and Messages," *Phi Delta Kappa,* November 1995, pp. 200–203; 206–209.

78. Howard Gardner, *Multiple Intelligences: The Theory in Practice,* Basic Books, New York, 1993.

79. Lou Russell, *The Accelerated Learning Fieldbook,* Jossey-Bass/Pfeiffer, San Francisco, 1999. Chapter 4 summarizes Gardner's MI and how to apply it for training in the workplace.

80. Frank L. Schmidt and John E. Hunter, "The Validity and Utility of Selection Methods in Personnel Psychology: Practical and Theoretical Implications of 85 Years of Research Findings," *Psychological Bulletin,* Vol. 124, No. 2, 1998, pp. 262–274. Also see Frank L. Schmidt and John E. Hunter, "Select on Intelligence," in Edwin A. Locke (Ed.), *The Blackwell Handbook of Principles of Organizational Behavior,* Blackwell, Oxford, UK, 2000, pp. 3–14.

81. P. Slovey and J. D. Mayer, "Emotional Intelligence," *Imagination, Cognition and Personality,* Vol. 9, No. 3, 1990, p. 189.

82. Daniel Goleman, *Working with Emotional Intelligence,* Bantam Books, New York, 1998, p. 317.

83. Nancy Gibbs, "The EQ Factor," *Time,* October 2, 1995, p. 61.

84. Daniel Goleman, *Emotional Intelligence,* Bantam Books, New York, 1995, p. xiii.

85. Goleman, *Working with Emotional Intelligence,* op. cit., p. 7.

86. For examples of the criticism see Bridget Murray, "Does Emotional Intelligence Matter in the Workplace," *The APA Monitor,* Vol. 29, No. 7, July 1998, pp. 1–3, and M. Davies, L. Stankov and R. D. Roberts, "Emotional Intelligence: In Search of an Elusive Construct," *Journal of Personality and Social Psychology,* October 1998, pp. 989–1015.

87. Reported in Kim Cameron, "Developing Emotional Intelligence at the Weatherhead School of Management," *Strategy: The Magazine of Weatherhead School of Management,* Winter 1999, pp. 2–3. Also see "The Feelgood Factor," *The Economist,* February 17, 2001, p. 59.

88. Goleman, Working with Emotional Intelligence, op. cit., p. 7.

89. See Davies, et al., op. cit., and A. Fisher, "Success Secret: A High Emotional IQ," *Fortune,* October 26, 1998, p. 294.

90. Goleman, *Working with Emotional Intelligence,* op. cit., pp. 4–5.

91. Ibid., p. 315.

92. Quy Nguyen Huy, "Emotional Capability, Emotional Intelligence, and Radical Change," *Academy of Management Review,* Vol. 24, No. 2, 1999, pp. 325–345.

93. For a summary of this literature, see Cameron, op. cit., pp. 2–3. Also see Robert Sternberg, *Successful Intelligence,* Simon & Schuster, New York, 1996.

94. Gibbs, op. cit., p. 64.

95. See J. Stuller, "EQ: Edging Toward Respectability," *Training,* June 1997, pp. 43–48; R. K. Cooper, "Applying Emotional Intelligence in the Workplace," *Training and Development,* December 1997, pp. 31–38; and "HR Pulse: Emotional Intelligence," *HR Magazine,* January 1998, p. 19.

96. Robert Kelley and Janet Caplan, "How Bell Labs Creates Star Performers," *Harvard Business Review,* July–August, 1993, pp. 128–139.

97. Gibbs, op. cit.

98. Schmidt and Hunter, "Select on Intelligence," op. cit., p. 3.

99. Reported in "Leadership: Older Bosses Are Best," *Management Review,* May 1999, p. 7.

100. Daniel Goleman, "Leadership that Gets Results," *Harvard Business Review,* March–April 2000, pp. 79–90. For an earlier article on leadership and EI, see Daniel Goleman, "What Makes a Leader?" *Harvard Business Review,* November–December, 1998, pp. 92–102.

101. Reported in Goleman, "Leadership that Gets Results," op. cit., p. 81.

102. See footnote 95 and "Unconventional Smarts," *Across the Board,* January 1998, pp. 22–23.

103. Presented at the Conference, "Emotional Intelligence: Optimizing Human Performance in the Workplace," September 28, 1999, Chicago Marriott Downtown. Also see Vanessa Urch Druskat and Steven B. Wolff, "Building the Emotional Intelligence of Groups," *Harvard Business Review,* March 2001, pp. 81–90.

104. Ibid.

105. J. Cheung, "Emotions' Class for Civil Servants," *South China Morning Post,* September 14, 1998, p. 3, and L. Yeung, "Stress-Busters Strive for Balance," *South China Morning Post,* October 18, 1998, p. 2. Reported in Steven L. McShane and Mary Ann Von Glinow, *Organizational Behavior,* Irwin/McGraw-Hill, Burr Ridge, Ill., 2000, p. 213.

106. Goleman, *Emotional Intelligence,* op. cit., p. 89, and Snyder, *Handbook of Hope,* op. cit., p. 15.

107. Albert Bandura, *Social Foundations of Thought and Action,* Prentice Hall, Upple Saddle River, N.J., 1986. For the many accolades for this landmark book, see: "Book Review Essays on Bandura's *Social Foundations of Thought and Action,*" *Psychological Inquiry,* Vol. 1, No. 1, 1990, pp. 86–100.

108. For a comprehensive summary of the body of knowledge see Albert Bandura, *Self-Efficacy: The Exercise of Control,* W. H. Freeman, New York, 1997. Also see J. E. Maddux, *Self-Efficacy, Adaptation and Adjustment: Theory, Research, and Application,* Plenum Press, New York, 1995.

109. For a summary of the various applications see Bandura, *Self-Efficacy: The Exercise of Control,* op. cit., and especially for research on the workplace see Alexander D. Stajkovic and Fred Luthans, "Self-Efficacy and Work-Related Performance: A Meta-Analysis," *Psychological Bulletin,* Vol. 124, No. 2, 1998, pp. 240–261.

110. See: Bandura, *Self-Efficacy: The Exercise of Control,* op. cit., and specifically Albert Bandura, "Social Cognitive Theory: An Agentic Perspective," *Asian Journal of Social Psychology,* Vol. 2, 1999, p. 21.

111. Albert Bandura, "Cultivate Self-Efficacy for Personal and Organizational Effectiveness," in Edwin A. Locke (Ed.), *The Blackwell Handbook of Principles of Organizational Behavior,* Blackwell, Oxford, U.K., 2000, p. 120.

112. Albert Bandura, "Self-Efficacy Mechanism in Human Agency," *American Psychologist,* Vol. 37, 1982, p. 122.

113. Alexander D. Stajkovic and Fred Luthans, "Social Cognitive Theory and Self-Efficacy: Going Beyond Traditional Motivational and Behavioral Approaches," *Organizational Dynamics,* Spring 1998, p. 66.

114. See: Stajkovic and Luthans, "Self-Efficacy and Work-Related Performance," op. cit., p. 244 for a review of the relationship and status of specific versus general efficacy. The discussion in this section mainly draws from this source.

115. For example, see D. Eden and Y. Zuk, "Seasickness as a Self-Fulfilling Prophecy: Raising Self-Efficacy to Boost Performance at Sea," *Journal of Applied Psychology,* Vol. 80, 1995, pp. 628–635, and M. Sherer, J. E. Maddux, B. Mercadante, S. Prentice-Dunn, B. Jacobs and R. W. Rogers, "The Self-Efficacy Scale: Construction and Validation," *Psychological Reports,* Vol. 51, 1982, pp. 663–671.

116. Bandura, *Social Foundations of Thought and Action,* op. cit., and Bandura, *Self-Efficacy: The Exercise of Control,* op. cit. For a similar conceptual argument see R. S. Lazarus, *Emotion and Adaptation,* Oxford University Press, New York, 1991, and R. S. Lazarus, "Vexing Research Problems Inherent in Cognitive Mediational Theories of Emotion—and Some Solutions," *Psychological Inquiry,* Vol. 6, 1995, pp. 183–196.

117. See: Eden and Zuk, op. cit., p. 629 and Sherer, et. al., op. cit., p. 664.

118. Bandura, *Self-Efficacy: The Exercise of Control,* op. cit., p. 42.

119. See: Bandura, *Self-Efficacy: The Exercise of Control,* op. cit., and D. Cervone, "Social-Cognitive Mechanisms and Personality Coherence: Self-Knowledge, Situational Beliefs, and Cross-Situational Coherence in Perceived Self-Efficacy," *Psychological Science,* Vol. 8, 1997, pp. 43–50.

120. See Stajkovic and Luthans, "Social Cognitive Theory and Self-Efficacy," op. cit., pp. 67–68 for a summary of the differences. This section's discussion is largely drawn from this source.

121. See: Donald G. Gardner and Jon L. Pierce, "Self-Esteem and Self-Efficacy Within the Organizational Context," *Group and Organization Management,* Vol. 23, No. 1, 1998, pp. 48–70.

122. See Stajkovic and Luthans, "Social Cognitive Theory and Self-Efficacy," op. cit., pp. 67–68.

123. Ibid., p. 68.

124. See Robert F. Mager, "No Self-Efficacy, No Performance," *Training,* April 1992, pp. 32, 34 for a summary of the effective of efficacy.

125. Bandura, "Cultivate Self-Efficacy for Personal and Organizational Effectiveness," op. cit., pp. 120–121.

126. Ibid., and E. A. Locke and G. P. Latham, *A Theory of Goal Setting and Task Performance,* Prentice Hall, Upper Saddle River, N.J., 1990.

127. For example, see: Fred Luthans, Alexander Stajkovic and Elina Ibrayeva, "Environmental and Psychological Challenges Facing Entrepreneurial Development in Transitional Economies," *Journal of World Business,* Vol. 35, No. 1, 2000, pp. 95–110.

128. Bandura, "Cultivate Self-Efficacy for Personal and Organizational Effectiveness," op. cit., p. 121.

129. In addition to Bandura's seminal book, *Self-Efficacy: The Exercise of Control,* op. cit., which is based on several hundred studies and his recent article aimed at performance, "Cultivate Self-Efficacy for Personal and Organizational Effectiveness," op. cit., see the following meta-analyses relating self-efficacy to performance: G. Holden, "The Relationship of Self-Efficacy Appraisals to Subsequent Health Related Outcomes: A Meta-Analysis," *Social Work in Health Care,* Vol. 16, 1991, pp. 53–93; G. Holden, M. S. Moncher, S. P. Schinke and K. M. Barker, "Self-Efficacy of Children and Adolescents: A Meta-Analysis," *Psychological Reports,* Vol. 66, 1990, pp. 1044–1060; K. D. Multon, S. D. Brown and

R. W. Lent, "Relation of Self-Efficacy Beliefs to Academic Outcomes: A Meta-Analytic Investigation," *Journal of Counseling Psychology,* Vol. 38, 1991, pp. 30–38; and Stajkovic and Luthans, "Self-Efficacy and Work-Related Performance," op. cit.

130. Albert Bandura, "Social Cognitive Theory of Personality," in L. Pervin and O. John (Eds.), *Handbook of Personality,* 2nd ed., Guilford, New York, 1999, p. 181.

131. Bandura, "Cultivate Self-Efficacy for Personal and Organizational Effectiveness," op. cit., p. 126, and Christine M. Shea and Jane M. Howell, "Efficacy-Performance Spirals: An Empirical Test," *Journal of Management,* Vol. 26, No. 4, 2000, pp. 791–812.

132. Bandura, "Social Cognitive Theory of Personality," op. cit., p. 181.

133. Robert F. Mager, "No Self-Efficacy, No Performance," *Training,* April 1992, p. 36.

134. Albert Bandura, "Self-Efficacy: Toward a Unifying Theory of Behavioral Change," *Psychological Review,* Vol. 84, 1977, p. 193.

135. For the full review including references on all the applications, see Daniel Cervone, "Thinking About Self-Efficacy," *Behavior Modification,* Vol. 24, No. 1, 2000, p. 33. Also see Bandura, *Self-Efficacy: The Exercise of Control,* op. cit.

136. Stajkovic and Luthans, "Self-Efficacy and Work-Related Performance: A Meta-Analysis," op. cit.

137. Ibid., p. 252.

138. R. E. Wood, A. J. Mento and E. A. Locke, "Task Complexity as a Moderator of Goal Effects: A Meta Analysis," *Journal of Applied Psychology,* Vol. 72, 1987, pp. 416–425.

139. A. N. Kluger and A. DeNisi, "The Effects of Feedback Interventions on Performance: A Historical Review, A Meta-Analysis, and A Preliminary Feedback Intervention Theory," *Psychological Bulletin,* Vol. 119, 1996, pp. 254–284.

140. Alexander D. Stajkovic and Fred Luthans, "A Meta-Analysis of the Effects of Organizational Behavior Modification on Task Performance," *Academy of Management Journal,* Vol. 40, 1997, pp. 1122–1149.

141. For the extensive review of the literature from which this conclusion is drawn, see Stajkovic and Luthans, "Self-Efficacy and Work-Related Performance: A Meta-Analysis," op. cit., p. 253.

142. Bandura, *Self-Efficacy: The Exercise of Control,* op. cit., Chapter 12.

143. Bandura, "Cultivate Self Efficacy for Personal and Organizational Effectiveness," op. cit.

144. See E. A. Locke, E. Frederick, C. Lee and P. Bobko, "Effects of Self-Efficacy, Goals and Task Strategies on Task Performance," *Journal of Applied Psychology,* Vol. 69, 1984, pp. 241–251, and Stajkovic and Luthans, "Social Cognitive Theory and Self-Efficacy," op. cit., pp. 68–69.

145. C. Lee and P. Bobko, "Self-Efficacy Beliefs: Comparison of Five Measures," *Journal of Applied Psychology,* Vol. 79, 1994, pp. 364–369.

146. Bandura, *Self-Efficacy: The Exercise of Control,* op. cit., p. 45.

147. See: Bandura, "Cultivate Self-Efficacy for Personal and Organizational Effectiveness," op. cit., pp. 126–133.

148. M. E. Gist, "The Influence of Training Method on Self-Efficacy and Idea Generation Among Managers," *Personnel Psychology,* Vol. 42, 1989, pp. 787–805.

149. Bandura, "Cultivating Self-Efficacy for Personal and Organizational Effectiveness," op. cit., p. 132, and Locke and Latham, op. cit.

150. Ibid., Gist, op. cit., M. E. Gist, A. G. Bavetta and C. K. Stevens, "Transfer Training Method," *Personnel Psychology,* Vol. 43, 1990, pp. 501–523.

151. For example, see S. M. Jex and P. D. Bliese, "Efficacy Beliefs as a Moderator of the Impact of Work-Related Stressors: A Multilevel Study," *Journal of Applied Psychology,* Vol. 84, 1999, pp. 349–361, and John Schaubroeck, Simon S. K. Lam, and Jia LinXie, "Collective Efficacy versus Self-Efficacy in Coping Responses to Stressors and Control," *Journal of Applied Psychology,* Vol. 85, No. 4, 2000, pp. 512–525.

152. H. K. S. Laschruger and J. Shamian, "Staff Nurses' and Nurse Managers' Perceptions of Job-Related Empowerment and Managerial Self-Efficacy," *Journal of Nursing Administration,* Vol. 24, 1994, pp. 38–47 and Steve Alper, Dean Tjosvold and Kenneth S. Law, "Conflict Management, Efficacy, and Performance in Organizational Teams," *Personnel Psychology,* Vol. 53, 2000, pp. 625–642.

153. For example, see Christina B. Gibson, Amy E. Randel and P. Christopher Earley, "Understanding Group Efficacy," *Group & Organization Management,* Vol. 25, No. 1, 2000, pp. 67–97, and C. B. Gibson, "Do They Do What They Believe They Can? Group Efficacy and Group Effectiveness Across Tasks and Cultures," *Academy of Management Journal,* Vol. 42, 1999, pp. 138–152.

154. S. K. Parker, "Enhancing Role Breadth Self-Efficacy: The Roles of Job Enrichment and Other Organizational Interventions," *Journal of Applied Psychology,* Vol. 83, 1998, pp. 835–852.

155. See P. C. Earley and T. R. Lituchy, "Delineating Goal and Efficacy Effects: A Test of Three Models," *Journal of Applied Psychology,* February 1991, pp. 81–98, and Locke and Latham, op. cit.

156. See House and Shamir, op. cit.

157. See Chemers, Watson and May, op. cit.

Chapter 10 Footnote References and Supplemental Readings

1. Fred Luthans, Richard M. Hodgetts and Stuart A. Rosenkrantz, *Real Managers,* Ballinger, Cambridge, Mass., 1988, p. 27 and Chap. 6.

2. Mzamo P. Mangaliso, "The Strategic Usefulness of Management Information as Perceived by Middle Managers," *Journal of Management,* Vol. 21, No. 2, 1995, pp. 231–250.

3. Chester I. Barnard, *The Functions of the Executive,* Harvard University Press, Cambridge, Mass., 1938, p. 90.

4. Ibid., pp. 175–181.

5. Eric M. Eisenberg and Marsha G. Witten, "Reconsidering Openness in Organizational Communication," *Academy of Management Review,* July 1987, pp. 418–426.

6. Fred Luthans and Janet K. Larsen, "How Managers Really Communicate," *Human Relations,* Vol. 39, No. 2, 1986, pp. 161–178.

7. Ibid.

8. Bernard J. Reilly and Joseph A. Di Angelo, Jr., "Communication: A Cultural System of Meaning and Value," *Human Relations,* February 1990, p. 129.

9. John M. Ivancevich and Michael T. Matteson, *Organizational Behavior and Management,* 3d ed., Irwin, Burr Ridge, Ill., 1993, p. 633.

10. Raymond S. Nickerson, "How We Know—And Sometimes Misjudge—What Others Know: Imputing One's Own Knowledge to Others," *Psychological Review,* Vol. 125, No. 6, 1999, pp. 737–759.

11. Aubrey Fisher, *Small Group Decision Making,* McGraw-Hill, New York, 1974, p. 23.

12. D. Clark, "Managing the Mountain," *Wall Street Journal,* June 21, 1999, p. R 4.

13. R. L. Daft and R. H. Lengel, "Information Richness: A New Approach to Managerial Behavior and Organizational Design," B. M. Staw and L. L. Cummings (Eds.), in *Research in Organizational Behavior.* JAI Press, Greenwich, Conn., 1984, p. 196.

14. Ibid, p. 197.

15. R. E. Rice and D. E. Shook, "Relationships of Job Categories and Organizational Levels to Use of Communication Channels, Including Electronic Mail: A Meta-Analysis and Extension," *Journal of Management Studies,* March 1990, pp. 195–229.

16. "Wireless-Communication Technology Exploding," *The New York Times,* reported in *Omaha World Herald,* September 21, 1993, p. 1.

17. "Wireless-Communication Technology Exploding," op. cit.

18. Randall L. Tobias, "Telecommunications in the 1990s," *Business Horizons,* January–February 1990, p. 82.

19. "Fogen's First Law," *Across the Board,* January 2000, p. 78.

20. Jenny C. McCune, "The Birth of Tech Terms," *Management Review,* February 1999, p. 11.

21. "Telecommuting: An Idea Whose Time Has Come," *HR Focus,* November 1995, p. 1.

22. See George M. Piskurich, "Making Telecommuting Work," *Training and Development,* February 1996, pp. 22–33.

23. Ibid, pp. 24–25.

24. Don Hellriegel, John W. Slocum, Jr. and Richard W. Woodman, *Organizational Behavior,* 4th ed., West, St. Paul, Minn., 1986, p. 221.

25. Paul Preston, *Communication for Managers,* Prentice Hall, Upper Saddle River, N.J., 1979, p. 161.

26. Martin G. Groder, "Incongruous Behavior: How to Read the Signals," *Bottom Line,* March 30, 1983, p. 13.

27. John T. Molloy, *Dress for Success,* Warner, New York, 1975, p. 46.

28. V. Hale Starr, quoted in "Expert: Non-Verbal Body Language Counts," *Omaha World Herald,* December 20, 1982, p. 2.

29. Daniel Goleman, *Emotional Intelligence,* Bantam, New York, 1995, and Nancy Gibbs, "The EQ Factor," *Time,* October 2, 1995, pp. 60–66.

30. See Robert S. Feldman, *Understanding Psychology,* 2d ed., McGraw-Hill, New York, 1990, pp. 329–330.

31. For an account of the work done in Albania, see Fred Luthans and Sang M. Lee, "There Are Lessons to Be Learned as Albania Undergoes a Paradigm Shift," *International Journal of Organizational Analysis,* Vol. 2, No. 1, 1994, pp. 5–17 and Fred Luthans and Laura Riolli, "Albania and Bora," *Academy of Management Executive,* August 1997, pp. 61–72.

32. Joanne Yates and Wanda J. Orlikowski, "Genres of Organizational Communication: A Structural Approach to Studying Communication and Media," *Academy of Management Review,* April 1992, p. 299.

33. James L. Heskett, *Managing in the Service Economy,* Harvard Business School Press, Boston, 1986, p. 127.

34. "Speaking to the Boss," *Training,* February 2000, p. 28.

35. For example, see James W. Smither, Manuel London, Nicholas L. Vasilopoulos, Richard R. Reilly, Roger E. Millsap, and Nat Salvemini, "An Examination of the Effects of an Upward Feedback Program over Time," *Personal Psychology,* Vol. 48, 1995, p. 432; A. N. Kluger and A. DeNisi, "The Effects of Feedback Interventions on Performance," *Psychological Bulletin,* Vol. 119, 1996, pp. 254–284; and Todd J. Maurer and Jerry K. Palmer, "Management Development Intentions

Following Feedback," *The Journal of Management Development,* Vol. 18, No. 9, 1999, pp. 733–751.

36. Patricia Schiff Estess, "Open-Book Policy," *Entrepreneur,* March 2000, pp. 130–131.

37. K. Denise Bane, "Gaining Control By Losing It? The Dilemma of Entrepreneurial Information," *Academy of Management Executive,* Vol. 11, No. 2, 1997, pp. 80–81.

38. See W. Tornow and M. London, *Maximizing the Value of 360-Degree Feedback: A Process for Successful Individual and Organizational Development,* Jossey-Bass, San Francisco, 1998, and Todd J. Maurer, Stephane Brutus, John Fleenor, and Manuel London, "Does 360-Degree Feedback Work in Different Industries?" *Journal of Management Development,* Vol. 17, No. 3, 1998, pp. 177–190.

39. Albert Bandura, *Social Foundations of Thought and Action,* Prentice Hall, Upper Saddle River, N.J., 1986; Alexander D. Stajkovic and Fred Luthans, "Social Cognitive Theory and Self-Efficacy," *Organizational Dynamics,* Vol. 26, No. 4, 1998, pp. 62–74; and Clive Fletcher and Caroline Baldry, "A Study of Individual Differences and Self-Awareness in the Context of Multi-Source Feedback," *Journal of Occupational and Organizational Psychology,* Vol. 73, 2000, pp. 303–319.

40. See the special issue on trust in *Academy of Management Review,* Vol. 23, No. 2, 1998.

41. See: Jennifer J. Salopek, "The Young and the Rest of Us," *Training and Development,* February 2000, pp. 26–30; Richard W. Oliver, "My Generation," *Management Review,* January 2000, pp. 12–13; and Charlene Marmer Solomon, "Ready or Not, Here Come the Net Kids," *Workforce,* February 2000, pp. 62–68.

42. Daniel Katz and Robert Kahn, *The Social Psychology of Organizations,* 2d ed., Wiley, New York, 1978, p. 440.

43. Ibid., p. 443.

44. See for example Reid Buckley, "When You Have to Put It to Them," *Across the Board,* October 1999, pp. 44–47 and Curtis Sittenfild, "How to WOW an Audience—Every Time," *Fast Company,* September 1999, p. 86.

45. Nelson W. Aldrich, Jr., "Lines of Communication," *Inc.,* June 1986, p. 142.

46. See David G. Myers, *Social Psychology,* 3d ed., McGraw-Hill, New York, 1990, p. 117.

47. "Manager's On-Line Design Keeps New Yorkers Rolling," *Computerworld,* December 10, 1984, p. 8.

48. Charles A. O'Reilly, "Individuals and Information Overload in Organizations," *Academy of Management Journal,* December 1980, pp. 684–696.

49. Donald F. Roberts, "The Nature of Communication Effects," in Wilbur Schramm and Donald F. Roberts (Eds.), *The Process and Effects of Mass Communica-*

tion, rev. ed., University of Illinois Press, Chicago, 1971, pp. 368–371.

50. Charles A. O'Reilly, "Supervisors and Peers as Information Sources, Group Supportiveness, and Individual Performance," *Journal of Applied Psychology,* October 1977, pp. 632–635 and Charles A. O'Reilly and Karlene H. Roberts, "Task Group Structure, Communication, and Effectiveness in Three Organizations," *Journal of Applied Psychology,* December 1977, pp. 674–681.

51. For example, see Victor J. Callan, "Subordinate–Manager Communication in Different Sex Dyads: Consequences for Job Satisfaction," *Journal of Occupational and Organizational Psychology,* March 1993, pp. 13–27.

52. Barbara Ettorre, "Communications Breakdown," *Management Review,* June 1996, p. 10.

53. Walter Kiechel, III, "Breaking Bad News to the Boss," *Fortune,* April 9, 1990, p. 111.

54. Lin Grensing-Pophal, "Talk to Me," *HR Magazine,* March 2000, p. 70.

55. Karlene H. Roberts and Charles A. O'Reilly, "Some Correlations of Communication Roles in Organizations," *Academy of Management Journal,* March 1979, pp. 42–57.

56. See Rich Teerlink and Lee Ozley, *More than a Motorcycle,* Harvard Business School Press, Boston, 2000.

57. Tom Peters, *Thriving on Chaos: Handbook for a Management Revolution,* Knopf, New York, 1987, p. 305.

58. Gary Yukl, *Skills for Managers and Leaders,* Prentice Hall, Upper Saddle River, N.J., 1990, pp. 111–115.

59. Katz and Kahn, op. cit., p. 446.

60. William G. Scott and Terence R. Mitchell, *Organization Theory,* rev. ed., Irwin, Burr Ridge, Ill., 1972, p. 147.

61. Luthans and Larsen, op. cit., p. 168.

62. Fred Luthans, Stuart A. Rosenkrantz and Harry W. Hennessey, "What Do Successful Managers Really Do? An Observational Study of Managerial Activities," *Journal of Applied Behavioral Science,* Vol. 21, No. 3, 1985, pp. 255–270.

63. J. Fulk and E. R. Wendler, "Dimensionality of Leader–Subordinate Interactions: A Path–Goal Investigation," *Organizational Behavior and Human Performance,* Vol. 30, 1982, pp. 241–264 and Larry E. Penley and Brian Hawkins, "Studying Interpersonal Communications in Organizations: A Leadership Application," *Academy of Management Journal,* June 1985, pp. 309–326.

64. Katz and Kahn, op. cit., p. 445.

65. Luthans, Hodgetts, and Rosenkrantz, op. cit., Chap. 4.

66. Gerald M. Goldhaber, *Organizational Communication,* Wm. C. Brown, Dubuque, Iowa, 1974, p. 121.

67. Henry C. Mishkoff, "The Network Nation Emerges," *Management Review,* August 1986, pp. 29–31.

68. Donna J. Abernathy, "An Intranet Renaissance," *Training and Development,* August 1999, p. 24.

69. Nancy M. Dixon, "The Hallways of Learning," *Organizational Dynamics,* Spring 1997, p. 23.

70. Nancy Adler, *International Dimensions of Organizational Behavior,* South-Western, Cincinnati, Ohio, 1997, p. 68.

71. Don Hellriegel, John W. Slocum and Richard W. Woodman, *Organizational Behavior,* 4th ed., West, St. Paul, Minn., 1986, p. 219.

72. See Thomas Siebel, "A Web of Misperceptions," *Across the Board,* June 1999, pp. 11–12.

73. Adler, op. cit., p. 72.

74. See C. Engholm, *When Business East Meets Business West,* Wiley, New York, 1991.

75. The answers for the cultural stereotype quiz are: 1. E; 2. D; 3. F; 4. A; 5. B; 6. C. These were drawn from R. E. Axtell, *The Do's and Taboos of International Trade,* Wiley, New York, 1991, pp. 83–84.

76. See Susan M. Adams, "Settling Cross-Cultural Disagreements Begins with 'Where' Not 'How,'" *Academy of Management Executive,* Vol. 13, No. 1, 1999, p. 109.

77. For example, see Margaret A. Shaffer, David Harrison and K. Matthew Gilley, "Dimensions, Determinants, and Differences in the Expatriate Adjustment Process," *Journal of International Business Studies,* Vol. 30, No. 3, 1999, pp. 557–581 and Mary F. Sully DeLuque and Steven M. Sommer, "The Impact of Culture on Feedback-Seeking Behavior: An Integrated Model and Propositions," *Academy of Management Review,* Vol. 25, No. 4, 2000, pp. 829–849.

78. "Lose That Thick Accent to Gain Career Ground," *Wall Street Journal,* January 4, 1990, p. B1.

79. Sully Taylor and Nancy Napier, "Working in Japan: Lessons from Women Expatriates," *Sloan Management Review,* Spring 1996, p. 82.

80. Ibid.

81. P. Christopher Earley, "Intercultural Training for Managers: A Comparison of Documentary and Interpersonal Methods," *Academy of Management Journal,* December 1987, pp. 685–698.

82. J. Stewart Black and Mark Mendenhall, "Cross-Cultural Training Effectiveness: A Review and a Theoretical Framework for Future Research," *Academy of Management Review,* January 1990, pp. 113–136.

83. Tomoko Yoshida and Richard W. Brislin, "Intercultural Skills and Recommended Behaviors," in Oded Shenkar (Ed.), *Global Perspectives of Human Resource Management,* Prentice Hall, Upper Saddle River, N.J., 1995, pp. 121–124.

84. Ibid.

Chapter 11 Footnote References and Supplemental Readings

1. Chester I. Barnard, *The Functions of the Executive,* Harvard University Press, Cambridge, Mass., 1938, p. 14.

2. Herbert A. Simon, *The New Science of Management Decision,* Harper, New York, 1960, p. 2.

3. Henry Mintzberg, Duru Raisin-ghani and André Theoret, "The Structure of 'Unstructured' Decision Processes," *Administrative Science Quarterly,* June 1976, pp. 246–275.

4. Richard L. Daft, *Organization Theory and Design,* West, St. Paul, Minn., 1983, pp. 357–358.

5. For example, see Kathleen M. Eisenhardt, "Strategy as Strategic Decision Making," *Sloan Management Review,* Spring 1999, pp. 65–72.

6. James W. Dean, Jr., and Mark P. Sharfman, "Does Decision Process Matter? A Study of Strategic Decision-Making Effectiveness," *Academy of Management Journal,* Vol. 39, No. 2, 1996, pp. 368–396 and Barbara A. Mellers, "Choice and the Relative Pleasure of Consequences," *Psychological Bulletin,* Vol. 126, No. 6, 2000, pp. 910–924.

7. See for example Paul C. Nutt, "Surprising but True: Half the Decisions in Organizations Fail," *Academy of Management Executive,* Vol. 13, No. 4, 1999, pp. 75–90.

8. See Gary Klein and Karl E. Weick, "Decisions: Making the Right Ones, Learning from the Wrong Ones," *Across the Board,* June 2000, pp. 16–22.

9. See Max H. Bazerman, *Judgement in Managerial Decision Making,* Wiley, New York, 1994 and David M. Messick and Max H. Bazerman, "Ethical Leadership and the Psychology of Decision Making," *Sloan Management Review,* Winter 1996, pp. 9–22.

10. See Madan M. Pillutla and Xiao-Ping Chen, "Social Norms and Cooperation in Social Dilemmas: The Effects of Context and Feedback," *Organizational Behavior and Human Decision Processes,* May 1999, pp. 81–103; Gerry McNamara and Philip Bromiley, "Risk and Return in Organizational Decision Making," *Academy of Management Journal,* Vol. 42, No. 3, 1999, pp. 330–339; and Stan Davis and Christopher Meyer, "Laying Off Risk," *Across the Board,* April 2000, pp. 33–37.

11. Herbert A. Simon, *Administrative Behavior,* 2d ed., Macmillan, New York, 1957, p. 64.

12. Ibid., pp. 76–77.

13. Ibid., p. xxiii.

14. For recent representative research that provides insights to factors that influence the pros and cons of the rational decision making process see Robert M. Wiseman and Luis R. Gomez-Mejia, "A Behavioral Agency Model of Managerial Risk Taking," *Academy of Management Review,* Vol. 23, No. 1, 1998, pp. 133–153; T. K. Das and Bing-Sheng Teng, "Managing Risks in Strategic Alliances," *Academy of Management Executive,* Vol. 13, No. 4, 1999, pp. 50–62; Theodore Modis, *Conquering Uncertainty,* McGraw-Hill, New York, 1998; and Gerry McNamara and Philip Bromiley, "Decision Making in an Organizational Setting: Cognitive and Organizational Influences on Risk Assessment in Commercial Lending," *Academy of Management Journal,* Vol. 40, No. 5, 1997, pp. 1063–1088.

15. Thomas J. Peters and Robert H. Waterman, Jr., *In Search of Excellence: Lessons from America's Best-Run Companies,* Harper & Row, New York, 1982, p. 29.

16. "The EVA Yardstick," *Management Review,* July 1995, p. 47 and Bruce B. Hanson, "What You Need to Know about Economic Value Added," *Compensation & Benefits Review,* March–April 1995, pp. 33–36.

17. Shawn Tully, "The Real Key to Creating Wealth," *Fortune,* September 20, 1993, p. 38.

18. Chuck Appleby, "The New Lingo of Added Value," *Hospitals & Health Networks,* February 5, 1997, pp. 50–52.

19. Paul Gray, "The Assault on Freud," *Time,* November 29, 1993, pp. 47–51.

20. For example, see Rajagopal Raghunathan and Michel Tuan Pham, "All Negative Moods Are Not Equal: Motivational Influences of Anxiety and Sadness on Decision Making," *Organizational Behavior and Human Decision Processes,* July 1999, pp. 56–77.

21. Solomon E. Asch, "Opinions and Social Pressure," *Scientific American,* November 1955, pp. 31–35.

22. Barry M. Staw and Jerry Ross, "Understanding Behavior in Escalation Situations," *Science,* October 1989, pp. 216–220. For recent research, see Donald A. Hantula and Jennifer L. DeNicolis Bragger, "The Effects of Equivocality on Escalation of Commitment: An Empirical Investigation of Decision Dilemma Theory," *Journal of Applied Social Psychology,* Vol. 29, No. 2, 1999, pp. 424–444.

23. For meta-analytic analyses of the complex impact of various human dynamics on decision making, see Jay J. J. Christensen-Szalanski and Cynthia Fobian Willham, "The Hindsight Bias: A Meta-Analysis," *Organizational Behavior and Human Decision Processes,* Vol. 48, 1991, pp. 147–168; Charles R. Schwenk, "Effects of Devil's Advocacy and Dialectical

Inquiry on Decision Making: A Meta-Analysis," *Organizational Behavior and Human Decision Processes,* Vol. 47, 1990, pp. 161–176; and Robert L. Cross and Susan E. Brodt, "How Assumptions of Consensus Undermine Decision Making," *MIT Sloan Management Review,* Winter 2001, pp. 86–94.

24. Fred Luthans and Robert Koester, "The Impact of Computer-Generated Information on the Choice Activity of Decision Makers," *Academy of Management Journal,* June 1976, pp. 328–332 and Robert Koester and Fred Luthans, "The Impact of the Computer on the Choice Activity of Decision Makers: A Replication with Actual Users of Computerized MIS," *Academy of Management Journal,* June 1979, pp. 416–422.

25. Simon, *Administrative Behavior,* op. cit., pp. xxv–xxvi.

26. E. Frank Harrison, *The Managerial Decision-Making Process,* Houghton Mifflin, Boston, 1975, p. 69.

27. The analysis of the judgmental heuristics model comes largely from Bazerman, *Management Decision Making,* op. cit.

28. For example, see D. Kahneman and A. Tversky, "Subjective Probability: A Judgment of Representativeness," *Cognitive Psychology,* Vol. 3, 1972, pp. 430–454; D. Kahneman and A. Tversky, "On the Psychology of Prediction," *Psychological Review,* Vol. 80, 1973, pp. 237–251; D. Kahneman and A. Tversky, "Prospect Theory: An Analysis of Decision under Risk," *Econometrica,* Vol. 47, 1979, pp. 263–291; A. Tversky and D. Kahneman, "Availability: A Heuristic for Judging Frequency and Probability," *Cognitive Psychology,* Vol. 5, 1973, pp. 207–232; and A. Tversky and D. Kahneman, "Judgment under Uncertainty: Heuristics and Biases," *Science,* Vol. 185, 1974, pp. 1124–1131.

29. See Gregory B. Northcraft and Margaret A. Neale, *Organizational Behavior,* Dryden, Chicago, 1990, p. 184.

30. See Max H. Bazerman, *Judgment in Management Decision Making,* Wiley, New York, 1986, 1990, 1994.

31. Tversky and Kahneman, "Availability: A Heuristic," op. cit., and Tversky and Kahneman, "Judgment under Uncertainty," op. cit.

32. Bazerman, *Judgement in Managerial Decision Making,* op. cit., p. 7.

33. Northcraft and Neale, op. cit., p. 185.

34. Kahneman and Tversky, "On the Psychology of Prediction," op. cit.

35. Bazerman, *Judgement in Managerial Decision Making,* op. cit., p. 7.

36. Northcraft and Neale, op. cit., p. 187.

37. Bazerman, *Judgement in Managerial Decision Making,* op. cit., p. 7.

38. Ibid., p. 28.

39. For example, see issues of the *Journal of Behavioral Decision Making* and the *Journal of Risk and*

Uncertainty, as well as the standard journals such as *Organizational Behavior and Human Decision Processes.*

40. See A. J. Rowe and R. O. Mason, *Managing with Style: A Guide to Understanding, Assessing and Improving Decision Making,* Jossey-Bass, San Francisco, 1987.

41. M. J. Dolinger and W. Danis, "Preferred Decision-Making Styles: A Cross-Cultural Comparison," *Psychological Reports,* 1998, pp. 255–261.

42. For example, see Robert S. Dooley and Gerald E. Fryxell, "Attaining Decision Quality and Commitment from Dissent: The Moderating Effects of Loyalty and Competence in Strategic Decision-Making Teams," *Academy of Management Journal,* Vol. 42, No. 4, 1999, pp. 389–402.

43. See: J. A. Wagner III, C. R. Lenna, E. A. Locke and D. M. Schweiger, "Cognitive and Motivational Frameworks in U.S. Research on Participation: A Meta-Analysis of Primary Effects," *Journal of Organizational Behavior,* Vol. 18, 1997, pp. 49–65.

44. David M. Schweiger and Carrie R. Leana, "Participation in Decision Making," in Edwin A. Locke (ed.), *Generalizing from Laboratory to Field Settings,* Lexington Books, Lexington, Mass., 1986, p. 148; Steve Alper, Dean Tjosvold and Kenneth S. Law, "Interdependence and Controversy in Group Decision Making: Antecedents to Effective Self-Managing Teams," *Organizational Behavior and Human Decision Processes,* April 1998, pp. 33–52; and David E. Drehmer, James A. Belohlav and Ray W. Coye, "An Exploration of Employee Participation Using a Scaling Approach," *Group and Organization Management,* Vol. 25, No. 4, 2000, pp. 397–418.

45. Stewart Black and Newton Margulies, "An Ideological Perspective on Participation: A Case for Integration," *Journal of Organizational Change Management,* Vol. 2, No. 1, 1989, pp. 13–34 and L. Alan Witt, "Exchange Ideology as a Moderator of the Relationships between Importance of Participation in Decision Making and Job Attitudes," *Human Relations,* Vol. 45, 1992, pp. 73–86.

46. Wagner, et al. op. cit.

47. John L. Cotton, David A. Vollrath, Kirk L. Froggatt, Mark L. Lengnick-Hall and Kenneth R. Jennings, "Employee Participation: Diverse Forms and Different Outcomes," *Academy of Management Review,* January 1988, pp. 8–22.

48. Alan R. Dennis, "Information Processing in Group Decision Making: You Can Lead a Group to Information, but You Can't Make It Think," *Academy of Management Best Papers Proceedings,* 1993, pp. 283–287.

49. Marshall Scott Poole, Michael Holmes, Richard Watson, and Gerardine DeSanctis, "Group Decision Support Systems and Group Communication," *Communication Research,* April 1993, pp. 176–213.

50. Jenny C. McCune, "The Call for Tech-Savvy Employees," *Management Review,* June 1999, pp. 10–12.

51. Teresa M. Amabile and Regina Conti, "Changes in the Work Environment for Creativity During Downsizing," *Academy of Management Journal,* Vol. 42, No. 6, 1999, pp. 630–640.

52. Teresa M. Amabile, "How to Kill Creativity," *Harvard Business Review,* September–October 1998, p. 78.

53. For a summary see Filiz Tabak, "Employee Creative Performance: What Makes It Happen," *Academy of Management Executive,* Vol. 11, No. 1, 1997, pp. 119–120. For the original research, see Greg R. Oldham and Anne Cummings, "Employee Creativity: Personal and Contextual Factors at Work," *Academy of Management Journal,* Vol. 39, 1996, pp. 607–634.

54. Robert Root-Bernstein and Michele Root-Bernstein, *Sparks of Genius,* Houghton Mifflin, Boston, 2000.

55. Lisa A. Burke and Monica K. Miller, "Taking the Mystery Out of Intuitive Decision Making," *Academy of Management Executive,* Vol. 13, No. 4, 1999, pp. 91–99.

56. Eric Berggren and Thomas Nacher, "Why Good Ideas Go Bust," *Management Review,* February 2000, pp. 32–36.

57. See E. M. Brockmann and W. P. Anthony, "The Influence of Tacit Knowledge and Collective Mind on Strategic Planning," *Journal of Managerial Issues,* Vol. 10, 1998, pp. 204–222, and D. Lenard and S. Sensiper, "The Role of Tacit Knowledge in Group Innovation," *California Management Review,* Vol. 40, 1998, pp. 112–132.

58. Marlene Piturro, "Mindshift," *Management Review,* May 1999, pp. 48–49.

59. See Ian Mitroff, *Smart Thinking for Crazy Times,* Berrett-Koehler, San Francisco, 1998, and Cameron M. Ford and Dennis A. Gioia, "Factors Influencing Creativity in the Domain of Managerial Decision Making," *Journal of Management,* Vol. 26, No. 4, 2000, pp. 705–732.

60. See for example, Warren Bennis and Patricia Ward Biederman, *Organizing Genius: The Secrets of Creative Collaboration,* Addison Wesley, Reading, Mass., 1997 and Ruth Palombo Weiss, "How to Foster Creativity at Work," *Training & Development,* February 2001, pp. 61–65.

61. Cheryl Comeau-Kirschner and Louisa Wah, "Who Has Time to Think?" *Management Review,* January 2000, pp. 16–23.

62. Suzy Wetlaufer, "Common Sense and Conflict: An Interview with Disney's Michael Eisner," *Harvard Business Review,* January–February 2000, p. 119.

63. Trish Hall, "When Budding MBAs Try to Save Kool-Aid. Original Ideas Are Scarce," *The Wall Street Journal,* November 25, 1986, p. 31.

64. M. D. Mumford and S. B. Gustafson, "Creativity Syndrome: Integration, Application, and Innovation," *Psychological Bulletin,* Vol. 103, 1988, pp. 27–43.

65. This description is part of a study reported in W. C. Ward, N. Kogan and E. Pankove, "Incentive Effects in Children's Creativity," *Child Development,* Vol. 43, 1972, pp. 669–676, and is found in Robert S. Feldman, *Understanding Psychology,* 2d ed., McGraw-Hill, New York, 1990, p. 243.

66. Feldman, op. cit., pp. 242–243.

67. Weston H. Agor, "Use of Intuitive Intelligence to Increase Productivity," *HR Focus,* September 1993, p. 9.

68. Min Basadur, "Managing Creativity: A Japanese Model," *Academy of Management Executive,* May 1992, pp. 29–42.

69. Allen Ward, Jeffrey K. Liker, John J. Cristiano and Durward K. Sobek II, "The Second Toyota Paradox: How Delaying Decisions Can Make Better Cars Faster," *Sloan Management Review,* Spring 1995, p. 43.

70. Dorothy Leonard and Jeffrey F. Rayport, "Spark Innovation Through Empathic Design," *Harvard Business Review,* November–December 1997, pp. 102–103. Also see Stefan Thomke, "Enlightened Experimentation: The New Imperative for Innovation," *Harvard Business Review,* February 2001, pp. 67–75.

71. See for example Gary Hamel and C. K. Prahalad, *Competing for the Future,* Harvard Business School Press, Boston, 1994, the more recent Gary Hamel, *Leading the Revolution,* Harvard Business School Press, Boston, 2000, and George M. Scott, "Top Priority Management Concerns about New Product Development," *Academy of Management Executive,* Vol. 13, No. 3, 1999, pp. 77–84.

72. Paco Underhill, *Why We Buy: The Science of Shopping,* Simon & Schuster, New York, 1999.

73. For some recent research on the complexity of risky decision making, see Anton Kühberger, "The Influence of Framing on Risky Decisions: A Meta-Analysis," *Organizational Behavior and Human Decision Processes,* Vol. 75, No. 1, 1998, pp. 23–55, Sim B. Sitkin and Laurie R. Weingart, "Determinants of Risky Decision-Making Behavior: A Test of the Mediating Role of Risk Perceptions and Propensity," *Academy of Management Journal,* Vol. 38, No. 6, 1995, pp. 1573–1592, and Richard L. Priem, David A. Harrison, and Nan Kanoff Muir, "Structured Conflict and Consensus Outcomes in Group Decision Making," *Journal of Management,* Vol. 21, No. 4, 1995, pp. 691–710.

74. For a recent review of this research see M. L. Ambrose and C. T. Kulik, "Old Friends, New Faces: Motivation Research in the 1990s," *Journal of Management,* Vol. 25, No. 3, 1999, pp. 267–268.

75. Spencer A. Rathus, *Psychology,* 4th ed., Holt, Rinehart & Winston, Fort Worth, Tex., 1990, pp. 634–635.

76. William S. Silver and Terence R. Mitchell, "The Status Quo Tendency in Decision Making," *Organizational Dynamics,* Spring 1990, pp. 45–46. Also see Paul B. Paulus and Huei-Chuan Yang, "Idea Generation in Groups: A Basis for Creativity in Organizations," *Organizational Behavior and Human Decision Processess,* Vol. 82, No. 1, 2000, pp. 76–87.

77. Paul B. Paulus and Mary T. Dzindolet, "Social Influence Processes in Group Brainstorming," *Journal of Personality and Social Psychology,* April 1993, pp. 575–586.

78. Andre L. Delbecq, Andrew H. Van deVen and David H. Gustafson, *Group Techniques for Program Planning,* Scott, Foresman, Glenview, Ill., 1975, p. 8.

79. A. H. Van deVen, *Group Decision-Making Effectiveness,* Kent State University Center for Business and Economic Research Press, Kent, Ohio, 1974.

80. John Rohrbaugh, "Improving the Quality of Group Judgment: Social Judgment Analysis and the Nominal Group Technique," *Organizational Behavior and Human Performance,* October 1981, pp. 272–288.

81. Thad B. Green, "An Empirical Analysis of Nominal and Interacting Groups," *Academy of Management Journal,* March 1975, pp. 63–73.

82. Alan R. Dennis and Joseph S. Valacich, "Group, Subgroup, and Nominal Group Idea Generation: New Rules for a New Media?" *Journal of Management,* Vol. 20, No. 4, 1994, pp. 723–736.

83. David R. Hampton, Charles E. Summer and Ross A. Webber, *Organizational Behavior and the Practice of Management,* 5th ed., Scott, Foresman, Glenview, Ill., 1987, p. 274.

Chapter 12 Footnote References and Supplemental Readings

1. "Stress: Can We Cope?" *Time,* June 6, 1983, p. 48.

2. See Marcie A. Cavanaugh, Wendy R. Boswell, Mark V. Roehling and John W. Boudreau, "An Empirical Examination of Self-Reported Work Stress Among U.S. Managers," *Journal of Applied Psychology,* Vol. 85, 2000, pp. 65–74.

3. Richard S. DeFrank, Robert Konopaske and John M. Ivancevich, "Executive Travel Stress: Perils of the

Road Warrior," *Academy of Management Executive,* Vol. 14, No. 2, 2000, pp. 58–71.

4. See Margaret L. Frank, "What's So Stressful About Job Relocation?" *Academy of Management Executive,* Vol. 14, No. 2, 2000, pp. 122–123, and Josh Martin, "New Moves," *Management Review,* March 2000, pp. 35–38.

5. Michelle M. Weil and Larry D. Rosen, "Don't Let Technology Enslave You," *Workforce,* February 1999, pp. 56–59.

6. Katharine Mieszkowski, "What a Disaster! Don't Panic," *Work Smarter, Not Harder,* Fast Company's Roadmap to Success, 2000, p. 20.

7. Debra L. Nelson and Ronald J. Burke, "Women Executives: Health, Stress, and Success," *Academy of Management Executive,* Vol. 14, No. 2, 2000, pp. 107–121.

8. Reported in "Heavy Overtime," *The Wall Street Journal,* March 29, 2000, p. A-1.

9. Quoted in Gail Dutton, "Cutting-Edge Stress Busters," *HR Focus,* September 1998, p. 11.

10. Reported in *HR Focus,* April 1999, p. 4.

11. John M. Ivancevich and Michael T. Matteson, *Organizational Behavior and Management,* Business Publications, Plano, Tex., 1987, p. 211.

12. See Terry A. Beehr, "The Current Debate about the Meaning of Job Stress," *Journal of Organizational Behavior Management,* Fall/Winter 1986, pp. 5–18. For a more recent analysis of the complexity and meaning of stress, see Jeffrey R. Edwards, "An Examination of Competing Versions of the Person-Environment Fit Approach to Stress," *Academy of Management Journal,* April 1996, pp. 292–339.

13. John M. Ivancevich and Michael T. Matteson, *Organizational Behavior and Management,* 3d ed., Irwin, Burr Ridge, Ill., 1993, p. 244.

14. Richard S. DeFrank and J. M. Ivancevich, "Stress on the Job: An Executive Update," *Academy of Management Executive,* August 1998, pp. 55–66.

15. T. A. Beehr and J. E. Newman, "Job Stress, Employee Health, and Organizational Effectiveness: A Facet Analysis, Model, and Literature Review," *Personnel Psychology,* Winter 1978, pp. 665–699.

16. This summary is based on Hans Selye, *Stress without Distress,* Lippincott, Philadelphia, 1974 and James C. Quick and Jonathan D. Quick, *Organizational Stress and Preventative Management,* McGraw-Hill, New York, 1984, pp. 8–9. Also see Debra L. Nelson and James Campbell Quick, *Organizational Behavior,* 3rd ed., South-Western, Cincinnati, Ohio, 2000, Chapter 7.

17. Daniel C. Ganster and John Schaubroeck, "Work, Stress and Employee Health," *Journal of Management,* Vol. 17, 1991, pp. 235–271.

18. For example, see Gilbert Sand and Anthony D. Miyazaki, "The Impact of Social Support on Salesperson Burnout and Burnout Components," *Psychology and Marketing,* Vol. 17, No. 1, 2000, pp. 13–26.

19. Quoted in Lin Grensing-Popbal, "Commuting HR Eases the Pain," *HR Magazine,* March 1999, p. 84.

20. Ibid.

21. Reported in Joanne Cole, "An Ounce of Prevention Beats Burnout," *HR Focus,* June 1999, p. 1.

22. Reported in Todd Balf, "Are You Burned Out?" *Work Smarter, Not Harder,* Fast Company's Roadmap to Success, 2000, p. 25.

23. Robert Kreitner, "Personal Wellness: It's Just Good Business," *Business Horizons,* May–June 1982, p. 28. Also see James Campbell Quick, Joanne H. Gavin, Cary L. Cooper and Jonathan D. Quick, "Executive Health: Building Strength, Managing Risks," *Academy of Management Executive,* Vol. 14, No. 2, 2000, pp. 34–46.

24. See: Hugh B. Price, "Age of Anxiety," *Leader to Leader,* Winter, 1997, pp. 15–17.

25. See William Atkinson, "Employee Fatigue," *Management Review,* October 1999, pp. 56–60.

26. Dawn S. Carlson and Pamela L. Perrewé, "The Role of Social Support in the Stressor-Strain Relationship: An Examination of Work Family Conflict," *Journal of Management,* Vol. 25, No. 4, 1999, pp. 513–540.

27. Defrank and Ivancevich, op. cit., pp. 55–56.

28. Juan I. Sanchez, Paul E. Spector and Cary L. Cooper, "Adapting to a Boundaryless World: A Developmental Expatriate Model," *Academy of Management Executive,* Vol. 14, No. 2, 2000, pp. 96–106.

29. T. H. Holmes and R. H. Rahe, "Social Readjustment Rating Scale," *Journal of Psychosomatic Research,* Vol. 11, 1967, pp. 213–218.

30. *Wall Street Journal,* December 23, 1986, p. 1.

31. Defrank and Ivancevich, op. cit., pp. 55–56.

32. For example, see Lisa Hope Pelled, Kathleen M. Eisenhardt and Katherine R. Xin, "Exploring the Black Box: An Analysis of Work Group Diversity, Conflict, and Performance," *Administrative Science Quarterly,* Vol. 44, 1999, pp. 1–28, and Sherry K. Schneider and Gregory B. Northcraft, "Three Social Dilemmas of Workforce Diversity in Organizations," *Human Relations,* Vol. 52, No. 11, 1999, p. 1445.

33. Nelson and Burke, op. cit., pp. 110–111.

34. Joseph J. Martocchio and Anne M. O'Leary, "Sex Differences in Occupational Stress: A Meta-Analytic Review," *Journal of Applied Psychology,* Vol. 74, No. 3, 1989, pp. 495–501.

35. Nelson and Burke, op. cit. and Wayne A. Hochwarter, Pamela L. Perrewe and Mark C. Dawkins, "Gender Differences in Perceptions of

Stress-Related Variables," *Journal of Managerial Issues,* Spring 1995, pp. 62–74.

36. R. Marens, "The Residential Environment," in A. Campbell, P. E. Converse and W. L. Rodgers (Eds.), *The Quality of American Life,* Russell Sage, New York, 1976, and Gary W. Evans and Dana Johnson, "Stress and Open-Office Noise," *Journal of Applied Psychology,* Vol. 85, No. 5, 2000, pp. 779–783.

37. Gail Dutton, "Cutting-Edge Stressbusters," *HR Focus,* September, 1998, p. 12.

38. See Defrank and Ivancevich, op. cit., p. 57.

39. See Atkinson, op. cit.

40. Jaclyn Fierman, "It's 2 A.M., Let's Go to Work," *Fortune,* August 21, 1995, p. 82.

41. John Schaubroeck and Daniel C. Ganster, "Chronic Demands and Responsivity to Challenge," *Journal of Applied Psychology,* February 1993, pp. 73–85.

42. Michael R. Manning, Conrad N. Jackson and Marcelline R. Fusilier, "Occupational Stress, Social Support, and the Costs of Health Care," *Academy of Management Journal,* June 1995, pp. 738–750.

43. Gerald R. Ferris, Dwight D. Frink, Maria Carmen Galang, Jing Zhou, K. Michele Kacmar and Jack L. Howard, "Perceptions of Organizational Politics: Prediction, Stress-Related Implications, and Outcomes," *Human Relations,* Vol. 49, No. 2, 1996, pp. 233–266.

44. Arthur P. Brief, Randall S. Schuler and Mary Van Sell, *Managing Job Stress,* Little, Brown, Boston, 1981, p. 94.

45. Meyer Friedman and Ray H. Rosenman, *Type A Behavior and Your Heart,* Knopf, New York, 1974.

46. John H. Howard, David A. Cunningham and Peter A. Rechnitzer, "Health Patterns Associated with Type A Behavior: A Managerial Population," *Journal of Human Stress,* March 1976, pp. 24–31.

47. Friedman and Rosenman, op. cit.

48. Brief, Schuler, and Van Sell, op. cit., pp. 11–12.

49. See: Edward Dolnick, "Hotheads and Heart Attacks," *Health,* July/August 1995, pp. 58–64.

50. "Heart Disease, Anger Linked Research Shows," *Lincoln Journal,* January 17, 1989, p. 4.

51. "Some Workers Just Stress-Prone," *The New York Times,* reported in *Lincoln Journal Star,* October 3, 1993, p. 3E.

52. See S. D. Bluen, J. Barling and W. Burns, "Predicting Sales Performance, Job Satisfaction, and Depression by Using the Achievement Striving and Impatience-Irritability Dimensions of Type A Behavior," *Journal of Applied Psychology,* April 1990, pp. 212–216, and C. Lee, L. F. Jamison and P. C. Earley, "Beliefs and Fears and Type A Behavior: Implications for Academic Performance and Psychiatric Health Disorder Symptoms," *Journal of Organizational Behavior,* March 1996, pp. 151–177.

53. Richard M. Steers, *Introduction to Organizational Behavior,* 2d ed., Scott, Foresman, Glenview, Ill., 1984, p. 518 and Ellen Van Velsor and Jean Brittain Leslie, "Why Executives Derail: Perspectives across Time and Cultures," *Academy of Management Executive,* November 1995, pp. 62–72.

54. Ronald E. Riggio, *Introduction to Industrial/ Organizational Psychology,* Scott, Foresman/Little, Brown, Glenview, Ill., 1990, p. 204.

55. S. E. Jackson, "Participation in Decision Making as a Strategy for Reducing Job Related Strain," *Journal of Applied Psychology,* Vol. 68, 1983, pp. 3–19.

56. "Jobs with Little Freedom Boost Heart Risk," *Lincoln Journal,* April 11, 1990, p. 1.

57. Marilyn L. Fox, Deborah J. Dwyer and Daniel C. Ganster, "Effects of Stressful Job Demands and Control on Physiological and Attitudinal Outcomes in a Hospital Setting," *Academy of Management Journal,* April 1993, pp. 289–318.

58. M. E. P. Seligman, *Helplessness: On Depression, Development, and Death,* Freeman, San Francisco, 1975.

59. S. Mineka and R. W. Henderson, "Controllability and Predictability in Acquired Motivation," *Annual Review of Psychology,* Vol. 36, 1985, pp. 495–529.

60. See L. Y. Abrahamson, J. Garber and M. E. P. Seligman, "Learned Helplessness in Humans: An Attributional Analysis," in J. Garber and M. E. P. Seligman (Eds.), *Human Helplessness: Theory and Applications,* Academic Press, New York, 1980; and summarized in Robert S. Feldman, *Understanding Psychology,* 2d ed., McGraw-Hill, New York, 1990, p. 525. Also see Mark J. Martinko and William L. Gardner, "Learned Helplessness: An Alternative Explanation for Performance Deficits," *Academy of Management Review,* Vol. 7, 1982, pp. 413–417.

61. S. C. Kobasa, "Stressful Life Events, Personality, and Health: An Inquiry into Hardiness," *Journal of Personality and Social Psychology,* Vol. 37, 1979, pp. 1–11 and S. C. Kobasa, S. R. Maddi and S. Kahn, "Hardiness and Health: A Perspective Study," *Journal of Personality and Social Psychology,* Vol. 42, 1982, pp. 168–177.

62. Brian O'Reilly, "Is Your Company Asking Too Much?" *Fortune,* March 12, 1990, p. 39.

63. Anne M. O'Leary-Kelly, Ricky Griffin, and David J. Glew, "Organizational-Motivated Aggression: A Research Framework," *Academy of Management Review,* January 1996, p. 225. Also see Pamela R. Johnson and Susan Gardner, "Domestic Violence and the Workplace," *Journal of Management Development,* Vol. 18, No. 7, 1999, pp. 590–597.

64. John Huey, "Managing in the Midst of Chaos," *Fortune,* April 5, 1993, p. 38.

65. Cliff Cheng, "Multi-Level Gender Conflict Analysis and Organizational Change," *Journal of Organizational Change Management,* Vol. 8, No. 6, 1996, pp. 26–38, and Cheryl Aavon-Corbin, "The Multiple-Role Balancing Act," *Management Review,* October 1999, p. 62.

66. Yitzhak et. al., "The Interactive Effect of Role Conflict and Role Ambiguity on Job Performance," *Journal of Occupational and Organizational Psychology,* Vol. 71, 1998, pp. 19–27, and Paul F. Buller, John J. Kohls and Kenneth S. Anderson, "When Ethics Collide: Managing Conflicts Across Cultures," *Organizational Dynamics,* Vol. 28, No. 4, 2000, pp. 52–66.

67. Brian O'Reilly, "Is Your Company Asking Too Much?" *Fortune,* March 12, 1990, p. 39.

68. Susan E. Jackson and Randall S. Schuler, "A Meta-Analysis and Conceptual Critique of Research on Role Ambiguity and Role Conflict in Work Settings," *Organizational Behavior and Human Decision Processes,* Vol. 36, 1985, pp. 16–78 and Cynthia D. Fisher and Richard Gitelson, "A Meta-Analysis of the Correlates of Role Conflict and Ambiguity," *Journal of Applied Psychology,* Vol. 68, No. 2, 1983, pp. 320–333.

69. Steven W. Floyd and Peter J. Lane, "Strategizing Throughout the Organization: Managing Role Conflict in Strategic Renewal," *Academy of Management Review,* Vol. 25, No. 1, 2000, pp. 154–177.

70. David A. Whetten and Kim S. Cameron, *Developing Management Skills,* 2d ed., Harper Collins, New York, 1991, pp. 397–399.

71. Ibid., p. 398.

72. Ibid., p. 399.

73. Ibid., pp. 400–402. These categories are based on some of the original work of Alan C. Filley, *Interpersonal Conflict Resolution,* Scott, Foresman. Glenview, Ill., 1975.

74. Jay W. Jackson, "Realistic Group Conflict Theory: A Review and Evaluation of the Theoretical and Empirical Literature," *The Psychological Record,* Summer 1993, p. 397.

75. See Gary Yukl, *Skills for Managers and Leaders,* Prentice Hall, Upper Saddle River, N.J., 1990, pp. 283–285.

76. Howard M. Guttman, "Conflict at the Top," *Management Review,* November 1999, pp. 49–50.

77. Tony L. Simons and Randall S. Peterson, "Task Conflict and Relationship Conflict in Top Management Teams: The Pivotal Role of Intragroup Trust," *Journal of Applied Psychology,* Vol. 85, No. 1, 2000, pp. 102–111.

78. Giuseppe Labianca, Daniel Brass and Barbara Gray, "Social Networks and Perceptions of Intergroup Conflict: The Role of Negative Relationships and Third Parties," *Academy of Management Journal,* Vol. 41, No. 1, 1998, pp. 55–67.

79. Richard L. Daft, *Organization Theory and Design,* West, St. Paul, Minn., 1983, pp. 424–425.

80. Joe Kelley, *Organizational Behavior,* rev. ed., Dorsey-Irwin, Burr Ridge, Ill., 1975, p. 555.

81. Ibid.

82. Jeanne M. Brett, Stephen B. Goldberg, and William L. Ury, "Designing Systems for Resolving Disputes in Organizations," *American Psychologist,* February 1990, pp. 162–170. Also see Donald E. Conlon and Daniel P. Sullivan, "Examining the Actions of Organizations in Conflict," *Academy of Management Journal,* Vol. 42, No. 3, 1999, pp. 319–329.

83. Howard M. Weiss, Daniel R. Ilgen and Michael E. Sharbaugh, "Effects of Life and Job Stress on Information Search Behaviors of Organizational Members," *Journal of Applied Psychology,* February 1982, pp. 60–62.

84. See Michael J. Burke, Arthur P. Brief and Jennifer M. George, "The Role of Negative Affectivity in Understanding Relations between Self-Reports of Stressors and Strains: A Comment on the Applied Psychology Literature," *Journal of Applied Psychology,* June 1993, pp. 402–412; John Schaubroeck, Daniel C. Ganster and Marilyn L. Fox, "Dispositional Affect and Work-Related Stress," *Journal of Applied Psychology,* Vol. 77, No. 3, 1992, pp. 322–335; and Paul E. Spector, Peter Y. Chen and Brian J. O'Connell, "A Longitudinal Study of Relations Between Job Stressors and Job Strains While Controlling for Prior Negative Affectivity and Strains," *Journal of Applied Psychology,* Vol. 85, No. 2, 2000, pp. 211–218.

85. Jenny Firth-Cozens, "Why Me? A Case Study of the Process of Perceived Occupational Stress," *Human Relations,* Vol. 45, No. 2, 1992, pp. 131–142.

86. Robert A. Baron, *Behavior in Organizations,* 2d ed., Allyn & Bacon, Boston, 1986, p. 223. Also, see the recent comprehensive study by Cavanaugh et.al, op. cit.

87. See: Defrank and Ivancevich, op. cit., p. 58.

88. Vernon Silver, "Heart Attacks Are a Way of Life for Wall Street," *Lincoln Journal Star,* January 4, 1998, p. 2E.

89. K. Bammer and B. H. Newberry (Eds.), *Stress and Cancer,* Hogrefe, Toronto, 1982.

90. John M. Ivancevich and Michael T. Matteson, *Stress and Work,* Scott, Foresman, Glenview, Ill., 1980, p. 92.

91. Peter Y. Chen and Paul E. Spector, "Relationships of Work Stressors with Aggression, Withdrawal, Theft and Substance Use: An Exploratory Study," *Journal of Occupational and Organizational Psychology,* September 1992, pp. 177–184. Also see Laurel R.

Goulet, "Modeling Aggression in the Workplace: The Role of Role Models," *Academy of Management Executive,* Vol. 11, No. 2, 1997, pp. 84–85.

92. J. E. McGrath, "Stress and Behavior in Organizations," in M. D. Dunnette (Ed.), *Handbook of Industrial and Organizational Psychology,* Rand McNally, Chicago, 1976.

93. Beehr and Newman, op. cit.; A. A. McLean, *Work Stress,* Addison-Wesley, Reading, Mass., 1980; and Cary L. Cooper and Judi Marshall, "Occupational Sources of Stress," *Journal of Occupational Psychology,* March 1976, pp. 11–28.

94. "Job Stress Said a 'Substantial Health Problem,'" *Lincoln Journal,* October 6, 1986, p. 15.

95. Robert L. Brady, "Stress-Related Claims: What Can You Do about Them?" *HR Focus,* December 1995, pp. 19–20.

96. David S. Allen, "Less Stress, Less Litigation," *Personnel,* January 1990, p. 33.

97. "Employees' Behavioral Health Neglected," *Management Review,* November 1999, p. 10.

98. Ivancevich and Matteson, *Stress and Work,* p. 96.

99. "Firm Hopes Breath Meter Curbs Workers' Drinking," *Lincoln Journal,* June 11, 1983, p. 13.

100. Ibid.

101. For example, see: A. J. Kinicki, F. M. McKee and K. J. Wade, "Annual Review, 1991–1995: Occupational Health," *Journal of Vocational Behavior,* October 1996, pp. 190–220, and J. R. Edwards and N. P. Rothbard, "Work and Family Stress and Well-Being," *Organizational Behavior and Human Decision Processes,* February 1999, pp. 85–129.

102. Jeffrey R. Edwards, "A Cybernetic Theory of Stress, Coping, and Well-Being in Organizations," *Academy of Management Review,* April 1992, pp. 238–274. Also see Susan Oakland and Alistair Ostell, "Measuring Coping: A Review and Critique," *Human Relations,* Vol. 49, No. 2, 1996, pp. 133–155.

103. Sean M. Lyden, "Stress Case," *Business Start-Ups,* March 2000, p. 62.

104. For example, see "Stress Management 101," *Management Review,* November 1999, p. 9 and Kathleen McLaughlin, "The Lighter Side of Learning," *Training,* February 2001, pp. 48–52.

105. Daniel C. Feldman and Hugh J. Arnold, *Managing Individual and Group Behavior in Organizations,* McGraw-Hill, New York, 1986, pp. 223–225. Also see Erik J. Van Slyke, "Resolve Conflict, Boost Creativity," *HR Magazine,* November 1999, pp. 132–137.

106. For example, see Kenneth Cloke and Joan Goldsmith, *Resolving Conflict at Work,* Jossey-Bass, San Francisco, 2000.

107. Christopher P. Neck and Kenneth H. Cooper, "The Fit Executive: Exercise and Diet Guidelines for

Enhancing Performance," *Academy of Management Executive,* Vol. 14, No. 2, 2000, pp. 72–83.

108. J. M. Smyth, A. A. Stone, A. Hurewitz and K. Kaell, "Effects of Writing About Stressful Experiences on Symptom Reduction in Patients with Asthma or Rheumatoid Arthritis," *Journal of the American Medical Association,* Vol. 281, 1999, pp. 1304–1329.

109. Robert K. Wallace and Herbert Benson, "The Physiology of Meditation," *Scientific American,* February 1972, pp. 84–90.

110. Terri Schultz, "What Science Is Discovering about the Potential Benefits of Meditation," *Today's Health,* April 1972, pp. 34–37.

111. "Executives Meditating to Success," *Omaha World-Herald,* February 11, 1986, p. 9.

112. An example of a recent study would be Vivien K. G. Lim, "Job Insecurity and Its Outcomes: Moderating Effects of Work-Based and Nonwork-Based Social Support," *Human Relations,* Vol. 49, No. 2, 1996, pp. 171–194. Also see Benedict Carey, "Don't Face Stress Alone," *Health,* April, 1997, pp. 74–76, 78.

113. Anson Seers, Gail W. McGee, Timothy T. Serey and George B. Graen, "The Interaction of Job Stress and Social Support: A Strong Inference Investigation," *Academy of Management Journal,* June 1983, pp. 273–284.

114. McLean, op. cit.

115. John Kotter, *The General Managers,* Free Press, New York, 1982.

116. Fred Luthans, Stuart A. Rosenkrantz and Harry W. Hennessey, "What Do Successful Managers Really Do? An Observation Study of Managerial Activities," *Journal of Applied Behavioral Science,* Vol. 21, No. 3, 1985, pp. 255–270.

117. Joanne Cole, "De-Stressing the Workplace," *HR Focus,* October 1999, pp. 1, 10–11.

118. Laurie Hays, "But Some Firms Try to Help," *Wall Street Journal,* April 24, 1987, p. 16D. Also see Helene Cooper, "Offering Aerobics, Karate, Aquatics, Hospitals Stress Business of 'Wellness,'" *Wall Street Journal,* August 9, 1993, pp. B1, B3 and Laura M. Litvan, "Preventive Medicine," *Nation's Business,* September 1995, pp. 32–36.

119. John M. Ivancevich, Michael T. Matteson, Sara M. Freedman and James S. Phillips, "Worksite Stress Management Interventions," *American Psychologist,* February 1990, pp. 252–261; John C. Erfurt, Andrea Foote and Max A. Heirich, "The Cost-Effectiveness of Worksite Wellness Programs for Hypertension Control, Weight Loss, Smoking Cessation, and Exercise," *Personnel Psychology,* Spring 1992, pp. 5–28; Shirley Reynolds, Emma Taylor and David A. Shapiro, "Session Impact in Stress Management

Training," *Journal of Occupational and Organizational Psychology,* June 1993, pp. 99–113; and Richard S. Lazarus, "Toward Better Research on Stress and Coping," *American Psychologist,* June 2000, pp. 665–673.

120. Todd Balf, "Out of Juice? Recharge," *Work Smarter, Not Harder,* Fast Company's Roadmap to Success, 2000, p. 24.

121. Stephenie Overman, "Make Family-Friendly Initiatives Fly," *HR Focus,* July 1999, p. 14.

122. Gary L. Wirt, "The ABCs of EAPs," *HR Focus,* November, 1998, p. S12.

123. "EAP: Another Element of Support," *HR Focus,* February, 1999, p. 8.

124. Janina C. Latack, Angelo J. Kinicki and Gregory E. Prussia, "An Integrative Process Model of Coping with Job Loss," *Academy of Management Review,* April 1995, pp. 311–342.

125. Nathan Bennett, Christopher L. Martin, Robert J. Bies and Joel Brockner, "Coping with a Layoff: A Longitudinal Study of Victims," *Journal of Management,* Vol. 21, No. 6, 1995, pp. 1025–1040.

126. Joel Brockner, Mary Konovsky, Rochelle Cooper-Schneider, Robert Folger, Christopher Martin and Robert Bies, "Interactive Effects of Procedural Justice and Outcome Negativity on Victims and Survivors of Job Loss," *Academy of Management Journal,* April 1994, pp. 397–409.

127. Roland E. Kidwell, "Pink Slips without Tears," *Academy of Management Executive,* May 1995, pp. 69–70.

128. Caudron, op. cit., p. 39.

129. Ibid., pp. 40–48.

130. Margaret A. Neale and Max H. Bazerman, "Negotiating Rationally: The Power and Impact of the Negotiator's Frame," *Academy of Management Executive,* August 1992, p. 42.

131. Whetten and Cameron, op. cit., p. 402.

132. Neale and Bazerman, op. cit., p. 43. Also see Deborah B. Basler and Robert N. Stern, "Resistance and Cooperation: A Response to Conflict over Job Performance," *Human Relations,* Vol. 52, No. 8, 1999, p. 1029.

133. Leigh Thompson, Erika Peterson, and Susan E. Brodt, "Team Negotiation: An Examination of Integrative and Distributive Bargaining," *Journal of Personality and Social Psychology,* Vol. 70, No. 1, 1996, pp. 66–78.

134. Whetten and Cameron, op. cit., p. 404.

135. Roger Fisher and William Ury, *Getting to Yes,* Penguin, New York, 1983, p. 4.

136. Ibid., p. 9.

137. See Whetten and Cameron, op. cit., p. 404 and research such as Laurie R. Weingart, Rebecca J. Bennett and Jeanne M. Brett, "The Impact of Consideration of Issues and Motivational Orientation on Group Negotiation Process and Outcome," *Journal of Applied Psychology,* June 1993, pp. 504–517.

138. Whetten and Cameron, op. cit., p. 404.

139. Gregory B. Northcraft and Margaret A. Neale, *Organizational Behavior,* Dryden, Chicago, 1990, pp. 247–248.

140. Robert Adler, Benson Rosen and Elliot Silverstein, "Thrust and Parry: The Art of Tough Negotiating," *Training and Development Journal,* March 1996, pp. 44–48.

141. Ibid., pp. 45–46. Also see Deborah M. Kolb and Judith Williams, "Breakthrough Bargaining" *Harvard Business Review,* February 2001, pp. 89–97.

142. Maurice E. Schweitzer and Jeffrey L. Kerr, "Bargaining Under the Influence: The Role of Alcohol in Negotiations," *Academy of Management Executive,* Vol. 14, No. 2, 2000, p. 47.

143. Fisher and Ury, op. cit., p. 11.

144. Ibid., p. 13.

145. Ibid., p. 14.

Chapter 13 Footnote References and Supplemental Readings

1. Rosabeth Moss Kanter, "Power Failure in Management Circuits," *Harvard Business Review,* July–August 1979, p. 65.

2. Max Weber, *The Theory of Social and Economic Organization,* A. M. Henderson and Talcott Parsons (trans. and Ed.), Free Press, New York, 1947, p. 152.

3. David Krackhardt, "Assessing the Political Landscape: Structure, Cognition, and Power in Organizations," *Administrative Science Quarterly,* Vol. 35, 1990, p. 343.

4. Jeffrey Pfeffer, *Managing with Power,* Harvard Business School Press, Boston, 1992, p. 30.

5. A. J. Grimes, "Authority, Power, Influence and Social Control: A Theoretical Synthesis," *Academy of Management Review,* October 1978, p. 725.

6. Jerald Greenberg and Robert A. Baron, *Behavior in Organizations: Understanding and Managing the Human Side of Work,* Prentice Hall, Upper Saddle River, N.J., 2000, p. 409.

7. Chester I. Barnard, *The Functions of the Executive,* Harvard University Press, Cambridge, Mass., 1938, p. 163.

8. Grimes, op. cit., p. 726.

9. John R. P. French, Jr., and Bertram Raven, "The Bases of Social Power," in D. Cartwright (Ed.), *Studies in Social Power*, University of Michigan, Institute for Social Research, Ann Arbor, 1959.

10. H. Joseph Reitz, *Behavior in Organizations*, 3d ed., Irwin, Burr Ridge, Ill., 1987, p. 435.

11. David G. Myers, *Social Psychology*, 3d ed., McGraw-Hill, New York, 1990, p. 240. Also see Serena Chen, Annette Y. Lee-Chai and John A. Bargh, "Relationship Orientation as a Moderator of the Effects of Social Power," *Journal of Personality and Social Psychology*, Vol. 80, No. 27, 2001, pp. 173–187.

12. Mitchell S. Nesler, Herman Aguinis, Brian M. Quigley and James T. Tedeschi, "The Effect of Credibility on Perceived Power," *Journal of Applied Social Psychology*, Vol. 23, No. 17, 1993, pp. 1407–1425.

13. Andrew S. Grove, "Breaking the Chains of Command," *Newsweek*, October 3, 1983, p. 23.

14. Kathryn M. Bartol and David C. Martin, "When Politics Pays: Factors Influencing Managerial Compensation Decisions," *Personnel Psychology*, Vol. 43, 1990, p. 599.

15. Herman Aguinis, Mitchell S. Nesler, Brian M. Quigley, Suk-Jae Lee and James T. Tedeschi, "Power Bases of Faculty Supervisors and Educational Outcomes for Graduate Students," *Journal of Higher Education*, May–June 1996, pp. 267–297.

16. Steven L. McShane and Mary Ann Von Glinow, *Organizational Behavior*, Boston, Irwin McGraw-Hill, 2000. Gary Yukl and Celia M. Falbe, "Importance of Different Power Sources in Downward and Lateral Relations," *Journal of Applied Psychology*, 1991, Vol. 76, pp. 416–423.

17. Herman Aguinis, Mitchell S. Nesler, Brian M. Quigley and James T. Tedeschi, "Perceptions of Power: A Cognitive Perspective," *Social Behavior and Personality*, Vol. 22, No. 4, 1994, pp. 377–384.

18. M. S. Nesler, H. Aguinis, B. M. Quigley, Suk-Jae Lee and J. T. Tedeschi, "The Development and Validation of a Scale Measuring Global Social Power Based on French and Raven's Power Taxonomy," *Journal of Applied Social Psychology*, Vol. 20 No. 4, 1999, pp. 750–771.

19. K. W. Mossholder, N. Bennett, E. R. Kemery and M. A. Wesolowski, "Relationships Between Bases of Power and Work Reactions: The Mediational Role of Procedural Justice," *Journal of Management*, Vol. 24, No. 4, 1998, pp. 533–552.

20. Pfeffer, op. cit., p. 69.

21. For example, see Herminia Ibarra and Steven B. Andrews, "Power, Social Influence, and Sense Making: Effects of Network Centrality and Proximity on Employee Perceptions," *Administrative Science Quarterly*, June 1993, pp. 277–303.

22. Stephen P. Robbins, *Organizational Behavior*, Prentice Hall, Upper Saddle River, N.J., 1979, p. 276.

23. Carol Stoak Saunders, "The Strategic Contingencies Theory of Power: Multiple Perspectives," *Journal of Management Studies*, January 1990, p. 4.

24. Daniel J. Brass and Marlene E. Burkhardt, "Potential Power and Power Use: An Investigation of Structure and Behavior," *Academy of Management Journal*, June 1993, pp. 441–470 and Chen et al., op. cit.

25. Adapted from Reitz, op. cit., pp. 441–443.

26. Ibid., pp. 442–443.

27. See Herbert C. Kelman, "Compliance, Identification, and Internalization: Three Processes of Attitude Change," *Journal of Conflict Resolution*, March 1958, pp. 51–60.

28. Robert J. Vandenberg, Robin M. Self and Jai Hyun Seo, "A Critical Examination of the Internalization, Identification, and Compliance Commitment Measures," *Journal of Management*, Vol. 20, No. 1, 1994, pp. 123–140.

29. David C. McClelland, "The Two Faces of Power," *Journal of International Affairs*, Vol. 24, No. 1, 1970, p. 36.

30. Ibid., p. 41.

31. Eugene M. Fodor and Terry Smith, "The Power Motive as an Influence on Group Decision Making," *Journal of Personality and Social Psychology*, January 1982, pp. 178–185.

32. W. Alan Randolph, "Navigating the Journey to Empowerment," *Organizational Dynamics*, Spring 1995, p. 20.

33. David L. Taylor and Ruth Karin Ramsey, "Empowering Employees to 'Just Do It,'" *Training and Development Journal*, May 1991, p. 71.

34. Kyle Dover, "Avoiding Empowerment Traps," *Management Review*, January, 1999, pp. 51–55.

35. Ibid.

36. Jeffrey B. Arthur, "Effects of Human Resource Systems on Manufacturing Performance and Turnover," *Academy of Management Journal*, June 1994, pp. 670–687.

37. Gretchen M. Spreitzer, "Social Structural Characteristics of Psychological Empowerment," *Academy of Management Journal*, April 1996, pp. 483–504.

38. Jay Klagge, "The Empowerment Squeeze-Views from the Middle Management Position, *Journal of Management Development*, Vol. 17, No. 8, 1998, pp. 548–558. Also see W. Alan Randolph, "Rethinking Empowerment: Why Is It So Hard to Achieve?" *Organizational Dynamics*, Vol. 29, No. 2, 2000, pp. 94–107.

39. Pasquale Gagliardi, "Theories Empowering For Action," *Journal of Management Inquiry*, Vol. 8, No. 2, 1999, pp. 143–147.

40. Monica Lee, "The Lie of Power: Empowerment as Impotence," *Human Relations*, Vol. 52, No. 2, 1999, pp. 225–235.

41. Randolph, op. cit., p. 22.

42. Taylor and Ramsey, op. cit., pp. 71–76.

43. Charley Braun, "Organizational Infidelity: How Violations of Trust Affect the Employee-Employer Relationship," *Academy of Management Executive,* Vol. 11, No. 4, 1997, pp. 94–96.

44. A. C. Wicks, S. L. Berman and T. M. Jones, "The Structure of Optimal Trust: Moral and Strategic Implications," *Academy of Management Review,* Vol. 24, No. 1, 1999, pp. 99–116.

45. Tom D'Aquanni and Gary Taylor, "Breaking The Political Stranglehold in the Executive Suite," *Management Review,* March 2000, pp. 42–46.

46. Oren Harari, "The Trust Factor," *Management Review,* January, 1999, pp. 28–31.

47. Laura Tiffany, "Let the Games Begin," *Business Start-Ups,* March 2000, p. 90.

48. David E. Bowen and Edward E. Lawler, "The Empowerment of Service Workers: What, Why, How, and When," *Sloan Management Review,* Spring 1992, pp. 36–39. Also see David E. Bowen and Edward E. Lawler III, "Empowering Service Employees," *Sloan Management Review,* Summer 1995, p. 73.

49. Alvin Toffler, "Powership—In the Workplace," *Personnel,* June 1990, p. 21.

50. Clifford M. Koen, Jr. and Stephen M. Crow, "Human Relations and Political Skills," *HR Focus,* December 1995, pp. 10–12.

51. Jeffrey Pfeffer, "Understanding Power in Organizations," *California Management Review,* Winter 1992, p. 29.

52. Walter Nord, "Dreams of Humanization and the Realities of Power," *Academy of Management Review,* July 1978, pp. 675–677.

53. Gerald R. Ferris and K. Michele Kacmar, "Perceptions of Organizational Politics," *Journal of Management,* Vol. 18, No. 1, 1992, p. 93.

54. "Labor Letter," *The Wall Street Journal,* December 23, 1986, p. 1.

55. Barbara Gray and Sonny S. Ariss, "Politics and Strategic Change across Organizational Life Cycles," *Academy of Management Review,* October 1985, p. 707.

56. Patricia M. Fandt and Gerald R. Ferris, "The Management of Information and Impressions: When Employees Behave Opportunistically," *Organizational Behavior and Human Decision Processes,* Vol. 45, 1990, p. 140. Also see Martin Gargiulo, "Two-Step Leverage: Managing Constraint in Organizational Politics," *Administrative Science Quarterly,* March 1993, pp. 1–19.

57. Robert H. Miles, *Macro Organizational Behavior,* Goodyear, Santa Monica, Calif., 1980, pp. 182–184.

58. Ibid., p. 182.

59. Jone L. Pearce and Robert A. Page, Jr., "Palace Politics: Resource Allocation in Radically Innovative Firms," *The Journal of High Technology Management Research,* Vol. 1, 1990, pp. 193–205.

60. Timothy A. Judge and Robert D. Bretz, Jr., "Political Influence Behavior and Career Success," *Journal of Management,* Vol. 20, No. 1, 1994, pp. 43–65. Also see Christopher P. Parker, Robert L. Dipboye and Stacy L. Jackson, "Perceptions of Organizational Politics: An Investigation of Antecedents and Consequences," *Journal of Management,* Vol. 21, No. 5, 1995, pp. 891–912, and K. M. Kacmar, D. P. Bozemen, D. S. Carlson and W. P Anthony, "An Examination of the Preceptions of Organizational Politics Model: Replication and Extension," *Human Relations,* Vol. 52, No. 3, 1999 p. 383.

61. Amy J. Hillman and Michael A. Hitt, "Corporate Political Strategy Formulation: A Model of Approach, Participation, and Strategy Decisions," *Academy of Management Review,* Vol. 24, No. 4, 1999, pp. 825–842.

62. Gary Yukl and Cecilia M. Falbe, "Influence Tactics and Objectives in Upward, Downward, and Lateral Influence Attempts," *Journal of Applied Psychology,* Vol. 75, 1990, pp. 132–140.

63. Gary Yukl and J. Bruce Tracey, "Consequences of Influence Tactics Used with Subordinates, Peers, and the Boss," *Journal of Applied Psychology,* August 1992, pp. 525–535.

64. Jeffrey Pfeffer, "Power and Resource Allocation in Organizations," in Barry M. Staw and Gerald R. Salancik (Eds.), *New Directions in Organizational Behavior,* St. Clair, Chicago, 1977, pp. 255–260.

65. Andrew Kakabadse, "Organizational Politics," *Management Decision,* Vol. 25, No. 1, 1987, pp. 35–36. Also see Gerald R. Ferris, Pamela L. Perrewe; William P. Anthony and David C. Gilmore, "Political Skill at Work," *Organizational Dynamics,* Vol. 28, No. 4, 2000, pp. 25–37.

66. Leonard Bierman, "Regulating Reindeer Games," *Academy of Management Executive,* Vol. 11, No. 4, 1997, p. 92.

67. These strategies are discussed fully in Andrew J. DuBrin, *Human Relations,* Reston, Reston, Va., 1978, pp. 113–122; DuBrin, in turn, abstracted them from the existing literature on power and politics. Also see Andrew J. DuBrin, *Winning Office Politics,* Prentice Hall, Upper Saddle River, N.J., 1990, Chaps. 8 and 9.

68. Nancy C. Morey and Fred Luthans, "The Use of Dyadic Alliances in Informal Organization: An Ethnographic Study," *Human Relations,* Vol. 44, 1991, pp. 597–618.

69. Anthony Jay, *Management and Machiavelli,* Holt, New York, 1967, p. 6.

70. Fred Luthans, Richard M. Hodgetts and Stuart A. Rosenkrantz, *Real Managers,* Ballinger, Cambridge, Mass., 1988.

71. Annette Simmons, *Territorial Games: Understanding & Ending Turf Wars at Work,* AMACOM, New York, 1998.

72. Christine M. Pearson and Judith A. Clair, "Reframing Crisis Management," *Academy of Management Review,* Vol. 23, No. 1, 1998, pp. 59–76.

73. John Whitney and Tina Packer, *Power Plays: Shakespeare's Lessons in Leadership and Management,* Simon & Schuster, New York, 2000, and Norma Augustine and Kenneth Adelman, *Shakespeare in Charge: The Bard's Guide to Leading and Succeeding on the Business Stage,* Hyperion, New York, 2000.

74. Exceptions would include studies such as Glenn R. Carroll and Albert C. Teo, "On the Social Networks of Managers," *Academy of Management Journal,* Vol. 39, No. 2, 1996, pp. 421–440, and Rahul Varman and Deepti Bhatnagar, "Power and Politics in Grievance Resolution: Managing Meaning of Due Process in an Organization," *Human Relations,* Vol. 52, No. 3, 1999, pp. 349–381.

75. Commerce Clearing House, SHRM/CCH Survey, Chicago, 1991.

76. M. Velasquez, D. J. Moberg, and G. F. Cavanaugh, "Organizational Statesmanship and Dirty Politics: Ethical Guidelines for the Organizational Politician," *Organizational Dynamics,* Vol. 11, 1982, pp. 65–79.

77. Gerald F. Cavanagh, Dennis J. Moberg and Manuel Velasquez, "The Ethics of Organizational Politics," *Academy of Management Review,* July 1981, p. 372.

78. Robert P. Vecchio, *Organizational Behavior,* Dryden, Chicago, 1988, p. 270.

79. Nina Gupta and G. Douglas Jenkins, Jr., "The Politics of Pay," *Compensation & Benefits Review,* March/April 1996, pp. 23–30.

80. Dennis Collins, "Death of a Gainsharing Plan: Power, Politics and Participatory Management," *Organizational Dynamics,* Summer 1995, pp. 23–37.

81. Luthans, Hodgetts, and Rosenkrantz, op. cit.

82. Fred Luthans, Dianne H. B. Welsh and Stuart A. Rosenkrantz, "What Do Russian Managers Really Do?" *Journal of International Business Studies,* Fourth Quarter 1993, pp. 741–761.

83. See George B. Weathersby, "You've Got the Power," *Management Review,* January 1999, p. 5.

84. See Marilyn Moats Kennedy, "Politics Lost," *Across the Board,* May, 2000, p. 67.

85. See Scott Thurm, "Taking the Hint: Microsoft's Behavior Is Helping Cisco Learn How to Avoid Trouble," *Wall Street Journal,* June 1, 2000, p. A14.

Chapter 14 Footnote References and Supplemental Readings

1. Clayton P. Alderfer, "Editor's Introduction: Contemporary Issues in Professional Work with Groups," *Journal of Applied Behavioral Science,* March 1992, p. 9.

2. Michael Hickins, "Duh! Gen Xers Are Cool With Teamwork," *Management Review,* March, 1999, p. 7.

3. John M. Ivancevich and Michael T. Matteson, *Organizational Behavior and Management,* 3d ed., Irwin, Burr Ridge, Ill., 1993, p. 286.

4. Dorthy A. Leonard and Walter C. Swap, *When Sparks Fly: Igniting Creativity in Groups,* Harvard Business School Press, Boston, 1999.

5. George C. Homans, *The Human Group,* Harcourt, Brace & World, New York, 1950, pp. 43–44.

6. Theodore M. Newcomb, *The Acquaintance Process,* Holt, New York, 1961.

7. John W. Thibaut and Harold H. Kelley, *The Social Psychology of Groups,* Wiley, New York, 1959.

8. See Bruce W. Tuckman, "Developmental Sequence in Small Groups," *Psychological Bulletin,* November 1965, pp. 384–399 and Bruce W. Tuckman and Mary Ann C. Jensen, "Stages of Small Group Development Revisited," *Group and Organization Studies,* December 1977, pp. 419–427.

9. Susan C. Hanlon, David C. Meyer and Robert R. Taylor, "Consequences of Gainsharing: A Field Experiment Revisited," *Group and Organizational Management,* Vol. 19, No. 1, 1994, pp. 87–111 and Michael Arndt, "A New Partnership: Sharing the Rewards," *Chicago Tribune,* August 18, 1996, pp. C1–C2.

10. E. Romanelli and E. Tushman, "Organizational Transformation as Punctuated Equilibrium: An Empirical Test," *Academy of Management Journal,* Vol. 37, No. 4, 1994, pp. 1141–1166.

11. Dora C. Lau and J. Keith Murnighan, "Demographic Diversity and Faultlines: The Compositional Dynamics of Organizational Groups," *Academy of Management Review,* Vol. 23, No. 2, 1998, pp. 325–340.

12. Cristina B. Gibson, "Do They Do What They Believe They Can? Group Efficacy and Group Effectiveness Across Tasks and Cultures," *Academy of Management Journal,* Vol. 42, No. 2, 1999, pp. 138–152.

13. Rocio Fernandez-Ballesteros, Juan Diez-Nicolas, G. V. Caparara, C. Barbaranelli and Albert Bandura, "Determinants and Structural Relation of Personal Efficacy to Collective Efficacy," working paper, 2000.

14. Ranjay Gulati, "Social Structure and Alliance Formation Patterns: A Longitudinal Analysis," *Administrative Science Quarterly,* Vol. 40, 1995, pp. 619–652.

15. William B. Stevenson, Jone L. Pearce and Lyman Porter, "The Concept of 'Coalition' in Organization Theory and Research," *Academy of Management Review,* April 1985, pp. 261–262.

16. Nancy C. Morey and Fred Luthans, "The Use of Dyadic Alliances in Informal Organization: An Ethnographic Study," *Human Relations,* Vol. 44, No. 6, 1991, pp. 597–618.

17. For a recent review of basic research on work groups, see Maureen L. Ambrose and Carol T. Kulik, "Old Friends, New Faces–Motivation Research in the 1990s," *Journal of Management,* Vol. 25, No. 1, 1999, pp. 269–273

18. David A. Nadler, J. Richard Hackman and Edward E. Lawler, *Managing Organizational Behavior,* Little, Brown, Boston, 1979, p. 102. Also see Alvin Zander, *Making Groups Effective,* 2d ed., Jossey-Bass, San Francisco, 1994 and Elizabeth Weldon, "The Development of Product and Process Involvements in Work Groups," *Group and Organization Management,* Vol. 25, No. 3, 2000, pp. 244–268.

19. Stanley Schachter, Norris Ellertson, Dorothy McBride, and Doris Gregory, "An Experimental Study of Cohesiveness and Productivity," *Human Relations,* August 1951, pp. 229–239.

20. Leonard Berkowitz, "Group Standards, Cohesiveness, and Productivity," *Human Relations,* Vol. 7, No. 4, 1954, pp. 509–519.

21. Brian Mullen and Carolyn Copper, "The Relation between Group Cohesiveness and Performance: An Integration," *Psychology Bulletin,* Vol. 115, No. 2, 1994, pp. 210–232.

22. D. A. Harrison, K. H. Price and M. P. Bell, "Beyond Relational Demography: Time and the Effects of Surface- and Deep-Level Diversity on Work Group Cohesion," *Academy of Management Journal,* Vol. 41, No. 1, 1998, pp. 96–107.

23. Barry W. Staw, "Organizational Psychology and the Pursuit of the Happy/Productive Worker," *California Management Review,* Summer 1986, p. 49.

24. Gregory P. Shea and Richard A. Guzzo, "Group Effectiveness: What Really Matters?" *Sloan Management Review,* Spring 1987, p. 25 and Gerben Van Der Vegt, Ben Emans and Evert Van De Vilert, "Team Members' Affective Responses to Patterns of Intragroup Interdependence and Job Complexity," *Journal of Management,* Vol. 26, No. 4, 2000, pp. 633–655.

25. Russ Forrester and Allan B. Drexler, "A Model for Team-Based Organization Performance," *Academy of Management Executive,* Vol 13, No. 3, 1999, p. 36.

26. Greg L. Steward and Murray R. Barrick, "Team Structure and Performance: Assessing the Mediating Role of Intrateam Process and the Moderating Role of Task Type," *Academy of Management Journal,* Vol. 43, No. 2, 2000, pp. 135–148.

27. Jane S. Prichard and Neville A. Stanton, "Testing Belbin's Team Role Theory of Effective Groups," *The Journal of Management Development,* Vol. 18, No. 8,

1999, pp. 652–665 and David Partington and Hilary Harris, "Team Role Balance and Team Performance: An Empirical Study," *The Journal of Management Development,* Vol. 18, No. 8, 1999, pp. 694–705.

28. Warren Bennis, "The Secrets of Great Groups," *Executive Forum,* Winter, 1997 pp. 29–32.

29. See Jean Lipman-Bluman and Harold J. Leavitt, "Hot Groups and the HR Manager," *HR Focus,* August, 1999, pp. 11–12 and Jean Lippman-Bluman and Harold J. Leavitt, "Hot Groups 'With Attitude': A New Organizational State of Mind," *Organizational Dynamics* Spring, 1999, p. 63.

30. Stefani L. Yorges, "The Impact of Group Formation and Perceptions of Fairness on Organizational Citizenship Behaviors," *Journal of Applied Social Psychology,* Vol. 29, No. 7, 1999, pp. 1444–1471.

31. Mary J. Waller, "The Timing of Adaptive Group Responses to Nonroutine Events," *Academy of Management Journal,* Vol. 42, No. 2, 1999, pp. 127–137.

32. Don Hellriegel, John W. Slocum, Jr. and Richard W. Woodman, *Organizational Behavior,* 5th ed., West, St. Paul, Minn., 1989, p. 216.

33. Glenn M. Parker, *Team Players and Teamwork,* Jossey-Bass, San Francisco, 1991, pp. 63–64.

34. Keith Davis and John W. Newstrom, *Human Behavior at Work,* 7th ed., McGraw-Hill, New York, 1985, p. 311.

35. Louis B. Barnes and Mark P. Kriger, "The Hidden Side of Organizational Leadership," *Sloan Management Review,* Fall 1986, p. 15.

36. Sandra L. Robinson and Anne M. O'Leary-Kelly, "Monkey See, Monkey Do: The Influence of Work Groups on the Antisocial Behavior of Employees," *Academy of Management Journal,* Vol. 41, No. 6, 1998, pp. 658–672.

37. Irving L. Janis, *Victims of Groupthink,* Houghton Mifflin, Boston, 1972, p. 9.

38. Carrie R. Leana, "A Partial Test of Janis' Groupthink Model: Effects of Group Cohesiveness and Leader Behavior on Defective Decision Making," *Journal of Management,* Vol. 11, No. 1, 1985, pp. 5–17.

39. See Sally Riggs Fuller and Ramon J. Aldag, "Organizational Tonypandy: Lessons from a Quarter Century of the Groupthink Phenomenon," *Organizational Behavior and Human Decision Processes,* Vol. 73, No. 2/3, 1998, pp. 163–184.

40. See Ibid, and Marlene E. Turner and Anthony R. Pratkanis, "Twenty-Five Years of Groupthink Theory and Research: Lessons from the Evaluation of a Theory," *Organizational Behavior and Human Decision Processes,* Vol. 73, No. 2/3, 1998, pp. 105–115.

41. The original research on risky shift goes back to a master's thesis by J. A. F. Stoner, "A Comparison of Individual and Group Decisions Involving Risk," Massachusetts Institute of Technology, Sloan School of Industrial Management, Cambridge, Mass., 1961.

42. See Daniel J. Isenberg, "Group Polarization: A Critical Review and Meta-Analysis," *Journal of Personality and Social Psychology,* Vol. 50, No. 6, 1986, pp. 1141–1151.

43. Richard A. Cosier and Charles R. Schwenk, "Agreement and Thinking Alike: Ingredients for Poor Decisions," *Academy of Management Executive,* February 1990, p. 70.

44. M. Erez and A. Somech, "Is Group Productivity Loss the Rule or the Exception? Effects of Culture and Group-Based Motivation," *Academy of Management Journal,* Vol. 39, No. 5, 1996, pp. 1513–1537.

45. T. A. Judge and T. D. Chandler, "Individual-Level Determinants of Employee Shirking," *Relations Industrielles,* Vol. 51, 1996, pp. 468–486.

46. Robal Johnson, "Effective Team Building," *HR Focus,* April 1996, p. 18.

47. Jon R. Katzenback and Douglas K. Smith, "The Discipline of Teams," *Harvard Business Review,* March–April 1993, p. 112.

48. Ibid., p. 113.

49. Laurie P. O'Leary, "Curing the Monday Blues: A U.S. Navy Guide for Structuring Cross-Functional Teams," *National Productivity Review,* Spring 1996, pp. 43–52.

50. Kenneth Labich, "Elite Teams Get the Job Done," *Fortune,* February 19, 1996, pp. 90–99.

51. David Chaudron, "How to Improve Cross-Functional Teams," *HR Focus,* August 1995, pp. 4–5.

52. See Deborah L. Duarte and Nancy Tennant, *Mastering Virtual Teams,* Jossey-Bass Publishers, San Francisco, 1999.

53. K. Kiser, "Building A Virtual Team," *Training,* March, 1999, p. 34.

54. K. A. Graetz, E. S. Boyle, C. E. Kimble, P. Thompson and J. L. Garloch, "Information Sharing in Face-to-Face, Teleconferencing, and Electronic Chat Groups," *Small Group Research,* December, 1998, pp. 714–743.

55. Dale E. Yeatts and Cloyd Hyten, *High-Performing Self-Managed Work Teams: A Comparison of Theory and Practice,* Sage, Thousand Oaks, Calif., 1998.

56. See Stratford Sherman, "Secrets of HP's 'Muddled' Team," *Fortune,* March 18, 1996, pp. 116–120, and Rich Teerlink and Lee Ozley, *More than a Motorcycle,* Harvard Business School Press, Boston, Mass., 2000.

57. Also see Ron Williams, "Self-Directed Work Teams: A Competitive Advantage," *Quality Digest,* November 1995, pp. 50–52.

58. See Yeatts and Hyten, op. cit., and Bradley L. Kirkman and Benson Rosen, "Beyond Self-Management: Antecedents and Consequences of Team Empower-ment," *Academy of Management Journal,* Vol. 42, No. 1, 1999, pp. 58–74.

59. See Paul S. Goodman, Rukmini Devadas and Terri L. Griffith Hughson, "Groups and Productivity: Analyzing the Effectiveness of Self-Managing Teams," in John P. Campbell, Richard J. Campbell, and Associates (Eds.), *Productivity in Organizations,* Jossey-Bass, San Francisco, 1988, pp. 295–327.

60. C. A. L. Pearson, "Autonomous Workgroups: An Evaluation at an Industrial Site," *Human Relations,* Vol. 45, No. 9, 1992, pp. 905–936.

61. "Work Teams Have Their Work Cut Out for Them," *HR Focus,* January 1993, p. 24.

62. Ibid.

63. Ibid., and John Beck and Neil Yeager, "Moving beyond Team Myths," *Training and Development,* March 1996, pp. S1–S5.

64. Joann S. Lublin, "My Colleague, My Boss," *Wall Street Journal,* April 12, 1995, p. R4.

65. See Daniel R. Ilgen, "Teams Embedded in Organizations," *American Psychologist,* February, 1999, pp. 129–137, and Frank Mueller, Stephen Proctor and David Buchanan, "Teamworking in Its Context(s): Antecedents, Nature and Dimension," *Human Relations,* Vol. 53, No. 11, 2000, pp. 1387–1424.

66. Evelyn F. Rogers, William Metlay, Ira T. Kaplan, and Terri Shapiro, "Self-Managing Work Teams: Do They Really Work?" *Human Resource Planning,* Vol. 18, No. 2, 1996, pp. 53–57.

67. James W. Bishop, K. Dow Scott and Susan H. Burroughs, "Support, Commitment, and Employee Outcomes in a Team Environment," *Journal of Management,* Vol. 26, No. 6, 2000, pp. 1113–1132 and P. Bordia, "Face-to-Face Versus Computer-Mediated Communication: A Synthesis of the Experimental Literature," *Journal of Business Communication,* Vol. 34, January, 1997, pp. 99–120.

68. B. Mullen and C. Copper, "The Relation Between Group Cohesiveness and Group Performance: An Integration," *Psychological Bulletin,* Vol. 115, 1994, pp. 210–227.

69. Melville Cottrill, "Give Your Work Teams Time and Training," *Academy of Management Executive,* Vol. 11, No. 3, 1997, p. 87.

70. Carla Joinson, "Teams at Work," *HR Magazine,* May, 1999, pp. 30–36.

71. Richard F. Schubert, "The Power of Partnership," *Leader to Leader,* Winter, 1997, pp. 9–10.

72. Svan Lembke and Marie G. Wilson, "Putting the 'Team' into Teamwork: Alternative Theoretical Contributions for Contemporary Management Practice," *Human Relations,* Vol. 51, No. 7, 1998, p. 927.

73. Kimball Fisher and Mareen Duncan Fisher, *The Distributed Mind,* AMACOM, New York, 1998.

74. Bradley L. Kirkman and Benson Rosen, "Powering Up Teams," *Organizational Dynamics,* Winter, 2000, pp. 48–66.

75. Kambiz Maani and Campbell Benton, "Rapid Team Learning: Lessons from Team New Zealand's America's

Cup Campaign," *Organizational Dynamics,* Spring 1999, pp. 48–62.

76. Howard Prager, "Cooking Up Effective Team Building," *Training and Development,* December 1999, pp. 14–15.

77. Paul E. Brauchle and David W. Wright, "Training Work Teams," *Training and Development,* March 1993, p. 68.

78. Victoria A. Hovemeyer, "How Effective Is Your Team?" *Training and Development,* September 1993, pp. 67–68.

79. Ralph D. Ward, *21st Century Corporate Board,* Wiley, New York, 1997.

80. "Creating an Outstanding Leadership Team," *Management Review,* February 2000, p. 8.

81. Ram Charan, *Boards at Work: How Corporate Boards Create Competitive Advantage,* Jossey-Bass, San Francisco, 1998.

82. Warren Bennis and Patricia Ward Biederman, *Organizing Genius: The Secrets of Creative Collaboration,* Addison-Wesley, Boston, 1997.

83. Avan R. Jasszwalla and Hemant C. Sashittal, "Building Collaborative Cross-Functional New Product Teams," *Academy of Management Executive,* Vol. 13, No. 3., 1999, p. 50.

84. Glenn Phelps, "The Relationship Between Manager Talent and the Performance of the Teams They Lead," *GRS,* Winter/Spring 2000, p. 17.

85. "Do We Really Need Bosses?" *Omaha World Herald,* July 12, 1998, p. 1-G.

86. Yochanan Altman and Paul Iles, "Learning, Leadership, Teams: Corporate Learning and Organisational Change," *Journal of Management Development,* Vol. 17, No. 1, 1998, pp. 44–55.

87. Sarah Heyward, "How I Taught My Team To Tango," *Across the Board,* July/August 2000, pp. 7–8.

88. Bradley L. Kirkman and Debra L. Shapiro, "The Impact of Cultural Values on Employee Resistance to Teams: Toward a Model of Globalized Self-Managing Work Team Effectiveness," *Academy of Management Review,* Vol. 22, No. 3, 1997, pp. 730–757.

89. Chantell E. Nicholls, H. W. Lane and M. B. Brechu, "Taking Self-Managed Teams to Mexico," *Academy of Management Executive.* Vol. 13, No. 3, 1999, p. 15.

90. Jane E. Salk and Mary Yoko Brannen, "National Culture, Networks, and Individual Influence in a Multinational Management Team," *Academy of Management Journal,* Vol. 43, No. 2, 2000, pp. 191–202.

91. P. Christopher Earley and Elaine Mosakowski, "Creating Hybrid Team Cultures: An Empirical Test of Transnational Team Functioning," *Academy of Management Journal,* Vol. 43, No. 1, 2000, pp. 26–49.

92. Ambrose and Kulik, op. cit. pp. 269–271.

Chapter 15 Footnote References and Supplemental Readings

1. Miguel A. Quinones, J. Kevin Ford and Mark S. Teachout, "The Relationship between Work Experience and Job Performance: A Conceptual and Meta-Analytic Review," *Personnel Psychology,* Vol. 48, 1995, p. 887.

2. "When Implementing Telecommuting Leave Nothing to Chance," *HRFocus,* October 1999, pp. 13–16; "The Basics of a Successful Telework Network," *HRFocus,* June 1999, pp. 9–10; and Wayne F. Cascio, "Managing a Virtual Workplace," *Academy of Management Executive,* Vol. 14, No. 3, 2000, pp. 81–90.

3. Garth R. Jones, *Organization Theory,* 3rd ed., Prentice-Hall, Upper Saddle River, N.J., 2001, pp. 320–321.

4. Michael A. Campion, Lisa Cheraskin and Michael J. Stevens, "Career Related Antecedents and Outcomes of Job Rotation," *Academy of Management Journal,* December 1996, pp. 1512–1542.

5. See Cynthia D. Fisher, "Boredom at Work: A Neglected Concept," *Human Relations,* March 1993, p. 395.

6. John B. Miner, *Organizational Behavior,* Random House, New York, 1988, p. 201.

7. Michael A. Campion and Carol L. McClelland, "Follow-Up and Extension of the Interdisciplinary Costs and Benefits of Enlarged Jobs," *Journal of Applied Psychology,* June 1993, pp. 339–351.

8. Greg R. Oldham and Anne Cummings, "Employee Creativity: Personal and Contextual Factors at Work," *Academy of Management Journal,* June 1996, pp. 607–634.

9. J. Richard Hackman and Greg R. Oldham, "Motivation through the Design of Work: Test of a Theory," *Organizational Behavior and Human Performance,* Vol. 16, 1976, pp. 250–279.

10. J. Richard Hackman, "Work Design," in J. Richard Hackman and J. Lloyd Suttle (eds.), *Improving Life at Work,* Goodyear, Santa Monica, Calif., 1977, p. 129.

11. Ibid., p. 130.

12. Robert W. Renn and Robert J. Vandenberg, "The Critical Psychological States: An Underrepresented Component in Job Characteristics Model Research," *Journal of Management,* Vol. 21, No. 2, 1995, pp. 279–303.

13. David Whitsett, "Where Are Your Enriched Jobs?" *Harvard Business Review,* January–February 1975, pp. 74–80.

14. J. Richard Hackman, Greg R. Oldham, Robert Janson and Kenneth Purdy, "A New Strategy for Job Enrichment," *California Management Review,* Summer 1975, pp. 55–71.

15. Ricky W. Griffin, "Work Redesign Effects on Employee Attitudes and Behaviors: A Long-Term Field Experiment," *Academy of Management Best Papers Proceedings,* 1989, pp. 216–217.

16. Y. Fried and G. R. Ferris, "The Validity of the Job Characteristics Model: A Review and Meta-Analysis," *Personnel Psychology,* Vol. 40, 1987, pp. 287–322 and Brian T. Loher, Robert A. Noe, Nancy L. Moeller and Michael P. Fitzgerald, "A Meta-Analysis of the Relation of Job Characteristics to Job Satisfaction," *Journal of Applied Psychology,* Vol. 70, No. 2, 1985, pp. 280–289.

17. Chi-Sum Wong, Chun Hiu and Kenneth S. Law, "A Longitudinal Study of the Job Perception-Job Satisfaction Relationship: A Test of the Three Alternative Specifications," *Journal of Occupational and Organizational Psychology,* Vol. 71, 1998, pp. 127–146.

18. For example, see Gary Johns, Jia Lin Xie and Yongqing Fang, "Mediating and Moderating Effects in Job Design," *Journal of Management,* Vol. 18, 1992, pp. 657–676; Robert Tiegs, Lois E. Tetrick and Yitzhak Fried, "Growth Need Strength and Context Satisfactions as Moderators of the Relations of the Job Characteristics Model," *Journal of Management,* Vol. 18, 1992, pp. 575–593; Joseph E. Champoux, "A Multivariate Analysis of Curvilinear Relationships among Job Scope, Work Context Satisfactions, and Affective Outcomes," *Human Relations,* January 1992, p. 87; and Yitzhak Fried, "Meta-Analytic Comparison of the Job Diagnostic Survey and Job Characteristics Inventory as Correlates of Work Satisfaction and Performance," *Journal of Applied Psychology,* Vol. 76, No. 5, 1991, pp. 690–697.

19. John Kelly, "Does Job Re-design Theory Explain Job Re-design Outcomes?" *Human Relations,* August 1992, pp. 753–774.

20. Dianne H. B. Welsh, Fred Luthans and Steven M. Sommer, "Managing Russian Factory Workers: The Impact of U.S.-Based Behavioral and Participative Techniques," *Academy of Management Journal,* February 1993, pp. 58–79.

21. Fred Luthans, Barbara Kemmerer, Robert Paul and Lew Taylor, "The Impact of a Job Redesign Intervention on Salespersons' Observed Performance Behaviors," *Group and Organization Studies,* March 1987, pp. 55–72.

22. Ibid.

23. Gregory Moorhead and Ricky W. Griffin, *Organizational Behavior,* 2d ed., Houghton Mifflin, Boston, 1989, p. 238.

24. William A. Kahn, "Psychological Conditions of Personal Engagement and Disengagement At Work," *Academy of Management Journal,* Vol. 33, No. 4, 1990, pp. 692–724.

25. See Edwin E. Lawler and D. T. Hall, "Relationships of Job Characteristics to Job Involvement, Satisfaction, and Intrinsic Motivation," *Journal of Applied Psychology,* Vol. 54, 1970, pp. 305–312; R. T. Mowday, L. W. Porter and R. M. Steers, *Employee-Organization Linkages: The Psychology of Commitment, Absenteeism, and Turnover,* Academic Press, New York, 1982; M. Seeman, "Alienation and Engagement," in A. Campbell and P. E. Converse (Eds.), *The Human Meaning of Social Change,* Russell Sage Foundation, New York, 1972.

26. Kahn, op. cit.

27. A. R. Hochschild, *The Managed Heart: Commercialization of Human Feeling,* University of California Press, Berkeley, Calif., 1983; C. Maslach, *Burnout: The Cost of Caring,* Prentice Hall, Upper Saddle River, N.J., 1982; and J. R. Hackman and G. R. Oldham, *Work Redesign,* Addison-Wesley, Reading, Mass., 1980.

28. Gerald Salancik and Jeffrey Pfeffer, "A Social Information Processing Approach to Job Attitudes and Task Design," *Administrative Science Quarterly,* June 1978, pp. 224–253.

29. See Gary J. Blau and Ralph Katerberg, "Toward Enhancing Research with the Social Information Processing Approach to Job Design," *Academy of Management Review,* October 1982, pp. 543–550; William H. Glick, G. Douglas Jenkins, and Nina Gupta, "Method versus Substance: How Strong Are Underlying Relationships between Job Characteristics and Attitudinal Outcomes?" *Academy of Management Journal,* September 1986, pp. 441–464; and Joe G. Thomas, "Sources of Social Information," *Human Relations,* Vol. 39, No. 9, 1986, pp. 855–870.

30. Joe Thomas and Ricky W. Griffin, "The Social Information Processing Model of Task Design: A Review of the Literature," *Academy of Management Review,* October 1983, pp. 672–682.

31. See Ricky W. Griffin, Thomas S. Bateman, Sandy J. Wayne and Thomas C. Head, "Objective and Social Factors as Determinants of Task Perceptions and Responses: An Integrated Perspective and Empirical Investigation," *Academy of Management Journal,* September 1987, pp. 501–523 and Donald J. Campbell, "Task Complexity: A Review and Analysis," *Academy of Management Review,* January 1988, pp. 40–52.

32. David A. Nadler and Edward E. Lawler III, "Quality of Work Life: Perspectives and Directions," *Organizational Dynamics,* Winter 1983, p. 26.

33. Mitchell W. Fields and James W. Thacker, "Influence of Quality of Work Life on Company and Union Commitment," *Academy of Management Journal,* June 1992, pp. 439–450.

34. Berth Jönsson and Alden G. Lank, "Volvo: A Report on the Workshop on Production Technology and

Quality of Working Life," *Human Resources Management,* Winter 1985, p. 463.

35. Brian Dumaine, "Who Needs a Boss?" *Fortune,* May 7, 1990, pp. 52–53; Ron Williams, "Self-Directed Work Teams: A Competitive Advantage," *Quality Digest,* November 1995, pp. 50–52; and Stratford Sherman, "Secrets of HP's 'Muddled' Team," *Fortune,* March 18, 1996, pp. 116–120.

36. D. P. Hanna, *Designing Organizations For High Performance,* Addison-Wesley, Reading, Mass., 1988.

37. Bradley L. Kirkman, Kevin B. Lowe and Dianne P. Young, *High Performance Work Organizations,* Center for Creative Leadership, Greensboro, N.C., 1999, p. 8.

38. D. A. Nadler and M. L. Tushman, *Strategic Organization Design,* 1988, Scott, Foresman, Glenview, Ill.

39. Arup Varma, Richard Beatty, Craig E. Schneier and David O. Ulrich, "High Performance Work Systems: Exciting Discovery or Passing Fad?" *Human Resource Planning,* Vol. 22, No. 1, 1999, pp. 26–37. Also see Mark Huselid, "The Impact of Human Resource Management Practices on Turnover, Productivity, and Corporate Financial Performance," *Academy of Management Journal,* Vol. 38, 1995, pp. 635–672, and Jeffrey R. Edwards, Judith A. Scully and Mary D. Brtelk, "The Nature and Outcomes of Work: A Replication and Extension of Interdisciplinary Work-Design Research," *Journal of Applied Psychology,* Vol. 85, No. 6, 2000, pp. 860–868.

40. Louisa Wah, "The Dear Cost of 'Scut Work,'" *Management Review,* June 1999, pp. 27–31.

41. Jean M. Phillips, "Effects of Realistic Job Previews on Multiple Organizational Outcomes," *Academy of Management Journal,* Vol. 41, No. 6, 1998, pp. 673–690 and Arthur F. Miller and Marlys Hanson, "Mismatches: The Problem Isn't Bad Employees. It's Good Employees in the Wrong Jobs," *Across The Board,* June, 2000, pp. 25–29.

42. Ron Zemke and Susan Zemke, "Putting Competencies To Work," *Training,* June 1999, pp. 70–76.

43. See Fred Luthans, Kyle W. Luthans, Richard M. Hodgetts and Brett C. Luthans, "Can HPWPs (High Performance Work Practices) Help in the Former Soviet Union? A Cross-Cultural Fit Analysis," *Business Horizons,* September-October 2000.

44. F. Trompenaars, *Riding the Ways of Culture,* 1995, Irwin, New York; F. Trompenaars and C. Hampden-Turner, *Riding the Waves of Culture,* 2nd ed., 1998, McGraw-Hill, New York.

45. Luthans, et. al, op. cit.

46. Edwin A. Locke, "Toward a Theory of Task Motivation and Incentives," *Organizational Behavior and Human Performance,* May 1968, pp. 157–189.

47. Edwin A. Locke, "The Ubiquity of the Technique of Goal Setting in Theories and Approaches to Employee Motivation," *Academy of Management Review,* July 1978, p. 600.

48. Edwin A. Locke, "The Ideas of Frederick W. Taylor: An Evaluation," *Academy of Management Review,* January 1982, p. 16.

49. Edwin A. Locke, "Personal Attitudes and Motivation," *Annual Review of Psychology,* Vol. 26, 1975, pp. 457–480, 596–598.

50. A. J. Mento, R. P. Steele and R. J. Karren, "A Meta-Analytic Study of the Effects of Goal Setting on Task Performance: 1966–1984," *Organizational Behavior and Human Decision Processes,* Vol. 39, 1987, pp. 52–83 and Terence R. Mitchell, Kenneth R. Thompson and Jane George-Falvy, "Goal Setting: Theory and Practice," in Cary L. Cooper and Edwin A. Locke, (Eds.), *Industrial and Organizational Psychology,* Blackwell, Oxford, U.K., 2000, pp. 216–249.

51. C. Lee and P. C. Earley, "Comparative Peer Evaluations of Organizational Behavior Theories," College of Business Administration, Northeastern University, Boston, 1988. This study is reported in Edwin A. Locke and Gary P. Latham, *A Theory of Goal Setting and Task Performance,* Prentice Hall, Upper Saddle River, N.J., 1990, p. 46.

52. Anthony J. Mento, Howard J. Klein and Edwin A. Locke, "Relationship of Goal Level to Valence and Instrumentality," *Journal of Applied Psychology,* August 1992, pp. 395–405 and K. Dow Scott and Anthony M. Townsend, "A Test of Eden's Expectancy/Goal Difficulty Model among Sales Representatives," *Academy of Management Best Papers Proceedings,* 1992, pp. 242–246.

53. Mark E. Tubbs, Donna M. Boehne and James G. Dahl, "Expectancy, Valence, and Motivational Force Functions in Goal-Setting Research: An Empirical Test," *Journal of Applied Psychology,* June 1993, pp. 361–373.

54. Locke, "Personnel Attitudes and Motivation," op. cit. pp. 457–480, 597–598.

55. Also see Manuel London and James W. Smither, "Can Multi-Source Feedback Change Perceptions of Goal Accomplishment, Self-Evaluations, and Performance-Related Outcomes? Theory-Based Applications and Directions for Research," *Personnel Psychology,* Vol. 48, 1995, pp. 803–839.

56. Edwin A. Locke, Gary P. Latham and Miriam Erez, "The Determinants of Goal Commitment," *Academy of Management Review,* January 1988, p. 24.

57. Mark E. Tubbs, "Commitment as a Moderator of the Goal-Performance Relation: A Case for Clearer Construct Definition," *Journal of Applied Psychology,* February 1993, pp. 86–97, and Beth Ann Martin and Donald J. Manning, Jr., "Combined Effects of Normative Information and Task Difficulty on the Goal

Commitment-Performance Relationship," *Journal of Management,* Vol. 21, No. 1, 1995, pp. 65–80.

58. J. C. Wofford, Vicki L. Goodwin and Steven Premack, "Meta-Analysis of the Antecedents of Personal Goal Level and of the Antecedents and Consequences of Goal Commitment," *Journal of Management,* September 1992, pp. 595–615.

59. See Edwin A. Locke, "The Myths of Behavior Mode in Organizations," *Academy of Management Review,* October 1977, pp. 543–553 and Edwin A. Locke, "Resolved: Attitudes and Cognitive Processes Are Necessary Elements in Motivational Models," in Barbara Karmel (ed.), *Point and Counterpoint in Organizational Behavior,* Dryden, Fort Worth, Tex., 1980, pp. 19–42.

60. Albert Bandura, *Social Foundations of Thought and Action,* Prentice Hall, Upper Saddle River, N.J., 1986.

61. Edwin A. Locke and Gary P. Latham, *A Theory of Goal Setting and Task Performance,* Prentice Hall, Upper Saddle River, N.J., 1990, pp. 23–24.

62. Locke, "Toward a Theory of Task Motivation and Incentives," summarizes the laboratory studies; Gary P. Latham and Gary A. Yukl, "A Review of the Research on the Application of Goal Setting in Organizations," *Academy of Management Journal,* December 1975, pp. 824–845, summarizes the field studies. Comprehensive summaries of this research can be found in Edwin A. Locke, Karylle A. Shaw, Lise M. Saari and Gary P. Latham, "Goal Setting and Task Performance: 1969–1980," *Psychological Bulletin,* July 1981, pp. 125–152; Gary P. Latham and Thomas W. Lee, "Goal Setting," in Edwin A. Locke (Ed.), *Generalizing from Laboratory to Field Settings,* Lexington Books, Lexington. Mass., 1986, pp. 101–117; Mark E. Tubbs, "Goal Setting: A Meta-Analytic Examination of the Empirical Evidence," *Journal of Applied Psychology,* Vol. 71, No. 3, 1986, pp. 474–483; and Faten M. Moussa, "Determinants, Process, and Consequences of Personal Goals and Performance," *Journal of Management,* Vol. 26, No.6, 2000, pp. 1259–1285.

63. G. P. Latham and E. A. Locke, "Self-regulation Through Goal Setting," *Organizational Behavior and Human Decision Processes,* Vol. 50, 1991, pp. 212–245.

64. P. C. Earley, C. E. Shalley and G. B. Northcraft, "I Think I Can, I Think I Can . . . Processing Time and Strategy Effects of Goal Acceptance/Rejection Decisions," *Organizational Behavior and Human Decision Processes,* Vol. 53, 1992, pp. 1–13.

65. D. J. Campbell and D. M. Furrer, "Goal Setting and Competition as Determinants of Task Performance," *Journal of Organizational Behavior,* Vol. 16, 1995, pp. 377–389; S. P. Allscheid and D. F. Cellar, "An Interactive Approach to Work Motivation: The Effects of Competition, Rewards, and Goal Difficulty on Task

Performance," *Journal of Business and Psychology,* Vol. 11, 1996, pp. 219–237.

66. R. H. Rasch and Henry L. Tosi, "Factors Affecting Software Developers' Performance: An Integrated Approach," *MIS Quarterly,* Vol. 16, 1992, pp. 395–413.

67. For example, see Gary P. Latham and Gary A. Yukl, "The Effects of Assigned and Participative Goal Setting on Performance and Job Satisfaction," *Journal of Applied Psychology,* April 1976, pp. 166–171 and Katherine I. Miller and Peter Monge, "Participation, Satisfaction, and Productivity: A Meta-Analytic Review," *Academy of Management Journal,* December 1986, pp. 727–753.

68. Maureen L. Ambrose and Carol T. Kulik, "Old Friends, New Faces: Motivation Research in the 1990s," *Journal of Management,* Vol. 25, No. 3, 1999, pp. 231–292.

69. J. C. Wofford, V. L Goodwin and S. Premack, "Meta-analysis of the Antecedents and Consequences of Goal Commitment," *Journal of Management,* Vol. 18, 1992, pp. 595–615.

70. E. A. Locke and P. G. Latham, "Work Motivation and Satisfaction: Light at the End of the Tunnel," *Psychological Science,* Vol. 1, 1990, pp. 240–246.

71. T. W. Lee, E. A. Locke and S. H. Phan, "Explaining the Assigned Goal-Incentive Interaction: The Role of Self-efficacy and Personal Goals," *Journal of Management,* Vol. 23, 1997, pp. 541–559.

72. For example, see Poppy Lauretta McLeod, Jeffrey K. Liker and Sharon A. Lobel, "Process Feedback in Task Groups: An Application of Goal Setting," *Journal of Applied Behavioral Science,* March 1992, pp. 15–41 and A. N. Kluger and Angelo De Nisi, "The Effects of Feedback Interventions on Performance," *Psychological Bulletin,* Vol. 119, 1996, pp. 254–284.

73. Leslie A. Wilk and William K. Redmon, "The Effects of Feedback and Goal Setting on the Productivity and Satisfaction of University Admissions Staff," *Journal of Organizational Behavior Management,* Vol. 18, No. 1, 1998, pp. 45–56.

74. See Richard D. Arvey, H. Dudley Dewhirst, and Edward M. Brown, "A Longitudinal Study of the Impact of Changes in Goal Setting on Employee Satisfaction," *Personnel Psychology,* Autumn 1978, pp. 595–608 and John R. Hollenbeck and Arthur P. Brief, "The Effects of Individual Differences and Goal Origin on Goal Setting and Performance," *Organizational Behavior and Human Decision Processes,* Vol. 40, 1987, pp. 392–414.

75. Gary P. Latham and Lise M. Saari, "Importance of Supportive Relationships in Goal Setting," *Journal of Applied Psychology,* April 1979, pp. 151–156.

76. Howard Garland, "Goal Level and Task Performance: A Compelling Replication of Some Compelling

Results," *Journal of Applied Psychology,* April 1982, pp. 245–248.

77. Howard J. Klein and Jay S. Kim, "A Field Study of the Influence of Situational Constraints, Leader-Member Exchange, and Goal Commitment on Performance," *Academy of Management Journal,* Vol. 41, No. 1, 1998, 88–95.

78. James T. Austin and Philip Bobko, "Goal Setting Theory: Unexplored Areas and Future Research Needs," *Journal of Occupational Psychology,* Vol. 58, No. 4, 1985, pp. 289–308.

79. Donald J. Campbell, "Task Complexity: A Review and Analysis," *Academy of Management Review,* January 1988, pp. 40–52 and Rich P. DeShon and Ralph A. Alexander, "Goal Setting Effects on Implicit and Explicit Learning of Complex Tasks," *Organizational Behavior and Human Decision Processes,* January 1996, pp. 18–36.

80. Maureen L. Ambrose and Carol T. Kulik, "Old Friends, New Faces: Motivation Research in the 1990s," *Journal of Management,* Vol. 25, No. 3, 1999, pp. 231–292.

81. Barry M. Staw and R. D. Boettger, "Task Revision: A Neglected Form of Work Performance," *Academy of Management Journal,* Vol. 33, No. 4, 1990, 534–559. 1990.

82. E. A. Locke and G. P. Latham, *Goal Setting: A Motivational Technique That Really Works,* Prentice Hall, Upper Saddle River, N.J., 1984, pp. 171–172.

83. Patrick M. Wright, Jennifer M. George, S. Regena Farnsworth and Gary C. McMahan, "Productivity and Extra-Role Behavior: The Effects of Goals and Incentives on Spontaneous Helping," *Journal of Applied Psychology,* June 1993, pp. 374–381.

84. Locke and Latham, *Goal Setting: A Motivational Technique,* op. cit., pp. 171–172, and Gary P. Latham, "Motivate Employee Performance through Goal Setting," in Edwin Locke (Ed.), *Handbook of Principles of Organizational Behavior,* Blackwood, Oxford, U.K., 2000, pp. 107–119.

85. Ibid.

86. Richard M. Hodgetts, *Blueprints for Continuous Improvement,* American Management Association, New York, 1993, pp. 108–109.

87. Donald J. Ford, "Benchmarking HRD," *Training and Development Journal,* June 1993, pp. 36–42.

88. Kenneth R. Thompson, Wayne A. Hochwarter and Nicholas J. Mathys, "Stretch Targets: What Makes Them Effective?" *Academy of Management Executive,* Vol. 11, No. 3, 1997, p. 48.

89. P. C. Earle, "Supervisors and Shop Stewards as Sources of Contextual Information in Goal Setting: A Comparison of the United States with England," *Journal of Applied Psychology,* Vol. 71, 1986, pp. 111–117.

90. Locke and Latham, *A Theory of Goal Setting,* op. cit., p. 15.

91. For example, see J. M. Ivancevich, "Changes in Performance in a Management by Objectives Program," *Administrative Science Quarterly,* Vol. 19, 1974, pp. 563–574; Jan P. Muczyk, "A Controlled Field Experiment Measuring the Impact of MBO on Performance Data," *Journal of Management Studies,* October 1978, pp. 318–329; and Kenneth R. Thompson. Fred Luthans and Will Terpening, "The Effects of MBO on Performance and Satisfaction in a Public Sector Organization," *Journal of Management,* Spring 1981, pp. 53–69.

92. Locke and Latham, *A Theory of Goal Setting,* op. cit., p. 244. Also see Raymond A. Katzell and Donna E. Thompson, "Work Motivation: Theory and Practice," *American Psychologist,* February 1990, pp. 149–150.

93. Robert Rodgers and John E. Hunter, "Impact of Management by Objectives on Organizational Productivity," *Journal of Applied Psychology,* Vol. 76, No. 2, 1991, pp. 322–336.

94. Christian M. Ellis and E. Michael Norman, "Real Change in Real Time," *Management Review,* February 1999, pp. 33–38.

95. Denise M. Rousseau, *Psychological Contracts In Organizations: Understanding Written and Unwritten Agreements,* Sage, Thousand Oaks, Calif., 1995, and Denise M. Rousseau and Michael B. Arthur, "The Boundaryless Human Resource Function," *Organizational Dynamics,* Spring 1999, pp. 7–18.

96. Elizabeth Wolfe Morrison and Sandra L. Robinson, "When Employees Feel Betrayed: A Model of How Psychological Contract Violation Develops," *Academy of Management Review,* Vol. 22, No. 1, 1997, pp. 226–256.

Chapter 16 Footnote References and Supplemental Readings

1. Aubrey C. Daniels, *Bringing Out the Best in People,* McGraw-Hill, New York, 2000, p. xiv.

2. See: David C. Palmer, "On Skinners's Rejection of S–R Psychology," *The Behavior Analyst,* Vol. 21, 1998, pp. 93–96.

3. For example, see Brian D. Till and Randi Lynn Priluck, "Stimulus Generalization in Classical Conditioning: An Initial Investigation and Extension," *Psychology and Marketing,* Vol. 17, No. 1, 2000, pp. 55–72.

4. B. F. Skinner, *The Shaping of a Behaviorist,* Knopf, New York, 1979, p. 143.

5. For example, see David W. Schaal, "Skinner May Be Difficult, But . . . " *The Behavior Analyst,* Vol. 21, No. 1, 1998, pp. 97–101.

6. Roy A. Moxley, "Why Skinner Is Difficult," *The Behavior Analyst,* Vol. 21, No. 1, 1998, pp. 73–91.

7. For example, see Valentin Dragoi and J. E. R. Staddon, "The Dynamics of Operant Conditioning," *Psychological Review,* Vol. 106, No. 1, 1999, pp. 20–61; Richard W. Malott, "Conceptual Behavior Analysis," *Journal of Organizational Behavior Management,* Vol. 19, No. 3, 1999, pp. 75–81; William M. Baum, "New Paradigm for Behavior Analysis," *The Behavior Analyst,* Vol. 20, No. 1, 1997, pp. 11–15; and John A. Bargh and Melissa J. Ferguson, "Beyond Behaviorism: On the Automaticity of Higher Mental Processes," *Psychological Bulletin,* Vol. 126, No. 6, 2000, pp. 925–945.

8. See David J. Murry, Andrea R. Kilgour and Louise Wasylkiw, "Conflicts and Missed Signals in Psychoananlysis, Behaviorism, and Gestalt Psychology," *American Psychologist,* April 2000, pp. 424–425 and Richard J. DeGrandpre, "A Science of Meaning: Can Behaviorism Bring Meaning to Psychological Science?" *American Psychologist,* July 2000, pp. 721–739.

9. See Gordon R. Foxall, "Radical Behaviorist Interpretation: Generating and Evaluating an Account of Consumer Behavior," *The Behavior Analyst,* Vol. 21, No. 2, 1998, pp. 321–354.

10. See Fred Luthans and Alexander D. Stajkovic, "Reinforce for Performance: The Need to Go Beyond Pay and Even Rewards," *Academy of Management Executive,* Vol. 13, No. 2, 1999, pp. 49–57; Jeanne Bursch and Adrianne Von Strander, "Well-Structured Employee Reward/Recognition Programs Yield Positive Results," *HR Focus,* November 1999, pp. 1, 14–15; Paul L. Brown, "Communicating the Benefits of the Behavioral Approach to the Business Community," *Journal of Organizational Behavior Management,* Vol. 20, Nos. 3/4, 2000, pp, 59–72; and Thomas C. Mawhinney, "OBM Today and Tomorrow: Then and Now," *Journal of Organizational Behavior Management,* Vol. 20, Nos. 3/4, 2000, pp. 73–137.

11. See Judith A. Ouellette and Wendy Wood, "Habit and Intention in Everyday Life: The Multiple Processes by Which Past Behavior Predicts Future Behavior," *Psychological Bulletin,* Vol. 124, No. 1, 1998, pp. 54–74.

12. For example, see Steven Kerr, "On the Folly of Rewarding A, while Hoping for B," *Academy of Management Executive,* February 1995, p. 7; Judith L. Komaki, "Toward Effective Supervision: An Operant Analysis and Comparison of Managers at Work," *Journal of Applied Psychology,* Vol. 71, No. 2, 1986,

pp. 270–279; Fred Luthans and Robert Kreitner, *Organizational Behavior Modification,* Scott, Foresman, Glenview, Ill., 1975; Fred Luthans and Robert Kreitner, *Organizational Behavior Modification and Beyond,* Scott, Foresman, Glenview, Ill., 1985; W. E. Scott, Jr. and P. M. Podsakoff, *Behavioral Principles in the Practice of Management,* Wiley, New York, 1985; Daniels, op. cit.; and Beth Sulzer-Azaroff, "Of Eagles and Worms: Changing Behavior in a Complex World," *Journal of Organizational Behavior Management,* Vol. 20, Nos. 3/4, 2000, pp. 139–163.

13. For example, see Paul Chance, "Where Does Behavior Come From?" *The Behavior Analyst,* Vol. 22, No. 2, 1999, pp. 161–163 and R. Epstein (Ed.), *Cognition, Creativity, and Behavior: Selected Essays,* Praeger, Westport, Conn., 1996.

14. Bertrand Russell, *An Outline of Philosophy,* Meridian, New York, 1960. (Original work published in 1927).

15. Robert Glaser, "The Reemergence of Learning Theory within Instructional Research," *American Psychologist,* January 1990, p. 29.

16. For example, see Dennis A. Gioia and Henry P. Sims, Jr., "Cognition–Behavior Connections: Attribution and Verbal Behavior in Leader–Subordinate Interactions," *Organizational Behavior and Human Decision Processes,* Vol. 37, 1986, pp. 197–229; Jeffrey L. Godwin, Christopher P. Neck and Jeffery D. Houghton, "The Impact of Thought Self-Leadership on Individual Goal Performance: A Cognitive Perspective," *The Journal of Management Development,* Vol. 18, No. 2, 1999, pp. 153–169; and Cheryl L. Rusting, "Personality, Mood, and Cognitive Processing of Emotional Information: Three Conceptual Frameworks," *Psychological Bulletin,* Vol. 124, No. 2, 1998, pp. 165–196.

17. Social learning and now social cognitive theory is mostly attributed to Albert Bandura, *Social Learning Theory,* Prentice Hall, Upper Saddle River, N.J., 1977; Albert Bandura, *Social Foundations of Thought and Action,* Prentice Hall, Upper Saddle River, N.J., 1986; and Albert Bandura, "Social Cognitive Theory: An Agentic Perspective," *Asian Journal of Social Psychology,* Vol. 2, 1999, pp. 21–41.

18. See Bandura *Social Foundations* and "Social Cognitive Theory" op.cit. and Alexander D. Stajkovic and Fred Luthans, "Social Cognitive Theory and Self Efficacy," *Organizational Dynamics,* Spring 1998, pp. 62–74.

19. Thomas C. Mawhinney, "Learning," in Dennis W. Organ and Thomas Bateman, *Organizational Behavior,* 3d ed., Business Publications, Plano, Tex., 1986, pp. 90–91.

20. Albert Bandura, "Social Learning Theory," In J. T. Spence, R. C. Carson and J. W. Thibaut (Eds.), *Behavioral Approaches to Therapy,* General Learning, Morristown, N.J., 1976, p. 5.

21. For a summary of this research, see Albert Bandura, *Social Foundations of Thought and Action: A Social-Cognitive View,* Prentice Hall, Upper Saddle River, N.J., 1986.

22. See Stajkovic and Luthans, op. cit., and Fred Luthans and Alexander D. Stajkovic, "Provide Recognition for Performance Improvement," in Edwin A. Locke (Ed.), *Handbook of the Principles of Organizational Behavior,* Blackwell, Oxford, UK, 2000, pp. 167–180.

23. Albert Bandura, *Self-Efficacy: The Exercise of Control,* W.H. Freeman, New York, 1997, p. 3.

24. Bandura, *Self-Efficacy: The Exercise of Control* and "Social Cognitive Theory: An Agentic Perspective," op. cit., and Stajkovic and Luthans, "Social Cognitive Theory and Self-Efficacy," op. cit.

25. Alexander D. Stajkovic and Fred Luthans, "Self-Efficacy and Work Related Performance: A Meta-Analysis," *Psychological Bulletin,* Vol. 24, No. 2, 1998, pp. 240–261.

26. A. Bandura, C. B. Taylor, S. C. Williams, I. N. Medford and J. D. Barchas, "Catecholamine Secretion as a Function of Perceived Coping Self-Efficacy," *Journal of Consulting and Clinical Psychology,* Vol. 53, 1985, pp. 406–414.

27. Bandura, *Self Efficacy: The Exercise of control* and "Social Cognitive Theory: An Agentic Perspective," op. cit., and Stajkovic and Luthans, "Social Cognitive Theory and Self-Efficacy," op. cit.

28. For example see: Alexander D. Stajkovic and Fred Luthans, "A Social Cognitive Model for Organizational Behavior Theory and Application," Paper presented at Organizational Behavior Division, Academy of Management, San Diego, 1998.

29. See Spencer A. Rathus, *Psychology* 4th Ed., Holt, Rinehart and Winston, Fort Worth, Tex., 1990, p. 201 for a more detailed discussion of the extinction process.

30. Gregory B. Northcraft and Margaret A. Neale, *Organizational Behavior,* Dryden, Chicago, 1990, p. 162.

31. See Chance, op. cit.

32. For example, see E. L. Deci, "The Effects of Contingent and Noncontingent Rewards and Controls on Intrinsic Motivation," *Organizational Behavior and Human Performance,* Vol. 8, 1972, pp. 217–229; E. L. Deci, *Intrinsic Motivation,* Plennum Press, New York, 1975; and E. L. Deci, "On the Nature and Functions of Motivation Theories," *Psychological Sciences,* Vol. 3, 1992, pp. 167–171.

33. See E. L. Deci and R. M. Ryan, *Intrinsic Motivation and Self Determination in Human Behavior.* Plennum Press, New York, 1985.

34. R. Eisenburger and J. Cameron, "Detrimental Effects of Reward: Reality or Myth?" *American Psychologist,* Vol. 51, 1996, p. 1157.

35. Ibid., p. 1153.

36. J. Cameron and W. D. Pierce, "Reinforcement, Reward and Intrinsic Motivation: A Meta-Analysis," *Review of Education Research,* Vol. 64, 1994, pp. 363–423.

37. John S. Carton, "The Differential Effects of Tangible Rewards and Praise on Intrinsic Motivation: A Comparison of Cognitive Evaluation Theory and Operant Theory," *The Behavior Analyst,* Vol. 19, 1996, pp. 237–255.

38. See: Alfie Kohn, *Punished By Rewards,* Houghton Mifflin, Boston, 1993 and Alfie Kohn, "Why Incentive Plans Cannot Work," *Harvard Business Review,* September–October, 1993, pp. 62–63.

39. Kohn, *Punished By Rewards,* op.cit., p. 119. For comprehensive critiques see: David Reitman, "Punished by Misunderstanding," *The Behavior Analyst,* Vol. 21, No. 1, 1998, pp. 143–157 and E. F. Montemayor, "Review of Punished by Rewards," *Personnel Psychology,* Vol. 48, 1995, pp. 941–945.

40. See Steve Kerr, "Practical, Cost-Neutral Alternatives that You May Know, but Don't Practice," *Organizational Dynamics,* Vol. 28, No. 1, 1999, pp. 61–70 and Jeffrey Pfeffer, *The Human Equation,* Harvard Business School Press, Boston, 1998.

41. Edward E. Lawler, *Strategic Pay,* Jossey-Bass, San Francisco, 1990.

42. See M. Bloom, "The Performance Effects of Pay Dispersion on Individuals and Organizations," *Academy of Management Journal,* March 1999, pp. 25–40 and Tim Gardner, "When Pay for Performance Works Too Well: The Negative Impact of Pay Dispersion," *Academy of Management Executive,* Vol. 13, No. 4, 1999, pp. 101–102.

43. Bandura, *Self-Efficacy: The Exercise of Control,* op. cit., p. 7.

44. Bandura, *Social Foundations,* op. cit., p. 228.

45. Robert A. Baron, *Behavior in Organizations,* Allyn & Bacon, Boston, 1986, p. 51.

46. Judy L. Agnew and William K. Redmon, "Contingency Specifying Stimuli: The Role of 'Rules' in Organizational Behavior Management," *Journal of Organizational Behavior Management,* Vol. 12, No. 2, 1992, pp. 67–76 and Richard W. Mallott, "A Theory of Rule-Governed Behavior," *Journal of Organizational Behavior Management,* Vol. 12, No. 2, 1992, pp. 45–65.

47. See: Judy L. Agnew, "The Establishing Operation in Organizational Behavior Management," *Journal of Organizational Behavior Management,* Vol. 18, No. 1, 1998, pp. 7–19, and J. Michael, "Establishing Operations," *The Behavior Analyst,* Vol. 16, No. 2, 1993, pp. 191–206. Establishing operation basically means there is enough motivation (e.g., the individual is not satiated) for the discriminative stimulus and the reinforcer to emit the behavior.

48. Aubrey Daniels, *Bringing out the Best in People,* McGraw-Hill, New York, 1995, p. 27.

49. For example, see: S. L. Rynes and B. Gerhart (Eds.), *Compensation in Organizations: Progress and Prospects.* New Lexington Press, San Francisco, 1999.

50. B. Gerhart, H. B. Minkoff and R. N. Olson, "Employee Compensation: Theory, Practice and Evidence," in G. R. Ferris, S. D. Rosen and D. T. Barnum (Eds.), *Handbook of Human Resource Management,* Blackwell, Cambridge, Mass., 1995.

51. Donald J. Campbell, Kathleen M. Campbell and Ho-Beng Chia, "Merit Pay, Performance Appraisal, and Individual Motivation: An Analysis and Alternative," *Human Resource Management,* Summer 1998, pp. 131–146, and Jeffrey Pfeffer, "Six Dangerous Myths About Pay," *Harvard Business Review,* May–June 1998, pp. 109–119.

52. Donald Brookes, "Merit Pay: Does It Help or Hinder Productivity?" *HR Focus,* January 1993, p. 13.

53. Atul Mitra, Nina Gupta and G. Douglas Jenkins, Jr., "The Case of the Invisible Merit Raise: How People See Their Pay Raises," *Compensation and Benefits Review,* May–June 1995, pp. 75–76.

54. For a recent analysis of pay for performance, see: Luthans and Stajkovic, "Reinforce for Performance," op. cit., pp. 49–57. For "New Pay" see Patricia K. Zingheim and Jay R. Schuster, "Introduction: How Are the New Pay Tools Being Deployed?" *Compensation and Benefits Review,* July–August, 1995, pp. 10–11 and Patricia K. Zingheim and Jay R. Schuster, *Pay People Right,* Jossey-Bass, San Francisco, 2000.

55. Virginia M. Gibson, "The New Employee Reward System," *Management Review,* February 1995, p. 18.

56. Alexander D. Stajkovic and Fred Luthans, "The Relative Effects of Incentive Motivators on Work Performance," *Academy of Management Journal,* Vol. 44, No. 3, 2001.

57. Melissa W. Barringer and George T. Milkovich, "A Theoretical Exploration of the Adoption and Design of Flexible Benefit Plans," *Academy of Management Review,* January 1998, pp. 305–324.

58. Jennifer Laabs, "Demand Performance for Benefits," *Workforce,* January 2000, pp. 45–46.

59. Bob Nelson, "Secrets of Successful Employee Recognition," *Quality Digest,* August 1996, p. 26.

60. This study was conducted by Gerald Graham and reported in ibid.

61. This is from Robert Half International and is reported in ibid.

62. Stajkovic and Luthans, "The Relative Effects," op. cit.

63. Luthans and Stajkovic, "Provide Recognition," op. cit., pp. 173–174.

64. Jerry L. McAdams, "Design, Implementation and Results: Employee Involvement and Performance Reward Plans," *Compensation and Benefits Review,* March–April 1995, p. 55.

65. Ibid., p. 54.

66. See S. J. Ashford and L. L. Cummings, "Feedback as an Individual Resource," *Organizational Behavior and Human Performance,* Vol. 32, 1983, pp. 370–398, and Mary F. Sully DeLuque and Steven Sommer, "The Impact of Culture on Feedback–Seeking Behavior," *Academy of Management Review,* Vol. 25, No. 4, 2000, pp. 829–849.

67. A. N. Kluger and Angelo DeNisi, "The Effects of Feedback Interventions on Performance: A Historical Review, a Meta-Analysis, and a Preliminary Feedback Intervention Theory," *Psychological Bulletin,* Vol. 119, 1996, pp. 254–248.

68. D. M. Prue and J. A. Fairbank, "Performance Feedback in Organizational Behavior Management: A Review," *Journal of Organizational Behavior Management,* Spring 1981, pp. 1–16.

69. Richard E. Kopelman, "Objective Feedback," in Edwin A. Locke (ed.), *Generalizing from Laboratory to Field Settings,* Lexington Books, Lexington, Mass., 1986, pp. 119–145.

70. Stajkovic and Luthans, "The Relative Effects," op. cit.

71. Fred Luthans, Richard M. Hodgetts and Stuart A. Rosenkrantz, *Real Managers,* Ballinger, Cambridge, Mass., 1988, pp. 141–142.

72. Daniel R. Ilgen, Cynthia D. Fisher and M. Susan Taylor, "Consequences of Individual Feedback on Behavior in Organizations," *Journal of Applied Psychology,* August 1979, pp. 349–371 and Locke and Latham, op. cit., pp. 185–189.

73. David A. Nadler, "The Effects of Feedback on Task Group Behavior: A Review of the Experimental Research," *Organizational Behavior and Human Performance,* June 1979, pp. 309–338.

74. John M. Ivancevich and J. Timothy McMahon, "The Effects of Goal Setting, External Feedback, and Self-Generated Feedback on Outcome Variables: A Field Experiment," *Academy of Management Journal,* June 1982, pp. 291–308.

75. Robert C. Linden and Terence R. Mitchell, "Reactions to Feedback: The Role of Attributions," *Academy of Management Journal,* June 1985, pp. 291–308.

76. Kenneth M. Nowack, "360-Degree Feedback: The Whole Story," *Training and Development,* January 1993, pp. 69–72.

77. David M. Herold, Robert C. Linden, and Marya L. Leatherwood, "Using Multiple Attributes to Assess Sources of Performance Feedback," *Academy of Management Journal,* December 1987, pp. 826–835.

78. For example, see Manuel London and James W. Smither, "Can Multisource Feedback Change Perceptions of Goal Accomplishment, Self-Evaluations, and

Performance-Related Outcomes? Theory-Based Applications and Directions for Research," *Personnel Psychology,* Vol. 48, 1995, pp. 803–839.

79. Steve Williams and Fred Luthans, "The Impact of Choice of Rewards and Feedback on Task Performance," *Journal of Organizational Behavior,* Vol. 13, 1992, pp. 653–666.

80. Robert Waldersee and Fred Luthans, "The Impact of Positive and Corrective Feedback on Customer Service Performance," *Journal of Organizational Behavior,* Vol. 14, 1993, pp. 83–95.

81. For example, academic models see J. Komaki, "Toward Effective Supervision: An Operant Analysis and Comparison of Managers at Work," *Journal of Applied Psychology,* Vol. 71, 1986, pp. 270–279 and W. E. Scott, Jr. and P. M. Podsakoff, *Behavioral Principles in the Practice of Management,* Wiley, New York, 1985. For consulting models see T. F. Gilbert, *Human Competence: Engineering Worthy Performance,* McGraw-Hill, New York, 1978; L. M. Miller, *Behavior Management: The New Science of Managing People at Work,* Wiley, New York, 1978; and Daniels, op. cit. For a comprehensive history see Alyce M. Dickinson, "The Historical Roots of Organizational Behavior Management in the Private Sector," *Journal of Organizational Behavior Management,* Vol. 20, Nos. 3/4, 2000, pp. 9–58.

82. Alexander D. Stajkovic and Fred Luthans, "A Meta-Analysis of the Effects of Organizational Behavior Modification on Task Performance, 1975–95," *Academy of Management Journal,* Vol. 40, No. 5, 1997, pp. 1122–1149.

83. See Fred Luthans, "Resolved: Functional Analysis Is the Best Technique for Diagnostic Evaluation of Organizational Behavior," in Barbara Karmel (Ed.), *Point and Counterpoint in Organizational Behavior,* Dryden, Fort Worth, Tex., 1980, pp. 48–60.

84. V. Mark Daniel, "Employee Absenteeism: A Selective Review of Antecedents and Consequences," *Journal of Organizational Behavior Management,* Spring/Summer 1985, p. 157.

85. Stajkovic and Luthans, "A Meta-Analysis," op. cit. and Stajkovic and Luthans, "The Relative Effects," op. cit.

86. Kenneth N. Wexley and Gary P. Latham, *Developing and Training Human Resources,* Scott, Foresman, Glenview, Ill., 1981, p. 78 and see Donna Goldwasser, "Beyond ROI," *Training,* January 2001, pp. 82–90.

87. Ibid., pp. 81–84.

88. See Lee W. Frederiksen (Ed.), *Handbook of Organizational Behavior Management,* Interscience Wiley, New York, 1982, pp. 12–14; these findings are summarized in Luthans and Kreitner, *Organizational Behavior Modification and Beyond,* op. cit., Chap. 8.

89. R. W. Kempen, "Absenteeism and Tardiness," in Frederiksen, op. cit., p. 372.

90. Fred Luthans and Terry L. Maris, "Evaluating Personnel Programs through the Reversal Technique," *Personnel Journal,* October 1979, pp. 696–697.

91. Dov Zohar and Nahum Fussfeld, "A System Approach to Organizational Behavior Modification: Theoretical Considerations and Empirical Evidence," *International Review of Applied Psychology,* October 1981, pp. 491–505.

92. Beth Sulzer-Azaroff, "Behavioral Approaches to Occupational Health and Safety," in Frederiksen, op. cit., pp. 505–538. Also see Robert A. Reber, Jerry A. Wallin and David L. Duhon, "Preventing Occupational Injuries through Performance Management," *Public Personnel Management,* Summer 1993, pp. 301–312.

93. See William Atkinson, "Behavior-Based Safety," *Management Review,* February 2000, pp. 41–45.

94. Thomas K. Connellan, *How to Improve Human Performance,* Harper & Row, New York, 1978, pp. 170–174.

95. Robert Mirman, "Performance Management in Sales Organizations," in Frederiksen, op. cit., pp. 427–475.

96. Mark J. Martinko, J. Dennis White and Barbara Hassell, "An Operant Analysis of Prompting in a Sales Environment," *Journal of Organizational Behavior Management,* Vol. 10, No. 1, 1989, pp. 93–107.

97. Fred Luthans, Robert Paul and Douglas Baker, "An Experimental Analysis of the Impact of Contingent Reinforcement on Salespersons Performance Behaviors," *Journal of Applied Psychology,* June 1981, pp. 314–323 and Fred Luthans, Robert Paul and Lew Taylor, "The Impact of Contingent Reinforcement on Retail Salespersons' Performance Behaviors: A Replicated Field Experiment," *Journal of Organizational Behavior Management,* Spring/Summer 1985, pp. 25–35.

98. See Kirk O'Hara, C. Merle Johnson and Terry A. Beehr, "Organizational Behavior Management in the Private Sector: A Review of Empirical Research and Recommendations for Further Investigation," *Academy of Management Review,* October 1985, pp. 848–864; Gerald A. Merwin, John A. Thompson and Eleanor E. Sanford, "A Methodology and Content Review of Organizational Behavior Management in the Private Sector 1978–1986," *Journal of Organizational Behavior Management,* Vol. 10, No. 1, 1989, pp. 39–57; Frank Andrasik, "Organizational Behavior Modification in Business Settings: A Methodological and Content Review," *Journal of Organizational Behavior Management,* Vol. 10, No. 1, 1989, pp. 59–77; and Timothy V. Nolan, Kimberly A. Jarema and John Austin, "An Objective Review of the Journal of Organizational Behavior Management: 1987–1997," *Journal of Organizational Behavior*

Management, Vol. 19, No. 3, 1999, pp. 83–114; and Maureen L. Ambrose and Carol T. Kulik, "Old Friends, New Faces: Motivation Research in the 1990s," *Journal of Management,* Vol. 25, No. 3, 1999, pp. 263–266.

99. Robert Ottemann and Fred Luthans, "An Experimental Analysis of the Effectiveness of an Organizational Behavior Modification Program in Industry," *Academy of Management Proceedings,* 1975, pp. 140–142; Fred Luthans and Jason Schweizer, "How Behavior Modification Techniques Can Improve Total Organizational Performance," *Management Review,* September 1979, pp. 43–50; and Fred Luthans, Walter S. Maciag and Stuart A. Rosenkrantz, "O.B. Mod.: Meeting the Productivity Challenge with Human Resource Management," *Personnel,* March–April 1983, pp. 28–36.

100. Luthans, Paul and Baker, op. cit.; Luthans, Paul and Taylor, op. cit.; and Charles A. Snyder and Fred Luthans, "Using O.B. Mod. to Increase Hospital Productivity," *Personnel Administrator,* August 1982, pp. 67–73.

101. Dianne H. B. Welsh, Fred Luthans and Steven M. Sommer, "Managing Russian Factory Workers: The Impact of U.S.-Based Behavioral and Participative Techniques," *Academy of Management Journal,* February 1993, pp. 58–79 and Dianne H. B. Welsh, Fred Luthans and Steven M. Sommer, "Organizational Behavior Modification Goes to Russia: Replicating an Experimental Analysis across Cultures and Tasks," *Journal of Organizational Behavior Management,* Vol. 13, No. 2, 1993, pp. 15–35.

102. Dianne H. B. Welsh, Steven M. Sommer and Nancy Birch, "Changing Performance among Russian Retail Workers: Effectively Transferring American Management Techniques," *Journal of Organizational Change Management,* Vol. 6, No. 2, 1993, pp. 34–50.

103. Alexander D. Stajkovic and Fred Luthans, "A Meta-Analysis of the Effects of Organizational Behavior Modification on Task Performance: 1975–1995," *Academy of Management Journal,* Vol. 40, No. 5, 1997, pp. 1122–1149.

104. Luthans and Stajkovic, "Reinforce for Performance," op. cit. p. 55.

Chapter 17 Footnote References and Supplemental Readings

1. Gary Gemmill and Judith Oakley, "Leadership: An Alienating Social Myth?" *Human Relations,* Vol. 45, No. 2, 1992, p. 113.

2. Warren Bennis, "The End of Leadership," *Organizational Dynamics,* Summer 1999, pp, 71–80. Also see Warren Bennis, "Leading in Unnerving Times," *MIT Sloan Management Review,* Winter 2001, pp. 97–103.

3. "It's the Manager, Stupid," *The Economist,* August 8, 1998, p. 54.

4. Stratford Sherman, "How Tomorrow's Best Leaders Are Learning Their Stuff," *Fortune,* November 27, 1995, pp. 91–92. Also see Donna Goldwasser, "Reinventing the Wheel: How American Home Products Transforms Senior Managers into Leaders," *Training,* February 2001, pp. 54–65.

5. For some basic research on influence, see Herman Aguinis, Mitchell S. Nesler, Megumi Hosoda and James T. Tedeschi, "The Use of Influence Tactics in Persuasion," *Journal of Social Psychology,* Vol. 124, No. 4, 1994, pp. 429–438.

6. Warren G. Bennis, "Managing the Dream: Leadership in the 21st Century," *Journal of Organizational Change Management,* Vol. 2, No. 1, 1989, p. 7. Also see W. Glenn Rowe, "Creating Wealth in Organizations: The Role of Strategic Leadership," *Academy of Management Executive,* Vol. 15, No. 1, 2001, pp. 81–94.

7. Bernard M. Bass, *Bass and Stogdill's Handbook of Leadership,* 3d ed., Free Press, New York, 1990, p. 11.

8. George B. Weathersby, "Commentary: Leadership vs. Management," *Management Review,* March 1999, p. 5.

9. Sherman, op. cit., p. 92.

10. Richard M. Hodgetts, "A Conversation with Warren Bennis on Leadership in the Midst of Downsizing," *Organizational Dynamics,* Summer 1996, p. 78.

11. Chester A. Schriesheim and Steven Kerr, "Theories and Measures of Leadership: A Critical Appraisal of Current and Future Directions," in James G. Hunt and Lars L. Larson (Eds.), *Leadership: The Cutting Edge,* Southern Illinois University Press, Carbondale, Ill. 1977, p. 22.

12. Daniel Goleman, *Emotional Intelligence,* Bantam, New York, 1995; Nancy Gibbs, "The EQ Factor," *Time,* October 2, 1995, pp. 60–66; and Martin P. Seligman, *Learned Optimism,* Pocket Books, New York, 1992.

13. Martin M. Chemers, Carl B. Watson and Stephen T. May, "Dispositional Affect and Leadership Effectiveness: A Comparison of Self-Esteem, Optimism, and Efficacy," *Personality and Social Psychology Bulletin,* Vol. 26, No. 3, 2000, pp. 267–277.

14. Robert Katz, "Skills of an Effective Administrator," *Harvard Business Review,* September–October 1974, pp. 90–101.

15. Gary A. Yukl, *Leadership in Organizations,* Prentice Hall, Upper Saddle River, N.J., 1981, p. 70.

16. See: R. J. House and R. N. Aditya, "The Social Scientific Study of Leadership: Quo Vadis," *Journal of Management,* Vol. 23, 1997, pp. 409–473; H. G. Gregersen, A. J. Morrison and J. S. Black, "Developing Leaders for the Global Frontier," *Solan Management Review,* Vol. 40, Fall 1998, pp. 21–32; and S. A. Kirkpatrick and E. A. Locke, "Leadership: Do Traits Matter?" *Academy of Management Executive,* Vol. 5, May 1991, pp. 48–60.

17. Bass, op. cit., p. 48.

18. Charles N. Greene, "The Reciprocal Nature of Influence between Leader and Subordinate," *Journal of Applied Psychology,* Vol. 60, 1975, pp. 187–193.

19. J. C. Barrow, "Worker Performance and Task Complexity as Casual Determinants of Leader Behavior Style and Flexibility," *Journal of Applied Psychology,* Vol. 61, 1976, pp. 433–440.

20. Charles N. Greene and Chester A. Schriesheim, "Leader-Group Interactions: A Longitudinal Field Investigation," *Journal of Applied Psychology,* February 1980, pp. 50–59.

21. Keith Davis and John Newstrom, *Human Behavior at Work: Organizational Behavior,* 7th ed., McGraw-Hill, New York, 1985, pp. 160, 182 and Ann Howard and James A. Wilson, "Leadership in a Declining Work Ethic," *California Management Review,* Summer 1982, pp. 33–46.

22. F. Dansereau, Jr., G. Graen and W. J. Haga, "A Vertical Dyad Linkage Approach to Leadership within Formal Organizations: A Longitudinal Investigation of the Role Making Process," *Organizational Behavior and Human Performance,* February 1975, pp. 46–78.

23. G. Graen, M. Novak and P. Sommerkamp, "The Effects of Leader-Member Exchange and Job Design and Productivity and Satisfaction: Testing a Dual Attachment Model," *Organizational Behavior and Human Performance,* Vol. 30, 1982, pp. 109–131.

24. Dansereau, Graen, and Haga, op. cit.

25. Fred Dansereau, Jr., Joseph A. Alutto, Steven E. Markham and MacDonald Dumas, "Multi-Plexed Supervision and Leadership: An Application of Within and Between Analysis," in James G. Hunt, Uma Sekaran and Chester A. Schriesheim (Eds.), *Leadership: Beyond Establishment Views,* Southern Illinois University Press, Carbondale, Ill. 1982, pp. 81–103.

26. Robert C. Liden and George Graen, "Generalizability of the Vertical Dyad Linkage Model of Leadership," *Academy of Management Journal,* September 1980, pp. 451–465 and Chester A Schriesheim, Linda L. Neider and Terri A. Scandura, "Delegation and Leader-Member Exchange: Main Effects, Moderators, and Measurement Issues," *Academy of Management Journal,* Vol. 41, No. 3, 1998, pp. 298–318.

27. Robert P. Vecchio, "A Further Test of Leadership Effect due to Between-Group Variation and Within-Group Variation," *Journal of Applied Psychology,* April 1982, pp. 200–208 and Richard M. Dienesch and Robert C. Liden, "Leader-Member Exchange Model of Leadership: A Critique and Further Development," *Academy of Management Review,* July 1986, pp. 618–634.

28. Pamela Tierney and Talya N. Bauer, "A Longitudinal Assessment of LMX on Extra-Role Behavior," *Academy of Management Best Paper Proceedings,* 1996, pp. 298–302.

29. Gary Yukl, "Managerial Leadership: A Review of Theory and Research," *Journal of Management,* Vol. 15, No. 2, 1989, p. 266.

30. Francis J. Yammarino and Alan J. Dubinsky, "Superior-Subordinate Relationships: A Multiple Levels of Analysis Approach," *Human Relations,* Vol. 45, No. 6, 1992, pp. 575–600.

31. Kenneth J. Dunegan, Dennis Duchon, and Mary Uhl-Bien, "Examining the Link between Leader-Member Exchange and Subordinate Performance: The Role of Task Analyzability and Variety of Moderators," *Journal of Management,* Vol. 18, No. 1, 1992, pp. 59–76.

32. Susan E. Murphy and Ellen A. Ensher, "The Effects of Leader and Subordinate Characteristics in the Development of Leader-Member Exchange Quality," *Journal of Applied Psychology,* Vol. 29, No. 7, 1999, pp. 1371–1394.

33. Elaine M. Engle and Robert G. Lord, "Implicit Theories, Self-Schemas, and Leader-Member Exchange," *Academy of Management Journal,* Vol. 40, No. 4, 1997, pp. 988–1010.

34. Susan E. Murphy and Ellen A. Ensher, "The Effects of Leader and Subordinate Characteristics in the Development of Leader-Member Exchange Quality," *Journal of Applied Psychology,* Vol. 29, No. 7, 1999, pp. 1371–1394.

35. George B. Graen and Mary Uhl-Bien, "Development of Leader-Member Exchange (LMX) Theory of Leadership over 25 Years: Applying a Multi-Level Multi-Domain Perspective," *Leadership Quarterly,* Vol. 6, No. 2, 1995, p. 225.

36. Raymond T. Sparrowe and Rober C. Liden, "Process and Structure in Leader-Member Exchange," *Academy of Management Review,* Vol. 22, No. 2, 1997, pp. 522–552.

37. Patrick T. Gibbons, "Impacts of Organizational Evolution on Leadership Roles and Behaviors," *Human Relations,* Vol. 45, No. 1, 1992, pp. 1–18 and Janet Z. Burns and Fred L. Otte, "Implications of Leader-Member Exchange Theory and Research for Human Resource Development Research," *Human Resource Development Quarterly,* Vol. 10, No. 3, Fall 1999, pp. 225–247.

38. Robert G. Lord, Douglas J. Brown and Steven J. Freiberg, "Understanding the Dynamics of Leadership: The Role of Follower Self-Concepts in the Leader/Follower Relationship," *Organizational Behavior and Human Decision Processes,* Vol. 78, No. 8, June 1999, pp. 167–203.

39. Fred E. Fiedler, *A Theory of Leadership Effectiveness,* McGraw-Hill, New York, 1967, pp. 13–144.

40. Ibid., p. 147.

41. Ibid.

42. Fred Fiedler and Martin M. Chemers, *Leadership and Effective Management,* Scott, Foresman, Glenview, Ill., 1974, p. 83.

43. Fred E. Fiedler and Linda Mahar, "The Effectiveness of Contingency Model Training: A Review of the Validation of Leader Match," *Personnel Psychology,* Spring 1979, p. 46.

44. Michael J. Strube and Joseph E. Garcia, "A Meta-Analytic Investigation of Fiedler's Contingency Model of Leadership Effectiveness," *Psychological Bulletin,* September 1981, pp. 307–321 and Lawrence H. Peters, Darrell D. Hartke and John T. Pohlman, "Fiedler's Contingency Theory of Leadership: An Application of the Meta-Analysis Procedures of Schmidt and Hunter," *Psychological Bulletin,* Vol. 97, No. 2, 1985, pp. 274–285.

45. Robert P. Vecchio, "Assessing the Validity of Fiedler's Contingency Model of Leadership Effectiveness: A Closer Look at Strube and Garcia," *Psychological Bulletin,* Vol. 93, No. 2, 1983, pp. 404–408.

46. Chester A. Schriesheim, Bennett J. Tepper and Linda A. Tetrault, "Least Preferred Co-worker Score, Situational Control, and Leadership Effectiveness: A Meta-Analysis of Contingency Model Performance Predictions," *Journal of Applied Psychology,* Vol. 79, No. 4, 1994, pp. 561–573.

47. Ronald E. Riggio, *Introduction to Industrial/Organizational Psychology,* Scott, Foresman/Little, Brown, Glenview, Ill., 1990, p. 293.

48. F. E. Fiedler, "The Contribution of Cognitive Resources to Leadership Performance," *Journal of Applied Social Psychology,* Vol. 16, 1986, pp. 532–548 and F. E. Fiedler and J. E. Garcia, *New Approaches to Leadership: Cognitive Resources and Organizational Performance,* Wiley, New York, 1987.

49. Fred E. Fiedler, Susan E. Murphy and Frederick W. Gibson, "Inaccurate Reporting and Inappropriate Variables: A Reply to Vecchio's Examination of Cognitive Resource Theory," *Journal of Applied Psychology,* Vol. 77, 1992, pp. 372–374.

50. Robert P. Vecchio, "Cognitive Resource Theory: Issues for Specifying a Test of the Theory," *Journal of Applied Psychology,* Vol. 77, 1992, pp. 375–376.

51. Basil S. Georgopoulos, Gerald M. Mahoney and Nyle W. Jones, "A Path–Goal Approach to Productivity,"

Journal of Applied Psychology, December 1957, pp. 345–353; Martin G. Evans, "The Effect of Supervisory Behavior on the Path–Goal Relationship," *Organizational Behavior and Human Performance,* May 1970, pp. 277–298; and Robert J. House, "A Path–Goal Theory of Leader Effectiveness," *Administrative Science Quarterly,* September 1971, pp. 321–338.

52. Robert J. House and Terence R. Mitchell, "Path–Goal Theory of Leadership," *Journal of Contemporary Business,* Autumn 1974, pp. 81–97.

53. Ibid.

54. Ibid.

55. Alan C. Filley, Robert J. House and Steven Kerr, *Managerial Process and Organizational Behavior,* 2d ed., Scott, Foresman, Gleview, Ill., 1976, p. 254.

56. House and Mitchell, op. cit.

57. Filley, House and Kerr, op. cit., pp. 256–260.

58. Chester A. Schriesheim and Angelo DeNisi, "Task Dimensions as Moderators of the Effects of Instrumental Leadership: A Two Sample Applicated Test of Path–Goal Leadership Theory," *Journal of Applied Psychology,* October 1981, pp. 589–597.

59. Julie Indvik, "Path–Goal Theory of Leadership: A Meta-Analysis," *Academy of Management Best Papers Proceedings,* 1986, pp. 189–192.

60. Robert A. Baron, *Behavior in Organizations,* 2d ed., Allyn & Bacon, Boston, 1986, p. 292.

61. Philip M. Podsakoff, Scott B. MacKenzie and Mike Ahearne, "Searching for a Needle in a Haystack: Trying to Identify the Illusive Moderators of Leadership Behaviors," *Journal of Management,* Vol. 21, No. 3, 1995, pp. 422–470.

62. R. J. House and J. L. Baetz, "Leadership: Some Empirical Generalizations and New Research Directions," in B. M. Staw (Ed.), *Research in Organizational Behavior,* Vol. 1, JAI Press, Greenwich, Conn., 1979, p. 399.

63. Robert J. House, "A 1976 Theory of Charismatic Leadership," in Hunt and Larson (Eds.), *Leadership: The Cutting Edge,* op. cit., pp. 189–207.

64. Ibid.

65. Bernard M. Bass, *Leadership and Performance Beyond Expectations,* Free Press, New York, 1985, pp. 54–61.

66. Patricia Sellers, "What Exactly Is Charisma?" *Fortune,* January 15, 1996, p. 68.

67. Stuart J. M. Weierter, "The Role of Self-Awareness and Self-Monitoring in Charismatic Relationships," *Journal of Applied Social Psychology,* Vol. 29, No. 6, 1999, pp. 1246–1262.

68. R. J. House, J. Woycke and E. M. Fodor, "Charismatic and Non Charismatic Leaders: Differences in Behavior and Effectiveness," in J. A. Conger and R. M. Kanungo (Eds.), *Charismatic Leadership: The Elusive Factor in Organizational Effectiveness,* Jossey-Bass, San Francisco, 1988, pp. 98–121 and

Robert J. House, William D. Spangler and James Woycke, "Personality and Charisma in the U.S. Presidency: A Psychological Theory of Leadership Effectiveness," *Academy of Management Best Papers Proceedings,* 1990, pp. 216–219.

69. Shelly A. Kirkpatrick and Edwin A. Locke, "Direct and Indirect Effects of Three Core Charismatic Leadership Components of Performance and Attitudes," *Journal of Applied Psychology,* Vol. 81, No. 1, 1996, pp. 36–51.

70. Boas Shamir, Eliav Zakay, Esther Breinin and Micha Popper, "Correlates of Charismatic Leader Behavior in Military Units: Subordinates' Attitudes, Unit Characteristics, and Superiors' Appraisals of Leader Performance," *Academy of Management Journal,* Vol. 41, No. 4, 1998, pp. 387–409.

71. J. A. Conger and R. Kanungo, "Toward a Behavioral Theory of Charismatic Leadership in Organizational Settings," *Academy of Management Review,* Vol. 12, 1987, pp. 637–647 and J. A. Conger and R. M. Kanungo, "Behavioral Dimensions of Charismatic Leadership," in Conger and Kanungo, *Charismatic Leadership,* op. cit., pp. 78–97.

72. Rajnandini Pillai, "Crisis and the Emergence of Charismatic Leadership in Groups: An Experimental Investigation," *Journal of Applied Social Psychology,* Vol. 26, No. 6, 1996, pp. 543–562.

73. Celia Romm and Nava Pliskin, "The Role of Charismatic Leadership in Diffusion and Implementation of E-mail." *The Journal of Management,* Vol. 18, No. 3, 1999, pp. 273–290.

74. Jane M. Howell and Bruce J. Avolio, "The Ethics of Charismatic Leadership: Submission or Liberation?" *Academy of Management Executive,* May 1992, pp. 43–54; Daniel Sankowsky, "The Charismatic Leader as Narcissist: Understanding the Abuse of Power," *Organizational Dynamics,* Spring 1995, pp. 57–71; and Fred Luthans, Suzanne Peterson and Elina Ibrayeva, "The Potential for the 'Dark Side' of Leadership in Post–Communist Countries," *Journal of World Business,* Vol. 33, No. 2, 1998, pp. 185–201.

75. Howell and Avolio, op. cit., p. 52. Also see F. Bird and J. Gandz, *Good Management: Business Ethics in Action,* Prentice-Hall, Toronto, 1991, p. 166.

76. Bass, *Bass & Stogdill's Handbook,* op. cit., p. 221.

77. J. M. Burns, *Leadership,* Harper & Row, New York, 1978.

78. Bernard M. Bass, "From Transactional to Transformational Leadership: Learning to Share the Vision," *Organizational Dynamics,* Winter 1990, pp. 19–31.

79. Yukl, "Managerial Leadership," op. cit., pp. 272–273.

80. Noel M. Tichy and Mary Anne Devanna, *The Transformational Leader,* Wiley, New York, 1986 and Noel M. Tichy and Mary Anne Devanna, "The Transformational Leader," *Training and Development Journal,* July 1986, pp. 30–32.

81. Bennett J. Tepper, "Patterns of Downward Influence and Follower Conformity in Transactional and Transformational Leadership," *Academy of Management Best Papers Proceedings,* 1993, pp. 267–271.

82. Robert T. Keller, "Transformational Leadership and the Performance of Research and Development Project Groups," *Journal of Management,* Vol. 18, 1992, pp. 489–501.

83. Francis J. Yammarino, Alan J. Dubinsky, Lucette B. Comer and Marvin A. Jolson, "Women and Transformational and Contingent Reward Leadership: A Multiple-Levels-of-Analysis Perspective," *Academy of Management Journal,* Vol. 40, No. 1, 1997, pp. 205–222.

84. Rajnandini Pillai, Chester A. Schriesheim and Eric S. Williams, "Fairness Perceptions and Trust as Mediators for Transformational and Transactional Leadership: A Two-Sample Study," *Journal of Management,* Vol. 25, No. 6, 1999, pp. 897–933, and Timothy A. Judge and Joyce E. Bono, "Five Factor Model of Personality and Transformational Leadership," *Journal of Applied Psychology,* Vol. 85, No. 5, 2000, pp. 751–765.

85. Badrinarayan Shankar Pawar and Kenneth K. Eastman, "The Nature and Implications of Contextual Influences on Transformational Leadership: A Conceptual Examination," *Academy of Management Review,* Vol. 22, No. 1, 1997, pp. 80–109.

86. See Tim R. V. Davis and Fred Luthans, "A Social Learning Approach to Organizational Behavior," *Academy of Management Review,* April 1980, pp. 281–290; Albert Bandura, *Social Foundations of Thought and Action: A Social Cognitive Theory,* Prentice Hall, Upper Saddle River, N.J., 1986; and Alexander D. Stajkovic and Fred Luthans, "Social Cognitive Theory and Self-Efficacy," *Organizational Dynamics,* Spring 1998, pp. 62–74.

87. See Fred Luthans, "Leadership: A Proposal for a Social Learning Theory Base and Observational and Functional Analysis Techniques to Measure Leader Behavior," in J. G. Hunt and L. L. Larson (Eds.), *Crosscurrents in Leadership,* Southern Illinois University Press, Carbondale and Edwardsville, Ill., 1979, pp. 201–208; Fred Luthans and Tim R. V. Davis, "Operationalizing a Behavioral Approach to Leadership," *Proceedings of the Midwest Academy of Management,* 1979, pp. 144–155; and Tim R. V. Davis and Fred Luthans," "Leadership Reexamined: A Behavioral Approach," *Academy of Management Review,* April 1979, pp. 237–248.

88. See Luthans, op. cit., for an expanded discussion.

89. Davis and Luthans, "Leadership Reexamined," p. 244.

90. Ibid., p. 245.

91. See Stajkovic and Luthans, op. cit. and Chemers, Watson and May, op. cit.

92. Steven Kerr and John M. Jermier, "Substitutes of Leadership: Their Meaning and Measurement," *Organizational Behavior and Human Performance,* December 1978, pp. 375–403. Also see Steven Kerr, "Substitutes for Leadership: Some Implications for Organizational Design," *Organization and Administrative Sciences,* Vol. 8, No. 1, 1977, p. 135, and Jon P. Howell, Peter Dorfman, and Steven Kerr, "Moderator Variables in Leadership Research," *Academy of Management Review,* Vol. 11, No. 1, 1986, pp. 88–102.

93. J. Jermier and L. Berkes, "Leader Behavior in a Police Command Bureaucracy: A Closer Look at the Quasi-Military Model," *Administrative Science Quarterly,* March 1979, pp. 1–23, and S. Kerr and J. W. Slocum, Jr., "Controlling the Performances of People in Organizations," in P. C. Nystrom and W. H. Starbuck (Eds.), *Handbook of Organizational Design,* Oxford, New York, 1981, pp. 116–134.

94. Kerr and Jermier, op. cit.

95. Robert H. Miles and M. M. Petty, "Leader Effectiveness in Small Bureaucracies," *Academy of Management Journal,* June 1977, pp. 238–250.

96. For example, see Robert House and Philip M. Podsakoff, "Leadership Effectiveness: Past Perspectives and Future Directions for Research," in Gerald Greenberg (Ed.), *Organizational Behavior: The State of the Science,* Erlbaum, Hillsdale, N.J., 1994, p. 53 and P. M. Podsakoff, B. P. Niehoff, S. B. MacKenzie and M. L. Williams, "Do Substitutes for Leadership Really Substitute for Leadership? An Empirical Examination of Kerr and Jermier's Situational Leadership Model," *Organizational Behavior and Human Decision Processes,* Vol. 54, 1993, pp. 1–44.

97. Jon P. Howell and Peter W. Dorfman, "Substitutes for Leadership: Test of a Construct," *Academy of Management Journal,* December 1981, pp. 714–728.

98. Jon P. Howell and Peter W. Dorfman, "Leadership and Substitutes for Leadership among Professionals and Nonprofessional Workers," *Journal of Applied Behavioral Science,* Vol. 22, No. 1, 1986, pp. 29–46.

99. Robert P. Vecchio, *Organizational Behavior,* Dryden, Chicago, Ill., 1988, p. 309.

100. Warren G. Bennis, "Managing the Dream: Leadership in the 21st Century," *Journal of Organizational Change Management,* Vol. 2, No. 1, 1989, p. 7.

101. M. Haire, E. E. Ghiselli and L. W. Porter, *Managerial Thinking: An International Study,* Wiley, New York, 1966.

102. F. A. Heller and B. Wilpert, *Competence and Power in Managerial Decision Making,* Wiley, London, 1981.

103. Dianne H. B. Welsh, Fred Luthans and Steven M. Sommer, "Managing Russian Factory Workers: The Impact of U.S.–Based Behavioral and Participative Techniques," *Academy of Management Journal,* Vol. 36, No. 1, 1993, pp. 58–79.

104. Fred Luthans, Richard M. Hodgetts and Stuart A. Rosenkrantz, *Real Managers,* Ballinger, Cambridge, Mass., 1988.

105. Fred Luthans, Dianne H. B. Welsh and Stuart A. Rosenkrantz, "What Do Russian Managers Really Do? An Observational Study with Comparisons to U.S. Managers," *Journal of International Business Studies,* 4th Quarter, 1993, pp. 741–761.

106. Ibid. Also see Manfred F. R. Kets De Vries, "A Journey into the 'Wild East': Leadership Style and Organizational Practices in Russia," *Organizational Dynamics,* Vol. 28, No. 4, 2000, pp. 67–81.

107. Abbas J. Ali and Rachid Wahabit, "Managerial Value System in Morocco," *International Studies of Management and Organization,* Vol. 25, No. 3, 1995, pp. 87–96.

108. Cynthia Pavett and Tom Morris, "Management Styles within A Multinational Corporation: A Five Country Comparative Study," *Human Relations,* Vol. 48, No. 10, 1995, pp. 1171–1191.

109. Andrew Myers, Andrew Kakabadse, and Colin Gordon, "Effectiveness of French Management," *Journal of Management Development,* Vol. 14, No. 6, 1995, pp. 56–72.

110. Richard L. Daft, *Management,* 2nd ed., 1991, Dryden, Fort Worth, Tex., p. 625.

111. Dong I. Jung and Bruce J. Avolio, "Effects of Leadership Style of Followers' Cultural Orientation on Performance in Group and Individual Task Conditions," *Academy of Management Journal,* Vol. 42, No. 2, 1999, pp. 208–218.

112. See: Fred Luthans, Paul A. Marsnik and Kyle W. Luthans, "A Contingency Matrix Approach to IHRM," *Human Resource Management,* Vol. 36, No. 2, 1997, pp. 183–199.

113. Project GLOBE, "Cultural Influences on Leadership and Organizations," *Advances in Global Leadership,* Vol. 1, 1999, JAI Press, Greenwich, Conn., pp. 171–233.

114. G. Hofstede, *Culture's Consequences: International Differences in Work Related Values,* Sage, London, 1980.

115. For example, see Mansour Javidan and Robert J. House, "Cultural Acumen for the Global Manager: Lessons from project GLOBE," *Organization Dynamics,* Vol. 29, No. 4, 2001.

116. Bernard M. Bass, "Does the Transactional-Transformational Leadership Paradigm Transcent Organizational and National Boundaries?" *American Psychologist,* Vol. 52, No. 2, 1997, pp. 130–139.

117. Allan H. Church and Janine Waclawski, "The Impact of Leadership Style on Global Management Practices," *Journal of Applied Social Psychology,* Vol. 29, No. 7, 1999, pp. 1416–1443.

118. Felix C. Brodbeck, et al., "Cultural Variation of Leadership Prototypes across 22 European Countries," *Journal of Occupational and Organizational Psychology,* Vol. 73, 2000, pp. 1–29.

Chapter 18 Footnote References and Supplemental Readings

1. Avis Johnson and Fred Luthans, "The Relationship between Leadership and Management: An Empirical Assessment," *Journal of Managerial Issues,* Spring 1990, pp. 13–25.

2. "Harley-Davidson: Going Whole Hog to Provide Stakeholder Satisfaction," *Management Review,* June 1993, p. 55. Also see Rich Teerlink and Lee Ozley, *More than a Motorcycle*; *The Leadership Journey at Harley-Davidson.* Harvard Business School Press, Boston, 2000.

3. Gregory G. Dess and Joseph C. Picken, "Changing Roles: Leadership in the 21st Century," *Organizational Dynamics,* Winter 2000, pp. 18–33.

4. *The State of Small Business,* 1997, pp. 50–56.

5. Marilyn Moats Kennedy, "The Decline of Management," *Across the Board,* July–August, 2000, pp. 57–58.

6. "GM's On-line Strategy," *HRFocus,* February, 1999, p. S11.

7. Geoffrey Colvin, "How to Be a Great E-CEO," *Fortune,* May 24, 1999, pp. 104–110; Peter Ellstrom, "The Power," *Business Week,* May 15, 2000; and "The Geek as Boss," *The Economist,* January 13, 2001, p. 66.

8. Alan Deutschman, "Steve Jobs' Next Big Gamble," *Fortune,* February 8, 1993, p. 99.

9. Alice H. Eagly, Steven J. Karau and Mona G. Makhijani, "Gender and the Effectiveness of Leaders: A Meta-Analysis," *Psychological Bulletin,* Vol. 117, No. 1, 1995, pp. 125–145; Alice H. Eagly, Mona G. Makhijani and Bruce G. Klonsky, "Gender and the Evaluation of Leaders: A Meta-Analysis," *Psychological Bulletin,* Vol. 111, No. 1, 1992, pp. 3–22; and Alice H. Eagly and Blair T. Johnson, "Gender and Leadership Style: A Meta-Analysis," *Psychological Bulletin,* Vol. 108, No. 2, 1993, pp. 233–256.

10. David A. Nadler and Michael L. Tushman, "Beyond the Charismatic Leader: Leadership and Organizational Change," *California Management Review,* Winter 1990, p. 83.

11. See Peter Burrows, "The Radical: Carly Fiorina's Bold Management Experiment at HP," *Business Week,* February 19, 2001, pp. 70–80.

12. "GE Chief Has Electric Presence," from *Wall Street Journal* reprinted in *The Honolulu Advisor,* April 17, 2000, p. 1.

13. "Changing Perspectives," *Wall Street Journal,* November 25, 1986, p. 1.

14. B. Joseph White, "Developing Leaders for the High-Performance Workplace," *Human Resource Management,* Spring 1994, p. 163.

15. Bennett J. Teper, "Consequences of Abusive Supervision," *Academy of Management Journal,* Vol. 43, No. 2, 2000, pp. 178–190.

16. Warren G. Bennis, "Managing the Dream: Leadership in the 21st Century," *Journal of Organizational Change Management,* Vol. 2, No. 1, 1989, p. 6. Also see Warren Bennis, "Leading in Unnerving Times," *MIT Sloan Management Review,* Winter 2001, pp. 97–103.

17. Robert Blake and Jane S. Mouton, "Should You Teach There's Only One Best Way to Manage?" *Training HRD,* April 1978, p. 24.

18. Robert Blake and Jane S. Mouton, "Management by Grid Principles or Situationalism: Which?" *Group and Organization Studies,* December 1981, pp. 439–455.

19. Paul Hersey and Kenneth H. Blanchard, *Management of Organizational Behavior,* 4th ed., Prentice Hall, Upper Saddle River, N.J., 1982.

20. For example, see: Jim Holt, "Bring Big Blue Back: Lessons From the Turnaround of a Faltering Giant," *Management Review,* September, 1999, p. 13, and Patricia Hunt Dirlam, "Taking CHARGE of Change," *Management Review,* September, 1999, p. 61.

21. Gary A. Yukl, *Leadership in Organizations,* Prentice Hall, Upper Saddle River, N.J., 1981, pp. 143–144.

22. Claude L. Graeff, "The Situational Leadership Theory: A Critical View," *Academy of Management Review,* April 1983, pp. 285–291.

23. Warren Blank, John R. Weitzel and Stephen G. Green, "A Test of the Situational Leadership Theory," *Personnel Psychology,* Vol. 43, 1990, pp. 579–597.

24. Robert House and Philip M. Podsakoff, "Leadership Effectiveness: Past Perspectives and Future Directions for Research," in Jerald Greenberg (Ed.), *Organizational Behavior: The State of the Science,* Erlbaum, Hillsdale, N.J., 1994, pp. 58–64.

25. Afsaneh Nahavandi and Ali R. Malekzadeh, "Leader Style in Strategy and Organizational Performance: An Integrative Framework," *Journal of Management Studies,* May 1993, pp. 405–426. Also see W. Glen Rowe, "Creating Wealth in Organizations: The Role of Strategic Leadership," *Academy of Management Executive,* Vol. 15, No. 1, 2001, pp. 81–94.

26. Matthew R. Redmond and Michael D. Mumford, "Putting Creativity to Work: Effects of Leader Behavior on Subordinate Creativity," *Organizational Behavior and Human Decision Processes,* June 1993, pp. 120–151.

27. Sabrina Salam, Jonathan Cox and Henry P. Sims, Jr., "How to Make a Team Work: Mediating Effects of

Job Satisfaction between Leadership and Team Citizenship," *Academy of Management Best Papers Proceedings,* 1996, p. 293.

28. See Richard M. Hodgetts, Fred Luthans and John W. Slocum, Jr., "Strategies and HRM Initiatives for the 00's Environment," *Organizational Dynamics,* Autumn 1999, pp. 18–20.

29. Bruce Avolio, Jane M. Howell and John J. Sosik, "A Funny Thing Happened on the Way to the Bottom Line: Humor as a Moderator of Leadership Style Effects," *Academy of Management Journal,* Vol. 42, No. 2, 1999, pp. 219–227.

30. The figure and following discussion are based on Henry Mintzberg, "The Managers' Job: Folklore and Fact," *Harvard Business Review,* July–August 1975, pp. 49–61.

31. Henry Mintzberg, "Retrospective Commentary on 'The Manager's Job: Folklore and Fact' " *Harvard Business Review,* March–April 1990, p. 170.

32. Stuart L. Hart and Robert E. Quinn, "Roles Executives Play: CEOs, Behavioral Complexity, and Firm Performance," *Human Relations,* May 1993, pp. 543–575.

33. Ibid.

34. Mansour Javidan and Ali Dastmalchian, "Assessing Senior Executives: The Impact of Context on Their Roles," *Journal of Applied Behavioral Science,* September 1993, pp. 328–342.

35. Ibid., p. 339.

36. The following sections are drawn from Fred Luthans, Richard M. Hodgetts and Stuart A. Rosenkrantz, *Real Managers,* Ballinger, Cambridge, Mass., 1988 and Fred Luthans, "Successful vs. Effective Real Managers," *Academy of Management Executive,* May 1988, pp. 127–132. The very extensive study took place over a four-year period.

37. See Henri Fayol, *General and Industrial Management* (Constance Storrs, trans.), Pitman, London, 1949.

38. See Henry Mintzberg, *The Nature of Managerial Work,* Harper & Row, New York, 1973 and Henry Mintzberg, "The Manager's Job: Folklore and Fact," op. cit., pp. 49–61.

39. See John Kotter, *The General Managers,* Free Press, New York, 1982; John Kotter, "What Do Effective General Managers Really Do?" *Harvard Business Review,* November–December 1982, pp. 156–167; and John P. Kotter, "What Effective General Managers Really Do," *Harvard Business Review,* March–April, 1999, pp. 145–159.

40. See Gary Yukl, *Leadership in Organizations,* 4th ed., Prentice Hall, Upper Saddle River, N.J., 1998, pp. 32–33.

41. Fred Luthans, Stuart Rosenkrantz and Harry Hennessey, "What Do Successful Managers Really Do?" *Journal of Applied Behavioral Science,* August 1985, pp. 255–270.

42. Arthur G. Bedian and Achilles A. Armenakis, "The Cesspool Syndrome: How Dreck Floats to the Top of Declining Organizations," *Academy of Management Executive,* Vol. 12, No. 1, 1998, p. 58.

43. Paul E. Mott, *The Characteristics of Effective Organizations,* Harper & Row, New York, 1972.

44. P. C. Smith, L. M. Kendall and C. L. Hulin, *The Measurement of Satisfaction in Work and Retirement,* Rand McNally, Chicago, 1969.

45. Richard T. Mowday, L. W. Porter and Richard M. Steers, *Employee–Organizational Linkages: The Psychology of Commitment, Absenteeism, and Turnover,* Academic Press, New York, 1982.

46. Luthans, Hodgetts and Rosenkrantz, op. cit., and Luthans, op. cit.

47. Fred Luthans, Dianne H. B. Welsh and Stuart A. Rosenkrantz, "What Do Russian Managers Really Do? An Observational Study with Comparisons to U.S. Managers," *Journal of International Business Studies,* Fourth Quarter, 1993, pp. 741–761.

48. Brooke Envick and Fred Luthans, "Identifying the Activities of Entrepreneur-Managers: An Idiographic Study," paper presented at the Academy of Entrepreneurship, Maui, Hawaii, October 10, 1996.

49. Fred Luthans, Suzanne J. Peterson and Elina Ibrayeva, "The Potential for the 'Dark Side' of Leadership in Post-Communist Countries," *Journal of World Business,* Vol. 33, No. 2, 1998, pp. 185–201.

50. Manfred F. R. Kets de Vries, "A Journey into the 'Wild East': Leadership Style and Organizational Practices in Russia," *Organizational Dynamics,* Vol. 28, No. 4, 2000, pp. 67–81.

51. David H. Gobeli, Krzysztof Pzybylowski and William Rudelius, "Customizing Management Training in Central and Eastern Europe: Mini-Shock Therapy," *Business Horizons,* Vol. 41, No. 3, May–June 1998, pp. 61–72.

52. Manfred F. R. Kets de Vries, Danny Miller, and Alain Noel, "Understanding the Leader-Strategy Interface: Application of the Strategic Relationship Interview Method," *Human Relations,* January 1993, pp. 5–21.

53. Michael J. Marquart and Dean W. Engel, "HRD Competencies for a Shrinking World," *Training and Development,* May 1993, pp. 62–64. Also see Robert M. Fullmer, Philip A. Gibbs and Marshall Goldsmith, "Developing Leaders: How Winning Companies Keep on Winning," *Sloan Management Review,* Fall 2000, pp. 49–59.

54. Rabindra M. Kanungo and Sasi Misra, "Managerial Resourcefulness: A Reconceptualization of Management Skills," *Human Relations,* December 1992, pp. 1311–1332.

55. David A. Whetten and Kim S. Cameron, *Developing Management Skills,* Harper Collins, New York, 1991, p. 8.

56. Ibid., p. 11.

57. Ibid., pp. 8–11.

58. Hugh P. Gunz, R. Michael Jalland and Martin G. Evans, "New Strategy, Wrong Managers? What You Need to Know about Career Streams," *Academy of Management Executive,* Vol. 12, No. 2, 1998, p. 21 and Charles H. Ferguson, "The Perfect CEO . . . Like Cinderella Is the Stuff of Fairy Tales. So Is Prince Charming," *Across the Board,* May, 2000, pp. 34–39.

59. Bernard Wysocki, Jr., "Yet Another Hazard of the New Economy: The Pied Piper Effect," *Wall Street Journal,* March 30, 2000, pp. A1, A6 and "Churning at the Top," *The Economist,* March 17, 2001, pp. 67–69.

60. Maury Peiperl and Yehuda Baruch, "Back to Square Zero: The Post-Corporate Career," *Organizational Dynamics,* Spring 1997, pp. 7–22.

61. "Of Executive Talent," *Management Review, July-August,* 1999, pp. 17–22.

62. Robert J. Grossman, "Heirs Apparent," *HR Magazine,* February, 1999, pp. 36–44.

63. Dale E. Zand, *The Leadership Triad,* Oxford University Press, New York, 1997.

64. William C. Byham, "How to Create a Reservoir of Ready-Made Leaders," *Training and Development,* March, 2000, pp. 29–32.

65. Leanne E. Atwater, Shelly D. Dionne, Bruce Avolio, John F. Camobreco and Alan W. Lau, "A Longitudinal Study of the Leadership Development Process: Individual Differences Predicting Leader Effectiveness," *Human Relations,* Vol. 52, No. 12, 1999, pp. 1543–1555.

66. Judity A. Kolb, "The Effect of Gender Role, Attitude Toward Leadership, and Self-Confidence on Leader Emergence: Implications for Leadership Development," *Human Resource Development Quarterly,* Vol. 10, No. 4, Winter, 1999, p. 305.

67. Jack Zenger, Dave Ulrich and Norm Smallwood, "The New Leadership Development," *Training and Development,* March, 2000, pp. 22–27.

68. Roni Drew and Louisa Wah, "Making Leadership Development Effective," *Management Review,* October, 1999, p. 8.

69. Jon P. Briscoe and Douglas T. Hall, "Using 'Competencies' to Groom and Pick Leaders: Are We on the Right Track?" *Organizational Dynamics,* Autumn 1999, pp. 37–52.

70. James Flaherty, *Coaching: Evoking Excellence In Others,* Butterworth, Heinemann, Boston, Mass., 1999.

71. Roger D. Evered and James C. Selman, "Coaching and the Art of Management," *Organizational Dynamics,* Autumn 1989, p. 16.

72. James P. Masciarelli, "Less Lonely at the Top," *Management Review,* April 1999, pp. 58–61.

73. Douglas T. Hall, Karen L. Otazo and George P. Hollenbeck, "Behind Closed Doors: What Really Happens in Executive Coaching," *Organizational Dynamics,* Winter, 1999, p. 39.

74. "Strategic Coaching: Five Ways to Get the Most Value," *HRFocus,* February, 1999, p. S7.

75. Dennis C. Carey and Dayton Odgen, *CEO Succession.* Oxford University Press, New York, 2000.

76. Anita Raghavan and Greg Steinmetz, "Bitter Sweets: Europe's Family Firms Become A Dying Breed Amid Succession Woes." *Wall Street Journal,* March 3, 2000, pp. A1, A20.

77. Jay A. Conger, "Personal Growth Training: Snake Oil or Pathway to Leadership?" *Organizational Dynamics,* Summer 1993, pp. 19–30.

78. Ibid., p. 19.

79. Kevin Cashman, *Leadership From the Inside Out,* Executive Excellence Publishing, Provo, Utah, 1998.

80. William Q. Judge, *The Leader's Shadow: Exploring and Developing the Executive Character,* Sage, Thousand Oaks, Calif., 1999.

81. See, for example, Jeffrey A. Tannenbaum, "Goldilocks, Management Guru," *The Wall Street Journal,* March 3, 2000, pp. B1, B6; James Krohe, "Leadership Books: Why Do We Buy Them?" *Across The Board,* January 2000, pp. 18–21; "You-re Fired, Capisce?: Managing Tips—Sopranos Style," *Fortune,* May 1, 2000, p. 41; and Jerry Cole, "Tough Love Supervision, *The American Management Association Journal,* March, 1997, p. A.

82. Jianping Shen, Van E. Cooley, Connie D. Ruhl-Smith and Nanette M. Keiser, "Quality and Impact of Educational Leadership Programs: A National Study," *The Journal of Leadership Studies,* Vol. 6, No. 1/2, 1999, pp. 1–16.

83. Deborah R. Rada, "Transformational Leadership and Urban Renewal," *The Journal of Leadership Studies,* Vol. 6, No. 3/4, 1999, pp. 18–33.

84. Randall H. Lucius and Karl Kuhnert, "Adult Development and Transformational Leader," *The Journal of Leadership Studies,* Vol. 6, No. 1/2, 1999, pp. 73–85.

85. See: William G. Lee, "The Society Builders," *Management Review,* September, 1999, pp. 52–57.

REFERENCES FOR BEST PRACTICE LEADER'S ADVICE, BOXES AND REAL CASES

CHAPTER 1

Best Practice Leader's Advice: The "Odd Couple" General Electric CEO Jack Welch and Sun Microsystems CEO Scott McNealy on the Interface Between the "New" and the "Old" Economy Source: Adapted from Brent Schlender, "The Odd Couple," *Fortune,* May 1, 2000, pp. 106–126.

OB in Action: The Four Horsemen of the New Economy Excerpted from Spencer Ante, "The Four Horsemen of the New Economy," *Business Week,* October 2, 2000. Reprinted by special permission, copyright © 2000 by McGraw-Hill, Inc.

Real Case: The Case for Optimism Excerpted from Christopher Farrell, "The Case for Optimism," *Business Week,* October 9, 2000, pp. 182, 184. Reprinted by special permission, copyright © 2000 by McGraw-Hill, Inc.

CHAPTER 2

Best Practice Leader's Advice: Intel's Andy Grove on the Impact of Information Technology and Globalization Source: Adapted from Sheila M. Puffer, "Global Executive: Intel's Andrew Grove on Competitiveness," *Academy of Management Executive,* Vol. 13, No. 1, 1999, pp. 22–23.

Technology Application: Get Wired or Get Whacked Sources: Samuel Greengard, "Technology Finally Advances HR," *Workforce,* January 2000, pp. 38–41; Scott Scherr, "Meeting HR Challenges with E-Business," *Workforce,* January 2000, p. 6; Michael Hickins, "It's an E-Buyer's Market," *Management Review,* June 1999, p. 6; and Steve Hamm and Marcia Stepanek, "From Reengineering to E-Engineering," *Business Week E Biz,* March 22, 1999, EB14–15, 18.

Application Example: It's the People, Stupid Excerpted from Robert D. Hof, "It's the People, Stupid," *Business Week,* October 23, 2000, p. EB138. Reprinted by special permission, copyright © 2000 by McGraw-Hill, Inc.

International Application Example: Cracks in Mexico's Glass Ceiling Excerpted from Elisabeth Malkin, "Cracks in Mexico's Glass Ceiling," *Business Week,* July 10, 2000, p. 116. Reprinted by special permission, copyright © 2000 by McGraw-Hill, Inc.

Real Case: Spread the Knowledge Excerpted from Marcia Stepanek, "Spread the Knowledge," *Business Week,* October 23, 2000, pp. EB52, 54, 56. Reprinted by special permission, copyright © 2000 by McGraw-Hill, Inc.

CHAPTER 3

Best Practice Leader's Advice: Admiral Louise Wilmot (Ret.) on Her Experiences in the Predominantly Male U.S. Navy Source: Adapted from Ellen Fagenson-Eland and Pamela J. Kidder, "A Conversation with Rear Admiral Louise Wilmot: Taking the Lead and Leading the Way," *Organizational Dynamics,* Winter 2000, pp. 80–91.

Diversity in Action: Equality Problems, Here, There and Everywhere Sources: Patrick McGeehan, "Morgan Stanley Is Cited for Discrimination Against Women," *New York Times,* June 6, 2000, pp. C1–2; Charles Gasparino and Randall Smith, "U.S. Agency Calls Morgan Stanley Biased Against Female Executives," *Wall Street Journal,* June 6, 2000, pp. C1, 15; Kevin G. Hall, "Chile Slow to Recognize Sexual Harassment," *Miami Herald,* April 30, 2000, p. 7A; Constance L. Hays, "Group of Black Employees Call for Boycott of Coca-Cola Products," *New York Times,* April 20, 2000, pp. C1–2; and Howard W. French, "Women Win a Battle, but Job Bias Still Rules Japan," *New York Times,* February 26, 2000, p. A3.

International Application Example: Is the Ethical Climate Getting Better or Worse? Sources: Skip Kaltenheuser, "Practicing What U.S. Preaches," *New York Times,* October 31, 1999, Business Section, p. 4; Seth Mydans, "Vietnam Awash in Graft Trials, but They Don't Clean Up Graft," *New York Times,* May 25, 1999, p. A5; and Seth Faison, "No. 1 Complaint of Chinese: All This Corruption!" *New York Times,* March 11, 1999, p. A3.

Diversity in Action: Some Progress, but Still a Long Way to Go Sources: Albert R. Hunt, "Major Progress Inequities Cross Three Generations," *Wall Street Journal,* June 22, 2000, pp. A9, 14; Brenda Paik Sunoo, "Around the World in HR Ways," *Workforce,* March 2000, pp. 54–58; and Minda Zetlin, "Nurturing Nonconformists," *Management Review,* October 1999, pp. 29–33.

Real Case: A World of Sweatshops Excerpted from Aaron Bernstein, Michael Shair, and Elisabeth Malkin, " A World of Sweatshops," *Business Week,* November 6, 2000, pp. 84, 86. Reprinted by special permission, copyright © 2000 by McGraw-Hill, Inc.

Real Case: Not Treating Everyone the Same Sources: Michele Galen, Ann Therese Palmer, Alice Cuneo, and Mark Maremont, "Work and Family," *Business Week,* June 28, 1993, pp. 80–88; Michelle Carpenter, "Aetna's Family-Friendly Executive," *Business Week,* June 28, 1993, p. 83; Sharon Allred Decker, "We Had to Recognize That People Have Lives," *Business Week,* June 28, 1993, p. 88; and Sue Shellenbarger, "Lessons from the Workplace: How Corporate Policies and Attitudes Lag behind Workers' Changing Needs," *Human Resource Management,* Fall 1992, pp. 157–169.

CHAPTER 4

Best Practice Leader's Advice: Harvard's Michael Porter's New Thinking on the Relation Between Strategy and Structure Source: Adapted from Richard M. Hodgetts, "A Conversation with Michael E. Porter: A 'Significant Extension' Toward Operational Improvement and Positioning," *Organizational Dynamics,* Summer 1999, pp. 24–33.

International Application Example: One Size Doesn't Fit All–Even Hamburgers Sources: Yumiko Ono, "U.S.

Superstores Find Japanese Are a Hard Sell," *Wall Street Journal,* February 14, 2000, pp. B1, 4; Andy Pasztor and Thomas Kamm, "Pardon My French, but It's English Only on the Flight Deck," *Wall Street Journal,* P. A1; and Robert Frank, "Big Boy's Adventures in Thailand," *Wall Street Journal,* April 12, 2000, pp. B1, 4.

Application Example: Cultural Clash of DaimlerChrysler vs. Mitsubishi Excerpted from Christine Tierney and Ben Bolson, "Mitsubishi: Conquest or Quicksand for Daimler?" *Business Week,* September 25, 2000, p. 62. Reprinted by special permission, copyright © 2000 by McGraw-Hill, Inc.

Real Case: Mike the Knife Excerpted from Kerry Capell, Heidi Dawley, Ariane Sains, and William Echickson, "What Does a Knife Do When the Cutting's Done," *Business Week,* October 23, 2000, p. 148H. Reprinted by special permission, copyright © 2000 by McGraw-Hill, Inc.

Real Case: A Fresh Face to Shake Up the Culture Excerpted from William Symonds, "A Fresh Face Could Do Wonders for Gillette," *Business Week,* November 6, 2000, p. 52. Reprinted by special permission, copyright © 2000 by McGraw-Hill, Inc.

CHAPTER 5

Best Practice Leader's Advice: CEO William Stavropoulos on Dow Chemical's Reward System Source: Adapted from Richard M. Hodgetts, "Dow Chemical's CEO William Stavropolous on Structure and Decision Making," *Academy of Management Executive,* Vol. 13, No. 4, 1999, pp. 33–34.

Application Example: Back to the Drawing Board Sources: Minda Zetlin, "Digitial Overhauls Its Pay Plan," *HR Focus,* December 1995, p. 17; Donald J. McNerney, "The Winner-Take-All Economy," *HR Focus,* October 1995, pp. 4–5; "It Pays to Be First," *Compensation Report,* September 1995, p. 17; and "Study Raises Questions of Executive Pay and Fairness," *Lincoln Journal Star,* August 30, 2000, p. 2A.

Organizational Behavior in Action: Some Easy Ways to Recognize Employees Sources: Neil Ruffolo, "Don't Forget to Provide Incentives for Your Middle Performers," *Workforce,* January 2000, pp. 62–64; Stephen Kerr, "Organizational Rewards: Practical, Cost-Neutral Alternatives that You May Know, but Don't Practice," *Organizational Dynamics,* Summer 1999, pp. 61–70; and Jeanne Bursch and Adrianne Van Strander, "Well-Structured Employee Reward/Recognition Programs Yield Positive Results," *HR Focus,* November 1999, pp. 1, 14.

Real Case: Rewarding Teamwork in the Plains Sources: Woodruff Imberman, "Gainsharing: A Lemon or Lemonade," *Business Horizons,* January–February 1996, pp. 36–40; Donald J. McNerney, "Case Study: Team Compensation," *Management Review,* February 1995, p. 16; and Donald J. McNerney, "Compensation Case Study: Rewarding Team Performance and Individual Skillbuilding," *HR Focus,* January 1995, pp. 1, 4–5.

Real Case: Different Strokes for Different Folks Sources: Many such examples of recognition are found in B. Nelson,

1001 Ways to Reward Employees, Workman, New York, 1994; B. Nelson, "Secrets of Successful Employee Recognition," *Quality Digest,* August 1996, pp. 26–28; and Jeanne Bursch and Adrianne Van Stander, "Well-Structured Employee Reward/Recognition Programs Yield Positive Results," *HR Focus,* November 1999, pp. 1, 14.

CHAPTER 6

Best Practice Leader's Advice: IBM's CEO Lou Gerstner Foretells the Bursting of the Dot-Com Bubble Source: Adapted from Louis V. Gerstner, "Blinded By Dot-Com Alchemy," *Business Week,* March 27, 2000, p. 40. Reprinted by special permission, copyright © 2000 by McGraw-Hill, Inc.

OB in Action: New CEOs Need to Overcome Perception Problems Sources: Katrina Brooker, "Can Anyone Replace Herb?" *Fortune,* April 17, 2000, pp. 186–192; Matt Murray, "Can House That Jack Built Stand When He Goes? Sure, Says Welch," *Wall Street Journal,* April 13, 2000, pp. A 1, 8; and Ram Charan and Geoffrey Colvin, "Why CEOs Fail," *Fortune,* June 21, 1999, pp. 69–78.

International Application Example: Sometimes It Doesn't Translate Sources: Betty Jane Punnett and David A. Ricks, *International Business,* PWS-Kent, Boston, 1992, pp. 340–341; Charles W. L. Hill, *International Business,* Irwin, Burr Ridge Ill., 1994, pp. 491–492; and Michael R. Czinkota and Ilkka A. Ronkainen, *International Marketing,* 3d ed., Dryden, Fort Worth, Tex., 1993, pp. 159–160.

OB in Action: Are You a Generation Xer? Sources: Andy Pasztor and Thomas Kamm, "Pardon My French, but It's English Only on the Flight Deck," *Wall Street Journal,* March 23, 2000; Richard D. Lewis, *When Cultures Collide,* Nicholas Brealey Publishing, London, 1999; and Bruce Stockler and Ross MacDonald, "Shorthand Revisited," *New York Times,* March 6, 1999, p. A27.

Real Case: Dressing Down for Success Excerpted from Anne Field, "What Is Business Casual?" *Business Week,* October 30, 2000, pp. 180, 182, 184, 186, 188, 190. Reprinted by special permission, copyright © 2000 by McGraw-Hill, Inc.

CHAPTER 7

Best Practice Leader's Advice: Insights into the Personalities and Attitudes of Virgin's Richard Branson and ABB's Percy Barnevik Source: Adapted from Manfred F. R. Kets DeVries, "Charisma in Action: The Transformational Abilities of Virgin's Richard Branson and ABB's Percy Barnevik," *Organizational Dynamics,* Winter 1998, pp. 10–15.

International Application Example: Gift Giving in Western Europe Sources: Roger Axtell, *Do's and Taboos around the World,* 2d ed., Wiley, New York, 1990; Philip R. Harris and Robert T. Moran, *Managing Cultural Differences,* 3d ed., Gulf Publishing, Houston, 1991, Chap. 16; and Richard M. Hodgetts and Fred Luthans, *International Management,* 2d ed., McGraw-Hill, New York, 1994, pp. 107–108.

International Application Example: The Mental Effects of the Demise of Japanese Lifetime Employment Policies Sources: Howard W. French, "A Postmodern Plague Ravages Japan's Workers," *New York Times,* February 21, 2000, p. A4; Stephanie Strom, "In Japan, from a Lifetime Job to No Job at All," *New York Times,* February 3, 1999, pp. A1, 6; and Sheryl WuDunn, "When Lifetime Jobs Die Prematurely," *New York Times,* June 12, 1996, pp. C1, 6.

Real Case: It's All a Matter of Personality Sources: "Working in Dilbert's World," *Newsweek,* August 12, 1996, p. 56; Andrew E. Serwer, "Huizenga's Third Act," *Fortune,* August 5, 1996, pp. 73–76; and Anne B. Fisher, "Corporate Reputations: Comebacks and Comeuppances," *Fortune,* March 6, 1996, pp. 90–98.

CHAPTER 8

Best Practice Leader's Advice: Disney's CEO Michael Eisner on the Challenge of Motivating Employees Source: Adapted from Suzy Wetlaufer, "Common Sense and Conflict," *Harvard Business Review,* January–February 2000, pp. 121–124.

Application Example: High Achievers in Action Sources: "Expert Advice: How to Reduce Your Risk as an Entrepreneur," *Working Woman,* January 1987, p. 62; Duncan Maxwell Anderson, "Inspire Yourself," *Success,* December 1993, pp. 58–59; Richard M. Hodgetts and Fred Luthans, *International Management,* 2d ed., McGraw-Hill, New York, 1994, pp. 401–406; and Richard M. Hodgetts, *Modern Human Relations at Work,* 5th ed., Dryden, Fort Worth, Tex., 1993, pp. 47–49.

Diversity in Action: Treating Customers and Employees Fairly Sources: Joseph B. Treaster, "Insurer Agrees It Overcharged Black Clients," *New York Times,* June 22, 2000, pp. A1, C22; "Pay Disparity Between Sexes Persists," *Miami Herald,* May 30, 2000, p. 7B; and Steven Greenhouse, "Sears Is Fined $325,000 by U.S. for Violating Child-Labor Laws," *New York Times,* May 15, 1999, p. A9.

Real Case: "I'm Outta Here!" Excerpted from Julie Forster and Ann Therese Palmer, "That's It, I'm Outta Here," *Business Week,* October 9, 2000, pp. 96, 98. Reprinted by special permission, copyright © 2000 by McGraw-Hill, Inc.

CHAPTER 9

Best Practice Leader's Advice: Daniel Goleman on the Importance of Employee Emotional Intelligence and Self-Confidence Source: Adapted from Jennifer J. Salopek, "Train Your Brain," *Training & Development,* October 1998, pp. 27–33.

Application Example: "Half-Empty"-"Half-Full" Sources: Adapted from Salvatore E. Maddi and Suzanne C. Kobasa, *The Hardy Executive: Health Under Stress,* Dow Jones-Irwin, Burr Ridge, IL, 1984; Patricia Sellers, "So You Fail. Now Bounce Back," *Fortune,* May 1, 1995; and Daniel Goleman, *Working with Emotional Intelligence,* Bantam Books, New York, 1988, pp. 126–127.

Real Case: High Tech–High Fear Sources: Adapted from "The New Economy: Untangling E-Conomics," *The Economist,* September 23, 2000, pp. 5–40; David J. Payne and William A. Minneman, "Apply a Human Solution to Electronic Fears," *HR Focus,* April 1999, pp. S1–S3; and T. McDonald and M. Siegall, "The Effects of Technological Self-Efficacy and Job Focus on Job Performance, Attitudes, and Withdrawal Behaviors," *The Journal of Psychology,* Vol. 126, 1992, pp. 465–475.

CHAPTER 10

Best Practice Leader's Advice: Cisco Systems CEO John Chambers on Meeting Communication Challenges Source: Adapted from Scott Thurm, "How to Drive an Express Train," *Wall Street Journal,* June 1, 2000, pp. B1, B4.

International Application Example: Nonverbal and Verbal Communication Sources: Philip R. Harris and Robert T. Moran, *Managing Cultural Differences,* 3d ed., Gulf Publishing, Houston, 1991, Chap. 16; Dara Khambata and Riad Ajami, *International Business: Theory and Practice,* Macmillan, New York, 1992, Chap. 13; Alan M. Rugman and Richard M. Hodgetts, *International Business,* McGraw-Hill, New York, 1995, Chap. 16; Karen Matthes, "Mind Your Manners When Doing Business in Europe," *Personnel,* January 1992, p. 19; and Roger E. Axtell, *Do's and Taboos around the World,* Wiley, New York, 1990.

International Application Example: Different Cultures, Different Meanings Sources: Jane Whitney Gibson, Richard M. Hodgetts, and Charles W. Blackwell, "Cultural Variations in Nonverbal Communication," Paper presented at the 55th Annual Business Communication meetings, San Antonio, Tex., Nov. 9, 1990; Philip R. Harris and Robert T. Moran, *Managing Cultural Differences,* 3d ed., Gulf Publishing, Houston, 1991, Chap. 2; and Betty Jane Punnett and David A. Ricks, *International Business,* PWS-Kent, Boston, 1992, Chap. 6.

Real Case: Online Communication to Share Knowledge Excerpted from Marcia Stepanek, "Spread the Knowledge," *Business Week,* October 23, 2000, pp. EB52, 54, 56. Reprinted by special permission, copyright © 2000 by McGraw-Hill, Inc.

CHAPTER 11

Best Practice Leader's Advice: Ford's CEO Jacques Nasser on Decisions Needed to Drive Change Source: Adapted from Suzy Wetlaufer, "Driving Change: An Interview with Ford Motor Company's Jacques Nasser," *Harvard Business Review,* March–April 1999, pp. 78–81.

Application Example: Ethics in the 21st Century: Matching the Competition or Driving Them Out? Sources: Nirihiko Shirouzu, "Driven by Necessity—and by Ford—Mazda Downsizes, U.S.-Style," *Wall Street Journal,* January 5, 2000, pp. A1, 8; Stephen Labaton and Laurence Zuckerman, "Airline Is Accused of Illegal Pricing," *New York Times,* May 14, 1999, pp. A1, C5; and Robert L. Simison, "Ford Rolls Out

New Model of Corporate Culture," *Wall Street Journal,* January 13, 1999, pp. B1, 4.

OB in Action: Creative Decision Making to Eliminate Downsizing Sources: Nancy Wong, "Partners Awaken Cultural Change," *Workforce,* March 2000, pp. 72–78; Marlene Piturro, "Alternatives to Downsizing," *Management Review,* October 1999, pp. 37–41; Sharon Machrone and Linda Dini Jenkins, "Creating Cultural Infrastructure: The Third Leg of the Success Stool," *HR Focus,* September 1999, pp. 13–14; and Kevin Walker, "Meshing Cultures in a Consolidation," *Training & Development Journal,* May 1998, pp. 83–90.

Real Case: Putting a Human Face on Rational Decisions Excerpted from Charles J. Whalen, "Putting a Human Face on Economics," *Business Week,* July 31, 2000, pp. 76–77. Reprinted by special permission, copyright © 2000 by McGraw-Hill, Inc.

Real Case: The Banker Who Can Say No Excerpted from Brian Bremner, "The Banker Who Can Say No," *Business Week,* October 23, 2000, p. 148. Reprinted by special permission, copyright © 2000 by McGraw-Hill, Inc.

CHAPTER 12

Best Practice Leader's Advice: Harvard's Robert H. Mnookin on Negotiation Strategies for Managers Source: Adapted from A. J. Vogl, "Negotiation: The Advanced Course," *Across the Board,* April 2000, pp. 21–23.

Application Example: Dealing with Conflicting Goals Sources: Alex Taylor III, "Speed! Power! Status! Mercedes and BMW Race Ahead," *Fortune,* June 10, 1996, pp. 46–58; Louis Kraar, "Daewoo's Daring Drive into Europe," *Fortune,* May 13, 1996, pp. 145–152; and Thomas A. Stewart, "The Nine Dilemmas Leaders Face," *Fortune,* March 18, 1996, pp. 112–113.

Application Example: Taking Time to Manage Time Sources: "Ten Tricks to Keep Time Eaters Away!" *Working Woman,* August 1986, p. 71; "Don't Manage Time, Manage Yourself," *Work Smarter, Not Harder,* Fast Company's Roadmap to Success, 2000, pp. 6–9; and James Gleick, "How Much Time," *Across the Board,* November–December 1999, pp. 9–10.

Real Case: When Workers Just Can't Cope Excerpted from Julie Forster, "When Workers Just Can't Cope," *Business Week,* October 30, 2000, pp. 100, 102. Reprinted by special permission, copyright © 2000 by McGraw-Hill, Inc.

Real Case: Round-the-Clock Stress Sources: Jaclyn Fierman, "It's 2 A.M., Let's Go to Work," *Fortune,* August 21, 1995, pp. 82–87; Sara Zeff Geber, "Pulling the Plug on Stress," *HR Focus,* April 1996, p. 12; and "Marriott Offers Hot Line for Low-Wage Employees," *Sunday Omaha World-Herald,* September 29, 1996, p. 18-G.

CHAPTER 13

Best Practice Leader's Advice: Ida Castro, Chairwoman of the Equal Employment Opportunity Commission, on the Power and Politics of Building an Effective EEOC Source: Adapted from "A New Era at the EEOC," *HR Magazine,* February 1999, pp. 55–58.

Application Example: Just Doing It Sources: Richard M. Hodgetts, *Blueprints for Continuous Improvement: Lessons from the Baldrige Winners,* American Management Association, New York, 1993, pp. 89–93; Shari Caudron, "How HR Drives TQM," *Personnel Journal,* August 1993, pp. 175–187; and Rhonda Thomas, "An Employee's View of Empowerment," *Personnel,* July 1993, pp. 14–15.

Application Example: Empowerment and Trust Can Go a Long Way Sources: Thomas A. Stewart, "Whom Can You Trust? It's Not So Easy to Tell," *Fortune,* June 12, 2000, pp. 331–334; Amy Zipkin, "The Wisdom of Thoughtfulness," *New York Times,* May 31, 2000, pp. C1, 10; and "Global Leader of the Future," *Management Review,* October 1999, p. 9.

Real Case: Fighting Back Sources: Donald M. Spero, "Patent Protection or Piracy—a CEO Views Japan," *Harvard Business Review,* September–October 1990, pp. 58–67; Fred Luthans and Richard M. Hodgetts, *Business,* 2d ed., Dryden, Fort Worth, Tex., 1993, pp. 640–641; and Donald F. Kuratko and Richard M. Hodgetts, *Entrepreneurship,* 2d ed., Dryden, Fort Worth, Tex., 1992, pp. 357–361.

CHAPTER 14

Best Practice Leader's Advice: Continental Airlines' CEO Gordon Bethune on the Value of Teams Source: Adapted from Sheila Puffer, "Continental Airlines' CEO Gordon Bethune on Teams and New Product Development," *Academy of Management Executive,* Vol. 13, No. 3, 1999, pp. 28–35.

Application Example: Greater Productivity through Cross-Functional Teams Sources: David Chaudron, "How to Improve Cross-Functional Teams," *HR Focus,* August 1995, pp. 4–5; Stratford Sherman. "Secrets of HP's 'Muddled' Team," *Fortune,* March 18, 1996, pp. 116–120; and Kenneth Labich, "Elite Teams Get the Job Done," *Fortune,* February 19, 1996, pp. 90–99.

Real Case: There Are Teams, and There Are Teams Sources: Howard W. French, "Japan Debates Culture of Covering Up," *New York Times,* May 2, 2000, p. A12; Yukimo Ono, "U.S. Superstores Find Japanese Are a Hard Sell," *Wall Street Journal,* February 14, 2000, pp. B1, 4; and Noboru Yoshimura and Philip Anderson, *Inside the Kaisa,* Harvard Business School Press, Boston, 1997.

CHAPTER 15

Best Practice Leader's Advice: GE's Steve Kerr on Designing Jobs and Setting Goals for Performance Improvement Sources: Adapted from Richard M. Hodgetts, "A Conversation with Steve Kerr," *Organizational Dynamics,* Spring 1996, pp. 69–77 and Strat Sherman, "Stretch Goals: The Dark Side of Asking for Miracles," *Fortune,* November 13, 1995, pp. 231–232.

Application Example: Using Stretch Goals Sources: Strat Sherman, "Stretch Goals: The Dark Side of Asking for Miracles," *Fortune,* November 13, 1995, pp. 231–232; Steven Kerr, "An Academy Classic: On the Folly of Rewarding A, While Hoping for B," *Academy of Management Executive,* February 1995, p. 7; Jerry L. McAdams, "Employee Involvement and Performance Reward Plans," *Compensation and Benefits Review,* March–April 1995, pp. 45–55; and Woodruff Imberman, "Gainsharing: A Lemon or Lemonade?" *Business Horizons,* January–February 1996, pp. 36–40.

Real Case: I Can't Believe They Redesigned the Whole Thing Excerpted from Jeff Green, "Why Workers Are Lining Up for Jobs at this GM Plant," *Business Week,* October 2, 2000, p. 152F. Reprinted by special permission, copyright © 2000 by McGraw-Hill, Inc.

Real Case: Making It a Nice Place to Work Sources: Joan O. C. Hamilton, Stephen Baker, and Bill Vlasic, "The New Workplace," *Business Week,* April 29, 1996, pp. 107–117; Richard M. Hodgetts, *Implementing TQM in Small and Medium-Sized Organizations,* Amacom, New York, 1996, Chap. 7; and Barbara Ettorre, "When the Walls Come Tumbling Down," *Management Review,* November 1995, pp. 33–37.

CHAPTER 16

Best Practice Leader's Advice: Ed Lawler, Director of the Center for Effective Organizations, on the Complexities of Using Pay in Performance Management Source: Adapted from "Keeping the Pay Demons at Bay," *Across the Board,* July–August 2000, pp. 10–11.

Real Case: Rewarding Big Time for Failure Excerpted from Dean Foust and Louis Lavelle, "CEO Pay: Nothing Succeeds Like Failure," *Business Week,* September 11, 2000, p. 46. Reprinted by special permission, copyright © 2000 by McGraw-Hill, Inc.

CHAPTER 17

Best Practice Leader's Advice: Learning Organization Guru Peter Senge on the Role of the Leadership Process Source: Adapted from "Why Organizations Still Aren't Learning," *Training,* September 1999, pp. 42–45.

Application Example: The "Right Stuff" Sources: "Confessor to the Boardroom," *Economist,* February 24, 1996, p. 74; Stratford Sherman, "How Tomorrow's Best Leaders Are Learning Their Stuff," *Fortune,* November 27, 1995, pp. 90–102; and Stanley Bing, "The Seven Habits of Highly Offensive People," *Fortune,* November 27, 1995, pp. 47–48.

International Application Example: Gauging Communications across Cultures Sources: Sheida Hodge, *Global Smarts,* John Wiley & Sons, New York, 2000; Richard M. Hodgetts and Fred Luthans, *International Management,* 4th edition, Irwin/McGraw, Burr Ridge, Ill.: 2000, Chapters 5–6; and Richard D. Lewis, *When Cultures Collide,* Nicholas Brealey Publishing, London, 1999.

Real Case: No Organization Chart and an 80 Blank Pages Policy Manual Excerpted from Pete Engardio, "Flextronics: Few Rules, Fast Responses," *Business Week,* October 23, 2000, p. 148F. Reprinted by special permission, copyright © 2000 by McGraw-Hill, Inc.

Real Case: Corporate Leaders: The Most Popular Is ... Excerpted from Robert Barker, "Jack, They Hardly Know Ye," *Business Week,* August 7, 2000, p. 38. Reprinted by special permission, copyright © 2000 by McGraw-Hill, Inc.

CHAPTER 18

Best Practice Leader's Advice: Leadership Guru Warren Bennis on Great Leaders vs. the Situation Source: Adapted from Richard M. Hodgetts, "A Conversation with Warren Bennis on Leadership in the Midst of Downsizing," *Organizational Dynamics,* Summer 1996, pp. 72–78.

OB in Action: With GenXer's, It's a Whole New Ballgame Sources: Richard W. Oliver, " 'My' Generation," *Management Review,* January 2000, pp. 12–13; Joanne Cole, "The Art of Wooing Gen Xers," *HR Focus,* November 1999, pp. 7–8; and "Gearing Up for Tomorrow's Workforce," *HR Focus,* February 1999, pp. 14–16.

International Application Example: Balancing People and Profits Sources: James B. Hayes, "Wanna Make a Deal in Moscow?" *Fortune,* October 22, 1990, pp. 113–118; "Such Good Friends with IBM," *Fortune,* October 4, 1993, p. 118; Tim Smart, Pete Engardio, and Geri Smith, "GE's Brave New World," *Business Week,* November 8, 1993, pp. 64–70; and "How to Negotiate with Really Tough Guys," *Fortune,* May 27, 1996, pp. 172–173.

Real Case: Jeanne P. Jackson: A Retailing Leader Excerpted from Wendy Zellmer, "Why Banana Republic's Star Jumped to Wal-Mart," *Business Week,* November 6, 2000, p. 112. Reprinted by special permission, copyright © 2000 by McGraw-Hill, Inc.

Real Case: He's the Best—Or Is He? Sources: Kenneth Labich, "Steve Wynn: A $2.5 Billion Wager," *Fortune,* July 22, 1996, pp. 80–86; Kenneth Labich, "Rethinking Almost Everything," *Fortune,* May 13, 1996, p. 179; and Betsy Morris, "The Brand's the Thing," *Fortune,* March 4, 1996, pp. 72–86.

INDEX

LAIRD LIBRARY
Glasgow College of Building & Printing
60 North Hanover Street
Glasgow G1 2BP
0141 566 4132